MICROSOFT®
VISUAL BASIC® 2015:
RELOADED

SIXTH EDITION

MICROSOFT®
VISUAL BASIC® 2015:
RELOADED

DIANE ZAK

Australia • Brazil • Mexico • Singapore • United Kingdom • United States

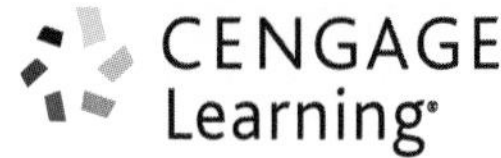

Microsoft® Visual Basic® 2015: RELOADED, Sixth Edition
Diane Zak

Product Director: Kathleen McMahon

Product Team Manager: Kristin McNary

Associate Product Manager: Megan Chrisman

Senior Content Developer: Alyssa Pratt

Product Assistant: Abigail Pufpaff

Marketing Manager: Eric LaScola

Senior Production Director: Wendy Troeger

Production Director: Patty Stephan

Senior Content Project Manager: Jennifer K. Feltri-George

Managing Art Director: Jack Pendleton

Cover image(s): © Rudchenko Liliia/Shutterstock.com

Unless otherwise noted all screenshots are courtesy of Microsoft Corporation

Open Clip art source: OpenClipArto.org

Library of Congress Control Number: 2015947713
ISBN: 978-1-285-86019-0

Cengage Learning
20 Channel Center Street
Boston, MA 02210
USA

Cengage Learning is a leading provider of customized learning solutions with employees residing in nearly 40 different countries and sales in more than 125 countries around the world. Find your local representative at **www.cengage.com**

Cengage Learning products are represented in Canada by Nelson Education, Ltd.

For your course and learning solutions, visit **www.cengage.com**

Purchase any of our products at your local college store or at our preferred online store **www.cengagebrain.com**

Printed in the United States of America
Print Number: 01 Print Year: 2016

Brief Contents

Contents

Preface

Microsoft Visual Basic 2015: RELOADED, Sixth Edition uses Visual Basic 2015, an object-oriented language, to teach programming concepts. This book is designed for a beginning programming course; however, it assumes students are familiar with basic Windows skills and file management.

Organization and Coverage

Microsoft Visual Basic 2015: RELOADED, Sixth Edition contains 14 chapters and five appendices (A through E). In the chapters, students with no previous programming experience learn how to plan and create their own interactive Windows applications. By the end of the book, students will have learned how to use TOE charts, pseudocode, and flowcharts to plan an application. They will also learn how to work with objects and write Visual Basic statements such as If...Then...Else, Select Case, Do...Loop, For...Next, and For Each...Next. Students will also learn how to manipulate variables, constants, strings, sequential access files, structures, and arrays. In Chapter 12, they will learn how to connect an application to a Microsoft Access database, and then use Language Integrated Query (LINQ) to query the database. Chapter 13 shows students how to create simple Web applications, and Chapter 14 shows them how to create their own classes and objects.

Approach

Like the previous editions, *Microsoft Visual Basic 2015: RELOADED, Sixth Edition* is distinguished from other textbooks because of its unique approach, which motivates students by demonstrating why they need to learn the concepts and skills presented. Each chapter begins with an introduction to one or more programming concepts. The concepts are illustrated with code examples and sample programs. The sample programs are provided to students to allow them to observe how the current concept can be utilized before they are introduced to the next concept. Following the concept portion in each chapter are two Programming Tutorials. Each Programming Tutorial guides students through the process of creating an application using the concepts covered in the chapter. A Programming Example follows the Programming Tutorials in each chapter. The Programming Example contains a completed application that demonstrates the chapter concepts. Following the Programming Example are the Summary, Key Terms, Review Questions, Exercises, and Case Projects sections.

Features

Microsoft Visual Basic 2015: RELOADED, Sixth Edition is an exceptional textbook because it also includes the following features:

READ THIS BEFORE YOU BEGIN This section is consistent with Cengage Learning's unequaled commitment to helping instructors introduce technology into the classroom. Technical considerations and assumptions about hardware, software, and default settings are listed in one place to help instructors save time and eliminate unnecessary aggravation.

DESIGNED FOR THE DIFFERENT LEARNING STYLES The three most common learning styles are visual, auditory, and kinesthetic. This book contains videos for visual and auditory learners, and Try It! files for kinesthetic learners.

OBJECTIVES The Review Questions, Exercises, and Case Projects are associated with one or more of the objectives listed at the beginning of the chapter.

VIDEOS These notes direct students to videos that explain and/or demonstrate one or more of the chapter's concepts, provide additional information about the concepts, or cover topics related to the concepts. The videos are available at *www.cengagebrain.com*. Search for the ISBN of your title (from the back cover of your book) using the search box at the top of the page. This will take you to the product page where free companion resources can be found.

TRY IT! FILES Each chapter has accompanying Try It! files that allow the student to practice a concept before moving on to the next concept.

MINI-QUIZZES Mini-Quizzes are strategically placed to test students' knowledge at various points in the chapter. Answers to the quiz questions are provided in Appendix A, allowing students to determine whether they have mastered the material covered thus far before continuing with the chapter.

HOW TO BOXES The How To boxes in each chapter summarize important concepts and provide a quick reference for students. The How To boxes that introduce new statements, functions, or methods contain the syntax and examples of using the syntax. Many of the How To boxes contain the steps for performing common tasks.

TIP These notes provide additional information about the current concept. Examples include alternative ways of writing statements or performing tasks, as well as warnings about common mistakes made when using a particular command and reminders of related concepts learned in previous chapters.

PROGRAMMING TUTORIALS Each chapter contains two Programming Tutorials that provide step-by-step instructions for using the chapter's concepts in an application. In most cases, the first tutorial in each chapter is easier than the second because it contains more detailed steps. Typically, one of the tutorial applications is a simple game, while the other is a business application. Game applications are used because research shows that the fun and exciting nature of games helps motivate students to learn.

PROGRAMMING EXAMPLE A Programming Example follows the Programming Tutorials in each chapter. The Programming Example shows the TOE chart and pseudocode used to plan the application. It also shows the user interface and Visual Basic code.

SUMMARY Each chapter contains a Summary section that recaps the concepts covered in the chapter.

KEY TERMS Following the Summary section in each chapter is a listing of the key terms introduced throughout the chapter, along with their definitions.

REVIEW QUESTIONS Each chapter contains Review Questions designed to test a student's understanding of the chapter's concepts.

PENCIL AND PAPER EXERCISES Following the Review Questions in each chapter are Pencil and Paper Exercises. The Exercises are designated as Modify This, Introductory, Intermediate, Advanced, Discovery, and Swat the Bugs. The Advanced and Discovery Exercises provide practice in applying cumulative programming knowledge. They also allow students to explore alternative solutions to programming tasks. The Swat the Bugs Exercises provide an opportunity for students to detect and correct errors in one or more lines of code.

COMPUTER EXERCISES The Computer Exercises, which follow the Pencil and Paper Exercises in each chapter, provide students with additional practice of the skills and concepts they learned in the chapter. The Exercises are designated as Modify This, Introductory, Intermediate, Advanced, Discovery, and Swat the Bugs. The Advanced and Discovery Exercises provide practice in applying cumulative programming knowledge. They also allow students to explore alternative solutions to programming tasks. The Swat the Bugs Exercises provide an opportunity for students to detect and correct errors in an existing application.

CASE PROJECTS At the end of each chapter are at least four Case Projects, one (or more) of which is a Think Tank Case Project. The Case Projects give the student the opportunity to independently synthesize and evaluate information, examine potential solutions, and make recommendations. Most of the Case Projects include a sample interface.

THINK TANK CASE PROJECTS Each chapter contains at least one Think Tank Case Project. These projects are more challenging than the other Case Projects.

New to this Edition!

NEW EXAMPLES, SAMPLE PROGRAMS, TUTORIALS, AND EXERCISES Each chapter has been updated with new examples, sample programs, tutorials, and/or exercises.

VIDEOS The videos that accompany the book have been updated from the previous edition.

VISUAL STUDIO COMMUNITY 2015 AND WINDOWS 10 The figures in the book and the steps in the Programming Tutorials assume you are using Visual Studio Community 2015 and a system running Microsoft Windows 10. Your screen and steps may be slightly different if you are using a different version of Visual Studio and/or Microsoft Windows.

STARTING AND CONFIGURING VISUAL STUDIO The How To boxes in Figures 1-1 and 1-2 in Chapter 1 contain the instructions for starting and configuring Visual Studio Community 2015 on a Windows 10 system. The instructions for starting Visual Studio Community on a Windows 8 system are contained in the VbReloaded2015\Chap01\Starting Using Windows 8.pdf file.

Instructor Resources

The following resources are available on the Instructor Companion Site (*sso.cengage.com*) to instructors who have adopted this book. Search for this title by ISBN, title, author, or keyword. From the Product Overview page, select the Instructor's Companion Site link to access your complementary resources.

INSTRUCTOR'S MANUAL The Instructor's Manual follows the text chapter by chapter to assist you in planning and organizing an effective, engaging course. The manual includes learning objectives, chapter overviews, ideas for classroom activities, and additional resources. A sample course **Syllabus** is also available.

TEST BANK Cengage Learning Testing Powered by Cognero is a flexible, online system that allows you to:

- author, edit, and manage test bank content from multiple Cengage Learning solutions
- create multiple test versions in an instant
- deliver tests from your LMS, your classroom or wherever you want

POWERPOINT PRESENTATIONS This book comes with Microsoft PowerPoint slides for each chapter. These are included as a teaching aid for classroom presentation, to make available to students on the network for chapter review, or to be printed for classroom distribution. Instructors are encouraged to customize the slides to fit their course needs, and may add slides to cover additional topics using the complete **Figure Files** from the text, also available on the Instructor Companion Site.

SOLUTION FILES Solutions to the Review Questions, Pencil and Paper Exercises, Computer Exercises, and Case Projects are available. The Solution Files also contain the sample programs that appear in the figures throughout the book.

DATA FILES Data Files are required to complete many of the computer activities in this book. They are available on the Instructor Companion Site as well as on CengageBrain.com.

Acknowledgments

Writing a book is a team effort rather than an individual one. I would like to take this opportunity to thank my team, especially Alyssa Pratt (Senior Content Developer), Heidi Aguiar (Project Manager), Jennifer Feltri-George (Senior Content Project Manager), Suzanne Huizenga (Proofreader), John Frietas (Quality Assurance), and the compositors at GEX. Thank you for your support, enthusiasm, patience, and hard work. Last, but certainly not least, I want to thank the following reviewers for their invaluable ideas and comments: Lorraine Bergkvist, University of Baltimore and Adam Lee, University of Maryland.

Diane Zak

Read This Before You Begin

Technical Information

Data Files

You will need data files to complete the computer activities in this book. Your instructor may provide the data files to you. You may obtain the files electronically at CengageBrain.com and then navigating to the page for this book.

Each chapter in this book has its own set of data files, which are stored in a separate folder within the VbReloaded2015 folder. The files for Chapter 1 are stored in the VbReloaded2015\Chap01 folder. Similarly, the files for Chapter 2 are stored in the VbReloaded2015\Chap02 folder. Throughout this book, you will be instructed to open files from or save files to these folders.

You can use a computer in your school lab or your own computer to complete the computer activities in this book.

Using Your Own Computer

To use your own computer to complete the computer activities in this book, you will need the following:

- A Pentium® 4 processor, 1.6 GHz or higher, personal computer running Microsoft Windows. This book was written using Microsoft Windows 10, and Quality Assurance tested using Microsoft Windows 8 and Microsoft Windows 10.
- Visual Studio Community 2015, Visual Studio Professional 2015, or Visual Studio Enterprise 2015 installed on your computer. This book was written and Quality Assurance tested using Visual Studio Community 2015. At the time of this writing, you can download a free copy of Visual Studio Community 2015 at *https://www.visualstudio.com/downloads/download-visual-studio-vs.*

To start and configure Visual Studio to match the figures and tutorial steps in this book:

1. Use the information in the How To box in Figure 1-1 (on page 10) to start Visual Studio Community 2015.
2. Use the information in the How To box in Figure 1-2 (on page 10) to configure Visual Studio Community 2015.

To install Microsoft Visual Basic PowerPacks 12.0:

1. Locate the vb_vbpowerpacks.exe file, which is contained in the VbReloaded2015\PowerPacks folder. Right-click the filename and then click Run as administrator. Click the Yes button.
2. Select the "I agree to the License Terms and Privacy Policy." check box. Either select or deselect the check box that asks if you want to join the Visual Studio Experience Improvement program. Click Install.
3. When the "Setup Successful!" message appears, click the Close button.
4. Start Visual Studio. Open the Toolbox window (if necessary) by clicking View on the menu bar and then clicking Toolbox. Right-click the Toolbox window and then click Add Tab. Type Visual Basic PowerPacks and press Enter.
5. Right-click the Visual Basic PowerPacks tab, and then click Choose Items. If necessary, click the .NET Framework Components tab in the Choose Toolbox Items dialog box.
6. In the Filter box, type PowerPacks. You may see one or more entries for the PrintForm control. Select all of Version 12's controls (PrintForm, DataRepeater, LineShape, OvalShape, and RectangleShape).
7. Click the OK button to close the Choose Toolbox Items dialog box. If the message "The following controls were successfully added to the toolbox but are not enabled in the active designer:" appears, click the OK button. The PowerPacks controls will not appear in the Toolbox window until you either create a new Visual Basic application or open an existing one. You will learn how to perform both of those tasks in Chapter 1.

Figures

The figures in this book reflect how your screen will look if you are using Visual Studio Community 2015 and a Microsoft Windows 10 system. Your screen may appear slightly different in some instances if you are using another version of either Visual Studio or Microsoft Windows.

Visit Our Web Site

Additional materials designed for this textbook might be available at CengageBrain.com. Search the site for more details.

To the Instructor

To complete the computer activities in this book, your students must use a set of data files. These files can be obtained on the Instructor Companion Site or at CengageBrain.com.

The material in this book was written using Visual Studio Community 2015 on a Microsoft Windows 10 system. It was Quality Assurance tested using Visual Studio Community 2015 on both a Windows 10 and a Windows 8 system.

OVERVIEW

An Introduction to Programming

After studying this Overview, you should be able to:

- Define the terminology used in programming
- Explain the tasks performed by a programmer
- Understand the employment opportunities for programmers and software developers
- Use the chapters effectively

Programming a Computer

In essence, the word **programming** means *giving a mechanism the directions to accomplish a task*. If you are like most people, you have already programmed several mechanisms, such as your digital video recorder (DVR), cell phone, or coffee maker. Like these devices, a computer is also a mechanism that can be programmed.

The directions (typically called instructions) given to a computer are called **computer programs** or, more simply, **programs**. The people who write programs are called **programmers**. Programmers use a variety of special languages, called **programming languages**, to communicate with the computer. Some popular programming languages are Visual Basic, C#, C++, and Java. In this book, you will use the Visual Basic programming language.

The Programmer's Job

When a company has a problem that requires a computer solution, typically it is a programmer who comes to the rescue. The programmer might be an employee of the company. Or, he or she might be a freelance programmer (or programming consultant), which is a programmer who works on temporary contracts rather than for a long-term employer.

Overview-Programmers

First the programmer meets with the user, who is the person (or people) responsible for describing the problem. In many cases, this person will also eventually use the solution. Depending on the complexity of the problem, multiple programmers may be involved, and they may need to meet with the user several times. Programming teams often contain subject matter experts, who may or may not be programmers. For example, an accountant might be part of a team working on a program that requires accounting expertise. The purpose of the initial meetings with the user is to determine the exact problem and to agree on the desired solution.

After the programmer and user agree on the solution, the programmer begins converting the solution into a computer program. During the conversion phase, the programmer meets periodically with the user to determine whether the program fulfills the user's needs and to refine any details of the solution. When the user is satisfied that the program does what he or she wants it to do, the programmer rigorously tests the program with sample data before releasing it to the user, who will test it further to verify that it correctly solves the problem. In many cases, the programmer also provides the user with a manual that explains how to use the program. As this process indicates, the creation of a good computer solution to a problem—in other words, the creation of a good program—requires a great deal of interaction between the programmer and the user.

Employment Opportunities

Overview-Programmer Qualities

When searching for a job in computer programming, you will encounter ads for "computer programmers" as well as for "computer software engineers." Although job titles and descriptions vary, computer software engineers typically are responsible for designing an appropriate solution to a user's problem, while computer programmers are responsible for translating the solution into a language that the computer can understand—a process called **coding**. Software engineering is a higher-level position that requires the ability to envision solutions. Using a construction analogy, software engineers are the architects, while programmers are the carpenters.

Keep in mind that depending on the employer as well as the size and complexity of the user's problem, the design and coding tasks may be performed by the same employee, no matter what his or her job title is. In other words, it's not unusual for a software engineer to code his or her solution or for a programmer to have designed the solution he or she is coding.

Programmers and software engineers need to have strong problem-solving and analytical skills, as well as the ability to communicate effectively with team members, end users, and other nontechnical personnel. Typically, software engineers are expected to have at least a bachelor's degree in software engineering, computer science, or mathematics, along with practical work experience, especially in the industry in which they are employed. Computer programmers usually need at least an associate's degree in computer science, mathematics, or information systems, as well as proficiency in one or more programming languages.

Computer programmers and software engineers are employed by companies in almost every industry, such as telecommunications companies, software publishers, financial institutions, insurance carriers, educational institutions, and government agencies. The Bureau of Labor Statistics predicts that employment of computer software engineers will increase by 22% from 2012 to 2022. The employment of computer programmers, on the other hand, will increase by 8% over the same period. In addition, consulting opportunities for freelance programmers and software engineers are expected to increase as companies look for ways to reduce their payroll expenses.

There is a great deal of competition for programming and software engineering jobs, so jobseekers will need to keep up to date with the latest programming languages and technologies. A competitive edge may be gained by obtaining vendor-specific or language-specific certifications, as well as knowledge of a prospective employer's business. More information about computer programmers and computer software engineers can be found on the U.S. Bureau of Labor Statistics Web site at *www.bls.gov.*

Using the Chapters Effectively

The chapters in this book teach you how to write programs using the Visual Basic programming language. Each chapter focuses on programming concepts, which are first introduced using simple examples and then utilized in larger applications at the end of the chapter.

Two Programming Tutorials follow the concepts section in each chapter. Each Programming Tutorial guides you through the process of creating an application using the concepts covered in the chapter. In most cases, the first tutorial in each chapter is easier than the second one because it contains more detailed steps. Some of the applications created in the Programming Tutorials are simple games, while others are business applications.

A Programming Example follows the Programming Tutorials in each chapter. The Programming Example contains a completed application that demonstrates the chapter concepts.

After reading the concepts section, be sure to complete one or both of the Programming Tutorials and the Programming Example. Doing this will help you complete the Computer Exercises and Case Projects at the end of the chapter. In addition, some of the Computer Exercises require you to modify the applications created in the Programming Tutorials and Programming Example.

Throughout each chapter, you will find How To boxes. Some How To boxes, like the one in Figure O-1, contain numbered steps that show you how to accomplish a task, such as how to open an existing solution in Visual Basic. You are not expected to follow the steps in these How To boxes while you are reading the chapter. Rather, these How To boxes are intended to provide a quick reference that you can use when completing the end-of-chapter Programming Tutorials, Programming Example, Exercises, and Case Projects. Feel free to skim these How To boxes and use them only if and when you need to do so. The same holds true for How To boxes containing bulleted items, like the one shown in Figure O-2.

HOW TO Open an Existing Solution

1. Click File on the menu bar and then click Open Project.
2. Locate and then open the application's solution folder. Click the solution filename, which ends with .sln. (The *sln* stands for *solution*.)
3. Click the Open button in the Open Project dialog box.
4. If the designer window is not open, click View on the menu bar and then click Designer. Or, you can right-click the form file's name in the Solution Explorer window and then click View Designer.

Note: To control the display of filename extensions, right-click the Start button on the Windows 10 taskbar, click Control Panel, click Appearance and Personalization, click File Explorer Options, and then click the View tab. Deselect the Hide extensions for known file types check box to show the extensions; or, select the check box to hide them.

Figure O-1 How to open an existing solution

HOW TO Start an Application

- Save the solution, click Debug on the menu bar, and then click Start Debugging.
- Save the solution and then press the F5 key on your keyboard.
- Save the solution and then click the Start button on the Standard toolbar.

Figure O-2 How to start an application

Other How To boxes contain information pertaining to a Visual Basic instruction. The How To box in Figure O-3, for example, contains the syntax and examples of assigning a value to an object's property while an application is running. You should study the information in these How To boxes while you are reading the chapter.

HOW TO Assign a Value to an Object's Property During Run Time

Syntax

object.property = expression

assignment operator

dot member access operator

Example 1

```
grossPayLabel.Width = 400
```

assigns the number 400 to the grossPayLabel's Width property

Example 2

```
companyLabel.Text = "Lakeside Hotels"
```

assigns the string "Lakeside Hotels" to the companyLabel's Text property

Example 3

```
goPictureBox.Visible = True
```

assigns the keyword `True` to the goPictureBox's Visible property

Figure 0-3 How to assign a value to an object's property during run time

The three most common learning styles are visual, auditory, and kinesthetic. Briefly, visual learners learn by watching, auditory learners learn by listening, and kinesthetic learners learn by doing. This book contains special elements designed specifically for each of the different learning styles. For example, each chapter contains videos for visual and auditory learners. The videos demonstrate and explain the concepts covered in the chapter. In addition to the Programming Tutorials, most chapters contain Try It! files for kinesthetic learners. The Try It! files allow the learner to practice with a concept before moving on to the next concept.

Overview Summary

- Programs are the step-by-step instructions that tell a computer how to perform a task.
- Programmers use various programming languages to communicate with the computer.
- In most cases, a programmer meets with the user several times to determine the exact problem to be solved and to agree on a solution. He or she also gets together periodically with the user to verify that the solution meets the user's needs and to refine any details.
- Programmers rigorously test a program with sample data before releasing the program to the user.
- It's not unusual for the same person to perform the duties of both a computer software engineer and a computer programmer.

Key Terms

Coding—the process of translating a solution into a language that the computer can understand

Computer programs—the directions given to computers; also called programs

Programmers—the people who write computer programs

Programming—the process of giving a mechanism the directions to accomplish a task

Programming languages—languages used to communicate with a computer

Programs—the directions given to computers; also called computer programs

CHAPTER 1

An Introduction to Visual Basic 2015

After studying Chapter 1, you should be able to:

1. Define some of the terms used in object-oriented programming
2. Create, start, and end a Visual Basic 2015 Windows Forms application
3. Manage the windows in the integrated development environment (IDE)
4. Set the properties of an object
5. Manipulate controls
6. Use label, button, and picture box controls
7. Use the options on the Format menu
8. Write Visual Basic code
9. Save, close, and open a solution
10. Run a project's executable file
11. Write an assignment statement
12. Print an application's code and interface
13. Find and correct a syntax error

Visual Basic 2015

In this book, you will learn how to create programs, called **applications**, using the Visual Basic 2015 programming language. Visual Basic 2015 is one of the languages built into Microsoft's newest integrated development environment: Visual Studio 2015. An **integrated development environment (IDE)** is an environment that contains all of the tools and features you need to create, run, and test your programs.

Visual Basic is an **object-oriented programming language**, which is a language that allows the programmer to use objects to accomplish a program's goal. An **object** is anything that can be seen, touched, or used. In other words, an object is nearly any *thing*. The objects in an object-oriented program can take on many different forms. Programs written for the Windows environment typically use objects such as check boxes, list boxes, and buttons. A payroll program, on the other hand, might utilize objects found in the real world, such as a time card object, an employee object, and a check object. Object-oriented programming is more simply referred to as **OOP**.

Every object in an object-oriented program is created from a **class**, which is a pattern that the computer uses to create the object. The class contains the instructions that tell the computer how the object should look and behave. An object created from a class is called an **instance** of the class and is said to be **instantiated** from the class. An analogy involving a cookie cutter and cookies is often used to describe a class and its objects: The class is the cookie cutter, and the objects instantiated from the class are the cookies. You will learn more about classes and objects throughout this book.

You can use Visual Basic to create applications for the Windows environment or for the Web. A Windows application has a Windows user interface and runs on a personal computer. A **user interface** is what the user sees and interacts with while an application is running. Examples of Windows applications include graphics programs, data-entry systems, and games. A Web application, on the other hand, has a Web user interface and runs on a server. You access a Web application using your computer's browser. Examples of Web applications include e-commerce applications available on the Internet and employee handbook applications accessible on a company's intranet. You can also use Visual Basic to create applications for tablet PCs and mobile devices, such as smartphones.

Starting and Configuring Visual Studio

Before you can create an application in Visual Basic, you must start Visual Studio. The steps for starting Visual Studio Community 2015 are listed in the How To box shown in Figure 1-1. Your steps may differ slightly if you are using a different edition of Visual Studio 2015. As mentioned in the Overview, you are not expected to follow the steps listed in a How To box right now. Rather, the steps are intended to be used as a quick reference while you are completing the Programming Tutorials, Programming Example, Exercises, and Case Projects located at the end of each chapter. For now, simply skim the How To box to see what it contains.

The Windows 10 Start button looks like this: ⊞.

HOW TO Start Visual Studio Community 2015

1. Click the Start button on the Windows 10 taskbar, click All apps, click the Visual Studio 2015 folder on the Start menu, and then click Visual Studio 2015.
2. *If the Choose Default Environment Settings dialog box appears*, click Visual Basic Development Settings and then click Start Visual Studio.

   If the Choose Default Environment Settings dialog box does not appear, you can select the appropriate settings (if necessary) as follows: click Tools on the menu bar, click Import and Export Settings, select the Reset all settings radio button, click the Next button, select the appropriate radio button, click the Next button, click Visual Basic, click the Finish button, and then click the Close button to close the Import and Export Settings Wizard dialog box.
3. To reset the IDE to the default layout for Visual Basic, click Window on the menu bar, click Reset Window Layout, and then click the Yes button.
4. To temporarily show/hide the underlined letters (called access keys) in the menu bar, press the Alt key on your keyboard. To permanently show/hide the access keys, right-click the Start button, click Control Panel, and then click Appearance and Personalization. In the Ease of Access Center section, click Turn on easy access keys. Select the Underline keyboard shortcuts and access keys check box, and then click the OK button. Close the Ease of Access Center window.

Note: The instructions for starting Visual Studio Community 2015 using Windows 8 are contained in the VbReloaded2015\Chap01\Starting Using Windows 8.pdf file.

Figure 1-1 How to start Visual Studio Community 2015

The How To box in Figure 1-2 contains the steps for configuring Visual Studio so that your screen and Programming Tutorial steps agree with the figures and tutorial steps in this book. You will be guided through performing these steps in Programming Tutorial 1 in this chapter. Figure 1-3 shows the Options dialog box mentioned in the steps.

HOW TO Configure Visual Studio Community 2015

1. Click Tools on the menu bar, and then click Options to open the Options dialog box. Click the Projects and Solutions node. Use the information shown in Figure 1-3 to select and deselect the appropriate check boxes.
2. Click the Debugging node and then deselect the Step over properties and operators (Managed only) check box. Also deselect the Enable Diagnostic Tools while debugging check box and the Show elapsed time PerfTip while debugging check box, which appear near the bottom of the list.
3. Click the OK button to close the Options dialog box.

Note: If you change your default environment settings *after* performing these three steps, you will need to perform the steps again.

Figure 1-2 How to configure Visual Studio Community 2015

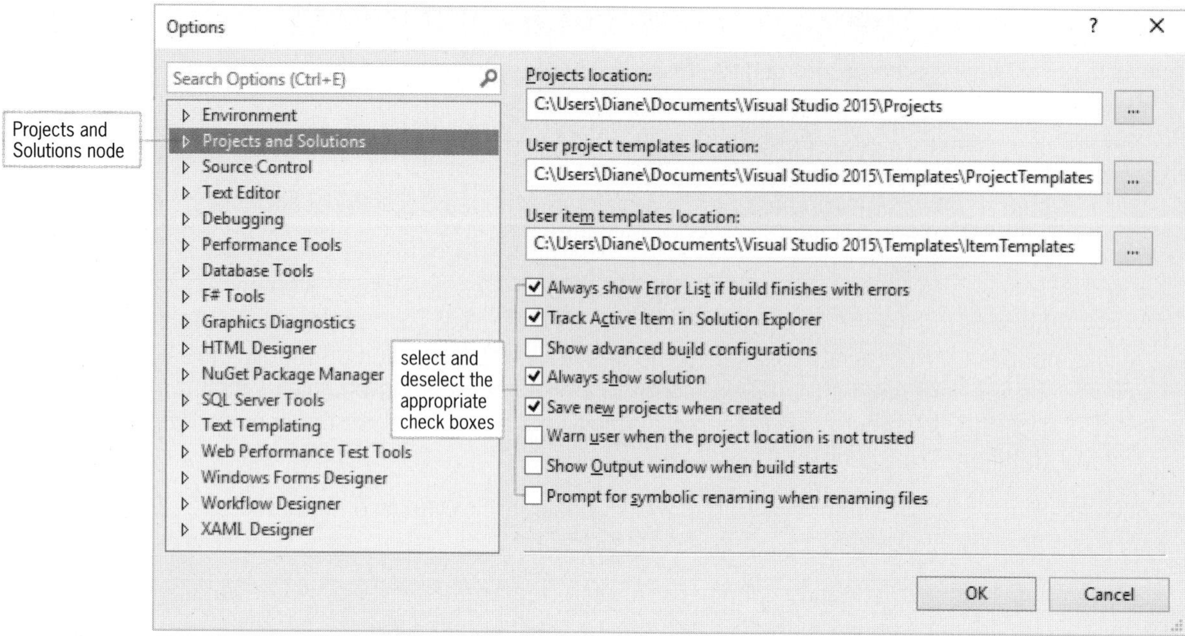

Figure 1-3 Options dialog box

When you start Visual Studio Community 2015, your screen will appear similar to Figure 1-4. However, your Recent list might include the names of projects or solutions with which you have recently worked. In addition, your menu bar may not contain the underlined letters, called access keys. As mentioned earlier in Figure 1-1, you can use the Alt key to temporarily display the access keys. You will learn about access keys in Chapter 2.

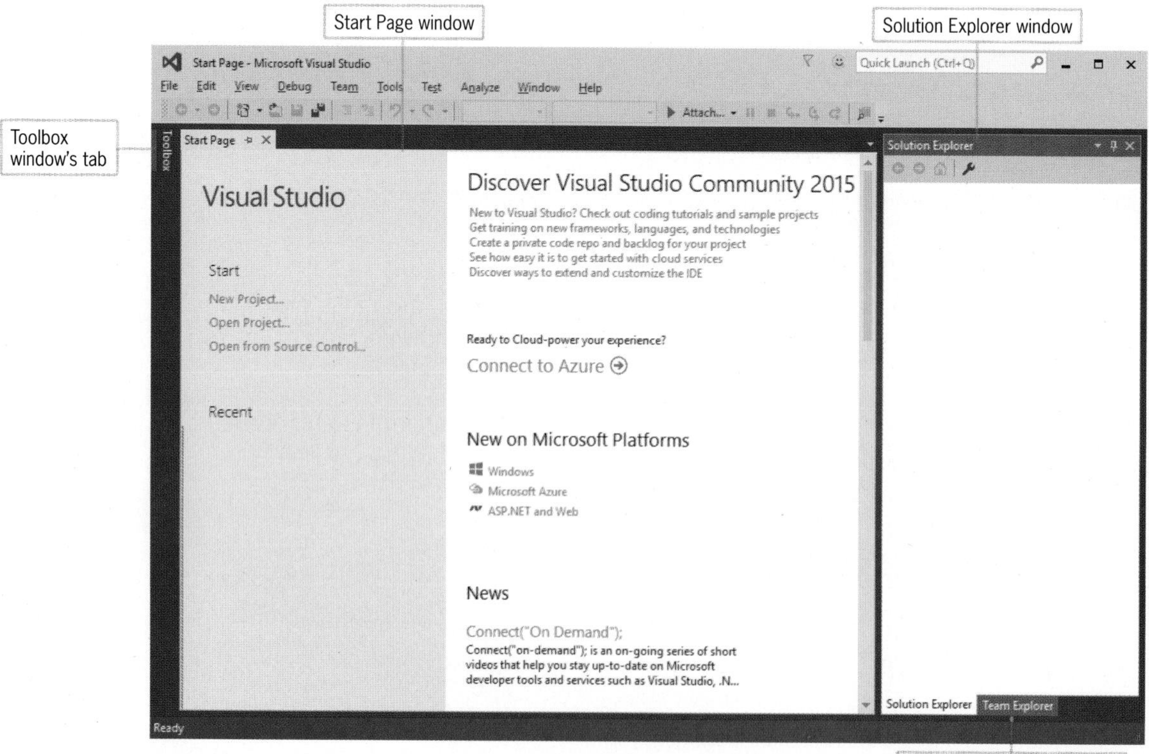

Figure 1-4 Microsoft Visual Studio Community 2015 startup screen

Creating a Visual Basic Windows Forms Application

Windows applications in Visual Basic are composed of solutions, projects, and files. A solution is a container that stores the projects and files for an entire application. Although the solutions in this book contain only one project, a solution can contain several projects. A project is also a container, but it stores only the files associated with that particular project.

The steps for creating a Visual Basic 2015 Windows Forms application are shown in Figure 1-5. Here again, you don't need to perform the steps right now; just glance over the figure to familiarize yourself with its contents. Figure 1-6 shows an example of the New Project dialog box mentioned in the steps.

HOW TO Create a Visual Basic 2015 Windows Forms Application

1. If necessary, start Visual Studio 2015.
2. Click File on the menu bar, and then click New Project to open the New Project dialog box.
3. If necessary, expand the Installed node and then expand the Templates node. Click the Visual Basic node in the Installed Templates list, and then click Windows Forms Application in the middle column of the dialog box.
4. Enter an appropriate name and location in the Name and Location boxes, respectively. (You can use the Browse button to enter the location.)
5. If necessary, select the Create directory for solution check box.
6. Enter an appropriate name in the Solution name box. Figure 1-6 shows an example of a completed New Project dialog box.
7. Click the OK button to close the New Project dialog box.

Figure 1-5 How to create a Visual Basic 2015 Windows Forms application

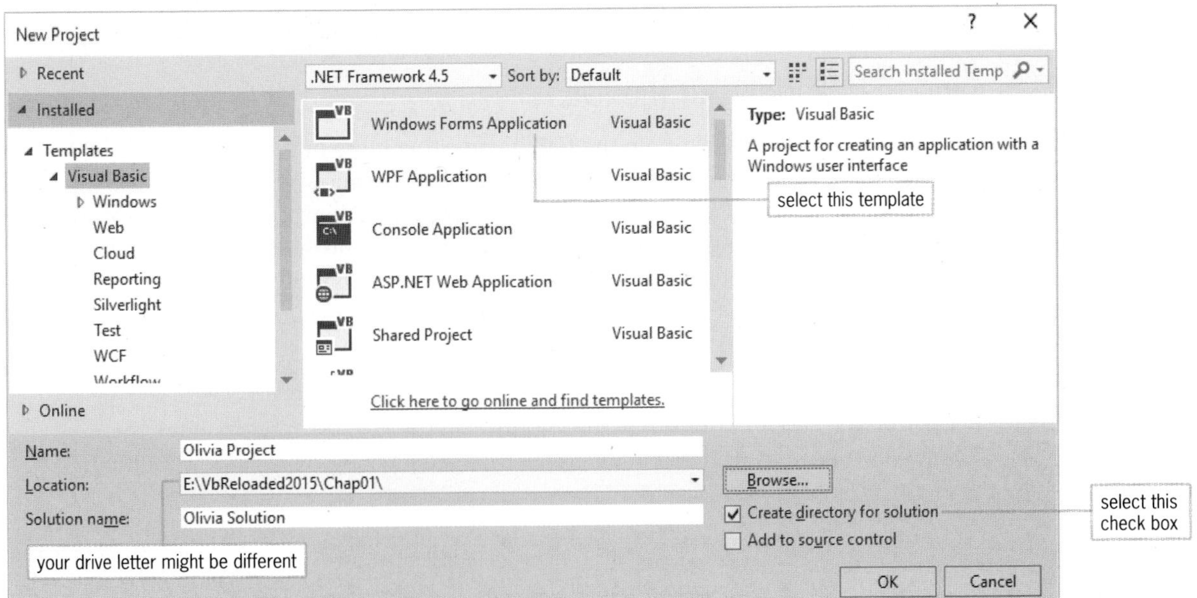

Figure 1-6 New Project dialog box

When you click the OK button in the New Project dialog box, the computer creates a solution and adds a Visual Basic project to the solution. The names of the solution and project appear in the Solution Explorer window, along with other information pertaining to the project, as shown in Figure 1-7. In addition to the windows shown earlier in Figure 1-4, three other windows appear in the IDE: Windows Form Designer, Properties, and Data Sources.

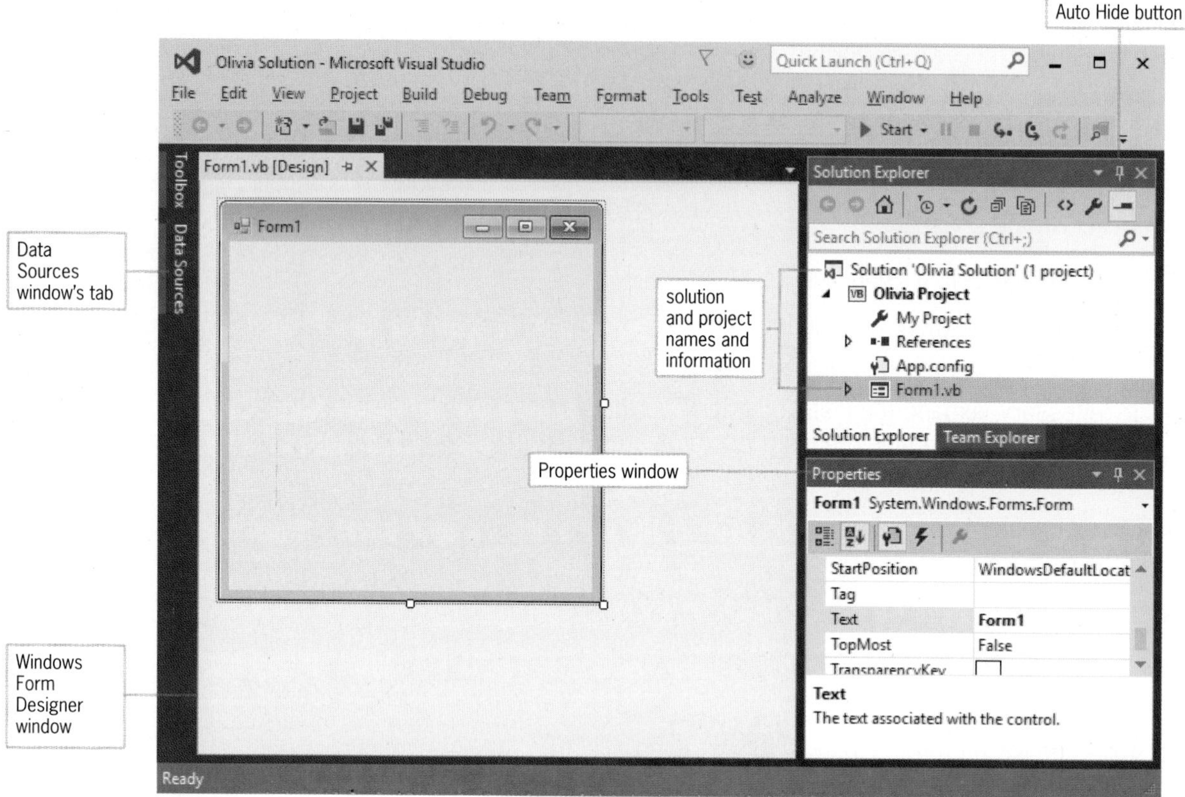

Figure 1-7 Solution and Visual Basic project

Managing the Windows in the IDE

Usually, you will find it easier to work in the IDE if you either close or auto-hide the windows you are not currently using. The easiest way to close an open window is to click the Close button on its title bar. In most cases, the View menu provides an appropriate option for opening a closed window. In addition to closing a window, you can also auto-hide it. You auto-hide a window using the Auto Hide button (refer to Figure 1-7) on the window's title bar. The Auto Hide button is a toggle button: Clicking it once activates it, and clicking it again deactivates it. When a window is auto-hidden, it appears as a tab on either the right or left border of the IDE. The Toolbox and Data Sources windows in Figure 1-7 are auto-hidden windows.

Figure 1-8 lists various ways of managing the windows in the IDE. As mentioned in the Overview, you don't need to read every bulleted item in a How To box right now. But you should browse the How To box to get familiar with its contents.

HOW TO Manage the Windows in the IDE

- To close an open window, click the Close button on its title bar.
- To open a closed window, use an option on the View menu.
- To auto-hide a window, click the Auto Hide (vertical pushpin) button on its title bar.
- To temporarily display an auto-hidden window, click the window's tab. To subsequently hide the window, click the tab again.
- To permanently display an auto-hidden window, click the Auto Hide (horizontal pushpin) button on its title bar.
- To reset the window layout, click Window on the menu bar, click Reset Window Layout, and then click the Yes button.

Figure 1-8 How to manage the windows in the IDE

In the next several sections, you will take a closer look at the Windows Form Designer, Solution Explorer, Properties, and Toolbox windows.

The Windows Form Designer Window

Figure 1-9 shows the **Windows Form Designer window**, where you create (or design) your application's graphical user interface, more simply referred to as a **GUI**. Only a Windows Form object appears in the designer window shown in the figure. A **Windows Form object**, or **form**, is the foundation for the user interface in a Windows application. You create the user interface by adding other objects, such as buttons and text boxes, to the form. Notice that a title bar appears at the top of the form. The title bar contains a default caption (Form1) along with Minimize, Maximize, and Close buttons.

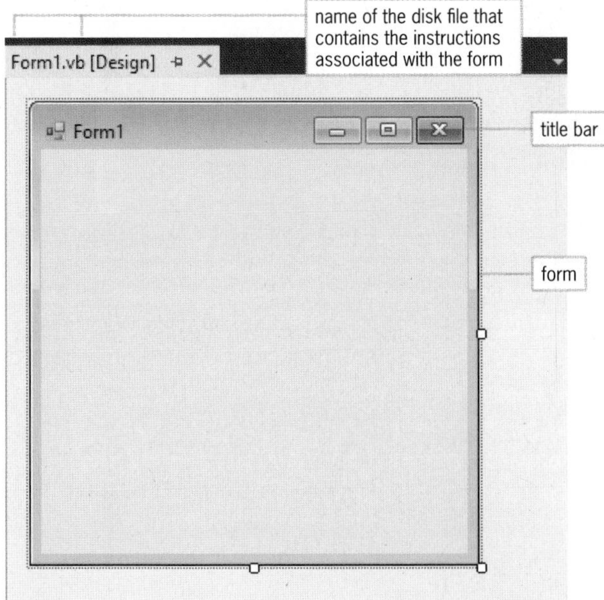

Figure 1-9 Windows Form Designer window

At the top of the designer window is a tab labeled Form1.vb [Design]. Form1.vb is the name of the file (on your computer's hard disk or on another device) that contains the Visual Basic instructions associated with the form, and [Design] identifies the window as the designer window.

As you learned earlier in this chapter, all objects in an object-oriented program are instantiated (created) from a class. A form, for example, is an instance of the Windows Form class. The form (an object) is automatically instantiated for you when you create a Windows application.

The Solution Explorer Window

The **Solution Explorer window** displays a list of the projects contained in the current solution and the items contained in each project. Figure 1-10 shows the Solution Explorer window for the Olivia Solution, which contains one project named Olivia Project. One of the items within the project is a file named Form1.vb. The .vb extension on the filename indicates that the file is a Visual Basic **source file**, which is a file that contains program instructions, called **code**. The Form1.vb file contains the code associated with the form displayed in the designer window. You can view the code using the Code Editor window, which you will learn about in the *The Code Editor Window* section of this chapter.

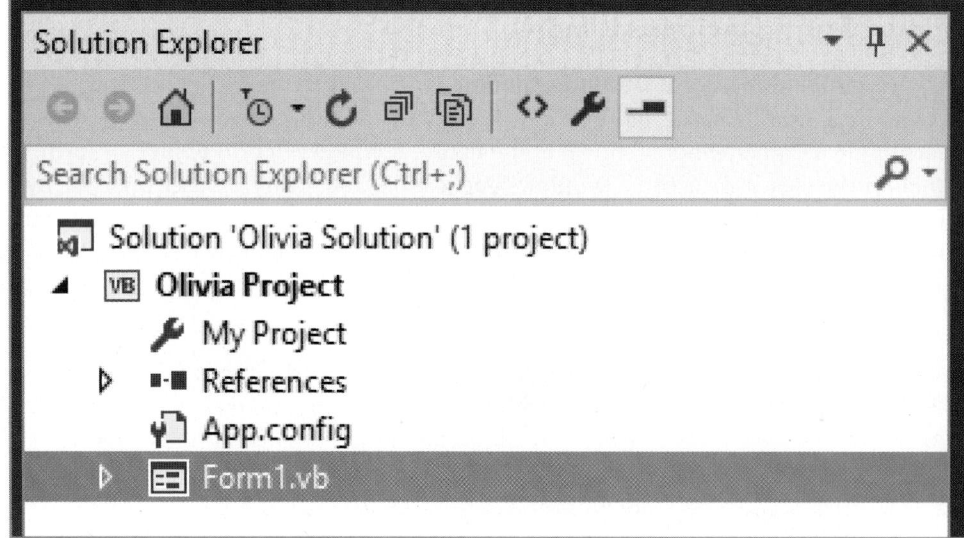

Figure 1-10 Solution Explorer window

The Form1.vb source file is referred to as a **form file** because it contains the code associated with a form. The code associated with the first form included in a project is automatically stored in a form file named Form1.vb. The code associated with the second form in the same project is stored in a form file named Form2.vb, and so on. Because a project can contain many forms and, therefore, many form files, it is a good practice to give each form file a more meaningful name. Doing this will help you keep track of the various form files in the project. You can use the Properties window to change the filename.

The Properties Window

Like everything in an object-oriented language, a file is an object. Each object has a set of attributes, called **properties**, that determine its appearance and behavior. When an object is created, a default value is assigned to each of its properties. The properties and their default values are listed in the **Properties window** when the object is selected in either the designer window or the Solution Explorer window.

The Properties window in Figure 1-11 shows the default values assigned to the properties of the Form1.vb file. The name of the selected object (in this case, the Form1.vb file) appears in the Properties window's Object box. The names of the properties are listed in the left column of the Properties list. The names can be viewed either alphabetically or by category. However, it's usually easier to work with the Properties window when the properties are listed in alphabetical order, as they are in Figure 1-11. A property's default (or current) value appears in the right column of the Properties list, called the Settings box.

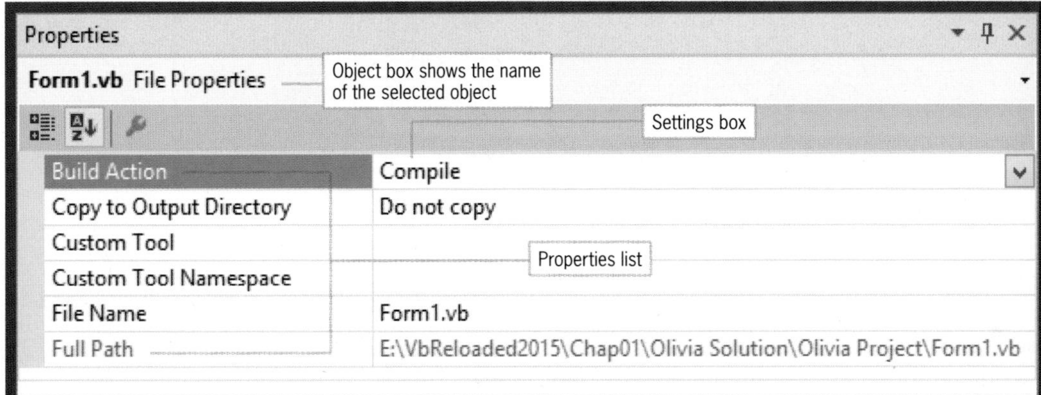

Figure 1-11 Properties window

In the context of OOP, the Properties window *exposes* an object's attributes (properties) to the programmer, allowing the programmer to change one or more default values.

To give a form file a more meaningful name (such as Main Form.vb), you click the File Name property in the Properties list, type Main Form.vb in the Settings box, and then press Enter. You can also right-click Form1.vb in the Solution Explorer window, click Rename on the context menu, type Main Form.vb, and then press Enter. Unlike the File Name property, some properties listed in the Properties window have predefined settings, and their values must be selected from a list, color palette, or dialog box. To restore a property to its default value, right-click the property in the Properties list and then click Reset on the context menu.

Properties of a Windows Form

Like a file, a Windows form also has a set of properties. The form's properties will appear in the Properties window when you select the form in the designer window. The Properties window in Figure 1-12 shows some of the properties of a Windows form. The vertical scroll bar on the Properties window indicates that there are more properties to view.

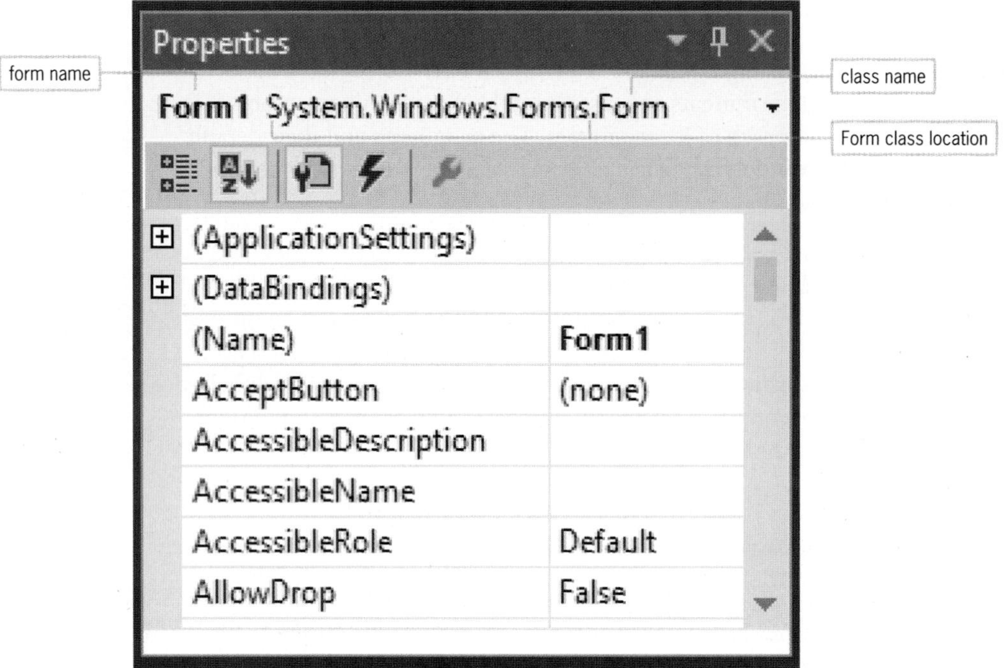

Figure 1-12 Partial list of the form's properties

Notice that *Form1 System.Windows.Forms.Form* appears in the Object box in Figure 1-12. *Form1* is the name of the form. The name is automatically assigned to the form when the form is instantiated (created). In *System.Windows.Forms.Form*, *Form* is the name of the class (pattern) used to instantiate the form. *System.Windows.Forms* is the namespace that contains the Form class definition. A **class definition** is a block of code that specifies (or defines) an object's appearance and behavior. All class definitions in Visual Basic are contained in namespaces, which you can picture as blocks of memory cells inside the computer. Each **namespace** contains the code that defines a group of related classes. The *System.Windows.Forms* namespace contains the definition of the Windows Form class. It also contains the class definitions for objects you add to a form, such as buttons and text boxes.

The period that separates each word in *System.Windows.Forms.Form* is called the **dot member access operator**. Similar to the backslash (\) in a folder path, the dot member access operator indicates a hierarchy, but of namespaces rather than folders. In other words, the backslash in the path *E:\VbReloaded2015\Chap01\Olivia Solution\Olivia Project\Form1.vb* indicates that the Form1.vb file is contained in (or is a member of) the Olivia Project folder, which is a member of the Olivia Solution folder, which is a member of the Chap01 folder, which is a member of the VbReloaded2015 folder, which is a member of the E: drive. Likewise, the name *System.Windows.Forms.Form* indicates that the Form class is a member of the Forms namespace, which is a member of the Windows namespace, which is a member of the System namespace. The dot member access operator allows the computer to locate the Form class in the computer's internal memory, similar to the way the backslash (\) allows the computer to locate the Form1.vb file on your computer's disk.

Name and Text Properties

As you do to a form file, you should assign a more meaningful name to a Windows form because doing so will help you keep track of the various forms in a project. But unlike a form file, a Windows form has a Name property rather than a File Name property. You use the name entered in an object's Name property to refer to the object in code, so each object must have a unique name. The name you assign to an object must begin with a letter and contain only letters, numbers, and the underscore character. The name cannot include punctuation characters or spaces.

There are several conventions for naming objects in Visual Basic. In this book, you will use a naming convention that begins each object's name with the object's purpose, followed by the name of its class. In addition, form names will be entered using **Pascal case**, which capitalizes the first letter in the name and the first letter of each subsequent word in the name. Following this naming convention, you might assign the name MainForm to the main form in an application. *Main* reminds you of the form's purpose, and *Form* indicates the class used to create the form. Similarly, a secondary form used to access an employee database might be named EmployeeDataForm or PersonnelForm.

In addition to changing the form's Name property, you should change its Text property, which controls the text displayed in the form's title bar. Form1 is the default value assigned to the Text property of the first form in a project. Better and more descriptive values for the Text property of a form include Commission Calculator and Employee Information.

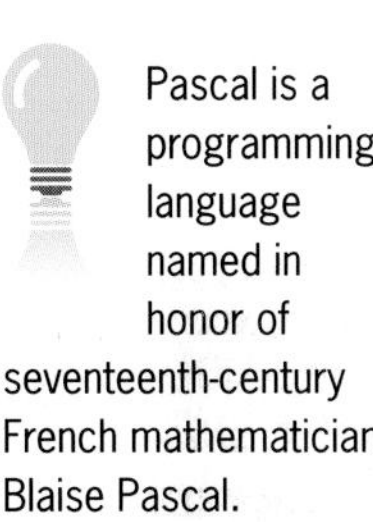

Pascal is a programming language named in honor of seventeenth-century French mathematician Blaise Pascal.

The Name and Text properties of a Windows form should always be changed to more meaningful values. The Name property is used by the programmer when coding the application. The Text property, on the other hand, is read by the user while the application is running.

StartPosition Property

When an application is started, the computer uses the form's StartPosition property to determine the form's initial position on the screen. To display a form in the middle of the screen, you change its StartPosition property from WindowsDefaultLocation to CenterScreen.

Font Property

A form's Font property determines the type, style, and size of the font used to display the text on the form. A font is the general shape of the characters in the text. Segoe UI, Tahoma, and Microsoft Sans Serif are examples of font types. Font styles include regular, bold, and italic. The numbers 9, 12, and 18 are examples of font sizes, which typically are measured in points, with one point (pt) equaling 1/72 of an inch. The recommended font for Windows applications is Segoe UI because it offers improved readability on a computer screen. Segoe is pronounced *SEE-go*, and UI stands for *user interface*. For most of the elements in the interface, you will use a 9-point font size. However, to make the figures in the book more readable, many of the interfaces created in this book will use a larger font size.

Size Property

As you can with any Windows object, you can size a form by selecting it and then dragging the sizing handles that appear around it. You can also size an object by selecting it and then pressing and holding down the Shift key as you press the up, down, right, or left arrow key on your keyboard. In addition, you can set the object's Size property. The Size property contains two numbers separated by a comma and a space, like this: 300, 250. The first number represents the object's width, and the second number represents its height. Both measurements are stated in pixels. A pixel, which is short for "picture element," is one spot in a grid of thousands of such spots that form an image either produced on the screen by a computer or printed on a page by a printer.

The answers to Mini-Quiz questions are located in Appendix A. Each question is associated with one or more objectives listed at the beginning of the chapter.

Mini-Quiz 1

1. Windows applications created in Visual Studio are composed of ____________. (2)
   a. solutions
   b. projects
   c. files
   d. all of the above
2. How do you auto-hide a window? (3)
3. How do you temporarily display an auto-hidden window? (3)
4. How do you reset the windows in the IDE? (3)
5. The value assigned to a form's ____________ property appears in the form's title bar. (4)
   a. Caption
   b. Name
   c. Text
   d. Title
6. You can display a form in the middle of the screen by setting the form's ____________ property to CenterScreen. (4)
   a. StartPosition
   b. ScreenLocation
   c. StartLocation
   d. CenterScreen

The Toolbox Window

Using OOP terminology, the control's Font property *inherits* the value stored in the form's Font property.

Figure 1-13 shows a portion of the Toolbox window that appears when you are using the Windows Form Designer. The **Toolbox window**, referred to more simply as the **toolbox**, contains the tools you use when creating your application's user interface. Each tool represents a class from which an object, such as a button or text box, can be instantiated. The instantiated objects, called **controls**, will appear on the form. Figure 1-14 lists the steps for adding a control to a form. If the added control has a Font property, it will be assigned the same value as the form's Font property.

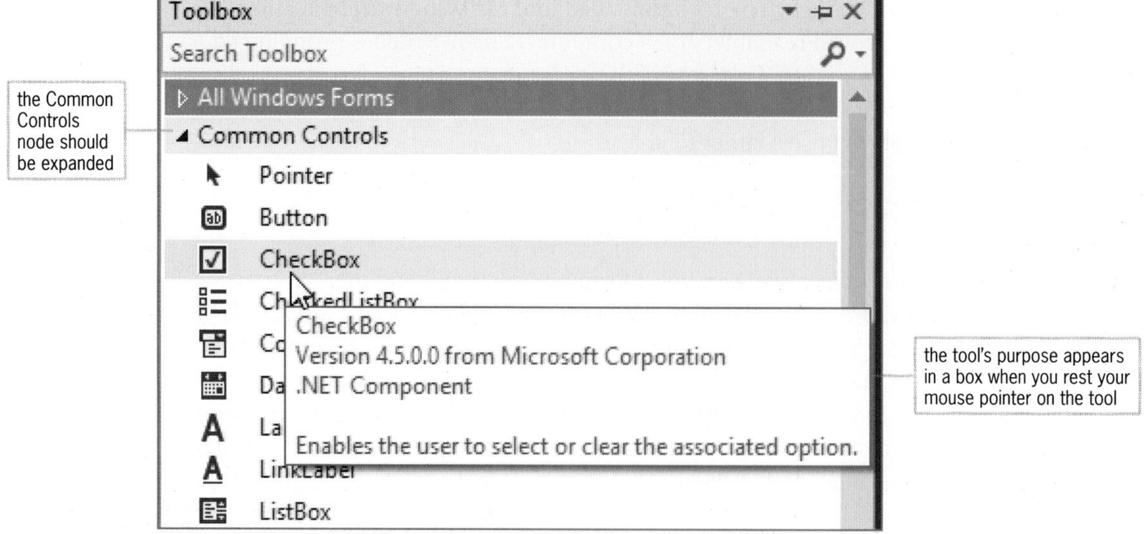

Figure 1-13 Toolbox window

Ch01-Adding a Control

HOW TO Add a Control to a Form

1. Click a tool in the toolbox, but do not release the mouse button.
2. Hold down the left mouse button as you drag the mouse pointer to the form. You will see a solid box, an outline of a rectangle, and a plus box following the mouse pointer.
3. Release the mouse button.

Additional ways:

- Click a tool in the toolbox and then click the form.
- Click a tool in the toolbox, place the mouse pointer on the form, and then press the left mouse button and drag the mouse pointer until the control is the desired size.
- Double-click a tool in the toolbox.

Figure 1-14 How to add a control to a form

Controls on a form can be selected, sized, moved, deleted, restored, locked, and unlocked. Locking a control prevents it from being moved inadvertently as you are working in the IDE. When a control is locked, a small lock appears in the upper-left corner of the control. Figure 1-15 summarizes the methods used to manipulate the controls on a form.

Ch01-Manipulating Controls

HOW TO Manipulate the Controls on a Form

- To select a control, click it in the designer window. You can also click the list arrow button in the Properties window's Object box and then click the control's name.
- To size a control, either drag the sizing handles that appear on the control when it is selected or set its Size property.
- To move a control, either drag the control to the desired location or set its Location property.
- To delete a control, select the control in the designer window and then press the Delete key on your keyboard. To restore the control, click Edit on the menu bar and then click Undo.
- To lock and unlock the controls, right-click the form (or any control on the form), and then click Lock Controls on the context menu. The Lock Controls option is a toggle option: Clicking it once activates it, and clicking it again deactivates it. You can also click Format on the menu bar and then click Lock Controls.

Figure 1-15 How to manipulate the controls on a form

In the next three sections, you will learn about the label, button, and picture box controls, which appear in the user interface shown in Figure 1-16. As you will learn in Programming Tutorial 1, the interface actually contains two picture boxes; one is hidden behind the other in the figure.

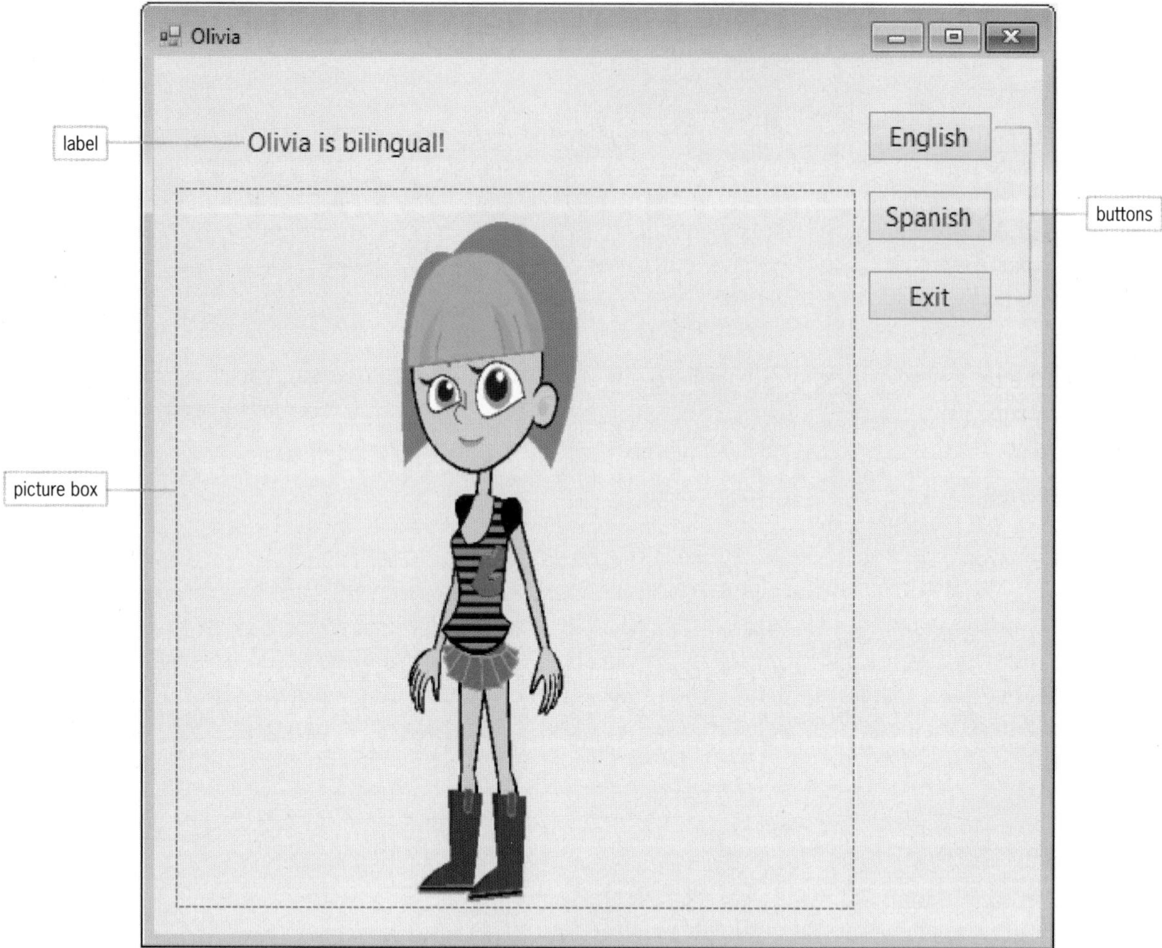

Figure 1-16 Olivia application's user interface

Image by Diane Zak; created with Reallusion CrazyTalk Animator

The Label Control

You use the Label tool to add a label control to a form. The purpose of a **label control** is to display text that the user is not allowed to edit while the application is running. Label controls are used in an interface to identify the contents of other controls, such as the contents of text boxes and list boxes. The label control in Figure 1-16 identifies the contents of a picture box control. Label controls are also used to display program output, such as the result of a calculation.

A label control's Name property allows you to give the control a more meaningful name, and its Text property allows you to specify the text to display inside the control. The Name property is used by the programmer when coding the application, whereas the Text property is read by the user while the application is running.

A label control's border is determined by its BorderStyle property, which is usually set to either None (the default) or FixedSingle. When the property is set to None, the label control does not have a border. Setting the property to FixedSingle surrounds the control with a thin line. The None setting is used for labels that identify other controls, whereas the FixedSingle setting is typically used for labels that display program output. (Although a label control's

BorderStyle property can also be set to Fixed3D, you should avoid doing so because in Windows applications, a control with a three-dimensional appearance implies that it can accept user input.)

A label control's AutoSize property determines whether the control either automatically sizes to fit its current contents (True) or remains static (False). This property is left at its default setting (True) for labels that identify other controls, but it is typically set to False for labels that display program output. A word of caution is in order at this point: If you remove the contents of a label's Text property when its AutoSize and BorderStyle properties are set to True and None, respectively, you will not see the label on the form. You will need to use the Properties window's Object box to access the label.

You can align the text that appears inside a label control using the control's TextAlign property. The property can be set to nine different values, such as TopLeft, MiddleCenter, and BottomRight.

Some programmers assign meaningful names to all of the label controls in an interface, while others do so only for label controls that display program output; this book follows the latter practice. In the naming convention used in this book, control names are made up of the control's purpose followed by the control's class (in this case, Label). Unlike form names, which are entered using Pascal case, control names are entered using **camel case**. This means that you enter the first word in the control's name in lowercase and then capitalize the first letter of each subsequent word in the name, like this: salesTaxLabel. Camel case refers to the fact that the uppercase letters appear as "humps" in the name because they are taller than the lowercase letters.

The Button Control

You use the Button tool to instantiate a **button control**, whose purpose is to perform an immediate action when clicked. The OK and Cancel buttons are examples of button controls found in many Windows applications. Each button in the interface shown earlier in Figure 1-16 will perform an action when it is clicked. The English and Spanish buttons will display different animated images of a character named Olivia, and the Exit button will close the application. Here too, you use the Name property to give a button control a more meaningful name. The name should end with the word *Button*, which is the class from which a button control is created. You use the Text property to specify the text to display on the button's face.

The Picture Box Control

The PictureBox tool instantiates a **picture box control** for displaying an image on the form, such as the image of Olivia shown earlier in Figure 1-16. You use the control's Name property to assign a more meaningful name (which should end with PictureBox) to the control, and use its Image property to specify the image to display. A PictureBox control's SizeMode property handles how the image will be displayed and can be set to Normal, StretchImage, AutoSize, CenterImage, or Zoom.

Using the Format Menu

The Format menu provides options for aligning and sizing two or more controls, as well as centering one or more controls on the form. Three of the options are listed and explained in Figure 1-17.

Ch01-Format menu

HOW TO Use the Format Menu to Align/Size/Center Controls

- To align/size two or more controls: Click the reference control, and then press and hold down the Ctrl (Control) key as you click the other controls you want to align/size. Click Format on the menu bar and then click one of the following options:
  - ✓ Align option: aligns two or more controls by their left, right, top, or bottom borders
  - ✓ Make Same Size option: makes two or more controls the same width and/or height
- To center one or more controls either horizontally or vertically on the form: Click a control that you want to center, and then (if necessary) press and hold down the Ctrl (Control) key as you click the other controls you want to center. Click Format on the menu bar, and then click the following option:
  - ✓ Center in Form option: centers one or more controls either horizontally or vertically on the form

Note: To select a group of controls on the form, place the mouse pointer slightly above and to the left of the first control you want to select. Press and hold down the left mouse button as you drag the mouse pointer. A dotted rectangle appears as you are dragging. When all of the controls you want to select are within (or at least touched by) the dotted rectangle, release the mouse button.

Figure 1-17 How to use the Format menu to align/size/center controls

When aligning and sizing controls, the first control you select should always be the one whose location and/or size you want to match. For example, to align the left border of the Label2 control with the left border of the Label1 control, you select the Label1 control first and then select the Label2 control. However, to make the Label1 control the same size as the Label2 control, you must select the Label2 control before selecting the Label1 control. The first control you select is referred to as the **reference control**. The reference control will have white sizing handles, whereas the other selected controls will have black sizing handles. You will experiment with the Format menu in both Programming Tutorials at the end of this chapter.

The answers to Mini-Quiz questions are located in Appendix A. Each question is associated with one or more objectives listed at the beginning of the chapter.

Mini-Quiz 2

1. How do you delete a control from the form? (5)
2. Amounts calculated by an application should be displayed in a ____________ control on the form. (4, 6)
   a. button
   b. form
   c. label
   d. text
3. Using the naming convention you learned in this book, which of the following is a valid name for a control? (4, 6)
   a. calcButton
   b. salesTaxLabel
   c. birthdayPictureBox
   d. all of the above

4. Which of the following properties determines the image that appears in a picture box? (4, 6)
   a. Icon
   b. Image
   c. Picture
   d. none of the above
5. If you want to use the Format menu to align the top border of the Label5 control with the top border of the Label4 control, which of the two controls should you select first? (7)
6. Which of the following properties determines the alignment of the text within a label control? (4, 6)
   a. Alignment
   b. AlignText
   c. TextAlign
   d. TextAlignment

The Code Editor Window

After creating your application's user interface, you can begin entering the Visual Basic instructions (code) that tell the controls how to respond to the user's actions. Those actions—such as clicking and double-clicking—are called **events**. You tell a control how to respond to an event by writing an **event procedure**, which is a set of Visual Basic instructions that are processed only when the event occurs. You enter the procedure's code in the **Code Editor window**. Figure 1-18 lists various ways to open the Code Editor window, and Figure 1-19 shows the Code Editor window opened in the IDE.

In OOP, an event is considered a behavior of an object because it represents an action to which the object can respond. The Code Editor window *exposes* an object's behaviors to the programmer.

HOW TO Open the Code Editor Window

- Right-click the form and then click View Code on the context menu.
- Verify that the designer window is the active window. Click View on the menu bar and then click Code.
- Verify that the designer window is the active window. Press the F7 key on your keyboard.
- Click the form or a control on the form, click the Events button in the Properties window, and then double-click the desired event.

Note: To display line numbers in the Code Editor window, click Tools on the menu bar and then click Options. Click the arrow next to Text Editor to expand the node, click Basic, select the Line numbers check box, and then click the OK button.

Figure 1-18 How to open the Code Editor window

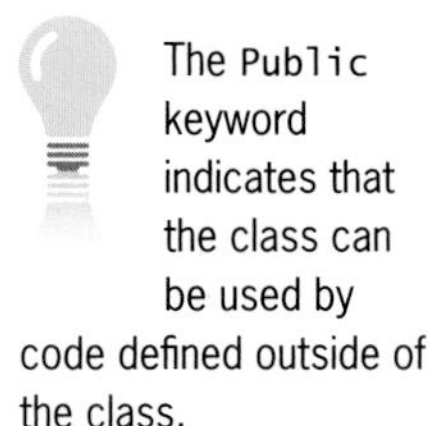

The Public keyword indicates that the class can be used by code defined outside of the class.

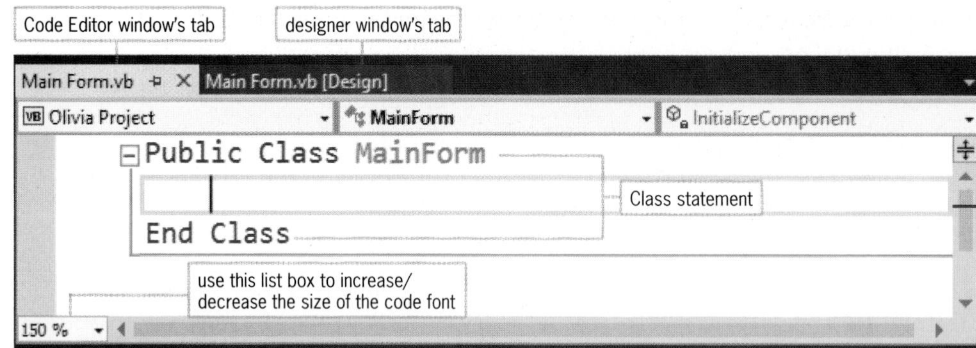

Figure 1-19 Code Editor window

The Code Editor window contains the Class statement, which is used to define a class in Visual Basic. Between the statement's Public Class and End Class clauses, you enter the code to tell the form and its objects how to react to the user's actions.

As Figure 1-20 indicates, the Code Editor window contains three dropdown list boxes named Project, Object, and Method. The Project box contains the name of the current project, Olivia Project. The Object box lists the names of the objects included in the user interface, and the Method box lists the events to which the selected object is capable of responding. You use the Object and Method list boxes to select the object and event, respectively, that you want to code. For example, to code the exitButton's Click event, you first select exitButton in the Object list box and then select Click in the Method list box. When you do this, a code template for the exitButton's Click event procedure appears in the Code Editor window, as shown in Figure 1-20. The code template helps you follow the rules of the Visual Basic language. The rules of a programming language are called its **syntax**.

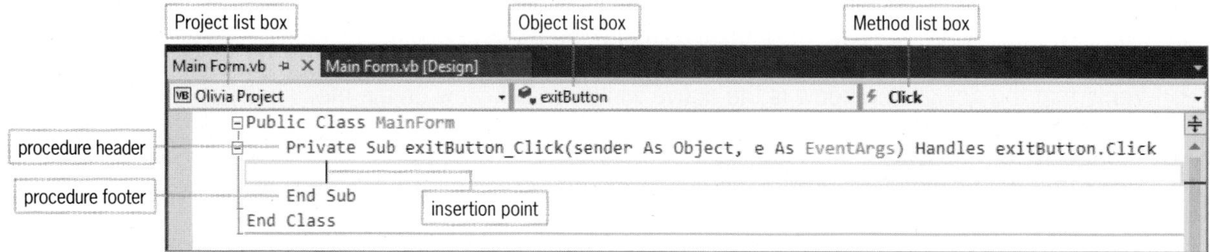

Figure 1-20 Code template for the exitButton_Click procedure

The first line in the code template is called the **procedure header**, and the last line is called the **procedure footer**. The procedure header begins with the two keywords `Private Sub`. A **keyword** is a word that has a special meaning in a programming language. Keywords appear in a different color from the rest of the code. The `Private` keyword in Figure 1-20 indicates that the button's Click event procedure can be used only within the current Code Editor window. The `Sub` keyword is an abbreviation of the term **sub procedure**, which is a block of code that performs a specific task.

Following the `Sub` keyword is the name of the object, an underscore, the name of the event, and parentheses containing some text. For now, you do not have to be concerned with the text that appears between the parentheses. After the closing parenthesis is the following Handles clause: `Handles exitButton.Click`. This clause indicates that the procedure handles (or is associated with) the exitButton's Click event. It tells the computer to process the procedure only when the exitButton is clicked.

The code template ends with the procedure footer, which contains the keywords `End Sub`. You enter your Visual Basic instructions at the location of the insertion point, which appears between the Private Sub and End Sub clauses in Figure 1-20. The Code Editor automatically indents the line between the procedure header and footer. Indenting the lines within a procedure makes the instructions easier to read and is a common programming practice.

When the user clicks an Exit button on a form, it usually indicates that he or she wants to end the application. You can stop an application using the `Me.Close()` instruction.

The `Me.Close()` Instruction

The `Me.Close()` instruction tells the computer to close the current form. If the current form is the only form in the application, closing it terminates the entire application. In the instruction, `Me` is a keyword that refers to the current form, and `Close` is one of the methods available in Visual Basic. A **method** is a predefined procedure that you can call (or invoke) when needed. If you want the computer to close the current form when the user clicks the Exit button, you enter the `Me.Close()` instruction in the button's Click event procedure, as shown in Figure 1-21. Notice the empty set of parentheses after the method's name in the instruction. The parentheses are required when calling some Visual Basic methods. However, depending on the method, the parentheses may or may not be empty. If you forget to enter the parentheses, the Code Editor will enter them for you when you move the insertion point to another line in the Code Editor window.

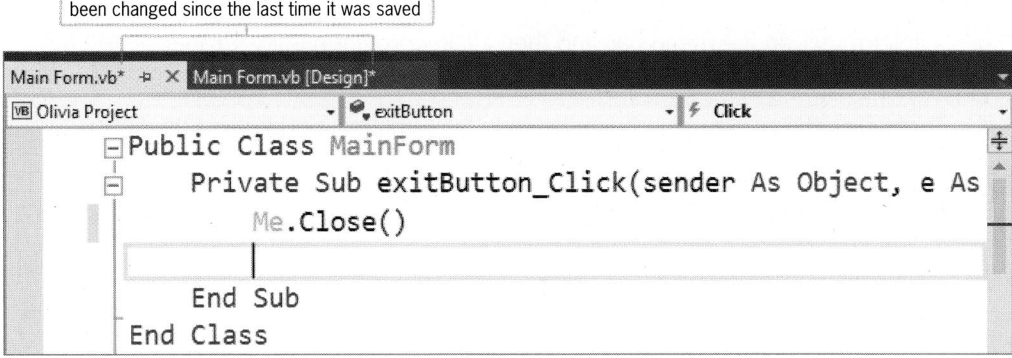

Figure 1-21 `Me.Close()` instruction entered in the exitButton_Click procedure

When the user clicks the Exit button while the application is running, the computer processes the instructions contained in the exitButton_Click procedure one after another in the order in which they appear in the procedure. In programming, this is referred to as **sequential processing** or as the **sequence structure**. (You will learn about two other programming structures, called selection and repetition, in later chapters.)

Saving a Solution

The asterisk (*) that appears on the designer and Code Editor tabs in Figure 1-21 indicates that a change was made to the solution since the last time it was saved. It is a good idea to save the current solution every 10 or 15 minutes so that you will not lose a lot of your work if a power outage unexpectedly occurs. When you save a solution, the computer saves any changes made to the files included in the solution. It also removes the asterisk that appears on the designer and Code Editor tabs. Figure 1-22 lists two ways to save a solution.

HOW TO Save a Solution

- Click File on the menu bar and then click Save All.
- Click the Save All button (the two disks) on the Standard toolbar.

Figure 1-22 How to save a solution

Starting and Ending an Application

Before you start an application for the first time, you should open the Project Designer window and verify the name of the **startup form**, which is the form that the computer automatically displays each time the application is started. Figure 1-23 shows the steps you follow to specify the startup form's name, and Figure 1-24 shows the name of the startup form (in this case, MainForm) selected in the Project Designer window.

HOW TO Specify the Startup Form

1. Use one of the following ways to open the Project Designer window:
   - ✓ Right-click My Project in the Solution Explorer window and then click Open on the context menu.
   - ✓ Click Project on the menu bar and then click <*project name*> Properties on the menu.
   - ✓ Right-click the project's name in the Solution Explorer window and then click Properties.
2. Click the Application tab, if necessary.
3. If the startup form's name does not appear in the Startup form list box, click the Startup form list arrow and then click the appropriate form name in the list.
4. Click the Close button on the Project Designer window.

Figure 1-23 How to specify the startup form

Figure 1-24 Project Designer window

Figure 1-25 shows various ways to start an application, and Figure 1-26 shows the result of starting the Olivia application. The computer automatically displays the startup form, which in this case is the MainForm. Notice that only the label and three buttons are visible when the application appears on the screen. As you will learn in Programming Tutorial 1, this is because the Visible properties of both picture boxes are set to False.

HOW TO Start an Application

- Save the solution, click Debug on the menu bar, and then click Start Debugging.
- Save the solution and then press the F5 key on your keyboard.
- Save the solution and then click the Start button on the Standard toolbar.

Figure 1-25 How to start an application

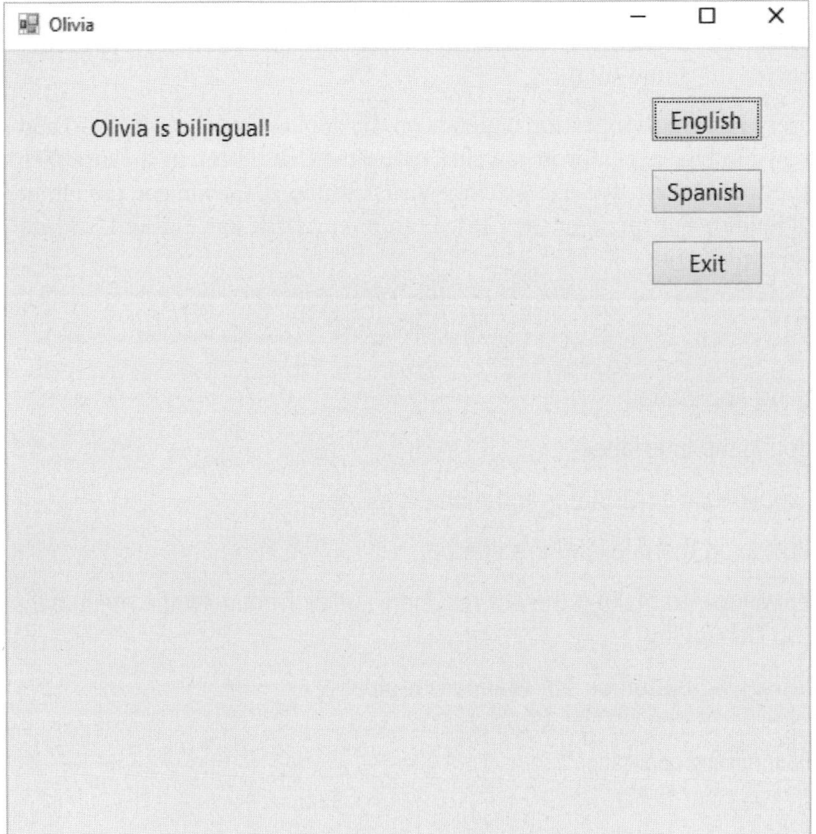

Figure 1-26 Result of starting the Olivia application

When you start a Visual Basic application, the computer creates an **executable file**, which is a file that can be run outside of the IDE. The executable file's name is the same as the project's name, except it ends with .exe. The name of the executable file for the Olivia Project, for example, is Olivia Project.exe. You can use the Project Designer window to change the executable file's name, or you can use Windows to rename the file. The steps for using the Project Designer window are listed in Figure 1-27.

HOW TO Change the Executable File's Name in the Project Designer Window

1. Open the Project Designer window using one of the ways listed earlier in Figure 1-23.
2. Click the Application tab, if necessary.
3. Replace the current name in the Assembly name box with the new name. For example, to change the executable file's name from Olivia Project.exe to Olivia.exe, replace the Olivia Project text in the Assembly name box with Olivia. Visual Basic will automatically append the .exe extension on the filename when the application is started.
4. Click the Close button on the Project Designer window.

Figure 1-27 How to change the executable file's name in the Project Designer window

The computer stores the executable file in the project's bin\Debug folder. In this case, the file will be stored in the VbReloaded2015\Chap01\Olivia Solution\Olivia Project\bin\Debug folder. When you are finished with an application, you typically give the user only the executable file because it does not allow the user to modify the application's code. To allow someone to modify the code, you need to provide the entire solution.

The way you end (or close) a running application depends on the application's interface. To end the Olivia application shown in Figure 1-26, you can click either the Exit button in the interface or the Close button on the application's title bar. To close Visual Studio 2015, you can use either the Exit option on Visual Studio's File menu or the Close button on its title bar. Figure 1-28 lists various ways of ending an application.

HOW TO End a Running Application

- Click an Exit button in the interface.
- Click File on the application's menu bar and then click Exit.
- Click the Close button on the application's title bar.
- Click the designer window to make it the active window, click Debug on the menu bar and then click Stop Debugging.
- Click the Stop Debugging button on the Standard toolbar.

Figure 1-28 How to end a running application

Assigning a Value to a Property During Run Time

As you learned earlier, you use the Properties window to set an object's properties during design time, which is when you are building the interface. You can also set an object's properties while an application is running by using an **assignment statement**, which is one of many different types of Visual Basic instructions. The purpose of an assignment statement is to assign a value to something (such as to the property of an object) during run time.

Figure 1-29 shows the syntax of an assignment statement that assigns a value to an object's property. In the syntax, *object* and *property* are the names of the object and property, respectively, to which you want the value of the *expression* assigned. You use the dot member access operator (a period) to separate the object name from the property name. The operator indicates that the *property* is a member of the *object*. You use an equal sign between the *object.property* information and the *expression*. The equal sign in an assignment statement is called the **assignment operator**.

HOW TO Assign a Value to an Object's Property During Run Time

Syntax
object.property = expression

assignment operator

dot member access operator

Example 1
```
grossPayLabel.Width = 400
```
assigns the number 400 to the grossPayLabel's Width property

Example 2
```
companyLabel.Text = "Lakeside Hotels"
```
assigns the string "Lakeside Hotels" to the companyLabel's Text property

Example 3
```
goPictureBox.Visible = True
```
assigns the keyword `True` to the goPictureBox's Visible property

Figure 1-29 How to assign a value to an object's property during run time

The expression in an assignment statement can be numeric, as shown in Example 1 in Figure 1-29. It can also be a string, as shown in Example 2. A **string** is zero or more characters enclosed in quotation marks. The expression can also be a keyword, as shown in Example 3 in the figure. When the computer processes an assignment statement, it assigns the value of the expression that appears on the right side of the assignment operator to the object and property that appear on the left side of the assignment operator.

Figure 1-30 shows the appropriate assignment statements entered in the Olivia application's Code Editor window. The englishButton's Click event procedure assigns the keyword `True` to the englishPictureBox's Visible property and assigns the keyword `False` to the spanishPictureBox's Visible property. (As mentioned earlier, the application's interface actually contains two picture boxes; one is hidden behind the other.) When an object's Visible property is set to True, the object is visible on the form while an application is running. Setting the property to False makes the object invisible during run time. The spanishButton's Click event procedure, on the other hand, assigns the keyword `True` to the spanishPictureBox's Visible property and assigns the keyword `False` to the englishPictureBox's Visible property. (You will create the Olivia application in Programming Tutorial 1.)

```
Public Class MainForm
    Private Sub englishButton_Click(sender As Object, e As EventArgs) Handles englishButton.Click
        englishPictureBox.Visible = True
        spanishPictureBox.Visible = False      assignment statements

    End Sub

    Private Sub exitButton_Click(sender As Object, e As EventArgs) Handles exitButton.Click
        Me.Close()

    End Sub

    Private Sub spanishButton_Click(sender As Object, e As EventArgs) Handles spanishButton.Click
        spanishPictureBox.Visible = True
        englishPictureBox.Visible = False      assignment statements

    End Sub
End Class
```

Figure 1-30 Assignment statements entered in the Code Editor window

Printing the Code and User Interface

You should always print a copy of your application's code and user interface because the printout will help you understand and maintain the application in the future. Figure 1-31 shows the steps for printing the code and the interface during design time. (In Chapter 2, you will learn how to print the interface during run time.)

Ch01-Snipping Tool

HOW TO Print the Code and Interface During Design Time

To print the code:

1. Make the Code Editor window the active window. Collapse any code that you do not want to print. You collapse the code by clicking the minus box that appears next to the code.
2. Click File on the menu bar, and then click Print to open the Print dialog box. If you don't want to print the collapsed code, select the Hide collapsed regions check box. To print line numbers, select the Include line numbers check box.
3. Click the OK button to begin printing.

To use the Windows Snipping Tool to print the interface during design time:

1. Make the designer window the active window.
2. Click the Start button on the Windows 10 taskbar, click All apps, click the Windows Accessories folder, and then click Snipping Tool.
3. Click the New button. Drag the cursor around the area you want to capture and then release the mouse button. Click File and then click Save As. Save the file as a .png file and then close the Snipping Tool window.
4. Use Windows to locate the .png file. Right-click the .png file and then click Print on the context menu. Select the appropriate printer (if necessary) and then click the Print button.

Figure 1-31 How to print the code and interface during design time

Closing the Current Solution

When you are finished working on a solution, you should close it using the steps listed in Figure 1-32. Closing a solution closes all projects and files contained in the solution.

HOW TO Close a Solution

1. Click File on the menu bar.
2. Click Close Solution.

Note: Be sure to use the Close Solution option rather than the Close option. The Close option does not close the solution. Instead, it closes only the open windows (such as the designer and Code Editor windows) in the IDE.

Figure 1-32 How to close a solution

Opening an Existing Solution

Figure 1-33 shows the steps you follow to open an existing solution. The names of solution files end with .sln. If a solution is already open in the IDE, you will be given the option of closing it before another solution is opened.

HOW TO Open an Existing Solution

1. Click File on the menu bar and then click Open Project.
2. Locate and then open the application's solution folder. Click the solution filename, which ends with .sln. (The *sln* stands for *solution.*)
3. Click the Open button in the Open Project dialog box.
4. If the designer window is not open, click View on the menu bar and then click Designer. Or, you can right-click the form file's name in the Solution Explorer window and then click View Designer.

Note: To control the display of filename extensions, right-click the Start button on the Windows 10 taskbar, click Control Panel, click Appearance and Personalization, click File Explorer Options, and then click the View tab. Deselect the Hide extensions for known file types check box to show the extensions; or, select the check box to hide them.

Figure 1-33 How to open an existing solution

Syntax Errors

As the amount of code you need to enter increases, so does the likelihood for errors. An error in a program's code is referred to as a **bug**. The process of locating and correcting any bugs in a program is called **debugging**. Program bugs are typically categorized as syntax errors, logic errors, or run time errors. In this chapter, you will learn about syntax errors only. Logic errors and run time errors are covered later in this book.

A **syntax error** occurs when you break one of the programming language's rules. Most syntax errors are a result of typing errors that occur when entering instructions, such as typing `Me.Clse()` instead of `Me.Close()`. The Code Editor detects most syntax errors as you enter the instructions. Figure 1-34 shows the result of typing `Me.Clse()` in the exitButton_Click procedure. The jagged red line below the statement indicates that the statement contains a syntax error. The jagged line is called a squiggle.

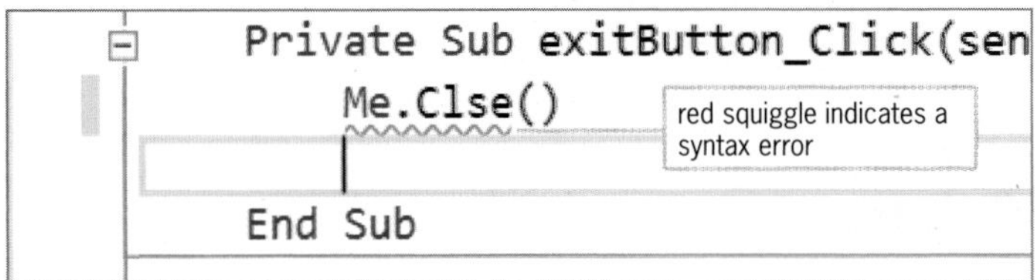

Figure 1-34 Syntax error in the exitButton_Click procedure

You can find out more information about the syntax error by positioning your mouse pointer on the mistyped instruction. When you do so, the Code Editor displays a box that contains an appropriate error message, as shown in Figure 1-35. In this case, the message indicates that the Code Editor does not recognize `Clse`.

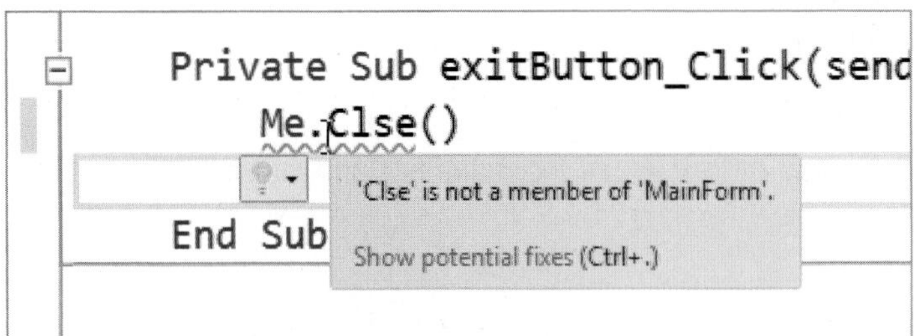

Figure 1-35 Result of placing the mouse pointer on the red squiggle

Usually, you correct any syntax errors before starting an application. However, if you inadvertently start an application that contains a syntax error, the dialog box shown in Figure 1-36 will appear. Clicking the No button opens the Error List window shown in Figure 1-37. The window provides both the description and location of the error in the code.

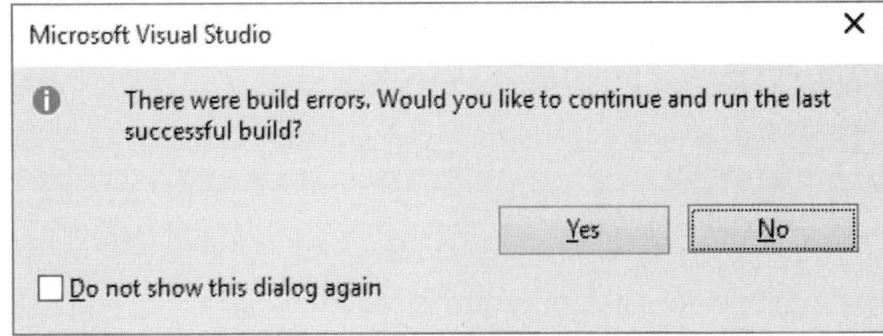

Figure 1-36 Message dialog box

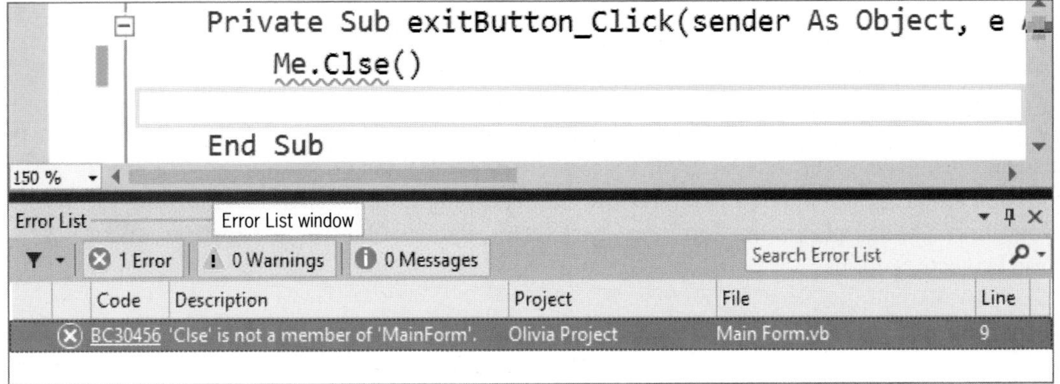

Figure 1-37 Result of starting an application that contains a syntax error

Mini-Quiz 3

The answers to Mini-Quiz questions are located in Appendix A. Each question is associated with one or more objectives listed at the beginning of the chapter.

1. The proper way to close a solution is to click the ____________ option on the File menu. (9)

   a. Close
   b. Close Solution
   c. Close All
   d. either a or b

2. The form that appears automatically when an application is started is called the ____________ form. (2)

   a. beginning
   b. main
   c. startup
   d. none of the above

3. Which of the following instructions can be used to end an application? (8)

   a. `Close.Me()`
   b. `Me.Close()`
   c. `Me.End()`
   d. `Me.Stop()`

4. Which of the following assigns the string "Nashville" to the cityLabel control? (4, 8, 11)
   a. `cityLabel.Label = "Nashville"`
   b. `cityLabel.String = "Nashville"`
   c. `cityLabel.Text = "Nashville"`
   d. none of the above

5. The process of locating and fixing the errors in a program is called ____________. (13)
   a. bug-proofing
   b. bug-eliminating
   c. debugging
   d. error removal

You have completed the concepts section of Chapter 1. The next section is the Programming Tutorial section, which contains two tutorials. The tutorials give you step-by-step instructions for completing applications that use the chapter's concepts. In most cases, the first tutorial in each chapter is easier than the second tutorial because it contains more detailed step-by-step instructions. A Programming Example follows the tutorials. The Programming Example is a completed program that demonstrates the concepts taught in the chapter. Following the Programming Example are the Summary, Key Terms, Review Questions, Exercises, and Case Projects sections.

PROGRAMMING TUTORIAL 1

Creating the Olivia Application

This tutorial contains the steps for creating, running, and testing the Olivia application from the chapter. The interface contains a label, two picture boxes, and three buttons. When clicked, two of the buttons will display (in the picture boxes) animated images of a character named Olivia, and the third button will end the application.

To begin creating the Olivia application:

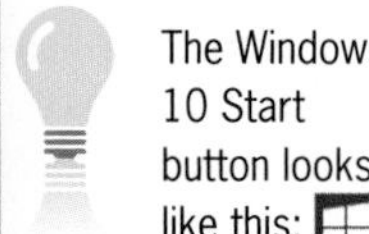

The Windows 10 Start button looks like this: ⊞.

1. Click the **Start** button on the Windows 10 taskbar, click **All apps**, click the **Visual Studio 2015** folder on the Start menu, and then click **Visual Studio 2015**.
2. *If the Choose Default Environment Settings dialog box appears*, click **Visual Basic Development Settings** and then click **Start Visual Studio**.

   If the Choose Default Environment Settings dialog box does not appear, click **Tools** on the menu bar, click **Import and Export Settings**, select the **Reset all settings** radio button, click the **Next** button, select the **No, just reset settings, overwriting my current settings** radio button, click the **Next** button, click **Visual Basic**, and then click the **Finish** button. Click the **Close** button to close the Import and Export Settings Wizard dialog box.
3. Click **Window** on the menu bar, click **Reset Window Layout**, and then click the **Yes** button. If you are using Visual Studio Community 2015, your screen will appear similar to Figure 1-38. Your screen may differ slightly if you are using a different edition of Visual Studio 2015.

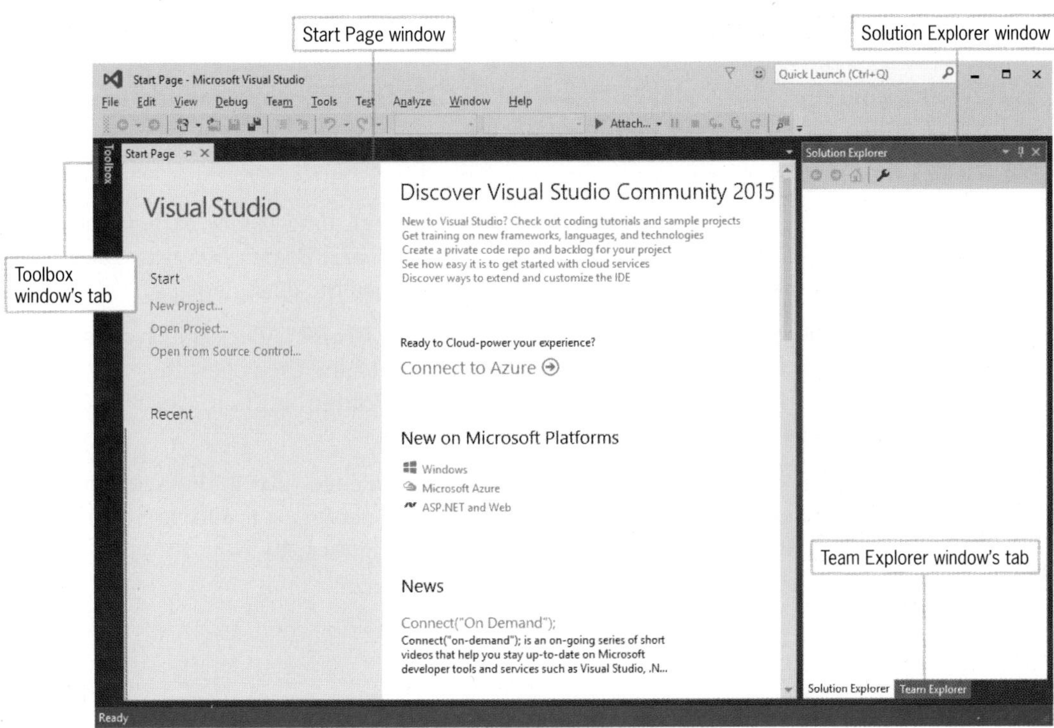

Figure 1-38 Startup screen for Visual Studio Community 2015

4. Now you will configure Visual Studio so that your screen and tutorial steps agree with the figures and tutorial steps in this book. Click **Tools** on the menu bar, click **Options**, and then click the **Projects and Solutions** node. Use the information shown in Figure 1-39 to select and deselect the appropriate check boxes.

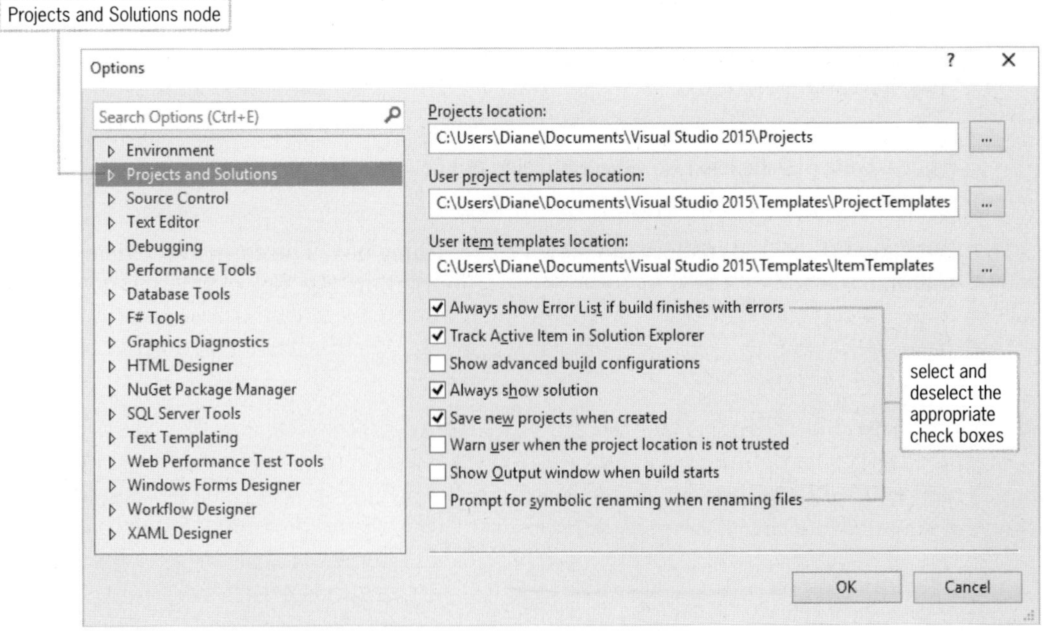

Figure 1-39 Options dialog box

5. Click the **Debugging** node and then deselect the **Step over properties and operators (Managed only)** check box. Also deselect the **Enable Diagnostic Tools while debugging** check box and the **Show elapsed time PerfTip while debugging** check box, which appear near the bottom of the list.
6. Click the **OK** button to close the Options dialog box.
7. Click **File** on the menu bar and then click **New Project**. If necessary, expand the **Installed** node and the **Templates** node. Click the **Visual Basic** node and then click **Windows Forms Application** in the middle column of the dialog box.
8. Change the name entered in the Name box to **Olivia Project**. Click the **Browse** button to open the Project Location dialog box. Locate and then click the **VbReloaded2015\Chap01** folder. Click the **Select Folder** button to close the Project Location dialog box.
9. If necessary, select the **Create directory for solution** check box in the New Project dialog box. Change the name entered in the Solution name box to **Olivia Solution**. The completed New Project dialog box is shown in Figure 1-40.

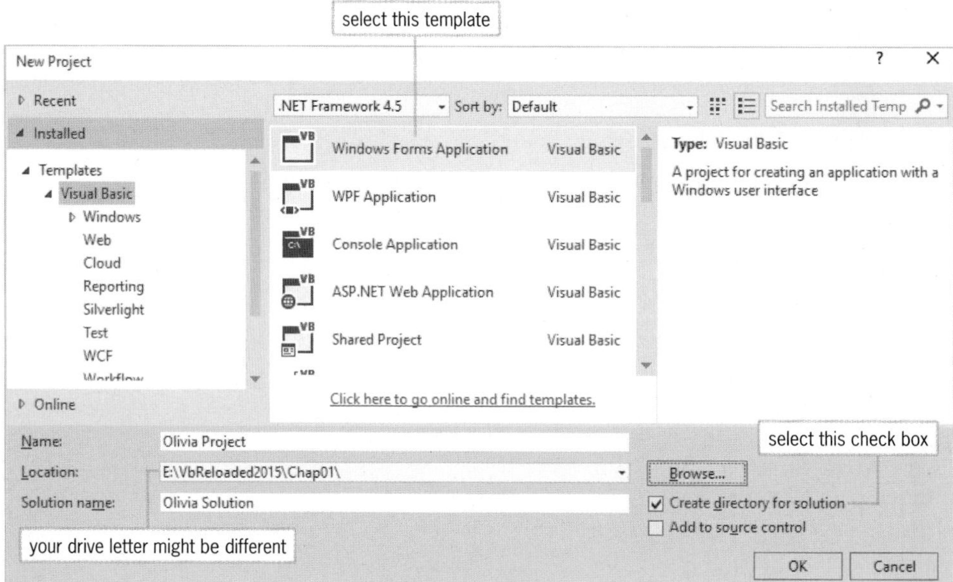

Figure 1-40 Completed New Project dialog box

10. Click the **OK** button to close the New Project dialog box. The computer creates a solution and adds a Visual Basic project to the solution. See Figure 1-41.

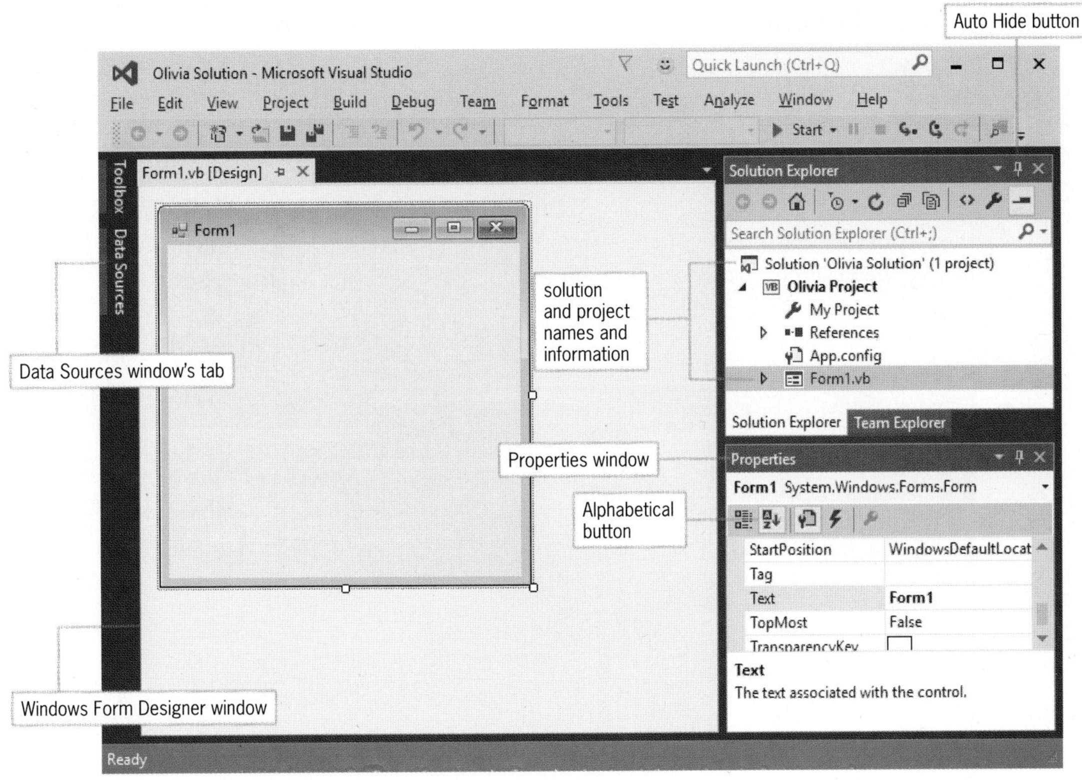

Figure 1-41 Solution and Visual Basic project

11. If necessary, click the **Alphabetical** button in the Properties window to display the property names in alphabetical order.

Managing the Windows in the IDE

In the next set of steps, you will practice closing, opening, auto-hiding, and displaying the windows in the IDE.

To close, open, auto-hide, and display the windows in the IDE:

1. Click the **Close** button on the Properties window's title bar to close the window. Then click **View** on the menu bar, and click **Properties Window** to open the window.
2. If your IDE contains the Team Explorer window, click the **Team Explorer** tab, and then click the **Close** button on the window's title bar.
3. Click the **Auto Hide** (vertical pushpin) button on the Solution Explorer window. The window is minimized and appears as a tab on the edge of the IDE.
4. To temporarily display the Solution Explorer window, click the **Solution Explorer** tab. Notice that the Auto Hide button is now a horizontal pushpin rather than a vertical pushpin. To return the Solution Explorer window to its auto-hidden state, click the **Solution Explorer** tab again.
5. If necessary, close the Data Sources window.
6. Finally, permanently display the Toolbox window by clicking its **tab** and then clicking its **Auto Hide** button. If necessary, collapse the All **Windows Form** node in the Toolbox window and expand the **Common Controls** node.

Adding and Manipulating Controls

In the next set of steps, you will add three buttons to the form. You will also practice sizing, moving, deleting, and restoring a control.

To add controls to the form and then manipulate them:

1. Click the **Button** tool in the toolbox, but do not release the mouse button. Hold down the left mouse button as you drag the mouse pointer to the lower-left corner of the form. The designer provides blue margin lines to assist you in spacing the controls properly on the form. See Figure 1-42.

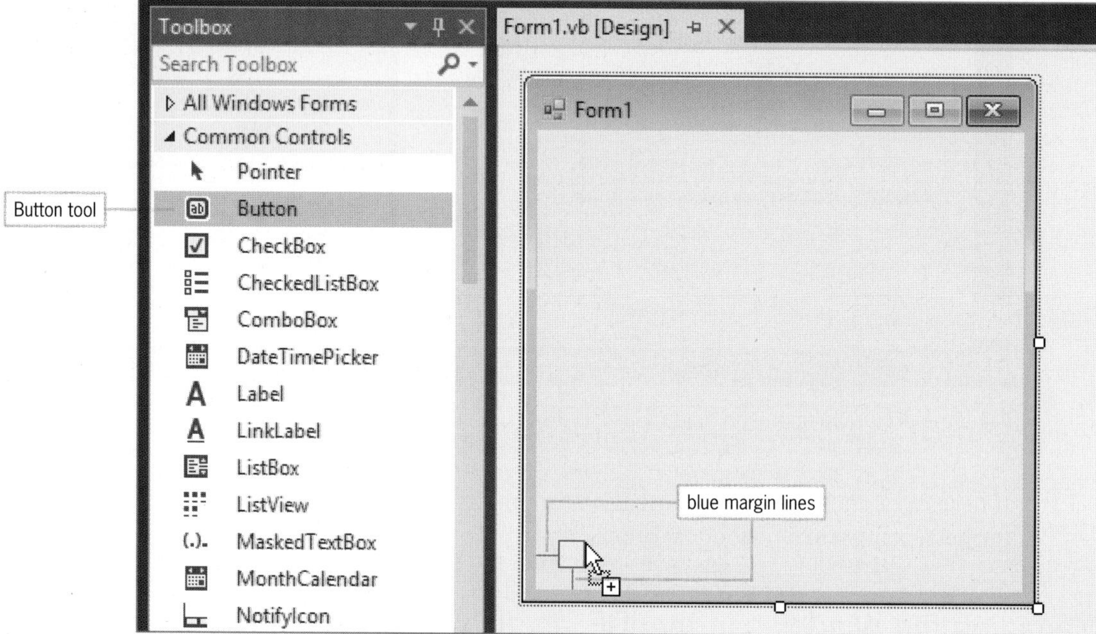

Figure 1-42 Button tool being dragged to the form

2. Release the mouse button. A button control appears on the form. The sizing handles on the button indicate that it is selected. You can use the sizing handles to make a control bigger or smaller. Use the middle sizing handle at the top of the button to make the button taller. See Figure 1-43.

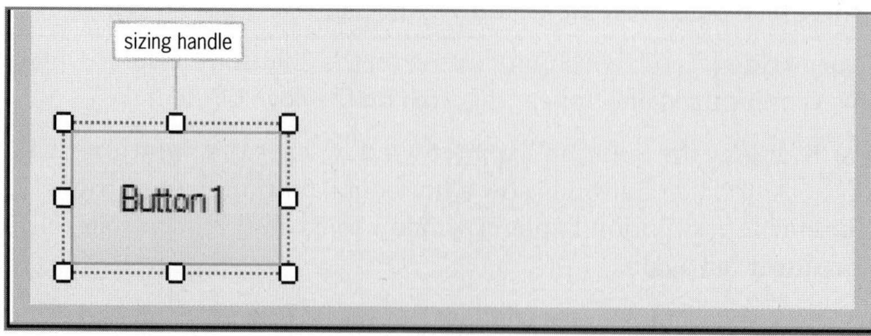

Figure 1-43 Button control added to the form

3. Now you will practice repositioning a control on the form. Place your mouse pointer on the center of the button. Press and hold down the left mouse button as you drag the button to another area of the form. Release the mouse button.
4. Next, you will practice deleting and then restoring a control. Press the **Delete** key on your keyboard to delete the button. Click **Edit** on the menu bar and then click **Undo** to reinstate the button.
5. Drag the button back to its original location in the lower-left corner of the form.
6. Another way to add a control to a form is by clicking the appropriate tool and then clicking the form. Click the **Button** tool in the toolbox and then click **anywhere on the form**.
7. Drag the second button until its top border is aligned with the top border of the first button, but don't release the mouse button. When the tops of both controls are aligned, the designer displays a blue snap line. See Figure 1-44.

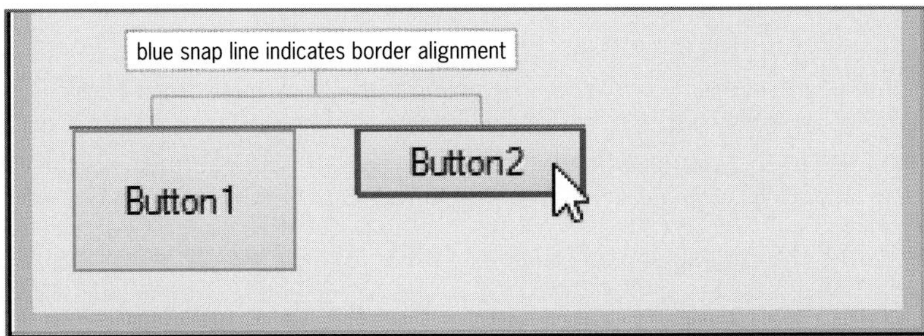

Figure 1-44 Controls aligned by their top borders

8. Now drag the second button down slightly, until the Button2 text is aligned with the Button1 text, but don't release the mouse button. When the text in both controls is aligned, the designer displays a pink snap line. See Figure 1-45.

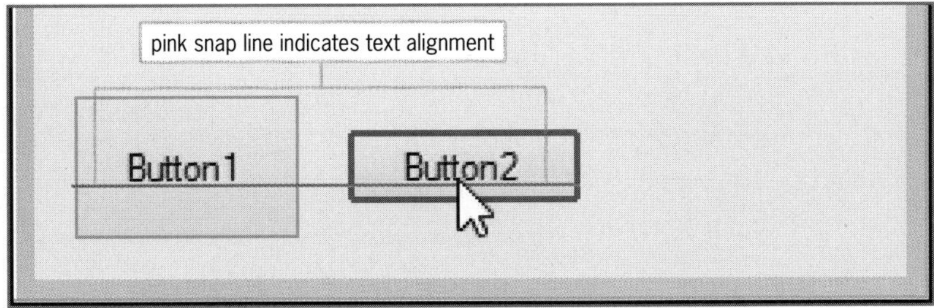

Figure 1-45 Controls aligned by their text

9. Release the mouse button.

10. You can also add a control to a form by clicking the appropriate tool, placing the mouse pointer on the form, and then pressing the left mouse button and dragging the mouse pointer until the control is the desired size. Click the **Button** tool in the toolbox and then place the mouse pointer anywhere on the form. Press the left mouse button, drag the mouse pointer until the control is the desired size, and then release the mouse button. (You do not need to worry about the exact location and size of the button.)
11. Click the **Button1** control to select it. Press and hold down the **Ctrl** (Control) key as you click the **Button2** and **Button3** controls. Press the **Delete** key to remove the three buttons from the form.

Using the Properties Window to Change an Object's Properties

Each object in Visual Basic has a set of properties that determine its appearance and behavior, and each property has a default value assigned to it when the object is created. You can use the Properties window to assign a different value to a property. In the next set of steps, you will change the form file object's File Name property. You will also change some of the properties of the form.

To change the properties of the form file and form:

1. Permanently display the Solution Explorer window. If the properties of the Form1.vb file do not appear in the Properties window, right-click **Form1.vb** in the Solution Explorer window and then click **Properties**.
2. Click **File Name** in the Properties list. Type **Main Form.vb** and then press **Enter**.
3. Click the **form** in the designer window. Sizing handles appear on the form to indicate that it is selected, and the form's properties appear in the Properties window.
4. First, you will change the type and size of the font used to display text in the controls on the form. (You will add the controls later in this tutorial.) Click **Font** in the Properties list and then click the **...** (ellipsis) button in the Settings box. When the Font dialog box opens, click **Segoe UI** in the Font box. Click **11** in the Size box and then click the **OK** button. (Do not be concerned if the size of the form changes.) When a control is subsequently added to the form, its Font property will be assigned the same value as the form's Font property.
5. Click **StartPosition** in the Properties list. This property determines the location of the form when the application is run and the form first appears on the screen. Click the **list arrow** in the Settings box and then click **CenterScreen**.
6. Click **Text** in the Properties list. This property specifies the text to display in the form's title bar. Type **Olivia** and press **Enter**.
7. Now you will give the form a more meaningful name. Scroll to the top of the Properties window and then click **(Name)** in the Properties list. Type **MainForm** and press **Enter**.
8. Finally, you will size the form. Either drag the form's right and bottom borders until the form is approximately the size shown in Figure 1-46, or set the form's Size property to **545, 545**. (Depending on your display screen, you may need to use slightly different values for your form's Size property.)

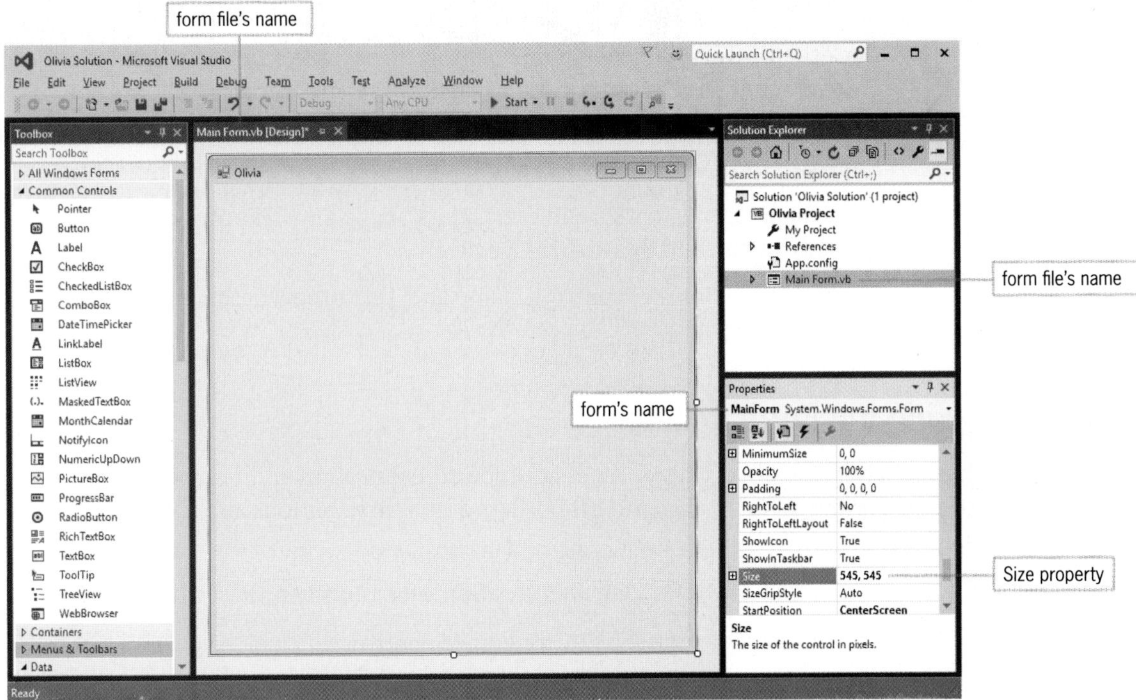

Figure 1-46 Correct size for the form

Adding Label and Button Controls to the Form

In the next set of steps, you will add label and button controls to the form and then set some of their properties.

To add controls to the form and then set some of their properties:

1. If necessary, collapse the **All Windows Forms** node in the toolbox and expand the **Common Controls** node. Add a label control and three buttons to the form. Position the controls as shown in Figure 1-47.

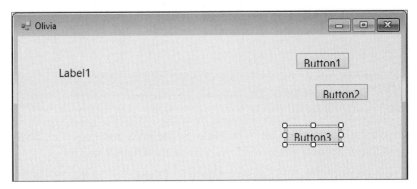

Figure 1-47 Label and buttons added to the form

2. Click the **Label1** control on the form. Verify that the label's Font property contains the same value as the form's Font property.
3. With the Label1 control still selected, click **Text** in the Properties list. Type **Olivia is bilingual!** and press **Enter**. The label's size automatically adjusts to fit its contents because the default value for the control's AutoSize property is True.

4. Click the **Button1** control on the form. Here again, verify that the button's Font property contains the same value as the form's Font property.
5. Set the Button1 control's Name property to **englishButton** and set its Text property to **English**. For now, do not worry about the size of the buttons on the form.
6. Click the **Button2** control and then set its Name and Text properties to **spanishButton** and **Spanish**, respectively.
7. Finally, set the Button3 control's Name and Text properties to **exitButton** and **Exit**, respectively.

Using the Format Menu

In this set of steps, you will set the English button's Location and Size properties. You then will use the Format menu to align the left borders of the three buttons and also make the buttons the same size.

To set the English button's size and location and then use the Format menu:

1. The English button will be the reference control, which is the control whose size and/or location you want the other buttons to match. Click the **English** button. Set its Size and Location properties to approximately **75, 30** and **425, 30**, respectively.
2. With the English button still selected, press and hold down the **Ctrl** (**Control**) key as you click the **Spanish** and **Exit** buttons, and then release the Ctrl key. The three buttons are now selected. You can tell that the English button is the reference control because its sizing handles are white; the sizing handles on the other selected controls are black. See Figure 1-48.

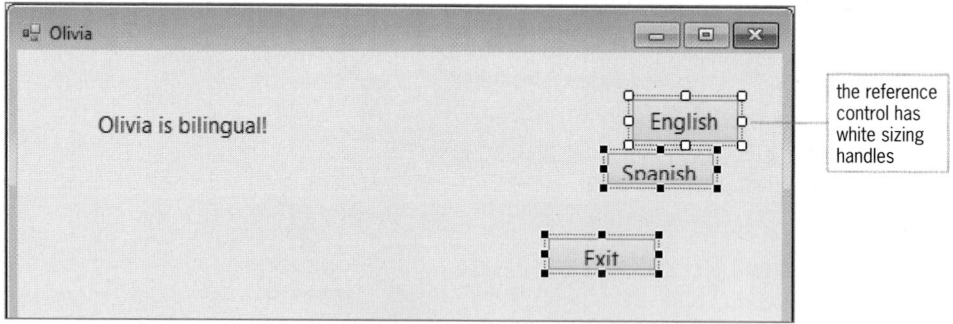

Figure 1-48 Buttons selected on the form

3. Click **Format** on the menu bar, point to **Make Same Size**, and then click **Both**. The Spanish and Exit buttons are now the same size as the English button.
4. Click **Format** on the menu bar, point to **Align**, and then click **Lefts**. The left borders of the Spanish and Exit buttons are now aligned with the left border of the English button.
5. On your own, use the Format menu to equalize the vertical spacing between the three buttons.
6. Click the **form** to deselect the buttons.

Coding the Exit Button's Click Event Procedure

When the user clicks the Exit button in the interface, the button's Click event procedure should end the application.

To code the Exit button's Click event procedure:

1. Right-click the **form** and then click **View Code** to open the Code Editor window.
2. Click the **Object** list arrow and then click **exitButton** in the list. Click the **Method** list arrow and then click **Click** in the list. The code template for the exitButton's Click event procedure appears in the Code Editor window. See Figure 1-49. You can use the sizing list box, which appears in the lower-left corner of the window, to either increase or decrease the size of the font used to display the code.

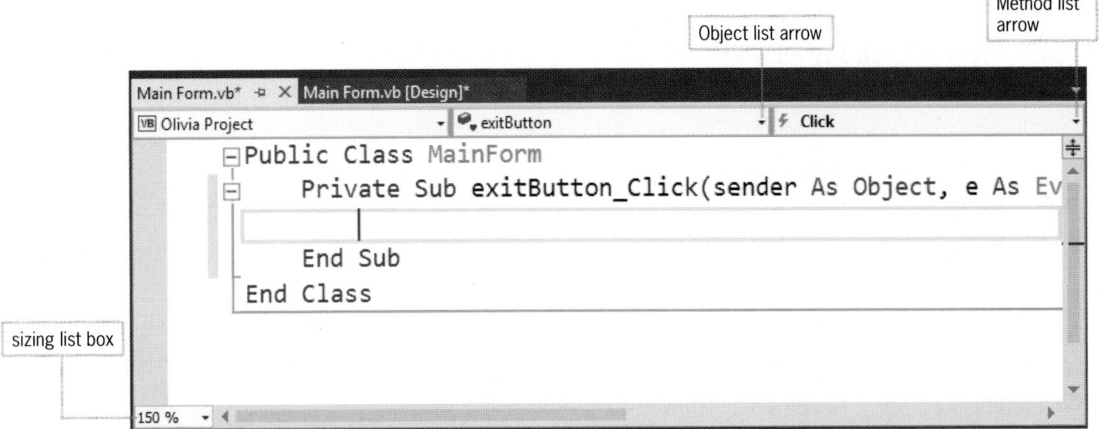

Figure 1-49 Code template for the exitButton's Click event procedure

3. The Exit button should end the application when it is clicked. Therefore, the appropriate instruction to enter in its Click event procedure is `Me.Close()`. You can type the instruction on your own or use the Code Editor window's IntelliSense feature. In this set of steps, you will use the IntelliSense feature. Type **me.** (be sure to type the period, but don't press Enter). When you type the period, the IntelliSense feature displays a list of properties, methods, and so on from which you can select.

   Note: If the list of choices does not appear, the IntelliSense feature may have been turned off on your computer system. To turn it on, click Tools on the menu bar, click Options, expand the Text Editor node, click Basic, select the Auto list members check box, and then click the OK button.

4. Type **clo** (but don't press Enter). The IntelliSense feature highlights the Close method in the list. See Figure 1-50. For now, do not be concerned about the LightBulb indicator or the red squiggle below `Me.clo`.

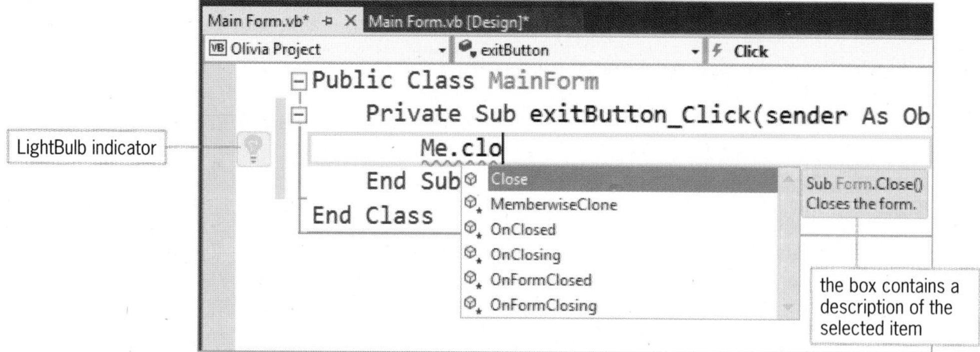

Figure 1-50 List displayed by the IntelliSense feature

5. Press the **Tab** key on your keyboard to include the Close method in the instruction, and then press **Enter**. See Figure 1-51.

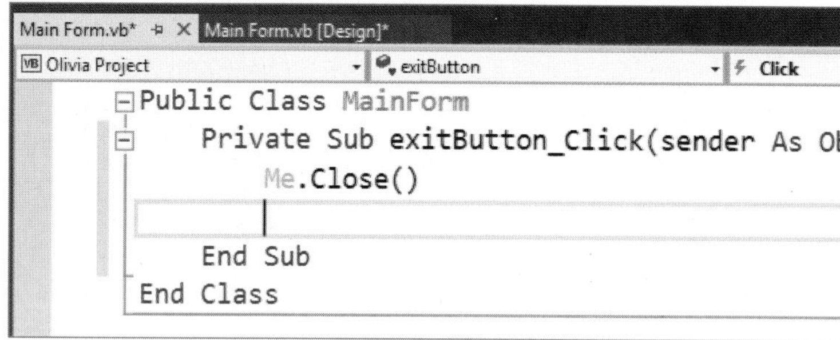

Figure 1-51 Completed exitButton_Click procedure

Adding a Picture Box Control to the Form

In the next set of steps, you will add a picture box to the form and then set some of its properties. (You will add the second picture box to the form later in this tutorial.)

To add a picture box to the form and then set some of its properties:

1. Click the **Main Form.vb [Design]** tab to return to the designer window. Add a picture box to the form. Position it as shown in Figure 1-52.

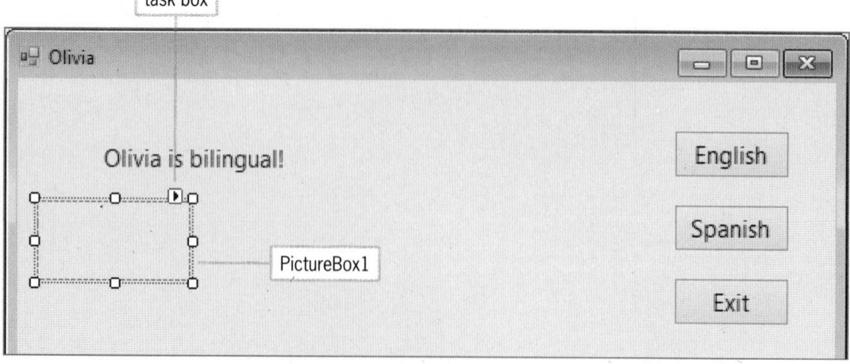

Figure 1-52 Picture box added to the form

2. Notice that a box containing a triangle appears in the upper-right corner of the control. The box is referred to as the task box because when you click it, it displays a list of the tasks associated with the control. Each task in the list is associated with one or more properties. You can set the properties using the task list or the Properties window. Click the **task box** on the PictureBox1 control. See Figure 1-53.

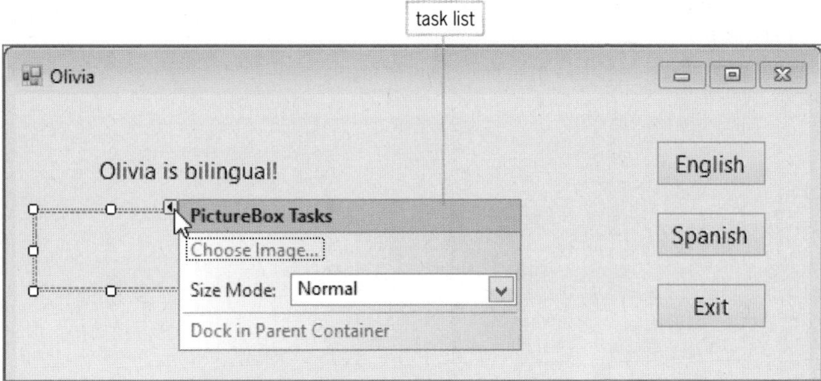

Figure 1-53 Open task list for the PictureBox1 control

3. Click **Choose Image** to open the Select Resource dialog box. The Choose Image task is associated with the Image property in the Properties window.
4. To include the image file within the project itself, the Project resource file radio button must be selected in the dialog box. Verify that the radio button is selected, and then click the **Import** button to open the Open dialog box.
5. Open the VbReloaded2015\Chap01 folder, if necessary. Click **English (English.gif)** in the list of filenames and then click the **Open** button. The completed Select Resource dialog box is shown in Figure 1-54.

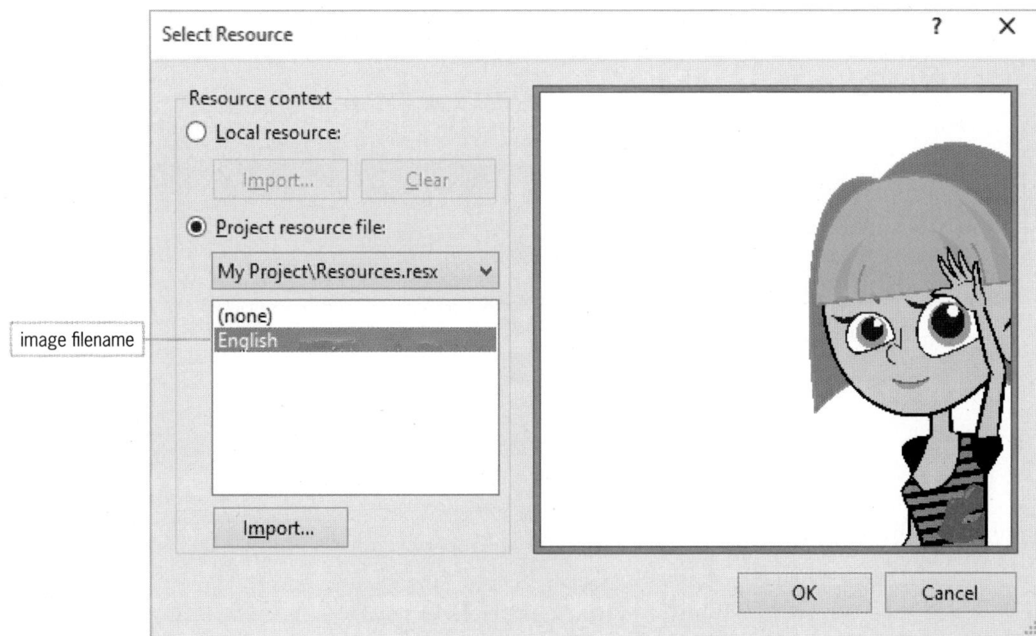

Figure 1-54 Completed Select Resource dialog box

Image by Diane Zak; created with Reallusion CrazyTalk Animator

PROGRAMMING TUTORIAL 1

6. Click the **OK** button to close the dialog box. If necessary, click the PictureBox1 control's **task box** to open the task list. Click the **list arrow** in the Size Mode box and then click **StretchImage** in the list. Click the **picture box** to close its task list. Drag the picture box's sizing handles until the picture box is approximately the size shown in Figure 1-55. Or, you can set its Size property to approximately **405, 415**. (Do not be concerned if the image in your picture box looks slightly different than the one shown in Figure 1-55.)

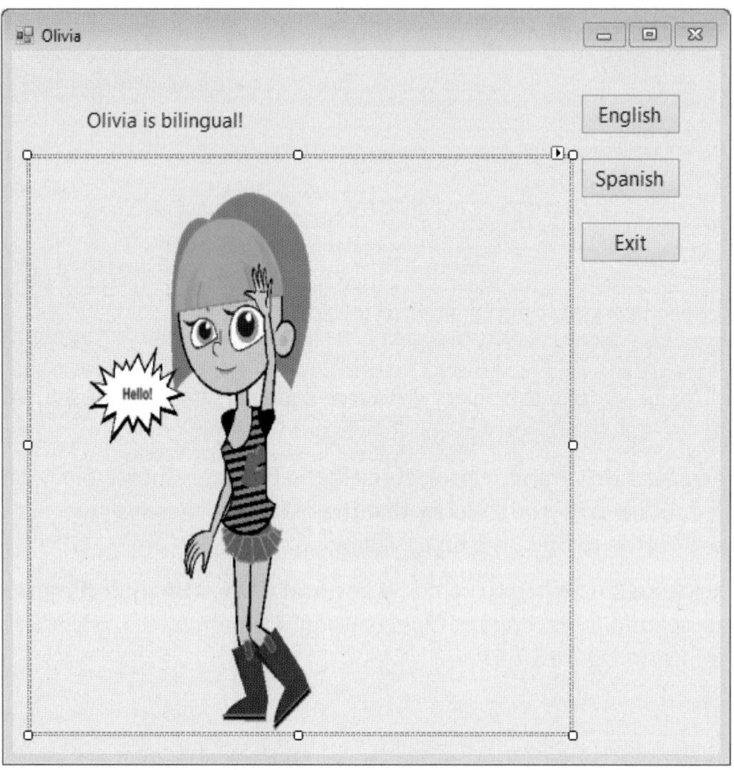

Figure 1-55 Correct size for the picture box
Image by Diane Zak; created with Reallusion CrazyTalk Animator

7. Use the Properties window to set the picture box's Name property to **englishPictureBox**.
8. When the application is started, the picture box control should be invisible. To view the control, the user will need to click the English button. Use the Properties window to set the picture box's Visible property to **False**.
9. Click **File** on the menu bar and then click **Save All**.

Coding the English and Spanish Buttons' Click Event Procedures

When the user clicks the English button, its Click event procedure should make the englishPictureBox visible. You can accomplish this task by assigning the keyword `True` to the picture box's Visible property, like this: `englishPictureBox.Visible = True`. When the user clicks the Spanish button, on the other hand, its Click event procedure should make the englishPictureBox invisible again. This is accomplished using the following assignment statement: `englishPictureBox.Visible = False`.

To begin coding the Click event procedures and then test the code:

1. Click the **Main Form.vb** tab to return to the Code Editor window. Use the Object and Method list boxes to open the code template for the englishButton's Click event procedure.
2. Type **eng** to highlight the englishPictureBox entry in the IntelliSense list. Press **Tab** to include the entry in the instruction.
3. The next character in the instruction is a period. Type **.** (a period) and then type the letter **v** to select the Visible entry in the list. Press **Tab** and then type = (an equal sign).
4. Type **tru** to select the True entry in the list. Press **Tab** and then press **Enter**. The procedure now contains the `englishPictureBox.Visible = True` assignment statement.
5. Open the code template for the spanishButton's Click event procedure. On your own, use the IntelliSense feature to enter the following assignment statement in the procedure:

   englishPictureBox.Visible = False
6. Save the solution by clicking **File** on the menu bar and then clicking **Save All**.
7. Now you will start the application and test the code entered so far. Recall that before you start the application the first time, you should verify the name of the startup form in the Project Designer window. Right-click **My Project** in the Solution Explorer window and then click **Open** on the context menu. If necessary, click the **Application** tab. If MainForm does not appear in the Startup form box, click the **Startup form** list arrow, click **MainForm** in the list, and then save the solution.
8. Close the Project Designer window by clicking the **Close** button on its tab.
9. Click **Debug** on the menu bar and then click **Start Debugging**. (Or you can simply press the **F5** key on your keyboard.) The interface appears on the screen. (Do not be concerned about any windows that appear at the bottom of the screen.) Notice that the picture box is invisible.
10. Click the **English** button to make the picture box visible, and then click the **Spanish** button to make it invisible. Click the **Exit** button to stop the application.

Completing the User Interface

In the next set of steps, you will complete the user interface.

To complete the user interface:

1. Return to the designer window. Add another picture box to the form. (You do not need to worry about the exact location.) Change its name to **spanishPictureBox**.
2. Click the spanishPictureBox's **task box**. Click **Choose Image** to open the Select Resource dialog box. Verify that the Project resource file radio button is selected, and then click the **Import** button to open the Open dialog box.
3. Open the VbReloaded2015\Chap01 folder, if necessary. Click **Spanish (Spanish.gif)** in the list of filenames, click the **Open** button, and then click the **OK** button.
4. If necessary, click the spanishPictureBox's **task box** to open the task list. Click the **list arrow** in the Size Mode box and then click **StretchImage** in the list. Click the **spanishPictureBox** to close its task list.
5. Use the Properties window to set the spanishPictureBox's Visible property to **False**.

6. Now you will make the spanishPictureBox the same size as the englishPictureBox, and then align their left and top borders. Click the **englishPictureBox** (the reference control) and then Ctrl+click the **spanishPictureBox**. Use the Format menu to make the spanishPictureBox the same height and width as the reference control. Also use the Format menu to align the left and top borders of the spanishPictureBox with the reference control.
7. Now that the interface is complete, you can lock the controls on the form. Right-click the **form** and then click **Lock Controls** on the context menu. Notice that a small lock appears in the upper-left corner of the form. (You can also lock the controls by clicking Format on the menu bar and then clicking Lock Controls.)
8. Click the **English** button. The small lock in the upper-left corner of the control indicates that the control is locked.
9. Try dragging one of the controls to a different location on the form. You will not be able to do so.

If you need to move a control after you have locked the controls in place, you can change the control's Location property setting in the Properties window. You can also unlock the control by changing its Locked property to False. Or, you can unlock all of the controls by clicking Format on the menu bar and then clicking Lock Controls. The Lock Controls option is a toggle option: Clicking it once activates it, and clicking it again deactivates it.

Completing the Code

In the next set of steps, you will finish coding the English and Spanish buttons' Click event procedures.

To complete the code and then test it:

1. Return to the Code Editor window. After making the englishPictureBox visible, the englishButton_Click procedure will make the spanishPictureBox invisible. Similarly, before making the englishPictureBox invisible, the spanishButton_Click procedure will make the spanishPictureBox visible.
2. Enter the two assignment statements shaded in Figure 1-56.

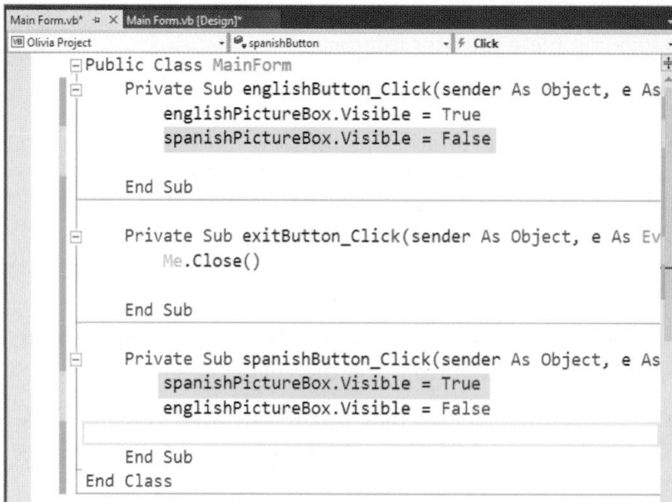

Figure 1-56 Completed Click event procedures

3. Click **File** on the menu bar and then click **Save All**. Press the **F5** key on your keyboard. (Or, click **Debug** on the menu bar and then click **Start Debugging**.)
4. Click the **English** button. After Olivia says *Hello!*, click the **Spanish** button. After Olivia says *Hola!*, click the **English** button again, and then click the **Spanish** button again. Click the **Exit** button.

Displaying Line Numbers in the Code Editor Window

At times, you may want to display line numbers in the Code Editor window.

To display line numbers in the Code Editor window:

1. Click **Tools** on the menu bar and then click **Options**. Expand the **Text Editor** node in the Options dialog box and then click **Basic**. Select the **Line numbers** check box and then click the **OK** button. See Figure 1-57.

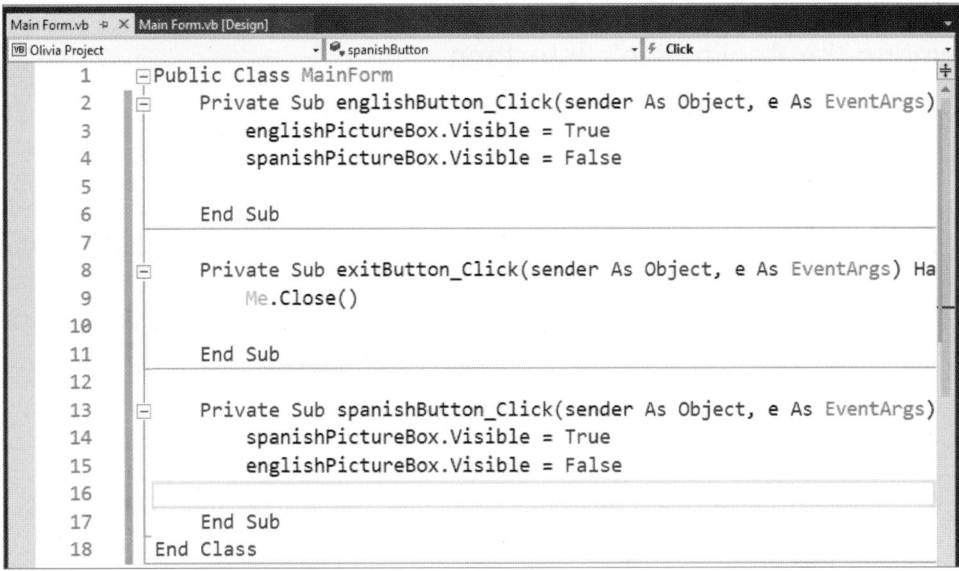

Figure 1-57 Line numbers shown in the Code Editor window

Closing the Current Solution

When you are finished working with a solution, you should use the Close Solution option on the File menu to close it. When you close a solution, all projects and files contained in the solution are also closed.

To close the current solution:

1. Close the Code Editor window. Click **File** on the menu bar and then click **Close Solution**.
2. Use the Solution Explorer window to verify that no solutions are open in the IDE.

Opening an Existing Solution

You can use the File menu to open an existing solution.

To open the Olivia Solution:

1. If necessary, permanently display the Solution Explorer window.
2. Click **File** on the menu bar and then click **Open Project** to open the Open Project dialog box.
3. Locate and then open the VbReloaded2015\Chap01\Olivia Solution folder. Click **Olivia Solution** (**Olivia Solution.sln**) in the list of filenames and then click the **Open** button. (Depending on how Windows is set up on your computer, you may or may not see the .sln extension on the filename. Refer to Figure 1-33 to learn how to show/hide the extensions on filenames.)
4. If you do not see the form in the designer window, click **View** on the menu bar and then click **Designer**.

Printing the Application's Interface

To print the application's interface during design time, the Windows Form Designer window must be the active window.

To print the Olivia application's interface:

1. Click the **Start** button on the Windows 10 taskbar, click **All apps**, click the **Windows Accessories** folder, and then click **Snipping Tool**.
2. Click the **New** button. Drag the cursor around the form and then release the mouse button.
3. Click **File** and then click **Save As**. Locate and then open the VbReloaded2015\Chap01\Olivia Solution folder. You can save the file using any one of the following formats: .png, .gif, .jpg, or .mht. In this case, you will save it as a .png file. If necessary, change the entry in the Save as type box to **Portable Network Graphic file (PNG) (*.PNG)**. Type **Olivia** in the File name box and then click the **Save** button. Close the Snipping Tool application.
4. If your computer is connected to a printer, use Windows to open the VbReloaded2015\Chap01\Olivia Solution folder. Right-click **Olivia.PNG** and then click **Print** on the context menu. Select the appropriate printer (if necessary) and then click the **Print** button.

Printing the Application's Code

For your future reference, you should always print a copy of the application's code. To print the code, the Code Editor window must be the active (current) window.

To print the application's code:

1. Open the Code Editor window by right-clicking the **form** and then clicking **View Code**.
2. First, you will remove the line numbers from the window. Click **Tools** on the menu bar and then click **Options**. Expand the **Text Editor** node in the Options dialog box and then click **Basic**. Deselect the **Line numbers** check box and then click the **OK** button.

3. Click **File** on the menu bar and then click **Print** to open the Print dialog box. If you select the Include line numbers check box, line numbers will be printed even if they do not appear in the Code Editor window. If the Include line numbers check box is not selected, no line numbers will appear on the printout, even though they may appear in the Code Editor window.
4. Select the **Include line numbers** check box.
5. If your computer is connected to a printer, click the **OK** button to begin printing; otherwise, click the **Cancel** button. If you clicked the OK button, your printer prints the code.
6. Auto-hide the Toolbox, Solution Explorer, and Properties windows.

Syntax Errors in Code

In this section, you will introduce a syntax error in the English button's Click event procedure. You then will debug the procedure by locating and fixing the error.

To introduce a syntax error in the code:

1. Locate the englishButton_Click procedure. Change the word `False` in the second assignment statement to **Flse** and then click the **blank line** below the assignment statement. The red squiggle that appears below the mistyped word indicates that the instruction contains a syntax error.
2. Position your mouse pointer on the red squiggle, as shown in Figure 1-58. The error message indicates that the Code Editor does not recognize the word `Flse`.

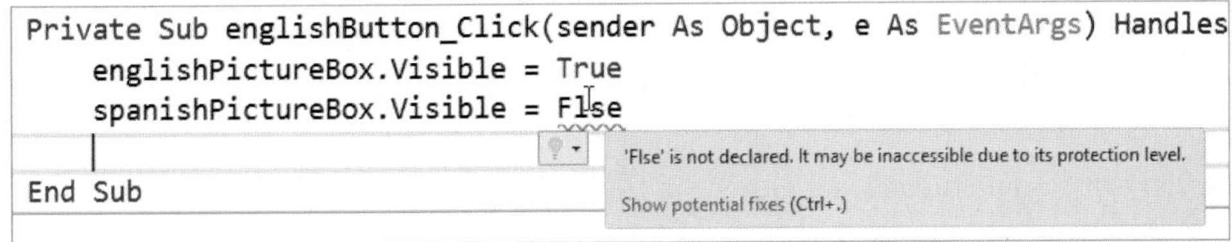
Private Sub englishButton_Click(sender As Object, e As EventArgs) Handles
englishPictureBox.Visible = True
spanishPictureBox.Visible = Flse
'Flse' is not declared. It may be inaccessible due to its protection level.
Show potential fixes (Ctrl+.)
End Sub

Figure 1-58 Red squiggle and message indicate a syntax error

3. Now observe what happens when you start the application without correcting the syntax error. Save the solution and then start the application. The message box shown in Figure 1-59 appears.

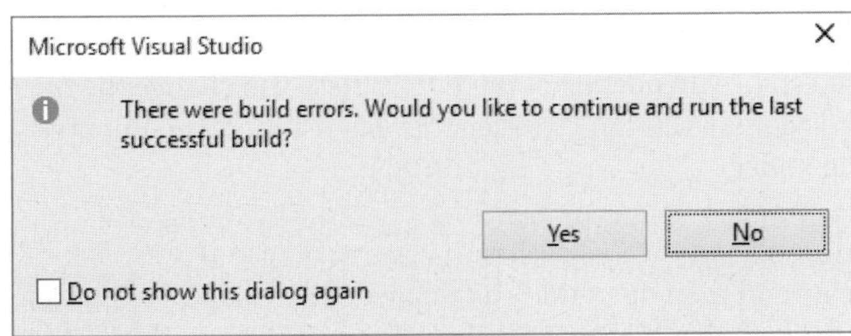
Microsoft Visual Studio
There were build errors. Would you like to continue and run the last successful build?
Yes
No
Do not show this dialog again

Figure 1-59 Result of running an application that contains a syntax error

4. Click the **No** button. The Error List window shown in Figure 1-60 opens. The window indicates that the code has one error, which occurs on Line 4.

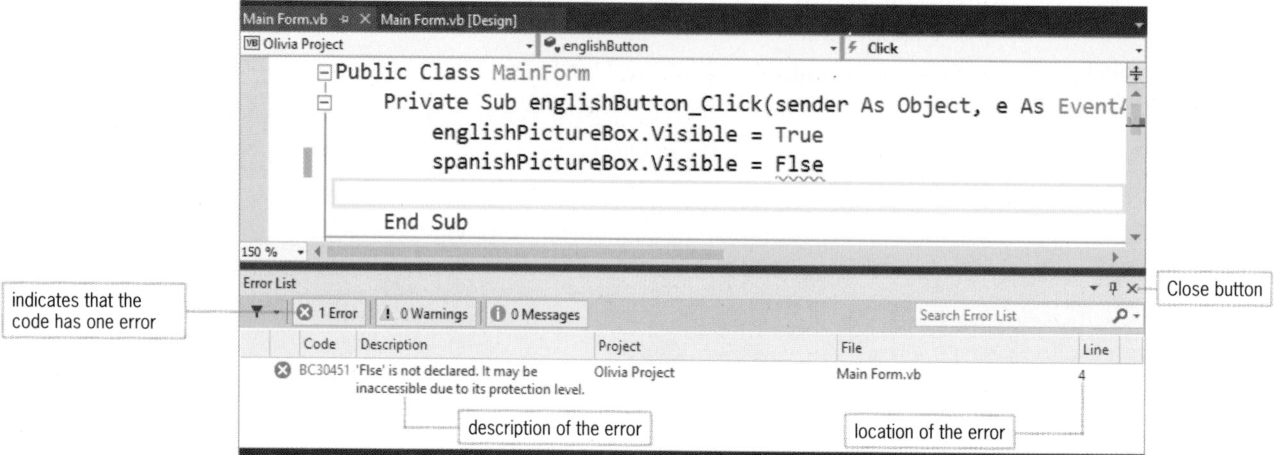

Figure 1-60 Error List window

5. Change `Flse` in Line 4's assignment statement to **False** and then click the **blank line** below the assignment statement. The Error List window shows that the code is now error-free.
6. Close the Error List window. Save the solution and then start the application. Click the **English** button to verify that it is working correctly.
7. Click the **Exit** button to end the application, and then close the Code Editor window.

Exiting Visual Studio 2015

You can exit Visual Studio using either the Close button on its title bar or the Exit option on its File menu.

To exit Visual Studio:

1. First, close the current solution. Click **File** on the menu bar and then click **Close Solution**.
2. Click **File** on the menu bar and then click **Exit**.

Running the Application's Executable File

Earlier you learned that when you start a Visual Basic application, the computer automatically creates an executable file that can be run outside of the IDE. Unless you change the file's name, it has the same name as the project, but with an .exe filename extension. The computer stores the file in the project's bin\Debug folder.

To run the Olivia Project.exe file:

1. Use Windows to locate and then open the VbReloaded2015\Chap01\Olivia Solution\Olivia Project\bin\Debug folder. Right-click **Olivia Project (Olivia Project.exe)** and then click **Open**.
2. The Olivia application's interface appears on the screen. Click the **English** and **Spanish** buttons to test the application, and then click the **Exit** button.

PROGRAMMING TUTORIAL 2

Creating the Cake Shoppe Application

In this tutorial, you will create the Cake Shoppe application shown in Figure 1-61. The interface contains a label, three picture boxes, and three buttons. The bdayPictureBox and weddingPictureBox controls contain images of cakes. The images are stored in the Bday.png and Wedding.png files contained in the VbReloaded2015\Chap01 folder. When clicked, the bdayButton and weddingButton controls will display one of the cake images in the displayPictureBox. Both will also display a word indicating the type of cake (either Birthday or Wedding) in the typeLabel control. The exitButton will end the application.

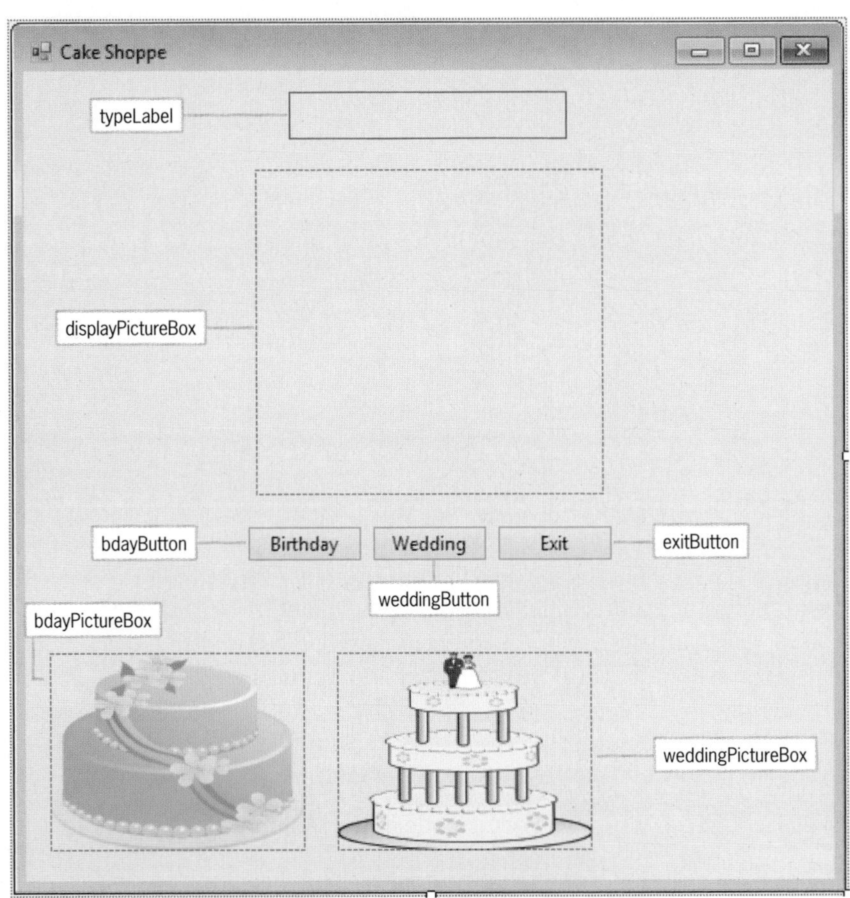

Figure 1-61 Cake Shoppe application's user interface

To begin creating the Cake Shoppe application:

1. Start Visual Studio 2015. If you need help, refer to the How To box shown earlier in Figure 1-1.
2. Click **Window** on the menu bar, click **Reset Window Layout**, and then click the **Yes** button.
3. If you did not complete Programming Tutorial 1, use the information shown earlier in Figures 1-2 and 1-3 to configure Visual Studio so that your screen and tutorial steps agree with the figures and tutorial steps in this book.

4. Use the **New Project** option on the File menu to create a Visual Basic Windows Forms application. Use the following names for the solution and project, respectively: **Cake Solution** and **Cake Project**. Save the solution in the VbReloaded2015\Chap01 folder. If you need help, refer to the How To box shown earlier in Figure 1-5.
5. Click **Form1.vb** in the Solution Explorer window. Use the Properties window to change the form file's name from Form1.vb to **Main Form.vb**.
6. Click the **form**. Change the form's name to **MainForm**. Also change the form's Font property to **Segoe UI, 9pt.**
7. Change the form's StartPosition property so that the form will be centered on the screen when the application is started.
8. Change the form's Text property to display "Cake Shoppe" (without the quotes) in its title bar.
9. Change the form's Size property to approximately **540, 535**.

Managing the Windows in the IDE

In the next set of steps, you will practice closing, opening, auto-hiding, and displaying the windows in the IDE. If you need help while performing the steps, refer to the How To box shown earlier in Figure 1-8.

To close, open, auto-hide, and display the windows in the IDE:

1. Close the Properties window and then open it again.
2. If necessary, close the Team Explorer and Data Sources windows.
3. Auto-hide the Solution Explorer window, and then temporarily display the window.
4. Permanently display the Solution Explorer and Toolbox windows.

Adding Controls to a Form

In the next set of steps, you will add the seven controls to the form. You will also size, move, delete, and undelete a control.

To add controls to the form and then manipulate the controls:

1. If necessary, collapse the **All Windows Forms** node in the toolbox and expand the **Common Controls** node.
2. Use the Label tool to add a label to the form. If you need help, refer to the How To box shown earlier in Figure 1-14.
3. Next, add three picture boxes and three buttons to the form. Position the controls as shown in Figure 1-62. If you need help, refer to the How To box shown earlier in Figure 1-15. (If necessary, use the form's sizing handles to make the form larger or smaller.)

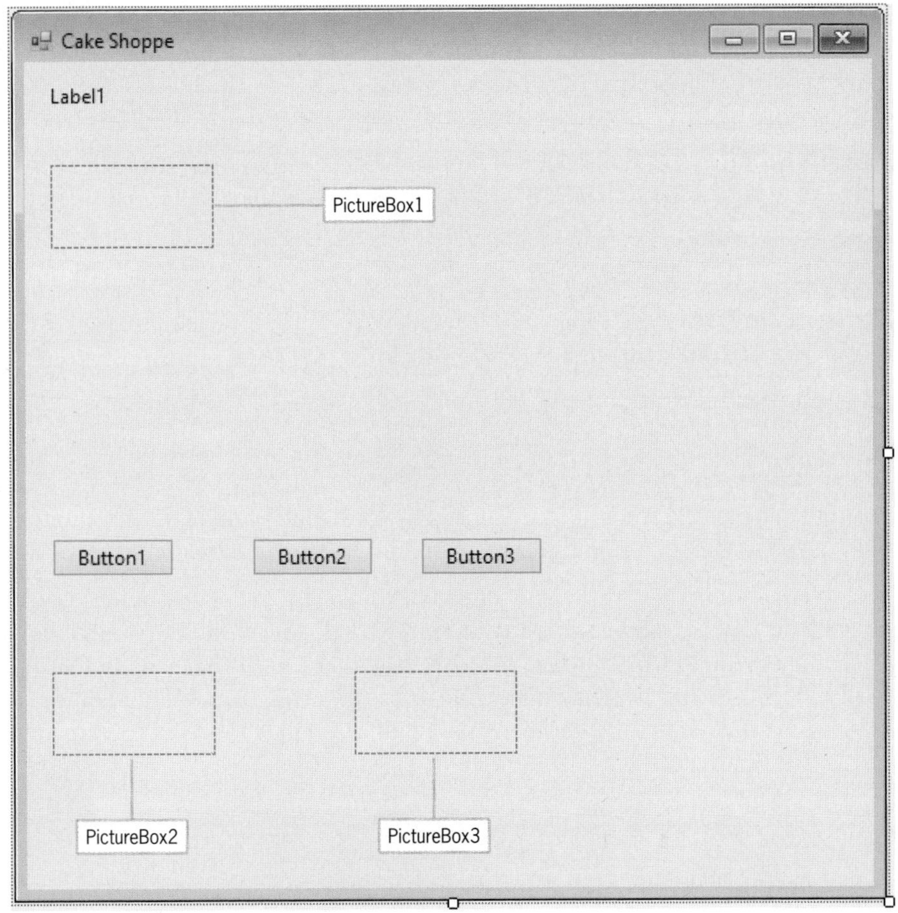

Figure 1-62 Controls added to the form

4. Click the **Label1** control. Change the label's name to **typeLabel**. Set its AutoSize and BorderStyle properties to **False** and **FixedSingle**, respectively.
5. Click **Text** in the label's Properties list, press the **Backspace** key, and then press **Enter** to remove the Label1 text from the control. Now change the label's Size property to **180, 30**.
6. Click **TextAlign** in the Properties list, click the **list arrow** in the Settings box, and then click the **rectangle** located in the second row, second column. This will center the text within the label control.
7. Click the **PictureBox2** control at the bottom of the form. Change its name to **bdayPictureBox**. Click the control's **task box** and then use its task list to display the image stored in the **Bday.png** file, which is contained in the VbReloaded2015\Chap01 folder. Also use the task list to set the Size Mode to **StretchImage**. If you need help, refer to the *Adding a Picture Box Control to the Form* section in Programming Tutorial 1.
8. Use the Properties window to set the bdayPictureBox control's Size property to **165, 125**.
9. Use the Make Same Size option on the Format menu to make the PictureBox3 control the same size as the bdayPictureBox. If you need help, refer to the How To box shown earlier in Figure 1-17.
10. Click the **form** to deselect the two picture boxes.

11. Click the **PictureBox3** control. Change its name to **weddingPictureBox**. Use the control's task list to display the image stored in the **Wedding.png** file, which is contained in the VbReloaded2015\Chap01 folder. Also use the task list to set the Size Mode to **StretchImage**.
12. Click the **PictureBox1** control at the top of the form. Set the control's Size property to **225, 205**. Set its Name and SizeMode properties to **displayPictureBox** and **StretchImage**, respectively.
13. Click the **Button1** control. Change its Name and Text properties to **bdayButton** and **Birthday**, respectively.
14. Change the Button2 control's Name and Text properties to **weddingButton** and **Wedding**, respectively.
15. Change the Button3 control's Name and Text properties to **exitButton** and **Exit**, respectively.
16. Just for practice, click the **bdayButton** on the form and then press the **Delete** key on your keyboard. To restore the control, click **Edit** on the menu bar and then click **Undo**.
17. Position the controls as shown in Figure 1-63. Use the Align option on the Format menu to align the top borders of the three buttons. Use the Center in Form option on the Format menu to center the label, horizontally, on the form. Then use it to center the displayPictureBox, horizontally, on the form. Select the three buttons and then use the Center in Form option to center them, horizontally, on the form. Click the **form** to deselect the buttons.

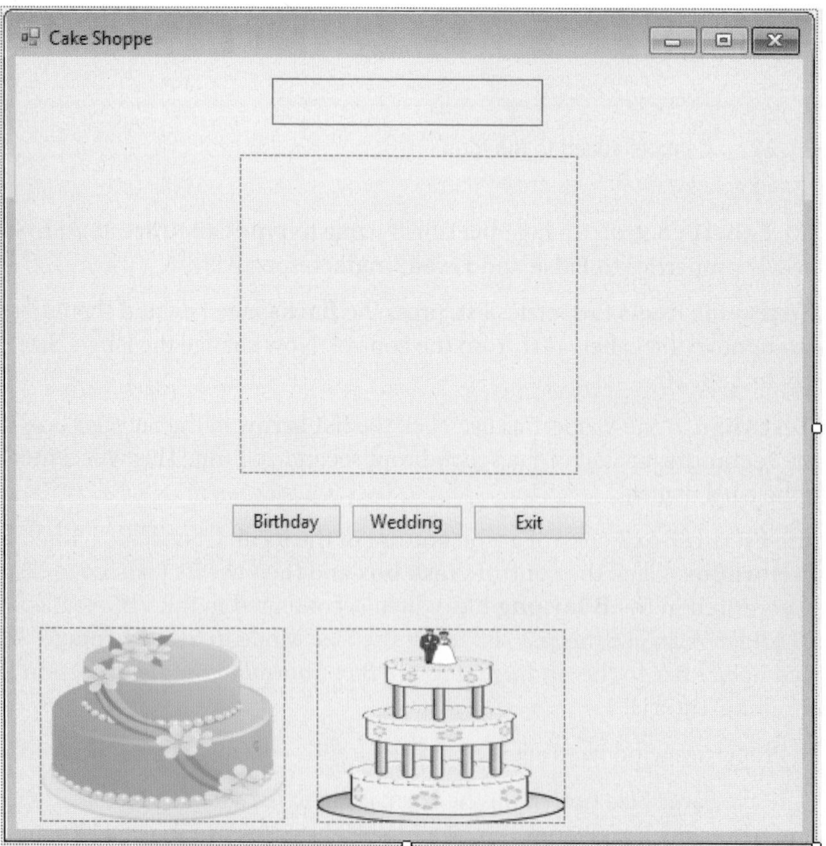

Figure 1-63 Completed user interface

18. Place your mouse pointer on the sizing handle that appears at the bottom of the form. Press and hold down the left mouse button as you drag the bottom border up. When you no longer see the bdayPictureBox and weddingPictureBox controls, release the mouse button.
19. Right-click the **form** and then click **Lock Controls**.
20. Save the solution. If you need help, refer to the How To box shown earlier in Figure 1-22.

Coding the Cake Shoppe Application

At this point, the buttons in the interface do not know the tasks they should perform when they are clicked by the user. You tell a button what to do by writing an event procedure for it in the Code Editor window.

To code the Exit button's Click event procedure:

1. Auto-hide the Toolbox, Solution Explorer, and Properties windows.
2. Open the Code Editor window. If you need help, refer to the How To box shown earlier in Figure 1-18.
3. Use the Object and Method list boxes to open the code template for the exitButton's Click event procedure.
4. The Exit button should end the application when it is clicked. Type **me.** (be sure to type the period, but don't press Enter). When you type the period, the Code Editor's IntelliSense feature displays a list of properties, methods, and so on from which you can select.

   Note: If the list of choices does not appear, the IntelliSense feature may have been turned off on your computer system. To turn it on, click Tools on the menu bar, click Options, expand the Text Editor node, click Basic, select the Auto list members check box, and then click the OK button.
5. Type **clo** (but don't press Enter). The IntelliSense feature highlights the Close method in the list.
6. Press the **Tab** key on your keyboard to include the Close method in the instruction, and then press **Enter**.

When the user clicks the Birthday button, the button's Click event procedure should display the image from the bdayPictureBox in the displayPictureBox. You can accomplish this task using an assignment statement that assigns the Image property of the bdayPictureBox to the Image property of the displayPictureBox, like this: `displayPictureBox.Image = bdayPictureBox.Image`. The Click event procedure should also display the word "Birthday" in the typeLabel. This task requires the following assignment statement, which assigns the string "Birthday" to the Text property of the typeLabel: `typeLabel.Text = "Birthday"`.

To code the Birthday button's Click event procedure:

1. Open the code template for the bdayButton's Click event procedure.
2. Type **disp** to select displayPictureBox in the list. Press **Tab** to enter displayPictureBox in the procedure.
3. Type **.** (a period) and then type the letter **i** to select the Image property in the list. Press **Tab** to include the Image property in the statement.

4. Type = **bdayp** to select bdayPictureBox in the list, and then press **Tab**. Type **.** (a period) and then type the letter **i** to select the Image property in the list. Press **Tab** and then press **Enter**. The procedure now contains the `displayPictureBox.Image = bdayPictureBox.Image` statement.
5. Next, use the IntelliSense feature to type the **typeLabel.Text** = **"Birthday"** statement in the procedure. Press **Enter** after typing the statement.

The Wedding button's Click event procedure should display the image from the weddingPictureBox in the displayPictureBox. It should also display the word "Wedding" in the typeLabel.

To code the Wedding button's Click event procedure:

1. Open the code template for the weddingButton's Click event procedure and then enter the appropriate assignment statements.
2. If line numbers do not appear in the Code Editor window, click **Tools** on the menu bar, click **Options**, expand the **Text Editor** node, click **Basic**, select the **Line numbers** check box, and then click the **OK** button. The completed code is shown in Figure 1-64.

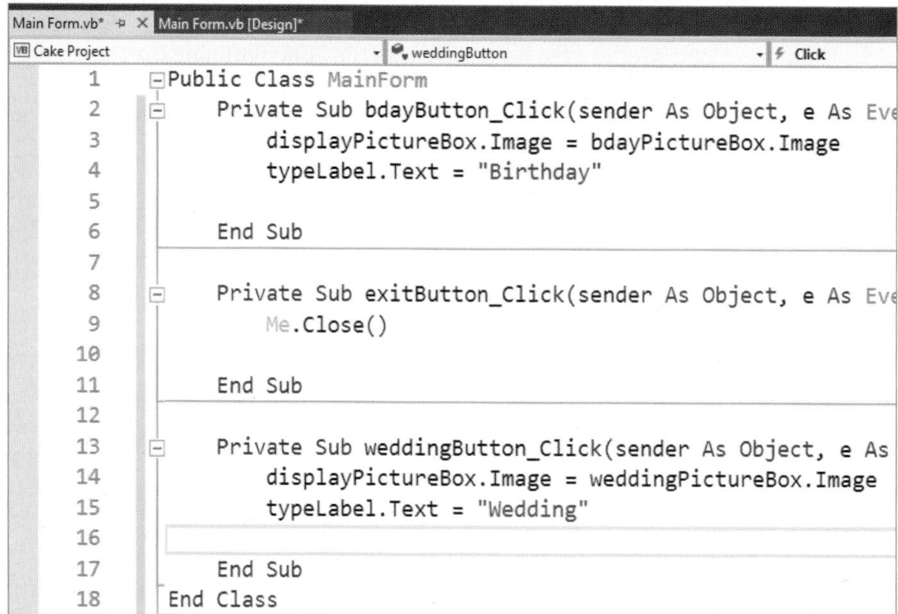

Figure 1-64 Cake Shoppe application's code

3. On your own, remove the line numbers from the Code Editor window.

Testing an Application

In the following set of steps, you will test the application to determine whether the buttons respond correctly to the user.

To start and end the current application:

1. Open the Project Designer window and verify that MainForm is the name of the startup form. Also change the executable file's name to **Cake Shoppe**. If you need help accomplishing either of these tasks, refer to the How To boxes shown earlier in Figures 1-23 and 1-27.

2. Save the solution and then close the Project Designer window.
3. Start the application. If you need help, refer to the How To box shown earlier in Figure 1-25. (Do not be concerned about any windows that appear at the bottom of the screen.)
4. Click the **Birthday** button. The birthday cake image appears in the displayPictureBox and the word "Birthday" appears in the label control. See Figure 1-65.

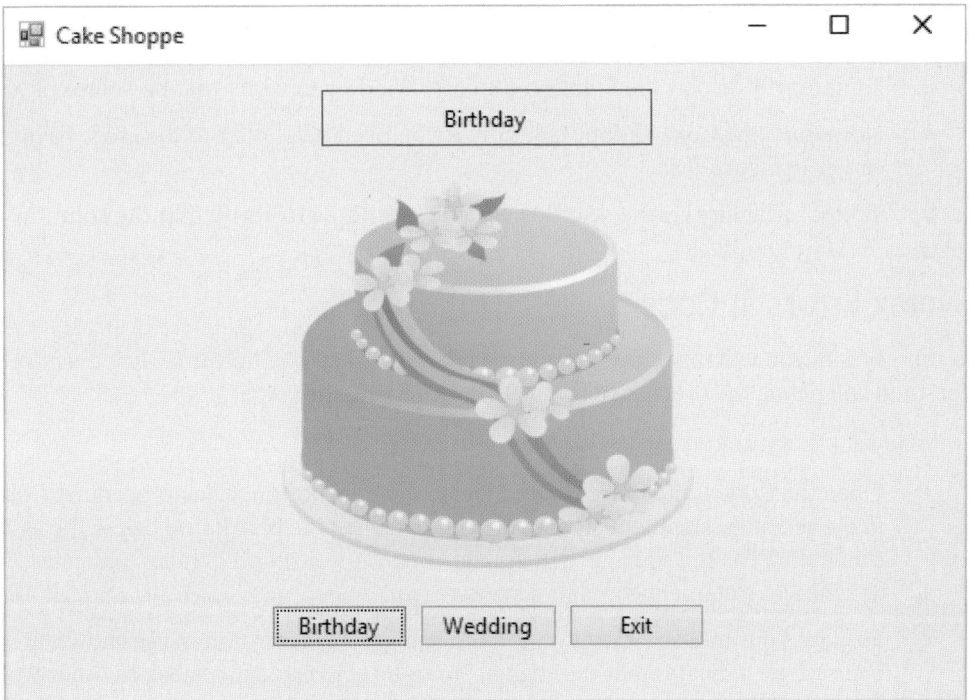

Figure 1-65 Sample run of the Cake Shoppe application

5. Click the **Wedding** button. The wedding cake image appears in the displayPictureBox and the word "Wedding" appears in the label control.
6. Click the **Exit** button.

Printing the Application's Code and Interface

For your future reference, you should always print a copy of the application's code and its interface. To print the code, the Code Editor window must be the active (current) window. To print the interface during design time, the Windows Form Designer window must be the active window.

To print the current application's code and interface:

1. If your computer is connected to a printer, print the code with line numbers. If you need help, refer to the How To box shown earlier in Figure 1-31.
2. If your computer is connected to a printer, print the application's interface. If you need help, refer to the How To box shown earlier in Figure 1-31.

Closing and Opening a Solution

When you are finished working with a solution, you should close it using the Close Solution option on the File menu. Closing a solution closes all projects and files contained in the solution. You can open an existing solution using the Open Project option on the File menu.

To close and then open the current solution:

1. First, close the Code Editor window.
2. Next, close the Cake Shoppe solution. If you need help, refer to the How To box shown earlier in Figure 1-32.
3. Temporarily display the Solution Explorer window to verify that no solutions are open.
4. Now, open the Cake Shoppe solution. If you need help, refer to the How To box shown earlier in Figure 1-33.
5. Temporarily display the Solution Explorer window to verify that the solution is open.

Syntax Errors in Code

In this section, you will introduce a syntax error in the Birthday button's Click event procedure. You then will debug the procedure by locating and fixing the error.

To introduce a syntax error in the code:

1. Open the Code Editor window and locate the bdayButton_Click procedure. Delete **.Text** in the second assignment statement and then click the **blank line** below the assignment statement. The red squiggle that appears below the string "Birthday" indicates that the assignment statement contains a syntax error.
2. Position your mouse pointer on the red squiggle. The error message shown in Figure 1-66 indicates that the string cannot be converted to a label. In other words, it cannot be assigned to the label itself. Instead, it must be assigned to one of the label's properties—in this case, its Text property.

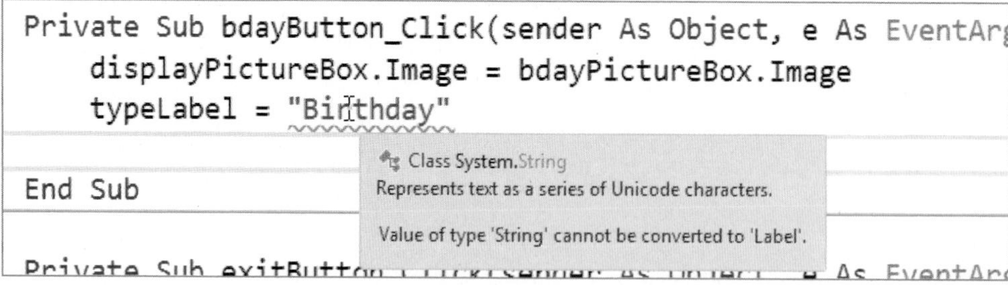

Figure 1-66 Red squiggle and message indicate a syntax error

3. Now observe what happens when you start the application without correcting the syntax error. Save the solution and then start the application. A message box appears and indicates that the code contains errors. The message asks whether you want to continue. Click the **No** button. The Error List window, which opens at the bottom of the IDE, indicates that Line 4 contains an error.
4. Type **.Text** after typeLabel to correct the error, and then click **another line** in the Code Editor window. The Error List window shows that the code is now error-free.
5. Close the Error List window. Save the solution and then start the application. Click the **Birthday** button to verify that it is working correctly.
6. Click the **Exit** button to end the application. Close the Code Editor window and then close the solution.

Exiting Visual Studio 2015

You can exit Visual Studio using either the Close button on its title bar or the Exit option on its File menu.

To exit Visual Studio:

1. Click **File** on the menu bar and then click **Exit** on the menu.

Running the Application's Executable File

Recall that when you start a Visual Basic application, the computer automatically creates an executable file that can be run outside of the IDE. The file's name ends with .exe. The computer stores the file in the project's bin\Debug folder.

To run the Cake Shoppe.exe file:

1. Use Windows to locate and then open the VbReloaded2015\Chap01\Cake Solution\Cake Project\bin\Debug folder. Right-click **Cake Shoppe** (**Cake Shoppe.exe**) and then click **Open**.
2. Click the **Birthday** and **Wedding** buttons to test the application, and then click the **Exit** button.

PROGRAMMING EXAMPLE

Academy Awards

Create an application that displays the winners of the Academy Award for Best Picture for the years 2012 through 2015. Use the following names for the solution and project, respectively: Academy Solution and Academy Project. Save the files in the VbReloaded2015\Chap01 folder. Change the form file's name to Main Form.vb. Remember to lock the controls in the interface. See Figures 1-67 through 1-69. The image in the picture box is contained in the VbReloaded2015\Chap01\Award.png file.

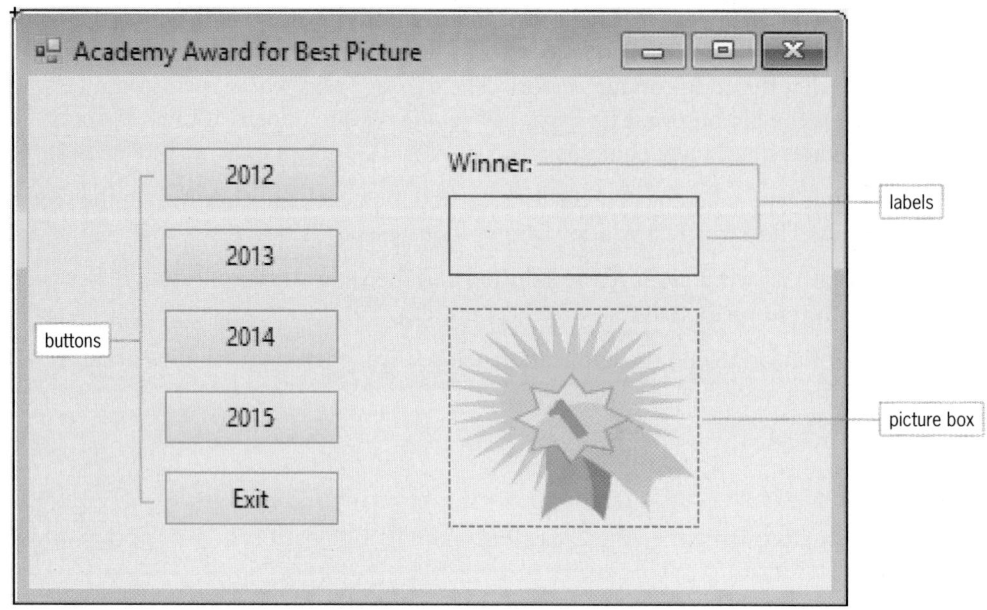

Figure 1-67 User interface

Object	Property	Setting
Form1	Name	MainForm
	Font	Segoe UI, 9pt
	StartPosition	CenterScreen
	Text	Academy Award for Best Picture
Button1	Name	year2012Button
	Text	2012
Button2	Name	year2013Button
	Text	2013
Button3	Name	year2014Button
	Text	2014
Button4	Name	year2015Button
	Text	2015
Button5	Name	exitButton
	Text	Exit
Label1	Text	Winner:
Label2	Name	winnerLabel
	AutoSize	False
	BorderStyle	FixedSingle
	Text	(empty)
	TextAlign	MiddleCenter
PictureBox1	Image	Award.png
	SizeMode	StretchImage

Figure 1-68 Objects, properties, and settings

```
Public Class MainForm
    Private Sub exitButton_Click(sender As Object, e As EventArgs
    ) Handles exitButton.Click
        Me.Close()
    End Sub

    Private Sub year2012Button_Click(sender As Object,
    e As EventArgs) Handles year2012Button.Click
        winnerLabel.Text = "The Artist"

    End Sub

    Private Sub year2013Button_Click(sender As Object,
    e As EventArgs) Handles year2013Button.Click
        winnerLabel.Text = "Argo"

    End Sub

    Private Sub year2014Button_Click(sender As Object,
    e As EventArgs) Handles year2014Button.Click
        winnerLabel.Text = "12 Years a Slave"

    End Sub

    Private Sub year2015Button_Click(sender As Object,
    e As EventArgs) Handles year2015Button.Click
        winnerLabel.Text = "Birdman"

    End Sub
End Class
```

Figure 1-69 Code

Chapter Summary

- An object-oriented programming language allows programmers to use objects to accomplish a program's goal.
- An object is anything that can be seen, touched, or used. Every object has attributes, called properties, that control its appearance and behavior.
- Every object in an object-oriented program is instantiated (created) from a class, which is a pattern that tells the computer how the object should look and behave. An object is referred to as an instance of the class.
- Applications created in Visual Studio are composed of solutions, projects, and files.
- You create your application's GUI in the Windows Form Designer window.
- A form is the foundation for the user interface in a Windows application.
- A Windows Form object is instantiated from the Windows Form class.

- The Solution Explorer window displays the names of projects and files contained in the current solution.
- The Properties window lists the selected object's properties.
- The *System.Windows.Forms* namespace contains the definition of the Windows Form class, as well as the class definitions for objects you add to a form.
- You use the value stored in an object's Name property to refer to the object in code.
- The value stored in the form's Text property appears in the form's title bar.
- The form's StartPosition property determines the position of the form when it first appears on the screen when the application is started.
- The recommended font for applications created for the Windows environment is the 9-point size of the Segoe UI font.
- The Toolbox window contains the tools you use when creating your application's GUI.
- It is helpful to change the form's Font property *before* adding controls to the form because the controls *inherit* the form's Font property setting.
- The value stored in a control's Text property appears inside the control.
- Controls on a form can be selected, sized, moved, deleted, restored, locked, and unlocked.
- A label control displays text that the user is not allowed to edit while the application is running.
- In most cases, an identifying label's BorderStyle and AutoSize properties are set to None and True, respectively. A label control that displays program output, on the other hand, usually has its BorderStyle and AutoSize properties set to FixedSingle and False, respectively.
- You can use a label control's TextAlign property to align the text that appears inside the label.
- Button controls are commonly used to perform an immediate action when clicked.
- You use a picture box control to display an image on the form.
- The Format menu provides options for aligning, sizing, and centering the controls on a form.
- You tell an object how to respond to an event by coding an event procedure. You enter the code in the Code Editor window.
- In the Code Editor window, you use the Object and Method list boxes to select the object and event, respectively, that you want to code.
- The Code Editor provides a code template for each of an object's event procedures. The code template begins with the Private Sub clause and ends with the End Sub clause. You enter your Visual Basic instructions between those clauses.
- You can use the `Me.Close()` instruction to terminate an application.
- You should save the solution every 10 or 15 minutes.
- When you start a Visual Basic application, the computer automatically creates an executable file and saves it in the project's bin\Debug folder. This is the file typically given to the user.
- You can use an assignment statement to assign a value to a property while an application is running.
- You should print an application's code and its user interface for future reference.
- Closing a solution closes all projects and files contained in the solution.
- The process of locating and correcting the errors (bugs) in a program is called debugging.

Key Terms

Applications—programs created for the Windows environment, the Web, or mobile devices

Assignment operator—the equal sign in an assignment statement

Assignment statement—an instruction that assigns a value to something, such as to the property of an object

Bug—an error in a program's code

Button control—the control commonly used to perform an immediate action when clicked

Camel case—the practice of entering the first word in an object's name in lowercase and then capitalizing the first letter of each subsequent word in the name

Class—the term used in object-oriented programming (OOP) to refer to a pattern that the computer uses to instantiate an object

Class definition—a block of code that specifies (or defines) an object's appearance and behavior

Code—program instructions

Code Editor window—the window in which you enter your application's code

Controls—objects (such as a label, a picture box, or a button) added to a form

Debugging—the process of locating and correcting the errors (bugs) in a program

Dot member access operator—a period; used to indicate a hierarchy

Event procedure—a set of Visual Basic instructions that tell an object how to respond to an event

Events—actions to which an object can respond; examples include clicking, double-clicking, and scrolling

Executable file—a file that can be run outside of the Visual Studio IDE; the file has an.exe extension on its filename

Form—the foundation for the user interface in a Windows application; also called a Windows form object

Form file—a file that contains the code associated with a Windows form

GUI—the acronym for a graphical user interface

IDE—the acronym for an integrated development environment

Instance—the term used in object-oriented programming (OOP) to refer to an object instantiated (created) from a class

Instantiated—the term used in object-oriented programming (OOP) to refer to the process of creating an object from a class

Integrated development environment—an environment that contains all of the tools and features needed to create, run, and test a program; also called an IDE

Keyword—a word that has a special meaning in a programming language

Label control—the control used to display text that the user is not allowed to edit during run time

Method—a predefined Visual Basic procedure that you can call (or invoke) when needed

Namespace—a block of memory cells inside the computer; the memory cells contain the code that defines a group of related classes

Object—in object-oriented programming (OOP), anything that can be seen, touched, or used

Object-oriented programming language—a language that allows the programmer to use objects to accomplish a program's goal

OOP—the acronym for object-oriented programming

Pascal case—the practice of capitalizing the first letter in a name and the first letter of each subsequent word in the name

Picture box control—the control used to display an image on a form

Procedure footer—the last line in a code template

Procedure header—the first line in a code template

Properties—the attributes that control an object's appearance and behavior

Properties window—the window that lists an object's attributes (properties)

Reference control—the first control selected in a group of controls; this is the control whose size and/or location you want the other selected controls to match

Sequence structure—refers to the fact that the computer processes a procedure's instructions one after another in the order in which they appear in the procedure; also referred to as sequential processing

Sequential processing—see sequence structure

Solution Explorer window—the window that displays a list of the projects contained in the current solution and the items contained in each project

Source file—a file that contains code

Startup form—the form that appears automatically when an application is started

String—zero or more characters enclosed in quotation marks

Sub procedure—a block of code that performs a specific task

Syntax—the rules of a programming language

Syntax error—occurs when an instruction in your code breaks one of a programming language's rules

Toolbox—see Toolbox window

Toolbox window—the window that contains the tools used when creating an interface; each tool represents a class; referred to more simply as the toolbox

User interface—what the user sees and interacts with while an application is running

Windows Form Designer window—the window in which you create your application's GUI

Windows Form object—the foundation for the user interface in a Windows application; referred to more simply as a form

Review Questions

> Each Review Question is associated with one or more objectives listed at the beginning of the chapter.

1. When a form has been modified since the last time it was saved, what appears on its tab in the designer window? (9)
   a. an ampersand (&)
   b. an asterisk (*)
   c. a percent sign (%)
   d. a plus sign (+)
2. Which of the following assigns the string "89.99" to the priceLabel control? (4, 8, 11)
   a. `priceLabel.Text = "89.99"`
   b. `priceLabel.String = "89.99"`
   c. `priceLabel.Text = '89.99'`
   d. `priceLabel = "89.99"`
3. Which of the following is a pattern for creating an object? (1)
   a. an attribute
   b. a behavior
   c. a class
   d. an instance
4. Which window is used to set the characteristics that control an object's appearance and behavior? (4)
   a. Characteristics
   b. Object
   c. Properties
   d. Toolbox
5. Which of the following instructions makes the helloLabel visible? (4, 8, 11)
   a. `helloLabel.Visible = False`
   b. `helloLabel.Visible = True`
   c. `helloLabel.Show = False`
   d. `hello.Show = True`
6. Which property contains the text that appears on the face of a button? (4, 6)
   a. Caption
   b. Label
   c. Name
   d. Text
7. Actions such as clicking and double-clicking are called ____________. (1)
   a. actionEvents
   b. events
   c. happenings
   d. procedures
8. The equal sign in an assignment statement is called the ____________ operator. (11)
   a. assignment
   b. dot member access
   c. equality
   d. equation

9. If a project is stored in the E:\Chap01\First Solution\First Project folder, where will the computer store the project's executable file? (2, 10)
   a. E:\Chap01\First Solution\First Project
   b. E:\Chap01\First Solution\First Project\bin\Debug
   c. E:\Chap01\First Solution\First Project\bin\Executable
   d. E:\Chap01\First Solution\First Project\Executable
10. Which property does the programmer use to refer to an object in code? (4, 8)
   a. Caption
   b. Label
   c. Name
   d. Text
11. Which property is used to put a border around a label control? (4, 6)
   a. Border
   b. BorderStyle
   c. Style
   d. StyleBorder

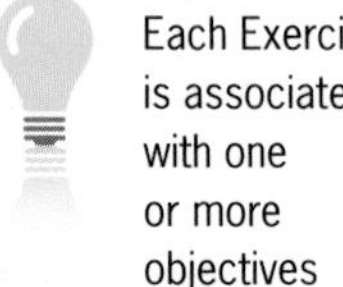

Each Exercise is associated with one or more objectives listed at the beginning of the chapter.

Exercises

Pencil and Paper

INTRODUCTORY 1. Explain the difference between an object's Text property and its Name property. (4, 6, 8)

INTRODUCTORY 2. Explain the process of using the Format menu to make the Button1 and Button2 controls the same size as the Button3 control. (5, 7)

INTERMEDIATE 3. Write an assignment statement to assign the string "Visual Basic" to the languageLabel control. (8, 11)

ADVANCED 4. Write an assignment statement to assign the contents of the firstLabel control to the secondLabel control. (8, 11)

SWAT THE BUGS 5. Correct the errors in the `myButton.Visibel = Yes` line of code. (4, 11, 13)

SWAT THE BUGS 6. Correct the errors in the `nameLabel = Jake Smith` line of code. (4, 11, 13)

Computer

MODIFY THIS 7. If necessary, create the Olivia application from this chapter's Programming Tutorial 1. Use Windows to make a copy of the Olivia Solution folder. Rename the copy Olivia Solution-ModifyThis. Open the Olivia Solution (Olivia Solution.sln) file contained in the Olivia Solution-ModifyThis folder. Add another button and picture box to the form; name the controls staticButton and staticPictureBox, respectively. The staticPictureBox control should display the image stored in the VbReloaded2015\Chap01\Static.png file. (The image was created using Reallusion CrazyTalk Animator.) Code the staticButton_Click procedure so that it displays the staticPictureBox's image before hiding the englishPictureBox and spanishPictureBox controls. Also make the appropriate modifications to the englishButton_Click and spanishButton_Click procedures. Test the application appropriately. Also test its .exe file. Print the application's code and interface. (1-12)

8. If necessary, create the Cake Shoppe application from this chapter's Programming Tutorial 2. Use Windows to make a copy of the Cake Solution folder. Rename the copy Cake Solution-ModifyThis. Open the Cake Solution (Cake Solution.sln) file contained in the Cake Solution-ModifyThis folder. Add another button and picture box to the form; name the controls generalButton and generalPictureBox, respectively. The generalPictureBox control should display the image stored in the VbReloaded2015\Chap01\General.png file. (The image is courtesy of OpenClipArt.org/vectorsme.) The generalButton_Click procedure should display the generalPictureBox's image in the displayPictureBox and display the word "General" in the typeLabel. Make the appropriate modifications to the application's interface and code. Test the application appropriately. Also test its .exe file. Print the application's code and interface. (1-12) MODIFY THIS

9. If necessary, create the Academy Awards application from this chapter's Programming Example. Use Windows to make a copy of the Academy Solution folder. Rename the copy Academy Solution-ModifyThis. Open the Academy Solution (Academy Solution.sln) file contained in the Academy Solution-ModifyThis folder. Change the text in the form's title bar to "Academy Award", and change the label's text to "Best Picture". Add four labels to the form. Change the name of two of the labels to actorLabel and actressLabel. Change the Text properties of the other two labels to "Best Actor:" and "Best Actress:". Use the Internet to determine the winners of the Best Actor and Best Actress awards for the years 2012 through 2015. Modify the application so that it displays the names of the winners in the actorLabel and actressLabel controls. Test the application appropriately. Also test its .exe file. (1-11) MODIFY THIS

10. In this exercise, you add one label, six picture boxes, and six button controls to a form. You also change the properties of the form and its controls. (1-11) INTERMEDIATE

    a. Create a Windows Forms application. Use the following names for the solution and project, respectively: Florist Solution and Florist Project. Save the application in the VbReloaded2015\Chap01 folder. Change the form file's name to Main Form.vb. Change the form's name to MainForm.

    b. Change the form's Font property to Segoe UI, 9pt. The form should be centered on the screen when it first appears.

    c. Create the interface shown in Figure 1-70. Assign meaningful names to the six buttons and six picture boxes, and set each picture box's SizeMode property to StretchImage. The images are stored in the following files, which are contained in the VbReloaded2015\Chap01 folder: Black.png, Blue.png, Brown.png, Green.png, and Purple.png.

    d. The Exit button should terminate the application when clicked. The other buttons should display the appropriate flower in the flowerPictureBox.

    e. Size the form to hide the five picture boxes that appear on the right side of the interface. Lock the controls on the form.

    f. Verify that MainForm is the project's startup form. Also, change the executable file's name to Florist. Close the Project Designer window. Test the application appropriately. Also test its .exe file.

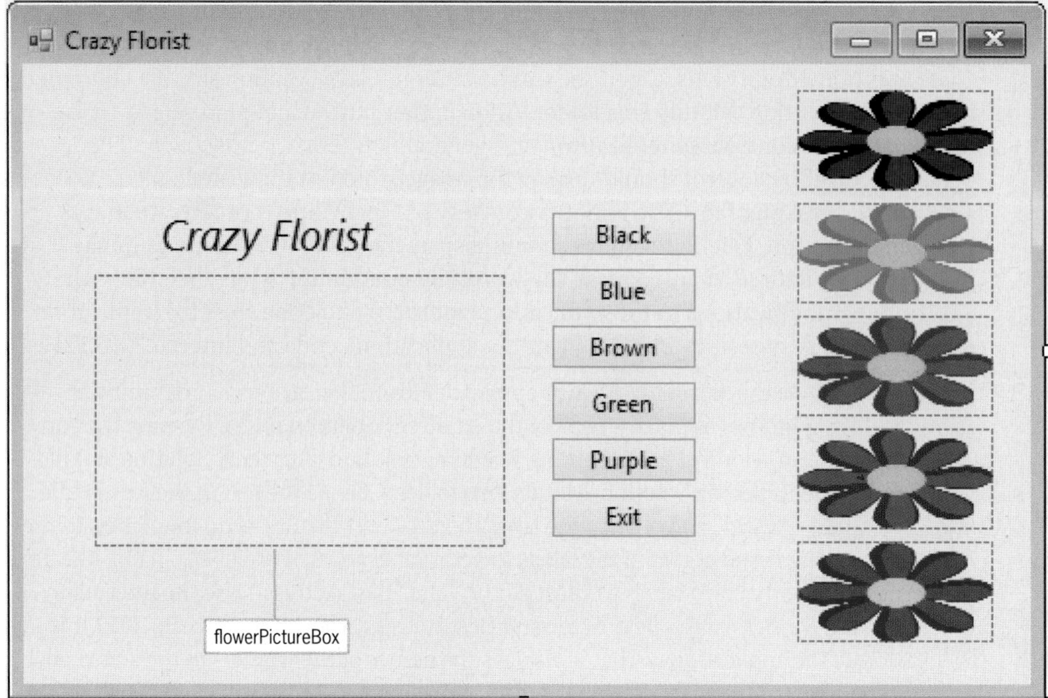

Figure 1-70 Sample interface for the Crazy Florist application

SWAT THE BUGS

11. Open the VbReloaded2015\Chap01\Debug Solution\Debug Solution (Debug Solution.sln) file. Start the application. Click the Exit button. Notice that the Exit button does not end the application. Click the Close button on the form's title bar to end the application. Open the Code Editor window. Locate and then correct the error. Save the solution and then start and test the application. Close the Code Editor window and then close the solution. (13)

Case Projects

Martin's Gymnasium

Create an application that displays the price of five sessions, 20 sessions, or 30 sessions of personal training. Use the following names for the solution and project, respectively: Gym Solution and Gym Project. Save the application in the VbReloaded2015\Chap01 folder. Change the form file's name to Main Form.vb. You can either create your own interface or create the one shown in Figure 1-71. Be sure to assign meaningful names to the form, the buttons, and the label that displays the price. Center the price within the label control. The image in the picture box is stored in the VbReloaded2015\Chap01\Gym.png file. Use your own prices for the sessions. (1-9, 11)

Figure 1-71 Sample interface for the Martin's Gymnasium application

Important Information

Create an application that displays a name and phone number. Use the following names for the solution and project, respectively: Info Solution and Info Project. Save the application in the VbReloaded2015\Chap01 folder. Change the form file's name to Main Form.vb. You can either create your own interface or create the one shown in Figure 1-72. Be sure to assign meaningful names to the form, the buttons, and the label controls that display the name and phone number. Center the names and phone numbers within their respective label controls. You provide the names and phone numbers. (1-9, 11)

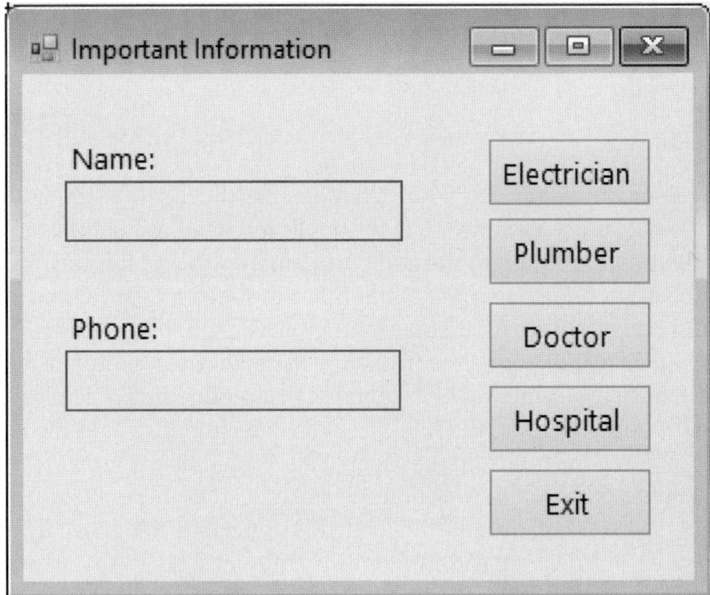

Figure 1-72 Sample interface for the Important Information application

Area Formulas

Create an application that displays the formulas for calculating the areas of different shapes. Use the following names for the solution and project, respectively: Area Solution and Area Project. Save the application in the VbReloaded2015\Chap01 folder. Change the form file's name to Main Form.vb. You can either create your own interface or create the one shown in Figure 1-73. Be sure to assign meaningful names to the form, the buttons, and the label control that displays the area. If necessary, use the Internet to determine the area formulas. Center the formula within the label control. (1-9, 11)

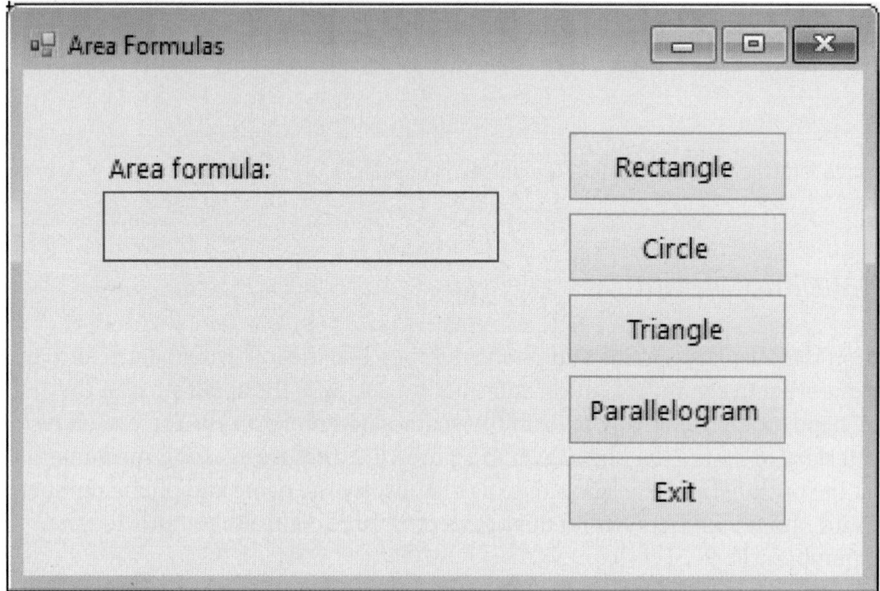

Figure 1-73 Sample interface for the Area Formulas application

Candice's Candy Shop

Create an eye-catching splash screen for the candy shop. A splash screen is the first image that appears when an application is started. It is used to introduce the application and to hold the user's attention while the application is being read into the computer's memory. You can use the tools you learned in this chapter, or you can experiment with other tools from the toolbox. For example, the Timer tool creates a timer control that you can use to close the splash screen after a specified period of time. (Hint: Research a timer control's Enabled and Interval properties and its Tick event.) You may also want to experiment with a control's BackColor and ForeColor properties. Be sure to include one or more images in the interface. You can either use your own image file(s) or download one or more free images from the Open Clip Art Library at *https://openclipart.org*. Use the following names for the solution and project, respectively: Candy Solution and Candy Project. Save the application in the VbReloaded2015\Chap01 folder. Change the form file's name to Main Form.vb. Print the application's code and interface. (1-9, 11, 12)

CHAPTER 2

Creating a User Interface

After studying Chapter 2, you should be able to:

1. Plan an application using a TOE chart
2. Use a text box
3. Follow the Windows standards regarding the layout and labeling of controls
4. Follow the Windows standards regarding the use of graphics, fonts, and color
5. Assign access keys to controls
6. Set the tab order
7. Designate a default button
8. Print the interface from code
9. Play an audio file

Planning an Application

Before you create the user interface for a Windows Forms application, you should plan the application. The plan should be developed jointly with the user to ensure that the application meets the user's needs. It cannot be stressed enough that the only way to guarantee the success of an application is to actively involve the user in the planning phase. Figure 2-1 lists the steps to follow when planning an application.

HOW TO Plan an Application

1. Identify the tasks the application needs to perform.
2. Identify the objects to which you will assign those tasks.
3. Identify the events required to trigger an object to perform its assigned tasks.
4. Design the user interface.

Figure 2-1 How to plan an application

You can use a TOE (Task, Object, Event) chart to record the application's tasks, objects, and events, which are identified in the first three steps of the planning phase. In the next several sections, you will complete a TOE chart for a small company named Say Cheese!.

Say Cheese! Company

The Say Cheese! company takes orders for cheesecakes by phone. The cheesecakes are priced at $25 each and are available in two flavors: vanilla bean and strawberry. The company's 10 salespeople record each order on a form that contains the customer's name and address and the number of each flavor of cheesecake ordered. The salespeople then calculate the total number of cheesecakes ordered and the total price of the order, including a 3% sales tax. The company's sales manager feels that having the salespeople manually perform the necessary calculations is much too time-consuming and prone to errors. She wants you to create a computerized application that will solve the problems of the current order-taking system. The first step in planning this application is to identify the application's tasks.

Identifying the Application's Tasks

Realizing that it is essential to involve the user when planning the application, you meet with the sales manager, Ms. Murphy, to determine her requirements. You ask Ms. Murphy to show you a sample of the current order form; the sample is shown in Figure 2-2. Viewing the company's current forms and procedures will help you better understand the application you need to create. You can also use the current form as a guide when designing the user interface.

Say Cheese!

ORDER FORM

Customer name: ______________________________

Address: ______________________________

City: ______________ State: _____ ZIP: __________

VANILLA BEAN	STRAWBERRY	TOTAL ORDERED	TOTAL PRICE

Figure 2-2 Current order form

When identifying the tasks an application needs to perform, it is helpful to ask the questions italicized in the following bulleted items. The answers pertaining to the Say Cheese! company's application follow each question.

- *What information will the application need to display on the screen and/or print on the printer?* The application should display and also print the customer information (name, street address, city, state, and ZIP code), the number of vanilla bean cheesecakes ordered, the number of strawberry cheesecakes ordered, the total number of cheesecakes ordered, and the total price of the order.
- *What information will the user need to enter into the user interface to display and/or print the desired information?* The salesperson (the user) must enter the customer information (name, street address, city, state, and ZIP code), the number of vanilla bean cheesecakes ordered, and the number of strawberry cheesecakes ordered.
- *What information will the application need to calculate to display and/or print the desired information?* The application needs to calculate the total number of cheesecakes ordered and the total price of the order.
- *How will the user end the application?* The application will provide an Exit button.
- *Will previous information need to be cleared from the screen before new information is entered?* The order information will need to be cleared from the screen before the next customer's information is entered.

Figure 2-3 shows the application's tasks listed in a TOE chart. The tasks do not need to be listed in any particular order. In this case, the data entry tasks are listed first, followed by the calculation tasks, the display and printing tasks, the application ending task, and the screen-clearing task.

Task	Object	Event
Get the following order information from the user: Customer name Street address City State ZIP code Number of vanilla bean ordered Number of strawberry ordered		
Calculate total ordered and total price		
Display the following information: Customer name Street address City State ZIP code Number of vanilla bean ordered Number of strawberry ordered Total ordered Total price		
Print the order form		
End the application		
Clear the screen for the next order		

Figure 2-3 Tasks entered in a TOE chart

Identifying the Objects

After completing the Task column of the TOE chart, you then assign each task to an object in the user interface. For this application, the only objects you will use besides the Windows form itself are the button, label, and text box controls. As you already know, you use a label control to display information that you do not want the user to change while the application is running, and you use a button control to perform an action immediately after the user clicks it. You use a **text box** to give the user an area in which to enter data.

The first task listed in the TOE chart gets the order information from the user. Because you need to provide the salesperson with areas in which to enter the information, you will assign the first task to seven text boxes—one for each item of information.

The TOE chart's second task calculates both the total number of cheesecakes ordered and the total price. So that the salesperson can calculate these amounts at any time, you will assign the task to a button named calcButton.

The third task in the TOE chart displays the order information, the total number of cheesecakes ordered, and the total price. The order information is displayed automatically when the user enters that information in the seven text boxes. The total ordered and total price, however, are not entered by the user. Instead, those amounts are calculated by the calcButton. Because the user should not be allowed to change the calculated results, you will have the calcButton display the total ordered and total price in two label controls named totalOrderedLabel and totalPriceLabel, respectively. If you look ahead to Figure 2-4, you will notice that "(from calcButton)" was added to the Task column for both display tasks.

The last three tasks listed in the TOE chart will be assigned to three buttons named printButton, exitButton, and clearButton. Assigning the tasks to buttons will give the user control over when the tasks are performed. Figure 2-4 shows the TOE chart with the Task and Object columns completed.

Task	Object	Event
Get the following order information from the user:		
Customer name	nameTextBox	
Street address	addressTextBox	
City	cityTextBox	
State	stateTextBox	
ZIP code	zipTextBox	
Number of vanilla bean ordered	vanillaTextBox	
Number of strawberry ordered	strawberryTextBox	
Calculate total ordered and total price	calcButton	
Display the following information:		
Customer name	nameTextBox	
Street address	addressTextBox	
City	cityTextBox	
State	stateTextBox	
ZIP code	zipTextBox	
Number of vanilla bean ordered	vanillaTextBox	
Number of strawberry ordered	strawberryTextBox	
Total ordered (from calcButton)	totalOrderedLabel	
Total price (from calcButton)	totalPriceLabel	
Print the order form	printButton	
End the application	exitButton	
Clear the screen for the next order	clearButton	

Figure 2-4 Tasks and objects entered in a TOE chart

Identifying the Events

After defining the application's tasks and assigning the tasks to objects in the interface, you then determine which event (if any) must occur for an object to carry out its assigned task. The seven text boxes listed in the TOE chart in Figure 2-4 are assigned the task of getting and displaying the order information. Text boxes accept and display information automatically, so no special event is necessary for them to carry out their assigned task.

The two label controls listed in the TOE chart are assigned the task of displaying the total number of cheesecakes ordered and the total price of the order. Label controls automatically display their contents; so, here again, no special event needs to occur. (Recall that the two label controls will get their values from the calcButton.)

The remaining objects listed in the TOE chart are the four buttons. You will have each button perform its assigned task(s) when the user clicks it. Figure 2-5 shows the completed TOE chart.

Task	**Object**	**Event**
Get the following order information from the user:		
Customer name	nameTextBox	None
Street address	addressTextBox	None
City	cityTextBox	None
State	stateTextBox	None
ZIP code	zipTextBox	None
Number of vanilla bean ordered	vanillaTextBox	None
Number of strawberry ordered	strawberryTextBox	None
Calculate total ordered and total price	calcButton	Click
Display the following information:		
Customer name	nameTextBox	None
Street address	addressTextBox	None
City	cityTextBox	None
State	stateTextBox	None
ZIP code	zipTextBox	None
Number of vanilla bean ordered	vanillaTextBox	None
Number of strawberry ordered	strawberryTextBox	None
Total ordered (from calcButton)	totalOrderedLabel	None
Total price (from calcButton)	totalPriceLabel	None
Print the order form	printButton	Click
End the application	exitButton	Click
Clear the screen for the next order	clearButton	Click

Figure 2-5 Completed TOE chart ordered by task

If the application you are creating is small, like the Say Cheese! company's application, you can use the TOE chart in its current form to help you write the Visual Basic code. When the application is large, however, it is often helpful to rearrange the TOE chart so that it is ordered by object rather than by task. Simply list all of the objects in the Object column of a new TOE chart, being sure to list each object only once, and then list each object's tasks and events in the Task and Event columns, respectively. Figure 2-6 shows the rearranged TOE chart ordered by object rather than by task.

Task	Object	Event
1. Calculate total ordered and total price 2. Display total ordered and total price in totalOrderedLabel and totalPriceLabel	calcButton	Click
Print the order form	printButton	Click
End the application	exitButton	Click
Clear the screen for the next order	clearButton	Click
Display total ordered (from calcButton)	totalOrderedLabel	None
Display total price (from calcButton)	totalPriceLabel	None
Get and display the order information	nameTextBox, addressTextBox, cityTextBox, stateTextBox, zipTextBox, vanillaTextBox, strawberryTextBox	None

Figure 2-6 Completed TOE chart ordered by object

Mini-Quiz 2-1

The answers to Mini-Quiz questions are located in Appendix A. Each question is associated with one or more objectives listed at the beginning of the chapter.

1. When planning an application, what is the first thing you need to identify? (1)
   a. code
   b. events
   c. objects
   d. tasks
2. Every object in a user interface needs an event to occur in order for it to perform its assigned task. (1)
   a. True
   b. False
3. The task of getting a sales tax rate from the user should be assigned to what type of control? (1, 2)
   a. button
   b. label
   c. text box
   d. either b or c

Designing the User Interface

A company's standards for interfaces used within the company supersede the Windows standards.

After completing the TOE chart, the next step is to design the user interface. Although the TOE chart lists the objects to include in the interface, it does not indicate *where* the objects should be placed on the form. While the design of an interface is open to creativity, there are some guidelines to which you should adhere so that your application is consistent with the

Windows standards. This consistency will give your interface a familiar look, which will make your application easier for users to both learn and use. The guidelines are referred to as GUI (graphical user interface) guidelines. The first GUI guidelines you will learn in this chapter relate to the placement of the controls in the interface.

Control Placement

In Western countries, the user interface should be organized so that the information flows either vertically or horizontally, with the most important information always located in the upper-left corner of the interface. In a vertical arrangement, the information flows from top to bottom: The essential information is located in the first column, while secondary information is placed in subsequent columns. In a horizontal arrangement, on the other hand, the information flows from left to right: The essential information is placed in the first row, with secondary information placed in subsequent rows.

Ch02-Container Controls

Related controls should be grouped together using either white (empty) space or one of the tools located in the Containers section of the toolbox. Examples of tools found in the Containers section include the GroupBox, Panel, and TableLayoutPanel tools.

Figures 2-7 and 2-8 show two different interfaces for the cheesecake company's application. In Figure 2-7, the information is arranged vertically, and white space is used to group related controls together. In Figure 2-8, the information is arranged horizontally, with related controls grouped together using a group box, panel, and table layout panel. Each box and button in both figures is labeled so the user knows its purpose. For example, the "Name:" label tells the user the type of information to enter in the text box that appears below it. Similarly, the "Calculate" caption on the first button indicates the action the button will perform when it is clicked.

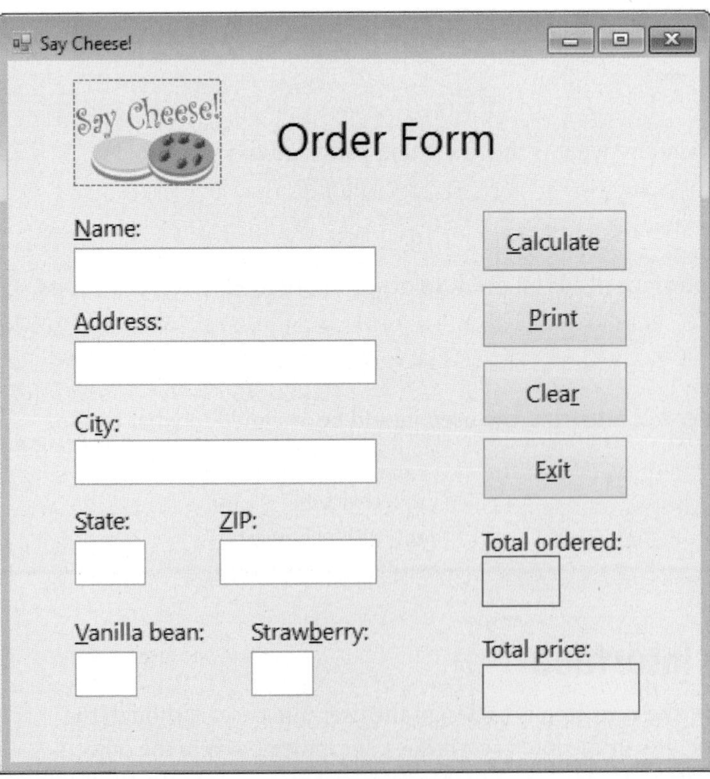

Figure 2-7 Vertical arrangement of the interface

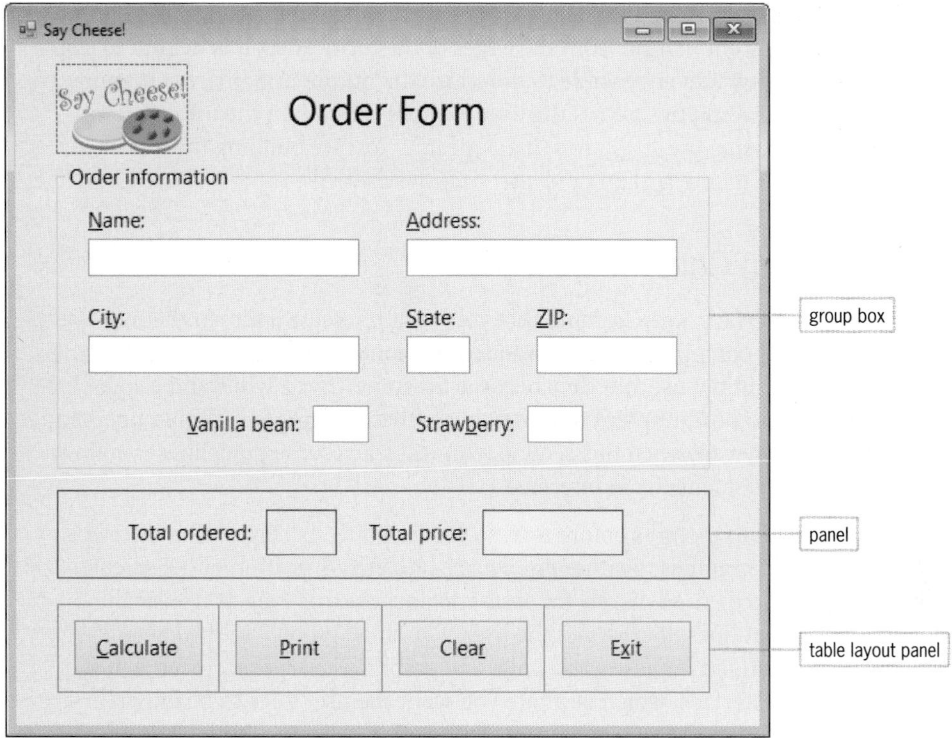

Figure 2-8 Horizontal arrangement of the interface.

Label controls that display program output, such as the result of calculations, should be labeled to make their contents obvious to the user. In the interfaces shown in Figures 2-7 and 2-8, the "Total ordered:" and "Total price:" labels identify the contents of the totalOrderedLabel and totalPriceLabel controls, respectively.

The text contained in a label control that identifies another control's contents should be meaningful and left-aligned within the label. In most cases, an identifying label should consist of one to three words only and appear on one line. In addition, the identifying label should be positioned either above or to the left of the control it identifies. An identifying label should end with a colon (:), which distinguishes it from other text in the user interface (such as the heading text "Order Form"). Some assistive technologies, which are technologies that provide assistance to individuals with disabilities, rely on the colons to make this distinction. The Windows standard is to use sentence capitalization for identifying labels. **Sentence capitalization** means you capitalize only the first letter in the first word and in any words that are customarily capitalized.

As you learned in Chapter 1, buttons are identified by the text that appears on the button's face. The text is often referred to as the button's caption. The caption should be meaningful, consist of one to three words only, and appear on one line. A button's caption should be entered using **book title capitalization**, which means you capitalize the first letter in each word, except for articles, conjunctions, and prepositions that do not occur at either the beginning or end of the caption.

If the buttons are stacked vertically, as they are in Figure 2-7, all the buttons should be the same height and width. If the buttons are positioned horizontally, as they are in Figure 2-8, all the buttons should be the same height, but their widths may vary if necessary. In a group of buttons, the most commonly used button typically appears first—either on the top (in a vertical arrangement) or on the left (in a horizontal arrangement).

When positioning the controls in the interface, place related controls close to each other, and be sure to maintain a consistent margin from the edges of the form. Also, it is helpful to align the borders of the controls wherever possible to minimize the number of different margins appearing in the interface. Doing this allows the user to more easily scan the information. You can align the borders using the snap lines that appear as you are building the interface. Or, you can use the Format menu to align (and also size) the controls.

Graphics, Fonts, and Color

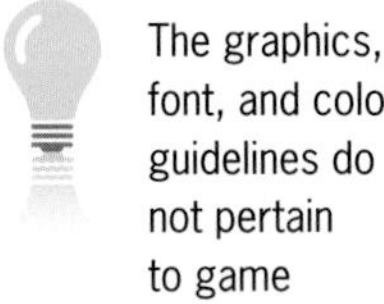
The graphics, font, and color guidelines do not pertain to game applications.

When designing a user interface, keep in mind that you want to create a screen that no one notices. Interfaces that contain a lot of different colors, fonts, and graphics may get *oohs* and *aahs* during their initial use, but they become tiresome after a while and also look unprofessional. The most important point to remember is that the interface should not distract the user from doing his or her work. In this section, you will learn some guidelines to follow regarding the use of these elements in an interface.

The human eye is attracted to pictures before text, so use graphics sparingly in an interface. Designers typically include graphics to either emphasize or clarify a portion of the screen. However, a graphic can also be used merely for aesthetic purposes, as long as it is small and placed in a location that does not distract the user. The small graphic in the cheesecake company's interfaces is included for aesthetics only. The graphic is purposely located in the upper-left corner of each interface, which is where you want the user's eye to be drawn first anyway. (Remember that the most important information usually begins there.) The graphic adds a personal touch to the order form without distracting the user.

As you learned in Chapter 1, an object's Font property determines the type, style, and size of the font used to display the object's text. You should use only one font type (typically Segoe UI) for all of the text in an interface, and use no more than two different font sizes. In addition, avoid using italics and underlining because both font styles make text difficult to read. The use of bold text should be limited to titles, headings, and key items that you want to emphasize.

The human eye is attracted to color before black and white; therefore, use color sparingly in an interface. It is a good practice to build the interface using black, white, and gray first, and then add color only if you have a good reason to do so. Keep the following three points in mind when deciding whether to include color in an interface:

1. People who have some form of either color blindness or color confusion will have trouble distinguishing colors.
2. Color is very subjective: A color that looks pretty to you may be hideous to someone else.
3. A color may have a different meaning in a different culture.

Usually, it is best to use black text on a white, off-white, or light gray background because dark text on a light background is the easiest to read. You should never use a dark color for the background or a light color for the text. This is because a dark background is hard on the eyes, and light-colored text can appear blurry.

If you are going to include color in the interface, limit the number of colors to three, not including white, black, and gray. Be sure that the colors you choose complement each other. Although color can be used to identify an important element in the interface, you should never use it as the only means of identification. In the cheesecake company's interfaces, for example, the colored box helps the salesperson quickly locate the total price. (You can change the background color of an object by setting its BackColor property.) However, color is not the only means of identifying the contents of that box; the box also has an identifying label (Total price:).

Mini-Quiz 2-2

1. The text on a button's face should be entered using ____________. (3)
   a. book title capitalization
   b. lowercase letters
   c. sentence capitalization
   d. uppercase letters
2. Which of the following controls can be used to group together other controls? (2, 3)
   a. group box
   b. panel
   c. table layout panel
   d. all of the above
3. The text in an identifying label should be entered using ____________. (3)
   a. book title capitalization
   b. lowercase letters
   c. sentence capitalization
   d. uppercase letters

The answers to Mini-Quiz questions are located in Appendix A. Each question is associated with one or more objectives listed at the beginning of the chapter.

Assigning Access Keys

The text in many of the controls shown in Figure 2-9 contains an underlined letter. The underlined letter is called an **access key**, and it allows the user to select an object using the Alt key in combination with a letter or number. For example, you can select the Exit button by pressing Alt+x because the letter x is the Exit button's access key. Access keys are not case sensitive. Therefore, you can select the Exit button by pressing either Alt+x or Alt+X. If you do not see the underlined access keys while an application is running, you can show them temporarily by pressing the Alt key. You can subsequently hide them by pressing the Alt key again. (To always display access keys, refer to Figure 1-1 in Chapter 1.)

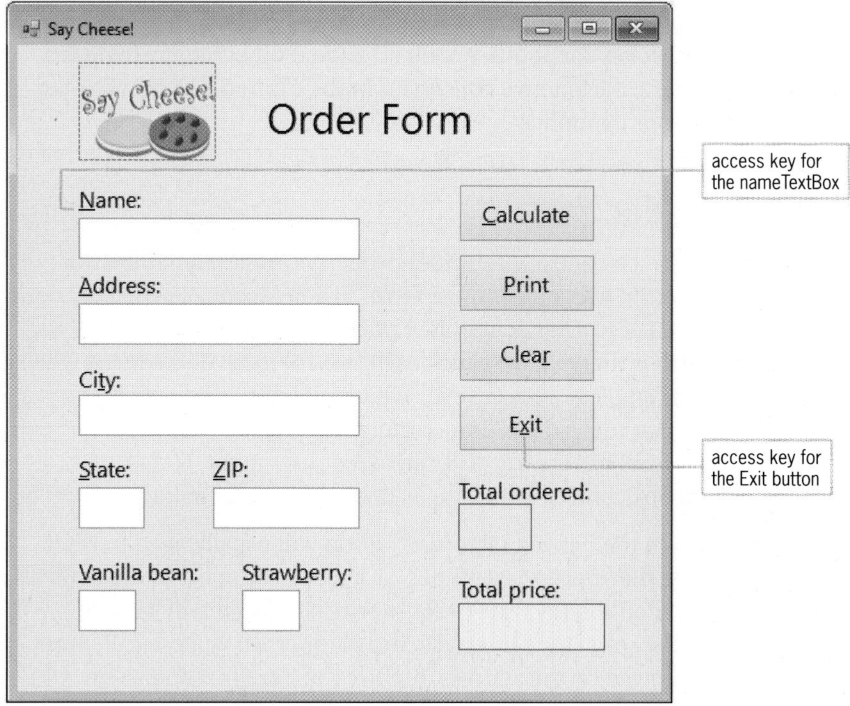

Figure 2-9 Say Cheese! application's interface

In an interface, you should assign access keys to each control that can accept user input, such as text boxes and buttons. This is because the user can enter information in a text box and click a button. The only exceptions to this rule are the OK and Cancel buttons, which typically do not have access keys in Windows applications. It is important to assign access keys to controls for the following reasons:

1. They allow users to work with the application even when their mouse becomes inoperative.
2. They allow users who are fast typists to keep their hands on the keyboard.
3. They allow people who cannot work with a mouse, such as people with disabilities, to use the application.

You assign an access key by including an ampersand (&) in the control's caption or identifying label. If the control is a button, you include the ampersand in the button's Text property, which is where a button's caption is stored. If the control is a text box, you include the ampersand in the Text property of its identifying label. (As you will learn later in this chapter, you must also set the TabIndex properties of the text box and its identifying label appropriately.) You enter the ampersand to the immediate left of the character you want to designate as the access key. To assign the letter x as the access key for the Exit button, you enter E&xit in the button's Text property. To assign the letter N as the access key for the nameTextBox, you enter &Name: in the Text property of its identifying label.

Notice that the Total ordered: and Total price: labels in Figure 2-9 do not have access keys. This is because those labels do not identify controls that accept user input; rather, they identify other label controls (totalOrderedLabel and totalPriceLabel). Users cannot access label controls while an application is running, so it is inappropriate to include an access key in their identifying labels.

Each access key in an interface should be unique. The first choice for an access key is the first letter of the caption or identifying label, unless another letter provides a more meaningful association. For example, the letter x is the access key for an Exit button because it provides a more meaningful association than does the letter E. If you can't use the first letter (perhaps because it is already used as the access key for another control) and no other letter provides a more meaningful association, then use a distinctive consonant in the caption or label. The last choices for an access key are a vowel or a number.

Controlling the Tab Order

When a text box has the focus, an insertion point appears inside it. When a button has the focus, a dotted rectangle appears inside its darkened border.

While you are creating the interface, each control's TabIndex property contains a number that represents the order in which the control was added to the form. The first control added to a form has a TabIndex value of 0; the second control has a TabIndex value of 1, and so on. The TabIndex values determine the tab order, which is the order in which each control receives the **focus** when the user either presses the Tab key or employs an access key while an application is running. A control whose TabIndex is 2 will receive the focus immediately after the control whose TabIndex is 1, and so on. When a control has the focus, it can accept user input. Not all controls have a TabIndex property; a picture box control, for example, does not have a TabIndex property.

Controls are rarely added to a form in the desired tab order, so you will usually need to reset their TabIndex values. To determine the appropriate values, you first make a list of the controls that can accept user input. The list should reflect the order in which the user will want to access the controls. In the cheesecake company's interface, the salesperson will typically want to access the nameTextBox first, followed by the addressTextBox, cityTextBox, and so on.

If a control that accepts user input is identified by a label control, you also include the label control in the list. (A text box is an example of a control that accepts user input and is identified by a label control.) You place the name of the label control immediately above the name of the control it identifies in the list. In the cheesecake company's interface, the Label1 control (which displays Name:) identifies the nameTextBox. Therefore, Label1 should appear immediately above nameTextBox in the list.

The names of controls that do not accept user input and are not used to identify controls that do should be placed at the bottom of the list; these names do not need to appear in any specific order. After listing the control names, you then assign a TabIndex value to each control in the list, beginning with the number 0. If a control does not have a TabIndex property, you do not assign it a value in the list. You can tell whether a control has a TabIndex property by viewing its Properties list.

Figure 2-10 shows the list of controls and TabIndex values for the cheesecake company's interface. Notice that the value assigned to each text box's identifying label is one number less than the value assigned to the text box itself. This is necessary for a text box's access key (which is defined in the identifying label) to work appropriately.

Controls that accept user input, along with their identifying labels	**TabIndex value**
Label1 (Name:)	0
nameTextBox	1
Label2 (Address:)	2
addressTextBox	3
Label3 (City:)	4
cityTextBox	5
Label4 (State:)	6
stateTextBox	7
Label5 (ZIP:)	8
zipTextBox	9
Label6 (Vanilla bean:)	10
vanillaTextBox	11
Label7 (Strawberry:)	12
strawberryTextBox	13
calcButton	14
printButton	15
clearButton	16
exitButton	17
Other controls	
Label10 (Order Form)	18
Label8 (Total ordered:)	19
totalOrderedLabel	20
Label9 (Total price:)	21
totalPriceLabel	22
PictureBox1	N/A

Figure 2-10 List of controls and TabIndex values

Although you can use the Properties window to set each control's TabIndex property, it is easier to use the Tab Order option on the View menu. Figure 2-11 shows the steps for using that option, and Figure 2-12 shows the correct TabIndex values for the cheesecake company's interface.

HOW TO Set the TabIndex Property Using the Tab Order Option

1. If necessary, make the designer window the active window.
2. Click View on the menu bar and then click Tab Order. The current TabIndex values appear in blue boxes on the form.
3. Click the first control you want in the tab order. The color of the box changes to white, and the number 0 appears in the box.
4. Click the second control you want in the tab order, and so on. If you make a mistake when specifying the tab order, press the Esc key to remove the boxes from the form, and then start over again.
5. When you have finished setting all of the TabIndex values, the color of the boxes will automatically change from white to blue. See Figure 2-12.
6. Press the Esc key to remove the blue boxes from the form. Or, click View on the menu bar and then click Tab Order.

Figure 2-11 How to set the TabIndex property using the Tab Order option

If you want to try setting the tab order, open the solution contained in the Try It 1! folder, and then use the information shown in Figures 2-11 and 2-12.

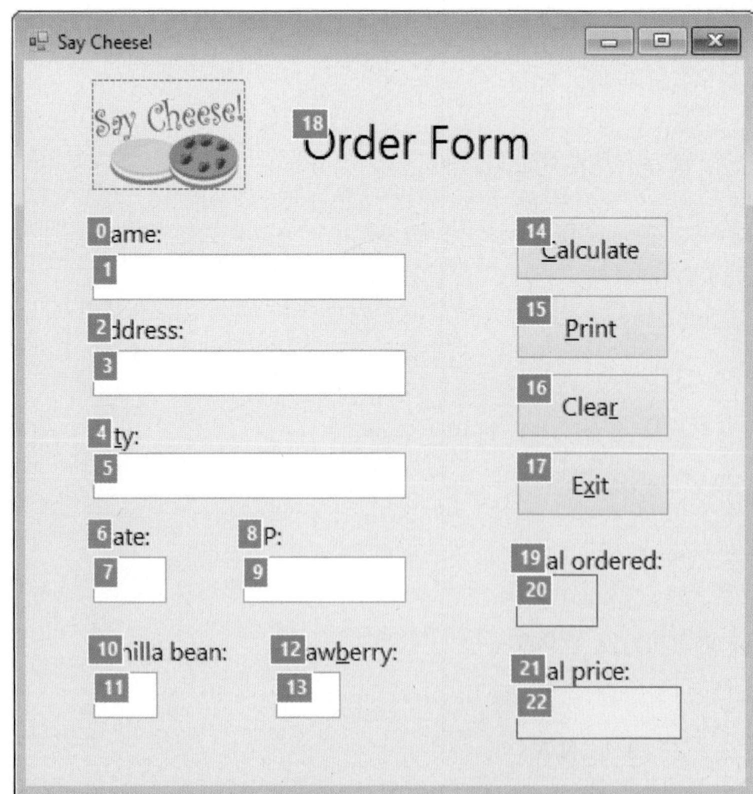

Figure 2-12 Correct TabIndex values

Mini-Quiz 2-3

1. What is the first TabIndex value on a form? (6)

   a. 0 b. 1

2. If a label's TabIndex value is 2, the TabIndex value of the text box it identifies should be ____________. (6)

   a. 1 b. 2 c. 3

3. You can select the Calculate Tax button by pressing ____________. (5)

   a. Shift+t c. Alt+t
   b. Ctrl+t d. none of the above

4. Every control in an interface has a TabIndex property. (5, 6)

   a. True b. False

The answers to Mini-Quiz questions are located in Appendix A. Each question is associated with one or more objectives listed at the beginning of the chapter.

Designating the Default Button on a Form

An interface can have one (and only one) **default button**, which is a button that can be selected by pressing the Enter key even when the button does not have the focus. The name of the default button is specified in the form's AcceptButton property. A form does not have to have a default button. However, if one is used, it should be the button that is most often selected by the user, except in cases where the tasks performed by the button are both destructive and irreversible. A button that deletes information should not be designated as the default button unless the interface provides a way for that information to be restored. The default button has a darkened border during design time, as shown in Figure 2-13, and also during run time.

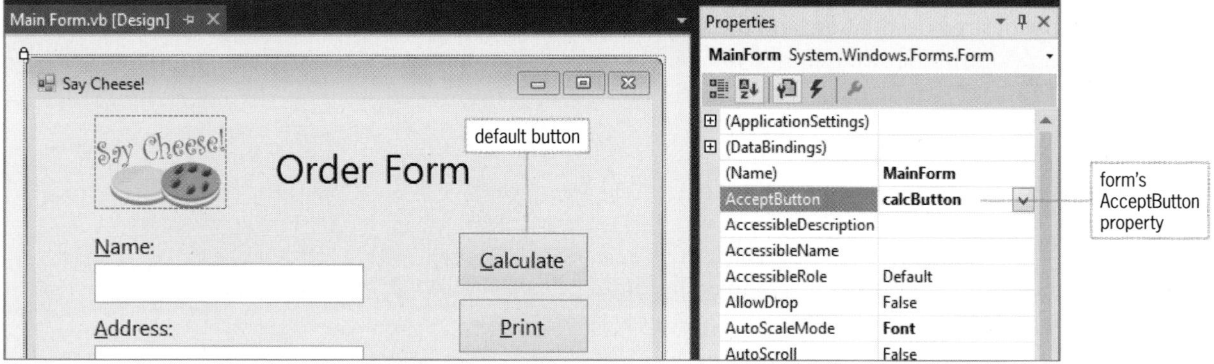

Figure 2-13 Default button on the MainForm

Printing an Interface from Code

Visual Basic provides the PrintForm tool for printing an interface from code. The tool is contained in the Visual Basic PowerPacks section of the toolbox. When you drag the PrintForm tool to a form, the instantiated print form control appears in the component tray, as shown in Figure 2-14. The component tray is a special area of the IDE; it stores controls that do not appear in the user interface during run time. The print form control's PrintAction property determines whether the printout is sent to a file, the Print preview window, or directly to the printer. You can set the property in either the Properties window or from code. To start the print operation, you need to enter the Print method in a procedure, using the following syntax: *printform*`.Print()`. In the syntax, *printform* is the name of the print form control.

If you want to try using the PrintForm tool, open the solution contained in the Try It 2! folder, and then use the information shown in Figures 2-14 and 2-15.

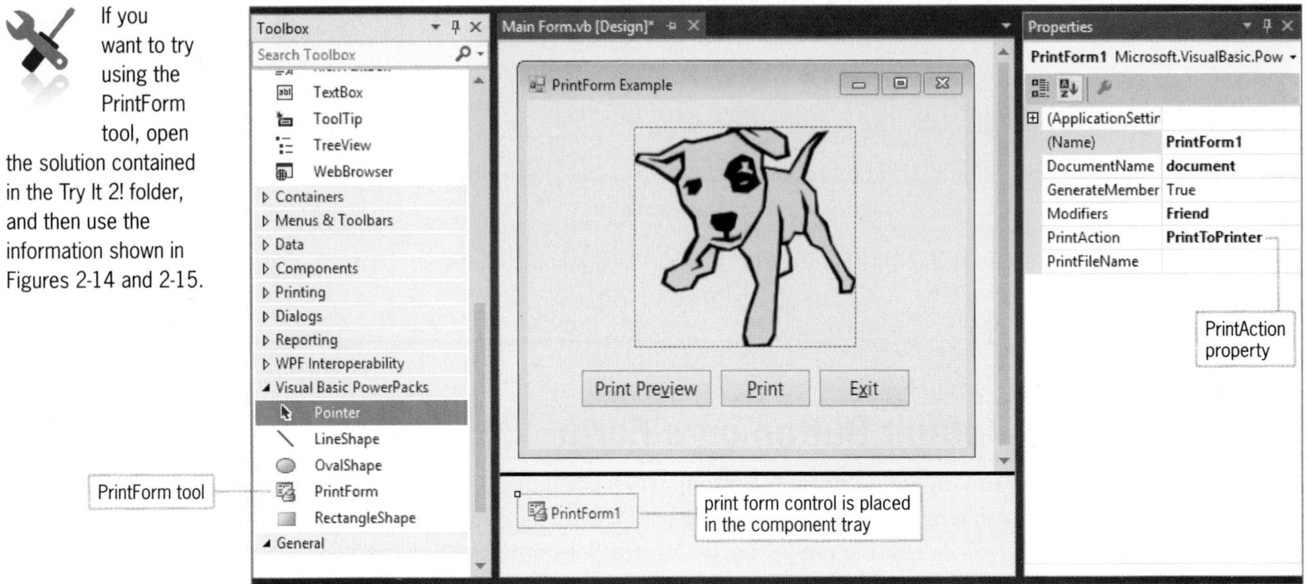

Figure 2-14 PrintForm Example application's interface

The Print Preview and Print buttons in Figure 2-14 send the printout to the Print preview window and printer, respectively. Figure 2-15 shows the code entered in the Click event procedures for both buttons. The first line in each procedure sets the PrintAction property to the desired destination, and the second line starts the print operation. If the interface contained only one of the two buttons, you could set the PrintAction property to the appropriate destination in the Properties window and then use only the Print method in the button's Click event procedure.

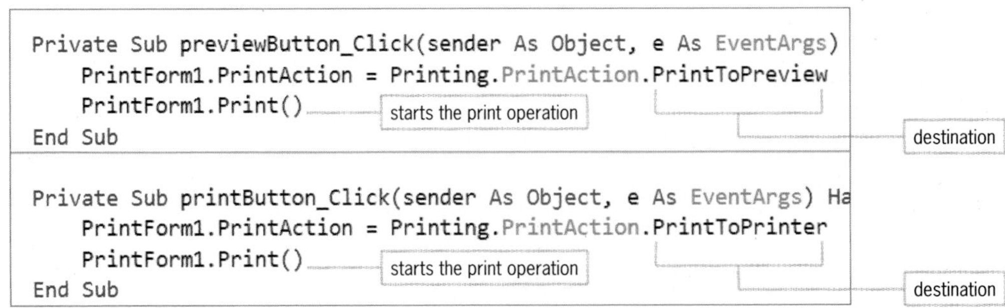

```
Private Sub previewButton_Click(sender As Object, e As EventArgs)
    PrintForm1.PrintAction = Printing.PrintAction.PrintToPreview
    PrintForm1.Print()
End Sub

Private Sub printButton_Click(sender As Object, e As EventArgs) Ha
    PrintForm1.PrintAction = Printing.PrintAction.PrintToPrinter
    PrintForm1.Print()
End Sub
```


Figure 2-15 Print Preview and Print buttons' Click event procedures

We will wrap up this chapter with a fun and easy topic, and one that you will use in this chapter's Programming Tutorial 1: playing audio files.

Playing Audio Files

Some applications contain an audio component, such as music, sound effects, or spoken text. Figure 2-16 shows the syntax you use to include audio in a Visual Basic application. The figure also contains an example of using the syntax to play an audio file named GoodMorning.wav. (As mentioned in the Overview, you should study the information in How To boxes that contain syntax and examples *while* you are reading the chapter.)

HOW TO Play an Audio File

Syntax
My.Computer.Audio.Play(*fileName*)

Example
```
My.Computer.Audio.Play("GoodMorning.wav")
```

Figure 2-16 How to play an audio file

If you want to try playing an audio file, open the solution contained in the Try It 3! folder, and then use the information shown in Figure 2-16. The GoodMorning.wav file is contained in the project's bin\Debug folder.

The keyword `My` in the syntax refers to Visual Basic's **My feature**—a feature that exposes a set of commonly used objects to the programmer. One of the objects exposed by the My feature is the Computer object, which represents your computer. The Computer object provides access to other objects available on your computer, such as your computer's Audio object. As the syntax shows, you use the Audio object's Play method to play an audio file.

Following the Play method in the syntax is a set of parentheses containing the text *fileName*. Items within parentheses after a method's name are called **arguments** and represent information that the method needs to perform its task. In this case, the *fileName* argument represents the name of the audio file you want played. The file must be a WAV file, which is an audio file whose filename extension is .wav. You enclose the WAV file's name in quotation marks. If the audio file is not in the project's bin\Debug folder, you will need to include the path to the file in the *fileName* argument.

Mini-Quiz 2-4

The answers to Mini-Quiz questions are located in Appendix A. Each question is associated with one or more objectives listed at the beginning of the chapter.

1. How can the default button on a form be selected? (7)
   a. by clicking it
   b. by pressing the Enter key when the button has the focus
   c. by pressing the Enter key when the button does *not* have the focus
   d. all of the above
2. If a form contains the PrintForm1 control, which of the following statements can be used to start the print operation? (8)
   a. `PrintForm1.Go()`
   b. `PrintForm1.Print()`
   c. `PrintForm1.Start()`
   d. none of the above

3. The My.Computer.Audio object can play which of the following types of files? (9)

a. .aud
b. .avi
c. .wav
d. .wmv

You have completed the concepts section of Chapter 2. The Programming Tutorial section is next. Recall that the first tutorial in each chapter contains more detailed step-by-step instructions than does the second tutorial.

PROGRAMMING TUTORIAL 1

Creating the Music Sampler Application

In this tutorial, you will create an application that allows the user to preview a song by playing several seconds of it. The application's TOE chart and MainForm are shown in Figures 2-17 and 2-18, respectively. The MainForm contains six labels and seven buttons.

Note: If you are in a computer lab, your instructor (or the lab supervisor) may not want you to play the audio files for this tutorial because doing so might be disruptive to other students. You may need to use earphones or mute your computer's speakers.

Task	Object	Event
Play an audio file that contains a preview of the song associated with the picture box	everythingPictureBox, invisiblePictureBox, magicPictureBox, threePictureBox, unclaimedPictureBox	Click
Send a printout of the interface to the Print preview window (use a print form control)	printPreviewButton	Click
End the application	exitButton	Click

Figure 2-17 TOE chart for the Music Sampler application

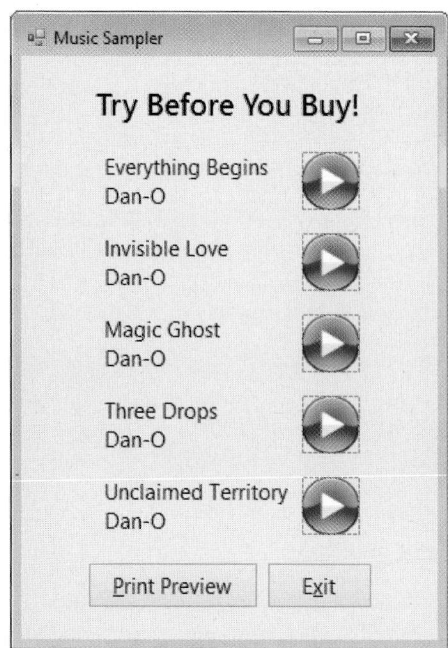

Figure 2-18 MainForm for the Music Sampler application
Music by Dan-O at DanoSongs.com

Completing the Interface and Adding a Print Form Control

Included in the data files for this book is a partially completed Music Sampler application. Before you begin coding the application, you will need to complete the interface and also add a print form control to the application.

To complete the interface and add a print form control:

1. Start Visual Studio and open the Solution Explorer window.
2. Open the **Music Solution** (**Music Solution.sln**) file contained in the VbReloaded2015\Chap02\Music Solution folder. If necessary, open the designer window. The partially completed MainForm appears on the screen. Missing from the interface are the last song title and artist name, which should be entered in the Label5 control.
3. Click the **Label5** control in the interface. Open the Properties window. Click the **Text** property and then click the **list arrow** in the property's Settings box. Replace the Label5 text in the box with the song title and artist name shown in Figure 2-19.

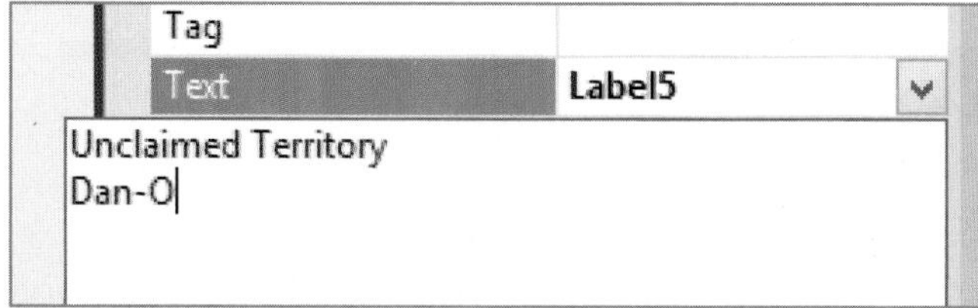

Figure 2-19 Song and artist names entered in the Label5 control's Text property

4. Click the **form** to close the box.

5. Now set the tab order for the controls. Click **View** on the menu bar and then click **Tab Order**. Use the information shown in Figure 2-20 to set each control's TabIndex property.

Figure 2-20 Correct TabIndex values
Music by Dan-O at DanoSongs.com

6. Press **Esc** to remove the tab order boxes from the form.
7. Open the Toolbox window. Click **PrintForm** in the Visual Basic PowerPacks section and then drag a print form control to the form. When you release the mouse button, the control appears in the component tray. See Figure 2-21.

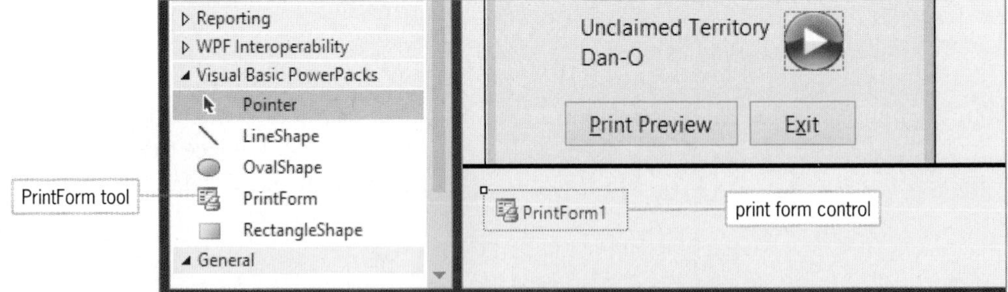

Figure 2-21 Print form control added to the component tray
Music by Dan-O at DanoSongs.com

Note: If your toolbox does not contain the Visual Basic PowerPacks section, refer to the Read This Before You Begin page in this book.

8. Auto-hide the Toolbox, Solution Explorer, and Properties windows, and then save the solution.

Coding the Picture Boxes

According to the TOE chart shown earlier in Figure 2-17, each picture box should play an audio file when it is clicked. The audio files are contained in the current project's bin\Debug folder.

Note: If you are in a computer lab, your instructor (or the lab supervisor) may not want you to play the audio files for this tutorial because doing so might be disruptive to other students. You may need to use earphones or mute your computer's speakers.

To code each picture box's Click event procedure:

1. Open the Code Editor window. The exitButton_Click procedure contains the `Me.Close()` instruction.
2. Open the code template for the everythingPictureBox's Click event procedure. Enter the Play method shown in Figure 2-22.

```
Private Sub everythingPictureBox_Click(sender As Object, e As EventArgs)
    My.Computer.Audio.Play("Everything-Begins-by-danosongs.com.wav")

End Sub
```

Figure 2-22 Play method entered in the everythingPictureBox_Click procedure

3. On your own, code the Click event procedures for the remaining four picture boxes. The names of the audio files associated with these picture boxes are listed in Figure 2-23.

Picture box	Audio file
invisiblePictureBox	Invisible-Love-by-danosongs.com.wav
magicPictureBox	Magic-Ghost-by-danosongs.com.wav
threePictureBox	Three-Drops-by-danosongs.com.wav
unclaimedPictureBox	Unclaimed-Territory-by-danosongs.com.wav

Figure 2-23 Audio files associated with four of the picture boxes

4. Save the solution and then start the application. Click **each of the buttons** to verify that the code you entered is working correctly.
5. Click the **Exit** button to end the application.

Coding the Print Preview Button

According to the application's TOE chart, the Print Preview button should send a printout of the interface to the Print preview window.

To code the Print Preview button's Click event procedure:

1. Click the **Main Form.vb [Design]** tab to make the designer window the active window. Click the **PrintForm1** control in the component tray and then temporarily display the Properties window. Set the control's PrintAction property to **PrintToPreview**.

2. Return to the Code Editor window and open the code template for the printPreviewButton_Click procedure. Now enter the instruction that tells the computer to start the print operation. Type **PrintForm1.Print()** and press **Enter**.

3. Save the solution and then start the application. Click the **Print Preview** button. The printout of the interface appears in the Print preview window. Click the **Zoom button** list arrow and then click **75%**. Use the window's borders to size the window, as shown in Figure 2-24.

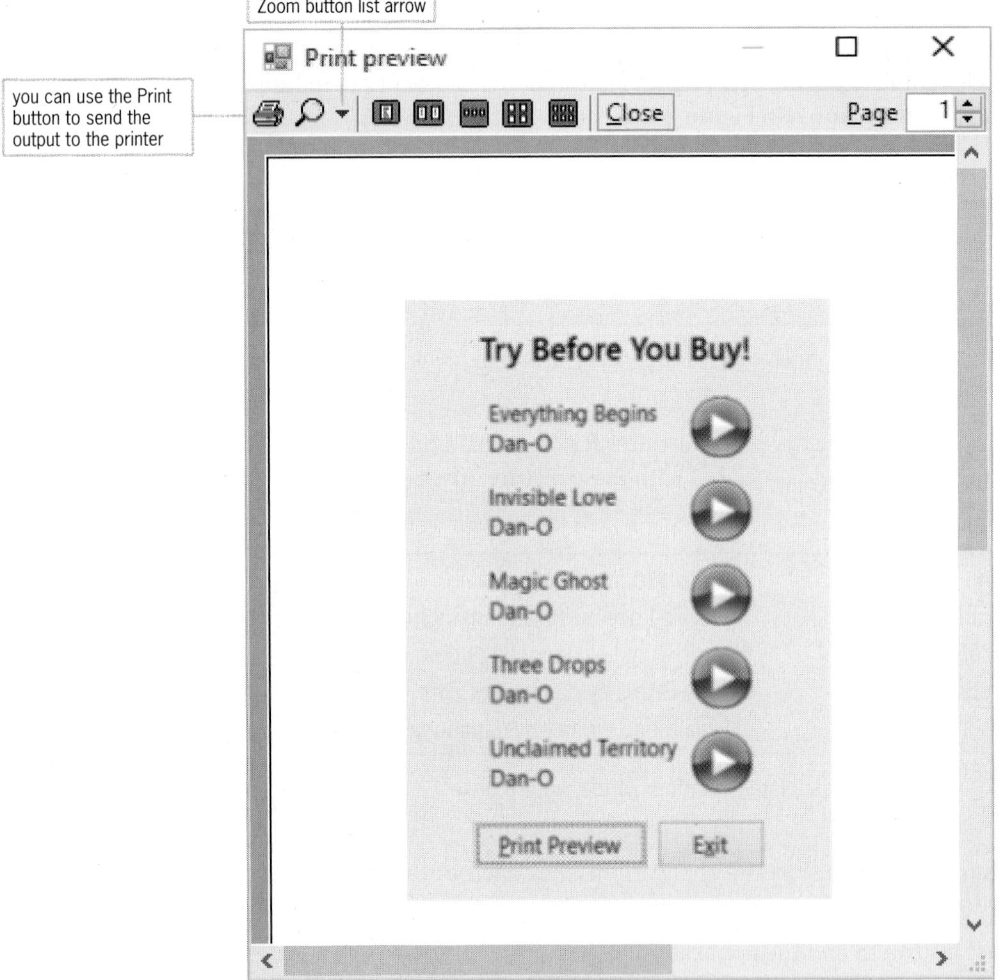

Figure 2-24 Print preview window
Music by Dan-O at DanoSongs.com

4. Click the **Close** button in the Print preview window and then click the **Exit** button.

5. Close the Code Editor window and then close the solution. Figure 2-25 shows the Music Sampler application's code.

```
Public Class MainForm
    Private Sub everythingPictureBox_Click(sender As Object,
    e As EventArgs) Handles everythingPictureBox.Click
        My.Computer.Audio.Play(
           "Everything-Begins-by-danosongs.com.wav")
    End Sub
    Private Sub exitButton_Click(sender As Object,
    e As EventArgs) Handles exitButton.Click
        Me.Close()
    End Sub
    Private Sub invisiblePictureBox_Click(sender As Object,
    e As EventArgs) Handles invisiblePictureBox.Click
        My.Computer.Audio.Play(
           "Invisible-Love-by-danosongs.com.wav")
    End Sub
    Private Sub magicPictureBox_Click(sender As Object,
    e As EventArgs) Handles magicPictureBox.Click
        My.Computer.Audio.Play(
           "Magic-Ghost-by-danosongs.com.wav")
    End Sub
    Private Sub printPreviewButton_Click(sender As Object,
    e As EventArgs) Handles printPreviewButton.Click
        PrintForm1.Print()
    End Sub
    Private Sub threePictureBox_Click(sender As Object,
    e As EventArgs) Handles threePictureBox.Click
        My.Computer.Audio.Play(
           "Three-Drops-by-danosongs.com.wav")
    End Sub
    Private Sub unclaimedPictureBox_Click(sender As Object,
    e As EventArgs) Handles unclaimedPictureBox.Click
        My.Computer.Audio.Play(
           "Unclaimed-Territory-by-danosongs.com.wav")
    End Sub
End Class
```

Figure 2-25 Music Sampler application's code

PROGRAMMING TUTORIAL 2

Creating the Alligator Inc. Application

Alligator Inc. pays each of the company's salespeople a monthly expense allowance of $200. In this tutorial, you will create an application that calculates and displays the total annual cost of these allowances. The application's TOE chart and MainForm are shown in Figures 2-26 and 2-27, respectively. The MainForm contains three labels, one text box, one picture box, and three buttons. You will code the Print Preview and Exit buttons in this tutorial. The Calculate button will be coded in Chapter 3.

Task	Object	Event
Get and display the number of salespeople	peopleTextBox	None
1. Calculate total annual allowance 2. Display total annual allowance in totalLabel	calcButton	Click
Display total annual allowance (from calcButton)	totalLabel	None
Send a printout of the interface to the Print preview window (use a print form control)	printPreviewButton	Click
End the application	exitButton	Click

Figure 2-26 TOE chart for the Alligator Inc. application

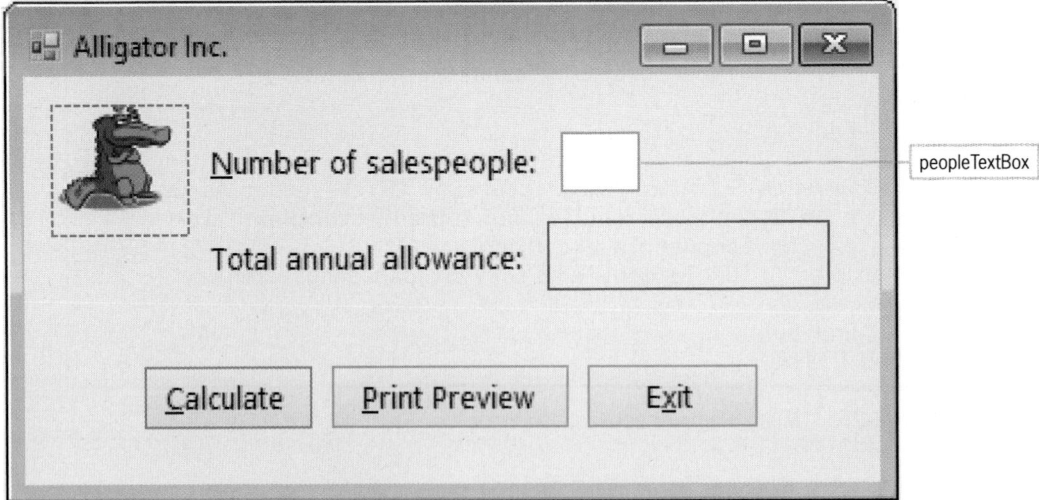

Figure 2-27 MainForm for the Alligator Inc. application

Completing the Interface and Adding a Print Form Control

Included in the data files for this book is a partially completed Alligator Inc. application. Before you begin coding the application, you will need to complete the interface and also add a print form control to the application.

To complete the interface and add a print form control:

1. Start Visual Studio and open the Solution Explorer window.
2. Open the **Alligator Solution** (**Alligator Solution.sln**) file contained in the VbReloaded2015\Chap02\Alligator Solution folder. If necessary, open the designer window. The partially completed MainForm appears on the screen. Missing from the interface are the access keys and the text box.
3. Open the Toolbox window. Use the TextBox tool to add a text box control to the form. Position and size the control as shown in Figure 2-27.
4. Change the text box's name to **peopleTextBox**.
5. Lock the controls on the form.
6. Assign the access keys shown in Figure 2-27 to the three buttons and the text box's identifying label.
7. The Calculate button should be the default button; set the appropriate property.
8. Use the information shown in Figure 2-28 to set the tab order for the controls.

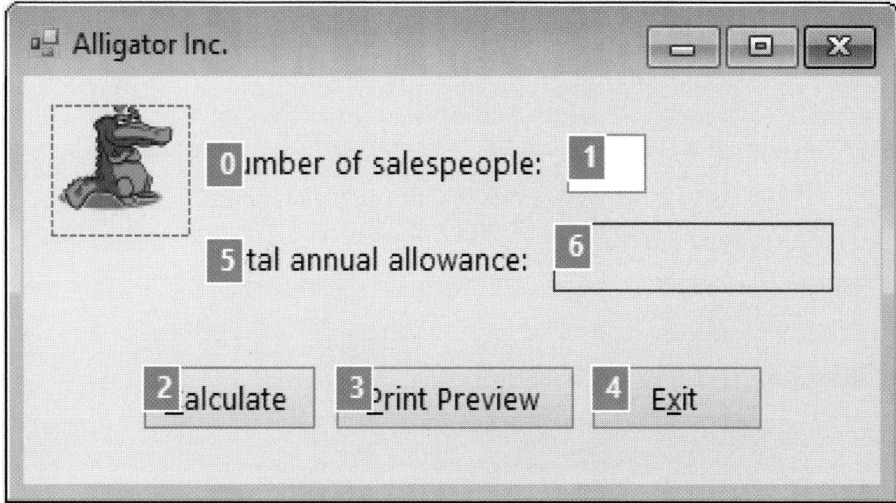

Figure 2-28 Correct tab order

9. Remove the tab order boxes from the form.
10. Click **PrintForm** in the Visual Basic PowerPacks section of the toolbox and then drag a print form control to the form. When you release the mouse button, the control appears in the component tray. (If your toolbox does not contain the Visual Basic PowerPacks section, refer to the Read This Before You Begin page in this book.)
11. Auto-hide the Toolbox and Solution Explorer windows, and then save the solution.

Coding the Print Preview and Exit Buttons

According to the application's TOE chart, you need to code the Click event procedures for the Print Preview and Exit buttons. (Recall that you will code the Calculate button in Chapter 3.)

To code both Click event procedures:

1. Click the **PrintForm1** control in the component tray. The control should send a printout of the interface to the Print preview window; set the appropriate property.
2. Open the Code Editor window and then open the code template for the printPreviewButton_Click procedure. Enter the instruction that tells the computer to start the print operation.
3. Open the code template for the exitButton_Click procedure. Enter the statement to end the application.
4. Save the solution and then start the application. Click the **Print Preview** button. The printout of the interface appears in the Print preview window. Click the **Zoom button** list arrow and then click **75%**.
5. Click the **Close** button in the Print preview window and then click the **Exit** button.
6. Close the Code Editor window and then close the solution. Figure 2-29 shows the Alligator Inc. application's code.

```
Public Class MainForm
    Private Sub exitButton_Click(sender As Object,
    e As EventArgs) Handles exitButton.Click
        Me.Close()

    End Sub

    Private Sub printPreviewButton_Click(sender As Object,
    e As EventArgs) Handles printPreviewButton.Click
        PrintForm1.Print()

    End Sub
End Class
```

Figure 2-29 Alligator Inc. application's code

PROGRAMMING EXAMPLE

VitaDrink Company

Create an interface that allows the user to enter the following customer information: company name, address, city, state, ZIP code, the number of cases of regular VitaDrink ordered, and the number of cases of sugar-free VitaDrink ordered. The interface will need to display the total number of cases ordered and the total price of the order. Use the following names for the solution and project, respectively: VitaDrink Solution and VitaDrink Project. Save the files in the VbReloaded2015\Chap02 folder. Change the form file's name to Main Form.vb. Remember to lock the controls on the form. See Figures 2-30 through 2-34. In this chapter, you will code only the Exit and Print Preview buttons' Click event procedures. You will code the Click event procedures for the Calculate and Clear buttons in Chapter 3.

Task	Object	Event
1. Calculate the total number of cases ordered and the total price of the order 2. Display the total number of cases ordered and the total price of the order in totalCasesLabel and totalPriceLabel	calcButton	Click
Send a printout of the order form to the Print preview window (use a print form control)	printPreviewButton	Click
Clear the screen for the next order	clearButton	Click
End the application	exitButton	Click
Display the total number of cases ordered (from calcButton)	totalCasesLabel	None
Display the total price of the order (from calcButton)	totalPriceLabel	None
Get and display the order information	nameTextBox, addressTextBox, cityTextBox, stateTextBox, zipTextBox, regularTextBox, sugarFreeTextBox	None

Figure 2-30 TOE chart

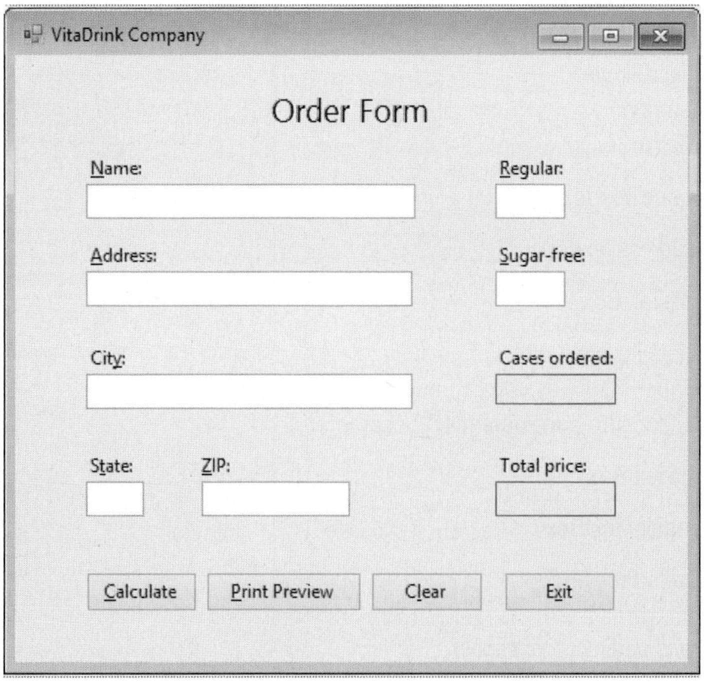

Figure 2-31 User interface

Object	Property	Setting
Form1	Name	MainForm
	AcceptButton	calcButton
	Font	Segoe UI, 9pt
	StartPosition	CenterScreen
	Text	VitaDrink Company
Label1	Font	Segoe UI, 16pt
	Text	Order Form
Label2	Text	&Name:
Label3	Text	&Address:
Label4	Text	Cit&y:
Label5	Text	S&tate:
Label6	Text	&ZIP:
Label7	Text	&Regular:
Label8	Text	&Sugar-free:
Label9	Text	Cases ordered:
Label10	Text	Total price:
Label11	Name	totalCasesLabel
	AutoSize	False
	BorderStyle	FixedSingle
	Text	(empty)
	TextAlign	MiddleCenter
Label12	Name	totalPriceLabel
	AutoSize	False
	BorderStyle	FixedSingle
	Text	(empty)
	TextAlign	MiddleCenter
TextBox1	Name	nameTextBox
TextBox2	Name	addressTextBox
TextBox3	Name	cityTextBox
TextBox4	Name	stateTextBox
	CharacterCasing	Upper (changes entry to uppercase)
	MaxLength	2 (accepts a maximum of 2 characters)
TextBox5	Name	zipTextBox
TextBox6	Name	regularTextBox
TextBox7	Name	sugarFreeTextBox

Figure 2-32 Objects, properties, and settings *(continues)*

(continued)

Button1	Name	calcButton
	Text	&Calculate
Button2	Name	printPreviewButton
	Text	&Print Preview
Button3	Name	clearButton
	Text	C&lear
Button4	Name	exitButton
	Text	E&xit
PrintForm1	PrintAction	PrintToPreview

Figure 2-32 Objects, properties, and settings

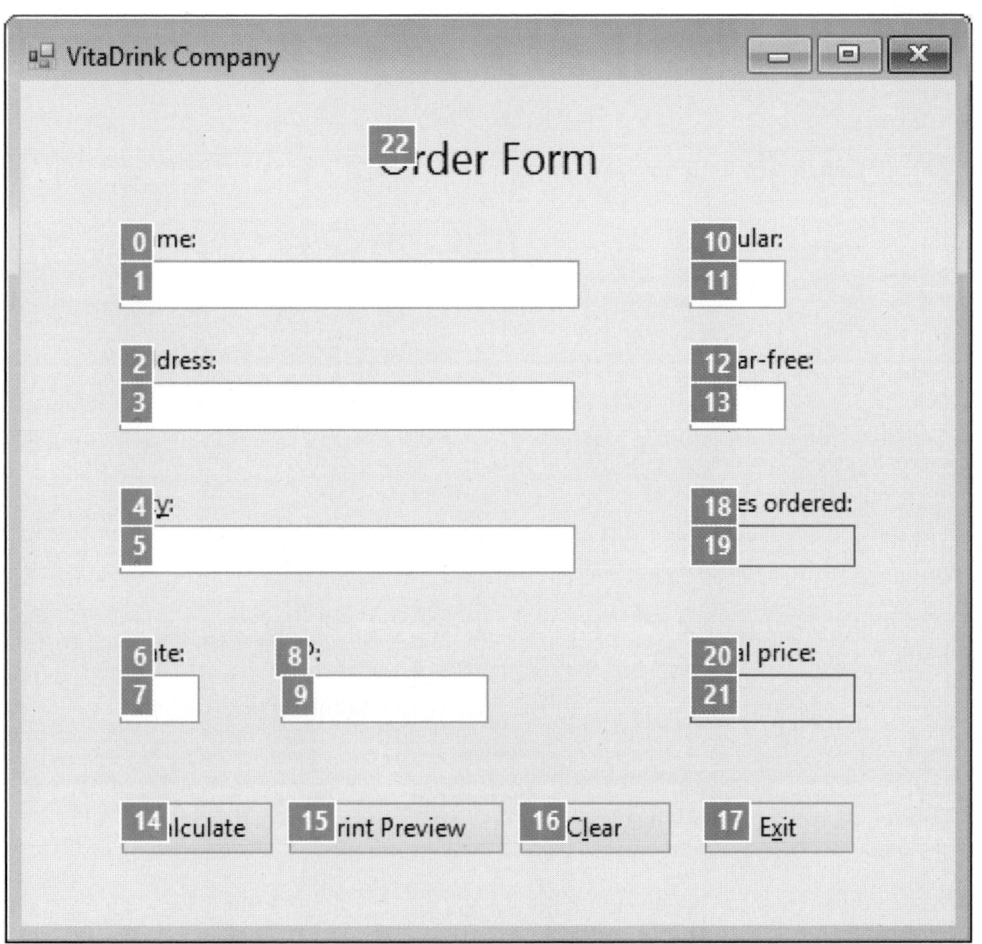

Figure 2-33 Tab order

```
Public Class MainForm
    Private Sub exitButton_Click(sender As Object, e As EventArgs) H
        Me.Close()

    End Sub

    Private Sub printPreviewButton_Click(sender As Object, e As Even
        PrintForm1.Print()

    End Sub
End Class
```

Figure 2-34 Code

Chapter Summary

- You should plan an application jointly with the user to ensure that the application meets the user's needs.
- Planning an application requires that you identify the application's tasks, objects, and events. You then build the interface. You can record the tasks, objects, and events in a TOE chart.
- Not all objects will need an event to occur for them to perform their assigned task(s).
- You use a text box control to give the user an area in which to enter data.
- In Western countries, you should organize the user interface so that the information flows either vertically or horizontally, with the most important information always located in the upper-left corner of the screen.
- You can group related controls together using either white (empty) space or one of the tools located in the Containers section of the toolbox.
- The text contained in identifying labels should be left-aligned within the label. Identifying labels should be positioned either above or to the left of the control they identify.
- Identifying labels and button captions should consist of one to three words, which should appear on one line.
- Identifying labels and button captions should be meaningful. Identifying labels should end with a colon and be entered using sentence capitalization. Button captions should be entered using book title capitalization.
- When positioning the controls, you should maintain a consistent margin from the edges of the form.
- Related controls are typically placed close together in the interface.
- When buttons are positioned horizontally on the form, all the buttons should be the same height; their widths, however, may vary. When buttons are stacked vertically on the form, all the buttons should be the same height and the same width.

- Align the borders of the controls wherever possible to minimize the number of different margins used in the interface.
- Graphics and color should be used sparingly in an interface.
- Avoid using italics and underlining in an interface, and limit the use of bold text to titles, headings, and key items that you want to emphasize.
- You should use only one font type and not more than two different font sizes for the text in an interface. Segoe UI (9 point) is the recommended font for Windows applications.
- You should assign access keys to each of the controls that can accept user input (such as text boxes and buttons). You assign an access key by including an ampersand (&) in the control's caption or identifying label.
- The TabIndex property determines the order in which a control receives the focus when the user either presses the Tab key or employs an access key during run time. A text box's TabIndex property should be set to a value that is one number more than the TabIndex value of its identifying label.
- You use a form's AcceptButton property to designate a default button. A form can have only one default button.
- The Visual Basic PowerPacks section of the toolbox provides the PrintForm tool for instantiating a print form control, which you can use to print the interface during run time. The instantiated control appears in the component tray in the IDE.
- You can use the Play method of the My.Computer.Audio object to play a WAV file during run time.

Key Terms

Access key—the underlined character in an object's identifying label or caption; allows the user to select the object using the Alt key in combination with the underlined character

Arguments—the items within parentheses after a method's name; represent information that the method needs to perform its task

Book title capitalization—the capitalization used for a button's caption; refers to capitalizing the first letter in each word, except for articles, conjunctions, and prepositions that do not occur at either the beginning or the end of the caption

Default button—a button that can be selected by pressing the Enter key even when it does not have the focus

Focus—indicates that a control is ready to accept user input

My feature—the Visual Basic feature that exposes a set of commonly used objects (such as the Computer object) to the programmer

Sentence capitalization—the capitalization used for identifying labels; refers to capitalizing only the first letter in the first word and in any words that are customarily capitalized

Text box—a control that provides an area in the form for the user to enter data

Review Questions

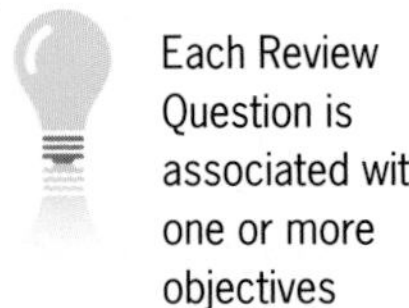
Each Review Question is associated with one or more objectives listed at the beginning of the chapter.

1. Which of the following statements is false? (3)
   a. A button's caption should appear on one line.
   b. A button's caption should consist of one to three words only.
   c. A button's caption should be entered using book title capitalization.
   d. A button's caption should end with a colon (:).
2. Which of the following statements is false? (3)
   a. The text that identifies a text box should be left-aligned within a label control.
   b. An identifying label should be positioned either above or to the left of the control it identifies.
   c. Labels that identify controls should be entered using book title capitalization.
   d. Labels that identify text boxes should end with a colon (:).
3. Which property determines the order in which a control receives the focus when the user presses the Tab key? (6)
   a. OrderTab
   b. SetOrder
   c. TabIndex
   d. TabOrder
4. Which property is used to assign an access key? (5)
   a. Access
   b. Caption
   c. KeyAccess
   d. Text
5. Which property is used to designate a default button on a form? (7)
   a. the button's AcceptButton
   b. the button's DefaultButton
   c. the form's AcceptButton
   d. the form's DefaultButton
6. If a text box's TabIndex value is 7, its identifying label's TabIndex value should be ____________. (5, 6)
   a. 6
   b. 7
   c. 8
   d. 9
7. Which of the following tells the PrintForm1 control to start the print operation? (8)
   a. `Print.PrintForm1()`
   b. `PrintForm1.BeginPrint()`
   c. `PrintForm1.Print()`
   d. `PrintForm1.Start()`

Each Exercise, except the DISCOVERY exercise, is associated with one or more objectives listed at the beginning of the chapter.

8. Which of the following tells the computer to play the Hello.wav file contained in the project's bin\Debug folder? (9)
   a. `My.Audio.Play("Hello.wav")`
   b. `My.Computer.Audio.Play("Hello.wav")`
   c. `My.Computer.Play.Audio("Hello.wav")`
   d. `My.Computer.Play.AudioFile("Hello.wav")`

Exercises

Pencil and Paper

1. Define the following two terms: book title capitalization and sentence capitalization. (3) INTRODUCTORY
2. List the four steps you should follow when planning a Visual Basic application. (1) INTRODUCTORY
3. Explain the procedure for choosing a control's access key. (5) INTRODUCTORY
4. Explain how you give users keyboard access to a text box. (5, 6) INTRODUCTORY
5. Write the Visual Basic instruction to specify that the PrintForm1 control should send a printout of the interface directly to the printer. (8) INTERMEDIATE
6. Correct the following line of code, which should play the Intro.wav file contained in the Music folder on the F drive: `My.Computer.Music.Play("Intro.wav")`. (9) SWAT THE BUGS

Computer

7. If necessary, create the Music Sampler application from this chapter's Programming Tutorial 1. Close the solution and then use Windows to make a copy of the Music Solution folder. Rename the copy Music Solution-ModifyThis. Open the Music Solution (Music Solution.sln) file contained in the Music Solution-ModifyThis folder. (3, 6, 9) MODIFY THIS
   a. Unlock the controls. Add a label and a picture box to the form, positioning them below the existing labels and picture boxes.
   b. Lock the controls and then verify that the tab order is correct.
   c. Name the picture box inkarnationPictureBox. The picture box should display the image stored in the VbReloaded2015\Chap02\PlayButton.png file. Enter Inkarnation on the first line in the label and Dan-O on the second line.
   d. Use Windows to copy the Inkarnation-by-danosongs.com.wav file from the VbReloaded2015\Chap02 folder to the project's bin\Debug folder.
   e. Code the inkarnationPictureBox_Click procedure so that it plays the music contained in the Inkarnation-by-danosongs.com.wav file. Test the application appropriately.
8. If necessary, create the Alligator Inc. application from this chapter's Programming Tutorial 2. Close the solution and then use Windows to make a copy of the Alligator Solution folder. Rename the copy Alligator Solution-ModifyThis. Open the Alligator Solution (Alligator Solution.sln) file contained in the Alligator Solution-ModifyThis folder. (2, 3, 8) MODIFY THIS
   a. Unlock the controls. Add a button to the form. Position the button between the Print Preview and Exit buttons. Change the button's Name and Text properties to printButton and Prin&t, respectively.
   b. Lock the controls and then verify that the tab order is correct.
   c. The Print button should send the printout directly to the printer. Code the button's Click event procedure. Also make the appropriate modification to the printPreviewButton_Click procedure. Test the application appropriately.

MODIFY THIS

9. If necessary, create the VitaDrink Company application from this chapter's Programming Example. Close the solution and then use Windows to make a copy of the VitaDrink Solution folder. Rename the copy VitaDrink Solution-ModifyThis. Open the VitaDrink Solution (VitaDrink Solution.sln) file contained in the VitaDrink Solution-ModifyThis folder. Add four labels to the form. Two of the labels will display the price of the order without any sales tax and the sales tax amount. The other two labels will be identifying labels. Use appropriate captions for the identifying labels. Size the form and reposition the controls as needed. Lock the controls and then verify that the tab order is correct. (You do not need to code the Calculate or Clear buttons.)

MODIFY THIS

10. Open the Time Solution (Time Solution.sln) file contained in the VbReloaded2015\Chap02\Time Solution folder. Organize the interface so that it follows all of the design guidelines specified in this chapter. (You do not need to code the Calculate Hours button.) Save the solution and then start the application. Click the Exit button and then close the solution. (3-6)

INTRODUCTORY

11. In this exercise, you will create an application that displays a person's net pay, given his or her gross pay, taxes, and insurance. Prepare a TOE chart ordered by object. Create a Windows Forms application. Use the following names for the solution and project, respectively: Net Solution and Net Project. Save the application in the VbReloaded2015\Chap02 folder. Change the form file's name to Main Form.vb. The button that calculates the net pay should be the default button. Code only the Exit button. (1-7)

INTRODUCTORY

12. Hillside Clothiers operates three retail stores. Create an application that the sales manager can use to enter each store's monthly sales amounts for three months. The application should calculate and display the total sales made during each month. Prepare a TOE chart ordered by object. Create a Windows Forms application. Use the following names for the solution and project, respectively: Hillside Solution and Hillside Project. Save the application in the VbReloaded2015\Chap02 folder. Change the form file's name to Main Form.vb. Code only the Exit button. (1-6)

INTERMEDIATE

13. The manager of Carson Carpets wants an application that calculates and displays the area of a rectangle in both square feet and square yards. The manager will enter the length and width of the rectangle in feet. The application should allow the manager to send a printout of the interface to the Print preview window. Prepare a TOE chart ordered by object. Create a Windows Forms application. Use the following names for the solution and project, respectively: Carson Solution and Carson Project. Save the application in the VbReloaded2015\Chap02 folder. Change the form file's name to Main Form.vb. The button that calculates the output should be the default button. Code only the Exit button and the button that sends the printout to the Print preview window. Test the application appropriately. (1-7)

ADVANCED

14. In this exercise, you will create a Windows Forms application that can be used to teach the Spanish names for nine different colors. Use the following names for the solution and project, respectively: Color Solution and Color Project. Save the application in the VbReloaded2015\Chap02 folder. Change the form file's name to Main Form.vb. Create the interface shown in Figure 2-35. When the user clicks a color button, the button's Click event procedure should display the corresponding Spanish word on the button's face. It should also change the button's ForeColor property to the appropriate color. For example, the Blue button's Click event procedure should change the button's Text property to Azul (the Spanish word for Blue), and change its ForeColor property to Color.Blue. The English button's Click event procedure should reinstate the English words on the buttons and also change their ForeColor properties to Color.Black. Code the application and then test it appropriately. (1, 3-6)

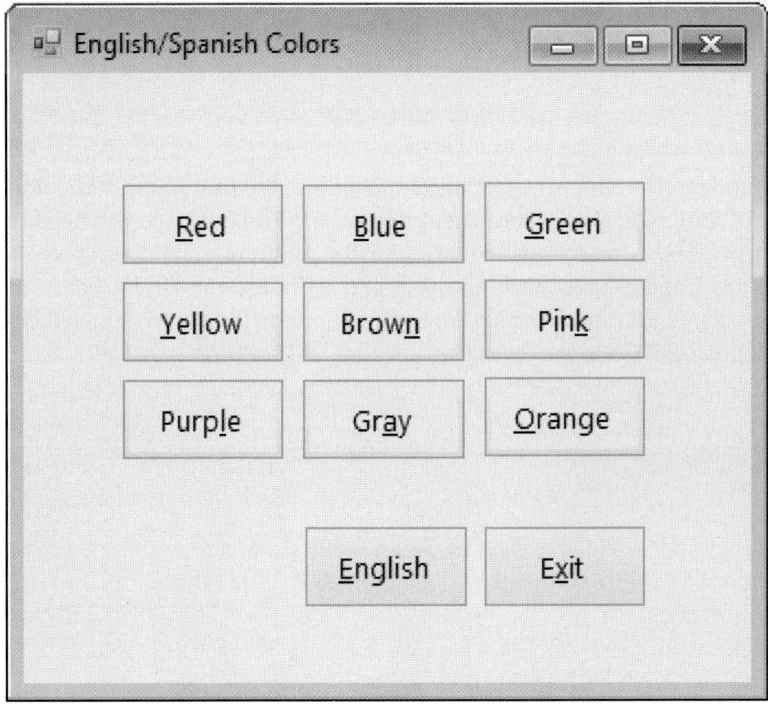

Figure 2-35 Interface for Exercise 14

15. In this exercise, you will create a Windows Forms application that plays five quotes from either a movie or a TV show. Use the following names for the solution and project, respectively: Quotes Solution and Quotes Project. Save the application in the VbReloaded2015\Chap02 folder. Change the form file's name to Main Form.vb. Download any five WAV files from the Internet. You can find free WAV files at *www.thefreesite.com/free_sounds/free_wavs/*. Code the application and then test it appropriately. (1, 3-6, 12) ADVANCED

16. In this exercise, you will learn how to bypass a control in the tab order when the user is tabbing. Open the Johnson Solution (Johnson Solution.sln) file contained in the VbReloaded2015\Chap02\Johnson Solution folder. Start the application. Press the Tab key several times, and notice where the focus is placed each time. Click the Exit button. Most of Johnson's customers are located in California. Enter CA in the stateTextBox's Text property. Find a property that will bypass (skip over) the stateTextBox when the user is tabbing. If the user needs to place the focus in the stateTextBox (for example, to change the control's contents), he or she will need to either click the control or use its access key. Test the application appropriately. DISCOVERY

17. Open the Debug Solution (Debug Solution.sln) file contained in the VbReloaded2015\Chap02\Debug Solution folder. Start the application. Test all of the access keys in the interface. So that you can test its access key, the Calculate Total button's Click event procedure contains a line of code. Notice that not all of the access keys are working. Stop the application. Correct the errors and then test the application again. (5, 6) SWAT THE BUGS

Case Projects

Eddy's

Create a TOE chart and interface for an application that allows the user to enter the number of hot dogs, hamburgers, and fountain drinks a customer orders. The interface will need to display the total price of the order. Use the following names for the solution and project, respectively: Eddy Solution and Eddy Project. Save the application in the VbReloaded2015\Chap02 folder. Change the form file's name to Main Form.vb. You can either create your own interface or create the one shown in Figure 2-36. Code the Print Preview and Exit buttons only. (1-7)

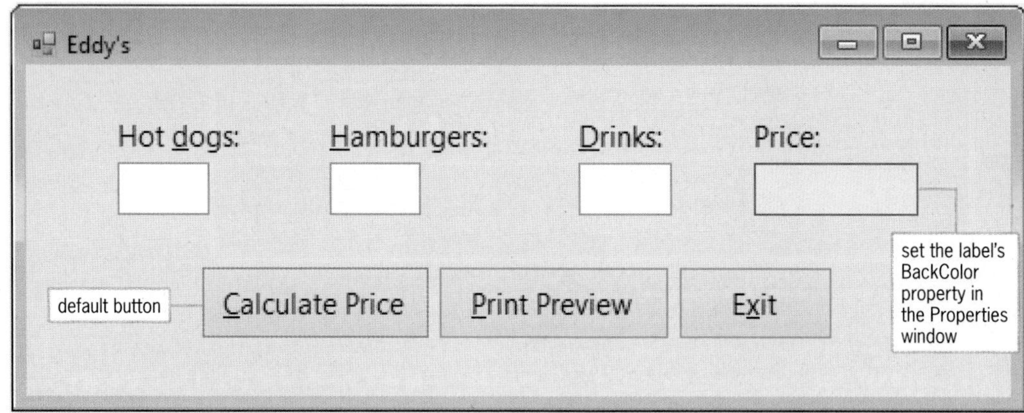

Figure 2-36 Sample interface for the Eddy's application

Football Scores

Create a TOE chart and interface for an application that calculates and displays a team's final score in a football game, given the numbers of the team's touchdowns, field goals, one-point conversions, two-point conversions, and safeties. Use the following names for the solution and project, respectively: Football Solution and Football Project. Save the application in the VbReloaded2015\Chap02 folder. Change the form file's name to Main Form.vb. You can either create your own interface or create the one shown in Figure 2-37. The image in the picture box is stored in the VbReloaded2015\Chap02\Football.png file. Code the Click event procedure for the Exit button only. (1-8)

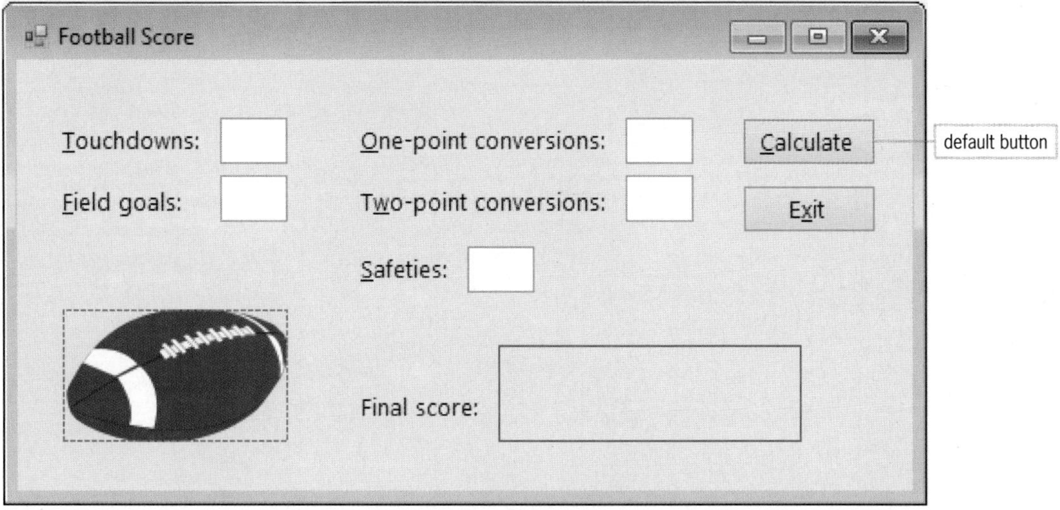

Figure 2-37 Sample interface for the Football Score application

Just Shirts

Create a TOE chart and interface for an application that allows the user to enter a customer's information (name, address, city, state, and ZIP code), the number of small shirts ordered, the number of medium shirts ordered, and the number of large shirts ordered. The interface will need to display the total number of shirts ordered and the total price of the order. Use the following names for the solution and project, respectively: Shirts Solution and Shirts Project. Save the solution in the VbReloaded2015\Chap02 folder. Change the form file's name to Main Form.vb. You can either create your own interface or create the one shown in Figure 2-38. Set the stateTextBox's CharacterCasing and MaxLength properties to Upper and 2, respectively. The Print Order button should send a printout of the interface to the Print preview window. Code the Click event procedures for the Print Order and Exit buttons only. (1-7)

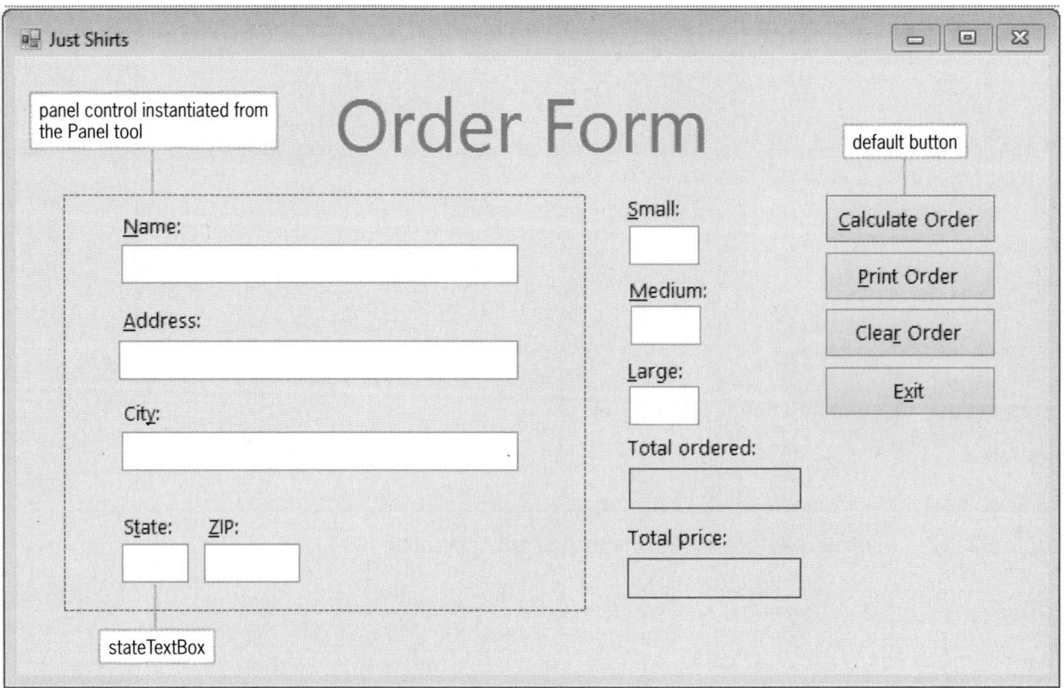

Figure 2-38 Sample interface for the Just Shirts application

Sophia's Italian Deli

Sophia's offers the following items on its lunch menu: Italian sub, meatball sandwich, slice of pizza, sausage sandwich, meatball/sausage combo, chicken fingers, ravioli plate, lasagna plate, bowl of soup, Caesar salad, calamari, spumoni, and cheesecake. Create a TOE chart and interface for an application that allows the user to enter a customer's lunch order. The interface will need to display the price of the order without sales tax, the sales tax amount, and the total price of the order. Use the following names for the solution and project, respectively: Sophia Solution and Sophia Project. Save the solution in the VbReloaded2015\Chap02 folder. Change the form file's name to Main Form.vb. Include Calculate, Clear, and Exit buttons in the interface. Code the Click event procedure for the Exit button only. (1-7)

CHAPTER 3

Memory Locations and Calculations

After studying Chapter 3, you should be able to:

1. Declare variables and named constants
2. Assign data to an existing variable
3. Convert data to the appropriate type using the TryParse method, Convert class methods, and a literal type character
4. Write and evaluate arithmetic expressions
5. Understand the scope and lifetime of variables and named constants
6. Understand the purpose of the Option statements
7. Use a TOE chart, pseudocode, and a flowchart to code an application
8. Format an application's numeric output
9. Clear the contents of a control's Text property during run time
10. Send the focus to a control during run time
11. Explain the different types of program errors

Internal Memory

The internal memory of a computer is composed of memory locations, with each memory location having a unique numeric address. It may be helpful to picture memory locations as shoe boxes, similar to the ones illustrated in Figure 3-1. As you know, shoe boxes come in different types and sizes. There are small boxes for children's sandals, larger boxes for adult sneakers, and even larger boxes for boots. The type and size of the footwear determine the appropriate type and size of the box.

Like shoe boxes, memory locations also come in different types and sizes. Here, too, the type and size of the item you want to store determine the appropriate type and size of the memory location. Examples of items stored in memory locations include numbers, strings, Boolean values, and Visual Basic instructions. Unlike the shoe boxes in Figure 3-1, however, each memory location inside a computer can hold only one item of data at a time.

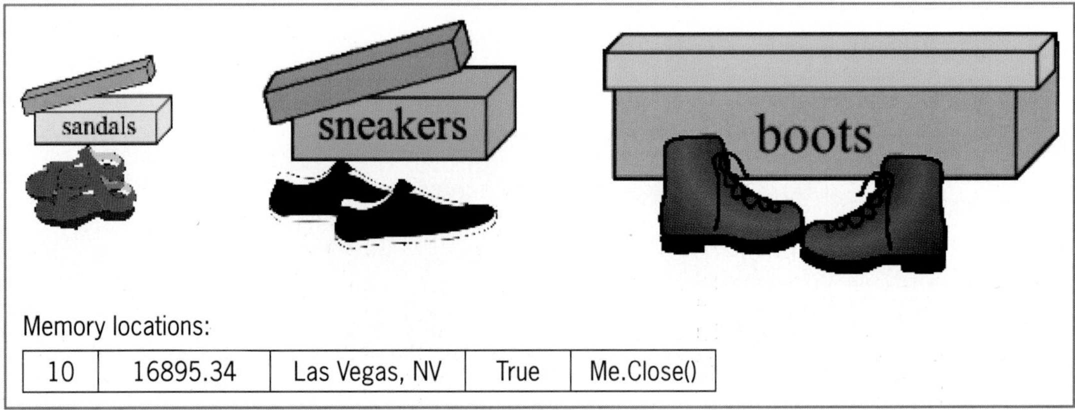

Figure 3-1 Illustration of shoe boxes and memory locations

Some of the memory locations inside the computer are automatically filled with data while you use your computer. For example, when you enter the number 10 at your keyboard, the computer saves the number 10 in a memory location for you. Likewise, when you start an application, each program instruction is placed in a memory location, where it awaits processing.

Memory locations can also be reserved by a programmer for use in a program. Reserving a memory location is also referred to as declaring the memory location. You declare a memory location using a Visual Basic instruction that assigns a name, a data type, and an initial value to the location. The name allows the programmer to refer to the memory location using one or more descriptive words, rather than a cryptic numeric address, in code. The **data type** indicates the type of data—for example, numeric or string—the memory location will store.

There are two types of memory locations that a programmer can declare: variables and named constants. You will learn about variables first. Named constants are covered in the *Named Constants* section in this chapter.

Variables

A **variable** is a computer memory location that a programmer uses to temporarily store data while an application is running. The data might be entered by the user at the keyboard. It also might be read from a file or be the result of a calculation made by the computer. The memory location is called a variable because its contents can change (vary) during run time.

The programmer must assign a name to each variable he or she wants to use in a program. The name, which is typically entered using camel case, should describe the variable's contents. It must also follow the rules listed in Figure 3-2, which shows examples of valid and invalid variable names.

HOW TO Name a Variable

1. The name must begin with a letter or an underscore.
2. The name can contain only letters, numbers, and the underscore character. No punctuation characters, special characters, or spaces are allowed in the name.
3. Although the name can contain thousands of characters, 32 characters is the recommended maximum number to use.
4. The name cannot be a reserved word, such as `Sub` or `Private`.

Valid names

`profit2018, firstName, janSales, taxRate, region1_2ndQtr`

Invalid names	Problem
`2018Profit`	the name must begin with a letter or an underscore
`first Name`	the name cannot contain a space
`jan.Sales`	the name cannot contain punctuation
`tax&Rate`	the name cannot contain a special character
`sub`	the name cannot be a reserved word
`r2Q`	although syntactically valid, the name does not describe the variable's contents

Figure 3-2 How to name a variable

The item that a memory location will accept for storage is determined by the location's data type, which the programmer assigns to the location when he or she declares it in code. Figure 3-3 describes most of the basic data types available in Visual Basic. Each data type listed in the figure is a class, which means that each data type is a pattern from which objects—in this case, variables—are instantiated.

Data type	Stores	Memory required
Boolean	a logical value (True, False)	2 bytes
Char	one Unicode character	2 bytes
Date	date and time information Date range: January 1, 0001 to December 31, 9999 Time range: 0:00:00 (midnight) to 23:59:59	8 bytes
Decimal	a number with a decimal place Range with no decimal place: +/–79,228,162,514,264,337,593,543,950,335 Range with a decimal place: +/–7.9228162514264337593543950335	16 bytes

Figure 3-3 Basic data types in Visual Basic *(continues)*

(continued)

Double	a number with a decimal place Range: +/–4.94065645841247 X 10^{-324} to +/–1.79769313486231 X 10^{308}	8 bytes
Integer	integer Range: –2,147,483,648 to 2,147,483,647	4 bytes
Long	integer Range: –9,223,372,036,854,775,808 to 9,223,372,036,854,775,807	8 bytes
Object	data of any type	4 bytes
Short	integer Range: –32,768 to 32,767	2 bytes
Single	a number with a decimal place Range: +/–1.401298 X 10^{-45} to +/–3.402823 X 10^{38}	4 bytes
String	text; 0 to approximately 2 billion characters	

Figure 3-3 Basic data types in Visual Basic

As Figure 3-3 indicates, variables assigned the Integer, Long, or Short data type can store **integers**, which are positive or negative numbers that do not have any decimal places. These three data types differ in the range of integers each can store and the amount of memory each needs to store the integers.

Decimal, Double, or Single variables can store **real numbers**, which are numbers that contain a decimal place. Here again, these three data types differ in the range of numbers each can store and the amount of memory each needs to store the numbers. However, calculations involving Decimal variables are not subject to the small rounding errors that may occur when using Double or Single variables. In most cases, these errors do not create any problems in an application. One exception to this is when the application contains complex equations involving money, where you need accuracy to the penny. In those cases, you should use the Decimal data type.

The Char data type can store one Unicode character, while the String data type can store from zero to approximately 2 billion Unicode characters. Unicode is the universal coding scheme that assigns a unique numeric value to each character used in the written languages of the world. (For more information, see The Unicode Consortium website at *http://unicode.org*.)

Also listed in Figure 3-3 are the Boolean, Date, and Object data types. You use a Boolean variable to store a Boolean value (either True or False) and a Date variable to store date and time information. The Object data type can store any type of data. However, your application will pay a price for this flexibility: It will run more slowly because the computer must determine the type of data currently stored in an Object variable. It is best to avoid using the Object data type.

The applications in this book will use the Integer data type for variables that will store integers used in calculations, even when the integers are small enough to fit into a Short variable. This is because a calculation containing Integer variables takes less time to process than the equivalent calculation containing Short variables. Either the Decimal data type or the Double data type will be used for numbers that contain decimal places and are used in calculations. The applications will use the String data type for variables that contain either text or numbers not used in calculations and the Boolean data type to store Boolean values (either True or False).

Declaring a Variable in Code

Figure 3-4 shows the syntax of the statement used to declare a variable. The declaration statement tells the computer to set aside a small section of its internal memory, and it allows the programmer to refer to the section by the variable's name. The size of the section is determined by the variable's data type. The {`Dim` | `Private` | `Static`} portion of the syntax indicates that you can select only one of the keywords appearing within the braces. In most instances, you declare a variable using the `Dim` keyword. (You will learn about the `Private` and `Static` keywords in the *Variables with Class Scope* and *Static Variables* sections, respectively, in this chapter.)

HOW TO Declare a Variable

Syntax
{**Dim** | **Private** | **Static**} *variableName* **As** *dataType* [= *initialValue*]

Example 1
```
Dim quantity As Integer
Dim price As Double
```
declares an Integer variable named `quantity` and a Double variable named `price`; the variables are automatically initialized to 0

Example 2
```
Dim tax As Decimal
```
declares a Decimal variable named `tax`; the variable is automatically initialized to 0

Example 3
```
Dim isDataOk As Boolean = True
```
declares a Boolean variable named `isDataOk` and initializes it using the keyword `True`

Example 4
```
Dim answer As String = "YES"
```
declares a String variable named `answer` and initializes it using the string "YES"

Figure 3-4 How to declare a variable

The keyword `Dim` comes from the word *dimension*, which is how programmers in the 1960s referred to the process of allocating the computer's memory. *Dimension* refers to the size of something.

As mentioned earlier, a variable is considered an object in Visual Basic. The variable is an instance of the class specified in the *dataType* portion of its declaration statement. The `Dim quantity As Integer` statement, for example, creates (instantiates) a variable (object) named `quantity`. The `quantity` variable (object) is an instance of the Integer class.

In the syntax, *initialValue* is the value you want stored in the variable when it is created in the computer's internal memory. The square brackets in the syntax indicate that the "= *initialValue*" part of a variable declaration statement is optional. If you do not assign an initial value to a variable when it is declared, the computer stores a default value in the variable. The default value depends on the variable's data type. A variable declared using one of the numeric data types is automatically initialized to—in other words, given a beginning value of—the number 0. The computer automatically initializes a Boolean variable using the keyword `False` and a Date variable to 1/1/0001 12:00:00 AM. Object and String variables are automatically initialized using the keyword `Nothing`. Variables initialized to `Nothing` do not actually contain the word *Nothing*; rather, they contain no data at all.

The answers to Mini-Quiz questions are located in Appendix A. Each question is associated with one or more objectives listed at the beginning of the chapter.

Mini-Quiz 3-1

1. A variable can store ____________ at a time. (1)
   a. only one item
   b. a maximum of two items
   c. an unlimited number of items
2. Which of the following is a valid name for a variable? (1)
   a. `first&lastNames`
   b. `10Percent_Rate`
   c. `sales_2018`
   d. `tax.rate5`
3. Write a Dim statement that declares a Double variable named `payRate`. (1)
4. Write a Dim statement that declares an Integer variable named `counter` and initializes it to the number 1. (1)

Assigning Data to an Existing Variable

In the previous chapters, you used an assignment statement to assign a value to a control's property during run time. You can also use an assignment statement to assign a value to a variable during run time; the syntax for doing this is shown in Figure 3-5. In the syntax, *expression* can contain items such as literal constants, object properties, variables, keywords, and arithmetic operators. A **literal constant** is an item of data whose value does not change while the application is running; examples include the numeric literal constant 23000 and the string literal constant "Miami". When the computer processes an assignment statement, it evaluates the expression that appears on the right side of the assignment operator (=) first. It then assigns the result to the variable that appears on the left side of the assignment operator, replacing the variable's existing data. (Recall that a variable can store only one item of data at a time.)

HOW TO Assign a Value to an Existing Variable

Syntax
variableName = *expression*

Example 1
```
Dim population As Integer
population = 23000
```
The assignment statement assigns the integer 23000 to the `population` variable.

Example 2
```
Dim city As String
city = "Miami"
```
The assignment statement assigns the string "Miami" to the `city` variable.

Figure 3-5 How to assign a value to an existing variable *(continues)*

(continued)

Example 3
```
Dim custName As String
custName = nameTextBox.Text
```
The assignment statement assigns the string contained in the nameTextBox's Text property to the `custName` variable.

Example 4
```
Dim taxRate As Double
taxRate = 0.035
```
The assignment statement assigns the Double number 0.035 to the `taxRate` variable.

Example 5
```
Dim taxRate As Decimal
taxRate = 0.035D
```
The assignment statement converts the Double number 0.035 to Decimal and then assigns the result to the `taxRate` variable.

Figure 3-5 How to assign a value to an existing variable

The data type of the expression assigned to a variable should be the same data type as the variable itself; this is the case in all of the examples included in Figure 3-5. The assignment statement in Example 1 stores the numeric literal constant 23000 (an integer) in an Integer variable named `population`. Similarly, the assignment statement in Example 2 stores the string literal constant "Miami" in a String variable named `city`. Notice that string literal constants are enclosed in quotation marks, but numeric literal constants and variable names are not. The quotation marks differentiate a string from both a number and a variable name. In other words, "23000" is a string, but 23000 is a number. Similarly, "Miami" is a string, but Miami (without the quotation marks) would be interpreted by the computer as the name of a variable. When the computer processes an assignment statement that assigns a string to a String variable, it assigns only the characters that appear between the quotation marks; it does not assign the quotation marks themselves.

The assignment statement in Example 3 assigns the string contained in the nameTextBox control's Text property to a String variable named `custName`. (Recall that the value stored in the Text property of an object is always treated as a string.) The assignment statement in Example 4 assigns the Double number 0.035 to a Double variable named `taxRate`. This is because a numeric literal constant that has a decimal place is automatically treated as a Double number in Visual Basic. When entering a numeric literal constant, you do not enter a comma or special characters, such as the dollar sign or percent sign. If you want to include a percentage in an assignment statement, you do so using its decimal equivalent; for example, you enter 0.035 rather than 3.5%. (If you enter .035 in the Code Editor window, the editor will change the number to 0.035 when you move the insertion point to a different line.)

Finally, the `taxRate = 0.035D` statement in Example 5 shows how you convert a numeric literal constant of the Double data type to the Decimal data type, and then assign the result to a Decimal variable. The D that follows the number 0.035 in the statement is one of the literal type characters in Visual Basic. A **literal type character** forces a literal constant to assume a data type other than the one its form indicates. In this case, the D forces the Double number 0.035 to assume the Decimal data type.

In all of the assignment statements in Figure 3-5, the expression's data type is the same as the variable's data type. At times, however, you may need to store a value of a different data type in a variable. You can change the value's data type to match the variable's data type using either the TryParse method or one of the methods in the Convert class.

Using the TryParse Method

As you learned earlier, each data type in Visual Basic is a class. Most classes have one or more methods that perform a specific task for the class. For example, all of the Visual Basic numeric data types (such as Double, Decimal, and Integer) have a **TryParse method** whose task is to convert a string to that particular data type.

Figure 3-6 shows the basic syntax of the TryParse method along with examples of using the method. In the syntax, *dataType* is one of the numeric data types available in Visual Basic. The dot member access operator in the syntax indicates that the TryParse method is a member of the *dataType* class. The method's arguments (*string* and *numericVariableName*) represent information that the method needs to perform its task. The *string* argument is the string you want converted to a number of the *dataType* type and typically is either the Text property of a control or the name of a String variable. The *numericVariableName* argument is the name of a numeric variable that the TryParse method can use to store the number. The numeric variable must have the same data type as specified in the *dataType* portion of the syntax.

Ch03-TryParse

HOW TO Use the Basic Syntax of the TryParse Method

Basic syntax
dataType.**TryParse(***string*, *numericVariableName***)**

Example 1
```
Dim price As Double
Double.TryParse(priceTextBox.Text, price)
```
If the string contained in the Text property can be converted to a Double number, the TryParse method converts the string and then stores the result in the `price` variable; otherwise, it stores the number 0 in the variable.

Example 2
```
Dim baseFee As Decimal
Decimal.TryParse(baseFeeLabel.Text, baseFee)
```
If the string contained in the Text property can be converted to a Decimal number, the TryParse method converts the string and then stores the result in the `baseFee` variable; otherwise, it stores the number 0 in the variable.

Example 3
```
Dim population As String = "23000"
Dim numPeople As Integer
Integer.TryParse(population, numPeople)
```
The TryParse method converts the string contained in the `population` variable to an Integer number and then stores the result (23000) in the `numPeople` variable.

Figure 3-6 How to use the basic syntax of the TryParse method

The TryParse method parses its *string* argument to determine whether the string can be converted to a number of the specified data type. In this case, the term *parse* means to look at each character in the string. If the string can be converted, the TryParse method converts the string to a number and then stores the number in the variable specified in the *numericVariableName* argument. If the TryParse method determines that the string cannot be converted to the appropriate data type, it assigns the number 0 to the variable.

Figure 3-7 shows how the TryParse method of the Double, Decimal, and Integer data types would convert various strings. As the figure indicates, the three methods can convert a string that contains only numbers. They can also convert a string that contains a leading sign as well as one that contains leading or trailing spaces. In addition, the Double.TryParse and Decimal.TryParse methods can convert a string that contains a decimal point or a comma. However, none of the three methods can convert a string that contains a dollar sign, a percent sign, a letter, or a space within the string, and none can convert an empty string. An **empty string**, also referred to as a **zero-length string**, is a set of quotation marks with nothing between them, like this: "".

	string	Double.TryParse	Decimal.TryParse	Integer.TryParse
can be converted	"62"	62	62	62
	–9	–9	–9	–9
	" 33 "	33	33	33
can be converted by only two of the methods	"12.55"	12.55	12.55	0
	"–4.23"	–4.23	–4.23	0
	"1,457"	1457	1457	0
cannot be converted	"$5"	0	0	0
	"7%"	0	0	0
	"122a"	0	0	0
	"1 345"	0	0	0
	empty string	0	0	0

Figure 3-7 Results of the TryParse method for the Double, Decimal, and Integer data types

Using the Convert Class Methods

At times, you may need to convert a number (rather than a string) from one data type to another. Visual Basic provides several ways of accomplishing this task. One way is to use the Visual Basic conversion functions, which are listed in Appendix D in this book. You can also use one of the methods defined in the **Convert class**. In this book, you will use the Convert class methods because they can be used in any of the languages built into Visual Studio. The conversion functions, on the other hand, can be used only in the Visual Basic language. The more commonly used methods in the Convert class are the ToDecimal, ToDouble, ToInt32, and ToString methods. The methods convert a value to the Decimal, Double, Integer, and String data types, respectively.

The syntax for using the Convert class methods is shown in Figure 3-8 along with examples of using the methods. The dot member access operator in the syntax indicates that the *method* is a member of the Convert class. In most cases, the *value* argument is a numeric value that you want converted either to the String data type or to a different numeric data type (for example, from Double to Decimal). Although you can use the Convert methods to convert a string to a numeric data type, the TryParse method is the recommended method to use for that task. This is because, unlike the Convert methods, the TryParse method does not produce an error when it tries to convert an empty string. Instead, the TryParse method assigns the number 0 to its *numericVariableName* argument.

HOW TO Use the Convert Class Methods

Syntax
Convert.*method***(***value***)**

Method	Purpose
ToDecimal	convert the *value* argument to the Decimal data type
ToDouble	convert the *value* argument to the Double data type
ToInt32	convert the *value* argument to the Integer data type
ToString	convert the *value* argument to the String data type

Example 1
```
Dim taxRate As Decimal
taxRate = Convert.ToDecimal(0.035)
```
The Convert method converts the Double number 0.035 to Decimal. (Recall that a number with a decimal place is automatically treated as a Double number in Visual Basic.) The assignment statement then assigns the result to the `taxRate` variable. You could also use the `taxRate = 0.035D` statement, as shown earlier in Figure 3-5.

Example 2
```
Dim totalScore As Integer
totalScore = 100
totalLabel.Text = Convert.ToString(totalScore)
```
The Convert method converts the integer stored in the `totalScore` variable to String. The assignment statement then assigns the result to the totalLabel's Text property.

Figure 3-8 How to use the Convert class methods

The answers to Mini-Quiz questions are located in Appendix A. Each question is associated with one or more objectives listed at the beginning of the chapter.

Mini-Quiz 3-2

1. Which of the following assigns the ID for the state of Tennessee to a String variable named `state`? (2)
   a. `state = 'TN'`
   b. `state = "TN"`
   c. `state = TN`
   d. `state As String = "TN"`
2. Which of the following assigns the number 21 to an Integer variable named `age`? (2)
   a. `age = '21'`
   b. `age = "21"`
   c. `age = 21`
   d. `age As Integer = 21`

3. Which of the following can be used to store the contents of a String variable named `inStock` in an Integer variable named `quantity`? (2, 3)
   a. `inStock.TryParse(String, quantity)`
   b. `Integer.TryParse(inStock, quantity)`
   c. `Integer.TryParse(quantity, inStock)`
   d. `quantity = TryParse(inStock)`

4. Which of the following assigns the number 75.63 to a Decimal variable named `price`? (2, 3)
   a. `price = Convert.ToDecimal(75.63)`
   b. `Convert.ToDecimal(75.63, price)`
   c. `price = TryParse.ToDecimal(75.63)`
   d. `TryParse.ToDecimal(75.63, price)`

Arithmetic Expressions

Most applications require the computer to perform at least one calculation. You instruct the computer to perform a calculation by writing an arithmetic expression, which is an expression that contains one or more arithmetic operators along with any of the following: variables, literal constants, named constants, or methods. When an expression contains either a variable or a named constant, the computer uses the value stored inside the memory location to process the expression.

Figure 3-9 lists the most commonly used arithmetic operators available in Visual Basic, along with their precedence numbers. The precedence numbers indicate the order in which the computer performs the operation in an expression. Operations with a precedence number of 1 are performed before operations with a precedence number of 2, and so on. However, you can use parentheses to override the order of precedence because operations within parentheses are always performed before operations outside parentheses.

Operator	Operation	Precedence number
^	exponentiation (raises a number to a power)	1
–	negation (reverses the sign of a number)	2
*, /	multiplication and division	3
\	integer division	4
Mod	modulus (remainder) arithmetic	5
+, –	addition and subtraction	6

Figure 3-9 Most commonly used arithmetic operators

Although the negation and subtraction operators listed in Figure 3-9 use the same symbol (a hyphen), there is a difference between them: the negation operator is *unary*, whereas the subtraction operator is *binary*. *Unary* and *binary* refer to the number of operands required by the operator. Unary operators require one operand. The expression –10, for example, uses the unary negation operator to turn its one operand (the positive number 10) into a negative number. Binary operators, on the other hand, require two operands. The expression 8 – 2, for instance, uses the binary subtraction operator to subtract its second operand (the number 2) from its first operand (the number 8).

Two of the arithmetic operators listed in Figure 3-9 might be less familiar to you: the integer division operator (\) and the modulus operator (Mod). You use the **integer division operator** to divide two integers (whole numbers) and then return the result as an integer. For instance, the expression 211 \ 4 results in 52, which is the integer result of dividing 211 by 4. (If you use the standard division operator [/] to divide 211 by 4, the result is 52.75 rather than 52.) You might use the integer division operator in a program that determines the number of quarters, dimes, and nickels to return as change to a customer. For example, if a customer should receive 53 cents in change, you could use the expression 53 \ 25 to determine the number of quarters to return; the expression evaluates to 2.

The **modulus operator** (sometimes referred to as the remainder operator) is also used to divide two numbers, but the numbers do not have to be integers. After dividing the numbers, the modulus operator returns the remainder of the division. For instance, 211 Mod 4 equals 3, which is the remainder of 211 divided by 4. A common use for the modulus operator is to determine whether a number is even or odd. If you divide the number by 2 and the remainder is 0, the number is even; if the remainder is 1, however, the number is odd. Figure 3-10 shows several examples of using the integer division and Mod operators.

HOW TO Use the Integer Division and Mod Operators

Examples	Results
211 \ 4	52
211 Mod 4	3
53 \ 25	2
53 Mod 25	3
75 \ 2	37
75 Mod 2	1
100 \ 2	50
100 Mod 2	0

Figure 3-10 How to use the integer division and Mod operators

You may have noticed that some of the operators listed in Figure 3-9, such as the addition and subtraction operators, have the same precedence number. When an expression contains more than one operator having the same priority, those operators are evaluated from left to right. In the expression 7 – 8 / 2 + 5 * 2, for instance, the division (/) is performed first, then the multiplication (*), then the subtraction (–), and then the addition (+). The result of the expression is the number 13, as shown in Example 1 in Figure 3-11. You can use parentheses to change the order in which the operators in an expression are evaluated. As Example 2 shows, the expression 7 – (8 / 2 + 5) * 2 evaluates to –11 rather than to 13. This is because the parentheses tell the computer to perform the division first, then the addition, then the multiplication, and then the subtraction.

Ch03-Expressions

HOW TO Evaluate Expressions Containing Operators with the Same Precedence

Example 1

Original expression	7 – 8 / 2 + 5 * 2
The division is performed first	7 – 4 + 5 * 2
The multiplication is performed second	7 – 4 + 10

Figure 3-11 How to evaluate expressions containing operators with the same precedence *(continues)*

(continued)

The subtraction is performed third	3 + 10
The addition is performed last	13
<u>Example 2</u>	
Original expression	7 – (8 / 2 + 5) * 2
The division is performed first	7 – (4 + 5) * 2
The addition is performed second	7 – 9 * 2
The multiplication is performed third	7 – 18
The subtraction is performed last	–11

Figure 3-11 How to evaluate expressions containing operators with the same precedence

You can save the result of an arithmetic expression by assigning it to a variable. The variable should have the same data type as the value being assigned to it, as shown in the examples in Figure 3-12.

If you want to practice writing assignment statements that contain arithmetic expressions, open the solution contained in the Try It 1! folder. For now, ignore the Option statements in the Code Editor window.

HOW TO Assign the Result of an Arithmetic Expression to a Variable

<u>Example 1</u>

```
Dim ordered As Integer = 76
ordered = ordered + 1
```

The assignment statement adds the integer 1 to the contents of the Integer `ordered` variable and then assigns the result (77) to the variable.

<u>Example 2</u>

```
Dim quarters As Integer
Dim change As Integer = 83
quarters = change \ 25
```

The assignment statement uses the integer division operator to divide the contents of the Integer `change` variable by the integer 25. The statement assigns the result (3) to the Integer `quarters` variable.

<u>Example 3</u>

```
Dim sales As Double = 5000
Dim commission As Double
commission = sales * 0.03
```

The assignment statement multiplies the contents of the Double `sales` variable by the Double number 0.03 and then assigns the result (150) to the Double `commission` variable.

<u>Example 4</u>

```
Dim price As Decimal = 20.75D
price = price * Convert.ToDecimal(1.04)
```

The Convert method converts the Double number 1.04 to Decimal. The assignment statement then multiplies the Decimal result by the contents of the Decimal `price` variable, assigning the result (21.58) to the variable.

Figure 3-12 How to assign the result of an arithmetic expression to a variable *(continues)*

(continued)

Example 5
```
Dim sales As Double = 234.5
bonusLabel.Text = Convert.ToString(sales * 0.1)
```
The assignment statement multiplies the contents of the Double `sales` variable by the Double number 0.1, giving 23.45. Next, the Convert method converts the number 23.45 to the String data type, giving "23.45". The assignment statement then assigns the string "23.45" to the bonusLabel's Text property.

Figure 3-12 How to assign the result of an arithmetic expression to a variable

Arithmetic Assignment Operators

In addition to the standard arithmetic operators listed earlier in Figure 3-9, Visual Basic provides several arithmetic assignment operators. You can use the **arithmetic assignment operators** to abbreviate an assignment statement that contains an arithmetic operator. However, the assignment statement must have the following format, in which *variableName* on both sides of the equal sign is the name of the same variable: *variableName = variableName arithmeticOperator value.* For example, you can use the addition assignment operator (+=) to abbreviate the statement `ordered = ordered + 1` as follows: `ordered += 1`. Both statements tell the computer to add the number 1 to the contents of the `ordered` variable and then store the result in the variable.

Figure 3-13 shows the syntax for using an arithmetic assignment operator. Notice that each operator listed in the figure consists of an arithmetic operator followed immediately by the assignment operator (=). The operators do not contain a space; including a space in an arithmetic assignment operator is a common syntax error. Figure 3-13 also includes examples of using arithmetic assignment operators to abbreviate assignment statements.

HOW TO Use the Arithmetic Assignment Operators

Syntax
variableName arithmeticAssignmentOperator value

Operator	Purpose
+=	addition assignment
-=	subtraction assignment
*=	multiplication assignment
/=	division assignment

Note: To abbreviate an assignment statement, remove the variable name that appears on the left side of the assignment operator (=), and then put the assignment operator immediately after the arithmetic operator.

Example 1
Original assignment statement: `ordered = ordered + 1`
Abbreviated statement: `ordered += 1`
Both statements add 1 to the number stored in the Integer `ordered` variable and then assign the result to the variable.

Figure 3-13 How to use the arithmetic assignment operators *(continues)*

(continued)

Example 2
Original assignment statement: `price = price - discount`
Abbreviated statement: `price -= discount`
Both statements subtract the number stored in the Decimal `discount` variable from the number stored in the Decimal `price` variable and then assign the result to the `price` variable.

Example 3
Original assignment statement: `sales = sales * 1.05`
Abbreviated statement: `sales *= 1.05`
Both statements multiply the number stored in the Double `sales` variable by 1.05 and then assign the result to the variable.

Example 4
Original assignment statement: `payment = payment / 2`
Abbreviated statement: `payment /= 2`
Both statements divide the number stored in the Double `payment` variable by 2 and then assign the result to the variable.

Figure 3-13 How to use the arithmetic assignment operators

Mini-Quiz 3-3

The answers to Mini-Quiz questions are located in Appendix A. Each question is associated with one or more objectives listed at the beginning of the chapter.

1. The expression 7 + 4 / 2 * 4.5 evaluates to which of the following? (4)
   a. 1.222222
   b. 7.444444
   c. 16
   d. 24.75

2. The expression 131 \ 4 evaluates to which of the following? (4)
   a. 3
   b. 32
   c. 32.75
   d. 33

3. The statement `counter = counter + 1` is equivalent to which of the following statements? (4)
   a. `counter += 1`
   b. `counter =+ 1`
   c. `1 += counter`
   d. both a and c

Variables can also have namespace scope and are referred to as namespace variables, public variables, or global variables. Such variables can lead to unintentional errors in a program and should be avoided, if possible. For this reason, they are not covered in this book.

Scope and Lifetime

Besides a name, a data type, and an initial value, every variable also has a scope and a lifetime. A variable's **scope** indicates where the variable can be used in an application's code, and its **lifetime** indicates how long the variable remains in the computer's internal memory. Variables can have class scope, procedure scope, or block scope. However, most of the variables used in an application will have procedure scope. This is because fewer unintentional errors occur in applications when the variables are declared using the minimum scope needed, which usually is procedure scope.

A variable's scope and lifetime are determined by where you declare the variable. Typically, you enter the declaration statement either in a procedure (such as an event procedure) or in the Declarations section of a form. A form's Declarations section is located between the Public Class and End Class clauses in the Code Editor window.

Variables declared in a form's Declarations section have class scope. Variables declared in a procedure, on the other hand, have either procedure scope or block scope, depending on where in the procedure they are declared. The `totalDue` variable, which is shaded in Figure 3-14, has class scope because its declaration statement appears in the form's Declarations section. The shaded `purchase` variable, on the other hand, has procedure scope because it is declared in the calcButton_Click procedure. You will learn more about class scope and procedure scope in the next two sections. Block scope is covered in Chapter 4.

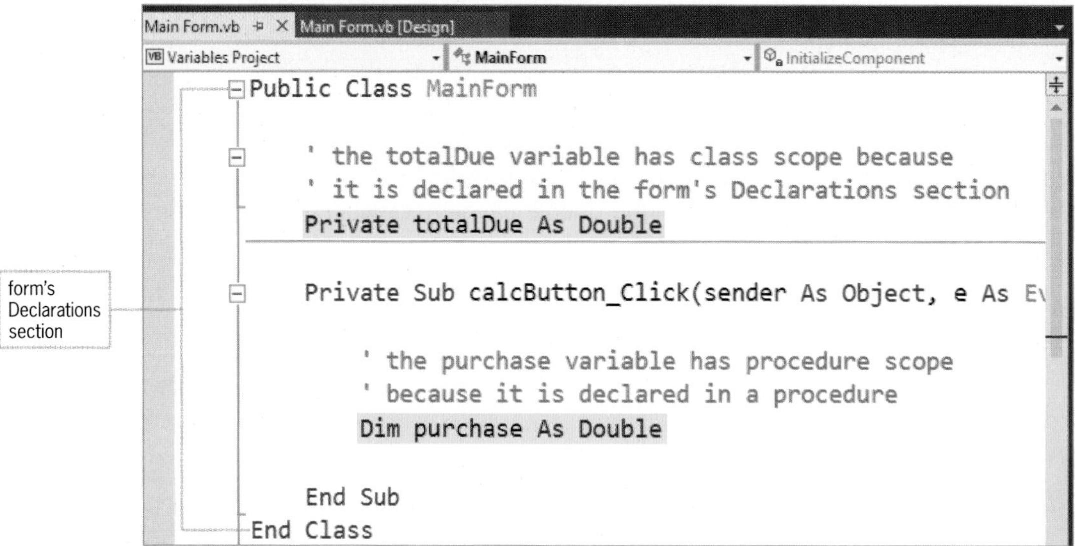

Figure 3-14 Variables declared in the form's Declarations section and calcButton_Click procedure

> Procedure-level variables are also called local variables and their scope is often referred to as local scope.

The green lines of text in Figure 3-14 are called comments. Programmers use **comments** to document a procedure's purpose and also to explain various sections of a procedure's code. Including comments in your code will make the code more readable and easier to understand by anyone viewing it. You create a comment by typing an apostrophe (`'`) before the text that represents the comment. The computer ignores everything that appears after the apostrophe on that line. Although it is not required, some programmers use a space to separate the apostrophe from the comment text, as shown in the figure.

> In the *Static Variables* section of this chapter, you will learn how to declare a procedure-level variable that remains in the computer's memory even when the procedure in which it is declared ends.

Variables with Procedure Scope

When you declare a variable in a procedure, the variable is called a **procedure-level variable**. Procedure-level variables have **procedure scope**, which means they can be used only by the procedure in which they are declared. Procedure-level variables are typically declared at the beginning of a procedure, and they remain in the computer's internal memory only while the procedure is running. Procedure-level variables are removed from memory when the procedure in which they are declared ends. In other words, a procedure-level variable has the same lifetime as the procedure that declares it. As mentioned earlier, most of the variables in your applications will be procedure-level variables.

The Discount Calculator application that you will view next illustrates the use of procedure-level variables. A sample run of the application is shown in Figure 3-15. The application provides a text box for the user to enter a sales amount. It then calculates and displays either a 15% discount or a 20% discount, depending on the button selected by the user.

If you want to experiment with the Discount Calculator application, open the solution contained in the Try It 2! folder. For now, ignore the Option statements in the Code Editor window.

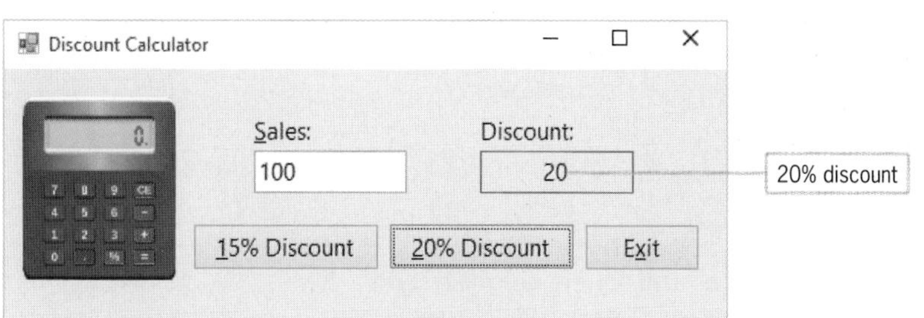

Figure 3-15 Sample run of the Discount Calculator application

Figure 3-16 shows the Click event procedures for the two discount buttons. The comments in the figure indicate the purpose of each line of code. (Be sure to read the comments before continuing with the chapter.) When each procedure ends, its procedure-level variables are removed from the computer's memory. The variables will be created again the next time the user clicks the button.

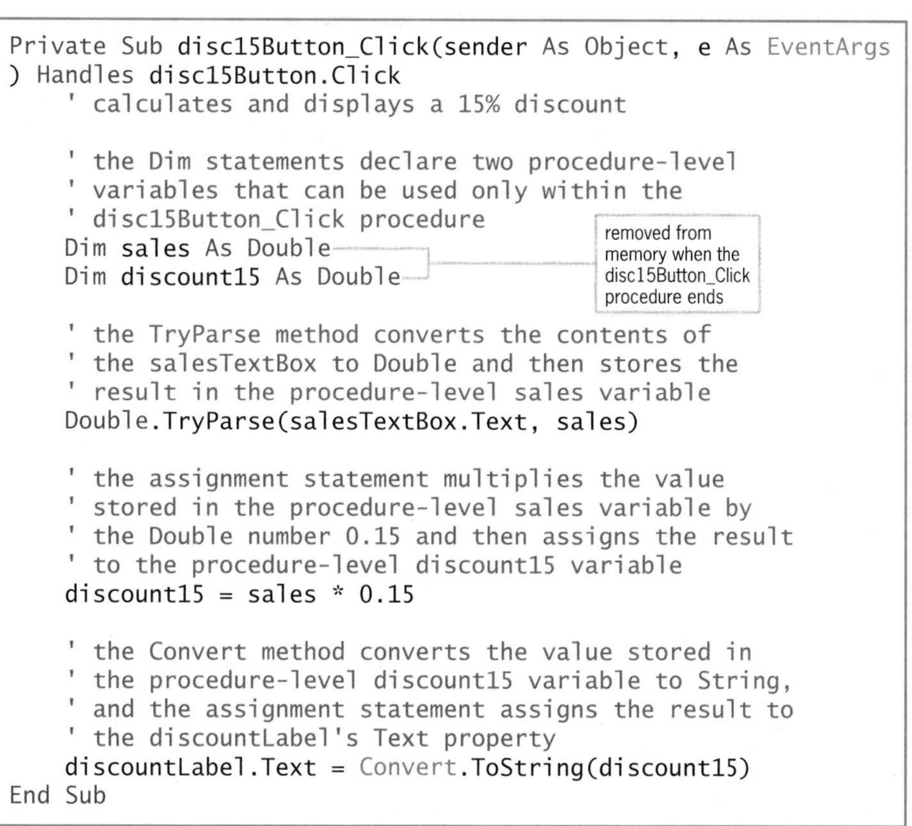

```
Private Sub disc15Button_Click(sender As Object, e As EventArgs
) Handles disc15Button.Click
    ' calculates and displays a 15% discount

    ' the Dim statements declare two procedure-level
    ' variables that can be used only within the
    ' disc15Button_Click procedure
    Dim sales As Double
    Dim discount15 As Double

    ' the TryParse method converts the contents of
    ' the salesTextBox to Double and then stores the
    ' result in the procedure-level sales variable
    Double.TryParse(salesTextBox.Text, sales)

    ' the assignment statement multiplies the value
    ' stored in the procedure-level sales variable by
    ' the Double number 0.15 and then assigns the result
    ' to the procedure-level discount15 variable
    discount15 = sales * 0.15

    ' the Convert method converts the value stored in
    ' the procedure-level discount15 variable to String,
    ' and the assignment statement assigns the result to
    ' the discountLabel's Text property
    discountLabel.Text = Convert.ToString(discount15)
End Sub
```


Figure 3-16 Click event procedures using procedure-level variables *(continues)*

(continued)

removed from memory when the disc20Button_Click procedure ends

```
Private Sub disc20Button_Click(sender As Object, e As EventArgs
) Handles disc20Button.Click
    ' calculates and displays a 20% discount

    ' the Dim statements declare two procedure-level
    ' variables that can be used only within the
    ' disc20Button_Click procedure
    Dim sales As Double
    Dim discount20 As Double

    ' the TryParse method converts the contents of
    ' the salesTextBox to Double and then stores the
    ' result in the procedure-level sales variable
    Double.TryParse(salesTextBox.Text, sales)

    ' the assignment statement multiplies the value
    ' stored in the procedure-level sales variable by
    ' the Double number 0.2 and then assigns the result
    ' to the procedure-level discount20 variable
    discount20 = sales * 0.2

    ' the Convert method converts the value stored in
    ' the procedure-level discount20 variable to String,
    ' and the assignment statement assigns the result to
    ' the discountLabel's Text property
    discountLabel.Text = Convert.ToString(discount20)
End Sub
```

Figure 3-16 Click event procedures using procedure-level variables

Notice that both procedures in Figure 3-16 declare a variable named `sales`. When you use the same name to declare a variable in more than one procedure, each procedure creates its own variable when the procedure is invoked. Each procedure also destroys its own variable when the procedure ends. In other words, even though they have the same name, each `sales` variable is located in a different section in the computer's internal memory, and each is an independent entity. This concept can be illustrated using the shoe box analogy from the beginning of the chapter. Just as both shoe boxes in Figure 3-17 have the same name (sneakers), both variables in the figure also have the same name (`sales`). However, like each shoe box, each variable has a different owner, different contents, and a different location.

Figure 3-17 Illustration of shoe boxes and variables

Variables with Class Scope

In addition to declaring a variable in a procedure, you can declare a variable in the form's Declarations section, which begins with the Public Class clause and ends with the End Class clause. When you declare a variable in the form's Declarations section, the variable is called a **class-level variable** and it has **class scope**. Class-level variables can be used by all of the procedures in the form, including the procedures associated with the controls contained on the form. Class-level variables retain their values and remain in the computer's internal memory until the application ends. In other words, a class-level variable has the same lifetime as the application itself.

Unlike a procedure-level variable, which is declared using the `Dim` keyword, you declare a class-level variable using the `Private` keyword. You typically use a class-level variable when you need more than one procedure in the same form to use the same variable. However, a class-level variable can also be used when a procedure needs to retain a variable's value after the procedure ends. The Total Calories application, which you will view next, illustrates this use of a class-level variable. A sample run of the application is shown in Figure 3-18. The application provides a text box for the user to enter the number of calories consumed in a day. Each time the user clicks the Add to Total button, the button's Click event procedure will add the daily amount to the grand total and then display the grand total in the interface.

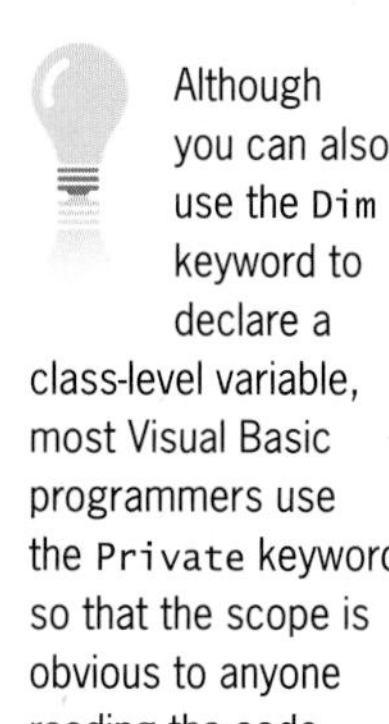

Although you can also use the `Dim` keyword to declare a class-level variable, most Visual Basic programmers use the `Private` keyword so that the scope is obvious to anyone reading the code.

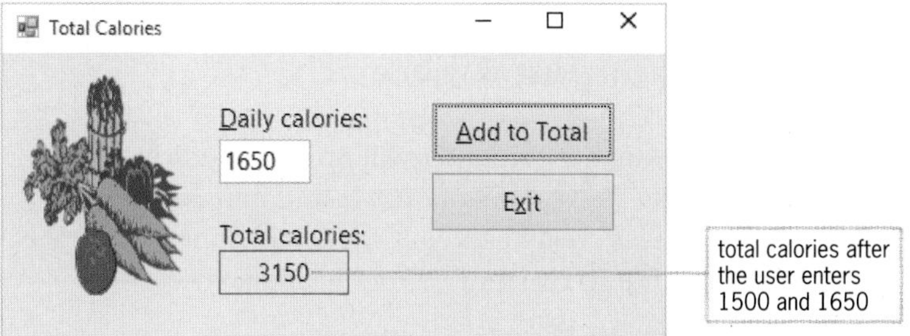

Figure 3-18 Sample run of the Total Calories application

Figure 3-19 shows most of the application's code. The addButton_Click procedure uses a class-level variable named `totalCalories` to accumulate (add together) the daily calorie amounts entered by the user. Class-level variables are declared after the Public Class clause in the form's Declarations section, but before the first Private Sub clause in that section. For now, do not be concerned about the three Option statements that appear in the code. You will learn about the Option statements later in this chapter. However, notice the comments at the beginning of the Code Editor window. The comments document the project's name and purpose, the programmer's name, and the date the program was either created or revised. The comments and Option statements are entered in the General Declarations section of the Code Editor window. Unlike the form's Declarations section, which is located *after* the Public Class clause, the General Declarations section is located *above* the Public Class clause.

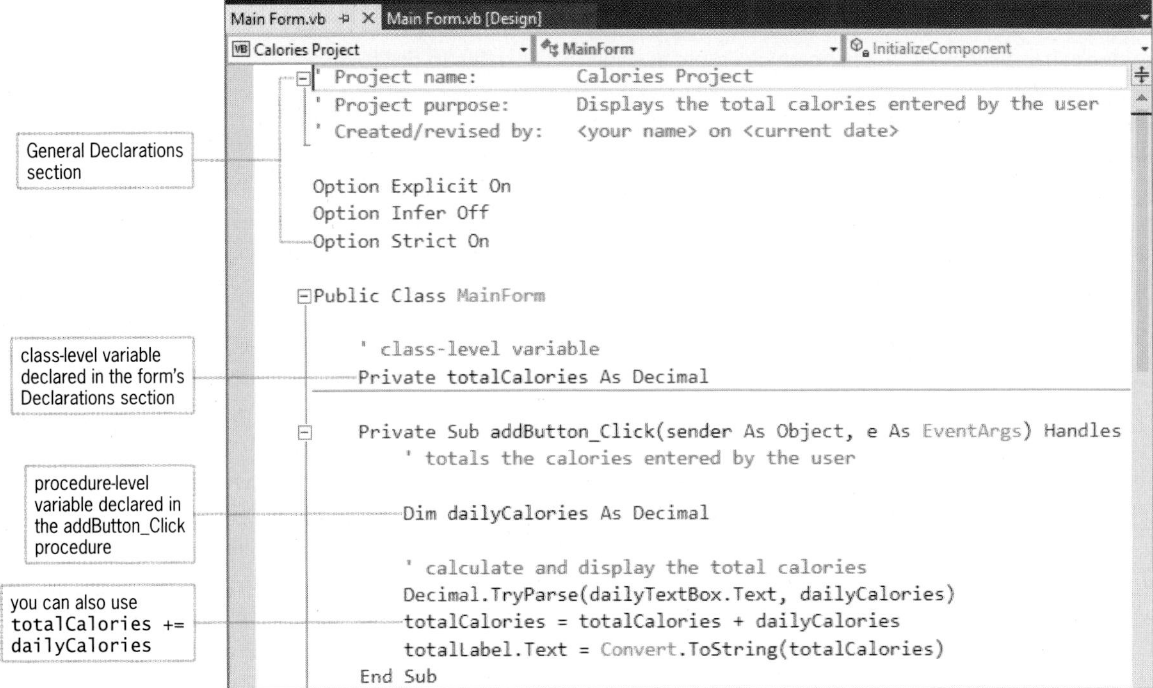

Figure 3-19 Total Calories application's code using a class-level variable

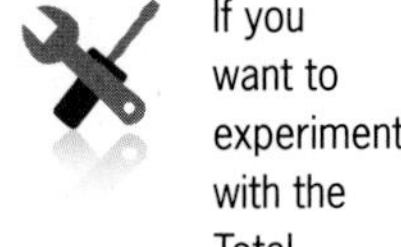

If you want to experiment with the Total Calories application, open the solution contained in the Try It 3! folder.

When the user starts the Total Calories application, the computer will process the Private statement in the form's Declarations section first. The statement creates and initializes the class-level `totalCalories` variable. The variable is created and initialized only once, when the application starts. It remains in the computer's internal memory until the application ends.

Each time the user clicks the Add to Total button, the button's Click event procedure creates and initializes a procedure-level variable named `dailyCalories`. The TryParse method then converts the contents of the dailyTextBox to Decimal, storing the result in the `dailyCalories` variable. The first assignment statement in the procedure adds the contents of the procedure-level `dailyCalories` variable to the contents of the class-level `totalCalories` variable. At this point, the `totalCalories` variable contains the sum of the daily calorie amounts entered so far.

The last assignment statement in the addButton_Click procedure converts the contents of the `totalCalories` variable to String and then assigns the result to the totalLabel. When the procedure ends, the computer removes the procedure-level `dailyCalories` variable from its memory. However, it does not remove the class-level `totalCalories` variable. The `totalCalories` variable is removed from the computer's memory only when the application ends.

Static Variables

As shown earlier in Figure 3-4, you can declare a variable using the `Dim`, `Private`, or `Static` keywords. You already know how to use the `Dim` and `Private` keywords to declare procedure-level and class-level variables, respectively. In this section, you will learn how to use the `Static` keyword to declare a special type of procedure-level variable, called a static variable.

A **static variable** is a procedure-level variable that remains in memory and also retains its value, even when the procedure in which it is declared ends. Like a class-level variable, a static variable is not removed from the computer's internal memory until the application ends. However, unlike a class-level variable, which can be used by all the procedures in a form, a static variable can be used only by the procedure in which it is declared. In other words, a static variable has a narrower (or more restrictive) scope than does a class-level variable. As mentioned earlier, you can prevent many unintentional errors from occurring in an application by declaring the variables using the minimum scope needed.

In the previous section, you viewed the interface and code for the Total Calories application, which uses a class-level variable to accumulate the daily calorie amounts entered by the user. Rather than using a class-level variable for that purpose, you can use a static variable, as shown in the code in Figure 3-20.

If you want to experiment with this version of the Total Calories application, open the solution contained in the Try It 4! folder.

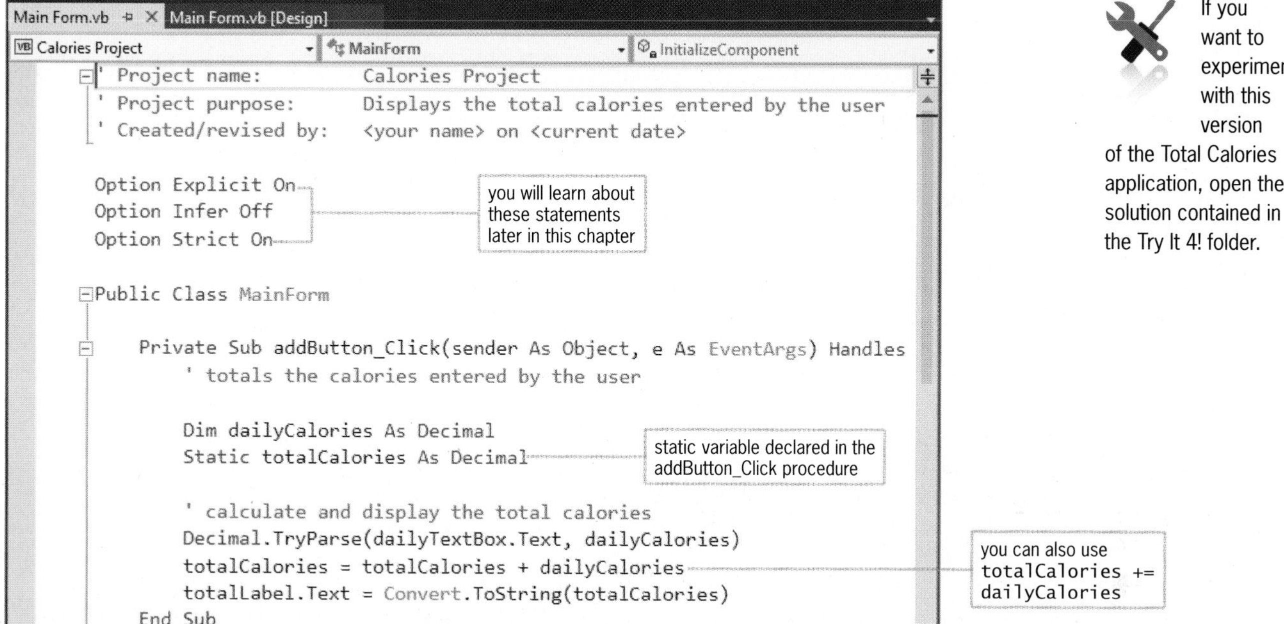

Figure 3-20 Total Calories application's code using a static variable

The first time the user clicks the Add to Total button in the application's interface, the button's Click event procedure creates and initializes a procedure-level variable named `dailyCalories` and a static variable named `totalCalories`. The TryParse method then converts the contents of the dailyTextBox to Decimal, storing the result in the `dailyCalories` variable. The first assignment statement in the procedure adds the contents of the `dailyCalories` variable to the contents of the `totalCalories` variable. The last assignment statement in the procedure converts the contents of the `totalCalories` variable to String and assigns the result to the totalLabel. When the procedure ends, the computer removes the variable declared using the `Dim` keyword (`dailyCalories`) from its internal memory. But it does not remove the variable declared using the `Static` keyword (`totalCalories`).

Each subsequent time the user clicks the Add to Total button, the computer re-creates and re-initializes the `dailyCalories` variable declared in the button's Click event procedure. However, it does not re-create or re-initialize the `totalCalories` variable because that variable, as well as its current value, is still in the computer's memory.

After re-creating and re-initializing the `dailyCalories` variable, the computer processes the remaining instructions contained in the button's Click event procedure. Here again, each time the procedure ends, the `dailyCalories` variable is removed from the computer's internal memory. The `totalCalories` variable is removed only when the application ends.

Ch03-Scope and Lifetime

Named Constants

In addition to using literal constants and variables in your code, you can use named constants. Like a variable, a **named constant** is a memory location inside the computer. However, unlike the value stored in a variable, the value stored in a named constant cannot be changed while the application is running.

You declare a named constant using the **Const statement**, whose syntax is shown in Figure 3-21. In the syntax, *expression* is the value you want stored in the named constant when it is created in the computer's internal memory. The expression's value must have the same data type as the named constant. The expression can contain a literal constant, another named constant, or an arithmetic operator; however, it cannot contain a variable or a method.

HOW TO Declare a Named Constant

Syntax
[Private] Const *constantName* **As** *dataType* = *expression*

Example 1
```
Const Pi As Double = 3.141593
```
declares `Pi` as a Double named constant and initializes it to the Double number 3.141593

Example 2
```
Const MinAge As Integer = 18
```
declares `MinAge` as an Integer named constant and initializes it to the integer 18

Example 3
```
Const Title As String = "Web Developer"
```
declares `Title` as a String named constant and initializes it to the string "Web Developer"

Example 4
```
Private Const TaxRate As Decimal = 0.035D
```
changes the number's data type from Double to Decimal

declares `TaxRate` as a Decimal named constant and initializes it to the Decimal number 0.035

Figure 3-21 How to declare a named constant

To differentiate the name of a constant from the name of a variable, many programmers enter the names of constants using Pascal case (rather than camel case), as shown in the examples in Figure 3-21. When entered in a procedure, the Const statements shown in the first three examples create procedure-level named constants. To create a class-level named constant, you precede the `Const` keyword with the `Private` keyword, as shown in Example 4. In addition, you enter the Const statement in the form's Declarations section. Notice that Example 4 uses the literal type character D to convert the Double number 0.035 to Decimal. The Convert.ToDecimal method was not used for this purpose because, as mentioned earlier, the expression assigned to a named constant cannot contain a method.

Named constants make code more self-documenting and easier to modify because they allow a programmer to use meaningful words in place of values that are less clear. The named constant `Pi`, for example, is much more meaningful than the number 3.141593, which is the value of pi rounded to six decimal places. Once you create a named constant, you can use the constant's name, rather than its value, in the application's code. For example, instead of using the statement `area = 3.141593 * radius * radius` to calculate the area of a circle, you can use `area = Pi * radius * radius`.

Unlike the value stored in a variable, the value stored in a named constant cannot be inadvertently changed while the application is running. Using a named constant to represent a value has another advantage: If the value changes in the future, you will need to modify only the Const statement in the program, rather than all the program statements that use the value.

Mini-Quiz 3-4

The answers to Mini-Quiz questions are located in Appendix A. Each question is associated with one or more objectives listed at the beginning of the chapter.

1. Most of the variables used in an application will have ____________ scope. (1, 5)
   a. block
   b. class
   c. general
   d. procedure
2. ____________ variables are declared in the form's Declarations section using the `Private` keyword. (1, 5)
   a. Block-level
   b. Class-level
   c. General-level
   d. Procedure-level
3. Which of the following declares a procedure-level variable that retains its value until the application ends? (1, 5)
   a. `Dim Static score As Integer`
   b. `Private Static score As Integer`
   c. `Static score As Integer`
   d. `Static Dim score As Integer`
4. Which of the following declares and initializes a class-level named constant called `Job`? (1, 5)
   a. `Private Const Job As String = "Coach"`
   b. `Static Job As String = "Coach"`
   c. `Const Private Job As String = "Coach"`
   d. `Const Class Job As String = "Coach"`

Note: You have learned a lot so far in this chapter. You may want to take a break at this point before continuing.

Option Statements

In the following two sections, you will learn about the Option statements shown earlier in Figures 3-19 and 3-20. As you may remember, the figures contain the code for both versions of the Total Calories application. Although not shown in any figures, the Option statements are also included in the code for the Discount Calculator application, which you viewed earlier in the chapter. You will learn about the Option Explicit and Option Infer statements first.

Option Explicit and Option Infer

It is important to declare every variable used in your code. This means every variable should appear in a declaration statement, such as a Dim, Static, or Private statement. The declaration statement is important because it allows you to control the variable's data type. Declaration statements also make your code more self-documenting. A word of caution is in order at this point: In Visual Basic, you can create variables "on the fly." This means that if a statement in your code refers to an undeclared variable, Visual Basic will create the variable for you and assign the Object data type to it. Recall that the Object type is not a very efficient data type, and its use should be limited.

Because it is so easy to forget to declare a variable—and so easy to misspell a variable's name while coding, thereby inadvertently creating an undeclared variable—Visual Basic provides a statement that tells the Code Editor to flag any undeclared variables in your code: `Option Explicit On`. You enter the statement in the General Declarations section (located above the Public Class clause) of the Code Editor window. When you also enter the `Option Infer Off` statement in the General Declarations section, the Code Editor ensures that every variable and named constant is declared with a data type. In other words, the statement tells the computer not to infer (or assume) a memory location's data type based on the data assigned to the memory location.

Option Strict

As you learned earlier, the data type of the value assigned to a memory location should be the same as the data type of the memory location itself. If the value's data type does not match the memory location's data type, the computer uses a process called **implicit type conversion** to convert the value to fit the memory location. For example, when processing the statement `Const Radius As Double = 9`, the computer converts the integer 9 to the Double number 9.0 before storing the value in the `Radius` constant. When a value is converted from one data type to another data type that can store either larger numbers or numbers with greater precision, the value is said to be **promoted**. In this case, if the `Radius` constant is used subsequently in a calculation, the results of the calculation will not be adversely affected by the implicit promotion of the number 9 to the number 9.0.

On the other hand, if you inadvertently assign a Double number to a memory location that can store only an integer, the computer converts the Double number to an integer before storing the value in the memory location. It does this by rounding the number to the nearest whole number and then truncating (dropping off) the decimal portion of the number. When processing the statement `Dim score As Integer = 75.3`, for example, the computer converts the Double number 75.3 to the integer 75 before storing the integer in the `score` variable. When a value is converted from one data type to another data type that can store only smaller numbers or numbers with less precision, the value is said to be **demoted**. If the `score` variable is used subsequently in a calculation, the implicit demotion of the number 75.3 to the number 75 will probably cause the calculated results to be incorrect.

With implicit type conversions, data loss can occur when a value is converted from one data type to a narrower data type, which is a data type with less precision or smaller capacity. (For instance, 0.3 is lost when 75.3 is demoted to 75.) You can eliminate the problems that occur as a result of implicit type conversions by entering the `Option Strict On` statement in the General Declarations section of the Code Editor window. When the `Option Strict On` statement appears in an application's code, the computer uses the type conversion rules listed in Figure 3-22. The figure also includes examples of these rules.

HOW TO Use the Type Conversion Rules with Option Strict On

Rules and examples

1. Strings will not be implicitly converted to numbers. The Code Editor will display a warning message when a statement attempts to use a string where a number is expected.

```
            Dim hours As Double
Incorrect:  hours = hoursTextBox.Text
Correct:    Double.TryParse(hoursTextBox.Text, hours)
```

2. Numbers will not be implicitly converted to strings. The Code Editor will display a warning message when a statement attempts to use a number where a string is expected.

```
            Const PayRate As Double = 12.75
Incorrect:  rateLabel.Text = PayRate
Correct:    rateLabel.Text = Convert.ToString(PayRate)
```

Note: As you will learn later in this chapter, you can also use `rateLabel.Text = PayRate.ToString`.

3. Wider data types will not be implicitly demoted to narrower data types. The Code Editor will display a warning message when a statement attempts to use a wider data type where a narrower data type is expected. (Recall that a number with a decimal place is assumed to be a Double number.)

```
Incorrect:  Const TaxRate As Decimal = 0.075
Correct:    Const TaxRate As Decimal = 0.075D
```

4. Narrower data types will be implicitly promoted to wider data types. In this case, the integer stored in the `hoursWkd` variable will be promoted to the Double data type before being multiplied by the Double number 9.85. The Double result will be assigned to the Double `pay` variable.

```
            Dim hoursWkd As Integer
            Dim pay As Double
Correct:    pay = hoursWkd * 9.85
```

Figure 3-22 How to use the type conversion rules with Option Strict On

According to the first rule, the computer will not implicitly convert a string to a number. As a result, the Code Editor will issue the warning message "Option Strict On disallows implicit conversions from 'String' to 'Double'" when your code contains the statement `hours = hoursTextBox.Text`. As you learned earlier, you should use the TryParse method to explicitly convert a string to the Double data type before assigning it to a Double variable. The appropriate TryParse method to use in this case is shown in Figure 3-22.

According to the second rule, the computer will not implicitly convert a number to a string. Therefore, the Code Editor will issue an appropriate warning message when your code contains the statement `rateLabel.Text = PayRate`. As Figure 3-22 indicates, you can use the Convert.ToString method to explicitly convert the number stored in the `PayRate` constant to the String data type before assigning it to the rateLabel's Text property.

The third rule states that wider data types will not be implicitly demoted to narrower data types. A data type is wider than another data type if it can store either larger numbers or numbers with greater precision. Because of this rule, a Double number will not be implicitly demoted to the Decimal or Integer data type. If your code contains the statement `Const TaxRate As Decimal = 0.075`, the Code Editor will issue an appropriate warning message because the statement assigns a Double number to a Decimal variable. As Figure 3-22 shows, you will need to use the literal type character D to convert the Double number to the Decimal data type.

According to the last rule listed in Figure 3-22, the computer will implicitly promote narrower data types to wider data types. This means that when processing the statement `pay = hoursWkd * 9.85`, the computer will implicitly promote the integer stored in the `hoursWkd` variable to Double before multiplying it by the Double number 9.85. The result, a Double number, will be assigned to the Double `pay` variable.

Figure 3-23 shows the three Option statements entered in the General Declarations section of the Code Editor window. If a project contains more than one form, the statements must be entered in each form's Code Editor window.

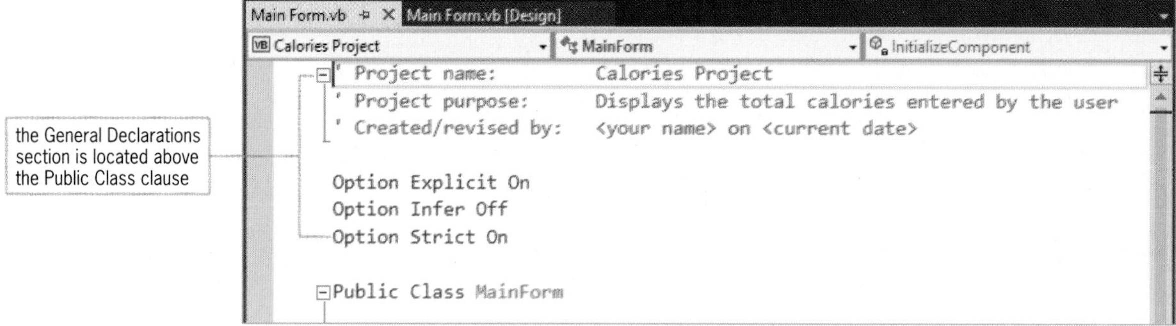

Figure 3-23 Option statements entered in the General Declarations section

Rather than entering the Option statements in the Code Editor window, you can set the options using either the Project Designer window or the Options dialog box. However, it is strongly recommended that you enter the Option statements in the Code Editor window because doing so makes your code more self-documenting and ensures that the options are set appropriately. The steps for setting the options in the Project Designer window and the Options dialog box are included in the Summary section at the end of this chapter. In Visual Basic 2015, the default setting for Option Explicit and Option Infer is On, whereas the default setting for Option Strict is Off.

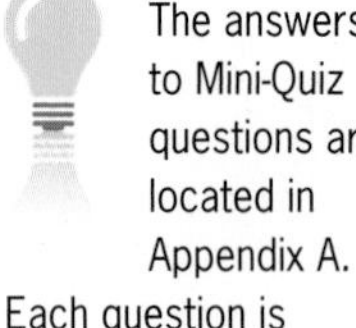

The answers to Mini-Quiz questions are located in Appendix A. Each question is associated with one or more objectives listed at the beginning of the chapter.

Mini-Quiz 3-5

1. When entered in the Code Editor window's General Declarations section, which of the following does not allow an undeclared variable in your code? (6)
   a. `Option Explicit On`
   b. `Option Infer On`
   c. `Option Undeclared Off`
   d. `Option Declared On`

2. If your code contains the `Option Strict On` statement, which of the following is the correct way to assign the contents of the salesTextBox to a Double variable named `sales`? (2, 3, 6)

   a. `sales = salesTextBox.Text`
   b. `sales = Double.TryParse(salesTextBox.Text)`
   c. `Double.TryParse(salesTextBox.Text, sales)`
   d. `Double.TryParse(sales, salesTextBox.Text)`

3. The `sales` and `commission` variables in the following assignment statement have the Double data type, whereas the `commRate` variable has the Decimal data type: `commission = sales * commRate`. If your code contains the `Option Strict On` statement, how will the computer process the assignment statement? (2, 4, 6)

Completing the Say Cheese! Company's Application

In this section, you will use what you learned about variables, constants, calculations, and the Option statements to complete the Say Cheese! company's application from Chapter 2. Recall that the company takes orders for cheesecakes by phone. The cheesecakes are priced at $25 each and are available in two flavors: vanilla bean and strawberry. The company's sales manager wants the application to calculate the total number of cheesecakes ordered by a customer and the total price of the order, including a 3% sales tax. The application's interface and TOE chart from Chapter 2 are shown in Figures 3-24 and 3-25, respectively.

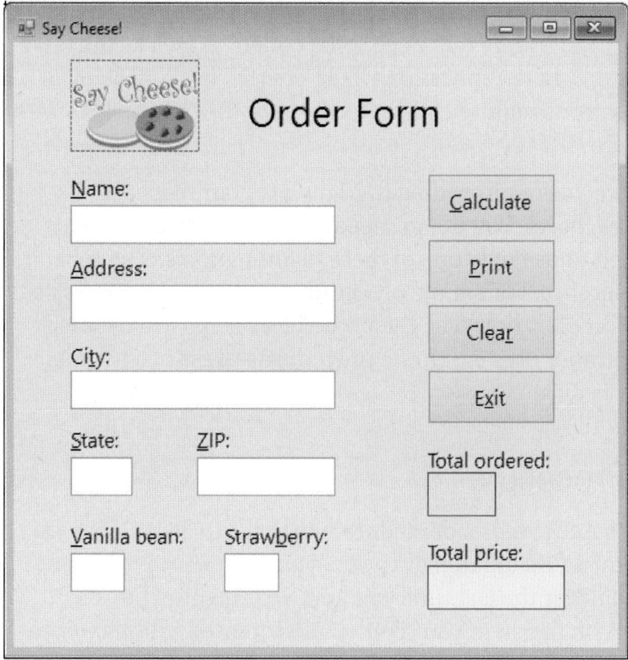

Figure 3-24 Interface from Chapter 2

Task	Object	Event
1. Calculate total ordered and total price 2. Display total ordered and total price in totalOrderedLabel and totalPriceLabel	calcButton	Click
Print the order form	printButton	Click
End the application	exitButton	Click
Clear the screen for the next order	clearButton	Click
Display total ordered (from calcButton)	totalOrderedLabel	None
Display total price (from calcButton)	totalPriceLabel	None
Get and display the order information	nameTextBox, addressTextBox, cityTextBox, stateTextBox, zipTextBox, vanillaTextBox, strawberryTextBox	None

Figure 3-25 TOE chart from Chapter 2

The next step after planning an application and building its interface is to code the application. You code an application so that the objects in the interface perform their assigned tasks when the appropriate event occurs. The objects and events that need to be coded, as well as the tasks assigned to each object and event, are listed in the application's TOE chart. The TOE chart in Figure 3-25 indicates that only the four buttons require coding, as they are the only objects with an event listed in the Event column.

You should always plan a procedure before you begin coding it. Many programmers use planning tools such as pseudocode or flowcharts. You do not need to create both a flowchart and pseudocode for a procedure; you need to use only one of these planning tools. The tool you use is really a matter of personal preference. For simple procedures, pseudocode works just fine. When a procedure becomes more complex, however, the procedure's steps may be easier to understand in a flowchart. The programmer uses either the procedure's pseudocode or its flowchart as a guide when coding the procedure.

Using Pseudocode to Plan a Procedure

Pseudocode uses short phrases to describe the steps a procedure must take to accomplish its goal. Even though the word *pseudocode* might be unfamiliar to you, you have already written pseudocode without even realizing it. Consider the last time you gave written directions to someone. You wrote each direction down on paper, in your own words; your directions were a form of pseudocode.

Figure 3-26 shows the pseudocode for the procedures that need to be coded in the Say Cheese! company's application. The printButton's Click event procedure will send a printout of the form to the Print preview window, and the exitButton's Click event procedure will simply end the application. The calcButton's Click event procedure will perform the appropriate calculations and then display the total number of cheesecakes ordered and the total price of the order. The clearButton's Click event procedure will prepare the screen for the next customer's order. It will do this by removing the current contents of the text boxes and also the calculated results from the two label controls. It will then send the focus to the nameTextBox so the user can begin entering the next customer's order.

```
printButton Click event procedure
send a printout of the form to the Print preview window

exitButton Click event procedure
end the application

calcButton Click event procedure
1. assign number of vanilla bean ordered and number of strawberry ordered
   to variables
2. total ordered = number of vanilla bean ordered + number of strawberry ordered
3. subtotal = total ordered * 25
4. sales tax = subtotal * 0.03
5. total price = subtotal + sales tax
6. display total ordered and total price in totalOrderedLabel and totalPriceLabel

clearButton Click event procedure
1. clear the Text property of the seven text boxes
2. clear the Text property of the totalOrderedLabel and totalPriceLabel
3. send the focus to the nameTextBox
```

Figure 3-26 Pseudocode for the Say Cheese! company's application

Using a Flowchart to Plan a Procedure

Unlike pseudocode, which consists of short phrases, a **flowchart** uses standardized symbols to show the steps a procedure must follow to reach its goal. Figure 3-27 shows the flowcharts for the procedures in the Say Cheese! company's application. The logic illustrated in the flowcharts is the same as the logic shown in the pseudocode in Figure 3-26.

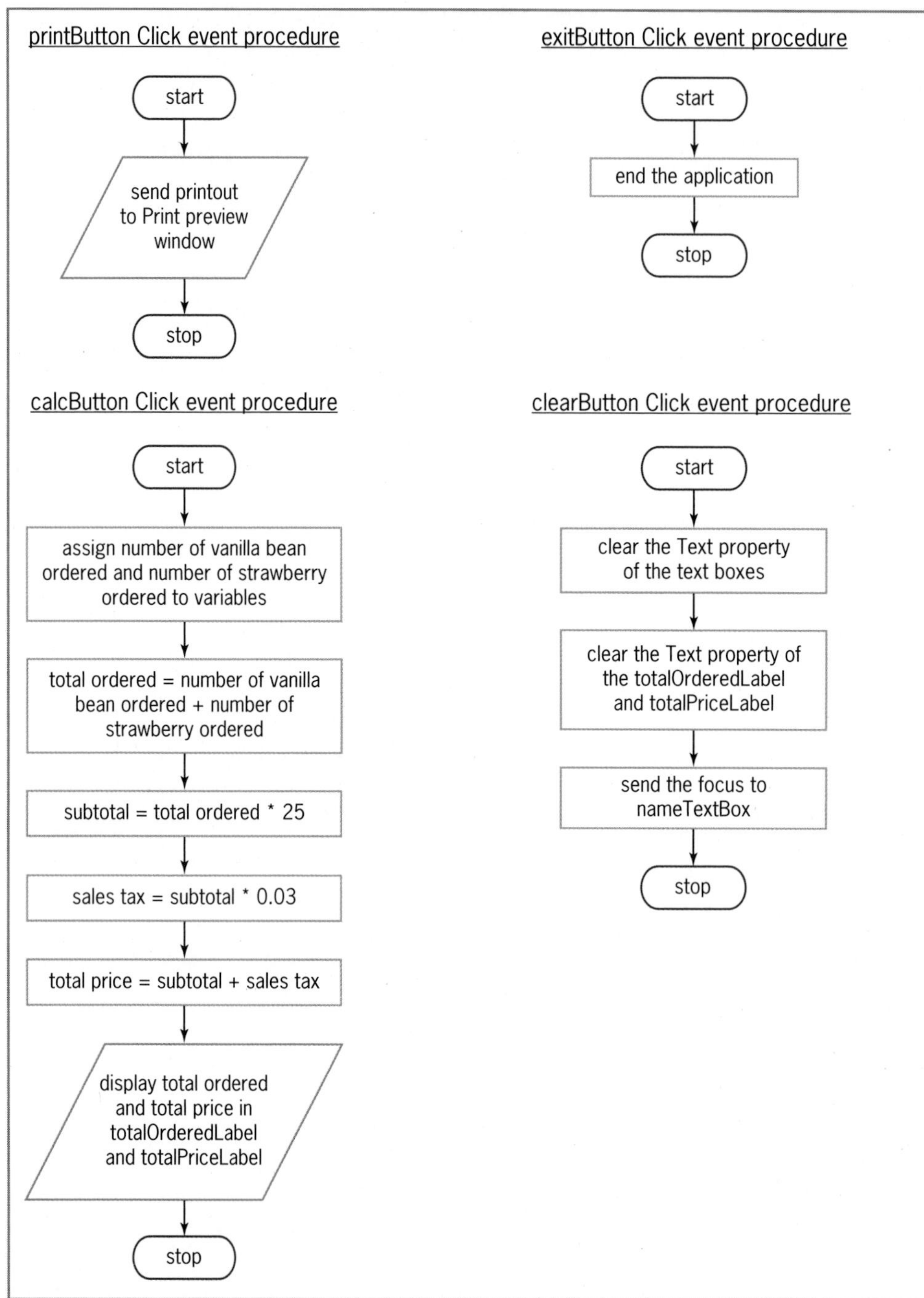

Figure 3-27 Flowcharts for the Say Cheese! company's application

The flowcharts in Figure 3-27 contain three different symbols: an oval, a rectangle, and a parallelogram. The oval symbol is called the **start/stop symbol**. The start and stop ovals indicate the beginning and end, respectively, of the flowchart. The rectangles are called **process symbols**. You use the process symbol to represent tasks such as making assignments and calculations. The parallelogram in a flowchart is called the **input/output symbol**, and it is used to represent input tasks (such as getting information from the user) and output tasks (such as displaying information). The parallelograms in Figure 3-27 represent output tasks. The lines connecting the symbols in a flowchart are called **flowlines**.

Coding the calcButton's Click Event Procedure

The programmer uses either the procedure's pseudocode or its flowchart as a guide when coding the procedure; in this chapter, you will use the pseudocode. The pseudocode for the calcButton's Click event procedure is shown in Figure 3-28.

```
calcButton Click event procedure
1. store number of vanilla bean ordered and number of strawberry ordered in variables
2. total ordered = number of vanilla bean ordered + number of strawberry ordered
3. subtotal = total ordered * 25
4. sales tax = subtotal * 0.03
5. total price = subtotal + sales tax
6. display total ordered and total price in totalOrderedLabel and totalPriceLabel
```

Figure 3-28 Pseudocode for the calcButton_Click procedure

Before you begin coding a procedure, you first study its pseudocode (or flowchart) to determine the variables and named constants (if any) the procedure will require. When determining the named constants, look for items whose value should be the same each time the procedure is invoked. In the calcButton's Click event procedure, two items will remain constant: the price of a cheesecake and the sales tax rate. You will assign the price to an Integer named constant and assign the sales tax rate to a Double named constant.

When determining a procedure's variables, look in the pseudocode (or flowchart) for items whose value is allowed to change during run time. In the calcButton's Click event procedure, the number of each flavor of cheesecake ordered will likely be different each time the procedure is processed. As a result, the total ordered, subtotal, sales tax, and total price values will also vary because they are based on the number of each flavor ordered. You will assign the number of vanilla bean ordered, the number of strawberry ordered, the total ordered, and the subtotal to Integer variables. The sales tax and total price will be assigned to Double variables because both will contain numbers with a decimal place. Figure 3-29 lists the memory locations that the procedure will use.

Named constants	**Data types**	**Values**
`Price`	Integer	25
`TaxRate`	Double	0.03 (the decimal equivalent of 3%)
Variables	**Data types**	**Value sources**
`vanillaBean`	Integer	user input (vanillaTextBox)
`strawberry`	Integer	user input (strawberryTextBox)
`totalOrdered`	Integer	procedure calculation
`subtotal`	Integer	procedure calculation
`salesTax`	Double	procedure calculation
`totalPrice`	Double	procedure calculation

Figure 3-29 Memory locations for the calcButton_Click procedure

Figure 3-30 shows the declaration statements entered in the procedure. The jagged lines, called squiggles, indicate that at this point, the named constants and variables do not appear in any other statement in the code.

```
Private Sub calcButton_Click(sender As Object, e
    ' determine total ordered and total price

    Const Price As Integer = 25
    Const TaxRate As Double = 0.03
    Dim vanillaBean As Integer
    Dim strawberry As Integer
    Dim totalOrdered As Integer
    Dim subtotal As Integer
    Dim salesTax As Double
    Dim totalPrice As Double

End Sub
```

green squiggle

Figure 3-30 Declaration statements entered in the procedure

Next, you code each of the steps in the pseudocode (or each symbol in the flowchart), one at a time. However, keep in mind that some steps (symbols) may require more than one line of code. The first step in the pseudocode shown earlier in Figure 3-28 stores the number of each cheesecake flavor ordered in variables. You can code the first step using the TryParse methods shown in Figure 3-31. The methods convert each text box's Text property to the Integer data type and then store the result in the appropriate variables.

```
    ' store numbers ordered in variables
    Integer.TryParse(vanillaTextBox.Text, vanillaBean)
    Integer.TryParse(strawberryTextBox.Text, strawberry)

End Sub
```

Figure 3-31 TryParse methods entered in the procedure

The second through fifth steps in the pseudocode calculate the total number ordered, the subtotal, the sales tax, and the total price. The appropriate assignment statements are shown in Figure 3-32. The three variables in the first assignment statement have the same data type: Integer. The two variables and the named constant in the second assignment statement also have the Integer data type. When processing the third assignment statement, the computer will implicitly promote the integer stored in the `subtotal` variable to Double before multiplying it by the Double `TaxRate` named constant; the result will be stored in the Double `salesTax` variable. Similarly, when processing the fourth assignment statement, the computer will implicitly promote the integer stored in the `subtotal` variable to Double before adding it to the Double `salesTax` variable. The computer will store the sum of both Double numbers in the Double `totalPrice` variable.

```
        ' perform calculations
        totalOrdered = vanillaBean + strawberry
        subtotal = totalOrdered * Price
        salesTax = subtotal * TaxRate
        totalPrice = subtotal + salesTax

        |
    End Sub
```

Figure 3-32 Calculation statements entered in the procedure

The last step in the pseudocode displays the total ordered and the total price in the totalOrderedLabel and totalPriceLabel controls, respectively. You accomplish this task using assignment statements along with the Convert.ToString method, as shown in Figure 3-33. The figure also shows a sample run of the application. Notice that the total price contains only one decimal place. You will learn how to fix that problem in the next section.

```
        ' display total ordered and total price
        totalOrderedLabel.Text = Convert.ToString(totalOrdered)
        totalPriceLabel.Text = Convert.ToString(totalPrice)
    End Sub
```

State: ZIP: Total ordered: 2

Vanilla bean: 1 Strawberry: 1 Total price: 51.5

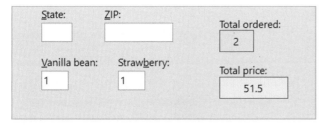

Figure 3-33 Display statements and a sample run

Formatting Numeric Output

In most applications, you will want the numeric output to contain a specific number of decimal places and perhaps an optional special character (such as a dollar sign). Specifying the number of decimal places and the special characters to display in a number is called **formatting**. You can format a number in Visual Basic using the ToString method.

Figure 3-34 shows the ToString method's syntax and includes examples of using the method. In the syntax, *name* is usually the name of a numeric variable; however, it can also be the name of a numeric named constant. The **ToString method** places a copy of the variable's or named constant's contents in a temporary memory location, where it converts the copy to a string. The method formats the string using the information in its *formatString* argument and then returns the result as a string. The *formatString* argument must take the form *"Axx"*, where *A* is an alphabetic character called the format specifier and *xx* is a sequence of digits called the precision specifier. The format specifier, which can be entered in either uppercase or lowercase, must be one of the built-in format characters. The most commonly used format characters are listed in Figure 3-34. When used with one of the format characters listed in the figure, the precision specifier determines the number of digits that will appear to the right of the decimal point in the formatted number. You can also use the ToString method without its *formatString* argument, as shown in Example 4 in the figure.

HOW TO Format a Number Using the ToString Method

Syntax
name.**ToString[(***formatString***)]**

Format specifier (Name)	Description
C or c (Currency)	displays the string with a dollar sign and includes a thousands separator (if appropriate); negative values are enclosed in parentheses
N or n (Number)	similar to the Currency format but does not include a dollar sign and negative values are preceded by a minus sign
F or f (Fixed-point)	same as the Number format but does not include a thousands separator
P or p (Percent)	multiplies the numeric variable's value by 100 and formats the result with a percent sign; negative values are preceded by a minus sign

Example 1
```
commission = 1250
commissionLabel.Text = commission.ToString("C0")
```
assigns the string "$1,250" to the commissionLabel's Text property

Example 2
```
total = 123.675
totalLabel.Text = total.ToString("N2")
```
assigns the string "123.68" to the totalLabel's Text property

Example 3
```
rate = 0.06
rateLabel.Text = rate.ToString("P0")
```
assigns the string "6 %" to the rateLabel's Text property

Example 4
```
population = 12560
peopleLabel.Text = population.ToString
```
the expression is equivalent to `Convert.ToString(population)`

assigns the string "12560" to the peopleLabel's Text property

Example 5
```
Const MaxPay As Double = 13.75
maxLabel.Text = MaxPay.ToString("C2")
```
assigns the string "$13.75" to the maxLabel's Text property

Figure 3-34 How to format a number using the ToString method

The calcButton_Click procedure in the Say Cheese! company's application will display the total price with a dollar sign, two decimal places, and a thousands separator (if necessary). This is accomplished by changing the `Convert.ToString(totalPrice)` expression in the last assignment statement to `totalPrice.ToString("C2")`. Figure 3-35 shows the modified statement and a sample run of the procedure.

```
    ' display total ordered and total price
    totalOrderedLabel.Text = Convert.ToString(totalOrdered)
    totalPriceLabel.Text = totalPrice.ToString("C2")
End Sub
```

ToString method

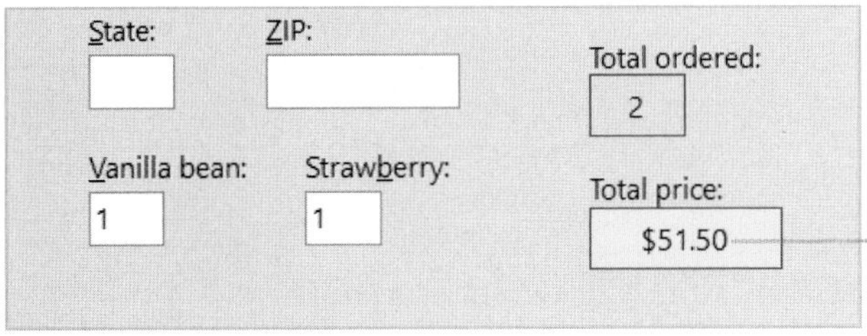

State: ZIP: Total ordered: 2

Vanilla bean: 1 Strawberry: 1 Total price: $51.50

formatted total price

Figure 3-35 Modified calcButton_Click procedure

Coding the clearButton's Click Event Procedure

The pseudocode for the clearButton's Click event procedure is shown in Figure 3-36. The procedure does not perform any tasks that require user input or calculations, so it will not need any named constants or variables.

```
clearButton Click event procedure
1. clear the Text property of the seven text boxes
2. clear the Text property of the totalOrderedLabel and totalPriceLabel
3. send the focus to the nameTextBox
```

Figure 3-36 Pseudocode for the clearButton_Click procedure

The first two steps in the pseudocode clear the Text property of various text boxes and labels in the interface. Figure 3-37 shows two ways of clearing the Text property of a control. Example 1 assigns an empty (or zero-length) string to the property. Example 2 assigns the value **String.Empty** to the property. The value represents the empty string in Visual Basic.

HOW TO Clear the Text Property of a Control

Example 1—assign the empty string

```
nameTextBox.Text = ""
totalOrderedLabel.Text = ""
```

Example 2—assign the String.Empty value

```
nameTextBox.Text = String.Empty
totalOrderedLabel.Text = String.Empty
```

Figure 3-37 How to clear the Text property of a control

The last step in the pseudocode sends the focus to the nameTextBox. You can accomplish this task using the **Focus method**. The method's syntax is shown in Figure 3-38 along with an example of using the method. In the syntax, *object* is the name of the object to which you want the focus sent.

HOW TO Send the Focus to a Control

Syntax
object.**Focus()**

Example
```
nameTextBox.Focus()
```

Figure 3-38 How to send the focus to a control

Figure 3-39 shows the code entered in the clearButton's Click event procedure.

```
Private Sub clearButton_Click(sender As Object,
    ' prepare screen for next order

    nameTextBox.Text = String.Empty
    addressTextBox.Text = String.Empty
    cityTextBox.Text = String.Empty
    stateTextBox.Text = String.Empty
    zipTextBox.Text = String.Empty
    vanillaTextBox.Text = String.Empty
    strawberryTextBox.Text = String.Empty
    totalOrderedLabel.Text = String.Empty
    totalPriceLabel.Text = String.Empty
    nameTextBox.Focus()
End Sub
```

Figure 3-39 clearButton_Click procedure

Coding the exitButton_Click and printButton_Click Procedures

According to their pseudocode (shown earlier in Figure 3-26), the exitButton's Click event procedure should end the application, and the printButton's Click event procedure should send a printout of the form to the Print preview window. You learned how to perform both of these tasks in Chapter 2. Recall that you can use the `Me.Close()` statement to end the application. If the PrintAction property of the application's PrintForm1 control is set to PrintToPreview, you can use the `PrintForm1.Print()` statement to code the printButton_Click procedure. Figure 3-40 shows the entire Say Cheese! company's program.

```
' Project name:       Cheese Project
' Project purpose:    Displays total ordered and total price
' Created/revised by: <your name> on <current date>

Option Explicit On
Option Strict On
Option Infer Off

Public Class MainForm
   Private Sub calcButton_Click(sender As Object, e As EventArgs) Handles calcButton.Click
       ' determine total ordered and total price

       Const Price As Integer = 25
       Const TaxRate As Double = 0.03
       Dim vanillaBean As Integer
       Dim strawberry As Integer
       Dim totalOrdered As Integer
       Dim subtotal As Integer
       Dim salesTax As Double
       Dim totalPrice As Double

       ' store numbers ordered in variables
       Integer.TryParse(vanillaTextBox.Text, vanillaBean)
       Integer.TryParse(strawberryTextBox.Text, strawberry)

       ' perform calculations
       totalOrdered = vanillaBean + strawberry
       subtotal = totalOrdered * Price
       salesTax = subtotal * TaxRate
       totalPrice = subtotal + salesTax

       ' display total ordered and total price
       totalOrderedLabel.Text = Convert.ToString(totalOrdered)
       totalPriceLabel.Text = totalPrice.ToString("C2")
   End Sub

   Private Sub clearButton_Click(sender As Object, e As EventArgs) Handles clearButton.Click
       ' prepare screen for next order

       nameTextBox.Text = String.Empty
       addressTextBox.Text = String.Empty
       cityTextBox.Text = String.Empty
       stateTextBox.Text = String.Empty
       zipTextBox.Text = String.Empty
       vanillaTextBox.Text = String.Empty
       strawberryTextBox.Text = String.Empty
       totalOrderedLabel.Text = String.Empty
       totalPriceLabel.Text = String.Empty
       nameTextBox.Focus()
   End Sub

```

Figure 3-40 Say Cheese! company's program *(continues)*

(continued)

```
    Private Sub exitButton_Click(sender As Object, e As EventArgs) Handles exitButton.Click
        Me.Close()
    End Sub

    Private Sub printButton_Click(sender As Object, e As EventArgs) Handles printButton.Click
        ' send printout to Print preview window
        PrintForm1.Print()
    End Sub
End Class
```

Figure 3-40 Say Cheese! company's program

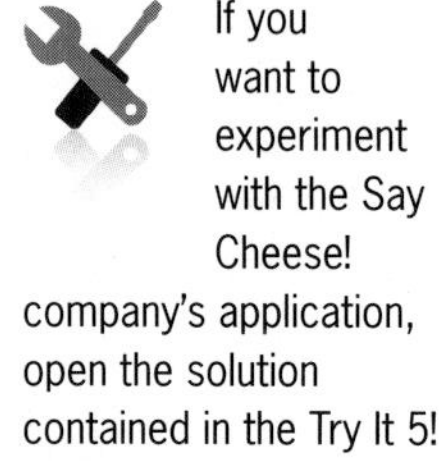

If you want to experiment with the Say Cheese! company's application, open the solution contained in the Try It 5! folder.

Testing and Debugging the Application

After coding an application, you must test it to verify that the code works correctly. You begin by choosing a set of sample data for the input values. You then use the sample data to manually compute the expected output. Next, you start the application and enter your sample data. You then compare the actual output with the expected output; both should be the same. If they are not the same, it indicates that your code contains one or more errors. You will need to locate and then correct the errors before giving the application to the user.

Recall that errors in a program's code are called bugs, and the process of locating and correcting the bugs is referred to as debugging. As you learned in Chapter 1, the bugs in a program are typically categorized as syntax errors, logic errors, or run time errors. You learned about syntax errors in Chapter 1. In this chapter, you will learn about logic errors and run time errors.

Unlike syntax errors, logic errors are much more difficult to find because they do not trigger an error message from the Code Editor. The only way to determine whether your code contains a logic error is by comparing its output with your manually calculated results. If they are not the same, chances are the code contains a logic error.

A **logic error** can occur for a variety of reasons, such as forgetting to enter an instruction or entering the instructions in the wrong order. Some logic errors occur as a result of calculation statements that are correct syntactically but incorrect mathematically. For example, consider the statement `numSquared = num + num`, which is supposed to square the number stored in the `num` variable. The statement's syntax is correct; however, the statement is incorrect mathematically because you square a value by multiplying it by itself, not by adding it to itself. For tips on finding and fixing logic errors, refer to the *Finding and Fixing Logic Errors* and *Setting Breakpoints* sections in Appendix E.

A **run time error** is an error that occurs while an application is running, and it causes the application to end abruptly with an error message. Run time errors are often the result of neglecting to set Option Strict to On and then attempting to assign the Text property of a control to a numeric variable. (When Option Strict is set to On, the Code Editor will flag that type of error for you.) A procedure that continues to run because it contains an endless loop will also eventually result in a run time error. You will learn more about this type of error in Chapter 6. For now, if a run time error occurs in your applications, click Debug on the Visual Studio menu bar and then click Stop Debugging.

The sample input values you use to test your applications should include both valid and invalid data. **Valid data** is data that the application is expecting the user to enter. **Invalid data**, which is typically the result of a typing error made by the user, is data that the application is *not* expecting the user to enter. The Say Cheese! company's application, for example, expects to find numbers in the Vanilla bean and Strawberry text boxes. It does not expect the boxes to contain letters or special characters. Therefore, you should test the application by entering one or more numbers, letters, and special characters in both boxes. Doing this helps to ensure that the application displays the correct output when valid data is entered and does not end abruptly when invalid data is entered.

Mini-Quiz 3-6

The answers to Mini-Quiz questions are located in Appendix A. Each question is associated with one or more objectives listed at the beginning of the chapter.

1. The rectangle in a flowchart is called the ____________ symbol. (7)
   a. input
   b. output
   c. process
   d. start/stop
2. Which of the following can be used to clear the contents of the salesTextBox? (9)
   a. `salesTextBox.Text = ""`
   b. `salesTextBox.Text = String.Empty`
   c. `salesTextBox.Text = String.Clear`
   d. both a and b
3. Which of the following sends the focus to the clearButton? (10)
   a. `clearButton.Focus()`
   b. `clearButton.SendFocus()`
   c. `clearButton.SetFocus()`
   d. none of the above
4. If the `bonus` variable contains the number 7504.2, which of the following assigns the string "$7,504.20" to the bonusLabel? (8)
   a. `bonusLabel.Text = bonus.Format("C2")`
   b. `bonusLabel.Text = bonus.ToString("C2")`
   c. `bonusLabel.Text = bonus.ToFormat("N2")`
   d. `bonusLabel.Text = bonus.ToString("N2")`

You have completed the concepts section of Chapter 3. The Programming Tutorial section is next.

PROGRAMMING TUTORIAL 1

Creating the Basketball Score Application

In this tutorial, you will create an application that calculates and displays a team's total score at the end of a basketball game. The user will enter the number of two-point baskets made, the number of three-point baskets made, and the number of free-throws made. (Free-throws are worth one point each.) The application's TOE chart and MainForm are shown in Figures 3-41 and 3-42, respectively. The MainForm contains five labels, three text boxes, three buttons, and one picture box.

Task	Object	Event
Get and display the number of 2-point baskets, number of 3-point baskets, and number of free-throw points	pt2TextBox, pt3TextBox, freeTextBox	None
End the application	exitButton	Click
1. Calculate the total score 2. Display the total score in totalLabel	calcButton	Click
Clear the screen	clearButton	Click
Display the total score (from calcButton)	totalLabel	None

Figure 3-41 TOE chart for the Basketball Score application

Figure 3-42 MainForm for the Basketball Score application

Including Comments and the Option Statements in the Code Editor window

In the Code Editor window's General Declarations section, many programmers include comments that document the project's name and purpose, the programmer's name, and the date the program was either created or revised.

To include comments in the General Declarations section:

1. Start Visual Studio. Open the **Basketball Solution** (**Basketball Solution.sln**) file contained in the VbReloaded2015\Chap03\Basketball Solution folder. If necessary, open the designer window.

2. Open the Code Editor window. The exitButton_Click procedure has already been coded for you.
3. Insert a blank line above the Public Class clause. Enter the comments shown in Figure 3-43 and then position the insertion point as shown in the figure. Be sure to replace <your name> and <current date> with your name and the current date, respectively.

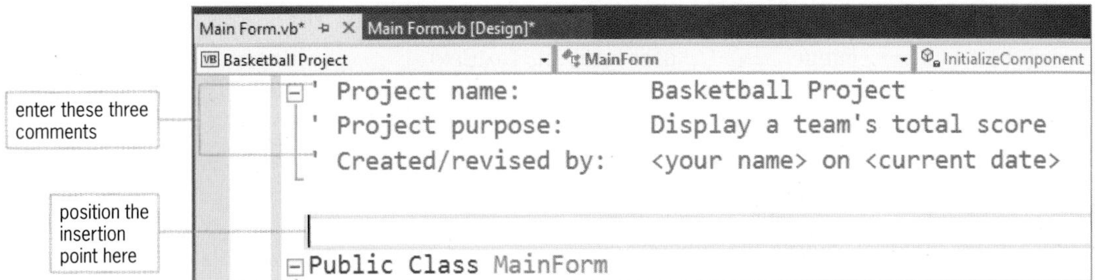

Figure 3-43 Comments entered in the General Declarations section

The application's code will use variables, so the General Declarations section should also contain the three Option statements covered in the chapter. Recall that the `Option Explicit On` and `Option Infer Off` statements tell the Code Editor to flag the name of an undeclared variable and warn you if a declaration statement does not contain a data type, respectively. The `Option Strict On` statement tells the computer not to implicitly demote any data.

To include the Option statements in the General Declarations section:

1. Enter the following three Option statements:

   Option Explicit On
   Option Infer Off
   Option Strict On

2. Save the solution.

Coding the calcButton_Click Procedure

According to the application's TOE chart, the calcButton's Click event procedure should calculate the total score and then display it in the totalLabel. The procedure's pseudocode is shown in Figure 3-44.

```
calcButton Click event procedure
1. store user input (number of 2-point baskets, number of 3-point baskets, and free-throw
   points) in variables
2. total for 2-point baskets = number of 2-point baskets * 2
3. total for 3-point baskets = number of 3-point baskets * 3
4. total score = total for 2-point baskets + total for 3-point baskets + free-throw points
5. display total score in totalLabel
```

Figure 3-44 Pseudocode for the calcButton_Click procedure

Before you begin coding a procedure, you first study the procedure's pseudocode (or flowchart) to determine the variables and named constants (if any) the procedure will require. In this case, the calcButton_Click procedure will not use any named constants. Although you could create named constants for the numbers 2 and 3, doing so is unnecessary because those values are already self-documenting and are unlikely to change. The procedure will use six Integer variables to store the user input and the calculated amounts. Integer variables are appropriate in this case because the user input and the calculated amounts will always be whole numbers. The variables are listed in Figure 3-45.

Variables	Data type	Value source
numPt2	Integer	user input (pt2TextBox)
numPt3	Integer	user input (pt3TextBox)
numFree	Integer	user input (freeTextBox)
totalPt2	Integer	procedure calculation
totalPt3	Integer	procedure calculation
totalScore	Integer	procedure calculation

Figure 3-45 Variables for the calcButton_Click procedure

To code the calcButton_Click procedure and then test it:

1. Open the code template for the calcButton's Click event procedure. Enter the comment and declaration statements shown in Figure 3-46, and then position the insertion point as shown in the figure.

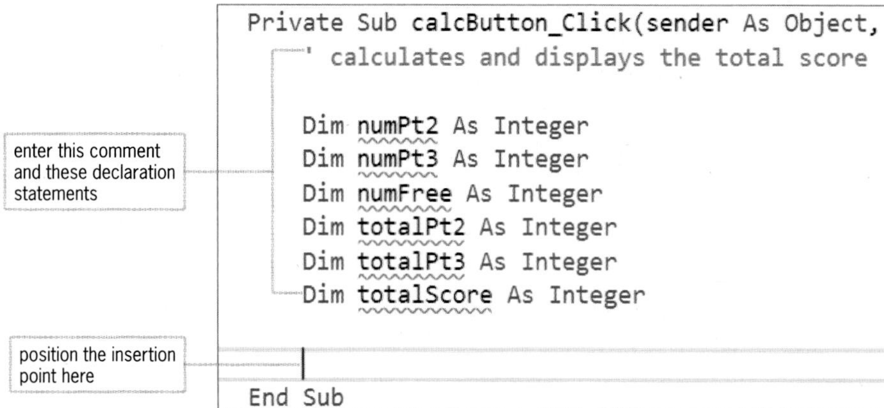

Figure 3-46 Comment and declaration statements entered in the procedure

2. The pseudocode begins by storing the user input, which is entered in the three text boxes, in three of the Integer variables. Enter the comment and three TryParse methods shown in Figure 3-47, and then position the insertion point as shown in the figure.

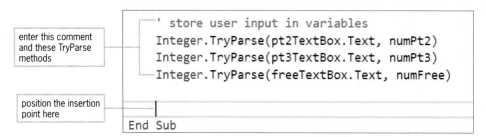

enter this comment and these TryParse methods

```
' store user input in variables
Integer.TryParse(pt2TextBox.Text, numPt2)
Integer.TryParse(pt3TextBox.Text, numPt3)
Integer.TryParse(freeTextBox.Text, numFree)

End Sub
```

position the insertion point here

Figure 3-47 Comment and TryParse methods entered in the procedure

3. The next three steps in the pseudocode calculate the total for the 2-point baskets, the total for the 3-point baskets, and the total score. Enter the comment and calculation statements shown in Figure 3-48, and then position the insertion point as shown in the figure.

```
    ' perform calculations
    totalPt2 = numPt2 * 2
    totalPt3 = numPt3 * 3
    totalScore = totalPt2 + totalPt3 + numFree

    |
End Sub
```

enter this comment and these assignment statements

position the insertion point here

Figure 3-48 Comment and calculation statements entered in the procedure

4. The last step in the pseudocode displays the total score in the totalLabel. Enter the comment and assignment statement shown in Figure 3-49.

```
    ' display total score
    totalLabel.Text = totalScore.ToString
    |
End Sub
```

Figure 3-49 Comment and assignment statement entered in the procedure

5. It is a good idea to test a procedure after you have coded it to verify that it works correctly. Save the solution and then start the application. Type **12** in the 2-point baskets box, type **5** in the 3-point baskets box, and type **2** in the Free-throw points box. Click the **Calculate** button. The total score is 41, as shown in Figure 3-50.

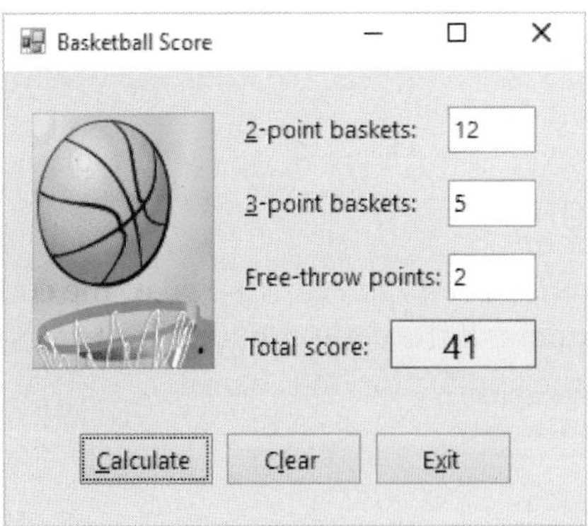

Figure 3-50 Sample run of the Basketball Score application

6. Click the **Exit** button to end the application.

Coding the clearButton_Click Procedure

According to the application's TOE chart, the clearButton's Click event procedure should clear the screen. The procedure's pseudocode is shown in Figure 3-51.

```
clearButton Click event procedure
1. clear the Text property of the three text boxes
2. clear the Text property of the totalLabel
3. send the focus to the pt2TextBox
```

Figure 3-51 Pseudocode for the clearButton_Click procedure

To code the clearButton_Click procedure and then test it:

1. Open the code template for the clearButton's Click event procedure. The first two steps in the pseudocode clear the contents of the three text boxes and the totalLabel. The last step sends the focus to the pt2TextBox. Enter the comment, the four assignment statements, and the Focus method shown in Figure 3-52.

```
Private Sub clearButton_Click(sender As Object,
    ' clear user input and total score

    pt2TextBox.Text = String.Empty
    pt3TextBox.Text = String.Empty
    freeTextBox.Text = String.Empty
    totalLabel.Text = String.Empty
    pt2TextBox.Focus()

End Sub
```

Figure 3-52 clearButton_Click procedure

2. Save the solution and then start the application. Type any three numbers in the text boxes and then click the **Calculate** button. Now, click the **Clear** button to remove the contents of the text boxes and totalLabel. Notice that the blinking insertion point appears in the 2-point baskets box.
3. Click the **Exit** button.

Testing and Debugging the Application

After you finish coding the entire application, you must test it to verify that all of the code works correctly. You should use both valid and invalid test data. If the code contains any errors, you will need to locate and then fix them before giving the application to the user.

To test the application:

1. Start the application. First, you will test the application without entering any data. Click the **Calculate** button. The total score is 0.
2. Next, you will test it using valid data. Click the **Clear** button. Type **25** in the 2-point baskets box, type **15** in the 3-point baskets box, and type **20** in the Free-throw points box. Click the **Calculate** button. The total score is 115.
3. Now, you will use invalid data to test the application. Click the **Clear** button. Type the letter **x** in each text box and then click the **Calculate** button. The total score is 0. (Recall that the TryParse method converts a letter to the number 0.)

4. Click the **Exit** button to end the application. Close the Code Editor window and then close the solution. Figure 3-53 shows the Basketball Score application's code.

```
' Project name:          Basketball Project
' Project purpose:       Display a team's total score
' Created/revised by:    <your name> on <current date>

Option Explicit On
Option Infer Off
Option Strict On

Public Class MainForm
   Private Sub calcButton_Click(sender As Object, e As EventArgs
   ) Handles calcButton.Click
       ' calculates and displays the total score

       Dim numPt2 As Integer
       Dim numPt3 As Integer
       Dim numFree As Integer
       Dim totalPt2 As Integer
       Dim totalPt3 As Integer
       Dim totalScore As Integer

       ' store user input in variables
       Integer.TryParse(pt2TextBox.Text, numPt2)
       Integer.TryParse(pt3TextBox.Text, numPt3)
       Integer.TryParse(freeTextBox.Text, numFree)

       ' perform calculations
       totalPt2 = numPt2 * 2
       totalPt3 = numPt3 * 3
       totalScore = totalPt2 + totalPt3 + numFree

       ' display total score
       totalLabel.Text = totalScore.ToString

   End Sub

   Private Sub clearButton_Click(sender As Object, e As EventArgs
   ) Handles clearButton.Click
       ' clear user input and total score

       pt2TextBox.Text = String.Empty
       pt3TextBox.Text = String.Empty
       freeTextBox.Text = String.Empty
       totalLabel.Text = String.Empty
       pt2TextBox.Focus()

   End Sub

   Private Sub exitButton_Click(sender As Object, e As EventArgs
   ) Handles exitButton.Click
       Me.Close()
   End Sub
End Class
```

Figure 3-53 Basketball Score application's code

PROGRAMMING TUTORIAL 2

Coding the Alligator Inc. Application

In Chapter 2's Programming Tutorial 2, you created the interface for the Alligator Inc. application. The interface is shown in Figure 3-54. You also coded the Click event procedures for the Print Preview and Exit buttons. You will code the Calculate button's Click event procedure in this tutorial.

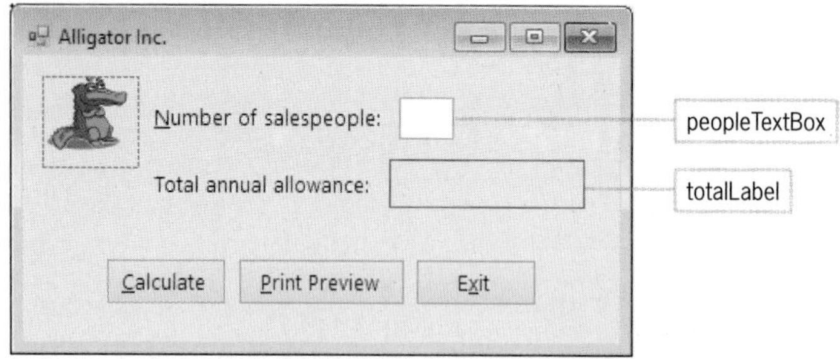

Figure 3-54 MainForm for the Alligator Inc. application

Including Comments and the Option Statements in the Code Editor Window

In the Code Editor window's General Declarations section, you will enter comments that document the project's name and purpose, the programmer's name, and the date the program was either created or revised. The application will use a named constant and variables, so you will also enter the three Option statements covered in the chapter.

To include comments and the Option statements in the General Declarations section:

1. Start Visual Studio. Copy the **Alligator Solution** folder from the VbReloaded2015\Chap02 folder to the VbReloaded2015\Chap03 folder.
2. Open the **Alligator Solution** (**Alligator Solution.sln**) file contained in the VbReloaded2015\Chap03\Alligator Solution folder. If necessary, open the designer window. The MainForm shown earlier in Figure 3-54 appears on the screen.
3. Open the Code Editor window. Enter the comments shown in Figure 3-55, and then position the insertion point as shown in the figure. Be sure to replace <your name> and <current date> with your name and the current date, respectively.

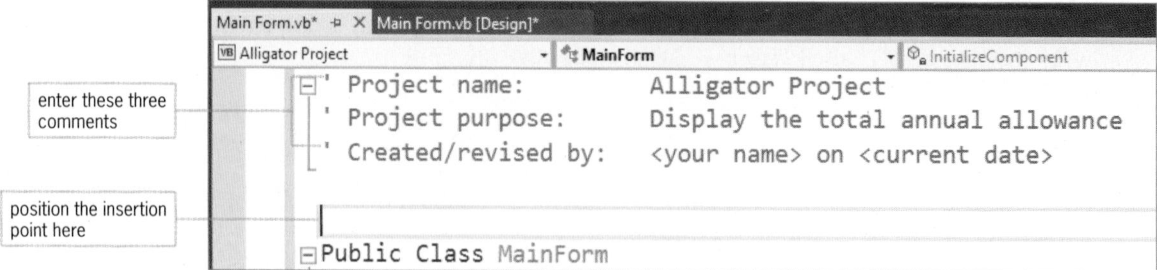

Figure 3-55 Comments entered in the General Declarations section

4. Enter the three Option statements covered in the chapter.
5. Save the solution.

Coding the calcButton_Click Procedure

As you may remember from Chapter 2, Alligator Inc. pays each of its salespeople a monthly expense allowance of $200. The calcButton_Click procedure is responsible for calculating and displaying the total annual cost of these allowances. The procedure's pseudocode is shown in Figure 3-56.

```
calcButton Click event procedure
1. store the number of salespeople in a variable
2. total annual allowance = number of salespeople * 200 * 12
3. display total annual allowance in totalLabel
```

Figure 3-56 Pseudocode for the calcButton_Click procedure

Before you begin coding a procedure, you first study the procedure's pseudocode (or flowchart) to determine the variables and named constants (if any) the procedure will require. In this case, the calcButton_Click procedure will use one named constant to store the monthly allowance amount: 200. It will also use two variables to store the number of salespeople and the total annual allowance cost. The named constant and variables are listed in Figure 3-57.

Named constant	Data type	Value
`MonthlyAllow`	Integer	200
Variables	**Data type**	**Value source**
`people`	Integer	user input (peopleTextBox)
`annualAllow`	Integer	procedure calculation

Figure 3-57 Memory locations for the calcButton_Click procedure

To code the calcButton_Click procedure and then test it:

1. Open the code template for the calcButton's Click event procedure. Type the following comment and then press **Enter** twice:

   ' calculate and display the total annual allowance

2. Now, enter the statements to declare the named constant and variables listed in Figure 3-57. Press **Enter** twice after typing the last declaration statement.
3. The first step in the procedure's pseudocode stores the number of salespeople in a variable. Type **' store user input in a variable** and press **Enter**. Now, enter a TryParse method that converts the contents of the peopleTextBox to Integer and then stores the result in the `people` variable. Press **Enter** twice after typing the method.
4. The second step in the pseudocode calculates the total annual allowance. Type **' calculate total annual allowance** and press **Enter**. Now, enter the appropriate assignment statement.
5. The third step in the pseudocode displays the total annual allowance in the totalLabel. Type **' display total annual allowance** and press **Enter**, and then enter the appropriate assignment statement. Display the annual allowance with a dollar sign and no decimal places.

6. Save the solution and then start the application. Type **10** in the text box and then click the **Calculate** button. The total annual allowance is $24,000. See Figure 3-58.

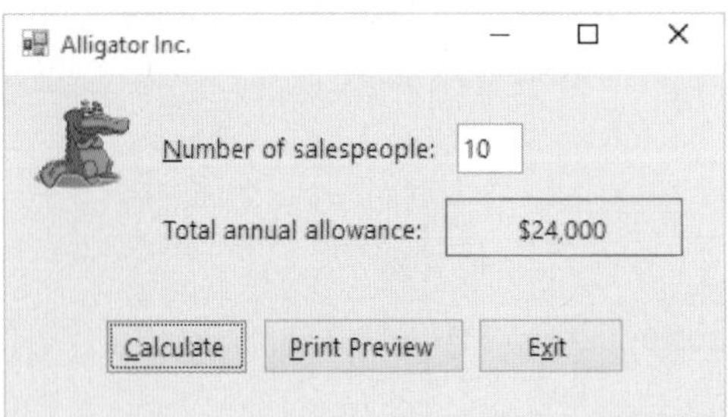

Figure 3-58 Sample run of the Alligator Inc. application

7. Click the **Exit** button. (You coded the exitButton_Click procedure in Chapter 2's Programming Tutorial 2.)

Testing and Debugging the Application

After you finish coding the entire application, you must test it to verify that all of the code works correctly. You should use both valid and invalid test data. If the code contains any errors, you will need to locate and then fix them before giving the application to the user.

To test the application:

1. Start the application. First, you will test the application without entering any data. Click the **Calculate** button. The total annual allowance is $0.
2. Next, you will test the application using valid data. Type **2** in the text box and then click the **Calculate** button. The total annual allowance is $4,800.
3. Finally, you will test the application using invalid data. Change the number of salespeople to the letter **z** and then click the **Calculate** button. The total annual allowance is $0. (Recall that the TryParse method converts a letter to the number 0.)
4. On your own, verify that the Print Preview button works correctly. (You coded the button in Chapter 2's Programming Tutorial 2.)
5. Click the **Exit** button to end the application. Close the Code Editor window and then close the solution. Figure 3-59 shows the Alligator Inc. application's code.

```
' Project name:          Alligator Project
' Project purpose:       Display the total annual allowance
' Created/revised by:    <your name> on <current date>

Option Explicit On
Option Infer Off
Option Strict On

```

Figure 3-59 Alligator Inc. application's code *(continues)*

(continued)

```
Public Class MainForm
    Private Sub calcButton_Click(sender As Object, e As EventArgs
    ) Handles calcButton.Click
        ' calculate and display the total annual allowance

        Const MonthlyAllow As Integer = 200
        Dim people As Integer
        Dim annualAllow As Integer

        ' store user input in a variable
        Integer.TryParse(peopleTextBox.Text, people)

        ' calculate total annual allowance
        annualAllow = people * MonthlyAllow * 12

        ' display total annual allowance
        totalLabel.Text = annualAllow.ToString("C0")

    End Sub

    Private Sub exitButton_Click(sender As Object, e As EventArgs
    ) Handles exitButton.Click
        Me.Close()

    End Sub

    Private Sub printPreviewButton_Click(sender As Object,
    e As EventArgs) Handles printPreviewButton.Click
        PrintForm1.Print()

    End Sub
End Class
```

Figure 3-59 Alligator Inc. application's code

PROGRAMMING EXAMPLE

Completing the VitaDrink Company Application

In Chapter 2's Programming Example, you created the interface for the VitaDrink Company application. The interface is shown in Figure 3-60. You also coded the Click event procedures for the Print Preview and Exit buttons. You will code the Click event procedures for the Calculate and Clear buttons in this Programming Example.

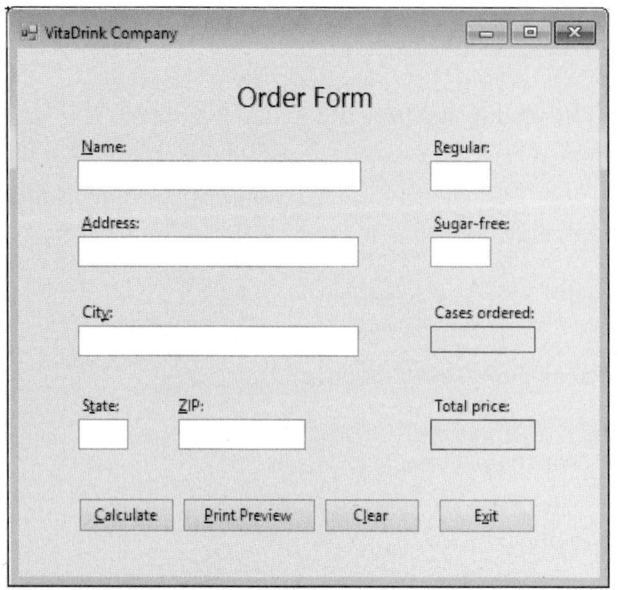

Figure 3-60 MainForm for the VitaDrink Company application

The pseudocode for the calcButton_Click and clearButton_Click procedures is shown in Figure 3-61. The calcButton_Click procedure is responsible for calculating and displaying the total number of cases ordered and the total price of the order. Each case costs $56.69. The clearButton_Click procedure is responsible for clearing the screen for the next order. Figure 3-61 also shows the memory locations used in the calcButton_Click procedure.

calcButton Click event procedure
1. store the number of regular cases and the number of sugar-free cases in variables
2. total cases = number of regular cases + number of sugar-free cases
3. total price = total cases * 56.69
4. display total cases and total price in totalCasesLabel and totalPriceLabel
5. send the focus to the printPreviewButton

Named constant	**Data type**	**Value**
`PricePerCase`	Double	56.69

Variables	**Data type**	**Value source**
`regular`	Integer	user input (regularTextBox)
`sugarFree`	Integer	user input (sugarFreeTextBox)
`totalCases`	Integer	procedure calculation
`totalPrice`	Double	procedure calculation

clearButton Click event procedure
1. clear the Text property of the seven text boxes
2. clear the Text property of the totalCasesLabel and totalPriceLabel
3. send the focus to the nameTextBox

Figure 3-61 Pseudocode and memory locations

Copy the VitaDrink Solution folder from the VbReloaded2015\Chap02 folder to the VbReloaded2015\Chap03 folder. Open the VitaDrink Solution (VitaDrink Solution.sln) file contained in the VbReloaded2015\Chap03\VitaDrink Solution folder. Open the designer window (if necessary) and then open the Code Editor window. In the General Declarations section, enter the comments and Option statements shown in Figure 3-62. Also enter the appropriate code in the Click event procedures for the clearButton and calcButton. Save the solution and then start and test the application. Figure 3-63 shows a sample run of the application.

```
' Project name:        VitaDrink Project
' Project purpose:     Display total cases ordered and total price
' Created/revised by:  <your name> on <current date>

Option Explicit On
Option Infer Off
Option Strict On

Public Class MainForm
   Private Sub calcButton_Click(sender As Object, e As EventArgs
   ) Handles calcButton.Click
       ' calculates total cases and total price

       Const PricePerCase As Double = 56.69
       Dim regular As Integer
       Dim sugarFree As Integer
       Dim totalCases As Integer
       Dim totalPrice As Double

       ' store input in variables
       Integer.TryParse(regularTextBox.Text, regular)
       Integer.TryParse(sugarFreeTextBox.Text, sugarFree)

       ' perform calculations
       totalCases = regular + sugarFree
       totalPrice = totalCases * PricePerCase

       ' display calculated results and set focus
       totalCasesLabel.Text = totalCases.ToString
       totalPriceLabel.Text = totalPrice.ToString("C2")
       printPreviewButton.Focus()

   End Sub

   Private Sub clearButton_Click(sender As Object, e As EventArgs
   ) Handles clearButton.Click
       ' prepare screen for next order

       nameTextBox.Text = String.Empty
       addressTextBox.Text = String.Empty
       cityTextBox.Text = String.Empty
       stateTextBox.Text = String.Empty
       zipTextBox.Text = String.Empty
       regularTextBox.Text = String.Empty
       sugarFreeTextBox.Text = String.Empty
       totalCasesLabel.Text = String.Empty
       totalPriceLabel.Text = String.Empty
       nameTextBox.Focus()

   End Sub

```

Figure 3-62 VitaDrink Company application's code *(continues)*

(continued)

```
    Private Sub exitButton_Click(sender As Object, e As EventArgs
    ) Handles exitButton.Click
        Me.Close()

    End Sub

    Private Sub printPreviewButton_Click(sender As Object,
    e As EventArgs) Handles printPreviewButton.Click
        PrintForm1.Print()

    End Sub
End Class
```

Figure 3-62 VitaDrink Company application's code

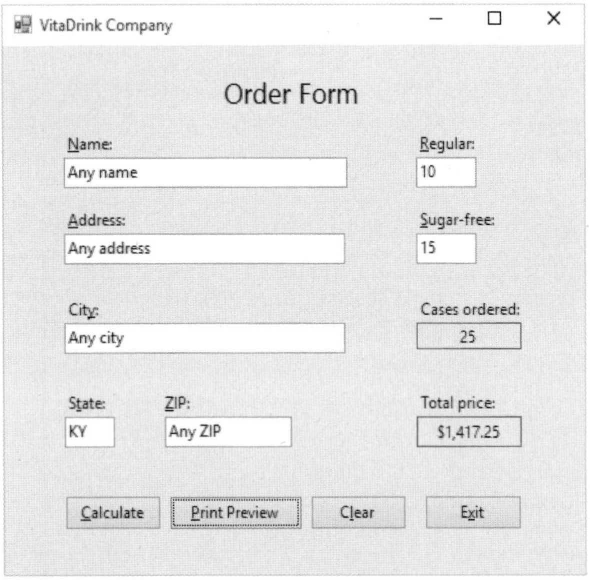

Figure 3-63 Sample run of the VitaDrink Company application

Chapter Summary

- Each memory location in the computer's internal memory can store only one item at a time.
- Variables and named constants are computer memory locations that the programmer uses to store data while an application is running. During run time, the contents of a variable can change, whereas the contents of a named constant cannot change.
- All variables and named constants have a name, data type, initial value, scope, and lifetime.
- The name assigned to a memory location (variable or named constant) should describe the memory location's contents.

- A variable declared in a procedure has procedure scope, and its declaration statement begins with either the keyword `Dim` or the keyword `Static`. A variable declared in a form's Declarations section has class scope, and its declaration statement begins with the keyword `Private`.
- You can use an assignment statement to assign a value to an existing variable during run time. The data type of the value should be the same as the data type of the variable.
- Unlike variables and named constants, which are computer memory locations, a literal constant is an item of data. The value of a literal constant does not change during run time.
- You can use the D literal type character to force a Double literal constant (number) to assume the Decimal data type.
- String literal constants are enclosed in quotation marks ("").
- You can use the TryParse method to convert a string to a number.
- The Convert class contains methods that convert values to a specified data type.
- When an arithmetic expression contains the name of a memory location (variable or named constant), the computer uses the value stored inside the memory location to process the expression.
- You can use the arithmetic assignment operators to abbreviate assignment statements that have the following format, in which *variableName* on both sides of the equal sign is the name of the same variable: *variableName = variableName arithmeticOperator value.*
- A procedure-level memory location can be used only by the procedure in which it is declared. Procedure-level variables declared with the `Dim` keyword are removed from memory when the procedure ends. Procedure-level variables declared with the `Static` keyword remain in memory and also retain their value until the application ends.
- A class-level memory location can be used by all the procedures in the form, including the procedures associated with the controls contained on the form. Class-level variables are removed from memory when the application ends.
- Programmers use comments to internally document an application's code. Comments begin with an apostrophe (`'`).
- You use the Const statement to declare a named constant.
- The `Option Explicit On` statement tells the Code Editor to flag the name of an undeclared variable in the code.
- The `Option Infer Off` statement tells the Code Editor to warn you if a declaration statement does not contain a data type.
- The `Option Strict On` statement tells the computer not to perform any implicit type conversions that demote data. Instead, it should follow the rules listed earlier in Figure 3-22.
- Programmers commonly use either pseudocode (short phrases) or a flowchart (standardized symbols) when planning a procedure's code.
- You can use the ToString method to format an application's numeric output so that it displays special characters (such as dollar signs and commas) and a specified number of decimal places. Every memory location declared using a numeric data type has a ToString method.
- While an application is running, you can remove the contents of a text box or label by assigning either the empty string ("") or the `String.Empty` value to the control's Text property.
- You can use the Focus method to move the focus to a control during run time.

- It is helpful to test a procedure immediately after coding it. By doing so, you will know where to look if the program contains an error.
- After you finish coding the entire application, you should test it to verify that the code is working correctly. Your sample data should include both valid and invalid values.
- Programs may contain syntax errors, logic errors, or run time errors.
- To use the Project Designer window to set Option Explicit, Option Strict, and Option Infer for the current project, right-click My Project in the Solution Explorer window, click Open, click the Compile tab, set the options, and then close the Project Designer window.
- To use the Options dialog box to set Option Explicit, Option Strict, and Option Infer for all of the projects you create, click Tools on the Visual Studio menu bar, click Options, expand the Projects and Solutions node, click VB Defaults, set the options, and then click the OK button.

Key Terms

Arithmetic assignment operators—composed of an arithmetic operator followed by the assignment operator; used to abbreviate an assignment statement that has the following format, in which *variableName* on both sides of the equal sign is the name of the same variable: *variableName = variableName arithmeticOperator value*

Class scope—the scope of a class-level variable; refers to the fact that the variable can be used by any procedure in the form

Class-level variable—a variable declared in the form's Declarations section; the variable has class scope

Comments—used to document a program internally; created by placing an apostrophe (') before the text you want to treat as a comment

Const statement—used to create a named constant

Convert class—contains methods that convert a value to a specified data type and then return the result

Data type—indicates the type of data a memory location (variable or named constant) can store

Demoted—the process of converting a value from one data type to another data type that can store only smaller numbers or numbers with less precision

Empty string—a set of quotation marks with nothing between them (""); also called a zero-length string

Flowchart—a planning tool that uses standardized symbols to show the steps a procedure must take to accomplish its goal

Flowlines—the lines connecting the symbols in a flowchart

Focus method—used to move the focus to a control during run time

Formatting—specifying the number of decimal places and the special characters to display in numeric output

Implicit type conversion—the process by which a value is automatically converted to fit the memory location to which it is assigned

Input/output symbol—the parallelogram in a flowchart; used to represent input and output tasks

Integer division operator—represented by a backslash (\); divides two integers and then returns the quotient as an integer

Integers—positive or negative numbers without any decimal places

Invalid data—data that an application is not expecting the user to enter

Lifetime—indicates how long a variable or named constant remains in the computer's internal memory

Literal constant—an item of data whose value does not change during run time

Literal type character—a character (such as the letter D) appended to a literal constant for the purpose of forcing the literal constant to assume a different data type (such as Decimal)

Logic error—occurs when you neglect to enter an instruction, when you enter the instructions in the wrong order, or as a result of calculation statements that are correct syntactically but incorrect mathematically

Modulus operator—represented by the keyword Mod; divides two numbers and then returns the remainder of the division

Named constant—a computer memory location whose contents cannot be changed during run time; created using the Const statement

Procedure scope—the scope of a procedure-level variable; refers to the fact that the variable can be used only within the procedure in which it is declared

Procedure-level variable—a variable declared in a procedure; the variable has procedure scope

Process symbols—the rectangle symbols in a flowchart; used to represent assignment and calculation tasks

Promoted—the process of converting a value from one data type to another data type that can store either larger numbers or numbers with greater precision

Pseudocode—a planning tool that uses phrases to describe the steps a procedure must take to accomplish its goal

Real numbers—numbers that contain a decimal place

Run time error—an error that occurs while an application is running

Scope—indicates where a memory location (variable or named constant) can be used in the application's code

Start/stop symbol—the oval symbol in a flowchart; used to indicate the beginning and end of the flowchart

Static variable—a procedure-level variable that remains in memory and also retains its value until the application (rather than the procedure) ends

String.Empty—the value that represents the empty string in Visual Basic

ToString method—formats a copy of a number stored in a numeric variable or named constant and then returns the result as a string

TryParse method—used to convert a string to a number

Valid data—data that an application is expecting the user to enter

Variable—a computer memory location where programmers can temporarily store data, as well as change the data, while an application is running

Zero-length string—a set of quotation marks with nothing between them (""); also called an empty string

Review Questions

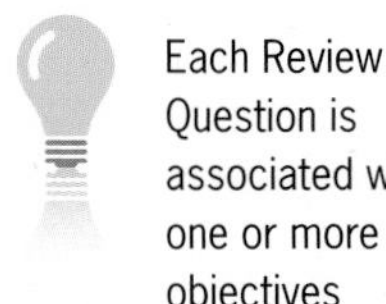

Each Review Question is associated with one or more objectives listed at the beginning of the chapter.

1. Every variable and named constant has ______________. (1, 5)
   a. a data type
   b. a lifetime
   c. a scope
   d. all of the above
2. Which of the following stores the string contained in the `inputPrice` variable in a Double variable named `price`? (2, 3)
   a. `Double.TryParse(price, inputPrice)`
   b. `Double.TryParse(inputPrice, price)`
   c. `number = Double.TryParse(inputPrice)`
   d. `number = TryParse.Double(inputPrice)`
3. What will be assigned to the Integer `answer` variable when the `answer = 31 Mod 2` statement is processed? (2, 4)
   a. 1
   b. 15
   c. 15.5
   d. none of the above
4. Static variables can be declared in ______________. (1, 5)
   a. the form's Declarations section
   b. the General Declarations section
   c. a procedure
   d. all of the above
5. Which of the following is a valid variable name? (1)
   a. `1stQtr`
   b. `sales.Jan`
   c. `tax_2018`
   d. all of the above
6. Which of the following displays the contents of the `price` variable with a dollar sign and two decimal places? (8)
   a. `priceTextBox.Text = Convert.ToString(price, "C2")`
   b. `priceTextBox.Text = ToString(price, "C2")`
   c. `priceTextBox.Text = price.ToString("C2")`
   d. none of the above
7. If an application contains the `Option Strict On` statement, which of the following will display the sum of the `janSales` and `febSales` variables in the sumTextBox? (2, 3, 4, 6)
   a. `answerTextBox.Text = Convert.ToString(janSales) + Convert.ToString(febSales)`
   b. `answerTextBox.Text = Convert.ToString(janSales + febSales)`
   c. `answerTextBox.Text = (janSales + febSales).ToString`
   d. both b and c

8. If an application contains the `Option Strict On` statement, which of the following can be used to declare the `Rate` named constant? (1, 3, 6)
   a. `Const Rate As Decimal = 0.09`
   b. `Const Rate As Decimal = Convert.ToDecimal(0.09)`
   c. `Const Rate As Decimal = 0.09D`
   d. both b and c
9. Which of the following statements adds the number 10.75 to the contents of the `price` variable? (2, 4)
   a. `price += 10.75`
   b. `price =+ 10.75`
   c. `10.75 += price`
   d. both a and c
10. Which of the following sends the focus to the test1TextBox? (10)
    a. `test1TextBox.Focus()`
    b. `test1TextBox.SendFocus()`
    c. `test1TextBox.SetFocus()`
    d. `SetFocus(test1TextBox)`

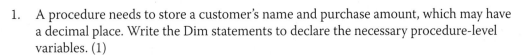

Each Exercise is associated with one or more objectives listed at the beginning of the chapter.

Exercises

Pencil and Paper

1. A procedure needs to store a customer's name and purchase amount, which may have a decimal place. Write the Dim statements to declare the necessary procedure-level variables. (1) INTRODUCTORY
2. Write an assignment statement that multiplies the contents of the `grossPay` variable by the contents of the `RaiseRate` constant and then assigns the result to the `raise` variable. The three memory locations have the Decimal data type. (2, 4) INTRODUCTORY
3. Write the statement to declare the procedure-level `InterestRate` constant whose data type and value are Double and 0.03, respectively. (1) INTRODUCTORY
4. Write the statement to store the contents of the orderedTextBox in an Integer variable named `ordered`. (2, 3) INTRODUCTORY
5. Write the statement to display the contents of an Integer variable named `grossPay` in the grossLabel. Display the output with a dollar sign and no decimal places. (8) INTRODUCTORY
6. Write the statement to declare the class-level `InterestRate` constant whose data type and value are Decimal and 0.04, respectively. (1, 3) INTRODUCTORY
7. Write the statement to declare a String variable that can be used by two procedures in the same form. Name the variable `storeName`. Also specify where you will need to enter the statement and whether the variable is a procedure-level or class-level variable. (1, 5) INTERMEDIATE

INTERMEDIATE

8. Write two versions of an assignment statement that multiplies the contents of the `price` variable by the number 1.5 and then assigns the result to the `price` variable. The `price` variable has the Decimal data type. Use the standard multiplication and assignment operators in one of the statements. Use the appropriate arithmetic assignment operator in the other statement. (2, 4)

ADVANCED

9. Write an assignment statement that adds together the contents of two Decimal variables named `store1Payroll` and `store2Payroll` and then assigns the sum to a String variable named `totalPayroll`. (2, 3, 4)

Computer

MODIFY THIS

10. If necessary, complete the Basketball Score application from this chapter's Programming Tutorial 1. Close the solution and then use Windows to make a copy of the Basketball Solution folder. Rename the copy Basketball Solution-ModifyThis. Open the Basketball Solution (Basketball Solution.sln) file contained in the Basketball Solution-ModifyThis folder. Locate the calcButton_Click procedure in the Code Editor window. Delete the `totalPt2` and `totalPt3` declaration statements and the statements that assign values to both variables. Now, modify the statement that calculates the total score. Test the application. (2, 4)

MODIFY THIS

11. If necessary, complete the Alligator Inc. application from this chapter's Programming Tutorial 2. Close the solution and then use Windows to make a copy of the Alligator Solution folder. Rename the copy Alligator Solution-ModifyThis. Open the Alligator Solution (Alligator Solution.sln) file contained in the Alligator Solution-ModifyThis folder. Modify the interface to allow the user to enter the number of salespeople who are paid a $200 monthly allowance and the number of salespeople who are paid a $150 monthly allowance. Make the appropriate modifications to the calcButton_Click procedure. Test the application using 10 and 15 as the number of salespeople who are paid $200 and $150, respectively. The total annual allowance is $51,000. (1–4)

MODIFY THIS

12. If necessary, complete the VitaDrink Company application from this chapter's Programming Example. Close the solution and then use Windows to make a copy of the VitaDrink Solution folder. Rename the copy VitaDrink Solution-ModifyThis. Open the VitaDrink Solution (VitaDrink Solution.sln) file contained in the VitaDrink Solution-ModifyThis folder. The company has lowered the price of a case of regular VitaDrink to $54.99. In addition, it now needs to charge customers a 3% sales tax and a $10 shipping charge. (Don't charge sales tax on the shipping.) Make the appropriate modifications to the calcButton_Click procedure. Test the application. (Hint: If the customer orders two cases of regular VitaDrink and three cases of sugar-free VitaDrink, the total price is $298.45.) Close the solution. (1, 2, 4)

INTRODUCTORY

13. Open the VbReloaded2015\Chap03\Static Solution\Static Solution (Static Solution.sln) file. Start the application. Click the Count button several times. The message indicates the number of times the Count button was clicked. Click the Exit button. Modify the application's code so that it uses a static variable rather than a class-level variable. Test the application. (1, 5)

INTRODUCTORY

14. If necessary, complete Computer Exercise 10 in Chapter 2. Close the solution and then copy the Time Solution folder from the VbReloaded2015\Chap02 folder to the VbReloaded2015\Chap03 folder. Open the VbReloaded2015\Chap03\Time Solution\Time Solution (Time Solution.sln) file. Open the Code Editor window and enter the

appropriate comments and Option statements in the General Declarations section. Complete the application by coding the Click event procedure for the Calculate Hours button. (1–6)

15. If necessary, complete Computer Exercise 11 in Chapter 2. Close the solution and then copy the Net Solution folder from the VbReloaded2015\Chap02 folder to the VbReloaded2015\Chap03 folder. Open the VbReloaded2015\Chap03\Net Solution\Net Solution (Net Solution.sln) file. Open the Code Editor window and enter the appropriate comments and Option statements in the General Declarations section. Complete the application by coding the Click event procedure for the button that calculates the net pay. Display the net pay with a dollar sign and two decimal places. (1–6, 8) INTRODUCTORY

16. If necessary, complete Computer Exercise 12 in Chapter 2. Close the solution and then copy the Hillside Solution folder from the VbReloaded2015\Chap02 folder to the VbReloaded2015\Chap03 folder. Open the VbReloaded2015\Chap03\Hillside Solution\Hillside Solution (Hillside Solution.sln) file. Open the Code Editor window and enter the appropriate comments and Option statements in the General Declarations section. Complete the application by coding the Click event procedure for the button that calculates the total sales made during each month. Display the total sales with a dollar sign and two decimal places. (1–6, 8) INTRODUCTORY

17. Open the Property Tax Solution (Property Tax Solution.sln) file contained in the VbReloaded2015\Chap03\Property Tax Solution folder. Open the Code Editor window and enter the appropriate Option statements. The application should calculate the annual property tax. Currently, the property tax rate is $1.02 for each $100 of a property's assessed value. Write the pseudocode for the Calculate button and then code the application. Display the tax with a dollar sign and two decimal places. Test the application. (1–8, 10) INTRODUCTORY

18. If necessary, complete Computer Exercise 13 in Chapter 2. Close the solution and then copy the Carson Solution folder from the VbReloaded2015\Chap02 folder to the VbReloaded2015\Chap03 folder. Open the VbReloaded2015\Chap03\Carson Solution\Carson Solution (Carson Solution.sln) file. Open the Code Editor window and enter the appropriate comments and Option statements in the General Declarations section. Complete the application by coding the Click event procedure for the button that calculates the area in both square feet and square yards. Display the area calculations with one decimal place. (1–6, 8) INTERMEDIATE

19. Colfax Industries needs an application that allows the shipping clerk to enter the quantity of an item in inventory and the quantity that can be packed in a box for shipping. When the shipping clerk clicks a button, the application should calculate and display the number of full boxes that can be packed and the number of items left over. Prepare a TOE chart ordered by object. Create a Windows Forms application. Use the following names for the solution and project, respectively: Colfax Solution and Colfax Project. Save the application in the VbReloaded2015\Chap03 folder. Change the form file's name to Main Form.vb. Build the interface. Write the pseudocode and then code the application. Be sure to include comments and the Option statements. Test the application. (Hint: If there are 45 skateboards in inventory and six fit into a box for shipping, the company will be able to ship seven full boxes, leaving three skateboards in inventory.) (1–8, 10) INTERMEDIATE

20. In this exercise, you will create an application that calculates the suggested amounts to tip a waiter at a restaurant. The interface should allow the user to enter the amount of the bill. The application should calculate and display a 10% tip, 15% tip, and 20% tip. INTERMEDIATE

Prepare a TOE chart ordered by object. Create a Windows Forms application. Use the following names for the solution and project, respectively: Tip Solution and Tip Project. Save the application in the VbReloaded2015\Chap03 folder. Change the form file's name to Main Form.vb. Build the interface. Write the pseudocode and then code the application. Be sure to include comments and the Option statements. Save the solution and then start and test the application. Close the solution. (1–8, 10)

INTERMEDIATE

21. Open the VbReloaded2015\Chap03\Mason Solution\Mason Solution (Mason Solution.sln) file. The application should calculate the projected sales for each sales region. Code the application. Display the calculated results with two decimal places. Be sure to include comments and the Option statements. (1–8, 10)

    a. Save the solution and then start the application. Test the application using the following valid data:

       Region 1 sales and percentage: 150000, 0.15
       Region 2 sales and percentage: 175500, 0.12
       Region 3 sales and percentage: 100300, 0.11

    b. Now, test the application without entering any data. Also test it using letters as the sales and percentage amounts.

    c. Close the solution.

INTERMEDIATE

22. The River Bend Hotel needs an application that calculates a customer's total bill. Each customer pays a room charge that is based on a per-night rate of $90. For example, if the customer stays two nights, the room charge is $180. Customers also may be billed a room service charge and a telephone charge. In addition, each customer pays an entertainment tax, which is 10% of the room charge only. The application's interface should allow the hotel manager to enter the number of nights, the total charge for room service, and the total charge for using the telephone. It should display the room charge, the entertainment tax, and the total bill. Prepare a TOE chart ordered by object. Create a Windows Forms application. Use the following names for the solution and project, respectively: River Bend Solution and River Bend Project. Save the application in the VbReloaded2015\Chap03 folder. Change the form file's name to Main Form.vb. Build the interface. Draw the flowcharts and then code the application. Test the application. (1–10)

ADVANCED

23. Create an application that allows the user to enter the number of pennies saved in a jar. The application should display the number of dollars, quarters, dimes, nickels, and pennies the user will receive when the pennies are cashed in at a bank. Use the following names for the solution and project, respectively: Pennies Solution and Pennies Project. Save the application in the VbReloaded2015\Chap03 folder. Change the form file's name to Main Form.vb. Build the interface. Be sure to include a button that will prepare the screen for the next calculation. Code the application and then test it. (1–10)

SWAT THE BUGS

24. Open the VbReloaded2015\Chap03\Debug Solution\Debug Solution (Debug Solution.sln) file. Start and then test the application. Correct any errors and then test the application again. (4, 11)

Case Projects

Eddy's

If necessary, complete the Eddy's application from the Case Projects section in Chapter 2. Copy the Eddy Solution folder from the VbReloaded2015\Chap02 folder to the VbReloaded2015\Chap03 folder. Open the VbReloaded2015\Chap03\Eddy Solution\Eddy Solution (Eddy Solution.sln) file. Code the Calculate Price button's Click event procedure. The prices of a hot dog, hamburger, and fountain drink are $1.79, $2.39, and $0.99, respectively. Be sure to include comments and the Option statements. (1–8)

Football Scores

If necessary, complete the Football Scores application from the Case Projects section in Chapter 2. Copy the Football Solution folder from the VbReloaded2015\Chap02 folder to the VbReloaded2015\Chap03 folder. Open the VbReloaded2015\Chap03\Football Solution\Football Solution (Football Solution.sln) file. Code the Calculate button's Click event procedure. The points for touchdowns, field goals, and safeties are 6, 3, and 2, respectively. Be sure to include comments and the Option statements. (1–8)

Just Shirts

If necessary, complete the Just Shirts application from the Case Projects section in Chapter 2. Copy the Shirts Solution folder from the VbReloaded2015\Chap02 folder to the VbReloaded2015\Chap03 folder. Open the VbReloaded2015\Chap03\Shirts Solution\Shirts Solution (Shirts Solution.sln) file. Code the Click event procedures for the Calculate Order and Clear Order buttons. The prices for the shirts in sizes small, medium, and large are $35.99, $35.99, and $37.99, respectively. Be sure to include comments and the Option statements. (1–9)

Pink Elephant Photo Studio

Create an application that allows the owner of the Pink Elephant Photo Studio to enter the studio's quarterly sales amount. The application should display the amount of state, county, and city sales taxes the studio must pay. It should also display the total sales tax. The sales tax rates for the state, county, and city are 2.5%, 0.5%, and 0.25%, respectively. Each sales tax is calculated by multiplying the appropriate rate by the quarterly sales amount. Use the following names for the solution and project, respectively: Pink Elephant Solution and Pink Elephant Project. Save the application in the VbReloaded2015\Chap03 folder. Change the form file's name to Main Form.vb. Display the sales taxes with a dollar sign and two decimal places. You can either create your own interface or create the one shown in Figure 3-64. Be sure to include comments and the Option statements. (1–8)

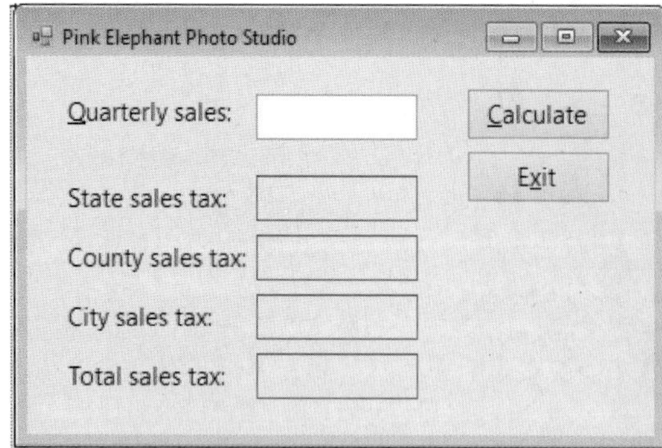

Figure 3-64 Sample interface for the Pink Elephant Photo Studio application

Credit Card Charges

Create an application that allows the user to enter the total monthly amount charged to his or her credit card for the following six categories of expenses: Merchandise, Restaurants, Gasoline, Travel/Entertainment, Services, and Supermarkets. The application should calculate and display each month's total charges, as well as the total annual amount the user charged. The application should also calculate and display the percentage that each category contributed to the total annual amount charged. Use the following names for the solution and project, respectively: Credit Solution and Credit Project. Save the application in the VbReloaded2015\Chap03 folder. Change the form file's name to Main Form.vb. You can either create your own interface or create the one shown in Figure 3-65. Be sure to include comments and the Option statements. (1–8)

Credit Card Charges
Merchandise Restaurants Gasoline Travel/ Entertainment Services Supermarkets Monthly Total Percentage
Jan: Feb: Mar: Apr: May: June: July: Aug: Sep: Oct: Nov: Dec:
Calculate Exit Annual charge:

Figure 3-65 Sample interface for the Credit Card Charges application

Flowerhill Resort

Create a reservation application for Flowerhill Resort. The application's interface should allow the user to enter the following information: the number of rooms to reserve, the length of stay (in nights), the number of adult guests, and the number of child guests. The resort charges $255.50 per room per night. It also charges a 10.75% sales and lodging tax, which is based on the room charge. In addition, there is a $22.50 resort fee per room per night. The application should display the total room charge, the sales and lodging tax, the total resort fee, and the total due. Use the following names for the solution and project, respectively: Flowerhill Solution and Flowerhill Project. Save the application in the VbReloaded2015\Chap03 folder. Change the form file's name to Main Form.vb. Code the application. Display the total room charge, the sales and lodging tax, and the total resort fee with two decimal places. Display the total due with a dollar sign and two decimal places. Be sure to include comments and the Option statements. (1–8)

CHAPTER 4

Making Decisions in a Program

After studying Chapter 4, you should be able to:

1. Include the selection structure in pseudocode and in a flowchart
2. Explain the difference between single-alternative and dual-alternative selection structures
3. Code a selection structure using the If...Then...Else statement
4. Include comparison and logical operators in a selection structure's condition
5. Verify that the denominator in an expression is not 0
6. Swap two values
7. Create a block-level variable
8. Concatenate strings
9. Use the ControlChars.NewLine constant
10. Change the case of a string
11. Include a check box in an interface
12. Generate random numbers

The Selection Structure

All of the procedures in an application are written using one or more of three basic control structures: sequence, selection, and repetition. The procedures in the previous chapters used the sequence structure only. When one of the procedures was invoked during run time, the computer processed its instructions sequentially—in other words, in the order the instructions appeared in the procedure. Every procedure you write will contain the sequence structure.

Many procedures also require the use of one or more selection structures. The **selection structure** (also called the decision structure) indicates that a decision needs to be made before any further processing can occur. The decision is based on a **condition** that must be evaluated to determine the next instruction to process. The condition must evaluate to either True or False only. A procedure that calculates an employee's gross pay, for example, would typically use a selection structure whose condition determines whether the employee worked more than 40 hours. If the condition evaluates to True, the computer would process the instruction that computes regular pay plus overtime pay. If the condition evaluates to False, on the other hand, the computer would process the instruction that computes regular pay only.

There are three types of selection structures: single-alternative, dual-alternative, and multiple-alternative. You will learn about single-alternative and dual-alternative selection structures in this chapter. Multiple-alternative selection structures are covered in Chapter 5.

Single-Alternative and Dual-Alternative Selection Structures

A **single-alternative selection structure** has a specific set of instructions to follow *only* when its condition evaluates to True. Example 1 in Figure 4-1 contains a single-alternative selection structure. A **dual-alternative selection structure**, on the other hand, has one set of instructions to follow when the condition evaluates to True, but a different set of instructions to follow when the condition evaluates to False. Examples 2 and 3 in Figure 4-1 contain a dual-alternative selection structure; both of these examples produce the same result.

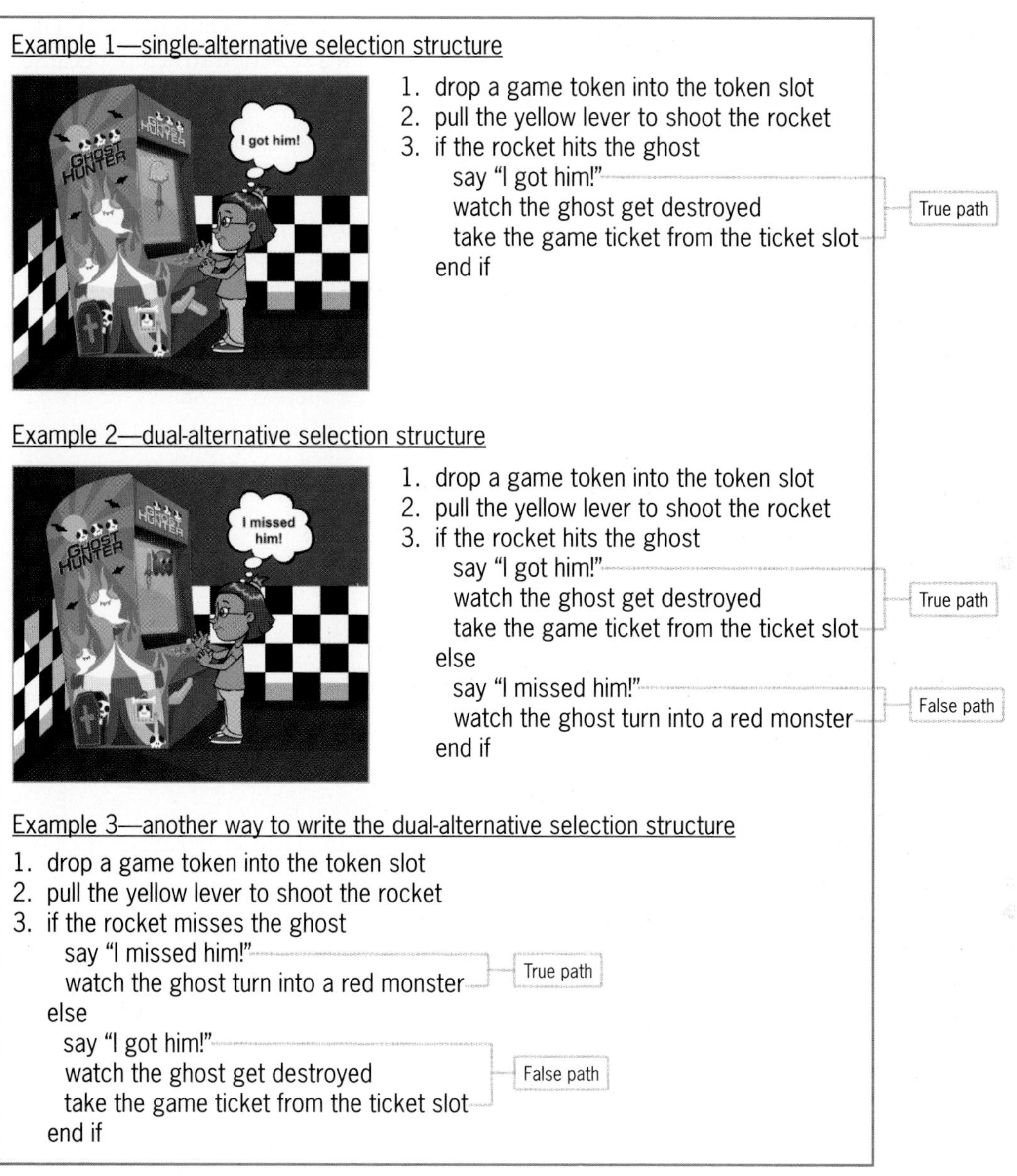

Figure 4-1 Single-alternative and dual-alternative selection structures
Image by Diane Zak; created with Reallusion CrazyTalk Animator

As indicated in Figure 4-1, the instructions to follow when the condition evaluates to True are called the **True path**. The instructions to follow when the condition evaluates to False are called the **False path**. When writing pseudocode, most programmers use the words *if* and *end if* to denote the beginning and end, respectively, of a selection structure, and they use the word *else* to denote the beginning of the structure's False path. Most programmers also indent the instructions within the selection structure, as shown in the figure.

The only way to determine whether a procedure requires a selection structure, and whether the structure should be single-alternative or dual-alternative, is by studying the problem specification. The first problem specification you will examine in this chapter is for Somerset Day Spa. The problem specification is shown in Figure 4-2 along with an appropriate interface.

The figure also includes the pseudocode for the Calculate button's Click event procedure. The procedure requires only the sequence structure. It does not need a selection structure because no decisions are necessary to calculate and display the total cost.

Problem specification
Create an application that displays the total cost of a three-hour spa party at the Somerset Day Spa. The cost per person is $195, which includes a one-hour European facial, a one-hour Swedish massage, and a one-hour Aromatherapy spa pedicure.

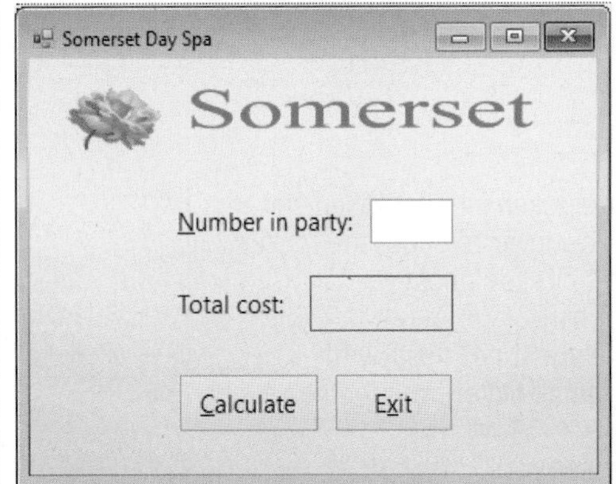

calcButton Click event procedure
1. store user input (number in party) in a variable
2. total cost = number in party * cost per person
3. display total cost in totalCostLabel

Figure 4-2 Somerset Day Spa application (sequence structure only)

Now we will make a slight change to the problem specification from Figure 4-2. Somerset Day Spa now offers a 10% discount when the party consists of more than six people. Consider the changes you will need to make to the pseudocode shown in Figure 4-2. The first two steps in the original pseudocode store the user input in a variable and then calculate the total cost by multiplying the number of party participants by the cost per person. The modified pseudocode will still need both of those steps.

Step 3 in the original pseudocode displays the total cost in the totalCostLabel. Before the modified procedure can display the total cost, it must determine whether there are more than six participants. It will make this determination using a selection structure whose condition compares the number of participants to the number 6. If the number of participants is greater than 6 (a True condition), the modified procedure should calculate the discount and then subtract the discount from the total cost.

The modified problem specification is shown in Figure 4-3 along with the pseudocode and flowchart for the Calculate button's Click event procedure, which contains a single-alternative selection structure. In this case, a single-alternative selection structure is appropriate because a special set of instructions needs to be followed *only* when the structure's condition (which is highlighted in the figure) evaluates to True.

Problem specification

Create an application that displays the total cost of a three-hour spa party at the Somerset Day Spa. The cost per person is $195, which includes a one-hour European facial, a one-hour Swedish massage, and a one-hour Aromatherapy spa pedicure. The spa offers a 10% discount for parties with more than six participants.

calcButton Click event procedure

1. store user input (number in party) in a variable
2. total cost = number in party * cost per person
3. if the number in party is more than 6
   discount = total cost * discount rate
   total cost = total cost – discount
   end if
4. display total cost in totalCostLabel

True path

calcButton Click event procedure

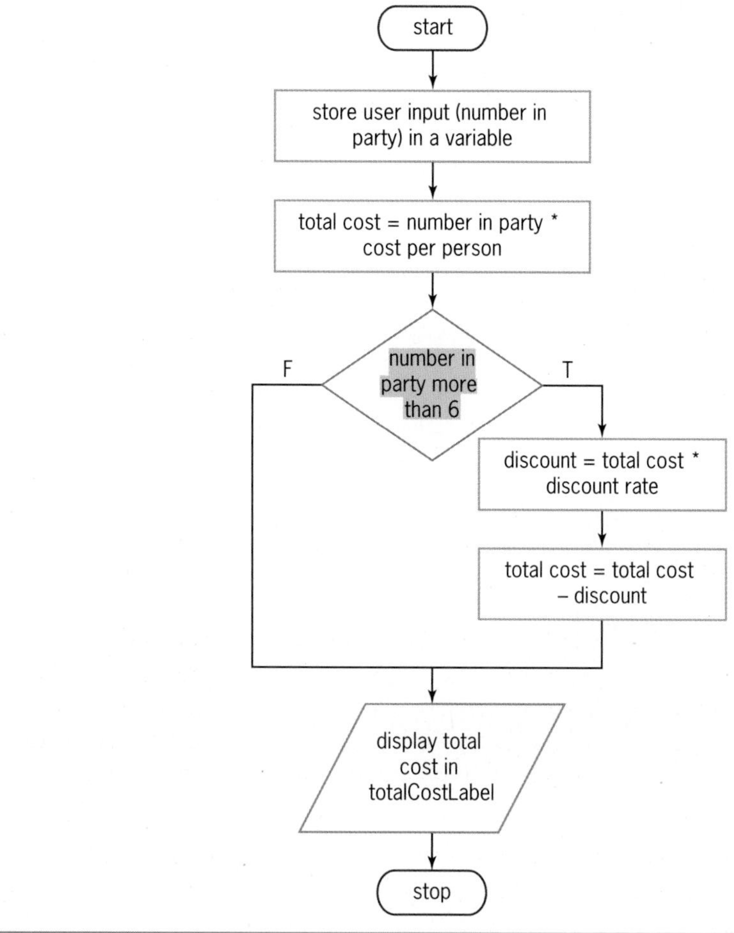

Figure 4-3 Modified Somerset Day Spa application (single-alternative selection structure)

The diamond is also used to represent the condition in a repetition structure, which is covered in Chapter 6.

You can also mark the flowlines with a Y and an N (for Yes and No).

Recall that the oval in a flowchart is the start/stop symbol, the rectangle is the process symbol, and the parallelogram is the input/output symbol. The diamond in a flowchart is called the **decision symbol** because it is used to represent the condition (decision) in the selection structure. The condition in Figure 4-3's diamond checks whether there are more than six people in the party, and it results in an answer of either True or False only.

Notice that the diamond in Figure 4-3 has one flowline entering it and two flowlines leaving it. One of the flowlines leading out of a diamond in a flowchart should be marked with a T (for True), and the other should be marked with an F (for False). The T flowline points to the next instruction to be processed when the condition evaluates to True. In Figure 4-3, the next instruction calculates the 10% discount. The F flowline points to the next instruction to be processed when the condition evaluates to False. In Figure 4-3, that instruction displays the total cost. You can tell that the selection structure in Figure 4-3 is a single-alternative selection structure because only its True path contains a special set of instructions.

Next, we'll modify the Somerset Day Spa problem specification one more time. In addition to the 10% discount for spa parties of more than six participants, the spa is now offering a 5% discount for parties of six or less. The modified problem specification, pseudocode, and flowchart are shown in Figure 4-4. The pseudocode and flowchart contain a dual-alternative selection structure. In this case, a dual-alternative selection structure is appropriate because the procedure needs the computer to follow one instruction when the condition evaluates to True but a different instruction when it evaluates to False. You can tell that the selection structure in Figure 4-4 is a dual-alternative selection structure because both of its paths contain a special instruction.

Problem specification

Create an application that displays the total cost of a three-hour spa party at the Somerset Day Spa. The cost per person is $195, which includes a one-hour European facial, a one-hour Swedish massage, and a one-hour Aromatherapy spa pedicure. The spa offers a 10% discount for parties with more than six participants and a 5% discount for parties of six or fewer.

calcButton Click event procedure

```
1. store user input (number in party) in a variable
2. total cost = number in party * cost per person
3. if the number in party is more than 6
True path ---- discount rate = 0.1
   else
False path --- discount rate = 0.05
   end if
4. discount = total cost * discount rate
5. total cost = total cost – discount
6. display total cost in totalCostLabel
```

Figure 4-4 Modified Somerset Day Spa application (dual-alternative selection structure) *(continues)*

(continued)

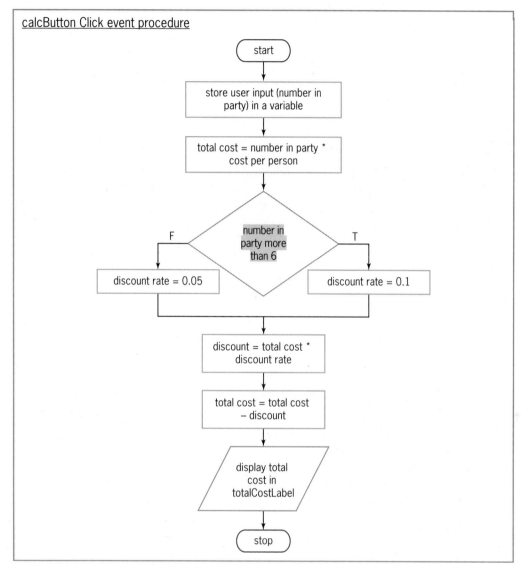

calcButton Click event procedure

start

store user input (number in party) in a variable

total cost = number in party * cost per person

number in party more than 6

F

T

discount rate = 0.05

discount rate = 0.1

discount = total cost * discount rate

total cost = total cost – discount

display total cost in totalCostLabel

stop

Figure 4-4 Modified Somerset Day Spa application (dual-alternative selection structure)

Mini-Quiz 4-1

The answers to Mini-Quiz questions are located in Appendix A. Each question is associated with one or more objectives listed at the beginning of the chapter.

1. Every procedure in an application contains the selection structure. (1)
   a. True
   b. False
2. A dual-alternative selection structure contains instructions in ____________. (2)
   a. its True path only
   b. its False path only
   c. both its True and False paths

3. In a flowchart, a hexagon is used to represent a selection structure's condition. (1)
   a. True b. False

4. Which of the following is the decision symbol in a flowchart? (1)
   a. diamond c. parallelogram
   b. oval d. rectangle

The If...Then...Else Statement

Visual Basic provides the **If...Then...Else statement** for coding single-alternative and dual-alternative selection structures. The statement's syntax is shown in Figure 4-5. The square brackets in the syntax indicate that the Else portion, referred to as the Else clause, is optional. Boldfaced items in a statement's syntax—in this case, the keywords `If`, `Then`, and `End If`, are required. The `Else` keyword is necessary only in a dual-alternative selection structure.

Italicized items in a statement's syntax indicate where the programmer must supply information. In the If...Then...Else statement, the programmer must supply the *condition* that the computer needs to evaluate before further processing can occur. The condition must be a Boolean expression, which is an expression that results in a Boolean value (either True or False). The programmer must also provide the statements to be processed in the True path and (optionally) in the False path. The set of statements contained in each path is referred to as a **statement block**.

Also included in Figure 4-5 are two examples of using the If...Then...Else statement. Example 1 shows how you use the statement to code the single-alternative selection structure shown earlier in Figure 4-3. Example 2 shows how you use the statement to code the dual-alternative selection structure shown earlier in Figure 4-4.

If you want to experiment with the Somerset Day Spa application, open the solution contained in the Try It 1! folder.

HOW TO Use the If...Then...Else Statement

Syntax
If *condition* **Then**
    statement block to be processed when the condition evaluates to True
[Else
    statement block to be processed when the condition evaluates to False]
End If

Example 1
```
Const CostPerPerson As Integer = 195
Const DiscountRate As Double = 0.1
Dim numInParty As Integer
Dim discount As Double
Dim totalCost As Double

Integer.TryParse(numberTextBox.Text, numInParty)
totalCost = numInParty * CostPerPerson
If numInParty > 6 Then
    discount = totalCost * DiscountRate
    totalCost = totalCost - discount
End If
totalCostLabel.Text = totalCost.ToString("C2")
```

single-alternative selection structure

Figure 4-5 How to use the If...Then...Else statement *(continues)*

(continued)

Example 2
```
Const CostPerPerson As Integer = 195
Dim discountRate As Double
Dim numInParty As Integer
Dim discount As Double
Dim totalCost As Double

Integer.TryParse(numberTextBox.Text, numInParty)
totalCost = numInParty * CostPerPerson
If numInParty > 6 Then
    discountRate = 0.1
Else
    discountRate = 0.05
End If
discount = totalCost * discountRate
totalCost = totalCost - discount
totalCostLabel.Text = totalCost.ToString("C2")
```
dual-alternative selection structure

Figure 4-5 How to use the If...Then...Else statement

An If...Then...Else statement's condition can contain variables, constants, properties, methods, keywords, and arithmetic operators. It can also contain comparison operators and logical operators, which you will learn about in this chapter.

Comparison Operators

Comparison operators (also referred to as relational operators) are used to compare two values, and the comparison always results in a Boolean value: either True or False. Figure 4-6 lists the most commonly used comparison operators in Visual Basic, along with examples of using the operators in an If...Then...Else statement's condition.

HOW TO Use Comparison Operators in a Condition

Operator	Operation
=	equal to
>	greater than
>=	greater than or equal to
<	less than
<=	less than or equal to
<>	not equal to

Note: Equal to (=) is the opposite of not equal to (<>), greater than (>) is the opposite of less than or equal to (<=), and less than (<) is the opposite of greater than or equal to (>=).

Example 1
```
If payRate = minWage Then
```
The condition evaluates to True when both variables contain the same value; otherwise, it evaluates to False.

Figure 4-6 How to use comparison operators in a condition *(continues)*

(continued)

Example 2
`If sales >= 3500 Then`
The condition evaluates to True when the value stored in the `sales` variable is greater than or equal to 3500; otherwise, it evaluates to False.

Example 3
`If price < 9.99D Then`
The condition evaluates to True when the value stored in the Decimal `price` variable is less than 9.99; otherwise, it evaluates to False. You can also write the condition as `price < Convert.ToDecimal(9.99)`.

Example 4
`If state <> "NM" Then`
The condition evaluates to True when the `state` variable does not contain the string "NM"; otherwise, it evaluates to False.

Figure 4-6 How to use comparison operators in a condition

Unlike arithmetic operators, comparison operators do not have an order of precedence. When an expression contains more than one comparison operator, the computer evaluates the comparison operators from left to right in the expression. Comparison operators are evaluated after any arithmetic operators in an expression. For example, when processing the expression 9 > 2 * 5, the computer first multiplies the number 2 by the number 5, giving 10. It then compares the number 9 with the number 10. Because 9 is not greater than 10, the expression evaluates to False, as shown in Figure 4-7. The figure also shows the evaluation steps for two other expressions that contain arithmetic and comparison operators.

HOW TO Evaluate Expressions Containing Arithmetic and Comparison Operators

Example 1	Result
Original expression	9 > 2 * 5
The multiplication is performed first	9 > 10
The > comparison is performed last	False

Example 2	Result
Original expression	7 + 6 / 3 < 3 * 4
The division is performed first	7 + 2 < 3 * 4
The multiplication is performed next	7 + 2 < 12
The addition is performed next	9 < 12
The < comparison is performed last	True

Example 3	Result
Original expression	10 * 2 + 6 * 3 – 4 >= 35
The first multiplication is performed first	20 + 6 * 3 – 4 >= 35
The remaining multiplication is performed next	20 + 18 – 4 >= 35
The addition is performed next	38 – 4 >= 35
The subtraction is performed next	34 >= 35
The >= comparison is performed last	False

Figure 4-7 How to evaluate expressions containing arithmetic and comparison operators

Checking the Denominator in an Expression

As you learned in Chapter 3, you can use either the division operator or the integer division operator to divide two numbers in an expression. The number to the left of the operator is called the numerator, and the number to the right of the operator is called the denominator. For example, in the expression 10 / 2, 10 is the numerator and 2 is the denominator; the expression evaluates to 5.

A problem occurs when the denominator in an expression is the number 0. The result of the expression depends on the operator (division or integer division), the data types of the numerator and denominator, and the numerator's value. The result could be NaN (which stands for *Not a Number*), Infinity (∞), or a run time error that abruptly ends the application. If it is possible that the denominator in an expression might contain the number 0, you should use a selection structure to verify its contents before allowing the computer to process the expression, as shown in Figure 4-8.

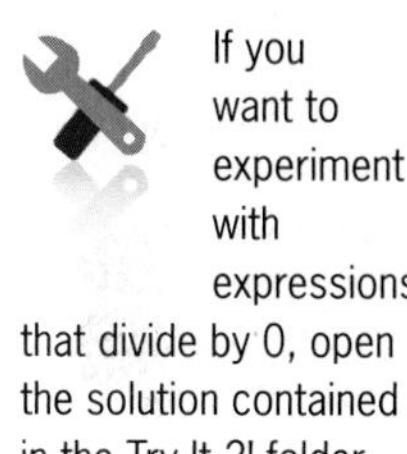

If you want to experiment with expressions that divide by 0, open the solution contained in the Try It 2! folder.

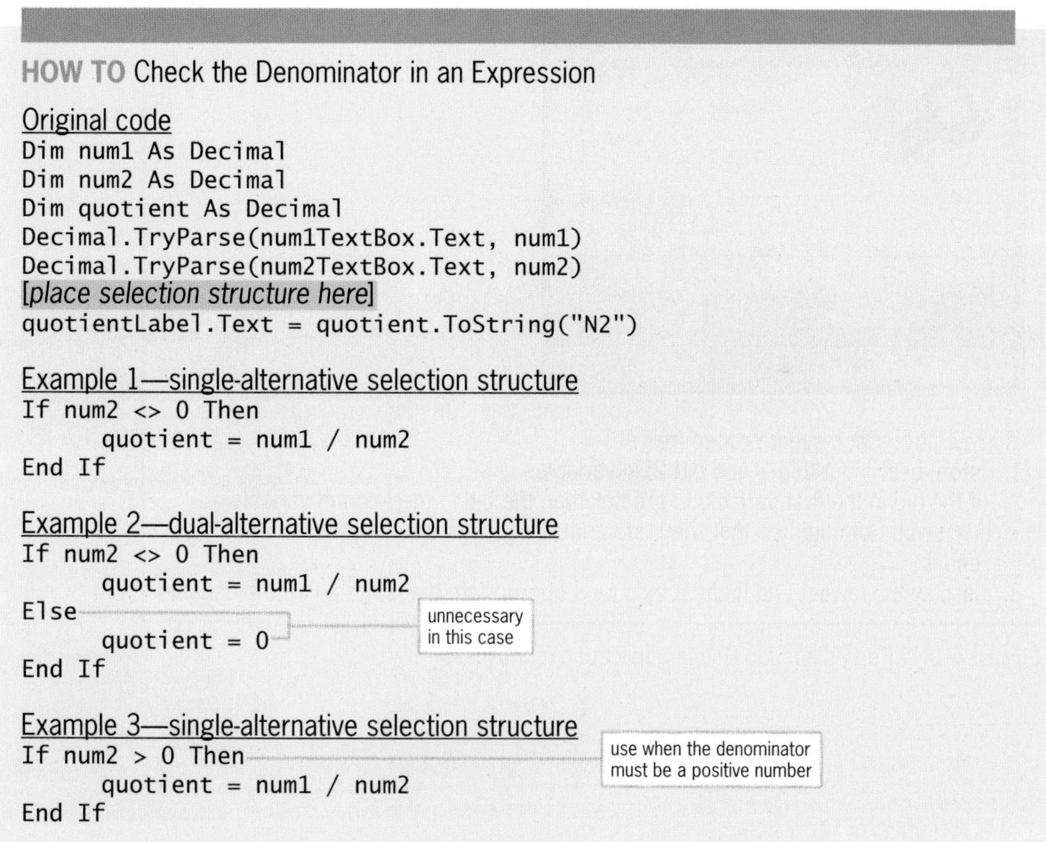

HOW TO Check the Denominator in an Expression

Original code
```
Dim num1 As Decimal
Dim num2 As Decimal
Dim quotient As Decimal
Decimal.TryParse(num1TextBox.Text, num1)
Decimal.TryParse(num2TextBox.Text, num2)
[place selection structure here]
quotientLabel.Text = quotient.ToString("N2")
```

Example 1—single-alternative selection structure
```
If num2 <> 0 Then
      quotient = num1 / num2
End If
```

Example 2—dual-alternative selection structure
```
If num2 <> 0 Then
      quotient = num1 / num2
Else
      quotient = 0
End If
```


Example 3—single-alternative selection structure
```
If num2 > 0 Then
      quotient = num1 / num2
End If
```


Figure 4-8 How to check the denominator in an expression

The single-alternative selection structure in Example 1 divides both numbers and assigns the result to the `quotient` variable *only* when the denominator (`num2`) does not contain the number 0. The dual-alternative structure in Example 2, on the other hand, *always* assigns a value to the `quotient` variable: either the result of the division or the number 0. Although the two selection structures will produce the same result, the Else portion in Example 2 is not really necessary in this case because the `quotient` variable already contains the number 0 from its

Dim statement. However, there is nothing wrong with using the dual-alternative structure; some programmers would argue that it makes the code clearer. In Example 3 in Figure 4-8, the single-alternative structure's condition uses the > (greater than) operator to determine whether the denominator's value is a positive number, which is a number that is greater than 0.

Swapping Numeric Values

Figure 4-9 shows a sample run of the Perry's Auction House application, which displays the lowest and highest of two bids entered by the user. The figure also includes the pseudocode and flowchart for the Display button's Click event procedure. The procedure contains a single-alternative selection structure whose condition determines whether the first bid entered by the user is greater than the second bid. If it is, the selection structure's True path takes the appropriate action.

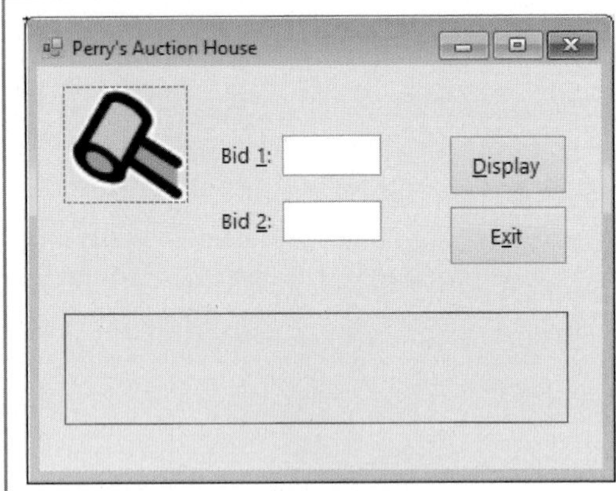

<u>displayButton Click event procedure</u>
1. store user input (bid 1 and bid 2) in variables
2. if the bid in the first variable is greater than the bid in the second variable
   swap both bids so that the first variable contains the lowest of the two bids
   end if
3. display the lowest and highest bids (and appropriate messages) in the bidsLabel

Figure 4-9 Perry's Auction House application *(continues)*

(continued)

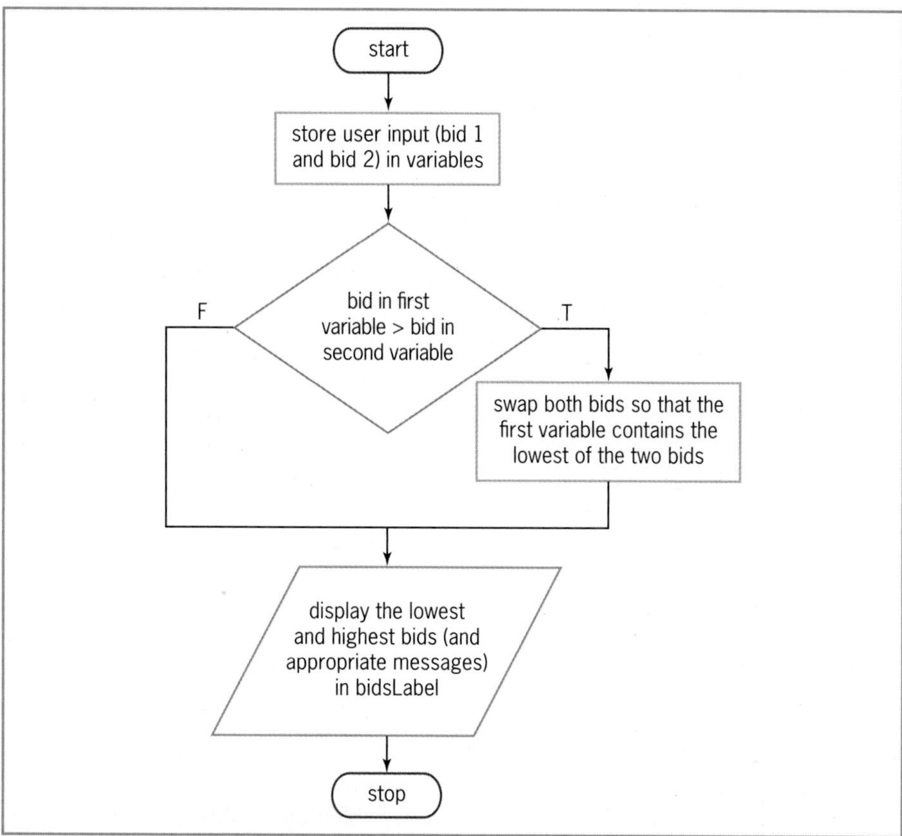

Figure 4-9 Perry's Auction House application

Figure 4-10 shows the code entered in the displayButton_Click procedure. The condition in the If clause compares the values stored in the `bid1` and `bid2` variables. If the value in the `bid1` variable is greater than the value in the `bid2` variable, the condition evaluates to True and the four instructions in the If...Then...Else statement's True path swap both values. Swapping the values places the smaller number in the `bid1` variable and places the larger number in the `bid2` variable. If the condition evaluates to False, on the other hand, the True path instructions are skipped over because the `bid1` variable already contains a number that is smaller than (or possibly equal to) the number stored in the `bid2` variable.

If you want to experiment with the Perry's Auction House application, open the solution contained in the Try It 3! folder.

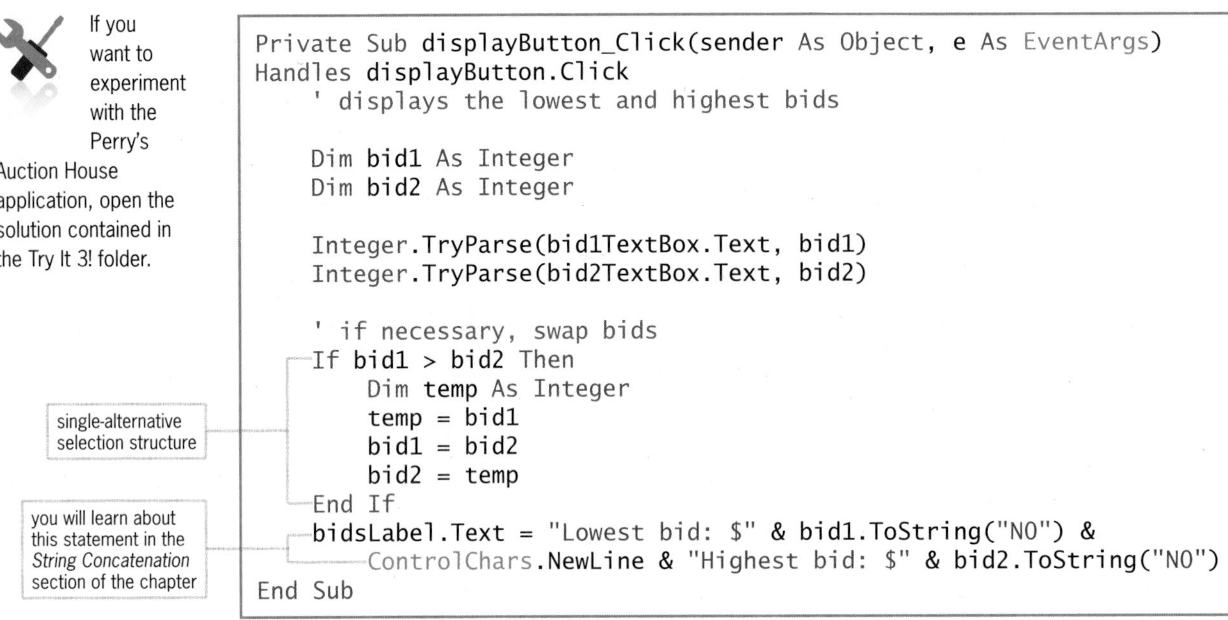


```
Private Sub displayButton_Click(sender As Object, e As EventArgs)
Handles displayButton.Click
    ' displays the lowest and highest bids

    Dim bid1 As Integer
    Dim bid2 As Integer

    Integer.TryParse(bid1TextBox.Text, bid1)
    Integer.TryParse(bid2TextBox.Text, bid2)

    ' if necessary, swap bids
    If bid1 > bid2 Then
        Dim temp As Integer
        temp = bid1
        bid1 = bid2
        bid2 = temp
    End If
    bidsLabel.Text = "Lowest bid: $" & bid1.ToString("N0") &
        ControlChars.NewLine & "Highest bid: $" & bid2.ToString("N0")
End Sub
```

Figure 4-10 displayButton_Click procedure

The first instruction in the If...Then...Else statement's True path declares and initializes a variable named `temp`. Like a variable declared at the beginning of a procedure, a variable declared within a statement block—referred to as a **block-level variable**—remains in memory until the procedure ends. However, unlike a variable declared at the beginning of a procedure, block-level variables have block scope rather than procedure scope. A variable that has **block scope** can be used only within the statement block in which it is declared. More specifically, it can be used only below its declaration statement within the statement block. In this case, the procedure-level `bid1` and `bid2` variables can be used anywhere below their Dim statements within the displayButton_Click procedure, but the block-level `temp` variable can be used only after its Dim statement within the If...Then...Else statement's True path.

You may be wondering why the `temp` variable was not declared at the beginning of the procedure, along with the other variables. Although there is nothing wrong with declaring the `temp` variable in that location, there is no reason to create the variable until it is needed, which (in this case) is only when a swap is necessary.

The second instruction in the If...Then...Else statement's True path assigns the value in the `bid1` variable to the `temp` variable. If you do not store the `bid1` variable's value in the `temp` variable, the value will be lost when the computer processes the `bid1 = bid2` statement, which replaces the contents of the `bid1` variable with the contents of the `bid2` variable. Finally, the `bid2 = temp` instruction assigns the `temp` variable's value to the `bid2` variable; this completes the swap.

Figure 4-11 lists the steps for swapping the contents of two variables. It also contains an example that illustrates the swapping concept, assuming the user enters the numbers 1200 and 900 in the bid1TextBox and bid2TextBox, respectively.

Ch04-Swapping

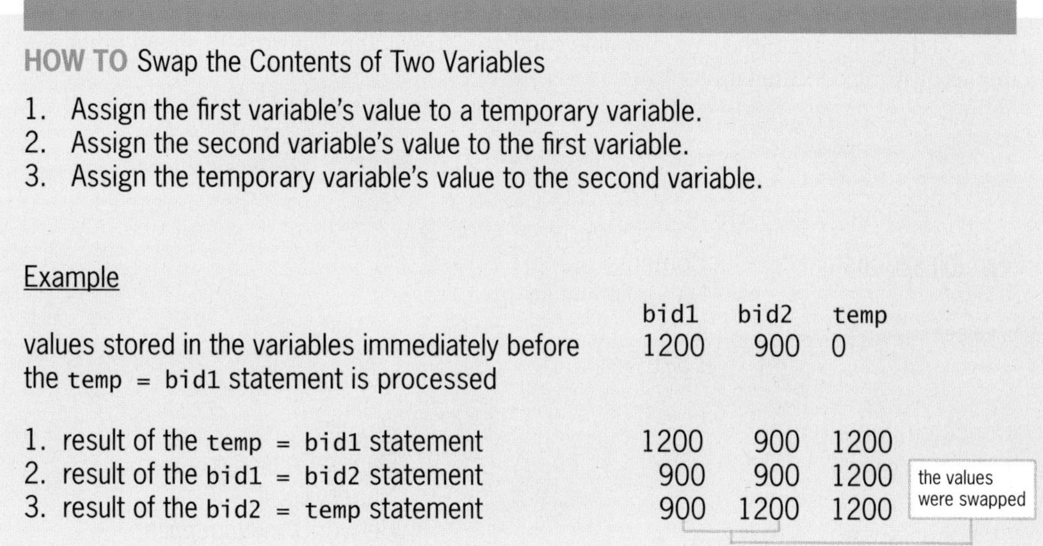

HOW TO Swap the Contents of Two Variables

1. Assign the first variable's value to a temporary variable.
2. Assign the second variable's value to the first variable.
3. Assign the temporary variable's value to the second variable.

Example

	bid1	bid2	temp
values stored in the variables immediately before the `temp = bid1` statement is processed	1200	900	0
1. result of the `temp = bid1` statement	1200	900	1200
2. result of the `bid1 = bid2` statement	900	900	1200
3. result of the `bid2 = temp` statement	900	1200	1200

the values were swapped

Figure 4-11 How to swap the contents of two variables

String Concatenation

The displayButton_Click procedure shown earlier in Figure 4-10 contains two items that were not covered in the previous three chapters: the `ControlChars.NewLine` constant and the concatenation operator. The assignment statement containing both items is shown in Figure 4-12 along with a sample run of the Perry's Auction House application.

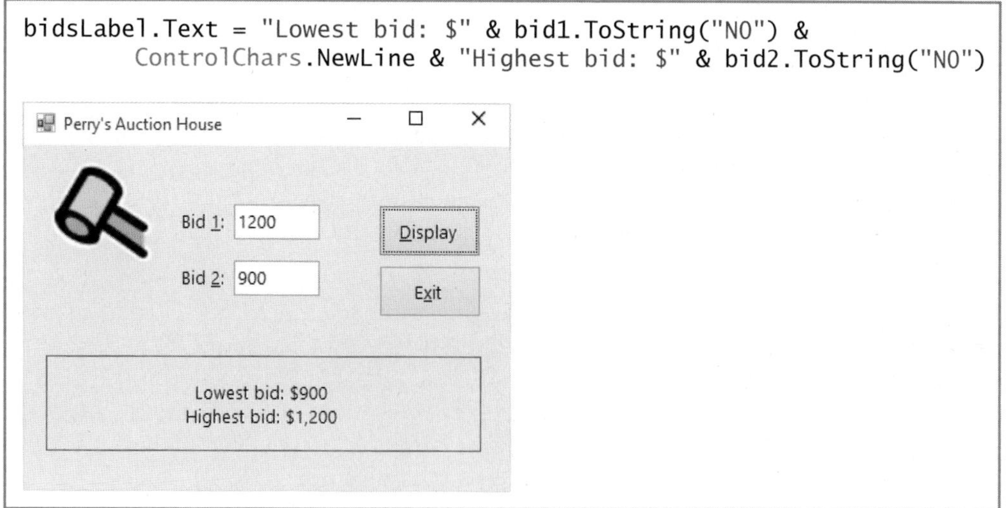

```
bidsLabel.Text = "Lowest bid: $" & bid1.ToString("N0") &
        ControlChars.NewLine & "Highest bid: $" & bid2.ToString("N0")
```


Figure 4-12 Assignment statement and sample run of the Perry's Auction House application

The **ControlChars.NewLine constant** in the statement advances the insertion point to the next line in the bidsLabel. The constant allows the procedure to display the "Highest: $1,200" text on the second line in the label. The **concatenation operator**, which is the ampersand (**&**), is used to concatenate (connect or link together) strings. For the Code Editor to recognize the ampersand as the concatenation operator, the ampersand must be both preceded and followed by a space. The assignment statement concatenates five strings: the string "Lowest bid: $", the contents of the `bid1` variable converted to a string, the `ControlChars.NewLine` constant, the string "Highest bid: $", and the contents of the `bid2` variable converted to a string. Figure 4-13 shows other examples of string concatenation.

If you want to practice concatenating strings, open the solution contained in the Try It 4! folder.

HOW TO Concatenate Strings

Variables/Constant	Contents
`city`	Naperville
`state`	IL
`rent`	1385

Concatenated string	Result
`city & state`	NapervilleIL
`city & ", " & state`	Naperville, IL
`"He works in " & city & "."`	He works in Naperville.
`"Rent: " & rent.ToString("C0")`	Rent: $1,385

Figure 4-13 How to concatenate strings

Comparing Strings

Each uppercase letter is stored in internal memory using a different Unicode value than its lowercase counterpart.

As is true in many programming languages, string comparisons in Visual Basic are case sensitive, which means that the uppercase letters of the alphabet are not equal to their lowercase counterparts. Because of this, each of the following three string comparisons will evaluate to False: `"A" = "a"`, `"Yes" = "yes"`, and `"12x" = "12X"`.

At times, your code may need to compare strings whose case cannot be determined until run time, such as strings either entered by the user or read from a file. When comparing two strings whose case is unknown, you can temporarily convert the strings to the same case (either uppercase or lowercase) and then use the converted strings in the comparison. Visual Basic provides the **ToUpper method** for temporarily converting a string to uppercase, and it provides the **ToLower method** for temporarily converting a string to lowercase. Both methods affect only letters of the alphabet because they are the only characters that have uppercase and lowercase forms.

Figure 4-14 shows the syntax of the ToUpper and ToLower methods and includes examples of using the methods. In each syntax, *string* is usually either the name of a String variable or the Text property of an object. Both methods copy the contents of the *string* to a temporary location in the computer's internal memory. The methods convert the temporary string to the appropriate case (if necessary) and then return the temporary string. Keep in mind that the ToUpper and ToLower methods do not change the contents of the original *string*; they change the contents of the temporary location only.

HOW TO Use the ToUpper and ToLower Methods

Syntax
string.**ToUpper**
string.**ToLower**

Example 1
```
If senior.ToUpper = "Y" Then
```
compares the uppercase version of the string stored in the `senior` variable with the uppercase letter Y

Example 2
```
If item1.ToUpper = item2.ToUpper Then
```
compares the uppercase version of the string stored in the `item1` variable with the uppercase version of the string stored in the `item2` variable

Example 3
```
If senior.ToLower <> "y" Then
```
compares the lowercase version of the string stored in the `senior` variable with the lowercase letter y

Example 4
```
If "madrid" = cityTextBox.Text.ToLower Then
```
compares the lowercase string "madrid" with the lowercase version of the string stored in the cityTextBox's Text property

Example 5
```
nameLabel.Text = customer.ToUpper
```
assigns the uppercase version of the string stored in the `customer` variable to the nameLabel's Text property

Example 6
```
firstName = firstName.ToUpper
stateTextBox.Text = stateTextBox.Text.ToLower
```
changes the contents of the `firstName` variable to uppercase, and changes the contents of the stateTextBox's Text property to lowercase

Figure 4-14 How to use the ToUpper and ToLower methods

When using the ToUpper method in a comparison, be sure that the strings you are comparing are uppercase, as shown in Examples 1 and 2; otherwise, the comparison will not evaluate correctly. Likewise, when using the ToLower method in a comparison, be sure that the strings you are comparing are lowercase, as shown in Examples 3 and 4. The statement in Example 5 temporarily converts the contents of the `customer` variable to uppercase and then assigns the result to the nameLabel. As Example 6 indicates, you can also use the ToUpper and ToLower methods to permanently convert the contents of either a String variable or a control's Text property to uppercase or lowercase, respectively.

Not all string comparisons involve letters of the alphabet, so not all will require either the ToUpper or ToLower method. The examples shown in Figure 4-15, for instance, compare strings that contain digits, hyphens, and parentheses.

HOW TO Compare Strings That Contain Digits and Special Characters

Examples

```
If zipCode = "60345" Then
If productIdTextBox.Text = "2047-5" Then
If phoneNum <> "(111)000-5555" Then
```

Figure 4-15 How to compare strings that contain digits and special characters

The Square Calculations Application

Figure 4-16 shows a sample run of the Square Calculations application, which displays either the area or the perimeter of a square whose side measurement is entered by the user. The figure also includes the pseudocode and flowchart for the Calculate button's Click event procedure. The procedure contains two dual-alternative selection structures: one to determine the formula to use for the calculation, and one to determine the number of decimal places to display in the answer.

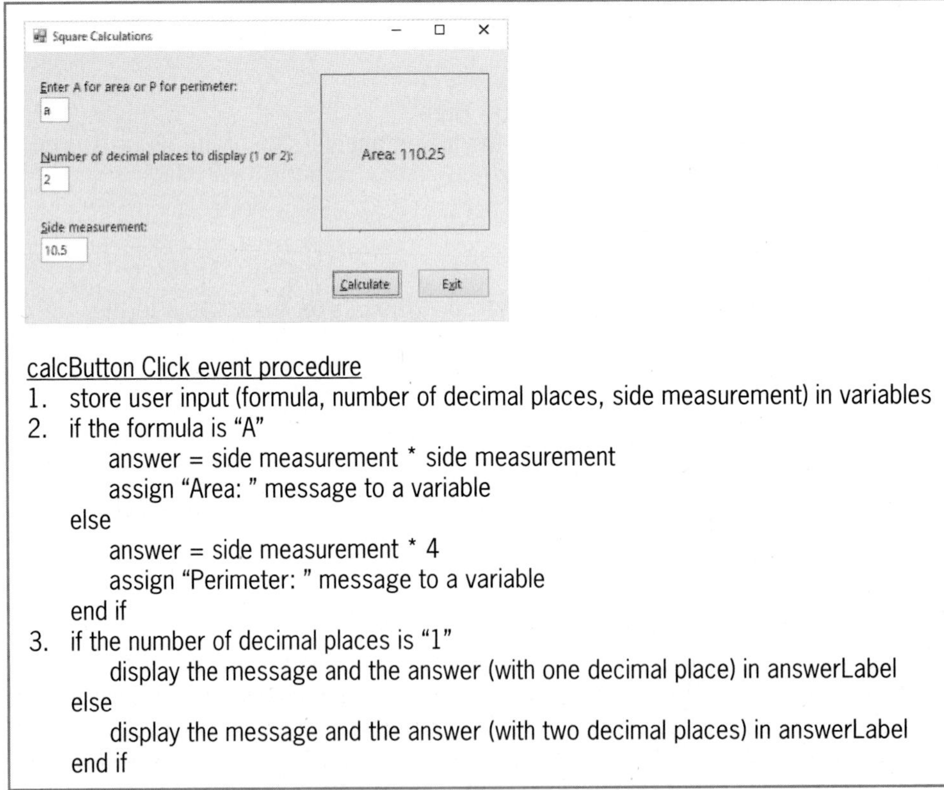

calcButton Click event procedure
1. store user input (formula, number of decimal places, side measurement) in variables
2. if the formula is "A"
   answer = side measurement * side measurement
   assign "Area: " message to a variable
   else
   answer = side measurement * 4
   assign "Perimeter: " message to a variable
   end if
3. if the number of decimal places is "1"
   display the message and the answer (with one decimal place) in answerLabel
   else
   display the message and the answer (with two decimal places) in answerLabel
   end if

Figure 4-16 Square Calculations application *(continues)*

(continued)

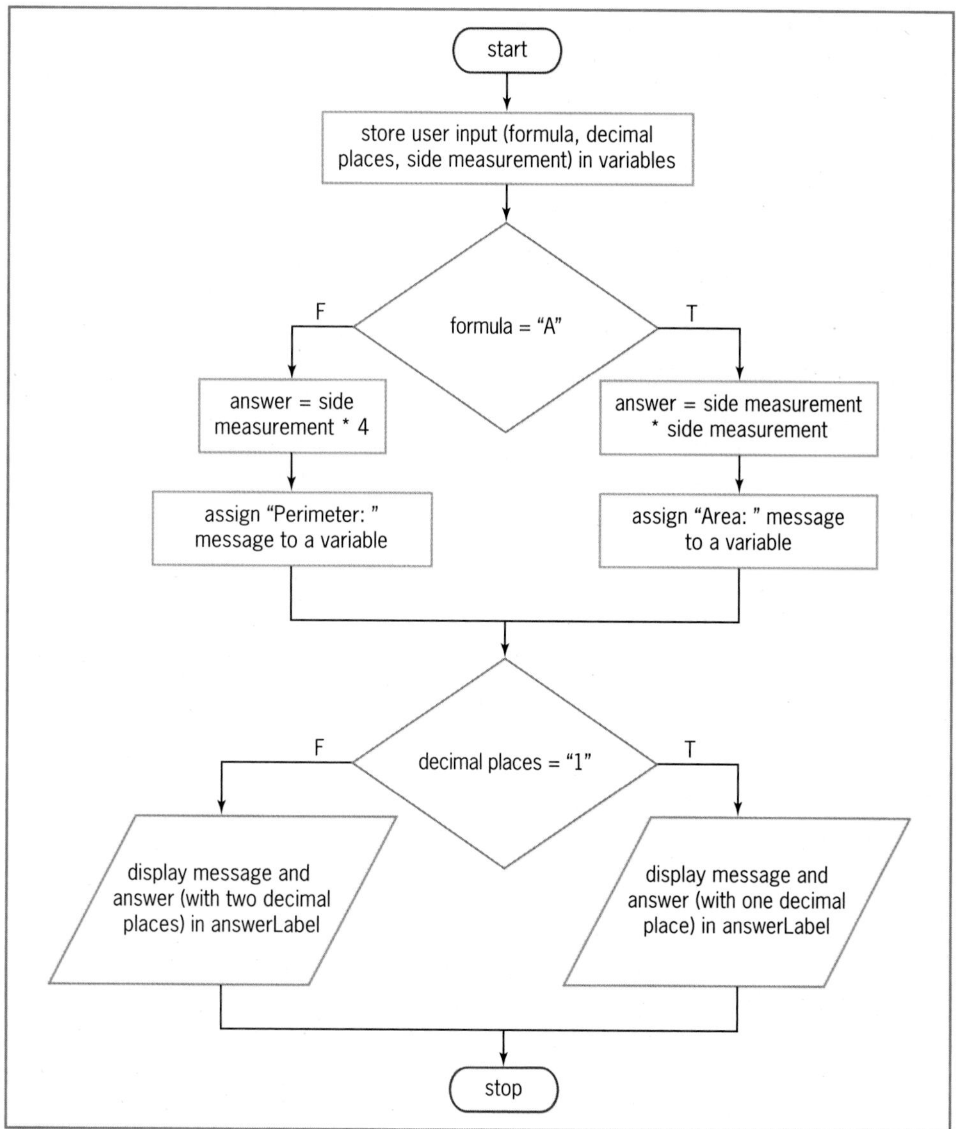

Figure 4-16 Square Calculations application

Figure 4-17 shows two versions of the calcButton_Click procedure. The ToUpper method is shaded in each version. In Version 1, the ToUpper method is included in the statement that assigns the text box value to the `formula` variable. After the statement is processed, the variable will contain an uppercase letter (assuming the user entered a letter). In Version 2, the ToUpper method is included in the If...Then...Else statement's condition. The `formula.ToUpper` portion of the condition will change the `formula` variable's value to uppercase only temporarily. After the comparison is made, the variable will still contain its original value. In this instance, neither version of the code is better than the other. Both simply represent two different ways of performing the same task.

If you want to experiment with the Square Calculations application, open the solution contained in the Try It 5! folder.

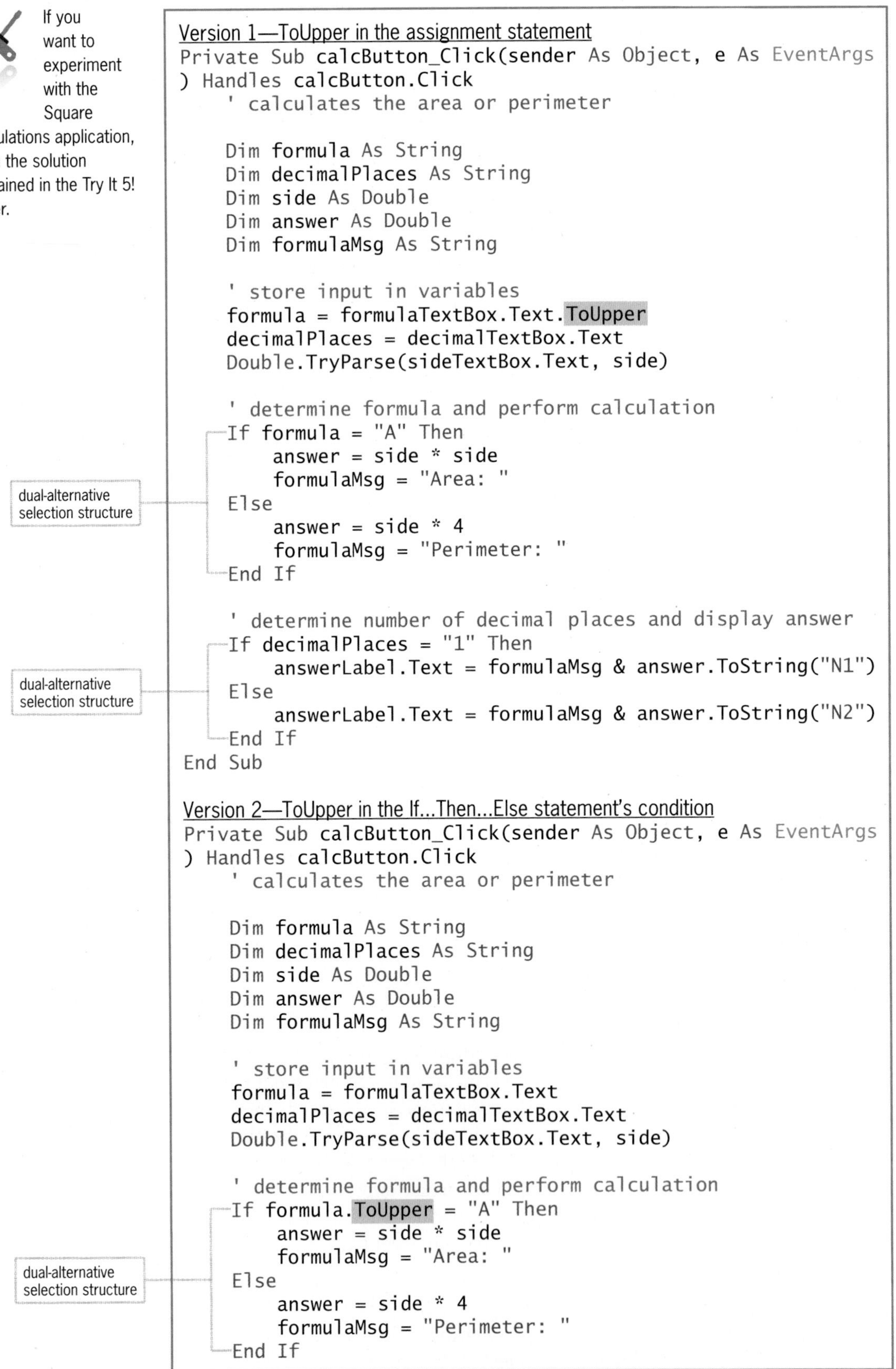

Version 1—ToUpper in the assignment statement

```
Private Sub calcButton_Click(sender As Object, e As EventArgs
) Handles calcButton.Click
    ' calculates the area or perimeter

    Dim formula As String
    Dim decimalPlaces As String
    Dim side As Double
    Dim answer As Double
    Dim formulaMsg As String

    ' store input in variables
    formula = formulaTextBox.Text.ToUpper
    decimalPlaces = decimalTextBox.Text
    Double.TryParse(sideTextBox.Text, side)

    ' determine formula and perform calculation
    If formula = "A" Then
        answer = side * side
        formulaMsg = "Area: "
    Else
        answer = side * 4
        formulaMsg = "Perimeter: "
    End If

    ' determine number of decimal places and display answer
    If decimalPlaces = "1" Then
        answerLabel.Text = formulaMsg & answer.ToString("N1")
    Else
        answerLabel.Text = formulaMsg & answer.ToString("N2")
    End If
End Sub
```

Version 2—ToUpper in the If...Then...Else statement's condition

```
Private Sub calcButton_Click(sender As Object, e As EventArgs
) Handles calcButton.Click
    ' calculates the area or perimeter

    Dim formula As String
    Dim decimalPlaces As String
    Dim side As Double
    Dim answer As Double
    Dim formulaMsg As String

    ' store input in variables
    formula = formulaTextBox.Text
    decimalPlaces = decimalTextBox.Text
    Double.TryParse(sideTextBox.Text, side)

    ' determine formula and perform calculation
    If formula.ToUpper = "A" Then
        answer = side * side
        formulaMsg = "Area: "
    Else
        answer = side * 4
        formulaMsg = "Perimeter: "
    End If
```

Figure 4-17 Two versions of the calcButton_Click procedure *(continues)*

(continued)

```
    ' determine number of decimal places and display answer
    If decimalPlaces = "1" Then
        answerLabel.Text = formulaMsg & answer.ToString("N1")
    Else
        answerLabel.Text = formulaMsg & answer.ToString("N2")
    End If
End Sub
```

dual-alternative selection structure

Figure 4-17 Two versions of the calcButton_Click procedure

You can also code the calcButton_Click procedure without using the ToUpper or ToLower methods. To do this, you simply need to change the formulaTextBox's CharacterCasing property (in the Properties window) from Normal to either Upper or Lower. A text box's **CharacterCasing property** indicates whether the text inside the control should remain as typed or be converted to either uppercase or lowercase as the user is typing. For example, if the formulaTextBox's CharacterCasing property is set to Upper, an uppercase letter A will appear in the text box even when the user types the lowercase letter a. As a result, the `formula = formulaTextBox.Text` statement will assign an uppercase letter A to the `formula` variable. The CharacterCasing property allows you to control the case of the input. (If you want to try using the CharacterCasing property, complete Computer Exercise 12 at the end of the chapter.)

Comparing Boolean Values

Figure 4-18 shows a sample run of a different version of the Square Calculations application. In this version, the interface provides two check boxes for specifying the desired output, which can be the square's area, its perimeter, or both its area and its perimeter.

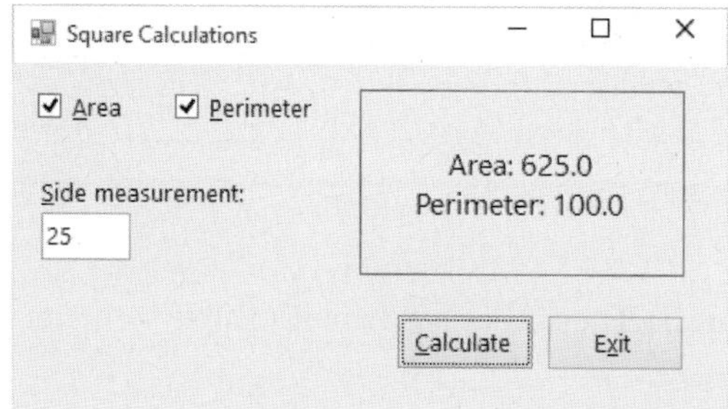

Figure 4-18 Sample run of a different version of the Square Calculations application

You add a check box to an interface using the CheckBox tool in the toolbox. In Windows applications, **check boxes** provide one or more independent and nonexclusive items from which the user can choose. An interface can contain any number of check boxes, and any number of them can be selected at the same time.

Each check box in an interface should be labeled to make its purpose obvious. You enter the label using sentence capitalization in the check box's Text property. Each check box should also have a unique access key. During run time, you can determine whether a check box is selected by looking at the Boolean value in its Checked property: A True value indicates that the check box is selected, whereas a False value indicates that it is not selected.

Figure 4-19 shows the calcButton_Click procedure, which contains two single-alternative selection structures. The condition in each selection structure is shaded in the figure. The condition in the first selection structure compares the value in the Checked property with the Boolean value True. However, because the Checked property contains a Boolean value, you can omit the = `True` in the condition, as shown in the second selection structure.

If you want to experiment with this version of the Square Calculations application, open the solution contained in the Try It 6! folder.

Version 1—single-alternative selection structure

```
Private Sub calcButton_Click(sender As Object, e As EventArgs
) Handles calcButton.Click
    ' calculates the area and/or perimeter

    Dim side As Double
    Dim answer As Double

    ' store input in a variable
    Double.TryParse(sideTextBox.Text, side)

    ' clear answerLabel
    answerLabel.Text = String.Empty

    ' perform calculation(s) and display answer(s)
    If areaCheckBox.Checked = True Then
        answer = side * side
        answerLabel.Text = "Area: " &
            answer.ToString("N1") & ControlChars.NewLine
    End If
    If perimeterCheckBox.Checked Then
        answer = side * 4
        answerLabel.Text = answerLabel.Text &
            "Perimeter: " & answer.ToString("N1")
    End If
End Sub
```

you can also use `If areaCheckBox.Checked`

you can also use `If perimeterCheckBox.Checked = True`

Figure 4-19 calcButton_Click procedure

The answers to Mini-Quiz questions are located in Appendix A. Each question is associated with one or more objectives listed at the beginning of the chapter.

Mini-Quiz 4-2

1. What is the scope of a variable declared in an If...Then...Else statement's False path? (3, 7)
   a. the entire application
   b. the procedure in which the If...Then...Else statement appears
   c. the entire If...Then...Else statement
   d. only the False path in the If...Then...Else statement

2. Which of the following determines whether the value contained in the `sales` variable is at least $450.67? (3, 4)
   a. `If sales >= 450.67 Then`
   b. `If sales <= 450.67 Then`
   c. `If sales > 450.67 Then`
   d. `If sales < 450.67 Then`

3. Which of the following concatenates the "Do they live in " message, the contents of the String `state` variable, and a question mark? (8)
   a. `"Do they live in " & state & "?"`
   b. `"Do they live in & state & ?"`
   c. `Do they live in & state & ?`
   d. `"Do they live in " # state # "?"`
4. Which of the following methods temporarily converts the string stored in the `item` variable to lowercase? (10)
   a. `item.Lower`
   b. `item.ToLower`
   c. `LowerCase(item)`
   d. `Lower(item)`
5. If a check box is selected, its ____________ property contains the Boolean value True. (11)
   a. Checked
   b. Checkbox
   c. Selected
   d. Selection

Logical Operators

As mentioned earlier, you can also include logical operators in an If...Then...Else statement's condition. **Logical operators** are used to combine two or more subconditions into one compound condition. The compound condition will always evaluate to a Boolean value: either True or False. You already are familiar with the concept of logical operators because you use logical operators—namely, *and* and *or*—in your daily conversations. Examples of this are shown in Figure 4-20.

Logical *and* and *or* examples
- If you finished your homework *and* you studied for tomorrow's exam, you can watch a movie.
- If your cell phone rings *and* (it's your spouse calling *or* it's your child calling), you should answer your phone.
- If you are driving your car *and* (it's raining *or* it's foggy *or* there is bug splatter on your windshield), you should turn on your car's wipers.

Figure 4-20 Examples of the English logical operators

The Visual Basic language provides six logical operators. The two most commonly used are listed in Figure 4-21 along with their order of precedence. The figure also contains examples of using the operators in an If...Then...Else statement's condition. Notice that the compound condition in each example evaluates to either True or False. Also notice that a complete expression appears on both sides of the logical operator.

HOW TO Use Logical Operators in a Condition

Logical operator	Operation	Precedence number
AndAlso	all subconditions must be true for the compound condition to evaluate to True	1
OrElse	only one of the subconditions needs to be true for the compound condition to evaluate to True	2

Example 1
```
Dim quantity As Integer
Integer.TryParse(quantityTextBox.Text, quantity)
If quantity > 0 AndAlso quantity < 50 Then
```
The compound condition evaluates to True when the number stored in the `quantity` variable is greater than 0 and, at the same time, less than 50; otherwise, it evaluates to False.

Example 2
```
Dim sales As Double
Double.TryParse(salesTextBox.Text, sales)
If bonusCheckBox.Checked AndAlso sales >= 500 Then
```
The compound condition evaluates to True when the bonusCheckBox is selected and, at the same time, the number stored in the `sales` variable is greater than or equal to 500; otherwise, it evaluates to False. (You can also write the first subcondition as `bonusCheckBox.Checked = True`.)

Example 3
```
Dim age As Integer
Integer.TryParse(ageTextBox.Text, age)
If age = 21 OrElse age > 55 Then
```
The compound condition evaluates to True when the number stored in the `age` variable is either equal to 21 or greater than 55; otherwise, it evaluates to False.

Example 4
```
Dim rating As Integer
Dim cost As Decimal
Integer.TryParse(ratingTextBox.Text, rating)
Decimal.TryParse(costTextBox.Text, cost)
If rating = 3 OrElse cost < 75.99D Then
```
The compound condition evaluates to True when either (or both) of the following is true: The number stored in the `rating` variable is 3 or the number stored in the `cost` variable is less than 75.99; otherwise, it evaluates to False.

Figure 4-21 How to use logical operators in a condition *(continues)*

(continued)

Example 5

```
Dim num As Integer
Dim state As String
Integer.TryParse(numTextBox.Text, num)
state = stateTextBox.Text.ToUpper
If state = "KY" OrElse num > 0 AndAlso num < 100 Then
```

The compound condition evaluates to True when either (or both) of the following is true: The `state` variable contains the string "KY" or the number stored in the `num` variable is between 0 and 100; otherwise, it evaluates to False. (The AndAlso operator is evaluated before the OrElse operator because it has a higher precedence.)

Figure 4-21 How to use logical operators in a condition

The tables shown in Figure 4-22, called **truth tables**, summarize how the computer evaluates expressions containing a logical operator. Notice that subcondition2 is not always evaluated. Because both subconditions combined with the **AndAlso operator** need to be True for the compound condition to be True, there is no need to evaluate subcondition2 when subcondition1 is False. Similarly, because only one of the subconditions combined with the **OrElse operator** needs to be True for the compound condition to be True, there is no need to evaluate subcondition2 when subcondition1 is True. The concept of evaluating subcondition2 based on the result of subcondition1 is referred to as **short-circuit evaluation**.

HOW TO Evaluate Expressions Containing a Logical Operator

Truth table for the AndAlso operator

subcondition1	subcondition2	subcondition1 AndAlso subcondition2
True	True	True
True	False	False
False	(not evaluated)	False

Truth table for the OrElse operator

subcondition1	subcondition2	subcondition1 OrElse subcondition2
True	(not evaluated)	True
False	True	True
False	False	False

Figure 4-22 How to evaluate expressions containing a logical operator

Using the Truth Tables

An application needs to display an employee's gross pay, given the number of hours worked and the hourly pay rate. The number of hours worked must be at least 0 but not more than 40. Before making the gross pay calculation, the calcButton_Click procedure should verify that the number of hours is within the expected range. Programmers refer to the process of verifying the input data as **data validation**. If the number of hours is valid, the procedure should calculate and display the gross pay; otherwise, it should display the "Incorrect number of hours" message. Figure 4-23 shows the problem specification and two partially completed If clauses that could be used to verify the number of hours. Missing from each If clause is the appropriate logical operator.

Problem specification
Create an application that displays an employee's weekly gross pay, given the number of hours worked and the hourly pay rate. The number of hours worked must be at least 0 but not more than 40. If the number of hours worked is not valid, the application should display the message "Incorrect number of hours".

If clause 1
```
If hours >= 0 ________ hours <= 40 Then
```

If clause 2
```
If hours < 0 ________ hours > 40 Then
```

Figure 4-23 Problem specification and partially completed If clauses

The first If clause contains two subconditions that determine whether the number of hours is *within* the expected range of 0 through 40. For the number of hours to be valid, both subconditions must be True at the same time. In other words, the number of hours must be greater than or equal to 0 and also less than or equal to 40. If both subconditions are not True, it means that the number of hours is *outside* the expected range. Which logical operator should you use to combine both subconditions into one compound condition? According to the truth tables shown in Figure 4-22, only the AndAlso operator evaluates the compound condition as True when both subconditions are True, while evaluating the compound condition as False when at least one of the subconditions is False. Therefore, the correct compound condition to use here is `hours >= 0 AndAlso hours <= 40`.

The second If clause in Figure 4-23 contains two subconditions that determine whether the number of hours is *outside* the expected range of 0 through 40. For the number of hours to be invalid, at least one of the subconditions must be True. In other words, the number of hours must be either less than 0 or greater than 40. If neither subcondition is True, it means that the number of hours is *within* the expected range. Which logical operator should you use to combine both subconditions into one compound condition? According to the truth tables, only the OrElse operator evaluates the compound condition as True when at least one of the subconditions is True, while evaluating the compound condition as False when both subconditions are False. Therefore, the correct compound condition to use here is `hours < 0 OrElse hours > 40`.

You can use either of the examples shown in Figure 4-24 to calculate and display the weekly gross pay. The compound condition is shaded in each example. Both examples produce the same result and simply represent two different ways of performing the same task. Figure 4-24 also includes two sample runs of the application: one using valid data and one using invalid data.

Example 1—using the AndAlso operator

```
Private Sub calcButton_Click(sender As Object, e As EventArgs
) Handles calcButton.Click
    ' calculates the gross pay

    Const RatePerHour As Double = 10.65
    Dim hours As Double
    Dim gross As Double

    Double.TryParse(hoursTextBox.Text, hours)
    If hours >= 0 AndAlso hours <= 40 Then
        gross = hours * RatePerHour
        grossLabel.Text = gross.ToString("C2")
    Else
        grossLabel.Text = "Incorrect number of hours"
    End If
End Sub
```

Example 2—using the OrElse operator

```
Private Sub calcButton_Click(sender As Object, e As EventArgs
) Handles calcButton.Click
    ' calculates the gross pay

    Const RatePerHour As Double = 10.65
    Dim hours As Double
    Dim gross As Double

    Double.TryParse(hoursTextBox.Text, hours)
    If hours < 0 OrElse hours > 40 Then
        grossLabel.Text = "Incorrect number of hours"
    Else
        gross = hours * RatePerHour
        grossLabel.Text = gross.ToString("C2")
    End If
End Sub
```

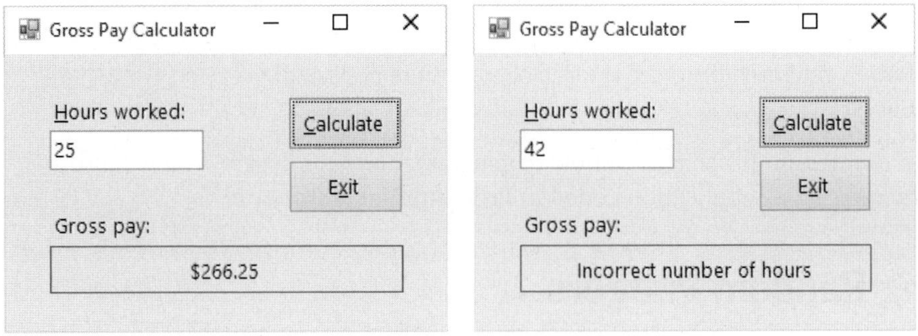

Gross Pay Calculator

Hours worked: 25

Calculate

Exit

Gross pay: $266.25

Gross Pay Calculator

Hours worked: 42

Calculate

Exit

Gross pay: Incorrect number of hours

Figure 4-24 calcButton_Click procedure and sample runs of the application

If you want to experiment with the Gross Pay Calculator application, open the solution contained in the Try It 7! folder.

Summary of Operators

Figure 4-25 shows the order of precedence for the arithmetic, concatenation, comparison, and logical operators you have learned so far. Recall that operators with the same precedence number are evaluated from left to right in an expression. Arithmetic operators are evaluated first, followed by the concatenation operator, comparison operators, and logical operators. As a result, the expression 12 > 0 AndAlso 12 < 10 * 2 evaluates to True, as shown in Figure 4-25. Keep in mind, however, that you can use parentheses to override the order of precedence.

Ch04-Operators

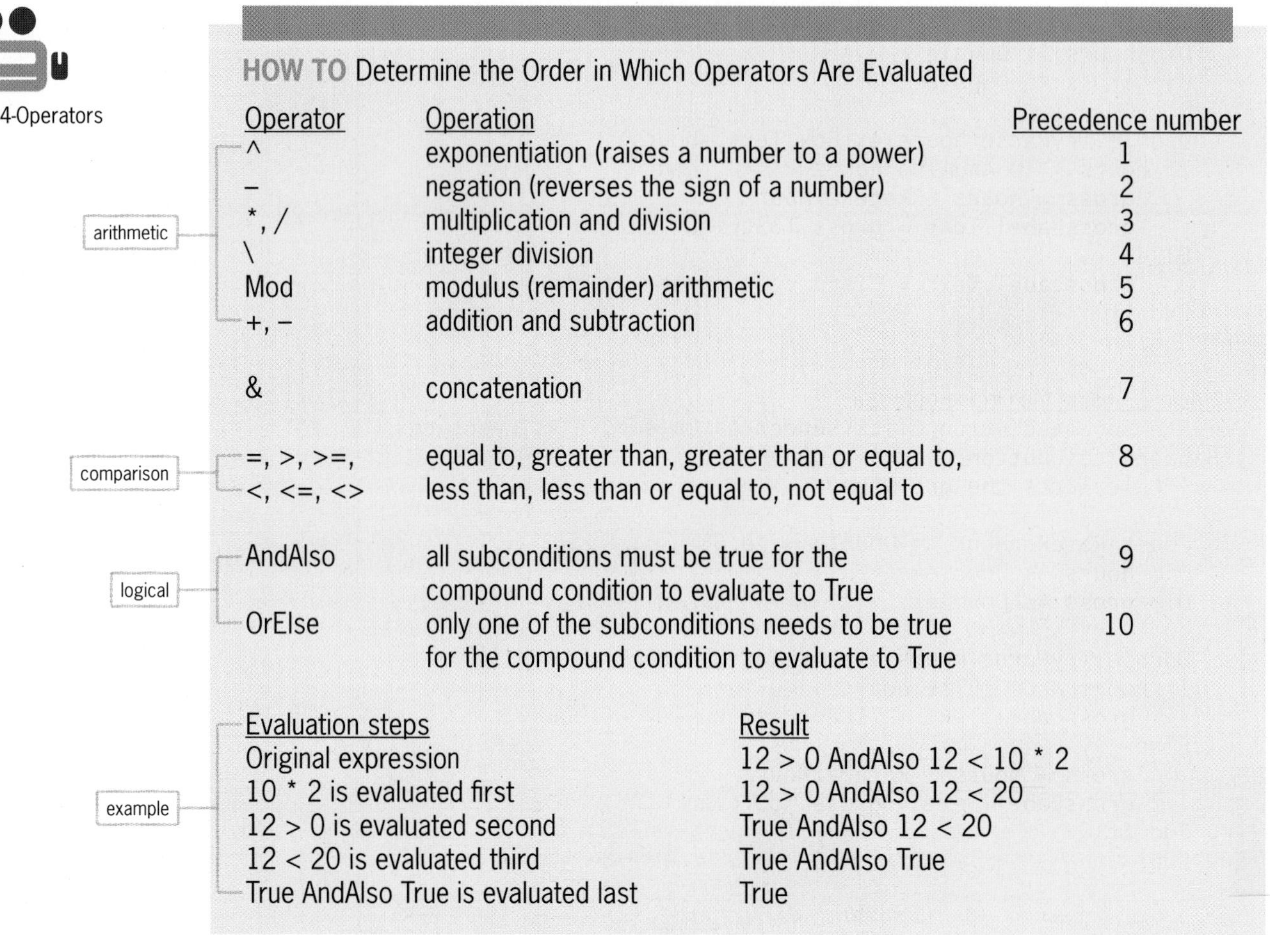

HOW TO Determine the Order in Which Operators Are Evaluated

	Operator	Operation	Precedence number
arithmetic	^	exponentiation (raises a number to a power)	1
	–	negation (reverses the sign of a number)	2
	*, /	multiplication and division	3
	\	integer division	4
	Mod	modulus (remainder) arithmetic	5
	+, –	addition and subtraction	6
	&	concatenation	7
comparison	=, >, >=, <, <=, <>	equal to, greater than, greater than or equal to, less than, less than or equal to, not equal to	8
logical	AndAlso	all subconditions must be true for the compound condition to evaluate to True	9
	OrElse	only one of the subconditions needs to be true for the compound condition to evaluate to True	10

	Evaluation steps	Result
example	Original expression	12 > 0 AndAlso 12 < 10 * 2
	10 * 2 is evaluated first	12 > 0 AndAlso 12 < 20
	12 > 0 is evaluated second	True AndAlso 12 < 20
	12 < 20 is evaluated third	True AndAlso True
	True AndAlso True is evaluated last	True

Figure 4-25 How to determine the order in which operators are evaluated

The last concept covered in this chapter is how to generate random integers. You will use random integers in the game application coded in Programming Tutorial 1.

Generating Random Integers

Many computer game programs use random numbers. The numbers can be integers or real numbers, which are numbers with a decimal place. In this section, you will learn how to generate random integers. If you want to learn how to generate random real numbers, refer to Computer Exercise 27 at the end of this chapter.

Most programming languages provide a **pseudo-random number generator**, which is a mathematical algorithm that produces a sequence of numbers that, although not completely random, are sufficiently random for practical purposes. The pseudo-random number generator in Visual Basic is represented by an object whose data type is Random.

Figure 4-26 shows the syntax for generating random integers in Visual Basic, and it includes examples of using the syntax. As the figure indicates, you first create a **Random object** to represent the pseudo-random number generator in your application's code. You create the Random object by declaring it in a Dim statement, which you enter in the procedure that will use the number generator. After the Random object is created, you can use the object's Random.Next method to generate random integers. In the method's syntax, *randomObjectName* is the name of the Random object. The *minValue* and *maxValue* arguments must be integers, and minValue must be less than maxValue. The **Random.Next method** returns an integer that is greater than or equal to minValue but less than maxValue.

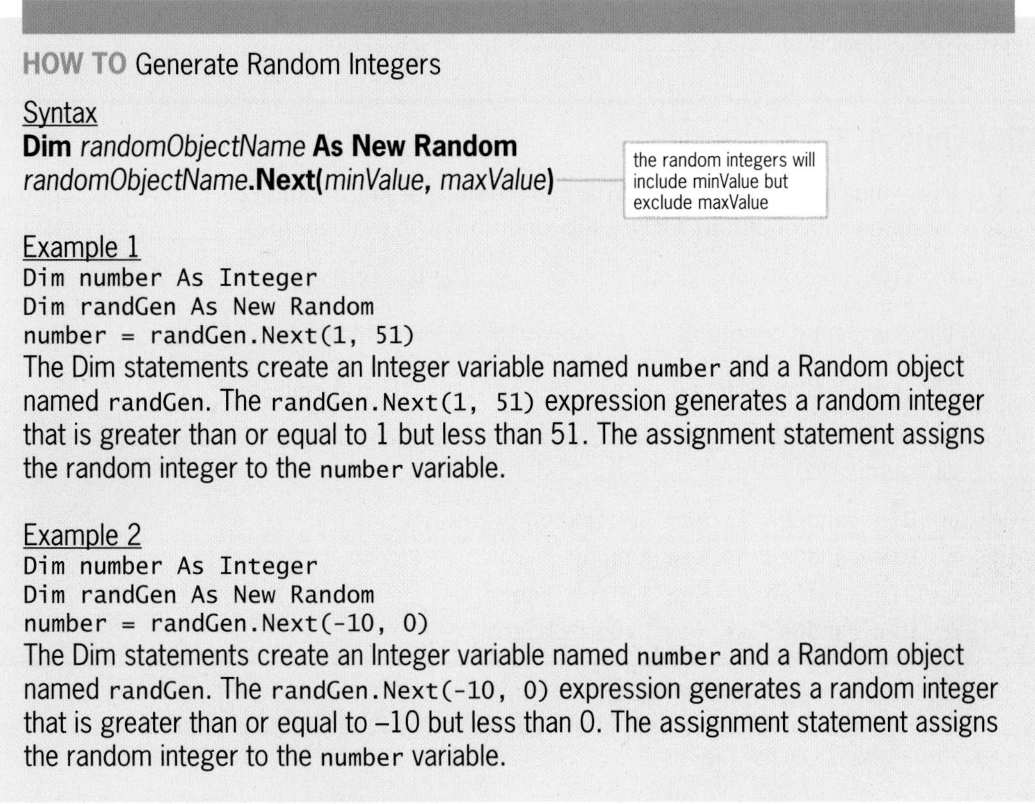

HOW TO Generate Random Integers

Syntax

Dim *randomObjectName* **As New Random**
randomObjectName.**Next(***minValue*, *maxValue***)**

the random integers will include minValue but exclude maxValue

Example 1

```
Dim number As Integer
Dim randGen As New Random
number = randGen.Next(1, 51)
```

The Dim statements create an Integer variable named `number` and a Random object named `randGen`. The `randGen.Next(1, 51)` expression generates a random integer that is greater than or equal to 1 but less than 51. The assignment statement assigns the random integer to the `number` variable.

Example 2

```
Dim number As Integer
Dim randGen As New Random
number = randGen.Next(-10, 0)
```

The Dim statements create an Integer variable named `number` and a Random object named `randGen`. The `randGen.Next(-10, 0)` expression generates a random integer that is greater than or equal to –10 but less than 0. The assignment statement assigns the random integer to the `number` variable.

Figure 4-26 How to generate random integers

Figure 4-27 shows a sample run of the Random Integer application. It also contains the code for the Generate Random Integer button's Click event procedure, which generates and displays a random number from 1 through 10.

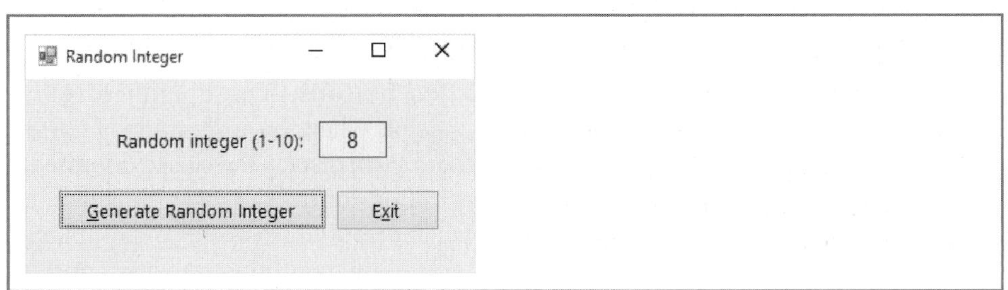

Figure 4-27 Sample run and code for the Random Integer application *(continues)*

If you want to experiment with the Random Integer application, open the solution contained in the Try It 8! folder.

(continued)

```
Private Sub generateButton_Click(sender As Object, e As EventArgs
) Handles generateButton.Click
    ' displays a random integer from 1 through 10

    Dim number As Integer
    Dim randGen As New Random

    number = randGen.Next(1, 11)
    randomLabel.Text = number.ToString
End Sub
```

Figure 4-27 Sample run and code for the Random Integer application

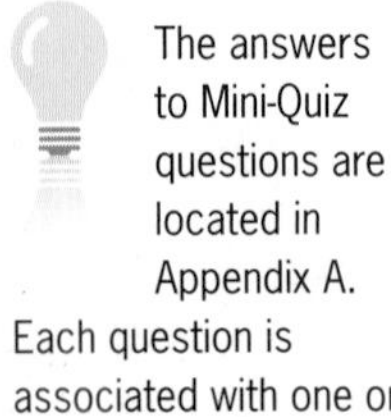

The answers to Mini-Quiz questions are located in Appendix A. Each question is associated with one or more objectives listed at the beginning of the chapter.

Mini-Quiz 4-3

1. If the value of subcondition1 is True and the value of subcondition2 is False, the compound condition subcondition1 OrElse subcondition2 will evaluate to ____________. (4)
   a. True
   b. False
2. The compound condition 7 > 3 AndAlso 5 < 2 will evaluate to ____________. (4)
3. The compound condition 3 + 4 * 2 > 12 AndAlso 4 < 15 will evaluate to ____________. (4)
4. Which of the following declares an object to represent the pseudo-random number generator? (12)
   a. `Dim randGen As New Generator`
   b. `Dim randGen As New Random`
   c. `Dim randGen As New RandomGenerator`
   d. `Dim randGen As New RandomObject`

You have completed the concepts section of Chapter 4. The Programming Tutorial section is next.

PROGRAMMING TUTORIAL 1

PROGRAMMING TUTORIAL 1

Creating the Find the Robot Application

In this tutorial, you will create the Find the Robot application. The application's TOE chart and MainForm are shown in Figures 4-28 and 4-29, respectively. The form's BackgroundImage property displays the image stored in the Room.png file, which is contained in the project's Resources folder. The form's BackgroundImageLayout property is set to Stretch.

The form contains six picture boxes, a label, and two buttons. The openPictureBox, robotPictureBox, and closedPictureBox controls will be invisible when the application is started. When the user clicks the Hide button, its Click event procedure will display the closed door image in the door1PictureBox, door2PictureBox, and door3PictureBox controls. It will also generate a random number from 1 through 3. The random number will indicate which of those three picture boxes will display the robot image when clicked. For example, if the random number is 1 and the user clicks the door1PictureBox, the robot image will appear in the picture box. However, if the user clicks the door2PictureBox, the open door image will appear in the picture box. The player's task is to find the robot, using as few guesses as possible.

Task	Object	Event
1. Generate a random integer from 1 through 3 2. Display the closed door image in door1PictureBox, door2PictureBox, and door3PictureBox	hideButton	Click
Use the random integer generated by the hideButton to display either the robot image or the open door image	door1PictureBox, door2PictureBox, door3PictureBox	Click
End the application	exitButton	Click
Store the closed door image	closedPictureBox	None
Store the open door image	openPictureBox	None
Store the robot image	robotPictureBox	None

Figure 4-28 TOE chart for the Find the Robot application

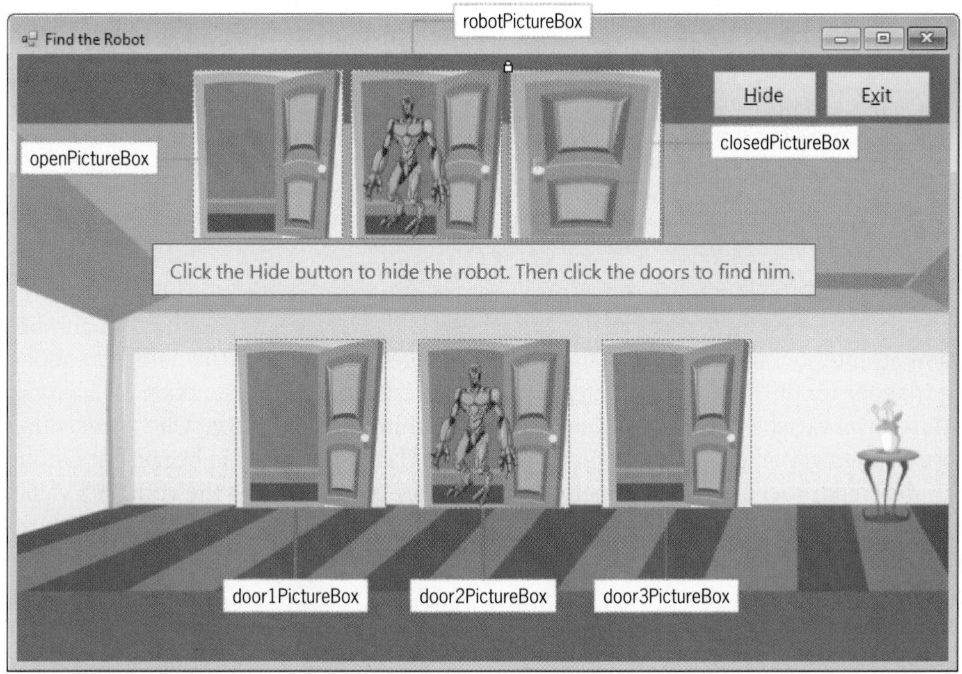

Figure 4-29 MainForm for the Find the Robot application
Image by Diane Zak; created with Reallusion CrazyTalk Animator

Coding the Find the Robot Application

According to the application's TOE chart, the Click event procedures for the hideButton, the exitButton, and three of the picture boxes need to be coded.

To begin coding the application:

1. Start Visual Studio. Open the **Robot Solution** (**Robot Solution.sln**) file contained in the VbReloaded2015\Chap04\Robot Solution folder. If necessary, open the designer window.
2. Open the Code Editor window. The exitButton's Click event procedure has already been coded for you. In the comments that appear in the General Declarations section, replace <your name> and <current date> with your name and the current date, respectively.
3. The application will use variables, so you should enter the appropriate Option statements in the General Declarations section. Click the **blank line** above the Public Class clause and then enter the following three statements:

   Option Explicit On
   Option Strict On
   Option Infer Off

The hideButton_Click procedure is responsible for generating a random integer from 1 through 3 and also displaying the closed door image in three of the picture boxes. Figure 4-30 shows the procedure's pseudocode.

```
hideButton Click event procedure
1. assign a random integer from 1 through 3 to a class-level Integer variable
2. assign the closed door image, which is contained in the closedPictureBox, to the
   door1PictureBox, door2PictureBox, and door3PictureBox controls
```

Figure 4-30 Pseudocode for the hideButton_Click procedure

The procedure will use two variables: a Random variable to represent the pseudo-random number generator and an Integer variable to store the random integer. You will use the names `randGen` and `randomInteger` for the Random and Integer variables, respectively. The `randGen` variable can be a procedure-level variable because it is needed only within the hideButton_Click procedure. The `randomInteger` variable, however, will need to be a class-level variable because it will be used by four different procedures: The hideButton_Click procedure will set the variable's value, and the door1PictureBox_Click, door2PictureBox_Click, and door3PictureBox_Click procedures will use the value to determine the appropriate image to display (either the robot image or the open door image).

To declare the class-level variable and then code the hideButton_Click procedure:

1. Click the **blank line** below the `' class-level variable` comment, and then enter the following Private statement:

   Private randomInteger As Integer

2. Locate the code template for the hideButton_Click procedure. Click the **blank line** above the End Sub clause. Type the following Dim statement and then press **Enter** twice:

   Dim randGen As New Random

3. The first step in the pseudocode assigns a random integer from 1 through 3 to the class-level variable. Enter the following comment and assignment statement:

```
' generate a random integer from 1 through 3
randomInteger = randGen.Next(1, 4)
```

4. The second step in the pseudocode assigns the image contained in the closedPictureBox to three picture boxes. Enter the following comment and assignment statements:

```
' display the closed door image
door1PictureBox.Image = closedPictureBox.Image
door2PictureBox.Image = closedPictureBox.Image
door3PictureBox.Image = closedPictureBox.Image
```

5. Save the solution.

According to the application's TOE chart, the door1PictureBox_Click procedure will use the random integer generated by the hideButton to display either the robot image or the closed door image in the picture box. The procedure's pseudocode is shown in Figure 4-31.

```
door1PictureBox Click event procedure
if the random integer generated by the hideButton is 1
    assign the image contained in the robotPictureBox to the door1PictureBox
else
    assign the image contained in the openPictureBox to the door1PictureBox
end if
```

Figure 4-31 Pseudocode for the door1PictureBox_Click procedure

To code the door1PictureBox_Click procedure:

1. Locate the code template for the door1PictureBox_Click procedure. Click the **blank line** above the End Sub clause, and then enter the following If...Then...Else statement. When you press Enter after typing the If clause, the Code Editor will automatically enter the End If clause for you.

```
If randomInteger = 1 Then
    door1PictureBox.Image = robotPictureBox.Image
Else
    door1PictureBox.Image = openPictureBox.Image
End If
```

2. Save the solution.

The door2PictureBox_Click and door3PictureBox_Click procedures will be almost identical to the door1PictureBox_Click procedure. The only exception is that the door2PictureBox_Click procedure will display the robot image in the door2PictureBox when the random integer is 2. Similarly, the door3PictureBox_Click procedure will display the robot image in the door3PictureBox when the random integer is 3.

To finish coding the application and then test it:

1. Copy the If...Then...Else statement from the door1PictureBox_Click procedure to the door2PictureBox_Click and door3PictureBox_Click procedures.

2. In the door2PictureBox_Click procedure, change the number 1 in the If...Then...Else statement's condition to **2**. Also change door1PictureBox in the statement's True and False paths to **door2PictureBox**.

3. On your own, make the appropriate modifications to the door3PictureBox_Click procedure.
4. Save the solution and then start the application. Click the **Hide** button. The closed door image appears in the three visible picture boxes, as shown in Figure 4-32.

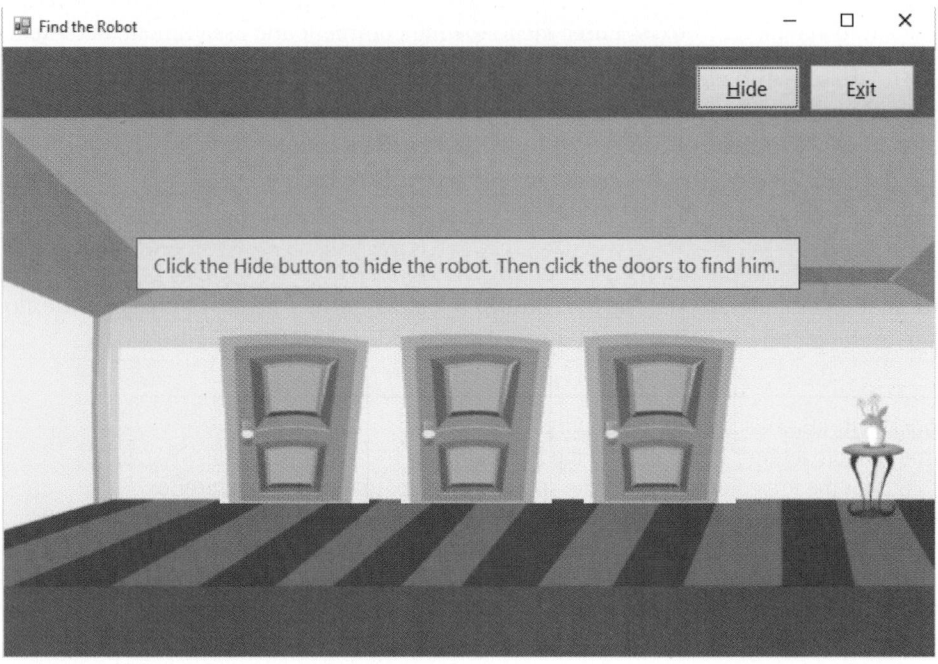

Figure 4-32 Result of clicking the Hide button
Image by Diane Zak; created with Reallusion CrazyTalk Animator

5. Click **one of the closed doors**. Either the robot image or the open door image appears.
6. Click **each of the remaining two doors**. Figure 4-33 shows a sample run of the application after all three doors were clicked. Because the application uses a random number, the robot image may be in a different location on your screen.

Figure 4-33 Sample run of the Find the Robot application
Image by Diane Zak; created with Reallusion CrazyTalk Animator

7. Click the **Hide** button. The closed door image appears in the three visible picture boxes. Try to find the robot again.

8. Click the **Exit** button. Close the Code Editor window and then close the solution. Figure 4-34 shows the application's code.

```
' Project name:       Robot Project
' Project purpose:    Guess where a robot is hiding
' Created/revised by: <your name> on <current date>

Option Explicit On
Option Strict On
Option Infer Off

Public Class MainForm

    ' class-level variable
    Private randomInteger As Integer

    Private Sub exitButton_Click(sender As Object,
    e As EventArgs) Handles exitButton.Click
        Me.Close()
    End Sub

    Private Sub hideButton_Click(sender As Object, e As EventArgs
    ) Handles hideButton.Click
        ' prepares the interface

        Dim randGen As New Random

```

Figure 4-34 Find the Robot application's code *(continues)*

(continued)

```
        ' generate a random integer from 1 through 3
        randomInteger = randGen.Next(1, 4)
        ' display the closed door image
        door1PictureBox.Image = closedPictureBox.Image
        door2PictureBox.Image = closedPictureBox.Image
        door3PictureBox.Image = closedPictureBox.Image

    End Sub

    Private Sub door1PictureBox_Click(sender As Object,
    e As EventArgs) Handles door1PictureBox.Click
        ' displays the appropriate image

        If randomInteger = 1 Then
            door1PictureBox.Image = robotPictureBox.Image
        Else
            door1PictureBox.Image = openPictureBox.Image
        End If
    End Sub

    Private Sub door2PictureBox_Click(sender As Object,
    e As EventArgs) Handles door2PictureBox.Click
        ' displays the appropriate image

        If randomInteger = 2 Then
            door2PictureBox.Image = robotPictureBox.Image
        Else
            door2PictureBox.Image = openPictureBox.Image
        End If
    End Sub

    Private Sub door3PictureBox_Click(sender As Object,
    e As EventArgs) Handles door3PictureBox.Click
        ' displays the appropriate image

        If randomInteger = 3 Then
            door3PictureBox.Image = robotPictureBox.Image
        Else
            door3PictureBox.Image = openPictureBox.Image
        End If
    End Sub
End Class
```

Figure 4-34 Find the Robot application's code

PROGRAMMING TUTORIAL 2

Coding the Bubbles Car Wash Application

In this tutorial, you will code the Bubbles Car Wash application, which calculates and displays the total cost of a car wash. The interface provides a text box for entering the basic fee. It also provides check boxes for specifying whether the customer wants one or both of the additional services: tire shine (for $2.50) or hand dry (for $3.50). The application's TOE chart and MainForm are shown in Figures 4-35 and 4-36, respectively. The MainForm contains three labels, one text box, two check boxes, two buttons, and a picture box.

Task	Object	Event
Get and display the basic fee	basicTextBox	None
Specify whether the customer wants additional services	tireCheckBox, handDryCheckBox	None
1. Calculate the total cost, which includes the basic fee and optional additional charges for tire shine and hand dry 2. Display the total cost in the costLabel	calcButton	Click
End the application	exitButton	Click
Display the total cost (from calcButton)	costLabel	None

Figure 4-35 TOE chart for the Bubbles Car Wash application

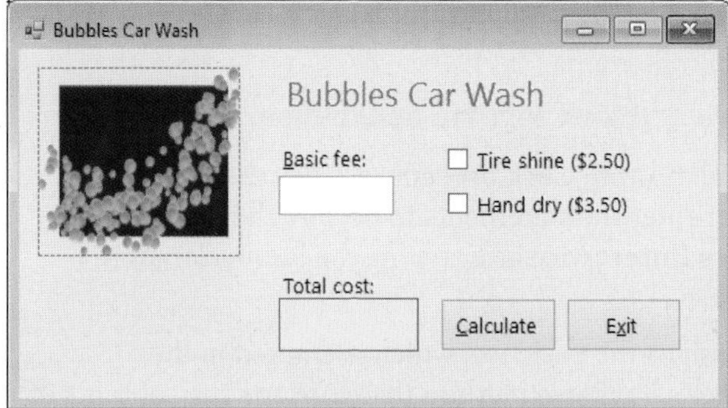

Figure 4-36 MainForm for the Bubbles Car Wash application

Coding the Bubbles Car Wash Application

According to the application's TOE chart, the Click event procedures for the calcButton and exitButton need to be coded.

To begin coding the application:

1. Start Visual Studio. Open the **Bubbles Solution** (**Bubbles Solution.sln**) file contained in the VbReloaded2015\Chap04\Bubbles Solution folder. If necessary, open the designer window.
2. Open the Code Editor window. The exitButton's Click event procedure has already been coded for you. In the comments that appear in the General Declarations section, replace <your name> and <current date> with your name and the current date, respectively.
3. Enter the appropriate Option statements in the General Declarations section.

The calcButton_Click procedure is responsible for calculating and displaying the total cost. Figure 4-37 shows the procedure's pseudocode along with the memory locations it requires.

calcButton Click event procedure
1. assign the basic fee, which is entered in the basicTextBox, as the total cost
2. if the Tire shine box is selected
      add the additional tire shine charge to the total cost
   end if
3. if the Hand dry check box is selected
      add the additional hand dry charge to the total cost
   end if
4. display the total cost in the costLabel

Named constants	Data type	Value
`TireShine`	Double	2.5
`HandDry`	Double	3.5

Variable	Data type	Value source
`totalCost`	Double	user input (basicTextBox) and procedure calculation

Figure 4-37 Pseudocode and memory locations for the calcButton_Click procedure

To code the calcButton_Click procedure and then test the application:

1. Locate the code template for the calcButton_Click procedure. Click the **blank line** above the End Sub clause, and then enter the statements to declare the three memory locations listed in Figure 4-37. Press **Enter** twice after typing the last declaration statement.
2. The first step in the pseudocode assigns the basic fee, which is entered in the basicTextBox, as the total cost. Enter a TryParse method that converts the contents of the text box to Double and then stores the result in the `totalCost` variable.
3. The second step in the pseudocode is a single-alternative selection structure that determines whether the Tire shine check box is selected. If it is selected, the selection structure's True path should add the tire shine charge to the total cost. Type **' add any additional charges to the total cost** and press **Enter**. Now enter the appropriate If...Then...Else statement.
4. Step 3 in the pseudocode is another single-alternative selection structure. This selection structure determines whether the Hand dry check box is selected. If it is selected, the selection structure's True path should add the applicable charge to the total cost. Insert a **blank line** between the End If clause and the End Sub clause, and then enter the appropriate If...Then...Else statement.
5. The last step in the pseudocode displays the total cost in the costLabel. Insert **a blank line** above the End Sub clause, and then enter the assignment statement to display the total cost formatted with a dollar sign and two decimal places.
6. Save the solution and then start the application. Type **9** in the Basic fee box and then click the **Tire shine** check box. Click the **Calculate** button. $11.50 appears in the Total cost box, as shown in Figure 4-38.

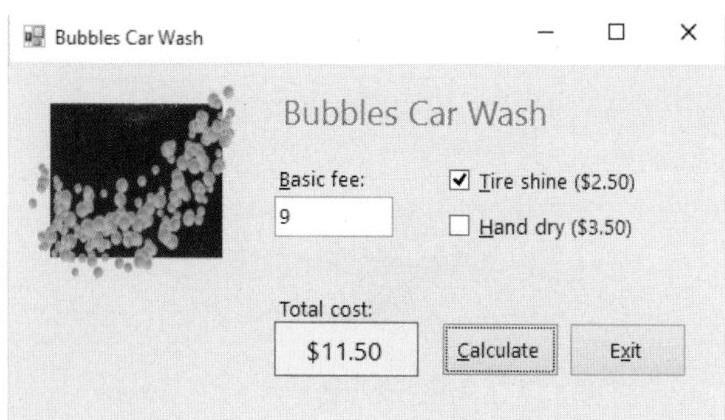

Figure 4-38 Sample run of the application

7. Click the **Hand dry** check box and then click the **Calculate** button. The total cost is now $15.00.
8. Click the **Tire shine** check box to deselect it, and then click the **Calculate** button. The total cost is now $12.50.
9. Click the **Hand dry** check box to deselect it, and then click the **Calculate** button. The total cost is now $9.00.
10. Click the **Exit** button to end the application. Close the Code Editor window and then close the solution.

Figure 4-39 shows the Bubbles Car Wash application's code. (You can also write the assignment statements in Lines 20 and 23 as `totalCost = totalCost + TireShine` and `totalCost = totalCost + HandDry`, respectively. You can also write the If clauses in Lines 19 and 22 as `If tireCheckBox.Checked = True Then` and `If handDryCheckBox.Checked = True Then`, respectively.)

```
 1 ' Project name:          Bubbles Project
 2 ' Project purpose:       Display the total cost of a car wash
 3 ' Created/revised by:    <your name> on <current date>
 4
 5 Option Explicit On
 6 Option Strict On
 7 Option Infer Off
 8
 9 Public Class MainForm
10     Private Sub calcButton_Click(sender As Object, e As EventArgs
       ) Handles calcButton.Click
11         ' calculates the cost of a car wash
12
13         Const TireShine As Double = 2.5
14         Const HandDry As Double = 3.5
15         Dim totalCost As Double
16
17         Double.TryParse(basicTextBox.Text, totalCost)
18         ' add any additional charges to the total cost
19         If tireCheckBox.Checked Then
20             totalCost += TireShine
```

Figure 4-39 Bubbles Car Wash application's code *(continues)*

(continued)

```
        End If
        If handDryCheckBox.Checked Then
            totalCost += HandDry
        End If
        costLabel.Text = totalCost.ToString("C2")

    End Sub

    Private Sub exitButton_Click(sender As Object, e As EventArgs
    ) Handles exitButton.Click
        Me.Close()
    End Sub
End Class
```

Figure 4-39 Bubbles Car Wash application's code

PROGRAMMING EXAMPLE

Edwards and Son Application

Create an interface that allows the user to enter a company's sales revenue and expenses. The interface will need to display either the company's net income (using a black font) or its net loss (using a red font). It should also display one of two messages: either "The company made a profit of *x*." or "The company experienced a loss of *x*." In both messages, *x* represents the amount of the company's profit or loss. Use the following names for the solution and project, respectively: Edwards Solution and Edwards Project. Save the application in the VbReloaded2015\Chap04 folder. Change the form file's name to Main Form.vb. See Figures 4-40 through 4-45. The image in the picture box in Figure 4-41 is stored in the VbReloaded2015\Chap04\EdwardsAndSon.png file.

Task	Object	Event
Get and display the revenue and expenses	revenueTextBox, expensesTextBox	None
1. Calculate the net income/loss 2. Display the net income (using a black font) or the net loss (using a red font) in the netLabel 3. Display an appropriate message in the messageLabel	calcButton	Click
End the application	exitButton	Click
Display the net income or net loss (from calcButton)	netLabel	None
Display the message (from calcButton)	messageLabel	None

Figure 4-40 TOE chart

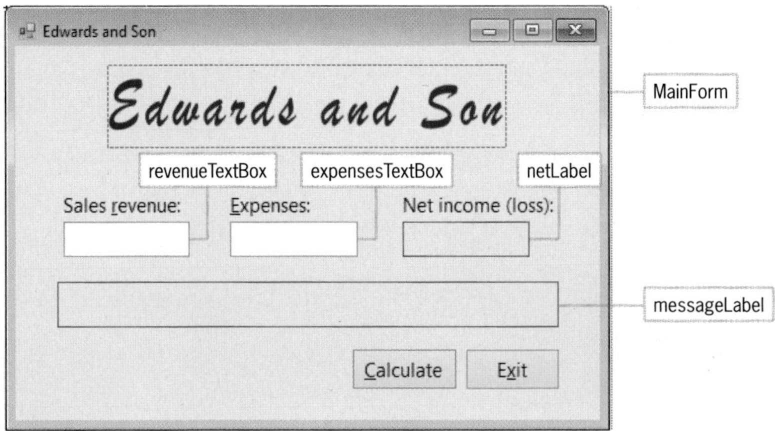

Figure 4-41 User interface

Object	Property	Setting
MainForm	AcceptButton	calcButton
	Font	Segoe UI, 11pt
	StartPosition	CenterScreen
	Text	Edwards and Son
netLabel	AutoSize	False
	BorderStyle	FixedSingle
	Text	(empty)
	TextAlign	MiddleCenter
messageLabel	AutoSize	False
	BorderStyle	FixedSingle
	Text	(empty)
	TextAlign	MiddleCenter

Figure 4-42 Objects, properties, and settings

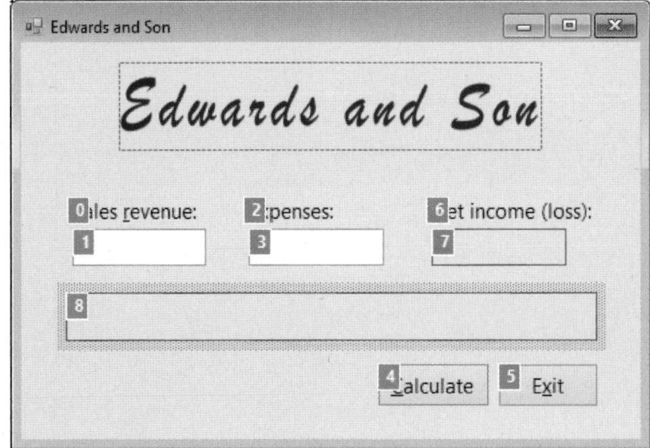

Figure 4-43 Tab order

```
calcButton Click event procedure
1. assign user input (revenue and expenses) to variables
2. calculate net = revenue – expenses
3. if net is less than 0
       display loss message and net in messageLabel
       change netLabel's font color to red
   else
       display profit message and net in messageLabel
       change netLabel's font color to black
   end if
4. display net in netLabel
```

Named constants	Data type	Value
`ProfitMsg`	String	"The company made a profit of "
`LossMsg`	String	"The company experienced a loss of "

Variables	Data type	Value source
`revenue`	Decimal	user input (revenueTextBox)
`expenses`	Decimal	user input (expensesTextBox)
`net`	Decimal	procedure calculation

Figure 4-44 Pseudocode and memory locations

```
' Project name:          Edwards Project
' Project purpose:       Display the net income or net loss
' Created/revised by:    <your name> on <current date>

Option Explicit On
Option Infer Off
Option Strict On

Public Class MainForm

  Private Sub exitButton_Click(sender As Object, e As EventArgs
  ) Handles exitButton.Click
      Me.Close()
  End Sub

  Private Sub calcButton_Click(sender As Object, e As EventArgs
  ) Handles calcButton.Click
      ' calculates and displays the annual net income

      Const ProfitMsg As String = "The company made a profit of "
      Const LossMsg As String = "The company experienced a loss of "
      Dim revenue As Decimal
      Dim expenses As Decimal
      Dim net As Decimal

      ' assign input to variables
      Decimal.TryParse(revenueTextBox.Text, revenue)
      Decimal.TryParse(expensesTextBox.Text, expenses)

```

Figure 4-45 Code *(continues)*

(continued)

```
        ' calculate net
        net = revenue - expenses

        ' display net using appropriate color
        If net < 0 Then
           messageLabel.Text = LossMsg & (-net).ToString("C2") & "."
           netLabel.ForeColor = Color.Red
        Else
           messageLabel.Text = ProfitMsg & net.ToString("C2") & "."
           netLabel.ForeColor = Color.Black
        End If
        netLabel.Text = net.ToString("C2")
     End Sub
  End Class
```

be sure to enter the negation operator

Figure 4-45 Code

Chapter Summary

- The selection structure allows a procedure to make a decision (based on some condition) and then take the appropriate action.
- There are three types of selection structures: single-alternative, dual-alternative, and multiple-alternative.
- The condition in a selection structure must evaluate to a Boolean value: either True or False. In a single-alternative selection structure, a specific set of tasks is performed *only* when the condition evaluates to True. In a dual-alternative selection structure, one set of tasks is performed when the condition evaluates to True, but a different set of tasks is performed when it evaluates to False.
- A selection structure's condition is represented in a flowchart by a diamond, which is called the decision symbol. The decision symbol has one flowline entering the symbol, and two flowlines (marked with a T and an F) leaving the symbol.
- Visual Basic provides the If...Then...Else statement for coding single-alternative and dual-alternative selection structures.
- All expressions containing a comparison operator evaluate to a Boolean value: either True or False.
- Comparison operators do not have an order of precedence in Visual Basic. If an expression contains more than one comparison operator, the comparison operators are evaluated from left to right. Comparison operators are evaluated after any arithmetic and concatenation operators in an expression.
- Variables declared in a statement block (for example, in the True or False path of a selection structure) have block scope and are referred to as block-level variables. A block-level variable can be used only within the statement block in which it is defined and only after its declaration statement.

- You connect (or link) strings together using the concatenation operator, which is the ampersand (&).
- The `ControlChars.NewLine` constant advances the insertion point to the next line in a control.
- String comparisons in Visual Basic are case sensitive. When comparing strings, you can use either the ToUpper method or the ToLower method to temporarily convert the strings to uppercase or lowercase, respectively.
- Check boxes provide the user with one or more independent and nonexclusive items from which to choose. The value in a check box's Checked property indicates whether the check box is selected (True) or unselected (False).
- Logical operators are used to combine two or more subconditions into one compound condition. The compound condition always evaluates to a Boolean value: either True or False.
- The AndAlso logical operator is evaluated before the OrElse logical operator in an expression.
- Logical operators are evaluated after any arithmetic, concatenation, and comparison operators in an expression.
- You use the pseudo-random number generator in Visual Basic to generate random numbers. The pseudo-random number generator is an object whose data type is Random.

Key Terms

&—the concatenation operator in Visual Basic

AndAlso operator—one of the logical operators in Visual Basic; when used to combine two subconditions, the resulting compound condition evaluates to True only when both subconditions evaluate to True

Block scope—the scope of a variable declared within a statement block; a variable with block scope can be used only within the statement block in which it is declared and only after its declaration statement

Block-level variable—a variable declared within a statement block; the variable has block scope

CharacterCasing property—indicates whether the case of the text in a text box should remain as typed or be converted to either uppercase or lowercase as the user is typing

Check boxes—used in an interface to provide one or more independent and nonexclusive choices

Comparison operators—used to compare values in an expression; also called relational operators

Concatenation operator—the ampersand (&); used to concatenate strings; must be both preceded and followed by a space character

Condition—specifies the decision that must be made before further processing can occur; must be phrased so that it evaluates to a Boolean value (either True or False)

ControlChars.NewLine constant—used to advance the insertion point to the next line in a control

Data validation—the process of verifying that a program's input data is within the expected range

Decision symbol—the diamond in a flowchart; used to represent the condition in selection and repetition structures

Dual-alternative selection structure—a selection structure that requires the computer to follow one set of instructions when the structure's condition evaluates to True but a different set of instructions when it evaluates to False

False path—contains the instructions to be processed when a selection structure's condition evaluates to False

If...Then...Else statement—used to code single-alternative and dual-alternative selection structures in Visual Basic

Logical operators—used to combine two or more subconditions into one compound condition

OrElse operator—one of the logical operators in Visual Basic; when used to combine two subconditions, the resulting compound condition evaluates to False only when both subconditions evaluate to False

Pseudo-random number generator—a mathematical algorithm that produces a sequence of numbers that meet certain statistical requirements for randomness; the pseudo-random number generator in Visual Basic is an object whose data type is Random

Random object—represents the pseudo-random number generator in Visual Basic

Random.Next method—used to generate a random integer that is greater than or equal to a minimum value but less than a maximum value

Selection structure—one of the three basic control structures; tells the computer to make a decision based on some condition and then select the appropriate action; also called the decision structure

Short-circuit evaluation—refers to the way the computer evaluates the second of two subconditions connected by a logical operator; when the logical operator is AndAlso, the computer does not evaluate subcondition2 when subcondition1 evaluates to False; when the logical operator is OrElse, the computer does not evaluate subcondition2 when subcondition1 evaluates to True

Single-alternative selection structure—a selection structure that requires the computer to follow a special set of instructions *only* when the structure's condition evaluates to True

Statement block—in a selection structure, the set of statements terminated by either an Else clause or an End If clause

ToLower method—temporarily converts a string to lowercase

ToUpper method—temporarily converts a string to uppercase

True path—contains the instructions to be processed when a selection structure's condition evaluates to True

Truth tables—tables that summarize how the computer evaluates the logical operators in an expression

Review Questions

Each Review Question is associated with one or more objectives listed at the beginning of the chapter.

1. Which of the following is a valid condition for an If...Then...Else statement? (3, 4, 10)
   a. `priceLabel.Text > 0 AndAlso priceLabel.Text < 10`
   b. `age > 30 OrElse < 50`
   c. `number > 100 AndAlso number <= 1000`
   d. `state.ToUpper = "Alaska" OrElse state.ToUpper = "Hawaii"`
2. Which of the following conditions should you use to compare the contents of the firstTextBox with the name Joe? Be sure the condition will handle Joe, JOE, joe, and so on. (3, 4, 10)
   a. `firstTextBox.Text = ToUpper("JOE")`
   b. `firstTextBox.Text = ToUpper("Joe")`
   c. `ToUpper(firstTextBox.Text) = "JOE"`
   d. `firstTextBox.Text.ToUpper = "JOE"`
3. The expression 3 < 6 AndAlso 7 > 4 evaluates to ____________. (4)
   a. True
   b. False
4. The computer will perform short-circuit evaluation when processing which of the following If clauses? (3, 4)
   a. `If 3 * 2 < 4 AndAlso 5 > 3 Then`
   b. `If 6 < 9 OrElse 5 > 3 Then`
   c. `If 12 > 4 * 4 AndAlso 6 < 2 Then`
   d. all of the above
5. The expression 7 >= 3 + 4 AndAlso 6 < 4 OrElse 2 < 5 evaluates to ____________. (4)
   a. True
   b. False
6. The expression 5 * 3 > 3 ^ 2 AndAlso True OrElse False evaluates to ____________. (4)
   a. True
   b. False
7. Which of the following generates a random integer from 10 to 55, inclusive? The Random object is named `randGen`. (12)
   a. `randGen.Next(10, 56)`
   b. `randGen.Next(10, 55)`
   c. `randGen.Next(9, 55)`
   d. `randGen.Next(9, 56)`
8. The `city` and `state` variables contain the strings "Boston" and "MA", respectively. Which of the following will display the string "Boston, MA" (the city, a comma, a space, and the state) in the addressLabel? (8)
   a. `addressLabel.Text = "city" & ", " & "state"`
   b. `addressLabel.Text = city $ ", " $ state`
   c. `addressLabel.Text = city & ", " & state`
   d. `addressLabel.Text = "city," & "state"`

9. A procedure contains an If...Then...Else statement. If the `x` variable is declared immediately after the statement's Else clause, where can the variable be used? (3, 7)
   a. in any instruction in the entire procedure
   b. in any instruction after the declaration statement in the procedure
   c. in any instruction in the False path
   d. in any instruction in the If...Then...Else statement
10. Which of the following conditions evaluates to True when the `initial` variable contains the letter A in either uppercase or lowercase? (4)
    a. `initial = "A" OrElse initial = "a"`
    b. `initial = "A" AndAlso initial = "a"`
    c. `initial = "A" OrElse "a"`
    d. `initial = "A" AndAlso "a"`

Each Exercise, except the DISCOVERY Exercise, is associated with one or more objectives listed at the beginning of the chapter.

Exercises

Pencil and Paper

INTRODUCTORY

1. Draw the flowchart that corresponds to the pseudocode shown in Figure 4-46. (1, 3, 4)

```
if the years employed are less than or equal to 2
   display "1 week vacation"
else
   display "2 weeks vacation"
end if
```

Figure 4-46 Pseudocode for Pencil and Paper Exercise 1

INTRODUCTORY

2. Write the If...Then...Else statement that corresponds to the partial flowchart shown in Figure 4-47. Use the following variable names: `sold` and `bonus`. Display the appropriate message and bonus amount (formatted with a dollar sign and two decimal places) in the messageLabel. (1, 3, 4)

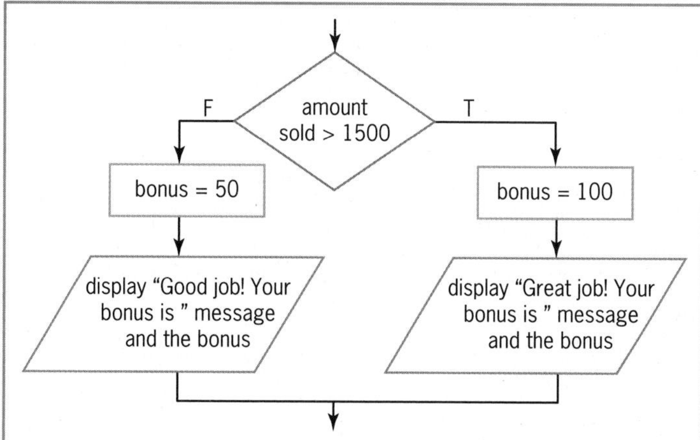

Figure 4-47 Partial flowchart

INTRODUCTORY

3. Write an If...Then...Else statement that displays the string "Fusion" in the carLabel when the carTextBox contains the string "Ford" (entered using any case). (3, 4, 10)

INTRODUCTORY

4. Write an If...Then...Else statement that displays the string "Reorder" in the messageLabel when the `quantity` variable's value is less than 25; otherwise, display the string "Sufficient quantity". (3, 4)

INTRODUCTORY

5. Write an If...Then...Else statement that assigns the number 0.05 to the `commissionRate` variable when the `sales` variable's value is less than or equal to $7000; otherwise, assign the number 0.23. (3, 4)

INTRODUCTORY

6. Write an If...Then...Else statement that assigns the number 100 to the `shipping` variable when the `state` variable contains either the string "Alaska" or the string "Hawaii" (both entered using any case); otherwise, assign the number 20. (3, 4, 10)

INTRODUCTORY

7. Write an If...Then...Else statement that assigns the number 50 to the `reward` variable when the `state` variable contains the string "FL" (entered using any case) and (at the same time) the `sales` variable contains a number that is greater than 2000; otherwise, assign the number 20. (3, 4, 10)

INTRODUCTORY

8. Write an If...Then...Else statement that displays the string "Winner" in the messageLabel when the `status` variable contains either the uppercase letter X or the uppercase letter Y. (3, 4, 10)

INTERMEDIATE

9. Write an If...Then...Else statement that displays the string "Please enter your name." in the messageLabel when the nameTextBox is empty. (3, 4)

INTERMEDIATE

10. Write an If...Then...Else statement that calculates a 5% sales tax when the `code` variable contains the string "3" and calculates a 4.5% sales tax when the `code` variable contains anything other than "3". Calculate the sales tax by multiplying the tax rate by the contents of the Double `sales` variable. Assign the sales tax to the Double `tax` variable. Also write the code to display the sales tax (formatted with a dollar sign and two decimal places) in the taxLabel. (3, 4)

Computer

MODIFY THIS

11. If necessary, complete the Bubbles Car Wash application from this chapter's Programming Tutorial 2, and then close the solution. Use Windows to make a copy of the Bubbles Solution folder. Rename the folder Bubbles Solution-ModifyThis. Open the Bubbles Solution (Bubbles Solution.sln) file contained in the Bubbles Solution-ModifyThis folder. Include an Undercarriage check box in the interface. The additional charge for an undercarriage wash is $5. Modify the application's code. Save the solution and then start and test the application. Close the solution. (3, 4, 11)

MODIFY THIS

12. Open the Square Solution (Square Solution.sln) file contained in the VbReloaded2015\Chap04\Square Solution folder. Change the formulaTextBox's CharacterCasing property to Upper. Open the Code Editor window and remove the ToUpper method from the assignment statement. Save the solution and then start and test the application. Close the solution. (10)

MODIFY THIS

13. Open the Random Swap Solution (Random Swap Solution.sln) file contained in the VbReloaded2015\Chap04\Random Swap Solution folder. The application should generate two random integers from 1 through 250 and then display the lowest and

highest integer in the interface. Draw the flowchart for the generateButton_Click procedure and then code the procedure. Save the solution and then start and test the application. Close the solution. (1–4, 6, 7, 12)

14. Open the Commission Solution (Commission Solution.sln) file contained in the VbReloaded2015\Chap04\Commission Solution folder. The application should calculate and display a salesperson's commission. The commission rate is 20% when the sales amount is at least $25,000; otherwise, the commission rate is 15%. Display the commission with a dollar sign and two decimal places. Write the pseudocode for the calcButton_Click procedure and then code the procedure. Save the solution and then start and test the application. Close the solution. (1–4) INTRODUCTORY

15. Open the Mount Rushmore Solution (Mount Rushmore Solution.sln) file contained in the VbReloaded2015\Chap04\Mount Rushmore Solution folder. The Display (AndAlso) and Display (OrElse) buttons should display the message "On Mount Rushmore" when the user enters the name of any of the four Mount Rushmore presidents; otherwise, they should display the message "Not on Mount Rushmore". The application should allow the user to enter the name using any combination of lowercase and uppercase letters. Use the AndAlso operator in the Display (AndAlso) button's Click event procedure. Use the OrElse operator in the Display (OrElse) button's Click event procedure. Save the solution and then start and test the application. Close the solution. (2–4, 10) INTRODUCTORY

16. Open the Computer Workshop Solution (Computer Workshop Solution.sln) file contained in the VbReloaded2015\Chap04\Computer Workshop Solution folder. Computer Workshop offers programming seminars to companies. The price per person depends on the number of people the company registers. The price for the first 10 registrants is $80 per person; thereafter, it is $70 per person. Display the total cost (formatted with a dollar sign and no decimal places) in the totalLabel. (Hint: If the company registers seven people, the total cost is $560. If the company registers 12 people, the total cost is $940.) Code the application. Save the solution and then start and test the application. Close the solution. (2–4) INTERMEDIATE

17. Open the Carley Solution (Carley Solution.sln) file contained in the VbReloaded2015\Chap04\Carley Solution folder. The application should display the amount of commission a salesperson earns for selling a car. The salesperson is paid 25% of the profit from the sale. The profit, which should be a positive number, is calculated by subtracting the dealer's costs from the selling price. However, in cases where the difference between the selling price and the dealer's costs is either 0 or less than 0, the salesperson is not paid a commission on the sale. Code the application. Save the solution and then start and test the application. Close the solution. (2–4) INTERMEDIATE

18. Tea Time Company wants an application that allows a clerk to enter the number of pounds of tea ordered. The price per pound is $11.25. Use a check box to specify whether the customer should receive a 10% discount on his or her purchase. Also use a check box to specify whether the customer should be charged a $5 shipping fee. The application should calculate and display the total amount the customer owes. Create a Windows Forms application. Use the following names for the solution and project, respectively: Tea Time Solution and Tea Time Project. Save the application in the VbReloaded2015\Chap04 folder. Change the form file's name to Main Form.vb. Code the application. Save the solution and then start and test the application. Close the Code Editor window and then close the solution. (1–4, 11) INTERMEDIATE

INTERMEDIATE

19. Create an application that generates and displays six lottery numbers. Each lottery number can range from 1 through 54 only. (An example of six lottery numbers would be: 4, 8, 35, 15, 20, 3.) Use the following names for the solution and project, respectively: Lottery Solution and Lottery Project. Save the application in the VbReloaded2015\Chap04 folder. Change the form file's name to Main Form.vb. Build an appropriate interface. Code the application. For now, do not worry if the lottery numbers are not unique. You will learn how to display unique numbers in Chapter 9 in this book. Save the solution and then start and test the application. Close the solution. (8, 12)

INTERMEDIATE

20. Create an application that determines whether a customer is entitled to free shipping when ordering from Savannah's website. Savannah's does not charge shipping when the customer uses his or her Savannah's credit card to pay for an order totaling $100 or more. Customers who do not meet these two requirements are charged $9 for shipping. The application should display the appropriate shipping charge: either $0 or $9. Use the following names for the solution and project, respectively: Savannah Solution and Savannah Project. Save the application in the VbReloaded2015\Chap04 folder. Change the form file's name to Main Form.vb. Create the interface. Use a check box to specify whether the customer is using his or her Savannah's credit card. Code the application. Save the solution and then start and test the application. Close the solution. (1–4, 11)

INTERMEDIATE

21. Create an application that determines whether a customer is entitled to free shipping when ordering from JimJoe's website. JimJoe's does not charge shipping on any order when the customer belongs to the JimJoe's Free Shipping Club. It also doesn't charge shipping for any order totaling $100 or more. The application should display one of the following messages: "Your shipping is free!" or "You will be charged for shipping." Use the following names for the solution and project, respectively: JimJoe Solution and JimJoe Project. Save the application in the VbReloaded2015\Chap04 folder. Change the form file's name to Main Form.vb. Create the interface. Use a check box to specify whether the customer belongs to the JimJoe's Free Shipping Club. Code the application. Save the solution and then start and test the application. Close the solution. (1–4, 11)

INTERMEDIATE

22. Open the Shipping Solution (Shipping Solution.sln) file contained in the VbReloaded2015\Chap04\Shipping Solution folder. The application should display the appropriate shipping charge. The shipping charge for the following ZIP codes is $32: 60618, 60620, and 60632. All other ZIP codes are charged $37.75. Code the application. Save the solution and then start and test the application. Close the solution. (2–4)

INTERMEDIATE

23. In this exercise, you modify the VitaDrink application from Chapter 3's Programming Example. Use Windows to copy the VitaDrink Solution folder from the VbReloaded2015\Chap03 folder to the VbReloaded2015\Chap04 folder, and then open the VitaDrink Solution (VitaDrink Solution.sln) file. Add a check box to the form. Change the check box's Name property to discountCheckBox and change its Text property to &20% discount. Modify the code to give customers a 20% discount when the check box is selected. Deselect the check box when the Clear button is clicked. Save the solution and then start and test the application. Close the solution. (2–4, 11)

INTERMEDIATE

24. Create an application that calculates and displays the area of a floor in either one or both of the following measurements: square feet or square yards. Use two check boxes to allow the user to select the measurement type: one labeled Square feet and one labeled Square yards. The user will enter the floor's measurements in feet. Use the following names for the solution and project, respectively: Carpet Solution and Carpet

Project. Save the application in the VbReloaded2015\Chap04 folder. Change the form file's name to Main Form.vb. Create the interface and then code the application. Save the solution and then start and test the application. Close the solution. (1–4, 11)

INTERMEDIATE

25. Create an application that calculates a customer's water bill for the Canton Water Department. The user will enter the current meter reading and the previous meter reading. The application should calculate and display the number of gallons of water used and the total charge for the water. The charge for water is $1.75 per 1000 gallons, or 0.00175 per gallon. However, there is a minimum charge of $19.50. In other words, every customer must pay at least $19.50. Display the total charge with a dollar sign and two decimal places. Use the following names for the solution and project, respectively: Canton Solution and Canton Project. Save the solution in the VbReloaded2015\Chap04 folder. Change the form file's name to Main Form.vb. Create the interface and then code the application. Save the solution and then start and test the application. Close the solution. (1–4)

INTERMEDIATE

26. Marcy's is having a BoGoHo (Buy One, Get One Half Off) sale. Create an application that allows the user to enter the prices of two items. The application should calculate the total owed and the amount the customer saved. The half-off should always be taken on the item having the lowest price. For example, if one item costs $24.99 and the second item costs $12.50, the $12.50 item would be half off. (In other words, the item would cost $6.25.) Use the following names for the solution and project, respectively: Marcy Solution and Marcy Project. Save the solution in the VbReloaded2015\Chap04 folder. Change the form file's name to Main Form.vb. Create the interface and then code the application. Save the solution and then start and test the application. Close the solution. (1–4)

DISCOVERY

27. In this exercise, you learn how to generate and display random real numbers, which are numbers that contain a decimal place. Open the Random Float Solution (Random Float Solution.sln) file contained in the VbReloaded2015\Chap04\Random Float Solution folder.

    a. You can use the Random.NextDouble method to return a random real number that is greater than or equal to 0.0 but less than 1.0. The method's syntax is *randomObjectName***.NextDouble**. Code the Display Random Number button's Click event procedure so that it displays a random real number in the numberLabel. Save the solution and then start the application. Click the Display Random Number button several times. Each time you click the button, a random number that is greater than or equal to 0.0 but less than 1.0 appears in the numberLabel. Click the Exit button to end the application.

    b. You can use the following formula to generate random real numbers within a specified range: **(***maxValue* – *minValue* + 1.0**)** * *randomObjectName***.NextDouble** + *minValue*. For example, the formula `(10.0 - 1.0 + 1.0) * randomGenerator.NextDouble + 1.0` generates real numbers that are greater than or equal to 1.0 but less than 11.0. Modify the Display Random Number button's Click event procedure so that it displays a random real number that is greater than or equal to 25.0 but less than 51.0. Display two decimal places in the number. Save the solution and then start the application. Click the Display Random Number button several times to verify that the code you entered is working correctly. Close the solution.

SWAT THE BUGS

28. Open the Debug Solution (Debug Solution.sln) file contained in the VbReloaded2015\Chap04\Debug Solution folder. Read the comments in the Code Editor window. Start and then test the application. Locate and then correct any errors. When the application is working correctly, close the solution. (3, 4)

Case Projects

Fuel Calculator

Josephine Miller owns two cars, referred to as Car 1 and Car 2. She wants to drive one of the cars to her vacation destination, but she's not sure which one (if any) would cost her the least amount in gas. Create an application that calculates and displays the total cost of the gas if she takes Car 1 as well as the total cost of the gas if she takes Car 2. It should also display a message that indicates which car she should take and approximately how much she will save by taking that car (show the savings with no decimal places). If the total cost of gas would be the same for both cars, Josephine should take Car 1 because that's her favorite car. Use the following names for the solution and project, respectively: Car Solution and Car Project. Save the application in the VbReloaded2015\Chap04 folder. Change the form file's name to Main Form.vb.

The application's interface should provide text boxes for Josephine to enter the following five items: the total miles she will drive, Car 1's miles per gallon (MPG), Car 2's miles per gallon, Car 1's cost per gallon of gas, and Car 2's cost per gallon of gas. (The cost per gallon of gas must be entered separately for each car because one car uses regular gas and the other uses premium gas.) You can either create your own user interface or create the one shown in Figure 4-48. Test the application using 1200 as the trip miles, 28 as Car 1's MPG, 35 as Car 2's MPG, 3.69 as Car 1's cost per gallon, and 3.38 as Car 2's cost per gallon. (Hint: The total costs for Car 1 and Car 2 are $158.14 and $115.89, respectively. By taking Car 2, Josephine will save approximately $42.) (1–4, 8)

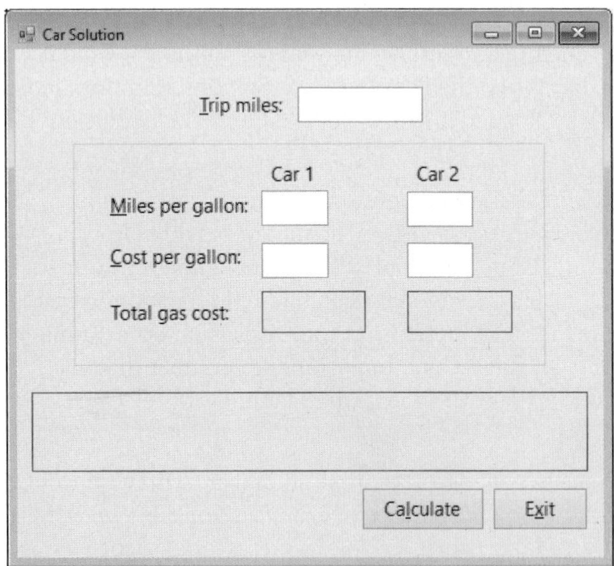

Figure 4-48 Sample interface for the Fuel Calculator application

Novelty Warehouse

Novelty Warehouse needs an application that allows the user to enter an item's price. When the user clicks a button in the interface, the button's Click event procedure should add the price to the total of the prices already entered; this amount represents the subtotal owed by the customer. The application should display the subtotal on the screen. It should also display a 3% sales tax, the shipping charge, and the total due from the customer. The total due is calculated by adding together the subtotal, the 3% sales tax, and a $15 shipping charge. For example, if the user enters 26.75 as the price and then clicks the button, the button's Click event procedure should display 26.75 as the subtotal, 0.80 as the sales tax, 15.00 as the shipping charge, and 42.55 as the total due. If the user subsequently enters 30 as the price and then clicks the button, the button's Click event procedure should display 56.75 as the subtotal, 1.70 as the sales tax, 15.00 as the shipping charge, and 73.45 as the total due. However, when the subtotal is at least 100, the shipping charge is 0 (zero). Use the following names for the solution and project, respectively: Novelty Solution and Novelty Project. Save the solution in the VbReloaded2015\Chap04 folder. Change the form file's name to Main Form.vb. You can either create your own user interface or create the one shown in Figure 4-49. (1–4)

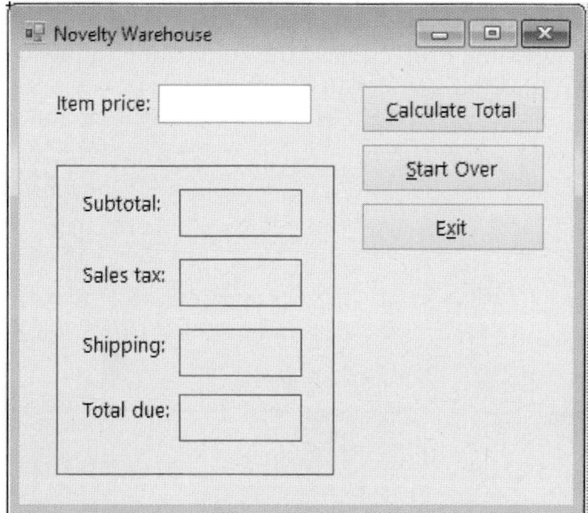

Figure 4-49 Sample interface for the Novelty Warehouse application

Multiplication Practice

Create an application that displays two random integers from 1 through 10 in the interface. The application should allow the user to enter the product of both numbers. It then should check whether the user's answer is correct. Display an appropriate message (or image) when the answer is correct. Also display an appropriate message (or image) when the answer is incorrect. Use the following names for the solution and project, respectively: Multiplication Solution and Multiplication Project. Save the solution in the VbReloaded2015\Chap04 folder. Change the form file's name to Main Form.vb. (1–4, 12)

Sunflower Resort

Create a reservation application for Sunflower Resort. The application should allow the user to enter the following information: the number of rooms to reserve, the length of stay (in nights), the number of adult guests, and the number of child guests. Each room can accommodate a maximum of six guests. If the number of rooms reserved is less than the number of rooms required, the application should display the message "You have exceeded the maximum guests per room." The resort charges $284 per room per night. It also charges a 15.25% sales and lodging tax, which is based on the room charge. In addition, there is a $15 resort fee per room per night. The application should display the total room charge, the sales and lodging tax, the resort fee, and the total due. Use the following names for the solution and project, respectively: Sunflower Solution and Sunflower Project. Save the solution in the VbReloaded2015\Chap04 folder. Change the form file's name to Main Form.vb. (1–4)

Wedding Reception

Create an application that displays the number of rectangular tables needed to seat the bridal party at a wedding reception, as well as the number of round tables required for the guests. Each rectangular table can accommodate a maximum of 10 people. Each round table can accommodate a maximum of 8 guests. The interface should provide text boxes for the user to enter the number of people in the bridal party and the number of guests. Display the numbers of rectangular and round tables in label controls. Use the following names for the solution and project, respectively: Wedding Solution and Wedding Project. Save the application in the VbReloaded2015\Chap04 folder. Change the form file's name to Main Form.vb. (1–4)

CHAPTER 5

More on the Selection Structure

After studying Chapter 5, you should be able to:

1. Determine whether a solution requires a nested selection structure
2. Include a nested selection structure in pseudocode and in a flowchart
3. Code a nested selection structure
4. Determine whether a solution requires a multiple-alternative selection structure
5. Include a multiple-alternative selection structure in pseudocode and in a flowchart
6. Code a multiple-alternative selection structure
7. Include radio buttons in an interface
8. Display a message in a message box
9. Use a message box's return value
10. Prevent the entry of invalid characters in a text box

Making More than One Decision

As you learned in Chapter 4, the True and False paths in a selection structure can include instructions that declare variables, perform calculations, and so on. Both paths can also include other selection structures. When either a selection structure's True path or its False path contains another selection structure, the inner selection structure is referred to as a **nested selection structure** because it is contained (nested) entirely within the outer selection structure.

A programmer determines whether a problem's solution requires a nested selection structure by studying the problem specification. The first problem specification you will examine in this chapter involves a basketball player named Derek. The problem specification and an illustration of the problem are shown in Figure 5-1 along with an appropriate solution. The solution requires a selection structure but not a nested one. This is because only one decision—whether the basketball went through the hoop—is necessary. The selection structure's condition is shaded in the figure.

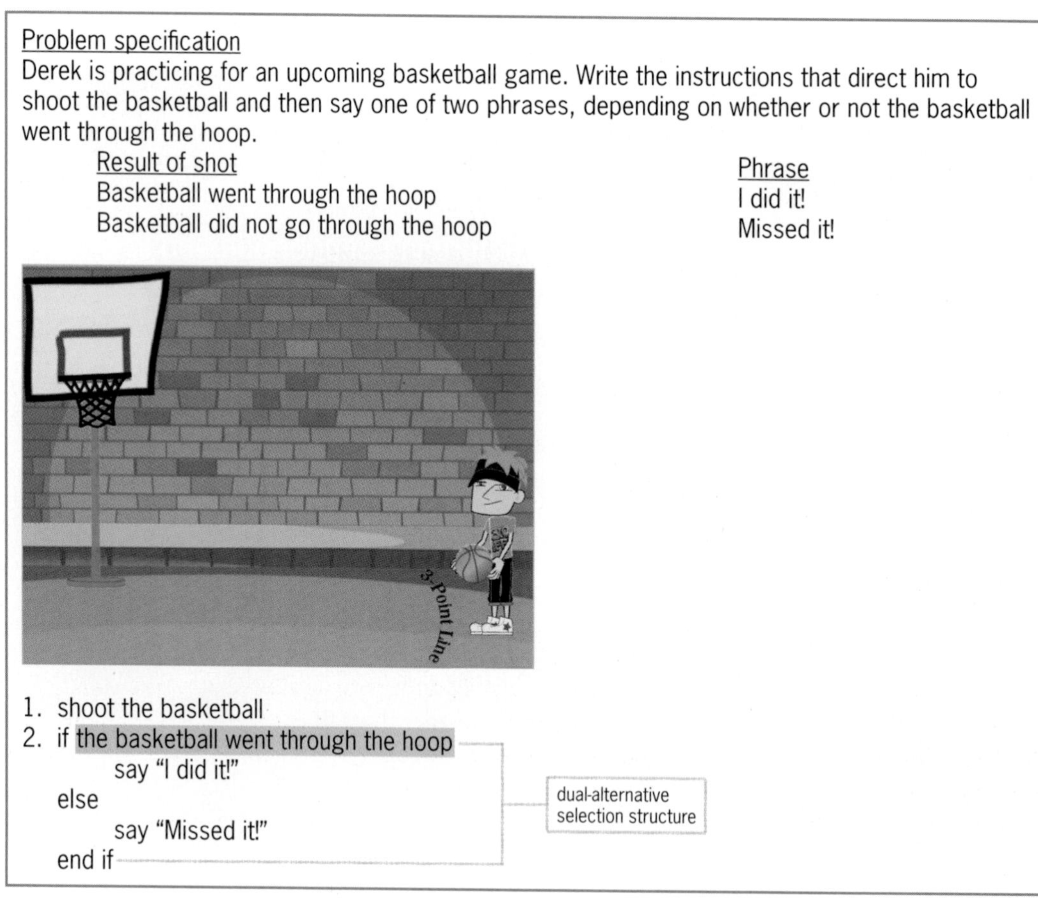

Problem specification
Derek is practicing for an upcoming basketball game. Write the instructions that direct him to shoot the basketball and then say one of two phrases, depending on whether or not the basketball went through the hoop.

Result of shot	Phrase
Basketball went through the hoop	I did it!
Basketball did not go through the hoop	Missed it!


```
1. shoot the basketball
2. if the basketball went through the hoop
        say "I did it!"
   else
        say "Missed it!"
   end if
```


Figure 5-1 A problem that requires a selection structure
Image by Diane Zak; created with Reallusion CrazyTalk Animator

Now we will make a slight change to the problem specification. This time, Derek should say either one or two phrases, depending not only on whether or not the ball went through the hoop but also on where he was standing when he made the basket. Figure 5-2 shows the modified problem specification and solution. The modified solution contains an outer dual-alternative selection structure and a nested dual-alternative selection structure. The conditions in both selection structures are shaded in the figure. For a nested selection structure to work correctly, it must be contained entirely within either the outer selection structure's True path (as it is in Figure 5-2) or its False path.

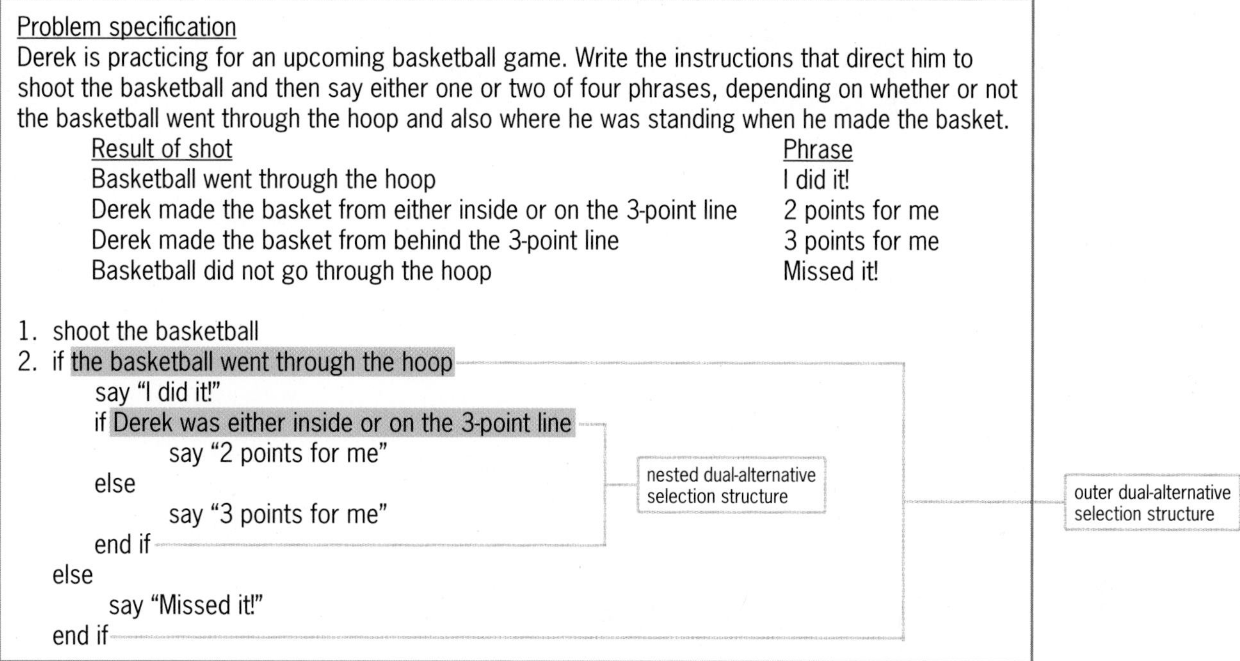
Problem specification
Derek is practicing for an upcoming basketball game. Write the instructions that direct him to shoot the basketball and then say either one or two of four phrases, depending on whether or not the basketball went through the hoop and also where he was standing when he made the basket.

Result of shot	Phrase
Basketball went through the hoop	I did it!
Derek made the basket from either inside or on the 3-point line	2 points for me
Derek made the basket from behind the 3-point line	3 points for me
Basketball did not go through the hoop	Missed it!

```
1. shoot the basketball
2. if the basketball went through the hoop
       say "I did it!"
       if Derek was either inside or on the 3-point line
              say "2 points for me"
       else
              say "3 points for me"
       end if
   else
        say "Missed it!"
   end if
```


Figure 5-2 A problem that requires a nested selection structure

Figure 5-3 shows a modified version of the previous problem specification, along with the modified solution. In this version of the problem, Derek should still say "Missed it!" when the basketball misses its target. However, if the basketball hits the rim, he should also say "So close". In addition to the nested dual-alternative selection structure from the previous solution, the modified solution also contains a nested single-alternative selection structure, which appears entirely within the outer selection structure's False path.

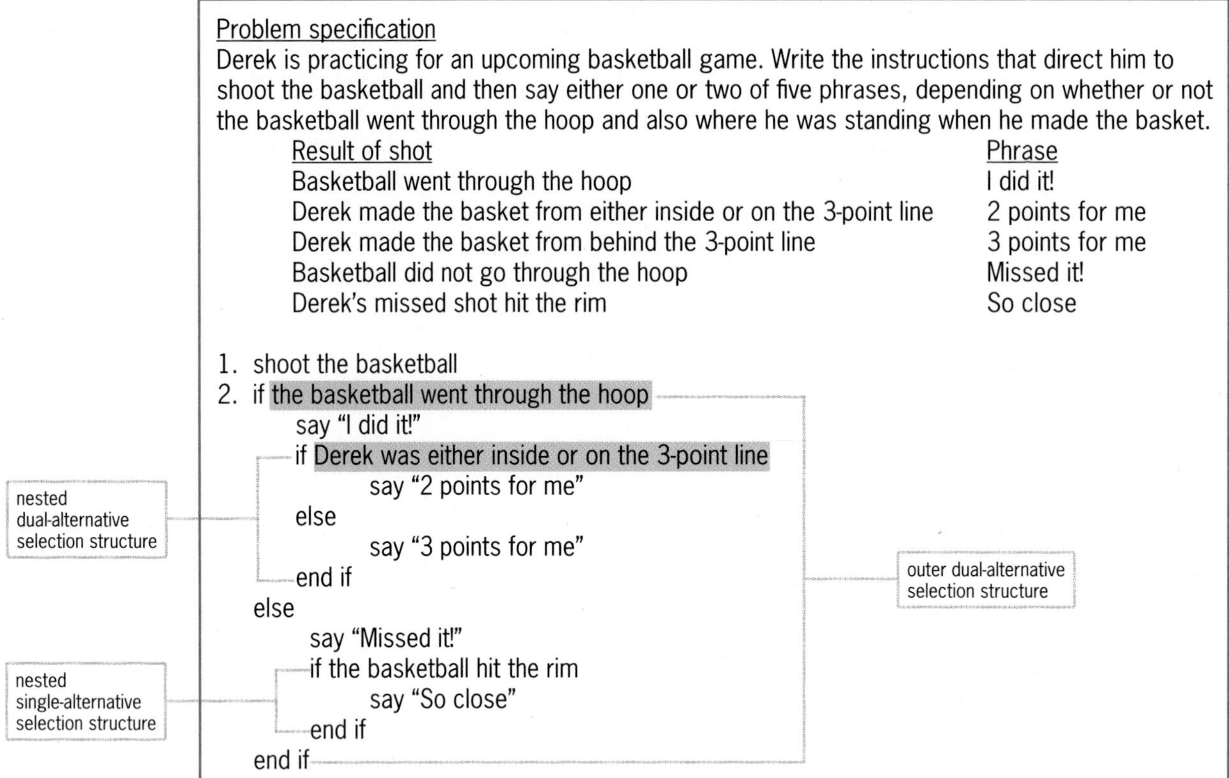

Problem specification
Derek is practicing for an upcoming basketball game. Write the instructions that direct him to shoot the basketball and then say either one or two of five phrases, depending on whether or not the basketball went through the hoop and also where he was standing when he made the basket.

Result of shot	Phrase
Basketball went through the hoop	I did it!
Derek made the basket from either inside or on the 3-point line	2 points for me
Derek made the basket from behind the 3-point line	3 points for me
Basketball did not go through the hoop	Missed it!
Derek's missed shot hit the rim	So close

```
1. shoot the basketball
2. if the basketball went through the hoop
       say "I did it!"
       if Derek was either inside or on the 3-point line
            say "2 points for me"
       else
            say "3 points for me"
       end if
   else
        say "Missed it!"
        if the basketball hit the rim
            say "So close"
        end if
   end if
```


Figure 5-3 A problem that requires two nested selection structures

The Cookie Palace Application

Figure 5-4 shows the problem specification for the Cookie Palace application, which calculates the total amount a customer owes. The discount rate depends on two items: the number of baskets ordered and the club membership. If the customer orders at least three baskets, the discount rate is 20%. If the order is for fewer than three baskets, the discount rate depends on whether the customer is a member of the Cookie Club. If the customer *is* a member, the discount rate is 15%; otherwise, it is 5%. Notice that determining the club membership status is important only *after* the number of baskets is determined. Because of this, the decision regarding the number of baskets is considered the primary decision, while the decision regarding the club membership status is considered the secondary decision because whether it needs to be made depends on the result of the primary decision. A primary decision is always made by an outer selection structure, while a secondary decision is always made by a nested selection structure.

Also included in Figure 5-4 is a correct solution to the problem shown in both pseudocode and a flowchart. The first diamond in the flowchart represents the outer selection structure's condition, which checks whether the customer ordered at least three baskets. If the condition evaluates to True, the outer selection structure's True path assigns 20% as the discount rate. If the outer selection structure's condition evaluates to False, on the other hand, the nested selection structure determines the customer's club membership status. The nested selection structure's condition is represented by the second diamond in the flowchart. If the customer is a club member, the nested selection structure's True path assigns 15% as the discount rate; otherwise, its False path assigns 5%. Notice that the nested selection structure is processed only when the outer selection structure's condition evaluates to False.

<u>Problem specification</u>

Cookie Palace sells baskets filled with a variety of gourmet cookies. Each basket costs $35.99. Create an application that allows the user to enter the number of baskets a customer orders. The application should calculate the subtotal, discount, and total owed. The subtotal is calculated by multiplying the number of baskets ordered by the price per basket. The discount is calculated by multiplying the subtotal by the appropriate discount rate. The total owed is calculated by subtracting the discount from the subtotal. The discount rates are shown here:

Discount rates	Criteria
20%	at least three baskets ordered
15%	fewer than three baskets ordered, but customer is a member of the Cookie Club
5%	fewer than three baskets ordered, and customer is not a member of the Cookie Club

```
1. store number of baskets in a variable
2. subtotal = number of baskets * price per basket
3. if number of baskets is at least 3
       discount rate = 20%
   else
       if club member
           discount rate = 15%
       else
           discount rate = 5%
       end if
   end if
4. discount = subtotal * discount rate
5. total = subtotal – discount
6. display total
```

Figure 5-4 Problem specification and a solution for the Cookie Palace application *(continues)*

(continued)

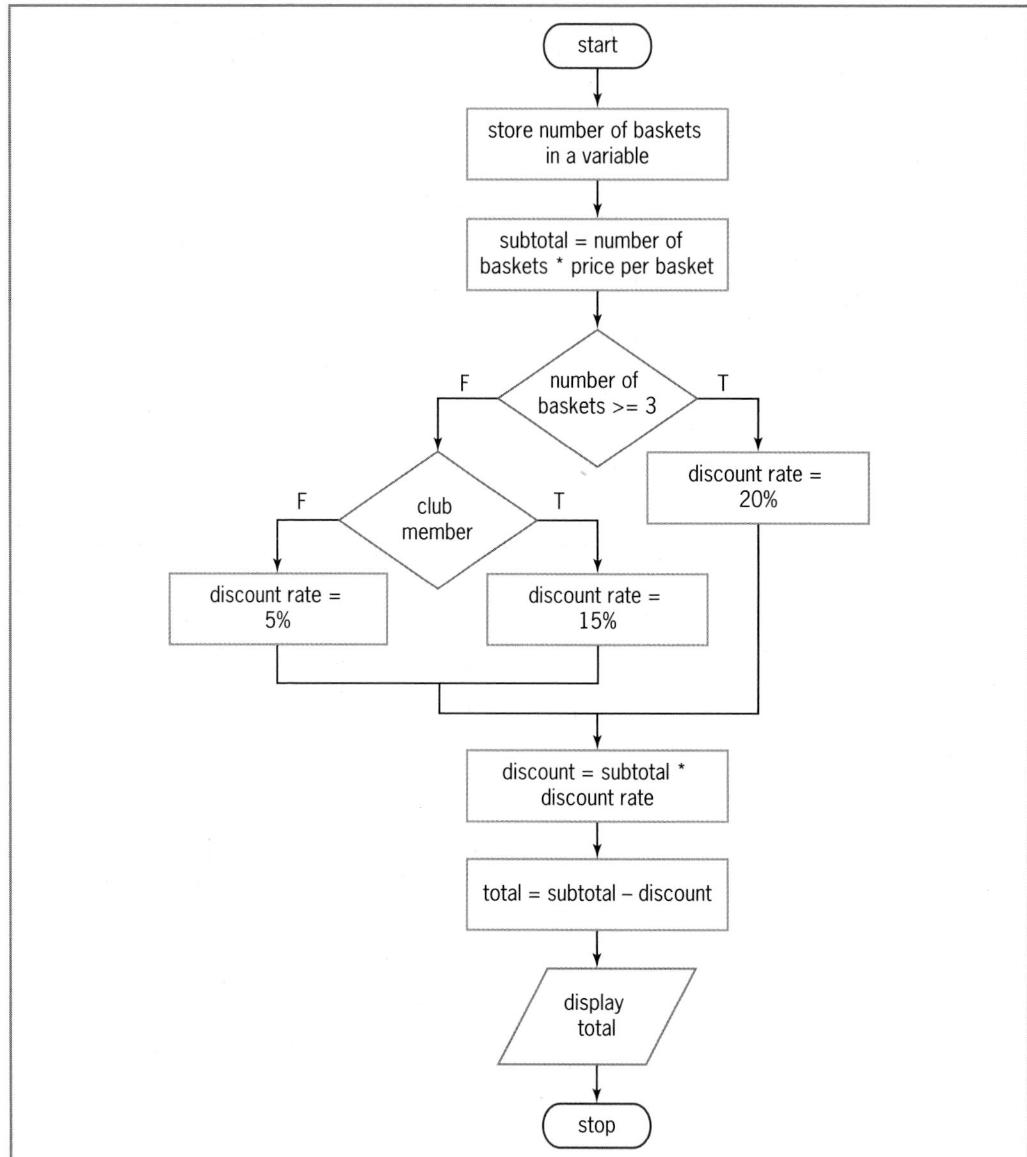

Figure 5-4 Problem specification and a solution for the Cookie Palace application

Even small procedures can have more than one solution. Figure 5-5 shows another correct solution for the Cookie Palace application. As in the previous solution, the outer selection structure in this solution determines the number of baskets ordered (the primary decision), and the nested selection structure determines the club membership status (the secondary decision). In this solution, however, the outer selection structure's condition is the opposite of the one in Figure 5-4: It checks whether the number of baskets is less than three, rather than checking if it is greater than or equal to three. (Recall that *less than* is the opposite of *greater than or equal to*.) In addition, the nested selection structure appears in the outer selection structure's True path in this solution, which means it will be processed only when the outer selection structure's condition evaluates to True. The solutions in Figures 5-4 and 5-5 produce the same result. Neither solution is better than the other; each simply represents a different way of solving the same problem.

Problem specification

Cookie Palace sells baskets filled with a variety of gourmet cookies. Each basket costs $35.99. Create an application that allows the user to enter the number of baskets a customer orders. The application should calculate the subtotal, discount, and total owed. The subtotal is calculated by multiplying the number of baskets ordered by the price per basket. The discount is calculated by multiplying the subtotal by the appropriate discount rate. The total owed is calculated by subtracting the discount from the subtotal. The discount rates are shown here:

Discount rates	Criteria
20%	at least three baskets ordered
15%	fewer than three baskets ordered, but customer is a member of the Cookie Club
5%	fewer than three baskets ordered, and customer is not a member of the Cookie Club

```
1. store number of baskets in a variable
2. subtotal = number of baskets * price per basket
3. if number of baskets is less than 3
       if club member
           discount rate = 15%
       else
           discount rate = 5%
       end if
   else
       discount rate = 20%
   end if
4. discount = subtotal * discount rate
5. total = subtotal – discount
6. display total
```

Figure 5-5 Another correct solution for the Cookie Palace application *(continues)*

(continued)

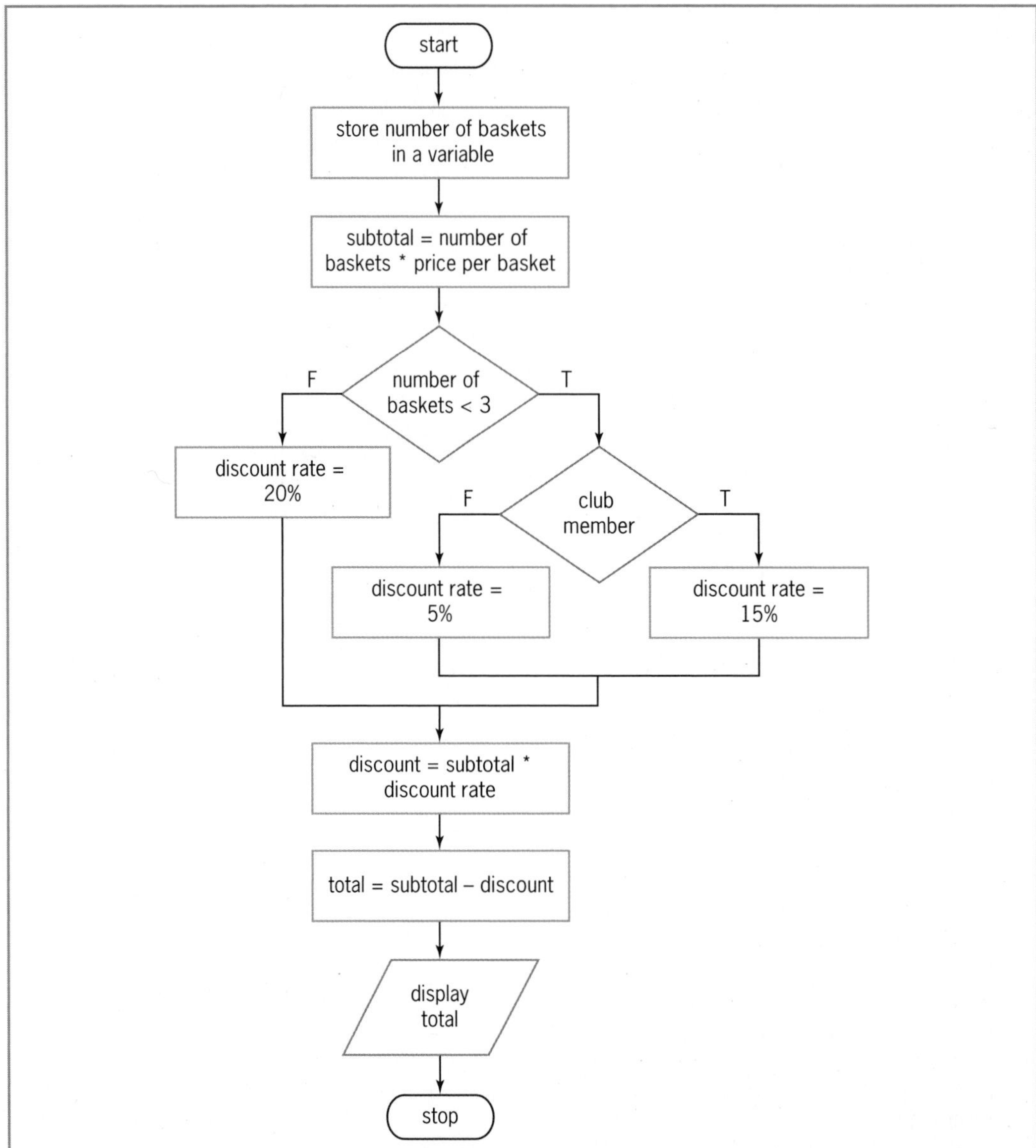

Figure 5-5 Another correct solution for the Cookie Palace application

Figure 5-6 shows the code corresponding to the solutions in Figures 5-4 and 5-5. It also includes a sample run of the application.

Example 1—code for the solution in Figure 5-4

```
Private Sub calcButton_Click(sender As Object, e As EventArgs
) Handles calcButton.Click
    ' calculates the total owed
```

Figure 5-6 Code and sample run for the solutions in Figures 5-4 and 5-5 *(continues)*

(continued)

```
    Const PricePerBasket As Double = 35.99
    Dim baskets As Integer
    Dim subtotal As Double
    Dim discountRate As Double
    Dim discount As Double
    Dim total As Double

    Integer.TryParse(basketsTextBox.Text, baskets)
    subtotal = baskets * PricePerBasket

    ' determine discount rate
    If baskets >= 3 Then
        discountRate = 0.2
    Else
        If memberCheckBox.Checked Then
            discountRate = 0.15
        Else
            discountRate = 0.05
        End If
    End If
    discount = subtotal * discountRate
    total = subtotal - discount
    totalLabel.Text = total.ToString("C2")
End Sub
```

nested selection structure in the False path

Example 2—code for the solution in Figure 5-5

```
Private Sub calcButton_Click(sender As Object, e As EventArgs
) Handles calcButton.Click
    ' calculates the total owed

    Const PricePerBasket As Double = 35.99
    Dim baskets As Integer
    Dim subtotal As Double
    Dim discountRate As Double
    Dim discount As Double
    Dim total As Double

    Integer.TryParse(basketsTextBox.Text, baskets)
    subtotal = baskets * PricePerBasket

    ' determine discount rate
    If baskets < 3 Then
        If memberCheckBox.Checked Then
            discountRate = 0.15
        Else
            discountRate = 0.05
        End If
    Else
        discountRate = 0.2
    End If
    discount = subtotal * discountRate
    total = subtotal - discount
    totalLabel.Text = total.ToString("C2")
End Sub
```

nested selection structure in the True path

Figure 5-6 Code and sample run for the solutions in Figures 5-4 and 5-5 *(continues)*

(continued)

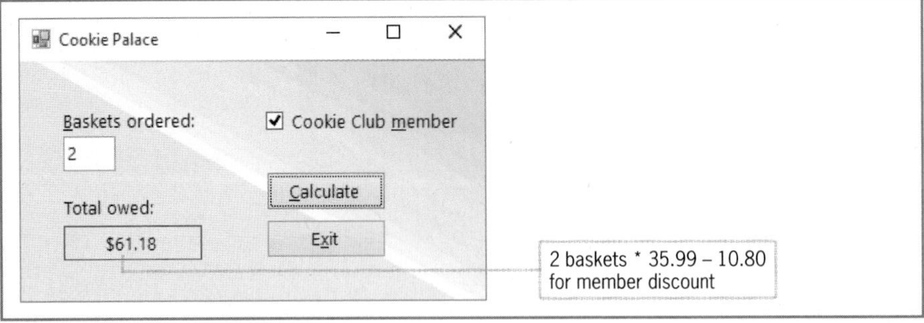

Figure 5-6 Code and sample run for the solutions in Figures 5-4 and 5-5

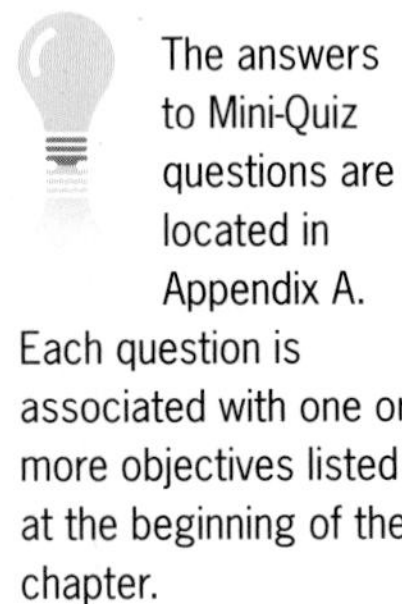

If you want to experiment with the Cookie Palace application, open the solution contained in the Try It 1! folder.

The answers to Mini-Quiz questions are located in Appendix A. Each question is associated with one or more objectives listed at the beginning of the chapter.

Mini-Quiz 5-1

1. The manager of a golf club wants an application that displays the appropriate fee to charge a golfer. Club members pay a $5 fee. Nonmembers golfing on Monday through Thursday pay $15. Nonmembers golfing on Friday through Sunday pay $25. The condition in the outer selection structure should check the _____________, while the condition in its nested selection structure should check the _____________. (1)
   a. membership status, day of the week
   b. day of the week, membership status
   c. membership status, fee
   d. fee, day of the week
2. Write the pseudocode for the outer and nested selection structures from Question 1. (2)
3. Draw a flowchart for the outer and nested selection structures from Question 1. (2)
4. Write the Visual Basic code corresponding to the selection structures from Questions 2 and 3. If the memberCheckBox in the interface is selected, it means that the person is a member. The day of the week is stored in an Integer variable named `dayNum`. The `dayNum` values range from 1 (Monday) through 7 (Sunday). Display the fee in the feeLabel. (3)

Multiple-Alternative Selection Structures

Figure 5-7 shows the problem specification for the Anderson Roofing application, which displays either the location of a company warehouse or an error message. The warehouse location is based on a code entered by the user; the valid codes are 1, 2, 3, 4, and 5. The figure also shows the pseudocode and flowchart for a procedure that will display the appropriate output. The procedure contains a **multiple-alternative selection structure**, which is a selection structure that can choose from several alternatives—in this case, from several codes. Multiple-alternative selection structures are also referred to as **extended selection structures**.

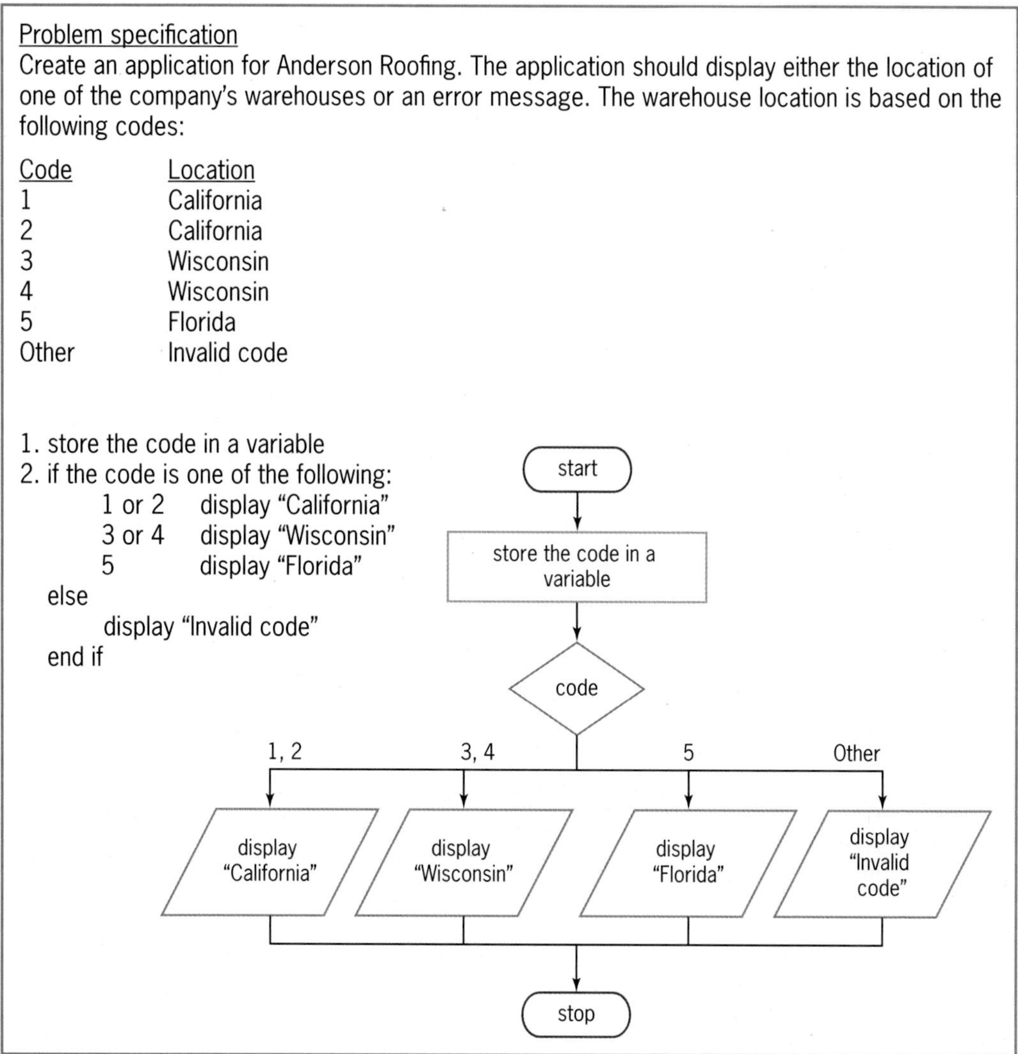

Problem specification
Create an application for Anderson Roofing. The application should display either the location of one of the company's warehouses or an error message. The warehouse location is based on the following codes:

Code	Location
1	California
2	California
3	Wisconsin
4	Wisconsin
5	Florida
Other	Invalid code

```
1. store the code in a variable
2. if the code is one of the following:
        1 or 2    display "California"
        3 or 4    display "Wisconsin"
        5         display "Florida"
   else
        display "Invalid code"
   end if
```


Figure 5-7 Problem specification and a solution for the Anderson Roofing application

The diamond in the flowchart in Figure 5-7 represents the multiple-alternative selection structure's condition. As you already know, the diamond is also used to represent the condition in both the single-alternative and dual-alternative selection structures. However, unlike the diamond in both of those selection structures, the diamond in a multiple-alternative selection structure has several flowlines (rather than only two flowlines) leading out of the symbol. Each flowline represents a possible path and must be marked appropriately, indicating the value(s) necessary for the path to be chosen.

Figure 5-8 shows two ways of using the If...Then...Else statement to code the pseudocode and flowchart from Figure 5-7. Both versions of the code produce the same result. The second version, which uses the keyword `ElseIf`, is simply a more convenient and compact way of writing a multiple-alternative selection structure.

Version 1—multiple-alternative selection structure

```
Private Sub displayButton_Click(sender As Object, e As EventArgs)
Handles displayButton.Click
    ' display the location of a warehouse

    Dim code As Integer
    Integer.TryParse(codeTextBox.Text, code)

    If code = 1 OrElse code = 2 Then
        locationLabel.Text = "California"
    Else
        If code = 3 OrElse code = 4 Then          you get here when the code is not 1 and not 2
            locationLabel.Text = "Wisconsin"
        Else
            If code = 5 Then                      you get here when the code is not 1, 2, 3, or 4
                locationLabel.Text = "Florida"
            Else
                locationLabel.Text = "Invalid code"   you get here when the code is not 1, 2, 3, 4, or 5
            End If
        End If          three End If clauses required
    End If
End Sub
```

Version 2—multiple-alternative selection structure

```
If code = 1 OrElse code = 2 Then
    locationLabel.Text = "California"
ElseIf code = 3 OrElse code = 4 Then
    locationLabel.Text = "Wisconsin"
ElseIf code = 5 Then
    locationLabel.Text = "Florida"
Else
    locationLabel.Text = "Invalid code"
End If          only one End If clause is required
```

Anderson Roofing

Code: 4 | Display Location | Exit

Location: Wisconsin

Figure 5-8 Code versions and sample run for the Anderson Roofing solution in Figure 5-7

If you want to experiment with the If...Then...Else statement in the Anderson Roofing application, open the solution contained in the Try It 2! folder.

The Select Case Statement

When a multiple-alternative selection structure has many paths from which to choose, it is often simpler and clearer to code the selection structure using the **Select Case statement** rather than several If...Then...Else statements. The Select Case statement's syntax is shown in Figure 5-9. The figure also shows how you can use the Select Case statement to code the multiple-alternative selection structure in the Anderson Roofing application from Figures 5-7 and 5-8.

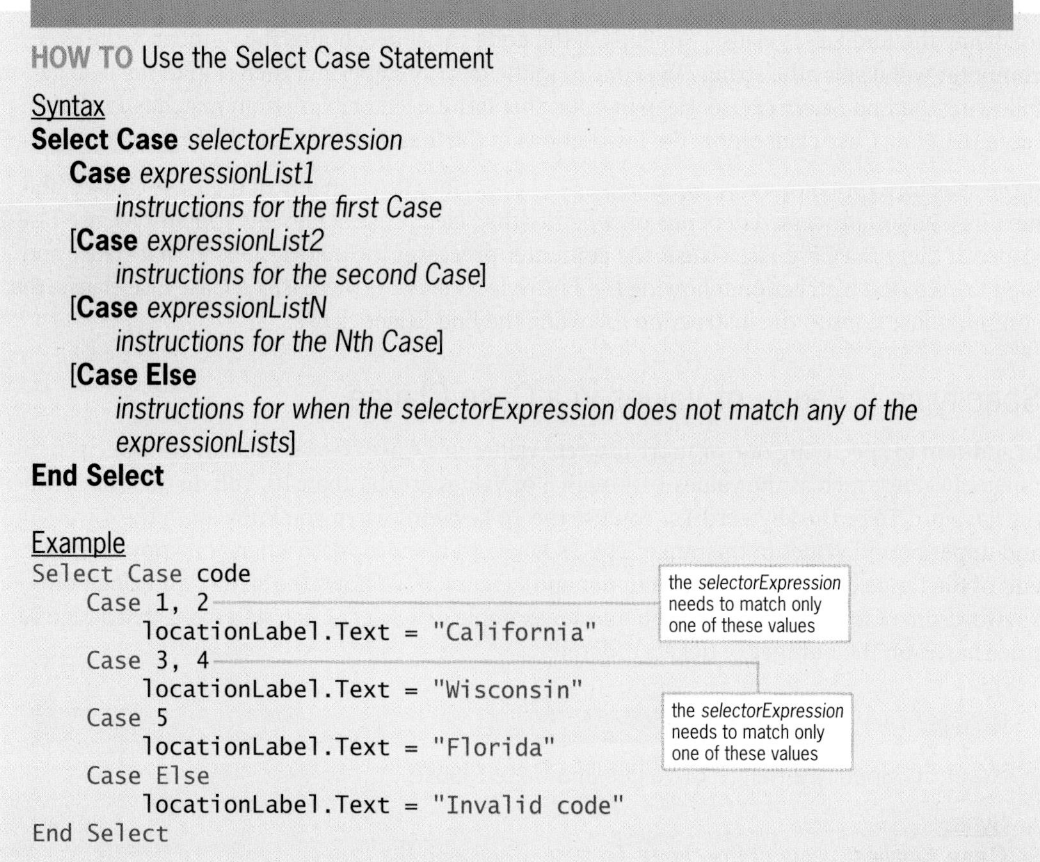

HOW TO Use the Select Case Statement

Syntax

Select Case *selectorExpression*
  Case *expressionList1*
    instructions for the first Case
  [**Case** *expressionList2*
    instructions for the second Case]
  [**Case** *expressionListN*
    instructions for the Nth Case]
  [**Case Else**
    instructions for when the selectorExpression does not match any of the expressionLists]
End Select

Example

```
Select Case code
    Case 1, 2
        locationLabel.Text = "California"
    Case 3, 4
        locationLabel.Text = "Wisconsin"
    Case 5
        locationLabel.Text = "Florida"
    Case Else
        locationLabel.Text = "Invalid code"
End Select
```


Figure 5-9 How to use the Select Case statement

If you want to experiment with the Select Case statement in the Anderson Roofing application, open the solution contained in the Try It 3! folder.

The *selectorExpression* in the Select Case clause can contain any combination of variables, constants, keywords, functions, methods, operators, and properties. In the example in Figure 5-9, the selectorExpression is an Integer variable named `code`. Each Case clause represents a different path that the computer can follow. It is customary to indent each Case clause and the instructions within each Case clause, as shown in the figure. You can have as many Case clauses as necessary. However, if the Select Case statement includes a Case Else clause, the Case Else clause must be the last clause in the statement.

Each of the individual Case clauses, except the Case Else clause, must contain an *expressionList*, which can include one or more expressions. To include more than one expression in an expressionList, you separate each expression with a comma, as in the expressionList `Case 1, 2`. The selectorExpression needs to match only one of the expressions listed in an expressionList. The data type of the expressions must be compatible with the data type of the selectorExpression. If the selectorExpression is numeric, the expressions in the Case clauses should be numeric. Likewise, if the selectorExpression is a string, the expressions should be strings. In the example in Figure 5-9, the selectorExpression (`code`) is an integer, and so are the expressions 1, 2, 3, 4, and 5.

The Select Case statement looks more complicated than it really is. When processing the statement, the computer simply compares the value of the selectorExpression with the value(s) listed in each of the Case clauses, one Case clause at a time beginning with the first. If the selectorExpression matches at least one of the values listed in a Case clause, the computer processes only the instructions contained in that clause. After the Case clause's instructions are processed, the Select Case statement ends and the computer skips to the instruction following the End Select clause. For instance, if the `code` variable in Figure 5-9 contains the number 2, the computer will display the string "California" in the locationLabel and then skip to the instruction following the End Select clause. Similarly, if the `code` variable contains the number 3, the computer will display the string "Wisconsin" in the locationLabel and then skip to the instruction following the End Select clause. Keep in mind that if the selectorExpression matches a value in more than one Case clause, only the instructions in the first match's Case clause are processed.

If the selectorExpression does *not* match any of the values listed in any of the Case clauses, the next instruction processed depends on whether the Select Case statement contains a Case Else clause. If there *is* a Case Else clause, the computer processes the instructions in that clause and then skips to the instruction following the End Select clause. If there *isn't* a Case Else clause, the computer just skips to the instruction following the End Select clause.

Specifying a Range of Values in a Case Clause

In addition to specifying one or more discrete values in a Case clause, you can also specify a range of values, such as the values 1 through 5 or values greater than 10. You do this using either the keyword `To` or the keyword `Is`. You use the `To` keyword when you know both the lower and upper bound values in the range. The `Is` keyword is appropriate when you know only one end of the range (either the lower or upper end). Figure 5-10 shows the syntax for using both keywords in a Case clause. It also contains an example of a Select Case statement that assigns a price based on the number of tickets ordered.

HOW TO Specify a Range of Values in a Case Clause

Syntax
Case *smallest value in the range* **To** *largest value in the range*
Case Is *comparisonOperator value*

Note: Be sure to test the Select Case statement thoroughly because the computer will not display an error message when the value preceding `To` in a Case clause is greater than the value following `To`. Instead, the statement will not give the correct results.

Example
The ABC Corporation's price chart is shown here:

Quantity ordered	Price per item
1–5	$25
6–10	$23
More than 10	$20
Fewer than 1	$0

```
Select Case quantity
    Case 1 To 5
        price = 25
    Case 6 To 10
        price = 23
    Case Is > 10
        price = 20
    Case Else
        price = 0
End Select
```

If you want to experiment with the Select Case statement in the ABC Corporation application, open the solution contained in the Try It 4! folder.

Figure 5-10 How to specify a range of values in a Case clause

According to the price chart shown in the figure, the price for 1 to 5 items is $25 each. Using discrete values, the first Case clause would look like this: `Case 1, 2, 3, 4, 5`. However, a more convenient way of writing that range of numbers is to use the `To` keyword, like this: `Case 1 To 5`. The expression `1 To 5` specifies the range of numbers from 1 to 5, inclusive. The expression `6 To 10` in the second Case clause in the example specifies the range of numbers from 6 through 10. Notice that both Case clauses state both the lower (1 and 6) and upper (5 and 10) values in each range.

The third Case clause, `Case Is > 10`, contains the `Is` keyword rather than the `To` keyword. Recall that you use the `Is` keyword when you know only one end of the range of values. In this case, you know only the lower end of the range: 10. The `Is` keyword is always used in combination with one of the following comparison operators: =, <, <=, >, >=, <>. The `Case Is > 10` clause specifies all numbers greater than the number 10. Because `quantity` is an Integer variable, you can also write this Case clause as `Case Is >= 11`. The Case Else clause in the example in Figure 5-10 is processed only when the `quantity` variable contains a value that is not included in any of the previous Case clauses.

Mini-Quiz 5-2

The answers to Mini-Quiz questions are located in Appendix A. Each question is associated with one or more objectives listed at the beginning of the chapter.

1. A Select Case statement's selectorExpression is a String variable named `colorCode`. Which of the following Case clauses will process the same instructions for color codes from 1 through 4? (6)
   a. `Case 1, 2, 3, 4`
   b. `Case "1", "2", "3", "4"`
   c. `Case "4" To "1"`
   d. both b and c

2. A Select Case statement's selectorExpression is an Integer variable named `colorCode`. Which of the following Case clauses will process the same instructions for color codes from 10 through 15? (6)
   a. `Case 10, 11, 12, 13, 14, 15`
   b. `Case 15 To 10`
   c. `Case Is >= 10 AndAlso <= 15`
   d. all of the above

3. You can code a multiple-alternative selection structure using either If...Then...Else statements or the Select Case statement. (6)
   a. True
   b. False

Using Radio Buttons in an Interface

You can also use a list box, checked list box, or combo box to limit the user to only one choice from a group of related but mutually exclusive choices.

Multiple-alternative selection structures are commonly used when coding applications whose interface contains radio buttons. You create a radio button using the RadioButton tool in the toolbox. **Radio buttons** allow you to limit the user to only one choice from a group of two or more related but mutually exclusive options. The interface shown in Figure 5-11 contains five radio buttons. Each radio button is labeled so the user knows the choice it represents. You enter the label using sentence capitalization in the radio button's Text property. Each radio button also has a unique access key that allows the user to select the button using the keyboard.

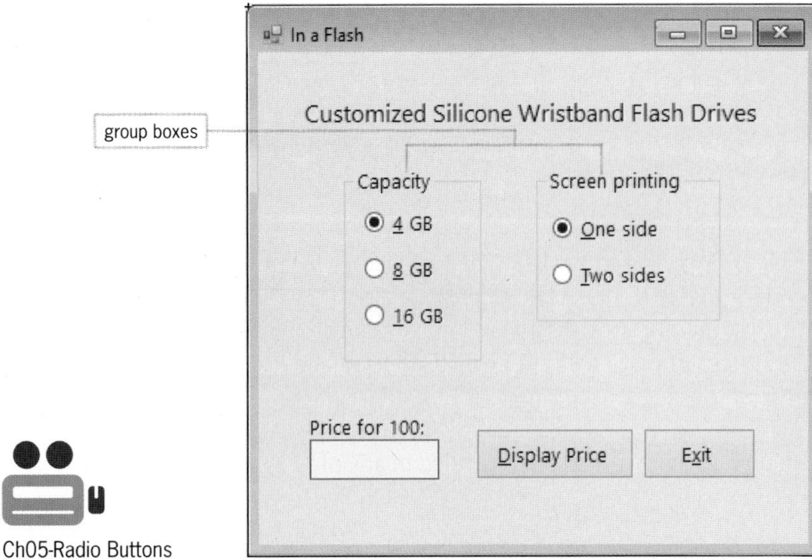

Ch05-Radio Buttons

Figure 5-11 Interface for the In a Flash application

The radio buttons in Figure 5-11 are separated into two groups: One group contains the three Capacity radio buttons, and one contains the two Screen printing radio buttons. To include two groups of radio buttons in an interface, at least one of the groups must be placed within a container, such as a group box, panel, or table layout panel. Otherwise, the radio buttons are considered to be in the same group, and only one can be selected at any one time.

You add a **group box** to a form using the GroupBox tool, which is located in the Containers section of the toolbox. Placing each group of radio buttons in a separate group box allows the user to select one button from each group. The minimum number of radio buttons in a group is two. This is because the only way to deselect a radio button is to select another radio button. The recommended maximum number of radio buttons in a group is seven.

It is customary in Windows applications to have one of the radio buttons in each group already selected when the interface first appears. The automatically selected button is called the **default radio button** and is either the radio button that represents the user's most likely choice or the first radio button in the group. You designate the default radio button by setting the button's Checked property to the Boolean value True. When you set the Checked property to True in the Properties window, a colored dot appears inside the button's circle to indicate that the button is selected. In Figure 5-11, the 4 GB and One side radio buttons are the default buttons in the Capacity and Screen printing groups, respectively. The Checked property is also used during run time to determine whether a radio button is selected (True) or unselected (False).

When the user clicks the Display Price button, the button's Click event procedure should display the appropriate price for 100 flash drives. The price information is shown in Figure 5-12 along with two versions of the Display Price button's code: one using If...Then...Else statements and one using the Select Case statement. Notice that both versions of the code use the Checked property to determine the radio button selected in each group. The figure also includes a sample run of the application.

In a Flash Price Chart

Capacity	Price for 100
4 GB	$459
8 GB	$499
16 GB	$725

Printing on two sides: additional $50

Version 1—If...Then...Else statements

```
Private Sub displayButton_Click(sender As Object, e As EventArgs
) Handles displayButton.Click
    ' displays the price for 100 flash drives

    Dim price As Integer

    ' determine capacity
    If gb4RadioButton.Checked Then
        price = 459
    ElseIf gb8RadioButton.Checked Then
        price = 499
    Else
        price = 725
    End If

    ' if necessary, add additional printing charge
    If twoRadioButton.Checked Then
        price += 50
    End If

    priceLabel.Text = price.ToString("C0")
End Sub
```

you can also use `If gb4RadioButton.Checked = True`

you can also use `If twoRadioButton.Checked = True`

Version 2—Select Case statement

```
Private Sub displayButton_Click(sender As Object, e As EventArgs
) Handles displayButton.Click
    ' displays the price for 100 flash drives

    Dim price As Integer

    ' determine capacity
    Select Case True
        Case gb4RadioButton.Checked
            price = 459
        Case gb8RadioButton.Checked
            price = 499
        Case Else
            price = 725
    End Select

    ' if necessary, add additional printing charge
    If twoRadioButton.Checked Then
        price += 50
    End If
```

you can also use `price = price + 50`

Figure 5-12 Price chart, displayButton_Click procedure, and a sample run of the In a Flash application *(continues)*

(continued)

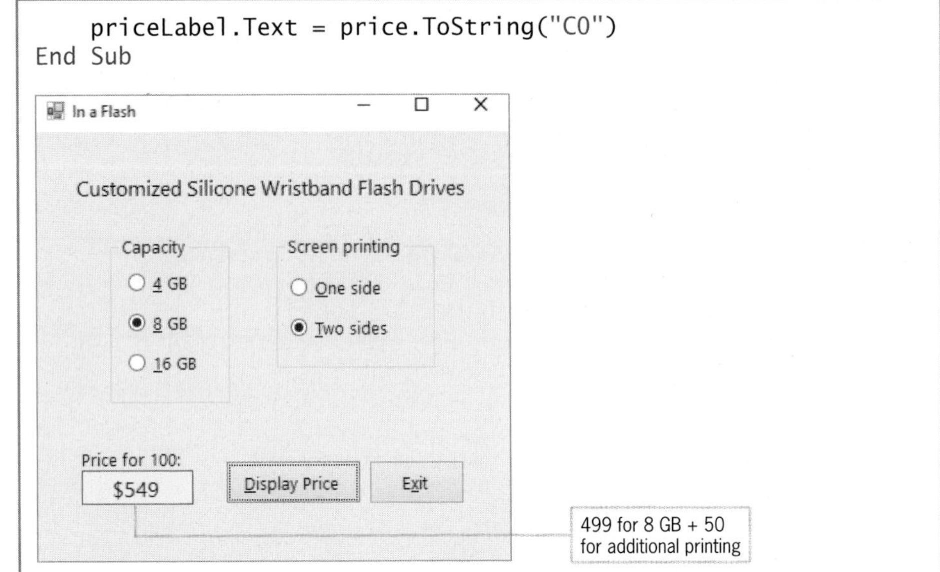

```
    priceLabel.Text = price.ToString("C0")
End Sub
```


If you want to experiment with the In a Flash application, open the solution contained in the Try It 5! folder.

Figure 5-12 Price chart, displayButton_Click procedure, and a sample run of the In a Flash application

The MessageBox.Show Method

At times, an application may need to communicate with the user during run time. One means of doing this is through a message box. You display a message box using the **MessageBox.Show method**. The message box contains text, one or more buttons, and an icon. Figure 5-13 shows the method's syntax and also lists the meaning of each argument. The figure also includes two examples of using the method. Figure 5-14 shows the message boxes created by the two examples.

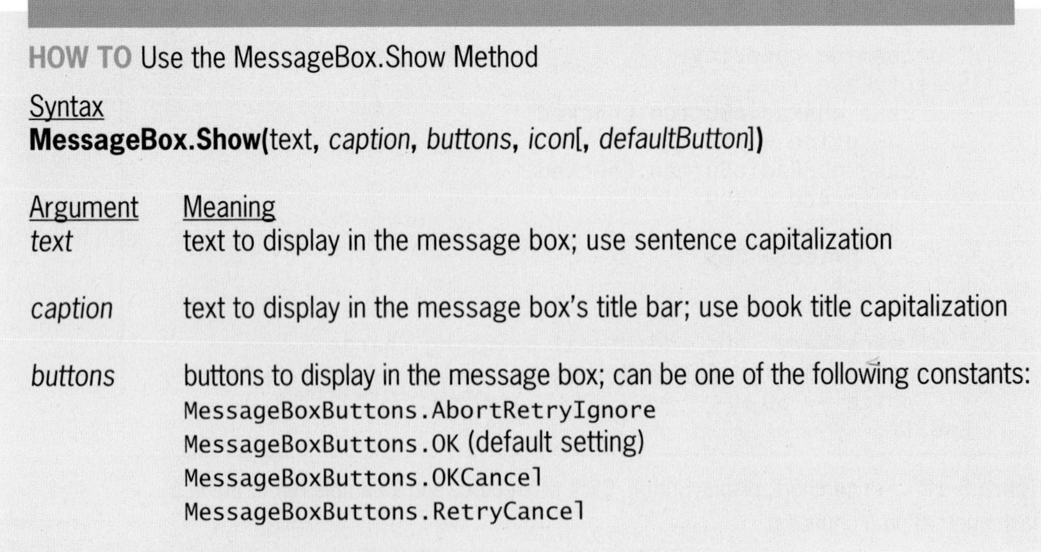

HOW TO Use the MessageBox.Show Method

Syntax
MessageBox.Show(text, *caption*, *buttons*, *icon*[, *defaultButton*]**)**

Argument	Meaning
text	text to display in the message box; use sentence capitalization
caption	text to display in the message box's title bar; use book title capitalization

buttons	buttons to display in the message box; can be one of the following constants:
	`MessageBoxButtons.AbortRetryIgnore`
	`MessageBoxButtons.OK` (default setting)
	`MessageBoxButtons.OKCancel`
	`MessageBoxButtons.RetryCancel`

Figure 5-13 How to use the MessageBox.Show method *(continues)*

(continued)

```
                MessageBoxButtons.YesNo
                MessageBoxButtons.YesNoCancel
```

icon	icon to display in the message box; typically, one of the following constants:
	`MessageBoxIcon.Exclamation`
	`MessageBoxIcon.Information`
	`MessageBoxIcon.Stop`

defaultButton	button automatically selected when the user presses Enter; can be one of the following constants:
	`MessageBoxDefaultButton.Button1` (default setting)
	`MessageBoxDefaultButton.Button2`
	`MessageBoxDefaultButton.Button3`

Example 1

```
MessageBox.Show("Record deleted.", "Payroll",
    MessageBoxButtons.OK, MessageBoxIcon.Information)
```

displays the information message box shown in Figure 5-14

Example 2

```
MessageBox.Show("Delete this record?", "Payroll",
    MessageBoxButtons.YesNo, MessageBoxIcon.Exclamation,
    MessageBoxDefaultButton.Button2)
```

displays the warning message box shown in Figure 5-14

Figure 5-13 How to use the MessageBox.Show method

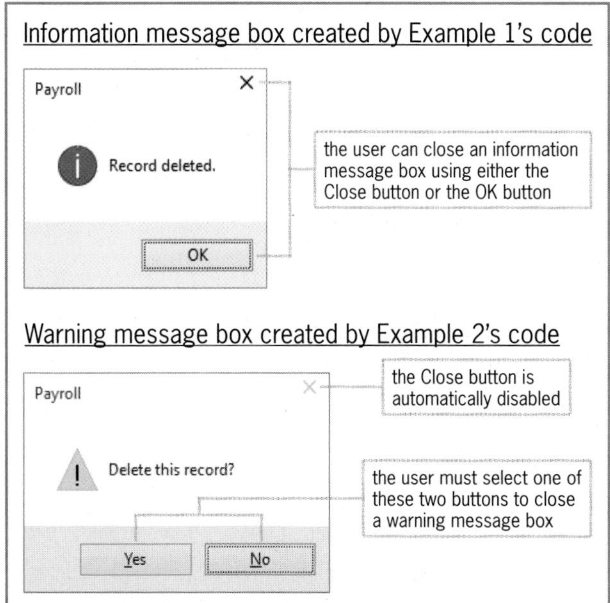

Figure 5-14 Message boxes created by the code in Figure 5-13

After displaying the message box, the MessageBox.Show method waits for the user to choose one of the buttons. It then closes the message box and returns an integer indicating the button chosen by the user. Sometimes you are not interested in the value returned by the method. This is the case when the message box is for informational purposes only, such as the first message box shown in Figure 5-14. Many times, however, the button selected by the user determines the next task performed by the application. Selecting the Yes button in the second message box shown in Figure 5-14 tells the application to delete the record; selecting the No button tells it *not* to delete the record.

Figure 5-15 lists the integer values returned by the MessageBox.Show method. Each value is associated with a button that can appear in a message box. The figure also lists the DialogResult values assigned to each integer as well as the meaning of the integers and values. As the figure indicates, the method returns the integer 6 when the user selects the Yes button. The integer 6 is represented by the DialogResult value `DialogResult.Yes`. When referring to the method's return value in code, you should use the DialogResult values rather than the integers because the values make the code more self-documenting and easier to understand. Figure 5-15 also shows two examples of using the method's return value.

HOW TO Use the MessageBox.Show Method's Return Value

Integer	DialogResult value	Meaning
1	`DialogResult.OK`	user chose the OK button
2	`DialogResult.Cancel`	user chose the Cancel button
3	`DialogResult.Abort`	user chose the Abort button
4	`DialogResult.Retry`	user chose the Retry button
5	`DialogResult.Ignore`	user chose the Ignore button
6	`DialogResult.Yes`	user chose the Yes button
7	`DialogResult.No`	user chose the No button

Example 1

```
Dim button As DialogResult
button =
    MessageBox.Show("Delete this record?", "Payroll",
    MessageBoxButtons.YesNo, MessageBoxIcon.Exclamation,
    MessageBoxDefaultButton.Button2)
If button = DialogResult.Yes Then
    ' instructions to delete the record
End If
```

Example 2

```
If MessageBox.Show("Play another game?", "Math Monster",
    MessageBoxButtons.YesNo, MessageBoxIcon.Exclamation) =
    DialogResult.Yes Then
    ' instructions to start another game
Else    ' No button
    ' instructions to close the game application
End If
```

If you want to experiment with the MessageBox.Show method, open the solution contained in the Try It 6! folder.

Figure 5-15 How to use the MessageBox.Show method's return value

In the first example in Figure 5-15, the MessageBox.Show method's return value is assigned to a DialogResult variable named `button`. The selection structure in the example compares the contents of the `button` variable with the `DialogResult.Yes` value. In the second example, the method's return value is not stored in a variable. Instead, the method appears in the selection structure's condition, where its return value is compared with the `DialogResult.Yes` value. The selection structure in Example 2 performs one set of tasks when the user selects the Yes button in the message box, and it performs a different set of tasks when the user selects the No button. Many programmers document the Else portion of the selection structure as shown in Example 2 because it clearly states that the Else portion is processed only when the user selects the No button.

Using the KeyPress Event

Earlier, in Figure 5-6, you viewed a sample run of the Cookie Palace application. The application's interface provides a text box for entering the number of baskets of cookies ordered. The user should enter the number of baskets as an integer. The number of baskets should not contain any letters, spaces, punctuation marks, or special characters. Unfortunately, you can't stop the user from trying to enter an inappropriate character into a text box. However, you can prevent the text box from accepting the character by coding the text box's KeyPress event procedure. As indicated in Figure 5-16, the procedure has two parameters, which appear within the parentheses in the procedure header: `sender` and `e`. A **parameter** represents information that is passed to the procedure when the event occurs.

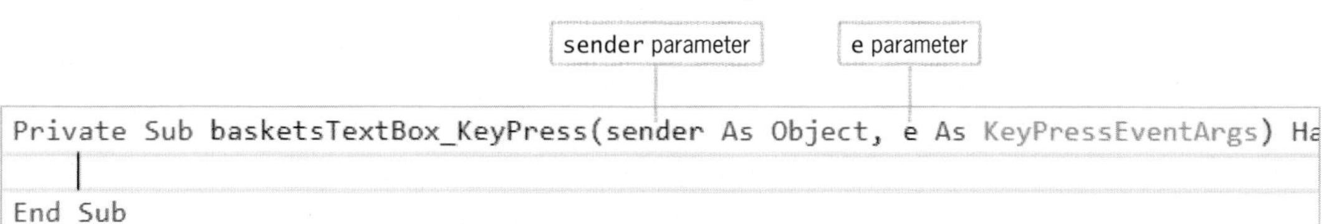

Figure 5-16 Code template for the basketsTextBox_KeyPress procedure

A control's **KeyPress event** occurs each time the user presses a key while the control has the focus. When the event occurs, a character corresponding to the pressed key is sent to the event's `e` parameter. For example, when the user presses the period (.) while entering data into a text box, the text box's KeyPress event occurs and a period is sent to the event's `e` parameter. Similarly, when the Shift key along with a lowercase letter is pressed, the uppercase version of the letter is sent to the `e` parameter.

To prevent a text box from accepting an inappropriate character, you first use the `e` parameter's **KeyChar property** to determine the pressed key. (*KeyChar* stands for *key character*.) You then use the `e` parameter's **Handled property** to cancel the key if it is an inappropriate one. You cancel the key by setting the `e` parameter's Handled property to True, like this: `e.Handled = True`.

In the Cookie Palace application, the basketsTextBox control's KeyPress event procedure should allow the text box to accept only numbers and the Backspace key, which is used for editing. Figure 5-17 shows two versions of the procedure's code. The If clause in both versions determines whether the value stored in the KeyChar property is inappropriate for the text box. In this case, an inappropriate value is one that is either less than "0" or greater than "9" and, at the same time, is not the Backspace key. You refer to the Backspace key on your keyboard using Visual Basic's **ControlChars.Back constant**. (The KeyPress event automatically allows the use of the Delete key for editing.)

HOW TO Use the KeyPress Event to Control the Characters Accepted by a Text Box

Version 1

```
Private Sub basketsTextBox_KeyPress(sender As Object,
e As KeyPressEventArgs) Handles basketsTextBox.KeyPress
    ' accept only numbers and the Backspace key

    If (e.KeyChar < "0" OrElse e.KeyChar > "9") AndAlso
        e.KeyChar <> ControlChars.Back Then
        e.Handled = True
    End If
End Sub
```

Version 2

```
Private Sub basketsTextBox_KeyPress(sender As Object,
e As KeyPressEventArgs) Handles basketsTextBox.KeyPress
    ' accept only numbers and the Backspace key

    If (e.KeyChar < "0" OrElse e.KeyChar > "9") _
        AndAlso e.KeyChar <> ControlChars.Back Then
        e.Handled = True
    End If
End Sub
```

line continuation character

If you want to experiment with the KeyPress event, open the solution contained in the Try It 7! folder.

Figure 5-17 How to use the KeyPress event to control the characters accepted by a text box

You can enter the entire If clause on one line in the Code Editor window. Or, you can split the clause into two lines, as shown in both versions in Figure 5-17. Depending on where you break a line of code, you may or may not need a line continuation character. The **line continuation character** is the underscore shown in Version 2. Examples of places where you can break a line of code without using the line continuation character include the following: after a comma, after an opening parenthesis, before a closing parenthesis, and after an operator (arithmetic, assignment, comparison, logical, or concatenation). The line continuation character must be immediately preceded by a space and appear at the end of a physical line of code in the Code Editor window.

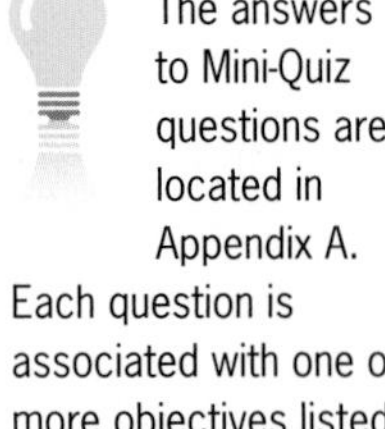

The answers to Mini-Quiz questions are located in Appendix A. Each question is associated with one or more objectives listed at the beginning of the chapter.

Mini-Quiz 5-3

1. Which of the following constants represents the Backspace key? (10)
   a. `Control.Back`
   b. `Control.Backspace`
   c. `ControlKey.Back`
   d. `ControlChars.Back`
2. You designate a default radio button by setting its ____________ property to True. (7)
   a. Checked
   b. Chosen
   c. Default
   d. Selected

3. The Abort button in a message box is represented by which of the following values? (8, 9)
    a. `Button.Abort`
    b. `Dialog.Abort`
    c. `DialogResult.Abort`
    d. `Result.Abort`

4. When entered in a text box's KeyPress event procedure, which of the following statements cancels the key pressed by the user? (10)
    a. `e.Cancel = True`
    b. `e.Handled = True`
    c. `e.KeyCancel = True`
    d. `e.KeyChar = True`

You have completed the concepts section of Chapter 5. The Programming Tutorial section is next.

PROGRAMMING TUTORIAL 1

Creating the Rock, Paper, Scissors Game Application

In this tutorial, you will create an application that simulates a game called Rock, Paper, Scissors. The game is meant to be played with two people. However, the application you create will allow one person to play against the computer. *Rock, Paper, Scissors* refers to the three choices each player can indicate using hand gestures. To play the game, the players face each other, call out *rock, paper, scissors, shoot,* and then make the hand gesture corresponding to their choice: a fist (rock), a flat hand (paper), or two fingers forming a V shape (scissors). The rules for determining a win are listed in Figure 5-18 along with the application's TOE chart. The application's MainForm is shown in Figure 5-19. The MainForm contains eight picture boxes, four labels, and one button.

Rules for the Rock, Paper, Scissors Game
Rock breaks scissors, so rock wins.
Paper covers rock, so paper wins.
Scissors cut paper, so scissors wins.

Task	Object	Event
1. Display the appropriate image in the playerPictureBox 2. Generate a random integer from 1 through 3 to represent the computer's choice 3. Use the random integer to display the appropriate image in the computerPictureBox 4. Determine whether the game is tied or there is a winner, and then display an appropriate message in the winnerLabel	playerRockPictureBox, playerPaperPictureBox, playerScissorsPictureBox	Click

Figure 5-18 Rules and TOE chart for the Rock, Paper, Scissors Game application *(continues)*

(continued)

Store the computer images	computerRockPictureBox, computerPaperPictureBox, computerScissorsPictureBox	None
End the application	exitButton	Click
Show the message that indicates either the winner or a tie game (from playerRockPictureBox, playerPaperPictureBox, or playerScissorsPictureBox)	winnerLabel	None
Show the image corresponding to the player's choice (from playerRockPictureBox, playerPaperPictureBox, or playerScissorsPictureBox)	playerPictureBox	None
Show the image corresponding to the computer's choice (from playerRockPictureBox, playerPaperPictureBox, or playerScissorsPictureBox)	computerPictureBox	None

Figure 5-18 Rules and TOE chart for the Rock, Paper, Scissors Game application

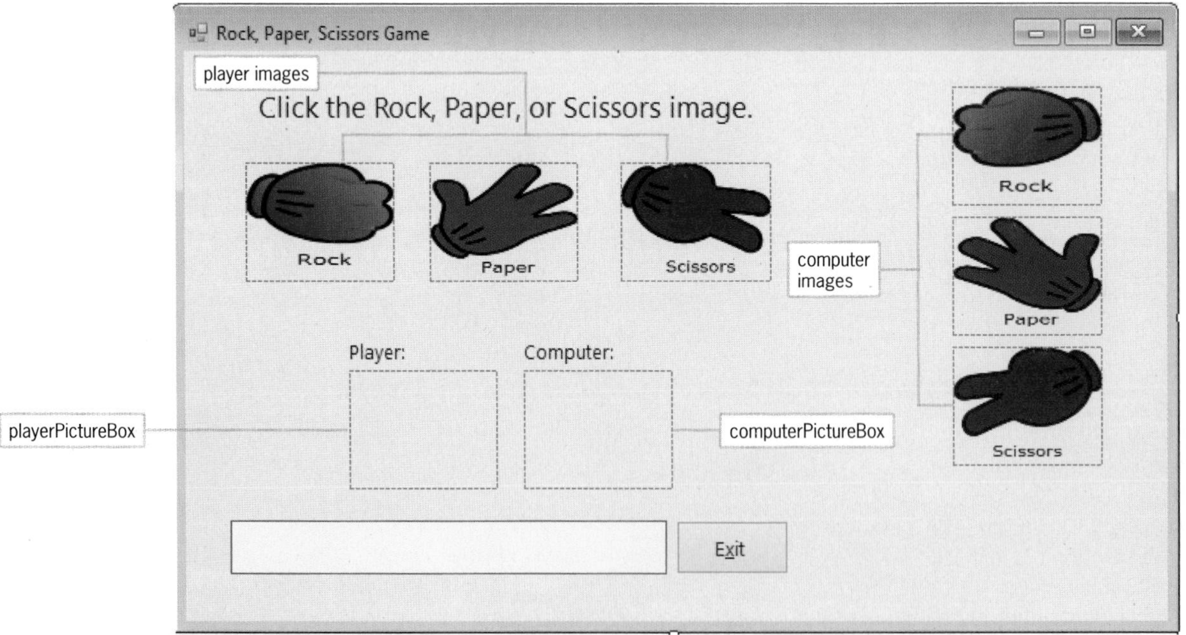

Figure 5-19 MainForm for the Rock, Paper, Scissors Game application

Coding the Rock, Paper, Scissors Game Application

According to the application's TOE chart, the Click event procedures for the exitButton and three of the picture boxes need to be coded.

To open the application:

1. Start Visual Studio. Open the **RockPaperScissors Solution** (**RockPaperScissors Solution.sln**) file contained in the VbReloaded2015\Chap05\RockPaperScissors Solution folder. If necessary, open the designer window.
2. Open the Code Editor window. The exitButton_Click procedure has already been coded for you. Replace <your name> and <current date> in the comments with your name and the current date, respectively.

Before coding the Click event procedures for the picture boxes, study closely the chart shown in Figure 5-20. The chart indicates the combinations that can occur when playing the game. It also shows the corresponding outcome of each combination.

Player's choice	Computer's choice	Outcome
Rock	Rock	Tie
	Paper	Computer wins because paper covers rock
	Scissors	Player wins because rock breaks scissors
Paper	Rock	Player wins because paper covers rock
	Paper	Tie
	Scissors	Computer wins because scissors cut paper
Scissors	Rock	Computer wins because rock breaks scissors
	Paper	Player wins because scissors cut paper
	Scissors	Tie

Figure 5-20 Chart showing the game combinations and outcomes

Now study the pseudocode shown in Figure 5-21. The pseudocode indicates the tasks to be performed by the playerRockPictureBox's Click event procedure.

```
playerRockPictureBox Click event procedure
1. display the playerRockPictureBox image, which represents the player's choice, in the
   playerPictureBox
2. generate a random integer from 1 through 3 to represent the computer's choice
3. if the random number is one of the following:
        1  display the computerRockPictureBox image in the computerPictureBox
           display "It's a tie." in the winnerLabel
        2  display the computerPaperPictureBox image in the computerPictureBox
           display "Computer wins because paper covers rock." in the winnerLabel
        3  display the computerScissorsPictureBox image in the computerPictureBox
           display "Player wins because rock breaks scissors." in the winnerLabel
   end if
```

Figure 5-21 Pseudocode for the playerRockPictureBox_Click procedure

To code and then test the playerRockPictureBox_Click procedure:

1. Open the code template for the playerRockPictureBox_Click procedure. Type the following comment and then press **Enter** twice:

   ' determines the winner or a tie game

2. The procedure will need a Random object to represent the pseudo-random number generator. It will also need an Integer variable to store the random number. Enter the following two Dim statements. Press **Enter** twice after typing the second Dim statement.

   Dim randGen As New Random
   Dim computerChoice As Integer

3. The first step in the pseudocode displays the playerRockPictureBox image, which represents the player's choice, in the playerPictureBox. Enter the following comment and assignment statement. Press **Enter** twice after typing the assignment statement.

   ' display the player' s choice
   playerPictureBox.Image = playerRockPictureBox.Image

4. The next step generates a random integer from 1 through 3. You will assign the random integer to the `computerChoice` variable. Enter the following comment and assignment statement:

   ' generate a random integer from 1 through 3
   computerChoice = randGen.Next(1, 4)

5. The last step in the pseudocode uses the random integer to display the appropriate image and message in the computerPictureBox and winnerLabel, respectively. Enter the following comment:

   ' display the computer's choice and the outcome

6. Now enter the Select Case statement shown in Figure 5-22.

```
Private Sub playerRockPictureBox_Click(sender As Object, e As EventArgs) Han
    ' determines the winner or a tie game

    Dim randGen As New Random
    Dim computerChoice As Integer

    ' display the player's choice
    playerPictureBox.Image = playerRockPictureBox.Image

    ' generate a random integer from 1 through 3
    computerChoice = randGen.Next(1, 4)
    ' display the computer's choice and the outcome
    Select Case computerChoice
        Case 1
            computerPictureBox.Image = computerRockPictureBox.Image
            winnerLabel.Text = "It's a tie."
        Case 2
            computerPictureBox.Image = computerPaperPictureBox.Image
            winnerLabel.Text = "Computer wins because paper covers rock."
        Case 3
            computerPictureBox.Image = computerScissorsPictureBox.Image
            winnerLabel.Text = "Player wins because rock breaks scissors."
    End Select
End Sub
```

enter the Select Case statement

Figure 5-22 playerRockPictureBox_Click procedure

7. Save the solution and then start the application. Click the **playerRockPictureBox** several times to verify that its Click event procedure is working properly. Figure 5-23 shows a sample run of the procedure. Because the procedure generates a random number for the computer's choice, a different image and message might appear in the computerPictureBox and winnerLabel controls on your screen.

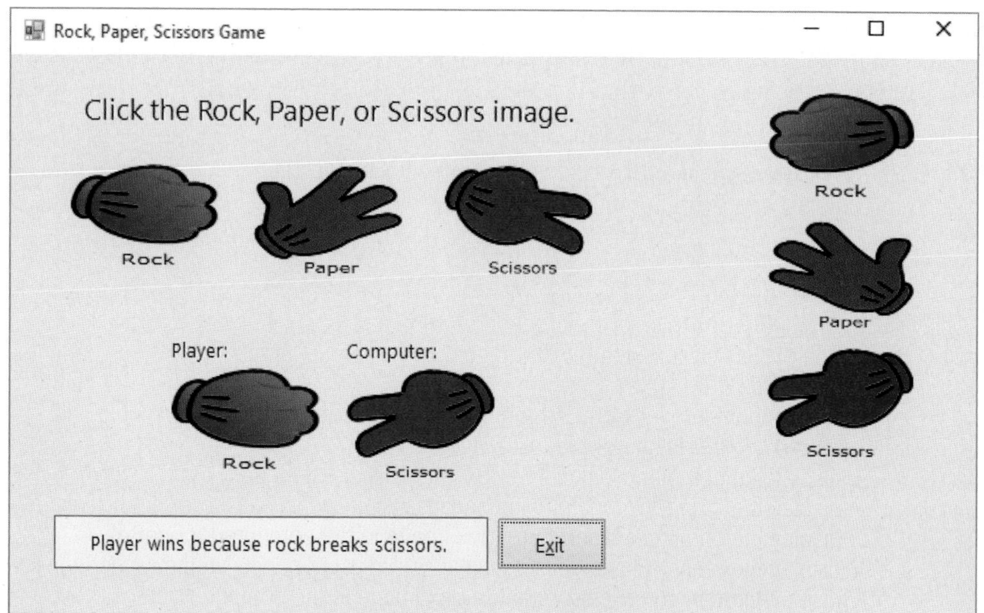

Figure 5-23 Sample run of the playerRockPictureBox_Click procedure

8. Click the **Exit** button to end the application.
9. Return to the designer window. The user does not need to see the three images that appear on the right side of the form. Drag the form's right border to the left in order to hide those images. (Or, expand the Size property in the Properties window, click Width, type 450 and press Enter.)
10. Lock the controls on the form, and then return to the Code Editor window.

Next, you will code the playerPaperPictureBox's Click event procedure. The procedure's pseudocode is shown in Figure 5-24.

```
playerPaperPictureBox Click event procedure
1. display the playerPaperPictureBox image, which represents the player's choice, in the
   playerPictureBox
2. generate a random integer from 1 through 3 to represent the computer's choice
3. if the random number is one of the following:
      1  display the computerRockPictureBox image in the computerPictureBox
         display "Player wins because paper covers rock." in the winnerLabel
      2  display the computerPaperPictureBox image in the computerPictureBox
         display "It's a tie." in the winnerLabel
      3  display the computerScissorsPictureBox image in the computerPictureBox
         display "Computer wins because scissors cut paper." in the winnerLabel
   end if
```

Figure 5-24 Pseudocode for the playerPaperPictureBox_Click procedure

PROGRAMMING TUTORIAL 1

To code and then test the playerPaperPictureBox_Click procedure:

1. Open the code template for the playerPaperPictureBox_Click procedure. Copy the comments and code from the playerRockPictureBox_Click procedure to the playerPaperPictureBox_Click procedure. (Do not copy the procedure header or footer.)
2. Using its pseudocode as a guide, make the appropriate modifications to the playerPaperPictureBox_Click procedure.
3. Save the solution and then start the application. Click the **playerPaperPictureBox** several times to verify that its Click event procedure is working properly, and then click the **Exit** button.

The last procedure you need to code is the playerScissorsPictureBox_Click procedure. The procedure's pseudocode is shown in Figure 5-25.

```
playerScissorsPictureBox Click event procedure
1. display the playerScissorsPictureBox image, which represents the player's choice, in the
   playerPictureBox
2. generate a random integer from 1 through 3 to represent the computer's choice
3. if the random number is one of the following:
       1  display the computerRockPictureBox image in the computerPictureBox
          display the string "Computer wins because rock breaks scissors." in the winnerLabel
       2  display the computerPaperPictureBox image in the computerPictureBox
          display the string "Player wins because scissors cut paper." in the winnerLabel
       3  display the computerScissorsPictureBox image in the computerPictureBox
          display the string "It's a tie." in the winnerLabel
   end if
```

Figure 5-25 Pseudocode for the playerScissorsPictureBox_Click procedure

To code and then test the scissorsPictureBox_Click procedure:

1. Open the code template for the playerScissorsPictureBox_Click procedure. Copy the comments and code from the playerRockPictureBox_Click procedure to the playerScissorsPictureBox_Click procedure. (Do not copy the procedure header or footer.)
2. Using its pseudocode as a guide, make the appropriate modifications to the playerScissorsPictureBox_Click procedure.
3. Save the solution and then start the application. Click the **playerScissorsPictureBox** several times to verify that its Click event procedure is working properly, and then click the **Exit** button.
4. Close the Code Editor window and then close the solution. Figure 5-26 shows the application's code.

```
' Project name:         RockPaperScissors Project
' Project purpose:      Simulates the Rock, Paper, Scissors game
' Created/revised by:   <your name> on <current date>

Option Explicit On
Option Strict On
Option Infer Off

Public Class MainForm
    Private Sub exitButton_Click(sender As Object, e As EventArgs
  ) Handles exitButton.Click
        Me.Close()
    End Sub

    Private Sub playerPaperPictureBox_Click(sender As Object,
    e As EventArgs) Handles playerPaperPictureBox.Click
        ' determines the winner or a tie game

        Dim randGen As New Random
        Dim computerChoice As Integer

        ' display the player's choice
        playerPictureBox.Image = playerPaperPictureBox.Image

        ' generate a random integer from 1 through 3
        computerChoice = randGen.Next(1, 4)
        ' display the computer's choice and the outcome
        Select Case computerChoice
            Case 1
                computerPictureBox.Image = computerRockPictureBox.Image
                winnerLabel.Text = "Player wins because paper covers
                rock."
            Case 2
                computerPictureBox.Image = computerPaperPictureBox
                .Image
                winnerLabel.Text = "It's a tie."
            Case 3
                computerPictureBox.Image = computerScissorsPictureBox
                .Image
                winnerLabel.Text = "Computer wins because scissors cut
                paper."
        End Select
    End Sub

    Private Sub playerRockPictureBox_Click(sender As Object,
    e As EventArgs) Handles playerRockPictureBox.Click
        ' determines the winner or a tie game

        Dim randGen As New Random
        Dim computerChoice As Integer

        ' display the player's choice
        playerPictureBox.Image = playerRockPictureBox.Image

```

Figure 5-26 Code for the Rock, Paper, Scissors Game application *(continues)*

(continued)

```
        ' generate a random integer from 1 through 3
        computerChoice = randGen.Next(1, 4)
        ' display the computer's choice and the outcome
        Select Case computerChoice
            Case 1
              computerPictureBox.Image = computerRockPictureBox.Image
              winnerLabel.Text = "It's a tie."
            Case 2
                computerPictureBox.Image = computerPaperPictureBox.Image
                winnerLabel.Text = "Computer wins because paper covers
                rock."
            Case 3
                computerPictureBox.Image = computerScissorsPictureBox
                .Image
                winnerLabel.Text = "Player wins because rock breaks
                scissors."
        End Select
    End Sub

    Private Sub playerScissorsPictureBox_Click(sender As Object,
    e As EventArgs) Handles playerScissorsPictureBox.Click
        ' determines the winner or a tie game

        Dim randGen As New Random
        Dim computerChoice As Integer

        ' display the player's choice
        playerPictureBox.Image = playerScissorsPictureBox.Image

        ' generate a random integer from 1 through 3
        computerChoice = randGen.Next(1, 4)
        ' display the computer's choice and the outcome
        Select Case computerChoice
            Case 1
                computerPictureBox.Image = computerRockPictureBox.Image
                winnerLabel.Text = "Computer wins because rock breaks
                scissors."
            Case 2
                computerPictureBox.Image = computerPaperPictureBox
                .Image
                winnerLabel.Text = "Player wins because scissors cut
                paper."
            Case 3
                computerPictureBox.Image = computerScissorsPictureBox
                .Image
                winnerLabel.Text = "It's a tie."
        End Select
    End Sub
End Class
```

Figure 5-26 Code for the Rock, Paper, Scissors Game application

PROGRAMMING TUTORIAL 2

Coding a Different Version of the Bubbles Car Wash Application

In this tutorial, you will code a different version of the Bubbles Car Wash application from Chapter 4. The application calculates and displays the total cost of a car wash. The new options offered by the car wash are shown in Figure 5-27 along with their corresponding prices. The figure also shows the application's MainForm. In this version of the application, the interface provides radio buttons for selecting the package type. The Basic radio button is the default button in the Package group. The interface also provides radio buttons for specifying whether the package is for the car's exterior only or for both its interior and exterior; the Exterior radio button is the default button in that group. The application will use a message box to ask the user whether the customer wants the additional Body Gloss service. Figure 5-28 shows the application's TOE chart.

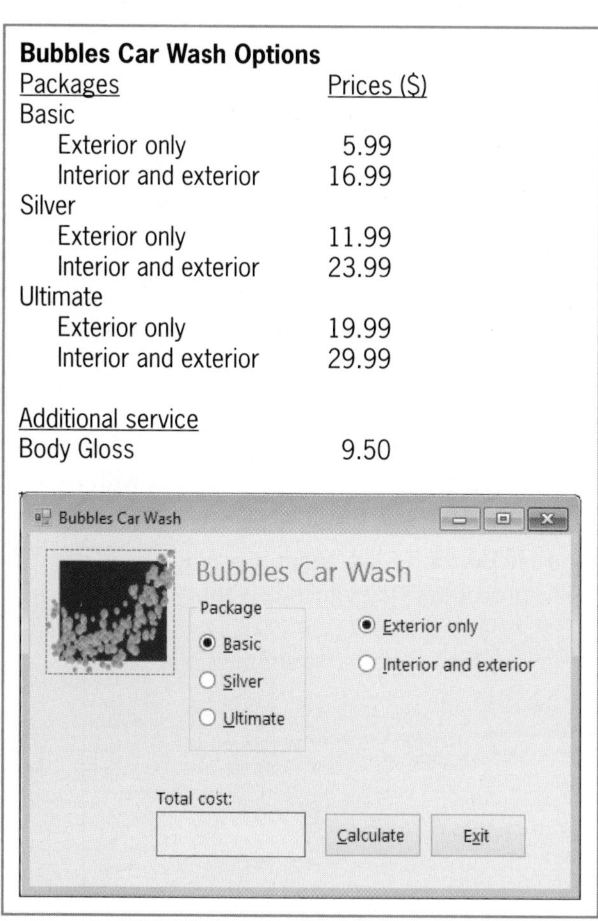

Bubbles Car Wash Options

Packages	Prices ($)
Basic	
Exterior only	5.99
Interior and exterior	16.99
Silver	
Exterior only	11.99
Interior and exterior	23.99
Ultimate	
Exterior only	19.99
Interior and exterior	29.99
Additional service	
Body Gloss	9.50

Figure 5-27 Options and MainForm

Task	Object	Event
Specify the package	basicRadioButton, silverRadioButton, ultimateRadioButton	None
Specify whether package is for exterior only or for both interior and exterior	exteriorRadioButton, interiorRadioButton	None
1. Calculate the total cost, which includes the package price and optional additional charge for the Body Gloss service; use a message box to determine whether to charge for the Body Gloss service 2. Display the total cost in the costLabel	calcButton	Click
End the application	exitButton	Click
Display the total cost (from calcButton)	costLabel	None

Figure 5-28 TOE chart for the Bubbles Car Wash application

Coding the Bubbles Car Wash Application

According to the application's TOE chart, the Click event procedures for the calcButton and exitButton need to be coded.

To open the application:

1. Start Visual Studio. Open the **Bubbles Solution** (**Bubbles Solution.sln**) file contained in the VbReloaded2015\Chap05\Bubbles Solution folder. If necessary, open the designer window.
2. Open the Code Editor window. The exitButton_Click procedure has already been coded for you. Replace <your name> and <current date> in the comments with your name and the current date, respectively.

The application's TOE chart indicates that the calcButton's Click event procedure is responsible for calculating and displaying the total cost. The procedure's pseudocode is shown in Figure 5-29.

```
calcButton Click event procedure
1. if the Basic package is selected
      if the Exterior radio button is selected
           total cost = price for Basic Exterior
      else
           total cost = price for Basic Interior and Exterior
      end if
   else if the Silver package is selected
      if the Exterior radio button is selected
           total cost = price for Silver Exterior
      else
           total cost = price for Silver Interior and Exterior
      end if
```

Figure 5-29 Pseudocode for the calcButton_Click procedure *(continues)*

(continued)

```
    else
       if the Exterior radio button is selected
            total cost = price for Ultimate Exterior
       else
            total cost = price for Ultimate Interior and Exterior
       end if
    end if
2. use a message box to ask the user whether the customer wants the Body Gloss service
3. if the customer wants the Body Gloss service
       add the additional Body Gloss price to the total cost
   end if
4. display the total cost in the costLabel
```

Figure 5-29 Pseudocode for the calcButton_Click procedure

As you know, before you begin coding a procedure, you first study the procedure's pseudocode (or flowchart) to determine any variables or named constants the procedure will require. The calcButton_Click procedure will use seven named constants to store the seven different prices shown earlier in Figure 5-28. It will also use a Double variable to keep track of the total cost and a DialogResult variable to determine the button selected in the message box. The named constants and variables are listed in Figure 5-30.

Named constants	Data type	Value
BasicExt	Double	5.99
BasicIntExt	Double	16.99
SilverExt	Double	11.99
SilverIntExt	Double	23.99
UltimateExt	Double	19.99
UltimateIntExt	Double	29.99
BodyGloss	Double	9.50
Variables	**Data type**	**Value source**
totalCost	Double	procedure calculation
button	DialogResult	user input (message box)

Figure 5-30 Memory locations for the calcButton_Click procedure

To code the calcButton_Click procedure and then test the procedure's code:

1. Locate the code template for the calcButton_Click procedure, and then click the **blank line** above the End Sub clause.
2. Enter the statements to declare the nine memory locations listed in Figure 5-30. Press **Enter** twice after typing the last declaration statement.
3. The first step in the pseudocode determines the radio button selected in the Package group and then assigns the appropriate price as the total cost. First, type **' determine package price** and press **Enter**. Then, enter a multiple-alternative selection structure to assign the appropriate price to the `totalCost` variable. Use the If...Then...Else statement.

4. The second step uses a message box to ask the user whether the customer wants to purchase the Body Gloss service. Type **' if necessary, add Body Gloss price** and press **Enter**. Now, enter an appropriate MessageBox.Show method. The method should display "Body Gloss?" as the prompt, "Bubbles Car Wash" as the title, Yes and No buttons, and the Exclamation icon.
5. The third step in the pseudocode determines whether the Body Gloss price should be added to the total cost. In this case, it should be added if the user chose the Yes button in the message box. Enter a single-alternative selection structure that adds the Body Gloss price to the total cost if the Yes button was selected.
6. The last step in the pseudocode displays the total cost in the costLabel. Enter an assignment statement to accomplish this task. Display the total cost with a dollar sign and two decimal places.
7. Save the solution and then start the application. Click the **Silver** radio button and then click the **Calculate** button. The message box shown in Figure 5-31 opens.

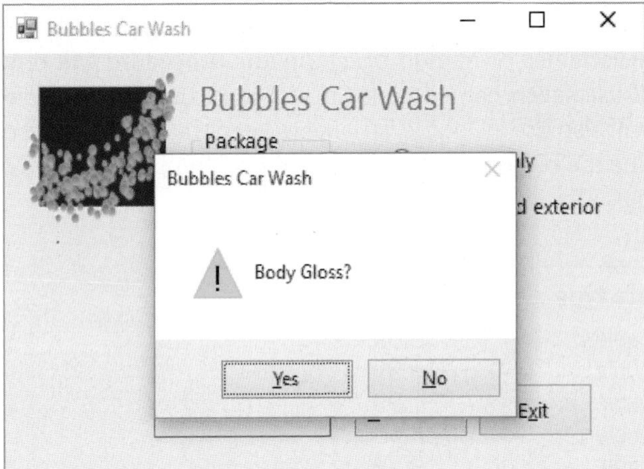

Figure 5-31 Message box asking the user about the Body Gloss service

8. Click the **No** button. $11.99 appears in the Total cost box.
9. Click the **Ultimate** radio button, and then click the **Interior and exterior** radio button. Click the **Calculate** button, and then click the **Yes** button in the message box. See Figure 5-32.

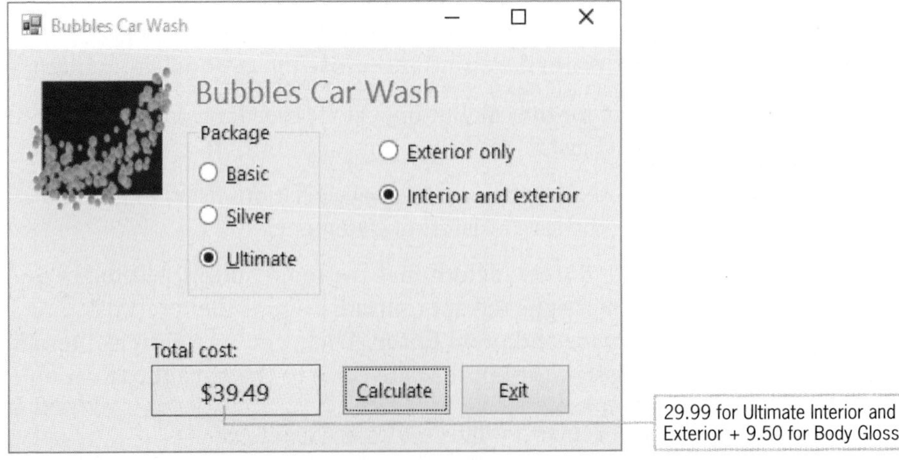

Figure 5-32 Total cost shown in the interface

PROGRAMMING TUTORIAL 2

10. On your own, test the other radio button combinations using both the Yes and No buttons in the message box. When you are finished, click the **Exit** button. Close the Code Editor window and then close the solution. Figure 5-33 shows the application's code.

```
' Project name:        Bubbles Project
' Project purpose:     Display the total cost of a car wash
' Created/revised by:  <your name> on <current date>

Option Explicit On
Option Strict On
Option Infer Off

Public Class MainForm
   Private Sub calcButton_Click(sender As Object, e As EventArgs
   ) Handles calcButton.Click
       ' calculates the cost of a car wash

       Const BasicExt As Double = 5.99
       Const BasicIntExt As Double = 16.99
       Const SilverExt As Double = 11.99
       Const SilverIntExt As Double = 23.99
       Const UltimateExt As Double = 19.99
       Const UltimateIntExt As Double = 29.99
       Const BodyGloss As Double = 9.5
       Dim totalCost As Double
       Dim button As DialogResult

       ' determine package price
       If basicRadioButton.Checked Then
           If exteriorRadioButton.Checked Then
               totalCost = BasicExt
           Else
               totalCost = BasicIntExt
           End If
       ElseIf silverRadioButton.Checked Then
           If exteriorRadioButton.Checked Then
               totalCost = SilverExt
           Else
               totalCost = SilverIntExt
           End If
       Else
           If exteriorRadioButton.Checked Then
               totalCost = UltimateExt
           Else
               totalCost = UltimateIntExt
           End If
       End If
       ' if necessary, add Body Gloss price
       button = MessageBox.Show("Body Gloss?",
                                "Bubbles Car Wash",
                                MessageBoxButtons.YesNo,
                                MessageBoxIcon.Exclamation)
       If button = DialogResult.Yes Then
           totalCost += BodyGloss
       End If
```

Figure 5-33 Code for the Bubbles Car Wash application *(continues)*

(continued)

```
        costLabel.Text = totalCost.ToString("C2")

    End Sub

    Private Sub exitButton_Click(sender As Object, e As EventArgs
    ) Handles exitButton.Click
        Me.Close()
    End Sub
End Class
```

Figure 5-33 Code for the Bubbles Car Wash application

PROGRAMMING EXAMPLE

Book Shack Application

The Book Shack store sells used books at discount prices. The store's price list is shown in Figure 5-34. Create an interface that provides a text box for the sales clerk to enter the number of books purchased. The text box should accept only numbers and the Backspace key. If the customer purchases more than six books, use a message box to determine whether he or she has a $1 coupon. Display the total price of the books in a label on the form. Use the following names for the solution and project, respectively: Book Solution and Book Project. Save the application in the VbReloaded2015\Chap05 folder. Change the form file's name to Main Form.vb. See Figures 5-34 through 5-39. The image in the picture box is contained in the VbReloaded2015\Chap05\Book.png file. Test the application using the data shown in Figure 5-38; the figure also shows the correct results.

Book Shack Price List

1–3 books	$2.99 per book
4–6 books	$2.49 per book
More than 6 books	$1.75 per book

Customers purchasing more than six books may have a $1 coupon.

Task	Object	Event
1. Calculate the total price, which may include a $1 coupon; use a message box to determine whether the customer has the coupon 2. Display the total price in totalLabel	calcButton	Click
End the application	exitButton	Click
Display the total price (from calcButton)	totalLabel	None
Get and display the number of books purchased Allow the text box to accept only numbers and the Backspace key	booksTextBox	None KeyPress

Figure 5-34 Price list and TOE chart

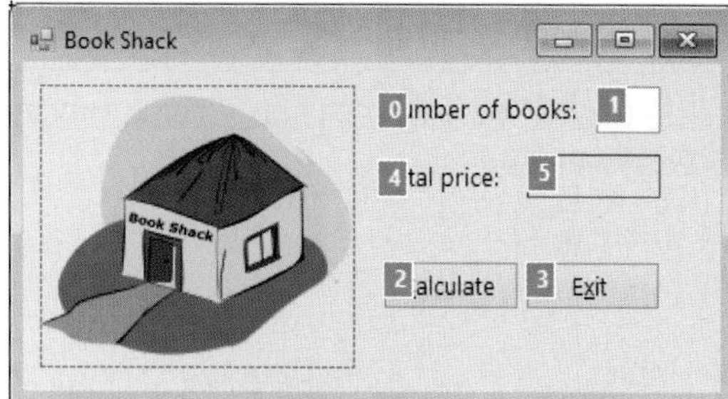

Figure 5-35 MainForm and tab order

Object	Property	Setting
MainForm	Font StartPosition Text	Segoe UI, 10pt CenterScreen Book Shack
totalLabel	AutoSize BorderStyle Text TextAlign	False FixedSingle (empty) MiddleCenter

Figure 5-36 Objects, properties, and settings

```
exitButton Click event procedure
close the application

booksTextBox KeyPress event procedure
if the user pressed a key that is not a number from 0 through 9 or the Backspace key
        cancel the key
end if

calcButton Click event procedure
1. assign user input (number of books) to a variable
2. number of books:
        1 to 3
                total price = price for 1 to 3 books * number of books
        4 to 6
                total price = price for 4 to 6 books * number of books
        More than 6 books
                total price = price for more than 6 books * number of books
                use a message box to determine whether the customer has a $1 coupon
                if the customer has a $1 coupon
                        subtract $1 from the total price
                end if
3. display the total price in totalLabel
4. send focus to booksTextBox
```

Figure 5-37 Pseudocode and memory locations *(continues)*

(continued)

calcButton Click event procedure—memory locations

Named constants	**Data type**	**Value**
`Price1To3`	Double	2.99
`Price4To6`	Double	2.49
`PriceOver6`	Double	1.75

Variables	**Data type**	**Value source**
`numBooks`	Integer	user input (booksTextBox)
`totalPrice`	Double	procedure calculation
`button`	DialogResult	user input (message box)

Figure 5-37 Pseudocode and memory locations

Number of books	Coupon	Total price
3		$8.97
4		$9.96
6		$14.94
7	Yes	$11.25
9	No	$15.75
0		$0.00

Figure 5-38 Test data and results

```
' Project name:          Book Project
' Project purpose:       Display the total price
' Created/revised by:    <your name> on <current date>

Option Explicit On
Option Strict On
Option Infer Off

Public Class MainForm
    Private Sub booksTextBox_KeyPress(sender As Object,
    e As KeyPressEventArgs) Handles booksTextBox.KeyPress
        ' accept only numbers and the Backspace key

        If (e.KeyChar < "0" OrElse e.KeyChar > "9") AndAlso
                e.KeyChar <> ControlChars.Back Then
            e.Handled = True
        End If
    End Sub

    Private Sub calcButton_Click(sender As Object, e As EventArgs
    ) Handles calcButton.Click
        ' calculate the total price

```

Figure 5-39 Code *(continues)*

(continued)

```
        Const Price1To3 As Double = 2.99
        Const Price4To6 As Double = 2.49
        Const PriceOver6 As Double = 1.75
        Dim numBooks As Integer
        Dim totalPrice As Double
        Dim button As DialogResult

        Integer.TryParse(booksTextBox.Text, numBooks)
        Select Case numBooks
            Case 1 To 3
                totalPrice = Price1To3 * numBooks
            Case 4 To 6
                totalPrice = Price4To6 * numBooks
            Case Is > 6
                totalPrice = PriceOver6 * numBooks
                button = MessageBox.Show("$1 coupon?", "Book Shack",
                         MessageBoxButtons.YesNo,
                         MessageBoxIcon.Exclamation)
                If button = DialogResult.Yes Then
                    totalPrice -= 1
                End If
        End Select
        totalLabel.Text = totalPrice.ToString("C2")
        booksTextBox.Focus()
    End Sub

    Private Sub exitButton_Click(sender As Object, e As EventArgs
    ) Handles exitButton.Click
        Me.Close()
    End Sub
End Class
```

Figure 5-39 Code

Chapter Summary

- You can nest a selection structure in either the True or False path of another selection structure.
- The primary decision is always made by an outer selection structure. The secondary decision is always made by a nested selection structure.
- You can code a multiple-alternative selection structure using either If...Then...Else statements or the Select Case statement.
- In a flowchart, a diamond is used to represent the condition in a multiple-alternative selection structure. The diamond has several flowlines leading out of the symbol, with each flowline representing a possible path.

- In a Select Case statement, the data type of the expressions in the Case clauses should match the data type of the statement's selectorExpression.
- A Case clause in a Select Case statement can contain more than one expression. The selectorExpression needs to match only one of the expressions for the instructions in that Case to be processed.
- You use the keyword `To` in a Case clause's expressionList when you know both the lower and upper bound values of the range you want to specify. You use the keyword `Is` when you know only one end of the range.
- Radio buttons allow you to limit the user to only one choice from a group of two or more related but mutually exclusive options.
- If you need to include two groups of radio buttons in an interface, at least one of the groups must be placed within a container, such as a group box, panel, or table layout panel.
- It is customary to have one radio button in each group of radio buttons selected when the interface first appears. The selected radio button is called the default radio button.
- If a radio button is selected, its Checked property contains the Boolean value True; otherwise, it contains the Boolean value False.
- The MessageBox.Show method allows an application to communicate with the user while the application is running.
- The MessageBox.Show method displays a message box that contains text, one or more buttons, and an icon. It returns an integer indicating the button chosen by the user. You should use the DialogResult value associated with the integer when referring to the return value in code.
- Use sentence capitalization for the text argument in the MessageBox.Show method, but use book title capitalization for the caption argument.
- You can code a text box's KeyPress event procedure to prevent the text box from accepting an inappropriate character. The character is stored in the `e` parameter's KeyChar property. To cancel the character, you set the `e` parameter's Handled property to True.

Key Terms

ControlChars.Back constant—the Visual Basic constant that represents the Backspace key on your keyboard

Default radio button—a radio button that is automatically selected when an interface first appears

Extended selection structures—another name for multiple-alternative selection structures

Group box—a control that is used to contain other controls; instantiated using the GroupBox tool, which is located in the Containers section of the toolbox

Handled property—a property of the KeyPress event procedure's `e` parameter; when set to True, it cancels the key pressed by the user

KeyChar property—a property of the KeyPress event procedure's `e` parameter; stores the character associated with the key pressed by the user

KeyPress event—occurs each time the user presses a key while a text box has the focus

Line continuation character—an underscore that is immediately preceded by a space and located at the end of a physical line of code; used to split a long instruction into two or more physical lines in the Code Editor window

MessageBox.Show method—displays a message box that contains text, one or more buttons, and an icon; allows an application to communicate with the user during run time

Multiple-alternative selection structure—a selection structure that contains several alternatives; also called an extended selection structure; can be coded using either If...Then...Else statements or the Select Case statement

Nested selection structure—a selection structure that is wholly contained (nested) within either the True or False path of another selection structure

Parameter—an item contained within parentheses in a procedure header; represents information passed to the procedure when the procedure is invoked

Radio buttons—used in an interface to limit the user to only one choice from a group of two or more related but mutually exclusive options

Select Case statement—used to code a multiple-alternative selection structure

Review Questions

Each Review Question is associated with one or more objectives listed at the beginning of the chapter.

1. A nested selection structure can appear in ____________ of another selection structure. (1–2)
   a. only the True path
   b. only the False path
   c. either the True path or the False path
2. If a Select Case statement's selectorExpression is an Integer variable named `code`, which of the following Case clauses is valid? (6)
   a. `Case Is > 7`
   b. `Case 3, 5`
   c. `Case 1 To 4`
   d. all of the above

Use the code shown in Figure 5-40 to answer Questions 3 through 5.

```
If number >= 0 AndAlso number <= 10 Then
     number += 4
Else
     If number > 10 OrElse number < 5 Then
          number *= 2
     Else
          number = -9999
     End If
End If
```

Figure 5-40 Code for Review Questions 3 through 5

3. If the `number` variable contains the number 9 before the code in Figure 5-40 is processed, what value will be in the variable after the code is processed? (3)

   a. –9999
   b. 13
   c. 18
   d. none of the above

4. If the `number` variable contains the number 12 before the code in Figure 5-40 is processed, what value will be in the variable after the code is processed? (3)

   a. –9999
   b. 16
   c. 24
   d. none of the above

5. If the `number` variable contains the number –3 before the code in Figure 5-40 is processed, what value will be in the variable after the code is processed? (3)

   a. –9999
   b. –6
   c. 1
   d. none of the above

Use the code shown in Figure 5-41 to answer Questions 6 through 9.

```
If code = "A" Then
    plan = "Standard"
ElseIf code = "C" OrElse code = "T" Then
    plan = "Deluxe"
ElseIf code = "R" Then
    plan = "Premier"
Else
    plan = "Invalid code"
End If
```

Figure 5-41 Code for Review Questions 6 through 9

6. What will the code in Figure 5-41 assign to the `plan` variable when the `code` variable contains the letter T? (6)

   a. Deluxe
   b. Premier
   c. Standard
   d. Invalid code

7. What will the code in Figure 5-41 assign to the `plan` variable when the `code` variable contains the letter R? (6)

   a. Deluxe
   b. Premier
   c. Standard
   d. Invalid code

8. What will the code in Figure 5-41 assign to the `plan` variable when the `code` variable contains the letter C? (6)

   a. Deluxe
   b. Premier
   c. Standard
   d. Invalid code

9. What will the code in Figure 5-41 assign to the `plan` variable when the `code` variable contains the letter X? (6)

   a. Deluxe
   b. Premier
   c. Standard
   d. Invalid code

Use the code shown in Figure 5-42 to answer Questions 10 through 12.

```
Select Case id
    Case 1
        city = "Chicago"
    Case 2, 8
        city = "San Francisco"
    Case 5 To 7
        city = "Boston"
    Case Else
        city = "N/A"
End Select
```

Figure 5-42 Code for Review Questions 10 through 12

10. What will the code in Figure 5-42 assign to the `city` variable when the `id` variable contains the number 8? (6)
    a. Boston
    b. Chicago
    c. San Francisco
    d. N/A
11. What will the code in Figure 5-42 assign to the `city` variable when the `id` variable contains the number 3? (6)
    a. Boston
    b. Chicago
    c. San Francisco
    d. N/A
12. What will the code in Figure 5-42 assign to the `city` variable when the `id` variable contains the number 6? (6)
    a. Boston
    b. Chicago
    c. San Francisco
    d. N/A
13. If the user clicks the Cancel button in a message box, the MessageBox.Show method returns the number 2, which is equivalent to which of the following values? (9)
    a. DialogResult.Cancel
    b. DialogResult.CancelButton
    c. MessageBox.Cancel
    d. MessageResult.Cancel
14. A Select Case statement's selectorExpression is an Integer variable. Which of the following Case clauses tells the computer to process the instructions when the Integer variable contains one of the following numbers: 1, 2, 3, 4, or 5? (6)
    a. `Case 1, 2, 3, 4, And 5`
    b. `Case 1 To 5`
    c. `Case Is > 1 And < 5`
    d. all of the above
15. A text box's ____________ event occurs when a user presses a key while the text box has the focus. (10)
    a. Key
    b. KeyPress
    c. Press
    d. PressKey

Exercises

Pencil and Paper

INTRODUCTORY

1. Carl is at a store's checkout counter. He'd like to pay for his purchase using either his credit card or his debit card, but preferably his credit card. However, he is not sure whether the store accepts either card. If the store doesn't accept either card, he will need to pay cash for the items. Write an appropriate solution, using only the instructions listed in Figure 5-43. An instruction can be used more than once. (1, 2)

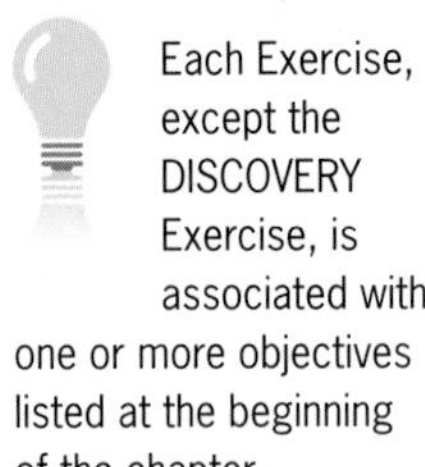

Each Exercise, except the DISCOVERY Exercise, is associated with one or more objectives listed at the beginning of the chapter.

```
else
end if
pay for your items using your credit card
pay for your items using your debit card
pay for your items using cash
if the store accepts your credit card
if the store accepts your debit card
ask the store clerk whether the store accepts your credit card
ask the store clerk whether the store accepts your debit card
```

Figure 5-43 Instructions for Exercise 1

INTRODUCTORY

2. Write the code to display the message "Entry error" in a message box when the value in the Integer `units` variable is less than or equal to 0. Otherwise, calculate the total owed and then display it in the totalLabel. The total owed is calculated as follows: If the value stored in the `units` variable is less than 20, multiply the value by $10; otherwise, multiply it by $5. Store the total owed in the `total` variable. Use the If...Then...Else statement. (1, 3, 4, 6, 8)

INTRODUCTORY

3. A procedure stores sales amounts in two Integer variables named `region1Sales` and `region2Sales`. Write the code to display the message "Both regions sold the same amount." when both variables contain the same number. If the variables contain different numbers, the code should compare the numbers and then display either the message "Region 1 sold more than region 2." or the message "Region 2 sold more than region 1." Use the If...Then...Else statement. Display the appropriate message in the msgLabel. (1, 3, 4, 6)

INTRODUCTORY

4. A selection structure needs to display the number of vacation weeks an employee has. The weeks are based on the number of years of employment, which is stored in an Integer variable named `yearsEmployed`. Employees who have been with the company for 1 to 3 years receive one week of vacation. Employees who have been with the company for 4 to 6 years receive two weeks of vacation. Employees who have been with the company over 6 years receive four weeks of vacation. Display the number of vacation weeks in the weeksLabel. Write two versions of the selection structure's code. In the first version, use the If...Then...Else statement. Use the Select Case statement in the second version. (4, 6)

INTRODUCTORY

5. Write two versions of the code to compare the contents of an Integer variable named `ordered` with the number 10. When the variable contains the number 10, display the string "Equal". When the variable contains a number that is greater than 10, display the string "Over 10". When the variable contains a number that is less than 10, display the string "Not over 10". Display the appropriate message in the msgLabel. In the first version, use the Select Case statement. Use the If...Then...Else statement in the second version. (1, 3, 4, 6)

6. Write two versions of the code to display the message "Great!" when a student's test score is at least 90. When the test score is from 70 through 89, display the message "Good job". For all other test scores, display the message "Retake the test". The test score is stored in an Integer variable named `score`. Display the appropriate message in the msgLabel. In the first version, use the If...Then...Else statement. Use the Select Case statement in the second version. (1, 3, 4, 6)

INTRODUCTORY

7. What will the solution in Figure 5-44 display if Derek was inside the 3-point line when the basketball went through the hoop? What will it display if Derek was behind the 3-point line when the basketball went through the hoop? What will it display if Derek was on the 3-point line when the basketball missed the hoop? What will it display if Derek was behind the 3-point line when the basketball missed the hoop? Does the solution in Figure 5-44 give you the same results as the solution shown in Figure 5-2 in the chapter? (2)

INTRODUCTORY

```
1. shoot the basketball
2. if the basketball went through the hoop and Derek was either inside or on the 3-point line
       say "I did it!"
       say "2 points for me"
   else
       if Derek was behind the 3-point line
             say "I did it!"
             say "3 points for me"
       else
             say "Missed it!"
       end if
   end if
```

Figure 5-44 Instructions for Exercise 7

8. What will the solution in Figure 5-45 display if Derek was inside the 3-point line when the basketball went through the hoop? What will it display if Derek was behind the 3-point line when the basketball went through the hoop? What will it display if Derek was on the 3-point line when the basketball missed the hoop? What will it display if Derek was behind the 3-point line when the basketball missed the hoop? Does the solution in Figure 5-45 give you the same results as the solution shown in Figure 5-2 in the chapter? (2)

INTRODUCTORY

```
1. shoot the basketball
2. if the basketball did not go through the hoop
       say "Missed it!"
   else
       say "I did it!"
       if Derek was either inside or on the 3-point line
              say "2 points for me"
       else
              say "3 points for me"
       end if
   end if
```

Figure 5-45 Instructions for Exercise 8

INTRODUCTORY

9. What will the solution in Figure 5-46 display if Derek was inside the 3-point line when the basketball went through the hoop? What will it display if Derek was behind the 3-point line when the basketball went through the hoop? What will it display if Derek was on the 3-point line when the basketball missed the hoop but hit the rim? What will it display if Derek was behind the 3-point line when the basketball missed the hoop? Does the solution in Figure 5-46 give you the same results as the solution shown in Figure 5-3 in the chapter? (2)

```
1. shoot the basketball
2. if the basketball hit the rim
         say "So close"
   else
         if the basketball went through the hoop
                  say "I did it!"
                  if Derek was behind the 3-point line
                           say "3 points for me"
                  else
                           say "2 points for me"
                  end if
         else
                  say "Missed it!"
         end if
   end if
```

Figure 5-46 Instructions for Exercise 9

INTRODUCTORY

10. What will the solution in Figure 5-47 display if Derek was inside the 3-point line when the basketball went through the hoop? What will it display if Derek was behind the 3-point line when the basketball went through the hoop? What will it display if Derek was on the 3-point line when the basketball missed the hoop but hit the rim? What will it display if Derek was behind the 3-point line when the basketball missed the hoop? Does the solution in Figure 5-47 give you the same results as the solution shown in Figure 5-3 in the chapter? (2)

```
1. shoot the basketball
2. if the basketball did not go through the hoop
          say "Missed it!"
          if the basketball hit the rim
                  say "So close"
          end if
   else
          say "I did it!"
          if Derek was behind the 3-point line
                  say "3 points for me"
          else
                  say "2 points for me"
          end if
   end if
```

Figure 5-47 Instructions for Exercise 10

11. A procedure uses a String variable named `department` and two Double variables named `salary` and `raise`. The `department` variable contains one of the following letters (entered in either uppercase or lowercase): A, B, C, or D. Employees in departments A and B are receiving a 2% raise. Employees in department C are receiving a 1.5% raise, and employees in department D are receiving a 3% raise. Write two versions of the code to calculate the appropriate raise amount. In the first version, use the Select Case statement. Use the If...Then...Else statement in the second version. Display the raise amount (with a dollar sign and two decimal places) in the raiseLabel. (4, 6) INTERMEDIATE

12. Code the partial flowchart shown in Figure 5-48. Use an Integer variable named `code` and two Double variables named `rate` and `bonus`. Display the bonus formatted with a dollar sign and two decimal places. Use the Select Case statement to code the multiple-alternative selection structure in the figure. (4–6) INTERMEDIATE

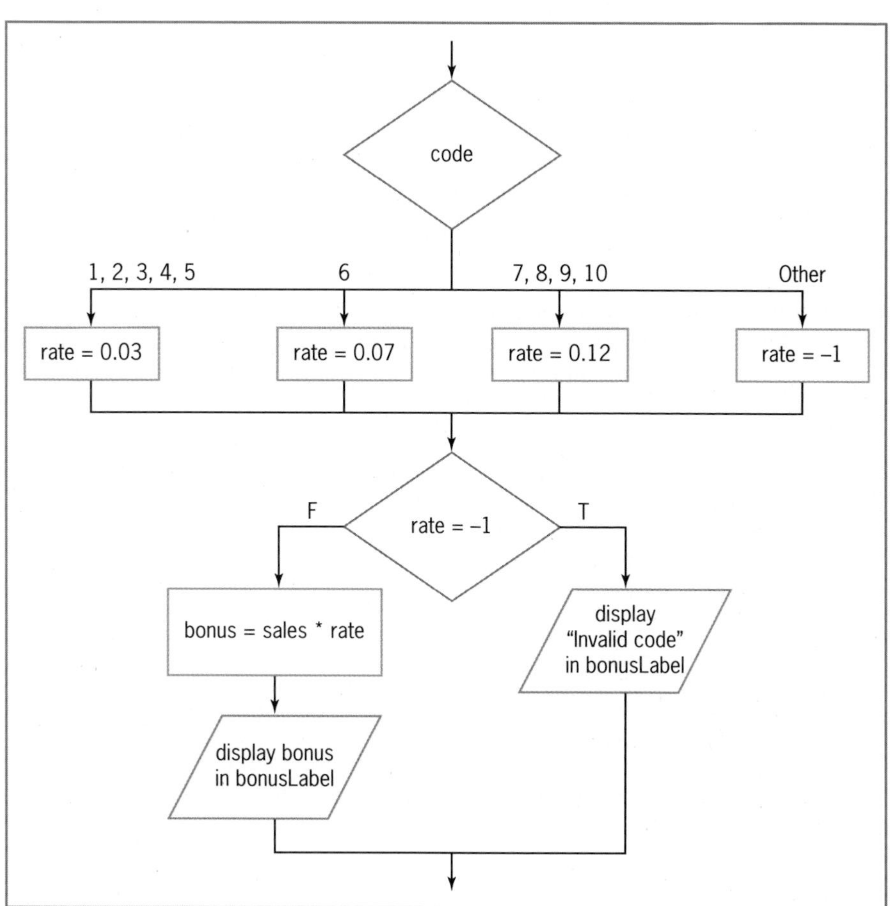

Figure 5-48 Flowchart for Exercise 12

13. The answerTextBox should accept only the letters Y, y, N, and n and the Backspace key. Write the appropriate selection structure for the text box's KeyPress event procedure. (10) ADVANCED

Computer

MODIFY THIS

14. If necessary, complete the Rock, Paper, Scissors Game application from this chapter's Programming Tutorial 1, and then close the solution. Use Windows to make a copy of the RockPaperScissors Solution folder. Rename the folder RockPaperScissors Solution-ModifyThis. Open the solution file contained in the RockPaperScissors Solution-ModifyThis folder. Change the Select Case statements to If...Then...Else statements. Save the solution and then start and test the application. Close the solution. (6)

MODIFY THIS

15. If necessary, complete the Bubbles Car Wash application from this chapter's Programming Tutorial 2, and then close the solution. Use Windows to make a copy of the Bubbles Solution folder. Rename the folder Bubbles Solution-ModifyThis. Open the solution file contained in the Bubbles Solution-ModifyThis folder. Change the multiple-alternative selection structure in the calcButton_Click procedure to a Select Case statement. Save the solution and then start and test the application. Close the solution. (6)

MODIFY THIS

16. If necessary, complete the Book Shack application from this chapter's Programming Example, and then close the solution. Use Windows to make a copy of the Book Solution folder. Rename the folder Book Solution-ModifyThis. Open the solution file contained in the Book Solution-ModifyThis folder. Before displaying the total price, use a message box to determine whether the customer is entitled to a 10% discount for being a member of the Book Shack Book Club. Save the solution and then start and test the application. Close the solution. (8, 9)

MODIFY THIS

17. Use Windows to make a copy of the AddSub Solution folder contained in the VbReloaded2015\Chap05 folder. Rename the folder AddSub Solution-ModifyThis. Open the solution file contained in the AddSub Solution-ModifyThis folder. (1, 3, 10)
    a. Set the operationTextBox's MaxLength property to 1.
    b. The operationTextBox should accept only the letters A, a, S, and s and the Backspace key. Code the appropriate event procedure.
    c. The num1TextBox and num2TextBox controls should accept only numbers, the period, and the Backspace key. Code the appropriate event procedure.
    d. Modify the calcButton_Click procedure to display "N/A" in the answerLabel when the operationTextBox is empty.
    e. Save the solution and then start and test the application. Close the solution.

MODIFY THIS

18. Use Windows to make a copy of the AddSub Solution folder contained in the VbReloaded2015\Chap05 folder. Rename the folder AddSub Solution-ModifyThis-RadioButtons. Open the solution file contained in the AddSub Solution-ModifyThis-RadioButtons folder. (7, 10)
    a. Provide the user with radio buttons, rather than a text box, for entering the mathematical operation. Make the appropriate modifications to the code.
    b. The num1TextBox and num2TextBox controls should accept only numbers, the period, and the Backspace key. Code the appropriate event procedures.
    c. Save the solution and then start and test the application. Close the solution.

19. Open the solution file contained in the VbReloaded2015\Chap05\Bonus Solution folder. (4, 6, 8, 10) INTRODUCTORY

    a. The user will enter the sales amount as an integer in the salesTextBox, which should accept only numbers and the Backspace key. Code the appropriate event procedure.

    b. The calcButton_Click procedure should display the salesperson's bonus. A salesperson with sales from $0 through $3,500 receives a 1% bonus. A salesperson with sales from $3,501 through $10,000 receives a 5% bonus. A salesperson whose sales are more than $10,000 receives a 10% bonus. The procedure should display the bonus, formatted with a dollar sign and two decimal places, in the bonusLabel. The procedure should not make any calculations when the salesTextBox is empty; rather, it should display an appropriate message in a message box. Code the procedure.

    c. Save the solution and then start and test the application. Close the solution.

20. Open the solution file contained in the VbReloaded2015\Chap05\Random Solution folder. The generateButton_Click procedure should generate two random integers from 1 through 10. It then should display one of the following messages in the messageLabel: *x* is equal to *y*, *x* is greater than *y*, or *x* is less than *y*. In each message, *x* and *y* are the first and second random integers, respectively, generated by the procedure. Draw the flowchart for the generateButton_Click procedure and then code the application. Save the solution and then start and test the application. Close the solution. (1–6) INTRODUCTORY

21. Open the solution file contained in the VbReloaded2015\Chap05\Turner Solution folder. Set the codeTextBox's MaxLength property to 1. The codeTextBox should accept only the numbers 1, 2, 3, and 4 and the Backspace key; code the appropriate event procedure. Code the displayButton_Click procedure to display the appropriate image in the displayPictureBox. The appropriate image is based on the code entered by the user. Display the house1PictureBox's image when the code is 1, and so on. If the codeTextBox is empty, set the displayPictureBox's Image property to the keyword `Nothing`. Size the form to hide the four picture boxes, and then lock the controls. Save the solution and then start and test the application. Close the solution. (1, 3, 4, 6, 10) INTRODUCTORY

22. Create a Windows Forms application. Use the following names for the solution and project, respectively: MacroTech Solution and MacroTech Project. Save the application in the VbReloaded2015\Chap05 folder. Change the form file's name to Main Form.vb. MacroTech sells a software package that is available in three editions. The application should display the price of the edition a customer wants to purchase. The retail prices for the Ultimate, Professional, and Student editions are $775.99, $499.99, and $149.99, respectively. Some customers may have a coupon worth 10% off the price of the Ultimate edition, while others may have a coupon worth 20% off the price of the Student edition. Create the interface shown in Figure 5-49, and then code the application. Save the solution and then start and test the application. Close the solution. (1, 3, 4, 6, 7) INTERMEDIATE

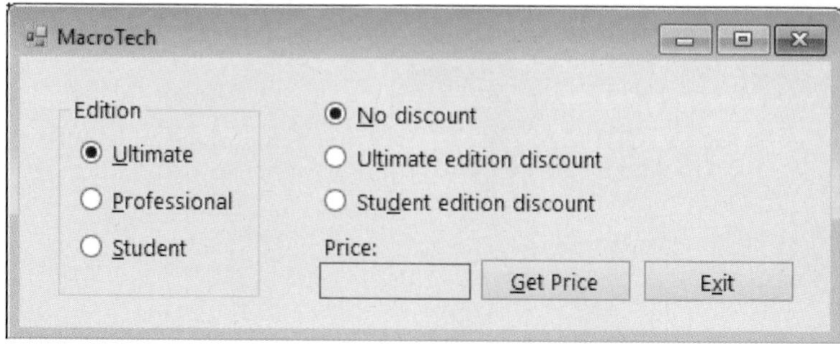

Figure 5-49 Interface for Exercise 22

INTERMEDIATE

23. Create a Windows Forms application. Use the following names for the solution and project, respectively: Currency Solution and Currency Project. Save the application in the VbReloaded2015\Chap05 folder. Change the form file's name to Main Form.vb. The application's interface should provide a text box for the user to enter the number of U.S. dollars. It should also provide radio buttons for the seven currencies listed in Figure 5-50. The text box should accept only numbers and the Backspace key. The interface should convert the U.S. dollars to the selected currency and then display the result (formatted to three decimal places). Use the Internet to determine the current exchange rates. Code the application. Save the solution and then start and test the application. Close the solution. (4–7, 10)

Currency
Canadian dollar
Euro
Indian rupee
Japanese yen
Mexican peso
South African rand
British pound

Figure 5-50 Currencies

ADVANCED

24. Open the solution file contained in the VbReloaded2015\Chap05\Blane Solution folder. Blane Ltd. sells economic development software to cities around the country. The company is having its annual user's forum next month. The price per person depends on the number of people a user registers. The first 3 people a user registers are charged $150 per person. Registrants 4 through 10 are charged $100 per person. Registrants over 10 are charged $60 per person. For example, if a user registers 8 people, then the total amount owed is $950. The $950 is calculated by first multiplying 3 by 150, giving 450. You then multiply 5 by 100, giving 500. You then add the 500 to the 450, giving 950. Display the total amount owed (formatted with a dollar sign and no decimal places) in the totalLabel. The numberTextBox should accept only numbers and the Backspace key. No calculations should be made when the numberTextBox is empty; rather, display an appropriate message. Save the solution and then start and test the application. Close the solution. (4, 6, 8, 10)

ADVANCED

25. Each salesperson at Marshall Sales Corporation receives a commission based on the amount of his or her sales. The commission rates are shown in Figure 5-51. If the salesperson has worked at the company for more than 10 years, he or she receives an additional $500. If the salesperson is classified as a traveling salesperson, he or she receives an additional $700. Create a Windows Forms application. Use the following names for the solution and project, respectively: Marshall Solution and Marshall Project. Save the application in the VbReloaded2015\Chap05 folder. Change the form file's name to Main Form.vb. Create the interface shown in Figure 5-51. The text box should accept only numbers, the period, and the Backspace key. Code the application. Save the solution and then start and test the application. Close the solution. (4, 6, 10)

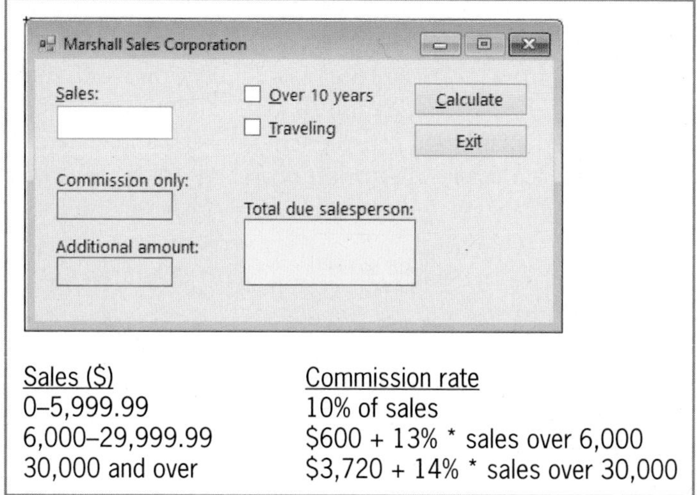

Sales ($)	Commission rate
0–5,999.99	10% of sales
6,000–29,999.99	$600 + 13% * sales over 6,000
30,000 and over	$3,720 + 14% * sales over 30,000

Figure 5-51 Interface and commission information for Exercise 25

26. If necessary, complete the Rock, Paper, Scissors Game application from this chapter's Programming Tutorial 1, and then close the solution. Use Windows to make a copy of the RockPaperScissors Solution folder. Rename the folder RockPaperScissors Solution-Advanced. Open the solution file contained in the RockPaperScissors Solution-Advanced folder. Modify the interface to display the number of times the player wins and the number of times the computer wins. Also make the appropriate modifications to the code. Save the solution and then start and test the application. Close the solution. (6) ADVANCED

27. In this exercise, you will learn about the SelectAll method and a text box's Enter event. DISCOVERY

    a. Open the Name Solution (Name Solution.sln) file contained in the VbReloaded2015\Chap05\Name Solution folder. Start the application. Type your first name in the First text box and then press Tab. Type your last name in the Last text box and then click the Concatenate Names button. Your full name appears in the Full name label.

    b. Press Tab twice to move the focus to the First text box. Notice that the insertion point appears after your first name in the text box. It is customary in Windows applications to have a text box's existing text selected (highlighted) when the text box receives the focus. You can select a text box's existing text by entering the text box's SelectAll method in the text box's Enter event procedure. The Enter event occurs when the text box receives the focus.

    c. Click the Exit button to end the application. Open the Code Editor window. Enter the SelectAll method in the Enter event procedures for the firstTextBox and lastTextBox controls. The method's syntax is *object*.SelectAll().

    d. Save the solution and then start the application. Type your first name in the First text box and then press Tab. Type your last name in the Last text box and then click the Concatenate Names button. Your full name appears in the Full name label. Press Tab twice to move the focus to the First text box. Notice that your first name is selected in the text box. Press Tab to move the focus to the Last text box. Notice that your last name is selected in the text box. Click the Exit button and then close the solution.

SWAT THE BUGS

28. Open the solution file contained in the VbReloaded2015\Chap05\Debug Solution folder. The application displays a shipping charge that is based on the total price entered by the user, as shown in Figure 5-52. Test the application using the following total prices: 100, 501, 1500, 500.75, 30, 1000.33, and 2000. Notice that the application does not always display the correct shipping charge. Correct the application's code. When the application is working correctly, close the solution. (6)

Total price	Shipping ($)
At least $100 but less than $501	10
At least $501 but less than $1,001	7
At least $1,001	5
Less than $100	13

Figure 5-52 Shipping information for Exercise 28

Case Projects

Kelvin's Department Store

Kelvin's Department Store wants an application that displays the number of reward points a customer earns each month. The reward points are based on the customer's membership type and total monthly purchase amount, as shown in Figure 5-53. Use the following names for the solution and project, respectively: Kelvin Solution and Kelvin Project. Save the solution in the VbReloaded2015\Chap05 folder. Change the form file's name to Main Form.vb. You can either create your own user interface or create the one shown in Figure 5-53. Display the number of reward points without any decimal places. (1–7, 10)

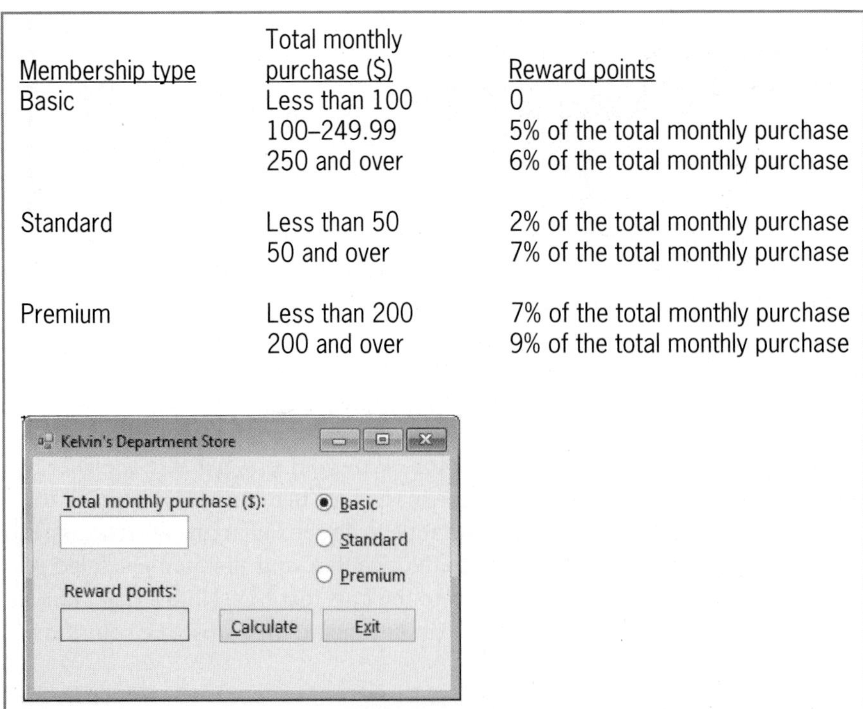

Membership type	Total monthly purchase ($)	Reward points
Basic	Less than 100	0
	100–249.99	5% of the total monthly purchase
	250 and over	6% of the total monthly purchase
Standard	Less than 50	2% of the total monthly purchase
	50 and over	7% of the total monthly purchase
Premium	Less than 200	7% of the total monthly purchase
	200 and over	9% of the total monthly purchase

Figure 5-53 Reward points chart and sample interface for Kelvin's Department Store

Asterwood Health Club

Asterwood Health Club offers personal training sessions to its members. The sessions are either 30 or 60 minutes in length, and members can sign up to meet either two or three times per week. Each 30-minute session costs $17.50; each 60-minute session costs $30. However, members who sign up for three 60-minute sessions per week receive a 10% discount. Additionally, members who are at least 60 years old receive a senior discount, which is an additional 5% off the total cost. Use the following names for the solution and project, respectively: Asterwood Solution and Asterwood Project. Save the application in the VbReloaded2015\Chap05 folder. Change the form file's name to Main Form.vb. You can either create your own user interface or create the one shown in Figure 5-54. The application should display the total cost for four weeks of personal training. (Hint: The monthly cost for a member who registers for three 60-minute sessions per week is $324.00. If the member is entitled to the senior discount, the cost is $307.80.) (1–7, 10)

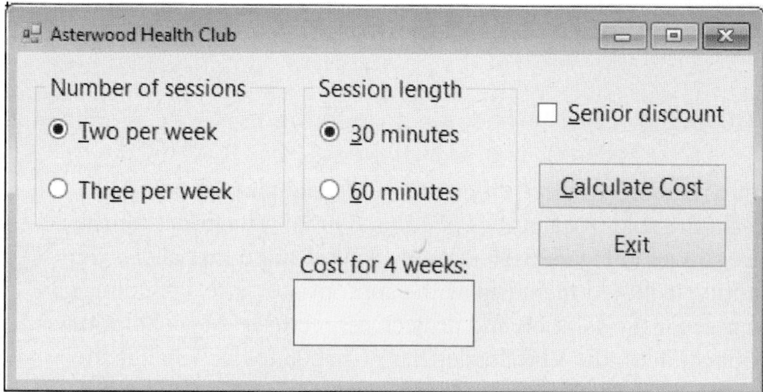

Figure 5-54 Sample interface for Asterwood Health Club

Campbell Tea Shoppe

Campbell Tea Shoppe sells tea by the box, with each box containing 30 tea bags. The tea comes in the following flavors: Breakfast Blend, Chamomile, Citrus Green, Earl Grey, and Spiced Chai. The price for a box of tea depends on the number of boxes ordered, as shown in Figure 5-55. The user will need to enter the number of boxes of each flavor ordered by the customer. He or she will also need to specify whether the customer should be charged a 5% sales tax. Use a message box to get the sales tax information. Create an application that displays the total number of boxes ordered, the sales tax (if any), and the total price of the order. Use the following names for the solution and project, respectively: Campbell Tea Solution and Campbell Tea Project. Save the application in the VbReloaded2015\Chap05 folder. Change the form file's name to Main Form.vb. You can either create your own user interface or create the one shown in Figure 5-55. The image in the picture box is stored in the VbReloaded2015\Chap05\Tea.png file. (1–10)

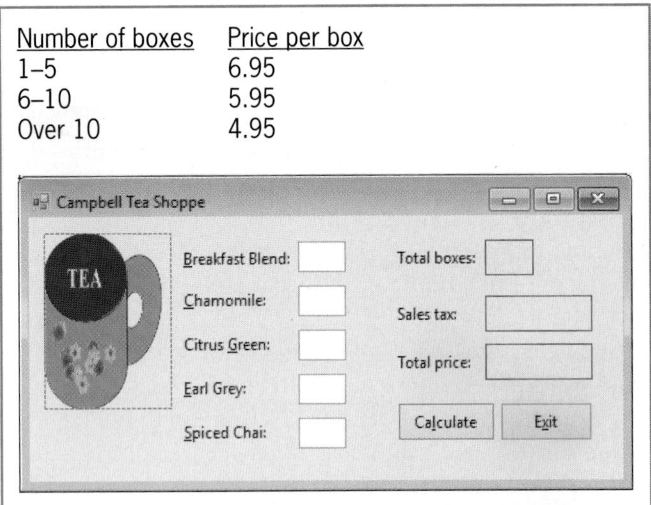

Number of boxes	Price per box
1–5	6.95
6–10	5.95
Over 10	4.95

Figure 5-55 Tea prices and a sample interface for Campbell Tea Shoppe

Steak Lovers Company

Steak Lovers Company sells filet mignons in three different sizes (weights): 4 ounces, 5 ounces, and 6 ounces. The steaks are sold in quantities of either 8 or 16. The prices for the various sizes and quantities are shown in Figure 5-56. Create an application that allows the user to enter the size and quantity; it should then display the appropriate price, including a 5% sales tax. Use the following names for the solution and project, respectively: Steak Solution and Steak Project. Save the application in the VbReloaded2015\Chap05 folder. Change the form file's name to Main Form.vb. You can either create your own user interface or create the one shown in Figure 5-56. The image used for the form's BackgroundImage property is stored in the VbReloaded2015\Chap05\BlueBack.gif file. You will also need to set the form's BackgroundImageLayout property to Stretch. (1–10)

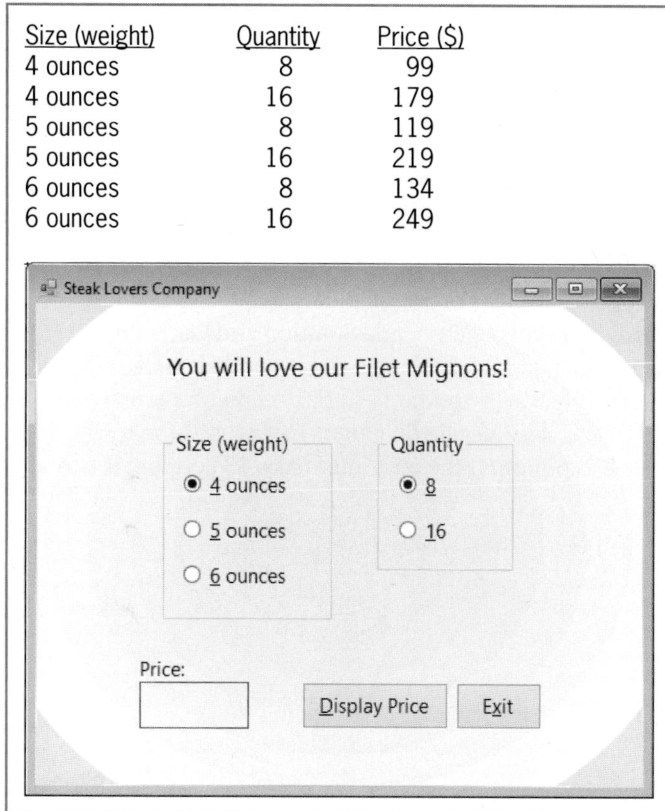

Size (weight)	Quantity	Price ($)
4 ounces	8	99
4 ounces	16	179
5 ounces	8	119
5 ounces	16	219
6 ounces	8	134
6 ounces	16	249

Figure 5-56 Steak prices and a sample interface for Steak Lovers Company

Just Tees

Just Tees sells organic cotton tee shirts for both men and women. The tees come in three sizes: S, M, and L. The women's tees are $17.75 each. The men's tees in size S are also $17.75; however, the men's tees in sizes M and L are $19.75. Each tee can be customized with a picture and/or a name. The additional charge for including a picture on a woman's tee is $5. The additional charge for including a picture on a man's tee in sizes S or M is also $5; however, the additional charge for a man's tee in size L is $6. The additional charge for including a name on a tee is $7.50. The application should allow the user to enter more than one of the same tee. Create an application that displays the total price of the tee(s), including a 2% sales tax. Use the following names for the solution and project, respectively: Just Tees Solution and Just Tees Project. Save the solution in the VbReloaded2015\Chap05 folder. Change the form file's name to Main Form.vb. (1–10)

  Carla's Pizzeria

Carla's Pizzeria sells three different stuffed pizzas: Mama Carla's, Papa Gino's, and Classic Veggie. The Mama Carla's pizza is $11.99. The Papa Gino's pizza is $12.99, and the Classic Veggie pizza is $9.99. However, the customer can request a gluten-free crust for $2 more per pizza. Periodically, Carla's Pizzeria e-mails customers a $3 coupon on the purchase of either a Mama Carla's pizza or a Papa Gino's pizza. Only one coupon can be used per order. Create an application that displays the total price of a customer's order, including a 6% sales tax. Use the following names for the solution and project, respectively: Carla Solution and Carla Project. Save the solution in the VbReloaded2015\Chap05 folder. Change the form file's name to Main Form.vb. (Hint: If the customer orders four pizzas—two Mama Carla's on regular crust, one Mama Carla's on gluten-free crust, and one Classic Veggie on gluten-free crust—the total price is $52.96 if the customer does not have a $3 coupon. If the customer has a $3 coupon, the total price is $49.78.) (1–10)

CHAPTER 6

Repeating Program Instructions

After studying Chapter 6, you should be able to:

1. Differentiate between a looping condition and a loop exit condition
2. Differentiate between a pretest loop and a posttest loop
3. Include pretest and posttest loops in pseudocode and in a flowchart
4. Write a Do...Loop statement
5. Utilize counters and accumulators
6. Display a dialog box using the InputBox function
7. Use a text box's Multiline, ReadOnly, and ScrollBars properties
8. Include a list box in an interface
9. Enable and disable a control
10. Refresh the screen and delay program execution
11. Use the Not logical operator (Programming Tutorial 1)

The Repetition Structure

Programmers use the **repetition structure**, referred to more simply as a **loop**, when they need the computer to repeatedly process one or more program instructions. The loop contains a condition that controls whether the instructions are repeated. Like the condition in a selection structure, the condition in a loop must evaluate to either True or False. The condition is evaluated with each repetition (or iteration) of the loop and can be phrased in one of two ways: It can either specify the requirement for repeating the instructions or specify the requirement for *not* repeating them. The requirement for repeating the instructions is referred to as the **looping condition** because it indicates when the computer should continue "looping" through the instructions. The requirement for *not* repeating the instructions is referred to as the **loop exit condition** because it tells the computer when to exit (or stop) the loop. Every looping condition has an opposing loop exit condition; one is the opposite of the other.

The examples in Figure 6-1 may help illustrate the difference between the looping condition and the loop exit condition. In each example, the looping condition indicates when to *continue* an action, while the loop exit condition indicates when to *stop* the action.

```
Keep your car's windshield wipers on
        while it is raining. (looping condition)
        until it stops raining. (loop exit condition)

At the end of the concert, clap your hands
        while the performers are on stage. (looping condition)
        until the performers leave the stage. (loop exit condition)

When playing musical chairs, walk around the chairs
        while the music is playing. (looping condition)
        until the music stops playing. (loop exit condition)
```

Figure 6-1 Examples of looping and loop exit conditions

In Chapter 5's Figure 5-1, you viewed a problem specification and solution involving a basketball player named Derek. The solution, which is shown in Figure 6-2, contains the sequence and selection structures only. In this chapter, we will make a slight change to the original problem specification. Now Derek should continue shooting the basketball until it goes through the hoop. Figure 6-2 shows the modified problem specification along with two solutions. Both solutions contain the sequence and repetition structures. The repetition structure in Solution 1 begins with the "repeat while the basketball did not go through the hoop" clause and ends with the "end repeat while" clause. The repetition structure in Solution 2 begins with the "repeat until the basketball goes through the hoop" clause and ends with the "end repeat until" clause. The instructions between both clauses are called the loop body, and they are indented to indicate that they are part of the repetition structure.

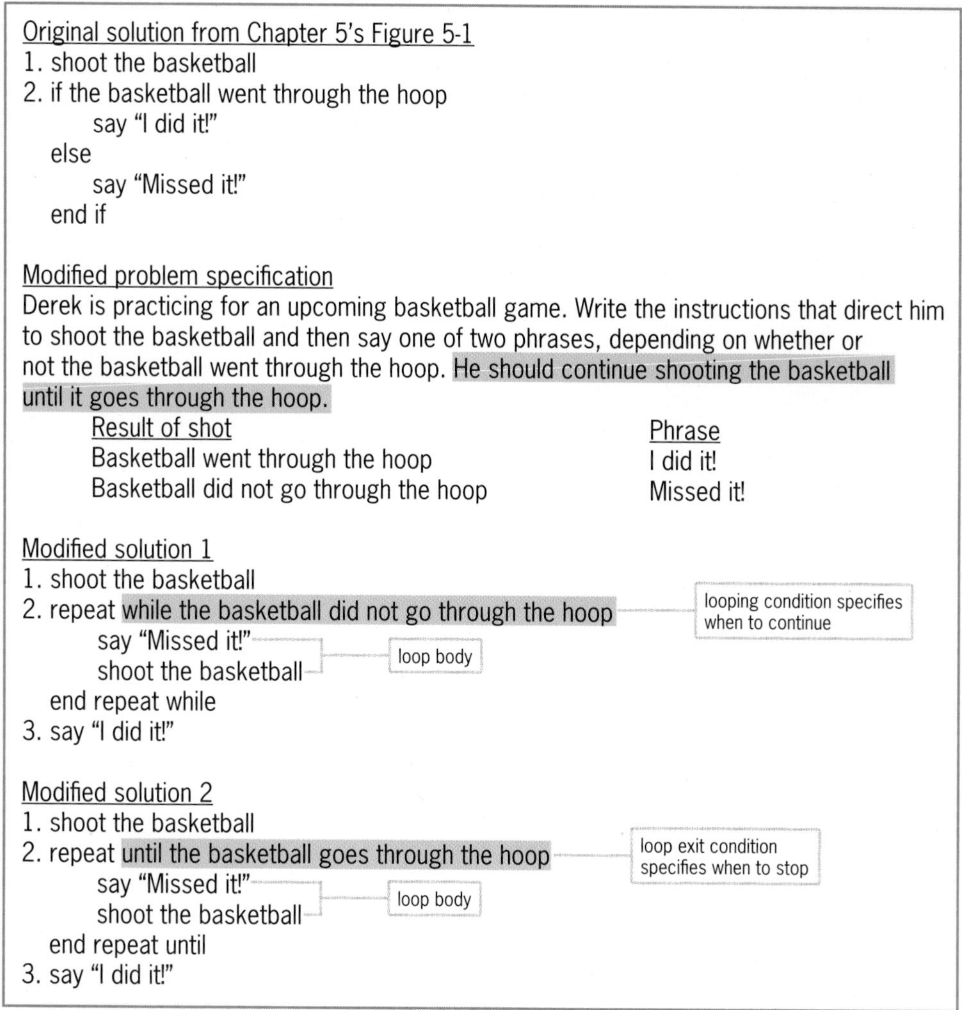

Figure 6-2 Original solution and modified problem specification and solutions

The shaded portion in each modified solution in Figure 6-2 specifies the repetition structure's condition. The condition in the first modified solution is phrased as a looping condition because it tells Derek when to *continue* repeating the instructions in the loop body. In this case, he should repeat the instructions as long as (or while) the basketball did not go through the hoop. The condition in the second modified solution is phrased as a loop exit condition because it tells Derek when to *stop* repeating the instructions in the loop body. In this case, he should stop when the basketball goes through the hoop. Notice that the loop exit condition is the opposite of the looping condition. Whether you use a looping condition or a loop exit condition, the condition must evaluate to a Boolean value (either True or False).

The Projected Sales Application

The programmer determines whether a problem's solution requires a loop by studying the problem specification. Figure 6-3 shows the problem specification for the Projected Sales application. It also includes the pseudocode and code for the calcButton's Click event procedure. The procedure requires only the sequence structure. It does not need a selection structure or a loop because no decisions need to be made and no instructions need to be repeated to display the projected sales for the following year. The figure also contains a sample run of the application.

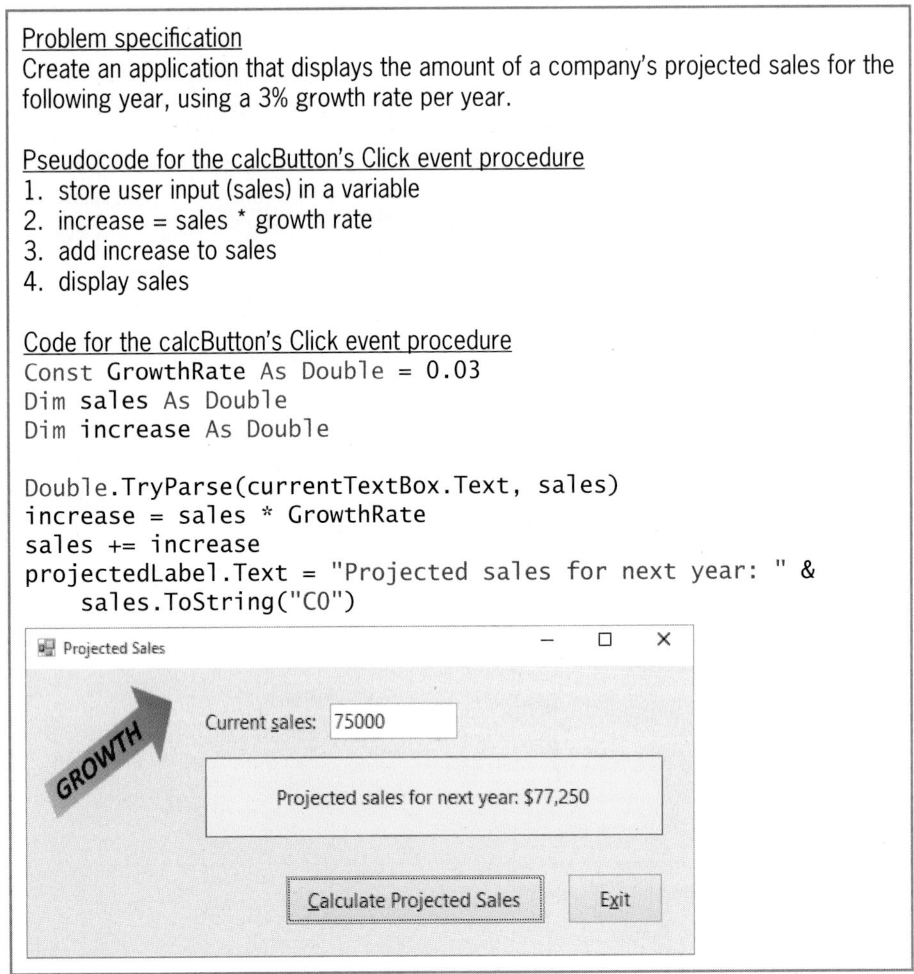

Problem specification
Create an application that displays the amount of a company's projected sales for the following year, using a 3% growth rate per year.

Pseudocode for the calcButton's Click event procedure
1. store user input (sales) in a variable
2. increase = sales * growth rate
3. add increase to sales
4. display sales

Code for the calcButton's Click event procedure

```
Const GrowthRate As Double = 0.03
Dim sales As Double
Dim increase As Double

Double.TryParse(currentTextBox.Text, sales)
increase = sales * GrowthRate
sales += increase
projectedLabel.Text = "Projected sales for next year: " &
    sales.ToString("C0")
```


Figure 6-3 Problem specification, pseudocode, code, and a sample run of the Projected Sales application

Now we will make a slight change to the problem specification from Figure 6-3. The application will now need to display the number of years required for the projected sales to reach at least $125,000. It will also need to display the projected sales amount at that time. Consider the changes you will need to make to the calcButton's original pseudocode.

The first step in the original pseudocode is to store the input item (sales) in a variable; the modified pseudocode will still need this step. Steps 2 and 3 calculate the projected increase and projected sales, respectively, for the following year. The modified pseudocode will need to repeat both steps either *while* the projected sales amount is less than $125,000 (looping condition) or *until* it is greater than or equal to $125,000 (loop exit condition). Here, too, notice that the loop exit condition is the opposite of the looping condition. The loop in the modified pseudocode will also need to keep track of the number of times the instructions in Steps 2 and 3 are processed because each time represents a year. The last step in the original pseudocode displays the projected sales amount. The modified pseudocode will need to display the projected sales amount as well as the number of years.

The modified problem specification is shown in Figure 6-4 along with four versions of the modified pseudocode for the calcButton's Click event procedure. (Here again, notice that even small procedures can have many solutions.) Only the loop is different in each version.

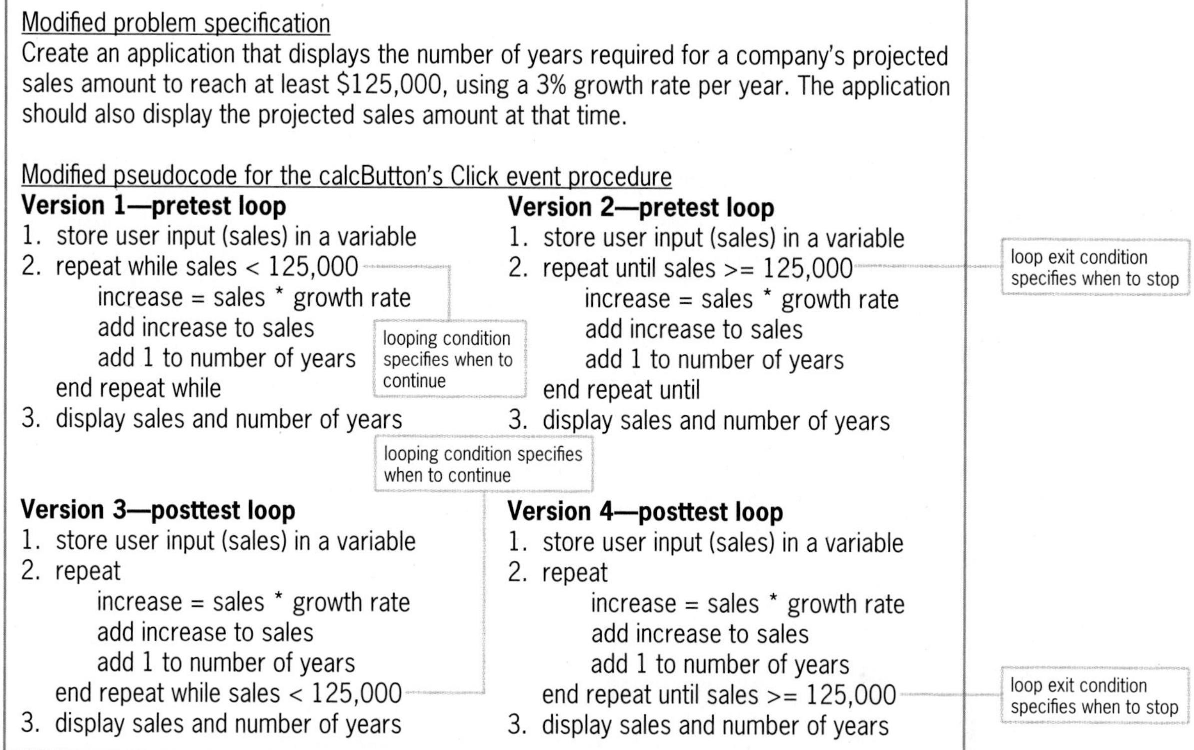

Modified problem specification
Create an application that displays the number of years required for a company's projected sales amount to reach at least $125,000, using a 3% growth rate per year. The application should also display the projected sales amount at that time.

Modified pseudocode for the calcButton's Click event procedure

Version 1—pretest loop
```
1. store user input (sales) in a variable
2. repeat while sales < 125,000
       increase = sales * growth rate
       add increase to sales
       add 1 to number of years
   end repeat while
3. display sales and number of years
```

Version 2—pretest loop
```
1. store user input (sales) in a variable
2. repeat until sales >= 125,000
       increase = sales * growth rate
       add increase to sales
       add 1 to number of years
   end repeat until
3. display sales and number of years
```

Version 3—posttest loop
```
1. store user input (sales) in a variable
2. repeat
       increase = sales * growth rate
       add increase to sales
       add 1 to number of years
   end repeat while sales < 125,000
3. display sales and number of years
```

Version 4—posttest loop
```
1. store user input (sales) in a variable
2. repeat
       increase = sales * growth rate
       add increase to sales
       add 1 to number of years
   end repeat until sales >= 125,000
3. display sales and number of years
```


Figure 6-4 Modified problem specification and pseudocode for the Projected Sales application

The loops in Versions 1 and 2 are pretest loops. In a **pretest loop**, the condition appears at the beginning of the loop, indicating that it is evaluated *before* the instructions within the loop are processed. The condition in Version 1 is a looping condition because it tells the computer when to continue repeating the loop instructions. Version 2's condition, on the other hand, is a loop exit condition because it tells the computer when to stop repeating the instructions. Depending on the result of the evaluation, the instructions in a pretest loop may never be processed. For example, if the sales amount entered by the user is greater than or equal to 125,000, the "while sales < 125,000" looping condition in Version 1 will evaluate to False and the loop instructions will be skipped over. Similarly, the "until sales >= 125,000" loop exit condition in Version 2 will evaluate to True, causing the loop instructions to be bypassed.

The loops in Versions 3 and 4 in Figure 6-4, on the other hand, are posttest loops. In a **posttest loop**, the condition appears at the end of the loop, indicating that it is evaluated *after* the instructions within the loop are processed. The condition in Version 3 is a looping condition, whereas the condition in Version 4 is a loop exit condition. Unlike the instructions in a pretest loop, the instructions in a posttest loop will always be processed at least once before the loop ends. Posttest loops should be used only when you are certain that the loop instructions should be processed one or more times.

Pretest and posttest loops are also called top-driven and bottom-driven loops, respectively.

The answers to Mini-Quiz questions are located in Appendix A. Each question is associated with one or more objectives listed at the beginning of the chapter.

Mini-Quiz 6-1

1. It's possible that the instructions in this type of loop may never be processed. (2)
   a. posttest
   b. pretest
2. The "repeat until your hair is clean" instruction is an example of which type of condition? (1)
   a. looping
   b. loop exit
3. Which condition indicates when the loop instructions should be repeated? (1)
   a. looping
   b. loop exit

The Visual Basic language provides three different statements for coding loops: Do...Loop, For...Next, and For Each...Next. The Do...Loop statement can be used to code both pretest and posttest loops, whereas the For...Next and For Each...Next statements are used only for pretest loops. You will learn about the Do...Loop statement in this chapter. The For...Next and For Each...Next statements are covered in Chapters 7 and 9, respectively.

The Do...Loop Statement

Figure 6-5 shows two versions of the syntax for the **Do...Loop statement**: one for coding a pretest loop and the other for coding a posttest loop. The {While | Until} portion in each syntax indicates that you can select only one of the keywords appearing within the braces. You follow the keyword with a *condition*, which can be phrased as either a looping condition or a loop exit condition. You use the `While` keyword in a looping condition to specify that the loop body should be processed while (in other words, as long as) the condition evaluates to True. You use the `Until` keyword in a loop exit condition to specify that the loop body should be processed until the condition becomes True, at which time the loop should stop.

Like the condition in an If...Then...Else statement, the condition in a Do...Loop statement can contain variables, constants, properties, methods, keywords, and operators; it also must evaluate to a Boolean value. The condition is evaluated with each repetition of the loop and determines whether the computer processes the loop body. Notice that the keyword (either `While` or `Until`) and the condition appear in the Do clause in a pretest loop, but they appear in the Loop clause in a posttest loop. The examples in Figure 6-5 show how you could use both syntax versions to display the numbers 1, 2, and 3 in a label control. The figure also includes a sample run of an application that contains either example.

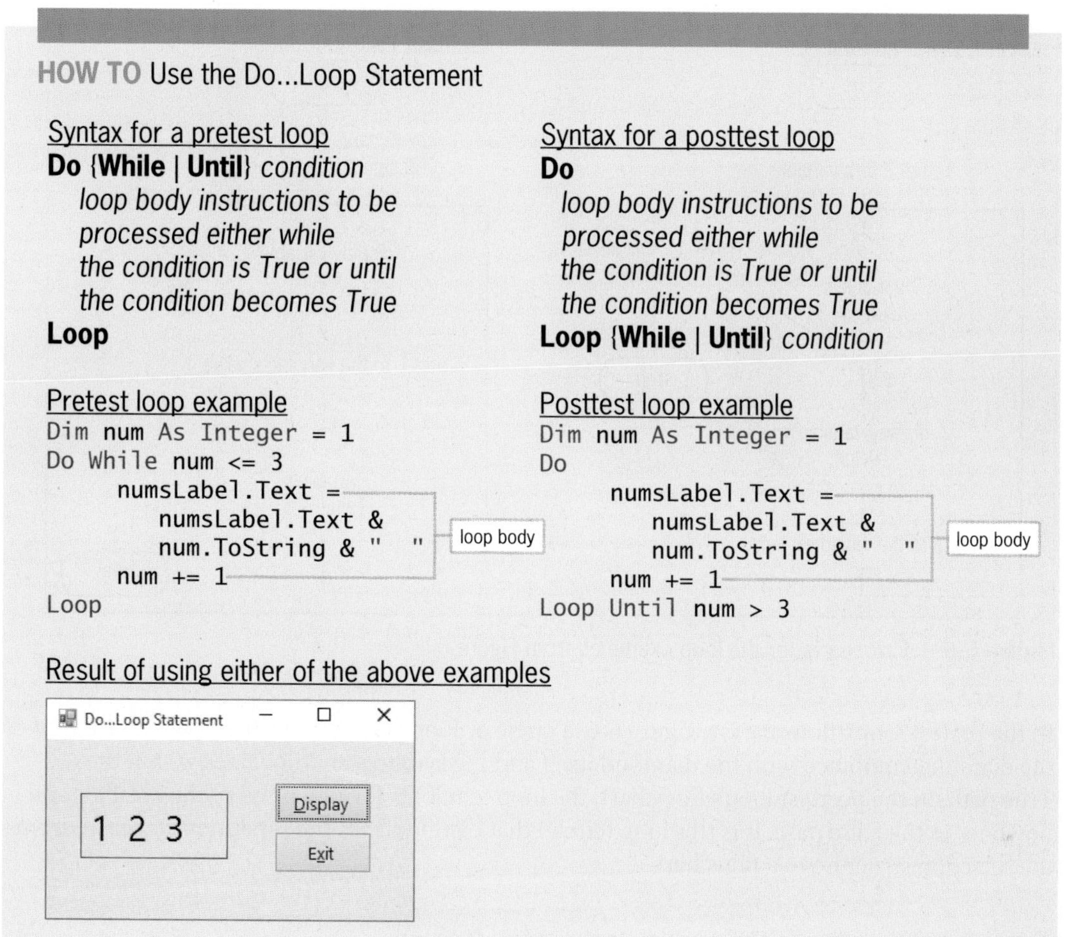

HOW TO Use the Do...Loop Statement

Syntax for a pretest loop
Do {**While** | **Until**} *condition*
loop body instructions to be processed either while the condition is True or until the condition becomes True
Loop

Syntax for a posttest loop
Do
loop body instructions to be processed either while the condition is True or until the condition becomes True
Loop {**While** | **Until**} *condition*

Pretest loop example

```
Dim num As Integer = 1
Do While num <= 3
    numsLabel.Text =
        numsLabel.Text &
        num.ToString & "  "
    num += 1
Loop
```

loop body

Posttest loop example

```
Dim num As Integer = 1
Do
    numsLabel.Text =
        numsLabel.Text &
        num.ToString & "  "
    num += 1
Loop Until num > 3
```

loop body

Result of using either of the above examples

Figure 6-5 How to use the Do...Loop statement

You can use the `Exit Do` statement to exit the Do...Loop statement before the loop has finished processing. You may need to do this if the computer encounters an error when processing the loop instructions.

If you want to experiment with the Do...Loop statement, open the solution contained in the Try It 1! folder.

Although both examples in Figure 6-5 produce the same results, pretest and posttest loops are not always interchangeable. For instance, if the `num` variable in the pretest loop in Figure 6-5 is initialized to 10 rather than to 1, the instructions in the pretest loop will not be processed because the `num <= 3` condition (which is evaluated before the instructions are processed) evaluates to False. However, if the `num` variable in the posttest loop is initialized to 10 rather than to 1, the instructions in the posttest loop will be processed one time because the `num > 3` condition is evaluated after (rather than before) the loop instructions are processed.

Ch06-Do Loop

Flowcharting a Loop

It's often easier to understand loops when viewed in flowchart form. Figure 6-6 shows the flowcharts associated with the loop examples from Figure 6-5. The diamond in each flowchart indicates the beginning of a repetition structure (loop). Like the diamond in a selection structure, the diamond in a repetition structure contains a condition that evaluates to either True or False only. The condition determines whether the instructions within the loop are processed. Also, like the diamond in a selection structure, the diamond in a repetition structure has one flowline entering the symbol and two flowlines leaving the symbol. The two flowlines leading out of the diamond should be marked so that anyone reading the flowchart can distinguish the True path from the False path. Typically, the flowlines are marked with a T (for True) and an F (for False); however, they can also be marked with a Y (for Yes) and an N (for No).

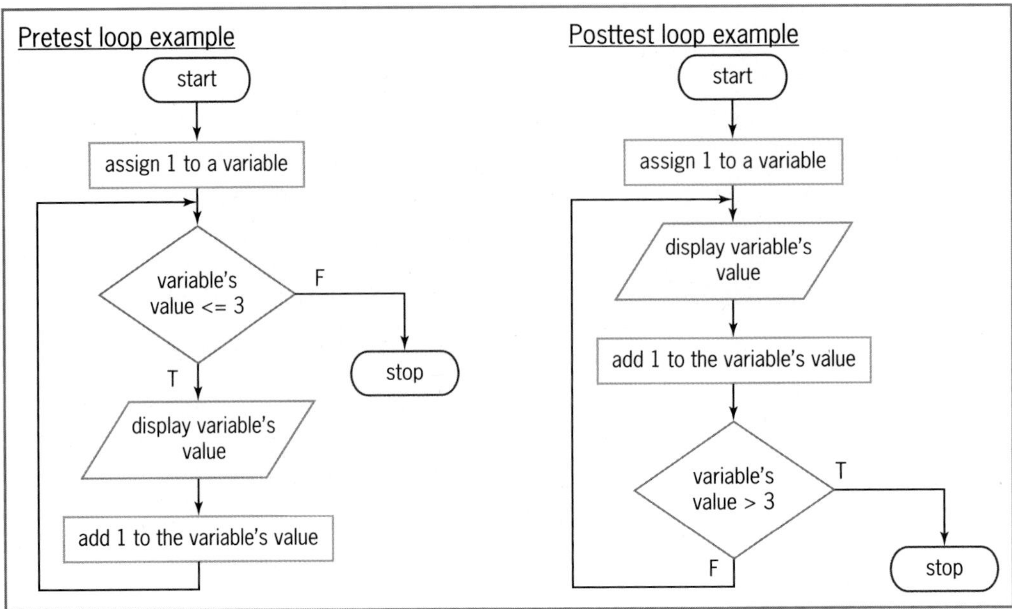

Figure 6-6 Flowcharts for the loop examples from Figure 6-5

In the pretest loop's flowchart in Figure 6-6, a circle or loop is formed by the flowline entering the diamond combined with the diamond itself and the symbols and flowlines within the True path. In the posttest loop's flowchart, the loop (circle) is formed by all of the symbols and flowlines in the False path. It is this loop (circle) that distinguishes the repetition structure from the selection structure in a flowchart.

Coding the Projected Sales Application

Figure 6-7 shows the modified pseudocode from Version 1 in Figure 6-4. It also shows the corresponding Visual Basic code and a sample run of the application. The changes made to the original pseudocode and code, which were shown earlier in Figure 6-3, are shaded in Figure 6-7. The looping condition in the Do...Loop statement tells the computer to repeat the loop body as long as (or while) the number in the `sales` variable is less than 125000.

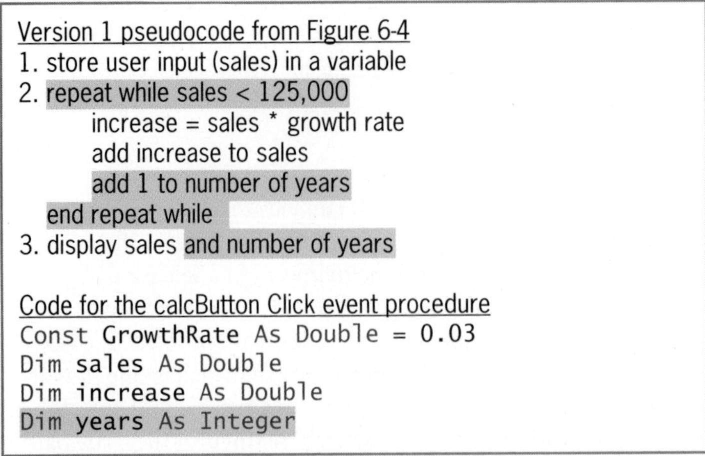

Version 1 pseudocode from Figure 6-4

```
1. store user input (sales) in a variable
2. repeat while sales < 125,000
        increase = sales * growth rate
        add increase to sales
        add 1 to number of years
   end repeat while
3. display sales and number of years
```

Code for the calcButton Click event procedure

```
Const GrowthRate As Double = 0.03
Dim sales As Double
Dim increase As Double
Dim years As Integer
```

Figure 6-7 Projected Sales application using a loop *(continues)*

(continued)

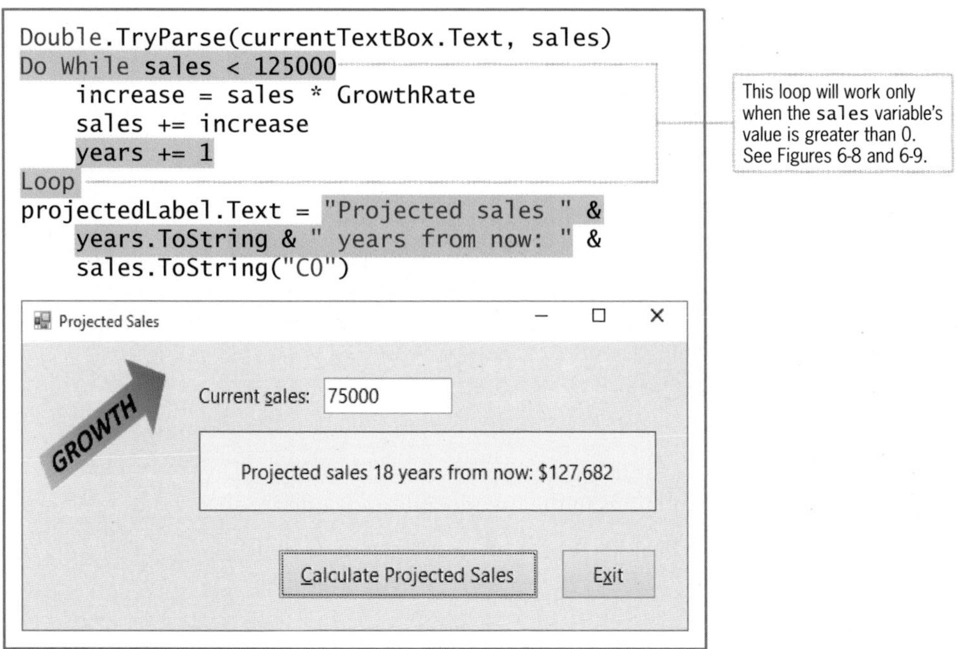

Figure 6-7 Projected Sales application using a loop

As you learned in previous chapters, it is important to test your code thoroughly, using both valid and invalid data. In this case, invalid data for the Current sales text box would include a letter, a space, or a special character. However, it would also be inappropriate for the text box to contain only the number 0 or no data at all. You can use the text box's KeyPress event procedure to prevent it from accepting letters, spaces, and special characters. However, you cannot use it to prevent the user from either entering only the number 0 or leaving the text box empty. If the user clicks the Calculate Projected Sales button when the text box is either empty or contains only the number 0, a run time error will occur and the message box shown in Figure 6-8 will appear.

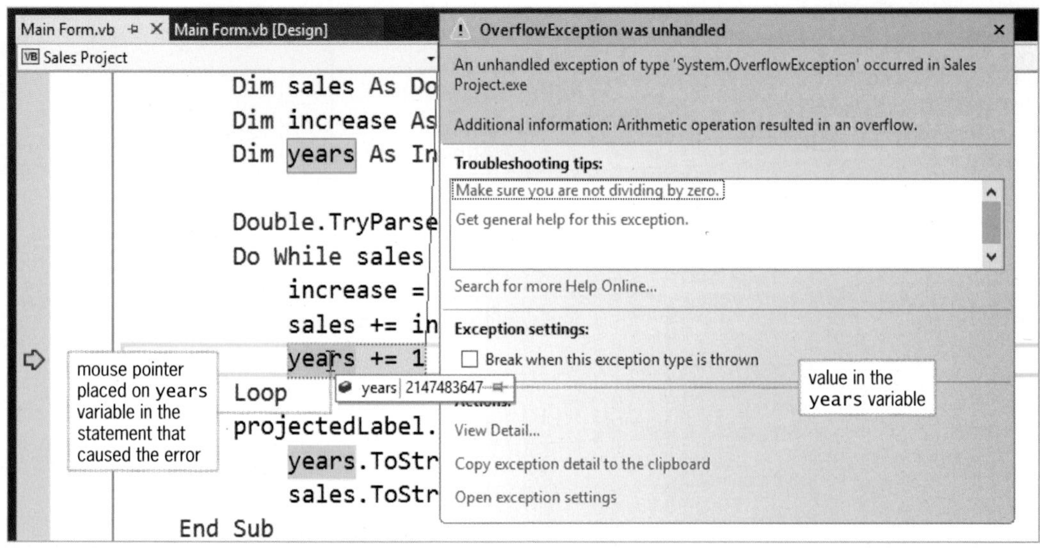

Figure 6-8 Error message box

The error message informs you that an arithmetic operation—in this case, adding 1 to the `years` variable—resulted in an overflow. An **overflow error** occurs when the value assigned to a memory location is too large for the location's data type. (An overflow error is similar to trying to fill an 8-ounce glass with 10 ounces of water.) In this case, the `years` variable already contains the highest value that can be stored in an Integer variable (2,147,483,647 according to Figure 3-3 in Chapter 3). Therefore, when the `years += 1` statement attempts to increase the variable's value by 1, an overflow error occurs.

But why does the `years` variable contain 2,147,483,647? When you do not provide an initial value for the current sales amount, the loop's condition (`sales < 125000`) will always evaluate to True; it will never evaluate to False, which is required for stopping the loop. A loop that has no way to end is called an **infinite loop** or an **endless loop**. You can stop a program that has an infinite loop by clicking Debug on the menu bar and then clicking Stop Debugging. Or, you can click the Stop Debugging button (the red square) on the Standard toolbar.

You can prevent the overflow error by using a compound condition in the Do clause, as shown in Figure 6-9. (The compound conditions in the pseudocode and code are shaded in the figure.) The figure also shows the result of clicking the Calculate Projected Sales button when the Current sales text box is empty.

If you want to experiment with the Projected Sales application, open the solution contained in the Try It 2! folder.

<u>Compound condition added to the pseudocode from Figure 6-7</u>

```
1. store user input (sales) in a variable
2. repeat while sales > 0 and sales < 125,000
       increase = sales * growth rate
       add increase to sales
       add 1 to number of years
   end repeat while
3. display sales and number of years
```

<u>Compound condition added to the calcButton Click event procedure</u>

```
Const GrowthRate As Double = 0.03
Dim sales As Double
Dim increase As Double
Dim years As Integer

Double.TryParse(currentTextBox.Text, sales)
Do While sales > 0 AndAlso sales < 125000
    increase = sales * GrowthRate
    sales += increase          accumulator
    years += 1                 counter
Loop
projectedLabel.Text = "Projected sales " &
    years.ToString & " years from now: " &
    sales.ToString("C0")
```

Figure 6-9 Final pseudocode and code for the calcButton_Click procedure *(continues)*

(continued)

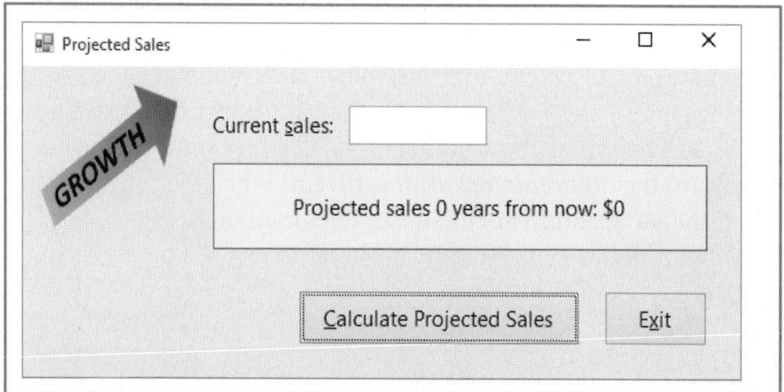

Figure 6-9 Final pseudocode and code for the calcButton_Click procedure

The Click event procedure in Figure 6-9 uses a counter (`years`) to keep track of the number of years. It also uses an accumulator (`sales`) to keep track of the projected sales amount. Counters and accumulators are covered in the next section.

Counters and Accumulators

Some procedures require you to calculate a subtotal, a total, or an average. You make these calculations using a loop that includes a counter, an accumulator, or both. A **counter** is a numeric variable used for counting something, such as the number of employees paid in a week. An **accumulator** is a numeric variable used for accumulating (adding together) something, such as the total dollar amount of a week's payroll. The `years` variable in the code shown earlier in Figure 6-9 is a counter because it keeps track of the number of years required for the projected sales amount to reach $125,000. The `sales` variable in the code is an accumulator because it adds together the projected increase amounts.

Two tasks are associated with counters and accumulators: initializing and updating. **Initializing** means assigning a beginning value to the counter or accumulator. Typically, counters and accumulators are initialized to the number 0. However, they can be initialized to any number depending on the value required by the procedure's code. The initialization task is performed before the loop is processed because it needs to be performed only once. The procedure shown earlier in Figure 6-9, for example, needs to start counting the number of years at 0 but start accumulating the projected increase amounts beginning with the current sales amount. The `years` variable in the code is initialized to 0 in its declaration statement. The `sales` variable is initialized to the current sales amount in the TryParse method.

Updating refers to the process of either adding a number to (called **incrementing**) or subtracting a number from (called **decrementing**) the value stored in the counter or accumulator. The number can be either positive or negative, integer or noninteger. A counter is always updated by a constant amount—typically the number 1. An accumulator, on the other hand, is usually updated by an amount that varies, and it is most times updated by incrementing rather than by decrementing. The assignment statement that updates a counter or an accumulator is placed in the body of the loop. This is because the update task must be performed each time the loop instructions are processed. In the code shown earlier in Figure 6-9, the last two assignment statements in the loop body update the `years` counter and `sales` accumulator: The counter is incremented by 1, and the accumulator is incremented by the projected increase amount.

Figure 6-10 shows the syntax used for updating counters and accumulators, and it includes examples of using the syntax. The syntax for counters tells the computer to add the *constantValue* to (or subtract the *constantValue* from) the *counterVariable* first and then place the result back in the *counterVariable*. If the `years` variable contains the number 1, then either of the following update statements will change the variable's contents to 2: `years = years + 1` or `years += 1`. The syntax for accumulators tells the computer to add the *value* to (or subtract the *value* from) the *accumulatorVariable* first and then place the result back in the *accumulatorVariable*. If the `sales` and `increase` variables contain the numbers 75000 and 2250, respectively, then either of the following update statements will change the `sales` variable's contents to 77250: `sales = sales + increase` or `sales += increase`.

HOW TO Update Counters and Accumulators

Syntax for counters
counterVariable = *counterVariable* {+ | –} *constantValue*
counterVariable {+= | –=} *constantValue*

Counter examples
```
years = years + 1
years += 1
students = students - 1
evenNum += 2
```

Syntax for accumulators
accumulatorVariable = *accumulatorVariable* {+ | –} *value*
accumulatorVariable {+= | –=} *value*

Accumulator examples
```
sales = sales + increase
sales += increase
sum = sum + num
totalSales += sales
```

Figure 6-10 How to update counters and accumulators

The answers to Mini-Quiz questions are located in Appendix A. Each question is associated with one or more objectives listed at the beginning of the chapter.

Mini-Quiz 6-2

1. Which of the following clauses will stop the loop when the `age` variable contains a number that is greater than 21? (1, 4)
   a. `Do While age <= 21`
   b. `Do Until age > 21`
   c. `Loop Until age > 21`
   d. all of the above
2. Write an assignment statement that updates an accumulator named `sum` by the value in the `score` variable. Both variables have the Double data type. (5)
3. Write an assignment statement that updates a counter named `numValues` by 5. (5)
4. Write an assignment statement that updates a counter named `numItems` by –1 (a negative 1). (5)

The InputBox Function

At times, a procedure may need to prompt the user to enter some specific information while an application is running; you can do this using the **InputBox function**. The function displays an input dialog box, which is one of the standard dialog boxes available in Visual Basic. An example of an input dialog box is shown in Figure 6-11. The message in the dialog box should prompt the user to enter the appropriate information in the input area. The user closes the dialog box by clicking the OK button, Cancel button, or Close button. The value returned by the InputBox function depends on the button the user chooses. If the user clicks the OK button, the function returns the value contained in the input area of the dialog box; the return value is always treated as a string. If the user clicks either the Cancel button in the dialog box or the Close button on the dialog box's title bar, the function returns an empty (or zero-length) string.

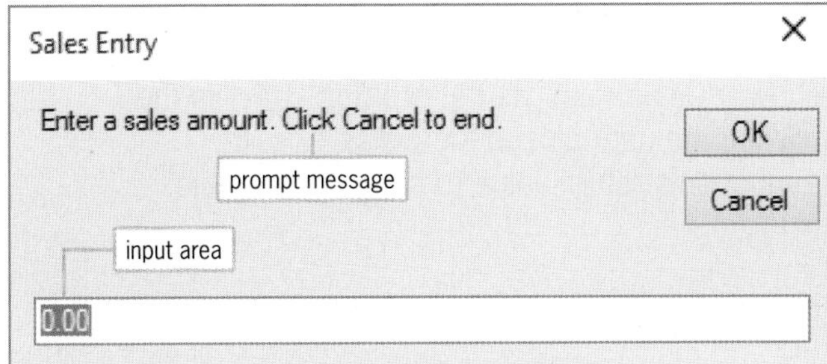

Figure 6-11 Example of an input dialog box

Figure 6-12 shows the basic syntax of the InputBox function. The *prompt* argument contains the message to display inside the dialog box. The optional *title* and *defaultResponse* arguments control the text that appears in the dialog box's title bar and input area, respectively. If you omit the *title* argument, the project name appears in the title bar. If you omit the *defaultResponse* argument, a blank input area appears when the dialog box opens. The *prompt, title,* and *defaultResponse* arguments can be string literal constants, String named constants, or String variables. The Windows standard is to use sentence capitalization for the prompt but book title capitalization for the title. The capitalization (if any) you use for the defaultResponse depends on the text itself. In most cases, you assign the value returned by the InputBox function to a String variable, as shown in the first three examples in Figure 6-12. However, you can also store the value in a numeric variable by first converting the value to the appropriate numeric data type, as shown in Example 4 in the figure. You will use the InputBox function to code the Average Seminar Registrants application in the next section.

HOW TO Use the InputBox Function

Syntax
InputBox(*prompt*[, *title*][, *defaultResponse*]**)**

Note: The InputBox function's syntax also includes optional *XPos* and *YPos* arguments for specifying the dialog box's horizontal and vertical positions, respectively. If both arguments are omitted, the dialog box appears centered on the screen.

Figure 6-12 How to use the InputBox function *(continues)*

(continued)

Example 1

```
Dim inputSales As String
inputSales =
    InputBox("Enter a sales amount. Click Cancel to end.",
    "Sales Entry", "0.00")
```

Displays the input dialog box shown in Figure 6-11. When the user closes the dialog box, the assignment statement assigns the function's return value to the `inputSales` variable.

Example 2

```
Dim city As String
city = InputBox("City name:", "City")
```

Displays an input dialog box that shows "City name:" as the prompt, "City" in the title bar, and an empty input area. When the user closes the dialog box, the assignment statement assigns the function's return value to the `city` variable.

Example 3

```
Const Message As String = "Hours worked:"
Const Title As String = "Hours"
Dim hours As String
hours = InputBox(Prompt, Title, "40.0")
```

Displays an input dialog box that shows the contents of the `Message` constant as the prompt, the contents of the `Title` constant in the title bar, and 40.0 in the input area. When the user closes the dialog box, the assignment statement assigns the function's return value to the `hours` variable.

Example 4

```
Dim age As Integer
Integer.TryParse(InputBox("How old are you?", "Age"), age)
```

Displays an input dialog box that shows "How old are you?" as the prompt, "Age" in the title bar, and an empty input area. When the user closes the dialog box, the TryParse method converts the function's return value from String to Integer and then stores the result in the `age` variable.

Figure 6-12 How to use the InputBox function

Average Seminar Registrants Application

Figure 6-13 shows the problem specification for the Average Seminar Registrants application, which uses a loop, a counter, and an accumulator to calculate the average number of people registered for one or more seminars. The figure also includes the pseudocode for the calcButton's Click event procedure.

Problem specification
Create an application that allows the user to enter the number of people registered for one or more seminars. Display each entry in the registrantsTextBox. Use a counter to keep track of the number of seminars entered and an accumulator to total the number of registrants. When the user has finished entering the data, the application should display the average number of registrants. Display the average as a whole number in the averageLabel. If the user did not enter any data, display the message "N/A" (for "not available") in the averageLabel.

calcButton Click event procedure

```
1. initialize a number of seminars counter to 0
2. initialize a total registrants accumulator to 0
3. clear the contents of the registrantsTextBox and averageLabel
4. get the number of registrants from the user                    priming read
5. repeat while the user entered the number of registrants
       display the number of registrants in the registrantsTextBox
       add 1 to the number of seminars counter
       add the number of registrants to the total registrants accumulator
       get the number of registrants from the user                update read
   end repeat while
6. if the value in the number of seminars counter is greater than 0
       average registrants = total registrants accumulator / number of seminars counter
       display the average registrants in the averageLabel
   else
       display "N/A" in the averageLabel
   end if
```

Figure 6-13 Problem specification and pseudocode for the Average Seminar Registrants application

Notice that the pseudocode contains two "get the number of registrants from the user" input instructions; both are shaded in the figure. One of the input instructions appears above the loop, and the other appears as the last instruction in the loop body. Programmers refer to the input instruction above the loop as the **priming read** because it is used to prime (prepare or set up) the loop. The priming read initializes the loop's condition by providing its first value. In this case, the priming read gets only the first number of registrants from the user. The first number is important because it determines whether the instructions in the loop body are processed at all.

If the loop body instructions *are* processed, the "get the number of registrants from the user" input instruction within the loop gets the second and subsequent (if any) numbers of registrants. Programmers refer to this instruction as the **update read** because it updates the value (in this case, the number of registrants) associated with the loop's condition. Typically, the update read is an exact copy of the priming read.

Figure 6-14 shows the flowchart for the calcButton's Click event procedure, with the priming and update reads shaded. Here, too, notice that the priming read appears above the loop, while the update read appears within the loop.

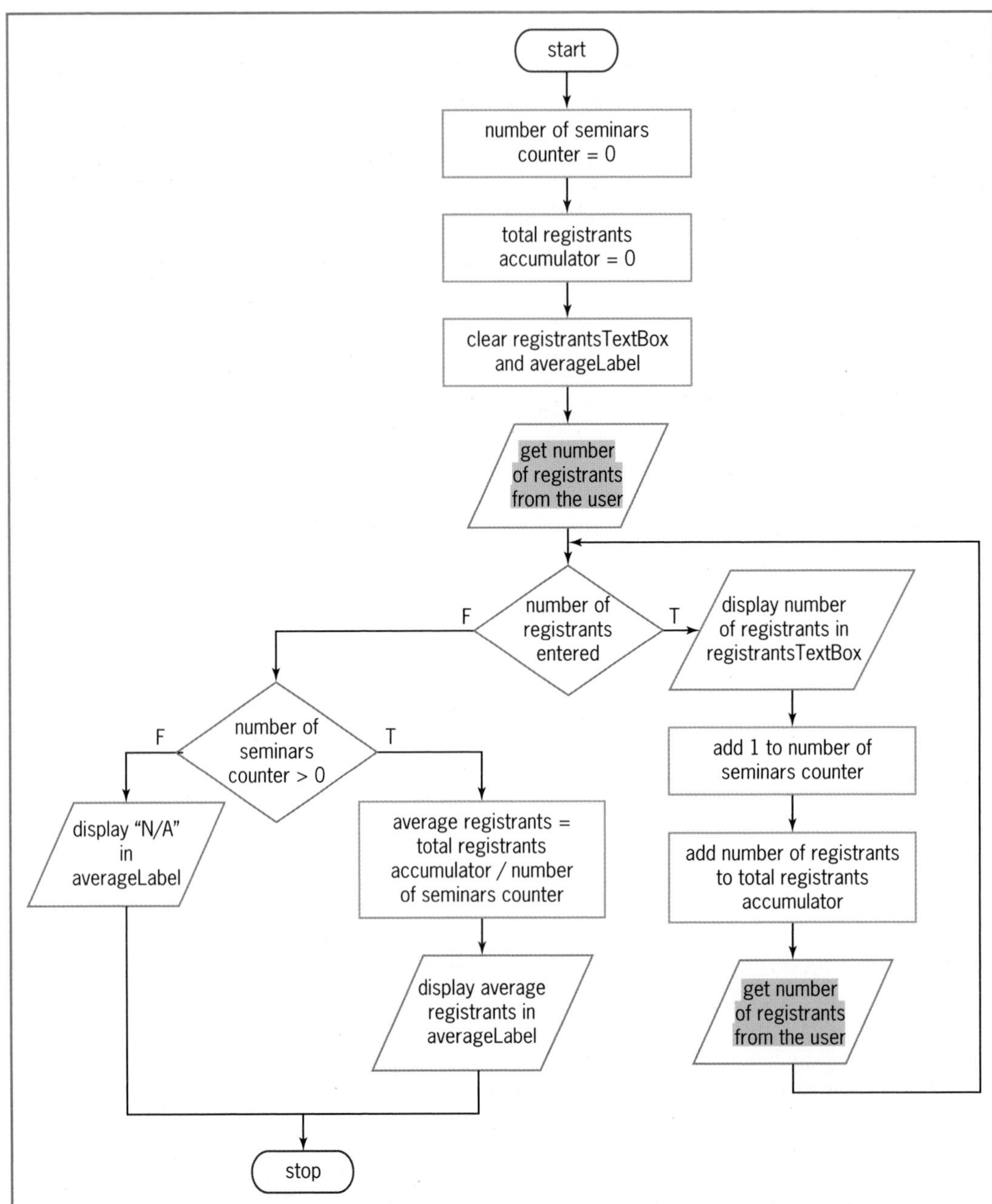

Figure 6-14 Flowchart for the calcButton_Click procedure

Figure 6-15 shows the code corresponding to the calcButton_Click procedure's pseudocode and flowchart. Notice that the InputBox function is used for both the priming read and the update read. The figure also includes a sample run of the application. The registrantsTextBox in the interface has its Multiline and ReadOnly properties set to True, and its ScrollBars property set to Vertical. When a text box's **Multiline property** is set to True, the text box can both accept and display multiple lines of text; otherwise, only one line of text can be entered in the text box. Changing a text box's **ReadOnly property** from its default value (False) to True prevents the user from changing the contents of the text box during run time. A text box's **ScrollBars property** specifies whether the text box has no scroll bars (the default), a horizontal scroll bar, a vertical scroll bar, or both horizontal and vertical scroll bars. The registrantsTextBox also has its TextAlign property set to Right.

```
Private Sub calcButton_Click(sender As Object, e As EventArgs
) Handles calcButton.Click
    ' calculates the average number of registrants

    Const Prompt As String = "Enter number of registrants. " &
        ControlChars.NewLine &
        "Click Cancel or leave blank to end."
    Const Title As String = "Number of Registrants"
    Dim inputRegistrants As String
    Dim registrants As Integer
    Dim numSeminars As Integer
    Dim totalRegistrants As Integer
    Dim avgRegistrants As Double

    ' clear text box and label
    registrantsTextBox.Text = String.Empty
    averageLabel.Text = String.Empty

    ' get first number of registrants
    inputRegistrants = InputBox(Prompt, Title)          priming read

    ' repeat as long as the user enters a value
    Do While inputRegistrants <> String.Empty
        ' display the input in the text box
        registrantsTextBox.Text = registrantsTextBox.Text &
         inputRegistrants & ControlChars.NewLine

        ' convert input to a number
        Integer.TryParse(inputRegistrants, registrants)
        ' update the counter and accumulator
        numSeminars += 1
        totalRegistrants += registrants

        ' get the next number of registrants
        inputRegistrants = InputBox(Prompt, Title)      update read
    Loop

    ' verify that the seminars counter is greater than 0
    If numSeminars > 0 Then
        avgRegistrants = totalRegistrants / numSeminars
        averageLabel.Text = avgRegistrants.ToString("N0")
    Else
        averageLabel.Text = "N/A"
    End If
End Sub
```

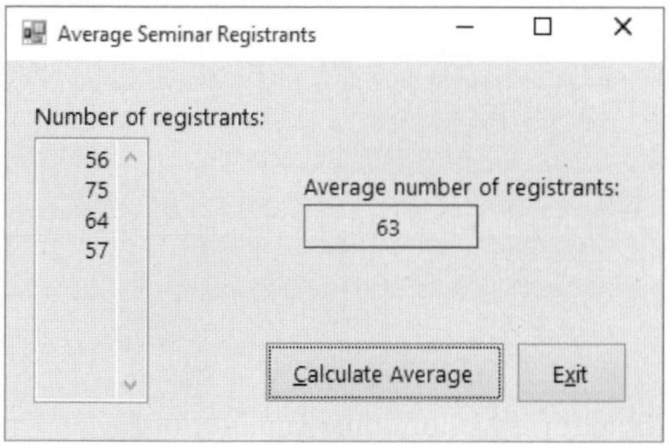

Figure 6-15 Code and a sample run of the Average Seminar Registrants application

If you want to experiment with the Average Seminar Registrants application, open the solution contained in the Try It 3! folder.

The importance of the update read cannot be stressed enough. If you do not include the update read in the loop body, there will be no way to enter a value that will stop the loop after it has been processed the first time. This is because the priming read is processed only once and gets only the first number of registrants from the user. Without the update read, the loop will have no way of stopping on its own. As you learned earlier, a loop that has no way to end is called an infinite (or endless) loop. Recall that you can stop an infinite loop by clicking Debug on the menu bar and then clicking Stop Debugging. Or, you can use the Stop Debugging button on the Standard toolbar.

The answers to Mini-Quiz questions are located in Appendix A. Each question is associated with one or more objectives listed at the beginning of the chapter.

Mini-Quiz 6-3

1. Which of the following properties allows a text box to accept and display multiple lines of text? (7)
   a. Multiline
   b. MultipleLine
   c. MultipleLines
   d. none of the above

2. The update read appears ____________ the loop. (4)
   a. above
   b. within

3. Which of the following statements prompts the user to enter a ZIP code and then assigns the user's response to a String variable named `zip`? (6)
   a. `InputBox("ZIP code:", "ZIP", zip)`
   b. `Input("ZIP code:", "ZIP", zip)`
   c. `zip = Input("ZIP code:", "ZIP")`
   d. `zip = InputBox("ZIP code:", "ZIP")`

Note: You have learned a lot so far in this chapter. You may want to take a break at this point before continuing.

Including a List Box in an Interface

The Do...Loop statement is often used to assign values to a list box. You add a list box to an interface using the ListBox tool in the toolbox. A **list box** displays a list of items from which the user can select zero items, one item, or multiple items. The number of items the user can select is controlled by the list box's **SelectionMode property**. The default value for the property, One, allows the user to select only one item at a time. (You can learn more about list boxes in Computer Exercises 35 and 36 at the end of this chapter.)

In most cases, a list box should be sized so that it displays at least three items but no more than eight items at a time. The control automatically displays a scroll bar for viewing any items that are not currently displayed. You should use a label control to provide keyboard access to the list box. For the access key to work correctly, you must set the label's TabIndex property to a value that is one number less than the list box's TabIndex value.

Adding Items to a List Box

The items in a list box belong to a collection called the **Items collection**. A **collection** is a group of individual objects treated as one unit. The first item in the Items collection appears as the first item in the list box. The second item in the collection appears as the second item in the list box, and so on. You can use the String Collection Editor window, which is shown in Figure 6-16, to specify the list box items during design time. You can open the window by clicking the ellipsis button in the list box's Items property in the Properties list. Or, you can click Edit Items on the list box's task list.

If you want to experiment with the Cities application, open the solution contained in the Try It 4! folder.

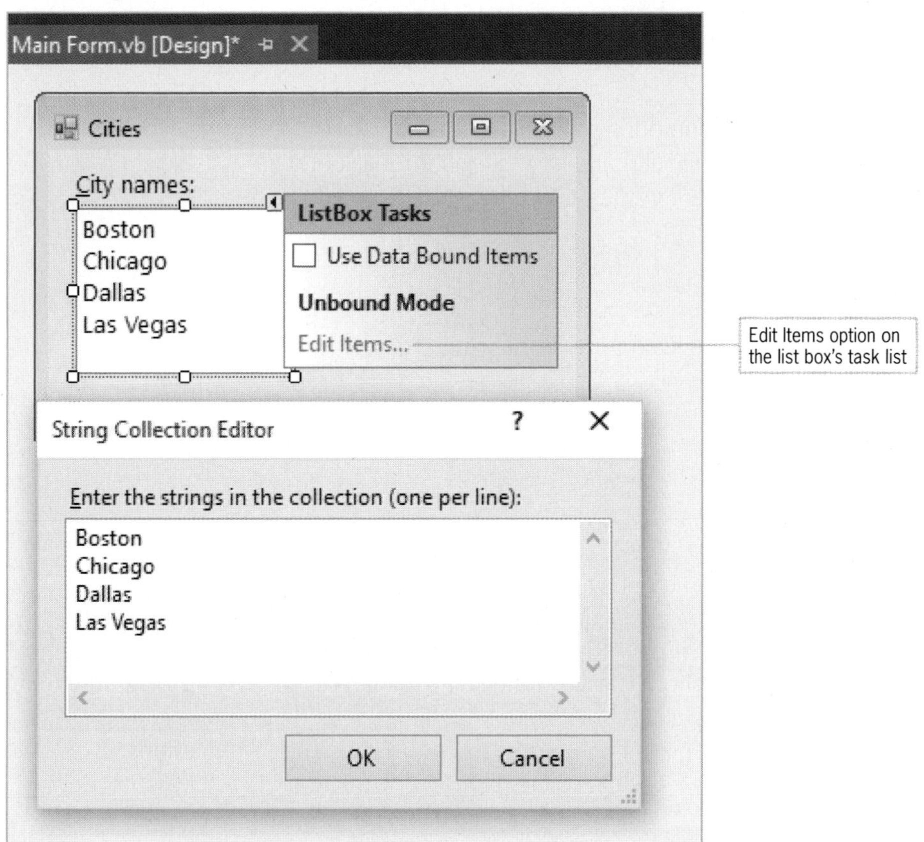

Figure 6-16 String Collection Editor window

Rather than using the String Collection Editor window to add items to a list box, you can use the Items collection's **Add method**. Figure 6-17 shows the method's syntax and includes examples and the results of using the method. In the syntax, *object* is the name of the list box control, and the *item* argument is the text you want added to the control's list.

HOW TO Use the Items Collection's Add Method

Syntax
object.**Items.Add(***item***)**

Example 1
```
statesListBox.Items.Add("Alaska")
statesListBox.Items.Add("Delaware")
statesListBox.Items.Add("Georgia")
statesListBox.Items.Add("Iowa")
```
The four Add methods add Alaska, Delaware, Georgia, and Iowa to the statesListBox, as shown here.

Figure 6-17 How to use the Items Collection's Add method *(continues)*

(continued)

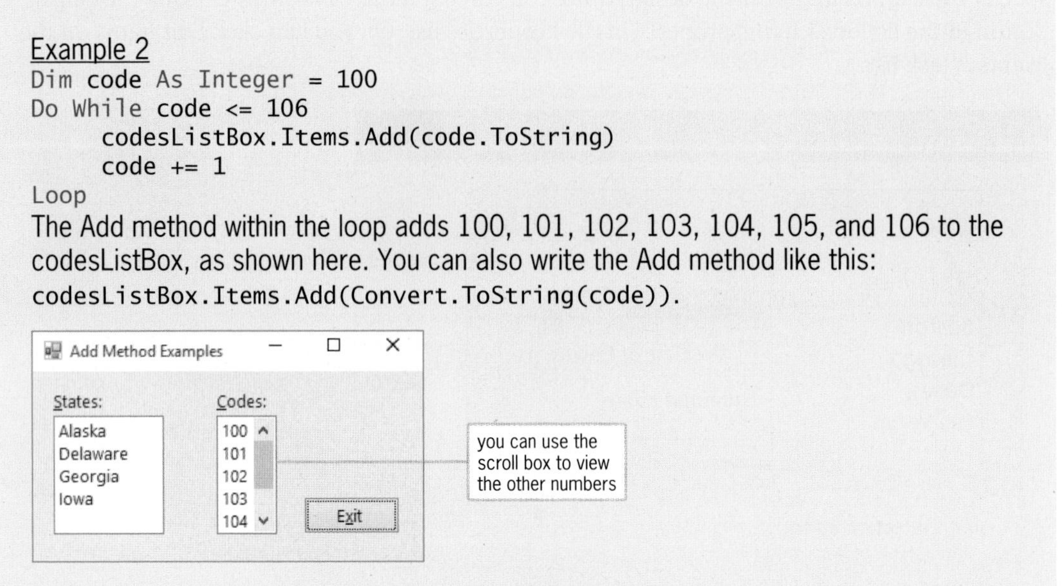

Example 2

```
Dim code As Integer = 100
Do While code <= 106
     codesListBox.Items.Add(code.ToString)
     code += 1
Loop
```

The Add method within the loop adds 100, 101, 102, 103, 104, 105, and 106 to the codesListBox, as shown here. You can also write the Add method like this: `codesListBox.Items.Add(Convert.ToString(code))`.

Figure 6-17 How to use the Items Collection's Add method

In most cases, you enter the Add methods in a form's Load event procedure, as shown in Figure 6-18. To open the Load event procedure, you click the Object list arrow in the Code Editor window and then click (*formName* Events) in the list, where *formName* is the name of your form. You then click the Method list arrow and click Load in that list. A form's **Load event** occurs when an application is started. Any code contained in the Load event procedure is processed before the form is displayed on the screen. In this case, the Add methods in Figure 6-18 ensure that the list boxes display their values when the interface comes into view.

If you want to experiment with the Add Method Examples application, open the solution contained in the Try It 5! folder.

```
Main Form.vb   Main Form.vb [Design]
Add Method Project      (MainForm Events)      Load
Public Class MainForm
    Private Sub MainForm_Load(sender As Object, e As EventArgs) Handles Me.Load

        ' add items to the statesListBox
        statesListBox.Items.Add("Alaska")
        statesListBox.Items.Add("Delaware")
        statesListBox.Items.Add("Georgia")
        statesListBox.Items.Add("Iowa")

        ' add items to the codesListBox
        Dim code As Integer = 100
        Do While code <= 106
            codesListBox.Items.Add(code.ToString)
            code += 1
        Loop
    End Sub
```

Figure 6-18 Add methods entered in the MainForm's Load event procedure

Depending on the application, you may need to allow the user to add items to a list box during run time. The Jasper's Food Hut application accomplishes this by providing a text box for entering an item and a button for adding the item to the list box. Figure 6-19 shows a sample run of the application. It also shows the addButton_Click procedure, which uses the Add method to add the contents of the nameTextBox to the workerListBox.

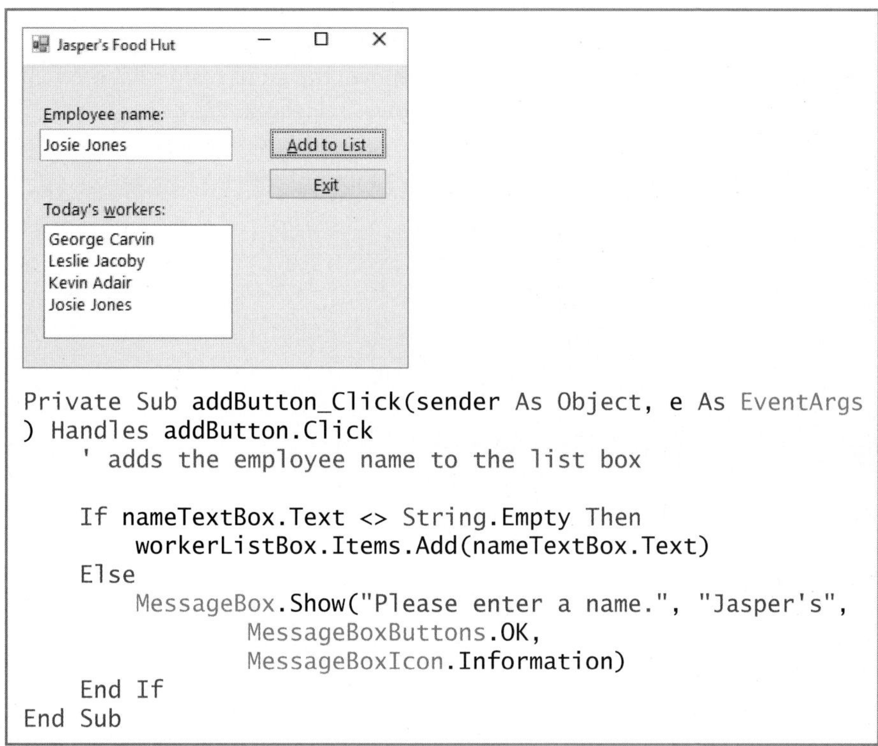


```
Private Sub addButton_Click(sender As Object, e As EventArgs
) Handles addButton.Click
    ' adds the employee name to the list box

    If nameTextBox.Text <> String.Empty Then
        workerListBox.Items.Add(nameTextBox.Text)
    Else
        MessageBox.Show("Please enter a name.", "Jasper's",
                MessageBoxButtons.OK,
                MessageBoxIcon.Information)
    End If
End Sub
```

Figure 6-19 Sample run and code for the Jasper's Food Hut application

If you want to experiment with the Jasper's Food Hut application, open the solution contained in the Try It 6! folder.

The Clark's Chicken application uses a different approach to allow the user to add items to a list box during run time. Figure 6-20 shows a sample run of the application. It also shows the enterButton_Click procedure, which uses the Add method along with a pretest loop and the InputBox function to add employee names to the list box.

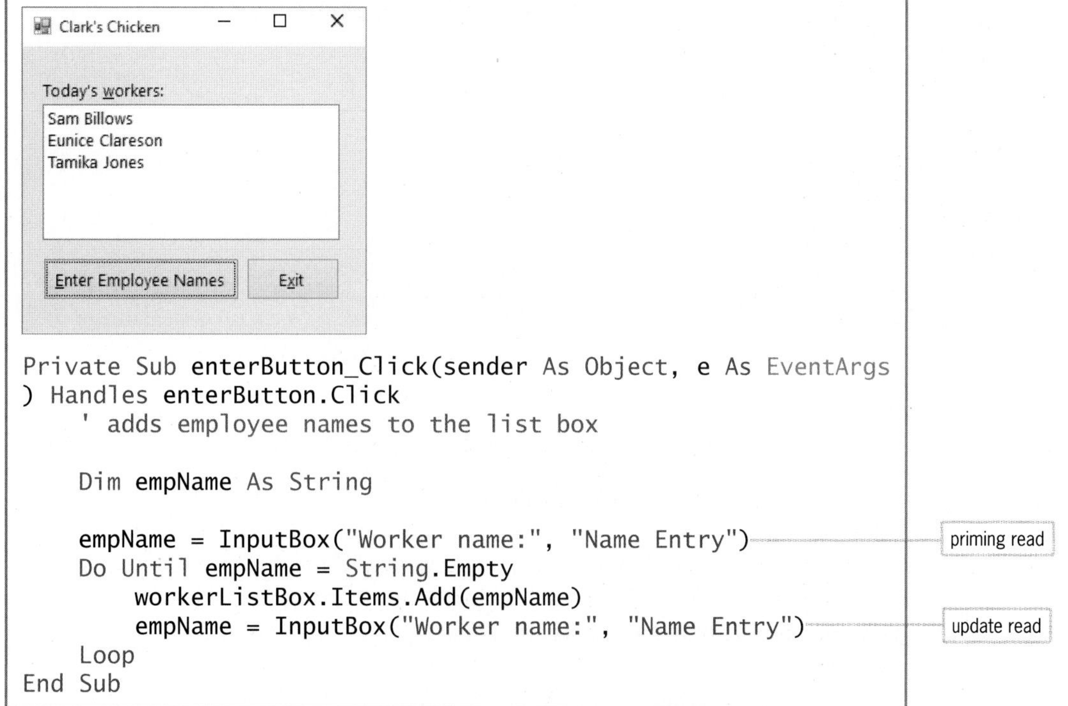


```
Private Sub enterButton_Click(sender As Object, e As EventArgs
) Handles enterButton.Click
    ' adds employee names to the list box

    Dim empName As String

    empName = InputBox("Worker name:", "Name Entry")
    Do Until empName = String.Empty
        workerListBox.Items.Add(empName)
        empName = InputBox("Worker name:", "Name Entry")
    Loop
End Sub
```

Figure 6-20 Sample run and code for the Clark's Chicken application

If you want to experiment with the Clark's Chicken application, open the solution contained in the Try It 7! folder.

Clearing the Items from a List Box

You can use the Items collection's **Clear method** to clear (remove) the items from a list box. The method's syntax and an example of using the method are shown in Figure 6-21.

HOW TO Clear (Remove) the Items from a List Box

Syntax
object.**Items.Clear()**

Example
```
statesListBox.Items.Clear()
```
clears (removes) all of the items from the statesListBox

Figure 6-21 How to clear (remove) the items from a list box

The Sorted Property

The position of an item in a list box depends on the value stored in the list box's **Sorted property**. When the property is set to False (the default value), the item is added at the end of the list. When it is set to True, the item is sorted along with the existing items and then placed in its proper position in the list.

Visual Basic sorts the list box items in dictionary order, which means that numbers are sorted before letters, and a lowercase letter is sorted before its uppercase equivalent. The items in a list box are sorted based on the leftmost characters in each item. As a result, the items "Personnel", "Inventory", and "Payroll" will appear in the following order when the deptListBox's Sorted property is set to True: Inventory, Payroll, Personnel. Likewise, the items 1, 2, 3, and 10 will appear in the following order when the numListBox's Sorted property is set to True: 1, 10, 2, 3. Both list boxes are shown in Figure 6-22.

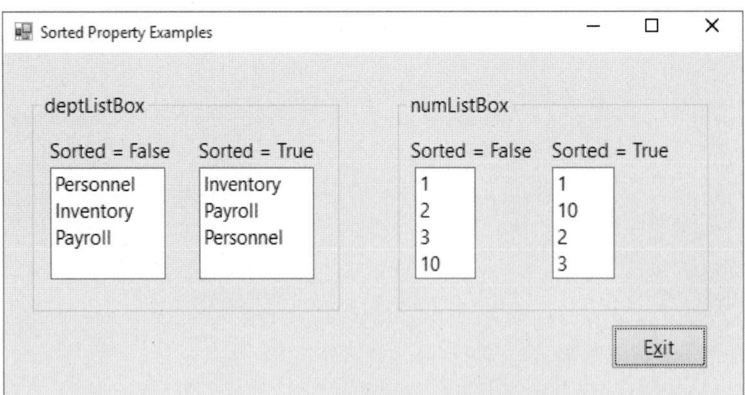

Figure 6-22 Examples of the list box's Sorted property

The requirements of the application you are creating determine whether you display the list box items in either sorted order or the order in which they are added to the list box. If several list items are selected much more frequently than other items, you typically leave the list box's Sorted property set to False and then add the frequently used items first to ensure that they appear at the beginning of the list. However, if the list box items are selected fairly equally, you usually set the list box's Sorted property to True because it is easier to locate items when they appear in a sorted order.

Accessing Items in a List Box

Each item in the Items collection is identified by a unique number, which is called an **index**. The first item in the collection (which is also the first item in the list box) has an index of 0. The second item's index is 1, and so on. The index allows you to access a specific item in the list box, as shown in the syntax and examples in Figure 6-23.

HOW TO Access an Item in a List Box

Syntax
object.**Items(***index***)**

Example 1
```
Dim state As String
state = Convert.ToString(statesListBox.Items(0))
```
or
```
state = statesListBox.Items(0).ToString
```
assigns the first item in the statesListBox to the `state` variable

Example 2
```
Dim code As Integer
code = Convert.ToInt32(codesListBox.Items(2))
```
or
```
Integer.TryParse(codesListBox.Items(2).ToString, code)
```
assigns the third item in the codesListBox to the `code` variable

Figure 6-23 How to access an item in a list box

Determining the Number of Items in a List Box

The number of items in a list box is stored in the Items collection's **Count property**. The property's value is always one number more than the list box's highest index; this is because the first index in a list box is 0. For example, the highest index in the statesListBox shown earlier in Figure 6-17 is 3, but the Count property contains the number 4. Figure 6-24 shows the syntax of the Count property and includes examples of using it.

HOW TO Determine the Number of Items in a List Box

Syntax
object.**Items.Count**

Example 1
```
Dim numStates As Integer
numStates = statesListBox.Items.Count
```
assigns the number 4, which is the number of items contained in the statesListBox from Figure 6-17, to the `numStates` variable

Figure 6-24 How to determine the number of items in a list box *(continues)*

(continued)

Example 2

```
Dim numCodes As Integer
Dim index As Integer
numCodes = codesListBox.Items.Count
Do While index < numCodes
    MessageBox.Show(codesListBox.Items(index).ToString)
    index += 1
Loop
```

displays the codesListBox items (100, 101, 102, 103, 104, 105, and 106) in message boxes (You can also use the Convert.ToString method rather than the ToString method.)

Figure 6-24 How to determine the number of items in a list box

The SelectedItem and SelectedIndex Properties

You can use either the **SelectedItem property** or the **SelectedIndex property** to determine whether an item is selected in a list box. When no item is selected, the SelectedItem property contains the empty string and the SelectedIndex property contains the number –1 (negative 1). Otherwise, the SelectedItem and SelectedIndex properties contain the value of the selected item and the item's index, respectively. Figure 6-25 shows examples of using both properties to determine the selected item in the list boxes shown earlier in Figure 6-17.

HOW TO Use the SelectedItem and SelectedIndex Properties

Example 1 (SelectedItem property)

```
stateLabel.Text = Convert.ToString(statesListBox.SelectedItem)
```

converts the selected item to String and then assigns the result to the stateLabel

Example 2 (SelectedItem property)

```
If Convert.ToInt32(codesListBox.SelectedItem) = 103 Then
```

converts the selected item to Integer and then compares the result with the integer 103

Example 3 (SelectedItem property)

```
If Convert.ToString(statesListBox.SelectedItem) = String.Empty Then
```

determines whether an item is selected in the list box

Example 4 (SelectedIndex property)

```
If codesListBox.SelectedIndex = -1 Then
```

determines whether an item is selected in the list box

Figure 6-25 How to use the SelectedItem and SelectedIndex properties *(continues)*

(continued)

Example 5 (SelectedIndex property)
```
Dim index As Integer
index = statesListBox.SelectedIndex
```
assigns the selected item's index to the `index` variable

Example 6 (SelectedIndex property)
```
If codesListBox.SelectedIndex = 0 Then
```
determines whether the first item is selected in the list box

Figure 6-25 How to use the SelectedItem and SelectedIndex properties

If a list box allows the user to make only one selection, it is customary in Windows applications to have one of the list box items already selected when the interface appears. The selected item, called the **default list box item**, should be either the item selected most frequently or the first item in the list. You can use either the SelectedItem property or the SelectedIndex property to select the default list box item from code, as shown in the examples in Figure 6-26. In most cases, you enter the appropriate code in the form's Load event procedure.

HOW TO Select the Default List Box Item

Example 1 (SelectedItem property)
```
statesListBox.SelectedItem = "Georgia"
```
selects the Georgia item in the statesListBox

Example 2 (SelectedIndex property)
```
codesListBox.SelectedIndex = 0
```
selects the first item in the codesListBox

Figure 6-26 How to select the default list box item

The SelectedValueChanged and SelectedIndexChanged Events

Each time either the user or a statement selects an item in a list box, the list box's **SelectedValueChanged event** occurs followed by its **SelectedIndexChanged event**. You can use the procedures associated with these events to perform one or more tasks when the selected item has changed, as shown in Figure 6-27. The figure also shows the form's Load event procedure, which fills the list boxes with items and then selects the default item in each list box. Selecting the default item will invoke the list box's SelectedValueChanged and SelectedIndexChanged events, causing the computer to process any code contained in the corresponding event procedures. The figure also contains a sample run of the ListBox Events application.

If you want to experiment with the ListBox Events application, open the solution contained in the Try It 8! folder.

selects the default item

SelectedValueChanged procedure

SelectedIndexChanged procedure

```
Private Sub MainForm_Load(sender As Object, e As EventArgs
) Handles Me.Load

    ' add items to the regionsListBox
    Dim region As Integer = 1
    Do While region <= 4
        regionsListBox.Items.Add(region.ToString)
        region += 1
    Loop

    ' add items to the titlesListBox
    titlesListBox.Items.Add("CEO")
    titlesListBox.Items.Add("COO")
    titlesListBox.Items.Add("CFO")


    ' select the default list box item
        regionsListBox.SelectedIndex = "3"
        titlesListBox.SelectedItem = 0
End Sub

Private Sub regionsListBox_SelectedValueChanged(
sender As Object, e As EventArgs
) Handles regionsListBox.SelectedValueChanged
    ' displays the shipping charge

    Dim region As String
    region = Convert.ToString(regionsListBox.SelectedItem)

    Select Case region
        Case "1"
            shippingLabel.Text = "$10"
        Case "2"
            shippingLabel.Text = "$12"
        Case "3"
            shippingLabel.Text = "$15"
        Case Else
            shippingLabel.Text = "$20"
    End Select
End Sub

Private Sub titlesListBox_SelectedIndexChanged(
sender As Object, e As EventArgs
) Handles titlesListBox.SelectedIndexChanged
    ' displays the title

    Select Case titlesListBox.SelectedIndex
        Case 0
            standsForLabel.Text = "Chief Executive Officer"
         Case 1
            standsForLabel.Text = "Chief Operations Officer"
        Case Else
            standsForLabel.Text = "Chief Financial Officer"
    End Select
End Sub
```

Figure 6-27 Code and a sample run for the ListBox Events application *(continues)*

(continued)

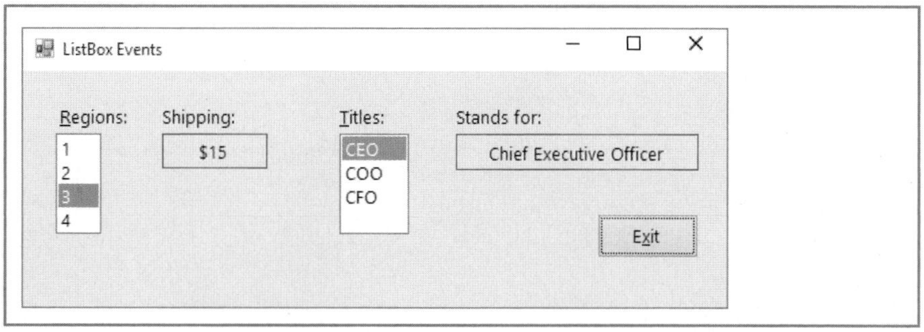

ListBox Events

Regions: 1 2 3 4 | Shipping: $15 | Titles: CEO COO CFO | Stands for: Chief Executive Officer | Exit

Figure 6-27 Code and a sample run for the ListBox Events application

The SelectedValueChanged procedure in Figure 6-27 uses the SelectedItem property to determine the item selected in the regionsListBox. It then uses that information to display the shipping charge associated with the selected item. You could also have entered this code in the regionsListBox's SelectedIndexChanged procedure.

The SelectedIndexChanged procedure in Figure 6-27 uses the SelectedIndex property to determine the index of the abbreviated title selected in the list box. It then uses that information to display the full title associated with the selected item. You could also have entered this code in the titlesListBox's SelectedValueChanged procedure.

When coding a list box's SelectedValueChanged procedure, you can use either the SelectedItem property (as shown in Figure 6-27) or the SelectedIndex property to determine the selected item. Similarly, you can use either the SelectedIndex property (as shown in Figure 6-27) or the SelectedItem property in the list box's SelectedIndexChanged procedure.

The Product Finder Application

The Product Finder application demonstrates most of what you learned about list boxes. It also provides another example of using a repetition structure. The problem specification is shown in Figure 6-28 along with the pseudocode for the displayButton_Click and idsListBox_SelectedIndexChanged procedures.

Problem specification
Create an application that searches a list box for the product ID entered by the user. If the ID is included in the list box, highlight (select) the ID in the list, and then have the list box's SelectedIndexChanged event procedure display the appropriate price. Otherwise, ensure that no ID is highlighted in the list box, and then display a message indicating that the ID was not found. The IDs and prices are listed here:

ID	Price
AB654	12.59
FX123	14.99
FX457	14.99
JH733	9.99
KVB419	23.79
KYT897	23.79
NK111	35.99
PQR333	35.99
UVP492	35.99

Figure 6-28 Problem specification and pseudocode for the Product Finder application *(continues)*

(continued)

```
displayButton Click event procedure
1. assign the ID entered by the user to a variable
2. assign the number of list box items to a variable
3. repeat while the list box item's index is less than the number of items in the list and
   the ID has not been found
      if the ID entered by the user is the same as the current item in the list box
            indicate that the ID was found by assigning True to a Boolean variable
      else
            continue the search by adding 1 to the list box index
      end if
   end repeat while
4. if the ID was found (indicated by a True value in the Boolean variable)
      select the ID in the list box
   else
      clear any selection in the list box
      display the "ID not found" message in a message box
   end if

idsListBox SelectedIndexChanged event procedure
1. selected index:
      0        assign 12.59 as the price
      1, 2     assign 14.99 as the price
      3        assign 9.99 as the price
      4, 5     assign 23.79 as the price
      6, 7, 8  assign 35.99 as the price
2. display the price in the priceLabel
```

Figure 6-28 Problem specification and pseudocode for the Product Finder application

Figure 6-29 shows most of the Product Finder application's code and includes two sample runs of the application.

If you want to experiment with the Product Finder application, open the solution contained in the Try It 9! folder.

```
Private Sub displayButton_Click(sender As Object, e As EventArgs
) Handles displayButton.Click
    ' Searches the list box for the product ID and then
    ' either selects the ID or deselects any ID and then
    ' displays a message. Selecting or deselecting an ID
    ' invokes the list box's SelectedIndexChanged event, which
    ' displays the price.

    Dim isFound As Boolean
    Dim index As Integer
    Dim numItems As Integer
    Dim id As String

    ' assign ID and number of list box items to variables
    id = idTextBox.Text.ToUpper
    numItems = idsListBox.Items.Count
```

Figure 6-29 Code and sample runs for the Product Finder application *(continues)*

(continued)

```
        ' search the list box, stopping either after the
        ' last item or when the ID is found
        Do While index < numItems AndAlso isFound = False
            If id = idsListBox.Items(index).ToString.ToUpper Then
                isFound = True
            Else
                index += 1
            End If
        Loop

        If isFound = True Then
            idsListBox.SelectedIndex = index
        Else
            idsListBox.SelectedIndex = -1
            MessageBox.Show("ID not found", "Product Finder",
               MessageBoxButtons.OK, MessageBoxIcon.Information)
        End If
    End Sub

    Private Sub idsListBox_SelectedIndexChanged(sender As Object, e As
    EventArgs) Handles idsListBox.SelectedIndexChanged
        ' displays the price of the selected ID

        Dim price As Double

        Select Case idsListBox.SelectedIndex
            Case 0   ' AB654
                price = 12.59
            Case 1, 2 ' FX123 and FX457
                price = 14.99
            Case 3 ' JH733
                price = 9.99
            Case 4, 5 ' KVB419 and KYT897
                price = 23.79
            Case 6 To 8 ' NK111, PQR333, and UVP492
                price = 35.99
        End Select
        priceLabel.Text = price.ToString("C2")
    End Sub

    Private Sub MainForm_Load(sender As Object, e As EventArgs) Handles
    Me.Load
        ' fills the list box with IDs

        idsListBox.Items.Add("AB654")
        idsListBox.Items.Add("FX123")
        idsListBox.Items.Add("FX457")
        idsListBox.Items.Add("JH733")
        idsListBox.Items.Add("KVB419")
        idsListBox.Items.Add("KYT897")
        idsListBox.Items.Add("NK111")
        idsListBox.Items.Add("PQR333")
        idsListBox.Items.Add("UVP492")
    End Sub
```

Figure 6-29 Code and sample runs for the Product Finder application *(continues)*

(continued)

Figure 6-29 Code and sample runs for the Product Finder application

The Color Viewer Application

The last concepts covered in this chapter involve enabling and disabling a control, refreshing the screen, and pausing program execution. You will use these concepts in the Color Viewer application coded in this section. You will also use the concepts in the game application coded in Programming Tutorial 1.

Figure 6-30 shows the MainForm in the Color Viewer application. When the user clicks the View Colors button, the viewButton_Click procedure should disable the button and then change the color of the colorOvalShape to blue, then to yellow, and then to red. You disable a control by changing its **Enabled property** from its default value (True) to False. When a control's Enabled property is set to False, the control appears dimmed (grayed out) during run time, indicating that it is not currently available to the user. The button will remain grayed out until the procedure enables it, which will occur immediately before the procedure ends.

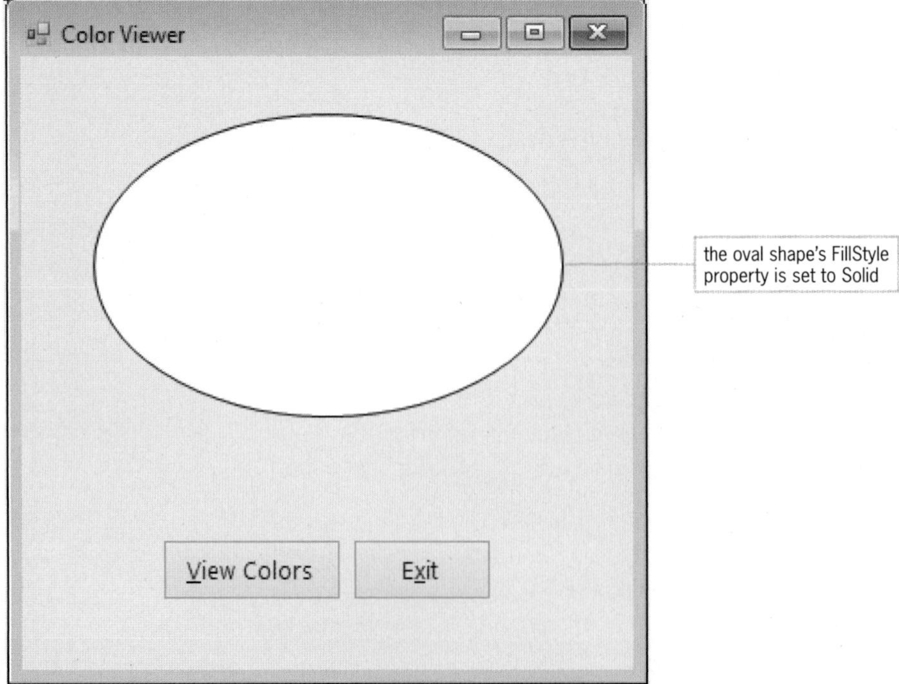

Figure 6-30 MainForm in the Color Viewer application

You can use the statement `colorOvalShape.FillColor = Color.Blue` to change the oval shape's color to blue. Similarly, you can change its color to yellow and red by setting its FillColor property to `Color.Yellow` and `Color.Red`, respectively. However, because the computer will process the color change instructions so rapidly, you will see only the last color (red) when you click the View Colors button. You can solve this problem by refreshing the interface and then delaying program execution each time (except for the final time) the FillColor property is changed. You refresh the interface by using the **Refresh method**, which tells the computer to process any previous lines of code that affect the interface's appearance. You delay program execution by using the **Sleep method**. Figure 6-31 shows each method's syntax. The `Me` keyword in the Refresh method refers to the current form. In the Sleep method, the *milliseconds* argument is the number of milliseconds to suspend the program. A millisecond is 1/1000 of a second; in other words, there are 1000 milliseconds in a second. Figure 6-31 also shows the viewButton_Click procedure.

If you want to experiment with the Color Viewer application, open the solution contained in the Try It 10! folder.

HOW TO Use the Refresh and Sleep Methods

Syntax
Me.Refresh()
System.Threading.Thread.Sleep(*milliseconds*)

```
Private Sub viewButton_Click(sender As Object, e As EventArgs
) Handles viewButton.Click
    ' changes the fill color of the colorOvalShape

    ' disable the View Colors button
    viewButton.Enabled = False

    ' change the color to blue
    colorOvalShape.FillColor = Color.Blue
    Me.Refresh()
    System.Threading.Thread.Sleep(1000)

    ' change the color to yellow
    colorOvalShape.FillColor = Color.Yellow
    Me.Refresh()
    System.Threading.Thread.Sleep(1000)

    ' change the color to red
    colorOvalShape.FillColor = Color.Red

    ' enable the View Colors button
    viewButton.Enabled = True
End Sub
```

Figure 6-31 How to use the Refresh and Sleep methods

Mini-Quiz 6-4

The answers to Mini-Quiz questions are located in Appendix A. Each question is associated with one or more objectives listed at the beginning of the chapter.

1. Items are added to a list box using which of the following methods? (8)
   a. Add
   b. AddList
   c. Item
   d. ItemAdd

2. The items in a list box belong to which of the following collections? (8)
   a. ItemList
   b. Items
   c. List
   d. ListItems

3. When an item is selected in a list box, the computer stores the item's index in which of the following properties? (8)
   a. Index
   b. ItemIndex
   c. SelectedIndex
   d. SelectedItem

4. Which of the following statements will delay program execution for two seconds? (10)
   a. `System.Threading.Thread.Sleep(2)`
   b. `System.Threading.Thread.Sleep(200)`
   c. `System.Threading.Thread.Sleep(2000)`
   d. `System.Threading.Thread.Sleep(20000)`

You have completed the concepts section of Chapter 6. The Programming Tutorial section is next.

PROGRAMMING TUTORIAL 1

Creating the Lucky Number Game Application

In this tutorial, you will create an application that simulates a dice game called Lucky Number. The game is played using two dice. Each time the player clicks the Roll 'Em button, the button's Click event procedure will generate two random integers from 1 through 6. The random integers represent the appropriate image to display in the firstDiePictureBox and secondDiePictureBox controls. For example, if the random numbers are 6 and 3, the application will display the image containing six dots in the firstDiePictureBox and display the image containing three dots in the secondDiePictureBox. The images in these two picture boxes correspond to a roll of the dice.

At the start of the game, the player is given 10 points. If the player rolls a 7 (in other words, the numbers of dots on both rolled dice total 7), the player's points are increased by 2; otherwise, they are reduced by 1. The game ends when the player loses all of his or her points. The interface also provides a Start Over button for starting a new game. Figures 6-32 and 6-33 show the application's TOE chart and MainForm, respectively. The images at the bottom of the MainForm represent the six sides of a die.

Task	Object	Event
1. Generate two random integers from 1 through 6 2. Use the random integers to display the appropriate images in the firstDiePictureBox and secondDiePictureBox 3. Determine whether the sum of the dots on the firstDiePictureBox and secondDiePictureBox controls equals 7, and then either add 2 points to the player's points or subtract 1 point from the player's points	rollButton	Click

Figure 6-32 TOE chart for the Lucky Number Game application *(continues)*

(continued)

4. If the player loses all of his or her points, display an appropriate message 5. Display the player's points in pointsLabel		
1. Set the player's points to 10 2. Display the player's points in pointsLabel 3. Remove images from firstDiePictureBox and secondDiePictureBox	startOverButton	Click
End the application	exitButton	Click
Display the player's points	pointsLabel	None
Display the number 7	numberLabel	None
Store the die images	dot1PictureBox, dot2PictureBox, dot3PictureBox, dot4PictureBox, dot5PictureBox, dot6PictureBox	None
Display the image corresponding to the first die (from rollButton)	firstDiePictureBox	None
Display the image corresponding to the second die (from rollButton)	secondDiePictureBox	None

Figure 6-32 TOE chart for the Lucky Number Game application

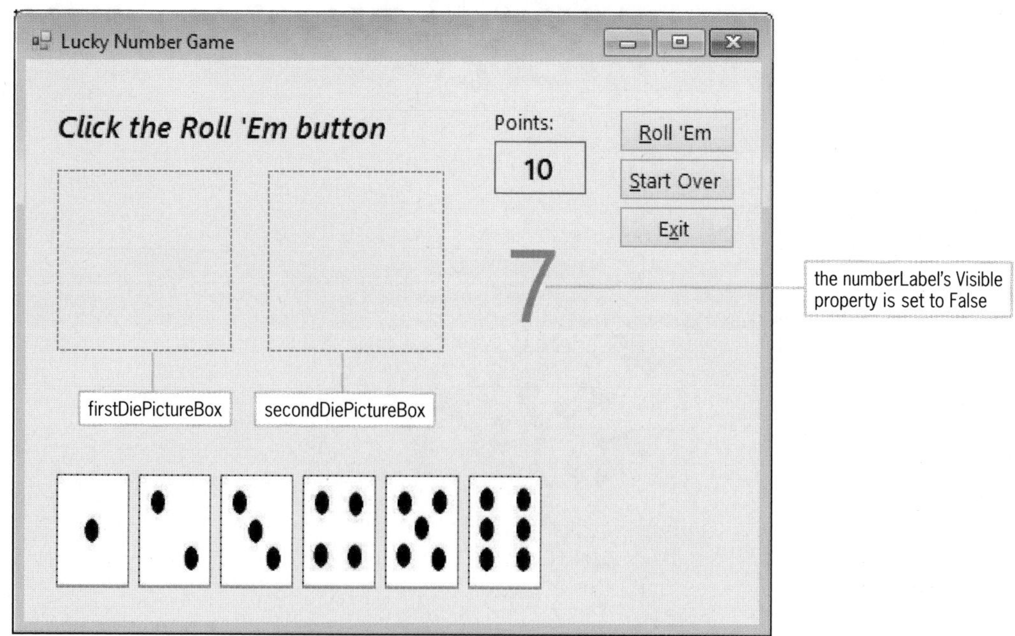

Figure 6-33 MainForm for the Lucky Number Game application

Coding the Lucky Number Game Application

According to the application's TOE chart, only the Click event procedures for the three buttons need to be coded.

To begin coding the application:

1. Start Visual Studio. Open the **Lucky Solution** (**Lucky Solution.sln**) file contained in the VbReloaded2015\Chap06\Lucky Solution folder. If necessary, open the designer window.
2. Open the Code Editor window. The exitButton_Click procedure has already been coded for you. In the comments that appear in the General Declarations section, replace <your name> and <current date> with your name and the current date, respectively.
3. The application will use a class-level variable to keep track of the player's points. A class-level variable is appropriate in this case because it will need to be used by two different procedures: rollButton_Click and startOverButton_Click. Click the **blank line** below the `' declare class-level variable` comment, and then enter the following declaration statement:

   Private points As Integer = 10

The first procedure you will code is the rollButton's Click event procedure. Figure 6-34 shows the procedure's pseudocode.

```
rollButton Click event procedure
1. generate two random integers from 1 through 6 and assign to variables
2. if the first random integer is one of the following:
       1  display dot1PictureBox image in firstDiePictureBox
       2  display dot2PictureBox image in firstDiePictureBox
       3  display dot3PictureBox image in firstDiePictureBox
       4  display dot4PictureBox image in firstDiePictureBox
       5  display dot5PictureBox image in firstDiePictureBox
       6  display dot6PictureBox image in firstDiePictureBox
   end if
3. if the second random integer is one of the following:
       1  display dot1PictureBox image in secondDiePictureBox
       2  display dot2PictureBox image in secondDiePictureBox
       3  display dot3PictureBox image in secondDiePictureBox
       4  display dot4PictureBox image in secondDiePictureBox
       5  display dot5PictureBox image in secondDiePictureBox
       6  display dot6PictureBox image in secondDiePictureBox
   end if
4. if the sum of both random integers is 7
       add 2 to the player's points
   else
       subtract 1 from the player's points
       if the player has no points left
           display "Sorry, you lost all of your points! Click the Start Over
           button to try again." message
       end if
   end if
5. display the player's points in pointsLabel
```

Figure 6-34 Pseudocode for the rollButton_Click procedure

To code and then test the rollButton_Click procedure:

1. Locate the code template for the rollButton_Click procedure. Click the **blank line** above the End Sub clause. The procedure will need a Random object to represent the pseudo-random number generator. It will also need two Integer variables to store the two random integers. Enter the following three Dim statements. Press **Enter** twice after typing the last Dim statement.

   Dim randGen As New Random
   Dim random1 As Integer
   Dim random2 As Integer

2. The first step in the pseudocode generates two random integers from 1 through 6. Enter the following comment and assignment statements. Press **Enter** twice after typing the last assignment statement.

   ' generate two random integers from 1 through 6
   random1 = randGen.Next(1, 7)
   random2 = randGen.Next(1, 7)

3. The second step in the pseudocode is a multiple-alternative selection structure. The structure uses the first random integer to display the appropriate image in the firstDiePictureBox. Enter the additional comment and code shown in Figure 6-35, and then position the insertion point as indicated in the figure.

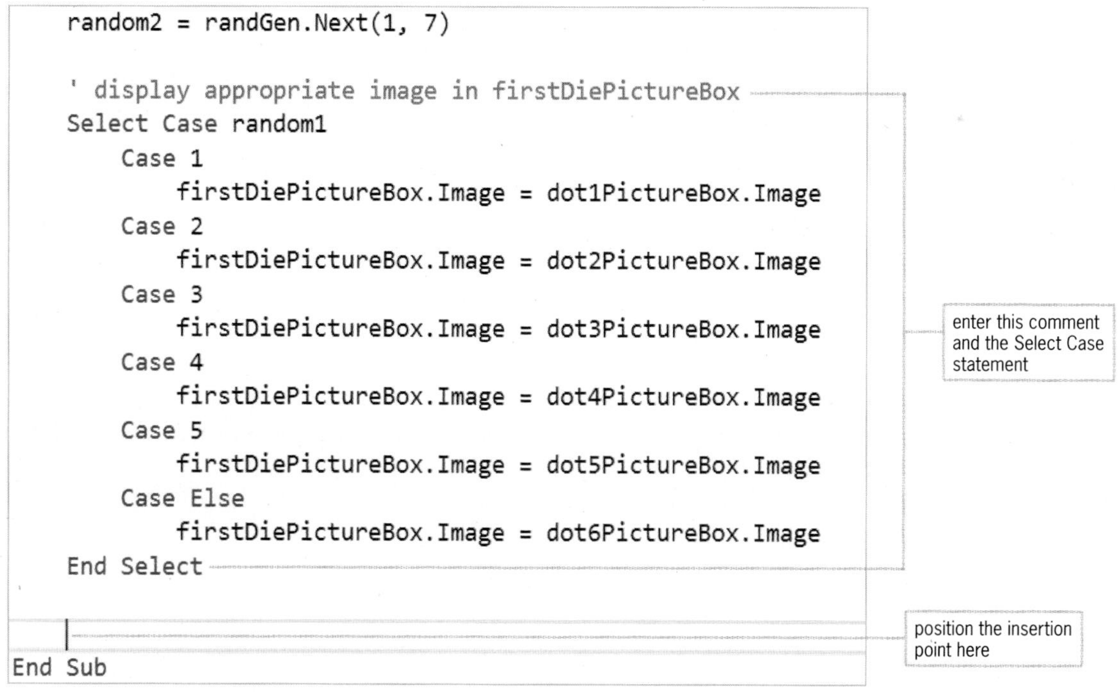

random2 = randGen.Next(1, 7)
' display appropriate image in firstDiePictureBox
Select Case random1
Case 1
firstDiePictureBox.Image = dot1PictureBox.Image
Case 2
firstDiePictureBox.Image = dot2PictureBox.Image
Case 3
firstDiePictureBox.Image = dot3PictureBox.Image
Case 4
firstDiePictureBox.Image = dot4PictureBox.Image
Case 5
firstDiePictureBox.Image = dot5PictureBox.Image
Case Else
firstDiePictureBox.Image = dot6PictureBox.Image
End Select
End Sub
enter this comment and the Select Case statement
position the insertion point here

Figure 6-35 First selection structure

4. The third step in the pseudocode is another multiple-alternative selection structure. This structure uses the second random number to display the appropriate image in the secondDiePictureBox. Enter the additional comment and code shown in Figure 6-36, and then position the insertion point as indicated in the figure.

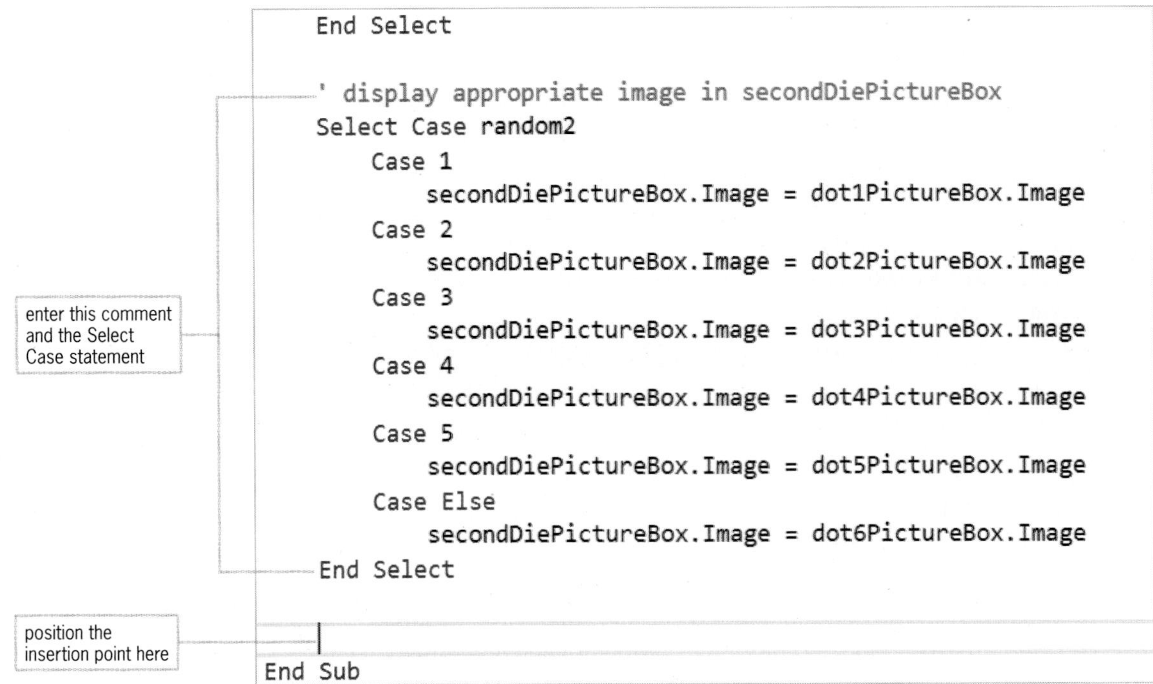
End Select
' display appropriate image in secondDiePictureBox
Select Case random2
Case 1
secondDiePictureBox.Image = dot1PictureBox.Image
Case 2
secondDiePictureBox.Image = dot2PictureBox.Image
Case 3
secondDiePictureBox.Image = dot3PictureBox.Image
Case 4
secondDiePictureBox.Image = dot4PictureBox.Image
Case 5
secondDiePictureBox.Image = dot5PictureBox.Image
Case Else
secondDiePictureBox.Image = dot6PictureBox.Image
End Select
End Sub
enter this comment and the Select Case statement
position the insertion point here

Figure 6-36 Second selection structure

5. The fourth step in the pseudocode is a single-alternative selection structure that compares the sum of both random integers with the number 7. If the sum equals 7, the selection structure's True path increases the player's points by 2. Type the following comment, If clause, and assignment statement:

   ' check sum of random numbers
   If random1 + random2 = 7 Then
   points += 2

6. If the sum of both random integers does not equal 7, the structure's False path subtracts the number 1 from the player's points. It then uses a nested selection structure to check whether the player has any points left. If the player is out of points, the nested structure's True path displays an appropriate message. Enter the additional code shown in Figure 6-37, and then position the insertion point as indicated in the figure.

enter the False path

position the insertion point here

```
        points += 2
    Else
        points -= 1
        If points = 0 Then
            MessageBox.Show("Sorry, you lost all of your points! " &
                            "Click the Start Over button to try again.",
                            "Lucky Number Game", MessageBoxButtons.OK,
                            MessageBoxIcon.Information)
        End If
    End If

End Sub
```

Figure 6-37 False path in the third selection structure

7. The last step in the pseudocode displays the player's points in the pointsLabel. Enter the following comment and assignment statement:

   ' display points
   pointsLabel.Text = points.ToString

8. Save the solution and then start the application. The Points box shows that the player has 10 points. Click the **Roll 'Em** button. Recall that the value in the Points box will increase by 2 whenever the sum of the dots on both dice equals 7; otherwise, the value will decrease by 1. The sum of the dots on Figure 6-38's dice does not equal 7, so the Points box indicates that the player now has only 9 points left. Because random integers determine the images assigned to the firstDiePictureBox and secondDiePictureBox controls, your controls might display different images than those shown in the figure. Also, if the sum of the dots on both of your dice equals 7, your Points box will contain the number 12 rather than the number 9.

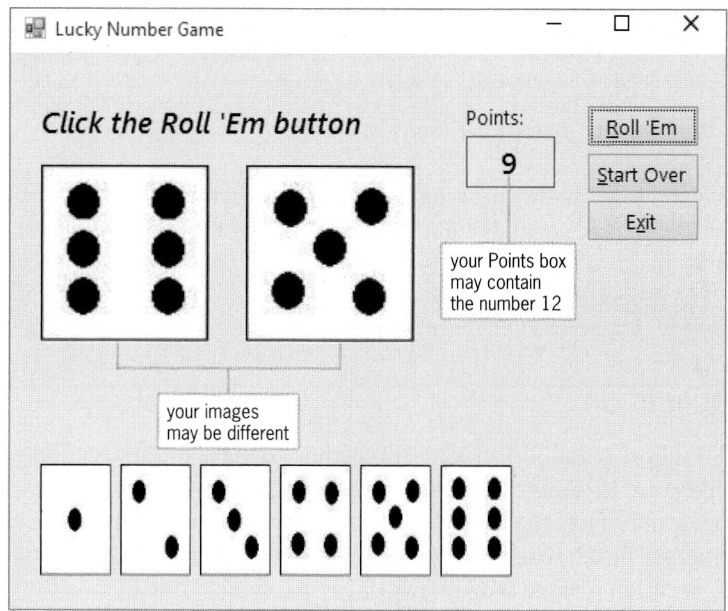

Figure 6-38 Sample run of the application

9. Click the **Exit** button to end the application.

Next, you will code the startOverButton's Click event procedure. According to the application's TOE chart, the procedure is responsible for setting the player's points to 10, then displaying the points in the pointsLabel, and then removing the images from the firstDiePictureBox and secondDiePictureBox controls. You can remove an image from a picture box by assigning the keyword `Nothing` to the control's Image property.

To code and then test the startOverButton_Click procedure:

1. Open the code template for the startOverButton_Click procedure. Type **' start a new game** and press **Enter** twice.

2. Enter the following four assignment statements:

   points = 10
   pointsLabel.Text = points.ToString
   firstDiePictureBox.Image = Nothing
   secondDiePictureBox.Image = Nothing

3. There is no need to show the six images at the bottom of the form during run time. Make the designer window the active window, and then unlock the controls on the form. Drag the form's bottom border until it hides the six images, and then lock the controls again.
4. Save the solution and then start the application. Click the **Roll 'Em** button until you run out of points. The "Sorry" message appears in a message box, as shown in Figure 6-39.

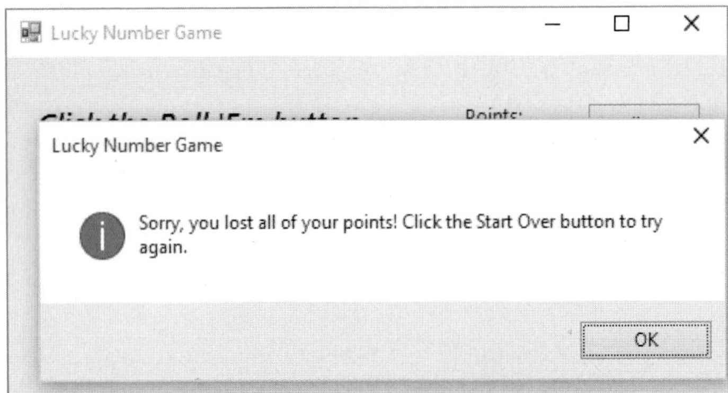

Figure 6-39 Message box showing the "Sorry" message

5. Click the **OK** button to close the message box, and then click the **Start Over** button. The firstDiePictureBox and secondDiePictureBox controls are now empty and the Points box shows the number 10.
6. Click the **Exit** button.

Modifying the Application

In this section, you will modify the rollButton_Click procedure to make the application a bit more exciting. The first modification involves three tasks: removing the previous images from the two picture boxes, refreshing the interface, and delaying (pausing) program execution before displaying the new images in the picture boxes. The delay will give the player a short time to anticipate the roll. You will delay the execution for one second, which is 1000 milliseconds.

To make the first modification to the procedure and then test it:

1. Make the Code Editor window the active window. Click the **blank line** below the last Dim statement in the rollButton_Click procedure, and then press **Enter** to insert a new blank line.
2. First, remove the images. Enter the following comment and assignment statements. Press **Enter** twice after typing the second assignment statement.

```
' remove images
firstDiePictureBox.Image = Nothing
secondDiePictureBox.Image = Nothing
```

3. Now, delay program execution. Enter the following comment and statements:

```
' refresh form and then delay execution
Me.Refresh()
System.Threading.Thread.Sleep(1000)
```

4. Save the solution and then start the application. Click the **Roll 'Em** button. Notice that there is a slight delay from when you click the button to when the dice images appear. Click the **Roll 'Em** button again, and then click the **Exit** button to end the application.

The disadvantage of the delay between clicking the button and the appearance of the dice images is that it might seem to the user that nothing is happening. And, as a result, he or she may click the Roll 'Em button again, before the dice images have a chance to appear. You can fix this problem by disabling the button after it has been clicked, and then enabling it after all of the code in its Click event procedure is processed.

To make the second modification to the procedure and then test it:

1. Click the **blank line** above the `' refresh form and then delay execution` comment, and then press **Enter** to insert a new blank line. Enter the following comment and assignment statement:

   ' disable Roll 'Em button
   rollButton.Enabled = False

2. Click the **blank line** above the End Sub clause, and then enter the following comment and assignment statement:

   ' enable Roll 'Em button
   rollButton.Enabled = True

3. Save the solution and then start the application. Click the **Roll 'Em** button. Notice that the button is disabled (grayed out) until after the dice images appear. Click the **Exit** button to end the application.

Finally, you will use a loop to make the numberLabel, which contains the red number 7, blink several times when the player rolls a 7. You can make a control blink by switching its Visible property from True to False and then back again several times. However, because the computer will process the switching instructions so rapidly, you won't notice that the control is blinking unless you refresh the form and then delay program execution each time you switch the Visible property's setting.

Figure 6-40 shows two versions of the third modification you will make to the rollButton_Click procedure. Version 2 uses the **Not logical operator**, which reverses the truth value of the numberLabel's Visible property. If the Visible property contains True when the `numberLabel.Visible = Not numberLabel.Visible` statement is processed, the `Not numberLabel.Visible` expression evaluates to False; as a result, the statement assigns False to the Visible property. On the other hand, if the Visible property contains False when the statement is processed, the `Not numberLabel.Visible` expression evaluates to True and the statement assigns True to the Visible property.

HOW TO Make a Control Blink

Version 1

```
Dim count As Integer = 1
Do While count <= 10
    If numberLabel.Visible = True Then
        numberLabel.Visible = False
    Else
        numberLabel.Visible = True
    End If
    Me.Refresh()
    System.Threading.Thread.Sleep(200)
    count += 1
Loop
```

Figure 6-40 How to make a control blink *(continues)*

(continued)

```
Version 2
Dim count As Integer = 1
Do While count <= 10
    numberLabel.Visible = Not numberLabel.Visible
    Me.Refresh()
    System.Threading.Thread.Sleep(200)
    count += 1
Loop
```

Figure 6-40 How to make a control blink

To finish modifying the rollButton_Click procedure and then test it:

1. Insert a blank line below the **If random1 + random2 = 7 Then** clause. Beginning in the blank line, enter either version of the code shown in Figure 6-40. (If you find the Not operator confusing, enter Version 1 of the code.)
2. Save the solution and then start the application. Play the game until you roll a 7, which causes the numberLabel to blink. (Be careful not to click the Roll 'Em button when it is grayed out because the button will still recognize the click. Computer Exercise 33 contains a hint as to how to get the button to ignore any clicks made when it is grayed out.)
3. Click the **Exit** button to end the application. Close the Code Editor window and then close the solution. Figure 6-41 shows the application's code. (The figure contains Version 2 of the code shown in Figure 6-40. Your code may contain Version 1.)

```
' Project name:          Lucky Project
' Project purpose:       Simulates the Lucky Number Game
' Created/revised by:    <your name> on <current date>

Option Explicit On
Option Strict On
Option Infer Off

Public Class MainForm
  ' declare class-level variable
  Private points As Integer = 10

  Private Sub exitButton_Click(sender As Object, e As EventArgs
  ) Handles exitButton.Click
      Me.Close()
  End Sub

  Private Sub rollButton_Click(sender As Object, e As EventArgs
  ) Handles rollButton.Click
      ' simulates the Lucky Number Game

```

Figure 6-41 Code for the Lucky Number Game application *(continues)*

(continued)

```
        Dim randGen As New Random
        Dim random1 As Integer
        Dim random2 As Integer

        ' remove images
        firstDiePictureBox.Image = Nothing
        secondDiePictureBox.Image = Nothing

        ' disable Roll 'Em button
        rollButton.Enabled = False

        ' refresh form and then delay execution
        Me.Refresh()
        System.Threading.Thread.Sleep(1000)

        ' generate two random integers from 1 through 6
        random1 = randGen.Next(1, 7)
        random2 = randGen.Next(1, 7)

        ' display appropriate image in firstDiePictureBox
        Select Case random1
            Case 1
                firstDiePictureBox.Image = dot1PictureBox.Image
            Case 2
                firstDiePictureBox.Image = dot2PictureBox.Image
            Case 3
                firstDiePictureBox.Image = dot3PictureBox.Image
            Case 4
                firstDiePictureBox.Image = dot4PictureBox.Image
            Case 5
                firstDiePictureBox.Image = dot5PictureBox.Image
            Case Else
                firstDiePictureBox.Image = dot6PictureBox.Image
       End Select

       ' display appropriate image in secondDiePictureBox
        Select Case random2
            Case 1
                secondDiePictureBox.Image = dot1PictureBox.Image
            Case 2
                secondDiePictureBox.Image = dot2PictureBox.Image
            Case 3
                secondDiePictureBox.Image = dot3PictureBox.Image
            Case 4
                secondDiePictureBox.Image = dot4PictureBox.Image
            Case 5
                secondDiePictureBox.Image = dot5PictureBox.Image
            Case Else
                secondDiePictureBox.Image = dot6PictureBox.Image
        End Select

```

Figure 6-41 Code for the Lucky Number Game application *(continues)*

(continued)

```
        ' check sum of random numbers
        If random1 + random2 = 7 Then
            Dim count As Integer = 1
            Do While count <= 10
                numberLabel.Visible = Not numberLabel.Visible
                Me.Refresh()
                System.Threading.Thread.Sleep(200)
                count += 1
            Loop
            points += 2
        Else
            points -= 1
            If points = 0 Then
               MessageBox.Show("Sorry, you lost all of your points! " &
                        "Click the Start Over button to try again.",
                        "Lucky Number Game", MessageBoxButtons.OK,
                        MessageBoxIcon.Information)
            End If
        End If
        ' display points
        pointsLabel.Text = points.ToString
        ' enable Roll 'Em button
        rollButton.Enabled = True

    End Sub

    Private Sub startOverButton_Click(sender As Object,
    e As EventArgs) Handles startOverButton.Click
        ' start a new game

        points = 10
        pointsLabel.Text = points.ToString
        firstDiePictureBox.Image = Nothing
        secondDiePictureBox.Image = Nothing

     End Sub
End Class
```

Figure 6-41 Code for the Lucky Number Game application

PROGRAMMING TUTORIAL 2

Coding the Just Birthdays Application

In this tutorial, you will create an application for the Just Birthdays store, which sells unique supplies for birthday parties. The application calculates and displays a customer's total charge, which is based on the type of birthday party and the number of guests. The application will also generate a set of test data that can be used when testing the application's code. The application's TOE chart is shown in Figure 6-42 along with the store's price list. The application's MainForm is shown in Figure 6-43.

Type of birthday party	Charge per guest ($)
Kid's	11
21st	20
40th	25
Other	15

Task	Object	Event
Get and display the number of guests	guestsTextBox	None
Allow the text box to accept only numbers and the Backspace key		KeyPress
Specify the birthday type	typeListBox	None
Display the birthday types in the typeListBox	MainForm	Load
1. Calculate the total charge 2. Display the total charge in totalLabel	calcButton	Click
Display the total charge (from calcButton)	totalLabel	None
End the application	exitButton	Click
Generate test data	testDataButton	Click
Display test data	testDataLabel	None

Figure 6-42 Just Birthdays price list and TOE chart

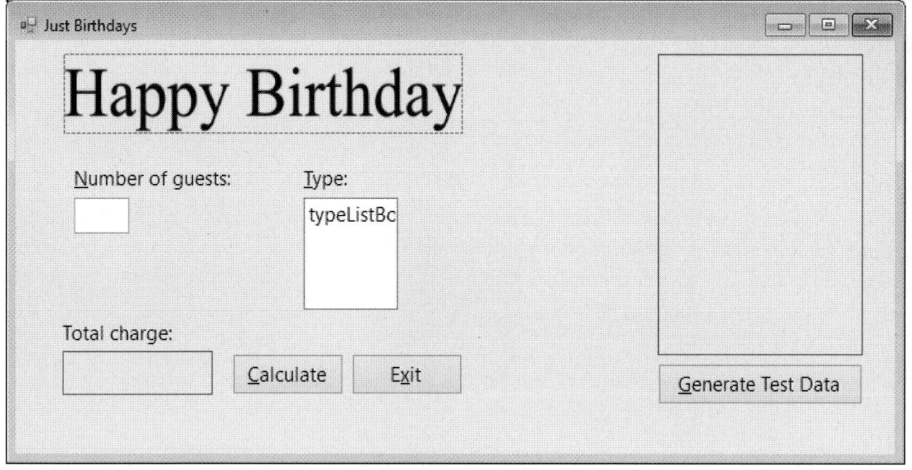

Figure 6-43 MainForm for the Just Birthdays application

Coding the Just Birthdays Application

According to the application's TOE chart, the guestsTextBox's KeyPress event procedure, the MainForm's Load event procedure, and the Click event procedures for the three buttons need to be coded.

To begin coding the application:

1. Start Visual Studio. Open the **Birthday Solution** (**Birthday Solution.sln**) file contained in the VbReloaded2015\Chap06\Birthday Solution folder. If necessary, open the designer window.
2. Open the Code Editor window. The exitButton_Click and the guestsTextBox_KeyPress procedures have already been coded for you. In the comments that appear in the General Declarations section, replace <your name> and <current date> with your name and the current date, respectively.
3. The MainForm's Load event procedure is responsible for displaying the birthday types in the typeListBox. Open the code template for the MainForm's Load event procedure. Recall that you do this by selecting (MainForm Events) in the Object list box and then selecting Load in the Method list box. Type the following comment and then press **Enter** twice:

   ' fills the list box and then selects the first item
4. Enter the following four Add methods:

   typeListBox.Items.Add("Kid's")
   typeListBox.Items.Add("21st")
   typeListBox.Items.Add("40th")
   typeListBox.Items.Add("Other")
5. Next, enter a statement that uses the SelectedIndex property to select the first item in the typeListBox.
6. Save the solution and then start the application. Four items appear in the Type list box. The first item in the list is selected (highlighted).
7. Click the **Exit** button to end the application.

The application's TOE chart indicates that the calcButton_Click procedure is responsible for calculating and displaying the total charge. The procedure's pseudocode is shown in Figure 6-44 along with the variables it requires.

```
calcButton Click event procedure
1. store the number of guests in a variable
2. store the index of the selected birthday type in a variable
3. if the birthday type index is one of the following:
       0 (Kid's)      price per guest = 11
       1 (21st)       price per guest = 20
       2 (40th)       price per guest = 25
       3 (Other)      price per guest = 15
   end if
4. total charge = number of guests * price per guest
5. display the total charge in totalLabel
```

Variables	Data types	Value sources
`guests`	Integer	user input (guestsTextBox)
`typeIndex`	Integer	user input (index of item selected in the typeListBox)
`guestPrice`	Integer	assigned in the procedure
`totalCharge`	Integer	procedure calculation

Figure 6-44 Pseudocode and variables for the calcButton_Click procedure

To code and then test the calcButton_Click procedure:

1. Open the code template for the calcButton_Click procedure. Type the following comment and then press **Enter** twice:

   ' displays the total charge

2. Enter the statements to declare the four variables listed in Figure 6-44. Press **Enter** twice after typing the last declaration statement.
3. The first step in the pseudocode stores the number of guests in a variable. Enter a TryParse method that will store the contents of the guestsTextBox in the `guests` variable.
4. The second step in the pseudocode stores the index of the selected birthday type in a variable. Enter an assignment statement that stores the index in the `typeIndex` variable. Press **Enter** twice after typing the assignment statement.
5. The third step in the pseudocode is a multiple-alternative selection structure that uses the birthday type index to determine the price per guest. Enter the following comment:

   ' determine the price per guest

6. Now, enter the appropriate Select Case statement. Assign the price per guest to the `guestPrice` variable. Use comments to make the Select Case statement more self-documenting. For example, enter `Case 0 ' Kid's` for the first Case clause.
7. The fourth step in the pseudocode calculates the total charge by multiplying the number of guests by the price per guest. If necessary, insert **two blank lines** between the End Select clause and the End Sub clause. In the blank line above the End Sub clause, enter the following comment:

   ' calculate and display the total charge

8. Now, enter the assignment statement to calculate the total charge. Assign the total charge to the `totalCharge` variable.
9. The last step in the pseudocode displays the total charge in the totalLabel. Enter the appropriate assignment statement. Display the total charge with a dollar sign and no decimal places.
10. Save the solution and then start the application. Type **10** as the number of guests and then click **40th** in the list box. Click the **Calculate** button. $250 appears in the Total charge box, as shown in Figure 6-45.

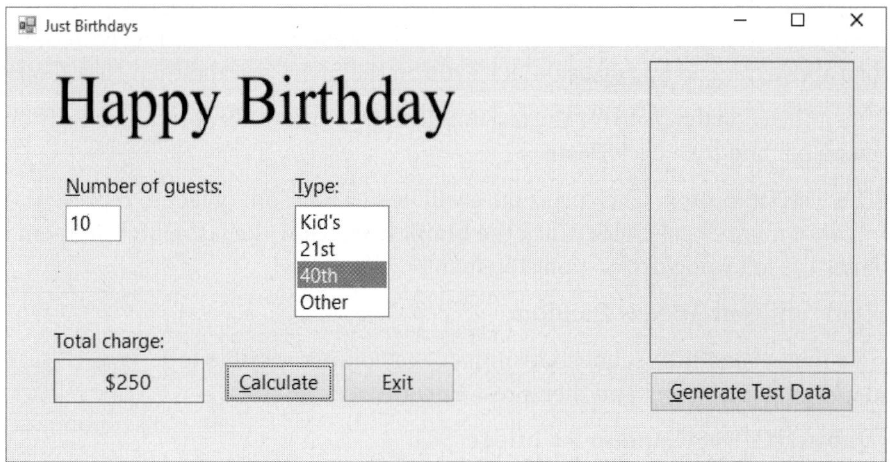

Figure 6-45 Total charge shown in the interface

11. On your own, test the application using different values for the number of guests and birthday types. When you are finished, click the **Exit** button to end the application.

Generating Test Data for the Just Birthdays Application

As you know, you should test an application as thoroughly as possible because you don't want to give the user an application that either produces incorrect output or ends abruptly with an error. For all of the applications you have created so far, you were either given the test data or expected to create your own test data. However, it's also possible to have the computer create a set of test data for you. As you will learn in the next set of steps, you do this using a loop and the random number generator. The Generate Test Data button's Click event procedure will be responsible for generating 10 sets of random test data. The procedure's pseudocode is shown in Figure 6-46.

```
testDataButton Click event procedure
1. initialize a counter variable to 1
2. clear the contents of the testDataLabel
3. repeat
       generate a random integer from 1 through 50 to represent the number of guests
       generate a random integer from 0 through 3 to represent the birthday type index
       if the birthday type index is one of the following:
              0 (Kid's)       price per guest = 11
              1 (21st)        price per guest = 20
              2 (40th)        price per guest = 25
              3 (Other)       price per guest = 15
       end if
       total charge = number of guests * price per guest
       display the birthday type index, number of guests, and total charge in the testDataLabel
       add 1 to the counter variable
   end repeat until the counter variable is greater than 10
```

Figure 6-46 Pseudocode for the testDataButton_Click procedure

To code the testDataButton_Click procedure and then test it:

1. Highlight the comments and code contained in the calcButton_Click procedure, beginning with the `Dim guests As Integer` statement and ending with the blank line above the End Sub clause. Click **Edit** on the menu bar and then click **Copy**.

2. Open the code template for the testDataButton_Click procedure. Click **Edit** on the menu bar and then click **Paste**.

3. The testDataButton_Click procedure will need a Random object to represent the random number generator. Click the **blank line** below the last Dim statement and then enter the following declaration statement:

   Dim randGen As New Random

4. The first step in the pseudocode initializes a counter variable to 1. Type the following declaration statement and then press **Enter** twice:

   Dim setsOfDataCounter As Integer = 1

5. The second step in the pseudocode clears the contents of the testDataLabel. Type the following assignment statement and then press **Enter** twice:

   testDataLabel.Text = String.Empty

6. The third step in the pseudocode contains a posttest loop. Type **Do** and press **Enter**. Change the Loop clause to **Loop Until setsOfDataCounter > 10**.

7. Delete the statement containing the TryParse method. Also delete the statement that assigns the SelectedIndex value to the `typeIndex` variable, as well as the blank line that follows that statement.

8. Now you can start coding the loop body. According to the pseudocode, the first instruction in the loop body generates a random integer from 1 through 50 to represent the number of guests. Click the **blank line** between the Do and Loop clauses, and then enter the following statement:

   guests = randGen.Next(1, 51)

9. The next instruction in the loop body generates a random integer from 0 through 3 to represent the birthday type index. Type the following statement, and then press **Enter** twice:

   typeIndex = randGen.Next(0, 4)

10. The procedure already contains the code corresponding to the selection structure and calculation task shown in the pseudocode. You just need to move that code into the loop. Highlight all of the comments and code, beginning with the `' determine the price per guest` comment and ending with the blank line below the last assignment statement. Click **Edit** on the menu bar and then click **Cut**.

11. Click the **blank line** above the Loop clause. Click **Edit** on the menu bar and then click **Paste**.

12. After calculating the total charge, the procedure will need to display the birthday type index, number of guests, and total charge in the testDataLabel. Change the `totalLabel.Text = totalCharge.ToString("C0")` statement in the loop body to the following (there are six spaces within the first two sets of quotation marks):

   testDataLabel.Text = testDataLabel.Text &
   typeIndex.ToString & "   " &
   guests.ToString & "   " &
   totalCharge.ToString("C0") &
   ControlChars.NewLine

13. The last instruction in the loop body should update the counter variable by 1. Enter the following statement in the blank line above the Loop clause:

   setsOfDataCounter += 1

14. If necessary, delete any blank lines between the Loop clause and the End Sub clause.

15. Save the solution and then start the application. Click the **Generate Test Data** button. The test data appears in the testDataLabel, as shown in Figure 6-47. Because random numbers are used for both the list box's index and the number of guests, your test data may be different from the test data shown in the figure.

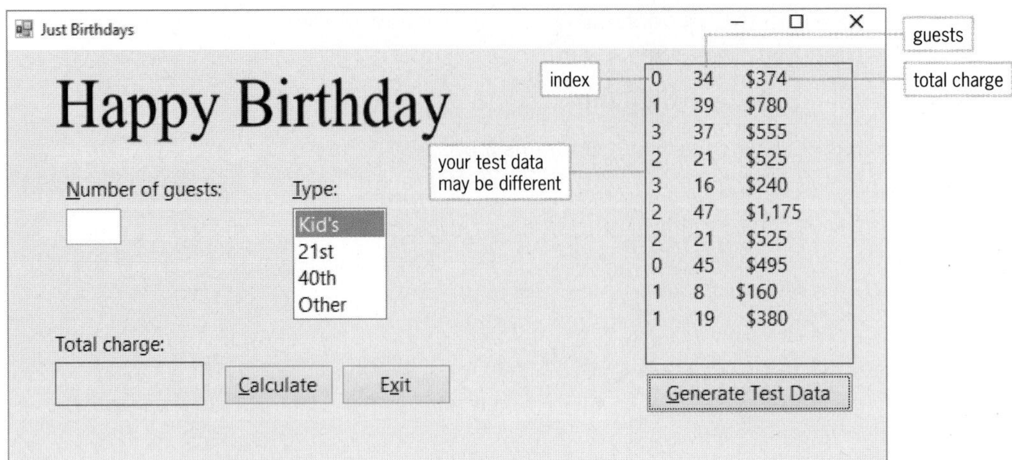

Figure 6-47 Test data generated by the testDataButton_Click procedure

16. Now, manually calculate the total charges using the values shown in the first two columns of the testDataLabel, and then compare your answers with the values in the third column. For example, in the first set of test data shown in Figure 6-47, the 0 and 34 indicate a Kid's birthday party and 34 guests, respectively. The price per guest for a Kid's birthday party is $11. If you multiply 34 by 11, the result is 374, which agrees with the value shown in the third column for this set of test data.

17. Click the **Exit** button. Close the Code Editor window and then close the solution. Figure 6-48 shows the code for the Just Birthdays application.

```
' Project name:         Birthday Project
' Project purpose:      Displays the total charge
' Created/revised by:   <your name> on <current date>

Option Explicit On
Option Strict On
Option Infer Off

Public Class MainForm
  Private Sub calcButton_Click(sender As Object, e As EventArgs
  ) Handles calcButton.Click
      ' displays the total charge

      Dim guests As Integer
      Dim typeIndex As Integer
      Dim guestPrice As Integer
      Dim totalCharge As Integer

      Integer.TryParse(guestsTextBox.Text, guests)
      typeIndex = typeListBox.SelectedIndex

      ' determine the price per guest
      Select Case typeIndex
          Case 0  ' Kid's
              guestPrice = 11
          Case 1  ' 21st
              guestPrice = 20
```

Figure 6-48 Code for the Just Birthdays application *(continues)*

PROGRAMMING TUTORIAL 2

(continued)

```
            Case 2  ' 40th
                guestPrice = 25
            Case 3  ' Other
                guestPrice = 15
        End Select

        ' calculate and display the total charge
        totalCharge = guests * guestPrice
        totalLabel.Text = totalCharge.ToString("C0")

    End Sub

    Private Sub exitButton_Click(sender As Object, e As EventArgs
    ) Handles exitButton.Click
        Me.Close()
   End Sub

    Private Sub guestsTextBox_KeyPress(sender As Object,
    e As KeyPressEventArgs) Handles guestsTextBox.KeyPress
        ' allows only numbers and the Backspace key

        If (e.KeyChar < "0" OrElse e.KeyChar > "9") AndAlso
            e.KeyChar <> ControlChars.Back Then
            e.Handled = True
        End If
    End Sub

    Private Sub MainForm_Load(sender As Object, e As EventArgs
    ) Handles Me.Load
        ' fills the list box and then selects the first item

        typeListBox.Items.Add("Kid's")
        typeListBox.Items.Add("21st")
        typeListBox.Items.Add("40th")
        typeListBox.Items.Add("Other")
        typeListBox.SelectedIndex = 0

    End Sub

    Private Sub testDataButton_Click(sender As Object,
    e As EventArgs) Handles testDataButton.Click
        Dim guests As Integer
        Dim typeIndex As Integer
        Dim guestPrice As Integer
        Dim totalCharge As Integer
        Dim randGen As New Random
        Dim setsOfDataCounter As Integer = 1

        testDataLabel.Text = String.Empty

        Do
            guests = randGen.Next(1, 51)
            typeIndex = randGen.Next(0, 4)

```

Figure 6-48 Code for the Just Birthdays application *(continues)*

(continued)

```
          ' determine the price per guest
          Select Case typeIndex
              Case 0  ' Kid's
                  guestPrice = 11
              Case 1  ' 21st
                  guestPrice = 20
              Case 2  ' 40th
                  guestPrice = 25
              Case 3  ' Other
                  guestPrice = 15
          End Select

          ' calculate and display the total charge
          totalCharge = guests * guestPrice
          testDataLabel.Text = testDataLabel.Text &
              typeIndex.ToString & "       " &
              guests.ToString & "       " &
              totalCharge.ToString("C0") &
              ControlChars.NewLine
          setsOfDataCounter += 1

      Loop Until setsOfDataCounter > 10
  End Sub
End Class
```

Figure 6-48 Code for the Just Birthdays application

PROGRAMMING EXAMPLE

Lockett Sales Application

Create an application that allows the sales manager to enter each salesperson's annual sales amount. When the sales manager has finished entering the sales amounts, the application should calculate and display the average sales amount. Use the following names for the solution and project, respectively: Lockett Project and Lockett Solution. Save the application in the VbReloaded2015\Chap06 folder. Change the form file's name to Main Form.vb. See Figures 6-49 through 6-53.

Task	Object	Event
1. Get the sales amounts 2. Display the sales amounts in salesListBox 3. Calculate the average sales amount 4. Display either the average sales amount or "N/A" (if the user didn't enter any sales amounts) in avgLabel	calcButton	Click
End the application	exitButton	Click
Display the sales amount (from calcButton)	salesListBox	None
Display either the average sales amount or "N/A" (from calcButton)	avgLabel	None
Clear the salesListBox and avgLabel	startOverButton	Click

Figure 6-49 TOE chart

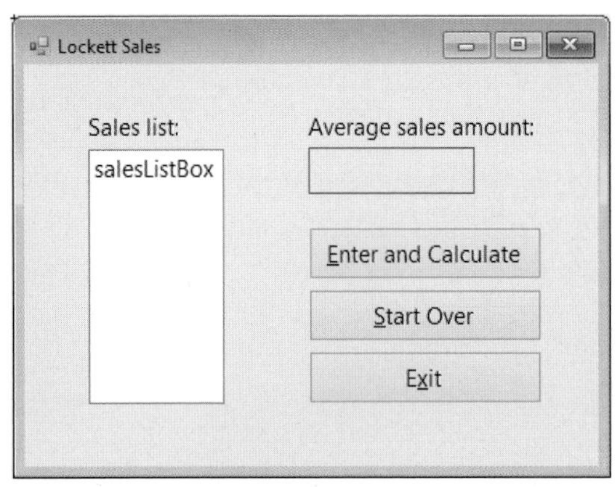

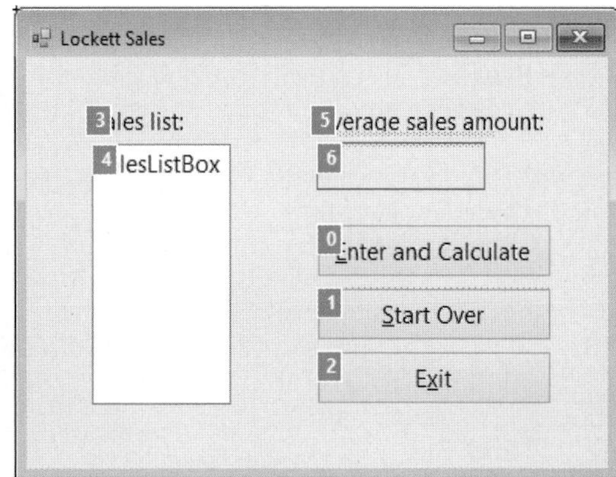

Figure 6-50 MainForm and tab order

Object	Property	Setting
MainForm	Font	Segoe UI, 11pt
	StartPosition	CenterScreen
	Text	Lockett Sales
salesListBox	Enabled	False
avgLabel	AutoSize	False
	BorderStyle	FixedSingle
	Text	(empty)
	TextAlign	MiddleCenter

Figure 6-51 Objects, properties, and settings

<u>exitButton Click event procedure</u>
close the application

<u>calcButton Click event procedure</u>
1. initialize number of sales counter to 0
2. initialize total sales accumulator to 0
3. get a sales amount from the user
4. repeat while the user entered a sales amount
        display the sales amount in the salesListBox
        add 1 to the number of sales counter
        add the sales amount to the total sales accumulator
        get a sales amount from the user
   end repeat while
5. if the value in the number of sales counter is greater than 0
      average sales amount = total sales accumulator / number of sales counter
      display the average sales amount in the avgLabel
   else
      display "N/A" in the avgLabel
   end if

<u>startOverButton Click event procedure</u>
1. clear the salesListBox
2. clear the avgLabel

Figure 6-52 Pseudocode

```
' Project name:         Lockett Project
' Project purpose:      Displays the average sales amount
' Created/revised by:   <your name> on <current date>

Option Explicit On
Option Strict On
Option Infer Off

Public Class MainForm
   Private Sub exitButton_Click(sender As Object, e As EventArgs) Handles exitButton.Click
       Me.Close()
   End Sub

   Private Sub calcButton_Click(sender As Object, e As EventArgs) Handles calcButton.Click
       ' calculates the average sales amount

       Const Prompt As String = "Enter a sales amount. " &
           ControlChars.NewLine &
           "Click Cancel or leave blank to end."
       Const Title As String = "Sales Entry"
       Dim inputSales As String
       Dim decSales As Decimal
       Dim numSales As Integer      ' counter
       Dim totalSales As Decimal    ' accumulator
       Dim avgSales As Decimal

       inputSales = InputBox(Prompt, Title, "0")
       ' repeat as long as the user enters a sales amount
       Do While inputSales <> String.Empty
           Decimal.TryParse(inputSales, decSales)
           salesListBox.Items.Add(decSales.ToString("N2"))
           numSales += 1
           totalSales += decSales
           inputSales = InputBox(Prompt, Title, "0")
       Loop

       ' verify that the counter is greater than 0
       If numSales > 0 Then
           avgSales = totalSales / numSales
           avgLabel.Text = avgSales.ToString("C2")
       Else
           avgLabel.Text = "N/A"
       End If
   End Sub

   Private Sub startOverButton_Click(sender As Object, e As EventArgs) Handles startOverButton.Click
       ' clear screen

       salesListBox.Items.Clear()
       avgLabel.Text = String.Empty
   End Sub
End Class
```

Figure 6-53 Code

Chapter Summary

- You use the repetition structure, also called a loop, to repeatedly process one or more program instructions either while the looping condition is true or until the loop exit condition has been met. A loop's condition must evaluate to either True or False only.
- A repetition structure can be either a pretest loop or a posttest loop. Depending on the loop's condition, the instructions in a pretest loop may never be processed. The instructions in a posttest loop, on the other hand, are always processed at least once.
- You can use the Do...Loop statement to code both pretest loops and posttest loops. The statement's condition must evaluate to a Boolean value.
- When used in the Do...Loop statement, the keyword `While` indicates that the loop instructions should be processed *while* (as long as) the condition evaluates to True. The keyword `Until` indicates that the loop instructions should be processed *until* the condition evaluates to True.
- In a flowchart, the loop's condition is represented by the decision symbol, which is a diamond.
- An overflow error occurs when the value assigned to a memory location is too large for the location's data type.
- A loop that has no way to end is called an infinite loop or an endless loop.
- You use a counter and/or an accumulator to calculate subtotals, totals, and averages.
- All counters and accumulators must be initialized and updated. The initialization is done outside of the loop that uses the counter or accumulator, and the updating is done within the loop. Counters are updated by a constant value, whereas accumulators are usually updated by an amount that varies.
- The input instruction located above a loop's condition is referred to as the priming read. The input instruction within the loop body is referred to as the update read. The priming read gets only the first value from the user. The update read gets the remaining values (if any).
- The InputBox function displays an input dialog box that can be used to prompt the user to enter some specific information. The function's return value is always treated as a string.
- In the InputBox function, you should use sentence capitalization for the prompt but book title capitalization for the title.
- You can use a text box's Multiline property to control whether the text box accepts and displays either one line of text or multiple lines of text. The value in a text box's ReadOnly property determines whether the user can edit the contents of the text box during run time. The value in a text box's ScrollBars property determines whether scroll bars appear on the text box.
- A list box displays a list of items from which the user can select zero items, one item (the default), or multiple items, depending on the value of its SelectionMode property.
- Use a label control to provide keyboard access to a list box. Set the label's TabIndex property to a value that is one number less than the list box's TabIndex value.
- You can use the String Collection Editor window to add items to a list box during design time. You can add items to a list box during run time using the Items collection's Add method. You can clear a list box using the Item collection's Clear method.
- The code contained in a form's Load event procedure will be processed before the form appears on the screen.

- List box items are either arranged by use, with the most used entries appearing first in the list, or sorted in ascending order.
- You use a list box item's index to access the item. The index of the first item in a list box is 0.
- The number of items in a list box is contained in the Items collection's Count property. The value in the Count property is always one number more than the list box's highest index.
- When an item is selected in a list box, the item appears highlighted in the list. The item's value is stored in the list box's SelectedItem property, and the item's index is stored in the list box's SelectedIndex property.
- If a list box allows the user to make only one selection at a time, then a default item is usually selected in the list box when the interface first appears. The default item should be either the item selected most frequently or the first item in the list.
- A list box's SelectedItem property and its SelectedIndex property can be used both to determine the item selected in the list box and to select a list box item from code.
- When you select an item in a list box, the list box's SelectedValueChanged and SelectedIndexChanged events occur.
- You use a control's Enabled property to enable or disable the control.
- You can use the Sleep method to delay (pause) program execution, and use the Refresh method to refresh (redraw) the form.

Key Terms

Accumulator—a numeric variable used for accumulating (adding together) something

Add method—the Items collection's method used to add items to a list box

Clear method—the Items collection's method used to clear the items from a list box

Collection—a group of individual objects treated as one unit

Count property—a property of the Items collection; stores an integer that represents the number of items contained in a list box

Counter—a numeric variable used for counting something

Decrementing—decreasing a value

Default list box item—the item automatically selected in a list box when the interface appears on the screen

Do...Loop statement—a Visual Basic statement that can be used to code both pretest loops and posttest loops

Enabled property—used to enable and display a control

Endless loop—a loop whose instructions are processed indefinitely; also called an infinite loop

Incrementing—increasing a value

Index—the unique number that identifies each item in a collection; used to access an item in a list box; the first index in a list box is 0

Infinite loop—another name for an endless loop

Initializing—the process of assigning a beginning value to a memory location, such as a counter variable or an accumulator variable

InputBox function—a Visual Basic function that displays an input dialog box containing a message, OK and Cancel buttons, and an input area

Items collection—the collection composed of the items in a list box

List box—a control used to display a list of items from which the user can select zero items, one item, or multiple items

Load event—the event that occurs when an application is started and the form is displayed the first time

Loop—another name for the repetition structure

Loop exit condition—the requirement that must be met for the computer to *stop* processing the loop body instructions

Looping condition—the requirement that must be met for the computer to *continue* processing the loop body instructions

Multiline property—determines whether a text box can accept and display only one line of text or multiple lines of text

Not logical operator—reverses the truth value of a condition

Overflow error—occurs when the value assigned to a memory location is too large for the location's data type

Posttest loop—a loop whose condition is evaluated *after* the instructions in its loop body are processed

Pretest loop—a loop whose condition is evaluated *before* the instructions in its loop body are processed

Priming read—the input instruction that appears above the loop that it controls; used to get the first input item from the user

ReadOnly property—determines whether the user is allowed to change the contents of a text box during run time

Refresh method—refreshes (redraws) a form

Repetition structure—the control structure used to repeatedly process one or more program instructions; also called a loop

ScrollBars property—a property of a text box; specifies whether the text box has scroll bars

SelectedIndex property—stores the index of the item selected in a list box

SelectedIndexChanged event—occurs when an item is selected in a list box

SelectedItem property—stores the value of the item selected in a list box

SelectedValueChanged event—occurs when an item is selected in a list box

SelectionMode property—determines the number of items that can be selected in a list box

Sleep method—used to delay program execution

Sorted property—specifies whether the list box items should appear in the order they are entered or in sorted order

Update read—the input instruction that appears within a loop and is associated with the priming read

Updating—the process of either adding a number to or subtracting a number from the value stored in a counter or accumulator variable

Review Questions

Each Review Question is associated with one or more objectives listed at the beginning of the chapter.

1. Which of the following clauses will stop the loop when the value in the `order` variable is less than the number 0? (1, 4)
   a. `Do While order >= 0`
   b. `Do Until order < 0`
   c. `Loop While order >= 0`
   d. all of the above

2. How many times will the MessageBox.Show method in the following code be processed? (1, 2, 4, 5)

```
Dim counter As Integer
Do While counter > 3
    MessageBox.Show("Hello")
    counter += 1
Loop
```

   a. 0
   b. 1
   c. 3
   d. 4

3. How many times will the MessageBox.Show method in the following code be processed? (1, 2, 4, 5)

```
Dim counter As Integer
Do
    MessageBox.Show("Hello")
    counter += 1
Loop While counter > 3
```

   a. 0
   b. 1
   c. 3
   d. 4

Refer to Figure 6-54 to answer Review Questions 4 through 7.

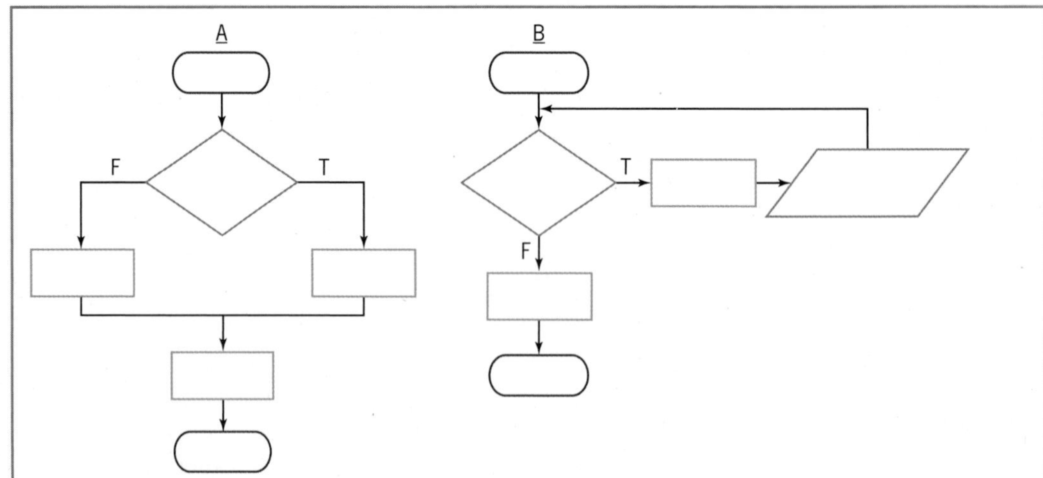

Figure 6-54 Flowcharts for Review Questions 4 through 7 *(continues)*

(continued)

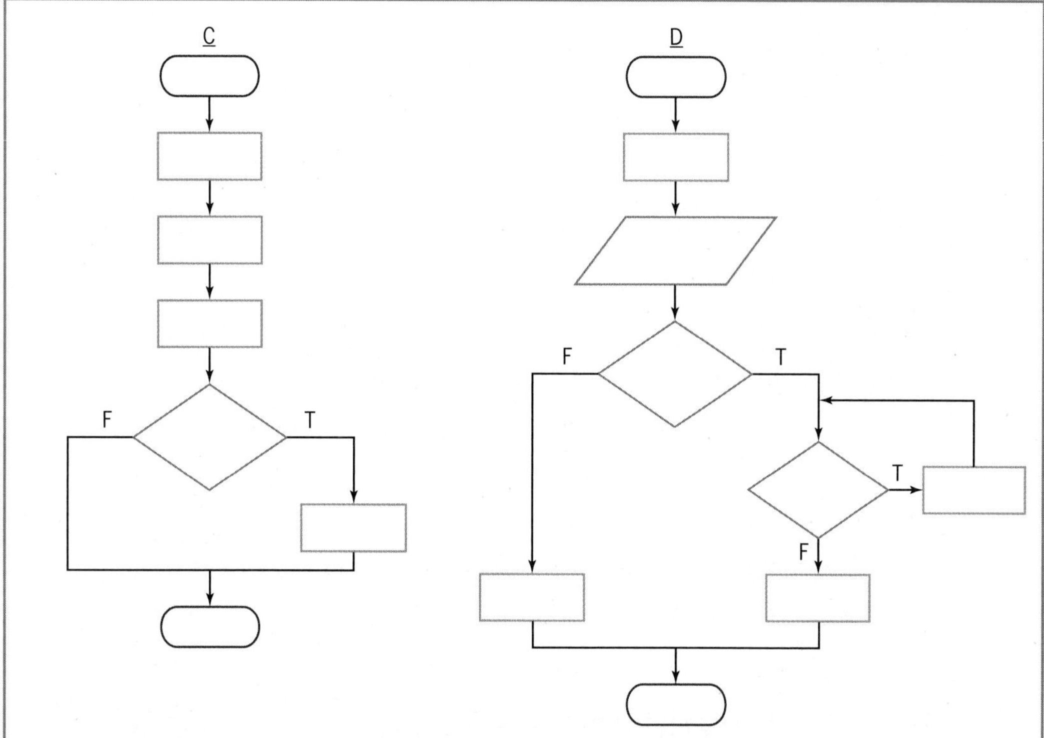

Figure 6-54 Flowcharts for Review Questions 4 through 7

4. In addition to the sequence structure, which of the following control structures are used in flowchart A in Figure 6-54? (3)
   a. selection
   b. repetition
   c. both selection and repetition
5. In addition to the sequence structure, which of the following control structures are used in flowchart B in Figure 6-54? (3)
   a. selection
   b. repetition
   c. both selection and repetition
6. In addition to the sequence structure, which of the following control structures are used in flowchart C in Figure 6-54? (3)
   a. selection
   b. repetition
   c. both selection and repetition

7. In addition to the sequence structure, which of the following control structures are used in flowchart D in Figure 6-54? (3)

   a. selection

   b. repetition

   c. both selection and repetition

8. What does the InputBox function return when the user clicks the Cancel button in its dialog box? (6)

   a. the number 0
   c. an error message

   b. the empty string
   d. none of the above

9. Which property stores the index of the item selected in a list box? (8)

   a. Index
   c. Selection

   b. SelectedIndex
   d. SelectionIndex

10. Which of the following selects the third item in the animalListBox? (8)

    a. `animalListBox.SelectedIndex = 2`

    b. `animalListBox.SelectedIndex = 3`

    c. `animalListBox.SelectedItem = 2`

    d. `animalListBox.SelectedItem = 3`

11. Which event occurs when the user selects an item in a list box? (8)

    a. SelectionChanged
    c. SelectedValueChanged

    b. SelectedItemChanged
    d. none of the above

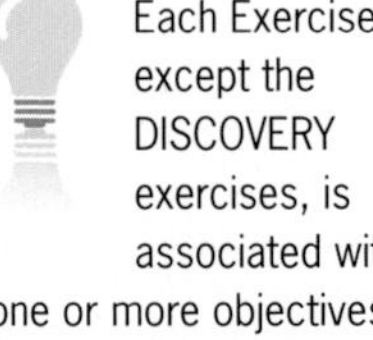

Each Exercise, except the DISCOVERY exercises, is associated with one or more objectives listed at the beginning of the chapter.

Exercises

Pencil and Paper

INTRODUCTORY

1. Write a Visual Basic Do clause that processes the loop instructions as long as the value in the `order` variable is greater than the number 100. Use the `While` keyword. Then rewrite the Do clause using the `Until` keyword. (1, 4)

INTRODUCTORY

2. Write a Visual Basic Do clause that stops the loop when the value in the `quantity` variable is less than or equal to the value in the `ordered` variable. Use the `Until` keyword. Then rewrite the Do clause using the `While` keyword. (1, 4)

INTRODUCTORY

3. Write an assignment statement that updates the `number` variable by 2. (5)

INTRODUCTORY

4. Write an assignment statement that updates the `number` variable by –3. (5)

INTRODUCTORY

5. Write an assignment statement that updates the `totalSales` variable by the value stored in the `quarterSales` variable. (5)

INTRODUCTORY

6. Write an assignment statement that updates the `sales` variable by subtracting the contents of the `returned` variable. (5)

7. Write a Visual Basic Loop clause that processes the loop instructions as long as the value in the `letter` variable is either Y or y. Use the `While` keyword. Then rewrite the Loop clause using the `Until` keyword. (1, 4) INTERMEDIATE

8. Write a Visual Basic Do clause that processes the loop instructions as long as the value in the `state` variable is not "Done" (in any case). Use the `Until` keyword. Then rewrite the Do clause using the `While` keyword. (1, 4) INTERMEDIATE

9. What will the following code display in message boxes? (1, 2, 4, 5) INTERMEDIATE

```
Dim x As Integer
Do While x < 5
    MessageBox.Show(x.ToString)
    x += 2
Loop
```

10. What will the following code display in message boxes? (1, 2, 4, 5) INTERMEDIATE

```
Dim x As Integer
Do
    MessageBox.Show(x.ToString)
    x += 3
Loop Until x > 5
```

11. What will the following code display in message boxes? (1, 2, 4, 5) INTERMEDIATE

```
Dim totalEmp As Integer
Do While totalEmp <= 6
    MessageBox.Show(totalEmp.ToString)
    totalEmp += 2
Loop
```

12. What will the following code display in message boxes? (1, 2, 4, 5) INTERMEDIATE

```
Dim totalEmp As Integer = 1
Do
    MessageBox.Show(totalEmp.ToString)
    totalEmp += 2
Loop Until totalEmp >= 3
```

13. Write two different statements that you can use to select the fifth item in the deptListBox. The fifth item is Security. (8) INTERMEDIATE

14. Write the Visual Basic code that corresponds to the flowchart shown in Figure 6-55. Display the calculated results in the numberListBox. (1–5) ADVANCED

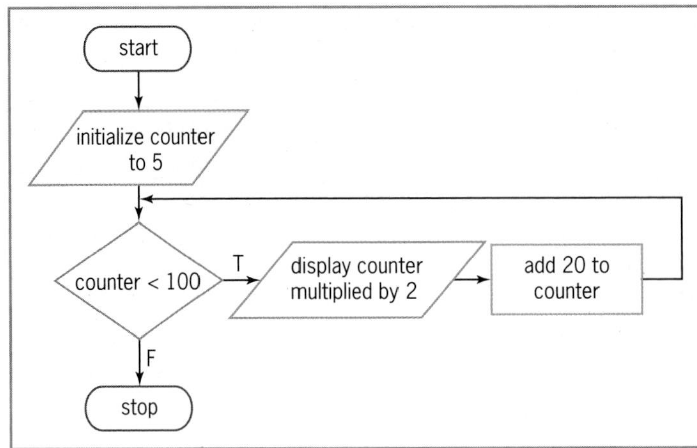

Figure 6-55 Flowchart for Exercise 14

SWAT THE BUGS

15. The following code should display the numbers 1 through 4, but it is not working correctly. Correct the code. (1, 2, 4, 5)

```
Dim number As Integer = 1
Do While number < 5
    MessageBox.Show(number.ToString)
Loop
```

SWAT THE BUGS

16. The following code should display the numbers 10 through 1, but it is not working correctly. Correct the code. (1, 2, 4, 5)

```
Dim number As Integer = 10
Do
    MessageBox.Show(number.ToString)
Loop Until number = 0
```

Computer

MODIFY THIS

17. If necessary, complete the Lucky Number Game application from this chapter's Programming Tutorial 1, and then close the solution. Use Windows to make a copy of the Lucky Solution folder. Rename the folder Lucky Solution-ModifyThis. Open the solution file contained in the Lucky Solution-ModifyThis folder. Change the Do clause to use a loop exit condition rather than a looping condition. Save the solution and then start and test the application. Close the solution. (1, 4)

MODIFY THIS

18. If necessary, complete the Just Birthdays application from this chapter's Programming Tutorial 2, and then close the solution. Use Windows to make a copy of the Birthday Solution folder. Rename the folder Birthday Solution-ModifyThis. Open the solution file contained in the Birthday Solution-ModifyThis folder. Modify the testDataButton_Click procedure so that it displays the type of birthday, rather than the type's index, in the testDataLabel. (In other words, display "Kid's" rather than 0.) Save the solution and then start and test the application. Close the solution. (8)

19. If necessary, complete the Lockett Sales application from this chapter's Programming Example, and then close the solution. Use Windows to make a copy of the Lockett Solution folder. Rename the folder Lockett Solution-ModifyThis. Open the solution file contained in the Lockett Solution-ModifyThis folder. Currently, the Do clause contains a looping condition. Change the Do clause to a loop exit condition. Save the solution and then start and test the application. Close the solution. (1, 4)

MODIFY THIS

20. Open the solution file contained in the VbReloaded2015\Chap06\Sales Solution-ModifyThis folder. Currently, the Do clause contains a looping condition. Change the Do clause to a loop exit condition. Also, rather than using $125,000 as the sales goal, the user should be able to enter any sales goal. Provide a text box for the user to enter the goal. Save the solution and then start and test the application. Close the solution. (1, 2, 4, 5)

MODIFY THIS

21. Open the solution file contained in the VbReloaded2015\Chap06\Go Team Solution folder. The Click Here button should disable itself and then blink the "Go Team!" message 10 times. Each time the message blinks, its font color should change from black to red and then back to black. After the message blinks 10 times, the button should enable itself. Code the button's Click event procedure. Save the solution and then start and test the application. Close the solution. (1, 2, 4, 5, 9, 10)

MODIFY THIS

22. Open the solution file contained in the VbReloaded2015\Chap06\Even Odd Solution folder. The pretestButton_Click procedure should clear the contents of the pretestListBox and then use a pretest loop to display the even integers from 2 through 10 in the list box. The posttestButton_Click procedure should clear the contents of the posttestListBox and then use a posttest loop to display the odd integers from 21 through 39 in the list box. Code both procedures. Save the solution and then start and test the application. Close the solution. (1, 2, 4, 5, 8)

INTRODUCTORY

23. Open the solution file contained in the VbReloaded2015\Chap06\Woodson Solution folder. The calcButton_Click procedure should allow the user to enter zero or more sales amounts. Use the InputBox function to get the sales amounts. Display the sales amounts in the salesListBox. When the user has completed entering the sales amounts, the procedure should display the total sales in the totalSalesLabel. It should also display a 10% bonus in the bonusLabel. Code the procedure. Save the solution and then start and test the application. Close the solution. (1, 2, 4–6, 8)

INTRODUCTORY

24. Open the solution file contained in the VbReloaded2015\Chap06\Calculator Solution folder. The addButton_Click procedure should perform the following three tasks: add the integer entered in the numTextBox to an accumulator, display the integer on a separate line in the numbersTextBox, and display the accumulator's value in the sumLabel. The startOverButton_Click procedure should clear the contents of both text boxes and the sumLabel. It should also start the accumulator at 0. Code the procedures. Save the solution and then start and test the application. Close the solution. (5, 7)

INTRODUCTORY

25. Open the solution file contained in the VbReloaded2015\Chap06\Average Solution folder. The calcButton_Click procedure should get from zero to five test scores from the user. Display the test scores in the scoresListBox. When the user has finished entering the scores, the procedure should calculate and display the average test score. Code the procedure. Save the solution and then start and test the application. Close the solution. (1, 2, 4–6, 8)

INTERMEDIATE

26. Create an application for General Dollar. Use the following names for the solution and project, respectively: General Solution and General Project. Save the application in the VbReloaded2015\Chap06 folder. Change the form file's name to Main Form.vb. The application's interface is shown in Figure 6-56. The interface allows the user to

INTERMEDIATE

enter an item's price, which should be displayed in the Prices entered text box. The Prices entered text box should have its Multiline, ReadOnly, ScrollBars, and TextAlign properties set to True, True, Vertical, and Right, respectively. The Add to Total button's Click event procedure should accumulate the prices entered by the user, always displaying the accumulated value plus a 3% sales tax in the Total due box. In other words, if the user enters the number 5 as the item's price, the Total due box should display $5.15. If the user subsequently enters the number 10, the Total due box should display $15.45. The Next Order button should allow the user to start accumulating the values for the next order. Code the application. Save the solution and then start and test the application. Close the solution. (1, 2, 4, 5, 7)

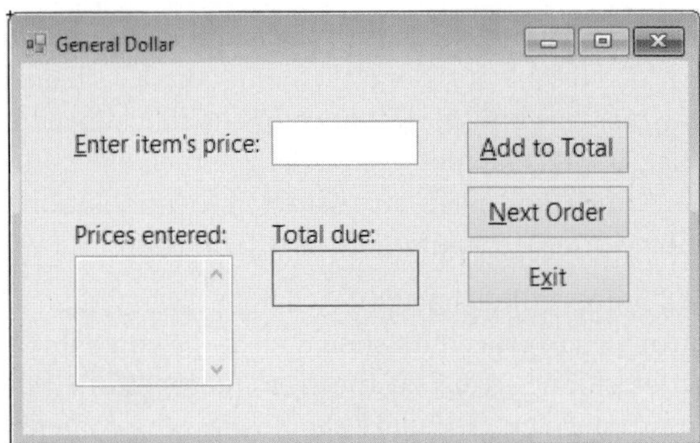

Figure 6-56 Interface for Exercise 26

INTERMEDIATE

27. Create an application for Premium Paper. Use the following names for the solution and project, respectively: Premium Solution and Premium Project. Save the solution in the VbReloaded2015\Chap06 folder. Change the form file's name to Main Form.vb. The application should allow the sales manager to enter the company's income and expense amounts. The number of income and expense amounts may vary each time the application is started. For example, the user may enter five income amounts and three expense amounts. Or, he or she may enter 20 income amounts and 30 expense amounts. The application should calculate and display the company's total income, total expenses, and profit (or loss). Use the InputBox function to get the individual income and expense amounts. (1–6)

    a. Design an appropriate interface. Use label controls to display the total income, total expenses, and profit (loss). Display the calculated amounts with a dollar sign and two decimal places. If the company experienced a loss, display the amount of the loss using a red font; otherwise, display the profit using a black font.

    b. Code the application. Keep in mind that the income and expense amounts may contain decimal places.

    c. Save the solution and then start the application. Test the application twice. For the first test, use 750.75 and 935.67 as the income amounts, and use 1995.65 as the expense amount. For the second test, use income amounts of 5000, 6000, 35000, and 78000, and use expense amounts of 1000, 2000, and 600. Close the solution.

28. Create an application that displays the ZIP code (or codes) corresponding to the city name selected in a list box. The city names and ZIP codes are shown in Figure 6-57. Use the following names for the solution and project, respectively: Zip Solution and Zip Project. Save the application in the VbReloaded2015\Chap06 folder. Change the form file's name to Main Form.vb. (8) INTERMEDIATE

   a. Create the interface shown in Figure 6-57. The items in the list box should be sorted; set the appropriate property.

   b. The form's Load event procedure should add the city names shown in Figure 6-57 to the list box and then select the first name in the list. Code the procedure.

   c. The citiesListBox_SelectedValueChanged procedure should assign the item selected in the list box to a variable, and then use the Select Case statement to display the city's ZIP code(s). Code the procedure.

   d. Save the solution and then start and test the application.

   e. Change the code you entered in the citiesListBox_SelectedValueChanged procedure to comments. Now, enter the code to assign the index of the selected item to a variable, and then use a Select Case statement to display the city's ZIP code(s).

   f. Save the solution and then start and test the application. Close the solution.

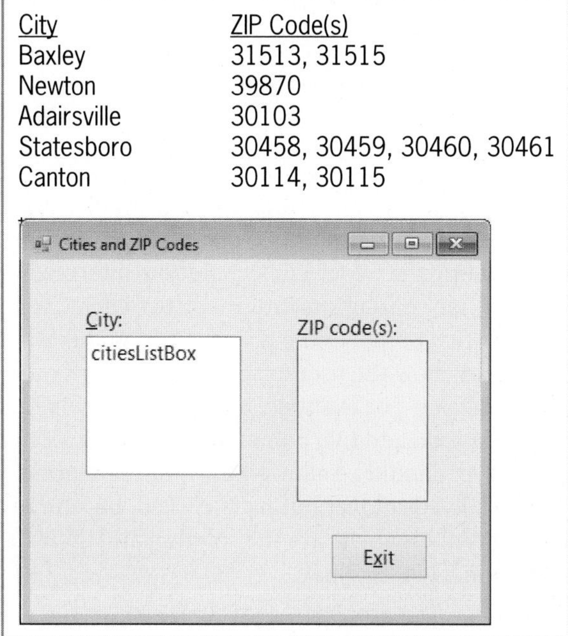

Figure 6-57 Cities, ZIP codes, and interface for Exercise 28

29. In this exercise, you will create a Windows application that displays a multiplication table. Use the following names for the solution and project, respectively: Multiplication Solution and Multiplication Project. Save the solution in the VbReloaded2015\Chap06 folder. Change the form file's name to Main Form.vb. Create the interface shown in Figure 6-58. The Number box should accept only numbers and the Backspace key. Code the application. Save the solution and then start and test the application. Close the solution. (1, 2, 4, 5, 7) INTERMEDIATE

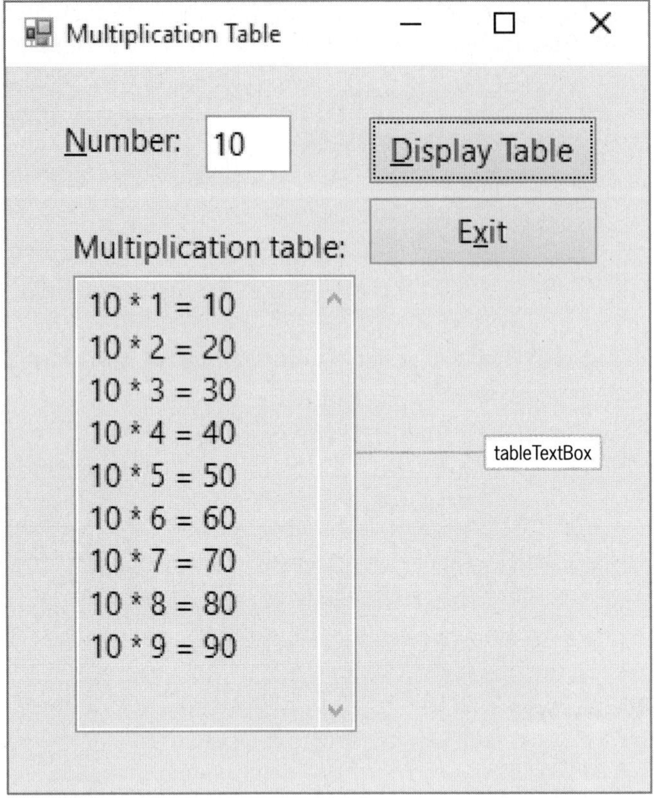

Figure 6-58 Interface for Exercise 29

INTERMEDIATE

30. If necessary, complete the Lucky Number Game application from this chapter's Programming Tutorial 1, and then close the solution. Use Windows to make a copy of the Lucky Solution folder. Rename the folder Lucky Solution-Intermediate. Open the solution file contained in the Lucky Solution-Intermediate folder. Currently, the rollButton_Click procedure adds two points to the player's total points when he or she rolls a 7. Modify the application to allow the user to specify a different number for the roll that increases the total point value. For example, if the player enters the number 3, the rollButton_Click procedure should add two points to the player's total points only when he or she rolls a 3. The player should be allowed to enter the number before the game begins and also each time the Start Over button is clicked. Be sure to also display the appropriate number in the numberLabel. Save the solution and then start and test the application. Close the solution. (1, 4–6, 9, 10)

ADVANCED

31. Open the solution file contained in the VbReloaded2015\Chap06\Fibonacci Solution folder. The application should display the first 10 Fibonacci numbers (1, 1, 2, 3, 5, 8, 13, 21, 34, and 55). Notice that beginning with the third number in the series, each Fibonacci number is the sum of the prior two numbers. In other words, 2 is the sum of 1 plus 1, 3 is the sum of 1 plus 2, 5 is the sum of 2 plus 3, and so on. Code the application. Save the solution and then start and test the application. Close the solution. (1, 2, 4, 5)

32. Create a Windows application. Use the following names for the solution and project, respectively: GPA Solution and GPA Project. Save the solution in the VbReloaded2015\Chap06 folder. Change the form file's name to Main Form.vb. Create an interface that uses list boxes for entering the gender (either F or M) and GPA (0.0 through 4.0) for any number of students. The application should calculate the average GPA for all students, the average GPA for male students, and the average GPA for female students. Code the application. Save the solution and then start and test the application. Close the solution. (1–5, 8)

ADVANCED

33. If necessary, complete the Lucky Number Game application from this chapter's Programming Tutorial 1, and then close the solution. Use Windows to make a copy of the Lucky Solution folder. Rename the folder Lucky Solution-Discovery33. Open the solution file contained in the Lucky Solution-Discovery33 folder. Start the application. Click the Roll 'Em button and then click it again while it is still grayed out. Notice that although the button is disabled, it still recognizes the second click. This problem is a result of setting the rollButton's Enabled property to True at the end of the rollButton_Click procedure. Modify the application so that it ignores the second click. (Hint: Research the Timer control, and then use a Timer control to set the rollButton's Enabled property to True.) Save the solution and then start and test the application. Close the solution.

DISCOVERY

34. If necessary, complete the Lucky Number Game application from this chapter's Programming Tutorial 1, and then close the solution. Use Windows to make a copy of the Lucky Solution folder. Rename the folder Lucky Solution-Discovery34. Open the solution file contained in the Lucky Solution-Discovery34 folder. Start the application. Click the Roll 'Em button until you run out of points, and then click it again several times. Notice that a negative number appears in the Points box. Modify the application to automatically start a new game when the number of points is 0. (Hint: Research a button's PerformClick method.) Save the solution and then start and test the application. Close the solution.

DISCOVERY

35. In this exercise, you learn how to create a list box that allows the user to select more than one item at a time. Open the solution file contained in the VbReloaded2015\Chap06\Multi Solution folder. The interface contains a list box named namesListBox. The list box's Sorted and SelectionMode properties are set to True and One, respectively.

DISCOVERY

   a. Open the Code Editor window. The MainForm_Load procedure adds five names to the namesListBox. Code the singleButton_Click procedure so that it displays, in the resultLabel, the item selected in the list box. For example, if the user clicks Debbie in the list box and then clicks the Single Selection button, the name Debbie should appear in the resultLabel. (Hint: Use the Convert.ToString method.)

   b. Save the solution and then start the application. Click Debbie in the list box, click Ahmad, and then click Bill. Notice that when the list box's SelectionMode property is set to One, you can select only one item at a time in the list. Click the Single Selection button. The name Bill appears in the resultLabel. Click the Exit button to end the application.

   c. Change the list box's SelectionMode property to MultiSimple. Save the solution and then start the application. Click Debbie in the list box, click Ahmad, click Bill, and then click Ahmad. Notice that when the list box's SelectionMode property is set to MultiSimple, you can select more than one item at a time in the list. Also notice that you click to both select and deselect an item. (You can also use Ctrl+click and Shift+click, as well as press the Spacebar, to select and deselect items when the list box's SelectionMode property is set to MultiSimple.) Click the Exit button.

d. Change the list box's SelectionMode property to MultiExtended. Save the solution and then start the application. Click Debbie in the list, and then click Jim. Notice that in this case, clicking Jim deselects Debbie. When a list box's SelectionMode property is set to MultiExtended, you use Ctrl+click to select multiple items in the list. You also use Ctrl+click to deselect items in the list. Click Debbie in the list, Ctrl+click Ahmad, and then Ctrl+click Debbie.

e. Next, click Bill in the list, and then Shift+click Jim; this selects all of the names from Bill through Jim. Click the Exit button.

f. As you know, when a list box's SelectionMode property is set to One, the item selected in the list box is stored in the SelectedItem property, and the item's index is stored in the SelectedIndex property. However, when a list box's SelectionMode property is set to either MultiSimple or MultiExtended, the items selected in the list box are stored in the SelectedItems property, and the indices of the items are stored in the SelectedIndices property. Code the multiButton_Click procedure so that it first clears the contents of the resultLabel. The procedure should then display the selected names (which are stored in the SelectedItems property) on separate lines in the resultLabel.

g. Save the solution and then start the application. Click Ahmad in the list box, and then Shift+click Jim. Click the Multi-Selection button. The five names should appear on separate lines in the resultLabel. Click the Exit button, and then close the solution.

DISCOVERY

36. In this exercise, you learn how to use the Items collection's Insert, Remove, and RemoveAt methods. Open the solution file contained in the VbReloaded2015\Chap06\Items Solution folder.

a. You can use the Items collection's Insert method to add an item at a desired position in a list box during run time. The Insert method's syntax is *object*`.Items.Insert`(*position*, *item*), where *position* is the index of the item. Code the insertButton_Click procedure so it adds your name as the fourth item in the list box.

b. You can use the Items collection's Remove method to remove an item from a list box during run time. The Remove method's syntax is *object*`.Items.Remove(`*item*`)`, where *item* is the item's value. Code the removeButton_Click procedure so it removes your name from the list box.

c. Like the Remove method, the Items collection's RemoveAt method also allows you to remove an item from a list box while an application is running. However, in the RemoveAt method, you specify the item's index rather than its value. The RemoveAt method's syntax is *object*`.Items.RemoveAt(`*index*`)`, where *index* is the item's index. Code the removeAtButton_Click procedure so it removes the second name from the list box.

d. Save the solution and then start and test the application. Close the solution.

SWAT THE BUGS

37. Open the Debug Solution (Debug Solution.sln) file contained in the VbReloaded2015\Chap06\Debug Solution folder. Open the Code Editor window and review the existing code. Start and then test the application. Locate and then correct any errors. When the application is working correctly, close the solution. (5, 6)

Case Projects

Martin Company

Create an application that the Martin Company's accountant can use to calculate an asset's annual depreciation. Use the following names for the solution and project, respectively: Martin Solution and Martin Project. Save the solution in the VbReloaded2015\Chap06 folder. Change the form file's name to Main Form.vb. You can either create your own interface or create the one shown in Figure 6-59. The figure shows a sample depreciation schedule for an asset with a cost of $100,000, a useful life of four years, and a salvage value of $15,000. The accountant will enter the asset's cost, useful life (in years), and salvage value (which is the value of the asset at the end of its useful life). Use a list box to allow the user to select the useful life. Display the numbers from 3 through 20 in the list box. The application should calculate the annual straight-line depreciation amounts using the Financial.SLN method. (*SLN* stands for *straight-line.*) The method's syntax is Financial.SLN (*cost, salvage, life*), in which *cost, salvage,* and *life* are the asset's cost, salvage value, and useful life, respectively. The method returns the depreciation amount as a Double number. The Asset cost and Salvage value text boxes shown in Figure 6-59 should accept only numbers, the period, and the Backspace key. The Depreciation Schedule image in the picture box is stored in the VbReloaded2015\Chap06\Martin.png file. (1–5, 7, 8)

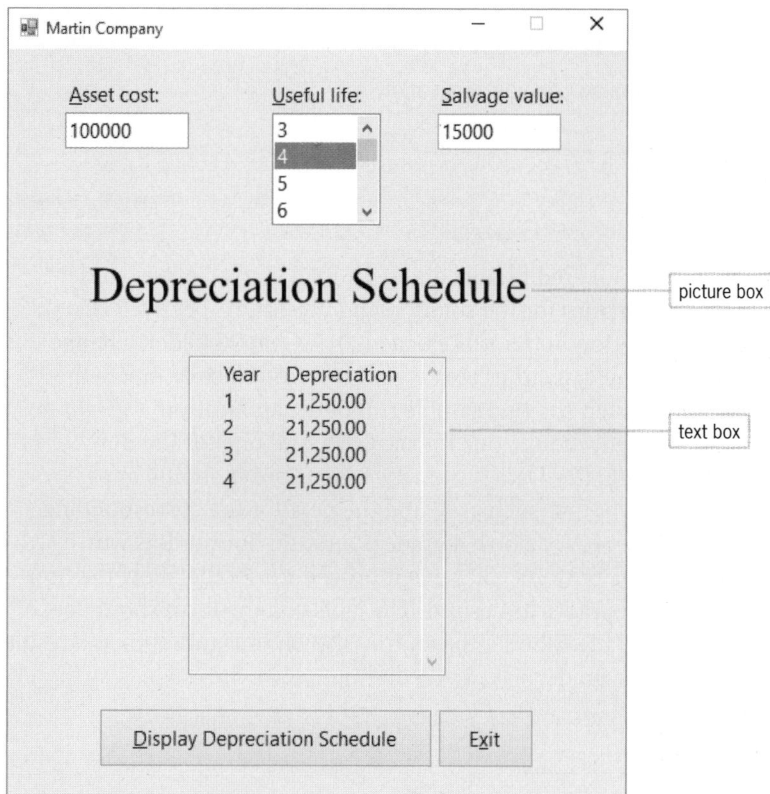

Figure 6-59 Sample run of the Martin Company application

Barclay Candies

Create an application for Barclay Candies. Use the following names for the solution and project, respectively: Barclay Solution and Barclay Project. Save the application in the VbReloaded2015\Chap06 folder. Change the form file's name to Main Form.vb. You can either create your own interface or create the one shown in Figure 6-60. The Calculate button's Click event procedure should use a loop and the InputBox function to get the prices of the candies purchased by the user. Each price should be displayed in the pricesListBox. The procedure should also accumulate the prices. When the user has finished entering the prices for the current order, the procedure should display the accumulated value plus a 5% sales tax in the Total due box. (1, 2, 4–8)

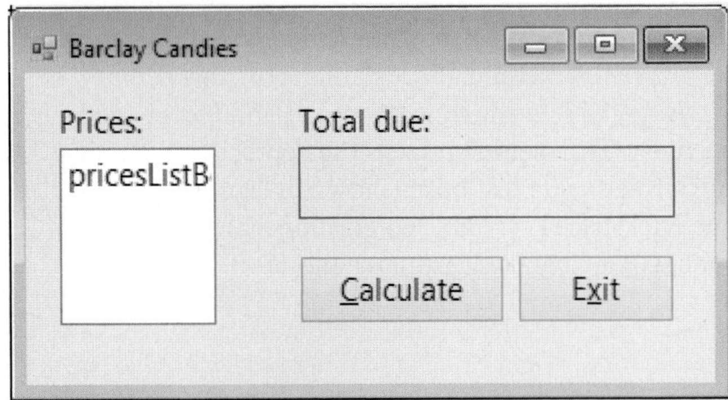

Figure 6-60 Sample interface for the Barclay Candies application

Cook College

Create an application that displays the total credit hours and GPA for a Cook College student during one semester. Use the following names for the solution and project, respectively: Cook Solution and Cook Project. Save the solution in the VbReloaded2015\Chap06 folder. Change the form file's name to Main Form.vb. You can either create your own interface or create the one shown in Figure 6-61. The figure, which shows a sample run of the application, uses three labels for the output: one for the total credit hours, one for the GPA, and one for the number of grades entered. When the user clicks the Enter Data button, two input boxes should appear in succession: one for the number of credit hours (such as 3) and the next for the corresponding letter grade (such as A). One credit hour of A is worth 4 grade points, an hour of B is worth 3 grade points, and so on. The Enter Data button's Click event procedure should allow the user to enter as many sets of credit hours and grades as desired. The labels on the form should be updated after the user enters the letter grade. The sample output shown in Figure 6-61 is a result of entering 3 as the credit hours, A as the grade, 5 as the credit hours, B as the grade, 3 as the credit hours, and B as the grade. (1–6)

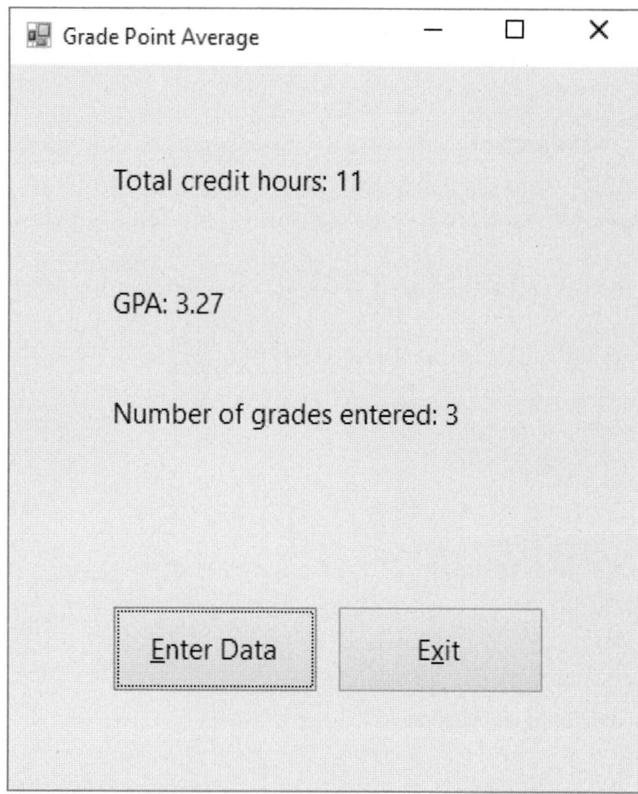

Figure 6-61 Sample run of the Cook College application

Zena Manufacturing

Zena Manufacturing has two warehouses, which the company refers to as warehouse A and warehouse B. Create an application that uses two list boxes to display the IDs of the company's products: one for products stored in warehouse A and one for products stored in warehouse B. Use the following names for the solution and project, respectively: Zena Solution and Zena Project. Save the solution in the VbReloaded2015\Chap06 folder. Change the form file's name to Main Form.vb. You can either create your own interface or create the one shown in Figure 6-62. The application should allow the user to enter a product ID, which will contain only letters and numbers. It then should use the Items collection's Contains method to determine whether the ID is listed in the Warehouse A list box; if it is, the application should display the letter A in the Location box. If the ID is not in the Warehouse A list box, the application should use the Contains method to determine whether it is listed in the Warehouse B list box; if it is, the application should display the letter B in the Location box. If the ID is not listed in either list box, the application should display N/A. (Hint: The syntax of the Contains method is *listbox*`.Items.Contains(`*value*`)`.) Use the following IDs to fill the Warehouse A list box: AB11, HY16, JK56, MM12, PY63, PY64, AB21, and AB14. Use the following IDs to fill the Warehouse B list box: AB20, JM17, PJ23, JK52, and TR16. (1–6, 8)

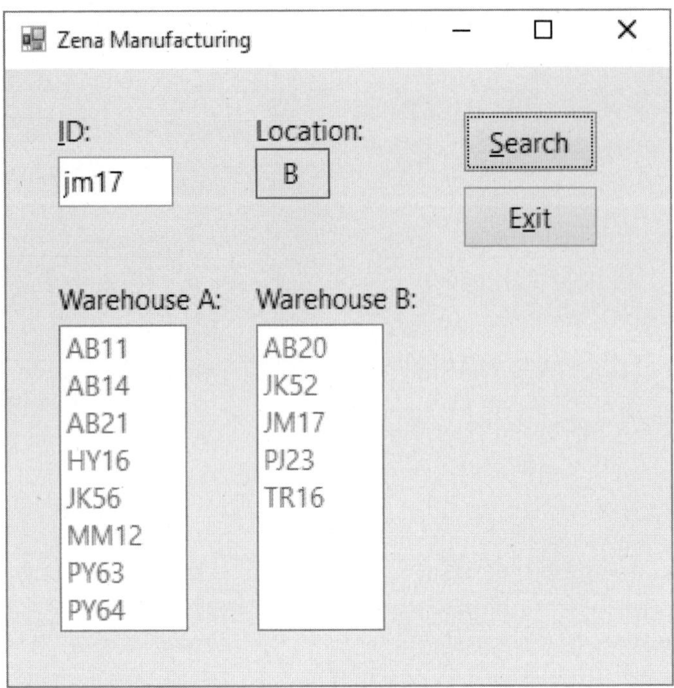

Figure 6-62 Sample run of the Zena Manufacturing application

Powder Skating Rink

Powder Skating Rink holds a weekly ice-skating competition. Competing skaters must perform a two-minute program in front of a panel of six judges. At the end of a skater's program, each judge assigns a score of 0 through 10 to the skater. The manager of the ice rink wants an application that calculates and displays a skater's average score. Use list boxes to allow the manager to select the names of the judges. (You will need to make up your own names to use.) Also use a list box to allow the manager to select the score. After a judge's score has been recorded, remove his/her name from the list box. Doing this will prevent the user from entering a judge's score more than once. (Hint: Complete Computer Exercise 36 before coding this application.) After displaying the skater's average, display each judge's name in the list box for the next skater's scores. Use the following names for the solution and project, respectively: Powder Solution and Powder Project. Save the solution in the VbReloaded2015\Chap06 folder. Change the form file's name to Main Form.vb. (1–5, 8)

CHAPTER 7

More on the Repetition Structure

After studying Chapter 7, you should be able to:

1. Code a counter-controlled loop
2. Nest repetition structures
3. Calculate a periodic payment using the Financial.Pmt method
4. Select the existing text in a text box
5. Code the Enter and TextChanged event procedures for a text box
6. Include a combo box in an interface
7. Code the TextChanged event procedure for a combo box
8. Store images in an image list control
9. Display an image stored in an image list control
10. Calculate the future value of an investment using the Financial.FV method (Programming Tutorial 2)

Counter-Controlled Loops

In Chapter 6, you learned about counters, which are numeric variables used for counting something, such as the number of items purchased by a customer. Programmers also use counters to control loops whose instructions must be processed a precise number of times; such loops are referred to as **counter-controlled loops**. The partial game program shown in Figure 7-1 uses a counter-controlled loop to process the loop instructions three times. As the figure indicates, a counter-controlled loop can be either a pretest loop or a posttest loop.

Ch07-Counter-Controlled Loops

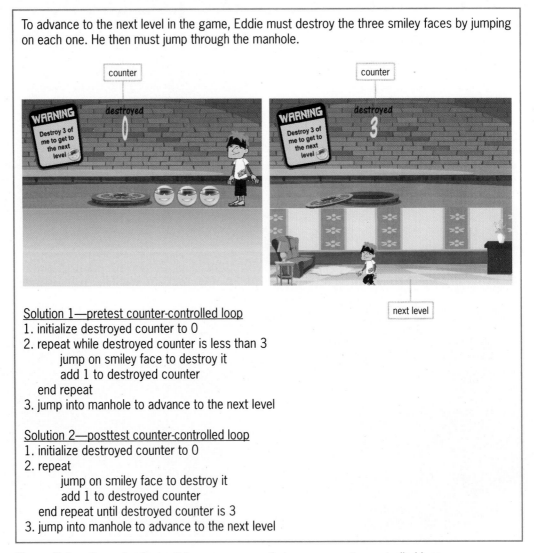

To advance to the next level in the game, Eddie must destroy the three smiley faces by jumping on each one. He then must jump through the manhole.

counter

counter

next level

<u>Solution 1—pretest counter-controlled loop</u>

1. initialize destroyed counter to 0
2. repeat while destroyed counter is less than 3
        jump on smiley face to destroy it
        add 1 to destroyed counter
    end repeat
3. jump into manhole to advance to the next level

<u>Solution 2—posttest counter-controlled loop</u>

1. initialize destroyed counter to 0
2. repeat
        jump on smiley face to destroy it
        add 1 to destroyed counter
    end repeat until destroyed counter is 3
3. jump into manhole to advance to the next level

Figure 7-1 Example of a partial game program that uses a counter-controlled loop
Image by Diane Zak; created with Reallusion CrazyTalk Animator

The For...Next Statement

In Visual Basic, posttest loops are coded using the Do...Loop statement, which you learned about in Chapter 6. Pretest counter-controlled loops, on the other hand, can be coded using either the Do...Loop statement or the For...Next statement. However, the **For...Next statement** provides a more convenient way to code that type of loop because it takes care of initializing and updating the counter and also evaluating the loop condition.

The For...Next statement's syntax is shown in Figure 7-2 along with examples of using the statement. The *counterVariableName* that appears in the For and Next clauses is the name of a numeric variable that the computer will use to keep track of (in other words, count) the number of times the loop body instructions are processed. Although, technically, you do not need to specify the name of the counter variable in the Next clause, doing so is highly recommended because self-documentation makes your code easier to understand. Figure 7-2 also shows the tasks performed by the computer when processing the statement.

You can use the `Exit For` statement to exit the For...Next statement before it has finished processing. You may need to do this if the computer encounters an error when processing the loop instructions.

HOW TO Use the For...Next Statement

Syntax

For *counterVariableName* [**As** *dataType*] = *startValue* **To** *endValue* [**Step** *stepValue*]
    loop body instructions
Next *counterVariableName*

stepValue	Loop body processed when	Loop ends when
positive number	counter's value <= *endValue*	counter's value > *endValue*
negative number	counter's value >= *endValue*	counter's value < *endValue*

Example 1

```
Dim sum As Integer
For num As Integer = 5 To 8
    sum += num
Next num
```

adds together the numbers 5, 6, 7, and 8, storing the sum in the `sum` variable

Example 2

```
Dim city As String
For x As Integer = 5 To 1 Step -1
    city = InputBox("City:", "City Entry")
    cityListBox.Items.Add(city)
Next x
```

adds the five city names entered by the user to the cityListBox

Example 3

```
Dim rate As Double
For rate = 0.05 To 0.1 Step 0.01
    rateListBox.Items.Add(rate.ToString("P0"))
Next rate
```

adds 5 %, 6 %, 7 %, 8 %, 9 %, and 10 % to the rateListBox

Figure 7-2 How to use the For...Next statement *(continues)*

(continued)

Processing tasks

1. If the counter variable is declared in the For clause, the variable is created and then initialized to the *startValue*; otherwise, it is just initialized to the *startValue*. The initialization is done only once, at the beginning of the loop.
2. The counter's value is compared with the *endValue* to determine whether the loop should end. If the *stepValue* is a positive number, the comparison determines whether the counter's value is greater than the *endValue*. If the *stepValue* is a negative number, the comparison determines whether the counter's value is less than the *endValue*. Notice that the computer evaluates the loop condition before processing the instructions within the loop.
3. If the comparison from Task 2 evaluates to True, the loop ends and processing continues with the statement following the Next clause. Otherwise, the loop body instructions are processed and then Task 4 is performed.
4. Task 4 is performed only when the comparison from Task 2 evaluates to False. In this task, the *stepValue* is added to the counter's value, and then Tasks 2, 3, and 4 are repeated until the loop condition evaluates to True.

Figure 7-2 How to use the For...Next statement

You can use the `As` *dataType* portion of the For clause to declare the counter variable, as shown in the first two examples in Figure 7-2. When you declare a variable in the For clause, the variable has block scope and can be used only within the For...Next loop. Alternatively, you can declare the counter variable in a Dim statement, as shown in Example 3. As you know, a variable declared in a Dim statement at the beginning of a procedure has procedure scope and can be used within the entire procedure. When deciding where to declare the counter variable, keep in mind that if the variable is needed only by the For...Next loop, then it is a better programming practice to declare the variable in the For clause. As mentioned in Chapter 3, fewer unintentional errors occur in applications when the variables are declared using the minimum scope needed. Block-level variables have the smallest scope, followed by procedure-level variables and then class-level variables. You should declare the counter variable in a Dim statement only when its value is required by statements outside the For...Next loop in the procedure.

The *startValue*, *endValue*, and *stepValue* items in the For clause control the number of times the loop body is processed. The startValue and endValue tell the computer where to begin and end counting, respectively. The stepValue tells the computer how much to count by—in other words, how much to add to the counter variable each time the loop body is processed. If you omit the stepValue, a stepValue of positive 1 is used. In Example 1 in Figure 7-2, the startValue is 5, the endValue is 8, and the stepValue (which is omitted) is 1. Those values tell the computer to start counting at 5 and, counting by 1s, stop at 8—in other words, count 5, 6, 7, and 8. The computer will process the instructions in Example 1's loop body four times.

The startValue, endValue, and stepValue items must be numeric and can be either positive or negative, integer or noninteger. As indicated in Figure 7-2, if the stepValue is a positive number, the startValue must be less than or equal to the endValue for the loop instructions to be processed. If, on the other hand, the stepValue is a negative number, then the startValue must be greater than or equal to the endValue for the loop instructions to be processed.

Figure 7-3 describes the steps the computer follows when processing the loop shown in Example 1 in Figure 7-2. As Task 2 indicates, the loop's condition is evaluated *before* the loop body is processed. This is because the loop created by the For...Next statement is a pretest loop. Notice that the num variable contains the number 9 when the For...Next statement ends. The number 9 is the first integer that is greater than the loop's endValue of 8.

Processing steps for the For...Next statement in Example 1
1. The For clause creates the num variable and initializes it to 5.
2. The For clause compares the num variable's value (5) with the endValue (8) to determine whether the loop should end. 5 is not greater than 8, so the computer adds 5 to the sum variable's value, giving 5. The For clause then increments the num variable's value by 1, giving 6.
3. The For clause compares the num variable's value (6) with the endValue (8) to determine whether the loop should end. 6 is not greater than 8, so the computer adds 6 to the sum variable's value, giving 11. The For clause then increments the num variable's value by 1, giving 7.
4. The For clause compares the num variable's value (7) with the endValue (8) to determine whether the loop should end. 7 is not greater than 8, so the computer adds 7 to the sum variable's value, giving 18. The For clause then increments the num variable's value by 1, giving 8.
5. The For clause compares the num variable's value (8) with the endValue (8) to determine whether the loop should end. 8 is not greater than 8, so the computer adds 8 to the sum variable's value, giving 26. The For clause then increments the num variable's value by 1, giving 9.
6. The For clause compares the num variable's value (9) with the endValue (8) to determine whether the loop should end. 9 is greater than 8, so the loop ends. Processing will continue with the statement following the Next clause.

Figure 7-3 Processing steps for the For...Next statement in Example 1 in Figure 7-2

The Projected Sales Application

Figure 7-4 shows the problem specification for a slightly different version of the Projected Sales application from Chapter 6. In this version, the Calculate Projected Sales button's Click event procedure will need to display the projected sales amount for each of four years, beginning with 2017. The figure also shows the procedure's pseudocode and flowchart. The procedure uses a counter-controlled loop to repeat the loop body instructions four times.

Problem specification
Create an application that displays the amount of a company's projected sales for each of four years, using a 3% growth rate per year and beginning with 2017.

Pseudocode and flowchart for the calcButton Click event procedure

```
1. store current sales in sales variable
2. display column headings (Year and Sales)
3. repeat for year from 2017 to 2020 in increments of 1
       increase = sales * growth rate
       add increase to sales
       display year and sales
   end repeat for
```

Figure 7-4 Problem specification, pseudocode, and flowchart for the Projected Sales application
(continues)

(continued)

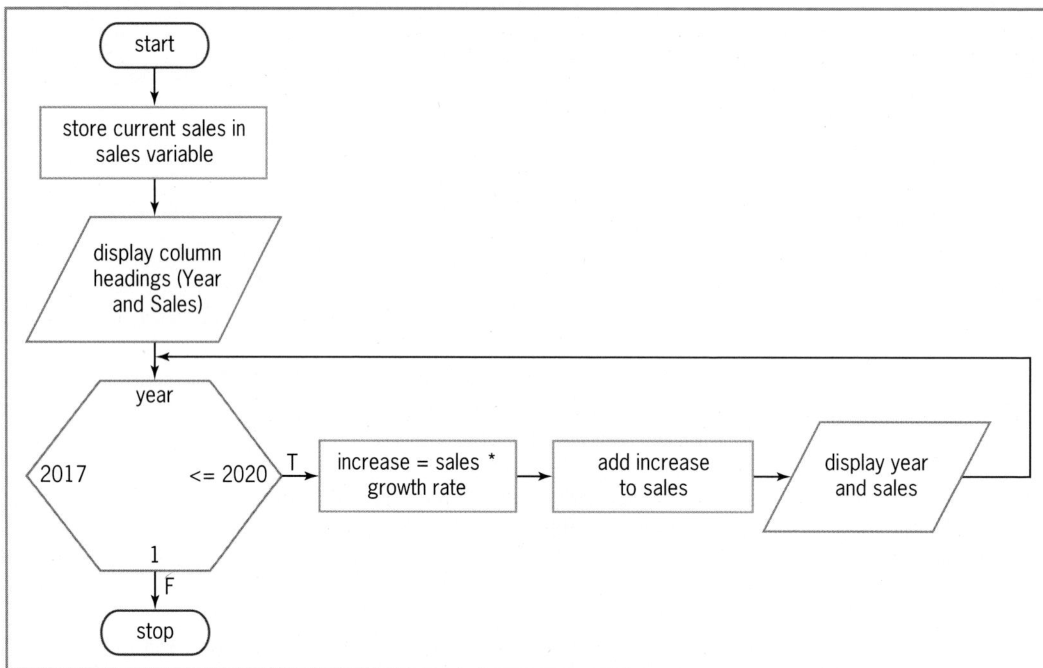

Figure 7-4 Problem specification, pseudocode, and flowchart for the Projected Sales application

Many programmers use a hexagon (a six-sided figure) to represent the For clause in a flowchart. Within the hexagon, you record the four items contained in the clause: *counterVariableName, startValue, endValue,* and *stepValue.* The counterVariableName and stepValue are placed at the top and bottom, respectively, of the hexagon. The startValue and endValue are placed on the left and right sides, respectively. The hexagon in Figure 7-4 indicates that the counterVariableName is `year`, the startValue is 2017, the endValue is 2020, and the stepValue is 1. The <= sign that precedes the endValue indicates that the loop body will be processed as long as the counter variable's value is less than or equal to 2020.

Figure 7-5 shows the code corresponding to the pseudocode and flowchart shown in Figure 7-4. It also includes a sample run of the Projected Sales application.

If you want to experiment with the Projected Sales application, open the solution contained in the Try It 1! folder.

```
Private Sub calcButton_Click(sender As Object, e As EventArgs
) Handles calcButton.Click
    ' display the projected sales

    Const GrowthRate As Double = 0.03
    Dim sales As Double
    Dim increase As Double

    Double.TryParse(currentTextBox.Text, sales)
    projectedLabel.Text = "Year      Sales" &
        ControlChars.NewLine
```

Figure 7-5 Code and sample run for the Projected Sales application *(continues)*

(continued)

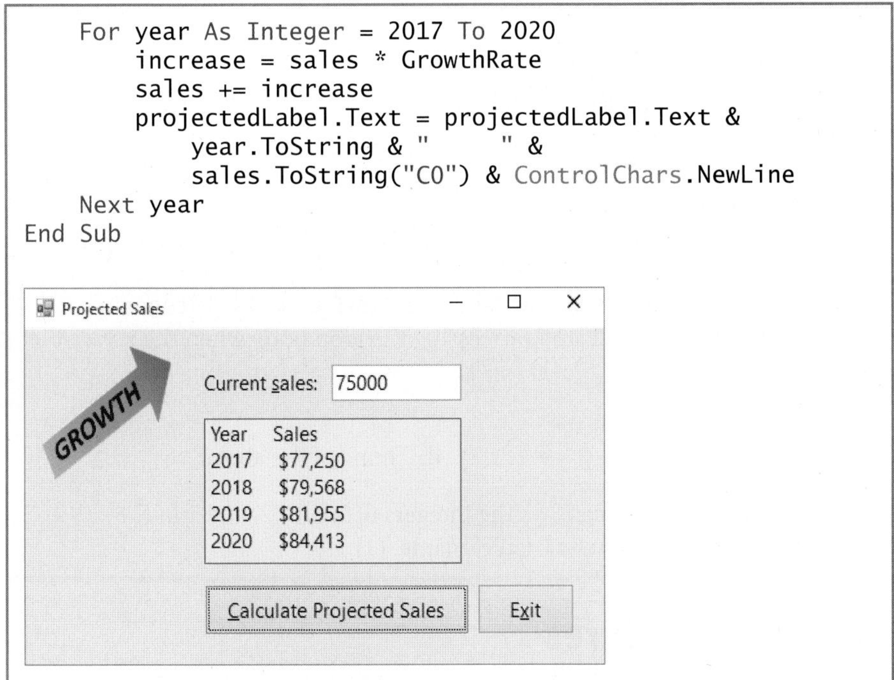

```
    For year As Integer = 2017 To 2020
        increase = sales * GrowthRate
        sales += increase
        projectedLabel.Text = projectedLabel.Text &
            year.ToString & "     " &
            sales.ToString("C0") & ControlChars.NewLine
    Next year
End Sub
```


Figure 7-5 Code and sample run for the Projected Sales application

Comparing the For...Next and Do...Loop Statements

As mentioned earlier, you can use either the For...Next statement or the Do...Loop statement to code a counter-controlled pretest loop; however, the For...Next statement is more convenient to use. Figure 7-6 shows an example of using both loops to display the string "Hi" three times. Notice that when using the Do...Loop statement to code a counter-controlled loop, you must include a statement to declare and initialize the counter variable as well as a statement to update the counter variable. In addition, you must include the appropriate comparison in the Do clause. In a For...Next statement, the declaration, initialization, update, and comparison tasks are handled by the For clause.

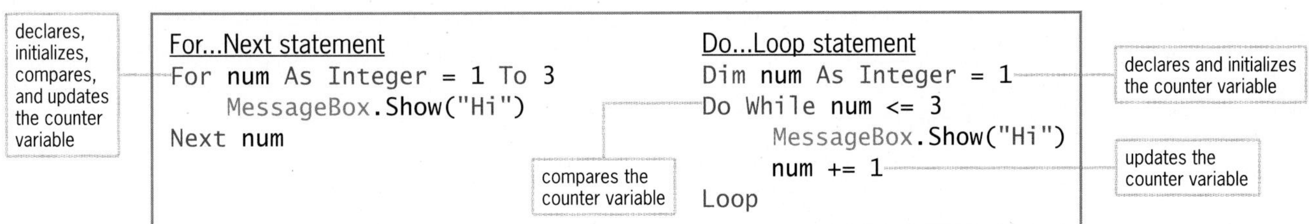

For...Next statement

```
For num As Integer = 1 To 3
    MessageBox.Show("Hi")
Next num
```

Do...Loop statement

```
Dim num As Integer = 1
Do While num <= 3
    MessageBox.Show("Hi")
    num += 1
Loop
```


Figure 7-6 Comparison of the For...Next and Do...Loop statements

The answers to Mini-Quiz questions are located in Appendix A. Each question is associated with one or more objectives listed at the beginning of the chapter.

Mini-Quiz 7-1

1. Which of the following For clauses processes the loop body as long as the `x` variable's value is less than or equal to the number 100? (1)
   a. `For x As Integer = 10 To 100 Step 10`
   b. `For x As Integer = 1 To 100`
   c. `For x As Integer = 3 To 100 Step 2`
   d. all of the above
2. A For...Next statement contains the following For clause: `For x As Integer = 5 To 11 Step 2`. The computer will stop processing the loop body when the `x` variable contains the number ____________. (1)
   a. 11
   b. 12
   c. 13
   d. none of the above
3. Write a For...Next statement that displays the integers 6, 5, 4, 3, 2, and 1 in the numListBox. Use `num` as the counter variable's name. (1)

Nested Repetition Structures

Like selection structures, repetition structures can be nested, which means you can place one loop (called the nested or inner loop) within another loop (called the outer loop). Both loops can be pretest loops, or both can be posttest loops. Or, one can be a pretest loop and the other a posttest loop.

A clock uses nested loops to keep track of the time. For simplicity, consider a clock's minute and second hands only. The second hand on a clock moves one position, clockwise, for every second that has elapsed. After the second hand moves 60 positions, the minute hand moves one position, also clockwise. The second hand then begins its journey around the clock again.

Figure 7-7 shows three versions of the logic used by a clock's minute and second hands. In each version, an outer loop controls the minute hand, while an inner (nested) loop controls the second hand. Notice that the entire nested loop is contained within the outer loop in each version. This must be true for the loop to be nested and for it to work correctly. The next iteration of the outer loop (which controls the minute hand) occurs only after the nested loop (which controls the second hand) has finished processing.

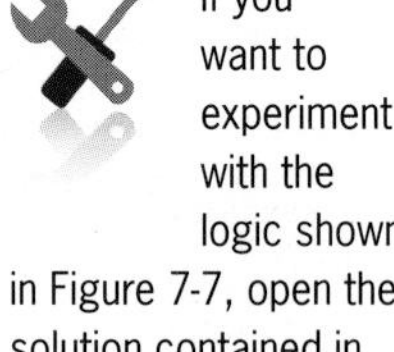

If you want to experiment with the logic shown in Figure 7-7, open the solution contained in the Try It 2! folder.

```
Version 1
repeat for minutes from 0 to 59
    repeat for seconds from 0 to 59
        move second hand 1 position, clockwise
    end repeat for seconds
    move minute hand 1 position, clockwise
end repeat for minutes
```

nested loop

Figure 7-7 Three versions of the logic used by a clock's minute and second hands *(continues)*

(continued)

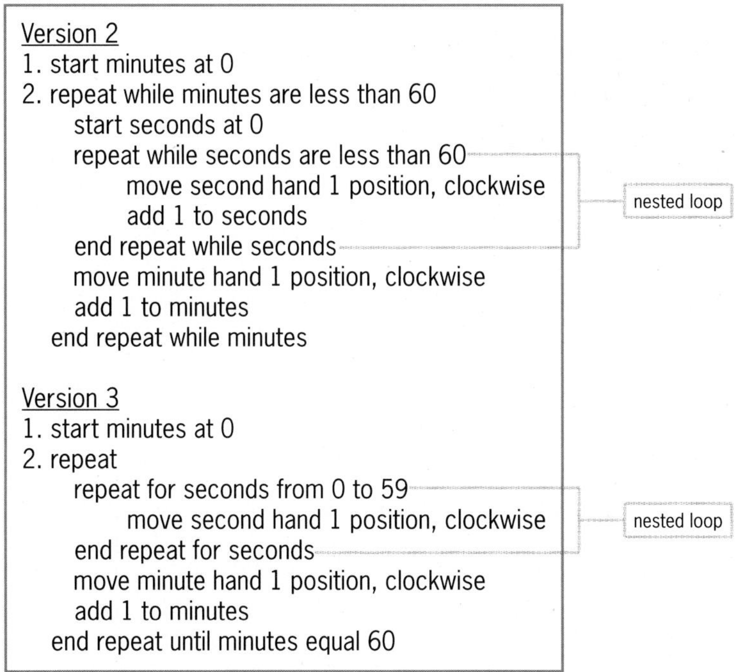

```
Version 2
1. start minutes at 0
2. repeat while minutes are less than 60
       start seconds at 0
       repeat while seconds are less than 60
              move second hand 1 position, clockwise
              add 1 to seconds
       end repeat while seconds
       move minute hand 1 position, clockwise
       add 1 to minutes
   end repeat while minutes

Version 3
1. start minutes at 0
2. repeat
       repeat for seconds from 0 to 59
              move second hand 1 position, clockwise
       end repeat for seconds
       move minute hand 1 position, clockwise
       add 1 to minutes
   end repeat until minutes equal 60
```


Figure 7-7 Three versions of the logic used by a clock's minute and second hands

You will use a nested loop to code a modified version of the Projected Sales application that you viewed earlier in the chapter. Rather than using a 3% annual growth rate to display the projected sales for each of four years, the modified application will use annual growth rates of 3%, 4%, and 5%. The modified problem specification and pseudocode are shown in Figure 7-8. The modifications made to the original pseudocode from Figure 7-4 are shaded. Notice that the outer loop keeps track of the growth rates, and the nested loop keeps track of the years.

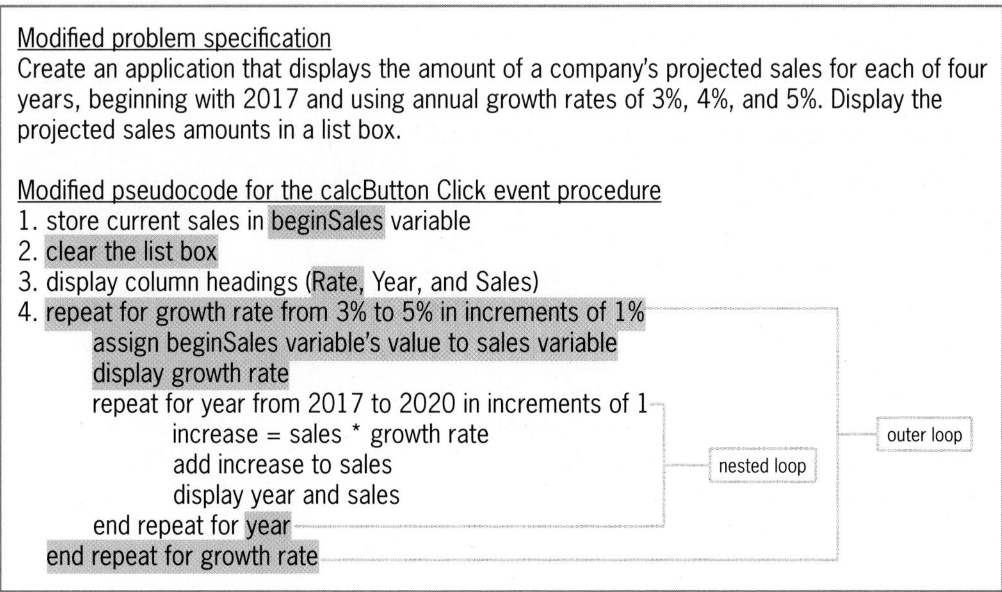

Modified problem specification
Create an application that displays the amount of a company's projected sales for each of four years, beginning with 2017 and using annual growth rates of 3%, 4%, and 5%. Display the projected sales amounts in a list box.

```
Modified pseudocode for the calcButton Click event procedure
1. store current sales in beginSales variable
2. clear the list box
3. display column headings (Rate, Year, and Sales)
4. repeat for growth rate from 3% to 5% in increments of 1%
       assign beginSales variable's value to sales variable
       display growth rate
       repeat for year from 2017 to 2020 in increments of 1
              increase = sales * growth rate
              add increase to sales
              display year and sales
       end repeat for year
   end repeat for growth rate
```


Figure 7-8 Problem specification and pseudocode for the modified Projected Sales application

Figure 7-9 shows two ways of coding the pseudocode shown in Figure 7-8. Version 1 uses two For...Next statements. Version 2 uses a Do...Loop statement in the outer loop and uses a For...Next statement in the nested loop. Figure 7-9 also includes a sample run of the modified application.

If you want to experiment with the modified Projected Sales application, open the solution contained in the Try It 3! and Try It 4! folders.

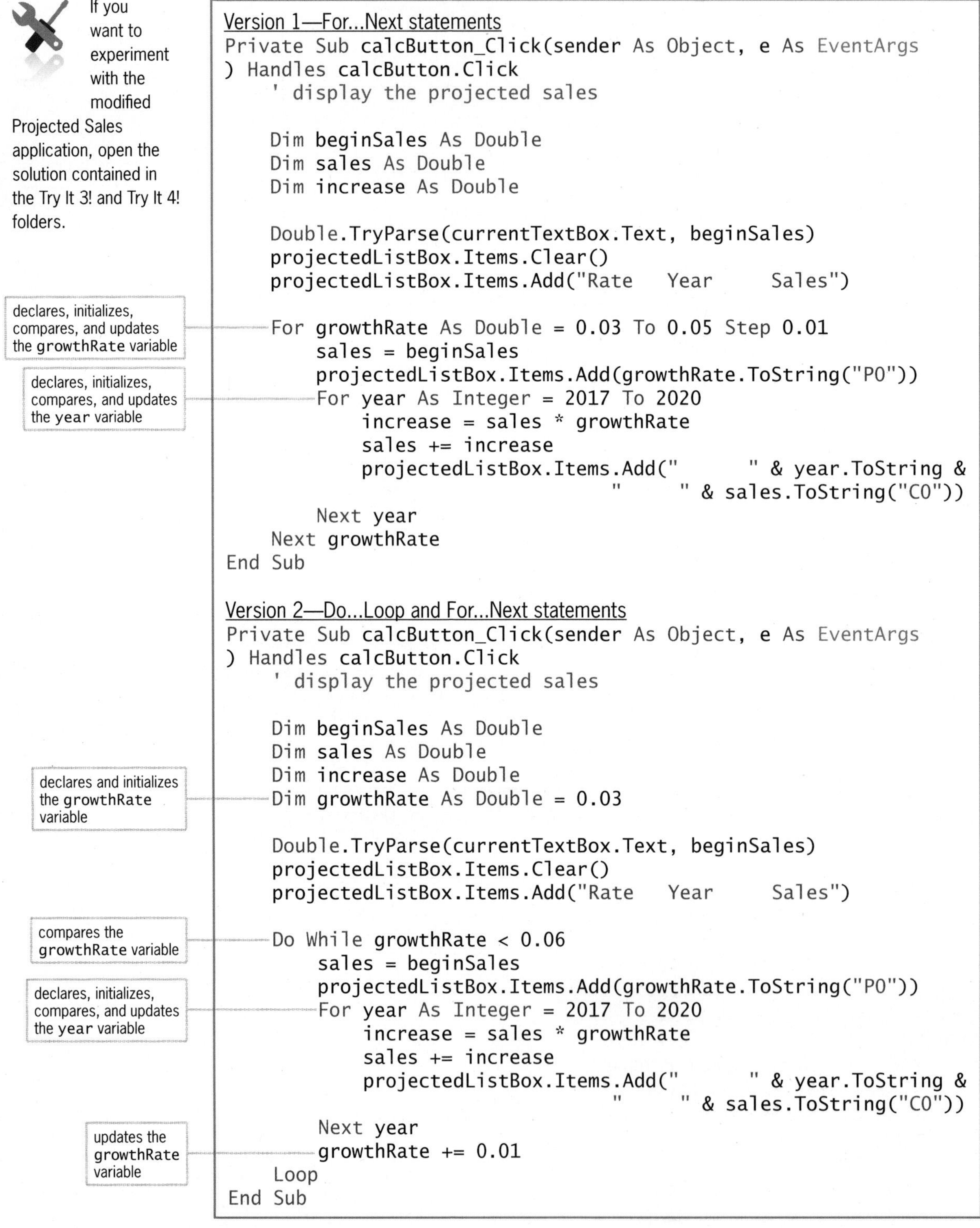

Version 1—For...Next statements

```
Private Sub calcButton_Click(sender As Object, e As EventArgs
) Handles calcButton.Click
    ' display the projected sales

    Dim beginSales As Double
    Dim sales As Double
    Dim increase As Double

    Double.TryParse(currentTextBox.Text, beginSales)
    projectedListBox.Items.Clear()
    projectedListBox.Items.Add("Rate   Year     Sales")

    For growthRate As Double = 0.03 To 0.05 Step 0.01
        sales = beginSales
        projectedListBox.Items.Add(growthRate.ToString("P0"))
        For year As Integer = 2017 To 2020
            increase = sales * growthRate
            sales += increase
            projectedListBox.Items.Add("      " & year.ToString &
                                  "     " & sales.ToString("C0"))
        Next year
    Next growthRate
End Sub
```

- declares, initializes, compares, and updates the growthRate variable (For growthRate ...)
- declares, initializes, compares, and updates the year variable (For year ...)

Version 2—Do...Loop and For...Next statements

```
Private Sub calcButton_Click(sender As Object, e As EventArgs
) Handles calcButton.Click
    ' display the projected sales

    Dim beginSales As Double
    Dim sales As Double
    Dim increase As Double
    Dim growthRate As Double = 0.03

    Double.TryParse(currentTextBox.Text, beginSales)
    projectedListBox.Items.Clear()
    projectedListBox.Items.Add("Rate   Year     Sales")

    Do While growthRate < 0.06
        sales = beginSales
        projectedListBox.Items.Add(growthRate.ToString("P0"))
        For year As Integer = 2017 To 2020
            increase = sales * growthRate
            sales += increase
            projectedListBox.Items.Add("      " & year.ToString &
                                  "     " & sales.ToString("C0"))
        Next year
        growthRate += 0.01
    Loop
End Sub
```

- declares and initializes the growthRate variable (Dim growthRate ...)
- compares the growthRate variable (Do While ...)
- declares, initializes, compares, and updates the year variable (For year ...)
- updates the growthRate variable (growthRate += 0.01)

Figure 7-9 Modified code and a sample run of the modified application *(continues)*

(continued)

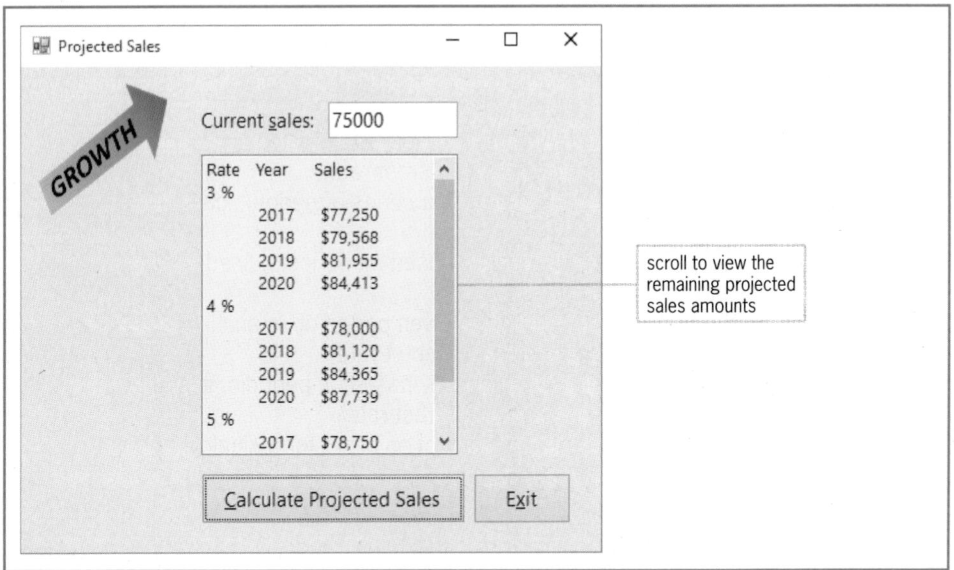

Figure 7-9 Modified code and a sample run of the modified application

Mini-Quiz 7-2

1. A nested loop can be ____________. (2)
   a. a pretest loop only
   b. a posttest loop only
   c. either a pretest loop or a posttest loop
2. For a(n) ____________ loop to work correctly, it must be contained entirely within the ____________ loop. (2)
   a. nested, outer
   b. outer, nested
3. A clock's hour hand is controlled by a(n) ____________ loop, while its minute hand is controlled by a(n) ____________ loop. (2)
   a. nested, outer
   b. outer, nested

The answers to Mini-Quiz questions are located in Appendix A. Each question is associated with one or more objectives listed at the beginning of the chapter.

The Financial.Pmt Method

Visual Basic's Financial class contains many methods that your applications can use to perform financial calculations. Figure 7-10 lists some of the more commonly used methods defined in the class. All of the methods return the result of their calculation as a Double number.

The Financial.FV method is covered in Programming Tutorial 2.

Method	Purpose
Financial.DDB	calculate the depreciation of an asset for a specific time period using the double-declining balance method
Financial.FV	calculate the future value of an annuity based on periodic, fixed payments and a fixed interest rate
Financial.IPmt	calculate the interest payment for a given period of an annuity based on periodic, fixed payments and a fixed interest rate
Financial.IRR	calculate the internal rate of return for a series of periodic cash flows (payments and receipts)
Financial.Pmt	calculate the payment for an annuity based on periodic, fixed payments and a fixed interest rate
Financial.PPmt	calculate the principal payment for a given period of an annuity based on periodic fixed payments and a fixed interest rate
Financial.PV	calculate the present value of an annuity based on periodic, fixed payments to be paid in the future and a fixed interest rate
Financial.SLN	calculate the straight-line depreciation of an asset for a single period
Financial.SYD	calculate the sum-of-the-years' digits depreciation of an asset for a specified period

Figure 7-10 Some of the methods defined in the Financial class

The Monthly Payment application, which you will view in the next section, will use the **Financial.Pmt method** to calculate the monthly payment on a loan. (*Pmt* stands for *payment.*) Figure 7-11 shows the method's basic syntax and lists the meaning of each argument. The *Rate* and *NPer* (number of periods) arguments must be expressed using the same units. If Rate is a monthly interest rate, then NPer must specify the number of monthly payments. Likewise, if Rate is an annual interest rate, then NPer must specify the number of annual payments. Figure 7-11 also includes examples of using the Financial.Pmt method.

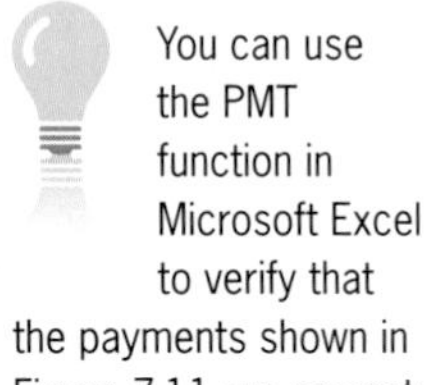
You can use the PMT function in Microsoft Excel to verify that the payments shown in Figure 7-11 are correct.

HOW TO Use the Financial.Pmt Method

Syntax
Financial.Pmt(*Rate*, *NPer*, *PV***)**

Argument	Meaning
Rate	interest rate per period
NPer	total number of payment periods in the term
PV	present value of the loan (the principal)

Example 1
```
Financial.Pmt(0.05, 3, 9000)
```
Calculates the annual payment for a loan of $9,000 for 3 years with a 5% interest rate. *Rate* is 0.05, *NPer* is 3, and *PV* is 9000. The annual payment returned by the method (rounded to the nearest cent) is –3304.88.

Figure 7-11 How to use the Financial.Pmt method *(continues)*

(continued)

Example 2
```
-Financial.Pmt(0.03 / 12, 15 * 12, 150000)
```
Calculates the monthly payment for a loan of $150,000 for 15 years with a 3% interest rate. *Rate* is 0.03 / 12, *NPer* is 15 * 12, and *PV* is 150000. The monthly payment returned by the method (rounded to the nearest cent and expressed as a positive number) is 1035.87.

Figure 7-11 How to use the Financial.Pmt method

Example 1 calculates the annual payment for a loan of $9,000 for 3 years with a 5% interest rate. As the example indicates, the annual payment returned by the method (rounded to the nearest cent) is –3304.88. This means that if you borrow $9,000 for 3 years at 5% interest, you will need to make three annual payments of $3,304.88 to pay off the loan. Notice that the Financial.Pmt method returns a negative number. You can change the negative number to a positive number by preceding the method with the negation operator, like this: `-Financial.Pmt(0.05, 3, 9000)`.

The Financial.Pmt method shown in Example 2 calculates the monthly payment for a loan of $150,000 for 15 years with a 3% interest rate. In this example, the Rate and NPer arguments are expressed in monthly terms rather than in annual terms. You change an annual rate to a monthly rate by dividing the annual rate by 12. You change the term from years to months by multiplying the number of years by 12. The monthly payment for the loan in Example 2, rounded to the nearest cent and expressed as a positive number, is 1035.87.

The Monthly Payment Application

Figure 7-12 shows the problem specification for the Monthly Payment application, which requires a loop and the Financial.Pmt method. The figure also contains the pseudocode and code for the calcButton's Click event procedure along with a sample run of the application.

Problem specification
Create an application that calculates the monthly payments on a car loan, using annual interest rates ranging from 3% to 6% in increments of 0.5%. The user will enter the loan amount and the term (in years). The term, which is the number of years the user has to pay off the loan, can be 2 years, 3 years, 4 years, or 5 years only. Display the payments in a list box.

Pseudocode for the calcButton Click event procedure
```
1. store user input (loan and term) in variables
2. clear the list box
3. repeat for rate from 0.03 to 0.06 in increments of 0.005
        calculate the monthly payment (using the loan, rate, term, and Financial.Pmt method)
        display rate and monthly payment amount
   end repeat for
4. send the focus to the loanTextBox
```

Figure 7-12 Problem specification, pseudocode, code, and sample run for the Monthly Payment application *(continues)*

(continued)

```
Private Sub calcButton_Click(sender As Object, e As EventArgs
) Handles calcButton.Click
    ' calculates the monthly payments on a loan using
    ' interest rates of 3% to 6% in increments of 0.5%

    Dim loan As Double
    Dim term As Integer
    Dim monthlyPayment As Double

    ' assign input to variables
    Double.TryParse(loanTextBox.Text, loan)
    term = Convert.ToInt32(termListBox.SelectedItem)

    paymentsListBox.Items.Clear()
    ' calculate and display monthly payments
    For rate As Double = 0.03 To 0.06 Step 0.005
        monthlyPayment =
            -Financial.Pmt(rate / 12, term * 12, loan)
            paymentsListBox.Items.Add(rate.ToString("P1") &
                      ":  " & monthlyPayment.ToString("C2"))
    Next rate
    loanTextBox.Focus()
End Sub
```

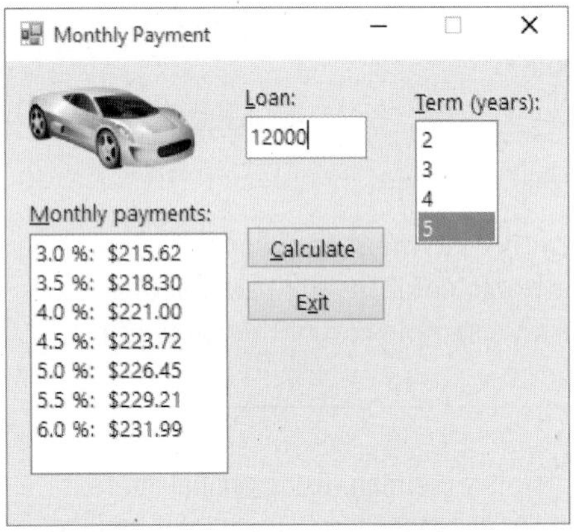

Figure 7-12 Problem specification, pseudocode, code, and sample run for the Monthly Payment application

Before the calcButton_Click procedure ends, it sends the focus to the loanTextBox. Doing this places the cursor after the existing text in the text box, as shown in Figure 7-12. However, it is customary in Windows applications to select (highlight) the existing text when a text box receives the focus.

Selecting the Existing Text in a Text Box

Visual Basic provides the **SelectAll method** for selecting a text box's existing text. The method's syntax is shown in Figure 7-13 along with an example of using the method.

HOW TO Use the SelectAll Method

Syntax

textBox.**SelectAll()**

Example

```
nameTextBox.SelectAll()
```

selects the contents of the nameTextBox

Figure 7-13 How to use the SelectAll method

In the Monthly Payment application, you can use the SelectAll method to select the contents of the Loan text box when the text box receives the focus. You do this by entering the method in the text box's Enter event procedure. A text box's **Enter event** occurs when the text box receives the focus, which can happen as a result of the user either tabbing to the control or using the control's access key. It also occurs when the Focus method is used to send the focus to the control. Figure 7-14 shows the Loan text box's Enter event procedure. It also shows the result of the computer processing the procedure's code. When the text is selected in the Loan text box, the user can remove the text simply by pressing a key on the keyboard, such as the number 2; the pressed key—in this case, the number 2—replaces the selected text.

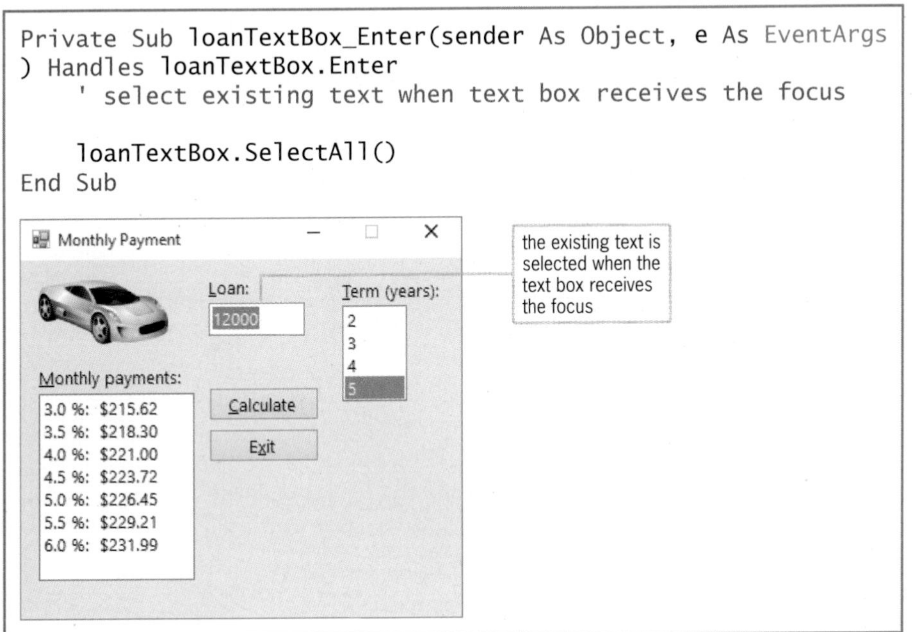

```
Private Sub loanTextBox_Enter(sender As Object, e As EventArgs
) Handles loanTextBox.Enter
    ' select existing text when text box receives the focus

    loanTextBox.SelectAll()
End Sub
```


Figure 7-14 Code and result of processing the loanTextBox_Enter procedure

Now consider what happens when the user enters the number 25000 in the Loan text box, as shown in Figure 7-15. Even though the loan amount has changed, the Monthly payments box still lists the monthly payments for a $12,000 loan. The monthly payments for a $25,000 loan will not appear until the user clicks the Calculate button. To prevent any confusion, it would be better to clear the contents of the Monthly payments box when the user enters a different loan amount. You can do this by coding the Loan text box's TextChanged event procedure.

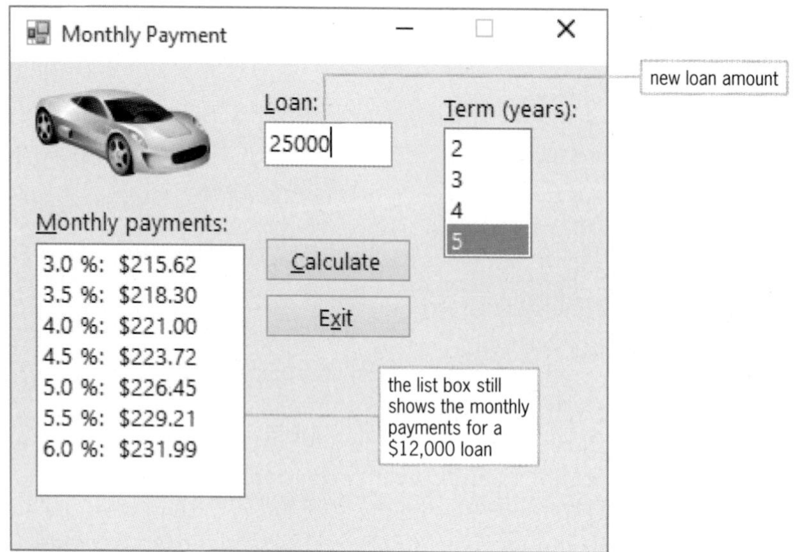

Figure 7-15 Result of entering a new loan amount

Coding the TextChanged Event Procedure

A control's **TextChanged event** occurs when a change is made to the contents of the control's Text property. This can happen as a result of either the user entering data into the control or the application's code assigning data to the control's Text property. In the Monthly Payment application, the loanTextBox_TextChanged procedure will remove the monthly payments from the Monthly payments box when the user changes the loan amount. Figure 7-16 shows the procedure's code and includes a sample run of the application. In the sample run, the user enters the number 2 in the Loan text box after calculating the monthly payments for a $12,000 loan. Notice that the monthly payments no longer appear in the Monthly payments box.

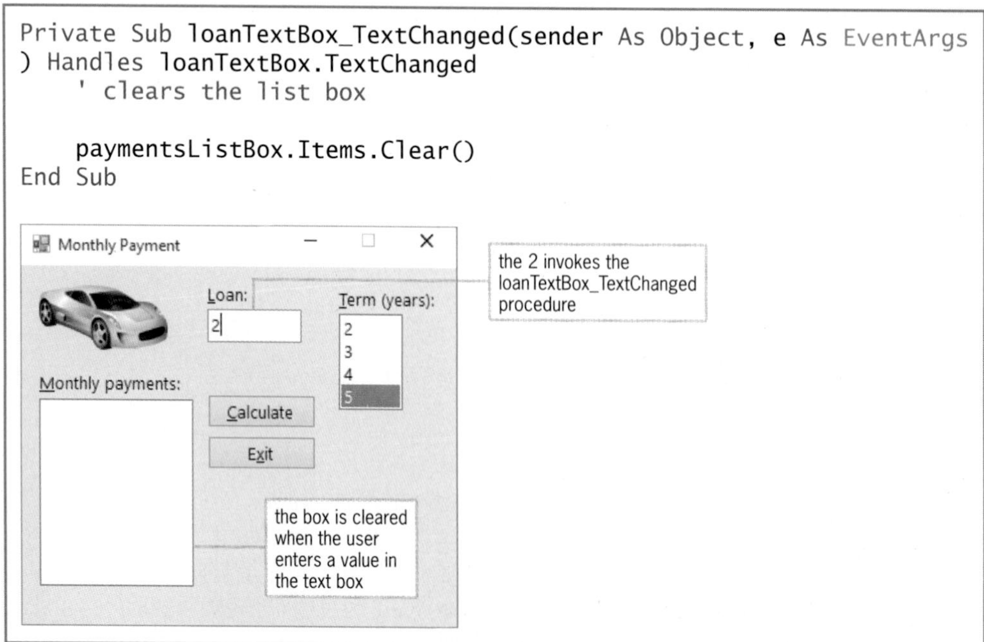

```
Private Sub loanTextBox_TextChanged(sender As Object, e As EventArgs
) Handles loanTextBox.TextChanged
    ' clears the list box

    paymentsListBox.Items.Clear()
End Sub
```


Figure 7-16 Code and result of processing the loanTextBox_TextChanged procedure

Coding the SelectedValueChanged and SelectedIndexChanged Event Procedures

In the Monthly Payment application, the Monthly payments box should also be cleared when the user selects a different term in the termListBox. You can accomplish this by entering the `paymentsListBox.Items.Clear()` statement in either the termListBox's SelectedValueChanged procedure or its SelectedIndexChanged procedure. Both procedures are shown in Figure 7-17; however, you need to enter the statement in only one of the procedures.

If you want to experiment with the Monthly Payment application, open the solution contained in the Try It 5! folder.

termListBox SelectedIndexChanged event procedure

```
Private Sub termListBox_SelectedIndexChanged(sender As Object,
e As EventArgs) Handles termListBox.SelectedIndexChanged
    ' clears the list box

    paymentsListBox.Items.Clear()
End Sub
```

termListBox SelectedValueChanged event procedure

```
Private Sub termListBox_SelectedValueChanged(sender As Object,
e As EventArgs) Handles termListBox.SelectedValueChanged
    ' clears the list box

    paymentsListBox.Items.Clear()
End Sub
```

you need to code only one of these procedures

Figure 7-17 termListBox's SelectedIndexChanged and SelectedValueChanged procedures

Mini-Quiz 7-3

The answers to Mini-Quiz questions are located in Appendix A. Each question is associated with one or more objectives listed at the beginning of the chapter.

1. Which of the following calculates the monthly payment on a $5,000 loan for 2 years with an annual interest rate of 4%? Payments should be expressed as a positive number. (3)
   a. `-Financial.Pmt(5000, .04 / 12, 24)`
   b. `-Financial.Pmt(24, .04 / 12, 5000)`
   c. `-Financial.Pmt(.04 / 12, 24, 5000)`
   d. `-Financial.Pmt(5000, 24, .04 / 12)`
2. Write the statement to select the contents of the cityTextBox. (4)
3. Which of the following will invoke the nameTextBox's Enter event? (5)
   a. the user tabbing to the nameTextBox
   b. the user employing the nameTextBox's access key
   c. the computer processing the statement `nameTextBox.Focus()`
   d. all of the above

Note: You have learned a lot so far in this chapter. You may want to take a break at this point before continuing.

Including a Combo Box in an Interface

In many interfaces, combo boxes are used in place of list boxes. You add a combo box to an interface by using the ComboBox tool in the toolbox. A **combo box** is similar to a list box in that it offers the user a list of choices from which to select. However, unlike a list box, the full list of choices in a combo box can be hidden, allowing you to save space on the form. Also, unlike a list box, a combo box contains a text field. Depending on the style of the combo box, the text field may or may not be editable by the user, as indicated in Figure 7-18. The style is controlled by the combo box's **DropDownStyle property**, which can be set to Simple, DropDown (the default), or DropDownList. Figure 7-18 also shows an example of each combo box style.

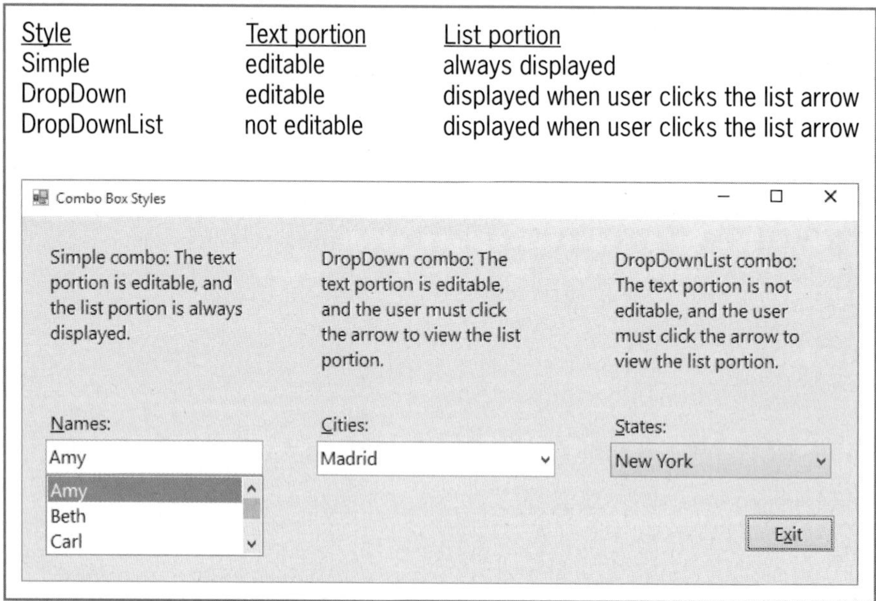

Style	Text portion	List portion
Simple	editable	always displayed
DropDown	editable	displayed when user clicks the list arrow
DropDownList	not editable	displayed when user clicks the list arrow

Figure 7-18 Combo box styles

You should use a label control to provide keyboard access to the combo box, as shown in Figure 7-18. For the access key to work correctly, the value in the label's TabIndex property must be one number less than the value in the combo box's TabIndex property. Like the items in a list box, the items in the list portion of a combo box are either arranged by use, with the most frequently used entries listed first, or sorted in ascending order. To sort the items in the list portion of a combo box, you set the combo box's **Sorted property** to True in the Properties window.

As you can with a list box, you can use the String Collection Editor window to specify the combo box items during design time. You can open the window by clicking Edit Items on the combo box's task list. Or, you can click the ellipsis button in the Items property in the Properties list. During run time, you use the Items collection's **Add method** to add an item to a combo box, as shown in the code in Figure 7-19. Like the first item in a list box, the first item in a combo box has an index of 0. You can use any of the following properties to select a default item, which will appear in the text portion of the combo box: SelectedIndex, SelectedItem, or Text. If no item is selected, the SelectedItem and Text properties contain the empty string, and the SelectedIndex property contains –1 (negative one).

If you want to experiment with the Combo Box Styles application, open the solution contained in the Try It 6! folder.

```
Private Sub MainForm_Load(sender As Object, e As EventArgs
) Handles Me.Load
    ' fills the combo boxes with values

    nameComboBox.Items.Add("Amy")
    nameComboBox.Items.Add("Beth")
    nameComboBox.Items.Add("Carl")
    nameComboBox.Items.Add("Dan")
    nameComboBox.Items.Add("Jan")
    nameComboBox.SelectedIndex = 0

    cityComboBox.Items.Add("London")
    cityComboBox.Items.Add("Madrid")
    cityComboBox.Items.Add("Paris")
    cityComboBox.SelectedItem = "Madrid"

    stateComboBox.Items.Add("Alabama")
    stateComboBox.Items.Add("Maine")
    stateComboBox.Items.Add("New York")
    stateComboBox.Items.Add("South Dakota")
    stateComboBox.Text = "New York"
End Sub
```

Items collection's Add method

you can use any of these three properties to select the default item in a combo box

Figure 7-19 Code for the combo boxes in Figure 7-18

It is easy to confuse a combo box's SelectedItem property with its Text property. The **SelectedItem property** contains the value of the item selected in the list portion of the combo box, whereas the **Text property** contains the value that appears in the text portion. A value can appear in the text portion as a result of the user either selecting an item in the list portion of the control or typing an entry in the text portion itself. It can also appear in the text portion as a result of a statement that assigns a value to the control's SelectedIndex, SelectedItem, or Text property.

If the combo box is a DropDownList style, where the text portion is not editable, you can use the SelectedItem and Text properties interchangeably. However, if the combo box is either a Simple or DropDown style, where the user can type an entry in the text portion, you should use the Text property because it contains the value either selected or entered by the user. When the value in the text portion of a combo box changes, the combo box's TextChanged event occurs.

If you need to determine the number of items in the list portion of a combo box, you can use the Items collection's **Count property**, like this: `nameComboBox.Items.Count`. The property's value will always be one number more than the combo box's highest index. You can use the Items collection's **Clear method** to clear the items from the list portion of the combo box, like this: `nameComboBox.Items.Clear()`.

Figure 7-20 shows a sample run of the Monthly Payment application using a DropDown combo box rather than a list box for the term. It also includes most of the application's code. Notice that the paymentsListBox is cleared when the combo box's TextChanged event occurs. (The figure does not show the exitButton_Click and loanTextBox_KeyPress procedures.)

If you want to experiment with this version of the Monthly Payment application, open the solution contained in the Try It 7! folder.

```
Private Sub MainForm_Load(sender As Object, e As EventArgs
) Handles Me.Load
    ' fills the termComboBox

    For term As Integer = 2 To 5
        termComboBox.Items.Add(term.ToString)
    Next term
    termComboBox.SelectedItem = "4"
End Sub

Private Sub calcButton_Click(sender As Object, e As EventArgs
) Handles calcButton.Click
    ' calculates the monthly payments on a loan using
    ' interest rates of 3% to 6% in increments of 0.5%

    Dim loan As Double
    Dim term As Integer
    Dim monthlyPayment As Double

    ' assign input to variables
    Double.TryParse(loanTextBox.Text, loan)
    term = Convert.ToInt32(termComboBox.Text)

    paymentsListBox.Items.Clear()
    ' calculate and display monthly payments
    For rate As Double = 0.03 To 0.06 Step 0.005
        monthlyPayment =
            -Financial.Pmt(rate / 12, term * 12, loan)
            paymentsListBox.Items.Add(rate.ToString("P1") &
                    ":  " & monthlyPayment.ToString("C2"))
    Next rate
    loanTextBox.Focus()
End Sub

Private Sub loanTextBox_Enter(sender As Object, e As EventArgs
) Handles loanTextBox.Enter
    ' select existing text when text box receives the focus

    loanTextBox.SelectAll()
End Sub

Private Sub loanTextBox_TextChanged(sender As Object,
e As EventArgs) Handles loanTextBox.TextChanged
    ' clears the list box

    paymentsListBox.Items.Clear()
End Sub

Private Sub termComboBox_TextChanged(sender As Object,
e As EventArgs) Handles termComboBox.TextChanged
    ' clears the list box

    paymentsListBox.Items.Clear()
End Sub
```

uses the combo box's Text property to determine the term

the combo box's TextChanged event procedure

Figure 7-20 Code and a sample run of the Monthly Payment application using a combo box *(continues)*

(continued)

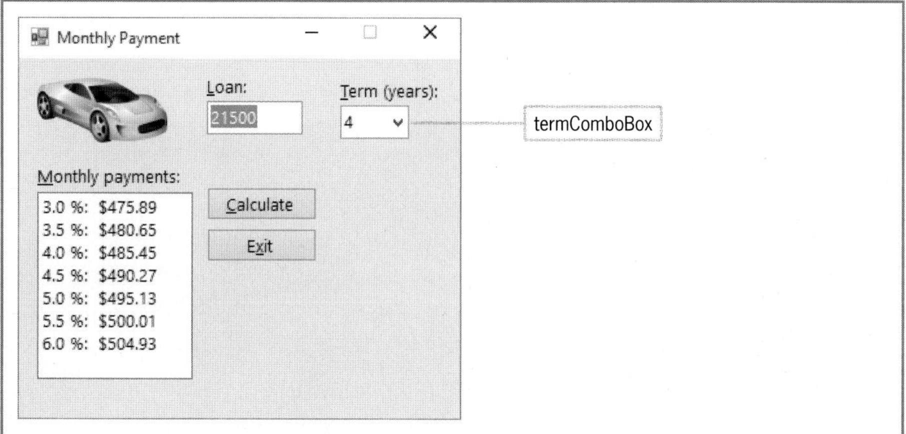

Figure 7-20 Code and a sample run of the Monthly Payment application using a combo box

The last concept covered in this chapter is how to use an image list control. You will use the control in the Slot Machine application coded in Programming Tutorial 1.

Using an Image List Control

The purpose of an **image list control** is to store a collection of images. The control is instantiated by using the ImageList tool, which is located in the Components section of the toolbox. An image list control does not appear on the form. Instead, it appears in the component tray, as shown in the Jumping Pixel Man application in Figure 7-21.

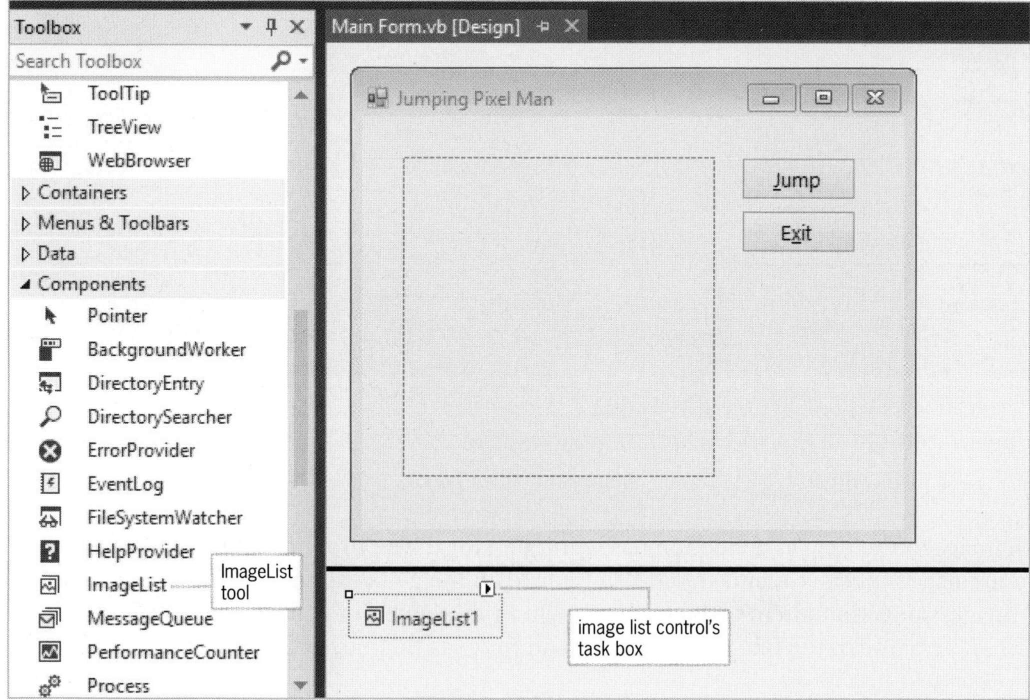

Figure 7-21 Jumping Pixel Man application

The images stored in an image list control belong to the **Images collection**. You add images to the collection using the Images Collection Editor window. The steps for doing this are listed in Figure 7-22. The figure also shows the completed Images Collection Editor window in the Jumping Pixel Man application.

HOW TO Add Images to an Image List Control's Images Collection

1. Select the image list control in the component tray. Open the Images Collection Editor window by clicking the control's task box and then clicking Choose images. Or, you can click Images in the Properties window and then click the ellipsis (...) button in the Settings box.
2. Click the Add button in the Images Collection Editor window to open the Open dialog box. Select the name(s) of the image file(s) you want to add to the collection, and then click the Open button.
3. When you are finished adding images, click the OK button to close the Images Collection Editor window.
4. If necessary, set the Image Size and Image Bit Depth items in the task list. Or, you can set the ColorDepth and ImageSize properties in the Properties windows.

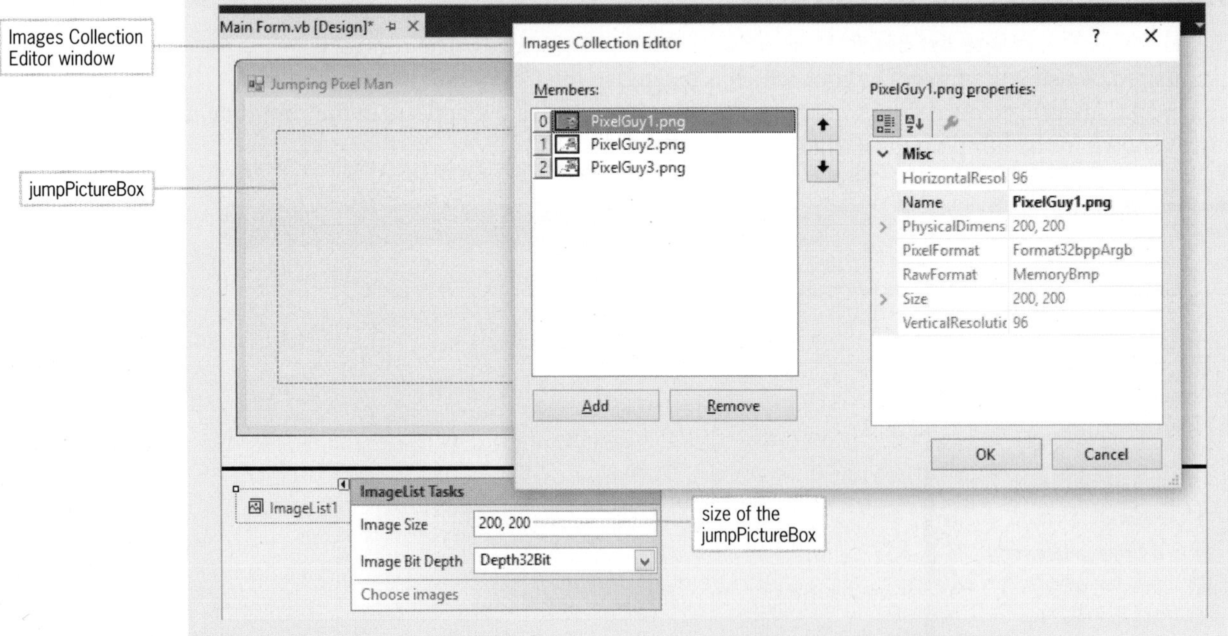

Figure 7-22 How to add images to an image list control's Images collection

Each image in the Images collection has a unique index. The first image's index is 0; the second image's index is 1, and so on. You refer to an image in the Images collection using the Images collection's Item property, as shown in the syntax in Figure 7-23. In the syntax, *object* is the name of the image list control, and *index* is the index of the image you want to access. Figure 7-23 also includes examples of using the syntax. Example 1 shows how you refer to the first image stored in the ImageList1 control's Images collection. Example 2 shows how you refer to the last image stored in the Images collection. The code in Example 2 uses the collection's Count property to determine the number of images stored in the collection. The index of the last image will always be one number less than the value in the collection's Count property.

HOW TO Refer to an Image in the Images Collection

Syntax

object.**Images.Item(***index***)**

Example 1

```
ImageList1.Images.Item(0)
```

refers to the first image stored in the ImageList1 control's Images collection

determines the number of images contained in the Images collection

Example 2

```
ImageList1.Images.Item(ImageList1.Images.Count - 1)
```

refers to the last image stored in the ImageList1 control's Images collection

Figure 7-23 How to refer to an image in the Images collection

An image list control merely stores images; it does not display them. To display the images, you need to use another control, such as a picture box. In the Jumping Pixel Man application, the jumpButton_Click procedure will display the images stored in the ImageList1 control, one at a time, in the jumpPictureBox. Figure 7-24 shows the procedure's code along with a sample run of the application.

```
Private Sub jumpButton_Click(sender As Object, e As EventArgs
) Handles jumpButton.Click
    ' view images, one at a time

    Dim numImages As Integer = ImageList1.Images.Count

    For index As Integer = 0 To numImages - 1
        jumpPictureBox.Image = ImageList1.Images.Item(index)
        Me.Refresh()
        System.Threading.Thread.Sleep(500)
    Next index
    jumpPictureBox.Image = ImageList1.Images.Item(0)
End Sub
```

Figure 7-24 Code and a sample run of the Jumping Pixel Man application *(continues)*

If you want to experiment with the Jumping Pixel Man application, open the solution contained in the Try It 8! folder.

(continued)

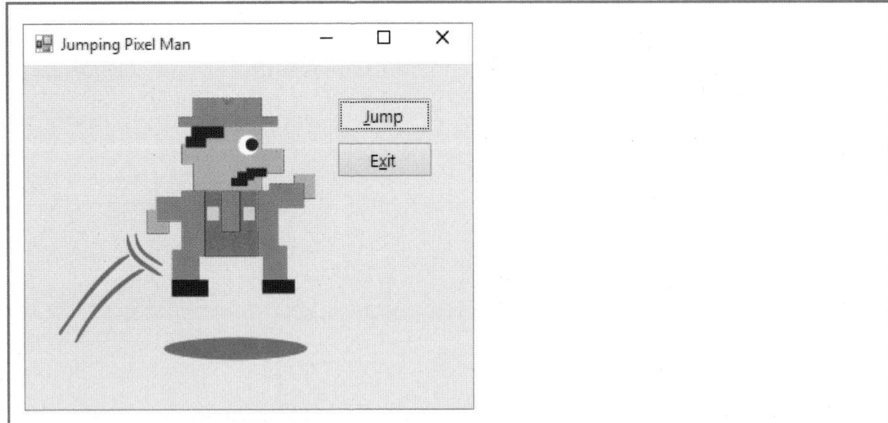

Figure 7-24 Code and a sample run of the Jumping Pixel Man application

The answers to Mini-Quiz questions are located in Appendix A. Each question is associated with one or more objectives listed at the beginning of the chapter.

Mini-Quiz 7-4

1. Which method is used to add items to a combo box? (6)
   a. Add
   b. AddItem
   c. AddList
   d. ItemAdd
2. The text portion of a combo box is always editable. (6)
   a. True
   b. False
3. Which of the following stores an integer that represents the number of items in the list portion of the stateComboBox? (6)
   a. `stateComboBox.Count`
   b. `stateComboBox.Count.Items`
   c. `stateComboBox.Items.Count`
   d. none of the above
4. Write the statement to refer to the second image stored in the ImageList1 control's Images collection. (8, 9)

You have completed the concepts section of Chapter 7. The Programming Tutorial section is next.

PROGRAMMING TUTORIAL 1

Creating the Slot Machine Application

In this tutorial, you will create an application that simulates a slot machine. Figure 7-25 shows the application's TOE chart and MainForm. The MainForm contains three picture boxes and two buttons. The application will store six different images in an image list control. When the user clicks the Click Here button, the button's Click event procedure will generate 10 sets of three random integers. The random integers will be used to select images from the image list control. The selected images will be displayed, one at a time, in the three picture boxes. If the final three random numbers are the same, the picture boxes will contain the same image and the Click event procedure will display the message "Congratulations!" in a message box. (The clickHereButton's BackgroundImage property displays the image stored in the ClickHere.png file. The button's BackgroundImageLayout property is set to Center and its Text property is empty.)

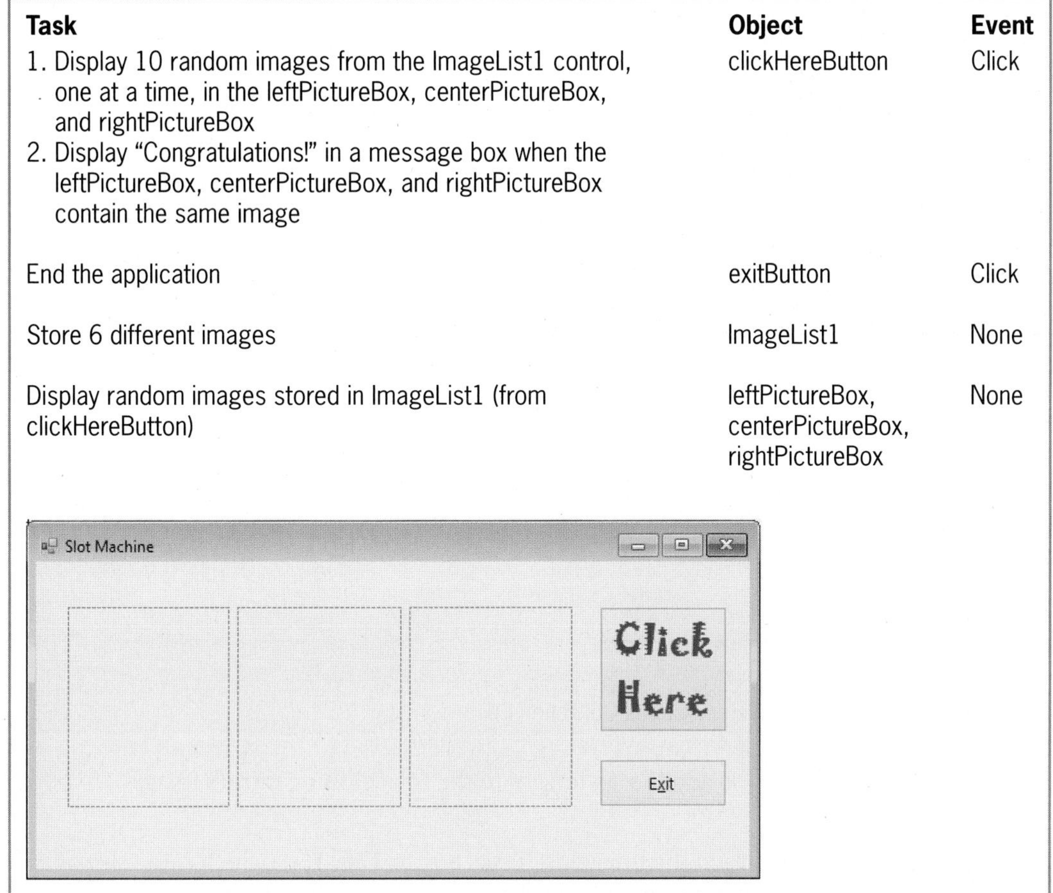

Task	Object	Event
1. Display 10 random images from the ImageList1 control, one at a time, in the leftPictureBox, centerPictureBox, and rightPictureBox 2. Display "Congratulations!" in a message box when the leftPictureBox, centerPictureBox, and rightPictureBox contain the same image	clickHereButton	Click
End the application	exitButton	Click
Store 6 different images	ImageList1	None
Display random images stored in ImageList1 (from clickHereButton)	leftPictureBox, centerPictureBox, rightPictureBox	None

Figure 7-25 TOE chart and Main Form for the Slot Machine application

Instantiating the ImageList1 Control

Before you begin coding the Slot Machine application, you will instantiate the ImageList1 control and then store six images in its Images collection.

To instantiate the ImageList1 control and then store images in its Images collection:

1. Start Visual Studio. Open the **Slot Machine Solution (Slot Machine Solution.sln)** file contained in the VbReloaded2015\Chap07\Slot Machine Solution folder. If necessary, open the designer window.

2. If necessary, open the Toolbox window and expand the Components section. Click **ImageList** and then drag an image list control to the form. Release the mouse button. The ImageList1 control appears in the component tray.

3. Click the ImageList1 control's **task box** and then click **Choose images** to open the Images Collection Editor window. Click the **Add** button, and then open the VbReloaded2015\Chap07 folder. Click **Apple.png** in the list of filenames, and then Ctrl+click the following filenames: **Banana.png**, **Cherries.png**, **Lemon.png**, **Pineapple.png**, and **Strawberry.png**. Click the **Open** button. The filenames and small images appear in the Members list section of the Images Collection Editor window, as shown in Figure 7-26.

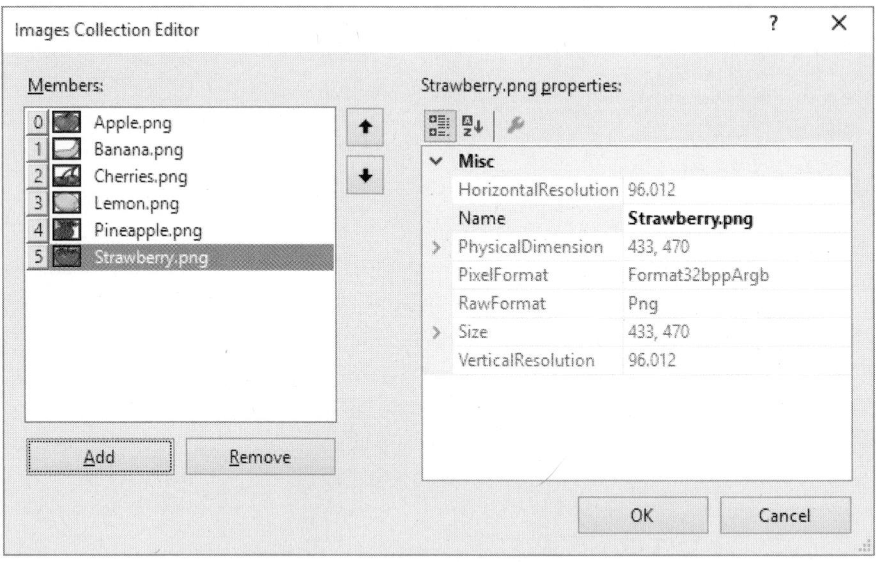

Figure 7-26 Completed Images Collection Editor window

4. Click the **OK** button to add the six images to the ImageList1 control's Images collection.
5. Change the Image Size in the ImageList Tasks box to **126, 150** (which is the size of the picture boxes on the form), and change the Image Bit Depth to **Depth32Bit**.
6. Click the **form** to close the ImageList Tasks box. Auto-hide the Toolbox window and then save the solution.

Coding the Slot Machine Application

According to the application's TOE chart, only the Click event procedures for the two buttons need to be coded.

To begin coding the application:

1. Open the Code Editor window. The exitButton_Click procedure has already been coded for you.
2. In the comments that appear in the General Declarations section, replace <your name> and <current date> with your name and the current date, respectively.

Figure 7-27 shows the pseudocode for the clickHereButton's Click event procedure. As the pseudocode indicates, the procedure will use random integers to display the appropriate images in the three picture boxes. It then will compare the random integers to determine whether the "Congratulations!" message should be displayed.

<u>clickHereButton Click event procedure</u>
1. disable the clickHereButton
2. repeat for spins from 1 through 10 in increments of 1
    generate a random integer from 0 through 5 and store it in a variable named leftIndex
    use the leftIndex variable to display the appropriate ImageList1 image in the leftPictureBox
    refresh the screen and pause the application
    generate a random integer from 0 through 5 and store it in a variable named centerIndex
    use the centerIndex variable to display the appropriate ImageList1 image in the centerPictureBox
    refresh the screen and pause the application
    generate a random integer from 0 through 5 and store it in a variable named rightIndex
    use the rightIndex variable to display the appropriate ImageList1 image in the rightPictureBox
    refresh the screen and pause the application
   end repeat for
3. if the leftIndex, centerIndex, and rightIndex variables contain the same integer
    display "Congratulations!" in a message box
   end if
4. enable the clickHereButton
5. send the focus to the clickHereButton

Figure 7-27 Pseudocode for the clickHereButton_Click procedure

To code and then test the clickHereButton_Click procedure:

1. Locate the clickHereButton_Click procedure. The procedure will need a Random object to represent the pseudo-random number generator. It will also need three Integer variables to store the random integers. Click the **blank line** above the End Sub clause and then enter the following four Dim statements. Press **Enter** twice after typing the last Dim statement.

   Dim randGen As New Random
   Dim leftIndex As Integer
   Dim centerIndex As Integer
   Dim rightIndex As Integer

2. The first step in the pseudocode disables the clickHereButton. Enter the following assignment statement:

   clickHereButton.Enabled = False

3. The second step in the pseudocode is a counter-controlled loop that repeats its loop body 10 times. Enter the following For clause:

   For spins As Integer = 1 To 10

4. Notice that the Code Editor enters the Next clause for you. Change the Next clause to **Next spins** and press **Enter**.

5. The first instruction in the loop body generates a random integer from 0 through 5 and stores it in the `leftIndex` variable. Click the **blank line** between the For and Next clauses, and then enter the following assignment statement:

   leftIndex = randGen.Next(0, 6)

6. The second instruction in the loop body uses the value in the `leftIndex` variable to display the appropriate image in the leftPictureBox. Enter the following assignment statement:

```
leftPictureBox.Image =
   ImageList1.Images.Item(leftIndex)
```

7. Next, you need to refresh the screen and then pause the application. Enter the following two statements. Press **Enter** twice after typing the second statement.

```
Me.Refresh()
System.Threading.Thread.Sleep(50)
```

8. The next three instructions in the pseudocode generate a random integer and store it in the `centerIndex` variable, then use the variable's value to display the appropriate image in the centerPictureBox, and then refresh the screen and pause the application. Enter the following statements. Press **Enter** twice after typing the last statement.

```
centerIndex = randGen.Next(0, 6)
centerPictureBox.Image =
  ImageList1.Images.Item(centerIndex)
Me.Refresh()
System.Threading.Thread.Sleep(50)
```

9. The last three instructions in the loop body generate a random integer and store it in the `rightIndex` variable, then use the variable's value to display the appropriate image in the rightPictureBox, and then refresh the screen and pause the application. Enter the following statements:

```
rightIndex = randGen.Next(0, 6)
rightPictureBox.Image =
  ImageList1.Images.Item(rightIndex)
Me.Refresh()
System.Threading.Thread.Sleep(50)
```

10. If necessary, delete the blank line above the `Next spins` clause.

11. The third step in the pseudocode is a single-alternative selection structure that determines whether the "Congratulations!" message should be displayed. Click the **blank line** above the End Sub clause and then press **Enter** to insert another blank line. Enter the following selection structure:

```
If leftIndex = centerIndex AndAlso
      leftIndex = rightIndex Then
  MessageBox.Show("Congratulations!", "Winner",
                  MessageBoxButtons.OK,
                  MessageBoxIcon.Information)
End If
```

12. The last two steps in the pseudocode enable the clickHereButton and then send the focus to the button. Click immediately after the letter **f** in the End If clause and then press **Enter**. Enter the following statements:

```
clickHereButton.Enabled = True
clickHereButton.Focus()
```

13. Save the solution and then start the application. Click the **Click Here** button. See Figure 7-28. Because random integers determine the images assigned to the three picture boxes, your application might display different images than those shown in the figure. In addition, the "Congratulations!" message may appear in a message box on your screen. If necessary, click the **OK** button to close the message box.

Figure 7-28 Sample runs of the application

14. If necessary, click the **Click Here** button until there is a winner. (You may need to click the button many times.) Then click the **OK** button to close the message box.

15. Click the **Exit** button to end the application. Close the Code Editor window and then close the solution. Figure 7-29 shows the application's code.

```
' Project name:         Slot Machine Project
' Project purpose:      Simulates a slot machine
' Created/revised by:   <your name> on <current date>

Option Explicit On
Option Infer Off
Option Strict On

Public Class MainForm
    Private Sub clickHereButton_Click(sender As Object,
    e As EventArgs) Handles clickHereButton.Click
        ' simulates a slot machine

        Dim randGen As New Random
        Dim leftIndex As Integer
        Dim centerIndex As Integer
        Dim rightIndex As Integer

        clickHereButton.Enabled = False
        For spins As Integer = 1 To 10
            leftIndex = randGen.Next(0, 6)
            leftPictureBox.Image =
                ImageList1.Images.Item(leftIndex)
            Me.Refresh()
            System.Threading.Thread.Sleep(50)

```

Figure 7-29 Code for the Slot Machine application *(continues)*

(continued)

```
            centerIndex = randGen.Next(0, 6)
            centerPictureBox.Image =
                ImageList1.Images.Item(centerIndex)
            Me.Refresh()
            System.Threading.Thread.Sleep(50)

            rightIndex = randGen.Next(0, 6)
            rightPictureBox.Image =
                ImageList1.Images.Item(rightIndex)
            Me.Refresh()
            System.Threading.Thread.Sleep(50)
        Next spins

        If leftIndex = centerIndex AndAlso
            leftIndex = rightIndex Then
            MessageBox.Show("Congratulations!", "Winner",
                            MessageBoxButtons.OK,
                            MessageBoxIcon.Information)
        End If
        clickHereButton.Enabled = True
        clickHereButton.Focus()

    End Sub

    Private Sub exitButton_Click(sender As Object,
    e As EventArgs) Handles exitButton.Click
        Me.Close()
    End Sub
End Class
```

Figure 7-29 Code for the Slot Machine application

PROGRAMMING TUTORIAL 2

Creating the College Savings Application

In this tutorial, you will create the College Savings application. The application displays the balance in a savings account at the end of 18 years, assuming the amount saved per month is $100, $150, $200, or $250, and the annual interest rate is 1.5%, 1.75%, or 2%. The application's TOE chart and MainForm are shown in Figure 7-30.

Task	**Object**	**Event**
1. Calculate the account balance at the end of 18 years, using fixed monthly deposits and fixed annual interest rates 2. Display the account balance in balanceListBox	calcButton	Click
Display the account balance (from calcButton)	balanceListBox	None
End the application	exitButton	Click

Figure 7-30 TOE chart and MainForm for the College Savings application *(continues)*

(continued)

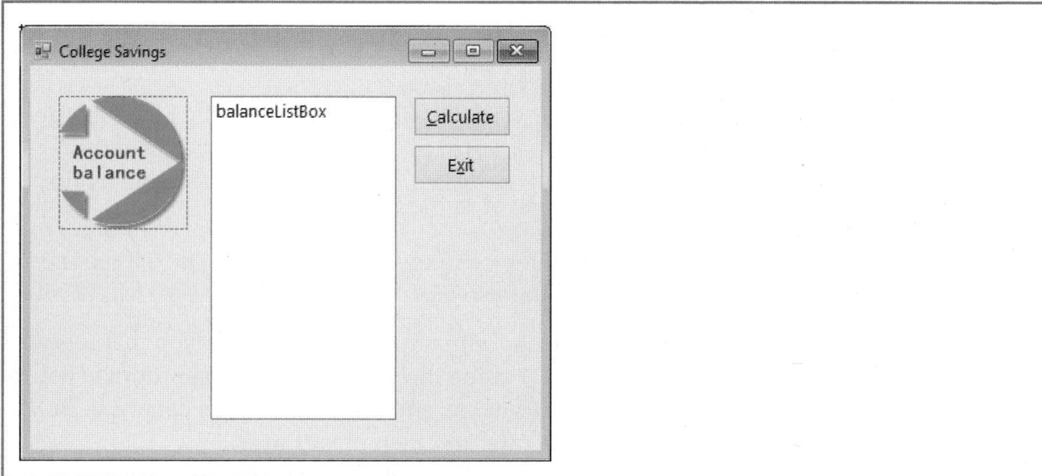

Figure 7-30 TOE chart and MainForm for the College Savings application

Coding the College Savings Application

According to the application's TOE chart, only the Click event procedures for the calcButton and exitButton need to be coded. The pseudocode for the calcButton's Click event procedure is shown in Figure 7-31 along with the memory locations the procedure will use.

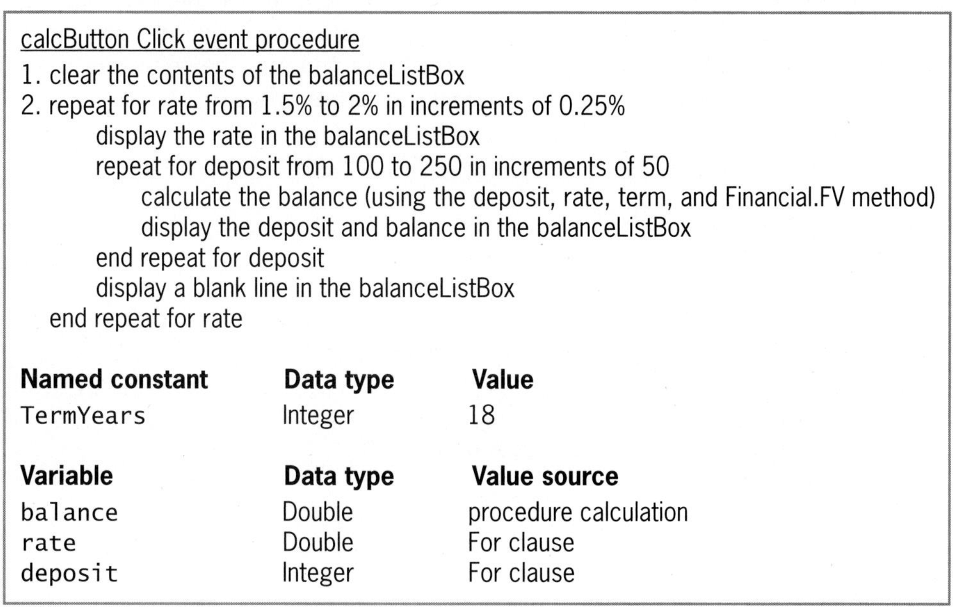

<u>calcButton Click event procedure</u>

```
1. clear the contents of the balanceListBox
2. repeat for rate from 1.5% to 2% in increments of 0.25%
        display the rate in the balanceListBox
        repeat for deposit from 100 to 250 in increments of 50
            calculate the balance (using the deposit, rate, term, and Financial.FV method)
            display the deposit and balance in the balanceListBox
        end repeat for deposit
        display a blank line in the balanceListBox
   end repeat for rate
```

Named constant	**Data type**	**Value**
`TermYears`	Integer	18

Variable	**Data type**	**Value source**
`balance`	Double	procedure calculation
`rate`	Double	For clause
`deposit`	Integer	For clause

Figure 7-31 Pseudocode and memory locations for the calcButton_Click procedure

To begin coding the application:

1. Start Visual Studio. Open the **College Savings Solution** (**College Savings Solution.sln**) file contained in the VbReloaded2015\Chap07\College Savings Solution folder. If necessary, open the designer window.

2. Open the Code Editor window. The exitButton's Click event procedure has already been coded for you. In the comments that appear in the General Declarations section, replace <your name> and <current date> with your name and the current date, respectively.
3. Locate the calcButton_Click procedure. Click the **blank line** above the End Sub clause and then enter the statements to declare the `TermYears` named constant and the `balance` variable, which are listed in Figure 7-31. Press **Enter** twice after typing the second declaration statement.
4. The first step in the pseudocode clears the contents of the balanceListBox. Type the appropriate statement and then press **Enter** twice.
5. The second step in the pseudocode begins with a counter-controlled loop that repeats its loop body three times—once for each of the three rates. Enter an appropriate For clause. Use `rate` as the counter variable's name, and use Double as its data type. Be sure to change the Next clause to **Next rate**, and then press **Enter**.
6. The first instruction in the loop body displays the rate in the balanceListBox. Click the **blank line** below the For clause. Type the following statement and then press **Enter**:

   balanceListBox.Items.Add(rate.ToString("P2"))
7. The second instruction in the loop body is a nested counter-controlled loop that repeats its loop body four times—once for each of the four deposit amounts. Enter the appropriate For and Next clauses. Use `deposit` and Integer as the counter variable's name and data type, respectively.

The first instruction in the nested loop calculates the savings account balance. To make the calculation, the procedure needs to use the current deposit amount, the current interest rate, the term, and the **Financial.FV method**. The Financial.FV method's syntax is shown in Figure 7-32 along with examples of using the method. (The *FV* stands for *future value.*)

HOW TO Use the Financial.FV Method

Syntax
Financial.FV(*Rate***,** *NPer***,** *Pmt***)**

Argument	Meaning
Rate	interest rate per period
NPer	total number of payment periods in the term
Pmt	periodic payment

Example 1
```
Financial.FV(0.05, 3, 9000)
```
Calculates the future value of an investment of $9,000 per year for 3 years with a 5% interest rate. *Rate* is 0.05, *NPer* is 3, and *Pmt* is 9000. The future value returned by the method is –28372.50.

Figure 7-32 How to use the Financial.FV method *(continues)*

(continued)

Example 2
```
-Financial.FV(0.03 / 12, 18 * 12, 100)
```
Calculates the future value of an investment of $100 per month for 18 years with a 3% interest rate. *Rate* is 0.03 / 12, *NPer* is 18 * 12, and *Pmt* is 100. The future value returned by the method (rounded to the nearest cent and expressed as a positive number) is 28594.03.

Figure 7-32 How to use the Financial.FV method

To finish coding the application:

1. Click the **blank line** below the nested For clause. The deposit amounts will be made monthly, so you will need to convert the annual interest rate to a monthly rate by dividing it by 12. You will also need to convert the 18-year term to months by multiplying it by 12. Type the following statement (be sure to include the negation operator) and then press **Enter**:

   balance =
   –Financial.FV(rate / 12, TermYears * 12, deposit)

2. The last instruction in the nested loop displays the deposit and balance in the balanceListBox. Enter the following statement (include three spaces between the second set of quotation marks):

   balanceListBox.Items.Add(deposit.ToString("C0") &
   "   " & balance.ToString("C2"))

3. If necessary, delete the blank line above the `Next deposit` clause.
4. Now, insert a **blank line** below the `Next deposit` clause.
5. The last instruction in the outer loop displays a blank line in the balanceListBox. Type the appropriate statement and then click the **blank line** below the `Next rate` clause.
6. Save the solution and then start the application. Click the **Calculate** button. The savings account balances appear in the balanceListBox, as shown in Figure 7-33.

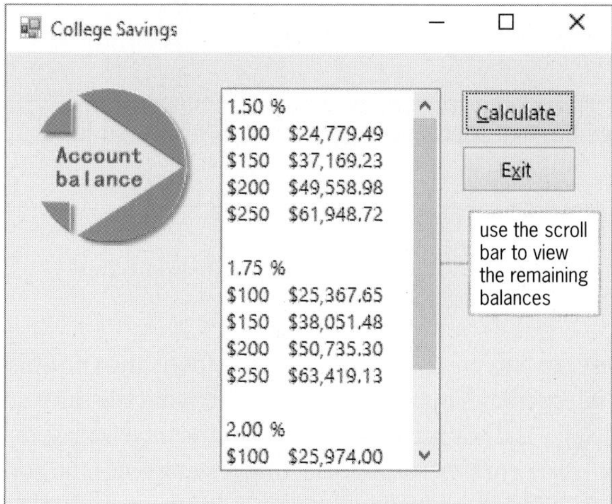

Figure 7-33 Savings account balances shown in the interface

PROGRAMMING TUTORIAL 2

7. Use the scroll bar to view the remaining account balances, and then click the **Exit** button to end the application. Close the Code Editor window and then close the solution. Figure 7-34 shows the application's code.

```
' Project name:         College Savings Project
' Project purpose:      Displays the balance in a savings account
' Created/revised by:   <your name> on <current date>

Option Explicit On
Option Strict On
Option Infer Off

Public Class MainForm
   Private Sub calcButton_Click(sender As Object,
   e As EventArgs) Handles calcButton.Click
       ' calculate the savings account balance at the end of 18
       ' years, using fixed monthly savings amounts and fixed
       ' annual interest rates

       Const TermYears As Integer = 18
       Dim balance As Double

       balanceListBox.Items.Clear()

       For rate As Double = 0.015 To 0.02 Step 0.0025
           balanceListBox.Items.Add(rate.ToString("P2"))
           For deposit As Integer = 100 To 250 Step 50
               balance =
                   -Financial.FV(rate / 12, TermYears * 12, deposit)
               balanceListBox.Items.Add(deposit.ToString("C0") &
                   "    " & balance.ToString("C2"))
           Next deposit
           balanceListBox.Items.Add(ControlChars.NewLine)
       Next rate

   End Sub

   Private Sub exitButton_Click(sender As Object,
   e As EventArgs) Handles exitButton.Click
       Me.Close()
   End Sub
End Class
```

Figure 7-34 Code for the College Savings application

PROGRAMMING EXAMPLE

Karlton Industries Application

Create an application that allows the user to enter a salesperson's sales amount and commission rate. The application should calculate the salesperson's commission by multiplying the sales amount by the commission rate. It should then display the commission amount in the interface. Provide a text box for entering the sales amount. Provide a combo box for selecting (or entering) the commission rate, which should be 10%, 15%, 20%, or 25%. Use the following names for the solution and project, respectively: Karlton Solution and Karlton Project. Save the application in the VbReloaded2015\Chap07 folder. Change the form file's name to Main Form.vb. See Figures 7-35 through 7-39.

Task	Object	Event
1. Fill the combo box with rates 2. Select the first rate in the combo box	MainForm	Load
1. Calculate the commission 2. Display the commission in commLabel	calcButton	Click
End the application	exitButton	Click
Display the commission (from calcButton)	commLabel	None
Get the sales amount Select the existing text Accept numbers, period, and Backspace Clear commLabel	salesTextBox	None Enter KeyPress TextChanged
Get the commission rate Accept numbers and Backspace Clear commLabel	rateComboBox	None KeyPress TextChanged

Figure 7-35 TOE chart

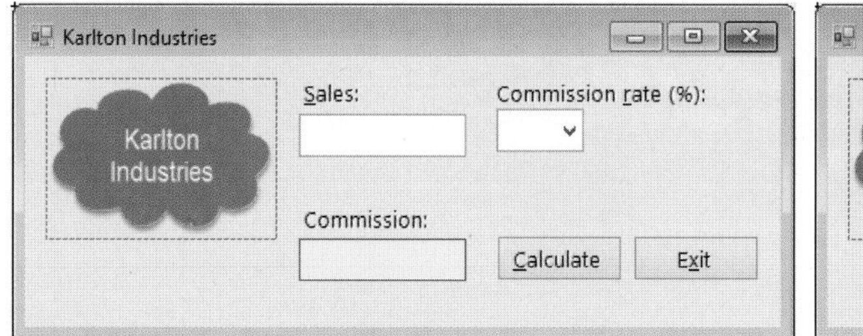

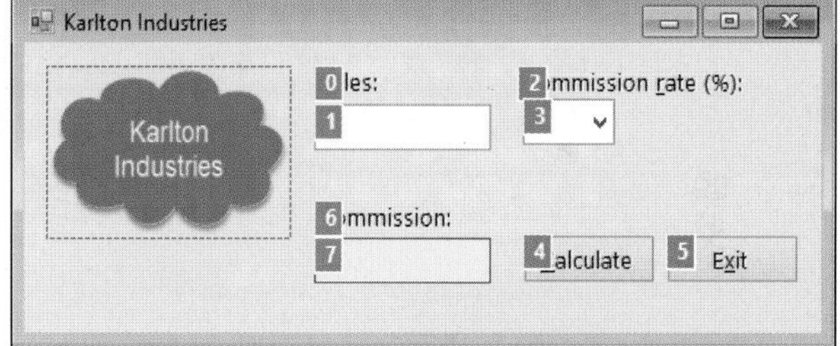

Figure 7-36 MainForm and tab order

Object	Property	Setting
MainForm	Font StartPosition Text	Segoe UI, 10pt CenterScreen Karlton Industries
rateComboBox	DropDownStyle	DropDown
commLabel	AutoSize BackColor BorderStyle Text TextAlign	False 255, 255, 192 FixedSingle (empty) MiddleCenter
PictureBox1	Image SizeMode	Karlton.png StretchImage

Figure 7-37 Objects, properties, and settings

<u>exitButton Click event procedure</u>
close the application

<u>MainForm Load event procedure</u>
1. repeat for rate from 10 to 25 in increments of 5
        add the current rate to the rateComboBox
   end repeat for
2. select the first rate in the rateComboBox

<u>salesTextBox Enter event procedure</u>
select the contents of the text box

<u>salesTextBox KeyPress event procedure</u>
allow only numbers, the period, and the Backspace key

<u>salesTextBox TextChanged event procedure</u>
clear the contents of the commLabel

<u>rateComboBox KeyPress event procedure</u>
allow only numbers and the Backspace key

<u>rateComboBox TextChanged event procedure</u>
clear the contents of the commLabel

<u>calcButton Click event procedure</u>
1. store user input (sales and commission rate) in variables
2. calculate the commission by multiplying the sales by the commission rate / 100
3. display the commission in commLabel
4. send the focus to the salesTextBox

Figure 7-38 Pseudocode

```
' Project name:        Karlton Project
' Project purpose:     Displays a commission amount
' Created/revised by:  <your name> on <current date>

Option Explicit On
Option Infer Off
Option Strict On

Public Class MainForm
   Private Sub calcButton_Click(sender As Object, e As EventArgs
   ) Handles calcButton.Click
       ' calculate the commission

       Dim sales As Decimal
       Dim commRate As Integer
       Dim commission As Decimal

       Decimal.TryParse(salesTextBox.Text, sales)
       Integer.TryParse(rateComboBox.Text, commRate)

```

Figure 7-39 Code *(continues)*

(continued)

```
        commission = sales * commRate / 100
        commLabel.Text = commission.ToString("C2")
        salesTextBox.Focus()
    End Sub

    Private Sub exitButton_Click(sender As Object, e As EventArgs
    ) Handles exitButton.Click
        Me.Close()
    End Sub

    Private Sub MainForm_Load(sender As Object, e As EventArgs
    ) Handles Me.Load
        ' fill combo box with commission rates

        For rate As Decimal = 10 To 25 Step 5
            rateComboBox.Items.Add(rate.ToString)
        Next rate
        ' select first rate
        rateComboBox.SelectedIndex = 0
    End Sub

    Private Sub rateComboBox_KeyPress(sender As Object,
    e As KeyPressEventArgs) Handles rateComboBox.KeyPress
        ' accept only numbers and the Backspace

        If (e.KeyChar < "0" OrElse e.KeyChar > "9") AndAlso
            e.KeyChar <> ControlChars.Back Then
            e.Handled = True
        End If
    End Sub

    Private Sub rateComboBox_TextChanged(sender As Object,
    e As EventArgs) Handles rateComboBox.TextChanged
        ' clear commission

        commLabel.Text = String.Empty
    End Sub

    Private Sub salesTextBox_Enter(sender As Object,
    e As EventArgs) Handles salesTextBox.Enter
        ' select existing text

        salesTextBox.SelectAll()
    End Sub

    Private Sub salesTextBox_KeyPress(sender As Object,
    e As KeyPressEventArgs) Handles salesTextBox.KeyPress
        ' accept only numbers, the period, and the Backspace

        If (e.KeyChar < "0" OrElse e.KeyChar > "9") AndAlso
            e.KeyChar <> "." AndAlso
            e.KeyChar <> ControlChars.Back Then
            e.Handled = True
        End If
    End Sub

```

Figure 7-39 Code *(continues)*

(continued)

```
    Private Sub salesTextBox_TextChanged(sender As Object,
    e As EventArgs) Handles salesTextBox.TextChanged
        ' clear commission

        commLabel.Text = String.Empty
    End Sub
End Class
```

Figure 7-39 Code

Chapter Summary

- You can use either the For...Next statement or the Do...Loop statement to code a pretest counter-controlled loop.
- A variable declared in a For clause has block scope and can be used only within the body of the For...Next statement.
- The For clause's startValue, stepValue, and endValue items can be positive or negative numbers, integer or noninteger.
- Many programmers use a hexagon to represent the For clause in a flowchart. The hexagon indicates the counter variable's name and its startValue, stepValue, and endValue.
- For a nested loop to work correctly, it must be contained entirely within an outer loop.
- You can use the Financial.Pmt method to calculate a periodic payment on a loan. You can use the Financial.FV method to calculate the future value of an investment.
- It is customary in Windows applications to highlight (select) the existing text in a text box when the text box receives the focus. You can do this by entering the SelectAll method in the text box's Enter event procedure.
- A control's TextChanged event occurs when either the user or the application's code changes the contents of the control's Text property.
- A list box's SelectedValueChanged and SelectedIndexChanged events occur when either the user or the application's code selects a different item in the list box.
- Combo boxes are similar to list boxes in that they allow the user to select from a list of choices. However, combo boxes also have a text field that may or may not be editable.
- Three styles of combo boxes are available. The style is specified in a combo box's DropDownStyle property. You can use a combo box to save space in an interface.
- You should use a label control to provide keyboard access to a combo box. Set the label's TabIndex property to a value that is one number less than the combo box's TabIndex value.
- You use the Items collection's Add method to add an item to a combo box during run time. You can use the String Collection Editor window to add an item to a combo box during design time.

- You can use the SelectedIndex, SelectedItem, or Text property to select the default item in a combo box.
- The number of items in the list portion of a combo box is stored in the Items collection's Count property.
- You can use the Sorted property to sort the items listed in a combo box.
- You can use the Items collection's Clear method to clear the items from the list portion of a combo box.
- A combo box's SelectedItem property contains the value of the item selected in the list portion of the combo box. A combo box's Text property contains the value that appears in the text portion of the combo box.
- A combo box's TextChanged event occurs when the user either selects an item in the list portion or types a value in the text portion.
- The images stored in an image list control belong to the Images collection. Each image in the collection has a unique index; the index of the first image is 0.
- You access an image in the Images collection using the collection's Item property along with the index of the image you want to access.
- You use the Images collection's Count property to determine the number of images in the collection.
- You need to use another control, such as a picture box, to display an image contained in an image list control.

Key Terms

Add method—the Items collection's method used to add items to a combo box

Clear method—the Items collection's method used to clear the items from a combo box

Combo box—a control that allows the user to select from a list of choices and also has a text field that may or may not be editable

Count property—a property of both the Items collection and the Images collection; stores an integer that represents the number of items contained in the list portion of a combo box, or stores an integer that represents the number of images contained in an image list control

Counter-controlled loops—loops whose processing is controlled by a counter; the loop body will be processed a precise number of times

DropDownStyle property—determines the style of a combo box

Enter event—occurs when a control receives the focus, which can happen as a result of the user either tabbing to the control or using the control's access key; also occurs when the Focus method sends the focus to the control

Financial.FV method—calculates the future value of an investment

Financial.Pmt method—calculates a periodic payment on either a loan or an investment

For...Next statement—used to code a pretest counter-controlled loop

Image list control—instantiated with the ImageList tool located in the Components section of the toolbox; stores the Images collection

Images collection—a collection composed of images

SelectAll method—used to select the contents of a text box

SelectedItem property—stores the value of the item selected in the list portion of a combo box

Sorted property—specifies whether the combo box items should appear in the order they are entered or in sorted order

Text property—stores the value of the item that appears in the text portion of a combo box

TextChanged event—occurs when a change is made to the contents of a control's Text property

Review Questions

Each Review Question is associated with one or more objectives listed at the beginning of the chapter.

1. How many times will the computer process the MessageBox.Show method in the following code? (1)

```
For counter As Integer = 4 To 13 Step 2
    MessageBox.Show("Hello")
Next counter
```

   a. 3
   b. 4
   c. 5
   d. 8

2. What `counter` value causes the loop in Review Question 1 to end? (1)
   a. 12
   b. 13
   c. 14
   d. 15

Use the code in Figure 7-40 to answer Review Questions 3 through 5.

```
For x As Integer = 1 To 2
    For y As Integer = 1 To 3
        msgLabel.Text = msgLabel.Text & "*"
    Next y
    msgLabel.Text = msgLabel.Text & ControlChars.NewLine
Next x
```

Figure 7-40 Code for Review Questions 3 through 5

3. What will the code in Figure 7-40 display in the msgLabel? (1, 2)

   a.
   ```
   ***
   ***
   ```
   b.
   ```
   ***
   ***
   ***
   ```
   c.
   ```
   **
   **
   **
   ```
   d.
   ```
   ****
   ****
   ****
   ****
   ```

4. What `x` value causes the outer loop in Figure 7-40 to end? (1, 2)
   a. 2
   b. 3
   c. 4
   d. none of the above
5. What `y` value causes the nested loop in Figure 7-40 to end? (1, 2)
   a. 2
   b. 3
   c. 4
   d. none of the above

Use the code in Figure 7-41 to answer Review Question 6.

```
Dim sum As Integer
Dim y As Integer
Do While y < 3
    For x As Integer = 1 To 4
        sum += x
    Next x
    y += 1
Loop
msgLabel.Text = sum.ToString
```

Figure 7-41 Code for Review Question 6

6. What number will the code in Figure 7-41 display in the msgLabel? (1, 2)
   a. 5
   b. 8
   c. 15
   d. 30
7. Which of the following calculates an annual payment on a $50,000 loan? The term is 10 years and the annual interest rate is 3%. (3)
   a. `-Financial.Pmt(.03 / 12, 10, 50000)`
   b. `-Financial.Pmt(.03 / 12, 10 * 12, 50000)`
   c. `-Financial.Pmt(.03, 10, 50000)`
   d. `-Financial.Pmt(.03, 10 * 12, 50000)`
8. Which of the following selects the "Paris" item, which is the sixth item in the cityComboBox? (6)
   a. `cityComboBox.SelectedIndex = 5`
   b. `cityComboBox.SelectedItem = "Paris"`
   c. `cityComboBox.Text = "Paris"`
   d. all of the above
9. The item entered by the user in the text field of a combo box is stored in which property? (6)
   a. SelectedItem
   b. SelectedValue
   c. Text
   d. TextItem

10. Which of the following refers to the second item in the ImageList1 control? (8, 9)
    a. `ImageList1.Image.Items(1)`
    b. `ImageList1.Image.Items(2)`
    c. `ImageList1.Images.Item(1)`
    d. `ImageList1.Images.Item(2)`

Each Exercise, except the DISCOVERY exercises, is associated with one or more objectives listed at the beginning of the chapter.

Exercises

Pencil and Paper

INTRODUCTORY

1. Put the For...Next statement's tasks in their proper order by placing the numbers 1 through 3 on the line to the left of the task. (1)

    _____ Adds the stepValue to the counter variable

    _____ Initializes the counter variable to the startValue

    _____ Checks whether the counter variable's value is greater (less) than the endValue

INTRODUCTORY

2. Create a chart (similar to the one shown earlier in Figure 7-3) that lists the processing steps for the code shown in Example 2 in Figure 7-2. (1)

INTRODUCTORY

3. Create a chart (similar to the one shown earlier in Figure 7-3) that lists the processing steps for the code shown in Example 3 in Figure 7-2. (1)

INTRODUCTORY

4. Write the code to calculate the annual payment on a loan of $30,000 for 4 years with a 6% interest rate. Payments should be expressed as a negative number. (3)

INTRODUCTORY

5. Write the statement to select the existing text in the priceTextBox. (4)

INTERMEDIATE

6. Write three different statements that you can use to select the first item in the movieComboBox. The first item is Frozen. (6)

INTERMEDIATE

7. Write the code to calculate the quarterly payment on a loan of $5,000 for 4 years with a 5% interest rate. Payments should be expressed as a positive number. (3)

INTERMEDIATE

8. Write the code for a pretest loop that lists the even integers from 2 through 10 in the numbersListBox. First, use the For...Next statement and an Integer variable named `evenNum`. Then rewrite the code using the Do...Loop statement. (1)

INTERMEDIATE

9. Write an assignment statement that displays (in the msgLabel) the number of images contained in the ImageList1 control. (8)

INTERMEDIATE

10. Write a For...Next statement that displays the images stored in the ImageList1 control. Display the images, one at a time, in the imagePictureBox. Display the images in reverse order; in other words, display the last image first. Refresh the screen and pause the application for 100 milliseconds between images. (1, 8, 9)

INTERMEDIATE

11. Write the code to display the following pattern of asterisks in the asterisksLabel. Use two For...Next statements. (1, 2)

```
*****
*****
*****
```

12. Rewrite the code from Exercise 11 using two Do...Loop statements. Both loops should be pretest loops. (1, 2)

INTERMEDIATE

13. Rewrite the code from Exercise 11 using two Do...Loop statements. Both loops should be posttest loops. (1, 2)

ADVANCED

14. Rewrite the code from Exercise 11 using a For...Next statement for the outer loop, and a Do...Loop statement for the nested loop. The nested loop should be a posttest loop. (1, 2)

ADVANCED

15. The following code should display three rows of percent signs in the msgLabel. The first row should contain one percent sign, the second row should contain two percent signs, and the third row should contain three percent signs. However, the code is not working correctly. Correct the code. (1, 2)

SWAT THE BUGS

```
For row As Integer = 1 To 3
    For percent As Integer = 1 To 3
        msgLabel.Text = msgLabel.Text & "%"
    Next percent
Next row
```

Computer

16. Use Windows to make a copy of the Sales Solution-Nested folder. Rename the folder Sales Solution-PretestDoLoop. Open the solution file contained in the Sales Solution-PretestDoLoop folder. Change both For...Next statements to pretest Do...Loop statements. Both loops should be pretest loops. Save the solution and then start and test the application. Close the solution. (1, 2)

MODIFY THIS

17. Use Windows to make a copy of the Sales Solution-Nested folder. Rename the folder Sales Solution-PosttestDoLoop. Open the solution file contained in the Sales Solution-PosttestDoLoop folder. Change both For...Next statements to posttest Do...Loop statements. Save the solution and then start and test the application. Close the solution. (1, 2)

MODIFY THIS

18. If necessary, complete the Slot Machine application from this chapter's Programming Tutorial 1, and then close the solution. Use Windows to make a copy of the Slot Machine Solution folder. Rename the folder Slot Machine Solution-Counter. Open the solution file contained in the Slot Machine Solution-Counter folder. Modify the code so that it uses a counter to keep track of the number of times the user clicked the Click Here button before the "Congratulations!" message appeared. Display the counter's value in a label on the form. Be sure to reset the counter after the user wins. Save the solution and then start and test the application. Close the solution. (1, 8, 9)

MODIFY THIS

19. If necessary, complete the College Savings application from this chapter's Programming Tutorial 2, and then close the solution. Use Windows to make a copy of the College Savings Solution folder. Rename the folder College Savings Solution-DoLoop. Open the solution file contained in the College Savings Solution-DoLoop folder. Change both For...Next statements to pretest Do...Loop statements. Save the solution and then start and test the application. Close the solution. (1, 2, 10)

MODIFY THIS

MODIFY THIS

20. If necessary, complete the College Savings application from this chapter's Programming Tutorial 2, and then close the solution. Use Windows to make a copy of the College Savings Solution folder. Rename the folder College Savings Solution-Nested. Open the solution file contained in the College Savings Solution-Nested folder. Currently, the calcButton_Click procedure displays the balances by deposit amount within interest rate. Modify the procedure to display the balances by interest rate within deposit amount. Save the solution and then start and test the application. Close the solution. (1, 2, 10)

MODIFY THIS

21. If necessary, complete the Karlton Industries application from this chapter's Programming Example, and then close the solution. Use Windows to make a copy of the Karlton Solution folder. Rename the folder Karlton Solution-DoLoop. Open the solution file contained in the Karlton Solution-DoLoop folder. Change the For...Next statement in the Load event procedure to a posttest Do...Loop statement. Save the solution and then start and test the application. Close the solution. (1, 4–7)

MODIFY THIS

22. To complete this exercise, you need to have completed the Lucky Number Game application from Chapter 6's Programming Tutorial 1. Use Windows to copy the Lucky Solution folder from the VbReloaded2015\Chap06 folder to the VbReloaded2015\Chap07 folder. Open the solution file contained in the Lucky Solution folder. Change the Do... Loop statement in the rollButton_Click procedure to a For...Next statement. Save the solution and then start and test the application. Close the solution. (1)

MODIFY THIS

23. To complete this exercise, you need to have completed the Just Birthdays application from Chapter 6's Programming Tutorial 2. Use Windows to copy the Birthday Solution folder from the VbReloaded2015\Chap06 folder to the VbReloaded2015\Chap07 folder. Open the solution file contained in the Birthday Solution folder. Change the Do...Loop statement in the testDataButton_Click procedure to a For...Next statement. Save the solution and then start and test the application. Close the solution. (1)

INTRODUCTORY

24. Open the Car Solution (Car Solution.sln) file contained in the VbReloaded2015\Chap07\Car Solution folder. When the user clicks the Click Me button, the "I WANT THIS CAR!" message should blink 10 times. In other words, it should disappear and then reappear, disappear and then reappear, and so on, 10 times. Code the button's Click event procedure using the For...Next statement. Save the solution and then start and test the application. Close the solution. (1)

INTERMEDIATE

25. Open the Odd Squares Solution (Odd Squares Solution.sln) file contained in the VbReloaded2015\Chap07\Odd Squares Solution folder. Code the Display button's Click event procedure so that it displays the squares of the odd integers from 1 through 9 in the squaresLabel. Display each square on a separate line in the control. Use the For...Next statement. Save the solution and then start and test the application. Close the solution. (1, 2)

INTERMEDIATE

26. In this exercise, you will create a Windows Forms application that displays a multiplication table. Use the following names for the solution and project, respectively: Multiplication Solution and Multiplication Project. Save the solution in the VbReloaded2015\Chap07 folder. Change the form file's name to Main Form.vb. Create the interface shown in Figure 7-42. The numberComboBox should list numbers from 1 through 15; however, the user should be allowed to enter a number in its text portion. The numberComboBox should accept only numbers and the Backspace key. Code the application using the For...Next statement. Save the solution and then start and test the application. Close the solution. (1, 6, 7)

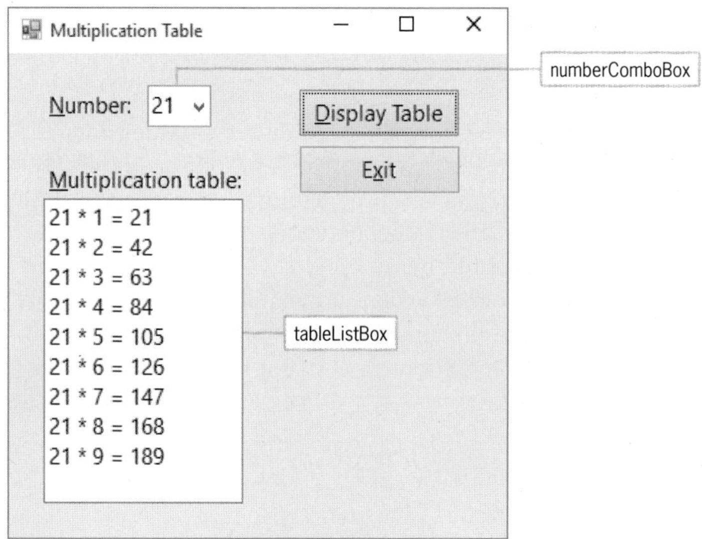

Figure 7-42 Sample run for Exercise 26

27. Create a Windows Forms application. Use the following names for the solution and project, respectively: Planets Solution and Planets Project. Save the application in the VbReloaded2015\Chap07 folder. Change the form file's name to Main Form.vb. The application's interface should provide a text box for the user to enter a person's weight on Earth. It should also provide a DropDownList combo box for selecting one of the following planet names: Mercury, Venus, Mars, Jupiter, Saturn, Uranus, and Neptune. When the user clicks a planet name, the application should convert the Earth weight to the weight on the selected planet and then display the converted weight in a label control. Use the Internet to research the formula for making the conversions. Save the solution and then start and test the application. Close the Code Editor window and then close the solution. (4–7) INTERMEDIATE

28. Create a Windows Forms application. Use the following names for the solution and project, respectively: New Salary Solution and New Salary Project. Save the application in the VbReloaded2015\Chap07 folder. Change the form file's name to Main Form.vb. Assume that at the beginning of every year, you receive a raise on your previous year's salary. The application's interface should provide a text box for you to enter your current salary. It should also provide a button that displays the amount of your annual raises and also your new salaries for the next five years, using raise rates of 1.5%, 2%, 2.5%, and 3%. You can display the output in a list box, a text box, or a label. Create a suitable interface and then code the application. Save the solution and then start and test the application. Close the Code Editor window and then close the solution. (1, 2, 4, 5) INTERMEDIATE

29. In this exercise, you code an application that allows the user to enter two integers. The application should display the sum of the odd numbers between both integers and the sum of the even numbers between both integers. (Don't include the two integers in the sums.) If the first integer entered by the user is greater than the second integer, the application will need to swap both integers before calculating the sums. Open the OddEven Solution (OddEven Solution.sln) file contained in the VbReloaded2015\Chap07\OddEven Solution folder. Code the application using the For...Next statement. Save the solution and then start the application. Test the application using the following integers: 6 and 25. The application should display the number 135 as the sum of the odd numbers and display the number 144 as the sum of the even numbers. Now test it again ADVANCED

using the following integers: 10 and 3. The application should display 21 as the sum of the odd numbers and display 18 as the sum of the even numbers. Close the solution. (1, 2, 4, 5)

ADVANCED

30. Open the Numbers Table Solution (Numbers Table Solution.sln) file contained in the VbReloaded2015\Chap07\Numbers Table Solution folder. Code the application so that it displays a table consisting of four rows and five columns. The first column should contain the numbers 10, 12, 14, and 16. The second and subsequent columns should contain the result of multiplying the number in the first column by the numbers 2 through 5. The table will look similar to the one shown in Figure 7-43. Use two For...Next statements. Save the solution and then start and test the application. Close the solution. (1, 2)

10	20	30	40	50
12	24	36	48	60
14	28	42	56	70
16	32	48	64	80

Figure 7-43 Sample output for Exercise 30

ADVANCED

31. Create a Windows Forms application. Use the following names for the solution and project, respectively: Car Depreciation Solution and Car Depreciation Project. Save the application in the VbReloaded2015\Chap07 folder. Change the form file's name to Main Form.vb. Typically, new cars depreciate—in other words, lose their value—by 15% to 25% per year. Create an application that displays the value of a new car at the end of each of five years, using annual depreciation rates of 15%, 20%, and 25%. Save the solution and then start and test the application. Close the solution. (1, 2, 4, 5)

DISCOVERY

32. If necessary, complete the Slot Machine application from this chapter's Programming Tutorial 1, and then close the solution. Use Windows to make a copy of the Slot Machine Solution folder. Rename the folder Slot Machine Solution-Discovery. Open the solution file contained in the Slot Machine Solution-Discovery folder. Open the Code Editor window and locate the clickHereButton_Click procedure. The procedure disables the button at the beginning of the procedure and then enables it at the end of the procedure. Start the application and then click the Click Here button; the button appears dimmed (grayed out) while its Click event procedure is running. If necessary, close the message box. Now, click the button, quickly, three times. Notice that even though the button appears dimmed, its Click procedure is still invoked each time you click the button. Modify the application so that it ignores the clicks when the button is disabled. (Hint: Use a Timer control to set the clickHereButton's Enabled property to True.) Save the solution and then start and test the application. Close the solution.

SWAT THE BUGS

33. Open the Debug Solution (Debug Solution.sln) file contained in the VbReloaded2015\Chap07\Debug Solution-Ex33 folder. Open the Code Editor window and review the existing code. Start and then test the application. Locate and then correct any errors. When the application is working correctly, close the solution. (1, 2)

SWAT THE BUGS

34. Open the Debug Solution (Debug Solution.sln) file contained in the VbReloaded2015\Chap07\Debug Solution-Ex34 folder. Start the application. The application should display the following commission rates: 3%, 4%, 5%, and 6%. However, it is not working correctly: It displays only 3%, 4%, and 5%. Correct the application's code. Save the solution and then start and test the application. Close the solution. (1)

Case Projects

Loan Calculator

Create an application that displays a monthly payment on a loan. The application should also display the amount applied to the loan's principal each month and the amount that represents interest. Use the following names for the solution and project, respectively: Loan Solution and Loan Project. Save the solution in the VbReloaded2015\Chap07 folder. Change the form file's name to Main Form.vb. The application should use annual interest rates from 2% through 10% in increments of 1%, and use terms from 1 through 30 years. You can use the Financial.PPmt method to calculate the portion of the payment applied to the principal each month. The method's syntax is `Financial.PPmt(`*Rate, Per, NPer, PV*`)`. In the syntax, *Rate* is the interest rate, *NPer* is the number of payment periods, and *PV* is the present value of the loan. The *Per* argument is the payment period for which you want to calculate the portion applied to the principal. The *Per* argument must be a number from 1 through *NPer*. The method returns the calculated value as a Double number. You can either create your own interface or create the one shown in Figure 7-44; the figure shows a sample run of the application. The combo box that gets the interest rate is the DropDown style. The combo box that gets the term is the DropDownList style. The text box that displays the output has its Multiline and ReadOnly properties set to True and its ScrollBars property set to Vertical. (1, 2, 4–7)

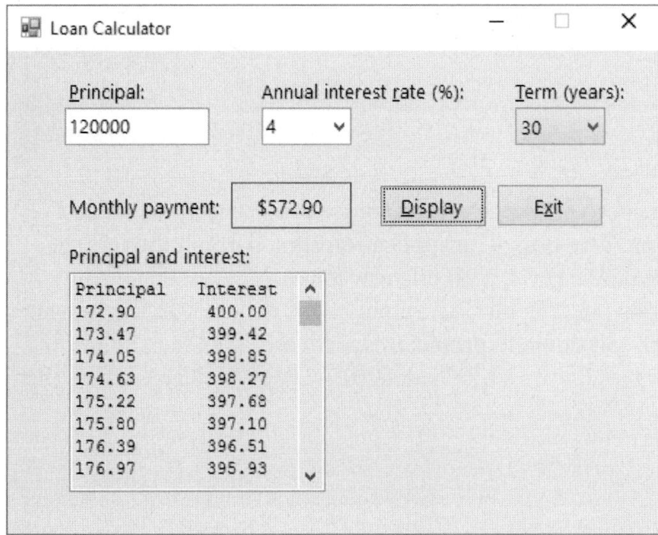

Figure 7-44 Sample run of the Loan Calculator application

Happy Temps

Happy Temps has hired you as a temporary worker for 10 days. The company offers you two pay options. Option 1 doubles your pay each day; however, the first day's pay is only $1. In other words, you would earn $1 the first day, $2 the second day, $4 the third day, $8 the fourth day, and so on. Option 2 is to be paid $100 per day. Create an application that calculates and displays your daily pay under each pay plan. Also display the total amount you would earn under each pay plan. Use the following names for the solution and project, respectively: Happy Temps Solution and Happy Temps Project. Save the solution in the VbReloaded2015\Chap07 folder. Change the form file's name to Main Form.vb. You can either create your own interface or create the one shown in Figure 7-45. (1, 2)

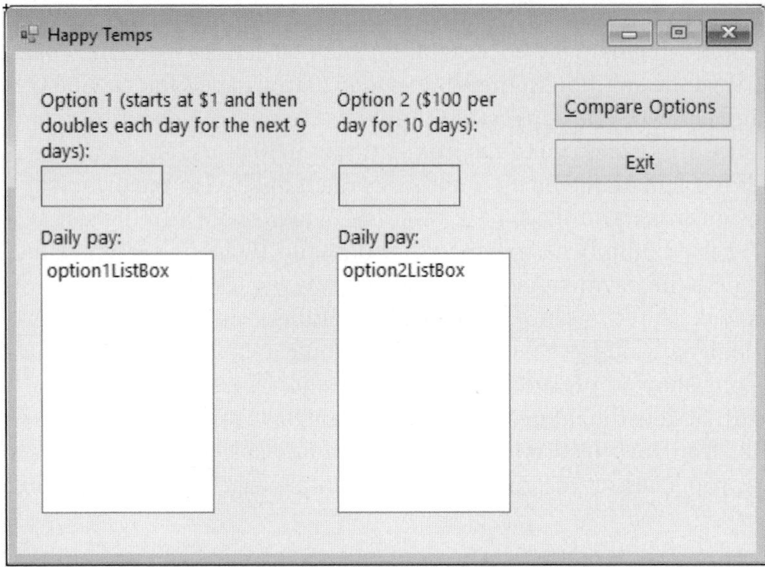

Figure 7-45 Sample interface for the Happy Temps application

Movie Ratings

Create an application that allows the user to enter the ratings for five different movies. Each rating should be a number from 1 through 10 only. The application should graph the ratings using a horizontal bar chart consisting of five rows, with one row for each movie. Each row should contain from one to 10 plus signs (+). The number of plus signs depends on the movie's rating. Use the following names for the solution and project, respectively: Bar Chart Solution and Bar Chart Project. Save the application in the VbReloaded2015\Chap07 folder. Change the form file's name to Main Form.vb. (1, 2)

Retirement Savings

Create an application that allows the user to enter a person's age (in years) and current salary. Both input items should be entered as integers. The application should display a person's total earnings before retirement at age 65, using annual raise rates of 3%, 4%, and 5%. Display the total earning amounts with a dollar sign and no decimal places. Use the following names for the solution and project, respectively: Retirement Solution and Retirement Project. Save the application in the VbReloaded2015\Chap07 folder. Change the form file's name to Main Form.vb. (1, 2, 4, 5)

Canton Manufacturing Company

Create an application for the accountant at Canton Manufacturing Company. The application should calculate an asset's annual depreciation (during its useful life) using the double-declining balance and sum-of-the-years' digits methods. Use the Internet to research Visual Basic's Financial.DDB and Financial.SYD methods. The accountant will enter the asset's cost, useful life (in years), and salvage value (which is the value of the asset at the end of its useful life). The interface should provide text boxes for entering the asset cost and salvage value. It should also provide a combo box for selecting the useful life, which ranges from 3 through 20 years. Display the depreciation amounts in two list boxes: one for the double-declining balance depreciation and one for the sum-of-the-years' digits depreciation. Use the following names for the solution and project, respectively: Canton Solution and Canton Project. Save the application in the VbReloaded2015\Chap07 folder. Change the form's file's name to Main Form.vb. (1, 4–7)

CHAPTER 8

Sub and Function Procedures

After studying Chapter 8, you should be able to:

1. Create and call an independent Sub procedure
2. Pass data to a procedure
3. Explain the difference between passing data *by value* and passing data *by reference*
4. Desk-check an application's code
5. Associate a procedure with more than one object and event
6. Explain the difference between Sub and Function procedures
7. Create and invoke a function
8. Convert an Object variable to a different type using the TryCast operator
9. Round a number
10. Code the CheckedChanged event procedure (Programming Tutorial 2)

Sub Procedures

There are two types of Sub procedures in Visual Basic: event procedures and independent Sub procedures. All of the procedures coded in the previous chapters were event procedures. As you already know, an event procedure is a Sub procedure that is associated with a specific object and event, such as a button's Click event or a text box's TextChanged event. The computer automatically processes an event procedure's code when the event occurs. An **independent Sub procedure**, on the other hand, is a procedure that is independent of any object and event. An independent Sub procedure is processed only when called (invoked) from code. Figure 8-1 lists several reasons for using independent Sub procedures in an application's code.

Reasons for using independent Sub procedures

1. Independent Sub procedures allow you to avoid duplicating code when different sections of a program need to perform the same task. Rather than entering the code in each of those sections, you can enter the code in a procedure and then have each section call the procedure to perform its task when needed.
2. If the task performed by the independent Sub procedure subsequently changes, you will need to make the modification in only the Sub procedure rather than in all of the sections that call the procedure.
3. If an event procedure must perform many tasks, you can prevent the procedure's code from getting unwieldy and difficult to understand by assigning some of the tasks to one or more independent Sub procedures. Doing this makes the event procedure easier to code because it allows you to concentrate on one small piece of the code at a time.
4. Independent Sub procedures are used extensively in large and complex programs, which typically are written by a team of programmers. The programming team will break up the program into small and manageable tasks, and then assign some of the tasks to different team members to be coded as independent Sub procedures. Doing this allows more than one programmer to work on the program at the same time, decreasing the time it takes to write the program.

Figure 8-1 Reasons programmers use independent Sub procedures

Figure 8-2 shows the syntax of an independent Sub procedure along with the syntax for calling (invoking) the procedure. As the figure indicates, you invoke an independent Sub procedure using a stand-alone statement (referred to as the **calling statement**) that includes the Sub procedure's name followed by zero or more arguments that are separated by commas and enclosed in parentheses. You learned about arguments in Chapter 2. In this case, the arguments represent information that the Sub procedure needs to perform its task. An argument can be a literal constant, a named constant, a keyword, or a variable; however, in most cases, the argument will be a variable. Figure 8-2 also shows examples of independent Sub procedures and their calling statements. Do not be concerned if you do not understand everything in the figure right now. The Sub procedures and calling statements will be explained further in the following sections.

HOW TO Create and Call an Independent Sub Procedure

Syntax of an independent Sub procedure

Private Sub *procedureName*(*[parameterList]*)
    statements
End Sub

Figure 8-2 How to create and call an independent Sub procedure *(continues)*

(continued)

<u>Syntax for calling (invoking) a Sub procedure</u>
procedureName(**[***argumentList***]**)

<u>Example 1 (no parameters/arguments)</u>
```
Private Sub ClearNet()
    netLabel.Text = String.Empty
End Sub
```
Calling statement: `ClearNet()`

<u>Example 2 (one parameter/argument passed *by value*)</u>
```
Private Sub ChangeColor(ByVal incomeOrLoss As Integer)
    ' change the font color

    If incomeOrLoss < 0 Then
        netLabel.ForeColor = Color.Red
    Else
        netLabel.ForeColor = Color.Black
    End If
End Sub
```
Calling statement: `ChangeColor(net)`

<u>Example 3 (three parameters/arguments: two passed *by value* and one passed *by reference*)</u>
```
Private Sub CalcNet(ByVal moneyIn As Integer,
                    ByVal moneyOut As Integer,
                    ByRef difference As Integer)
    difference = moneyIn - moneyOut
End Sub
```
Calling statement: `CalcNet(income, expenses, net)`

Figure 8-2 How to create and call an independent Sub procedure

Like event procedures, independent Sub procedures have a procedure header and footer. The rules for naming an independent Sub procedure are the same as those for naming a variable; however, procedure names are usually entered using Pascal case. The Sub procedure's name should indicate the task the procedure performs. It is a common practice to begin the name with a verb, such as ClearNet, DisplayNet, or CalculateOvertime.

Following the procedure name in the procedure header is a set of parentheses that contains an optional *parameterList*, which lists the data type and name of one or more parameters. A parameter is simply a memory location. Each parameter in the parameterList has procedure scope and each stores an item of data that it receives from the calling statement's *argumentList*. The number of arguments should agree with the number of parameters. If the parameterList contains one parameter, then the argumentList should have one argument. Similarly, a procedure that contains three parameters in its procedure header requires three arguments in the calling statement that invokes it. If the parameterList does not contain any parameters, then an empty set of parentheses follows the procedure name in the calling statement.

In addition to having the same number of arguments as parameters, the data type and order (or position) of each argument should agree with the data type and order (position) of its corresponding parameter. If the first parameter has a data type of String and the second has a data type of Double, then the first argument in the calling statement should have the String data type and the second should have the Double data type. This is because when the procedure is called, the computer associates the first argument with the first parameter, the second argument with the second parameter, and so on.

In the next several sections, you will view applications that create and call the independent Sub procedures from Figure 8-2. An independent Sub procedure can be entered anywhere between the Public Class and End Class clauses in the Code Editor window, as long as it is outside of any other procedure. In this book, the independent Sub procedures will be entered above the first event procedure.

The Gillian Company Application

Figure 8-3 shows the problem specification for the Gillian Company application, which calculates and displays the company's net income (or loss). The figure also shows some of the application's code and includes two sample runs of the application. The code uses an independent Sub procedure named ClearNet to clear the contents of the netLabel when a change is made to the contents of either the incomeTextBox or the expensesTextBox. The procedure header indicates that the procedure does not need any information from the calling statement in order to accomplish its goal. Therefore, the `ClearNet()` statement, which appears in the two TextChanged event procedures, does not contain any arguments.

If you want to experiment with the Gillian Company application, open the solution contained in the Try It 1! folder.

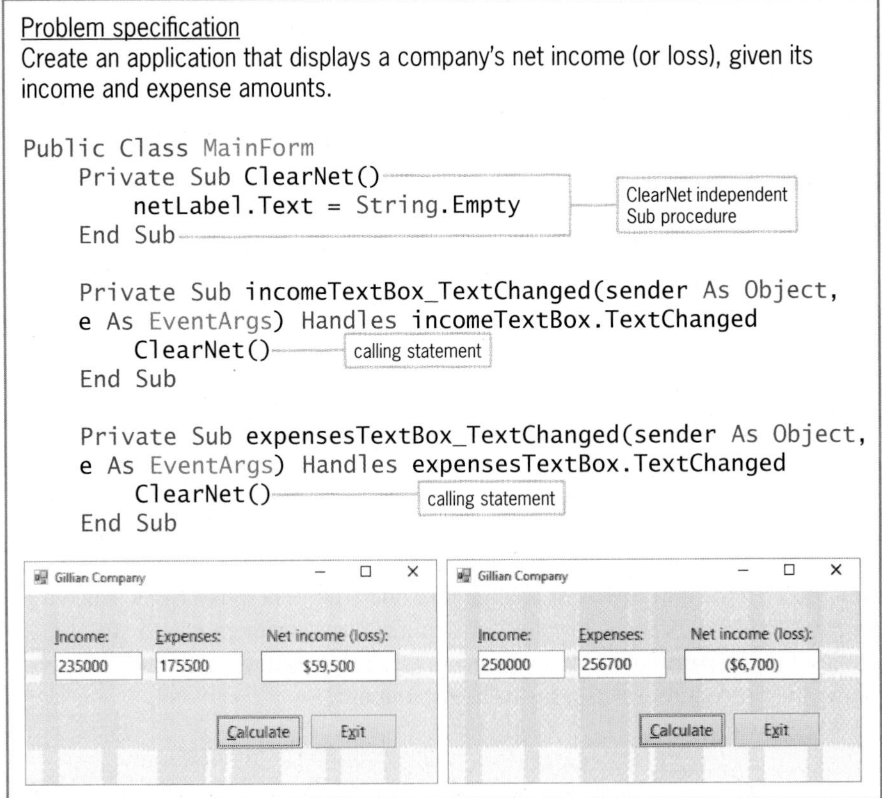

Figure 8-3 Partial code and sample runs for the Gillian Company application

Although you could enter the `netLabel.Text = String.Empty` instruction in each TextChanged event procedure, entering it in the ClearNet procedure has a distinct advantage: If you subsequently need to modify the statement—for example, you may need to assign the string "0" rather than the empty string to the netLabel—you need to make the change in only one place in the code.

When the computer processes the `ClearNet()` statement in the incomeTextBox_TextChanged procedure, it temporarily leaves the event procedure to process the code in the ClearNet procedure. The assignment statement in the ClearNet procedure removes the contents of the netLabel. After processing the assignment statement, the computer processes the ClearNet procedure's End Sub clause, which ends the procedure. The computer then returns to the incomeTextBox_TextChanged procedure and processes the line of code located immediately below the calling statement—in this case, the event procedure's End Sub clause. A similar process is followed when the expensesTextBox_TextChanged event occurs: The computer temporarily leaves the event procedure to process the code contained in the independent Sub procedure. When the independent Sub procedure ends, the computer returns to the event procedure and processes the code immediately below the calling statement.

Mini-Quiz 8-1

The answers to Mini-Quiz questions are located in Appendix A. Each question is associated with one or more objectives listed at the beginning of the chapter.

1. An event procedure is a Sub procedure that is associated with a specific object and event. (1)
   a. True
   b. False
2. Which of the following is the correct way to write a procedure header that does not require a parameterList? (1)
   a. `Private Sub DisplayMessage`
   b. `Private Sub DisplayMessage()`
   c. `Private Sub DisplayMessage(none)`
   d. `Private Sub DisplayMessage[]`
3. Which of the following invokes the DisplayMessage procedure from Question 2? (1)
   a. `DisplayMessage`
   b. `Sub DisplayMessage()`
   c. `DisplayMessage(none)`
   d. `DisplayMessage()`

Passing Variables

The internal memory of a computer is similar to a large post office. Like each post office box, each memory cell has a unique address.

As mentioned earlier, the arguments in the statements that invoke independent Sub procedures can be literal constants, named constants, keywords, or variables; however, in most cases, the arguments will be variables. Each variable declared in a program has both a value and a unique address that represents the location of the variable in the computer's internal memory. Visual Basic allows you to pass either a copy of the variable's value or its address to the receiving procedure. Passing a copy of the variable's value is referred to as **passing by value**, whereas passing its address is referred to as **passing by reference**. The method you choose—*by value* or

Ch08-Passing Variables

by reference—depends on whether you want the receiving procedure to have access to the variable in memory. In other words, it depends on whether you want to allow the receiving procedure to change the variable's contents.

Passing Variables by Value

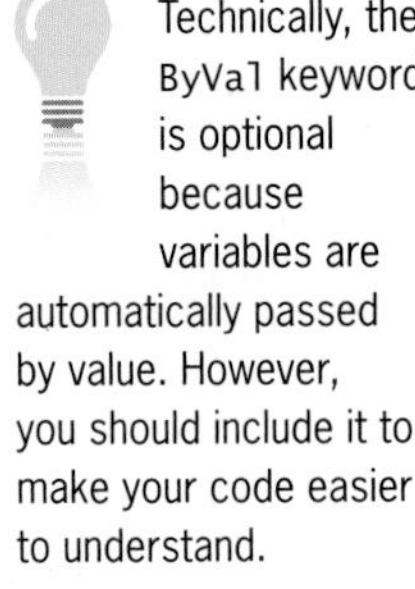
Technically, the `ByVal` keyword is optional because variables are automatically passed by value. However, you should include it to make your code easier to understand.

To pass a variable *by value*, you include the keyword `ByVal` before the name of its corresponding parameter in the receiving procedure's parameterList. When you pass a variable *by value*, the computer passes a copy of the variable's contents to the receiving procedure. When only a copy of the contents is passed, the receiving procedure is not given access to the variable in memory. Therefore, it cannot change the value stored inside the variable. It is appropriate to pass a variable *by value* when the receiving procedure needs to *know* the variable's contents but does not need to *change* the contents.

To demonstrate passing *by value*, we will make a slight change to the problem specification from Figure 8-3. If Gillian Company experiences a net loss, the amount should now be displayed using a red font; otherwise, a black font is still appropriate. The modified problem specification and code are shown in Figure 8-4 along with two sample runs of the application. The parameterList (in the ChangeColor procedure header) and the argumentList (in the calling statement) are shaded in the figure.

If you want to experiment with the modified Gillian Company application, open the solution contained in the Try It 2! folder.

Modified problem specification
Create an application that displays a company's net income (or loss), given its income and expense amounts. Display the net loss using a red font; otherwise, use a black font.

```
Private Sub ChangeColor(ByVal incomeOrLoss As Integer)
    ' change the font color

    If incomeOrLoss < 0 Then
        netLabel.ForeColor = Color.Red
    Else
        netLabel.ForeColor = Color.Black
    End If
End Sub

Private Sub calcButton_Click(sender As Object, e As EventArgs
) Handles calcButton.Click
    ' calculates net income or net loss

    Dim income As Integer
    Dim expenses As Integer
    Dim net As Integer

    Integer.TryParse(incomeTextBox.Text, income)
    Integer.TryParse(expensesTextBox.Text, expenses)

    net = income - expenses
    ChangeColor(net)
    netLabel.Text = net.ToString("C2")
End Sub
```

ChangeColor independent Sub procedure

calling statement

Figure 8-4 Partial code and sample runs for the modified Gillian Company application *(continues)*

(continued)

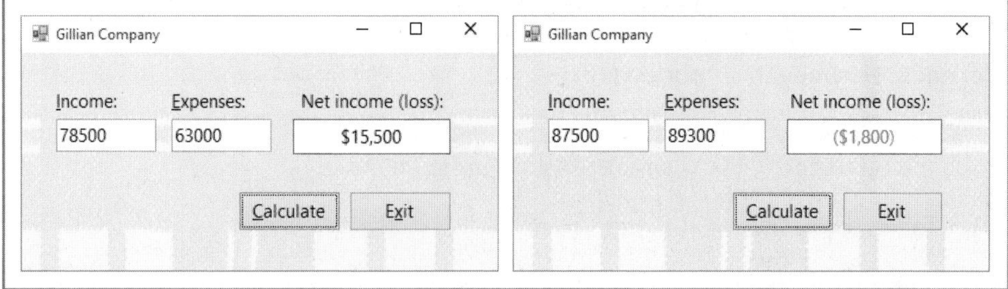

Figure 8-4 Partial code and sample runs for the modified Gillian Company application

The calling statement in the calcButton_Click procedure passes the `net` variable *by value* to an independent Sub procedure named ChangeColor. The variable is passed *by value* because the ChangeColor procedure does not need to change the value stored in the variable. You can tell that the variable is passed *by value* because the keyword `ByVal` appears before its corresponding parameter (`incomeOrLoss`) in the ChangeColor procedure header. Notice that the data type of the argument matches the data type of the corresponding parameter. Also notice that the argument's name does not need to be identical to the parameter's name. In fact, to avoid confusion, you should use different names for an argument and its corresponding parameter.

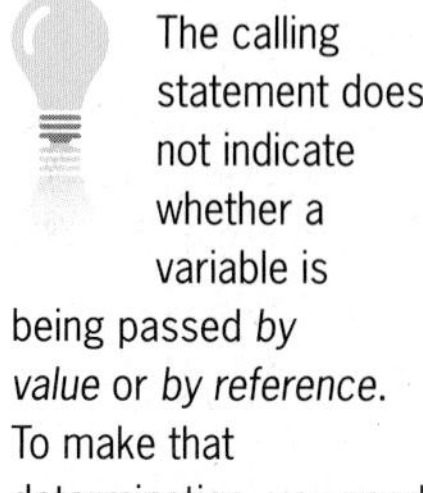

The calling statement does not indicate whether a variable is being passed *by value* or *by reference*. To make that determination, you need to look at the receiving procedure's header.

When the ChangeColor procedure receives the `net` variable's value from the calling statement, it stores the value in its `incomeOrLoss` parameter. (Recall that a parameter is simply a memory location.) The selection structure in the procedure compares the value in the `incomeOrLoss` parameter with the number 0. If the parameter's value is less than 0, the netLabel control's ForeColor property is set to `Color.Red`; otherwise, it is set to `Color.Black`. When the ChangeColor procedure ends, processing continues with the instruction immediately below the calling statement in the calcButton_Click procedure. That instruction displays the `net` variable's value in the netLabel.

Passing Variables by Reference

Instead of passing a copy of a variable's value to a procedure, you can pass its address. In other words, you can pass the variable's location in the computer's internal memory. As you learned earlier, passing a variable's address is referred to as passing *by reference*, and it gives the receiving procedure access to the variable being passed. You pass a variable *by reference* when you want the receiving procedure to change the contents of the variable. To pass a variable *by reference* in Visual Basic, you include the keyword `ByRef` before the name of the corresponding parameter in the receiving procedure's header. The `ByRef` keyword tells the computer to pass the variable's address rather than a copy of its contents.

We can use the Gillian Company application from the previous section to demonstrate passing *by reference*. Figure 8-5 shows the code entered in two of the procedures in the application: the calcButton_Click event procedure and the CalcNet procedure. The `CalcNet(income, expenses, net)` statement in the calcButton_Click procedure invokes the CalcNet procedure, passing it three items of data. `ByVal` in the parameterList indicates that the first two items are passed to the procedure *by value*, whereas `ByRef` indicates that the third item is passed *by reference*.

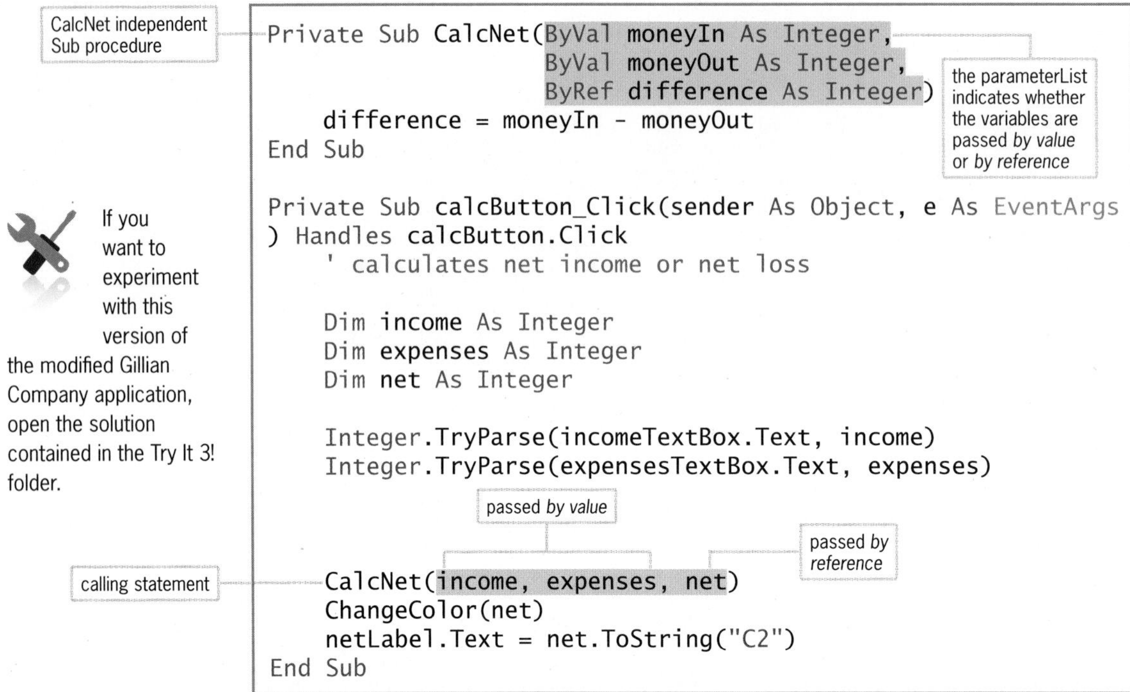


```
Private Sub CalcNet(ByVal moneyIn As Integer,
                    ByVal moneyOut As Integer,
                    ByRef difference As Integer)
    difference = moneyIn - moneyOut
End Sub

Private Sub calcButton_Click(sender As Object, e As EventArgs
) Handles calcButton.Click
    ' calculates net income or net loss

    Dim income As Integer
    Dim expenses As Integer
    Dim net As Integer

    Integer.TryParse(incomeTextBox.Text, income)
    Integer.TryParse(expensesTextBox.Text, expenses)

    CalcNet(income, expenses, net)
    ChangeColor(net)
    netLabel.Text = net.ToString("C2")
End Sub
```

If you want to experiment with this version of the modified Gillian Company application, open the solution contained in the Try It 3! folder.

Figure 8-5 CalcNet and calcButton_Click procedures in the Gillian Company application

Notice that the number, data type, and order (position) of the arguments in the calling statement match the number, data type, and order (position) of the corresponding parameters in the CalcNet procedure header. Also notice that the names of the arguments are not identical to the names of their corresponding parameters. Finally, notice that the calling statement does not indicate the way a variable is being passed; that information is found only in the receiving procedure's header.

Desk-checking the procedures shown in Figure 8-5 will help clarify the difference between passing *by value* and passing *by reference.* **Desk-checking** refers to the process of reviewing the program instructions while seated at your desk rather than in front of the computer. Desk-checking is also called **hand-tracing** because you use a pencil and paper to follow each of the instructions by hand.

Before you begin the desk-check, you first choose a set of sample data for the input values, which you then use to manually compute the expected output values. You will desk-check Figure 8-5's procedures using 78500 and 63000 as the income and expense amounts, respectively. The net income should be 15500.

When the user clicks the Calculate button after entering 78500 and 63000 in the appropriate text boxes, the Dim statements in the calcButton_Click procedure create and initialize three Integer variables. The two TryParse methods convert the user's input to the Integer data type, storing the results in the `income` and `expenses` variables. Figure 8-6 shows the contents of the variables before the next statement, which is the first calling statement, is processed.

income	expenses	net
~~0~~	~~0~~	0
78500	63000	

these three variables belong to the calcButton_Click procedure

Figure 8-6 Desk-check table before the first calling statement is processed

The computer processes the first calling statement next. The statement invokes the CalcNet procedure, passing it three arguments. At this point, the computer temporarily leaves the calcButton_Click procedure to process the code contained in the CalcNet procedure, beginning with the procedure header. The `ByVal` keyword indicates that the first two parameters are receiving values from the calling statement—in this case, copies of the numbers stored in the `income` and `expenses` variables. As a result, the computer creates the `moneyIn` and `moneyOut` variables listed in the parameterList and stores the numbers 78500 and 63000, respectively, in the variables.

The `ByRef` keyword indicates that the third parameter is receiving the address of a variable. When you pass a variable's address to a procedure, the computer uses the address to locate the variable in its internal memory. It then assigns the parameter name to the same memory location. In this case, the computer locates the `net` variable in memory and assigns the name `difference` to it. As indicated in the desk-check table shown in Figure 8-7, the memory location now has two names: one assigned by the calcButton_Click procedure and one assigned by the CalcNet procedure. Although both procedures can access the memory location, each procedure uses a different name to do so: The calcButton_Click procedure uses the name `net`, whereas the CalcNet procedure uses the name `difference`.

The names in black indicate memory locations that belong to the calcButton_Click procedure. The names in red indicate memory locations that belong to the CalcNet procedure.

this memory location belongs to both procedures

income	expenses	difference net
~~0~~	~~0~~	0
78500	63000	
moneyIn	moneyOut	
78500	63000	

Figure 8-7 Desk-check table after the first calling statement and CalcNet procedure header are processed

After processing the CalcNet procedure header, the computer processes the assignment statement contained in the procedure. The statement subtracts the `moneyOut` variable's value (63000) from the `moneyIn` variable's value (78500) and assigns the result (15500) to the `difference` variable, as shown in Figure 8-8. Notice that changing the value in the `difference` variable also changes the value in the `net` variable. This is because both variable names refer to the same location in the computer's internal memory.

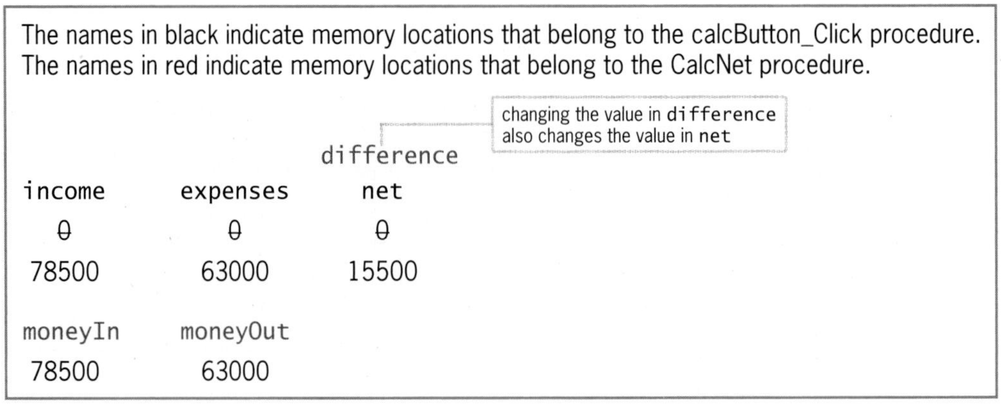

The names in black indicate memory locations that belong to the calcButton_Click procedure.
The names in red indicate memory locations that belong to the CalcNet procedure.

changing the value in difference also changes the value in net

income	expenses	difference net
~~0~~	~~0~~	~~0~~
78500	63000	15500
moneyIn	moneyOut	
78500	63000	

Figure 8-8 Desk-check table after the assignment statement in the CalcNet procedure is processed

The CalcNet procedure's End Sub clause is processed next and ends the procedure. At this point, the computer removes the `moneyIn` and `moneyOut` variables from its internal memory. It also removes the `difference` name from the appropriate location in memory, as indicated in Figure 8-9. The `net` memory location now has only one name: the name assigned to it by the calcButton_Click procedure.

The names in black indicate memory locations that belong to the calcButton_Click procedure.
The names in red indicate memory locations that belong to the CalcNet procedure.

income	expenses	~~difference~~ net
~~0~~	~~0~~	~~0~~
78500	63000	15500
~~moneyIn~~	~~moneyOut~~	
~~78500~~	~~63000~~	

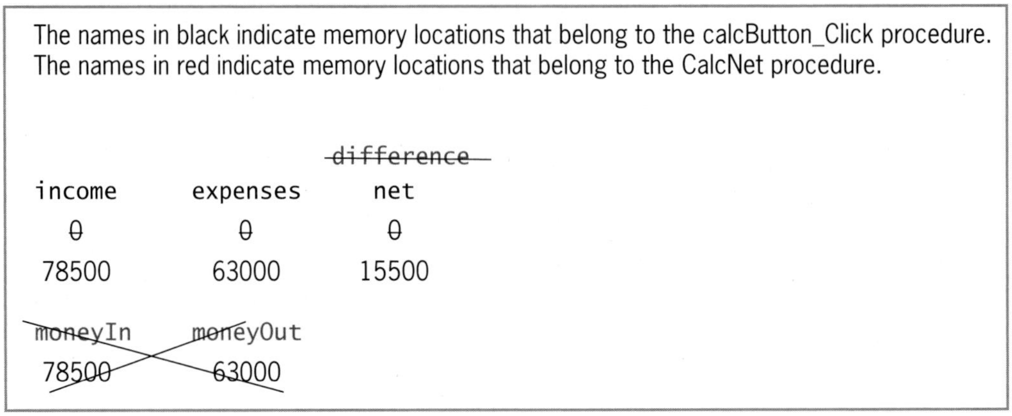

Figure 8-9 Desk-check table after the CalcNet procedure ends

After the CalcNet procedure ends, the computer returns to the calcButton_Click procedure to finish processing the event procedure's code. More specifically, it returns to the `ChangeColor(net)` statement, which invokes the ChangeColor procedure, passing it the `net` variable *by value*. The variable's value is not less than 0, so the ChangeColor procedure assigns `Color.Black` to the netLabel's ForeColor property. The last statement in the calcButton_Click procedure displays the contents of the `net` variable in the netLabel, as shown earlier in Figure 8-4. Finally, the computer processes the Click event procedure's End Sub clause, which ends the procedure. The computer then removes the procedure's variables (`income`, `expenses`, and `net`) from memory.

Mini-Quiz 8-2

The answers to Mini-Quiz questions are located in Appendix A. Each question is associated with one or more objectives listed at the beginning of the chapter.

1. Which of the following indicates that the procedure receives a copy of the values stored in two String variables? (2, 3)
   a. `Private Sub Display(ByRef x As String, ByRef y As String)`
   b. `Private Sub Display(ByVal x As String, ByVal y As String)`
   c. `Private Sub Display(ByValue x As String, ByValue y As String)`
   d. `Private Sub Display(ByCopy x As String, ByCopy y As String)`

2. Which of the following indicates that the procedure will receive two items of data: an integer and the address of a Double variable? (2, 3)
   a. `Private Sub Calc(ByVal x As Integer, ByRef y As Double)`
   b. `Private Sub Calc(Value x As Integer, Address y As Double)`
   c. `Private Sub Calc(ByInt x As Integer, ByAdd y As Double)`
   d. `Private Sub Calc(ByCopy x As Integer, ByAdd y As Double)`

3. Which of the following invokes the Calc procedure from Question 2, passing it an Integer variable named `sales` and a Double variable named `bonus`? (2, 3)
   a. `Calc(ByVal sales, ByRef bonus)`
   b. `Calc(sales, bonus)`
   c. `Calc(bonus, sales)`
   d. both b and c

Associating a Procedure with Different Objects and Events

As you learned in Chapter 1, the Handles clause in an event procedure's header indicates the object and event associated with the procedure. The Handles clause in Figure 8-10 indicates that the procedure is associated with the TextChanged event of the incomeTextBox. As a result, the procedure will be processed when the incomeTextBox's TextChanged event occurs.

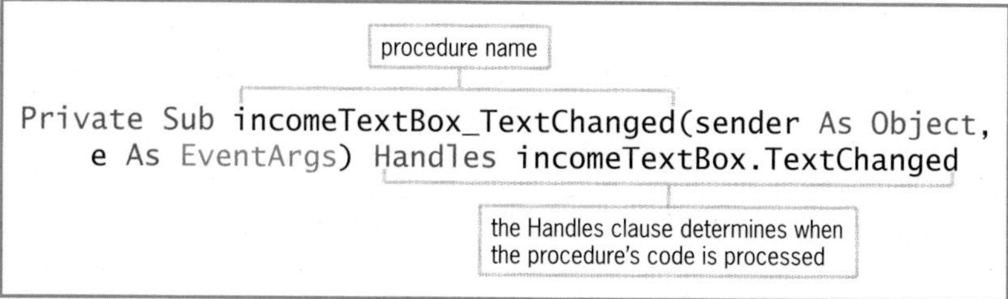

Figure 8-10 TextChanged event procedure associated with the incomeTextBox

Although an event procedure's name contains the names of its associated object and event separated by an underscore, this is not a requirement. You can change the name of an event procedure to any name that follows the naming rules for procedures. Unlike variable names, however, procedure names are usually entered using Pascal case. For example, you can change the name incomeTextBox_TextChanged to ClearNet and the procedure will still work correctly. This is because the Handles clause, rather than the event procedure's name, determines when the procedure is invoked.

You can associate a procedure with more than one object and event as long as each event contains the same parameters in its procedure header; Figure 8-11 shows the steps for doing this. The figure also includes an example of a procedure that is associated with two events: incomeTextBox.TextChanged and expensesTextBox.TextChanged. The ClearNet procedure will be processed when either of these events occurs.

If you want to experiment with the code shown in Figure 8-11, open the solution contained in the Try It 4! folder.

HOW TO Associate a Procedure with Different Objects and Events

1. Open the code template for one of the events with which you want to associate a procedure.
2. Change the event procedure's name to one that describes the procedure's task.
3. Verify that the parameterList in each event you want to associate is the same as the parameterList in the code template opened in Step 1. (If necessary, you can open the code templates for the other events to view their parameterLists.)
4. In the procedure's Handles clause, list each object and event that you want to associate. Separate the object and event with a period, like this: *object.event*. Use a comma to separate each *object.event* from the next *object.event*.

Example

```
Private Sub ClearNet(sender As Object, e As EventArgs
            ) Handles incomeTextBox.TextChanged,
            expensesTextBox.TextChanged
    netLabel.Text = String.Empty
End Sub
```

Figure 8-11 How to associate a procedure with different objects and events

To see the advantage of associating a procedure with more than one object and event, compare the code shown earlier in Figure 8-3 with the code shown in Figure 8-11. Figure 8-3's code contains three procedures: ClearNet, incomeTextBox_TextChanged, and expensesTextBox_TextChanged. You can replace those three procedures with one procedure: the ClearNet procedure shown in Figure 8-11. Although it is only one procedure, it is associated with two objects and events.

Function Procedures

In addition to creating Sub procedures in Visual Basic, you can also create Function procedures. The difference between both types of procedures is that a **Function procedure** returns a value after performing its assigned task, whereas a Sub procedure does not return a value. Function procedures are referred to more simply as **functions**. The illustrations shown in Figure 8-12 may help clarify the difference between a function and a Sub procedure. In Illustration A, Helen is at the ticket counter in her local movie theater, requesting a senior ticket for the current movie. Helen gives the ticket agent a $5 bill and expects a senior ticket in return. The ticket agent is similar to a function in that he performs his task (fulfilling Helen's request for a ticket) and then returns a value (a senior ticket) to Helen. Compare that with Illustration B, where Helen and her granddaughter, Penelope, are at the Blast Off Games arcade. Helen wants Penelope to have fun, so she gives Penelope a $5 bill to play some games. But, unlike with the ticket agent, Helen expects nothing from Penelope in return. This is similar to the way a Sub procedure works. Penelope performs her task (having fun by playing games) but doesn't need to return any value to her grandmother.

Illustration A - function

Helen:
1. ask ticket agent for a senior ticket
2. give ticket agent $5
3. receive senior ticket from ticket agent

Ticket agent (function):
1. take $5 from Helen
2. give Helen a senior ticket

Illustration B - Sub procedure

Helen:
1. tell Penelope to have fun playing games
2. give Penelope $5

Penelope (Sub procedure):
1. take $5 from Helen
2. buy game tickets with the $5
3. play games and have fun

Figure 8-12 Illustrations of the difference between a function and a Sub procedure

Image by Diane Zak; created with Reallusion CrazyTalk Animator

Figure 8-13 shows the syntax and examples of functions in Visual Basic. Unlike a Sub procedure, a function's header and footer contain the `Function` keyword rather than the `Sub` keyword. A function's header also includes the `As` *dataType* section, which specifies the data type of the value the function will return. The value is returned by the **Return statement**, which typically is the last statement within a function. The statement's syntax is `Return` *expression*, where *expression* represents the one and only value that the function will return to the statement that invoked it. The data type of the *expression* must agree with the data type specified in the `As` *dataType* section of the header. Like a Sub procedure, a function can receive information either *by value* or *by reference*. The information it receives is listed in its parameterList.

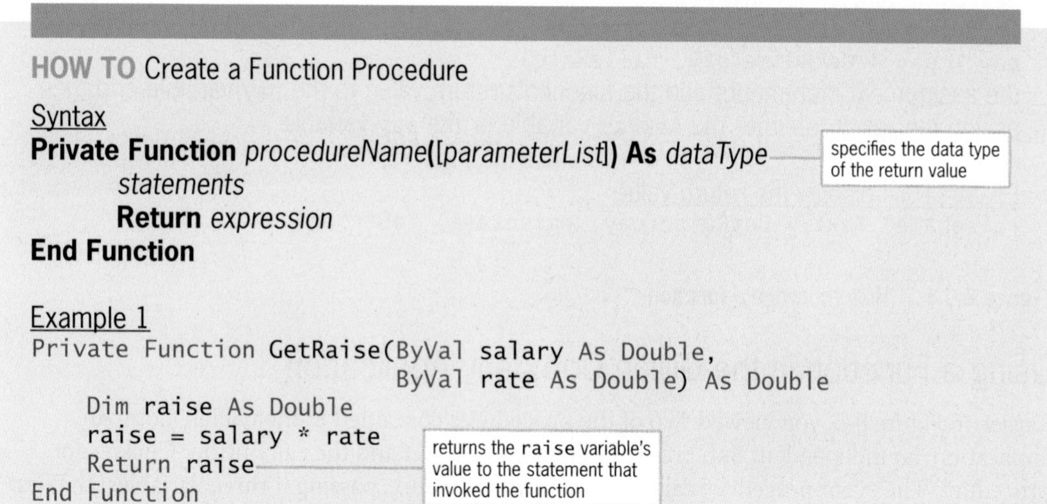

HOW TO Create a Function Procedure

Syntax

Private Function *procedureName***(**[*parameterList*]**) As** *dataType* — specifies the data type of the return value

    statements
    Return *expression*
End Function

Example 1

```
Private Function GetRaise(ByVal salary As Double,
                          ByVal rate As Double) As Double
    Dim raise As Double
    raise = salary * rate
    Return raise
End Function
```

returns the `raise` variable's value to the statement that invoked the function

Figure 8-13 How to create a Function procedure *(continues)*

(continued)

Example 2
```
Private Function GetRaise(ByVal salary As Double,
                          ByVal rate As Double) As Double
    Return salary * rate
End Function
```
calculates and returns the raise to the statement that invoked the function

Figure 8-13 How to create a Function procedure

As with Sub procedures, you can enter your functions anywhere in the Code Editor window as long as you enter them between the Public Class and End Class clauses and outside of any other procedure. In this book, the functions will be entered above the first event procedure in the Code Editor window. Like Sub procedure names, function names are entered using Pascal case and typically begin with a verb. The name should indicate the task the function performs.

You can invoke a function from one or more places in an application's code. You invoke a function that you create in exactly the same way that you invoke one of Visual Basic's built-in functions, such as the InputBox function. You do this by including the function's name and arguments (if any) in a statement. The number, data type, and position of the arguments should agree with the number, data type, and position of the function's parameters. In most cases, the statement that invokes a function assigns the function's return value to a variable. However, it also may use the return value in a calculation or simply display the return value.

Figure 8-14 shows examples of invoking the GetRaise function from Figure 8-13. The `GetRaise(pay, raiseRate)` entry in each example invokes the function, passing it the values stored in the `pay` and `raiseRate` variables.

HOW TO Invoke a Function

Example 1—assign the return value to a variable
```
increase = GetRaise(pay, raiseRate)
```

Example 2—use the return value in a calculation
```
newPay = pay + GetRaise(pay, raiseRate)
```
or
```
pay = pay + GetRaise(pay, raiseRate)
```
the assignment statements add the function's return value to the `pay` variable and then assign the result to either the `newPay` variable or the `pay` variable

Example 3—display the return value
```
raiseLabel.Text = GetRaise(pay, raiseRate).ToString("C2")
```

Figure 8-14 How to invoke a function

Using a Function in the Gillian Company Application

Earlier, in Figure 8-5, you viewed two of the procedures contained in the Gillian Company application: an independent Sub procedure named CalcNet and the calcButton_Click event procedure. The event procedure calls the CalcNet procedure, passing it three variables: the first two (`income` and `expenses`) *by value* and the third (`net`) *by reference*. Figure 8-15 shows how you could code the application using a function rather than an independent Sub procedure.

Here, too, the event procedure calls the CalcNet procedure (function); however, it passes only two variables (`income` and `expenses`) *by value*. When the function has completed its task, the `net = CalcNet(income, expenses)` statement in the event procedure assigns the function's return value to the `net` variable. The modified lines of code are shaded in the figure, which also includes two sample runs of the program.

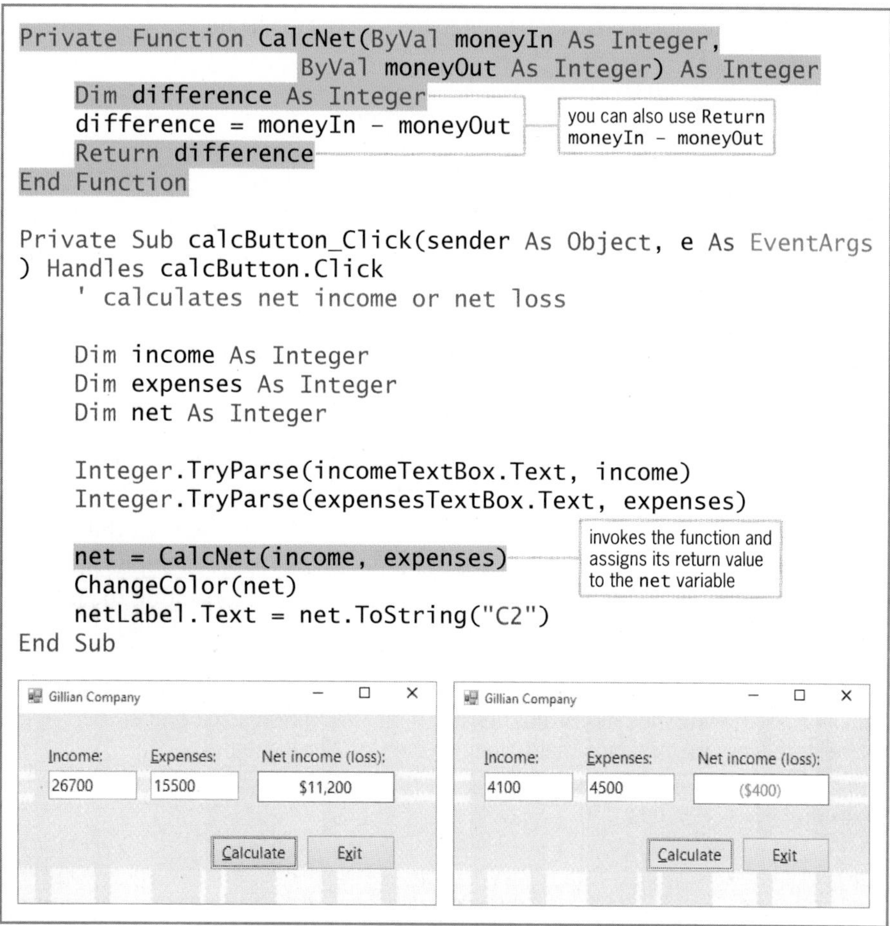

```
Private Function CalcNet(ByVal moneyIn As Integer,
                         ByVal moneyOut As Integer) As Integer
    Dim difference As Integer
    difference = moneyIn - moneyOut
    Return difference
End Function

Private Sub calcButton_Click(sender As Object, e As EventArgs
) Handles calcButton.Click
    ' calculates net income or net loss

    Dim income As Integer
    Dim expenses As Integer
    Dim net As Integer

    Integer.TryParse(incomeTextBox.Text, income)
    Integer.TryParse(expensesTextBox.Text, expenses)

    net = CalcNet(income, expenses)
    ChangeColor(net)
    netLabel.Text = net.ToString("C2")
End Sub
```


Figure 8-15 Gillian Company application using a function

If you want to experiment with this version of the Gillian Company application, open the solution contained in the Try It 5! folder.

We will desk-check the procedures shown in Figure 8-15 using 4100 and 4500 as the income and expenses amounts, respectively. Using these amounts, the company experienced a net loss of 400.

When the user clicks the Calculate button after entering 4100 and 4500 in the appropriate text boxes, the Dim statements in the calcButton_Click procedure create and initialize three Integer variables. The two TryParse methods convert the user's input to the Integer data type, storing the results in the `income` and `expenses` variables. The statement that invokes the CalcNet function is processed next. At this point, the computer temporarily leaves the calcButton_Click procedure to process the code contained in the function, beginning with the function header. The `ByVal` keyword before each parameter indicates that the function is receiving values from the statement that invoked it—in this case, copies of the numbers stored in the `income` and `expenses` variables. As a result, the computer creates the `moneyIn` and `moneyOut` variables listed in the parameterList and stores the numbers 4100 and 4500, respectively, in the variables.

After processing the CalcNet function header, the computer processes the code contained in the function. The Dim statement creates and initializes a variable named `difference`. The next statement subtracts the `moneyOut` variable's value (4500) from the `moneyIn` variable's value (4100) and assigns the result (–400) to the `difference` variable, as shown in Figure 8-16.

The names in black indicate memory locations that belong to the calcButton_Click procedure.
The names in red indicate memory locations that belong to the CalcNet function.

income	expenses	net
~~0~~	~~0~~	0
4100	4500	

moneyIn	moneyOut	difference
4100	4500	~~0~~
		–400

Figure 8-16 Desk-check table before the function's Return statement is processed

The `Return difference` statement returns the contents of the `difference` variable to the statement that invoked the function. That statement is the `net = CalcNet(income, expenses)` statement in the calcButton_Click procedure. The statement assigns the function's return value to the `net` variable. The End Function clause is processed next and ends the CalcNet function. At this point, the computer removes the function's variables from its internal memory. Figure 8-17 shows the desk-check table after the function ends. Notice that the `net` variable now contains the amount of the company's net loss.

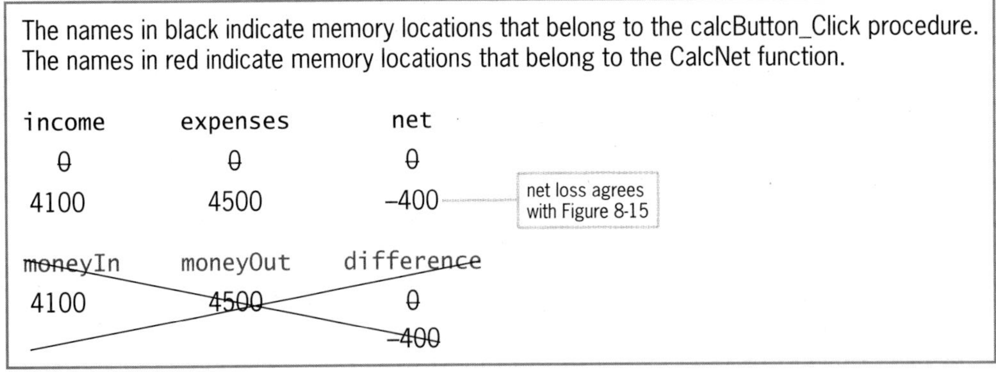

Figure 8-17 Desk-check table after the CalcNet function ends

After the CalcNet function ends, the computer returns to the calcButton_Click procedure to finish processing the event procedure's code. More specifically, it returns to the `ChangeColor(net)` statement, which invokes the ChangeColor procedure, passing it the `net` variable *by value*. The variable's value is less than 0, so the ChangeColor procedure assigns `Color.Red` to the netLabel's ForeColor property. The last statement in the calcButton_Click procedure displays the contents of the `net` variable in the netLabel, as shown earlier in Figure 8-15. Finally, the computer processes the Click event procedure's End Sub clause, which ends the procedure. The computer then removes the procedure's variables (`income`, `expenses`, and `net`) from memory.

The last concepts covered in this chapter are how to convert Object variables to a different data type and how to round numbers.

Converting Object Variables

Every event procedure contains the `sender As Object` code in its procedure header. The code creates a variable named `sender` and assigns the Object data type to it. As you learned in Chapter 3, an Object variable can store any type of data. In this case, the `sender` variable contains a copy of the object that raised the event.

Unlike variables declared using the String and numeric data types, variables declared using the Object data type do not have a set of properties. This is because there are no common attributes for all of the different types of data that can be stored in an Object variable. If you need to access the properties of the object stored in the `sender` variable, you must convert the variable to the appropriate data type. The process of converting a variable from one data type to another is sometimes referred to as **type casting** or, more simply, as **casting**.

You can cast a variable from the Object data type to a different data type by using the **TryCast operator**. The operator's syntax is shown in Figure 8-18 along with an example of using the operator in the Full Name application's code. Instead of entering the SelectAll method in each text box's Enter event procedure, the code enters the SelectAll method in a Sub procedure named SelectText and then associates the procedure with each text box's Enter event. When a text box receives the focus, the TryCast operator in the assignment statement converts the `sender` argument to the text box whose Enter event was invoked. The statement then assigns the result to the `thisTextBox` variable. The SelectAll method then selects the text box's existing text.

If you want to experiment with the Full Name application, open the solution contained in the Try It 6! folder.

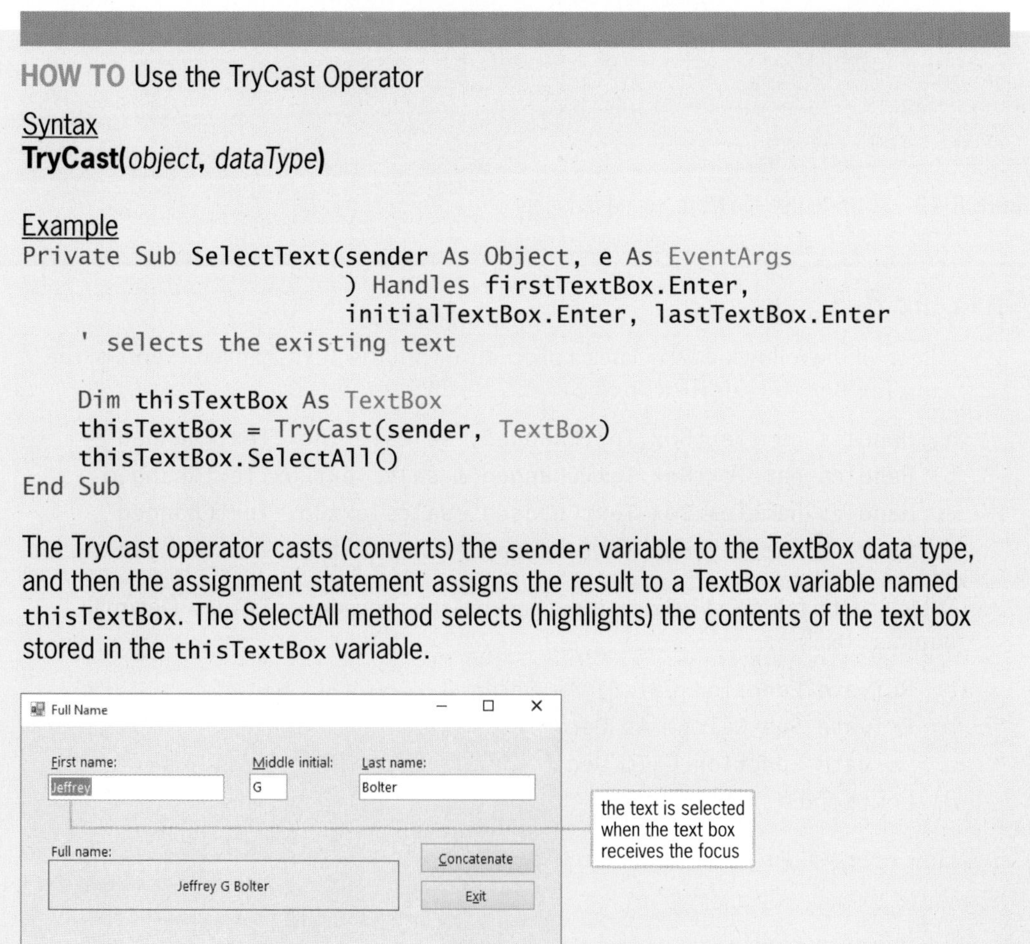

HOW TO Use the TryCast Operator

Syntax
TryCast(*object*, *dataType***)**

Example

```
Private Sub SelectText(sender As Object, e As EventArgs
                       ) Handles firstTextBox.Enter,
                       initialTextBox.Enter, lastTextBox.Enter
    ' selects the existing text

    Dim thisTextBox As TextBox
    thisTextBox = TryCast(sender, TextBox)
    thisTextBox.SelectAll()
End Sub
```

The TryCast operator casts (converts) the `sender` variable to the TextBox data type, and then the assignment statement assigns the result to a TextBox variable named `thisTextBox`. The SelectAll method selects (highlights) the contents of the text box stored in the `thisTextBox` variable.

Figure 8-18 How to use the TryCast operator

Rounding Numbers

You can use the **Math.Round function** to return a number rounded to a specific number of decimal places. The function's syntax and examples are shown in Figure 8-19. In the syntax, *value* is a numeric expression and *digits* (which is optional) is an integer indicating how many places to the right of the decimal point are included in the rounding. If the *digits* argument is omitted, the function returns an integer.

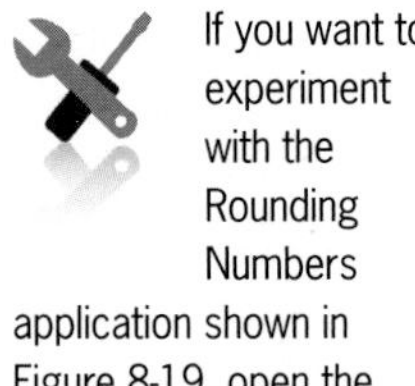

If you want to experiment with the Rounding Numbers application shown in Figure 8-19, open the solution contained in the Try It 7! folder.

HOW TO Use the Math.Round Function

Syntax

Math.Round(*value*[, *digits*]**)**

Examples	Result
`Math.Round(3.235, 2)`	3.24
`Math.Round(6.517, 1)`	6.5
`Math.Round(8.99)`	9

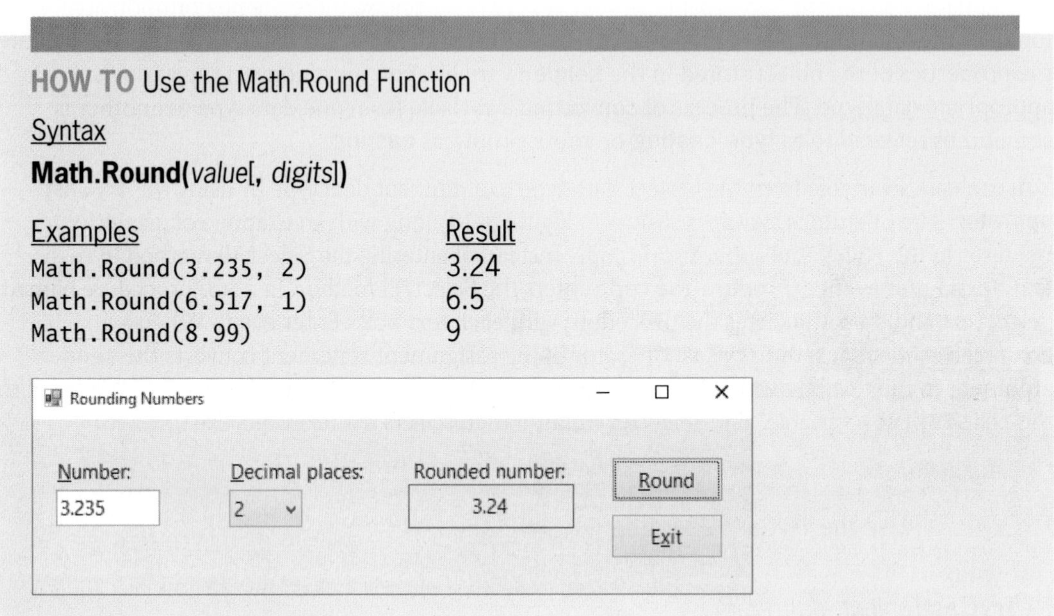

Figure 8-19 How to use the Math.Round function

The answers to Mini-Quiz questions are located in Appendix A. Each question is associated with one or more objectives listed at the beginning of the chapter.

Mini-Quiz 8-3

1. Which of the following associates a procedure with the TextChanged events of the nameTextBox and salesTextBox? (5)
   a. `Handles nameTextBox_TextChanged, salesTextBox_TextChanged`
   b. `Handles nameTextBox.TextChanged & salesTextBox.TextChanged`
   c. `Handles nameTextBox-TextChanged, salesTextBox-TextChanged`
   d. `Handles nameTextBox.TextChanged, salesTextBox.TextChanged`

2. Which of the following headers indicates that the procedure returns a Decimal number? (6, 7)
   a. `Private Function Calc() As Decimal`
   b. `Private Sub Calc() As Decimal`
   c. `Private Function Calc(Decimal)`
   d. both a and b

3. How many values can a function return? (6, 7)
   a. zero or more values
   b. one or more values
   c. one value only

4. Which of the following converts the `sender` parameter to the Label data type, assigning the result to a Label variable named `currentLabel`? (8)
   a. `TryCast(sender, Label, currentLabel)`
   b. `currentLabel = TryCast(sender, Label)`
   c. `currentLabel = TryCast(Label, sender)`
   d. `sender = TryCast(currentLabel, Label)`
5. Which of the following rounds the contents of the `number` variable to three decimal places? (9)
   a. `Math.Round(number, 3)`
   b. `Math.Round(3, number)`
   c. `Round.Math(number 3)`
   d. `Num.Round(3, number)`

You have completed the concepts section of Chapter 8. The Programming Tutorial section is next.

PROGRAMMING TUTORIAL 1

Coding the Addition Practice Application

In this tutorial, you will code an application that allows the user to enter the answer to a random addition problem (using numbers from 1 to 12) displayed on the screen. The application will verify the user's answer and then display one of two messages (either "Correct!" or "Try again.") in a message box. Figure 8-20 shows the application's TOE chart and MainForm.

Task	**Object**	**Event**
End the application	exitButton	Click
Display an addition problem using numbers from 1 to 12	newButton	Click
1. Determine sum 2. Compare the user's answer to the sum 3. If the user's answer does not match the sum, display "Try again." message 4. If the user's answer matches the sum, display "Correct!" message and a new addition problem using numbers from 1 to 12	checkButton	Click
Select the existing text Allow only numbers and the Backspace key	answerTextBox	Enter KeyPress
Display random integers	firstLabel, secondLabel	None

Figure 8-20 TOE chart and MainForm for the Addition Practice application *(continues)*

(continued)

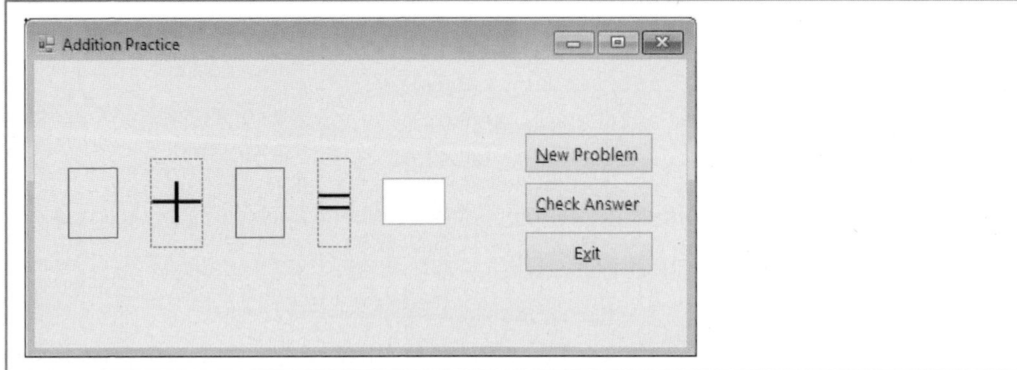

Figure 8-20 TOE chart and MainForm for the Addition Practice application

Coding the Application

According to the application's TOE chart, five procedures need to be coded.

To open the Addition Practice application:

1. Start Visual Studio. Open the **Addition Solution** (**Addition Solution.sln**) file contained in the VbReloaded2015\Chap08\Addition Solution folder. If necessary, open the designer window.
2. Open the Code Editor window. The exitButton_Click, answerTextBox_Enter, and answerTextBox_KeyPress procedures have already been coded for you.
3. In the comments that appear in the General Declarations section, replace <your name> and <current date> with your name and the current date, respectively.

Figure 8-21 shows the pseudocode for the newButton_Click procedure along with the pseudocode for an independent Sub procedure named DisplayAdditionProblem. As the figure indicates, the Click event procedure will call the independent Sub procedure to display two random integers in the firstLabel and secondLabel controls.

```
newButton Click event procedure
1. call the DisplayAdditionProblem procedure to display two random integers
2. send the focus to the answerTextBox

DisplayAdditionProblem procedure
1. assign two random integers from 1 to 12 to variables
2. display the two random integers in firstLabel and secondLabel
```

Figure 8-21 Pseudocode for the newButton_Click and DisplayAdditionProblem procedures

To code the newButton_Click and DisplayAdditionProblem procedures:

1. Click the **blank line** below the Public Class clause, and then enter the DisplayAdditionProblem procedure shown in Figure 8-22.

```
Public Class MainForm
    Private Sub DisplayAdditionProblem()
        ' displays random integers from 1 to 12

        Dim randGen As New Random
        Dim num1 As Integer
        Dim num2 As Integer

        num1 = randGen.Next(1, 13)
        num2 = randGen.Next(1, 13)

        firstLabel.Text = num1.ToString
        secondLabel.Text = num2.ToString
    End Sub
```

enter the DisplayAdditionProblem procedure

Figure 8-22 DisplayAdditionProblem procedure

2. Locate the newButton_Click procedure, and then click the **blank line** above its End Sub clause. Enter the following two lines of code:

   DisplayAdditionProblem()
   answerTextBox.Focus()

3. If necessary, delete the **blank line** above the End Sub clause.
4. Save the solution and then start the application. Click the **New Problem** button. A random addition problem appears, as shown in Figure 8-23.

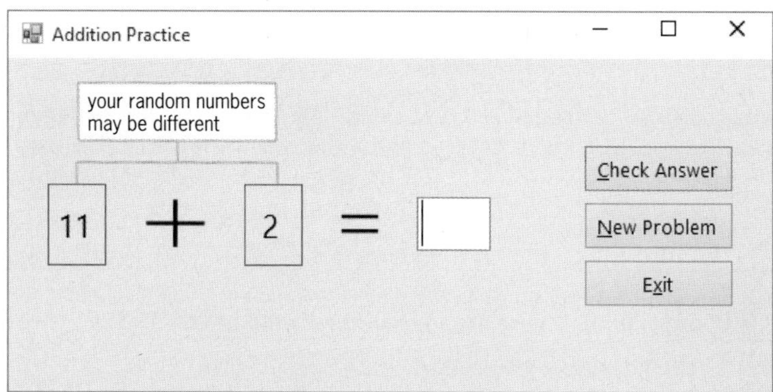

Figure 8-23 Random addition problem displayed in the interface

5. Click the **New Problem** button several times. Each time you do so, a new random addition problem appears in the interface.
6. Click the **Exit** button.

Figure 8-24 shows the pseudocode for the checkButton_Click procedure along with the pseudocode for a function named GetCorrectAnswer. As the figure indicates, the Click event procedure will invoke the function, passing it the two random numbers contained in the current addition problem. The function will return the sum of both random numbers. If the user's answer matches the function's return value, the checkButton_Click procedure will display the "Correct!" message before calling the DisplayAdditionProblem procedure to display a new problem. If the user's answer does not match the sum returned by the function, the checkButton_Click procedure will display the "Try again." message.

```
checkButton Click event procedure
1. assign the random numbers from the firstLabel and secondLabel controls to variables
2. assign the user's answer to a variable
3. correct answer = invoke the GetCorrectAnswer function, passing it the two random numbers
4. if the user's answer matches the correct answer
        display "Correct!" in a message box
        call the DisplayAdditionProblem procedure to display two random integers
   else
        display the "Try again." message in a message box
   end if
5. select the contents of the answerTextBox
6. send the focus to the answerTextBox

GetCorrectAnswer function (receives two random numbers)
return the sum of both random numbers
```

Figure 8-24 Pseudocode for the checkButton_Click procedure and GetCorrectAnswer function

To code the GetCorrectAnswer function and checkButton_Click procedure:

1. Click the **blank line** below the DisplayAdditionProblem procedure's End Sub clause, and then press **Enter** to insert another blank line. Enter the GetCorrectAnswer function shaded in Figure 8-25.

```
    secondLabel.Text = num2.ToString
End Sub

Private Function GetCorrectAnswer(ByVal num1 As Integer, ByVal num2 As Integer) As Integer
    ' calculates and returns the sum

    Return num1 + num2
End Function

Private Sub newButton_Click(sender As Object, e As EventArgs) Handles newButton.Click
```

Figure 8-25 GetCorrectAnswer function

2. Locate the checkButton_Click procedure, and then click the **blank line** above the SelectAll method. The procedure will use two Integer variables to store the random numbers contained in the firstLabel and secondLabel controls. It will also use an Integer variable to store the value returned by the GetCorrectAnswer function and an Integer variable to store the user's answer to the addition problem. Enter the following declaration statements. Press **Enter** twice after typing the last declaration statement.

   Dim firstNum As Integer
   Dim secondNum As Integer
   Dim correctAnswer As Integer
   Dim userAnswer As Integer

3. The first step in the pseudocode assigns the random numbers from the firstLabel and secondLabel controls to variables. Enter the following TryParse methods:

   Integer.TryParse(firstLabel.Text, firstNum)
   Integer.TryParse(secondLabel.Text, secondNum)

4. The second step in the pseudocode assigns the user's answer to a variable. Type the following TryParse method and then press **Enter** twice.

   Integer.TryParse(answerTextBox.Text, userAnswer)

5. The third step in the pseudocode invokes the GetCorrectAnswer function and assigns its return value to the `correctAnswer` variable. The procedure will need to pass the function the random numbers stored in the `firstNum` and `secondNum` variables. Enter the following assignment statement:

   correctAnswer = GetCorrectAnswer(firstNum, secondNum)

6. The fourth step in the pseudocode is a dual-alternative selection structure whose condition determines whether the user's answer matches the correct answer. If the selection structure's condition evaluates to True, its True path displays the "Correct!" message before calling the DisplayAdditionProblem procedure to display another addition problem. Otherwise, its False path displays the "Try again." message. Enter the If...Then...Else statement shown in Figure 8-26.

```
correctAnswer = GetCorrectAnswer(firstNum, secondNum)
If userAnswer = correctAnswer Then
    MessageBox.Show("Correct!", "Addition Practice",
          MessageBoxButtons.OK,
          MessageBoxIcon.Information)
    DisplayAdditionProblem()
Else
    MessageBox.Show("Try again.", "Addition Practice",
        MessageBoxButtons.OK,
        MessageBoxIcon.Information)
End If
```

enter the If...Then... Else statement

Figure 8-26 Selection structure entered in the checkButton_Click procedure

7. The last two steps in the pseudocode have already been coded for you. Save the solution and then start the application. Click the **New Problem** button. In the answerTextBox, type the correct answer to the problem, and then press **Enter**. The "Correct!" message appears in a message box. Drag the message box to the location shown in Figure 8-27.

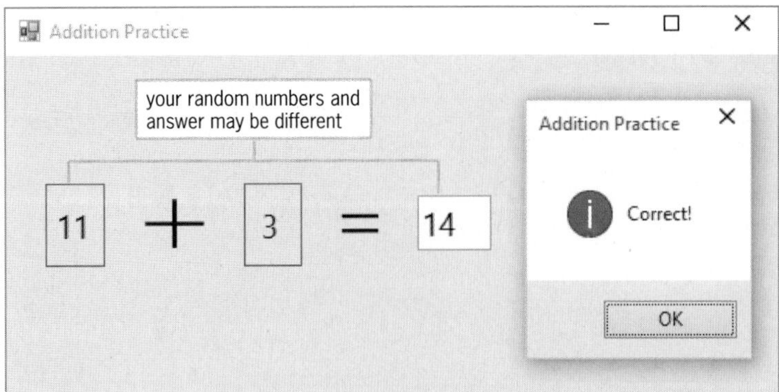

Figure 8-27 Message box that appears when the user's answer is correct

8. Press **Enter** to close the message box. A new addition problem appears in the interface.
9. Type an incorrect answer to the addition problem, and then press **Enter**. The "Try again." message appears in a message box. Press **Enter** to close the message box. The same addition problem still appears in the interface. Type the correct answer and then press **Enter**. Press **Enter** again to close the message box.
10. If you want to change the addition problem that appears on the screen, click the **New Problem** button.
11. Click the **Exit** button to end the application. Close the Code Editor window, and then close the solution. Figure 8-28 shows the application's code.

```
' Project name:         Addition Project
' Project purpose:      Displays random addition problems
'                       using numbers from 1 to 12
' Created/revised by:   <your name> on <current date>

Option Explicit On
Option Strict On
Option Infer Off

Public Class MainForm
   Private Sub DisplayAdditionProblem()
       '  displays random integers from 1 to 12

       Dim randGen As New Random
       Dim num1 As Integer
       Dim num2 As Integer

       num1 = randGen.Next(1, 13)
       num2 = randGen.Next(1, 13)

       firstLabel.Text = num1.ToString
       secondLabel.Text = num2.ToString
   End Sub

   Private Function GetCorrectAnswer(ByVal num1 As Integer,
                             ByVal num2 As Integer) As Integer
       ' calculates and returns the sum

```

Figure 8-28 Code for the Addition Practice application *(continues)*

(continued)

```
        Return num1 + num2
    End Function

    Private Sub newButton_Click(sender As Object, e As EventArgs
    ) Handles newButton.Click
        ' display new addition problem

        DisplayAdditionProblem()
        answerTextBox.Focus()
    End Sub

    Private Sub checkButton_Click(sender As Object, e As EventArgs
    ) Handles checkButton.Click
        ' check user's answer

        Dim firstNum As Integer
        Dim secondNum As Integer
        Dim correctAnswer As Integer
        Dim userAnswer As Integer

        Integer.TryParse(firstLabel.Text, firstNum)
        Integer.TryParse(secondLabel.Text, secondNum)
        Integer.TryParse(answerTextBox.Text, userAnswer)

        correctAnswer = GetCorrectAnswer(firstNum, secondNum)
        If userAnswer = correctAnswer Then
            MessageBox.Show("Correct!", "Addition Practice",
                  MessageBoxButtons.OK,
                  MessageBoxIcon.Information)
            DisplayAdditionProblem()
        Else
            MessageBox.Show("Try again.", "Addition Practice",
                MessageBoxButtons.OK,
                MessageBoxIcon.Information)
        End If
        answerTextBox.SelectAll()
        answerTextBox.Focus()
    End Sub

    Private Sub answerTextBox_Enter(sender As Object,
    e As EventArgs) Handles answerTextBox.Enter
        answerTextBox.SelectAll()
    End Sub

    Private Sub answerTextBox_KeyPress(sender As Object,
    e As KeyPressEventArgs) Handles answerTextBox.KeyPress
        ' allow only numbers and the Backspace key

        If (e.KeyChar < "0" OrElse e.KeyChar > "9") AndAlso
          e.KeyChar <> ControlChars.Back Then
            e.Handled = True
        End If
    End Sub

```

Figure 8-28 Code for the Addition Practice application *(continues)*

(continued)

```
    Private Sub exitButton_Click(sender As Object, e As EventArgs
    ) Handles exitButton.Click
        Me.Close()
    End Sub
End Class
```

Figure 8-28 Code for the Addition Practice application

PROGRAMMING TUTORIAL 2

Coding the Sumner Electric Application

In this tutorial, you will code an application for Sumner Electric. Figure 8-29 shows the application's TOE chart and MainForm. The interface allows the user to enter three items of data: the rate code, previous meter reading, and current meter reading. When the user clicks the Calculate button, the button's Click event procedure should verify that the current meter reading is greater than or equal to the previous meter reading. If it is, the application should calculate and display the number of electrical units used during the month and also the total charge. The total charge is based on the number of units used and the rate code. Residential customers are charged $0.09 per unit, with a minimum charge of $17.65. Commercial customers are charged $0.12 per unit, with a minimum charge of $21.75. If the current meter reading is less than the previous meter reading, the application should display an appropriate message.

Task	Object	Event
End the application	exitButton	Click
Get the rate code	residentialRadioButton, commercialRadioButton	None
Get and display the current meter reading and previous meter reading	currentTextBox, previousTextBox	None
Select the existing text	currentTextBox, previousTextBox	Enter
Allow only numbers and the Backspace key	currentTextBox, previousTextBox	KeyPress
Clear usageLabel and totalLabel	currentTextBox, previousTextBox	TextChanged
	residentialRadioButton, commercialRadioButton	CheckedChanged
1. Determine whether the current meter reading is greater than or equal to the previous meter reading 2. If necessary, calculate the monthly usage and total charge and then display the results in usageLabel and totalLabel, respectively	calcButton	Click

Figure 8-29 TOE chart and MainForm for Sumner Electric *(continues)*

(continued)

3. If necessary, display "The current reading must be greater than or equal to the previous reading." message in a message box		
Display monthly usage (from calcButton)	usageLabel	None
Display total charge (from calcButton)	totalLabel	None

Figure 8-29 TOE chart and MainForm for Sumner Electric

Coding the Application

According to the application's TOE chart, each button's Click event procedure and each radio button's CheckedChanged event procedure need to be coded. The **CheckedChanged event** occurs when the value in the Checked property of either a radio button or a check box changes. Each text box's Enter, KeyPress, and TextChanged event procedures also need to be coded.

To open the Sumner Electric application:

1. Start Visual Studio. Open the **Sumner Solution** (**Sumner Solution.sln**) file contained in the VbReloaded2015\Chap08\Sumner Solution folder. If necessary, open the designer window.
2. Open the Code Editor window. The exitButton_Click procedure has already been coded for you. The KeyPress event procedures for the text boxes have also been coded and are associated with the CancelKeys procedure.
3. In the comments that appear in the General Declarations section, replace <your name> and <current date> with your name and the current date, respectively.

First, you will code the Enter event procedures for both text boxes. The procedures should select the text box's existing text when the text box receives the focus. You can code each text box's Enter event procedure individually. Or, you can enter the code in a Sub procedure and then associate both Enter events with the procedure; this is the method you will use.

To code each text box's Enter event:

1. Open the code template for the currentTextBox's Enter event procedure. In the procedure header, change currentTextBox_Enter to **SelectText**.
2. Change the Handles clause in the procedure header to the following:

   Handles currentTextBox.Enter, previousTextBox.Enter
3. In the blank line below the procedure header, type **' select existing text** and then press **Enter** twice.

4. Now, enter the appropriate Dim statement, TryCast operator, and SelectAll method. Use `thisTextBox` as the name of the TextBox variable.
5. If necessary, delete the **blank line** above the SelectText procedure's End Sub clause.
6. Save the solution and then start the application. Type **12** in the Previous reading box, press **Tab**, and then type **200** in the Current reading box. Press **Tab** four times to move the focus to the Previous reading box; doing this selects the text entered in the box. Press **Tab** again to move the focus to the Current reading box, which selects that box's text.
7. Click the **Exit** button.

Next, you will code the TextChanged event procedures for both text boxes and also the CheckedChanged event procedures for both radio buttons. The procedures should clear the contents of the usageLabel and totalLabel. Here, too, you can code each event procedure individually. Or, you can enter the code in a Sub procedure that is associated with the events.

To code the TextChanged and CheckedChanged event procedures:

1. Open the code template for the currentTextBox's TextChanged event procedure. In the procedure header, change currentTextBox_TextChanged to **ClearLabels**.
2. Now, modify the Handles clause to associate the procedure with the TextChanged events for both text boxes and the CheckedChanged events for both radio buttons.
3. In the blank line below the procedure header, type the following comment and then press **Enter** twice:

   ' clear calculated values
4. Now, enter the code to assign the String.Empty value to the usageLabel and totalLabel controls.
5. If necessary, delete the **blank line** above the ClearLabels procedure's End Sub clause.
6. Save the solution. You won't be able to test the ClearLabels procedure until the calcButton_Click procedure is coded.

Completing the Application's Code

Figure 8-30 shows the pseudocode for the calcButton's Click event procedure. The procedure will use an independent Sub procedure to calculate the total charge for residential customers. It will use a function to calculate the total charge for commercial customers. A Sub procedure and function were chosen, rather than two Sub procedures or two Function procedures, simply to allow you to practice with both types of procedures. The pseudocode for both procedures is included in Figure 8-30.

```
calcButton Click event procedure
1. assign user input (previous reading and current reading) to variables
2. if current reading is greater than or equal to previous reading
       usage = current reading – previous reading

       if the residentialRadioButton is selected
            call the CalcResidentialTotal procedure to calculate the total charge; pass the
            procedure the usage value and a variable in which to store the total charge
       else
```

Figure 8-30 Pseudocode for three procedures in the application *(continues)*

(continued)

```
            total charge = invoke the GetCommercialTotal function; pass the function the usage
            value
        end if
        display the usage and total charge in usageLabel and totalLabel

    else
        display message in a message box
    end if

CalcResidentialTotal procedure (receives the usage value and the address of a variable in which to
store the total charge)
1. declare constants to store the unit charge (0.09) and the minimum fee (17.65)
2. total charge = usage value * unit charge
3. if total charge is less than the minimum fee
        total charge = minimum fee
   end if

GetCommercialTotal function (receives the usage value)
1. declare constants to store the unit charge (0.12) and the minimum fee (21.75)
2. declare a variable to store the total charge
3. total charge = usage value * unit charge
4. if total charge is less than the minimum fee
        total charge = minimum fee
   end if
5. return total charge
```

Figure 8-30 Pseudocode for three procedures in the application

The CalcResidentialTotal Sub procedure will be coded first. According to its pseudocode, the procedure will receive two items of data from the statement that calls it: the usage value and the address of a variable where the total charge can be placed after it has been calculated. The procedure will store the data it receives in two parameters named `units` and `charge`.

To code the CalcResidentialTotal Sub procedure:

1. Scroll to the top of the Code Editor window. Click the **blank line** below the Public Class clause. Enter the appropriate procedure header. The `units` parameter should have the Integer data type. The `charge` parameter should have the Double data type. (Keep in mind that the `units` parameter will be receiving a number, whereas the `charge` parameter will be receiving the address of a variable.)
2. In the blank line below the procedure header, type the following comment and then press **Enter** twice:

   ' calculates the total charge for a residential customer
3. The first step in the procedure's pseudocode declares constants to store the unit charge (0.09) and minimum fee (17.65). Enter the appropriate declaration statements, using the names `UnitCharge` and `MinFee`. Press **Enter** twice after typing the second declaration statement.
4. The second step in the pseudocode calculates the total charge by multiplying the usage value by the unit charge. The usage value is stored in the `units` parameter. Enter an assignment statement that calculates the total charge and assigns it to the `charge` parameter.

5. The final step in the procedure's pseudocode is a single-alternative selection structure whose condition compares the total charge with the minimum fee. If the total charge is less than the minimum fee, the selection structure's True path assigns the minimum fee as the total charge. Enter the appropriate selection structure.
6. If necessary, delete the **blank line** above the End If clause. Save the solution.

The GetCommercialTotal function will be coded next. According to its pseudocode, the function will receive one item of data from the statement that calls it: the usage value. The function will store the usage value in a parameter named `units`.

To code the GetCommercialTotal function:

1. Click the **blank line** below the CalcResidentialTotal procedure's End Sub clause, and then press **Enter**.
2. Enter the appropriate function header. The function will return a Double number. (Do not be concerned about the green squiggle that appears below the End Function clause; it will disappear when you enter the Return statement.)
3. In the blank line below the function header, type the following comment and then press **Enter** twice:

   ' calculates the total charge for a commercial customer
4. The first step in the pseudocode declares constants to store the unit charge (0.12) and minimum fee (21.75). Enter the appropriate declaration statements, using the names `UnitCharge` and `MinFee`.
5. The second step in the pseudocode declares a variable to store the total charge. Type the appropriate declaration statement, using the name `charge`, and then press **Enter** twice.
6. The third step in the pseudocode calculates the total charge by multiplying the usage value by the unit charge. The usage value is stored in the `units` parameter. Enter an assignment statement that calculates the total charge and assigns it to the `charge` variable.
7. The fourth step in the pseudocode is a single-alternative selection structure whose condition compares the total charge with the minimum fee. If the total charge is less than the minimum fee, the selection structure's True path assigns the minimum fee as the total charge. Enter the appropriate selection structure.
8. If necessary, delete the **blank line** above the End If clause.
9. The final step in the procedure's pseudocode returns the total charge. Insert a **blank line** below the procedure's End If clause and then enter the appropriate Return statement.
10. If necessary, delete the **blank line** above the End Function clause.
11. Now, insert a **blank line** below the End Function clause, and then save the solution.

The calcButton's Click event procedure is the last procedure you need to code.

To code and then test the calcButton_Click procedure:

1. Open the code template for the calcButton_Click procedure. Type the following comment and then press **Enter** twice:

   ' displays the monthly usage and total charge

2. The procedure will use three Integer variables to store the previous reading, current reading, and usage amount. It will also use a Double variable to store the total charge. Enter the appropriate declaration statements, using the names `previous`, `current`, `usage`, and `total`. Press **Enter** twice after typing the last declaration statement.

3. The first step in the procedure's pseudocode assigns the user input (previous reading and current reading) to variables. Enter the appropriate TryParse methods. Press **Enter** twice after typing the last TryParse method.

4. The second step in the pseudocode is a dual-alternative selection structure whose condition determines whether the current reading is greater than or equal to the previous reading. If the selection structure's condition evaluates to True, the first instruction in the True path calculates the usage amount by subtracting the previous reading from the current reading. Enter the code shown in Figure 8-31, and then position the insertion point as shown in the figure.

enter these lines of code

```
    If current >= previous Then
        usage = current - previous
        |
    End If
End Sub
```

position the insertion point here

Figure 8-31 Additional code entered in the calcButton_Click procedure

5. The next instruction in the True path is a nested dual-alternative selection structure whose condition determines whether the residentialRadioButton is selected. If the condition evaluates to True, the nested structure's True path calls the CalcResidentialTotal procedure, passing it the `usage` variable *by value* and the `total` variable *by reference*. If the condition evaluates to False, on the other hand, the nested structure's False path invokes the GetCommercialTotal function, passing it the `usage` variable *by value*; it then assigns the function's return value to the `total` variable. Enter the nested selection structure shown in Figure 8-32, and then position the insertion point as shown in the figure.

```
    If current >= previous Then
        usage = current - previous
        If residentialRadioButton.Checked Then
            CalcResidentialTotal(usage, total)
        Else
            total = GetCommercialTotal(usage)
        End If
        |
    End If
End Sub
```

enter the nested selection structure

position the insertion point here

Figure 8-32 Nested selection structure entered in the calcButton_Click procedure

6. The last instruction in the outer selection structure's True path displays the usage and total charge in the usageLabel and totalLabel, respectively. Enter the appropriate assignment statements. Display the usage using the "N0" format. Display the total charge using the "C2" format.

7. According to the procedure's pseudocode, the outer selection structure's False path should display a message in a message box. Enter the additional code shown in Figure 8-33.

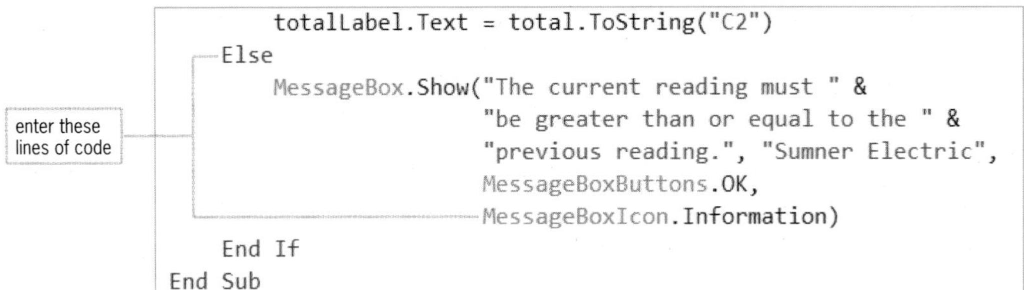


```
        totalLabel.Text = total.ToString("C2")
    Else
        MessageBox.Show("The current reading must " &
                        "be greater than or equal to the " &
                        "previous reading.", "Sumner Electric",
                        MessageBoxButtons.OK,
                        MessageBoxIcon.Information)
    End If
End Sub
```

Figure 8-33 Outer selection structure's False path entered in the calcButton_Click procedure

8. Save the solution and then start the application. Type **7350** in the Previous reading box, and then type **9275** in the Current reading box. Click the **Calculate** button. The monthly usage and total charge appear in the interface, as shown in Figure 8-34.

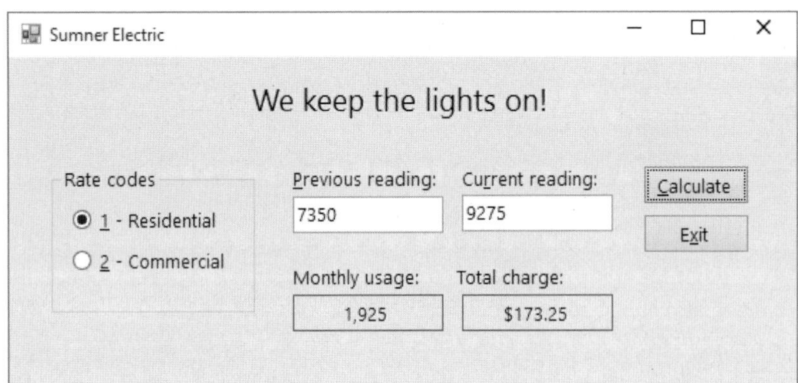

Figure 8-34 Interface showing the monthly usage and total charge

9. Click the **2 - Commercial** radio button. The ClearLabels procedure, which is associated with the radio button's CheckedChanged event, clears the contents of the Monthly usage and Total charge boxes. Click the **Calculate** button. The interface shows that the monthly usage and total charge are 1,925 and $231.00, respectively.
10. Press **Tab** three times to place the focus in the Previous reading box. The SelectText procedure, which is associated with the previousTextBox's Enter event, selects the text box's existing text.
11. Type **4**. The ClearLabels procedure, which is associated with the previousTextBox's TextChanged event, clears the contents of the Monthly usage and Total charge boxes. Click the **Calculate** button.
12. Click the **1 – Residential** radio button. The ClearLabels procedure, which is associated with the radio button's CheckedChanged event, clears the contents of the Monthly usage and Total charge boxes. Click the **Calculate** button.
13. Press **Tab** four times to place the focus in the Current reading box. The SelectText procedure, which is associated with the currentTextBox's Enter event, selects the text box's existing text.
14. Type **2**. The ClearLabels procedure, which is associated with the currentTextBox's TextChanged event, clears the contents of the Monthly usage and Total charge boxes. Click the **Calculate** button.

15. The message “The current reading must be greater than or equal to the previous reading.” appears in a message box. Close the message box.

16. Change the 2 in the Current reading box to **6**, and then click the **Calculate** button. The monthly usage and total charge are 2 and $17.65 (the minimum residential fee), respectively.

17. Click the **2 – Commercial** radio button, and then click the **Calculate** button. The monthly usage and total charge are 2 and $21.75 (the minimum commercial fee), respectively.

18. Click the **Exit** button to end the application. Close the Code Editor window, and then close the solution. Figure 8-35 shows the application’s code.

```
' Project name:         Sumner Project
' Project purpose:      Displays a monthly electric bill
' Created/revised by:   <your name> on <current date>

Option Explicit On
Option Strict On
Option Infer Off

Public Class MainForm
    Private Sub CalcResidentialTotal(ByVal units As Integer,
    ByRef charge As Double)
        ' calculates the total charge for a residential customer

        Const UnitCharge As Double = 0.09
        Const MinFee As Double = 17.65

        charge = units * UnitCharge
        If charge < MinFee Then
            charge = MinFee
        End If
    End Sub

    Private Function GetCommercialTotal(ByVal units As Integer
    ) As Double
        ' calculates the total charge for a commercial customer

        Const UnitCharge As Double = 0.12
        Const MinFee As Double = 21.75
        Dim charge As Double

        charge = units * UnitCharge
        If charge < MinFee Then
            charge = MinFee
        End If
        Return charge
    End Function

    Private Sub CancelKeys(sender As Object, e As KeyPressEventArgs
    ) Handles currentTextBox.KeyPress, previousTextBox.KeyPress
        ' allow only numbers and the Backspace

```

Figure 8-35 Code for the Sumner Electric application *(continues)*

(continued)

```
        If (e.KeyChar < "0" OrElse e.KeyChar > "9") AndAlso
            e.KeyChar <> ControlChars.Back Then
            e.Handled = True
        End If
    End Sub

    Private Sub SelectText(sender As Object, e As EventArgs
    ) Handles currentTextBox.Enter, previousTextBox.Enter
        ' select existing text

        Dim thisTextBox As TextBox
        thisTextBox = TryCast(sender, TextBox)
        thisTextBox.SelectAll()
    End Sub

    Private Sub exitButton_Click(sender As Object, e As EventArgs
    ) Handles exitButton.Click
        Me.Close()
    End Sub

    Private Sub ClearLabels(sender As Object, e As EventArgs
    ) Handles currentTextBox.TextChanged,
      previousTextBox.TextChanged,
      residentialRadioButton.CheckedChanged,
      commercialRadioButton.CheckedChanged
        ' clear calculated values

        usageLabel.Text = String.Empty
        totalLabel.Text = String.Empty
    End Sub

    Private Sub calcButton_Click(sender As Object, e As EventArgs
    ) Handles calcButton.Click
        ' displays the monthly usage and total charge

        Dim previous As Integer
        Dim current As Integer
        Dim usage As Integer
        Dim total As Double

        Integer.TryParse(previousTextBox.Text, previous)
        Integer.TryParse(currentTextBox.Text, current)

        If current >= previous Then
            usage = current - previous
            If residentialRadioButton.Checked Then
                CalcResidentialTotal(usage, total)
            Else
                total = GetCommercialTotal(usage)
            End If
            usageLabel.Text = usage.ToString("N0")
            totalLabel.Text = total.ToString("C2")
        Else
```

Figure 8-35 Code for the Sumner Electric application *(continues)*

(continued)

```
            MessageBox.Show("The current reading must " &
                            "be greater than or equal to the " &
                            "previous reading.", "Sumner Electric",
                            MessageBoxButtons.OK,
                            MessageBoxIcon.Information)
        End If
    End Sub
End Class
```

Figure 8-35 Code for the Sumner Electric application

PROGRAMMING EXAMPLE

Danada Sales Application

Create an application that allows the user to enter the sales amounts made in four sales regions. The application should calculate the total sales and the percentage that each region contributed to the total sales. Use the following names for the solution and project, respectively: Danada Solution and Danada Project. Save the application in the VbReloaded2015\Chap08 folder. Change the form file's name to Main Form.vb. See Figures 8-36 through 8-40.

Task	Object	Event
1. Calculate the total sales 2. Calculate the percentage that each region contributed to the total sales 3. Calculate the total percentage 4. Display each region's percentage in aPercentLabel, bPercentLabel, cPercentLabel, and dPercentLabel 5. Display the total sales and total percentage in totalSalesLabel and totalPercentLabel, respectively	calcButton	Click
End the application	exitButton	Click
Display total sales and total percentage (from calcButton)	totalSalesLabel, totalPercentLabel	None
Display each region's percentage (from calcButton)	aPercentLabel, bPercentLabel, cPercentLabel, dPercentLabel	None
Get and display each region's sales Select the existing text Allow numbers and Backspace key Clear totalSalesLabel, totalPercentLabel, aPercentLabel, bPercentLabel, cPercentLabel, dPercentLabel	aTextBox, bTextBox, cTextBox, dTextBox	None Enter KeyPress TextChanged

Figure 8-36 TOE chart

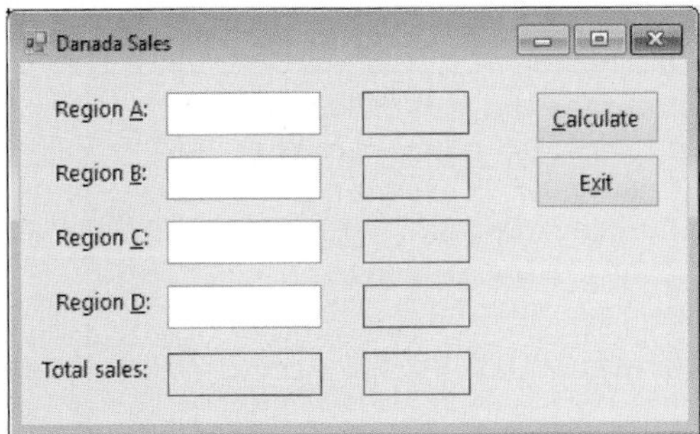

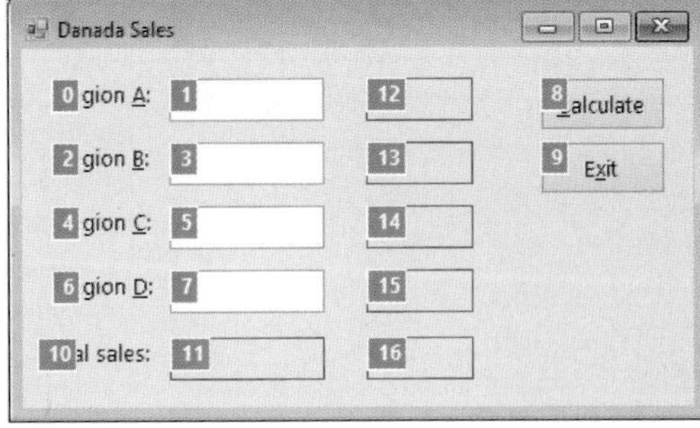

Figure 8-37 MainForm and tab order

Object	Property	Setting
MainForm	Font StartPosition Text	Segoe UI, 10pt CenterScreen Danada Sales
totalSalesLabel, totalPercentLabel, aPercentLabel, bPercentLabel, cPercentLabel, dPercentLabel	AutoSize BorderStyle Text TextAlign	False FixedSingle (empty) MiddleCenter

Figure 8-38 Objects, properties, and settings

<u>exitButton Click event procedure</u>
close the application

<u>aTextBox, bTextBox, cTextBox, dTextBox Enter event procedures</u>
select the existing text

<u>aTextBox, bTextBox, cTextBox, dTextBox KeyPress event procedures</u>
allow only numbers and the Backspace key

<u>aTextBox, bTextBox, cTextBox, dTextBox TextChanged event procedures</u>
clear the contents of totalSalesLabel, totalPercentLabel, aPercentLabel, bPercentLabel, cPercentLabel, and dPercentLabel

<u>calcButton Click event procedure</u>
1. assign each region's sales amounts to variables
2. calculate the total sales by adding together each region's sales amounts
3. calculate each region's contribution percentage
4. calculate the total of each region's contribution percentages
5. display each region's contribution percentage in aPercentLabel, bPercentLabel, cPercentLabel, and dPercentLabel
6. display the total sales in totalSalesLabel
7. display the total contribution percentage in totalPercentLabel

Figure 8-39 Pseudocode

```
' Project name:         Danada Project
' Project purpose:      Displays total sales and the percentage
'                       that each region contributed to the total
' Created/revised by:   <your name> on <current date>

Option Explicit On
Option Strict On
Option Infer Off

Public Class MainForm
   Private Sub SelectText(sender As Object, e As EventArgs
                       ) Handles aTextBox.Enter, bTextBox.Enter,
                        cTextBox.Enter, dTextBox.Enter
       ' select existing text

       Dim thisTextBox As TextBox
       thisTextBox = TryCast(sender, TextBox)
       thisTextBox.SelectAll()
   End Sub

   Private Sub CancelKeys(sender As Object, e As KeyPressEventArgs
                     ) Handles aTextBox.KeyPress, bTextBox.KeyPress,
                       cTextBox.KeyPress, dTextBox.KeyPress
       ' allow only numbers and the Backspace

       If (e.KeyChar < "0" OrElse e.KeyChar > "9") AndAlso
               e.KeyChar <> ControlChars.Back Then
           e.Handled = True
       End If
   End Sub

   Private Sub exitButton_Click(sender As Object, e As EventArgs
   ) Handles exitButton.Click
       Me.Close()
   End Sub

   Private Sub ClearLabels(sender As Object, e As EventArgs
                       ) Handles aTextBox.TextChanged,
                       bTextBox.TextChanged, cTextBox.TextChanged,
                       dTextBox.TextChanged
       ' clear calculated results

       totalSalesLabel.Text = String.Empty
       totalPercentLabel.Text = String.Empty
       aPercentLabel.Text = String.Empty
       bPercentLabel.Text = String.Empty
       cPercentLabel.Text = String.Empty
       dPercentLabel.Text = String.Empty
   End Sub

   Private Sub calcButton_Click(sender As Object, e As EventArgs
   ) Handles calcButton.Click
       ' calculate total sales and region percentages

```

Figure 8-40 Code *(continues)*

(continued)

```
        Dim aSales As Integer
        Dim bSales As Integer
        Dim cSales As Integer
        Dim dSales As Integer
        Dim aPercent As Double
        Dim bPercent As Double
        Dim cPercent As Double
        Dim dPercent As Double
        Dim totalSales As Integer
        Dim totalPercent As Double

        Integer.TryParse(aTextBox.Text, aSales)
        Integer.TryParse(bTextBox.Text, bSales)
        Integer.TryParse(cTextBox.Text, cSales)
        Integer.TryParse(dTextBox.Text, dSales)

        totalSales = aSales + bSales + cSales + dSales
        aPercent = Math.Round(aSales / totalSales, 3)
        bPercent = Math.Round(bSales / totalSales, 3)
        cPercent = Math.Round(cSales / totalSales, 3)
        dPercent = 1 - (aPercent + bPercent + cPercent)
        totalPercent = aPercent + bPercent + cPercent + dPercent

        aPercentLabel.Text = aPercent.ToString("P1")
        bPercentLabel.Text = bPercent.ToString("P1")
        cPercentLabel.Text = cPercent.ToString("P1")
        dPercentLabel.Text = dPercent.ToString("P1")

        totalSalesLabel.Text = totalSales.ToString("C0")
        totalPercentLabel.Text = totalPercent.ToString("P1")
    End Sub
End Class
```

Figure 8-40 Code

Chapter Summary

- An event procedure is a Sub procedure that is associated with one or more objects and events.
- Independent Sub procedures and functions are not associated with any specific object or event. The names of independent Sub procedures and functions typically begin with a verb.
- The difference between a Sub procedure and a function is that a function returns a value, whereas a Sub procedure does not return a value.
- Procedures allow programmers to avoid duplicating code in different parts of a program. They also allow the programmer to concentrate on one small piece of a program at a time. In addition, they allow a team of programmers to work on large and complex programs.

- When calling (invoking) a procedure, the number of arguments listed in the argumentList should agree with the number of parameters listed in the parameterList in the procedure header. Also, the data type and position of each argument in the argumentList should agree with the data type and position of its corresponding parameter in the parameterList.
- You can pass information to a Sub procedure or a function either *by value* or *by reference.* To pass a variable *by value,* you precede the variable's corresponding parameter with the keyword `ByVal`. To pass a variable *by reference,* you precede the variable's corresponding parameter with the keyword `ByRef`. The procedure header indicates whether a variable is being passed *by value* or *by reference.*
- When you pass a variable *by value,* only a copy of the variable's contents is passed. When you pass a variable *by reference,* the variable's address is passed.
- Variables that appear in the parameterList in a procedure header have procedure scope, which means they can be used only by the procedure.
- You can use an event procedure's Handles clause to associate the procedure with more than one object and event.
- You invoke a function by including its name and any arguments in a statement. Usually the statement assigns the function's return value to a variable. However, it also may use the return value in a calculation or display the return value.
- You can use the TryCast operator to convert an Object variable to a different data type.
- You can use the Math.Round function to round a number to a specific number of decimal places. The function's syntax is `Math.Round(`*value*`[, `*digits*`])`, where *value* is a numeric expression and *digits* (which is optional) is an integer indicating how many places to the right of the decimal point are included in the rounding. If the *digits* argument is omitted, the function returns an integer.

Key Terms

Calling statement—the statement used to invoke an independent Sub procedure in a Visual Basic program

Casting—another term for type casting

CheckedChanged event—occurs when the value in the Checked property of either a radio button or a check box changes

Desk-checking—the process of manually walking through your code, using sample data; also called hand-tracing

Function procedure—a procedure that returns a value after performing its assigned task; also called a function

Functions—another term for Function procedures

Hand-tracing—another term for desk-checking

Independent Sub procedure—a procedure that is not associated with any specific object or event and is processed only when invoked (called) from code

Math.Round function—rounds a number to a specific number of decimal places

Passing by reference—refers to the process of passing a variable's address to a procedure so that the value in the variable can be changed

Passing by value—refers to the process of passing a copy of a variable's value to a procedure

Return statement—returns a function's value to the statement that invoked the function

TryCast operator—used to convert an Object variable to a different data type

Type casting—the process of converting a variable from one data type to another; also called casting

Review Questions

Each Review Question is associated with one or more objectives listed at the beginning of the chapter.

1. To determine whether a variable is being passed to a procedure *by value* or *by reference*, you will need to examine _____________. (2, 3)
   a. the calling statement
   b. the receiving procedure's header
   c. the statements entered in the procedure
   d. either a or b
2. Which of the following invokes the CalcArea Sub procedure, passing it two variables *by value*? (1–3)
   a. `CalcArea(length, width)`
   b. `CalcArea(ByVal length, ByVal width)`
   c. `CalcArea ByVal(length, width)`
   d. `CalcArea(length, width) As Double`
3. Which of the following is a valid header for a procedure that receives an integer followed by a number with a decimal place? (1–3)
   a. `Private Sub CalcFee(base As Integer, rate As Number)`
   b. `Private Sub CalcFee(ByRef base As Integer, ByRef rate As Decimal)`
   c. `Private Sub CalcFee(ByVal base As Integer, ByVal rate As Decimal)`
   d. none of the above
4. Which of the following Handles clauses indicates that a procedure should be processed when either the num1TextBox or the num2TextBox receives the focus? (5)
   a. `Handles num1TextBox.Enter OrElse num2TextBox.Enter`
   b. `Handles num1TextBox.Enter AndAlso num2TextBox.Enter`
   c. `Handles num1TextBox_Enter, num2TextBox_Enter`
   d. `Handles num1TextBox.Enter, num2TextBox.Enter`
5. Which of the following is false? (1–3)
   a. The position of the arguments listed in the calling statement should agree with the position of the parameters listed in the receiving procedure's parameterList.
   b. The data type of each argument in the calling statement should match the data type of its corresponding parameter in the receiving procedure's parameterList.

c. The name of each argument in the calling statement should be identical to the name of its corresponding parameter in the receiving procedure's parameterList.

d. When you pass items of data to a procedure *by value*, the procedure stores the value of each item it receives in a separate memory location.

6. Which of the following instructs a function to return the contents of the `grossPay` variable? (7)

   a. `Return grossPay`
   b. `Return grossPay ByVal`
   c. `Return ByVal grossPay`
   d. `Return ByRef grossPay`

7. Which of the following is a valid header for a procedure that receives the value stored in an Integer variable first and the address of a Decimal variable second? (1–3)

   a. `Private Sub CalcFee(ByVal base As Integer, ByAdd rate As Decimal)`

   b. `Private Sub CalcFee(base As Integer, rate As Decimal)`

   c. `Private Sub CalcFee(ByVal base As Integer, ByRef rate As Decimal)`

   d. none of the above

8. Which of the following is false? (2–4)

   a. When you pass a variable *by reference*, the receiving procedure can change its contents.

   b. To pass a variable *by reference* in Visual Basic, you include the keyword `ByRef` before the variable's name in the calling statement.

   c. When you pass a variable *by value*, the receiving procedure creates a procedure-level variable that it uses to store the value passed to it.

   d. At times, a computer memory location may have more than one name.

9. A Sub procedure named CalcEnd is passed four Integer variables named `begin`, `sales`, `purchases`, and `ending`. The procedure should calculate the ending inventory using the beginning inventory, sales, and purchase amounts passed to the procedure. The result should be stored in the `ending` variable. Which of the following procedure headers is correct? (1–3)

   a. `Private Sub CalcEnd(ByVal b As Integer, ByVal s As Integer, ByVal p As Integer, ByRef final As Integer)`

   b. `Private Sub CalcEnd(ByVal b As Integer, ByVal s As Integer, ByVal p As Integer, ByVal final As Integer)`

   c. `Private Sub CalcEnd(ByRef b As Integer, ByRef s As Integer, ByRef p As Integer, ByVal final As Integer)`

   d. `Private Sub CalcEnd(ByRef b As Integer, ByRef s As Integer, ByRef p As Integer, ByRef final As Integer)`

10. Which of the following statements should you use to call the CalcEnd procedure described in Review Question 9? (1–3)
    a. `CalcEnd(begin, sales, purchases, ending)`
    b. `CalcEnd(ByVal begin, ByVal sales, ByVal purchases, ByRef ending)`
    c. `CalcEnd(ByRef begin, ByRef sales, ByRef purchases, ByRef ending)`
    d. `CalcEnd(ByVal begin, ByVal sales, ByVal purchases, ByVal ending)`
11. Which of the following rounds the contents of the `num` variable to two decimal places? (9)
    a. `Math.Round(num, 2)`
    b. `Math.Round(2, num)`
    c. `Round.Math(num, 2)`
    d. `Round.Math(2, num)`

Each Exercise is associated with one or more objectives listed at the beginning of the chapter.

Exercises

Pencil and Paper

INTRODUCTORY

1. Explain the difference between a Sub procedure and a function. (6)

INTRODUCTORY

2. Explain the difference between passing a variable *by value* and passing it *by reference.* (3)

INTRODUCTORY

3. Explain the difference between invoking a Sub procedure and invoking a function. (1, 6, 7)

INTRODUCTORY

4. Write the code for a Sub procedure that receives a Double number passed to it. The procedure should multiply the number by 2 and then display the result in the numLabel. Name the procedure MultiplyByTwo. Then write a statement to invoke the procedure, passing it the number 15. (1–3)

INTRODUCTORY

5. Write the code for a Sub procedure named GetState. The procedure should prompt the user to enter the name of a state. It should store the user's response in its String parameter, which is named `stateName`. Then write a statement to invoke the procedure, passing it the `state` variable. (1–3)

INTRODUCTORY

6. Write the code for a function named GetState. The function should prompt the user to enter the name of a state and then return the user's response. Then write a statement to invoke the function. Display the function's return value in a message box. (2, 3, 7)

INTRODUCTORY

7. Write the code for a Sub procedure that receives three Decimal variables: the first two *by value* and the last one *by reference.* The procedure should multiply the first variable by the second variable and then store the result in the third variable. Name the procedure CalcProduct. (1–3)

INTRODUCTORY

8. Write the code for a function that receives a copy of the value stored in an Integer variable. The procedure should divide the value by 2 and then return the result, which may contain a decimal place. Name the function GetQuotient. Then write an appropriate statement to invoke the function, passing it the `number` variable. Assign the function's return value to the `answer` variable. (2, 3, 7)

9. Write the code for a function that receives a copy of the contents of four Integer variables. The function should calculate the average of the four integers and then return the result, which may contain a decimal place. Name the function GetAverage. Then write a statement to invoke the function, passing it the `num1`, `num2`, `num3`, and `num4` variables. Assign the function's return value to a Double variable named `average`. (2, 3, 7) INTERMEDIATE

10. Write the code for a Sub procedure that receives four Integer variables: the first two *by value* and the last two *by reference*. The procedure should calculate both the sum of and the difference between the two variables passed *by value*, and then store the results in the variables passed *by reference*. When calculating the difference, subtract the contents of the second variable from the contents of the first variable. Name the procedure GetSumAndDiff. Then write an appropriate statement to invoke the procedure, passing it the `first`, `second`, `sum`, and `difference` variables. (1–3) INTERMEDIATE

11. Write the procedure header for a Sub procedure named CalculateTax. The procedure should be invoked when any of the following occurs: the rate1Button's Click event, the rate2Button's Click event, and the salesListBox's SelectedValueChanged event. (5) INTERMEDIATE

12. Write the statement to convert the `sender` parameter to a radio button. Assign the result to a RadioButton variable named `currentRadioButton`. (8) INTERMEDIATE

Computer

13. In this exercise, you experiment with passing variables *by value* and *by reference*. (1–3) MODIFY THIS
    a. Open the Passing Solution (Passing Solution.sln) file contained in the VbReloaded2015\Chap08\Passing Solution folder. Open the Code Editor window and review the existing code. Notice that the `myName` variable is passed *by value* to the GetName procedure. Start the application. Click the Display Name button. When prompted to enter a name, type your name and press Enter. Explain why the displayButton_Click procedure does not display your name in the nameLabel. Stop the application.
    b. Modify the code so that it passes the `myName` variable *by reference* to the GetName procedure. Save the solution and then start the application. Click the Display Name button. When prompted to enter a name, type your name and press Enter. This time, your name appears in the nameLabel. Explain why the displayButton_Click procedure now works correctly. Stop the application and close the solution.

14. If necessary, complete the Addition Practice application from this chapter's Programming Tutorial 1, and then close the solution. Use Windows to make a copy of the Addition Solution folder. Rename the folder Addition Solution-ModifyThis. Open the solution file contained in the Addition Solution-ModifyThis folder. Change the GetCorrectAnswer function to a Sub procedure named CalcCorrectAnswer, and then make the appropriate modifications to the checkButton_Click procedure. Save the solution and then start and test the application. Close the solution. (1–3, 6, 7) MODIFY THIS

15. If necessary, complete the Sumner Electric application from this chapter's Programming Tutorial 2, and then close the solution. Use Windows to make a copy of the Sumner Solution folder. Rename the folder Sumner Solution-ModifyThis. Open the solution file contained in the Sumner Solution-ModifyThis folder. Change the CalcResidentialTotal Sub procedure to a function named GetResidentialTotal. Also change the GetCommercialTotal MODIFY THIS

function to a Sub procedure named CalcCommercialTotal. Make the appropriate modifications to the calcButton_Click procedure. Save the solution and then start and test the application. Close the solution. (1–3, 6, 7)

MODIFY THIS

16. If necessary, complete the Danada Sales application from this chapter's Programming Example, and then close the solution. Use Windows to make a copy of the Danada Solution folder. Rename the folder Danada Solution-ModifyThis. Open the solution file contained in the Danada Solution-ModifyThis folder. Create two functions named GetTotalSales and GetTotalPercent. The GetTotalSales function should return the sum of the four sales amounts passed to it. The GetTotalPercent function should return the sum of the four percentages passed to it. Make the appropriate modifications to the calcButton_Click procedure. Save the solution and then start and test the application. Close the solution. (1–3, 6, 7)

INTRODUCTORY

17. Open the Bonus Calculator Solution (Bonus Calculator Solution.sln) file contained in the VbReloaded2015\Chap08\Bonus Calculator Solution folder. Code the application, using a Sub procedure to both calculate and display a 10% bonus. Also use a Sub procedure named ClearLabel to clear the contents of the bonusLabel when the TextChanged event occurs for either text box. In addition, associate each text box's Enter event with a procedure that selects the contents of the text box. Save the solution and then start and test the application. Close the solution. (1–3, 5, 8)

INTRODUCTORY

18. Open the Gross Pay Solution (Gross Pay Solution.sln) file contained in the VbReloaded2015\Chap08\Gross Pay Solution-Sub folder. The application should display an employee's gross pay. Employees receive time and one-half for the hours worked over 40. Use a Sub procedure to calculate the gross pay. Display the gross pay with a dollar sign and two decimal places. Save the solution and then start and test the application. Close the solution. (1–3)

INTRODUCTORY

19. Open the Gross Pay Solution (Gross Pay Solution.sln) file contained in the VbReloaded2015\Chap08\Gross Pay Solution-Function folder. The application should display an employee's gross pay. Employees receive time and one-half for the hours worked over 40. Use a function to calculate and return the gross pay. Display the gross pay with a dollar sign and two decimal places. Save the solution and then start and test the application. Close the solution. (2, 3, 7)

INTERMEDIATE

20. Open the Circle Solution (Circle Solution.sln) file contained in the VbReloaded2015\Chap08\Circle Solution-Sub folder. The application should display either a circle's area or its diameter, given its radius. Use 3.141593 as the value of pi. Create two independent Sub procedures: one to calculate the area and one to calculate the diameter. Display the result with two decimal places. Save the solution and then start and test the application. Close the solution. (1–3)

INTERMEDIATE

21. Open the Circle Solution (Circle Solution.sln) file contained in the VbReloaded2015\Chap08\Circle Solution-Function folder. The application should display either a circle's area or its diameter, given its radius. Use 3.141593 as the value of pi. Create two functions: one to calculate the area and one to calculate the diameter. Display the result with two decimal places. Save the solution and then start and test the application. Close the solution. (2, 3, 7)

INTERMEDIATE

22. Open the Conversion Solution (Conversion Solution.sln) file contained in the VbReloaded2015\Chap08\Conversion Solution-Sub folder. Code the application so it uses two independent Sub procedures: one to convert a measurement from inches to

centimeters, and one to convert a measurement from centimeters to inches. Display the result with two decimal places. Save the solution and then start and test the application. Close the solution. (1–3)

23. Open the Conversion Solution (Conversion Solution.sln) file contained in the VbReloaded2015\Chap08\Conversion Solution-Function folder. Code the application so it uses two independent functions: one to convert a measurement from inches to centimeters, and one to convert a measurement from centimeters to inches. Display the result with two decimal places. Save the solution and then start and test the application. Close the solution. (1–3)

INTERMEDIATE

24. Open the Translator Solution (Translator Solution.sln) file contained in the VbReloaded2015\Chap08\Translator Solution-Function folder. Code the application so that it uses three functions to translate the English words into French, Spanish, or Italian. (Hint: If the Code Editor indicates that a String variable is being passed before it has been assigned a value, assign the String.Empty value to the variable in its Dim statement.) Clear the label when a different radio button is selected. Save the solution and then start and test the application. Close the solution. (2, 3, 7)

INTERMEDIATE

25. Open the Translator Solution (Translator Solution.sln) file contained in the VbReloaded2015\Chap08\Translator Solution-Sub folder. Code the application so that it uses three independent Sub procedures to translate the English words into French, Spanish, or Italian. (Hint: If the Code Editor indicates that a String variable is being passed before it has been assigned a value, assign the String.Empty value to the variable in its Dim statement.) Clear the label when a different radio button is selected. Save the solution and then start and test the application. Close the solution. (1–3)

INTERMEDIATE

26. Create an application that displays the subtotal, discount, and total due for concert tickets purchased from Concert-Mania Inc. Use the following names for the solution and project, respectively: Concert Solution and Concert Project. Save the solution in the VbReloaded2015\Chap08 folder. Change the form file's name to Main Form.vb. The company's ticket prices are shown in Figure 8-41. Use a text box to get the number of tickets purchased, and use radio buttons to determine whether the tickets are Standard or VIP tickets. The text box should accept only integers and the Backspace key. Use a function to get the appropriate discount rate. Be sure to clear the calculated results when a change is made to the number of tickets. Also clear the calculated results when the user selects a different radio button. Create the interface and then code the application. Save the solution and then start and test the application. Close the solution. (2, 3, 5, 7)

INTERMEDIATE

Type	Price
Standard	$32
VIP	$75

Number of tickets purchased	Discount
3 or fewer	None
4 or 5	3%
6 or more	10%

Figure 8-41 Ticket information for Exercise 26

ADVANCED

27. If necessary, complete the Sumner Electric application from this chapter's Programming Tutorial 2, and then close the solution. Use Windows to make a copy of the Sumner Solution folder. Rename the folder Sumner Solution-Sub. Open the solution file contained in the Sumner Solution-Sub folder. Replace the CalcResidentialTotal Sub procedure and the GetCommercialTotal function with a Sub procedure named CalcTotal. Modify the calcButton_Click procedure so that it uses the CalcTotal procedure for both residential and commercial customers. Save the solution and then start and test the application. Close the solution. (1–3)

ADVANCED

28. If necessary, complete the Sumner Electric application from this chapter's Programming Tutorial 2, and then close the solution. Use Windows to make a copy of the Sumner Solution folder. Rename the folder Sumner Solution-Function. Open the solution file contained in the Sumner Solution-Function folder. Replace the CalcResidentialTotal Sub procedure and the GetCommercialTotal function with a function named GetTotal. Modify the calcButton_Click procedure so that it uses the GetTotal function for both residential and commercial customers. Save the solution and then start and test the application. Close the solution. (2, 3, 7)

SWAT THE BUGS

29. Open the Debug Solution (Debug Solution.sln) file contained in the VbReloaded2015\Chap08\Debug Solution folder. Open the Code Editor window and review the existing code. Start and then test the application. Locate and then correct any errors. When the application is working correctly, close the solution. (2)

Case Projects

Car Shoppers Inc.

In an effort to boost sales, Car Shoppers Inc. is offering buyers a choice of either a large cash rebate or an extremely low financing rate, much lower than the rate most buyers would pay by financing the car through their local bank. Jake Miller, the manager of Car Shoppers Inc., wants you to create an application that helps buyers decide whether to take the lower financing rate from his dealership or take the rebate and then finance the car through their local bank. (Hint: Use the Financial.Pmt method to calculate the payments.) Use the following names for the solution and project, respectively: Car Solution and Car Project. Save the solution in the VbReloaded2015\Chap08 folder. Change the form file's name to Main Form.vb. You can either create your own interface or create the one shown in Figure 8-42. Be sure to use one or more independent Sub or Function procedures in the application. (1–3, 5–7)

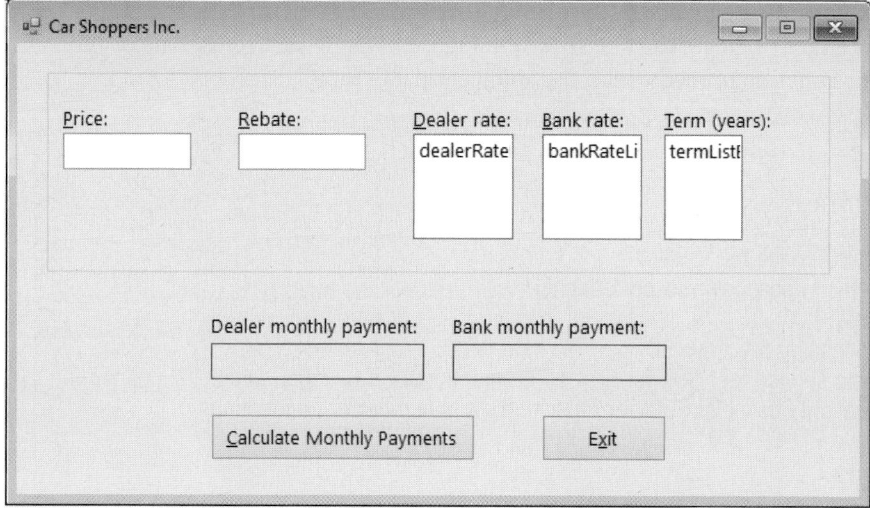

Figure 8-42 Sample interface for the Car Shoppers Inc. application

 Wallpaper Warehouse

Last year, Johanna Liu opened a new wallpaper store named Wallpaper Warehouse. Johanna would like you to create an application that the salesclerks can use to quickly calculate and display the number of single rolls of wallpaper required to cover a room. Use the following names for the solution and project, respectively: Wallpaper Solution and Wallpaper Project. Save the solution in the VbReloaded2015\Chap08 folder. Change the form file's name to Main Form.vb. You can either create your own interface or create the one shown in Figure 8-43, which uses combo boxes to get the user's input. Be sure to use one or more independent Sub or Function procedures in the application. (1–3, 5–7)

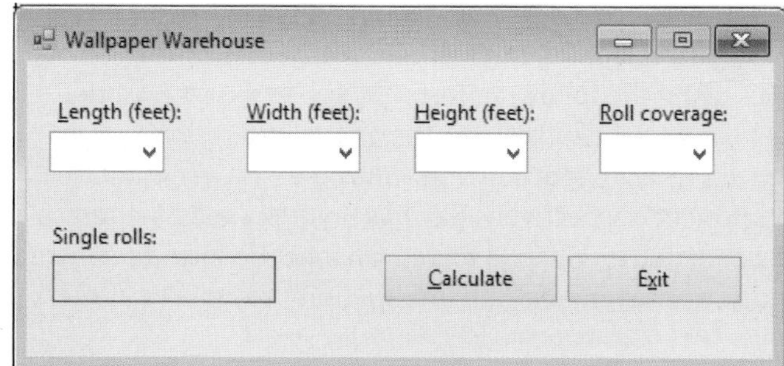

Figure 8-43 Sample interface for the Wallpaper Warehouse application

 Cable Direct

Sharon Barrow, the billing supervisor at Cable Direct (a local cable company), has asked you to create an application that calculates and displays a customer's bill. The cable rates are shown in Figure 8-44. Business customers must have at least one connection. Use the following names for the solution and project, respectively: Cable Solution and Cable Project. Save the solution in the

VbReloaded2015\Chap08 folder. Change the form file's name to Main Form.vb. You can either create your own interface or create the one shown in Figure 8-44. Be sure to use one or more independent Sub or Function procedures in the application. (1–3, 5–7)

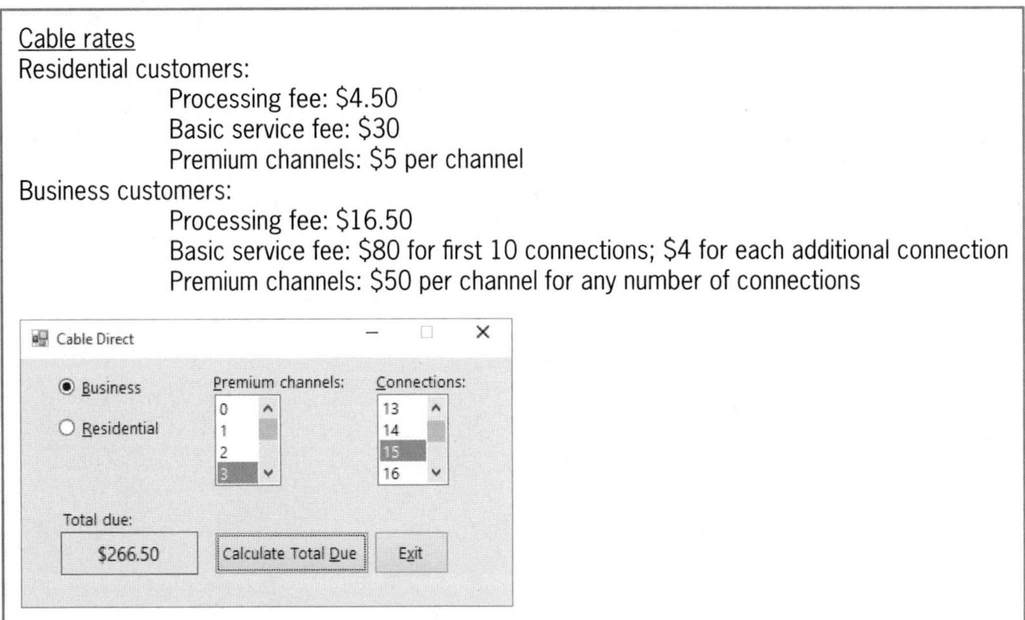

Cable rates
Residential customers:
Processing fee: $4.50
Basic service fee: $30
Premium channels: $5 per channel
Business customers:
Processing fee: $16.50
Basic service fee: $80 for first 10 connections; $4 for each additional connection
Premium channels: $50 per channel for any number of connections
Cable Direct
Business
Residential
Premium channels:
0
1
2
3
Connections:
13
14
15
16
Total due:
$266.50
Calculate Total Due
Exit

Figure 8-44 Cable rates and a sample run of the Cable Direct application

Savings Account

Create an application that allows the user to enter the initial deposit made into a savings account. If no additional deposits or withdrawals are made, how much money will be in the account at the end of one through five years using annual interest rates of 2%, 3%, and 4%? You can calculate the savings account balances using the following formula: $b = p * (1 + r)^n$. In the formula, p is the principal (the amount of the initial deposit), r is the annual interest rate, n is the number of years, and b is the balance in the savings account at the end of the nth year. Use the following names for the solution and project, respectively: Savings Solution and Savings Project. Save the application in the VbReloaded2015\Chap08 folder. Change the form file's name to Main Form.vb. Be sure to use one or more independent Sub or Function procedures in the application. (1–3, 5–7)

Mats-R-Us

Mats-R-Us sells three different types of mats: Standard ($99), Deluxe ($129), and Premium ($179). All of the mats are available in blue, red ($10 extra), and pink ($15 extra). There is also an extra $25 charge if the customer wants the mat to be foldable. Create an application that displays the price of a mat. Use the following names for the solution and project, respectively: Mats Solution and Mats Project. Save the application in the VbReloaded2015\Chap08 folder. Change the form file's name to Main Form.vb. Be sure to use one or more independent Sub or Function procedures in the application. (1–3, 5–7)

Harvey Industries

Khalid Patel, the payroll manager at Harvey Industries, has asked you to create an application that displays an employee's weekly gross pay, Social Security and Medicare (FICA) tax, federal withholding tax (FWT), and net pay. Use the following names for the solution and project, respectively: Harvey Industries Solution and Harvey Industries Project. Save the solution in the VbReloaded2015\Chap08 folder. Change the form file's name to Main Form.vb. Create an appropriate interface. Employees at Harvey Industries are paid every Friday. All employees are paid on an hourly basis, with time and one-half paid for the hours worked over 40. The amount of FICA tax to deduct from an employee's weekly gross pay is calculated by multiplying the gross pay amount by 7.65%. The amount of FWT to deduct from an employee's weekly gross pay is based on the employee's filing status—either single (including head of household) or married—and his or her weekly taxable wages. You calculate the weekly taxable wages by first multiplying the number of withholding allowances by $76.90 (the value of a withholding allowance in 2015), and then subtracting the result from the weekly gross pay. For example, if your weekly gross pay is $400 and you have two withholding allowances, your weekly taxable wages are $246.20. You use the weekly taxable wages, along with the filing status and the appropriate weekly Federal Withholding Tax table, to determine the amount of FWT to withhold. The weekly tax tables for the year 2015 are shown in Figure 8-45. Be sure to use one or more independent Sub or Function procedures in the application. (1–4, 5, 7, 9)

FWT Tables—Weekly Payroll Period

Single person (including head of household)

If the taxable wages are: **Over**	The amount of income tax to withhold is: **But not over**	**Base amount**	**Percentage**	**Of excess over**
	$ 44	0		
$ 44	$ 222	0	10%	$ 44
$ 222	$ 764	$ 17.80 plus	15%	$ 222
$ 764	$1,789	$ 99.10 plus	25%	$ 764
$1,789	$3,685	$ 355.35 plus	28%	$1,789
$3,685	$7,958	$ 886.23 plus	33%	$3,685
$7,958	$7,990	$2,296.32 plus	35%	$7,958
$7,990		$2,307.52 plus	39.6%	$7,990

Married person

If the taxable wages are: **Over**	The amount of income tax to withhold is: **But not over**	**Base amount**	**Percentage**	**Of excess over**
	$ 165	0		
$ 165	$ 520	0	10%	$ 165
$ 520	$1,606	$ 35.50 plus	15%	$ 520
$1,606	$3,073	$ 198.40 plus	25%	$1,606
$3,073	$4,597	$ 565.15 plus	28%	$3,073
$4,597	$8,079	$ 991.87 plus	33%	$4,597
$8,079	$9,105	$2,140.93 plus	35%	$8,079
$9,105		$2,500.03 plus	39.6%	$9,105

Figure 8-45 Weekly FWT tables

CHAPTER 9

Arrays

After studying Chapter 9, you should be able to:

1. Declare and initialize one-dimensional and two-dimensional arrays
2. Store and access data in an array
3. Determine the number of array elements and the highest subscript
4. Traverse an array
5. Code a loop using the For Each...Next statement
6. Compute the total and average of an array's contents
7. Find the highest value in an array
8. Associate a list box with a one-dimensional array
9. Use a one-dimensional array as an accumulator or a counter
10. Sort a one-dimensional array
11. Search an array

Arrays

All of the variables you have used so far have been simple variables. A **simple variable**, also called a **scalar variable**, is one that is unrelated to any other variable in memory. At times, however, you will encounter situations in which some of the variables *are* related to each other. In those cases, it is easier and more efficient to treat the related variables as a group.

You already are familiar with the concept of grouping. The clothes in your closet are probably separated into groups, such as coats, sweaters, shirts, and so on. Grouping your clothes in this manner allows you to easily locate your favorite sweater because you need to look only through the sweater group rather than through the entire closet. You may also have the songs on your MP3 player grouped by either music type or artist. If the songs are grouped by artist, it will take only a few seconds to find all of your Maroon 5 songs and, depending on the number of Maroon 5 songs you own, only a short time after that to locate a particular song.

When you group together related variables, the group is referred to as an array of variables or, more simply, an **array**. You might use an array of 50 variables to store the population of each U.S. state. Or, you might use an array of four variables to store the sales made in each of your company's four sales regions. Storing data in an array increases the efficiency of a program because data can be both stored in and retrieved from the computer's internal memory much faster than it can be written to and read from a file on a disk. In addition, after the data is entered into an array, which typically is done at the beginning of a program, the program can use the data as many times as necessary without having to enter the data again. Your company's sales program, for example, can use the sales amounts stored in an array to calculate the total company sales and the percentage that each region contributed to the total sales. It also can use the sales amounts in the array either to calculate the average sales amount or to simply display the sales made in a specific region. As you will learn in this chapter, the variables in an array can be used just like any other variables. You can assign values to them, use them in calculations, display their contents, and so on.

The most commonly used arrays in business applications are one-dimensional and two-dimensional. You will learn about one-dimensional and two-dimensional arrays in this chapter. Arrays having more than two dimensions are beyond the scope of this book.

At this point, it is important to point out that arrays are one of the more challenging topics for beginning programmers. Therefore, it is important for you to read and study each section in this chapter thoroughly before moving on to the next section. If you still feel overwhelmed by the end of the chapter, try reading the chapter again, paying particular attention to the examples and procedures shown in the figures.

One-Dimensional Arrays

The variables in an array are stored in consecutive locations in the computer's internal memory. Each variable in an array is referred to as an **element**, and each has the same name and data type. You distinguish one element in a **one-dimensional array** from another element in the same array by using a unique number. The unique number, which is always an integer, is called a subscript. The **subscript** indicates the element's position in the array and is assigned by the computer when the array is created in internal memory. The first element in a one-dimensional array is assigned a subscript of 0, the second a subscript of 1, and so on.

You refer to each element in an array by the array's name and the element's subscript, which is specified in a set of parentheses immediately following the array name. Figure 9-1 illustrates a one-dimensional array named `scientists` that contains three elements. You use `scientists(0)`—read "`scientists` sub zero"—to refer to the first element. You use `scientists(1)` to refer to the second element, and you use `scientists(2)` to refer to the third (and last) element. The last subscript in an array is always one number less than the total number of elements in the array; this is because array subscripts in Visual Basic (and in many other programming languages) start at 0.

Figure 9-1 Illustration of the one-dimensional `scientists` array
Image by Diane Zak; created with Reallusion CrazyTalk Animator

Declaring a One-Dimensional Array

Before you can use an array in a program, you must declare (create) it using one of the two syntax versions shown in Figure 9-2. The {Dim | Private | Static} portion in each version indicates that you can select only one of the keywords appearing within the braces. The appropriate keyword depends on whether you are creating a procedure-level array or a class-level array. *ArrayName* is the name of the array, and *dataType* is the type of data the array elements will store. In syntax Version 1, *highestSubscript* is an integer that specifies the highest subscript in the array. Because the first element in a one-dimensional array has a subscript of 0, the array will contain one element more than the number specified in the highestSubscript argument. In other words, an array whose highest subscript is 2 will contain three elements. In syntax Version 2, *initialValues* is a comma-separated list of values you want assigned to the array elements. Also included in Figure 9-2 are examples of using both versions of the syntax.

HOW TO Declare a One-Dimensional Array

Syntax—Version 1
{**Dim** | **Private** | **Static**} *arrayName*(*highestSubscript*) **As** *dataType*

Syntax—Version 2
{**Dim** | **Private** | **Static**} *arrayName*() **As** *dataType* = {*initialValues*}

Example 1
```
Dim states(49) As String
```
declares a 50-element procedure-level array named `states`; each element is automatically initialized using the keyword `Nothing`

Figure 9-2 How to declare a one-dimensional array *(continues)*

(continued)

Example 2
```
Static numbers(4) As Integer
```
declares a static, five-element procedure-level array named `numbers`; each element is automatically initialized to 0

Example 3
```
Dim tvSeries() As String = {"Aquarius",
                            "House of Cards",
                            "Sense8",
                            "Wayward Pines"}
```
declares and initializes a four-element procedure-level array named `tvSeries`

Example 4
```
Private rates() As Double = {1.75, 3.6, 4.3, 5.1, 7.3}
```
declares and initializes a five-element class-level array named `rates` (Note: Like class-level variables, class-level arrays are declared in the form's Declarations section.)

Figure 9-2 How to declare a one-dimensional array

When you use syntax Version 1, the computer automatically initializes each element when the array is created. If the array's data type is String, each element is initialized using the keyword `Nothing`. As you learned in Chapter 3, variables initialized to `Nothing` do not actually contain the word *Nothing*; rather, they contain no data at all. Elements in a numeric array are initialized to the number 0, and elements in a Boolean array are initialized using the Boolean keyword `False`. Date array elements are initialized to 12:00 AM January 1, 0001.

Rather than having the computer use a default value to initialize each array element, you can use syntax Version 2 to specify each element's initial value when the array is declared. Assigning initial values to an array is often referred to as **populating the array**. You list the initial values in the initialValues section of the syntax, using commas to separate the values, and you enclose the list of values in braces ({}).

Notice that syntax Version 2 does not include the highestSubscript argument; instead, an empty set of parentheses follows the array name. The computer automatically calculates the highest subscript based on the number of values listed in the initialValues section. Because the first subscript in a one-dimensional array is the number 0, the highest subscript is always one number less than the number of values listed in the initialValues section. The Dim statement in Example 3 in Figure 9-2, for instance, creates a four-element array with subscripts of 0, 1, 2, and 3. Similarly, the Private statement in Example 4 creates a five-element array with subscripts of 0, 1, 2, 3, and 4. The arrays are initialized as shown in Figure 9-3.

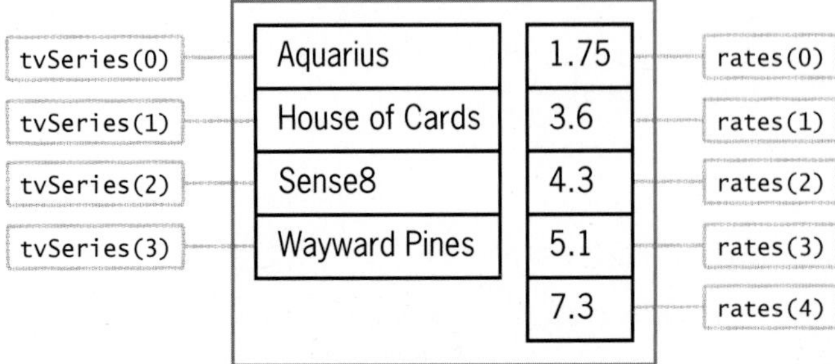

Figure 9-3 Illustration of the `tvSeries` and `rates` arrays

Storing Data in a One-Dimensional Array

After an array is declared, you can use another statement to store a different value in an array element. Examples of such statements include assignment statements and statements that contain the TryParse method. Figure 9-4 shows examples of both types of statements.

HOW TO Store Data in a One-Dimensional Array

Example 1
```
states(0) = "Alabama"
```
assigns the string "Alabama" to the first element in the `states` array

Example 2
```
For x As Integer = 1 To 5
    numbers(x - 1) = x ^ 2
Next x
```
assigns the squares of the numbers from 1 through 5 to the `numbers` array

Example 3
```
Dim subscript As Integer
Do While subscript < 5
    numbers(subscript) = 100
    subscript += 1
Loop
```
assigns the number 100 to each of the five elements in the `numbers` array

Example 4
```
rates(1) *= 1.5
```
multiplies the contents of the second element in the `rates` array by 1.5 and then assigns the result to the element; you can also write this statement as `rates(1) = rates(1) * 1.5`

Example 5
```
Double.TryParse(rateTextBox.Text, rates(2))
```
assigns either the value entered in the rateTextBox (converted to Double) or the number 0 to the third element in the `rates` array

Figure 9-4 How to store data in a one-dimensional array

Determining the Number of Elements in an Array

The number of elements in a one-dimensional array is stored as an integer in the array's **Length property**. Figure 9-5 shows the property's syntax and includes an example of using the property. The Length property is shaded in the example.

HOW TO Determine the Number of Elements in an Array

Syntax
arrayName.**Length**

Example
```
Dim cities(12) As String
Dim numElements As Integer
numElements = cities.Length
```
assigns the number 13 to the `numElements` variable

Figure 9-5 How to determine the number of elements in an array

Determining the Highest Subscript in a One-Dimensional Array

As you learned earlier, the highest subscript in a one-dimensional array is always one number less than the number of array elements. Therefore, one way to determine the highest subscript is by subtracting the number 1 from the array's Length property, like this: `cities.Length - 1`. However, you can also use the array's GetUpperBound method, as shown in Figure 9-6. The **GetUpperBound method**, which is shaded in the example, returns an integer that represents the highest subscript in the specified dimension in the array. When used with a one-dimensional array, the specified dimension (which appears between the parentheses after the method's name) is always 0.

HOW TO Determine the Highest Subscript in a One-Dimensional Array

Syntax
arrayName.**GetUpperBound(0)**

the specified dimension for a one-dimensional array is always 0

Example
```
Dim cities(12) As String
Dim highestSub As Integer
highestSub = cities.GetUpperBound(0)
```
assigns the number 12 to the `highestSub` variable

Figure 9-6 How to determine the highest subscript in a one-dimensional array

The answers to Mini-Quiz questions are located in Appendix A. Each question is associated with one or more objectives listed at the beginning of the chapter.

Mini-Quiz 9-1

1. Which of the following declares a four-element, one-dimensional String array named `letters`? (1)
   a. `Dim letters(3) As String`
   b. `Dim letters() As String = "A", "B", "C", "D"`
   c. `Dim letters(3) As String = {"A", "B", "C", "D"}`
   d. all of the above

2. Which of the following assigns the number of elements contained in a one-dimensional array named `items` to the `numElements` variable? (3)
   a. `numElements = items.Length`
   b. `numElements = items.GetUpperBound(0) + 1`
   c. `numElements = items.GetNumItems(0)`
   d. both a and b

3. Which of the following assigns the string "Scottsburg" to the fifth element in a one-dimensional array named `cities`? (2)
   a. `cities(4) = "Scottsburg"`
   b. `cities(5) = "Scottsburg"`
   c. `cities[4] = "Scottsburg"`
   d. `cities[5] = "Scottsburg"`

Traversing a One-Dimensional Array

At times, you may need to traverse an array, which means to look at each array element, one by one, beginning with the first element and ending with the last element. You traverse an array using a loop. Figure 9-7 shows two examples of loops that traverse the `tvSeries` array, displaying each element's value in the seriesListBox, as shown in the figure.

If you want to experiment with the TV Series application, open the solution contained in the Try It 1! folder.

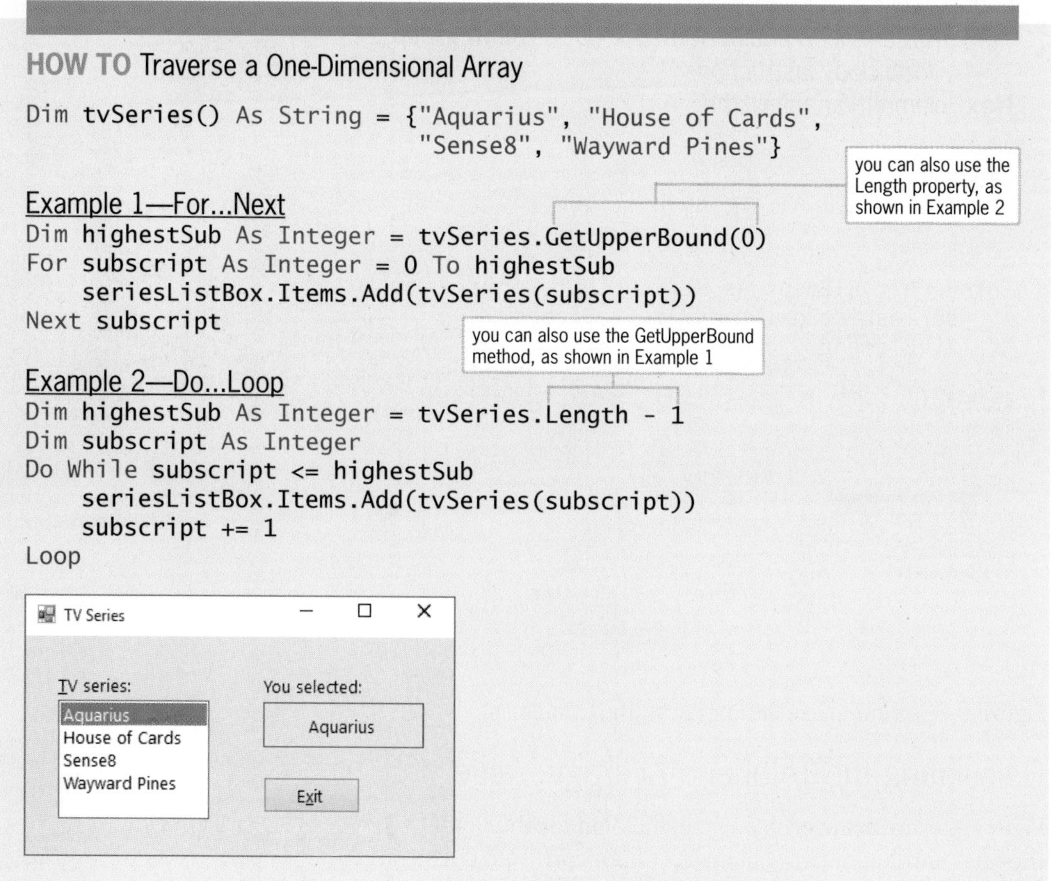

HOW TO Traverse a One-Dimensional Array
Dim tvSeries() As String = {"Aquarius", "House of Cards",
"Sense8", "Wayward Pines"}
Example 1—For...Next
Dim highestSub As Integer = tvSeries.GetUpperBound(0)
For subscript As Integer = 0 To highestSub
seriesListBox.Items.Add(tvSeries(subscript))
Next subscript
you can also use the Length property, as shown in Example 2
Example 2—Do...Loop
Dim highestSub As Integer = tvSeries.Length - 1
Dim subscript As Integer
Do While subscript <= highestSub
seriesListBox.Items.Add(tvSeries(subscript))
subscript += 1
Loop
you can also use the GetUpperBound method, as shown in Example 1
TV Series
TV series:
Aquarius
House of Cards
Sense8
Wayward Pines
You selected:
Aquarius
Exit

Figure 9-7 How to traverse a one-dimensional array

The For Each...Next Statement

In addition to coding loops by using the Do...Loop and For...Next statements, which you learned about in Chapter 8, you can also use the For Each...Next statement. The **For Each... Next statement** provides a convenient way of coding a loop whose instructions you want processed for each element in a group, such as for each element in an array. An advantage of using the For Each...Next statement to process an array is that your code does not need to keep track of the array subscripts or even know the number of array elements. However, unlike the loop instructions in a Do...Loop or For...Next statement, the instructions in a For Each...Next statement can only read the array values; they cannot permanently modify the values.

Figure 9-8 shows the For Each...Next statement's syntax. The *elementVariableName* that appears in the For Each and Next clauses is the name of a variable that the computer can use to keep track of each element in the *group*. The variable's data type is specified in the `As` *dataType* portion of the For Each clause and must be the same as the group's data type. A variable declared in the For Each clause has block scope and is recognized only by the instructions within the For Each...Next loop. The example in Figure 9-8 shows how to write the loops from Figure 9-7 using the For Each...Next statement. (Although, technically, you do not need to specify the *elementVariableName* in the Next clause, doing so is highly recommended because it makes your code more self-documenting.)

If you want to experiment with this version of the TV Series application, open the solution contained in the Try It 2! folder.

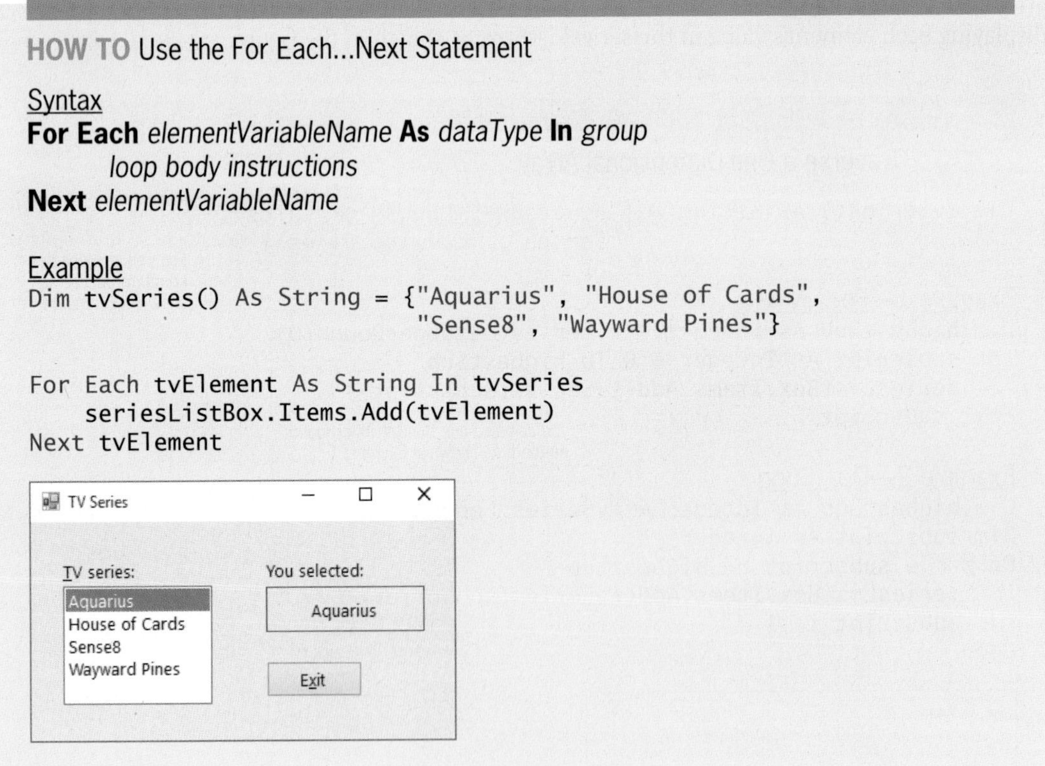

HOW TO Use the For Each...Next Statement

Syntax
For Each *elementVariableName* **As** *dataType* **In** *group*
    loop body instructions
Next *elementVariableName*

Example
```
Dim tvSeries() As String = {"Aquarius", "House of Cards",
                             "Sense8", "Wayward Pines"}

For Each tvElement As String In tvSeries
    seriesListBox.Items.Add(tvElement)
Next tvElement
```


Figure 9-8 How to use the For Each...Next statement

Calculating the Total and Average Values

Figure 9-9 shows the problem specification for the Popcorn Factory application, which displays the total number of two-gallon tins of popcorn sold during a 12-month period and the average number sold each month. It also shows most of the application's code and includes a sample run of the application.

Note: In most applications, the array values are either entered by the user at the keyboard or read from a file. However, for convenience, many of the examples in this chapter fill the array with values in its declaration statement.

Problem specification
Create an application for the Popcorn Factory store. The application should display two items: the total number of two-gallon tins of popcorn sold during a 12-month period and the average number sold each month. Last year, the monthly sales amounts were as follows: 300, 350, 363, 375, 380, 350, 368, 347, 410, 402, 405, and 410. The application should store the monthly amounts in a 12-element one-dimensional array. The total number sold is calculated by accumulating the array values. The average number sold is calculated by dividing the total number sold by the number of array elements. Display the average number with no decimal places.

```
Private sold() As Integer = {300, 350, 363, 375,
                             380, 350, 368, 347,
                             410, 402, 405, 410}
```

class-level array declared in the form's Declarations section

```
Private Sub forNextButton_Click(sender As Object, e As EventArgs
) Handles forNextButton.Click
    ' displays the total and average sold

    Dim highSub As Integer = sold.GetUpperBound(0)
    Dim total As Integer
    Dim average As Double

    ' accumulate numbers sold
    For subscript As Integer = 0 To highSub
        total += sold(subscript)
    Next subscript
    ' calculate average
    average = total / sold.Length

    totalLabel.Text = total.ToString("N0")
    avgLabel.Text = average.ToString("N0")
End Sub

Private Sub doLoopButton_Click(sender As Object, e As EventArgs
) Handles doLoopButton.Click
    ' displays the total and average sold

    Dim highSub As Integer = sold.GetUpperBound(0)
    Dim total As Integer
    Dim average As Double
    Dim subscript As Integer

    ' accumulate numbers sold
    Do While subscript <= highSub
        total += sold(subscript)
        subscript += 1
    Loop
    ' calculate average
    average = total / sold.Length

    totalLabel.Text = total.ToString("N0")
    avgLabel.Text = average.ToString("N0")
End Sub
```

Figure 9-9 Problem specification, code, and sample run for the Popcorn Factory application *(continues)*

If you want to experiment with the Popcorn Factory application, open the solution contained in the Try It 3! folder.

(continued)

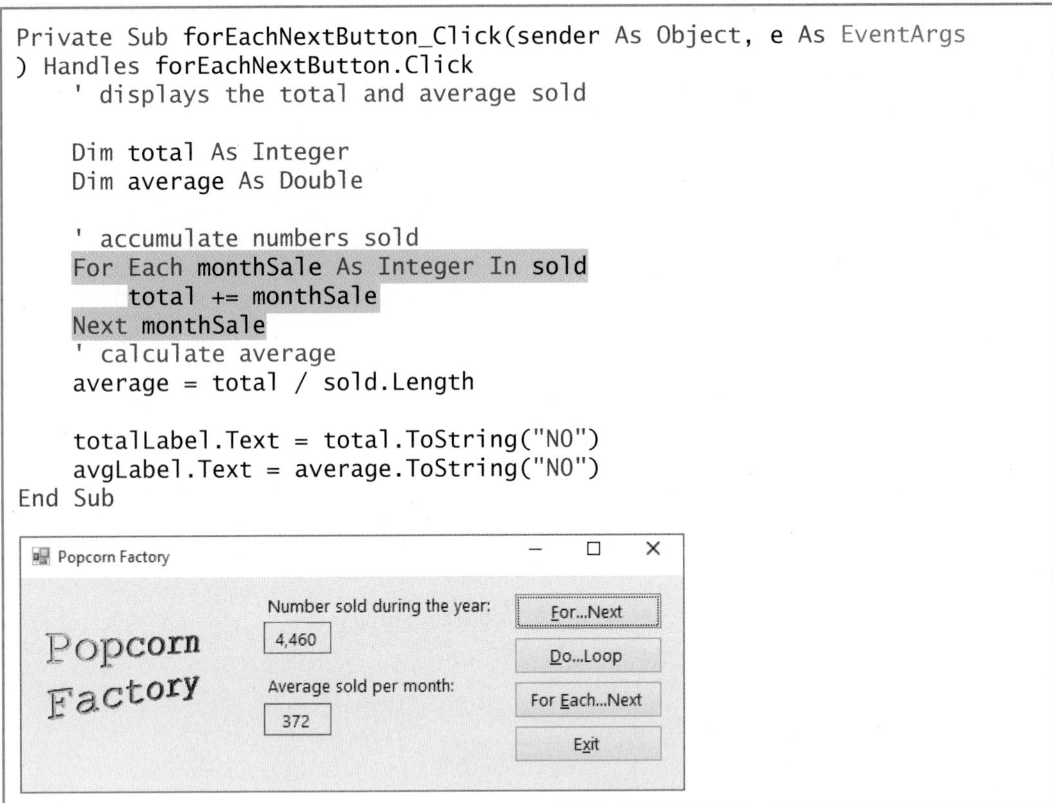

```
Private Sub forEachNextButton_Click(sender As Object, e As EventArgs
) Handles forEachNextButton.Click
    ' displays the total and average sold

    Dim total As Integer
    Dim average As Double

    ' accumulate numbers sold
    For Each monthSale As Integer In sold
        total += monthSale
    Next monthSale
    ' calculate average
    average = total / sold.Length

    totalLabel.Text = total.ToString("N0")
    avgLabel.Text = average.ToString("N0")
End Sub
```


Figure 9-9 Problem specification, code, and sample run for the Popcorn Factory application

The Private statement in the MainForm's Declarations section declares and initializes a class-level Integer array named `sold`. Each button's Click event procedure uses a loop to traverse the 12-element `sold` array, adding each array element's value to the `total` variable. The code pertaining to each loop is shaded in Figure 9-9. Notice that you need to specify the highest array subscript in the For...Next and Do...Loop statements but not in the For Each...Next statement. The For...Next and Do...Loop statements must also keep track of the array subscripts; this task is not necessary in the For Each...Next statement, thereby making it easier to use.

After accumulating the array values, each button's Click event procedure calculates the average number sold by dividing the value stored in the `total` variable by the number of array elements. Each procedure then displays the total and average amounts in the interface.

Finding the Highest Value

Figure 9-10 shows the problem specification for a different Popcorn Factory application. This application displays the highest number of two-gallon tins sold during the year and the number of months in which that sales amount occurred. The figure also shows most of the application's code and includes a sample run of the application.

If you want to experiment with this version of the Popcorn Factory application, open the solution contained in the Try It 4! folder.

Problem specification
Create an application for the Popcorn Factory store. The application should display two items: the highest number of two-gallon tins of popcorn sold during a 12-month period and the number of months in which that sales amount occurred. Last year, the monthly sales amounts were as follows: 300, 350, 363, 375, 380, 350, 368, 347, 410, 402, 405, and 410. The application should store the monthly amounts in a 12-element one-dimensional array. It should then examine each element in the array, looking for the highest amount. A counter variable should be used to keep track of the number of months in which the highest sales amount occurred.

```
Private sold() As Integer = {300, 350, 363, 375,
                             380, 350, 368, 347,
                             410, 402, 405, 410}

Private Sub findButton_Click(sender As Object, e As EventArgs
) Handles findButton.Click
    ' finds the highest number sold and the number of
    ' months in which that sales amount occurred

    Dim lastSub As Integer = sold.GetUpperBound(0)
    Dim highestSold As Integer = sold(0)
    Dim numMonths As Integer = 1

    For subscript As Integer = 1 To lastSub
        If sold(subscript) = highestSold Then
            numMonths += 1
        Else
            If sold(subscript) > highestSold Then
                highestSold = sold(subscript)
                numMonths = 1
            End If
        End If
    Next subscript

    highestLabel.Text = highestSold.ToString
    monthsLabel.Text = numMonths.ToString
End Sub
```

class-level array declared in the form's Declarations section

assigns the first array element's value and the number 1 to variables

searches the second through the last array elements

Popcorn Factory		
Popcorn Factory	Highest number sold: 410	Find Highest
	Number of months: 2	Exit

Figure 9-10 Problem specification, code, and sample run for another version of the Popcorn Factory application

The Private statement declares and initializes a 12-element, class-level Integer array named `sold`. The first Dim statement in the findButton_Click procedure declares an Integer variable named `lastSub` and initializes it to the highest subscript in the `sold` array (11). The second Dim statement declares an Integer variable named `highestSold` and initializes it to the value stored in the first array element. The procedure will use the `highestSold` variable to keep track of the highest value in the array.

The numMonths variable declared in the third Dim statement in Figure 9-10 will be used as a counter to keep track of the number of elements (months) whose value matches the amount stored in the highestSold variable. The numMonths variable is initialized to 1 because, at this point, only one element (the first one) contains the number stored in the highestSold variable.

Notice that the loop in Figure 9-10 searches the second through the last element in the sold array. The first element is not included in the search because its value is already contained in the highestSold variable. The loop body contains an outer selection structure and a nested selection structure. The outer selection structure's condition compares the value stored in the current array element with the value stored in the highestSold variable. If both values are equal, the outer selection structure's True path adds 1 to the numMonths counter; otherwise, the nested selection structure in its False path is processed.

The nested selection structure's condition determines whether the value stored in the current array element is greater than the value stored in the highestSold variable. If it is, the nested structure's True path assigns the current array element's value to the variable. It also assigns the number 1 to the numMonths counter because, at this point, only one element (the current one) contains the value stored in the highestSold variable.

After both selection structures end, the loop proceeds to the next element in the array. When the loop has finished processing, the last two assignment statements in the procedure display the highest number sold (410) and the number of months in which that sales amount occurred (2).

You may be wondering why the sold array in Figure 9-10 is declared as a class-level array in the form's Declarations section rather than as a procedure-level array in the findButton_Click procedure. If you declare the array in the procedure, it will remain in the computer's internal memory only while the procedure is being processed. The array will be removed from memory when the procedure ends. As a result, it will need to be recreated each time the user selects the Find Highest button. Using a procedure-level array is fine when the array contains only a few elements. However, having the computer recreate a large array every time a button is clicked is very inefficient. Since most arrays used in business applications are large, a better approach is to use a class-level array. Like class-level variables, class-level arrays remain in memory until the application ends.

Arrays and Collections

It is not uncommon for programmers to associate the values in an array with the items in a list box. This is because the items in a list box belong to a collection (namely, the Items collection), and collections and arrays have several things in common. First, each is a group of individual objects treated as one unit. Second, each individual object in the group is identified by a unique number, which is called an index when referring to a collection but a subscript when referring to an array. Third, both the first index in a collection and the first subscript in an array are 0. These commonalities allow you to associate the list box items and array elements by their positions within their respective groups. In other words, you can associate the first item in a list box with the first element in an array, the second item with the second element, and so on.

To associate a list box with an array, you first add the appropriate items to the list box. You then store each item's related value in its corresponding position in the array. Figure 9-11 shows the problem specification for the Presidents – Vice Presidents application, which uses a list box name presidentsListBox and a one-dimensional array name vicePresidents. The figure also illustrates the relationship between the list box items and the array elements. In addition, the figure shows most of the application's code and includes a sample run of the application.

If you want to experiment with the Presidents – Vice Presidents application, open the solution contained in the Try It 5! folder.

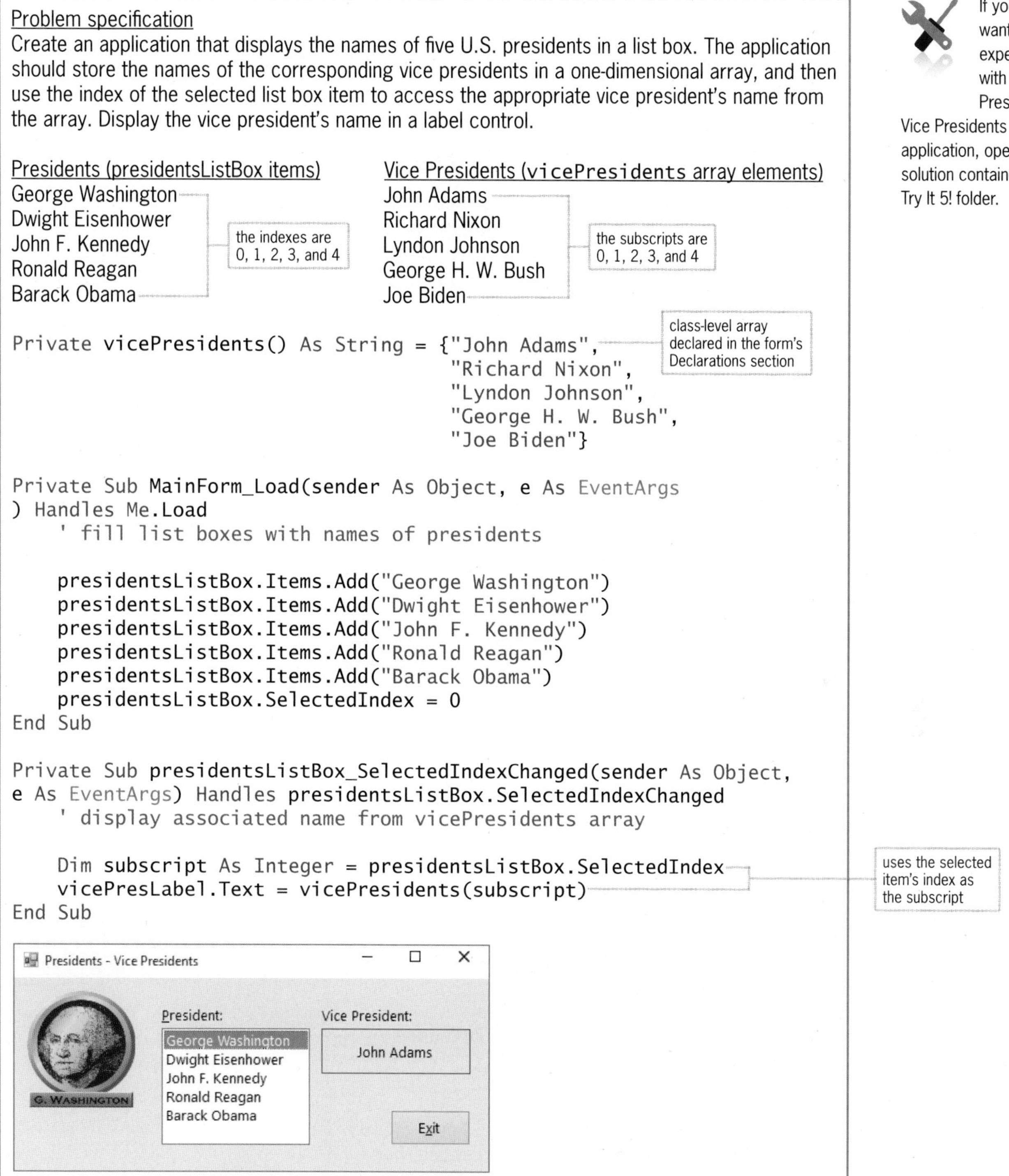


```
Private vicePresidents() As String = {"John Adams",
                                      "Richard Nixon",
                                      "Lyndon Johnson",
                                      "George H. W. Bush",
                                      "Joe Biden"}

Private Sub MainForm_Load(sender As Object, e As EventArgs
) Handles Me.Load
    ' fill list boxes with names of presidents

    presidentsListBox.Items.Add("George Washington")
    presidentsListBox.Items.Add("Dwight Eisenhower")
    presidentsListBox.Items.Add("John F. Kennedy")
    presidentsListBox.Items.Add("Ronald Reagan")
    presidentsListBox.Items.Add("Barack Obama")
    presidentsListBox.SelectedIndex = 0
End Sub

Private Sub presidentsListBox_SelectedIndexChanged(sender As Object,
e As EventArgs) Handles presidentsListBox.SelectedIndexChanged
    ' display associated name from vicePresidents array

    Dim subscript As Integer = presidentsListBox.SelectedIndex
    vicePresLabel.Text = vicePresidents(subscript)
End Sub
```

Figure 9-11 Problem specification, code, and sample run for the Presidents – Vice Presidents application

The MainForm's Load event procedure adds the names of the five presidents to the presidentsListBox and then selects the first item in the list. The Private statement in the form's Declarations section initializes the first element in the `vicePresidents` array to John Adams, which is the name of the vice president associated with the first item in the list box (George Washington). The remaining array elements are initialized to the names of the vice presidents associated with their list box items.

The Dim statement in the list box's SelectedIndexChanged procedure assigns the index of the item selected in the list box to the `subscript` variable. The assignment statement in the procedure uses the value in the `subscript` variable to access the appropriate element in the `vicePresidents` array.

Accumulator and Counter Arrays

One-dimensional arrays are often used to either accumulate or count related values. These arrays are commonly referred to as **accumulator arrays** and **counter arrays**, respectively. The Allen School application, whose problem specification is shown in Figure 9-12, uses an accumulator array. The figure also shows most of the application's code and includes a sample run of the application.

If you want to experiment with the Allen School application, open the solution contained in the Try It 6! folder.

Problem specification
Allen School is having its annual Cookie Fund Raiser event. Students sell boxes of the following five types of cookies: Chunky Chocolate, Macadamia, Peanut Butter, Snickerdoodle, and Sugar. The school principal wants an application that allows him to enter the number of boxes of each cookie type sold by each student. The application's interface should provide a list box for selecting the cookie type and a text box for entering the number of boxes sold. The application should use a five-element one-dimensional array to accumulate the number of boxes sold for each cookie type, and then display that information in label controls in the interface.

```
Private Sub MainForm_Load(sender As Object, e As EventArgs
) Handles Me.Load
    ' fill the list box with values

    cookieListBox.Items.Add("Chunky Chocolate")
    cookieListBox.Items.Add("Macadamia")
    cookieListBox.Items.Add("Peanut Butter")
    cookieListBox.Items.Add("Snickerdoodle")
    cookieListBox.Items.Add("Sugar")
    cookieListBox.SelectedIndex = 0
End Sub

Private Sub addButton_Click(sender As Object, e As EventArgs
) Handles addButton.Click
    ' add amount sold to the appropriate total

    ' declare array and variables
    Static totalBoxesSold(4) As Integer    [static procedure-level array]
    Dim sold As Integer
    Dim subscript As Integer

    Integer.TryParse(soldTextBox.Text, sold)
    subscript = cookieListBox.SelectedIndex

    ' update array value
    totalBoxesSold(subscript) += sold    [uses the selected item's index as the array subscript]
```

Figure 9-12 Problem specification, code, and sample run for the Allen School application *(continues)*

(continued)

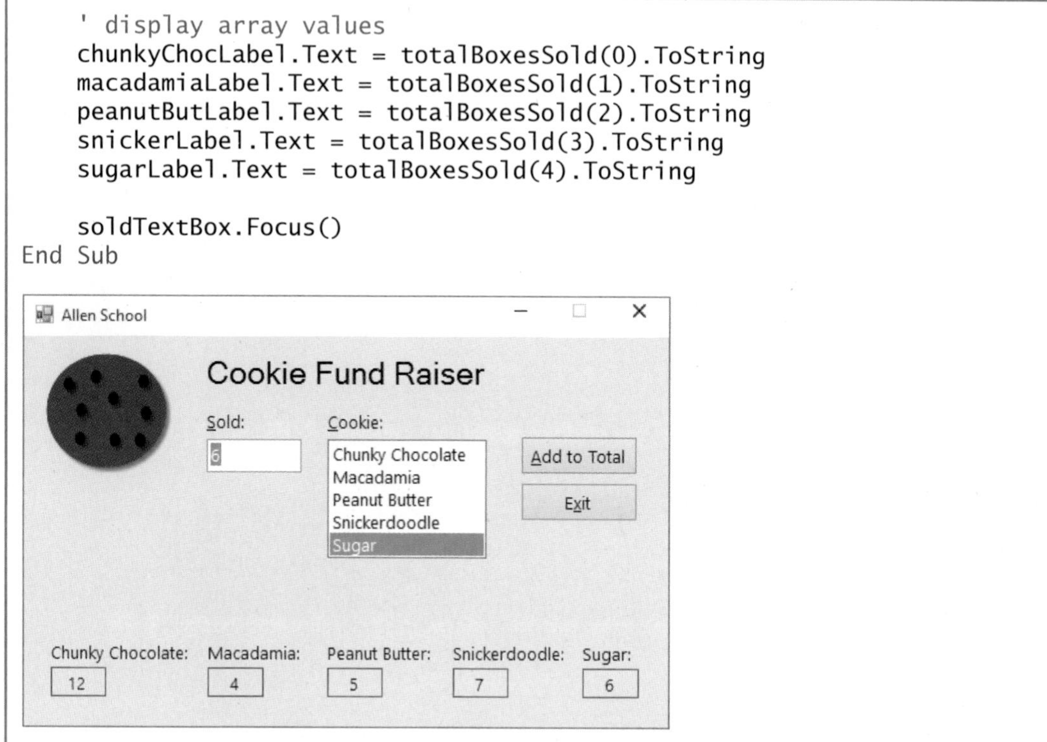

```
    ' display array values
    chunkyChocLabel.Text = totalBoxesSold(0).ToString
    macadamiaLabel.Text = totalBoxesSold(1).ToString
    peanutButLabel.Text = totalBoxesSold(2).ToString
    snickerLabel.Text = totalBoxesSold(3).ToString
    sugarLabel.Text = totalBoxesSold(4).ToString

    soldTextBox.Focus()
End Sub
```


Figure 9-12 Problem specification, code, and sample run for the Allen School application

The MainForm's Load event procedure adds the five cookie types to the cookieListBox and then selects the first type in the list. The Static statement in the addButton_Click procedure declares a procedure-level Integer array named `totalBoxesSold`. The array has five elements, each corresponding to an item listed in the cookieListBox. Each array element will be used to accumulate the sales of its corresponding list box item. Like static variables, which you learned about in Chapter 3, static arrays remain in memory and retain their values until the application ends.

Rather than using a static array, you can use a class-level array.

The two Dim statements in the addButton_Click procedure in Figure 9-12 declare and initialize two Integer variables named `sold` and `subscript`. The TryParse method stores the contents of the soldTextBox, converted to Integer, in the `sold` variable. The first assignment statement in the procedure assigns the index of the item selected in the list box to the `subscript` variable. The second assignment statement uses the number stored in the `subscript` variable to locate the appropriate element in the `totalBoxesSold` array; it then adds the contents of the `sold` variable to the element's contents. The last five assignment statements in the procedure display the contents of the array in the interface. The last statement in the procedure sends the focus to the soldTextBox.

Sorting a One-Dimensional Array

In some applications, you might need to arrange the contents of a one-dimensional array in either ascending or descending order. Arranging data in a specific order is called **sorting**. You can use the **Array.Sort method** to sort the values in a one-dimensional array in ascending order. To sort the values in descending order, you first use the Array.Sort method to sort the values in ascending order, and then you use the **Array.Reverse method** to reverse the values. Figure 9-13 shows the syntax of both methods. In each syntax, *arrayName* is the name of a one-dimensional array.

If you want to experiment with the code shown in Figure 9-13, open the solution contained in the Try It 7! folder.

HOW TO Use the Array.Sort and Array.Reverse Methods

Syntax
Array.Sort(*arrayName***)**
Array.Reverse(*arrayName***)**

Example 1
```
Dim pays() As Double = {9.75, 12.5, 10.75, 8.35}
Array.Sort(pays)
```
sorts the contents of the array in ascending order, as follows: 8.35, 9.75, 10.75, and 12.5

Example 2
```
Dim pays() As Double = {9.75, 12.5, 10.75, 8.35}
Array.Reverse(pays)
```
reverses the contents of the array, placing the values in the following order: 8.35, 10.75, 12.5, and 9.75

Example 3
```
Dim pays() As Double = {9.75, 12.5, 10.75, 8.35}
Array.Sort(pays)
Array.Reverse(pays)
```
sorts the contents of the array in ascending order and then reverses the contents, placing the values in descending order as follows: 12.5, 10.75, 9.75, and 8.35

Figure 9-13 How to use the Array.Sort and Array.Reverse methods

The answers to Mini-Quiz questions are located in Appendix A. Each question is associated with one or more objectives listed at the beginning of the chapter.

Mini-Quiz 9-2

1. Which of the following will total the values contained in a five-element Integer array named scores? (4–6)

   a.
   ```
   For Each scoreElement As Integer In scores
         total += scores(scoreElement)
   Next scoreElement
   ```
   b.
   ```
   For Each scoreElement As Integer In scores
         total += scoreElement
   Next scoreElement
   ```
   c.
   ```
   For Each score As Integer In scores
         total = scores(score) + score
   Next score
   ```
   d.
   ```
   For Each element As Array In scores
         total = total + scores(element)
   Next element
   ```

2. Rewrite the code from Question 1 using a For...Next statement. Use `subscript` as the counter variable's name in the For clause. (3, 4, 6)
3. Rewrite the code from Question 2 using a Do...Loop statement. (3, 4, 6)
4. Write the code to sort the `scores` array in ascending order. (10)

Ch09-One-Dimensional Arrays

Note: You have learned a lot so far in this chapter. You may want to take a break at this point before continuing.

Two-Dimensional Arrays

As you learned earlier, the most commonly used arrays in business applications are one-dimensional and two-dimensional. You can visualize a one-dimensional array as a column of variables in memory. A **two-dimensional array**, on the other hand, resembles a table in that the variables (elements) are in rows and columns. You can determine the number of elements in a two-dimensional array by multiplying the number of its rows by the number of its columns. An array that has four rows and three columns, for example, contains 12 elements.

Each element in a two-dimensional array is identified by a unique combination of two subscripts that the computer assigns to the element when the array is created. The subscripts specify the element's row and column positions in the array. Elements located in the first row in a two-dimensional array are assigned a row subscript of 0, elements in the second row are assigned a row subscript of 1, and so on. Similarly, elements located in the first column in a two-dimensional array are assigned a column subscript of 0, elements in the second column are assigned a column subscript of 1, and so on.

You refer to each element in a two-dimensional array by the array's name and the element's row and column subscripts, with the row subscript listed first and the column subscript listed second. The subscripts are separated by a comma and specified in a set of parentheses immediately following the array name. For example, to refer to the element located in the first row, first column in a two-dimensional array named `songs`, you use `songs(0, 0)`—read "`songs` sub zero comma zero." Similarly, to refer to the element located in the second row, fourth column, you use `songs(1, 3)`. Notice that the subscripts are one number less than the row and column in which the element is located. This is because the row and column subscripts start at 0 rather than at 1. You will find that the last row subscript in a two-dimensional array is always one number less than the number of rows in the array. Likewise, the last column subscript is always one number less than the number of columns in the array. Figure 9-14 illustrates the elements contained in the two-dimensional `songs` array.

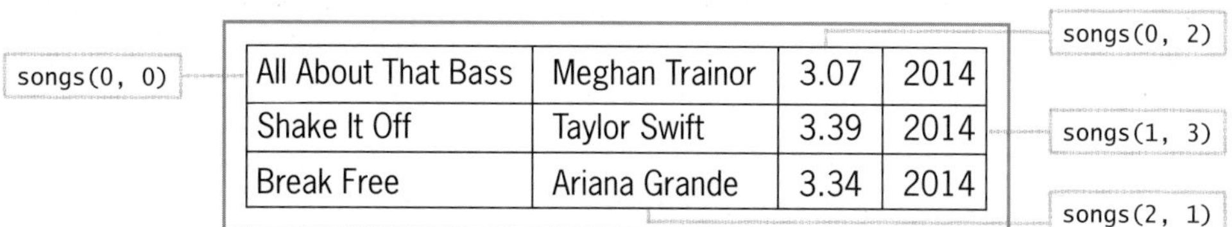

Figure 9-14 Names of some of the elements in the `songs` array

Figure 9-15 shows two versions of the syntax for declaring a two-dimensional array. The figure also includes examples of using both syntax versions. In each version, *dataType* is the type of data the array variables will store.

HOW TO Declare a Two-Dimensional Array

Syntax—Version 1
{**Dim** | **Private** | **Static**} *arrayName*(*highestRowSub*, *highestColumnSub*) **As** *dataType*

Syntax—Version 2
{**Dim** | **Private** | **Static**} *arrayName*(,) **As** *dataType* = {{*initialValues*},...{*initialValues*}}

Example 1
```
Dim states(49, 1) As String
```
declares a 50-row, two-column procedure-level array named `states`; each element is automatically initialized using the keyword `Nothing`

Example 2
```
Static totals(4, 3) As Integer
```
declares a static, five-row, four-column procedure-level array named `totals`; each element is automatically initialized to 0

Example 3
```
Private prices(3, 1) As Double = {{9.99, 8.99},
                                  {6.75, 4.5},
                                  {8.99, 12.99},
                                  {2.75, 15.99}}
```
declares and initializes a four-row, two-column class-level array named `prices`

Example 4
```
Private songs(,) As String =
      {{"All About That Bass", "Meghan Trainor", "3.07", "2014"},
       {"Shake It Off", "Taylor Swift", "3.39", "2014"},
       {"Break Free", "Ariana Grande", "3.34", "2014"}}
```
declares and initializes a three-row, four-column class-level array named `songs` (the array is illustrated in Figure 9-14)

Figure 9-15 How to declare a two-dimensional array

In Version 1's syntax, *highestRowSub* and *highestColumnSub* are integers that specify the highest row and column subscripts, respectively, in the array. When the array is created, it will contain one row more than the number specified in the highestRowSub argument and one column more than the number specified in the highestColumnSub argument. This is because the first row and column subscripts in a two-dimensional array are 0. When you declare a two-dimensional array using Version 1's syntax, the computer automatically initializes each element in the array when the array is created.

You would use Version 2's syntax when you want to specify each variable's initial value. You do this by including a separate *initialValues* section, enclosed in braces, for each row in the array. If the array has six rows, then the statement that declares and initializes the array should have six initialValues sections. Within the individual initialValues sections, you enter one or more values separated by commas. The number of values to enter corresponds to the number of columns in the array. If the array contains 10 columns, then each individual initialValues section should contain 10 values. In addition to the set of braces enclosing each individual initialValues section, Version 2's syntax also requires all of the initialValues sections to be enclosed in a set of braces.

When using Version 2's syntax, be sure to include a comma within the parentheses that follow the array's name. The comma indicates that the array is a two-dimensional array. (Recall that a comma is used to separate the row subscript from the column subscript in a two-dimensional array.)

After a two-dimensional array is declared, you can use another statement to store a different value in an array element. Examples of such statements include assignment statements and statements that contain the TryParse method. Figure 9-16 shows examples of both types of statements, using three of the arrays from Figure 9-15.

HOW TO Store Data in a Two-Dimensional Array

Example 1
```
states(0, 0) = "AL"
states(0, 1) = "Montgomery"
```
assigns the strings "AL" and "Montgomery" to the elements located in the first row in the `states` array; "AL" is assigned to the first column, and "Montgomery" is assigned to the second column

Example 2
```
For row As Integer = 0 To 4
    For column As Integer = 0 To 3
        totals(row, column) += 1
    Next column
Next row
```
adds the number 1 to the contents of each element in the `totals` array

Example 3
```
Dim row As Integer
Dim column As Integer
Do While row <= 3
    column = 0
    Do While column <= 1
        prices(row, column) *= 1.2
        column += 1
    Loop
    row += 1
Loop
```
increases the contents of each element in the `prices` array by 20%; you can also write the calculation statement as `prices(row, column) = prices(row, column) * 1.2`

Example 4
```
prices(2, 1) += 2.25
```
adds 2.25 to the value stored in the third row, second column in the `prices` array and then assigns the result to the element; you can also write this statement as `prices(2, 1) = prices(2, 1) + 2.25`

Example 5
```
Double.TryParse(priceTextBox.Text, prices(0, 0))
```
assigns either the value entered in the priceTextBox (converted to Double) or the number 0 to the element located in the first row, first column in the `prices` array

Figure 9-16 How to store data in a two-dimensional array

Earlier, you learned how to use the GetUpperBound method to determine the highest subscript in a one-dimensional array. You can also use the GetUpperBound method to determine the highest row and column subscripts in a two-dimensional array, as shown in Figure 9-17. The GetUpperBound methods are shaded in the example shown in the figure.

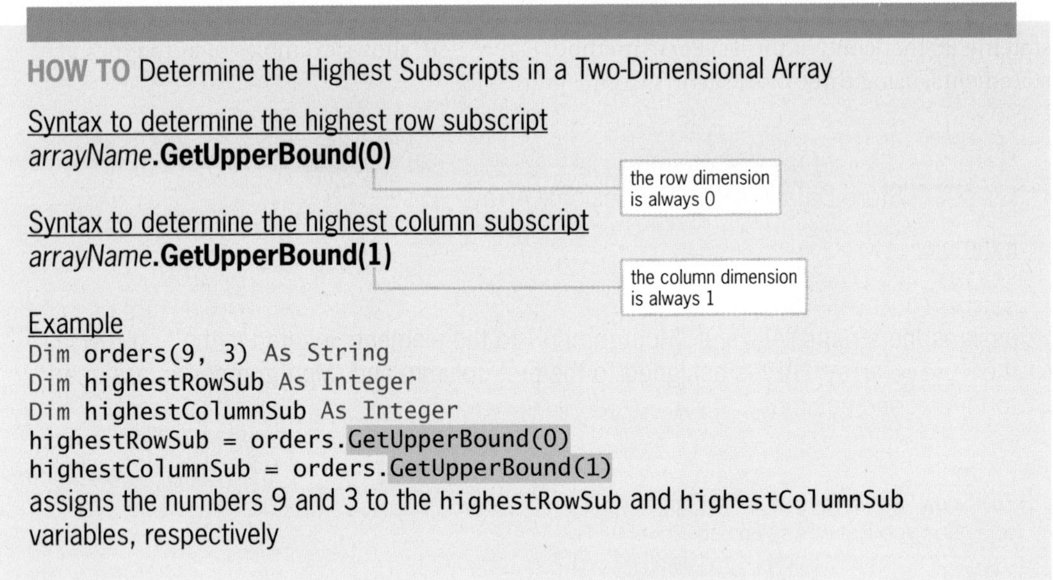

HOW TO Determine the Highest Subscripts in a Two-Dimensional Array

Syntax to determine the highest row subscript
arrayName.**GetUpperBound(0)**

Syntax to determine the highest column subscript
arrayName.**GetUpperBound(1)**

the row dimension is always 0
the column dimension is always 1

Example

```
Dim orders(9, 3) As String
Dim highestRowSub As Integer
Dim highestColumnSub As Integer
highestRowSub = orders.GetUpperBound(0)
highestColumnSub = orders.GetUpperBound(1)
```

assigns the numbers 9 and 3 to the `highestRowSub` and `highestColumnSub` variables, respectively

Figure 9-17 How to determine the highest subscripts in a two-dimensional array

Traversing a Two-Dimensional Array

Recall that you use a loop to traverse a one-dimensional array. To traverse a two-dimensional array, you typically use two loops: an outer loop and a nested loop. One of the loops keeps track of the row subscript, and the other keeps track of the column subscript. You can code the loops using either the For...Next statement or the Do...Loop statement. Rather than using two loops to traverse a two-dimensional array, you can also use one For Each...Next loop. However, recall that the instructions in a For Each...Next loop can only read the array values; they cannot permanently modify the values.

Figure 9-18 shows examples of loops that traverse the `months` array, displaying each element's value in the monthsListBox. Both loops in Example 1 are coded using the For...Next statement. However, either one of the loops could be coded using the Do...Loop statement instead. Or, both loops could be coded using the Do...Loop statement, as shown in Example 2. The loop in Example 3 is coded using the For Each...Next statement.

If you want to experiment with the code shown in Figure 9-18, open the solution contained in the Try It 8! folder.

HOW TO Traverse a Two-Dimensional Array

```
Private months(,) As String = {{"Jan", "31"},
                               {"Feb", "28"},
                               {"Mar", "31"}}
```

Example 1

```
Dim highRow As Integer = months.GetUpperBound(0)
Dim highCol As Integer = months.GetUpperBound(1)
For row As Integer = 0 To highRow
    For col As Integer = 0 To highCol
        monthsListBox.Items.Add(months(row, col))
    Next col
Next row
```

displays the contents of the `months` array in the monthsListBox; the contents are displayed row by row, as shown in Illustration A

Example 2

```
Dim highRow As Integer = months.GetUpperBound(0)
Dim highCol As Integer = months.GetUpperBound(1)
Dim row As Integer
Dim col As Integer
Do While col <= highCol
    row = 0
    Do While row <= highRow
        monthsListBox.Items.Add(months(row, col))
        row += 1
    Loop
    col += 1
Loop
```

displays the contents of the `months` array in the monthsListBox; the contents are displayed column by column, as shown in Illustration B

Example 3

```
For Each monthElement As String In months
    monthsListBox.Items.Add(monthElement)
Next monthElement
```

displays the contents of the `months` array in the monthsListBox; the contents are displayed as shown in Illustration A

Illustration A

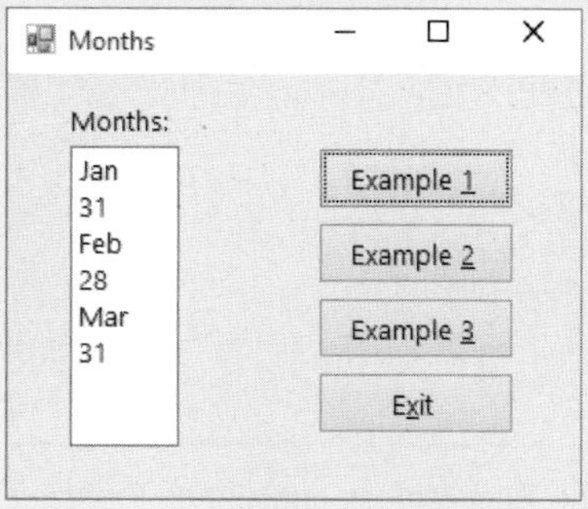

Months
Months:
Jan
31
Feb
28
Mar
31
Example 1
Example 2
Example 3
Exit

Illustration B

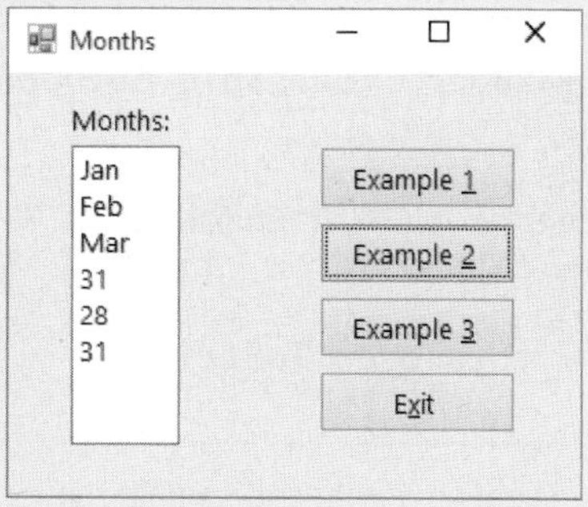

Months
Months:
Jan
Feb
Mar
31
28
31
Example 1
Example 2
Example 3
Exit

Figure 9-18 How to traverse a two-dimensional array

Totaling the Values Stored in a Two-Dimensional Array

Figure 9-19 shows the problem specification for the Tyler Motors application, which displays the total number of new cars sold, the total number of used cars sold, and the total number of cars sold. The figure also shows most of the application's code and includes a sample run of the application.

If you want to experiment with the Tyler Motors application, open the solution contained in the Try It 9! folder.

Problem specification
Tyler Motors sells new and used cars in each of its three dealerships. Create an application that displays the total number of new cars sold, the total number of used cars sold, and the total number of cars sold in the previous month. The numbers sold for the previous month are shown here. Store the numbers sold in a two-dimensional array that has three rows (one for each dealership) and two columns. The first column should contain the number of new cars sold, and the second column should contain the number of used cars sold. Calculate the total number of new cars sold by accumulating the values stored in the first column. Similarly, calculate the total number of used cars sold by accumulating the values stored in the second column. Calculate the total number of cars sold by accumulating the values stored in the entire array.

	New cars sold	Used cars sold
Dealership 1	100	50
Dealership 2	84	35
Dealership 3	87	22

```
Private carsSold(,) As Integer = {{100, 50},
                                  {84, 35},
                                  {87, 22}}
```

class-level array declared in the form's Declarations section

```
Private Sub newButton_Click(sender As Object, e As EventArgs
) Handles newButton.Click
    ' calculates the number of new cars sold

    Dim highRow As Integer = carsSold.GetUpperBound(0)
    Dim totalNew As Integer

    For row As Integer = 0 To highRow
        totalNew += carsSold(row, 0)
    Next row
    newLabel.Text = totalNew.ToString
End Sub
```

accumulates the first column's values

```
Private Sub usedButton_Click(sender As Object, e As EventArgs
) Handles usedButton.Click
    ' calculates the number of used cars sold

    Dim highRow As Integer = carsSold.GetUpperBound(0)
    Dim totalUsed As Integer

    For row As Integer = 0 To highRow
        totalUsed += carsSold(row, 1)
    Next row
    usedLabel.Text = totalUsed.ToString
End Sub
```

accumulates the second column's values

Figure 9-19 Problem specification, code, and sample run for the Tyler Motors application *(continues)*

(continued)

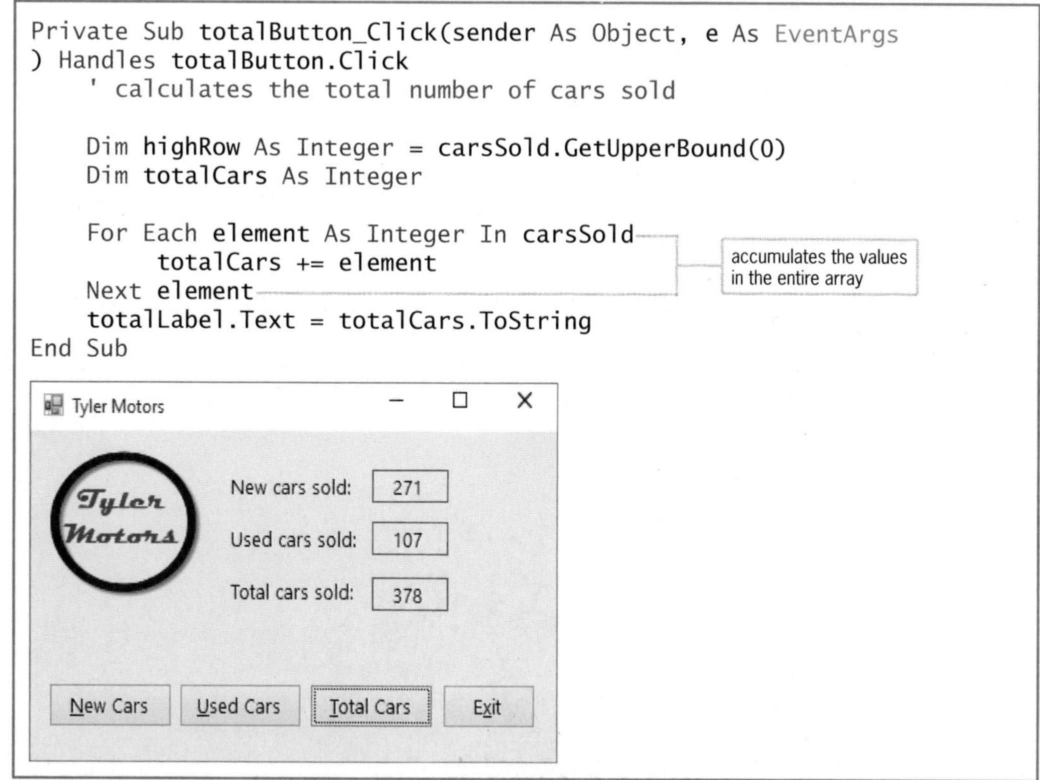

```
Private Sub totalButton_Click(sender As Object, e As EventArgs
) Handles totalButton.Click
    ' calculates the total number of cars sold

    Dim highRow As Integer = carsSold.GetUpperBound(0)
    Dim totalCars As Integer

    For Each element As Integer In carsSold
         totalCars += element
    Next element
    totalLabel.Text = totalCars.ToString
End Sub
```


Figure 9-19 Problem specification, code, and sample run for the Tyler Motors application

The newButton_Click and usedButton_Click procedures use the For...Next statement to accumulate the values in the first and second columns, respectively. The totalButton_Click procedure uses the For Each...Next statement to accumulate all of the array values.

Searching a Two-Dimensional Array

Figure 9-20 shows the problem specification for the O'Reilly Studios application, which displays the amount a customer owes for artwork. The figure also shows most of the application's code and includes a sample run of the application.

Problem specification
O'Reilly Studios sells paintings for local artists. Create an application that allows the studio manager to enter the number of paintings a customer orders. The application should display the total cost of the order. The price per painting depends on the number of paintings ordered, as shown in the chart below. Notice that each price in the chart is associated with a range of values. The minimum value in the first range is 1, and the maximum value is 5. The minimum and maximum values in the second range are 6 and 10, respectively. The third range has only a minimum value, 11. The application should store each range's minimum value and price in a two-dimensional array that has three rows and two columns. The first column will contain the minimum values for the three ranges, entered in descending order: 11, 6, and 1. The second column will contain the prices associated with the minimum values: 75, 90, and 100. The application should search the first column in the array, row by row, looking for the first minimum value that is less than or equal to the quantity ordered. The appropriate price can be found in the same row as that minimum value, but in the second column.

If you want to experiment with the O'Reilly Studios application, open the solution contained in the Try It 10! folder.

Figure 9-20 Problem specification, code, and sample run for the O'Reilly Studios application *(continues)*

(continued)

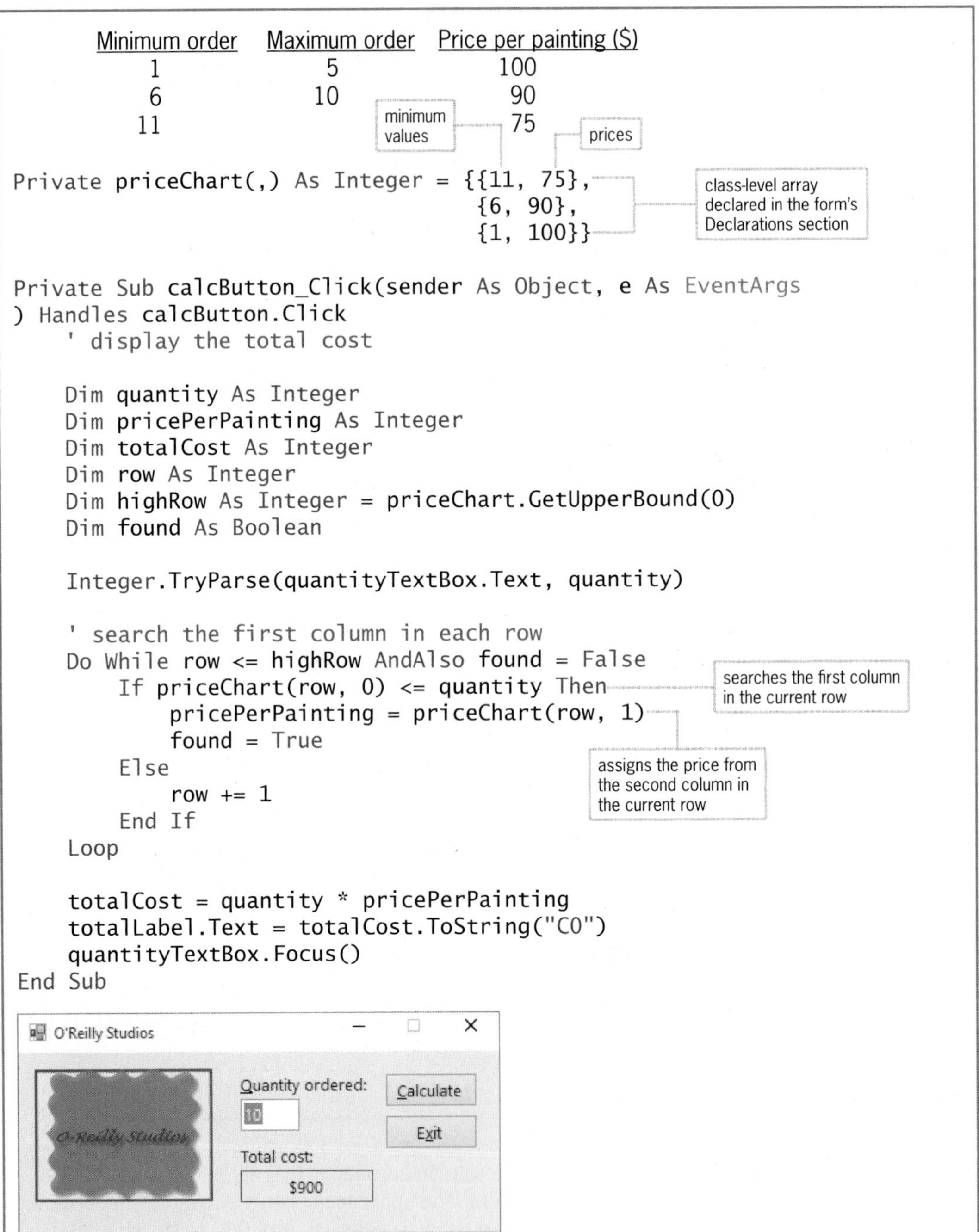

Minimum order	Maximum order	Price per painting ($)
1	5	100
6	10	90
11		75

```
Private priceChart(,) As Integer = {{11, 75},
                                    {6, 90},
                                    {1, 100}}

Private Sub calcButton_Click(sender As Object, e As EventArgs
) Handles calcButton.Click
    ' display the total cost

    Dim quantity As Integer
    Dim pricePerPainting As Integer
    Dim totalCost As Integer
    Dim row As Integer
    Dim highRow As Integer = priceChart.GetUpperBound(0)
    Dim found As Boolean

    Integer.TryParse(quantityTextBox.Text, quantity)

    ' search the first column in each row
    Do While row <= highRow AndAlso found = False
        If priceChart(row, 0) <= quantity Then
            pricePerPainting = priceChart(row, 1)
            found = True
        Else
            row += 1
        End If
    Loop

    totalCost = quantity * pricePerPainting
    totalLabel.Text = totalCost.ToString("C0")
    quantityTextBox.Focus()
End Sub
```


Figure 9-20 Problem specification, code, and sample run for the O'Reilly Studios application

The Private statement in the form's Declarations section declares and initializes the three-row, two-column `priceChart` array. Notice that the minimum values, which appear in ascending order in the chart shown in Figure 9-20, are entered in the array in descending order.

The first three Dim statements in the calcButton_Click procedure declare and initialize variables to store the quantity ordered, the price per painting, and the total cost. The next three Dim statements declare the variables that will be used to search the array. The `row` variable will keep track of the row subscripts in the array, and the `highRow` variable will store the highest row subscript in the array. The Boolean `found` variable, which is automatically initialized to False, will keep track of whether the appropriate minimum value is located in the first column in the array.

After the variables are declared, the TryParse method converts the contents of the quantityTextBox to Integer and stores the result in the `quantity` variable. The Do clause then tells the computer to repeat the loop body while the current row subscript is less than or equal to the highest row subscript and, at the same time, the `found` variable contains False.

Within the loop body is a dual-alternative selection structure whose condition compares the value stored in the first column in the current row of the array with the quantity ordered. If the array value is less than or equal to the quantity ordered, the selection structure's True path assigns the price from the second column in the current row to the `pricePerPainting` variable. It also assigns the Boolean value True to the `found` variable to indicate that the appropriate range was located. On the other hand, if the array value is *greater* than the quantity ordered, the instruction in the selection structure's False path updates the row subscript by 1, allowing the loop to search the next row in the array. When the loop ends, the procedure calculates the total price and then displays the result in the interface. As shown earlier in Figure 9-20, the procedure displays $900 when the user enters 10 in the Quantity ordered box.

Mini-Quiz 9-3

The answers to Mini-Quiz questions are located in Appendix A. Each question is associated with one or more objectives listed at the beginning of the chapter.

1. Which of the following declares a four-row, two-column String array named `letters`? (1)
   a. `Dim letters(3, 1) As String`
   b. `Private letters(3, 1) As String`
   c. `Dim letters(,) As String = {{"A", "B"}, {"C", "D"}, {"E", "F"}, {"G", "H"}}`
   d. all of the above

2. Which of the following assigns the Boolean value True to the element located in the third row, first column of a two-dimensional Boolean array named `testAnswers`? (2)
   a. `testAnswers(0, 2) = True`
   b. `testAnswers(2, 0) = True`
   c. `testAnswers(3, 1) = True`
   d. `testAnswers(1, 3) = True`

3. An application uses a two-dimensional array named `population`. Which of the following assigns the array's highest column subscript to the `highCol` variable? (3)
   a. `highCol = population.GetUpperBound(0)`
   b. `highCol = population.GetUpperBound(1)`
   c. `highCol = population.GetUpperColumn(0)`
   d. `highCol = population.UpperColumn(1)`

You have completed the concepts section of Chapter 9. The Programming Tutorial section is next.

PROGRAMMING TUTORIAL 1

Coding the Lottery Game Application

In this tutorial, you will code the Lottery Game application. Figure 9-21 shows the application's TOE chart and MainForm. When the user clicks the Get Numbers button, the button's Click event procedure should generate and display six unique random numbers that range from 1 to 54 only.

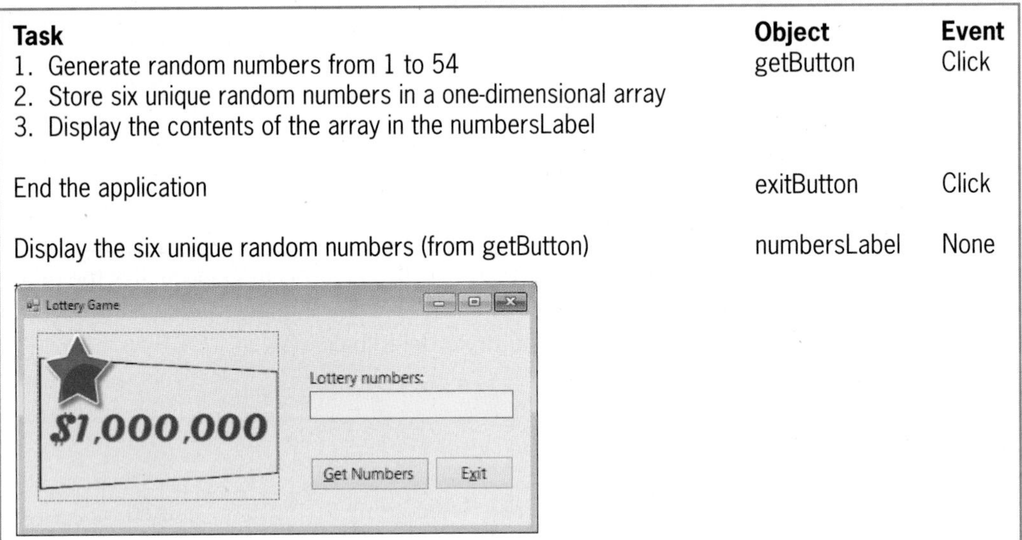

Task	Object	Event
1. Generate random numbers from 1 to 54 2. Store six unique random numbers in a one-dimensional array 3. Display the contents of the array in the numbersLabel	getButton	Click
End the application	exitButton	Click
Display the six unique random numbers (from getButton)	numbersLabel	None

Figure 9-21 TOE chart and MainForm for the Lottery Game application

Coding the Application

According to the application's TOE chart, only the Click event procedures for the two buttons need to be coded.

To open the Lottery Game application:

1. Start Visual Studio. Open the **Lottery Solution** (**Lottery Solution.sln**) file contained in the VbReloaded2015\Chap09\Lottery Solution folder. If necessary, open the designer window.
2. Open the Code Editor window. The exitButton_Click procedure has already been coded for you. In the comments that appear in the General Declarations section, replace <your name> and <current date> with your name and the current date, respectively.

Figure 9-22 shows the pseudocode for the getButton_Click procedure, which is responsible for generating and displaying six unique random numbers.

```
getButton Click event procedure
1. declare a six-element Integer array named numbers
2. generate a random number from 1 to 54 and then store it in the first array element
3. repeat until all of the remaining array elements contain a unique random number
       generate a random number from 1 to 54

       search the array elements that already contain numbers

       if the random number is not already in the array
              store the random number in the current array element and
              then continue with the next array element
       end if
   end repeat

4. display the contents of the array in the numbersLabel
```

Figure 9-22 Pseudocode for the getButton_Click procedure

To begin coding the getButton_Click procedure:

1. Locate the getButton_Click procedure. The procedure will store the six unique random numbers in a one-dimensional Integer array that has six elements. Click the **blank line** above the End Sub clause and then enter the following Dim statement:

   Dim numbers(5) As Integer

2. Next, you need to declare a Random object to represent the pseudo-random number generator in the procedure. Enter the following Dim statement:

   Dim randGen As New Random

3. The procedure will store the random numbers generated by the pseudo-random number generator in an Integer variable named `randomNum`. Enter the following Dim statement:

   Dim randomNum As Integer

4. While the procedure's loop is filling the array with values, it will use an Integer variable to keep track of the array subscripts. Enter the following Dim statement:

   Dim subscript As Integer

5. The procedure's loop will use another Integer variable to keep track of the array subscripts while the array is being searched. Enter the following Dim statement:

   Dim searchSubscript As Integer

6. The procedure will use a Boolean variable to indicate whether the current random number is already contained in the array. Enter the following Dim statement:

   Dim found As Boolean

7. The last variable you need to declare will store the array's highest subscript. Type the following statement and then press **Enter** twice:

   Dim highestSub As Integer = numbers.GetUpperBound(0)

8. The first step in the procedure's pseudocode (shown earlier in Figure 9-22) is to declare the `numbers` array; that step has already been coded. The second step is to generate a random number from 1 to 54 and then store it in the first array element. Enter the following comments and assignment statement. Press **Enter** twice after typing the assignment statement.

   ' store a random number in the first array element
   numbers(0) = randGen.Next(1, 55)

9. Next, the procedure should fill the remaining array elements, which have subscripts of 1 through 5, with unique random numbers. Enter the following comment and lines of code. (The Code Editor will automatically enter the Loop clause for you.)

' fill remaining elements with unique random numbers
subscript = 1
Do While subscript <= highestSub

10. Now, generate another random number and store it in the `randomNum` variable. Enter the following assignment statement:

randomNum = randGen.Next(1, 55)

11. Save the solution.

Before storing the `randomNum` variable's value in the array, the procedure needs to search the array to verify that it does not contain that value. Only the array elements that already contain numbers need to be searched. Those elements have subscripts starting with 0 and ending with the subscript that is one less than the current subscript. In other words, if the current subscript is 1, you need to search only the `numbers(0)` element because that is the only element that contains a number. Similarly, if the current subscript is 4, you need to search only the array elements with subscripts of 0, 1, 2, and 3.

To finish coding the getButton_Click procedure and then test the code:

1. Enter the following comments:

' search the array for the random number
' stop the search when there are no more
' elements or when the random number is found

2. The search should begin with the first array element. Enter the following statement:

searchSubscript = 0

3. Before the search begins, the procedure will assume that the newly generated random number (which is stored in the `randomNum` variable) is not already in the array. Enter the following statement:

found = False

4. The procedure should continue searching as long as there are array elements to search and, at the same time, the random number has not been found in the array. Enter the additional comments and code indicated in Figure 9-23, and then position the insertion point as shown in the figure.

```
        found = False
        Do While searchSubscript < subscript AndAlso found = False
            ' if the random number is in the current array
            ' element, assign True to found; otherwise,
            ' examine the next element
            If numbers(searchSubscript) = randomNum Then
                found = True
            Else
                searchSubscript += 1
            End If
        Loop

        |
    Loop
End Sub
```

enter these comments and lines of code

position the insertion point here

Figure 9-23 Additional comments and code entered in the getButton_Click procedure

5. If the newly generated random number is *not* in the array, the procedure should assign the random number to the current array element and then prepare to fill the next element. Enter the following comments and selection structure:

```
' if the random number is not in the array, assign it
' to the current element and move to the next element
If found = False Then
    numbers(subscript) = randomNum
    subscript += 1
End If
```

6. The last step in the procedure's pseudocode displays the contents of the `numbers` array, which contains six unique random numbers. Insert **two blank lines** between the outer Loop clause and the End Sub clause. In the blank line above the End Sub clause, enter the following comment and code. Be sure to include two spaces between the quotation marks. Also be sure to change the Next clause to `Next num`.

```
' display the contents of the array
numbersLabel.Text = String.Empty
For Each num As Integer In numbers
     numbersLabel.Text = numbersLabel.Text &
          "  " & num.ToString
Next num
```

7. Save the solution and then start the application. Click the **Get Numbers** button. Six unique numbers appear in the Lottery numbers box. See Figure 9-24.

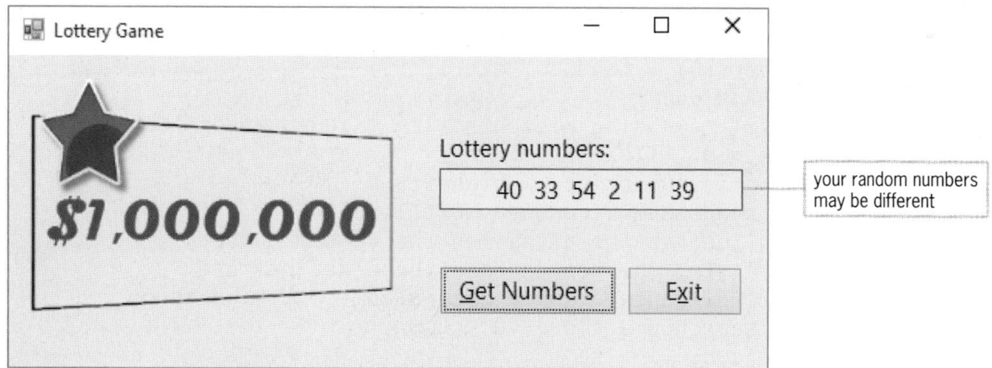

Figure 9-24 Sample run of the Lottery Game application

8. Click the **Get Numbers** button several times to continue testing the code. When you are finished, click the **Exit** button. Close the Code Editor window and then close the solution. Figure 9-25 shows the application's code.

```
' Project name:         Lottery Project
' Project purpose:      Displays six unique random
'                       numbers from 1 through 54
' Created/revised by:   <your name> on <current date>

Option Explicit On
Option Strict On
Option Infer Off

Public Class MainForm
   Private Sub exitButton_Click(sender As Object, e As EventArgs
   ) Handles exitButton.Click
       Me.Close()
   End Sub

   Private Sub getButton_Click(sender As Object, e As EventArgs
   ) Handles getButton.Click
       ' generates and displays six unique random
       ' numbers from 1 through 54

       Dim numbers(5) As Integer
       Dim randGen As New Random
       Dim randomNum As Integer
       Dim subscript As Integer
       Dim searchSubscript As Integer
       Dim found As Boolean
       Dim highestSub As Integer = numbers.GetUpperBound(0)

       ' store a random number in the first array element
       numbers(0) = randGen.Next(1, 55)

       ' fill remaining elements with unique random numbers
       subscript = 1
       Do While subscript <= highestSub
           randomNum = randGen.Next(1, 55)
           ' search the array for the random number
           ' stop the search when there are no more
           ' elements or when the random number is found
           searchSubscript = 0
           found = False
           Do While searchSubscript < subscript AndAlso found = False
               ' if the random number is in the current array
               ' element, assign True to found; otherwise,
               ' examine the next element
               If numbers(searchSubscript) = randomNum Then
                   found = True
               Else
                   searchSubscript += 1
               End If
           Loop

```

Figure 9-25 Code for the Lottery Game application *(continues)*

(continued)

```
            ' if the random number is not in the array, assign it
            ' to the current element and move to the next element
            If found = False Then
                numbers(subscript) = randomNum
                subscript += 1
            End If
        Loop

        ' display the contents of the array
        numbersLabel.Text = String.Empty
        For Each num As Integer In numbers
            numbersLabel.Text = numbersLabel.Text &
                "  " & num.ToString
        Next num
    End Sub
End Class
```

Figure 9-25 Code for the Lottery Game application

PROGRAMMING TUTORIAL 2

Coding the Jenkins Gym Application

In this tutorial, you will code an application for Jenkins Gym. The application displays the 3-month, 6-month, and 12-month fees for three different membership types: Single, Couple, and Family. The appropriate fees are listed in Figure 9-26 along with the application's TOE chart and MainForm.

Membership type	3 months	6 months	12 months
Single	$225	$420	$750
Couple	$400	$750	$1,250
Family	$575	$950	$1,400

Task	**Object**	**Event**
Declare and initialize a class-level array named feeTable that has three rows and three columns	MainForm	Declarations section
1. Fill the membershipListBox with the membership types 2. Select the first membership type in the membershipListBox		Load
End the application	exitButton	Click
Specify the membership type Use the index of the item selected in the membershipListBox to display the fees in the month3Label, month6Label, and month12Label	membershipListBox	None SelectedIndexChanged
Display the fees (from membershipListBox)	month3Label, month6Label, month12Label	None

Figure 9-26 Membership fees, TOE chart, and MainForm for the Jenkins Gym application *(continues)*

(continued)

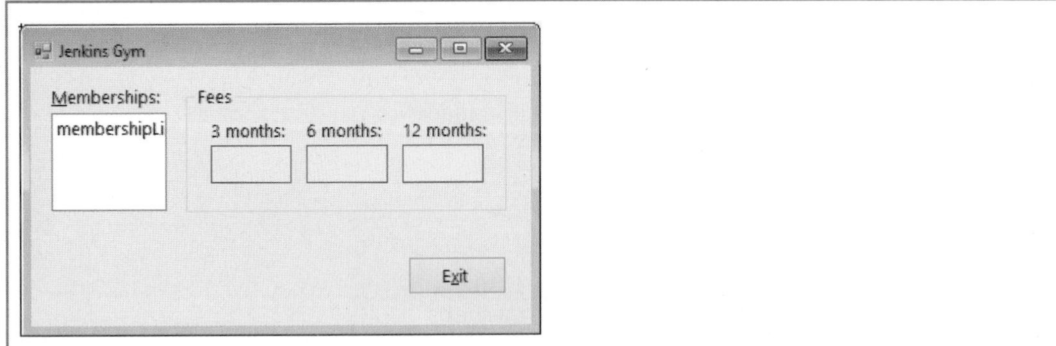

Figure 9-26 Membership fees, TOE chart, and MainForm for the Jenkins Gym application

Coding the Application

According to the application's TOE chart, three procedures need to be coded: MainForm_Load, exitButton_Click, and membershipListBox_SelectedIndexChanged. You also need to declare and initialize a two-dimensional array in the MainForm's Declarations section.

To begin coding the application:

1. Start Visual Studio. Open the **Gym Solution** (**Gym Solution.sln**) file contained in the VbReloaded2015\Chap09\Gym Solution folder. If necessary, open the designer window.
2. Open the Code Editor window. The exitButton_Click procedure has already been coded for you. In the comments that appear in the General Declarations section, replace <your name> and <current date> with your name and the current date, respectively.
3. First, you will complete the MainForm_Load procedure, which is responsible for filling the membershipListBox with the three membership types and then selecting the first type. Locate the MainForm_Load procedure, and then click the **blank line** above its End Sub clause.
4. Enter the statements to add the following three membership types to the membershipListBox: Single, Couple, and Family.
5. Now, enter the statement to select the first membership type in the list box.
6. Save the solution and then start the application. The three membership types appear in the list box, with the first type selected in the list.
7. Click the **Exit** button to end the application.

Next, you will declare the `feeTable` array in the MainForm's Declarations section. The array should have three rows and three columns. Each row represents a membership type (Single, Couple, and Family), and each column represents the length of the membership (3 months, 6 months, and 12 months).

To declare and initialize the array:

1. Click the **blank line** below the `' class-level array` comment, and then enter the statement to declare a three-row, three-column Integer array named `feeTable`. Initialize the array using the fees shown earlier in Figure 9-26.
2. Save the solution.

Finally, you will code the list box's SelectedIndexChanged event procedure.

To code and then test the membershipListBox_SelectedIndexChanged procedure:

1. Locate the membershipListBox_SelectedIndexChanged procedure, and then click the **blank line** above its End Sub clause.
2. Enter the statement to declare an Integer variable named `row`. The statement should initialize the variable to the index of the item selected in the list box.
3. Now, enter the code to assign the appropriate fees to the month3Label, month6Label, and month12Label controls. Format the fees with a dollar sign and no decimal places.
4. Save the solution and then start the application. The fees for a Single membership appear in the interface, as shown in Figure 9-27.

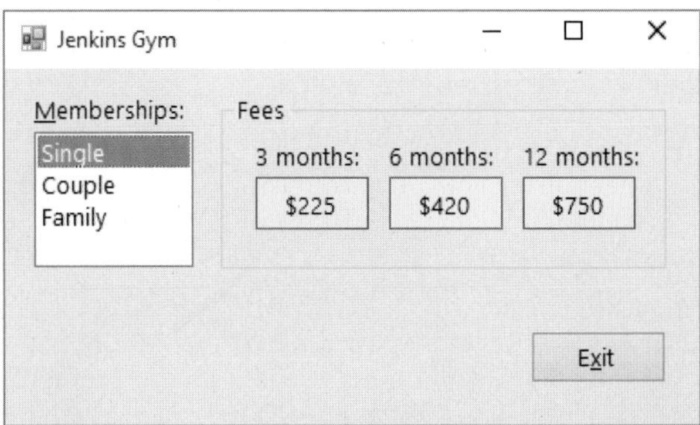

Figure 9-27 Sample run of the Jenkins Gym application

5. Click **Couple** in the list box. The fees for a Couple membership ($400, $750, and $1,250) appear in the interface.
6. Click **Family** in the list box. The fees for a Family membership ($575, $950, and $1,400) appear in the interface.
7. Click the **Exit** button. Close the Code Editor window and then close the solution. Figure 9-28 shows the code for the Jenkins Gym application.

```
' Project name:          Gym Project
' Project purpose:       Display 3-month, 6-month, and 12-month
'                        membership fees
' Created/revised by:    <your name> on <current date>

Option Explicit On
Option Strict On
Option Infer Off

Public Class MainForm
    ' class-level array
    Private feeTable(,) As Integer = {{225, 420, 750},
                                      {400, 750, 1250},
                                      {575, 950, 1400}}

```

Figure 9-28 Code for the Jenkins Gym application *(continues)*

(continued)

```
    Private Sub MainForm_Load(sender As Object, e As EventArgs
    ) Handles Me.Load
        ' fills the list box

        membershipListBox.Items.Add("Single")
        membershipListBox.Items.Add("Couple")
        membershipListBox.Items.Add("Family")
        membershipListBox.SelectedIndex = 0

    End Sub

    Private Sub membershipListBox_SelectedIndexChanged(
    sender As Object, e As EventArgs
    ) Handles membershipListBox.SelectedIndexChanged
        ' display membership fees

        Dim row As Integer = membershipListBox.SelectedIndex
        month3Label.Text = feeTable(row, 0).ToString("C0")
        month6Label.Text = feeTable(row, 1).ToString("C0")
        month12Label.Text = feeTable(row, 2).ToString("C0")
    End Sub

    Private Sub exitButton_Click(sender As Object, e As EventArgs
    ) Handles exitButton.Click
        Me.Close()
    End Sub
End Class
```

Figure 9-28 Code for the Jenkins Gym application

PROGRAMMING EXAMPLE

Professor Coleman Application

Create an interface that allows Professor Coleman to select one of the following letter grades from a list box: A, B, C, D, or F. The application should display the names of the students who earned the selected letter grade. Store each student's name and letter grade in a two-dimensional array that has 11 rows (one for each student) and two columns. Store the student names in the first column, and store the grades in the second column. Use the following names for the solution and project, respectively: Coleman Solution and Coleman Project. Save the application in the VbReloaded2015\Chap09 folder. Change the form file's name to Main Form.vb. See Figures 9-29 through 9-33.

Task	Object	Event
Declare and initialize a class-level array named studentInfo that has 11 rows and two columns	MainForm	Declarations section
1. Fill the gradeListBox with the letter grades 2. Select the first letter grade in the gradeListBox		Load
End the application	exitButton	Click
Specify the letter grade Clear the namesListBox	gradeListBox	None SelectedIndexChanged

Figure 9-29 TOE chart *(continues)*

(continued)

1. Search the studentInfo array for the letter grade selected in the gradeListBox 2. Display the names of students who earned the selected letter grade in the namesListBox	findButton	Click
Display the names of students who earned the grade selected in the gradeListBox (from findButton)	namesListBox	None

Figure 9-29 TOE chart

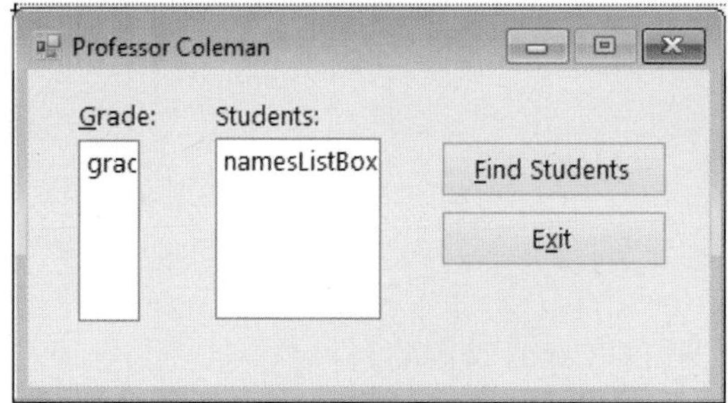

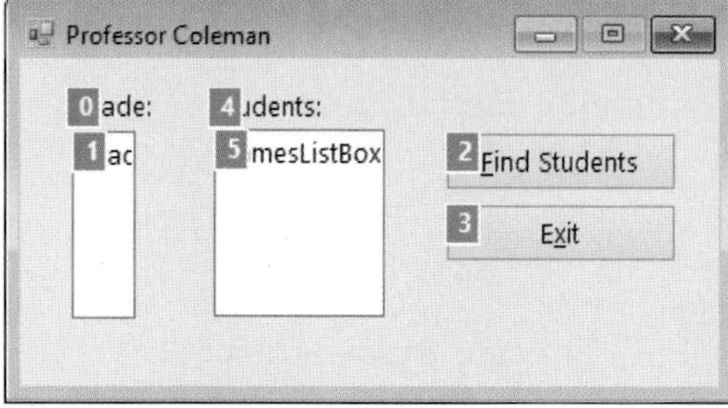

Figure 9-30 MainForm and tab order

Object	Property	Setting
MainForm	Font	Segoe UI, 10 point
	MaximizeBox	False
	StartPosition	CenterScreen
	Text	Professor Coleman
namesListBox	SelectionMode	None

Figure 9-31 Objects, properties, and settings

```
exitButton Click event procedure
close the application

MainForm Load event procedure
1. fill the gradeListBox with the following letter grades: A, B, C, D, and F
2. select the first letter grade in the gradeListBox

gradeListBox SelectedIndexChanged event procedure
clear the namesListBox

findButton Click event procedure
1. assign the grade selected in the gradeListBox to a variable named searchGrade
2. repeat for array rows from 0 to the highest row subscript
        if the grade stored in the second column in the current row matches
        the grade stored in the searchGrade variable
                add the student name, which is stored in the first column in
                the current row, to the namesListBox
        end if
   end repeat for
```

Figure 9-32 Pseudocode *(continues)*

PROGRAMMING EXAMPLE

(continued)

3. if the namesListBox does not contain any names
      display "NONE" in the namesListBox
   end if

Figure 9-32 Pseudocode

```
' Project name:         Coleman Project
' Project purpose:      Display the names of students
'                       who earned a specific grade
' Created/revised by:   <your name> on <current date>

Option Explicit On
Option Strict On
Option Infer Off

Public Class MainForm

    Private studentInfo(,) As String = {{"Carol", "A"},
                          {"Toby", "C"}, {"George", "A"},
                          {"Elaine", "B"}, {"Francisco", "C"},
                          {"Khalid", "B"}, {"Jack", "C"},
                          {"Carl", "F"}, {"Susan", "B"},
                          {"Mark", "A"}, {"Monica", "B"}}

    Private Sub exitButton_Click(sender As Object, e As EventArgs
    ) Handles exitButton.Click
        Me.Close()
    End Sub

    Private Sub gradeListBox_SelectedIndexChanged(
    sender As Object, e As EventArgs
    ) Handles gradeListBox.SelectedIndexChanged
        namesListBox.Items.Clear()
    End Sub

    Private Sub MainForm_Load(sender As Object,
    e As EventArgs) Handles Me.Load
        gradeListBox.Items.Add("A")
        gradeListBox.Items.Add("B")
        gradeListBox.Items.Add("C")
        gradeListBox.Items.Add("D")
        gradeListBox.Items.Add("F")
        gradeListBox.SelectedIndex = 0
    End Sub

    Private Sub findButton_Click(sender As Object, e As EventArgs
    ) Handles findButton.Click
        ' displays the names of students who earned the
        ' grade selected in the gradeListBox

        Dim highRowSub As Integer = studentInfo.GetUpperBound(0)
        Dim searchGrade As String

```

Figure 9-33 Code *(continues)*

(continued)

```
        searchGrade = gradeListBox.SelectedItem.ToString
        For row As Integer = 0 To highRowSub
            If studentInfo(row, 1) = searchGrade Then
                namesListBox.Items.Add(studentInfo(row, 0))
            End If
        Next row

        If namesListBox.Items.Count = 0 Then
            namesListBox.Items.Add("NONE")
        End If
    End Sub
End Class
```

Figure 9-33 Code

Chapter Summary

- Programmers use arrays to temporarily store related data in the internal memory of the computer.
- All of the elements in an array have the same name and data type. However, each has a different subscript (one-dimensional array) or subscripts (two-dimensional array).
- When declaring a one-dimensional array, you provide either the highest subscript or the initial values.
- Each element in a one-dimensional array is identified by a unique subscript that appears in parentheses after the array's name. The first subscript in a one-dimensional array is 0.
- You refer to an element in a one-dimensional array using the array's name followed by the element's subscript, which is enclosed in parentheses.
- Examples of statements that you can use to change the data stored in an array include assignment statements and statements that contain the TryParse method.
- A one-dimensional array's Length property contains an integer that represents the number of elements in the array. The number of elements is always one number more than the array's highest subscript.
- A one-dimensional array's GetUpperBound method returns an integer that represents the highest subscript in the array. The highest subscript is always one number less than the number of array elements.
- You use a loop to traverse a one-dimensional array. You can code the loop using the For... Next, Do...Loop, or For Each...Next statements. However, keep in mind that the instructions within a For Each...Next loop can only read the array values; the instructions cannot permanently change the values.
- You can associate the items in a list box with the elements in an array. You do this using the list box's index and the array's subscript, both of which start at 0.

- You can use the elements in an array as accumulators or counters.
- The Array.Sort method sorts the elements in a one-dimensional array in ascending order. The Array.Reverse method reverses the order of the elements in a one-dimensional array.
- A two-dimensional array resembles a table in that the elements are in rows and columns.
- When declaring a two-dimensional array, you provide either the highest row and column subscripts or the initial values.
- The number of rows in a two-dimensional array is one number more than its highest row subscript. Likewise, the number of columns is one number more than its highest column subscript.
- You can determine the number of elements in a two-dimensional array by multiplying the number of its rows by the number of its columns.
- Each element in a two-dimensional array is identified by a unique combination of two subscripts: a row subscript and a column subscript. The subscripts appear in parentheses after the array's name. You list the row subscript first, followed by a comma and the column subscript. The first row subscript in a two-dimensional array is 0. Likewise, the first column subscript also is 0.
- You can use a two-dimensional array's GetUpperBound method to determine the highest row subscript and highest column subscript in the array.
- You can traverse a two-dimensional array using either two loops (coded with the For...Next or Do...Loop statements) or one loop (coded with the For Each...Next statement). However, recall that the instructions in a For Each...Next loop can only read the array values; they cannot permanently change the values.

Key Terms

Accumulator arrays—arrays whose elements are used to accumulate (add together) values

Array—a group of related variables that have the same name and data type and are distinguished by one or more subscripts

Array.Reverse method—reverses the order of the elements in a one-dimensional array

Array.Sort method—sorts the elements in a one-dimensional array in ascending order

Counter arrays—arrays whose elements are used for counting something

Element—a variable in an array

For Each...Next statement—used to code a loop whose instructions you want processed for each element in a group

GetUpperBound method—returns an integer that represents the highest subscript in a specified dimension; the dimension is 0 for a one-dimensional array; for a two-dimensional array, the dimension is 0 for the row subscript but 1 for the column subscript

Length property—one of the properties of a one-dimensional array; stores an integer that represents the number of array elements

One-dimensional array—an array whose elements are identified by a unique subscript

Populating the array—refers to the process of initializing the elements in an array

Scalar variable—another term for a simple variable

Simple variable—a variable that is unrelated to any other variable in the computer's internal memory; also called a scalar variable

Sorting—the process of arranging data in a specific order

Subscript—a unique number that identifies the position of an element in an array

Two-dimensional array—an array made up of rows and columns; each element has the same name and data type and is identified by a unique combination of two subscripts: a row subscript and a column subscript

Review Questions

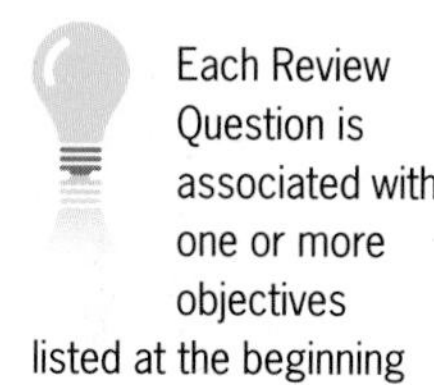

Each Review Question is associated with one or more objectives listed at the beginning of the chapter.

1. Which of the following declares a five-element array named `prices`? (1)
   a. `Dim prices(4) As Decimal`
   b. `Dim prices(5) As Decimal`
   c. `Dim prices() As Decimal = {3.55D, 6.7D, 8D, 4D, 2.34D}`
   d. both a and c
2. The `items` array is declared using the `Dim items(20) As String` statement. The `x` variable keeps track of the array subscripts and is initialized to 0. Which of the following Do clauses will process the loop instructions for each element in the array? (3, 4)
   a. `Do While x > items.GetUpperBound(0)`
   b. `Do While x < items.GetUpperBound(0)`
   c. `Do While x >= items.GetUpperBound(0)`
   d. `Do While x <= items.GetUpperBound(0)`

Use the information shown in Figure 9-34 to answer Review Questions 3 through 7.

```
Dim sales() As Integer = {10000, 12000, 900, 500, 20000}
```

Figure 9-34 Code for Review Questions 3 through 7

3. The `sales(3) += 10` statement will replace the number ____________. (2)
   a. 500 with 10
   b. 500 with 510
   c. 900 with 10
   d. 900 with 910
4. The `sales(4) = sales(4 - 2)` statement will replace the number ____________. (2)
   a. 20000 with 900
   b. 20000 with 19998
   c. 500 with 12000
   d. 500 with 498

5. Which of the following If clauses verifies that the array subscript stored in the `x` variable is valid for the `sales` array? (3)
   a. `If sales(x) >= 0 AndAlso sales(x) < 4 Then`
   b. `If sales(x) >= 0 OrElse sales(x) <= 4 Then`
   c. `If x >= 0 AndAlso x <= sales.GetUpperBound(0) Then`
   d. `If x >= 0 AndAlso x < sales.GetUpperBound(0) Then`

6. Which of the following will correctly add 100 to each element in the `sales` array? The `x` variable was declared using the `Dim x As Integer` statement. (2–4, 9)
   a.
   ```
   Do While x <= sales.GetUpperBound(0)
       x += 100
   Loop
   ```
   b.
   ```
   Do While x <= sales.GetUpperBound(0)
       sales += 100
   Loop
   ```
   c.
   ```
   Do While sales < sales.Length
       sales(x) += 100
   Loop
   ```
   d.
   ```
   Do While x < sales.Length
       sales(x) += 100
       x += 1
   Loop
   ```

7. Which of the following statements sorts the `sales` array in ascending order? (10)
   a. `Array.Sort(sales)`
   b. `sales.Sort()`
   c. `Sort(sales)`
   d. `SortArray(sales)`

Use the information shown in Figure 9-35 to answer Review Question 8.

```
Dim numbers() As Double = {10, 5, 7, 2}
Dim x As Integer
Dim total As Double
Dim avg As Double
```

Figure 9-35 Code for Review Question 8

8. Which of the following will correctly calculate the average of the elements included in the `numbers` array? (2–4, 6)

   a.
```
Do While x < numbers.Length
     numbers(x) = total + total
     x += 1
Loop
avg = total / x
```

   b.
```
Do While x < numbers.Length
     total += numbers(x)
     x += 1
Loop
avg = total / x
```

   c.
```
Do While x < numbers.Length
     total += numbers(x)
     x += 1
Loop
avg = total / x - 1
```

   d.
```
Do While x < numbers.Length
     total += numbers(x)
     x += 1
Loop
avg = total / (x - 1)
```

9. Which of the following statements creates an array that contains three rows and four columns? (1)

   a. `Dim temps(2, 3) As Decimal`

   b. `Dim temps(3, 4) As Decimal`

   c. `Dim temps(3, 2) As Decimal`

   d. `Dim temps(4, 3) As Decimal`

Use the information shown in Figure 9-36 to answer Review Questions 10 and 11.

```
Dim sales(,) As Integer = {{1000, 1200, 900, 500, 2000},
                            {350, 600, 700, 800, 100}}
```

Figure 9-36 Code for Review Questions 10 and 11

10. The `sales(1, 3) += 10` statement will replace the number ____________. (2)

    a. 900 with 910

    b. 500 with 510

    c. 700 with 710

    d. 800 with 810

11. Which of the following If clauses verifies that the array subscripts stored in the `r` and `c` variables are valid for the `sales` array? (3)

    a.
    ```
    If sales(r, c) >= 0 AndAlso
        sales(r, c) <= sales.UpperBound(0) Then
    ```

    b.
    ```
    If sales(r, c) >= 0 AndAlso
        sales(r, c) < sales.Length Then
    ```

    c.
    ```
    If r >= 0 AndAlso r < sales.Length AndAlso
        c >= 0 AndAlso c < sales.Length Then
    ```

    d.
    ```
    If r >= 0 AndAlso r <= sales.GetUpperBound(0) AndAlso
        c >= 0 AndAlso c <= sales.GetUpperBound(1) Then
    ```

12. Which of the following assigns the string "California" to the variable located in the third column, fifth row of the `states` array? (2)

    a. `states(3, 5) = "California"`

    b. `states(5, 3) = "California"`

    c. `states(4, 2) = "California"`

    d. `states(2, 4) = "California"`

Each Exercise, except the DISCOVERY exercise, is associated with one or more objectives listed at the beginning of the chapter.

Exercises

Pencil and Paper

INTRODUCTORY

1. Write a Dim statement that declares a 20-element, one-dimensional Integer array named `ordered`. Then write the statement to store the number 9500 in the fourth element in the array. (1, 2)

INTRODUCTORY

2. Write the code to display the contents of the `ordered` array from Pencil and Paper Exercise 1 in the orderedListBox. Use the For Each...Next statement. Then rewrite the code using the For...Next statement. (3–5)

INTRODUCTORY

3. Write a Private statement that declares and initializes a four-element, one-dimensional Double array named `prices`. Use the following numbers to initialize the array: 7.99, 8.99, 10.75, and 12.5. (1)

INTRODUCTORY

4. Write the code to display the contents of the `prices` array from Pencil and Paper Exercise 3 in the pricesListBox. Use the Do...Loop statement. Then rewrite the code using the For Each...Next statement. (3–5)

INTRODUCTORY

5. Write a statement that assigns the number of elements in the one-dimensional `rates` array to an Integer variable named `numRates`. (3)

INTRODUCTORY

6. Write a statement that assigns the highest subscript in the one-dimensional `rates` array to an Integer variable named `highSub`. (3)

INTRODUCTORY

7. The `nums` array is a one-dimensional Integer array. Write the code to multiply the value stored in the array's fifth element by 2. Assign the result to the `numDoubled` variable. (2)

INTRODUCTORY

8. Write the code to add together the numbers stored in the first and second elements in a one-dimensional Integer array named `ordered`. Display the sum in the sumLabel. (2)

9. Write a Private statement that declares a three-row, four-column Double array named `balances`. (1) INTRODUCTORY

10. Write the code to display the contents of a two-dimensional String array named `products` in the productsListBox. Use the For Each...Next statement. Then rewrite the code using two For...Next statements to display the array, row by row. (2–5) INTERMEDIATE

11. The `schools` array is a two-dimensional String array. Write the statements that assign the highest row subscript and the highest column subscript to Integer variables named `highRow` and `highColumn`, respectively. (3) INTERMEDIATE

12. The `schools` array is a two-dimensional String array. Write the statement that assigns the number of array elements to an Integer variable named `numSchools`. (3) INTERMEDIATE

13. Write the code to subtract the number 1 from each element in a one-dimensional Integer array named `numbers`. Use the Do...Loop statement. (2–4, 9) INTERMEDIATE

14. The `commission` array is a two-dimensional Double array. Write the statement to total the values stored in the following three array elements: the first row, second column; the third row, fourth column; and the fifth row, third column. Assign the sum to the `total` variable. (2) INTERMEDIATE

15. The `ordered` array is a two-dimensional Integer array. Write the code to subtract the number 1 from each array element. Use two For...Next statements. (2–4, 9) INTERMEDIATE

16. The `population` array is a two-dimensional Integer array. Write the code to determine the largest number stored in the first column of the array. Use the For...Next statement. (2–4, 7) ADVANCED

Computer

17. Open the Popcorn Solution (Popcorn Solution.sln) file contained in the VbReloaded2015\Chap09\Popcorn Solution-LowHigh folder. Modify the interface and code so that each button (except the Exit button) also displays the lowest and highest values stored in the `sold` array. Save the solution and then start and test the application. Close the solution. (2–5, 7) MODIFY THIS

18. Open the Popcorn Solution (Popcorn Solution.sln) file contained in the VbReloaded2015\Chap09\Popcorn Solution-Highest folder. Replace the For...Next statement in the code with the For Each...Next statement. Save the solution and then start and test the application. Close the solution. (2, 4, 5, 7) MODIFY THIS

19. If necessary, complete the Jenkins Gym application from this chapter's Programming Tutorial 2, and then close the solution. Use Windows to make a copy of the Gym Solution folder. Rename the folder Gym Solution-ModifyThis. Open the solution file contained in the Gym Solution-ModifyThis folder. The gym has just announced two new membership types: Senior Single and Senior Couple. The fees for the 3-month, 6-month, and 12-month Senior Single memberships are $180, $336, and $600, respectively. The fees for the 3-month, 6-month, and 12-month Senior Couple memberships are $320, $600, and $1,000, respectively. Modify the interface and code to accommodate the new membership types. Save the solution and then start and test the application. Close the solution. (2, 8) MODIFY THIS

INTRODUCTORY

20. In this exercise, you code an application that sums the values contained in a two-dimensional array. Open the Inventory Solution (Inventory Solution.sln) file contained in the VbReloaded2015\Chap09\Inventory Solution folder. Code the displayButton_Click procedure so that it adds together the values stored in the `inventory` array. Display the sum in the totalLabel. (2–6)

INTRODUCTORY

21. Open the Retail Solution (Retail Solution.sln) file contained in the VbReloaded2015\Chap09\Retail Solution folder. Open the Code Editor window. The code declares and initializes a class-level array named `wholesale`. The retailButton_Click procedure should ask the user for a percentage amount and then use that amount to increase each price stored in the array. The increased prices should be displayed in the retailListBox. Save the solution and then start the application. Click the Retail Price button. Increase each price by 10%. Close the solution. (1–5, 8)

INTRODUCTORY

22. Open the Tips Solution (Tips Solution.sln) file contained in the VbReloaded2015\Chap09\Tips Solution folder. (The image in the picture box is courtesy of OpenClipArt.org/antontw.) Declare a class-level, one-dimensional array containing the following tip amounts: 75, 40, 35, and 80. The forNextButton_Click procedure should use the For...Next statement to calculate the average tip. The doLoopButton_Click procedure should use the Do...Loop statement to calculate the average tip. The forEachNextButton_Click procedure should use the For Each...Next statement to calculate the average tip. Code the procedures, which should display the average tip (with two decimal places) in the avgLabel. Save the solution and then start and test the application. Close the solution. (1–6)

INTERMEDIATE

23. In this exercise, you modify the application from Computer Exercise 21. The modified application will allow the user to update a specific price. Use Windows to make a copy of the Retail Solution folder. Rename the folder Retail Solution-Specific. Open the solution file contained in the Retail Solution-Specific folder. Modify the retailButton_Click procedure so that it also asks the user to enter a number from 1 through 10. If the user enters the number 1, the procedure should update the first price in the array. If the user enters the number 2, the procedure should update the second price in the array, and so on. Save the solution and then start the application. Click the Retail Price button. Increase the second price by 10%. Then, increase the tenth price by 5%. (The second price in the list box should still reflect the 10% increase.) Close the solution. (1–5, 8)

INTERMEDIATE

24. In this exercise, you code an application that displays a grade based on the number of points entered by the user. The grading scale is shown in Figure 9-37. Open the Chang Solution (Chang Solution.sln) file contained in the VbReloaded2015\Chap09\Chang Solution folder. Declare two class-level arrays: a one-dimensional Integer array named `minPoints` and a one-dimensional String array named `grades`. Store the minimum points in the `minPoints` array, and store the corresponding grades in the `grades` array. The displayButton_Click procedure should search the `minPoints` array for the number of points entered by the user and then display the corresponding grade from the `grades` array. Code the procedure. Save the solution and then start the application. Enter 455 in the Points box and then click the Display Grade button. The letter B appears in the Grade box. Enter 210 in the Points box and then click the Display Grade button. The letter F appears in the Grade box. Close the solution. (2–4, 11)

Minimum points	Maximum points	Grade
0	299	F
300	349	D
350	414	C
415	464	B
465	500 or more	A

Figure 9-37 Grading scale for Exercise 24

25. In this exercise, you code an application that displays the highest score earned on the midterm exam and the highest score earned on the final exam. Open the Highest Solution (Highest Solution.sln) file contained in the VbReloaded2015\Chap09\Highest Solution folder. Code the displayButton_Click procedure so that it displays (in the appropriate label controls) the highest score earned on the midterm exam and the highest score earned on the final exam. Save the solution and then start and test the application. Close the solution. (2–4, 7, 11) INTERMEDIATE

26. Open the Shipping Solution (Shipping Solution.sln) file contained in the VbReloaded2015\Chap09\Shipping Solution folder. Declare a class-level, two-dimensional Decimal array to store the minimum order amounts and shipping charges shown in Figure 9-38. The displayButton_Click procedure should display the appropriate shipping charge with a dollar sign and two decimal places. Save the solution and then start and test the application. Close the solution. (1–4, 11) INTERMEDIATE

Minimum order	Maximum order	Shipping
1	5	10.99
6	10	7.99
11	20	3.99
21	No maximum	0

Figure 9-38 Order amounts and shipping charges for Exercise 26

27. Open the Sales Solution (Sales Solution.sln) file contained in the VbReloaded2015\Chap09\Sales Solution folder. The interface allows the user to enter a sales amount. Code the searchButton_Click procedure so that it displays the number of salespeople selling at least that amount. The sales amounts are stored in the `sales` array. Save the solution and then start and test the application. Close the solution. (2–5, 11) INTERMEDIATE

28. Open the Tyler Solution (Tyler Solution.sln) file contained in the VbReloaded2015\Chap09\Tyler Solution folder. Modify the newButton_Click procedure so that it also displays (in a message box) the dealership that sold the most new cars and the dealership that sold the fewest new cars. Modify the usedButton_Click procedure so that it also displays (in a message box) the dealership that sold the most used cars and the dealership that sold the fewest used cars. Modify the totalButton_Click procedure so that it also displays (in a message box) the dealership that sold the most cars and the dealership that sold the fewest cars. Save the solution and then start and test the application. Close the solution. (2–4, 7, 11) ADVANCED

ADVANCED

29. In this exercise, you code an application that displays the number of salespeople earning a specific commission. Open the Commission Solution (Commission Solution.sln) file contained in the VbReloaded2015\Chap09\Commission Solution folder. The displayButton_Click procedure should prompt the user to enter a commission amount from 0 through 1000. It then should display (in a message box) the number of salespeople who earned that commission. Code the procedure. Save the solution and then start the application. Use the application to answer the following questions: How many salespeople earned a commission of $100? How many salespeople earned a commission of $300? How many salespeople earned a commission of $50? How many salespeople earned a commission of $900? Close the solution. (1–5, 11)

ADVANCED

30. In this exercise, you modify the application from Computer Exercise 29. The modified application will allow the user to display the number of salespeople earning a commission within a specific range. Use Windows to make a copy of the Commission Solution folder. Rename the folder Commission Solution-Range. Open the solution file contained in the Commission Solution-Range folder. Modify the displayButton_Click procedure to prompt the user to enter a minimum commission amount and a maximum commission amount. The procedure should then display (in a message box) the number of salespeople who earned a commission within that range. Save the solution and then start the application. Use the application to answer the following questions: How many salespeople earned a commission from 100 through 300? How many salespeople earned a commission from 700 through 800? How many salespeople earned a commission from 0 through 200? Close the solution. (1–5, 11)

ADVANCED

31. In this exercise, you code an application that displays the number of times a specific value appears in a two-dimensional array. Open the Count Solution (Count Solution.sln) file contained in the VbReloaded2015\Chap09\Count Solution folder. Code the Display button's Click event procedure so that it displays the number of times each of the numbers from 1 through 9 appears in the `numbers` array. (Hint: Store the counts in a one-dimensional array.) Save the solution and then start and test the application. Close the solution. (1–4, 9, 11)

DISCOVERY

32. Research the Visual Basic ReDim statement. What is the purpose of the statement? What is the purpose of the `Preserve` keyword? Open the solution file contained in the VbReloaded2015\Chap09\ReDim Solution folder.

    a. Open the Code Editor window and locate the displayButton_Click procedure. Study the existing code, and then modify the procedure so that it stores any number of sales amounts in the `sales` array. (Hint: Declare the array using empty sets of parentheses and braces. Use the ReDim statement to add an element to the array.)

    b. Save the solution and then start the application. Click the Display Sales button and then enter the following sales amounts, one at a time: 700, 550, and 800. Click the Cancel button in the input box. The three sales amounts should appear in the list box.

    c. Click the Display Sales button again and then enter the following sales amounts, one at a time: 5, 9, 45, 67, 8, and 0. Click the Cancel button in the input box. This time, six sales amounts should appear in the list box. Close the solution.

SWAT THE BUGS

33. Open the Debug Solution (Debug Solution.sln) file contained in the VbReloaded2015\Chap09\Debug Solution folder. Open the Code Editor window and review the existing code. Correct the syntax errors. When the application is working correctly, close the solution. (1–4)

Case Projects

JM Sales

JM Sales employs five salespeople. The sales manager wants an application that allows him to enter any number of sales amounts for each of the five salespeople. The application should accumulate the sales amounts in a one-dimensional array. The application should also display a report similar to the one shown in Figure 9-39. The report contains each salesperson's ID and total sales. It also contains the total company sales. Use the following names for the solution and project, respectively: JM Sales Solution and JM Sales Project. Save the application in the VbReloaded2015\Chap09 folder. Change the form file's name to Main Form.vb. You can either create your own interface or create the one shown in Figure 9-39. The text box that displays the report has its BorderStyle property set to Fixed3D, its Font property set to Courier New 10pt, its MultiLine and ReadOnly properties set to True, and its ScrollBars property set to Vertical. (1–4, 6, 8, 9)

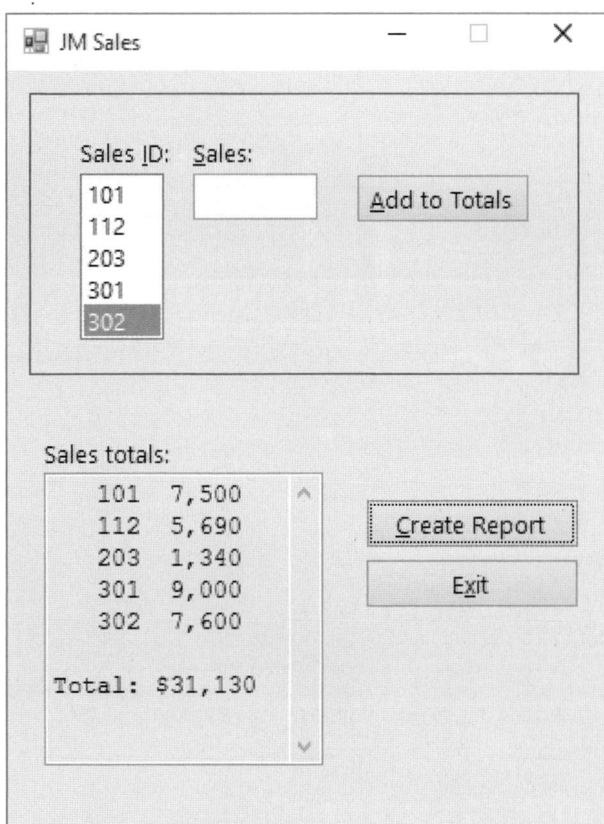

Figure 9-39 Sample run of the JM Sales application

Waterglen Horse Farms

Each year, Sabrina Cantrell, the owner of Waterglen Horse Farms, enters four of her horses in five local horse races. She uses the table shown in Figure 9-40 to keep track of her horses' performances in each race. In the table, a 1 indicates that the horse won the race, a 2 indicates second place, and a 3 indicates third place. A 0 indicates that the horse did not finish in the top three places. Sabrina wants an application that displays a summary of each horse's individual performance, as well as the performances of all the horses. For example, according to the table shown in Figure 9-40, horse 1 won one race, finished second in one race, finished third in one race, and didn't finish in the top three in two races. Overall, Sabrina's horses won four races, finished second in three races, finished third in three races, and didn't finish in the top three in 10 races. Be sure to use one or more arrays in the application. Use the following names for the solution and project, respectively: Waterglen Solution and Waterglen Project. Save the application in the VbReloaded2015\Chap09 folder. Change the form file's name to Main Form.vb. You can either create your own interface or create the one shown in Figure 9-41. The horse image is stored in the VbReloaded2015\Chap09 folder. (1–4, 6)

	1	2	3	4	5
1	0	1	0	3	2
2	1	0	2	0	0
3	0	3	0	1	0
4	3	2	1	0	0

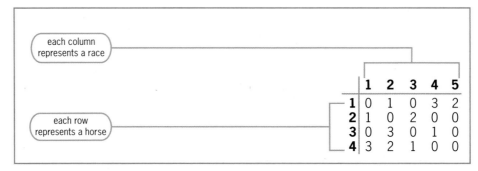

Figure 9-40 Horse race results for Waterglen Horse Farms

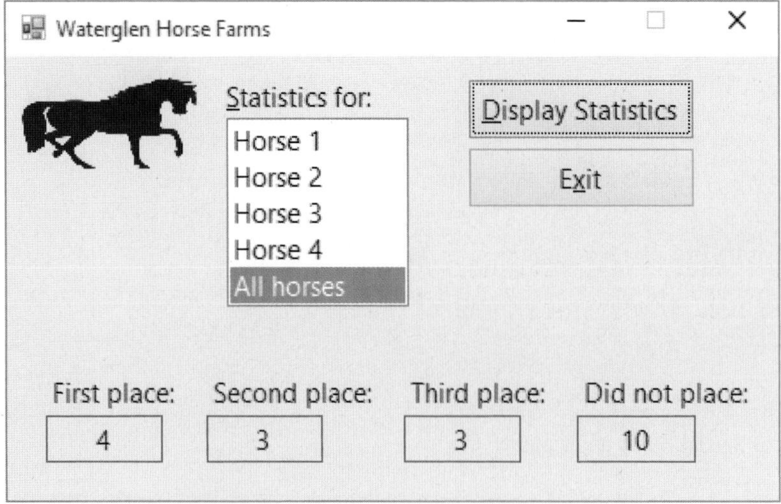

Figure 9-41 Sample run of the Waterglen Horse Farms application

Conway Enterprises

Conway Enterprises has both domestic and international sales operations. The company's sales manager wants an application that she can use to display the total domestic, total international, and total company sales made during a six-month period. The sales amounts are listed in Figure 9-42. Be sure to use one or more arrays in the application. Use the following names for the solution and project, respectively: Conway Solution and Conway Project. Save the application in the VbReloaded2015\Chap09 folder. Change the form file's name to Main Form.vb. You can either create your own interface or create the one shown in Figure 9-43. (1–4, 6)

Month	Domestic	International
1	100,000	150,000
2	90,000	120,000
3	75,000	210,000
4	88,000	50,000
5	125,000	220,000
6	63,000	80,000

Figure 9-42 Sales amounts for Conway Enterprises

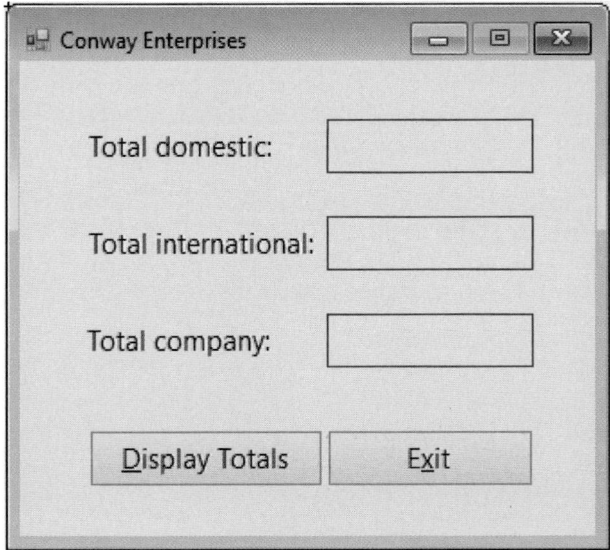

Figure 9-43 Sample interface for Conway Enterprises

Modified Harvey Industries

Before you can complete this Case Project, you need to complete the Harvey Industries Case Project from Chapter 8. After doing so, use Windows to copy the Harvey Industries Solution folder from the VbReloaded2015\Chap08 folder to the VbReloaded2015\Chap09 folder. Open the solution file contained in the Harvey Industries Solution folder. Store the weekly Federal Withholding Tax (FWT) tables in two two-dimensional arrays, and then make the appropriate modifications to the code. The FWT tables are shown in Figure 8-45 in Chapter 8. (1–4, 11)

Tic-Tac-Toe

Create an application that simulates the Tic-Tac-Toe game, which requires two players. Be sure to use one or more arrays in the application. Use the following names for the solution and project, respectively: TicTacToe Solution and TicTacToe Project. Save the application in the VbReloaded2015\Chap09 folder. Change the form file's name to Main Form.vb. (Hint: You may find it helpful to create an array of Label controls.) (1–5)

CHAPTER 10

String Manipulation and Menus

After studying Chapter 10, you should be able to:

1. Determine the number of characters in a string
2. Remove characters from a string
3. Insert characters in a string
4. Align the characters in a string
5. Search a string
6. Access characters in a string
7. Compare strings using pattern matching
8. Add a menu to a form
9. Code a menu item's Click event procedure

Working with Strings

In many cases, an application's code will need to manipulate (process) string data in some way. For example, it may need to look at the first character in a part number to determine the part's location in the warehouse. It may also need to search an address to determine the street name. Or, it may need to verify that the input entered by the user is in the expected format. In this chapter, you will learn several ways of manipulating strings in Visual Basic. You will begin by learning how to determine the number of characters in a string.

Determining the Number of Characters in a String

If an application expects the user to enter a seven-digit phone number or a five-digit ZIP code, you should verify that the user's entry contains the required number of characters. The number of characters contained in a string is stored as an integer in the string's **Length property**. Figure 10-1 shows the property's syntax and includes examples of using the property. In the syntax, *string* can be a String variable, a String named constant, or the Text property of a control.

HOW TO Determine the Number of Characters in a String

Syntax
string.**Length**

Example 1
```
Dim state As String = "Oklahoma"
Dim numChars As Integer = state.Length
```
assigns the number 8 to the `numChars` variable

Example 2
```
Dim numChars As Integer
numChars = cityTextBox.Text.Length
```
assigns the number of characters in the cityTextBox's Text property to the `numChars` variable

Example 3
```
Dim zip As String
Do
    zip = InputBox("5-digit ZIP code", "ZIP")
Loop Until zip.Length = 5
```
continues prompting the user for a ZIP code until the user enters exactly five characters

Figure 10-1 How to determine the number of characters in a string

To learn more about the Trim method, as well as its companion TrimStart and TrimEnd methods, complete Computer Exercise 35 at the end of this chapter.

Removing Characters from a String

Visual Basic provides two methods for removing characters from a string. The **Trim method** removes (trims) any space characters from both the beginning and the end of a string. The **Remove method**, on the other hand, removes a specified number of characters located anywhere in a string. Figure 10-2 shows the syntax of both methods and includes examples of using the methods. In each syntax, *string* can be a String variable, a String named constant, or the Text property of a control. When processing either method, the computer first makes a temporary copy of the *string* in memory. It then performs the specified removal on the copy only. Neither method removes any characters from the original *string*. Both methods return a string with the appropriate characters removed.

The *startIndex* argument in the Remove method is the index of the first character you want removed from the copy of the *string*. A character's index is an integer that indicates the character's position in the string. The first character in a string has an index of 0; the second character has an index of 1, and so on. The optional *numCharsToRemove* argument is the number of characters you want removed. To remove only the first character from a string, you use 0 as the startIndex and 1 as the numCharsToRemove. To remove the fourth through eighth characters, you use 3 as the startIndex and 5 as the numCharsToRemove. If the numCharsToRemove argument is omitted, the Remove method removes all of the characters from the startIndex position through the end of the string, as indicated in Example 3 in Figure 10-2.

HOW TO Remove Characters from a String

Syntax
string.**Trim**
string.**Remove(***startIndex*[, *numCharsToRemove*]**)**

Example 1
```
Dim state As String
state = stateTextBox.Text.Trim
```
assigns the contents of the stateTextBox's Text property, excluding any leading and trailing spaces, to the `state` variable

Example 2
```
Dim cityState As String = "Louisville, KY"
stateTextBox.Text = cityState.Remove(0, 12)
```
assigns the string "KY" to the stateTextBox's Text property

Example 3
```
Dim cityState As String = "Louisville, KY"
cityTextBox.Text = cityState.Remove(10)
```
assigns the string "Louisville" to the cityTextBox's Text property; you can also write the assignment statement as `cityTextBox.Text = cityState.Remove(10, 4)`

Example 4
```
Dim firstName As String = "Jose"
firstName = firstName.Remove(2, 1)
```
assigns the string "Joe" to the `firstName` variable

Figure 10-2 How to remove characters from a string

Inserting Characters in a String

Visual Basic's **Insert method** allows you to insert characters anywhere in a string. The method's syntax is shown in Figure 10-3 along with examples of using the method. In the syntax, *string* can be a String variable, a String named constant, or the Text property of a control. When processing the Insert method, the computer first makes a temporary copy of the *string* in memory. It then performs the specified insertion on the copy only. The Insert method does not affect the original *string*. The method's *startIndex* argument is an integer that specifies where in the string's copy you want the *value* inserted. The integer represents the character's index—in other words, its position in the string. To insert the value at the beginning of a string, you use a startIndex of 0, as shown in Example 1 in Figure 10-3. To insert the value beginning with the sixth character in the string, you use a startIndex of 5, as shown in Example 2. The Insert method returns a string with the appropriate characters inserted.

If you want to experiment with the Length property and the Trim, Remove, and Insert methods, open the solution contained in the Try It 1! folder.

HOW TO Insert Characters in a String

Syntax
string.**Insert(***startIndex*, *value***)**

Example 1
```
Dim phone As String = "111-2222"
phoneTextBox.Text = phone.Insert(0, "(877) ")
```
assigns the string "(877) 111-2222" to the phoneTextBox's Text property

Example 2
```
Dim fullName As String = "Ella Jacoby"
fullName = fullName.Insert(5, "C. ")
```
assigns the string "Ella C. Jacoby" to the `fullName` variable

Figure 10-3 How to insert characters in a string

The answers to Mini-Quiz questions are located in Appendix A. Each question is associated with one or more objectives listed at the beginning of the chapter.

Mini-Quiz 10-1

1. Which of the following assigns the number of characters stored in the stateTextBox to the `numChars` variable? (1)
   a. `numChars = stateTextBox.Text.Length`
   b. `numChars = stateTextBox.Length.Text`
   c. `numChars = Len(stateTextBox.Text)`
   d. `numChars = Length(stateTextBox.Text)`
2. Which of the following changes the contents of the `state` variable from California to Ca? (2)
   a. `state = state.Remove(2)`
   b. `state = state.Remove(2, 8)`
   c. `state = state.Remove(1, 8)`
   d. all of the above
3. Which of the following changes the contents of the `state` variable from Carolina to North Carolina? (3)
   a. `state = state.Insert("North ", 0)`
   b. `state = state.Insert(0, "North ")`
   c. `state = state.Insert(1, "North ")`
   d. `state = state.Insert("North", 1)`

Aligning the Characters in a String

You can use Visual Basic's PadLeft and PadRight methods to align the characters in a string. The methods do this by inserting (padding) the string with zero or more characters until the string is a specified length; each method then returns the padded string. The **PadLeft method** pads the string on the left, which means it inserts the padded characters at the beginning of the string, thereby right-aligning the characters within the string. The **PadRight method**, on the other hand, pads the string on the right, which means it inserts the padded characters at the end of the string and left-aligns the characters within the string.

Figure 10-4 shows the syntax of both methods and includes examples of using them. In each syntax, *string* can be a String variable, a String named constant, or the Text property of a control. When processing the PadLeft and PadRight methods, the computer first makes a temporary copy of the *string* in memory; it then pads the copy only. The *totalChars* argument in each syntax is an integer that represents the total number of characters you want the string's copy to contain. The optional *padCharacter* argument is the character that each method uses to pad the string until the desired number of characters is reached. If the padCharacter argument is omitted, the default padding character is the space character.

If you want to experiment with the PadLeft and PadRight methods, open the solution contained in the Try It 2! folder.

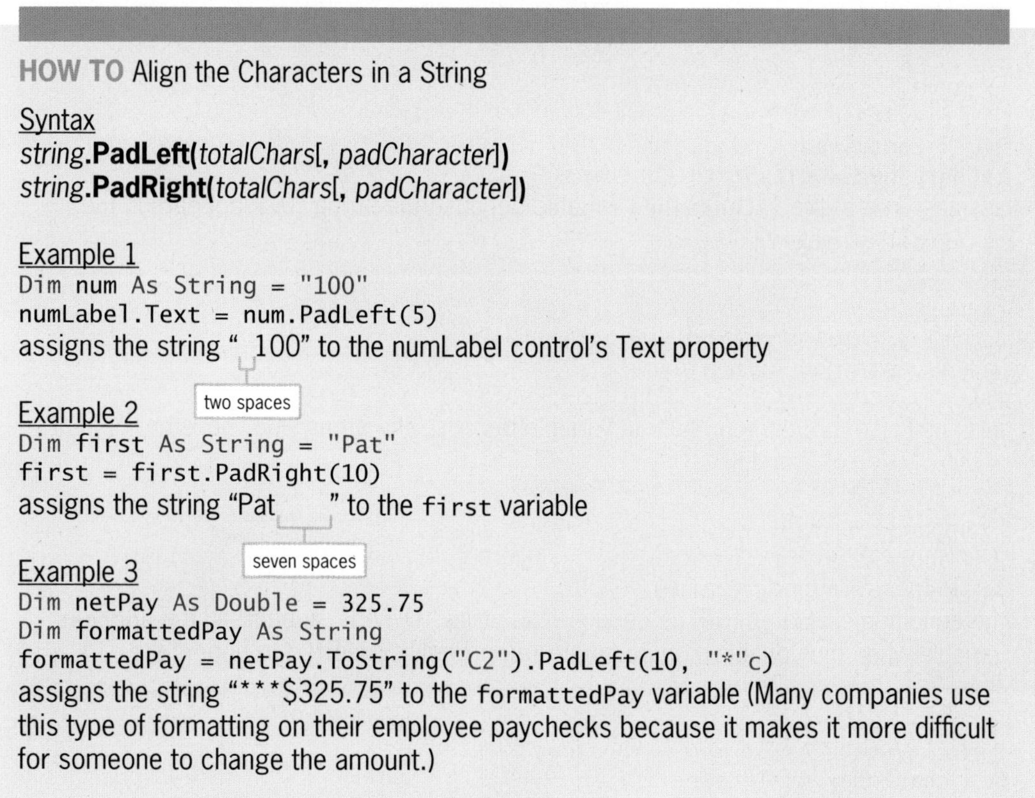

HOW TO Align the Characters in a String

Syntax
string.**PadLeft(***totalChars*[**,** *padCharacter*]**)**
string.**PadRight(***totalChars*[**,** *padCharacter*]**)**

Example 1
```
Dim num As String = "100"
numLabel.Text = num.PadLeft(5)
```
assigns the string " 100" to the numLabel control's Text property

Example 2
```
Dim first As String = "Pat"
first = first.PadRight(10)
```
assigns the string "Pat   " to the `first` variable

Example 3
```
Dim netPay As Double = 325.75
Dim formattedPay As String
formattedPay = netPay.ToString("C2").PadLeft(10, "*"c)
```
assigns the string "***$325.75" to the `formattedPay` variable (Many companies use this type of formatting on their employee paychecks because it makes it more difficult for someone to change the amount.)

Figure 10-4 How to align the characters in a string

Notice that the expression in Example 3 contains the ToString and PadLeft methods. When an expression contains more than one method, the computer processes the methods from left to right. In this case, the computer will process the ToString method before processing the PadLeft method. Also notice the letter c that appears at the end of the padCharacter argument in Example 3. The letter c is one of the literal type characters in Visual Basic. As you learned in

Chapter 3, a literal type character forces a literal constant to assume a data type other than the one its form indicates. In this case, the letter c forces the "*" string in the padCharacter argument to assume the Char (character) data type.

Searching a String

You can use either the Contains method or the IndexOf method to determine whether a string contains a specific sequence of characters. Figure 10-5 shows the syntax of both methods. In each syntax, *string* can be a String variable, a String named constant, or the Text property of a control. The *subString* argument in each syntax represents the sequence of characters for which you are searching. Both methods perform a case-sensitive search, which means the case of the subString must match the case of the string in order for both to be considered equal.

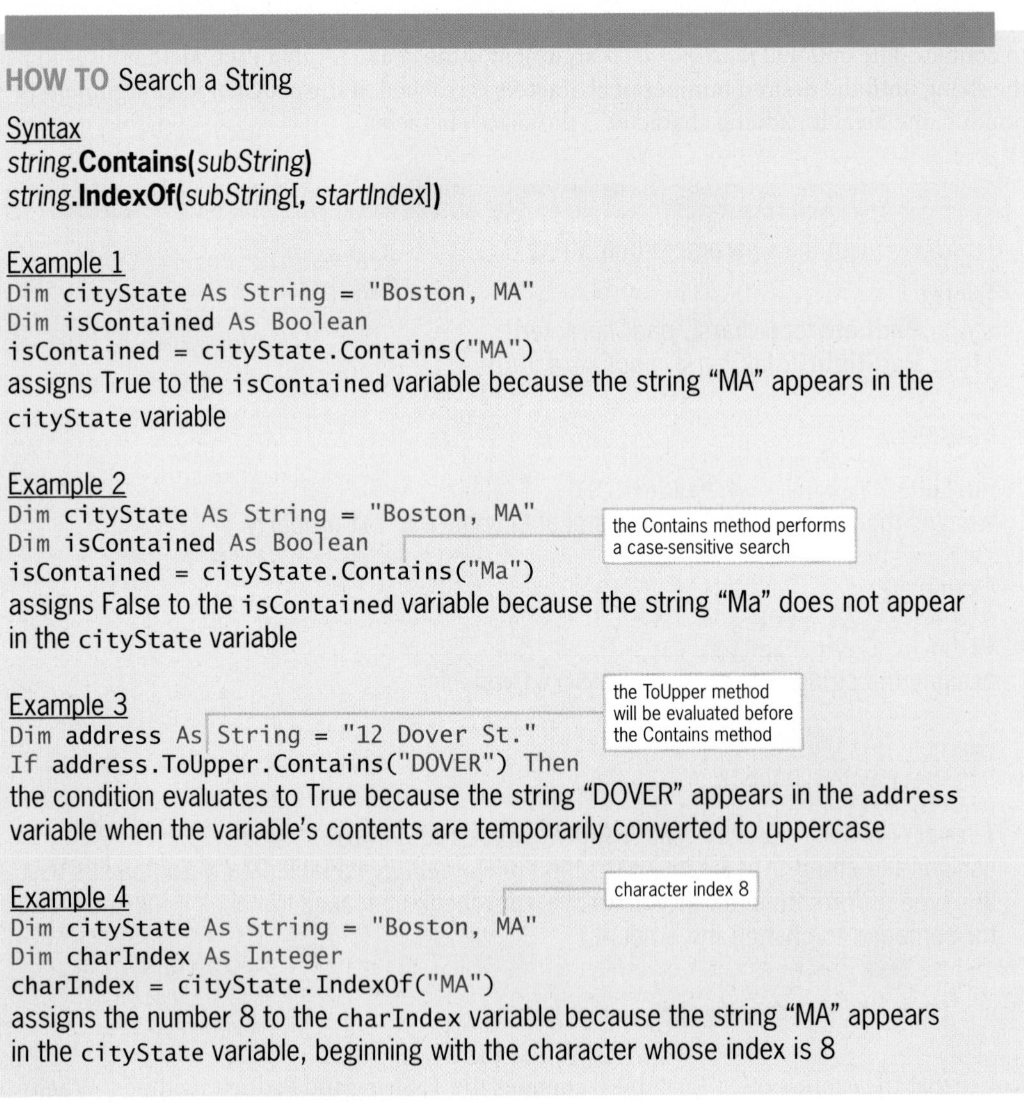

HOW TO Search a String

Syntax
string.**Contains(***subString***)**
string.**IndexOf(***subString*[, *startIndex*]**)**

Example 1
```
Dim cityState As String = "Boston, MA"
Dim isContained As Boolean
isContained = cityState.Contains("MA")
```
assigns True to the `isContained` variable because the string "MA" appears in the `cityState` variable

Example 2
```
Dim cityState As String = "Boston, MA"
Dim isContained As Boolean
isContained = cityState.Contains("Ma")
```
the Contains method performs a case-sensitive search
assigns False to the `isContained` variable because the string "Ma" does not appear in the `cityState` variable

Example 3
```
Dim address As String = "12 Dover St."
If address.ToUpper.Contains("DOVER") Then
```
the ToUpper method will be evaluated before the Contains method
the condition evaluates to True because the string "DOVER" appears in the `address` variable when the variable's contents are temporarily converted to uppercase

Example 4
```
Dim cityState As String = "Boston, MA"
Dim charIndex As Integer
charIndex = cityState.IndexOf("MA")
```
character index 8
assigns the number 8 to the `charIndex` variable because the string "MA" appears in the `cityState` variable, beginning with the character whose index is 8

Figure 10-5 How to search a string *(continues)*

(continued)

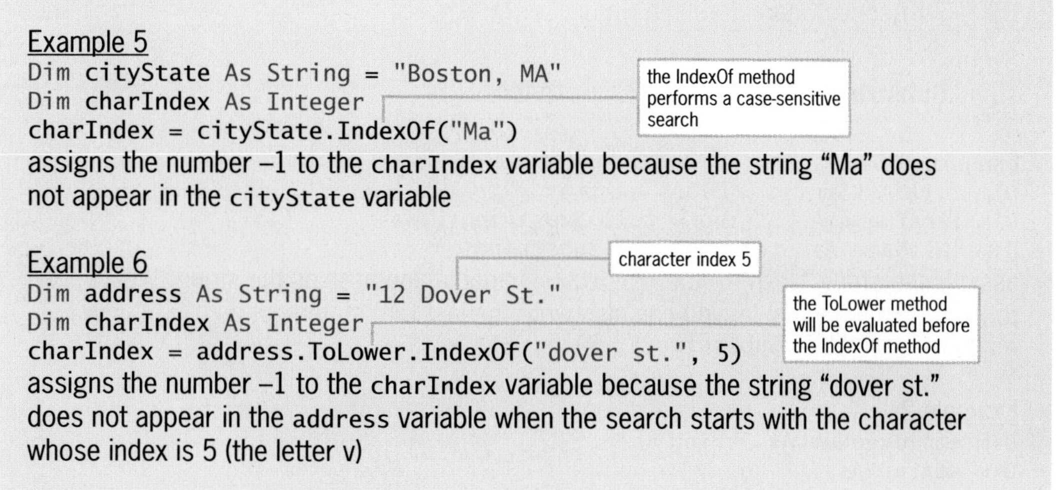
Example 5
Dim cityState As String = "Boston, MA"
Dim charIndex As Integer
charIndex = cityState.IndexOf("Ma")
the IndexOf method performs a case-sensitive search
assigns the number –1 to the charIndex variable because the string "Ma" does not appear in the cityState variable
Example 6
character index 5
Dim address As String = "12 Dover St."
Dim charIndex As Integer
charIndex = address.ToLower.IndexOf("dover st.", 5)
the ToLower method will be evaluated before the IndexOf method
assigns the number –1 to the charIndex variable because the string "dover st." does not appear in the address variable when the search starts with the character whose index is 5 (the letter v)

Figure 10-5 How to search a string

The **Contains method**, which appears in Examples 1 through 3, returns the Boolean value True when the subString is contained anywhere in the string; otherwise, it returns the Boolean value False. The Contains method always begins the search with the first character in the string.

The **IndexOf method**, which appears in Examples 4 through 6, returns an integer: either –1 or a number that is greater than or equal to 0. The –1 indicates that the subString is not contained in the string. A number other than –1 is the character index of the subString's starting position in the string. Unless you specify otherwise, the IndexOf method starts the search with the first character in the string. To specify a different starting location, you use the optional *startIndex* argument.

Notice that the expression in Example 3 contains two methods: ToUpper and Contains. Two methods also appear in the expression in Example 6: ToLower and IndexOf. Recall that when an expression contains more than one method, the computer processes the methods from left to right. In this case, the computer will process the ToUpper method before the Contains method in Example 3, and it will process the ToLower method before the IndexOf method in Example 6.

Accessing the Characters in a String

Visual Basic provides the **Substring method** for accessing any number of characters in a string. Figure 10-6 shows the method's syntax and includes examples of using the method. In the syntax, *string* can be a String variable, a String named constant, or the Text property of a control. The *startIndex* argument is the index of the first character you want to access in the string. As you already know, the first character in a string has an index of 0. The optional *numCharsToAccess* argument specifies the number of characters you want to access. The Substring method returns a string that contains the number of characters specified in the numCharsToAccess argument, beginning with the character whose index is startIndex. If you omit the numCharsToAccess argument, the Substring method returns all characters from the startIndex position through the end of the string.

If you want to experiment with the Contains, IndexOf, and Substring methods, open the solution contained in the Try It 3! folder.

HOW TO Access Characters in a String

Syntax
string.**Substring(***startIndex*[, *numCharsToAccess*]**)**

Example 1

character index 0 / character index 5

```
Dim full As String = "Josh Wentworth"
Dim firstName As String = full.Substring(0, 4)
Dim lastName As String = full.Substring(5)
```

assigns the string "Josh" to the `firstName` variable and assigns the string "Wentworth" to the `lastName` variable; you can also write the last Dim statement as `Dim lastName As String = full.Substring(5, 9)`

Example 2

character index 2

```
Dim employeeNum As String = "38F45"
Dim status As String
status = employeeNum.Substring(2, 1)
```

assigns the string "F" to the `status` variable

Figure 10-6 How to access characters in a string

The answers to Mini-Quiz questions are located in Appendix A. Each question is associated with one or more objectives listed at the beginning of the chapter.

Mini-Quiz 10-2

1. If the `hotel` variable contains the string "Jefferson Express", what will the `hotel.ToUpper.Contains("Jefferson")` method return? (5)
   a. 0
   b. 1
   c. True
   d. False

2. If the `hotel` variable contains the string "Jefferson Express", what will the `hotel.ToUpper.IndexOf("EXPRESS")` method return? (5)
   a. 9
   b. 10
   c. True
   d. False

3. If the `restaurant` variable contains the string "Monica's Polish Deli", which of the following assigns the string "Polish" to the `foodType` variable? (6)
   a. `foodType = restaurant.Substring(8)`
   b. `foodType = restaurant.Substring(8, 6)`
   c. `foodType = restaurant.Substring(9)`
   d. `foodType = restaurant.Substring(9, 6)`

4. Which of the following changes the contents of the `grade` variable from A to A++++? (3, 4)
   a. `grade = grade.Insert(1, "++").PadRight(5, "+"c)`
   b. `grade = grade.PadRight(5, "+"c)`
   c. `grade = grade.Insert(1, "++++")`
   d. all of the above

Using Pattern Matching to Compare Strings

The **Like operator** allows you to use pattern-matching characters to determine whether one string is equal to another string. Figure 10-7 shows the operator's syntax and examples of using the operator. In the syntax, *string* can be a String variable, a String named constant, or the Text property of a control. *Pattern* is a String expression containing one or more of the pattern-matching characters listed in the figure.

If you want to experiment with the Like operator, open the solution contained in the Try It 4! folder.

HOW TO Use Pattern Matching to Compare Strings

Syntax
string **Like** *pattern*

Pattern-matching characters	Matches in *string*
?	any single character
*	zero or more characters
#	any single digit (0 through 9)
[*characterList*]	any single character in the *characterList* (for example, "[A9M]" matches A, 9, or M, whereas "[a-z]" matches any lowercase letter)
[!*characterList*]	any single character *not* in the *characterList* (for example, "[!A9M]" matches any character other than A, 9, or M, whereas "[!a-z]" matches any character that is not a lowercase letter)

Example 1

```
If firstName.ToUpper Like "B?LL" Then
```

The condition evaluates to True when the string stored in the `firstName` variable (converted to uppercase) begins with the letter B followed by one character and then the two letters LL; otherwise, it evaluates to False. Examples of strings that would make the condition evaluate to True include "Bill", "Ball", "bell", and "bull". Examples of strings for which the condition would evaluate to False include "BPL", "BLL", and "billy".

Example 2

```
If stateTextBox.Text Like "K*" Then
```

The condition evaluates to True when the contents of the stateTextBox's Text property begins with the letter K followed by zero or more characters; otherwise, it evaluates to False. Examples of strings that would make the condition evaluate to True include "KANSAS", "Ky", and "Kentucky". Examples of strings for which the condition would evaluate to False include "kansas" and "ky".

Example 3

```
Do While id Like "###*"
```

The condition evaluates to True when the string stored in the `id` variable begins with three digits followed by zero or more characters; otherwise, it evaluates to False. Examples of strings that would make the condition evaluate to True include "178" and "983Ab". Examples of strings for which the condition would evaluate to False include "X34" and "34Z5".

Figure 10-7 How to use pattern matching to compare strings *(continues)*

(continued)

Example 4

```
If firstName.ToUpper Like "T[OI]M" Then
```

The condition evaluates to True when the string stored in the `firstName` variable (converted to uppercase) is either "TOM" or "TIM". When the variable does not contain "TOM" or "TIM"—for example, when it contains "Tam" or "Tommy"—the condition evaluates to False.

Example 5

```
If letter Like "[a-z]" Then
```

The condition evaluates to True when the string stored in the `letter` variable is one lowercase letter; otherwise, it evaluates to False.

Example 6

```
Dim fullName As String
Dim currentChar As String
Dim nonLetter As Integer
fullName = nameTextBox.Text
For index As Integer = 0 To fullName.Length - 1
    currentChar = fullName.Substring(index, 1)
    If currentChar Like "[!a-zA-Z]" Then
        nonLetter += 1
    End If
Next index
```

The loop compares each character contained in the `fullName` variable with the lowercase and uppercase letters of the alphabet, and counts the number of characters that are not letters.

Example 7

```
If rateTextBox.Text Like "*.*" Then
```

The condition evaluates to True when a period appears anywhere in the rateTextBox's Text property; otherwise, it evaluates to False.

Example 8

```
If partNum.ToUpper Like "[A-Z][A-Z]##" Then
```

The condition evaluates to True when the string stored in the `partNum` variable (converted to uppercase) is two letters followed by two numbers; otherwise, it evaluates to False.

Figure 10-7 How to use pattern matching to compare strings

As Figure 10-7 indicates, the question mark (?) character in a pattern represents one character only, whereas the asterisk (*) character represents zero or more characters. To represent a single digit in a pattern, you use the number sign (#). The last two pattern-matching characters listed in the figure contain a *characterList*, which is simply a listing of characters. "[A9M]" is a characterList that contains three characters: A, 9, and M. You can also include a range of values in a characterList. You do this by using a hyphen to separate the lowest value in the range from the highest value in the range. For example, to include all lowercase letters in a characterList, you use "[a-z]". To include both lowercase and uppercase letters in a characterList, you use "[a-zA-Z]".

The Like operator performs a case-sensitive comparison of the string to the pattern. If the string matches the pattern, the Like operator returns the Boolean value True; otherwise, it returns the Boolean value False.

Mini-Quiz 10-3

The answers to Mini-Quiz questions are located in Appendix A. Each question is associated with one or more objectives listed at the beginning of the chapter.

1. Which of the following evaluates to True when the `modelNum` variable contains the string "45Y32Z"? (7)
   a. `modelNum Like "99[A-Z]99[A-Z]"`
   b. `modelNum Like "##[A-Z]##[A-Z]"`
   c. `modelNum Like "[##]A-Z[##]A-Z"`
   d. `modelNum Like "[99][[A-Z][99][A-Z]"`
2. Which of the following determines whether a comma appears anywhere in the salesTextBox's Text property? (7)
   a. `salesTextBox.Text Like "*,*"`
   b. `salesTextBox.Text Like ","`
   c. `salesTextBox.Text Like "[*,*]"`
   d. none of the above
3. Which of the following determines whether a percent sign (%) appears as the last character in the rateTextBox's Text property? (7)
   a. `rateTextBox.Text Like "%"`
   b. `rateTextBox.Text Like "*%*"`
   c. `rateTextBox.Text Like "*%"`
   d. none of the above

Adding a Menu to a Form

The Menus & Toolbars section of the toolbox contains a MenuStrip tool for instantiating a menu strip control. You use a **menu strip control** to include one or more menus on a Windows form. Each menu contains a menu title, which appears on the menu bar at the top of the form. When you click a menu title, its corresponding menu opens and displays a list of options, called menu items. The menu items can be commands (such as Open or Exit), separator bars, or submenu titles. As in all Windows applications, clicking a command on a menu executes the command, and clicking a submenu title opens an additional menu of options. Each of the options on a submenu is referred to as a submenu item. You can use a separator bar to visually group together related items on a menu or submenu. Figure 10-8 identifies the location of these menu elements. Although you can create many levels of submenus, it is best to use only one level in your application because including too many layers of submenus can confuse the user.

Ch10-Menus

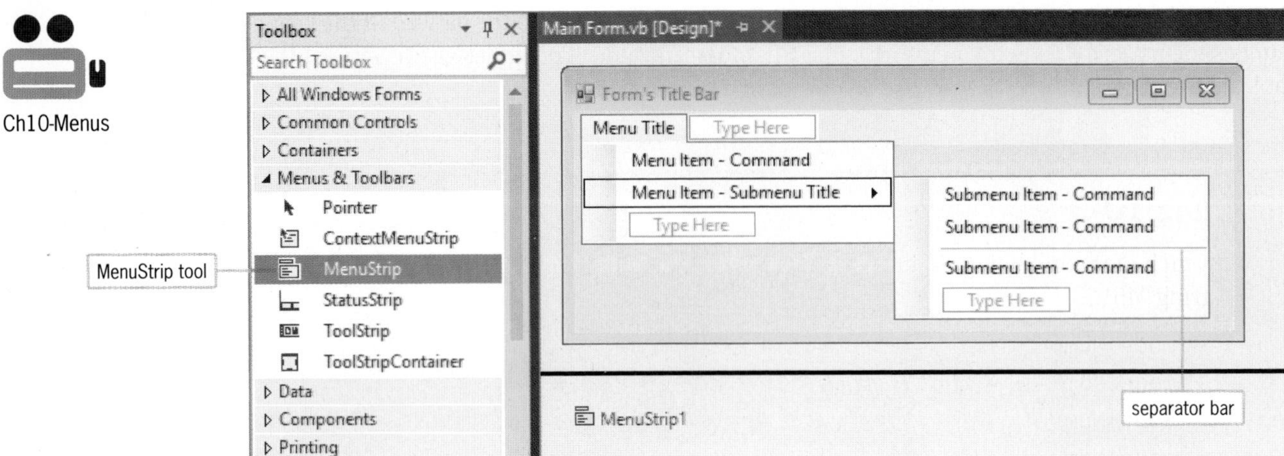

Figure 10-8 Location of menu elements

Each menu element is considered an object and has a set of properties associated with it. The most commonly used properties for a menu element are the Name and Text properties. The programmer uses the Name property to refer to the menu element in code. The Text property stores the menu element's caption, which is the text that the user sees when he or she is working with the menu. The caption indicates the menu element's purpose. Examples of familiar captions for menu elements include Edit, Save As, Copy, and Exit.

Menu title captions should be one word only, with only the first letter capitalized. Each menu title should have a unique access key. The access key allows the user to open the menu by pressing the Alt key in combination with the access key. Unlike the captions for menu titles, the captions for menu items typically consist of one to three words and are entered using book title capitalization. Each menu item should have an access key that is unique within its menu. The access key allows the user to select the item by pressing the access key when the menu is open. If a menu item requires additional information from the user, the Windows standard is to place an ellipsis (...) at the end of the caption. The ellipsis alerts the user that the menu item requires more information before it can perform its task.

Commonly used menu items should be assigned shortcut keys. The **shortcut keys** appear to the right of a menu item and allow the user to select the item without opening the menu. Examples of familiar shortcut keys include Ctrl+X and Ctrl+V. In Windows applications that have an Edit menu, Ctrl+X and Ctrl+V can be used to select the Cut and Paste commands, respectively, when the Edit menu is closed. You specify a menu item's shortcut keys in its ShortcutKeys property in the Properties window.

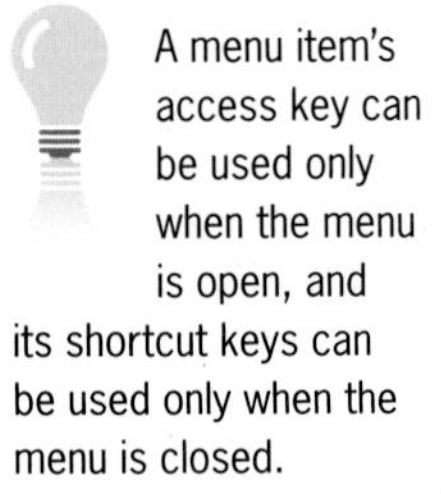

A menu item's access key can be used only when the menu is open, and its shortcut keys can be used only when the menu is closed.

Figure 10-9 shows the File menu you will create in Programming Tutorial 1. The menu contains two menu items: New Game and Exit. The menu title and both menu items have access keys. In addition, shortcut keys are provided for the New Game menu item.

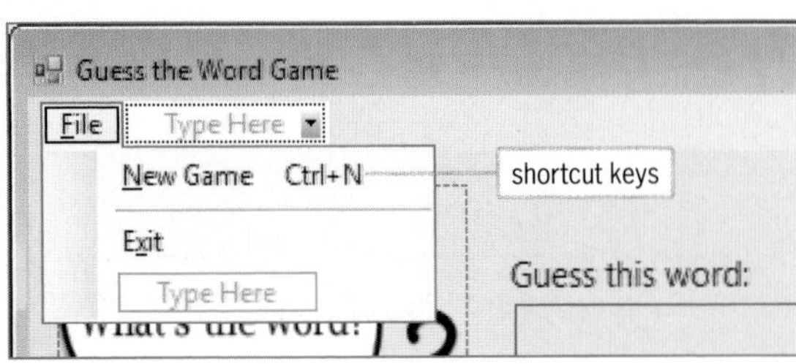

Figure 10-9 File menu

If an item on a menu or submenu is a command, you enter the appropriate instructions in the item's Click event procedure. Figure 10-10 shows the Click event procedure for the Exit command from Figure 10-9.

```
Private Sub fileExitMenuItem_Click(sender As Object, e As EventArgs
) Handles fileExitMenuItem.Click
    Me.Close()
End Sub
```

Figure 10-10 Exit command's Click event procedure

You have completed the concepts section of Chapter 10. The Programming Tutorial section is next.

PROGRAMMING TUTORIAL 1

Completing the Guess the Word Game Application

In this tutorial, you will complete the Guess the Word Game application, which is played by two people. Figures 10-11 and 10-12 show the application's TOE chart and MainForm, respectively. The MainForm contains seven labels, one picture box, one text box, and one button. It also contains a File menu that has two options: New Game and Exit. When the user clicks the New Game option, the option's Click event procedure will prompt player 1 to enter a six-letter word. Player 2 will then be given seven chances to guess the word, letter by letter. The game is over when player 2 either guesses all of the letters in the word or makes seven incorrect guesses, whichever comes first. If player 2 guesses the word, the application will display the "Great guessing!" message. If player 2 does not guess the word, the application will display the message "Sorry, the word is" followed by the word.

Task	Object	Event
1. Clear wordLabel, incorrectLabel, and letterTextBox 2. Set incorrect guess counter to 0 3. Assign 7 to remainingLabel 4. Get a 6-letter word from player 1, trim spaces, and convert to uppercase 5. Determine whether the word contains 6 letters 6. If the word contains 6 letters, display 6 dashes in wordLabel, enable checkButton, and send the focus to letterTextBox 7. If the word doesn't contain 6 letters, display "6 letters are required" in a message box and disable checkButton	fileNewMenuItem	Click
1. Search the word for the letter entered by player 2 2. If the letter is contained in the word, replace the appropriate dashes in wordLabel; if there aren't any other dashes in the word, the game is over because player 2 guessed the word, so display "Great guessing!" in a message box and disable checkButton	checkButton	Click

Figure 10-11 TOE chart for the Guess the Word Game application *(continues)*

(continued)

3. If the letter is not contained in the word, display the letter in incorrectLabel, add 1 to the incorrect guesses counter, and update the value in the remainingLabel; if player 2 made 7 incorrect guesses, the game is over, so display "Sorry, the word is *word*." in a message box and disable checkButton 4. Clear letterTextBox and send the focus to it		
End the application	fileExitMenuItem	Click
Accept only letters and the Backspace key	letterTextBox	KeyPress
Display dashes and letters (from fileNewMenuItem and checkButton)	wordLabel	None
Display the incorrect letters (from checkButton)	incorrectLabel	None
Display number of incorrect guesses remaining (from fileNewMenuItem and checkButton)	remainingLabel	None

Figure 10-11 TOE chart for the Guess the Word Game application

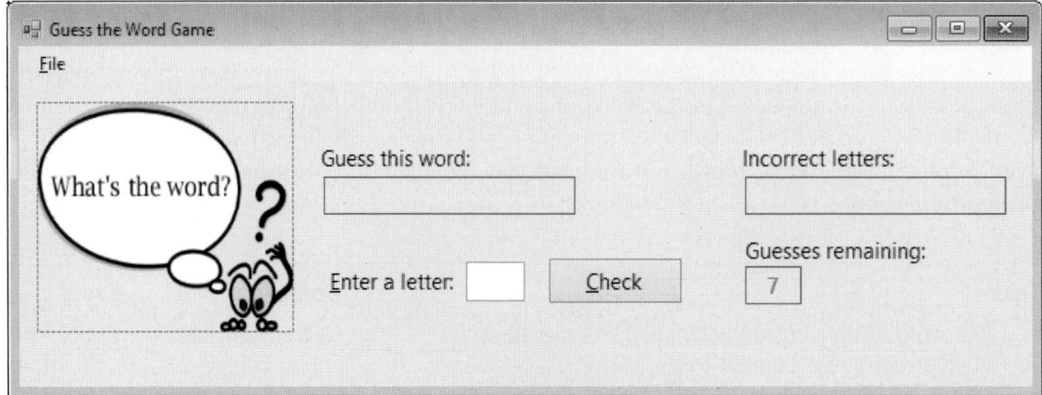

Figure 10-12 MainForm for the Guess the Word Game application

Completing the Interface

Before you can code the application, you need to complete its interface.

To complete the application's interface:

1. Start Visual Studio. Open the **Word Solution** (**Word Solution.sln**) file contained in the VbReloaded2015\Chap10\Word Solution folder. If necessary, open the designer, Toolbox, and Properties windows.
2. Click **MenuStrip** in the Menus & Toolbars section of the toolbox. Drag the mouse pointer to the form and then release the mouse button. A MenuStrip control named MenuStrip1 appears in the component tray, and the words *Type Here* appear in a box below the form's title bar. See Figure 10-13.

PROGRAMMING TUTORIAL 1

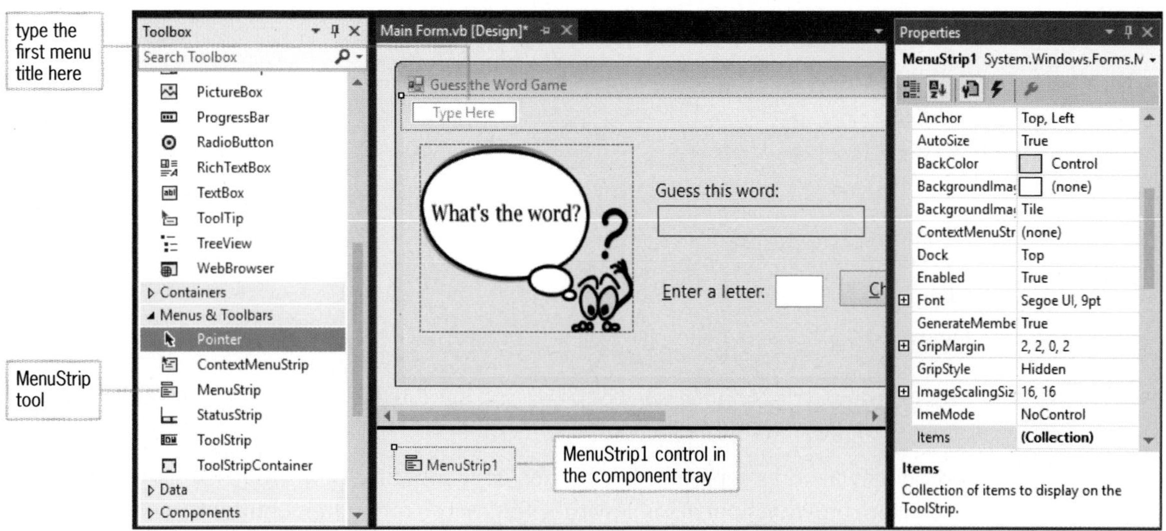

Figure 10-13 MenuStrip control added to the form

3. Auto-hide the toolbox. Click the **Type Here** box on the menu bar and then type **&File**. See Figure 10-14. You use the Type Here box that appears below the menu title to add a menu item to the File menu. You use the Type Here box that appears to the right of the menu title to add another menu title to the menu bar.

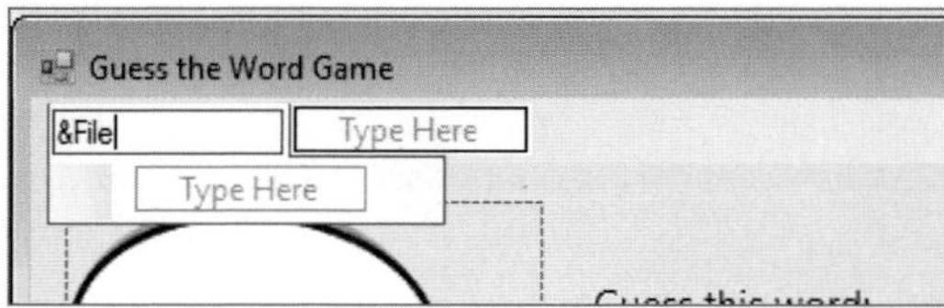

Figure 10-14 Menu title included on the form

4. Press **Enter** and then click the **File** menu title. Scroll the Properties window until you see the Text property, which contains &File. Now, scroll to the top of the Properties window and then click **(Name)**. Type **fileMenuTitle** and then press **Enter**.
5. Click the **Type Here** box that appears below the File menu title. Type **&New Game** and then press **Enter**. Click the **New Game** menu item, and then change its name to **fileNewMenuItem**.
6. Next, you will assign Ctrl+N as the shortcut keys for the New Game menu item. Click **ShortcutKeys** in the Properties window and then click the **list arrow** in the Settings box. A box opens and allows you to specify a modifier and a key. In this case, the modifier and the key will be Ctrl and N, respectively. Click the **Ctrl** check box to select it, and then click the **list arrow** that appears in the Key combo box. An alphabetical list of keys appears. Scroll the list until you see the letter N, and then click **N** in the list. See Figure 10-15.

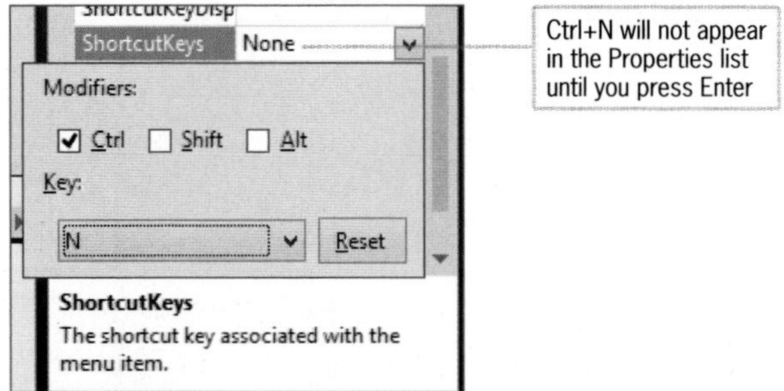

Figure 10-15 Shortcut keys specified in the ShortcutKeys box

7. Press **Enter**. Ctrl+N appears in the ShortcutKeys property in the Properties list. It also appears to the right of the New Game menu item.
8. Now, you will add a separator bar to the File menu. Place your mouse pointer on the Type Here box that appears below the New Game menu item, but don't click the box. Instead, click the **list arrow** that appears inside the box. See Figure 10-16.

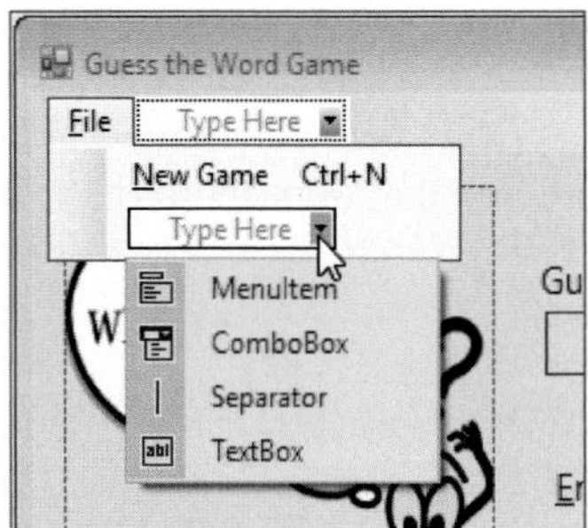

Figure 10-16 Drop-down list

9. Click **Separator** in the list. A horizontal line, called a separator bar, appears below the New Game menu item.
10. Click the **Type Here** box that appears below the separator bar. Type **E&xit** and then press **Enter**. Click the **Exit** menu item, and then change its name to **fileExitMenuItem**.
11. Auto-hide the Properties window. Save the solution and then start the application. Click **File** on the menu bar. The menu opens and offers two options separated by a separator bar, as shown in Figure 10-17.

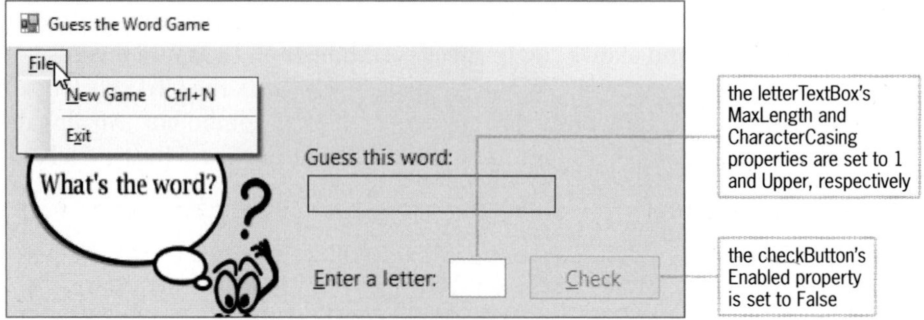

Figure 10-17 File menu opened during run time

12. Click the **Close** button on the form's title bar.

Coding the File Menu's Exit Option

According to the application's TOE chart, the Click event procedures for the two menu items and the checkButton need to be coded. The KeyPress event procedure for the letterTextBox also needs to be coded. You'll begin by coding the fileExitMenuItem_Click procedure.

To code the fileExitMenuItem_Click procedure:

1. Open the Code Editor window, which already contains most of the application's code. In the comments that appear in the General Declarations section, replace <your name> and <current date> with your name and the current date, respectively.
2. Open the code template for the fileExitMenuItem_Click procedure. Type **Me.Close()** and press **Enter**.

Coding the letterTextBox's KeyPress Event

As indicated earlier in Figure 10-17, the letterTextBox's MaxLength and CharacterCasing properties are set to 1 and Upper, respectively. As a result, the text box will accept one character only. If the character is a letter of the alphabet, it will be converted to uppercase. In the next set of steps, you will prevent the text box from accepting a character that is not either a letter of the alphabet or the Backspace key. You can do this by using an If...Then...Else statement with the following condition: `e.KeyChar Like "[!A-Za-z]" AndAlso e.KeyChar <> ControlChars.Back`. The subcondition on the left side of the AndAlso operator will evaluate to True if the user's entry is not one of the uppercase or lowercase letters of the alphabet. The subcondition on the right side of the AndAlso operator will evaluate to True if the user's entry is not the Backspace key. If both subconditions evaluate to True, the compound condition will evaluate to True and the text box should not accept the user's entry.

To code and then test the letterTextBox_KeyPress procedure:

1. Open the code template for the letterTextBox_KeyPress procedure, and then type the comment and selection structure shown in Figure 10-18. (Be sure to type the exclamation point in the Like operator's characterList.)

```
Private Sub letterTextBox_KeyPress(sender As Object
    ' allows only letters and the Backspace key

    If e.KeyChar Like "[!A-Za-z]" AndAlso
          e.KeyChar <> ControlChars.Back Then
        e.Handled = True
    End If
End Sub
```

enter this comment and selection structure

Figure 10-18 letterTextBox_KeyPress procedure

2. Save the solution and then start the application. Type **a** in the text box. Notice that the letter is changed to its uppercase equivalent, A. Press the **Backspace** key to delete the letter A.
3. Next, try to enter a character other than a letter of the alphabet or the Backspace key; you won't be able to do so. Also try to enter more than one letter; here, too, you won't be able to do so.
4. Click **File** on the game application's menu bar and then click **Exit** to end the application.

Coding the File Menu's New Game Option

The fileNewMenuItem_Click procedure is invoked when the user either clicks the New Game option on the File menu or presses Ctrl+N (the option's shortcut keys). The procedure should get a six-letter word from player 1 and then verify that the word contains exactly six letters. The procedure's pseudocode is shown in Figure 10-19.

```
fileNewMenuItem Click event procedure
1. clear contents of wordLabel, incorrectLabel, and letterTextBox
2. assign 0 to the counter variable that keeps track of the number of incorrect letters
3. assign 7 to the remainingLabel
4. get a 6-letter word from player 1, trim leading and trailing spaces, and convert to uppercase
5. if the word contains 6 letters
      display 6 dashes in wordLabel
      enable checkButton
      send the focus to letterTextBox
   else
      display "6 letters are required" message in a message box
      disable checkButton
   end if
```

Figure 10-19 Pseudocode for the fileNewMenuItem_Click procedure

To begin coding the fileNewMenuItem_Click procedure:

1. First, scroll to the top of the Code Editor window. The form's Declarations section declares two class-level variables. The `secretWord` variable will store the word entered by player 1. The `numIncorrect` variable will keep track of the number of incorrect letters entered by player 2.
2. Now, open the code template for the fileNewMenuItem_Click procedure. Type the following comment and then press **Enter** twice:

   ' start a new game
3. According to its pseudocode, the procedure should begin by clearing the contents of the wordLabel, incorrectLabel, and letterTextBox. Enter the following assignment statements:

   wordLabel.Text = String.Empty
   incorrectLabel.Text = String.Empty
   letterTextBox.Text = String.Empty
4. Next, the procedure should reset the variable that keeps track of the number of incorrect letters to 0. It should also assign the number 7, which is the total number of incorrect guesses player 2 is allowed per game, to the remainingLabel. (Each time player 2 makes an incorrect guess, the checkButton_Click procedure updates the value displayed in the remainingLabel.) Type the following assignment statements and then press **Enter** twice:

   numIncorrect = 0
   remainingLabel.Text = "7"

5. The fourth step in the pseudocode gets a word that contains six letters from player 1. The procedure should trim any leading and trailing spaces from the word and also convert the word to uppercase. Enter the following comment and lines of code. Press **Enter** twice after typing the last line.

   ' get a 6-letter word from player 1
   ' trim and convert to uppercase
   secretWord = InputBox("Enter a 6-letter word:",
   "Guess the Word Game").Trim.ToUpper

Next, the procedure should verify that player 1's word contains exactly six letters. Figure 10-20 shows two ways of accomplishing this task. Example 1 uses the Length property and the Substring method; both are shaded in the figure. Example 2 uses the Like operator, which is also shaded in the figure. Although the code in both examples produces the same result, Example 2's code is much more concise and easier to understand.

Example 1

```
Dim validWord As Boolean

' determine whether the word contains 6 letters
validWord = True   ' assume word is valid
If word.Length <> 6 Then
    validWord = False
Else
    Dim index As Integer
    Do While index < 6 AndAlso validWord = True
        If word.Substring(index, 1) Like "[!A-Z]" Then
            validWord = False
        End If
        index += 1
    Loop
End If

If validWord = True Then
      instructions to be processed when the word is valid
Else
      instructions to be processed when the word is not valid
End If
```

Example 2

```
If word Like "[A-Z][A-Z][A-Z][A-Z][A-Z][A-Z]" Then
      instructions to be processed when the word is valid
Else
      instructions to be processed when the word is not valid
End If
```

Figure 10-20 Two ways of determining whether the word contains six letters

To complete and then test the fileNewMenuItem_Click procedure:

1. Enter the following comment and If clause:

   ' determine whether the word contains 6 letters
   If secretWord Like "[A-Z][A-Z][A-Z][A-Z][A-Z][A-Z]" Then

2. If player 1's word contains six letters, the selection structure's True path should display six dashes (one for each letter in the word) in the wordLabel. It then should enable the checkButton and send the focus to the letterTextBox. Enter the following comments and lines of code:

```
' display 6 dashes
wordLabel.Text = "------"
' enable button and set focus
checkButton.Enabled = True
letterTextBox.Focus()
```

3. Next, you need to code the selection structure's False path. According to the pseudocode, the False path should display a message and disable the checkButton when player 1's word does not contain six letters. Enter the following lines of code:

```
Else
    MessageBox.Show("6 letters are required",
                    "Guess the Word Game",
                    MessageBoxButtons.OK,
                    MessageBoxIcon.Information)
checkButton.Enabled = False
```

4. If necessary, delete the **blank line** above the End If clause.

5. Save the solution and then start the application. Click **File** on the menu bar and then click **New Game**. A dialog box opens and prompts you to enter a word that contains six letters. Type **summer** in the dialog box and then press **Enter**. Six dashes appear in the Guess this word box. In addition, the Check button is enabled for the user. See Figure 10-21.

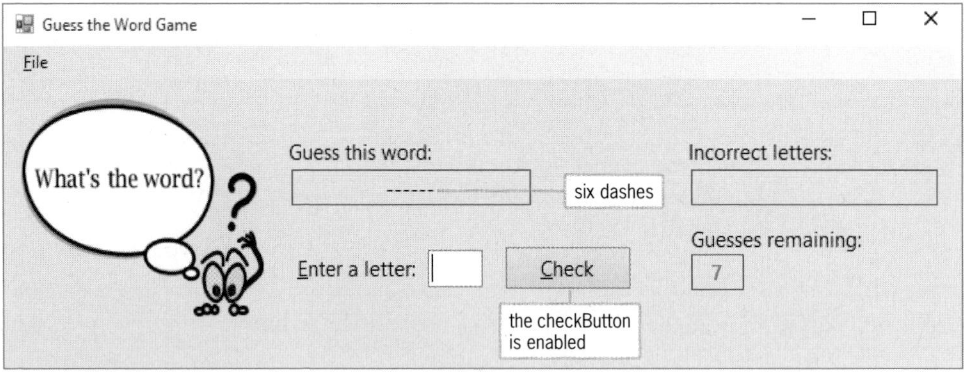

Figure 10-21 Result of entering a valid word

6. Next, you will enter a word that contains fewer than six letters. Press **Ctrl+n**, which are the shortcut keys for the New Game option. Type **fall** in the dialog box and then press **Enter**. The message "6 letters are required" appears in a message box. Close the message box. Notice that the Check button is now disabled.

7. On your own, test the procedure using a word that has more than six letters. Also test it using a word that has five characters followed by a number. In both cases, the message "6 letters are required" appears in a message box. When you are finished testing the procedure, click the **Exit** option on the game application's File menu.

Completing the Check Button's Click Event Procedure

Figure 10-22 shows the pseudocode for the checkButton_Click procedure. It also shows the pseudocode for an independent Sub procedure named DetermineGameOver, which is used by the checkButton_Click procedure.

```
checkButton Click event procedure
1. repeat for each letter in player 1's word
        if the current letter is the same as the letter entered by player 2
              replace the corresponding dash in wordLabel
              assign True to the dashReplaced variable
        end if
   end repeat
2. if the dashReplaced variable contains True
        call the DetermineGameOver procedure to determine whether player 2 guessed
        the word; pass the dashReplaced variable
   else
        display player 2's letter in incorrectLabel
        add 1 to the counter variable that keeps track of the number of incorrect letters
        display remaining number of guesses in remainingLabel
        call the DetermineGameOver procedure to determine whether player 2 made
        7 incorrect guesses; pass the dashReplaced variable
   end if
3. clear letterTextBox and send the focus to it

DetermineGameOver procedure
if a dash was replaced in player 1's word
        if there aren't any other dashes in the word
              display "Great guessing!" in a message box
              disable checkButton
        end if
else
        if the user entered 7 incorrect letters
              display "Sorry, the word is word." in a message box
              disable checkButton
        end if
end if
```

Figure 10-22 Pseudocode for the checkButton_Click and DetermineGameOver procedures

The DetermineGameOver procedure has already been coded for you. The Code Editor window also contains most of the code for the checkButton_Click procedure. You will complete the procedure in the next set of steps.

To complete the checkButton_Click procedure:

1. Locate the checkButton_Click procedure. The first step in the procedure's pseudocode is a loop that performs its instructions for each letter in player 1's word. The word, which is stored in the class-level `secretWord` variable, contains six letters whose indexes are 0, 1, 2, 3, 4, and 5. Click the **blank line** below the `' look at each letter in the word` comment and then enter the following For clause:

   For index As Integer = 0 To 5

2. Change the Next clause to **Next index** and then click the **blank line** below the For clause.
3. The first instruction in the loop is a selection structure that compares the current letter in the `secretWord` variable with the letter entered by player 2. As you learned in the concepts section of the chapter, you can use the Substring method to access an individual character in a string. The method's *startIndex* argument is the index of the first character you want to access, and its optional *numCharsToAccess* argument specifies the number of characters you want to access. Enter the following If clause:

   If secretWord.Substring(index, 1) = letter Then
4. If the current letter in the `secretWord` variable matches player 2's letter, the selection structure's True path should replace the corresponding dash in the wordLabel with player 2's letter. You can use the Remove and Insert methods to make the replacement. Enter the following comment and assignment statements:

   ' replace corresponding dash with letter
   wordLabel.Text =
   wordLabel.Text.Remove(index, 1)
   wordLabel.Text =
   wordLabel.Text.Insert(index, letter)
5. Finally, the selection structure's True path should assign the Boolean value True to the `dashReplaced` variable to indicate that a replacement was made. Type **dashReplaced = True** and then click the **blank line** below the `Next index` clause.
6. Save the solution.

Before testing the checkButton_Click procedure, review the code contained in the DetermineGameOver procedure. Notice that the procedure uses the Contains method to determine whether there are any dashes in the wordLabel.

To test the checkButton_Click procedure:

1. Start the application. Click **File** and then click **New Game**. Type **summer** in the input dialog box, and then press **Enter**.
2. Type **m** in the Enter a letter text box, and then press **Enter**. The letter M replaces two of the dashes in the Guess this word box.
3. Type **x** in the text box, and then press **Enter**. The letter X appears in the Incorrect letters box. In addition, the number 6 (rather than 7) now appears in the Guesses remaining box.
4. Type the following letters in the text box, pressing **Enter** after typing each one: **a**, **e**, **s**, **r**, **i**, and **u**. With each incorrect guess, the value in the Guesses remaining box is decreased by 1.
5. When the Game Over message box opens, drag it to the location shown in Figure 10-23.

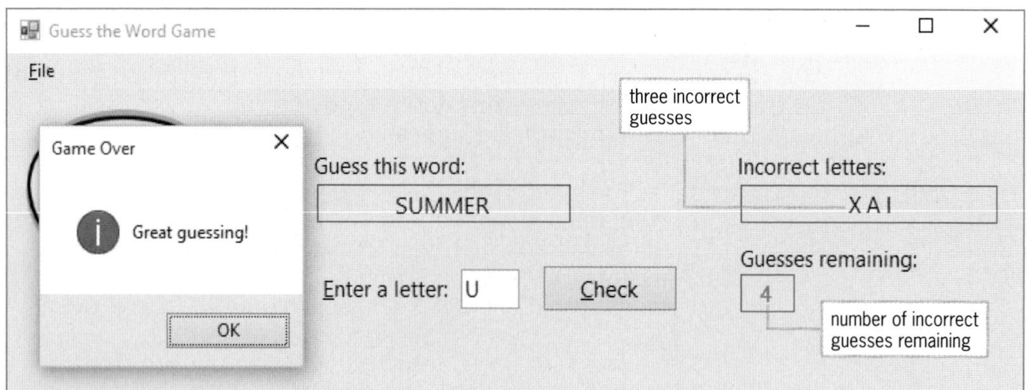

Figure 10-23 Result of guessing the word entered by player 1

6. Close the message box, and then press **Ctrl+n**. Type **winter** in the input dialog box, and then press **Enter**. Type the following letters in the text box, pressing **Enter** after typing each one: **c**, **e**, **t**, **y**, **a**, **b**, **x**, **z**, and **k**.
7. When the Game Over message box opens, drag it to the location shown in Figure 10-24.

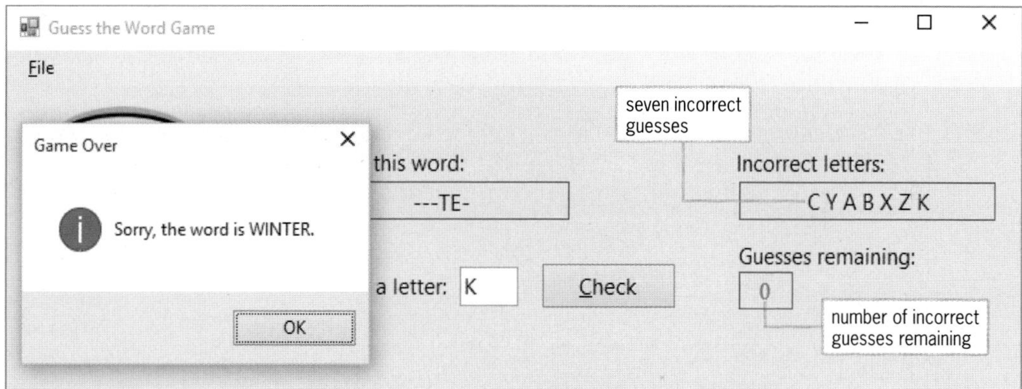

Figure 10-24 Result of not guessing the word entered by player 1

8. Close the message box. Click **File** on the application's menu bar and then click **Exit**. Close the Code Editor window and then close the solution. Figure 10-25 shows the application's code.

```
' Project name:          Word Project
' Project purpose:       A game that allows the user to guess a
'                        word letter-by-letter
' Created/revised by:    <your name> on <current date>

Option Explicit On
Option Strict On
Option Infer Off

Public Class MainForm
    Private secretWord As String
    Private numIncorrect As Integer

```

Figure 10-25 Code for the Guess the Word Game application *(continues)*

(continued)

```
    Private Sub DetermineGameOver(ByVal aDashWasReplaced As Boolean)
        ' determine whether the game is over and
        ' take the appropriate action

        If aDashWasReplaced Then
            ' if the word does not contain any dashes, the game
            ' is over because player 2 guessed the word
            If wordLabel.Text.Contains("-") = False Then
                MessageBox.Show("Great guessing!", "Game Over",
                                MessageBoxButtons.OK,
                                MessageBoxIcon.Information)
                checkButton.Enabled = False
            End If
        Else
            ' if 7 incorrect guesses, the game is over
            If numIncorrect = 7 Then
                MessageBox.Show("Sorry, the word is " &
                                secretWord & ".", "Game Over",
                                MessageBoxButtons.OK,
                                MessageBoxIcon.Information)
                checkButton.Enabled = False
            End If
        End If
    End Sub

    Private Sub checkButton_Click(sender As Object, e As EventArgs) Handles checkButton.Click
        ' check if the letter appears in the word

        Dim letter As String
        Dim dashReplaced As Boolean

        letter = letterTextBox.Text

        ' look at each letter in the word
        For index As Integer = 0 To 5
            If secretWord.Substring(index, 1) = letter Then
                ' replace corresponding dash with letter
                wordLabel.Text =
                    wordLabel.Text.Remove(index, 1)
                wordLabel.Text =
                    wordLabel.Text.Insert(index, letter)
                dashReplaced = True
            End If
        Next index

        If dashReplaced Then
            Call DetermineGameOver(dashReplaced)
        Else  ' no dash was replaced
            incorrectLabel.Text =
                incorrectLabel.Text & " " & letter
            numIncorrect += 1
            remainingLabel.Text = (7 - numIncorrect).ToString
            Call DetermineGameOver(dashReplaced)
        End If

```

Figure 10-25 Code for the Guess the Word Game application *(continues)*

(continued)

```
        ' clear text box and set focus
        letterTextBox.Text = String.Empty
        letterTextBox.Focus()
    End Sub

   Private Sub fileExitMenuItem_Click(sender As Object,
   e As EventArgs) Handles fileExitMenuItem.Click
        Me.Close()

    End Sub

    Private Sub letterTextBox_KeyPress(sender As Object,
    e As KeyPressEventArgs) Handles letterTextBox.KeyPress
        ' allows only letters and the Backspace key

        If e.KeyChar Like "[!A-Za-z]" AndAlso
                e.KeyChar <> ControlChars.Back Then
            e.Handled = True
        End If
    End Sub

    Private Sub fileNewMenuItem_Click(sender As Object,
    e As EventArgs) Handles fileNewMenuItem.Click
        ' start a new game

        wordLabel.Text = String.Empty
        incorrectLabel.Text = String.Empty
        letterTextBox.Text = String.Empty
        numIncorrect = 0
        remainingLabel.Text = "7"

        ' get a 6-letter word from player 1
        ' trim and convert to uppercase
        secretWord = InputBox("Enter a 6-letter word:",
                              "Guess the Word Game").Trim.ToUpper

        ' determine whether the word contains 6 letters
        If secretWord Like "[A-Z][A-Z][A-Z][A-Z][A-Z][A-Z]" Then
            ' display 6 dashes
            wordLabel.Text = "------"
            ' enable button and set focus
            checkButton.Enabled = True
            letterTextBox.Focus()
        Else
            MessageBox.Show("6 letters are required",
                            "Guess the Word Game",
                            MessageBoxButtons.OK,
                            MessageBoxIcon.Information)
            checkButton.Enabled = False
        End If
    End Sub
End Class
```

Figure 10-25 Code for the Guess the Word Game application

PROGRAMMING TUTORIAL 2

Creating the Bucky's Burgers Application

In this tutorial, you will code an application for the manager of the Bucky's Burgers restaurant. The application's interface provides a text box for entering the names of employees who worked the previous day. Each name is added, using proper case, to a list box. Proper case means that the first and last names begin with an uppercase letter, while the remaining letters in the names are lowercase. The application also allows the manager to print the interface. The application's TOE chart and MainForm are shown in Figure 10-26.

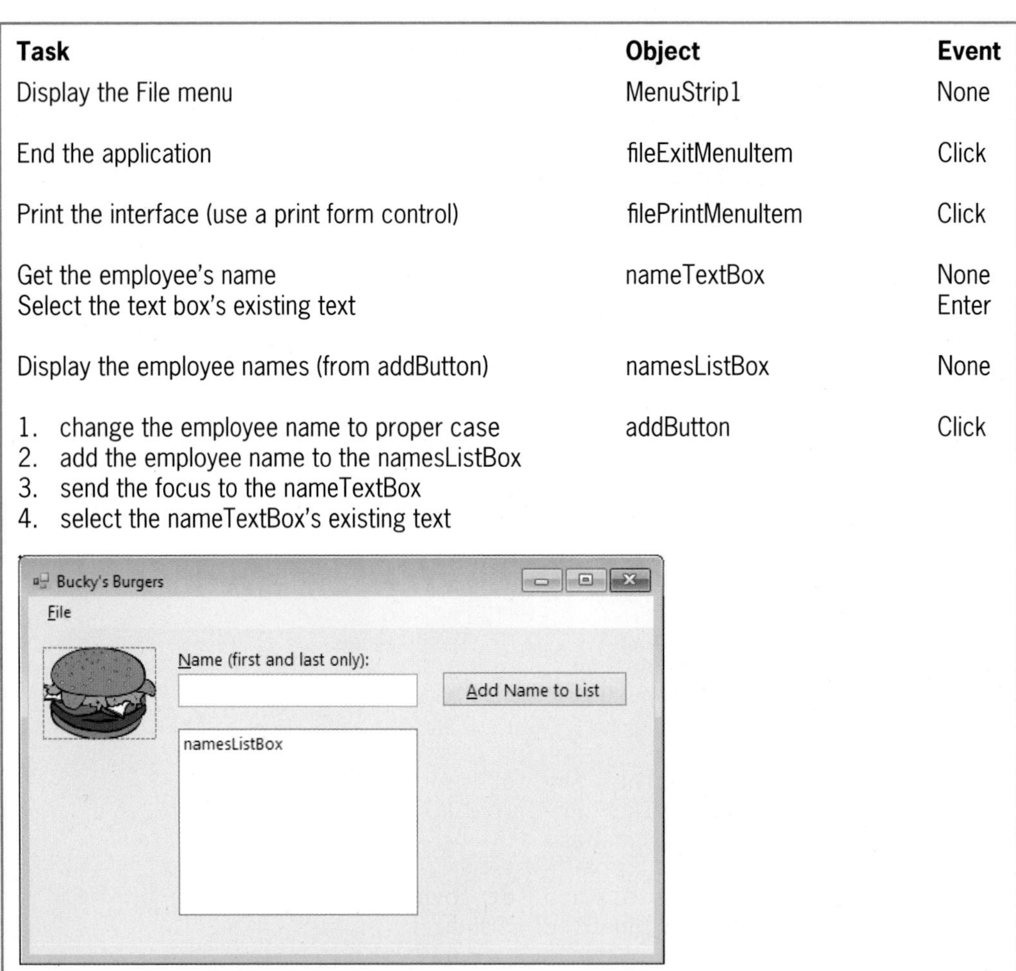

Task	Object	Event
Display the File menu	MenuStrip1	None
End the application	fileExitMenuItem	Click
Print the interface (use a print form control)	filePrintMenuItem	Click
Get the employee's name Select the text box's existing text	nameTextBox	None Enter
Display the employee names (from addButton)	namesListBox	None
1. change the employee name to proper case 2. add the employee name to the namesListBox 3. send the focus to the nameTextBox 4. select the nameTextBox's existing text	addButton	Click

Figure 10-26 TOE chart and MainForm for the Bucky's Burgers application

Completing the Interface

Before you can code the application, you need to add a print form control and the File menu to the form.

To add a print form control and the File menu to the form:

1. Start Visual Studio. Open the **Bucky Solution** (**Bucky Solution.sln**) file contained in the VbReloaded2015\Chap10\Bucky Solution folder. If necessary, open the designer window.

2. Click **PrintForm** in the Visual Basic PowerPacks section of the toolbox. Drag the mouse pointer to the form and then release the mouse button. The PrintForm1 control appears in the component tray. Change the control's PrintAction property to **PrintToPreview**.
3. Click **MenuStrip** in the Menus & Toolbars section of the toolbox. Drag the mouse pointer to the form and then release the mouse button. The MenuStrip1 control appears in the component tray.
4. Create the menu shown in Figure 10-27. Use the following names for the menu title and menu items: fileMenuTitle, filePrintMenuItem, and fileExitMenuItem.

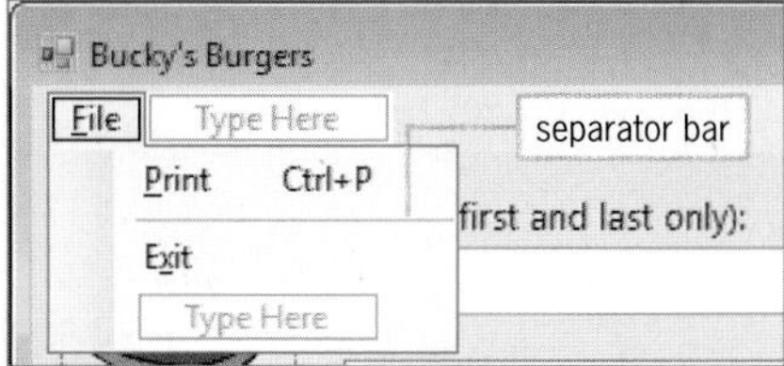

Figure 10-27 File menu

5. Save the solution and then start the application. Click **File** on the application's menu bar. The menu opens and offers two options separated by a separator bar.
6. Click the **Close** button on the form's title bar.

Coding the Application

According to the application's TOE chart, four event procedures need to be coded: the Click event procedures for the two menu items, the text box's Enter event procedure, and the addButton's Click event procedure. You will begin by coding the Click event procedures for the two menu items.

To code the two menu items and then test the code:

1. Open the Code Editor window. The nameTextBox_Enter procedure has already been coded for you. In the comments that appear in the General Declarations section, replace <your name> and <current date> with your name and the current date, respectively.
2. Open the code template for the fileExitMenuItem_Click procedure, and then enter the following statement:

   Me.Close()
3. Open the code template for the filePrintMenuItem_Click procedure. Enter the following comment and statement:

   ' sends the printout to the Print preview window
   PrintForm1.Print()
4. Save the solution and then start the application. Click **File** on the application's menu bar and then click **Print**. An image of the interface appears in the Print preview window. Close the Print preview window.
5. Click **File** on the application's menu bar and then click **Exit**.

Next, you will code the addButton's Click event procedure. The procedure's pseudocode is shown in Figure 10-28.

```
addButton Click event procedure
1. assign user input (full name), excluding any leading or trailing spaces, to a variable
2. if the variable is empty
       display the "Please enter a name" message in a message box
   else
       use the IndexOf method to search for the space in the full name; assign
       the space's index to a variable
       if the full name contains a space
             use the location of the space to separate the first and last
             names; assign the first and last names to separate variables
             change the first name to proper case
             change the last name to proper case
             concatenate the first name, a space, and the last name
       else
             change the full name to proper case
       end if
       add the full name to the namesListBox
   end if
3. send the focus to the nameTextBox
4. select the nameTextBox's existing text
```

Figure 10-28 Pseudocode for the addButton_Click procedure

To code and then test the addButton_Click procedure:

1. Open the code template for the addButton's Click procedure. Type the following comment and then press **Enter** twice:

   ' adds names in proper case to the list box

2. The procedure will use three String variables to store the full name, first name, and last name. Enter the appropriate Dim statements, using the names `fullName`, `firstName`, and `lastName`.
3. The procedure will use an Integer variable to store the index of the space that separates the first name from the last name. Type the appropriate Dim statement, using the name `index`, and then press **Enter** twice.
4. The first step in the pseudocode assigns the user input, excluding any leading and trailing spaces, to a variable. Enter a statement that assigns the contents of the nameTextBox, excluding any leading and trailing spaces, to the `fullName` variable.
5. The second step in the pseudocode is a dual-alternative selection structure whose condition determines whether the `fullName` variable is empty. If it is empty, the selection structure's True path should display the "Please enter a name" message in a message box. Enter an appropriate If clause and MessageBox.Show method.
6. Type **Else** and press **Enter**. If the `fullName` variable is not empty, the selection structure's False path should use the IndexOf method to search for the space in the variable. The space's index should be assigned to the `index` variable. Type **' locate the space** and then press **Enter**. Now, enter the appropriate assignment statement.
7. The next instruction in the False path is a nested dual-alternative selection structure whose condition determines whether the `fullName` variable contains a space. Type the following If clause and then press **Enter**:

   If index > –1 Then

8. If the `fullName` variable contains a space, the nested structure's True path should use the location of the space to separate the first and last names. Type **' separate first and last names** and then press **Enter**. Now, enter a statement that uses the Substring method to assign the first name to the `firstName` variable. (Hint: The first name starts with index 0 in the `fullName` variable. The `index` variable's value indicates the number of characters contained in the first name.)
9. Next, enter a statement that uses the Substring method to assign the last name to the `lastName` variable. (Hint: The last name starts with the character immediately after the space in the `fullName` variable.)
10. The next two instructions in the nested structure's True path should change the first and last names to proper case, which means the first letter in each name should be uppercase and the remaining letters should be lowercase. Type **' change first name to proper case** and then press **Enter**. Now, enter the appropriate code to change the first name to proper case. (Hint: You will need to use the Substring, ToUpper, and ToLower methods and the concatenation operator.)
11. Next, type **' change last name to proper case** and then press **Enter**. Now, enter the appropriate code to change the last name to proper case.
12. The last instruction in the nested structure's True path concatenates the first name, a space, and the last name. Type **' concatenate first, space, and last** and then press **Enter**. Enter a statement that performs the concatenation and assigns the result to the `fullName` variable.
13. It is possible that the user may enter only an employee's first or last name in the nameTextBox. In that case, the `fullName` variable will not contain a space, and the nested structure's False path should simply change the variable's contents to proper case. Type **Else** and press **Tab** twice. Type **' no space in name** and press **Enter**. Now, enter the code to change the contents of the `fullName` variable to proper case.
14. If necessary, delete the **blank line** above the nested End If clause.
15. The last instruction in the outer selection structure's False path adds the full name to the namesListBox. Insert a **blank line** between the two End If clauses. Type **' add full name to list box** and then press **Enter**. Now, enter the appropriate statement.
16. If necessary, delete the **blank line** above the outer End If clause.
17. The last two instructions in the pseudocode send the focus to the nameTextBox and also select the text box's existing text. Insert a **blank line** above the End Sub clause and then enter the appropriate statements.
18. If necessary, delete the **blank line** above the End Sub clause.
19. Save the solution and then start the application. Click the **Add Name to List** button. The "Please enter a name" message appears in a message box. Close the message box.
20. Type **jennifer swansky** in the text box and then press **Enter** to select the Add Name to List button, which is the form's default button. The name appears (in proper case) in the list box.
21. Type **cher** in the text box and then press **Enter**. The name "Cher" appears in the list box. See Figure 10-29.

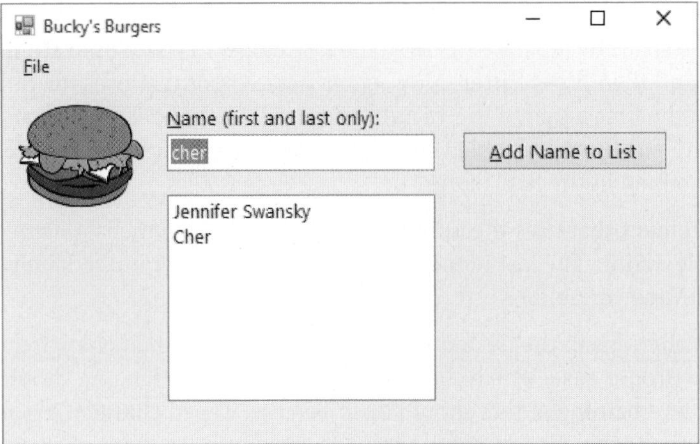

Figure 10-29 Sample run of the Bucky's Burgers application

22. Click **File** on the application's menu bar and then click **Exit**. Close the Code Editor window and then close the solution. Figure 10-30 shows the application's code.

```
' Project name:          Bucky Project
' Project purpose:       Add names in proper case to a list
'                        box and print the interface
' Created/revised by:    <your name> on <current date>

Option Explicit On
Option Strict On
Option Infer Off

Public Class MainForm
   Private Sub addButton_Click(sender As Object, e As EventArgs
   ) Handles addButton.Click
       ' adds names in proper case to the list box

       Dim fullName As String
       Dim firstName As String
       Dim lastName As String
       Dim index As Integer

       fullName = nameTextBox.Text.Trim
       If fullName = String.Empty Then
           MessageBox.Show("Please enter a name",
                           "Bucky's Burgers",
                           MessageBoxButtons.OK,
                           MessageBoxIcon.Information)
       Else
           ' locate the space
           index = fullName.IndexOf(" ")
           If index > -1 Then
               ' separate first and last names
               firstName = fullName.Substring(0, index)
               lastName = fullName.Substring(index + 1)
               ' change first name to proper case
               firstName = firstName.Substring(0, 1).ToUpper &
                   firstName.Substring(1).ToLower
```

Figure 10-30 Code for the Bucky's Burgers application *(continues)*

(continued)

```
                ' change last name to proper case
                lastName = lastName.Substring(0, 1).ToUpper &
                    lastName.Substring(1).ToLower
                ' concatenate first, space, and last
                fullName = firstName & " " & lastName
            Else    ' no space in name
                fullName = fullName.Substring(0, 1).ToUpper &
                    fullName.Substring(1).ToLower
            End If
            ' add full name to list box
            namesListBox.Items.Add(fullName)
        End If
        nameTextBox.Focus()
        nameTextBox.SelectAll()
    End Sub

    Private Sub fileExitMenuItem_Click(sender As Object,
    e As EventArgs) Handles fileExitMenuItem.Click
        Me.Close()

    End Sub

    Private Sub filePrintMenuItem_Click(sender As Object,
    e As EventArgs) Handles filePrintMenuItem.Click
        ' sends the printout to the Print preview window
        PrintForm1.Print()

    End Sub

    Private Sub nameTextBox_Enter(sender As Object, e As EventArgs
    ) Handles nameTextBox.Enter
        nameTextBox.SelectAll()
    End Sub
End Class
```

Figure 10-30 Code for the Bucky's Burgers application

PROGRAMMING EXAMPLE

Carlton Fencing Application

Create an interface that allows the user to display a report in a list box, but only if the user enters the appropriate password. The password must begin with two uppercase letters, followed by one digit, either an asterisk or a dollar sign, the number 3, a lowercase letter from a through g, and a digit. Examples of valid passwords include GK7$3g9 and HY6*3c2. The report should list the names of the Carlton Fencing salespeople in the first column, and each salesperson's commission amount in the second column. The names and commission amounts are shown in Figure 10-31. Store the names in a class-level one-dimensional array named `salespeople`. Store the commission amounts in a class-level one-dimensional array named `commAmts`. Use the following names for the solution and project, respectively: Carlton Solution and Carlton Project. Save the application in the VbReloaded2015\Chap10 folder. Change the form file's name to Main Form.vb. See Figures 10-31 through 10-36.

Salesperson	Commission
Rory Jenkins	2,500
Sophia Mendez	2,250
Peter Harvey	1,560
Susan Cheng	2,800
Colbin Haily	1,780

Figure 10-31 Salespeople and commission amounts

Task	Object	Event
1. Declare and initialize a class-level, 5-element String array named salespeople 2. Declare and initialize a class-level, 5-element Integer array named commAmts	MainForm	Declarations section
End the application	exitButton	Click
1. Get the password from the user 2. Determine whether the password is valid 3. If the password is valid, display the report in reportListBox; otherwise display the "Invalid password" message in a message box	displayButton	Click
Display the report (from displayButton)	reportListBox	None

Figure 10-32 TOE chart

Figure 10-33 MainForm and tab order

Object	Property	Setting
MainForm	Font StartPosition Text	Segoe UI, 10pt CenterScreen Carlton Fencing
reportListBox	Font SelectionMode TabStop	Courier New, 10pt None False

Figure 10-34 Objects, properties, and settings

<u>exitButton Click event procedure</u>
close the application

<u>reportButton Click event procedure</u>
1. clear the reportListBox
2. store the user's input (password) in a variable
3. if the password is valid
      display the "Name" and "Commission ($)" column headers
      repeat for each element in the salespeople and commAmts arrays
            concatenate the current element in both arrays and
            then add the result to the reportListBox
      end repeat for
   else
      display the "Invalid password" message in a message box
   end if

Figure 10-35 Pseudocode

```
' Project name:         Carlton Project
' Project purpose:      Displays a report, but only if
'                       the user enters a valid password
' Created/revised by:   <your name> on <current date>

Option Explicit On
Option Strict On
Option Infer Off

Public Class MainForm
    Private salespeople() As String = {"Rory Jenkins",
                                       "Sophia Mendez",
                                       "Peter Harvey",
                                       "Susan Cheng",
                                       "Colbin Haily"}
    Private commAmts() As Integer = {2500, 2250, 1560, 2800, 1780}

    Private Sub exitButton_Click(sender As Object, e As EventArgs
 ) Handles exitButton.Click
        Me.Close()
    End Sub

    Private Sub displayButton_Click(sender As Object, e As EventArgs
    ) Handles displayButton.Click
        ' display the report

        Const NameHead As String = "Name"
        Const CommHead As String = "Commission ($)"
        Dim passWord As String
        Dim line As String

        ' clear list box
        reportListBox.Items.Clear()
        ' get password
        passWord = InputBox("Password:", "Password Entry")

```

Figure 10-36 Code *(continues)*

(continued)

```
        ' determine whether password is valid
        If passWord Like "[A-Z][A-Z]#[*$]3[a-g]#" Then
            ' display column headers and report
            reportListBox.Items.Add(NameHead.PadRight(15) &
                                    CommHead.PadLeft(8))
            For x As Integer = 0 To salespeople.GetUpperBound(0)
                line = salespeople(x).PadRight(15) &
                    commAmts(x).ToString("N0").PadLeft(8)
                reportListBox.Items.Add(line)
            Next x
        Else
            MessageBox.Show("Invalid password",
                            "Password Error",
                            MessageBoxButtons.OK,
                            MessageBoxIcon.Information)
        End If
    End Sub
End Class
```

Figure 10-36 Code

Chapter Summary

- You use a menu strip control to add one or more menus to a form.
- Each menu title and menu item should have an access key. Commonly used menu items should be assigned shortcut keys.
- Figure 10-37 contains a summary of the string manipulation techniques covered in the chapter.

Technique	Syntax	Purpose
Length property	*string*.**Length**	stores an integer that represents the number of characters contained in a string
Trim method	*string*.**Trim**	removes any spaces from both the beginning and the end of a string
Remove method	*string*.**Remove(***startIndex*[, *numCharsToRemove*]**)**	removes characters from a string
Insert method	*string*.**Insert(***startIndex*, *value***)**	inserts characters in a string
Contains method	*string*.**Contains(***subString***)**	determines whether a string contains a specific sequence of characters; returns a Boolean value

Figure 10-37 String manipulation techniques *(continues)*

(continued)

IndexOf method	*string*.**IndexOf(***subString*[**,** *startIndex*]**)**	determines whether a string contains a specific sequence of characters; returns either –1 or an integer that indicates the starting position of the characters in the string
Substring method	*string*.**Substring(***startIndex*[**,** *numCharsToAccess*]**)**	accesses one or more characters in a string
PadLeft method	*string*.**PadLeft(***totalChars*[**,** *padCharacter*]**)**	pads the beginning of a string with a character until the string has the specified number of characters; right-aligns the string
PadRight method	*string*.**PadRight(***totalChars*[**,** *padCharacter*]**)**	pads the end of a string with a character until the string has the specified number of characters; left-aligns the string
Like operator	*string* **Like** *pattern*	uses pattern matching to compare strings
Important note: The following additional methods are covered in the Discovery Exercises at the end of this chapter: Replace, StartsWith, EndsWith, Trim (full syntax), TrimStart, and TrimEnd.		

Figure 10-37 String manipulation techniques

Key Terms

Contains method—determines whether a string contains a specific sequence of characters; returns a Boolean value

IndexOf method—determines whether a string contains a specific sequence of characters; returns either –1 (if the string does not contain the sequence of characters) or an integer that represents the starting position of the sequence of characters

Insert method—inserts characters anywhere in a string

Length property—stores an integer that represents the number of characters contained in a string

Like operator—uses pattern-matching characters to determine whether one string is equal to another string

Menu strip control—located in the Menus & Toolbars section of the toolbox; used to include one or more menus on a form

PadLeft method—right-aligns a string by inserting characters at the beginning of the string

PadRight method—left-aligns a string by inserting characters at the end of the string

Remove method—removes a specified number of characters located anywhere in a string

Shortcut keys—appear to the right of a menu item and allow the user to select the item without opening the menu

Substring method—used to access any number of characters contained in a string

Trim method—removes spaces from both the beginning and end of a string

Review Questions

Each Review Question is associated with one or more objectives listed at the beginning of the chapter.

1. The `state` variable contains the letters N and M followed by two spaces. Which of the following assigns only the letters N and M to the variable? (2)
   a. `state = state.Trim`
   b. `state = Trim(state)`
   c. `state = Trim(state, " ")`
   d. `state = Trim(2, 2)`
2. Which of the following assigns the first four characters in the `item` variable to the `warehouse` variable? (6)
   a. `warehouse = item.Assign(0, 4)`
   b. `warehouse = item.Assign(1, 4)`
   c. `warehouse = item.Substring(0, 4)`
   d. `warehouse = item.Substring(1, 4)`
3. Which of the following changes the contents of the `lastName` variable from Carlson to Carl? (2)
   a. `lastName = lastName.Remove(0, 4)`
   b. `lastName = lastName.Remove(4, 3)`
   c. `lastName = lastName.Remove(5, 3)`
   d. `lastName = lastName.Remove(5)`
4. Which of the following changes the contents of the `zip` variable from 60521 to 60561? (2, 3)
   a.
   ```
   zip = zip.Insert(3, "6")
   zip = zip.Remove(4, 1)
   ```
   b.
   ```
   zip = zip.Insert(4, "6")
   zip = zip.Remove(3, 1)
   ```
   c. `zip = zip.Remove(3, 1).Insert(3, "6")`
   d. all of the above
5. If the `president` variable contains the string "Abraham Lincoln", what value will the `president.IndexOf("Lincoln")` method return? (5)
   a. −1
   b. 8
   c. 9
   d. True
6. Which of the following assigns the sixth character in the `item` variable to the `letter` variable? (6)
   a. `letter = item.Substring(4, 1)`
   b. `letter = item.Substring(5, 1)`
   c. `letter = item.Substring(5)`
   d. none of the above

7. Which of the following expressions evaluates to True when the `partNum` variable contains ABC73? (7)
   a. `partNum Like "[A-Z]99"`
   b. `partNum Like "[A-Z]##"`
   c. `partNum Like "[A-Z][A-Z][A-Z]##"`
   d. none of the above
8. If the `msg` variable contains the string "The picnic is Saturday.", which of the following assigns the number 14 to the `num` variable? (5)
   a. `msg.Substring(0, "S")`
   b. `msg.Contains("S")`
   c. `msg.IndexOf("S")`
   d. `msg.IndexOf(0, "S")`
9. Which of the following changes the contents of the `amount` variable from 76.89 to 76.89!!!! (the number 76.89 followed by four exclamation points)? (3, 4)
   a. `amount = amount.PadRight(4, "!"c)`
   b. `amount = amount.PadRight(9, "!"c)`
   c. `amount = amount.PadLeft(4, "!"c)`
   d. none of the above
10. Which of the following determines whether the `userEntry` variable contains a dollar sign? (5)
    a. `userEntry.Contains("$")`
    b. `userEntry.IndexOf("$")`
    c. `userEntry.IndexOf("$", 0)`
    d. all of the above
11. Which of the following allows you to access a menu item without opening the menu? (8)
    a. an access key
    b. a menu key
    c. shortcut keys
    d. none of the above
12. Which of the following is false? (8)
    a. Menu titles should be one word only.
    b. Each menu title should have a unique access key.
    c. You should assign shortcut keys to commonly used menu titles.
    d. Menu items should be entered using book title capitalization.

Each Exercise, except the DISCOVERY exercises, is associated with one or more objectives listed at the beginning of the chapter.

Exercises

Pencil and Paper

INTRODUCTORY

1. Write a statement that uses the Trim method to remove the leading and trailing spaces from the addressTextBox. (2)

INTRODUCTORY

2. Write a statement that uses the Insert method to change the contents of the `firstName` variable from Jon to John. (3)

INTRODUCTORY

3. The `productId` variable contains XY573K. Write a statement that assigns only the Y57 portion of the `productId` variable's contents to the `code` variable. (6)

INTRODUCTORY

4. Write a statement that assigns the number of characters contained in the `customerName` variable to the numCharsLabel control. (1)

INTRODUCTORY

5. Write a statement that uses the Insert method to change the string stored in the `word` variable from "out" to "sprout". (3)

INTRODUCTORY

6. Write a statement that uses the PadLeft method to change the string stored in the `pay` variable from "123.45" to "****123.45". (3, 4)

INTRODUCTORY

7. Write the code that uses the Remove method to change the string stored in the `amount` variable from "36,123,560" to "36123560". (2)

INTRODUCTORY

8. Write a statement that determines whether the `address` variable contains the street name "Main Street" (entered in uppercase, lowercase, or a combination of uppercase and lowercase). Use the Contains method and assign the method's return value to a Boolean variable named `isContained`. (5)

INTRODUCTORY

9. Write a statement that determines whether the `address` variable contains the street name "George Street" (entered in uppercase, lowercase, or a combination of uppercase and lowercase). Use the IndexOf method and assign the method's return value to an Integer variable named `indexNum`. (5)

INTERMEDIATE

10. Write the code to change the contents of the `pet` variable from dog to frog. (2, 3)

INTERMEDIATE

11. Write the code to change the contents of the `word` variable from home to hose. (2, 3)

INTERMEDIATE

12. Write the code to change the string stored in the `amount` variable from "36123560" to "$36,123,560". (3)

INTERMEDIATE

13. Write an If clause that determines whether the state name stored in the `state` variable is one of the following (entered using any case): New York, New Jersey, or New Mexico. Use the Like operator. (7)

INTERMEDIATE

14. Write a Do clause that processes the loop body when the `userEntry` variable begins with the letter X (entered using any case) followed by two characters. Use the Like operator. (7)

INTERMEDIATE

15. Write an If clause that determines whether the name stored in the `lastName` variable is either Smith or Smyth (entered using any case). Use the Like operator. (7)

ADVANCED

16. Write the code to determine the number of lowercase letters stored in the `message` variable. Assign the result to an Integer variable named `numLower`. (6, 7)

ADVANCED

17. Write an If clause that determines whether the last character in the rateTextBox's Text property is a percent sign (%). (7)

ADVANCED

18. Write the code to determine the number of commas in the salesTextBox's Text property. Assign the result to an Integer variable named `numCommas`. (6)

Computer

MODIFY THIS

19. If necessary, complete the Guess the Word Game application from this chapter's Programming Tutorial 1, and then close the solution. Use Windows to make a copy of the Word Solution folder. Rename the folder Word Solution-ModifyThis. Open the solution file contained in the Word Solution-ModifyThis folder. Modify the code to

allow player 1 to enter a word that contains any number of letters, up to a maximum of 10 letters. Save the solution and then start and test the application. Close the solution. (1, 5–7)

20. If necessary, complete the Bucky's Burgers application from this chapter's Programming Tutorial 2, and then close the solution. Use Windows to make a copy of the Bucky Solution folder. Rename the folder Bucky Solution-ModifyThis. Open the solution file contained in the Bucky Solution-ModifyThis folder. The modified application should allow the user to enter the employee's first, middle, and last names. First, remove the "(first and last only)" text from the Label1 control's Text property. Next, modify the code to display the names using proper case. Save the solution and then start and test the application. Close the solution. (5, 6) MODIFY THIS

21. If necessary, complete the Carlton Fencing application from this chapter's Programming Example, and then close the solution. Use Windows to make a copy of the Carlton Solution folder. Rename the folder Carlton Solution-ModifyThis. Open the solution file contained in the Carlton Solution-ModifyThis folder. Passwords should now begin with either two uppercase letters or two lowercase letters, followed by two digits, any two lowercase letters, the @ symbol, and a digit. Modify the application's code. Save the solution and then start and test the application. Close the solution. (7) MODIFY THIS

22. Open the Item Prices Solution (Item Prices Solution.sln) file contained in the VbReloaded2015\Chap10\Item Prices Solution folder. Modify the MainForm_Load procedure so that it right-aligns the prices listed in the rightComboBox and then selects the first price. Save the solution and then start the application. Close the solution. (4) INTRODUCTORY

23. Open the Date Solution (Date Solution.sln) file contained in the VbReloaded2015\Chap10\Date Solution folder. The interface provides a text box for entering the date. The displayButton_Click procedure should verify that the date was entered in the correct format, which is two numbers followed by a slash, two numbers, a slash, and two numbers. If the date was entered in the correct format, the procedure should change the year number from *yy* to 20*yy* before displaying the date in the dateLabel. Save the solution and then start the application. Close the solution. (1, 3, 7) INTRODUCTORY

24. Open the Zip Solution (Zip Solution.sln) file contained in the VbReloaded2015\Chap10\Zip Solution folder. The displayButton_Click procedure should display the correct shipping charge based on the ZIP code entered by the user. To be valid, the ZIP code must contain exactly five digits, and the first three digits must be either "605" or "606". The shipping charge for "605" ZIP codes is $25. The shipping charge for "606" ZIP codes is $30. Display an appropriate message if the ZIP code is invalid. Code the procedure. Save the solution and then start the application. Test the application using the following ZIP codes: 60677, 60511, 60344, and 7130. Close the solution. (7) INTRODUCTORY

25. Open the Commission Solution (Commission Solution.sln) file contained in the VbReloaded2015\Chap10\Commission Solution folder. Add a File menu and a Calculate menu to the form. Include an Exit menu item on the File menu. Include two menu items on the Calculate menu: 5% Commission and 7% Commission. Assign shortcut keys to the items on the Calculate menu. The Exit menu item should end the application when it is clicked. The two items on the Calculate menu should calculate and display the appropriate commission amount: either 5% of the sales amount or 7% of the sales amount. Code the appropriate procedures. Save the solution and then start and test the application. Close the solution. (8, 9) INTRODUCTORY

INTERMEDIATE

26. Open the Tax Solution (Tax Solution.sln) file contained in the VbReloaded2015\Chap10\Tax Solution folder. The interface provides a text box and a combo box for entering a sales amount and a tax rate, respectively. The calcButton_Click procedure should remove the percent sign and the space that precedes it from the tax rate before using the rate to calculate the sales tax. Finish coding the procedure. Save the solution and then start the application. Close the solution. (1, 6)

INTERMEDIATE

27. Open the Social Security Solution (Social Security Solution.sln) file contained in the VbReloaded2015\Chap10\Social Security Solution-Remove folder. The interface provides a text box for entering a Social Security number. The removeButton_Click procedure should verify that the Social Security number contains three numbers followed by a hyphen, two numbers, a hyphen, and four numbers. If the Social Security number is in the correct format, the procedure should remove the hyphens from the number before displaying the number in the numberLabel; otherwise, it should display an error message. Code the procedure. Save the solution and then start the application. Close the solution. (1, 6)

INTERMEDIATE

28. Open the Color Solution (Color Solution.sln) file contained in the VbReloaded2015\Chap10\Color Solution folder. The displayButton_Click procedure should display the color of the item whose item number is entered by the user. All items are available in four colors: blue, green, red, and purple. All item numbers contain exactly five characters: two numbers followed by a letter and two numbers. The letter indicates the item's color, as follows: a b or B indicates blue, a g or G indicates green, an r or R indicates red, and a p or P indicates purple. If the item number is not in the correct format, or if the third character is not one of the valid color characters, the procedure should change the colorLabel to white and display "Invalid item number" in the colorLabel. However, if the item number is in the correct format and the third character is valid, the procedure should change the colorLabel's background to the appropriate color and also remove any message from the colorLabel. Code the procedure. Save the solution and then start the application. Test the application using the following item numbers: 12x, 12b45, 67b555, 99g44, abg55, 78p99, 93r6a, and 23r12. Close the solution. (1, 6, 7)

INTERMEDIATE

29. Open the Reverse Name Solution (Reverse Name Solution.sln) file contained in the VbReloaded2015\Chap10\Reverse Name Solution folder. The interface provides a text box for entering a person's first name followed by a space and the person's last name. Code the reverseButton_Click procedure to display the name as follows: the last name followed by a comma, a space, and the first name. Save the solution and then start and test the application. Close the solution. (5, 6)

ADVANCED

30. Open the Search Name Solution (Search Name Solution.sln) file contained in the VbReloaded2015\Chap10\Search Name Solution folder. The interface provides text boxes for entering a name (first name followed by a space and the last name) and the search text. If the last name (entered in any case) begins with the search text (entered in any case), the displayButton_Click procedure should display the message "The last name begins with" followed by a space and the search text. If the characters in the last name come before the search text, display the message "The last name comes before" followed by a space and the search text. Finally, if the characters in the last name come after the search text, display the message "The last name comes after" followed by a space and the search text. Code the procedure. Save the solution and then start the application. To test the application, enter Helga Swanson as the name and then use the following strings for the search text: g, ab, he, s, SY, sw, swan, and wan. Close the solution. (1, 5, 6)

31. Open the Sales Tax Solution (Sales Tax Solution.sln) file contained in the VbReloaded2015\Chap10\Sales Tax Solution folder. The interface provides text boxes for entering a sales amount and a tax rate. The Calculate button's Click event procedure should remove any dollar signs, spaces, and commas from the sales amount. It should also verify that the tax rate begins with a period. Code the procedure. Save the solution and then start and test the application. Close the solution. (1, 2, 6, 7) ADVANCED

32. Open the Sales Bonus Solution (Sales Bonus Solution.sln) file contained in the VbReloaded2015\Chap10\Sales Bonus Solution folder. The interface provides a text box for entering a sales amount. The text box's KeyPress event procedure allows the text box to accept only numbers, the period, and the Backspace key. The Calculate button's Click event procedure should verify that the sales amount contains either no periods or one period. If the sales amount contains more than one period, the procedure should display an appropriate message; otherwise, it should display a 10% bonus. Code the procedure. Save the solution and then start and test the application. Close the solution. (1, 6) ADVANCED

33. Open the Delivery Solution (Delivery Solution.sln) file contained in the VbReloaded2015\Chap10\Delivery Solution folder. The interface provides a text box for entering a product ID, which should consist of two numbers followed by either one or two letters. The letter(s) represent the delivery method, as follows: SM represents Standard Mail, PM represents Priority Mail, FS represents FedEx Standard, FO represents FedEx Overnight, and U represents UPS. Code the Select Delivery button's Click event procedure so that it selects the appropriate delivery method in the list box; use the Like operator. Display an appropriate message when the product ID does not contain two numbers followed by one or two letters, or when the letter(s) do not represent a valid delivery method. Save the solution and then start the application. Test the application using the following product IDs: 73pm, 34fs, 12u, 78h, 9FO, and 34sm. Close the solution. (7) ADVANCED

34. If necessary, complete the Guess the Word Game application from this chapter's Programming Tutorial 1, and then close the solution. Use Windows to make a copy of the Word Solution folder. Rename the folder Word Solution-Advanced. Open the solution file contained in the Word Solution-Advanced folder. Replace the Contains method in the DetermineGameOver procedure with the Like operator. Save the solution and then start and test the application. Close the solution. (7) ADVANCED

35. Research Visual Basic's Trim, TrimStart, and TrimEnd methods, and then open the Trim Methods Solution (Trim Methods Solution.sln) file contained in the VbReloaded2015\Chap10\Trim Methods Solution folder. Code the Trim, TrimStart, and TrimEnd buttons' Click event procedures. Save the solution and then start and test the application. Close the solution. DISCOVERY

36. Research Visual Basic's Replace method, and then open the Replace Method Solution (Replace Method Solution.sln) file contained in the VbReloaded2015\Chap10\Replace Method Solution folder. Code the Replace button's Click event procedure. Save the solution and then start and test the application. Close the solution. DISCOVERY

37. Research Visual Basic's StartsWith and EndsWith methods, and then open the StartsWith EndsWith Solution (StartsWith EndsWith Solution.sln) file contained in the VbReloaded2015\Chap10\StartsWith EndsWith Solution folder. Code the StartsWith and EndsWith buttons' Click event procedures. Save the solution and then start and test the application. Close the solution. DISCOVERY

SWAT THE BUGS

38. Open the Debug Solution (Debug Solution.sln) file contained in the VbReloaded2015\Chap10\Debug Solution 1 folder. Open the Code Editor window and review the existing code. Start and then test the application. Locate and then correct any errors. When the application is working correctly, close the solution. (5, 6)

SWAT THE BUGS

39. Open the Debug Solution (Debug Solution.sln) file contained in the VbReloaded2015\Chap10\Debug Solution 2 folder. Open the Code Editor window and review the existing code. Start and then test the application. Locate and then correct any errors. When the application is working correctly, close the solution. (2)

SWAT THE BUGS

40. Open the Debug Solution (Debug Solution.sln) file contained in the VbReloaded2015\Chap10\Debug Solution 3 folder. Open the Code Editor window and review the existing code. Start and then test the application. Locate and then correct any errors. When the application is working correctly, close the solution. (1, 6)

Case Projects

Credit Card Verifier

Create an application that uses the steps shown in Figure 10-38 to verify a credit card number that contains 12 digits. The interface should provide a text box for the user to enter the 12-digit number. The application should display either the "Valid number" message or the "Invalid number" message. Use the following names for the solution and project, respectively: Credit Solution and Credit Project. Save the application in the VbReloaded2015\Chap10 folder. Change the form file's name to Main Form.vb. (1, 6, 7)

Steps for verifying a credit card number:

1. Beginning with the first digit in the credit card number, multiply every other digit by 2.
2. If the product of a multiplication contains two digits, add both digits together.
3. Add all of the digits together. If the sum of the digits is evenly divisible by 10, the credit card number is valid; otherwise, it is not valid.

Invalid credit card number example:

the sum is not evenly divisible by 10

Number	3	0	7	8	6	7	4	2	8	1	2	1	
Step 1	6		14		12		8		16		4		
Step 2			5		3				7				
Step 3	6	0	5	8	3	7	8	2	7	1	4	1	52

Figure 10-38 Information for the Credit Card Verifier application *(continues)*

(continued)

Valid credit card number example:

Number	7	1	3	2	8	4	6	3	0	5	3	8	
Step 1	14		6		16		12		0		6		
Step 2	5				7		3						
Step 3	5	1	6	2	7	4	3	3	0	5	6	8	50

the sum is evenly divisible by 10

Figure 10-38 Information for the Credit Card Verifier application

Password Creator

Create an application that allows the user to enter any five words. The application should create and display a password using the rules specified in Figure 10-39. Use the following names for the solution and project, respectively: Password Solution and Password Project. Save the application in the VbReloaded2015\Chap10 folder. Change the form file's name to Main Form.vb. (1–3, 6, 7)

Rules for creating a password:
1. Assign the first letter in each of the five words as the password.
2. Insert a dollar sign as the second character in the password.
3. Insert a percent sign as the fourth character in the password.
4. Insert a comma as the seventh character in the password.
5. Reverse all of the characters in the password.

Figure 10-39 Information for the Password Creator application

Rembrandt Auto-Mart

Each salesperson at Rembrandt Auto-Mart is assigned an ID number that consists of five characters. The first three characters are numbers. The fourth character is a letter: either the letter N if the salesperson sells new cars or the letter U if the salesperson sells used cars. The fifth character is also a letter: either the letter F if the salesperson is a full-time employee or the letter P if the salesperson is a part-time employee. The application should allow the sales manager to enter the ID and the number of cars sold for as many salespeople as needed. The calcButton_Click procedure should display the total number of cars sold by each of the following four categories of employees: full-time employees, part-time employees, employees selling new cars, and employees selling used cars. Use the following names for the solution and project, respectively: Rembrandt Solution and Rembrandt Project. Save the application in the VbReloaded2015\Chap10 folder. Change the form file's name to Main Form.vb. You can either create your own interface or create the one shown in Figure 10-40. (1, 6, 7)

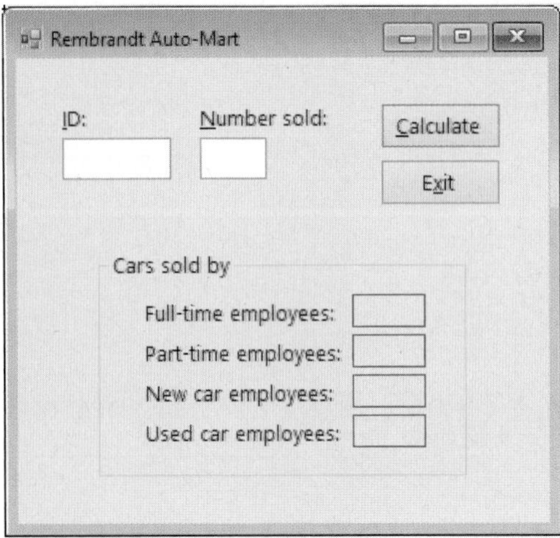

Figure 10-40 Sample interface for the Rembrandt Auto-Mart application

Pig Latin

Create an application that allows the user to enter a word that contains one or more letters only. The application should use the rules shown in Figure 10-41 to convert the word to Pig Latin. It should then display the word in Pig Latin form. Use the following names for the solution and project, respectively: Pig Latin Solution and Pig Latin Project. Save the application in the VbReloaded2015\Chap10 folder. Change the form file's name to Main Form.vb. (1–3, 6, 7)

Rules for converting a word to Pig Latin:

1. If the word begins with a vowel (A, E, I, O, or U), add the string "way" to the end of the word. For example, the Pig Latin form of the word "ant" is "antway".
2. If the word does not begin with a vowel, continue moving the first character in the word to the end of the word until the first character is the letter A, E, I, O, U, or Y. Then add the string "ay" to the end of the word. For example, the Pig Latin form of the word "chair" is "airchay".

Figure 10-41 Pig Latin rules

CHAPTER 11

Structures and Sequential Files

After studying Chapter 11, you should be able to:

1. Define a structure
2. Declare and use a structure variable
3. Pass a structure variable to a procedure
4. Create an array of structure variables
5. Write data to a sequential access file
6. Close a sequential access file
7. Read data from a sequential access file
8. Use the Exists and Peek methods
9. Code the FormClosing event procedure
10. Remove an item from a list box
11. Align columns of information
12. Use the Strings.Space method
13. Write and read records
14. Use the Split function

Structures

The data types used in previous chapters, such as Integer and Double, are built into the Visual Basic language. You can also create your own data types in Visual Basic by using the **Structure statement**, whose syntax is shown in Figure 11-1. Data types created by the Structure statement are referred to as **user-defined data types** or **structures**.

HOW TO Define a Structure

Syntax
Structure *structureName*
  Public *memberVariableName1* **As** *dataType*
  [**Public** *memberVariableNameN* **As** *dataType*]
End Structure

Example
```
Structure Employee
    Public id As String
    Public firstName As String
    Public lastName As String
    Public pay As Double
End Structure
```

Figure 11-1 How to define a structure

Most programmers use the Class statement (rather than the Structure statement) to create data types that contain procedures. The Class statement is covered in Chapter 14.

You can also include an array in a structure. This topic is explored in Computer Exercises 31 and 32 at the end of the chapter.

The structures you create are composed of members, which are defined between the Structure and End Structure clauses. The members can be variables, constants, or procedures. However, in most cases the members will be variables; such variables are referred to as **member variables**. The *dataType* in the member variable definition identifies the type of data the member variable will store, and it can be any of the standard data types available in Visual Basic; it can also be another structure (user-defined data type). The Structure statement is typically entered in the form's Declarations section, which begins with the Public Class clause and ends with the End Class clause. The structure's name is usually entered using Pascal case, whereas the member variable names are entered using camel case.

The Structure statement allows the programmer to group related items into one unit: a structure. However, keep in mind that the Structure statement merely defines the structure members. It does not reserve any memory locations inside the computer. You reserve member locations by declaring a structure variable.

Declaring and Using a Structure Variable

After entering the Structure statement in the Code Editor window, you then can use the structure to declare a variable. Variables declared using a structure are often referred to as **structure variables**. The syntax for creating a structure variable is shown in Figure 11-2. The figure also includes examples of declaring structure variables using the Employee structure from Figure 11-1.

HOW TO Declare a Structure Variable

Syntax
{**Dim** | **Private**} *structureVariableName* **As** *structureName*

Example 1
```
Dim hourly As Employee
```
declares a procedure-level Employee structure variable named `hourly`

Example 2
```
Private salaried As Employee
```
declares a class-level Employee structure variable named `salaried`

Figure 11-2 How to declare a structure variable

Similar to the way the `Dim taxRate As Double` instruction declares a Double variable named `taxRate`, the `Dim hourly As Employee` instruction in Example 1 declares an Employee variable named `hourly`. However, unlike the `taxRate` variable, the `hourly` variable contains four member variables. In code, you refer to the entire structure variable by its name—in this case, `hourly`. You refer to a member variable by preceding its name with the name of the structure variable in which it is defined. You use the dot member access operator (a period) to separate the structure variable's name from the member variable's name, like this: `hourly.id`, `hourly.firstName`, `hourly.lastName`, and `hourly.pay`. The dot member access operator indicates that `id`, `firstName`, `lastName`, and `pay` are members of the `hourly` structure variable.

The `Private salaried As Employee` instruction in Example 2 in Figure 11-2 declares a class-level structure variable named `salaried`. The names of the member variables within the `salaried` variable are `salaried.id`, `salaried.firstName`, `salaried.lastName`, and `salaried.pay`. Figure 11-3 illustrates the Employee structure and the `hourly` and `salaried` structure variables.

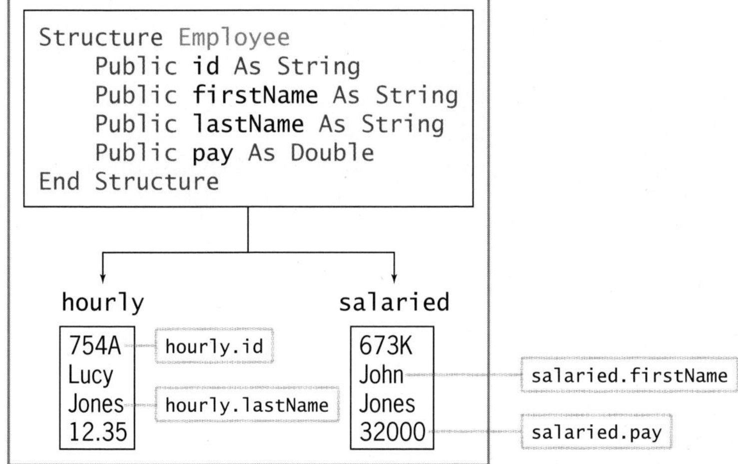

Figure 11-3 Illustration of the structure and structure variables

The member variables in a structure variable can be used just like any other variables. You can assign values to them, use them in calculations, display their contents, and so on. Figure 11-4 shows examples of statements that perform these tasks using the member variables contained in the `hourly` and `salaried` structure variables.

HOW TO Use a Member Variable

Example 1
```
hourly.lastName = "Loritz"
```
assigns the string "Loritz" to the `hourly.lastName` member variable

Example 2
```
hourly.pay *= 1.05
```
multiplies the contents of the `hourly.pay` member variable by 1.05 and then assigns the result to the member variable; you can also write the statement as
```
hourly.pay = hourly.pay * 1.05
```

Example 3
```
salaryLabel.Text = salaried.pay.ToString("C2")
```
formats the value contained in the `salaried.pay` member variable and then displays the result in the salaryLabel

Figure 11-4 How to use a member variable

Programmers use structure variables when they need to pass a group of related items to a procedure for further processing. This is because it's easier to pass one structure variable rather than many individual variables. Programmers also use structure variables to store related items in an array, even when the members have different data types. In the next two sections, you will learn how to pass a structure variable to a procedure and also how to store a structure variable in an array.

Passing a Structure Variable to a Procedure

Figure 11-5 shows the problem specification for Painters Paradise. It also shows most of the application's code, which does not use a structure. Notice that the calcButton_Click procedure calls the GetCostOfGoodsSold function, passing it three variables *by value*. The function uses the values to calculate the cost of goods sold. It then returns the result as a Double number to the calcButton_Click procedure, which assigns the value to the `costGoodsSold` variable.

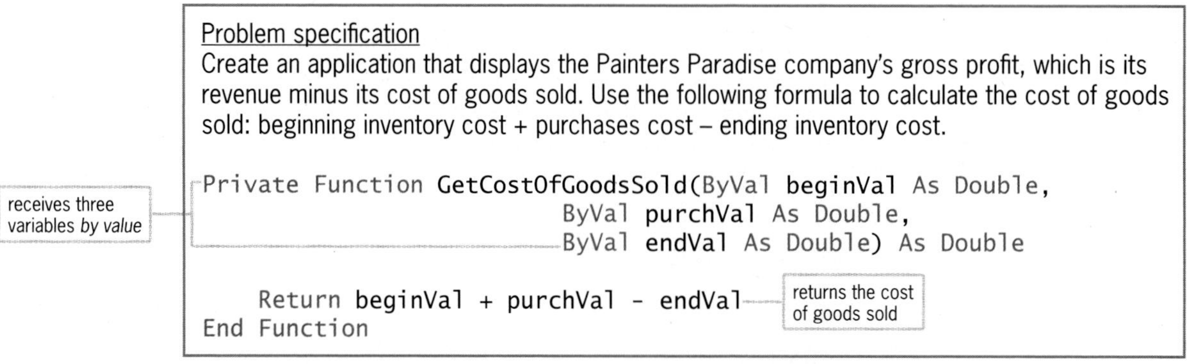

Problem specification
Create an application that displays the Painters Paradise company's gross profit, which is its revenue minus its cost of goods sold. Use the following formula to calculate the cost of goods sold: beginning inventory cost + purchases cost – ending inventory cost.

```
Private Function GetCostOfGoodsSold(ByVal beginVal As Double,
                                    ByVal purchVal As Double,
                                    ByVal endVal As Double) As Double

    Return beginVal + purchVal - endVal
End Function
```

receives three variables *by value*
returns the cost of goods sold

Figure 11-5 Paradise Painters application (without a structure) *(continues)*

(continued)

```
Private Sub calcButton_Click(sender As Object, e As EventArgs
) Handles calcButton.Click
    ' calculate the gross profit

    Dim revenue As Double
    Dim costBegin As Double
    Dim costPurch As Double
    Dim costEnd As Double
    Dim costGoodsSold As Double
    Dim grossProfit As Double

    Double.TryParse(revenueTextBox.Text, revenue)
    Double.TryParse(beginTextBox.Text, costBegin)
    Double.TryParse(purchasesTextBox.Text, costPurch)
    Double.TryParse(endingTextBox.Text, costEnd)

    ' calculate cost of goods sold
    costGoodsSold =
        GetCostOfGoodsSold(costBegin, costPurch, costEnd)

    ' calculate gross profit
    grossProfit = revenue - costGoodsSold

    costGoodsSoldLabel.Text = costGoodsSold.ToString("N2")
    grossProfitLabel.Text = grossProfit.ToString("C2")
End Sub
```

declares three variables to store the input data pertaining to the cost of goods sold

stores data in the three variables

passes three variables to the GetCostOfGoodsSold function

Painters Paradise

Revenue: 32000

Beginning inventory ($): 22500

Purchases ($): 2600

Ending inventory ($): 12300

Cost of goods sold: 12,800.00

Gross profit: $19,200.00

Calculate

Exit

Figure 11-5 Paradise Painters application (without a structure)

If you want to experiment with the Painters Paradise application, open the solution contained in the Try It 1! folder.

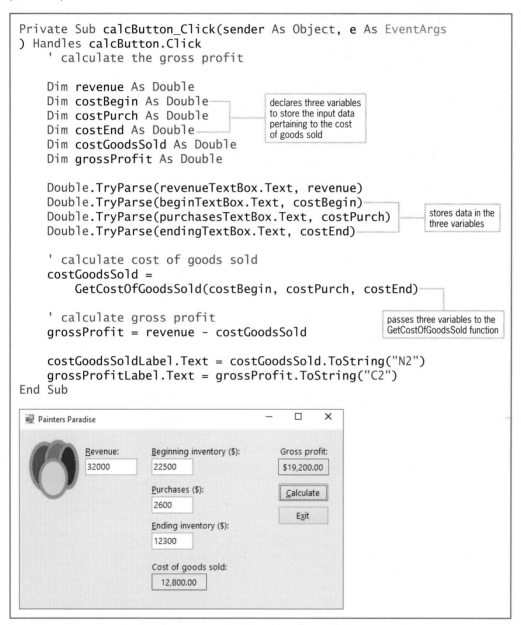

Figure 11-6 shows a more convenient way of writing the code for the Painters Paradise application. This version of the code contains a structure named CostOfGoodsSold. The structure groups together the three input items involved in the cost of goods calculation. The Structure statement that defines the structure is entered in the MainForm's Declarations section, and it contains three member variables: `beginVal`, `purchVal`, and `endVal`. The code pertaining to the structure is shaded in the figure.

If you want to experiment with this version of the Painters Paradise application, open the solution contained in the Try It 2! folder.

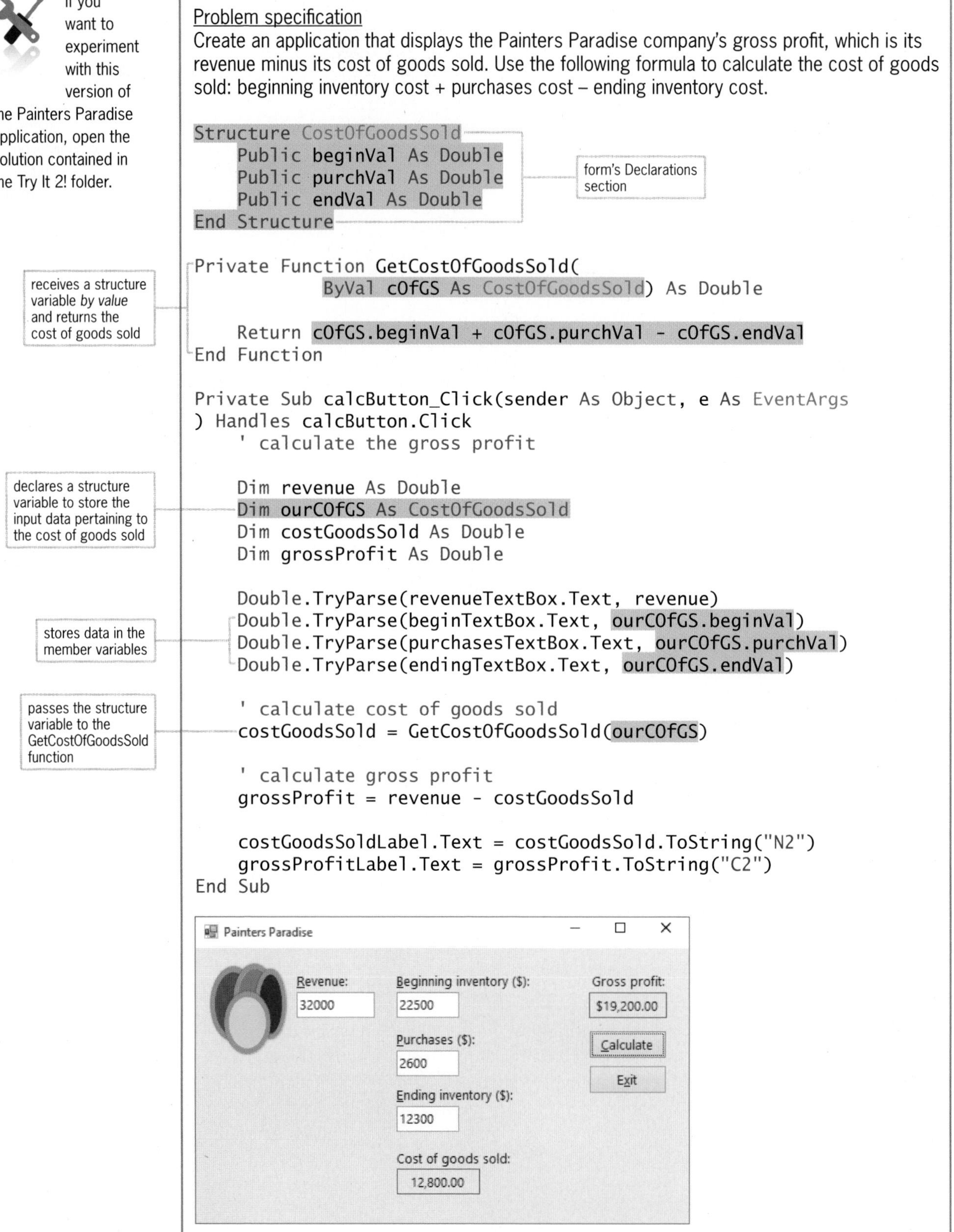

Problem specification

Create an application that displays the Painters Paradise company's gross profit, which is its revenue minus its cost of goods sold. Use the following formula to calculate the cost of goods sold: beginning inventory cost + purchases cost – ending inventory cost.

```
Structure CostOfGoodsSold
    Public beginVal As Double
    Public purchVal As Double
    Public endVal As Double
End Structure

Private Function GetCostOfGoodsSold(
            ByVal cOfGS As CostOfGoodsSold) As Double

    Return cOfGS.beginVal + cOfGS.purchVal - cOfGS.endVal
End Function

Private Sub calcButton_Click(sender As Object, e As EventArgs
) Handles calcButton.Click
    ' calculate the gross profit

    Dim revenue As Double
    Dim ourCOfGS As CostOfGoodsSold
    Dim costGoodsSold As Double
    Dim grossProfit As Double

    Double.TryParse(revenueTextBox.Text, revenue)
    Double.TryParse(beginTextBox.Text, ourCOfGS.beginVal)
    Double.TryParse(purchasesTextBox.Text, ourCOfGS.purchVal)
    Double.TryParse(endingTextBox.Text, ourCOfGS.endVal)

    ' calculate cost of goods sold
    costGoodsSold = GetCostOfGoodsSold(ourCOfGS)

    ' calculate gross profit
    grossProfit = revenue - costGoodsSold

    costGoodsSoldLabel.Text = costGoodsSold.ToString("N2")
    grossProfitLabel.Text = grossProfit.ToString("C2")
End Sub
```

form's Declarations section
receives a structure variable *by value* and returns the cost of goods sold
declares a structure variable to store the input data pertaining to the cost of goods sold
stores data in the member variables
passes the structure variable to the GetCostOfGoodsSold function
Painters Paradise
Revenue:
32000
Beginning inventory ($):
22500
Purchases ($):
2600
Ending inventory ($):
12300
Cost of goods sold:
12,800.00
Gross profit:
$19,200.00
Calculate
Exit

Figure 11-6 Paradise Painters application (with a structure)

The second Dim statement in the calcButton_Click procedure declares a CostOfGoodsSold structure variable named `ourCOfGS`, and the last three TryParse methods fill the member variables with values. The `costGoodsSold = GetCostOfGoodsSold(ourCOfGS)` statement calls the GetCostOfGoodsSold function, passing it the `ourCOfGS` structure variable *by value*. When you pass a structure variable, all of the member variables are automatically passed. The GetCostOfGoodsSold function uses the values stored in the member variables to calculate the cost of goods sold, which it returns as a Double number. The calcButton_Click procedure assigns the function's return value to the `costGoodsSold` variable.

Compare the calcButton_Click procedure in Figure 11-5 with the same procedure shown in Figure 11-6. Notice that the procedure in Figure 11-5 uses three scalar variables to store the input data, while the procedure in Figure 11-6 uses only one structure variable for this purpose. The procedure in Figure 11-5 also passes three scalar variables (rather than one structure variable) to the GetCostOfGoodsSold function, which uses three scalar variables (rather than one structure variable) to accept the data. If the data to be passed consisted of 20 items rather than just three items, consider how much easier it would be to pass one structure variable rather than 20 scalar variables.

Creating an Array of Structure Variables

As mentioned earlier, another advantage of using a structure is that a structure variable can be stored in an array, even when its members have different data types. The West Coast Emporium application can be used to illustrate this concept. The problem specification is shown in Figure 11-7, along with most of the application's code. The figure also includes a sample run of the application.

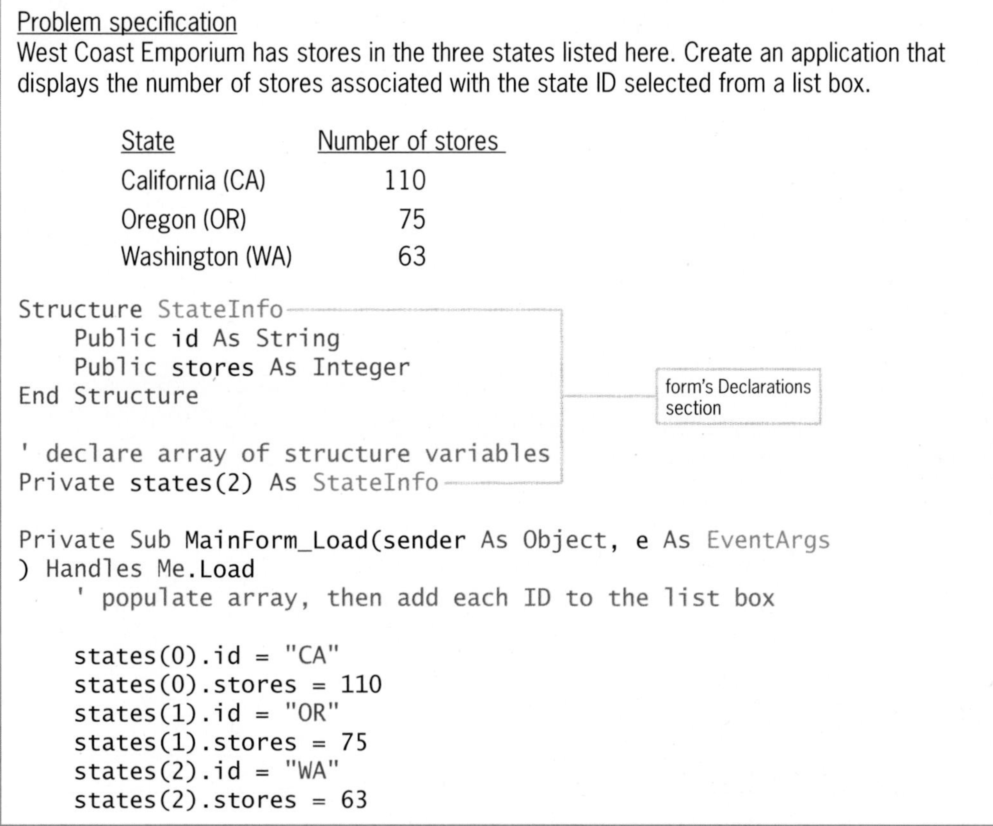

Problem specification
West Coast Emporium has stores in the three states listed here. Create an application that displays the number of stores associated with the state ID selected from a list box.

State	Number of stores
California (CA)	110
Oregon (OR)	75
Washington (WA)	63

```
Structure StateInfo
    Public id As String
    Public stores As Integer
End Structure

' declare array of structure variables
Private states(2) As StateInfo

Private Sub MainForm_Load(sender As Object, e As EventArgs
) Handles Me.Load
    ' populate array, then add each ID to the list box

    states(0).id = "CA"
    states(0).stores = 110
    states(1).id = "OR"
    states(1).stores = 75
    states(2).id = "WA"
    states(2).stores = 63
```

If you want to experiment with the West Coast Emporium application, open the solution contained in the Try It 3! folder.

Figure 11-7 West Coast Emporium application (with a structure) *(continues)*

(continued)

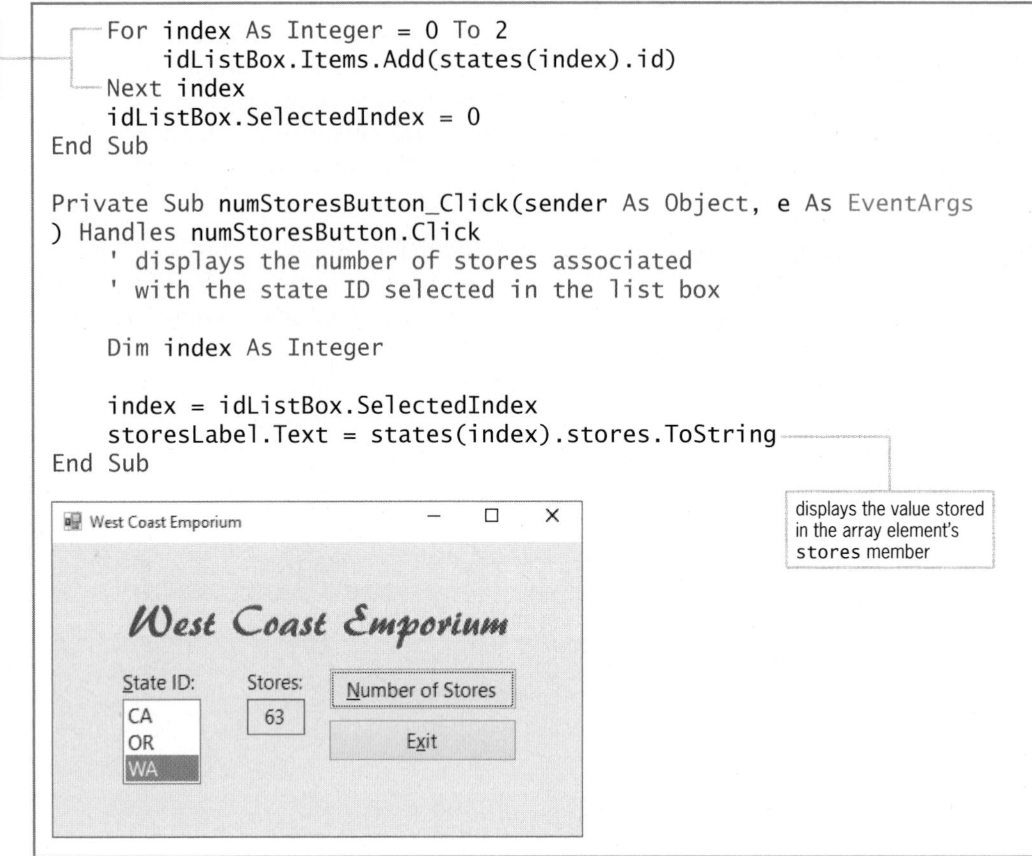

```
    For index As Integer = 0 To 2
        idListBox.Items.Add(states(index).id)
    Next index
    idListBox.SelectedIndex = 0
End Sub

Private Sub numStoresButton_Click(sender As Object, e As EventArgs
) Handles numStoresButton.Click
    ' displays the number of stores associated
    ' with the state ID selected in the list box

    Dim index As Integer

    index = idListBox.SelectedIndex
    storesLabel.Text = states(index).stores.ToString
End Sub
```


Figure 11-7 West Coast Emporium application (with a structure)

The MainForm's Declarations section defines a structure named StateInfo and then uses the structure to declare a three-element one-dimensional array named `states`. Each element in the `states` array is a structure variable that contains two member variables: a String variable named `id` and an Integer variable named `stores`. You refer to a member variable in an array element using the syntax shown in Figure 11-8.

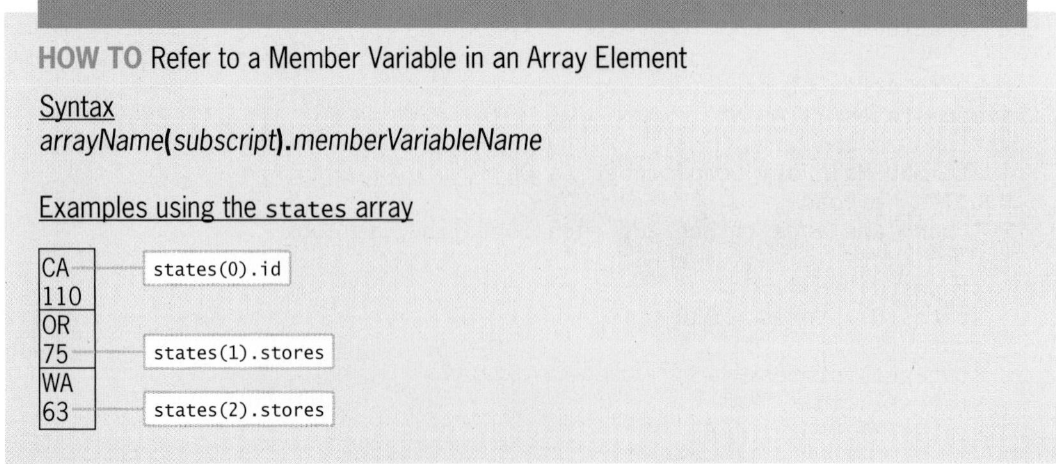

HOW TO Refer to a Member Variable in an Array Element
Syntax
arrayName(*subscript*).*memberVariableName*
Examples using the states array
CA
110
OR
75
WA
63
states(0).id
states(1).stores
states(2).stores

Figure 11-8 How to refer to a member variable in an array element

After the array is declared, the MainForm_Load procedure in Figure 11-7 populates the array with the appropriate IDs and numbers of stores. The procedure also adds each state ID stored in the array to the idListBox. The numStoresButton_Click procedure displays the number of stores associated with the ID selected in the list box.

Mini-Quiz 11-1

The answers to Mini-Quiz questions are located in Appendix A. Each question is associated with one or more objectives listed at the beginning of the chapter.

1. In most applications, the Structure statement is entered in the form's ____________ (1).
   a. Declarations section
   b. Definition section
   c. Load event procedure
   d. User-defined section
2. Which of the following assigns the string "Miami" to the `city` member variable within a structure variable named `address`? (2)
   a. `address&city = "Miami"`
   b. `address.city = "Miami"`
   c. `city.address = "Miami"`
   d. none of the above
3. An array is declared using the statement `Dim inventory(4) As Product`. Which of the following assigns the number 100 to the `quantity` member variable contained in the last array element? (4)
   a. `inventory.quantity(4) = 100`
   b. `inventory(4).Product.quantity = 100`
   c. `inventory(3).quantity = 100`
   d. `inventory(4).quantity = 100`

The values stored in an array usually come from a file on the computer's disk, and they are assigned to the array after it is declared. In many cases, the file is a sequential access file. You will learn about sequential access files in the next several sections.

Sequential Access Files

In addition to getting data from the keyboard and sending data to the computer screen, an application can also get data from and send data to a file on a disk. Files to which data is written are called **output files** because the files store the output produced by an application. Files that are read by the computer are called **input files** because an application uses the data in these files as input.

Most input and output files are composed of lines of text that are both read and written in consecutive order, one line at a time, beginning with the first line in the file and ending with the last line in the file. Such files are referred to as **sequential access files** because of the manner in which the lines of text are accessed. They are also called **text files** because they are composed of lines of text. Examples of text stored in sequential access files include an employee list, a memo, and a sales report.

Writing Data to a Sequential Access File

An item of data—such as the string "Jacob"—is viewed differently by a human being and by a computer. To a human being, the string represents a person's name; to a computer, it is merely a sequence of characters. Programmers refer to a sequence of characters as a **stream of characters**.

In Visual Basic, you use a **StreamWriter object** to write a stream of characters to a sequential access file. Before you create the object, you first declare a variable to store the object in the computer's internal memory. Figure 11-9 shows the syntax and an example of declaring a StreamWriter variable. The IO in the syntax stands for Input/Output.

HOW TO Declare a StreamWriter Variable

Syntax
{**Dim** | **Private**} *streamWriterVariableName* **As IO.StreamWriter**

Example
```
Dim outFile As IO.StreamWriter
```
declares a StreamWriter variable named `outFile`

Figure 11-9 How to declare a StreamWriter variable

After declaring a StreamWriter variable, you can use the syntax shown in Figure 11-10 to create a StreamWriter object. As the figure indicates, creating a StreamWriter object involves opening a sequential access file using either the CreateText method or the AppendText method. You use the **CreateText method** to open a sequential access file for output. When you open a file for output, the computer creates a new, empty file to which data can be written. If the file already exists, the computer erases the contents of the file before writing any data to it. You use the **AppendText method** to open a sequential access file for append. When a file is opened for append, new data is written after any existing data in the file. If the file does not exist, the computer creates the file for you. In addition to opening the file, both methods automatically create a StreamWriter object to represent the file in the application. You assign the StreamWriter object to a StreamWriter variable, which you use to refer to the file in code.

Because sequential access files contain text, programmers typically name them using the filename extension *txt*, which is short for *text*.

HOW TO Create a StreamWriter Object

Syntax
IO.File.*method***(***fileName***)**

method	Description
CreateText	opens a sequential access file for output
AppendText	opens a sequential access file for append

Example 1
```
outFile = IO.File.CreateText("memo.txt")
```
opens the memo.txt file for output; creates a StreamWriter object and assigns it to the `outFile` variable

Example 2
```
outFile = IO.File.AppendText("F:\Chap11\pay.txt")
```
opens the pay.txt file for append; creates a StreamWriter object and assigns it to the `outFile` variable

Figure 11-10 How to create a StreamWriter object

When processing the statement in Example 1, the computer searches for the memo.txt file in the default folder, which is the current project's bin\Debug folder. If the file exists, its contents are erased and the file is opened for output; otherwise, a new, empty file is created and opened for output. The statement then creates a StreamWriter object and assigns it to the `outFile` variable.

Unlike the *fileName* argument in Example 1, the *fileName* argument in Example 2 contains a folder path. When processing the statement in Example 2, the computer searches for the pay.txt file in the Chap11 folder on the F drive. If the computer locates the file, it opens the file for append. If it does not find the file, it creates a new, empty file and then opens the file for append. Like the statement in Example 1, the statement in Example 2 creates a StreamWriter object and assigns it to the `outFile` variable. When deciding whether to include the folder path in the fileName argument, keep in mind that a USB drive may have a different letter designation on another computer. Therefore, you should specify the folder path only when you are sure that it will not change.

After opening a file for either output or append, you can begin writing data to it using either the **Write method** or the **WriteLine method**. The difference between the methods is that the WriteLine method writes a newline character after the data. Figure 11-11 shows the syntax and an example of both methods. As the figure indicates, when using the Write method, the next character written to the file will appear immediately after the letter o in the string "Hello". When using the WriteLine method, however, the next character written to the file will appear on the line immediately below the string. You do not need to include the file's name in either method's syntax because the data will be written to the file associated with the StreamWriter variable.

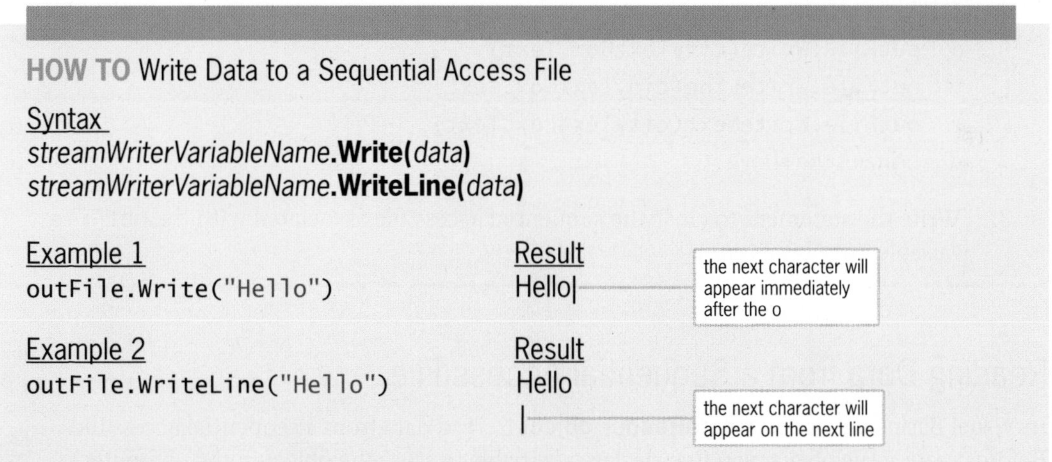

HOW TO Write Data to a Sequential Access File
Syntax
streamWriterVariableName.Write(data)
streamWriterVariableName.WriteLine(data)
Example 1
outFile.Write("Hello")
Result
Hello|
the next character will appear immediately after the o
Example 2
outFile.WriteLine("Hello")
Result
Hello
|
the next character will appear on the next line

Figure 11-11 How to write data to a sequential access file

Closing an Output Sequential Access File

You should use the **Close method** to close an output sequential access file as soon as you are finished using it. This ensures that the data is saved, and it makes the file available for use elsewhere in the application. The syntax to close an output sequential access file is shown in Figure 11-12, along with an example of using the method. Here, again, notice that you use the StreamWriter variable to refer to the file in code.

A run time error will occur if a program statement attempts to open a file that is already open.

HOW TO Close an Output Sequential Access File

Syntax
streamWriterVariableName.**Close()**

Example
`outFile.Close()`
closes the file associated with the `outFile` variable

Figure 11-12 How to close an output sequential access file

The answers to Mini-Quiz questions are located in Appendix A. Each question is associated with one or more objectives listed at the beginning of the chapter.

Mini-Quiz 11-2

1. A procedure needs to write information to a sequential access file. Which of the following methods can be used to open the file? (5)
   a. AppendText
   b. CreateText
   c. OpenText
   d. both a and b
2. Which of the following writes the contents of the cityTextBox's Text property, followed by the newline character, to the sequential access file associated with the `outFile` variable? (5)
   a. `outFile.Write(cityTextBox.Text)`
   b. `outFile.WriteLine(cityTextBox.Text)`
   c. `outFile.WriteNext(cityTextBox.Text)`
   d. none of the above
3. Write the statement to close the sequential access file associated with the `outFile` variable. (6)

Reading Data from a Sequential Access File

In Visual Basic, you use a **StreamReader object** to read data from a sequential access file. Before creating the object, you first declare a variable to store the object in the computer's internal memory. Figure 11-13 shows the syntax and an example of declaring a StreamReader variable. As mentioned earlier, the IO in the syntax stands for Input/Output.

HOW TO Declare a StreamReader Variable

Syntax
{**Dim** | **Private**} *streamReaderVariableName* **As IO.StreamReader**

Example
`Dim inFile As IO.StreamReader`
declares a StreamReader variable named `inFile`

Figure 11-13 How to declare a StreamReader variable

After declaring a StreamReader variable, you can use the **OpenText method** to open a sequential access file for input, which will automatically create a StreamReader object. When a file is opened for input, the computer can read the lines of text stored in the file. Figure 11-14 shows the OpenText method's syntax along with an example of using the method. The *fileName* argument in the example does not include a folder path, so the computer will search for the memo.txt file in the default folder, which is the current project's bin\Debug folder. If the computer finds the file, it opens the file for input. If the computer does not find the file, a run time error occurs. You assign the StreamReader object created by the OpenText method to a StreamReader variable, which you use to refer to the file in code.

HOW TO Create a StreamReader Object

Syntax
IO.File.OpenText(*fileName*)

Example
```
inFile = IO.File.OpenText("memo.txt")
```
opens the memo.txt file for input; creates a StreamReader object and assigns it to the `inFile` variable

Figure 11-14 How to create a StreamReader object

The run time error that occurs when the computer cannot locate the file you want opened for input will cause the application to end abruptly. You can use the Exists method to avoid this run time error. Figure 11-15 shows the method's syntax and includes an example of using the method. If the *fileName* argument does not include a folder path, the computer searches for the file in the current project's bin\Debug folder. The **Exists method** returns the Boolean value True if the file exists; otherwise, it returns the Boolean value False.

HOW TO Determine Whether a File Exists

Syntax
IO.File.Exists(*fileName*)

Example
```
If IO.File.Exists("memo.txt") Then
```
determines whether the memo.txt file exists in the current project's bin\Debug folder; you can also write the If clause as `If IO.File.Exists("memo.txt") = True Then`

Figure 11-15 How to determine whether a file exists

After opening a file for input, you can use the **ReadLine method** to read the file's contents, one line at a time. A **line** is defined as a sequence (stream) of characters followed by the newline character. The ReadLine method returns a string that contains only the sequence of characters in the current line. The returned string does not include the newline character at the end of the line. In most cases, you assign the returned string to a String variable. Figure 11-16 shows the ReadLine method's syntax and includes an example of using the method. The method does not require you to provide the file's name because it uses the file associated with the StreamReader variable.

HOW TO Read Data from a Sequential Access File

Syntax
streamReaderVariableName.**ReadLine**

Example
```
Dim lineOfText As String
lineOfText = inFile.ReadLine
```
reads a line of text from the sequential access file associated with the `inFile` variable and assigns the line, excluding the newline character, to the `lineOfText` variable

Figure 11-16 How to read data from a sequential access file

In most cases, an application will need to read each line of text contained in a sequential access file, one line at a time. You can do this using a loop along with the **Peek method**, which "peeks" into the file to determine whether the file contains another character to read. If the file contains another character, the Peek method returns the character; otherwise, it returns the number −1 (a negative 1). The Peek method's syntax is shown in Figure 11-17 along with an example of using the method. The Do clause in the example tells the computer to process the loop instructions until the Peek method returns the number −1, which indicates that there are no more characters to read. In other words, the Do clause tells the computer to process the loop instructions until the end of the file is reached.

HOW TO Use the Peek Method

Syntax
streamReaderVariableName.**Peek**

Example
```
Dim lineOfText As String
Do Until inFile.Peek = -1
    lineOfText = inFile.ReadLine
    MessageBox.Show(lineOfText)
Loop
```
reads each line of text from the sequential access file associated with the `inFile` variable, line by line; each line (excluding the newline character) is assigned to the `lineOfText` variable and is then displayed in a message box

Figure 11-17 How to use the Peek method

Closing an Input Sequential Access File

A run time error will occur if a program statement attempts to open a file that is already open.

Just as you do with an output sequential access file, you should use the Close method to close an input sequential access file as soon as you are finished using it. Doing this makes the file available for use elsewhere in the application. The syntax to close an input sequential access file is shown in Figure 11-18 along with an example of using the method. Notice that you use the StreamReader variable to refer to the file in code.

HOW TO Close an Input Sequential Access File

Syntax
streamReaderVariableName.**Close()**

Example
`inFile.Close()`
closes the file associated with the `inFile` variable

Figure 11-18 How to close an input sequential access file

Mini-Quiz 11-3

The answers to Mini-Quiz questions are located in Appendix A. Each question is associated with one or more objectives listed at the beginning of the chapter.

1. A procedure needs to read information from a sequential access file. Which of the following methods can be used to open the file? (7)
   a. AppendText
   b. CreateText
   c. OpenText
   d. both b and c
2. Which of the following reads a line of text from the sequential access file associated with the `inFile` variable and assigns the line of text (excluding the newline character) to the `msg` variable? (7)
   a. `msg = inFile.Read`
   b. `msg = inFile.ReadLine`
   c. `inFile.ReadLine(msg)`
   d. none of the above
3. Write the statement to close the sequential access file associated with the `inFile` variable. (6)
4. What does the Peek method return when a sequential access file contains another character to read? (8)

The FormClosing Event

As you already know, you can close a form using either the `Me.Close()` statement or the Close button on the form's title bar. When a form is about to be closed, its **FormClosing event** occurs. Figure 11-19 shows examples of code you might enter in the FormClosing event procedure. Example 1 writes the contents of the membersListBox to a sequential access file named members.txt. Example 2 displays the "Do you want to exit?" message in a message box, along with Yes and No buttons. If the user clicks the No button, it indicates that he or she does not want to exit the application. In that case, the MainForm_FormClosing procedure stops the computer from closing the MainForm by setting the **Cancel property** of the procedure's `e` parameter to True.

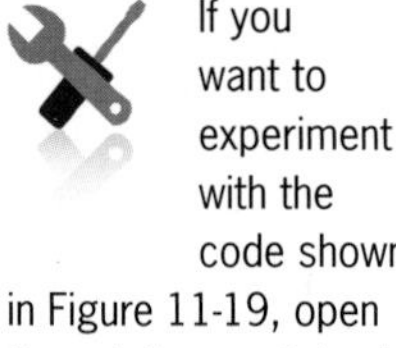

If you want to experiment with the code shown in Figure 11-19, open the solution contained in the Try It 4! folder.

HOW TO Use the FormClosing Event Procedure

Example 1—writes information to a sequential access file

```
Private Sub MainForm_FormClosing(sender As Object,
e As FormClosingEventArgs) Handles Me.FormClosing

    Dim outFile As IO.StreamWriter
    outFile = IO.File.CreateText("members.txt")
    For Each member As String In membersListBox.Items
        outFile.WriteLine(member)
    Next member
    outFile.Close()
End Sub
```

Example 2—verifies that the user wants to exit the application

```
Private Sub MainForm_FormClosing(sender As Object,
e As FormClosingEventArgs) Handles Me.FormClosing

    Dim button As DialogResult
    button = MessageBox.Show("Do you want to exit?",
                             "Exit Verification",
                             MessageBoxButtons.YesNo,
                             MessageBoxIcon.Exclamation,
                             MessageBoxDefaultButton.Button2)

    If button = DialogResult.No Then
        e.Cancel = True
    End If
End Sub
```

Figure 11-19 How to use the FormClosing event procedure

The Kettleson Club Application

The Kettleson Club application uses what you have learned so far about sequential access files and the FormClosing event. The application's problem specification is shown in Figure 11-20 along with most of the application's code. The code pertaining to the sequential access file is shaded in the figure. The figure also includes a sample run of the application, as well as the contents of the members.txt file. You can open a sequential access file in the IDE by clicking File on the menu bar and then clicking Open File. When the Open File dialog box opens, click the name of the file you want to open and then click the Open button. (Recall that unless you specify otherwise, the sequential access file is saved in the project's bin\Debug folder.)

If you want to experiment with the Kettleson Club application, open the solution contained in the Try It 5! folder.

Problem specification
Create an application for the Kettleson Club. When the application is started, it should display the contents of the members.txt sequential access file in a list box. The application should allow the user to add names to the list box and also delete names from the list box. When the user exits the application, it should save the contents of the list box in the members.txt file.

Figure 11-20 Kettleson Club application *(continues)*

(continued)

```
Private Sub MainForm_Load(sender As Object, e As EventArgs
) Handles Me.Load
    ' reads names from a sequential access file
    ' and displays them in the list box

    Dim inFile As IO.StreamReader
    Dim name As String

    ' clear previous names from the list box
    membersListBox.Items.Clear()

    ' determine whether the file exists
    If IO.File.Exists("members.txt") Then
        ' open the file for input
        inFile = IO.File.OpenText("members.txt")
        ' process loop instructions until end of file
        Do Until inFile.Peek = -1
            ' read a name
            name = inFile.ReadLine
            ' add name to list box
            membersListBox.Items.Add(name)
        Loop
        ' close the file
        inFile.Close()
    End If
End Sub

Private Sub MainForm_FormClosing(sender As Object,
e As FormClosingEventArgs) Handles Me.FormClosing
    ' saves the contents of the list box
    ' to a sequential access file

    ' declare a StreamWriter variable
    Dim outFile As IO.StreamWriter
    ' open the file for output
    outFile = IO.File.CreateText("members.txt")
    ' write each name on a separate line in the file
    For Each member As String In membersListBox.Items
        outFile.WriteLine(member)
    Next member
    ' close the file
    outFile.Close()
End Sub

Private Sub addButton_Click(sender As Object, e As EventArgs
) Handles addButton.Click
    ' adds a name to the list box

    nameTextBox.Text = nameTextBox.Text.Trim
    If nameTextBox.Text <> "" Then
        membersListBox.Items.Add(nameTextBox.Text)
    End If
    nameTextBox.Focus()
    nameTextBox.SelectAll()
End Sub
```

reads the file

writes to the file

adds a name to the list box

Figure 11-20 Kettleson Club application *(continues)*

(continued)

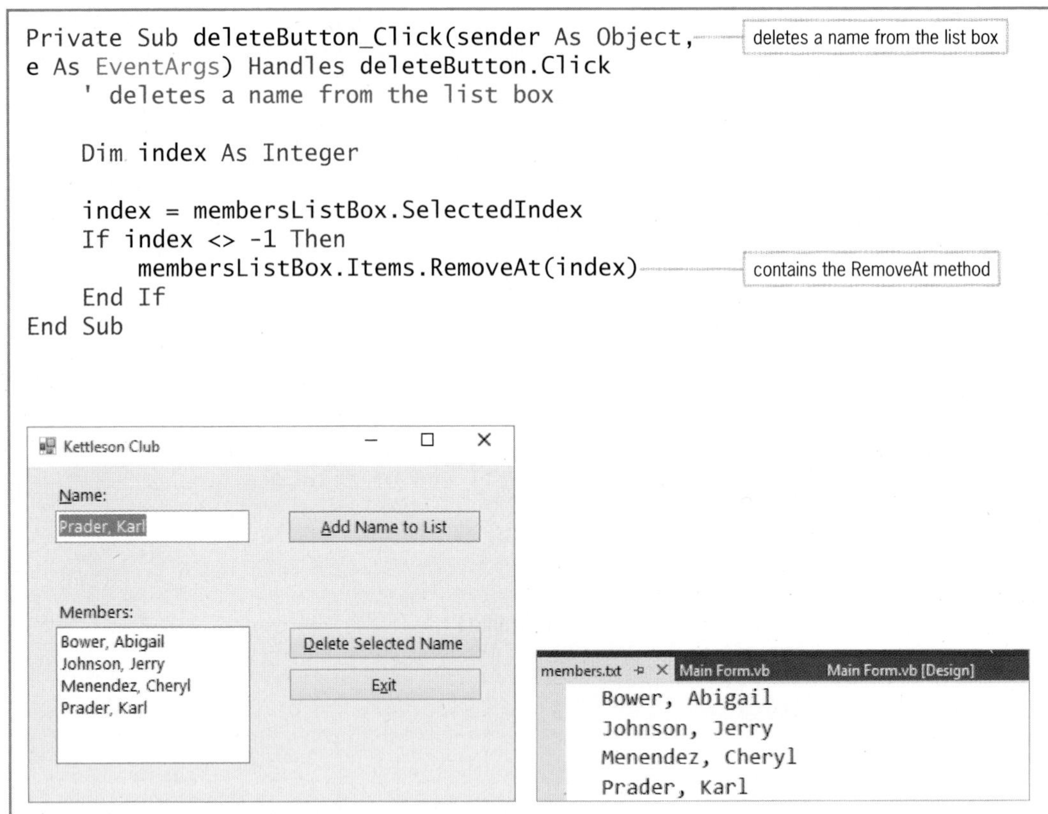

```
Private Sub deleteButton_Click(sender As Object,
e As EventArgs) Handles deleteButton.Click
    ' deletes a name from the list box

    Dim index As Integer

    index = membersListBox.SelectedIndex
    If index <> -1 Then
        membersListBox.Items.RemoveAt(index)
    End If
End Sub
```


Figure 11-20 Kettleson Club application

When the application is started, the MainForm_Load procedure reads the names contained in the members.txt file and displays them in the membersListBox. The addButton_Click procedure adds the name entered in the Name box to the list box. The deleteButton_Click procedure deletes the selected name from the list box. When the user clicks either the Exit button or the Close button on the form's title bar, the MainForm_FormClosing procedure saves the contents of the list box to the members.txt file.

Notice the `membersListBox.Items.RemoveAt(index)` statement in the deleteButton_Click procedure. The statement uses the Items collection's **RemoveAt method** to remove the selected item from the membersListBox. The method's syntax is shown in Figure 11-21 along with the syntax of the Items collection's **Remove method**, which can also be used to remove the selected item. In the RemoveAt method's syntax, *index* is the item's index. In the Remove method's syntax, *item* is the item's value.

HOW TO Remove an Item from a List Box or Combo Box

Syntax
object.**Items.RemoveAt(***index***)**
object.**Items.Remove(***item***)**

Figure 11-21 How to remove an item from a list box or combo box *(continues)*

(continued)

Example 1—RemoveAt
```
index = membersListBox.SelectedIndex
membersListBox.Items.RemoveAt(index)
```
uses the selected item's index to remove the item from the membersListBox

Example 2—RemoveAt
```
membersListBox.Items.RemoveAt(0)
```
removes the first item from the membersListBox

Example 3—Remove
```
membersListBox.Items.Remove("Johnson, Jerry")
```
removes the "Johnson, Jerry" item from the membersListBox

Example 4—Remove
```
name = membersListBox.SelectedItem
membersListBox.Items.Remove(name)
```
uses the selected item's value to remove the item from the membersListBox

Figure 11-21 How to remove an item from a list box or combo box

Aligning Columns of Information

In Chapter 10, you learned how to use the PadLeft and PadRight methods to pad a string with a character until the string is a specified length. Figure 11-22 shows the syntax of each method, along with examples of using the methods to align columns of information.

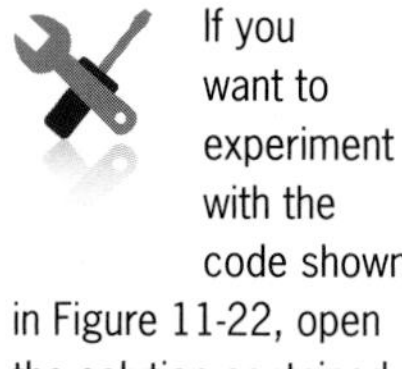

If you want to experiment with the code shown in Figure 11-22, open the solution contained in the Try It 6! folder.

HOW TO Align Columns of Information

Syntax
string.**PadLeft(***totalChars*[, *padCharacter*]**)**
string.**PadRight(***totalChars*[, *padCharacter*]**)**

Example 1
```
Dim priceOfItem As String
For price As Double = 9 To 11 Step 0.5
    priceOfItem = price.ToString("N2").PadLeft(5)
    pricesListBox.Items.Add(priceOfItem)
Next price
```

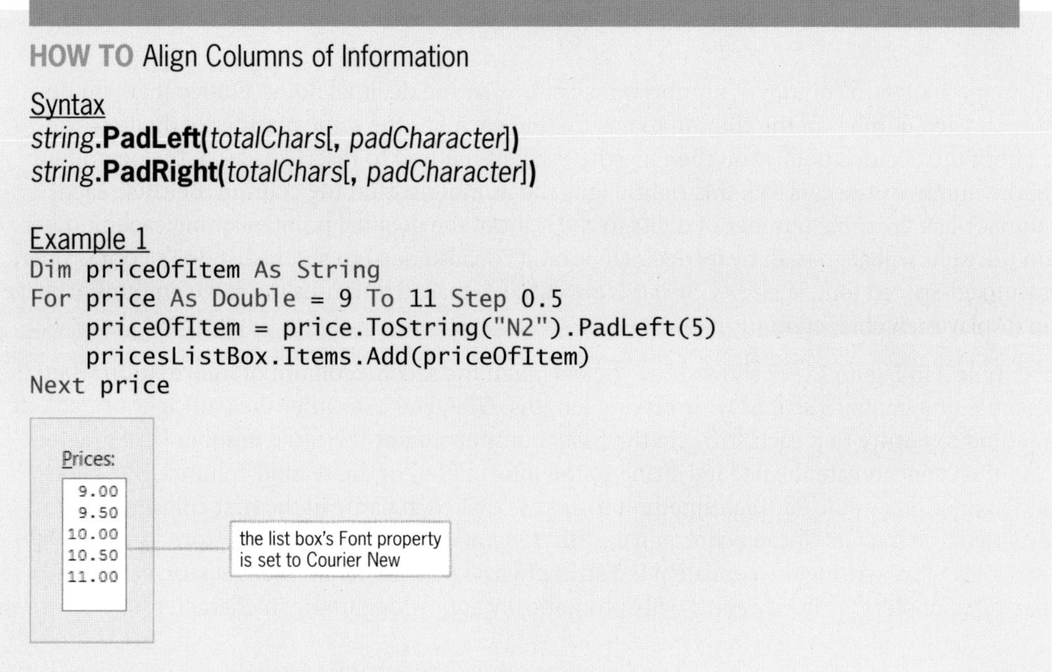

Figure 11-22 How to align columns of information *(continues)*

(continued)

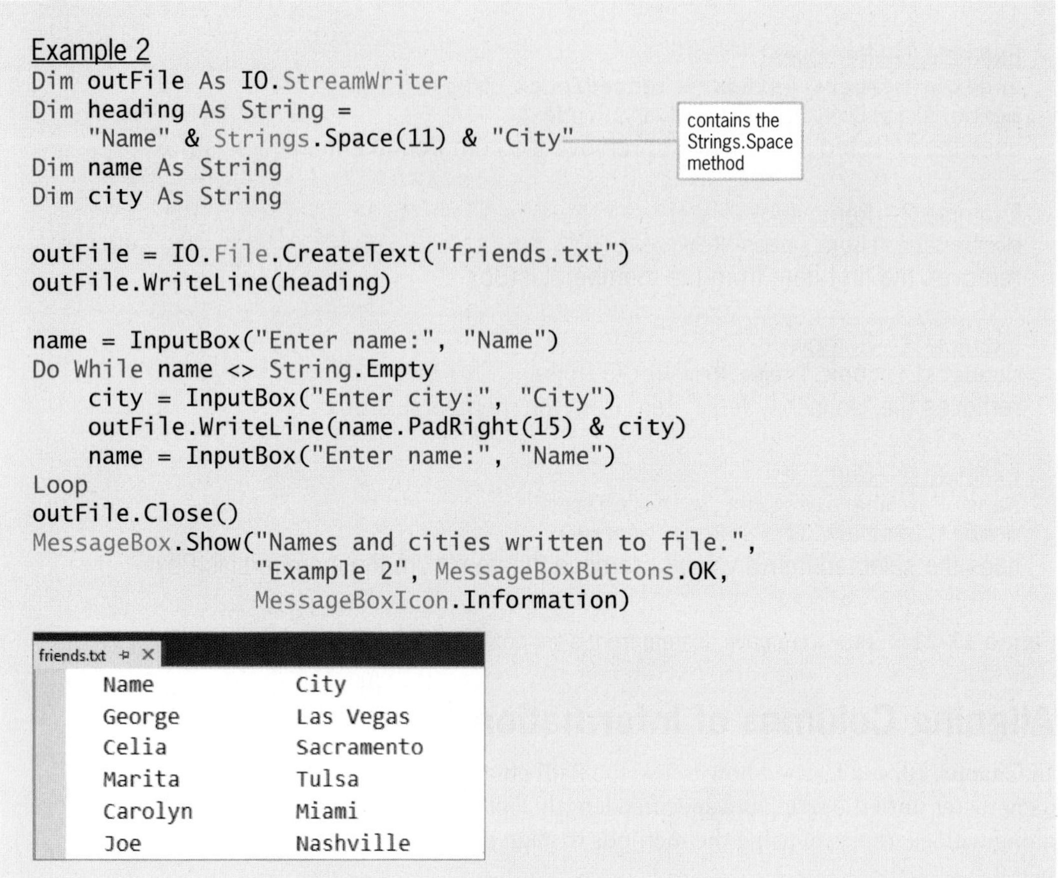

Example 2

```
Dim outFile As IO.StreamWriter
Dim heading As String =
    "Name" & Strings.Space(11) & "City"
Dim name As String
Dim city As String

outFile = IO.File.CreateText("friends.txt")
outFile.WriteLine(heading)

name = InputBox("Enter name:", "Name")
Do While name <> String.Empty
    city = InputBox("Enter city:", "City")
    outFile.WriteLine(name.PadRight(15) & city)
    name = InputBox("Enter name:", "Name")
Loop
outFile.Close()
MessageBox.Show("Names and cities written to file.",
                "Example 2", MessageBoxButtons.OK,
                MessageBoxIcon.Information)
```


Figure 11-22 How to align columns of information

Example 1 aligns a column of numbers in a list box by the decimal point. Notice that you first format each number in the column to ensure that each has the same number of digits to the right of the decimal point. You then use the PadLeft method to insert spaces at the beginning of the number (if necessary); this right-aligns the number within the column. Because each number has the same number of digits to the right of the decimal point, aligning each number on the right will align each by its decimal point. (You also need to set the list box's Font property to a fixed-spaced font, such as Courier New. A fixed-spaced font uses the same amount of space to display each character.)

Example 2 in Figure 11-22 shows how you can align the second column of information when the first column contains strings with varying lengths. First, you use either the PadRight or PadLeft method to ensure that each string in the first column contains the same number of characters. You then concatenate the padded string to the information in the second column. The code in Example 2 uses the PadRight method to ensure that each name in the first column contains exactly 15 characters. It then concatenates the 15 characters with the string stored in the `city` variable before writing the concatenated string to a sequential access file. Because each name has 15 characters, each city entry will automatically appear beginning in character position 16 in the file. Example 2 also shows how you can use the **Strings.Space method** to include a specific number of space characters in a string. The method's syntax is `Strings.Space(`*number*`)`, in which *number* is an integer that represents the number of spaces to include.

Writing and Reading Records

In some applications, a sequential access file is used to store fields and records. A **field** is a single item of information about a person, place, or thing. Examples of fields include a name, a salary, a Social Security number, and a price. A **record** is a group of related fields that contain all of the necessary data about a specific person, place, or thing.

When writing records to a sequential access file, programmers typically write each record on a separate line in the file. They use a special character, called a **delimiter character**, to separate each field. Commonly used delimiter characters include the comma and the number (or hash) sign (#). Figure 11-23 shows examples of writing records to a sequential access file. The WriteLine method in Example 1 writes a record that contains two fields separated by a comma. The WriteLine method in Example 2 writes a record that contains three fields, with each field separated by a number sign.

HOW TO Write Records to a Sequential Access File

Example 1

```
Dim city As String = "Pierre"
Dim state As String = "South Dakota"
outFile.WriteLine(city & "," & state)
```

writes the following record on a separate line in the file associated with the `outFile` variable: Pierre,South Dakota

Example 2

```
Dim salesperson As String = "Amelia Johnson"
Dim sales As Integer = 9500
Dim bonus As Integer = 750
outSalesFile.WriteLine(salesperson & "#" &
    sales.ToString & "#" & bonus.ToString)
```

writes the following record on a separate line in the file associated with the `outSalesFile` variable: Amelia Johnson#9500#750

Figure 11-23 How to write records to a sequential access file

You can use the **Split function** to read records from a sequential access file. The function's syntax is shown in Figure 11-24. In the syntax, *arrayName* is the name of a one-dimensional String array, and *streamReaderVariableName* is the name of the StreamReader variable associated with the sequential access file. The *delimiterChar* argument specifies the delimiter character that separates the fields in each record. Figure 11-24 also includes examples of using the Split function to read the records from Figure 11-23.

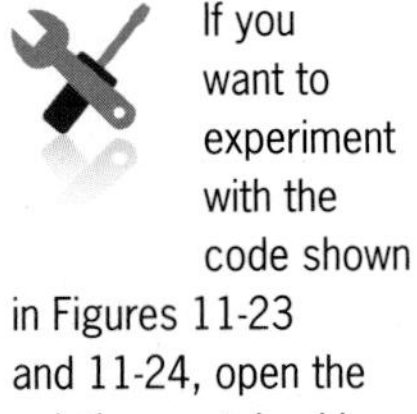

If you want to experiment with the code shown in Figures 11-23 and 11-24, open the solution contained in the Try It 7! folder.

HOW TO Read Records from a Sequential Access File

Syntax

arrayName = *streamReaderVariableName*.**ReadLine.Split(***delimiterChar***)**

Example 1

```
Dim cityState(1) As String
cityState = inFile.ReadLine.Split(","c)
```

reads a record from the file associated with the `inFile` variable and assigns each field to an element in the `cityState` array

Result (using the record written in Example 1 in Figure 11-23)

Field	Element
Pierre	`cityState(0)`
South Dakota	`cityState(1)`

Example 2

```
Dim salesInfo(2) As String
salesInfo = inSalesFile.ReadLine.Split("#"c)
```

reads a record from the file associated with the `inSalesFile` variable and assigns each field to an element in the `salesInfo` array

Result (using the record written in Example 2 in Figure 11-23)

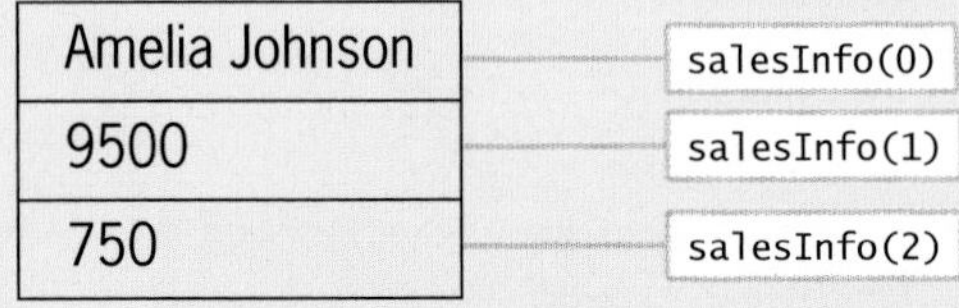

Figure 11-24 How to read records from a sequential access file

In Example 1, the ReadLine method reads a line of text from the file associated with the `inFile` variable. Then, using the delimiter character as a guide, the Split function splits the line of text into two fields and assigns each field to an element in the `cityState` array. In Example 2, the ReadLine method reads a line of text associated with the `inSalesFile` variable. The Split function then uses the number (hash) sign as a guide when dividing the line of text. In this case, the Split function divides the line of text into three fields and assigns each field to an element in the `salesInfo` array.

Notice the letter c that appears after the delimiterChar argument in each example in Figure 11-24. As you learned in Chapter 10, the letter c is one of the literal type characters in Visual Basic. Recall that a literal type character forces a literal constant to assume a data type other than the one its form indicates. In this case, the letter c forces the `","` and `"#"` delimiter characters, which are strings, to assume the Char (character) data type.

Mini-Quiz 11-4

The answers to Mini-Quiz questions are located in Appendix A. Each question is associated with one or more objectives listed at the beginning of the chapter.

1. Which of the following concatenates the contents of the `city` variable, 10 spaces, and the contents of the `state` variable and then assigns the result to the `address` variable? (12)
   a. `address = city & Space(10) & state`
   b. `address = city & Spaces(10) & state`
   c. `address = city & Strings.Space(10) & state`
   d. `address = city & String.Space(10) & state`
2. When entered in the FormClosing event procedure, which of the following prevents the computer from closing the form? (9)
   a. `e.Cancel = True`
   b. `e.Close = False`
   c. `e.Closing = False`
   d. `e.Open = True`
3. A sequential access file contains records whose fields are separated by a dollar sign. Which of the following reads a record from the file and assigns the fields to the `customer` array? (13, 14)
   a. `customer = inFile.ReadLine.Split($)`
   b. `customer = inFile.ReadLine.Split("$"c)`
   c. `customer = inFile.Split("$")`
   d. `customer = inFile.Split.ReadLine("$"c)`

You have completed the concepts section of Chapter 11. The Programming Tutorial section is next.

PROGRAMMING TUTORIAL 1

Modifying the Guess the Word Game Application

In this tutorial, you will modify the Guess the Word Game application from Chapter 10's Programming Tutorial 1. The modified application will use the secret words contained in a sequential access file named words.txt.

Creating the words.txt File

Before modifying the application's code, you will create the words.txt file.

To open the Guess the Word Game application and then create the words.txt file:

1. Start Visual Studio. Open the **Word Solution** (**Word Solution.sln**) file contained in the VbReloaded2015\Chap11\Word Solution folder. If necessary, open the designer window.
2. Rather than using a StreamWriter object and the WriteLine method to create the words.txt file, you can use the Add New Item option on the Project menu. Click **Project** on the menu bar, and then click **Add New Item** to open the Add New Item dialog box. Click **Common Items** in the Installed list (if necessary) and then click **Text File** in the middle column of the dialog box. Change the name in the Name box to **words**, and then click the **Add** button. The words.txt window opens in the IDE.

3. Enter the 10 words shown in Figure 11-25.

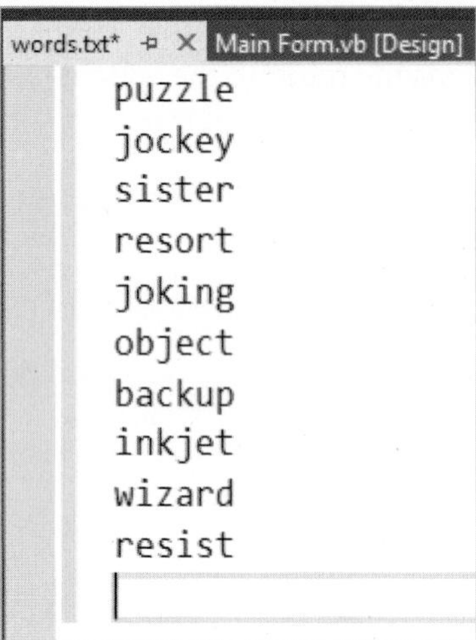

Figure 11-25 10 words entered in the words.txt sequential access file

4. Save the words.txt file and then close the words.txt window.
5. Use Windows to move the words.txt file from the Word Solution\Word Project folder to the Word Solution\Word Project\bin\Debug folder.

Coding the MainForm_Load Procedure

The MainForm_Load procedure will read the 10 words from the words.txt file. It will store each word in a class-level, 10-element String array named `words`.

To begin coding the MainForm_Load procedure:

1. Open the Code Editor window. In the comments that appear in the General Declarations section, replace <your name> and <current date> with your name and the current date, respectively.
2. First, you need to declare the class-level `words` array. Click the **blank line** above the DetermineGameOver procedure's header, and then enter the following declaration statement:

   Private words(9) As String

3. Open the code template for the MainForm_Load procedure. Type **' fill array with secret words from file** and press **Enter** twice.
4. The procedure will need a StreamReader variable to read the contents of the words.txt file, line by line. It will also use a String named constant to store the filename and use an Integer variable to keep track of the array subscripts. Enter the following Dim and Const statements. Press **Enter** twice after typing the last Dim statement.

   Dim inFile As IO.StreamReader
   Const FileName As String = "words.txt"
   Dim subscript As Integer

PROGRAMMING TUTORIAL 1

5. Next, you will use the Exists method to determine whether the words.txt file exists. Enter the following If clause. (The Code Editor will automatically enter the End If clause for you.)

   If IO.File.Exists(FileName) Then

6. If the file exists, the selection structure's True path should open the file for input. Enter the following statement:

   inFile = IO.File.OpenText(FileName)

7. Now, you will use a loop to read each word in the file, assigning each (in uppercase) to an element in the `words` array. Enter the following lines of code. (The Code Editor will automatically enter the Loop clause for you.)

```
Do Until inFile.Peek = -1
   words(subscript) = inFile.ReadLine.ToUpper
   subscript += 1
```

8. If necessary, delete the **blank line** above the Loop clause.

9. Recall that you should close a sequential access file as soon as you are finished using it. Insert a **blank line** after the Loop clause, and then enter the following statement:

   inFile.Close()

10. If the words.txt file does not exist, the selection structure's False path will display an appropriate message. Enter the following lines of code:

```
Else
   MessageBox.Show("Can't find " & FileName,
                   "Missing File", MessageBoxButtons.OK,
                    MessageBoxIcon.Information)
```

11. If necessary, delete the **blank line** above the End If clause.

12. Save the solution.

Modifying the New Game Option's Click Event Procedure

In the next set of steps, you will modify the fileNewMenuItem_Click procedure so that it gets a word from the `words` array rather than from the user. The word will be chosen randomly by the procedure.

To modify the fileNewMenuItem_Click procedure:

1. Locate the fileNewMenuItem_Click procedure. The procedure will use the random number generator to generate a random number from 0 to 9. The random number will be used to select one of the 10 words stored in the `words` array.

2. Click the **blank line** below the `' start a new game` comment, and then press **Enter**. Enter the following Dim statements:

```
Dim randGen As New Random
Dim randomNum as Integer
```

3. In the `' get a 6-letter word from player 1` comment, change `player 1` to **array**.

4. Replace the `' trim and convert to uppercase` comment with the following statement:

   randomNum = randGen.Next(0, 10)

5. In the assignment statement that assigns the InputBox function's return value to the `secretWord` variable, replace the entire InputBox function with **words(randomNum)**.
6. Delete the `' determine whether the word contains 6 letters` comment.
7. Delete the **If clause**, but leave the instructions in the True path.
8. Delete the **Else clause**, the **two instructions in the False path**, and the **End If clause**.
9. Save the solution and then start the application. The MainForm_Load procedure assigns the 10 words stored in the words.txt file to the `words` array.
10. Click **File** on the application's menu bar, and then click **New Game**. The fileNewMenuItem_Click procedure selects one of the 10 words from the `words` array. It also displays six dashes (hyphens) in the Guess this word box.
11. Type the letter **e** in the Enter a letter box, and then press **Enter**. Depending on the word selected from the array, the letter e appears in either the Guess this word box or the Incorrect letters box.
12. Continue guessing letters until you have either guessed the word or made seven incorrect guesses. Figure 11-26 shows two sample runs of the application.

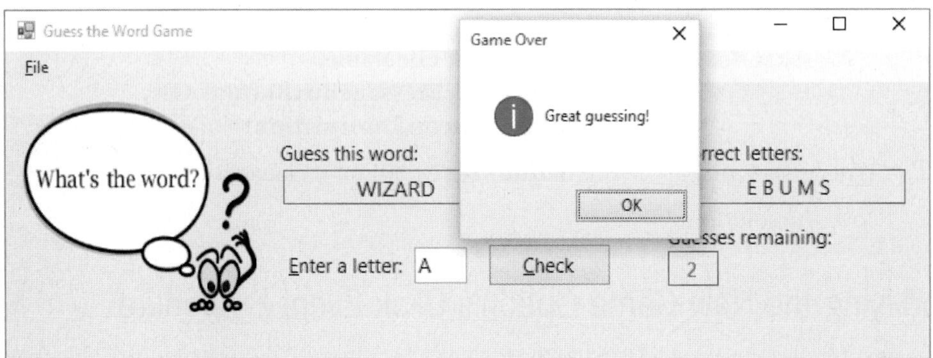

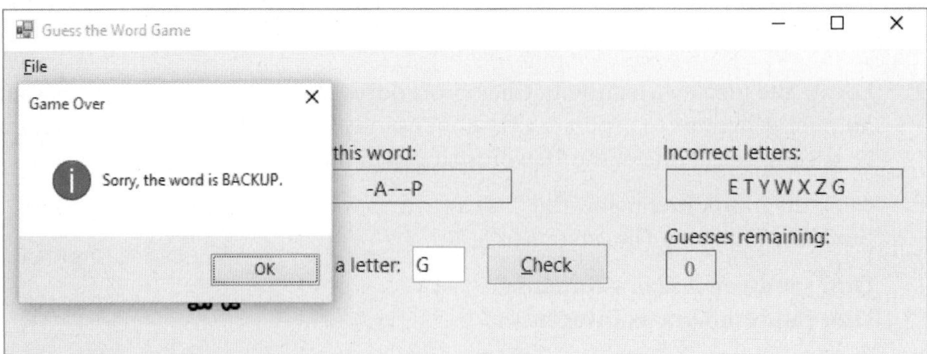

Figure 11-26 Sample runs of the Guess the Word Game application

13. Close the message box. Test the application several more times. When you are finished testing the application, close the Code Editor window and then close the solution. Figure 11-27 shows the application's code. The changes made to the original code shown in Figure 10-25 in Chapter 10 are shaded in the figure.

```
' Project name:          Word Project
' Project purpose:       A game that allows the user to guess a
'                        word letter-by-letter
' Created/revised by:    <your name> on <current date>

Option Explicit On
Option Strict On
Option Infer Off

Public Class MainForm
    Private secretWord As String
    Private numIncorrect As Integer
    Private words(9) As String

    Private Sub DetermineGameOver(ByVal aDashWasReplaced As Boolean)
        ' determine whether the game is over and
        ' take the appropriate action

        If aDashWasReplaced Then
            ' if the word does not contain any dashes, the game
            ' is over because player 2 guessed the word
            If wordLabel.Text.Contains("-") = False Then
                MessageBox.Show("Great guessing!", "Game Over",
                                MessageBoxButtons.OK,
                                MessageBoxIcon.Information)
                 checkButton.Enabled = False
            End If
        Else
            ' if 7 incorrect guesses, the game is over
            If numIncorrect = 7 Then
                MessageBox.Show("Sorry, the word is " &
                                secretWord & ".", "Game Over",
                                MessageBoxButtons.OK,
                                MessageBoxIcon.Information)
                checkButton.Enabled = False
            End If
        End If
    End Sub

    Private Sub checkButton_Click(sender As Object, e As EventArgs
    ) Handles checkButton.Click
        ' check if the letter appears in the word

        Dim letter As String
        Dim dashReplaced As Boolean

        letter = letterTextBox.Text

```

Figure 11-27 Guess the Word Game application's code *(continues)*

(continued)

```
        ' look at each letter in the word
        For index As Integer = 0 To 5
            If secretWord.Substring(index, 1) = letter Then
              ' replace corresponding dash with letter
                wordLabel.Text =
                    wordLabel.Text.Remove(index, 1)
                wordLabel.Text =
                    wordLabel.Text.Insert(index, letter)
                dashReplaced = True
            End If
        Next index

        If dashReplaced Then
            Call DetermineGameOver(dashReplaced)
        Else  ' no dash was replaced
            incorrectLabel.Text =
                incorrectLabel.Text & " " & letter
            numIncorrect += 1
            remainingLabel.Text = (7 - numIncorrect).ToString
            Call DetermineGameOver(dashReplaced)
        End If

        ' clear text box and set focus
        letterTextBox.Text = String.Empty
        letterTextBox.Focus()
    End Sub

    Private Sub fileExitMenuItem_Click(sender As Object,
    e As EventArgs) Handles fileExitMenuItem.Click
        Me.Close()

    End Sub

    Private Sub letterTextBox_KeyPress(sender As Object,
    e As KeyPressEventArgs) Handles letterTextBox.KeyPress
        ' allows only letters and the Backspace key

        If e.KeyChar Like "[!A-Za-z]" AndAlso
                e.KeyChar <> ControlChars.Back Then
            e.Handled = True
        End If
    End Sub

    Private Sub fileNewMenuItem_Click(sender As Object,
    e As EventArgs) Handles fileNewMenuItem.Click
        ' start a new game

        Dim randGen As New Random
        Dim randomNum As Integer

        wordLabel.Text = String.Empty
        incorrectLabel.Text = String.Empty
        letterTextBox.Text = String.Empty
        numIncorrect = 0
        remainingLabel.Text = "7"

```

Figure 11-27 Guess the Word Game application's code *(continues)*

(continued)

```
        ' get a 6-letter word from array
        randomNum = randGen.Next(0, 10)
        secretWord = words(randomNum)

        ' display 6 dashes
        wordLabel.Text = "------"
        ' enable button and set focus
        checkButton.Enabled = True
        letterTextBox.Focus()
    End Sub

    Private Sub MainForm_Load(sender As Object, e As EventArgs
    ) Handles Me.Load
        ' fill array with secret words from file

        Dim inFile As IO.StreamReader
        Const FileName As String = "words.txt"
        Dim subscript As Integer

        If IO.File.Exists(FileName) Then
            inFile = IO.File.OpenText(FileName)
            Do Until inFile.Peek = -1
                words(subscript) = inFile.ReadLine.ToUpper
                subscript += 1
            Loop
            inFile.Close()
        Else
            MessageBox.Show("Can't find " & FileName,
                            "Missing file", MessageBoxButtons.OK,
                            MessageBoxIcon.Information)
        End If
    End Sub
End Class
```

Figure 11-27 Guess the Word Game application's code

PROGRAMMING TUTORIAL 2

Coding the eBooks Collection Application

In this tutorial, you will code an application that keeps track of a person's collection of eBooks. The application will save each eBook's title, its author's name, and its price in a sequential access file named eBooks.txt. When it is started, the application will display the contents of the file in a list box. It will also allow the user to add information to the list box and file, as well as remove information from the list box and file. The application's TOE chart and MainForm are shown in Figures 11-28 and 11-29, respectively. Figure 11-30 shows the contents of the eBooks.txt file, which is contained in the project's bin\Debug folder.

Task	Object	Event
Read the eBooks.txt file and assign its contents to eBooksListBox Save the contents of the eBooksListBox in the eBooks.txt file	MainForm	Load FormClosing
End the application	exitButton	Click
1. Get title, author, and price 2. Add title, author, and price to eBooksListBox	addButton	Click
Remove the selected eBook from eBooksListbox	removeButton	Click
Display the title, author, and price	eBooksListBox	None

Figure 11-28 TOE chart for the eBooks Collection application

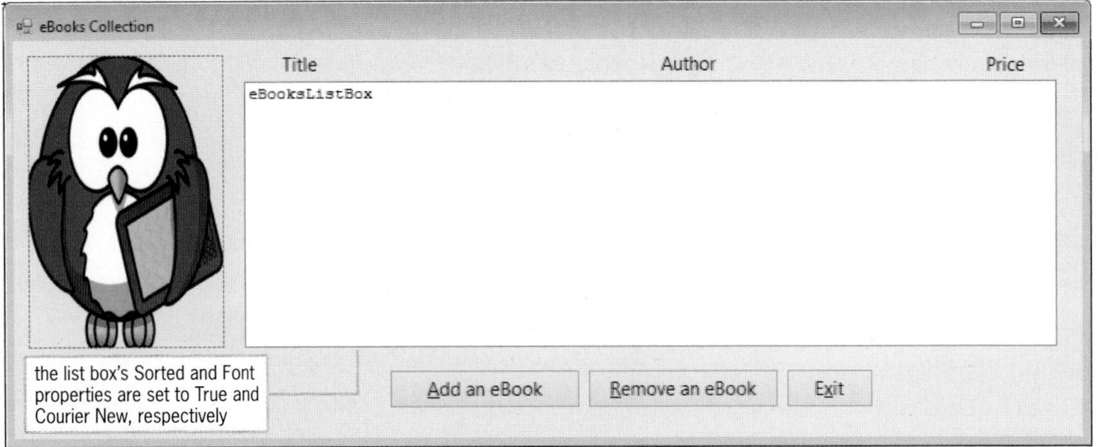

Figure 11-29 MainForm for the eBooks Collection application

```
eBooks.txt
Allegiant                         Veronica Roth                  3.99
Divergent                         Veronica Roth                  2.99
Gone Girl                         Gillian Flynn                  2.99
If I Stay                         Gayle Forman                   2.99
Insurgent                         Veronica Roth                  6.99
Orphan Train                      Christina Baker Kline          6.99
The Fault in Our Stars            John Green                     2.99
The Goldfinch                     Donna Tartt                    6.99
The Husband's Secret              Liane Moriarty                 9.99
Interview with the Vampire        Anne Rice                      7.99
```

Figure 11-30 Contents of the eBooks.txt file

Coding the MainForm_Load Procedure

According to the application's TOE chart, five event procedures need to be coded: the Click event procedures for the three buttons, and the MainForm's Load and FormClosing event procedures. You will code the MainForm_Load procedure first. The procedure's pseudocode is shown in Figure 11-31.

```
MainForm Load event procedure
if the eBooks.txt file exists
     open the file for input
     repeat until the end of the file
          read a line from the file
          add the line to the eBooksListBox
     end repeat
     close the file
     select the first line in the eBooksListBox
else
     display the "Can't find the eBooks.txt file" message in a message box
end if
```

Figure 11-31 Pseudocode for the MainForm_Load procedure

To code and then test the MainForm_Load procedure:

1. Start Visual Studio. Open the **Ebook Solution** (**Ebook Solution.sln**) file contained in the VbReloaded2015\Chap11\Ebook Solution folder. If necessary, open the designer window.
2. Open the Code Editor window. The exitButton_Click procedure has already been coded for you. In the comments that appear in the General Declarations section, replace <your name> and <current date> with your name and the current date, respectively.
3. Locate the MainForm_Load procedure, and then click the **blank line** above the End Sub clause. The procedure will use a StreamReader variable named `inFile`. Enter the appropriate Dim statement.
4. The procedure will store the eBooks.txt filename in a String named constant. Enter the appropriate Const statement, using the name `FileName`. Initialize the named constant to **"eBooks.txt"**.
5. While reading the eBooks.txt file, the procedure will use a String variable named `eBookInfo` to store each line of text. Type the appropriate Dim statement and then press **Enter** twice.
6. According to its pseudocode, the procedure should verify that the eBooks.txt file exists. Type **' verify that the file exists** and then press **Enter**. Then, enter the appropriate If clause, using the Exists method. (Recall that the filename is stored in the `FileName` named constant.)
7. If the eBooks.txt file exists, the selection structure's True path should open the file for input. Type **' open the file for input** and then press **Enter**. Now, enter the appropriate statement to open the file.

8. The next instruction in the selection structure's True path is a loop that repeats its instructions until the end of the file is reached. Type **' process loop body until end of file** and then press **Enter**. Now, enter the appropriate Do clause, using the `Until` keyword and the Peek method.

9. The first instruction in the loop body reads a line from the file. Type **' read a line from the file** and then press **Enter**. Now, enter a statement that reads the line and assigns it to the `eBookInfo` variable.

10. The next instruction in the loop body adds the line to the eBooksListBox. Type **' add the line to the list box** and then press **Enter**. Then, enter the appropriate statement.

11. If necessary, delete the **blank line** above the Loop clause.

12. Next, the procedure needs to close the file. Insert a **blank line** below the Loop clause, and then enter the appropriate statement.

13. Next, type **' select the first line in the list box** and then press **Enter**, and then enter the appropriate statement.

14. If the eBooks.txt file does not exist, the selection structure's False path should display the "Can't find the eBooks.txt file" message in a message box. Type **Else** and then press **Enter**. Now, enter the appropriate MessageBox.Show method.

15. If necessary, delete the **blank line** above the End If clause.

16. Save the solution and then start the application. The information contained in the eBooks.txt file appears in the eBooksListBox, as shown in Figure 11-32.

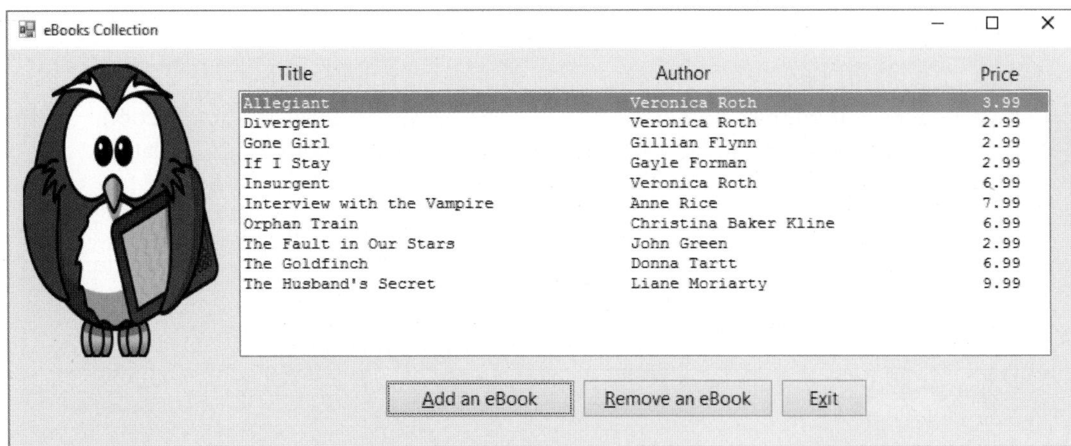

Figure 11-32 Contents of the eBooks.txt file added to the list box

17. Click the **Exit** button to end the application.

Coding the addButton_Click Procedure

According to the application's TOE chart, the addButton_Click procedure should get the eBook information from the user and then add it to the eBooksListBox. Figure 11-33 shows the procedure's pseudocode.

addButton Click event procedure
1. use the InputBox function to get the eBook's title, author, and price
2. concatenate the title, author, and price
3. add the concatenated string to the eBooksListBox

Figure 11-33 Pseudocode for the addButton_Click procedure

To code and then test the addButton_Click procedure:

1. Locate the addButton_Click procedure, and then click the **blank line** below the `' declare variables` comment. The procedure will use three String variables to store the title, author's name, and price. It will also use a String variable to store the concatenated string. Enter the appropriate Dim statements, using `title`, `author`, `price`, and `concatenatedInfo` as the variable names.
2. The procedure will use a Double variable to store the eBook's price after it has been converted from String to Double. Enter a Dim statement that declares a Double variable named `tempPrice`.
3. The first step in the procedure's pseudocode uses the InputBox function to get the title, author's name, and price. Click the **blank line** below the `' get the eBook information` comment, and then enter the appropriate InputBox functions. Assign the functions' return values to the appropriate variables.
4. The second step in the pseudocode concatenates the title, author's name, and price. Click the **blank line** below the `' characters for the price` comment. First, enter a statement that uses the TryParse method to convert the `price` variable's value to Double, storing the result in the `tempPrice` variable.
5. Next, enter an assignment statement that formats the `tempPrice` variable's value to "N2" and assigns the result to the `price` variable. (Recall that the `price` variable's data type is String.)
6. Finally, enter an assignment statement that concatenates the contents of the following three variables: `title`, `author`, and `price`. Use the PadRight method to ensure that the title and author's name contain 40 and 35 characters, respectively. Use the PadLeft method to ensure that the price contains five characters. The assignment statement should assign the concatenated string to the `concatenatedInfo` variable.
7. The third step in the pseudocode adds the concatenated string to the eBooksListBox. Click the **blank line** below the `' add the information to the list box` comment. Enter a statement that adds the contents of the `concatenatedInfo` variable to the eBooksListBox.
8. Save the solution and then start the application.
9. Click the **Add an eBook** button. Type **Death on the Nile** as the title and then press **Enter**. Type **Agatha Christie** as the author and then press **Enter**. Type **7.99** as the price and then press **Enter**. The addButton_Click procedure adds the eBook information to the list box. The list box's Sorted property is set to True, so the information you entered appears in the second line of the list box, as shown in Figure 11-34.

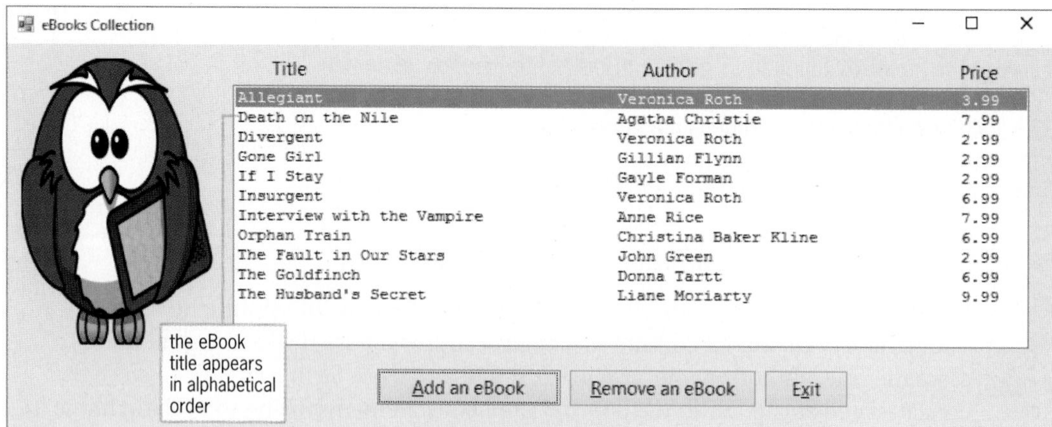

Figure 11-34 New eBook information added to the list box

10. Click the **Exit** button to end the application.

Coding the removeButton_Click Procedure

According to the application's TOE chart, the removeButton_Click procedure should remove the selected eBook from the eBooksListBox. The procedure's pseudocode is shown in Figure 11-35.

```
removeButton Click event procedure
if an eBook is selected in the eBooksListBox
     remove the eBook from the eBooksListBox
end if
```

Figure 11-35 Pseudocode for the removeButton_Click procedure

To code and then test the removeButton_Click procedure:

1. Locate the removeButton_Click procedure, and then click the **blank line** above the End Sub clause. The procedure will use an Integer variable to store the index of the eBook selected in the eBooksListBox. Enter a Dim statement that declares an Integer variable named `index`. Initialize the variable using the list box's SelectedIndex property.
2. The procedure's pseudocode contains a selection structure whose condition determines whether an eBook is selected in the eBooksListBox. Recall that when no item is selected in a list box, the list box's SelectedIndex property contains the number –1. Enter the following If clause:

   If index <> – 1 Then
3. As you learned in the chapter, a list box's Items collection has a RemoveAt method that you can use to remove an item from the list box. Enter the statement to remove the selected eBook from the eBooksListBox.
4. If necessary, delete the **blank line** above the End If clause in the procedure.

5. Save the solution and then start the application. Notice that the eBook information you entered in the previous section does not appear in the list box. This is because you haven't yet entered the instructions to save the list box items to the eBooks.txt file. Those instructions will be entered in the MainForm_FormClosing procedure, which you will code in the next section.

6. Click **Gone Girl** in the list box and then click the **Remove an eBook** button. The button's Click event procedure removes the Gone Girl eBook from the list box. Click the **Exit** button to end the application.

Coding the MainForm_FormClosing Procedure

According to the application's TOE chart, the MainForm_FormClosing procedure is responsible for saving the contents of the eBooksListBox to the eBooks.txt file. The procedure's pseudocode is shown in Figure 11-36.

```
MainForm_FormClosing event procedure
1. open the eBooks.txt file for output
2. repeat for each eBook in the list box
       write the eBook information to the file
   end repeat
3. close the file
```

Figure 11-36 Pseudocode for the MainForm_FormClosing procedure

To code and then test the MainForm_FormClosing procedure:

1. Locate the MainForm_FormClosing procedure, and then click the **blank line** below the `' declare a StreamWriter variable` comment. Enter a Dim statement that declares a StreamWriter variable named `outFile`.

2. The first step in the procedure's pseudocode opens the eBooks.txt file for output. Click the **blank line** below the `' open the file for output` comment, and then enter a statement that uses the CreateText method to open the file.

3. The second step in the pseudocode is a loop that repeats its instructions for each eBook in the list box. Click the **blank line** below the `' write each line in the list box` comment, and then enter the following For Each clause:

   For Each eBook As String In eBooksListBox.Items

4. Change the Next clause to **Next eBook**.

5. The instruction in the loop body should write the eBook information to the file. Click the **blank line** below the For Each clause, and then enter a statement that uses the WriteLine method to write the contents of the `eBook` variable to the eBooks.txt file.

6. If necessary, delete the **blank line** above the `Next eBook` clause.

7. The third step in the pseudocode closes the file. Click the **blank line** below the `' close the file` comment, and then enter the appropriate statement.

8. If necessary, delete the **blank line** above the End Sub clause in the procedure.

9. Save the solution and then start the application. Click the **Add an eBook** button. Use the input dialog boxes to enter the following eBook: **Death on the Nile**, **Agatha Christie**, and **7.99**. The addButton_Click procedure adds the eBook information to the list box.

10. Click the **Exit** button. The computer processes the `Me.Close()` statement in the button's Click event procedure; doing this invokes the form's FormClosing event. The instructions in the MainForm_FormClosing procedure save the contents of the list box to the eBooks.txt file.

11. Start the application again. Notice that the eBook information you entered appears as the second eBook in the list box. Click **Death on the Nile** and then click the **Remove an eBook** button. The button's Click event procedure removes the selected eBook information from the list box.

12. Click the **Exit** button. Start the application again. Notice that the *Death on the Nile* eBook does not appear in the list box. Click the **Exit** button.

13. Close the Code Editor window and then close the solution. Figure 11-37 shows the code for the eBooks Collection application.

```
' Project name:         Ebook Project
' Project purpose:      Adds and deletes list box entries
'                       Reads information from a sequential access file
'                       Writes information to a sequential access file
' Created/revised by: <your name> on <current date>

Option Explicit On
Option Strict On
Option Infer Off

Public Class MainForm
   Private Sub MainForm_Load(sender As Object, e As EventArgs
   ) Handles Me.Load
      ' fills the list box with data from
      ' a sequential access file

      Dim inFile As IO.StreamReader
      Const FileName As String = "eBooks.txt"
      Dim eBookInfo As String

      ' verify that the file exists
      If IO.File.Exists(FileName) Then
          ' open the file for input
          inFile = IO.File.OpenText(FileName)
          ' process loop body until end of file
          Do Until inFile.Peek = -1
             ' read a line from the file
             eBookInfo = inFile.ReadLine
             ' add the line to the list box
             eBooksListBox.Items.Add(eBookInfo)
          Loop
          inFile.Close()
          ' select the first line in the list box
          eBooksListBox.SelectedIndex = 0
      Else
          MessageBox.Show("Can't find the eBooks.txt file",
                  "eBooks", MessageBoxButtons.OK,
                  MessageBoxIcon.Information)
```

Figure 11-37 Code for the eBooks Collection application *(continues)*

(continued)

```
        End If
    End Sub

    Private Sub addButton_Click(sender As Object, e As EventArgs
    ) Handles addButton.Click
        ' adds eBook information to the list box

        ' declare variables
        Dim title As String
        Dim author As String
        Dim price As String
        Dim concatenatedInfo As String
        Dim tempPrice As Double

        ' get the eBook information
        title = InputBox("Title:", "eBooks")
        author = InputBox("Author:", "eBooks")
        price = InputBox("Price:", "eBooks")

        ' format the price, then concatenate the input
        ' items, using 40 characters for the title,
        ' 35 characters for the author, and 5
        ' characters for the price
        Double.TryParse(price, tempPrice)
        price = tempPrice.ToString("N2")
        concatenatedInfo = title.PadRight(40) &
           author.PadRight(35) & price.PadLeft(5)

        ' add the information to the list box
        eBooksListBox.Items.Add(concatenatedInfo)

    End Sub

    Private Sub removeButton_Click(sender As Object, e As EventArgs
    ) Handles removeButton.Click
        ' removes the selected line from the list box

        ' if a line is selected, remove the line
        Dim index As Integer = eBooksListBox.SelectedIndex
        If index <> -1 Then
            eBooksListBox.Items.RemoveAt(index)
        End If
    End Sub

    Private Sub MainForm_FormClosing(sender As Object,
    e As FormClosingEventArgs) Handles Me.FormClosing
        ' save the list box information

        ' declare a StreamWriter variable
        Dim outFile As IO.StreamWriter

        ' open the file for output
        outFile = IO.File.CreateText("eBooks.txt")

```

Figure 11-37 Code for the eBooks Collection application *(continues)*

(continued)

```
        ' write each line in the list box
        For Each eBook As String In eBooksListBox.Items
            outFile.WriteLine(eBook)
        Next eBook

        ' close the file
        outFile.Close()
    End Sub

    Private Sub exitButton_Click(sender As Object, e As EventArgs
    ) Handles exitButton.Click
        Me.Close()
    End Sub
End Class
```

Figure 11-37 Code for the eBooks Collection application

PROGRAMMING EXAMPLE

Glovers Industries Application

Glovers Industries stores the item numbers and prices of its products in a sequential access file named itemInfo.txt. Create an application that displays the item numbers in a list box. When the user selects an item number, the application should display the item's price. Use the following names for the solution and project, respectively: Glovers Solution and Glovers Project. Save the application in the VbReloaded2015\Chap11 folder. Change the form file's name to Main Form.vb. You will also need to create the itemInfo.txt sequential access file. If necessary, use Windows to move the itemInfo.txt file to the project's bin\Debug folder. See Figures 11-38 through 11-43.

Task	Object	Event
1. Create a Product structure that has two members: a String member named number and a Decimal member named price 2. Declare and initialize a class-level, five-element Product array named items	MainForm	Declarations section
1. Fill the items array with the item numbers and prices stored in the itemInfo.txt file 2. Fill the numbersListBox with the item numbers stored in the itemInfo.txt file		Load
Display the item numbers	numbersListBox	None
Display (in the priceLabel) the price associated with the selected item number		SelectedIndexChanged
End the application	exitButton	Click
Display the price (from numbersListBox)	priceLabel	None

Figure 11-38 TOE chart

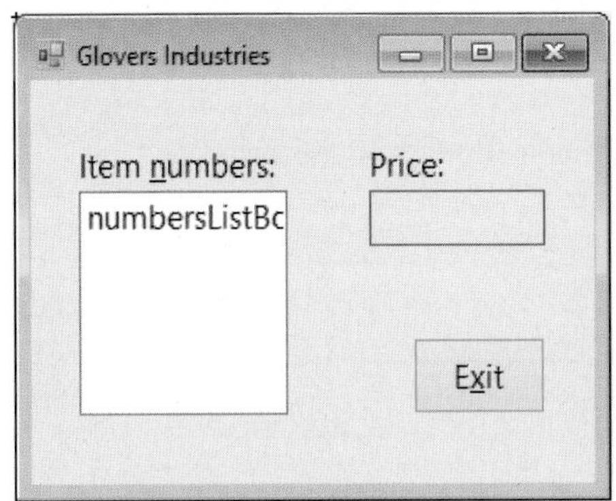

Figure 11-39 MainForm and tab order

Object	**Property**	**Setting**
MainForm	Font StartPosition Text	Segoe UI, 11pt CenterScreen Glovers Industries
priceLabel	AutoSize BorderStyle TextAlign	False FixedSingle MiddleCenter

Figure 11-40 Objects, properties, and settings

```
12AVX,5
23ABC,8.97
23TWT,4.69
34ZAB,12.5
91BAN,34.67
```

Figure 11-41 Contents of the itemInfo.txt sequential access file

```
MainForm Load event procedure
if the itemInfo.txt file exists
    open the file for input
    repeat until the end of the file
        read a line from the file and separate the item number from the price
        assign the item number and the price to the current element in the items array
        add the item number to the numbersListBox
        add 1 to the variable that keeps track of the array subscript and list box index
    end repeat
    close the file
    select the first item in the numbersListBox
else
    display an appropriate error message
end if
```

Figure 11-42 Pseudocode *(continues)*

PROGRAMMING EXAMPLE

(continued)

<u>numbersListBox SelectedIndexChanged event procedure</u>
use the index of the selected item to access the appropriate price from the items array, and then display the price in the priceLabel

<u>exitButton Click event procedure</u>
close the application

Figure 11-42 Pseudocode

```
' Project name:         Glovers Project
' Project purpose:      Display the price of an item
' Created/revised by:   <your name> on <current date>

Option Explicit On
Option Strict On
Option Infer Off

Public Class MainForm
    ' define the Product structure
    Structure Product
        Public number As String
        Public price As Decimal
    End Structure

    ' declare class-level array
    Private items(4) As Product

    Private Sub MainForm_Load(sender As Object, e As EventArgs
    ) Handles Me.Load
        ' fills the items array and numbersListBox with
        ' the data stored in a sequential access file

        Dim inFile As IO.StreamReader
        Const FileName As String = "itemInfo.txt"
        Dim x As Integer   ' subscript and index
        Dim fields(1) As String

        If IO.File.Exists(FileName) Then
            inFile = IO.File.OpenText(FileName)
            Do Until inFile.Peek = -1
                ' separate item number from price
                fields = inFile.ReadLine.Split(","c)
                ' assign item number and price to the array
                items(x).number = fields(0)
                items(x).price = Convert.ToDecimal(fields(1))
                ' add item number to the list box
                numbersListBox.Items.Add(items(x).number)

                ' update variable that keeps track of the
                ' array subscript and list box index
                x += 1
```

Figure 11-43 Code *(continues)*

(continued)

```
            Loop
            inFile.Close()
            numbersListBox.SelectedIndex = 0
        Else
            MessageBox.Show("Can't find " & FileName,
                "Glovers Industries", MessageBoxButtons.OK,
                MessageBoxIcon.Information)
        End If
    End Sub

    Private Sub numbersListBox_SelectedIndexChanged(
    sender As Object, e As EventArgs
    ) Handles numbersListBox.SelectedIndexChanged
        ' displays the price corresponding to the
        ' item selected in the list box

        Dim index As Integer = numbersListBox.SelectedIndex
        priceLabel.Text = items(index).price.ToString("N2")
    End Sub

    Private Sub exitButton_Click(sender As Object, e As EventArgs
    ) Handles exitButton.Click
        Me.Close()
    End Sub
End Class
```

Figure 11-43 Code

Chapter Summary

- You can use Visual Basic's Structure statement to define a user-defined data type, also called a structure. You typically enter the Structure statement in the form's Declarations section in the Code Editor window.
- After defining a structure, you can use the structure to declare a structure variable. A structure variable contains one or more member variables. You access a member variable using the structure variable's name followed by the dot member access operator and the member variable's name.
- The member variables contained in a structure variable can be used just like any other variables.
- When a structure variable is passed to a procedure, all of its members are automatically passed.
- You can create an array of structure variables. You access a member variable in an array element using the array's name followed by the element's subscript enclosed in parentheses, the dot member access operator, and the member variable's name, like this: *arrayName*(*subscript*).*memberVariableName.*

- An application can write information to a file (called an output file) and also read information from a file (called an input file).
- The information in a sequential access file (also referred to as a text file) is always accessed sequentially, which means it is accessed in consecutive order from the beginning of the file through the end of the file.
- You can write data to a sequential access file by first declaring a StreamWriter variable and then using either the CreateText method or the AppendText method to open the file. You assign the appropriate method's return value to the StreamWriter variable. You then use either the Write method or the WriteLine method to write the data to the file.
- You can read data from a sequential access file by first declaring a StreamReader variable. Before opening the file, you should use the Exists method to determine whether the file exists. If the file exists, you use the OpenText method to open the file, assigning the method's return value to the StreamReader variable. You then use the Peek and ReadLine methods to read the data from the file.
- When a procedure is finished using a sequential access file, it should use the Close method to close the file.
- The FormClosing event occurs when a form is about to be closed. You can prevent a form from being closed by setting the Cancel property of the FormClosing event procedure's e parameter to True.
- You can use the Items collection's RemoveAt method or its Remove method to remove an item from a list box or combo box.
- You can use the PadLeft and PadRight methods to align columns of information that appear in the interface. You can also use the methods to align information written to a sequential access file.
- You can use the Strings.Space method to include a specific number of space characters in a string.
- When writing records to a file, programmers typically write each record on a separate line in the file. They use a delimiter character to separate the fields in each record.
- You can use the Split function to read delimited records from a file.

Key Terms

AppendText method—used with a StreamWriter variable to open a sequential access file for append

Cancel property—a property of the e parameter in the FormClosing event procedure; when set to True, it prevents the form from closing

Close method—used with either a StreamWriter variable or a StreamReader variable to close a sequential access file

CreateText method—used with a StreamWriter variable to open a sequential access file for output

Delimiter character—a character used to separate the fields in a record

Exists method—used to determine whether a file exists

Field—a single item of information about a person, place, or thing

FormClosing event—occurs when a form is about to be closed, which can happen as a result of the computer processing the `Me.Close()` statement or the user clicking the Close button on the form's title bar

Input files—files from which an application reads data

Line—a sequence (stream) of characters followed by the newline character

Member variables—the variables contained in a structure

OpenText method—used with a StreamReader variable to open a sequential access file for input

Output files—files to which an application writes data

Peek method—used with a StreamReader variable to determine whether a file contains another character to read

ReadLine method—used with a StreamReader variable to read a line of text from a sequential access file

Record—a group of related fields that contain all of the necessary data about a specific person, place, or thing

Remove method—a method of the Items collection; uses the item's value to remove the item from a list box or combo box

RemoveAt method—a method of the Items collection; uses the item's index to remove the item from a list box or combo box

Sequential access files—files composed of lines of text that are both read and written sequentially; also called text files

Split function—separates (splits) a string into substrings based on a delimiter character and then assigns the substrings to a one-dimensional array

Stream of characters—a sequence of characters

StreamReader object—used to read a sequence (stream) of characters from a sequential access file

StreamWriter object—used to write a sequence (stream) of characters to a sequential access file

Strings.Space method—can be used to include a specific number of spaces in a string

Structure statement—used to create user-defined data types, called structures

Structure variables—variables declared using a structure as the data type

Structures—data types created by the Structure statement; allow the programmer to group related items into one unit; also called user-defined data types

Text files—another term for sequential access files

User-defined data types—data types created by the Structure statement; see Structures

Write method—used with a StreamWriter variable to write data to a sequential access file; differs from the WriteLine method in that it does not write a newline character after the data

WriteLine method—used with a StreamWriter variable to write data to a sequential access file; differs from the Write method in that it writes a newline character after the data

Review Questions

Each Review Question is associated with one or more objectives listed at the beginning of the chapter.

1. Which of the following declares a Vehicle variable named `car`? (2)
   a. `Private car As Vehicle`
   b. `Dim car As Vehicle`
   c. `Dim Vehicle As car`
   d. both a and b
2. Which of the following assigns the string "Jaguar" to the `maker` member of a Vehicle variable named `car`? (2)
   a. `car.maker = "Jaguar"`
   b. `Vehicle.maker = "Jaguar"`
   c. `Vehicle.car.maker = "Jaguar"`
   d. `maker.car = "Jaguar"`
3. An application uses a structure named Employee. Which of the following statements creates a five-element array of Employee structure variables? (4)
   a. `Dim workers As Employee(4)`
   b. `Dim workers As Employee(5)`
   c. `Dim workers(4) As Employee`
   d. `Dim workers(5) As Employee`
4. Each structure variable in the `states` array contains a String member named `id` and an Integer member named `population`. Which of the following assigns the string "RI" to the first element in the array? (4)
   a. `states(0).id = "RI"`
   b. `states(1).id = "RI"`
   c. `states.id(0) = "RI"`
   d. `states.id(1) = "RI"`
5. Which of the following opens the cities.txt file and allows the computer to write new data to the end of the file's existing data? (5)
   a. `outFile = IO.File.AddText("cities.txt")`
   b. `outFile = IO.File.AppendText("cities.txt")`
   c. `outFile = IO.File.InsertText("cities.txt")`
   d. `outFile = IO.File.OpenText("cities.txt")`
6. If the file to be opened does not exist, the ____________ method results in an error when it is processed by the computer. (7)
   a. AppendText
   b. CreateText
   c. OpenText
   d. WriteText
7. Which of the following reads a line of text from a sequential access file and assigns the line (excluding the newline character) to the `lineOfText` variable? (7)
   a. `lineOfText = inFile.ReadLine`
   b. `lineOfText = ReadLine(inFile)`
   c. `inFile.Read(lineOfText)`
   d. `inFile.ReadLine(lineOfText)`

8. What does the Peek method return when the end of the file is reached? (8)

   a. 0
   b. –1
   c. the last character in the file
   d. the newline character

9. Which of the following If clauses determines whether the employ.txt file exists? (8)

   a. `If IO.File.Exists("employ.txt") Then`
   b. `If IO.File("employ.txt").Exists Then`
   c. `If IO.Exists("employ.txt") = True Then`
   d. `If IO.Exists.File("employ.txt") = True Then`

10. The OpenText method creates a ____________ object. (7)

    a. File
    b. SequenceReader
    c. StreamReader
    d. StreamWriter

11. The AppendText method creates a ____________ object. (5)

    a. File
    b. SequenceReader
    c. StreamReader
    d. StreamWriter

12. Which of the following reads a record from a sequential access file and assigns the fields in each record to the `songs` array? The fields are delimited by a space character. (13, 14)

    a. `songs = inFile.ReadLine.Split(" "c)`
    b. `songs = inFile.ReadLine.SplitBy(" "c)`
    c. `songs = inFile.ReadLine.SplitInto(" "c)`
    d. `songs = inFile.ReadLine.SplitUsing(" "c)`

13. The ____________ event occurs when the computer processes the `Me.Close()` statement or when the user clicks the Close button on the form's title bar. (9)

    a. FormClosing
    b. FormFinish
    c. Finish
    d. none of the above

Each Exercise, except the DISCOVERY exercises, is associated with one or more objectives listed at the beginning of the chapter.

Exercises

Pencil and Paper

INTRODUCTORY

1. Write a Structure statement that defines a structure named SongInfo. The structure contains two String member variables named `title` and `artist` and a Decimal member variable named `cost`. Then, write a Private statement that declares a SongInfo variable named `hiphop`. (1, 2)

INTRODUCTORY

2. Write a Structure statement that defines a structure named Dvd. The structure contains two String member variables named `movieName` and `yearReleased`. It also contains an Integer member variable named `price`. Then, write a Dim statement that declares a Dvd variable named `myDvds`. (1, 2)

INTRODUCTORY

3. An application contains the Structure statement shown here. Write a Dim statement that declares a Computer variable named **homeUse**. Then, write an assignment statement that assigns the string "App75" to the **model** member. Finally, write an assignment statement that assigns the number 1650 to the **cost** member. (1, 2)

```
Structure Computer
    Public model As String
    Public cost As Decimal
End Structure
```

INTRODUCTORY

4. An application contains the Structure statement shown here. Write a Dim statement that declares a MyFriend variable named **school**. Then, write assignment statements that assign the value in the firstTextBox to the **first** member and assign the value in the lastTextBox to the **last** member. Finally, write assignment statements that assign the value in the **last** member to the lastLabel and assign the value in the **first** member to the firstLabel. (1, 2)

```
Structure MyFriend
    Public last As String
    Public first As String
End Structure
```

INTRODUCTORY

5. Write the code to declare a variable named **outFile** that can be used to write data to a sequential access file. Then, write the statement to open a sequential access file named sales.txt for output. (5)

INTRODUCTORY

6. Write the code to declare a variable named **inFile** that can be used to read data from a sequential access file. Then, write the statement to open a sequential access file named sales.txt for input. (7)

INTRODUCTORY

7. Write the code to close the sequential access file associated with a StreamWriter variable named **outFile**. (6)

INTRODUCTORY

8. Write an If clause that determines whether a sequential access file exists. The file's name is sales.txt. (8)

INTRODUCTORY

9. Write a Do clause that determines whether the end of a sequential access file has been reached. The file is associated with a StreamReader variable named **inFile**. (8)

INTERMEDIATE

10. An application contains the Structure statement shown here. Write a Private statement that declares a 10-element one-dimensional array of Computer variables. Name the array **business**. Then, write an assignment statement that assigns the string "Tosh7400" to the **model** member contained in the first array element. Finally, write an assignment statement that assigns the number 4560 to the **cost** member contained in the first array element. (4)

```
Structure Computer
    Public model As String
    Public cost As Decimal
End Structure
```

INTERMEDIATE

11. An application contains the Structure statement shown here. Write a Private statement that declares a five-element one-dimensional array of Worker variables. Name the array **coWorkers**. Then, write an assignment statement that assigns the value in the

name1TextBox to the `first` member contained in the last array element. Finally, write an assignment statement that assigns the value in the name2TextBox to the `last` member contained in the last array element. (4)

```
Structure Worker
    Public last As String
    Public first As String
End Structure
```

12. A sequential access file named travel.txt contains records whose four fields are delimited by a comma. Write a Dim statement to declare a one-dimensional String array named `travelInfo`. Then, write a statement that reads a line of text from the file and assigns the fields to the array. The file is associated with a StreamReader variable named `inFile`. (13, 14) INTERMEDIATE

13. A sequential access file named vacations.txt contains records whose three fields are delimited by a comma. The application that uses the file defines a structure named TravelInfo. The TravelInfo structure contains three members: a String member named `location`, an Integer member named `lengthOfStay`, and a Double member named `cost`. (4, 13, 14) ADVANCED
    a. Write a Private statement to declare a one-dimensional TravelInfo array named `myVacations`. The array should contain 10 elements.
    b. Write a Dim statement to declare a one-dimensional String array named `fields`.
    c. Write a statement that reads a line of text from the vacations.txt file and assigns the fields to the `fields` array. The file is associated with a StreamReader variable named `inFile`.
    d. Write the statements to assign the fields contained in the first element in the `fields` array to the appropriate members in the first element in the `myVacations` array.

Computer

14. If necessary, complete the Guess the Word Game application from this chapter's Programming Tutorial 1, and then close the solution. Use Windows to make a copy of the Word Solution folder. Rename the folder Word Solution-ModifyThis. Open the solution file contained in the Word Solution-ModifyThis folder. Add 10 more six-letter words to the words.txt file, and then make the appropriate modifications to the application's code. Save the solution and then start and test the application. Close the solution. (5, 7) MODIFY THIS

15. If necessary, complete the eBooks Collection application from this chapter's Programming Tutorial 2, and then close the solution. Use Windows to make a copy of the Ebook Solution folder. Rename the folder Ebook Solution-ModifyThis. Open the solution file contained in the Ebook Solution-ModifyThis folder. The MainForm_FormClosing procedure should verify that the user wants to save the changes made to the list box. It should then take the appropriate action based on the user's response. The removeButton_Click procedure should verify that the user wants to remove the selected eBook from the list box. Use the message "Do you want to remove the *x* eBook?", in which *x* is the name of the eBook. The procedure should take the appropriate action based on the user's response. Modify the code accordingly. Save the solution and then start and test the application. Close the solution. (9, 10) MODIFY THIS

MODIFY THIS

16. In this exercise, you will modify the West Coast Emporium application from Figure 11-7 in the chapter. Open the West Coast Solution (West Coast Solution.sln) file contained in the VbReloaded2015\Chap11\West Coast Solution-ModifyThis folder. The modified application should display the number of stores in the selected state and also the name of the regional manager for the state. The names of the regional managers are shown in Figure 11-44. Make the appropriate modifications to the interface and code. Save the solution and then start and test the application. Close the solution. (4)

State	Regional manager
California (CA)	Perry Johanson
Oregon (OR)	Sally Cranston
Washington (WA)	Pat Ippolito

Figure 11-44 Information for Exercise 16

INTRODUCTORY

17. Open the Employee List Solution (Employee List Solution.sln) file contained in the VbReloaded2015\Chap11\Employee List Solution folder. The Write button should write the contents of the employTextBox (excluding any leading or trailing spaces) to a sequential access file named employees.txt. Each name should appear on a separate line in the file. Save the file in the project's bin\Debug folder. The Read button should read the names from the employees.txt file and display each in the list box. Code the appropriate event procedures. Save the solution and then start the application. Test the application by writing five names to the file, and then end the application. Open the employees.txt file to verify that it contains five names. Close the employees.txt window and then close the solution. (5–8)

INTRODUCTORY

18. Open the Memo Solution (Memo Solution.sln) file contained in the VbReloaded2015\Chap11\Memo Solution folder. The Write button should write the contents of the memoTextBox to a sequential access file named memo.txt. Save the file in the project's bin\Debug folder. Save the solution and then start the application. Test the application by writing the memo shown in Figure 11-45 to the file, and then end the application. Open the memo.txt file to verify that it contains the memo. Close the memo.txt window and then close the solution. (5, 6)

> To all employees:
>
> The annual picnic will be held at Jeffers Park on Saturday, August 21. Bring your family for a day full of fun!
>
> Peter Mulcahey
> Personnel Manager

Figure 11-45 Memo for Exercise 18

INTRODUCTORY

19. Open the City Solution (City Solution.sln) file contained in the VbReloaded2015\Chap11\City Solution folder. Locate the displayButton_Click procedure. The procedure should display the contents of the array of structure variables in the list box, using the following format: the city name followed by a comma, a space, and the state name. Modify the code and then test the application. Close the solution. (4)

INTRODUCTORY

20. Open the Report Solution (Report Solution.sln) file contained in the VbReloaded2015\Chap11\Report Solution folder. The application stores three names and commission amounts in an array. Code the application so that it creates the report shown in

Figure 11-46. Save the report in a sequential access file named report.txt. Use hyphens for the underline. Use an accumulator to total the commission amounts. Save the solution and then start and test the application. End the application. Open the report.txt file to verify that it contains the report. Close the report.txt window and then close the solution. (5, 6)

```
Commission Report

Salesperson          Commission ($)
Karen Klementz       12,600
Jack Harper             900
Tim Harris            5,750
                     ------
Total               $19,250
```

Figure 11-46 Report for Exercise 20

21. Open the Name Solution (Name Solution.sln) file contained in the VbReloaded2015\Chap11\Name Solution folder. Open the names.txt file contained in the project's bin\Debug folder. The sequential access file contains five names. Close the names.txt window. The Display button should read the five names from the names.txt file and store each in a five-element array. It should sort the array in descending order and then display the contents of the array in the list box. Code the button's Click event procedure. Save the solution and then start and test the application. Close the solution. If you need to recreate the names.txt file, open the file in a window in the IDE, delete the contents of the file (if necessary), and then enter the following five names: Joanne, Zelda, Abby, Ben, and Linda. (6–8) INTRODUCTORY

22. Open the Chang Solution (Chang Solution.sln) file contained in the VbReloaded2015\Chap11\Chang Solution folder. The application should display a grade based on the number of points entered by the user. The grading scale is shown in Figure 11-47. Create a structure that contains two members: an Integer variable for the minimum points and a String variable for the grades. Use the structure to declare a class-level one-dimensional array that has five elements. The MainForm_Load procedure should store the minimum points and grades in the array. The application should search the array for the number of points earned and then display the appropriate grade from the array. Code the application. Save the solution and then start and test the application. Close the solution. (4, 9) INTERMEDIATE

Minimum points	Maximum points	Grade
0	299	F
300	349	D
350	414	C
415	464	B
465	500	A

Figure 11-47 Grading scale for Exercise 22

23. If necessary, complete Computer Exercise 17, and then close the solution. Use Windows to make a copy of the Employee List Solution folder. Rename the folder Employee List Solution-Intermediate. Open the solution file contained in the Employee List Solution-Intermediate folder. (5, 6, 8) INTERMEDIATE

    a. Use Windows to delete the employees.txt file contained in the project's bin\Debug folder.

b. The first time the Write button's Click event procedure is processed, it should determine whether the employees.txt file exists. If the file exists, the procedure should use the MessageBox.Show method to ask the user whether the existing file should be replaced. Include Yes and No buttons in the message box. If the user clicks the Yes button, replace the existing file; otherwise, append to the existing file.

c. Save the solution and then start the application. Type Helen in the Name box and then click the Write button. End the application.

d. Start the application again. Type Ginger in the Name box and then click the Write button. The application should ask whether you want the existing file replaced. Click the No button and then end the application.

e. Open the employees.txt file. The file should contain two names: Helen and Ginger. Close the employees.txt window.

f. Start the application again. Type George in the Name box and then click the Write button. Click the Yes button and then end the application.

g. Open the employees.txt file. The file should contain one name: George. Close the employees.txt window and then close the solution.

INTERMEDIATE

24. Open the Salary Solution (Salary Solution.sln) file contained in the VbReloaded2015\Chap11\Salary Solution folder. Open the Code Editor window and study the existing code. The application displays the salary amount associated with the code entered by the user. Currently, the Private statement stores the six salary amounts in the `salaries` array. Modify the application so that it reads the salary amounts from the salary.txt file contained in the project's bin\Debug folder and stores each in the array. Save the solution and then start and test the application. Close the solution. (6–8)

INTERMEDIATE

25. If necessary, complete the eBooks Collection application from this chapter's Programming Tutorial 2, and then close the solution. Use Windows to make a copy of the Ebook Solution folder. Rename the folder Ebook Solution-Undo. Open the solution file contained in the Ebook Solution-Undo folder. Add an Undo Remove button to the interface. Set its Enabled property to False. The button's Click event procedure should restore the last line removed by the Remove button. Make the necessary modifications to the code. Save the solution and then start and test the application. Close the solution. (10)

INTERMEDIATE

26. If necessary, complete the eBooks Collection application from this chapter's Programming Tutorial 2, and then close the solution. Use Windows to make a copy of the Ebook Solution folder. Rename the folder Ebook Solution-Structure. Open the solution file contained in the Ebook Solution-Structure folder. Create a structure and then use the structure in the addButton_Click procedure. Save the solution and then start and test the application. Close the solution. (1, 2)

INTERMEDIATE

27. Open the Friends Solution (Friends Solution.sln) file contained in the VbReloaded2015\Chap11\Friends Solution folder. The Add button should add the name entered in the text portion of the combo box control to the list portion of the control, but only if the name is not already in the list. The Remove button should remove (from the list portion of the combo box) the name either entered in the text portion or selected in the list portion. The form's FormClosing event procedure should save the combo box items in a sequential access file named myFriends.txt. The form's Load event procedure should read the names from the myFriends.txt file and add each name to the combo box. Code the application. Save the solution and then start and test the application. Close the solution. (5–10)

28. Open the Vacation Solution (Vacation Solution.sln) file contained in the VbReloaded2015\Chap11\Vacation Solution folder. The tripInfo.txt file contains 10 records whose three fields are separated by a number (#) sign. Define a structure that contains a member for each of the three fields in the tripInfo.txt file. Use the following member names: `location`, `oneWeekPrice`, and `twoWeekPrice`. Store the records in a class-level one-dimensional array that contains 10 elements. Use a list box to display each of the locations from the file. When the user selects a location from the list box, the application should display the prices for a one-week stay and a two-week stay. Code the appropriate procedures. Save the solution and then start and test the application. (1, 2, 4, 6–8, 13, 14) ADVANCED

29. Open the Test Scores Solution (Test Scores Solution.sln) file contained in the VbReloaded2015\Chap11\Test Scores Solution folder. The Save button should save the contents of the nameTextBox and scoreTextBox to a sequential access file named scores.txt. Save each student's record on a separate line. The Display button should use the InputBox function to prompt the user to enter a test score. It then should display the names of the students earning that test score. Save the solution and then start the application. Test the application by entering the student records shown in Figure 11-48. Click the Save button after entering each record. Then, click the Display button. Enter 95 and then press Enter. The names of the students whose test score is 95 appear in the list box. Close the solution. (5–8, 13, 14) ADVANCED

Name	Test score
John Jones	80
Phillip Hawking	95
Kevin Carley	83
Ellie Mayfield	78
Rachael Smith	95
Susan Carkley	99
Harriet Chu	95

Figure 11-48 Student records for Exercise 29

30. If necessary, complete the eBooks Collection application from this chapter's Programming Tutorial 2, and then close the solution. Use Windows to make a copy of the Ebook Solution folder. Rename the folder Ebook Solution-No Duplicate. Open the solution file contained in the Ebook Solution-No Duplicate folder. Before prompting the user to enter the author's name and the price, the addButton_Click procedure should determine whether the eBook's title is already included in the list box. If the list box contains the title, the procedure should display an appropriate message, and it should not add the eBook to the list. Save the solution and then start and test the application. Close the solution. DISCOVERY

31. Open the Grades Solution (Grades Solution.sln) file contained in the VbReloaded2015\Chap11\Grades Solution folder. The application should display a student's name and the grades earned on two tests. DISCOVERY

    a. Open the Code Editor window. Create a structure named StudentInfo. The structure should contain two members: a String variable for the student's name and a String array for the grades. An array contained in a structure cannot be assigned an initial size, so you will need to include an empty set of parentheses after the array name.

b. In the getButton_Click procedure, use the StudentInfo structure to declare a structure variable.

c. Research the Visual Basic ReDim statement. Use the ReDim statement to declare the array's size in the getButton_Click event procedure. In this case, the array should have two elements. (Keep in mind that the array belongs to the structure variable.)

d. The getButton_Click procedure should use three InputBox functions to get the student's name and both grades. (Store each grade in the array.)

e. The getButton_Click procedure should display the student's name and grades in the reportLabel.

f. Save the solution and then start the application. Enter your name and the grades A and B. Your name and both grades appear in the reportLabel. Close the solution.

DISCOVERY

32. If necessary, complete Computer Exercise 31, and then close the solution. Use Windows to make a copy of the Grades Solution folder. Rename the folder Grades Solution-Modified. Open the solution file contained in the Grades Solution-Modified folder. The getButton_Click procedure should allow the user to enter the names and grades for five students. (Hint: You will need to use an array of structure variables.) Display the five student names and their grades in the reportLabel. You will need to make the reportLabel larger. Save the solution and then start and test the application. Close the solution.

SWAT THE BUGS

33. Open the Debug Solution (Debug Solution.sln) file contained in the VbReloaded2015\Chap11\Debug Solution folder. Open the Code Editor window and review the existing code. Start the application and then test it using Sue and 1000, and then using Pete and 5000. A run time error occurs. Read the error message. Click Debug on the menu bar and then click Stop Debugging. Open the bonus.txt file contained in the project's bin\Debug folder. Notice that the file is empty. Close the bonus.txt window. Locate and then correct the errors in the code. When the application is working correctly, close the solution. (5, 6)

Case Projects

Jackson High School

This year, three students are running for senior class president: Tyler Tomkins, Kate Gonzo, and John Chang. Create an application that keeps track of the voting. Save the voting information in a sequential access file. The application should display the number of votes per candidate. Use the following names for the solution and project, respectively: Jackson Solution and Jackson Project. Save the application in the VbReloaded2015\Chap11 folder. Change the form file's name to Main Form.vb. You can either create your own interface or create the one shown in Figure 11-49. (5–8)

Figure 11-49 Sample interface for the Jackson High School application

 KJPR-Radio

Each year, KJPR-Radio polls its audience to determine the best Super Bowl commercial. The choices are as follows: Cheerios, Doritos, T-Mobile, and RadioShack. Create an application that the station manager can use to save each caller's choice in a sequential access file. The application should display the number of votes for each commercial as well as the percentage of the total contributed by each choice. Use the following names for the solution and project, respectively: Commercial Solution and Commercial Project. Save the application in the VbReloaded2015\Chap11 folder. Change the form file's name to Main Form.vb. You can either create your own interface or create the one shown in Figure 11-50. (5–8)

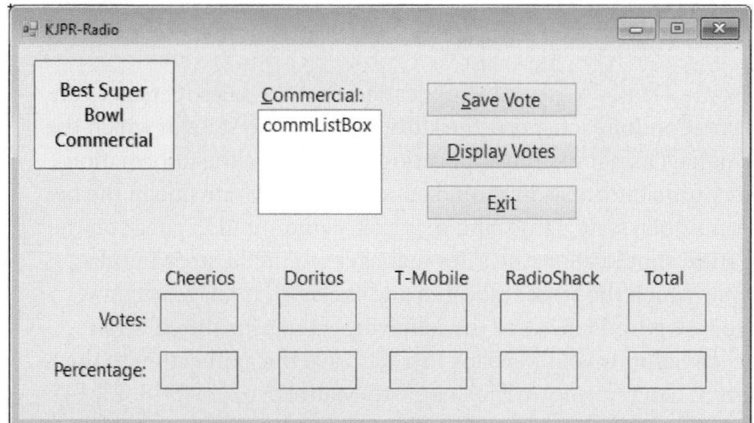

Figure 11-50 Sample interface for the KJPR-Radio application

 Political Awareness Organization

During July and August of each year, the Political Awareness Organization (PAO) sends a questionnaire to the voters in its district. The questionnaire asks the voter for his or her political party (Democratic, Republican, or Independent) and age. The age should contain only numbers, and the minimum age for a respondent is 18. From the returned questionnaires, the organization's secretary tabulates the number of Democrats, Republicans, and Independents in the district. The secretary wants an application that she can use to save each respondent's information (political party and age) to a sequential access file. The application should calculate and display the number of voters in each political party. When the user clicks the Exit button, the application should verify that the user wants to exit the application. Use the following names for the solution and project, respectively: PAO Solution and PAO Project. Save the application in the VbReloaded2015\Chap11 folder. Change the form file's name to Main Form.vb. You can either create your own interface or create the one shown in Figure 11-51. (5–9)

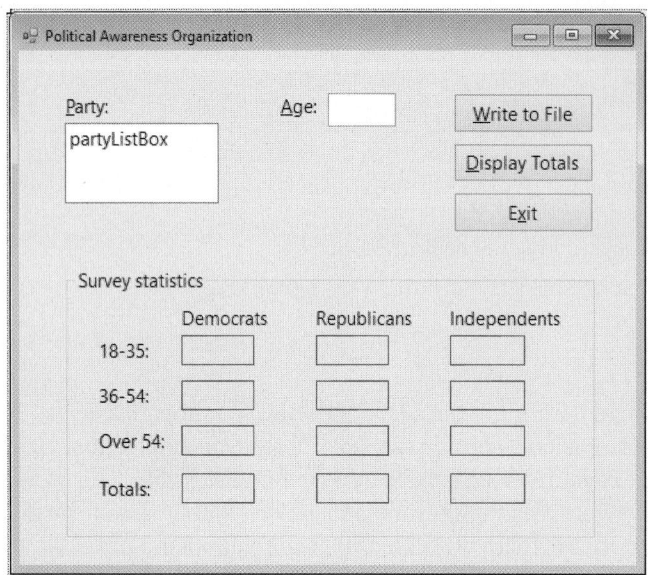

Figure 11-51 Sample interface for the Political Awareness Organization application

Revellos

Revellos has stores located in several states. Create an application that the sales manager can use to enter the following information for each store: the store number, the state in which the store is located, and the store manager's name. The application should save the information in a sequential access file. Each store's information should appear on a separate line in the file. In other words, the first store's number, state name, and manager name should appear on the first line in the file. The application should allow the sales manager to enter a store number, and then display both the state in which the store is located and the store manager's name. The store information is shown in Figure 11-52. Use the following names for the solution and project, respectively: Revellos Solution and Revellos Project. Save the application in the VbReloaded2015\Chap11 folder. Change the form file's name to Main Form.vb. (5–8, 13, 14)

Number	State	Manager
1004	Texas	Jeffrey Jefferson
1005	Texas	Paula Hendricks
1007	Arizona	Jake Johansen
1010	Arizona	Henry Abernathy
1011	California	Barbara Millerton
1013	California	Inez Baily
1015	California	Sung Lee
1016	California	Lou Chan
1017	California	Homer Gomez
1019	New Mexico	Ingrid Nadkarni

Figure 11-52 Information for the Revellos application

CHAPTER 12

Access Databases and LINQ

After studying Chapter 12, you should be able to:

1. Define the terms used when talking about databases
2. Connect an application to a Microsoft Access database
3. Bind table and field objects to controls
4. Explain the purpose of the DataSet, BindingSource, TableAdapter, TableAdapterManager, and BindingNavigator objects
5. Customize a DataGridView control
6. Handle errors using the Try...Catch statement
7. Position the record pointer in a dataset
8. Access the value stored in a field object
9. Query a dataset using LINQ
10. Customize a BindingNavigator control
11. Use the LINQ aggregate operators

Database Terminology

In order to maintain accurate records, most businesses store information about their employees, customers, and inventory in computer databases. A **computer database** is an electronic file that contains an organized collection of related information. Many products exist for creating computer databases; such products are called database management systems (or DBMSs). Some of the most popular database management systems are Microsoft Access, Microsoft SQL Server, and Oracle. You can use Visual Basic to access the data stored in databases created by these database management systems. As a result, companies can use Visual Basic to create a standard interface that allows employees to access information stored in a variety of database formats. Instead of learning each DBMS's user interface, the employee needs to know only one interface. The actual format of the database is unimportant and will be transparent to the user.

In this chapter, you will learn how to access the data stored in Microsoft Access databases. Databases created using Microsoft Access are relational databases. A **relational database** stores information in tables composed of columns and rows, similar to the format used in a spreadsheet. The databases are called relational because the information in the tables can be related in different ways.

Each column in a relational database's table represents a field, and each row represents a record. As you learned in Chapter 11, a field is a single item of information about a person, place, or thing—such as a name, a salary amount, a Social Security number, or a price. A record is a group of related fields that contain all of the necessary data about a specific person, place, or thing. The college you are attending keeps a student record on you. Examples of fields contained in your student record include your Social Security number, name, address, phone number, credits earned, and grades earned.

A group of related records is called a **table**. Each record in a table pertains to the same topic and contains the same type of information. In other words, each record in a table contains the same fields.

A relational database can contain one or more tables. A one-table database would be a good choice for storing information about the college courses you have taken. An example of such a table is shown in Figure 12-1. Each record in the table contains four fields: an ID field that indicates the department name and course number, a course title field, a field listing the number of credit hours, and a grade field.

ID	Title	Hours	Grade
ACC110	Accounting Procedures	3	A
ENG101	English Composition I	3	B
CIS110	Introduction to Programming	3	A
BIO111	Environmental Biology	3	C

Figure 12-1 Example of a one-table relational database

Most tables have a **primary key**, which is a field that uniquely identifies each record. In the table shown in Figure 12-1, you could use either the ID field or the Title field as the primary key because the data in those fields will be unique for each record.

You might use a two-table database to store information about a CD (compact disc) collection. You would store the general information about each CD, such as the CD's name and the artist's name, in the first table. The information about the songs on each CD, such as their title and track number, would be stored in the second table. You would need to use a common field—for example, a CD number—to relate the records contained in both tables.

Figure 12-2 shows an example of a two-table database that stores CD information. The first table is referred to as the **parent table**, and the second table is referred to as the **child table**. The CdNum field is the primary key in the parent table because it uniquely identifies each record in the table. The CdNum field in the child table is used solely to link the song title and track information to the appropriate CD in the parent table. In the child table, the CdNum field is called the **foreign key**.

Parent and child tables are also referred to as master and detail tables, respectively.

CdNum	Name	Artist
01	For You	Selena Gomez
02	1989	Taylor Swift

the two tables are related by the CdNum field

CdNum	SongTitle	Track
01	The Heart Wants What It Wants	1
01	Come & Get It	2
01	Love You Like a Love Song	3
02	Welcome to New York	1
02	Blank Space	2
02	Style	3

Figure 12-2 Example of a two-table relational database

Storing data in a relational database offers many advantages. The computer can retrieve data stored in a relational format both quickly and easily, and the data can be displayed in any order. The information in the CD database, for example, can be arranged by artist name, song title, and so on. You can also control the amount of information you want to view from a relational database. You can view all of the information in the CD database, only the information pertaining to a certain artist, or only the names of the songs contained on a specific CD.

Mini-Quiz 12-1

The answers to Mini-Quiz questions are located in Appendix A. Each question is associated with one or more objectives listed at the beginning of the chapter.

1. A ____________ is an organized collection of related information stored in a computer file. (1)

   a. database
   b. dataset
   c. field
   d. record

2. A ____________ database stores information in tables. (1)

   a. columnar
   b. relational
   c. sorted
   d. tabular

3. Which of the following statements is true about a relational database? (1)
   a. Data stored in a relational database can be retrieved both quickly and easily by the computer.
   b. Data stored in a relational database can be displayed in any order.
   c. A relational database stores data in a column and row format.
   d. all of the above

Connecting an Application to a Microsoft Access Database

In the concepts portion of this chapter, you will use a Microsoft Access database named Stores. The database contains one table, which is named tblStores. The table data is shown in Figure 12-3. The table contains five fields and 20 records. The StoreNum field is the primary key because it uniquely identifies each record in the table. The Ownership field indicates whether the store is company-owned (C) or a franchisee (F).

StoreNum	City	State	Sales	Ownership
100	San Francisco	CA	236,700	C
101	San Diego	CA	125,900	C
102	Burbank	CA	96,575	F
103	Chicago	IL	135,400	C
104	Chicago	IL	108,000	F
105	Denver	CO	212,600	C
106	Atlanta	GA	123,500	C
107	Louisville	KY	178,500	C
108	Lexington	KY	167,450	F
109	Nashville	TN	205,625	C
110	Atlanta	GA	198,600	F
111	Denver	CO	45,900	F
112	Miami	FL	175,300	C
113	Las Vegas	NV	245,675	C
114	New Orleans	LA	213,400	C
115	Louisville	KY	68,900	F
116	Las Vegas	NV	110,340	F
117	Indianapolis	IN	97,500	C
118	Raleigh	NC	86,400	C
119	San Francisco	CA	65,975	F

field names

records

Figure 12-3 Data contained in the tblStores table

Before an application can access the data stored in a database, it needs to be connected to the database. You can make the connection using the Data Source Configuration Wizard. The basic procedure for doing this is shown in Figure 12-4. (More detailed steps can be found in Programming Tutorial 1.) The wizard allows you to specify the data you want to access. The computer makes a copy of the specified data and stores the copy in its internal memory. The copy of the data you want to access is called a **dataset**.

HOW TO Connect an Application to an Access Database

1. Open the application's solution file.
2. If necessary, open the Data Sources window by clicking View on the menu bar, pointing to Other Windows, and then clicking Data Sources.
3. Click Add New Data Source in the Data Sources window to start the Data Source Configuration Wizard, which displays the Choose a Data Source Type screen. If necessary, click Database.
4. Click the Next button to display the Choose a Database Model screen. If necessary, click Dataset.
5. Click the Next button to display the Choose Your Data Connection screen. Click the New Connection button. At this point, either the Choose Data Source dialog box or the Add Connection dialog box will open. If the Choose Data Source dialog box opens, click Microsoft Access Database File in the Data source box, select the Always use this selection check box, and then click the Continue button to open the Add Connection dialog box.
6. In the Add Connection dialog box, verify that Microsoft Access Database File (OLE DB) appears in the Data source box. If it does not, click the Change button, click Microsoft Access Database File, select the Always use this selection check box, and then click the OK button.
7. Click the Browse button in the Add Connection dialog box to open the Select Microsoft Access Database File dialog box. Locate and then click the database filename. Click the Open button.
8. Click the Test Connection button, and then close the "Test connection succeeded." message box.
9. Click the OK button to close the Add Connection dialog box. Click the Next button, and then click the Yes button to add the database file to the application's project folder.
10. If necessary, select the "Yes, save the connection as" check box in the Save the Connection String to the Application Configuration File screen.
11. Click the Next button to display the Choose Your Database Objects screen. Select the appropriate table and/or field objects, and then click the Finish button.

Figure 12-4 How to connect an application to an Access database

Figure 12-5 shows the result of using the wizard to connect the Adalene Fashions application to the Stores database. The database file's name appears in the Solution Explorer window, and the dataset's name appears in the Data Sources window. The StoresDataSet contains one table object and five field objects.

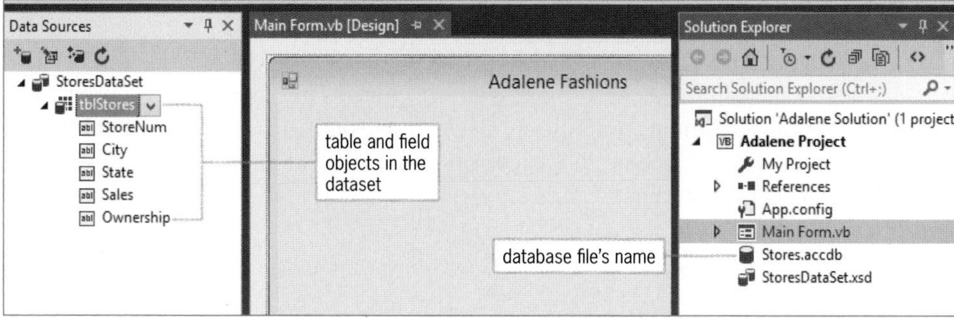

Figure 12-5 Result of running the Data Source Configuration Wizard

After an application is connected to a database, you can use the procedure shown in Figure 12-6 to view the fields and records stored in the dataset. The figure also includes a sample Preview Data window showing the contents of the StoresDataSet. Notice the information that appears in the Select an object to preview box. StoresDataSet is the name of the dataset in the application, and tblStores is the name of the table included in the dataset. Fill and GetData are methods. The Fill method populates an existing table with data, while the GetData method creates a new table and populates it with data.

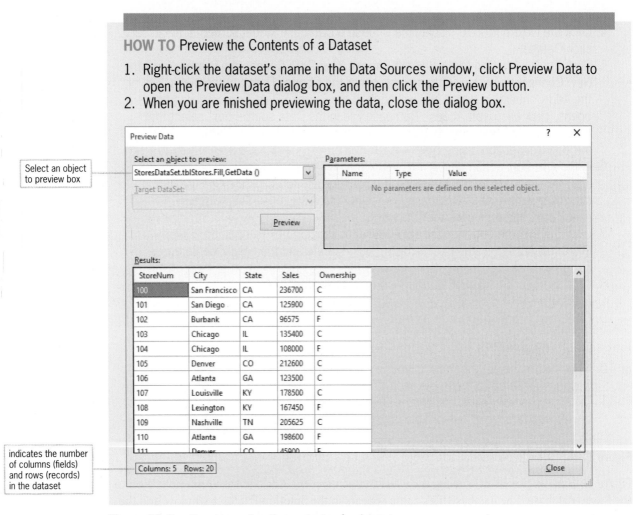

HOW TO Preview the Contents of a Dataset

1. Right-click the dataset's name in the Data Sources window, click Preview Data to open the Preview Data dialog box, and then click the Preview button.
2. When you are finished previewing the data, close the dialog box.

StoreNum	City	State	Sales	Ownership
100	San Francisco	CA	236700	C
101	San Diego	CA	125900	C
102	Burbank	CA	96575	F
103	Chicago	IL	135400	C
104	Chicago	IL	108000	F
105	Denver	CO	212600	C
106	Atlanta	GA	123500	C
107	Louisville	KY	178500	C
108	Lexington	KY	167450	F
109	Nashville	TN	205625	C
110	Atlanta	GA	198600	F
111	Denver	CO	45900	F

Figure 12-6 How to preview the contents of a dataset

Binding the Objects in a Dataset

Bound controls are also referred to as data-aware controls.

For the user to view the contents of a dataset while an application is running, you need to connect one or more objects in the dataset to one or more controls in the interface. Connecting an object to a control is called **binding**, and the connected controls are called **bound controls**. As indicated in Figure 12-7, you can bind the object either to a control that the computer creates for you or to an existing control in the interface.

HOW TO Bind an Object in a Dataset

To have the computer create a control and then bind an object to it:
In the Data Sources window, click the object you want to bind. If necessary, use the object's list arrow to change the control type. Drag the object to an empty area on the form and then release the mouse button.

To bind an object to an existing control:
In the Data Sources window, click the object you want to bind. Drag the object to the control on the form and then release the mouse button. Alternatively, you can click the control on the form and then use the Properties window to set the appropriate property or properties. (Refer to the *Binding to an Existing Control* section later in this chapter.)

Figure 12-7 How to bind an object in a dataset

Having the Computer Create a Bound Control

When you drag an object from a dataset to an empty area on the form, the computer creates a control and automatically binds the object to it. The icon that appears before the object's name in the Data Sources window indicates the type of control the computer will create. The icon next to tblStores in Figure 12-8 indicates that a DataGridView control will be created when you drag the tblStores table object to the form. A DataGridView control displays the table data in a row-and-column format, similar to a spreadsheet. You will learn more about the DataGridView control in the next section. The icon next to each of the five field objects, on the other hand, indicates that the computer creates a text box when a field object is dragged to the form.

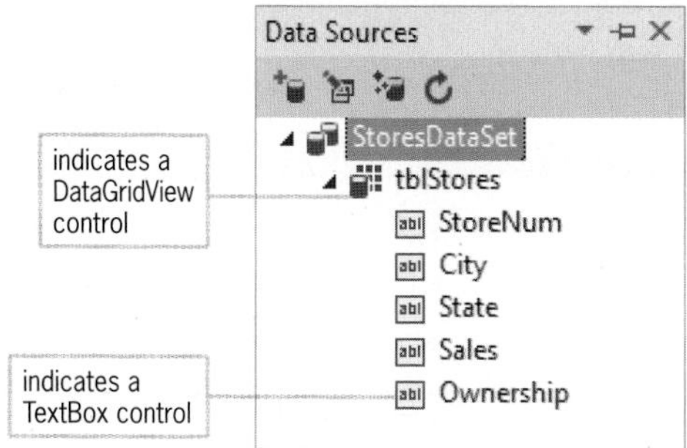

Figure 12-8 Icons in the Data Sources window

When an object is selected in the Data Sources window, you can use the list arrow that appears next to the object's name to change the type of control the computer creates. For example, to display the table data in separate text boxes rather than in a DataGridView control, you click tblStores in the Data Sources window and then click the tblStores list arrow, as shown in Illustration A in Figure 12-9. Clicking Details in the list tells the computer to create a separate control for each field in the table. Similarly, to display the City field's data in a label control rather than in a text box, you first click City in the Data Sources window. You then click the field's list arrow, as shown in Illustration B in Figure 12-9, and then click Label in the list.

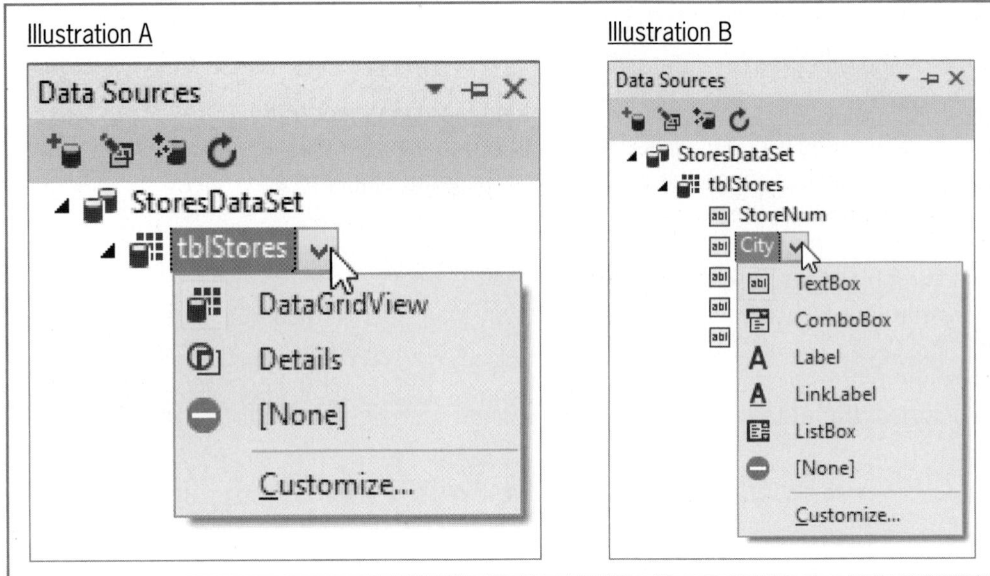

Figure 12-9 Result of clicking an object's list arrow

Figure 12-10 shows the result of dragging the tblStores object from the Data Sources window to the MainForm, using the default control type for a table. Besides adding a DataGridView control to the form, the computer also adds a BindingNavigator control. When an application is running, you can use the **BindingNavigator control** to move from one record to the next in the dataset, as well as to add or delete a record and save any changes made to the dataset. The computer also places five objects in the component tray: a DataSet, BindingSource, TableAdapter, TableAdapterManager, and BindingNavigator. As you learned in Chapter 2, the component tray stores objects that do not appear in the user interface while an application is running. An exception to this is the BindingNavigator object, which appears as the BindingNavigator control during both design time and run time.

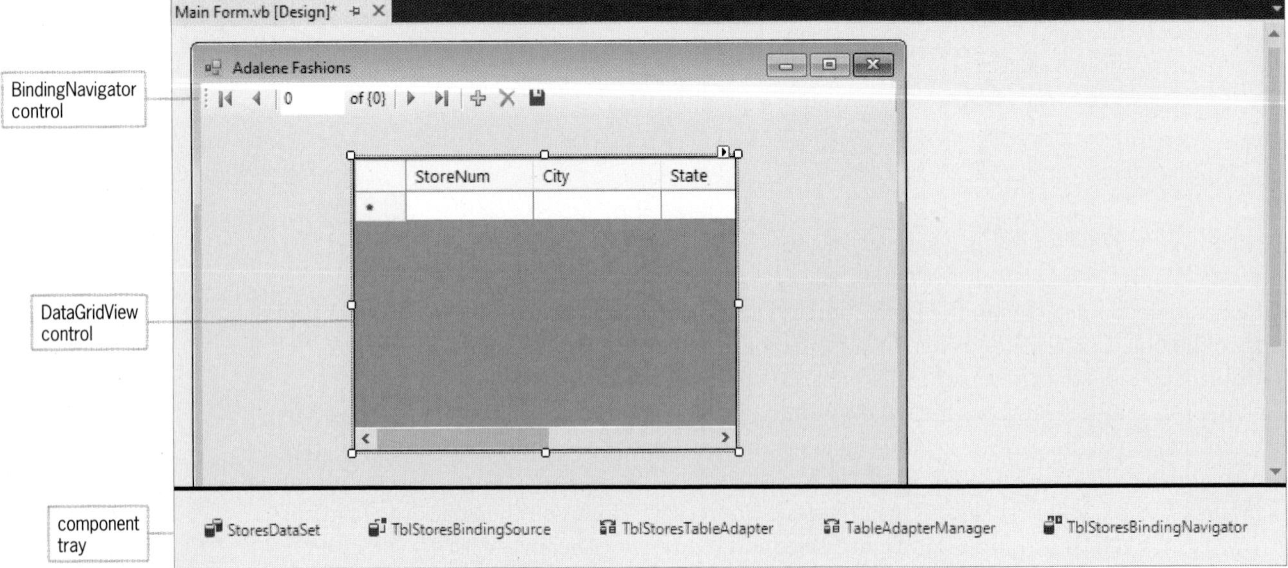

Figure 12-10 Result of dragging the table object to the form

The **TableAdapter object** connects the database to the **DataSet object**, which stores the information you want to access from the database. The TableAdapter is responsible for retrieving the appropriate information from the database and storing it in the DataSet. It can also be used to save to the database any changes made to the data contained in the DataSet. However, in most cases, you will use the **TableAdapterManager object** to save the changes because it can handle saving data to multiple tables in the DataSet.

The **BindingSource object** provides the connection between the DataSet and the bound controls on the form. The TblStoresBindingSource in Figure 12-10, for example, connects the StoresDataSet to two bound controls: a DataGridView control and a BindingNavigator control. The TblStoresBindingSource allows the DataGridView control to display the data contained in the StoresDataSet. It also allows the BindingNavigator control to access the records stored in the StoresDataSet. Figure 12-11 illustrates the relationships among the database, the objects in the component tray, and the bound controls on the form.

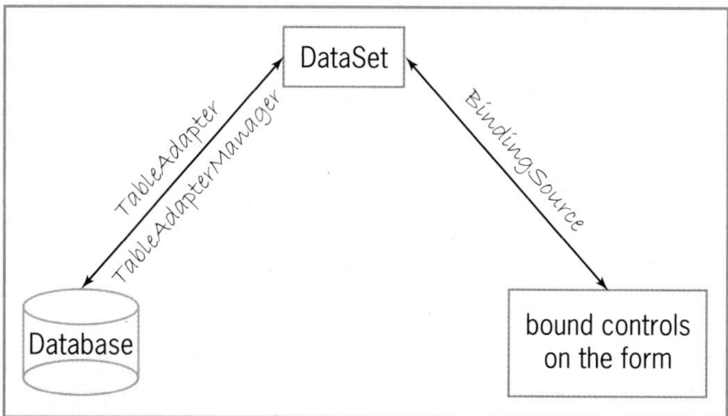

Figure 12-11 Illustration of the relationships among the database, the objects in the component tray, and the bound controls

If a table object's control type is changed from DataGridView to Details, the computer automatically provides the appropriate controls (such as text boxes, labels, and so on) when you drag the table object to the form. It also adds the BindingNavigator control to the form and the five objects to the component tray. The appropriate controls and objects are also automatically included when you drag a field object to an empty area on the form.

The DataGridView Control

The **DataGridView control** is one of the most popular controls for displaying table data because it allows you to view a great deal of information at the same time. The control displays the data in a row and column format, similar to a spreadsheet. Each row represents a record, and each column represents a field. The intersection of a row and a column in a DataGridView control is called a **cell**.

The control's **AutoSizeColumnsMode property**, which has seven different settings, determines the way the column widths are sized in the control. The Fill setting automatically adjusts the column widths so that all of the columns exactly fill the display area of the control. The ColumnHeader setting, on the other hand, adjusts the column widths based on the header text.

Like the PictureBox control, the DataGridView control has a task list. The task list is shown in Figure 12-12 along with a description of each task.

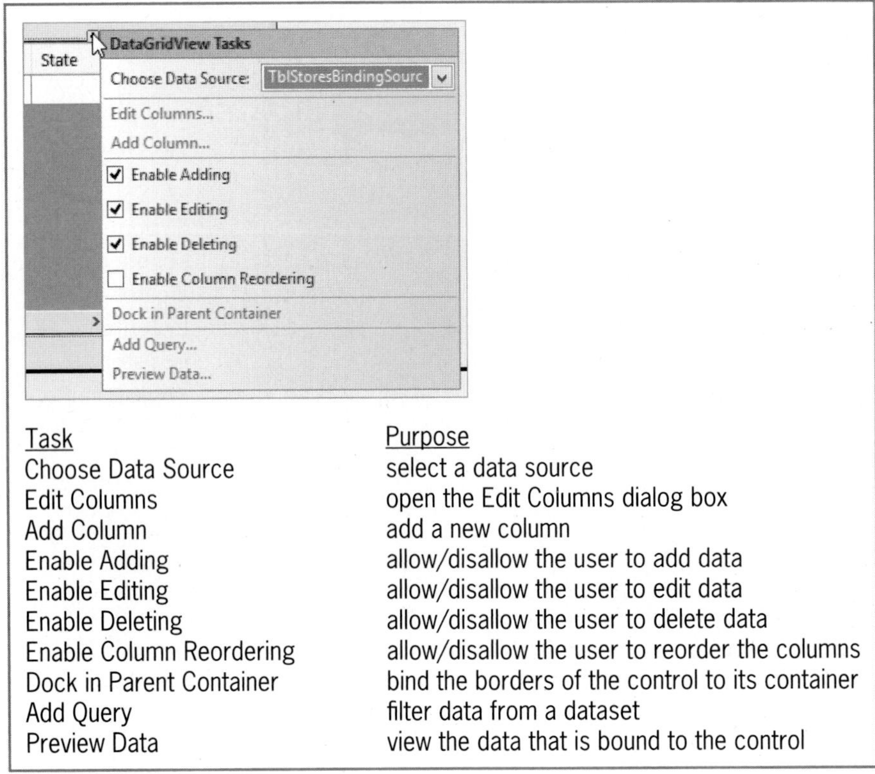

Task	Purpose
Choose Data Source	select a data source
Edit Columns	open the Edit Columns dialog box
Add Column	add a new column
Enable Adding	allow/disallow the user to add data
Enable Editing	allow/disallow the user to edit data
Enable Deleting	allow/disallow the user to delete data
Enable Column Reordering	allow/disallow the user to reorder the columns
Dock in Parent Container	bind the borders of the control to its container
Add Query	filter data from a dataset
Preview Data	view the data that is bound to the control

Figure 12-12 DataGridView control's task list

Figure 12-13 shows the Edit Columns dialog box, which opens when you click Edit Columns on the DataGridView control's task list. You can use the Edit Columns dialog box during design time to add columns to the control, remove columns from the control, and reorder the columns. You can also use it to set the properties of the bound columns. For example, you can use a column's DefaultCellStyle property to format the column's data as well as to change the column's width and alignment. You can use a column's HeaderText property to change a column's heading.

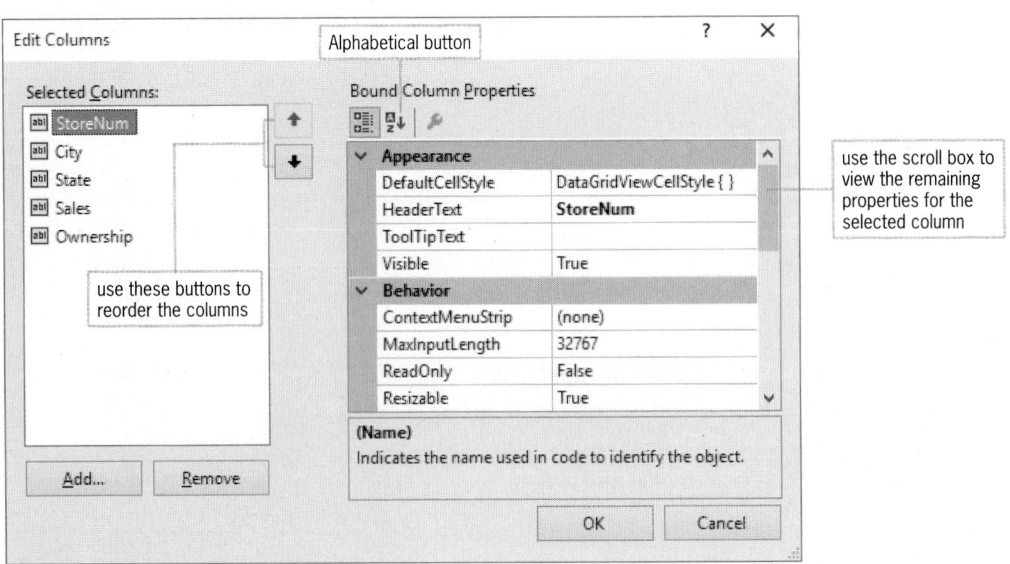

Figure 12-13 Edit Columns dialog box

Figure 12-14 shows a sample run of the Adalene Fashions application. The DataGridView control is docked in its parent container, which is the MainForm. The Edit Columns dialog box was used to change the header text in the first column. It was also used to format and align the data in the Sales column. The Properties window was used to set the control's AutoSizeColumnsMode property to Fill.

Adalene Fashions

1 of 20 — Save Data button

Store	City	State	Sales	Ownership
100	San Francisco	CA	$236,700	C
101	San Diego	CA	$125,900	C
102	Burbank	CA	$96,575	F
103	Chicago	IL	$135,400	C
104	Chicago	IL	$108,000	F
105	Denver	CO	$212,600	C
106	Atlanta	GA	$123,500	C
107	Louisville	KY	$178,500	C
108	Lexington	KY	$167,450	F
109	Nashville	TN	$205,625	C
110	Atlanta	GA	$198,600	F
111	Denver	CO	$45,900	F
112	Miami	FL	$175,300	C
113	Las Vegas	NV	$245,675	C
114	New Orleans	LA	$213,400	C
115	Louisville	KY	$68,900	F

Figure 12-14 DataGridView control after setting some of its properties

Notice that the first cell in the DataGridView control is highlighted (selected). You can use the arrow keys on your keyboard to move the highlight to a different cell in the control. When a cell is highlighted, you can modify its contents by simply typing the new data.

Visual Basic Code

In addition to adding the appropriate controls and objects to the application when a table or field object is dragged to the form, Visual Basic also enters two event procedures in the Code Editor window. Both procedures are shown in Figure 12-15.

```
Private Sub TblStoresBindingNavigatorSaveItem_Click(sender As Object, e As EventArgs
            ) Handles TblStoresBindingNavigatorSaveItem.Click
    Me.Validate()
    Me.TblStoresBindingSource.EndEdit()
    Me.TableAdapterManager.UpdateAll(Me.StoresDataSet)

End Sub
```

```
Private Sub MainForm_Load(sender As Object, e As EventArgs) Handles MyBase.Load
    'TODO: This line of code loads data into the
    'StoresDataSet.tblStores' table. You can move, or remove it, as needed.
    Me.TblStoresTableAdapter.Fill(Me.StoresDataSet.tblStores)

End Sub
```

Figure 12-15 Procedures automatically entered in the Code Editor window

The MainForm_Load procedure uses the TableAdapter object's Fill method to retrieve the data from the database and store it in the StoresDataSet. In most applications, the code to fill a dataset belongs in this procedure. However, as the comments in the procedure indicate, you can either move or delete the code.

The TblStoresBindingNavigatorSaveItem_Click procedure is processed when you click the Save Data button (the disk) on the BindingNavigator control. The procedure's code validates the changes made to the data before saving the data to the database. Two methods are involved in the save operation: the BindingSource object's EndEdit method and the TableAdapterManager's UpdateAll method. The EndEdit method applies any pending changes (such as new records, deleted records, or changed records) to the dataset, and the UpdateAll method commits the changes to the database. Because it is possible for an error to occur when saving data to a database, you should add error handling code to the Save Data button's Click event procedure.

Handling Errors in the Code

When an error occurs in a procedure's code during run time, programmers say that the procedure "threw an exception."

An error that occurs while an application is running is called an **exception**. If your code does not contain specific instructions for handling the exceptions that may occur, Visual Basic handles them for you. Typically, it does this by displaying an error message and then abruptly terminating the application. You can prevent your application from behaving in such an unfriendly manner by taking control of the exception handling in your code; you can do this by using the **Try...Catch statement**.

Figure 12-16 shows the basic syntax of the Try...Catch statement and includes examples of using the syntax. The basic syntax contains only a Try block and a Catch block. Within the Try block, you place the code that could possibly generate an exception. When an exception occurs in the Try block's code, the computer processes the code contained in the Catch block and then skips to the code following the End Try clause. A description of the exception that occurred is stored in the Message property of the Catch block's `ex` parameter. You can access the description by using the code `ex.Message`, as shown in Example 1 in the figure. Or, you can display your own message, as shown in Example 2. Keep in mind that the Catch block's code is processed only when an error occurs in the Try block.

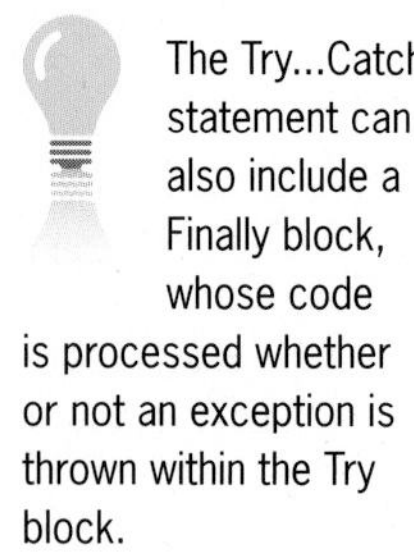

The Try...Catch statement can also include a Finally block, whose code is processed whether or not an exception is thrown within the Try block.

HOW TO Use the Try...Catch Statement

Basic syntax

Try
one or more statements that might generate an exception
Catch ex As Exception
one or more statements to execute when an exception occurs
End Try

Example 1

```
Private Sub TblStoresBindingNavigatorSaveItem_Click(
sender As Object, e As EventArgs
) Handles TblStoresBindingNavigatorSaveItem.Click
    Try
        Me.Validate()
        Me.TblStoresBindingSource.EndEdit()
        Me.TableAdapterManager.UpdateAll(Me.StoresDataSet)
```

Figure 12-16 How to use the Try...Catch statement *(continues)*

(continued)

```
        MessageBox.Show("Changes saved", "Adalene Fashions",
               MessageBoxButtons.OK, MessageBoxIcon.Information)
    Catch ex As Exception
        MessageBox.Show(ex.Message, "Adalene Fashions",
               MessageBoxButtons.OK, MessageBoxIcon.Information)
    End Try
End Sub
```

Example 2

```
Private Sub displayButton_Click(sender As Object, e As EventArgs
) Handles displayButton.Click
    Dim inFile As IO.StreamReader
    Dim line As String

    Try
        inFile = IO.File.OpenText("names.txt")
        Do Until inFile.Peek = -1
            line = inFile.ReadLine
            namesListBox.Items.Add(line)
        Loop
        inFile.Close()
    Catch ex As Exception
        MessageBox.Show("Sequential file error", "JK's",
               MessageBoxButtons.OK, MessageBoxIcon.Information)
    End Try
End Sub
```

Figure 12-16 How to use the Try...Catch statement

If an exception occurs in Example 1's Try block, the computer will display a description of the exception and then skip to the code following the End Try clause; otherwise, it will display the "Changes saved" message before processing the code that follows the End Try clause. If an exception occurs in Example 2's Try block, the computer will display the message "Sequential file error" and then skip to the code following the End Try clause.

The Copy to Output Directory Property

When the Data Source Configuration Wizard connected the Adalene Fashions application to the Stores database, it added the database file (Stores.accdb) to the application's project folder. (You can verify that the file was added to the project folder by viewing the Solution Explorer window shown earlier in Figure 12-5.) A database file contained in a project is referred to as a local database file. The way Visual Basic saves the changes to a local database file is determined by the file's **Copy to Output Directory property**. Figure 12-17 lists the values that can be assigned to the property.

If you want to experiment with the DataGridView version of the Adalene Fashions application, open the solution contained in the Try It 1! folder. The database file's Copy to Output Directory property is set to Copy if newer.

HOW TO Use the Copy to Output Directory Property

Property setting	Meaning
Do not copy	The file in the project folder is not copied to the bin\Debug folder when the application is started.
Copy always	The file in the project folder is copied to the bin\Debug folder each time the application is started.
Copy if newer	When an application is started, the computer compares the date on the file in the project folder with the date on the file in the bin\Debug folder. The file from the project folder is copied to the bin\Debug folder only when its date is newer.

Figure 12-17 How to use the Copy to Output Directory property

When a file's Copy to Output Directory property is set to its default setting (Copy always), the file is copied from the project folder to the project folder's bin\Debug folder each time you start the application. In this case, the Stores.accdb file is copied from the Adalene Project folder to the Adalene Project\bin\Debug folder. As a result, the file will appear in two different folders in the solution. When you click the Save Data button on the BindingNavigator control, any changes made in the DataGridView control are recorded only in the file stored in the bin\Debug folder; the file stored in the project folder is not changed. The next time you start the application, the file in the project folder is copied to the bin\Debug folder, overwriting the file that contains the changes. You can change this behavior by setting the database file's Copy to Output Directory property to Copy if newer. The Copy if newer setting tells the computer to compare the dates on both files to determine which file has the newer (i.e., more current) date. If the database file in the project folder has a newer date, the computer should copy it to the bin\Debug folder; otherwise, it should not copy it.

Binding to an Existing Control

As indicated earlier in Figure 12-7, you can bind an object in a dataset to an existing control on the form. The easiest way to do this is by dragging the object from the Data Sources window to the control. However, you can also click the control and then set one or more properties in the Properties window. The appropriate property (or properties) to set depends on the control you are binding. To bind a DataGridView control, you use the DataSource property. However, you use the DataSource and DisplayMember properties to bind a ListBox control. To bind label and text box controls, you use the DataBindings/Text property.

When you drag an object from the Data Sources window to an existing control, the computer does not create a new control; instead, it binds the object to the existing control. Because a new control does not need to be created, the computer ignores the control type specified for the object in the Data Sources window. Therefore, it is not necessary to change the control type in the Data Sources window to match the existing control's type. For example, you can drag an object that is associated with a text box in the Data Sources window to a label control on the form. The computer will bind the object to the label, but it will not change the label to a text box.

Figure 12-18 shows a different version of the Adalene Fashions application. In this version, the StoreNum, Sales, and Ownership field objects were dragged from the Data Sources window to the storeLabel, salesLabel, and ownerLabel controls, respectively; doing this binds each field object to its respective label control. In addition to binding the field objects to the controls, the computer also adds the DataSet, BindingSource, TableAdapter, and TableAdapterManager objects to the component tray.

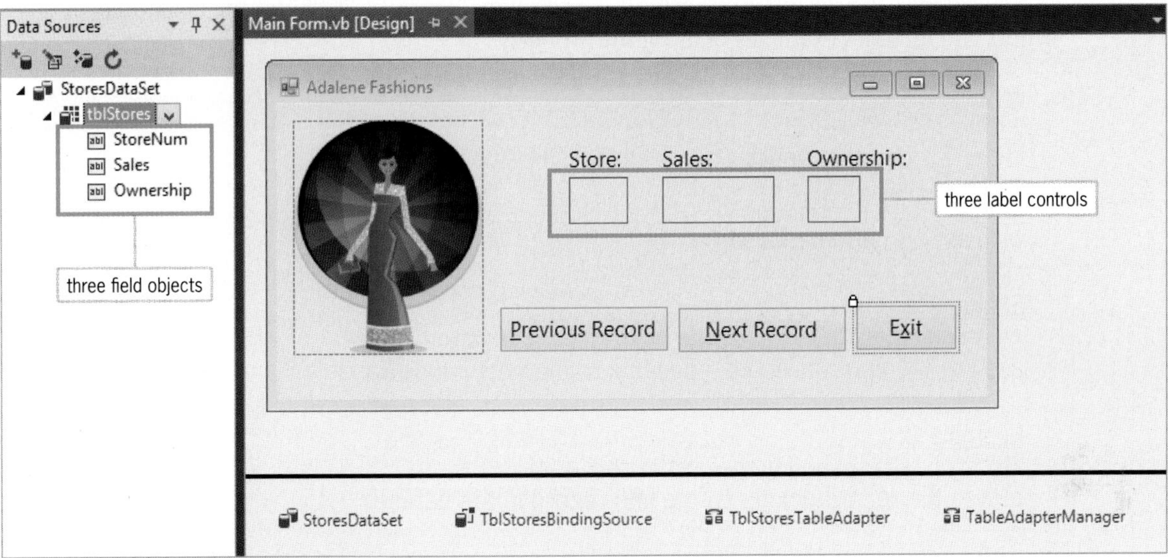

Figure 12-18 Result of dragging field objects to existing label controls

Notice that when you drag an object from the Data Sources window to an existing control, the computer does not add a BindingNavigator object to the component tray, nor does it add a BindingNavigator control to the form. You can use the BindingNavigator tool, which is located in the Data section of the toolbox, to add a BindingNavigator control and object to the application. You then would set the control's DataSource property to the name of the BindingSource object (in this case, TblStoresBindingSource).

Besides adding the objects shown in Figure 12-18 to the component tray, the computer also enters (in the Code Editor window) the Load event procedure shown earlier in Figure 12-15. Recall that the procedure uses the TableAdapter object's Fill method to retrieve the data from the database and store it in the DataSet object.

Figure 12-19 shows a sample run of this version of the Adalene Fashions application. Only the first record in the dataset appears in the interface. Because the interface does not contain a BindingNavigator control, which would allow you to move from one record to the next, you will need to code the Next Record and Previous Record buttons to view the remaining records.

Figure 12-19 First record displayed in the interface

Coding the Next Record and Previous Record Buttons

The BindingSource object uses an invisible record pointer to keep track of the current record in the dataset. It stores the position of the record pointer in its **Position property**. The first record is in position 0, the second is in position 1, and so on. Figure 12-20 shows the Position property's syntax and includes examples of using the property.

HOW TO Use the BindingSource Object's Position Property

Syntax
bindingSourceName.**Position**

Example 1
```
recordNum = TblStoresBindingSource.Position
```
assigns the current record's position to the `recordNum` variable

Example 2
```
TblStoresBindingSource.Position = 4
```
moves the record pointer to the fifth record in the dataset

Example 3
```
TblStoresBindingSource.Position += 1
```
moves the record pointer to the next record in the dataset; you can also write the statement as follows:
```
TblStoresBindingSource.Position = TblStoresBindingSource.Position + 1
```

Figure 12-20 How to use the BindingSource object's Position property

Rather than using the Position property to position the record pointer in a dataset, you can use the BindingSource object's **Move methods** to move the record pointer to the first, last, next, or previous record in the dataset. Figure 12-21 shows each Move method's syntax and includes examples of using two of the methods.

HOW TO Use the BindingSource Object's Move Methods

Syntax
bindingSourceName.**MoveFirst()**
bindingSourceName.**MoveLast()**
bindingSourceName.**MoveNext()**
bindingSourceName.**MovePrevious()**

Example 1
```
TblStoresBindingSource.MoveFirst()
```
moves the record pointer to the first record in the dataset

Example 2
```
TblStoresBindingSource.MoveNext()
```
moves the record pointer to the next record in the dataset

Figure 12-21 How to use the BindingSource object's Move methods

When the user clicks the Next Record button in the Adalene Fashions interface, the button's Click event procedure should move the record pointer to the next record in the dataset. Similarly, when the user clicks the Previous Record button, the button's Click event procedure should move the record pointer to the previous record in the dataset. You can use the TblStoresBindingSource object's MoveNext and MovePrevious methods to code the procedures, as shown in Figure 12-22.

```
Private Sub nextButton_Click(sender As Object, e As Eve
    ' moves the record pointer to the next record

    TblStoresBindingSource.MoveNext()
End Sub

Private Sub previousButton_Click(sender As Object, e As
    ' moves the record pointer to the previous record

    TblStoresBindingSource.MovePrevious()
End Sub
```

Figure 12-22 nextButton_Click and previousButton_Click procedures

If you want to experiment with the Labels version of the Adalene Fashions application, open the solution contained in the Try It 2! folder. The database file's Copy to Output Directory property is set to Copy always.

Accessing the Value Stored in a Field

At times, you may need to access the value stored in a field in a dataset. You can do so using the syntax shown in Figure 12-23. The figure also includes examples of accessing some of the fields in the StoresDataSet.

HOW TO Access the Value Stored in a Field

Syntax
dataSetObjectName.*tableName*(*recordNumber*).*fieldName*

Example 1
```
Dim storeCity As String
storeCity = StoresDataSet.tblStores(0).City
```
assigns the value stored in the first record's City field (San Francisco) to the `storeCity` variable

Example 2
```
Dim storeSales As Integer
storeSales = StoresDataSet.tblStores(4).Sales
```
assigns the value stored in the fifth record's Sales field (108000) to the `storeSales` variable

Figure 12-23 How to access the value stored in a field

The answers to Mini-Quiz questions are located in Appendix A. Each question is associated with one or more objectives listed at the beginning of the chapter.

Mini-Quiz 12-2

1. Which of the following objects connects a database to a DataSet object? (4)
   a. BindingSource
   b. DataBase
   c. DataGridView
   d. TableAdapter

2. An application contains the following objects: FriendsDataSet, TblFriendsBindingSource, TblFriendsTableAdapter, TableAdapterManager, and TblFriendsBindingNavigator. Which of the following statements retrieves data from the Friends database and stores it in the FriendsDataSet? (4)
   a. `Me.FriendsDataSet.Fill(Friends.accdb)`
   b. `Me.TblFriendsBindingSource.Fill(Me.FriendsDataSet)`
   c. `Me.TblFriendsBindingNavigator.Fill(FriendsDataSet.tblFriends)`
   d. `Me.TblFriendsTableAdapter.Fill(Me.FriendsDataSet.tblFriends)`

3. If an application contains the `Catch ex As Exception` clause, which of the following can be used to access the exception's description? (6)
   a. `ex.Description`
   b. `ex.Exception`
   c. `ex.Message`
   d. `Exception.Description`

4. If the current record is the second record in the dataset, which of the following statements will position the record pointer on the first record? (7)
   a. `TblStoresBindingSource.Position = 0`
   b. `TblStoresBindingSource.Position -= 1`
   c. `TblStoresBindingSource.MoveFirst()`
   d. all of the above

Creating a Query

The records in the StoresDataSet can be arranged in any order, such as by store number, city name, and so on. You can also control the number of records you want to view at any one time. You can view all of the records in the StoresDataSet, or you can choose to view only the records for the company-owned stores. You use a **query** to specify both the records to select and the order in which to arrange the records. You can create a query in Visual Basic using a feature called **Language Integrated Query** or, more simply, **LINQ**.

Figure 12-24 shows the basic syntax of LINQ when used to select and arrange records in a dataset. In the syntax, *variableName* and *elementName* can be any names you choose as long as the name follows the naming rules for variables. In other words, there is nothing special about the `records` and `store` names used in the examples. The Where and Order By clauses are optional parts of the syntax. You use the **Where clause**, which contains a *condition*, to limit the records you want to view. Similar to the condition in the If...Then...Else and Do...Loop statements, the condition in a Where clause specifies a requirement that must be met for a record to be selected. The **Order By clause** is used to arrange (sort) the records in either ascending (the default) or descending order by one or more fields.

HOW TO Use LINQ to Select and Arrange Records in a Dataset

Basic syntax

Dim *variableName* = **From** *elementName* **In** *dataset.table*
  [**Where** *condition*]
  [**Order By** *elementName.fieldName1* [**Ascending** | **Descending**]
    [, *elementName.fieldNameN* [**Ascending** | **Descending**]]]
  Select *elementName*

Example 1

```
Dim records = From store In StoresDataSet.tblStores
              Select store
```

selects all of the records from the dataset

Example 2

```
Dim records = From store In StoresDataSet.tblStores
              Order By store.Sales
              Select store
```

selects all of the records from the dataset and arranges them in ascending order by the Sales field

Example 3

```
Dim records = From store In StoresDataSet.tblStores
              Where store.Ownership.ToUpper = "F"
              Select store
```

selects only the franchisees' records from the dataset

Example 4

```
Dim records = From store In StoresDataSet.tblStores
              Where store.Sales > 100000
              Select store
```

selects from the dataset only the records for stores that have more than $100,000 in sales

Example 5

```
Dim records = From store In StoresDataSet.tblStores
              Where store.State.ToUpper Like "C*"
              Order By store.City Descending
              Select store
```

selects from the dataset only the records whose State field begins with the letter C and arranges them in descending order by the City field

Figure 12-24 How to use LINQ to select and arrange records in a dataset

Notice that the syntax shown in Figure 12-24 does not require you to specify the data type of the variable in the Dim statement. Instead, the syntax allows the computer to infer the data type from the value being assigned to the variable. However, for this inference to take place, you must set Option Infer to On (rather than to Off, as you have been doing). You can do this by entering the Option Infer On statement in the General Declarations section of the Code Editor window.

Figure 12-24 also includes examples of using the LINQ syntax. The statement in Example 1 selects all of the records from the dataset and assigns them to the `records` variable. The statement in Example 2 performs the same task; however, the records are assigned in ascending order by the Sales field. If you are sorting records in ascending order, you do not need to include the keyword `Ascending` in the Order By clause because `Ascending` is the default sort order. The statement in Example 3 assigns only the franchisees' records to the `records` variable. The statement in Example 4 assigns only the records for stores that have more than $100,000 in sales. The statement in Example 5 uses the Like operator and the asterisk pattern-matching character to select only records whose State field begins with the letter C followed by zero or more characters. (You learned about the Like operator and pattern-matching characters in Chapter 10.) The selected records are then arranged in descending order by the City field.

The syntax and examples in Figure 12-24 merely assign the selected and/or arranged records to a variable. To actually view the records, you need to assign the variable's contents to the DataSource property of a BindingSource object. The syntax for doing this is shown in Figure 12-25 along with an example of using the syntax. Any control that is bound to the BindingSource object will display the appropriate field(s) when the application is started.

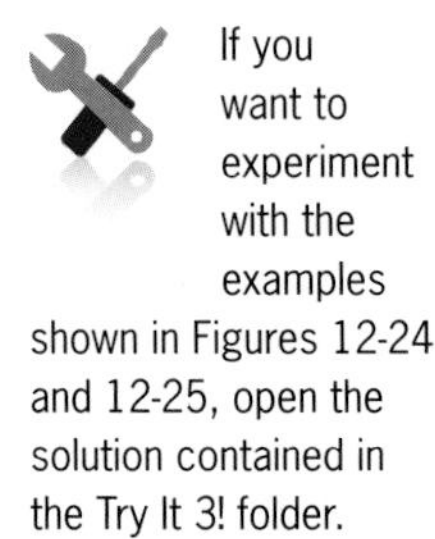

If you want to experiment with the examples shown in Figures 12-24 and 12-25, open the solution contained in the Try It 3! folder.

HOW TO Assign the Contents of a LINQ Variable to a BindingSource Object

Basic syntax
bindingSource.**DataSource** = *variableName*.**AsDataView**

Example
```
TblStoresBindingSource.DataSource = records.AsDataView
```
assigns the contents of the `records` variable (from Figure 12-24) to the TblStoresBindingSource object

Figure 12-25 How to assign the contents of a LINQ variable to a BindingSource object

Customizing a BindingNavigator Control

The BindingNavigator control contains buttons that allow you to move to a different record in the dataset, add or delete a record, and save any changes made to the dataset. At times, you may want to include additional items on the control, such as another button, a text box, or a drop-down button. The steps for adding and deleting items are shown in Figure 12-26.

HOW TO Customize a BindingNavigator Control

To add an item to a BindingNavigator control:
1. Click the BindingNavigator control's task box, and then click Edit Items to open the Items Collection Editor window (shown at the end of this How To box).
2. If necessary, click the "Select item and add to list below" arrow in the Items Collection Editor window.
3. Click the item you want to add to the BindingNavigator control, and then click the Add button.
4. Click the Alphabetical button to display the property names in alphabetical order. Provide appropriate values for the item's Name, DisplayStyle, and Text properties.
5. If necessary, you can use the up and down arrows to reposition the item.

Figure 12-26 How to customize a BindingNavigator control *(continues)*

(continued)

To delete an item from a BindingNavigator control:

1. Click the BindingNavigator control's task box, and then click Edit Items to open the Items Collection Editor window, which is shown below.
2. In the Members list, click the item you want to remove, and then click the *X* button.

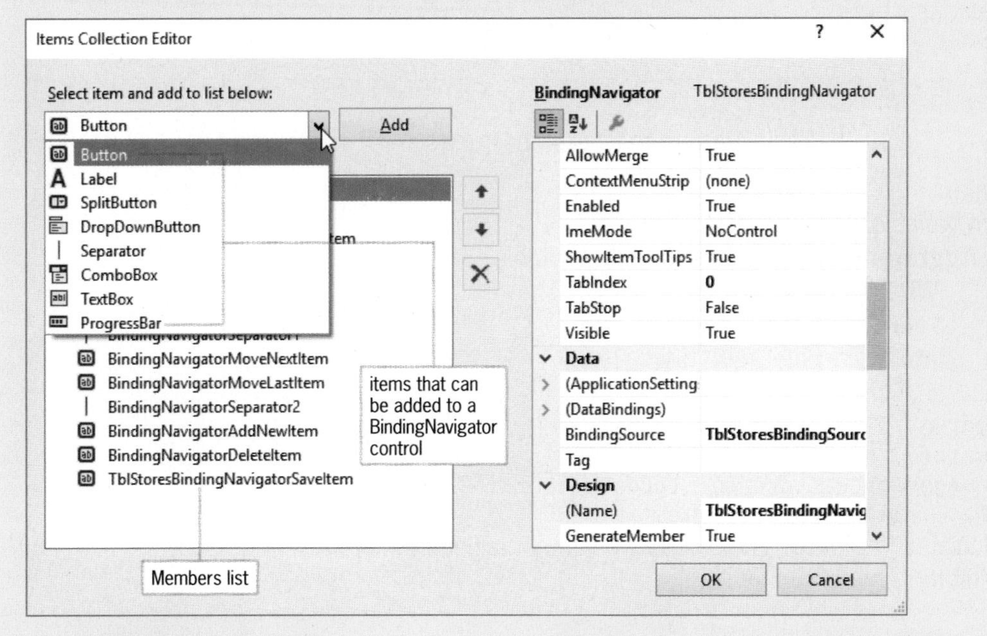

Figure 12-26 How to customize a BindingNavigator control

Figure 12-27 shows a DropDownButton on the Adalene Fashions BindingNavigator control during design time. The DropDownButton, whose caption is Total Sales, offers a menu that contains three items. The menu items allow the user to determine the total sales for all stores, company-owned stores, or franchisees. (You will learn how to calculate these values in the next section.)

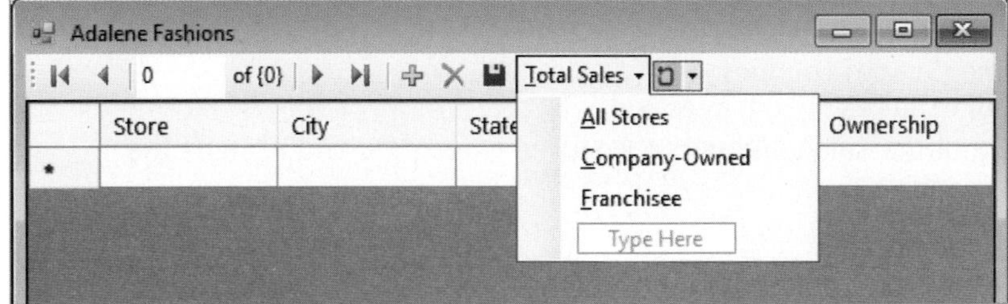

Figure 12-27 DropDownButton added to the BindingNavigator control

Using the LINQ Aggregate Operators

LINQ provides several aggregate operators—such as Average, Count, Max, Min, and Sum—that you can use when querying a dataset. An **aggregate operator** returns a single value from a group of values. The Sum operator, for example, returns the sum of the values in the group, whereas the Min operator returns the smallest value in the group. You include an aggregate operator in a LINQ statement using the syntax shown in Figure 12-28. The figure also includes examples of using the syntax.

If you want to experiment with the code shown in Figure 12-28, open the solution contained in the Try It 4! folder.

HOW TO Use the LINQ Aggregate Operators

Syntax

Dim *variableName* [**As** *dataType*] =
    Aggregate *elementName* **In** *dataset.table*
        [**Where** *condition*]
        Select *elementName.fieldName*
        Into *aggregateOperator*

Example 1

```
Dim total As Integer =
    Aggregate store In StoresDataSet.tblStores
        Select store.Sales Into Sum
```

calculates the total of the sales amounts contained in the dataset and assigns the result to the `total` variable

Example 2

```
Dim highCompanyOwned As Integer
highCompanyOwned =
    Aggregate store In StoresDataSet.tblStores
        Where store.Ownership.ToUpper = "C"
        Select store.Sales Into Max
```

finds the highest sales amount for a company-owned store and assigns the result to the `highCompanyOwned` variable

Example 3

```
Dim average As Double =
    Aggregate store In StoresDataSet.tblStores
        Where store.State.ToUpper = "GA"
        Select store.Sales Into Average
```

calculates the average of the sales amounts for stores in Georgia and assigns the result to the `average` variable

Example 4

```
Dim counter As Integer =
    Aggregate store In StoresDataSet.tblStores
        Where store.City.ToUpper = "CHICAGO"
        Into Count
```

counts the number of stores in the city of Chicago and assigns the result to the `counter` variable (The Count operator is the only operator that does not need the Select clause.)

Figure 12-28 How to use the LINQ aggregate operators

Figure 12-29 shows the code associated with the three menu items shown earlier in Figure 12-27. Figure 12-30 shows the result of starting the Adalene Fashions application and then selecting the Franchisee item from the Total Sales DropDownButton.

```
Private Sub allMenuItem_Click(sender As Object, e As EventArgs
) Handles allMenuItem.Click
    ' displays the total sales for all stores

    Dim total As Integer =
        Aggregate store In StoresDataSet.tblStores
            Select store.Sales Into Sum

    MessageBox.Show("Total sales for all stores: " &
            total.ToString("C0"), "Adalene Fashions",
            MessageBoxButtons.OK,
            MessageBoxIcon.Information)
End Sub

Private Sub companyMenuItem_Click(sender As Object,
e As EventArgs) Handles companyMenuItem.Click
    ' displays the total sales for company-owned stores

    Dim total As Integer =
        Aggregate store In StoresDataSet.tblStores
            Where store.Ownership.ToUpper = "C"
            Select store.Sales Into Sum

    MessageBox.Show("Total sales for company-owned stores: " &
            total.ToString("C0"), "Adalene Fashions",
            MessageBoxButtons.OK,
            MessageBoxIcon.Information)
End Sub

Private Sub franchiseeMenuItem_Click(sender As Object,
e As EventArgs) Handles franchiseeMenuItem.Click
    ' displays the total sales for franchisees

    Dim total As Integer =
        Aggregate store In StoresDataSet.tblStores
            Where store.Ownership.ToUpper = "F"
            Select store.Sales Into Sum

    MessageBox.Show("Total sales for franchisees: " &
            total.ToString("C0"), "Adalene Fashions",
            MessageBoxButtons.OK,
            MessageBoxIcon.Information)
End Sub
```

Figure 12-29 Code associated with the three items on the DropDownButton

If you want to experiment with the LINQ aggregate operator version of the Adalene Fashions application, open the solution contained in the Try It 5! folder.

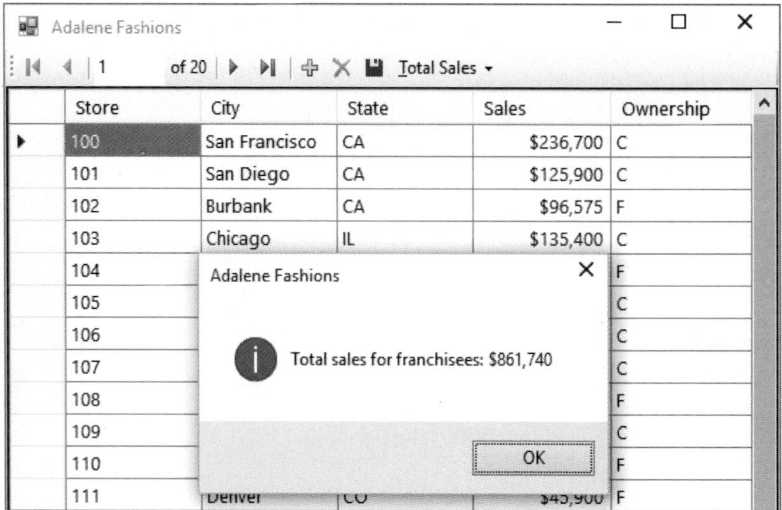

Figure 12-30 Result of selecting the Franchisee item from the Total Sales DropDownButton

The answers to Mini-Quiz questions are located in Appendix A. Each question is associated with one or more objectives listed at the beginning of the chapter.

Mini-Quiz 12-3

1. Which of the following will select only records whose City field begins with the letter L? (9)

   a.
   ```
   Dim records = From StoresDataSet.tblStores
        Select City.ToUpper Like "L*"
   ```
   b.
   ```
   Dim records = From tblStores
        Where tblStores.City.ToUpper Like "L*"
        Select city
   ```
   c.
   ```
   Dim records =
        From store In StoresDataSet.tblStores
        Where store.City.ToUpper Like "L*"
        Select store
   ```
   d.
   ```
   Dim records =
        From store In StoresDataSet.tblStores
        Where tblStores.City.ToUpper Like "L*"
        Select store
   ```

2. The tblCities table contains a numeric field named Population. Which of the following calculates the total population of all the cities in the table? (11)

   a.
   ```
   Dim total As Integer =
        Aggregate city In CitiesDataSet.tblCities
            Select city.Population Into Sum
   ```
   b.
   ```
   Dim total As Integer =
        Sum city In CitiesDataSet.tblCities
            Select city.Population Into total
   ```
   c.
   ```
   Dim total As Integer =
        Aggregate CitiesDataSet.tblCities.city
            Select city.Population Into Sum
   ```
   d.
   ```
   Dim total As Integer =
        Sum city In CitiesDataSet.tblCities.population
   ```

3. In a LINQ statement, which clause is used to sort the selected records? (9)
    a. Arrange
    b. Order By
    c. Sort
    d. Where

You have completed the concepts section of Chapter 12. The Programming Tutorial section is next.

PROGRAMMING TUTORIAL 1

Completing the Trivia Game Application

In this tutorial, you will complete an application that displays trivia questions and answers. The questions and answers are stored in a Microsoft Access database named Trivia.accdb. The database contains one table, which is named tblGame. The table contains nine records. Each record has six fields named Question, AnswerA, AnswerB, AnswerC, AnswerD, and CorrectAnswer. The application keeps track of the number of incorrect responses made by the user, and it displays that information after all nine questions have been answered. Figures 12-31 and 12-32 show the application's TOE chart and MainForm, respectively.

Task	Object	Event
End the application	exitButton	Click
Fill the dataset with data	MainForm	Load
1. Compare the user's answer with the correct answer 2. Keep track of the number of incorrect answers 3. Display the next question and answers from the dataset 4. Display the number of incorrect answers	submitButton	Click
Display questions from the dataset	questionTextBox	None
Display answers from the dataset	aTextBox, bTextBox, cTextBox, dTextBox	None
Get the user's answer	aRadioButton, bRadioButton, cRadioButton, dRadioButton	None

Figure 12-31 TOE chart for the Trivia Game application

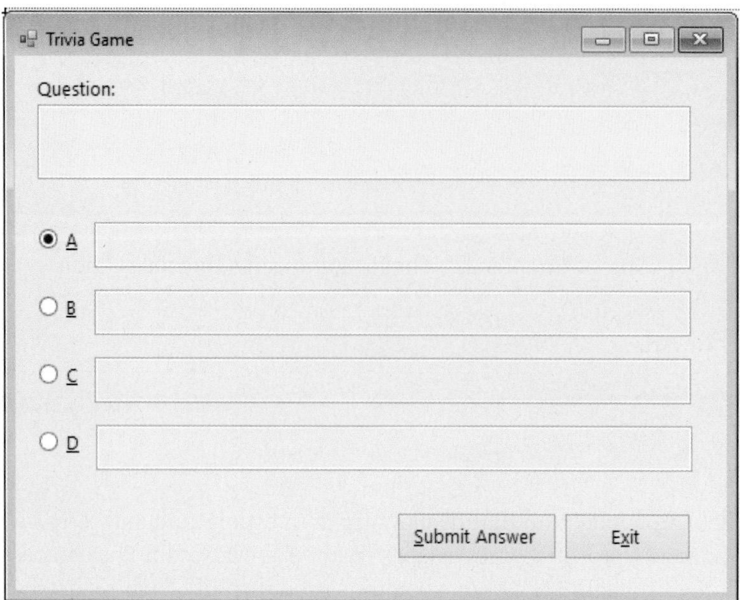

Figure 12-32 MainForm for the Trivia Game application

Connecting the Application to the Trivia Database

First, you need to open the Trivia Game application and connect it to the Trivia database.

To open the application and then connect it to the database:

1. Start Visual Studio. Open the **Trivia Solution** (**Trivia Solution.sln**) file contained in the VbReloaded2015\Chap12\Trivia Solution folder. If necessary, open the designer window.
2. If necessary, auto-hide the toolbox and Properties windows, and permanently display the Solution Explorer window.
3. If necessary, open the Data Sources window by clicking **View** on the menu bar, pointing to **Other Windows**, and then clicking **Data Sources**. If necessary, click the **Auto Hide** button to permanently display the window.
4. Click **Add New Data Source** in the Data Sources window to start the Data Source Configuration Wizard. If necessary, click **Database** on the Choose a Data Source Type screen.
5. Click the **Next** button to display the Choose a Database Model screen. If necessary, click **Dataset**.
6. Click the **Next** button to display the Choose Your Data Connection screen. Click the **New Connection** button. At this point, you will see either the Choose Data Source dialog box or the Add Connection dialog box.
7. If the Add Connection dialog box opens, skip to Step 8. However, if the Choose Data Source dialog box opens, click **Microsoft Access Database File** in the Data source box, select the **Always use this selection** check box, and then click the **Continue** button to open the Add Connection dialog box.
8. If Microsoft Access Database File (OLE DB) does not appear in the Data source box, click the **Change** button to open the Change Data Source dialog box, click **Microsoft Access Database File**, select the **Always use this selection** check box, and then click the **OK** button.

9. Click the **Browse** button in the Add Connection dialog box. Open the VbReloaded2015\Chap12\Access Databases folder and then click **Trivia.accdb** in the list of filenames. Click the **Open** button. Figure 12-33 shows the completed Add Connection dialog box.

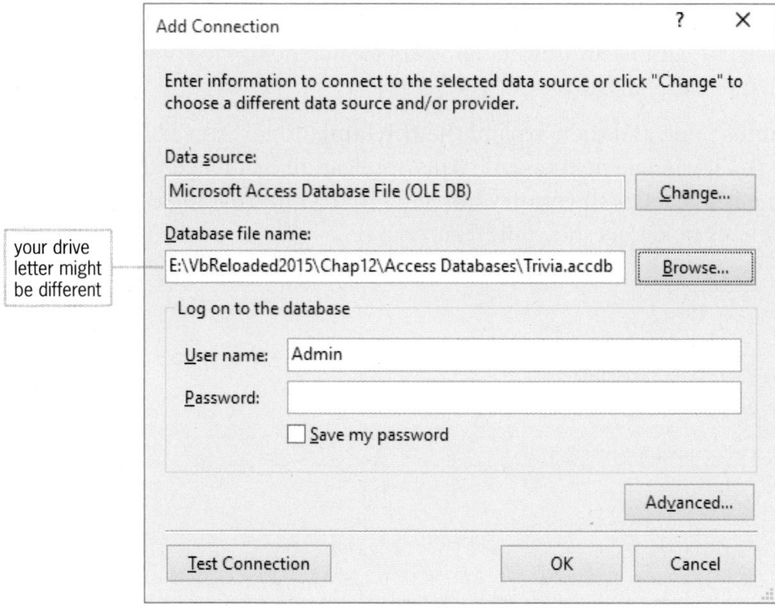

Figure 12-33 Completed Add Connection dialog box

10. Click the **Test Connection** button. The "Test connection succeeded." message appears in a message box. Close the message box.

11. Click the **OK** button to close the Add Connection dialog box. Trivia.accdb appears in the Choose Your Data Connection screen. Click the **Next** button. The message box shown in Figure 12-34 opens. The message asks whether you want to include the database file in the current project. By including the file in the current project, you can more easily copy the application and its database to another computer.

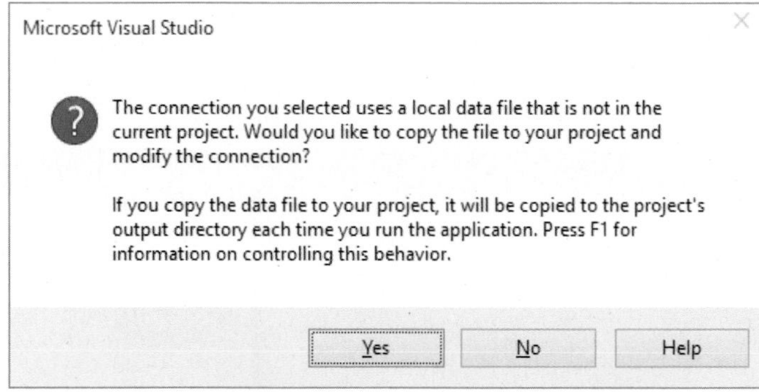

Figure 12-34 Message regarding copying the database file

12. Click the **Yes** button to add the Trivia.accdb file to the application's project folder in the Solution Explorer window. The Save the Connection String to the Application Configuration File screen appears next. The name of the connection string, TriviaConnectionString, appears on the screen. If necessary, select the **Yes, save the connection as** check box.

13. Click the **Next** button to display the Choose Your Database Objects screen. You use this screen to select the table and/or field objects to include in the dataset, which is automatically named TriviaDataSet.

14. Expand the **Tables** node and then expand the **tblGame** node. (You expand a node by clicking the small triangle next to it.) In this application, you need the dataset to include all of the fields. Click the **empty box** next to tblGame. Doing this selects the table and field check boxes, as shown in Figure 12-35.

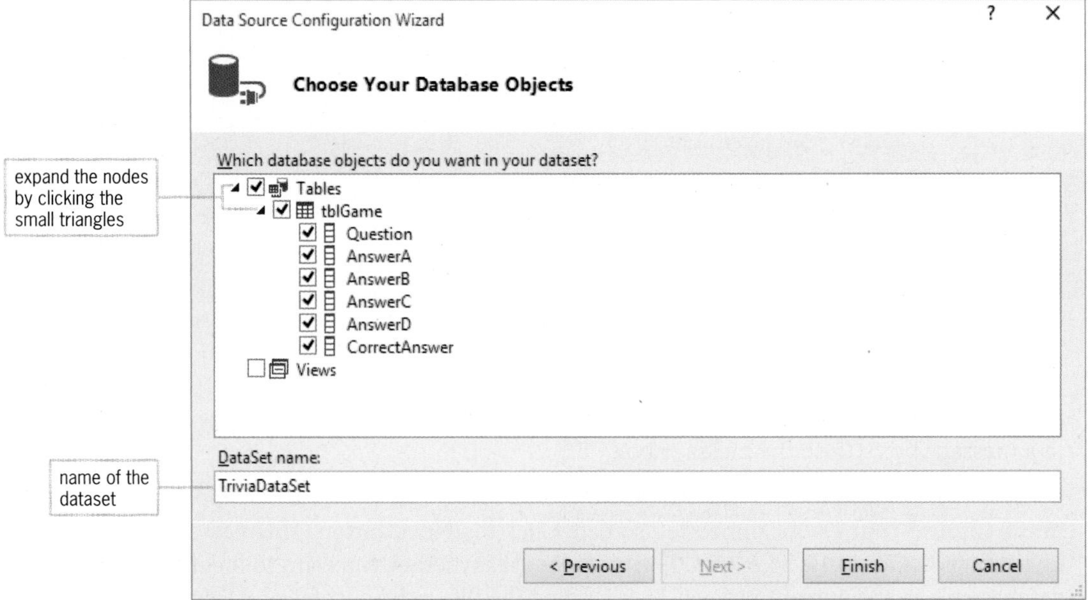

Figure 12-35 Objects selected in the Choose Your Database Objects screen

15. Click the **Finish** button. The computer adds the TriviaDataSet to the Data Sources window. Expand the **tblGame** node in the Data Sources window. The dataset contains one table object and six field objects, as shown in Figure 12-36.

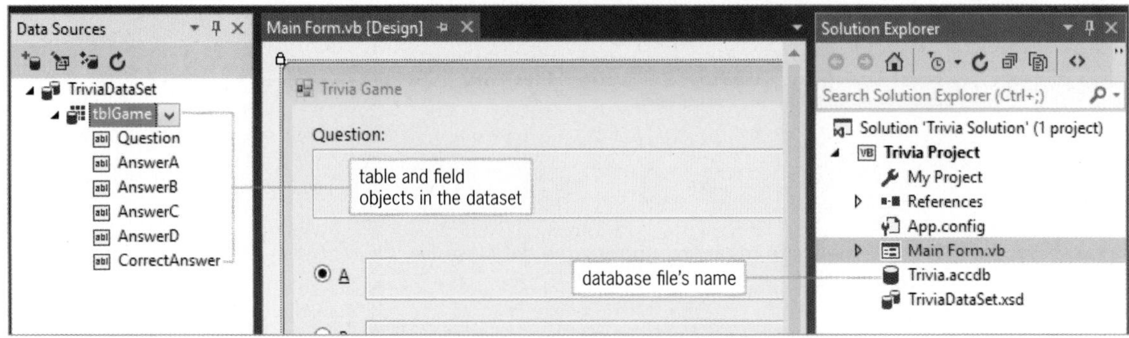

Figure 12-36 Result of running the Data Source Configuration Wizard

16. Now, preview the data contained in the dataset. Right-click **TriviaDataSet** in the Data Sources window, and then click **Preview Data** to open the Preview Data dialog box. Click the **Preview** button. See Figure 12-37.

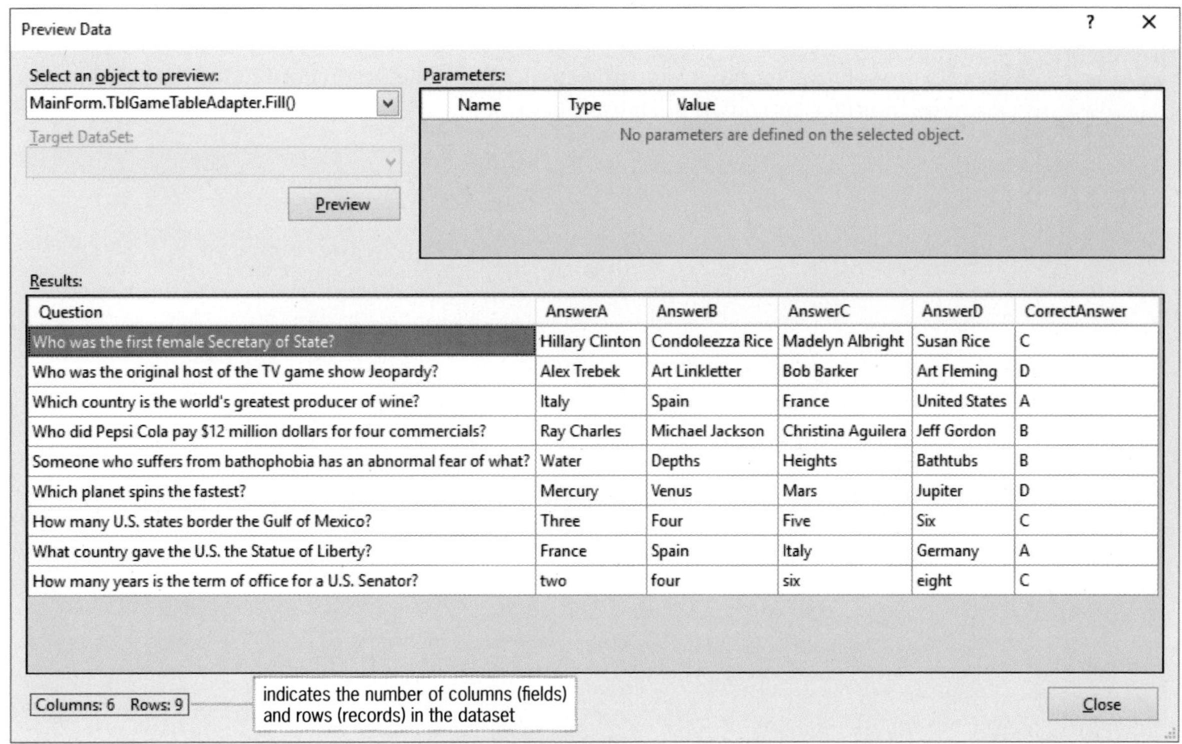

Question	AnswerA	AnswerB	AnswerC	AnswerD	CorrectAnswer
Who was the first female Secretary of State?	Hillary Clinton	Condoleezza Rice	Madelyn Albright	Susan Rice	C
Who was the original host of the TV game show Jeopardy?	Alex Trebek	Art Linkletter	Bob Barker	Art Fleming	D
Which country is the world's greatest producer of wine?	Italy	Spain	France	United States	A
Who did Pepsi Cola pay $12 million dollars for four commercials?	Ray Charles	Michael Jackson	Christina Aguilera	Jeff Gordon	B
Someone who suffers from bathophobia has an abnormal fear of what?	Water	Depths	Heights	Bathtubs	B
Which planet spins the fastest?	Mercury	Venus	Mars	Jupiter	D
How many U.S. states border the Gulf of Mexico?	Three	Four	Five	Six	C
What country gave the U.S. the Statue of Liberty?	France	Spain	Italy	Germany	A
How many years is the term of office for a U.S. Senator?	two	four	six	eight	C

Figure 12-37 Data displayed in the Preview Data dialog box

17. Click the **Close** button to close the Preview Data dialog box.

Note: In this application, the user will not be adding, deleting, or modifying the records in the dataset, so you do not need to change the database file's Copy to Output Directory property from "Copy always" to "Copy if newer."

Binding the Field Objects to the Text Boxes

Next, you will bind the field objects in the dataset to the appropriate text boxes on the form.

To bind the field objects to the text boxes and then test the application:

1. Click the **Question** field object in the Data Sources window, and then drag the field object to the questionTextBox, but don't release the mouse button. See Figure 12-38.

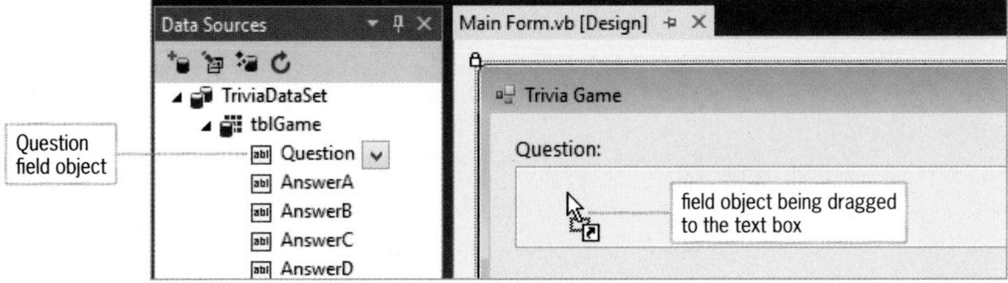

Figure 12-38 Question field object being dragged to the questionTextBox

2. Release the mouse button. The computer binds the Question field object to the questionTextBox. It also adds the TriviaDataSet, TblGameBindingSource, TblGameTableAdapter, and TableAdapterManager objects to the component tray.
3. Drag the AnswerA, AnswerB, AnswerC, and AnswerD field objects to the appropriate text boxes.
4. Save the solution and then start the application. The first record in the dataset appears in the interface, as shown in Figure 12-39.

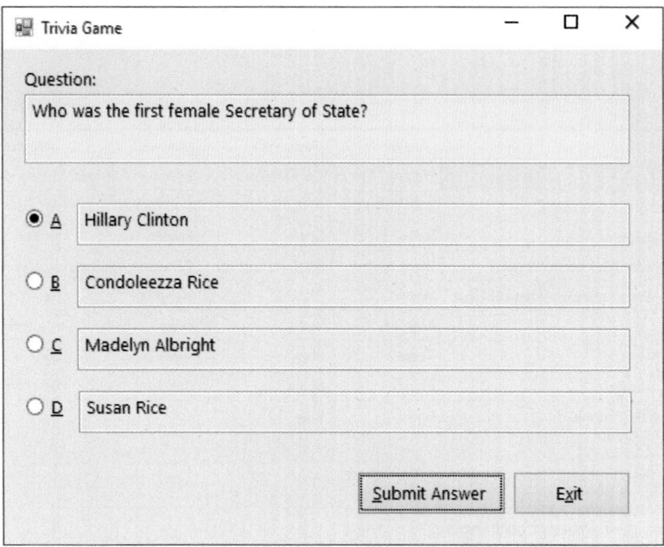

Figure 12-39 Interface showing the first record

5. Click the **Exit** button to end the application. Auto-hide the Data Sources and Solution Explorer windows.

Coding the Trivia Game Application

According to the application's TOE chart (shown earlier in Figure 12-31), only three event procedures need to be coded: exitButton_Click, MainForm_Load, and submitButton_Click. The exitButton_Click procedure has already been coded for you. The MainForm_Load procedure also contains the appropriate code. Recall that the computer automatically enters the code in the Load event procedure when you drag an object from the Data Sources window to the interface. Therefore, the only procedure you need to code is the submitButton_Click procedure. The procedure's pseudocode is shown in Figure 12-40.

```
submitButton Click event procedure
1. store the position of the record pointer in a variable
2. determine the selected radio button and assign its Text property (without the leading ampersand
   that designates the access key) to a variable named userAnswer
3. if the value in the userAnswer variable does not match the value stored in the current record's
   CorrectAnswer field
       add 1 to a counter variable that keeps track of the number of incorrect answers
   end if
4. if the record pointer is not pointing to the last record
       move the record pointer to the next record in the dataset
   else
       display the number of incorrect answers in a message box
   end if
```

Figure 12-40 Pseudocode for the submitButton_Click procedure

To code and then test the submitButton_Click procedure:

1. Open the Code Editor window. In the General Declarations section, replace <your name> and <current date> in the comments with your name and the current date, respectively.

2. Open the code template for the submitButton's Click event procedure. Enter the following comments. Press **Enter** twice after typing the last comment.

```
' determines whether the user's answer is correct
' and the number of incorrect answers
```

3. The procedure will use an Integer variable to keep track of the record pointer's position in the dataset. It will also use a String variable to store the user's answer (A, B, C, or D) to the current question. Enter the following Dim statements:

```
Dim ptrPosition As Integer
Dim userAnswer As String
```

4. The procedure will use a static Integer variable to keep track of the number of incorrect answers made by the user. Type the following Static statement and then press **Enter** twice:

```
Static numIncorrect As Integer
```

5. The first step in the pseudocode stores the record pointer's position in a variable. Enter the following comment and assignment statement. Press **Enter** twice after typing the assignment statement.

```
' store record pointer's position
ptrPosition = TblGameBindingSource.Position
```

6. Next, the procedure needs to determine the selected radio button, and then assign its Text property (without the leading ampersand) to the `userAnswer` variable. Enter the following comment and Select Case statement:

```
' determine selected radio button
Select Case True
  Case aRadioButton.Checked
    userAnswer = aRadioButton.Text.Substring(1, 1)
  Case bRadioButton.Checked
    userAnswer = bRadioButton.Text.Substring(1, 1)
```

```
    Case cRadioButton.Checked
        userAnswer = cRadioButton.Text.Substring(1, 1)
    Case Else
        userAnswer = dRadioButton.Text.Substring(1, 1)
End Select
```

7. The next step in the pseudocode is a single-alternative selection structure that compares the value in the `userAnswer` variable with the value in the current record's CorrectAnswer field. If both values are not the same, the procedure should add the number 1 to the value in the `numIncorrect` variable. Insert **two blank lines** after the End Select clause. Beginning in the blank line above the End Sub clause, enter the following comment and selection structure:

```
' if necessary, update the number of incorrect answers
If userAnswer <>
        TriviaDataSet.tblGame(ptrPosition).CorrectAnswer Then
    numIncorrect += 1
End If
```

8. The last step in the pseudocode is a dual-alternative selection structure that determines whether the record pointer is pointing to the last record in the dataset. If it is not, the procedure should move the record pointer to the next record; doing this will display that record's question and answers. However, if the record pointer is pointing to the last record, it means that there are no more questions and answers to display. In that case, the procedure should display the number of incorrect answers made by the user. Insert **two blank lines** after the End If clause. Beginning in the blank line above the End Sub clause, enter the following selection structure:

```
If ptrPosition < 8 Then
    TblGameBindingSource.MoveNext()
Else
    MessageBox.Show("Number incorrect: " &
                    numIncorrect.ToString, "Trivia Game",
                    MessageBoxButtons.OK,
                    MessageBoxIcon.Information)
End If
```

9. Save the solution and then start the application. You will answer the first question correctly. Click the **C** radio button and then click the **Submit Answer** button.

10. You will answer the second question incorrectly. Click the **A** radio button and then click the **Submit Answer** button.

11. Answer the remaining seven questions on your own. When you have submitted the answer for the last question, the submitButton_Click procedure displays the number of incorrect responses in a message box.

12. Close the message box and then click the **Exit** button. Close the Code Editor window and then close the solution. Figure 12-41 shows the Trivia Game application's code.

```
' Project name:          Trivia Project
' Project purpose:       Displays trivia questions and
'                        answers and the number of incorrect
'                        answers made by the user
' Created/revised by:    <your name> on <current date>

Option Explicit On
Option Strict On
Option Infer Off

Public Class MainForm
    Private Sub exitButton_Click(sender As Object, e As EventArgs
    ) Handles exitButton.Click
        Me.Close()
    End Sub

    Private Sub MainForm_Load(sender As Object, e As EventArgs
    ) Handles MyBase.Load
        'TODO: This line of code loads data into the
         'TriviaDataSet.tblGame' table. You can move,
         or remove it, as needed.
        Me.TblGameTableAdapter.Fill(Me.TriviaDataSet.tblGame)

    End Sub

    Private Sub submitButton_Click(sender As Object, e As EventArgs
    ) Handles submitButton.Click
        ' determines whether the user's answer is correct
        ' and the number of incorrect answers

        Dim ptrPosition As Integer
        Dim userAnswer As String
        Static numIncorrect As Integer

        ' store record pointer's position
        ptrPosition = TblGameBindingSource.Position

        ' determine selected radio button
        Select Case True
            Case aRadioButton.Checked
                userAnswer = aRadioButton.Text.Substring(1, 1)
            Case bRadioButton.Checked
                userAnswer = bRadioButton.Text.Substring(1, 1)
            Case cRadioButton.Checked
                userAnswer = cRadioButton.Text.Substring(1, 1)
            Case Else
                userAnswer = dRadioButton.Text.Substring(1, 1)
        End Select

        ' if necessary, update the number of incorrect answers
        If userAnswer <>
                TriviaDataSet.tblGame(ptrPosition).CorrectAnswer Then
            numIncorrect += 1
        End If

```

Figure 12-41 Code for the Trivia Game application *(continues)*

(continued)

```
        If ptrPosition < 8 Then
            TblGameBindingSource.MoveNext()
        Else
            MessageBox.Show("Number incorrect: " &
                            numIncorrect.ToString, "Trivia Game",
                            MessageBoxButtons.OK,
                            MessageBoxIcon.Information)
        End If
    End Sub
End Class
```

Figure 12-41 Code for the Trivia Game application

PROGRAMMING TUTORIAL 2

Creating the Games Galore Application

In this tutorial, you will create an application for the Games Galore store, which sells new and used video games. The video game information is contained in a Microsoft Access database named Games. The Games database is stored in the Games.accdb file and contains one table named tblGames. The application will display the records in a DataGridView control. The store manager will be allowed to add records to the database, delete records from the database, and modify the existing records. In addition, he or she can use the application to display only the games for a specific platform (Xbox, PlayStation, or Wii) as well as the total value of the games in the store. Figure 12-42 shows the contents of the tblGames table.

ID	Title	Platform	Rating	Price	NewUsed	Quantity
1	Dead Space	XB	M	$59.99	N	5
2	Dead Space	PS	M	$59.99	N	4
3	Just Dance	WII	E10+	$37.50	N	3
4	Just Dance	XB	E10+	$37.35	N	4
5	Just Dance	PS	E10+	$34.39	N	4
6	Call of Duty: Black Ops II	XB	M	$49.44	N	2
7	Call of Duty: Black Ops II	PS	M	$52.43	N	2
8	Halo	XB	M	$39.99	N	2
9	Halo	XB	M	$33.55	U	1
10	LEGO Batman: DC Super Heroes	WII	E10+	$19.99	N	4
11	LEGO Batman: DC Super Heroes	WII	E10+	$10.39	U	2
12	LEGO Batman: DC Super Heroes	XB	E10+	$19.99	N	3
13	LEGO Batman: DC Super Heroes	XB	E10+	$17.50	U	1

Figure 12-42 Contents of the tblGames table in the Games database *(continues)*

(continued)

14	LEGO Batman: DC Super Heroes	PS	E10+	$19.99	N	2
15	LEGO Batman: DC Super Heroes	PS	E10+	$17.75	U	1
16	The Sims Pets	XB	T	$19.99	N	4
17	The Sims Pets	XB	T	$7.99	U	1
18	The Sims Pets	PS	T	$17.65	N	3
19	The Sims Pets	PS	T	$8.50	U	2
20	Madden NFL 16	XB	E	$39.99	N	8
21	Madden NFL 16	XB	E	$35.50	U	2
22	Madden NFL 16	PS	E	$35.50	N	6
23	Madden NFL 16	PS	E	$33.50	U	2
24	Madden NFL 15	WII	E	$35.99	U	3
25	Madden NFL 14	WII	E	$29.97	U	1
26	Resident Evil	PS	M	$27.60	N	3
27	Resident Evil	PS	M	$25.98	U	1
28	Resident Evil	XB	M	$27.59	N	3
29	Resident Evil	XB	M	$15.95	U	1
30	NBA 2K16	XB	E	$43.80	N	9
31	NBA 2K16	XB	E	$37.71	U	1
32	NBA 2K16	PS	E	$43.99	N	6
33	NBA 2K15	PS	E	$42.00	U	1
34	NBA 2K16	WII	E	$33.99	N	7
35	NBA 2K15	WII	E	$29.99	U	3

Figure 12-42 Contents of the tblGames table in the Games database

Connecting the Application to the Games Database

First, you need to open the Games Galore application and connect it to the Games database.

To open the application and then connect it to the database:

1. Start Visual Studio. Open the **Games Solution** (**Games Solution.sln**) file contained in the VbReloaded2015\Chap12\Games Solution folder. If necessary, open the designer and Data Sources windows.
2. Click **Add New Data Source** in the Data Sources window to start the Data Source Configuration Wizard. Use the wizard to connect the application to the Games database, which is stored in the Games.accdb file. The file is contained in the VbReloaded2015\Chap12\Access Databases folder. In this application, you need the dataset to include all of the fields in the tblGames table.

The user will be allowed to add, delete, and modify the records in the dataset, so you will need to change the database file's Copy to Output Directory property.

To change the database file's Copy to Output Directory property:

1. Click **Games.accdb** in the Solution Explorer window.
2. Use the Properties window to change the Copy to Output Directory property to **Copy if newer**.

Displaying the Records in a DataGridView Control

The application will display the records in a DataGridView control.

To display the records in a DataGridView control:

1. Drag the tblGames table object from the Data Sources window to the upper-left corner of the form and then release the mouse button.
2. In the Properties window, set the TblGamesDataGridView control's AutoSizeColumnsMode to **Fill**.
3. Click the TblGamesDataGridView control's **task box**, and then click **Dock in Parent Container** on the task list.
4. Click **Edit Columns** on the task list to open the Edit Columns dialog box. Click the **Alphabetical** button to display the properties in alphabetical order.
5. Change the ID column's AutoSizeMode property to **DisplayedCells**. Also change the Title column's AutoSizeMode property to **DisplayedCells**.
6. Click the **OK** button to close the Edit Columns dialog box.

Customizing the TblGamesBindingNavigator Control

In this section, you will add a label, a text box, and two buttons to the TblGamesBindingNavigator control. The label, text box, and one of the buttons will be used to display the games for a specific platform. The second button will be used to display the total value of the games in the store.

To customize the TblGamesBindingNavigator control:

1. Click the **TblGamesBindingNavigator** control, and then click its **task box**. Click **Edit Items** on the task list.
2. Click the **down arrow** in the "Select item and add to list below" box, and then click **Label** in the list. Click the **Add** button.
3. Click the **Alphabetical** button to display the property names in alphabetical order. Click **Text** in the properties list, and then type **&Platform:** and press **Enter**.
4. Click the **down arrow** in the "Select item and add to list below" box, and then click **TextBox** in the list. Click the **Add** button. Change the text box's name to **platformTextBox**.
5. Next, you will add a button that, when clicked, will display the games whose platform designation is entered in the text box. Click the **down arrow** in the "Select item and add to list below" box, and then click **Button** in the list. Click the **Add** button. Change the button's name to **goButton**. Also change its DisplayStyle and Text properties to **Text** and **&Go**, respectively.

6. Finally, you will add a button for displaying the total value of the games. Click the **Add** button again to add another button to the BindingNavigator control. Change the button's name to **totalButton**. Also change its DisplayStyle and Text properties to **Text** and **&Total Value**, respectively. Figure 12-43 shows the completed Items Collection Editor dialog box.

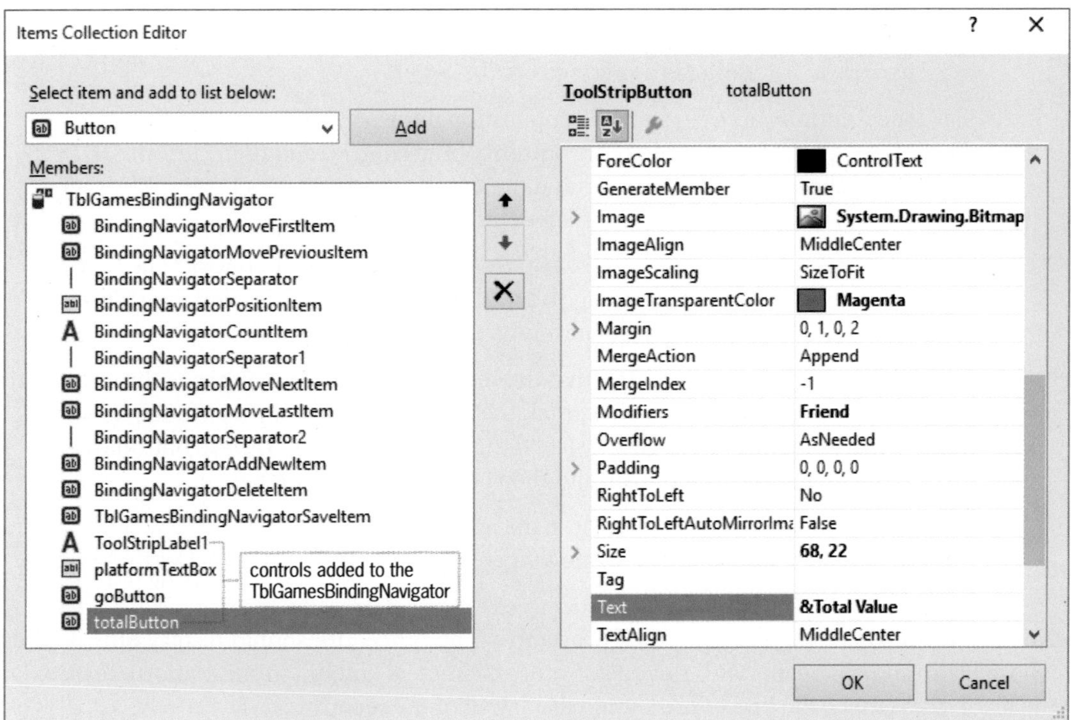

Figure 12-43 Completed Items Collection Editor dialog box

7. Click the **OK** button to close the dialog box, and then click the form's **title bar**. The four controls you added appear on the BindingNavigator control, as shown in Figure 12-44.

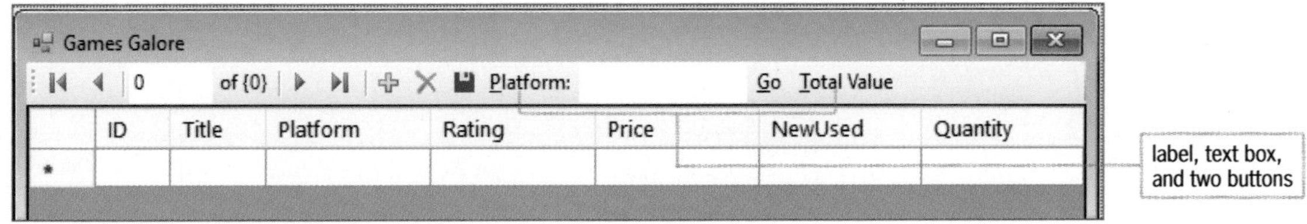

Figure 12-44 Four controls added to the TblGamesBindingNavigator

Coding the Application

The application allows the store manager to save the changes (additions, deletions, and edits) made to the database. Therefore, you should enter an appropriate Try...Catch statement in the TblGamesBindingNavigatorSaveItem_Click procedure.

To begin coding the application:

1. Lock the controls on the form, and then open the Code Editor window. In the comments that appear in the General Declarations section, replace <your name> and <current date> with your name and the current date, respectively.
2. Include an appropriate Try...Catch statement in the TblGamesBindingNavigatorSaveItem_Click procedure. If an error occurs in the procedure, display a description of the error in a message box; otherwise, display the "Changes saved" message in a message box.
3. Save the solution and then start the application to display the records in the DataGridView control. Scroll to the bottom of the control, and then click the **ID column** in the empty row. Type **36** and press **Tab**. Type **NBA 2K17**, **PS**, **E**, **49.99**, **N**, and **5** in the remaining fields, and then press **Enter**.
4. Click the **Save Data** button (the disk) on the BindingNavigator control. The "Changes saved" message appears in a message box. Close the message box, and then close the application by clicking the **Close** button on the form's title bar.
5. Start the application again. Verify that the record you entered appears as the last record in the DataGridView control. Now, click the **empty box** that appears to the left of the last record; doing this highlights (selects) the record. Click the **Delete** button (the **X**) on the BindingNavigator control, and then click the **Save Data** button.
6. Close the message box, and then close the application. Now, start the application again. Verify that the record you deleted no longer appears in the TblGamesDataGridView control. Close the application.

Next, you will code the goButton_Click procedure. The procedure should display only records whose Platform field begins with the one or more characters entered in the platformTextBox. If the text box is empty, the procedure should display all of the records.

To code and then test the goButton_Click procedure:

1. The goButton_Click procedure will use LINQ to select the appropriate records. Therefore, you will need to set Option Infer to On. Locate the `Option Infer Off` statement in the General Declarations section, and then change Off to **On**. Press **Tab** and then type **' using LINQ**.
2. Open the code template for the goButton_Click procedure. Enter the comment and code shown in Figure 12-45.

```
Private Sub goButton_Click(sender As Object, e As EventArgs) Hand
    ' display records for a specific platform

    Dim records = From game In GamesDataSet.tblGames
                  Where game.Platform.ToUpper Like
                      platformTextBox.Text.ToUpper & "*"
                  Select game
    TblGamesBindingSource.DataSource = records.AsDataView
End Sub
```

Figure 12-45 goButton_Click procedure

3. Save the solution and then start the application. The 35 records appear in the DataGridView control.

4. Click the **Platform** text box (or press **Alt+p**), and then type the letter **w**. Click the **Go** button (or press **Alt+g**). The DataGridView control shows only the seven games for the Wii. See Figure 12-46.

Games Galore

1 of 7 Platform: w Go Total Value

ID	Title	Platform	Rating	Price	NewUsed	Quantity
3	Just Dance	WII	E10+	37.5	N	3
10	LEGO Batman: DC Super Heroes	WII	E10+	19.99	N	4
11	LEGO Batman: DC Super Heroes	WII	E10+	10.39	U	2
24	Madden NFL 15	WII	E	35.99	U	3
25	Madden NFL 14	WII	E	29.97	U	1
34	NBA 2K16	WII	E	33.99	N	7
35	NBA 2K15	WII	E	29.99	U	3

Figure 12-46 Games for the Wii

5. Delete the letter **w** from the Platform text box, and then click the **Go** button. The 35 records appear in the DataGridView control.

6. Click the **Close** button on the form's title bar to stop the application.

The totalButton_Click procedure should display the total value of the games in the store. The total value is calculated by multiplying the value in each game's Quantity field by the value in its Price field, using the Sum aggregate operator to accumulate the results.

To code and then test the totalButton_Click procedure:

1. Open the code template for the totalButton_Click procedure. Enter the comment and code shown in Figure 12-47.

```
Private Sub totalButton_Click(sender As Object, e As EventArgs) H
    ' display the total value of the games

    Dim total As Double =
        Aggregate game In GamesDataSet.tblGames
            Select game.Quantity * game.Price
                Into Sum
    MessageBox.Show("Total value: " &
                    total.ToString("C2"),
                    "Games Galore",
                    MessageBoxButtons.OK,
                    MessageBoxIcon.Information)
End Sub
```

Figure 12-47 totalButton_Click procedure

2. Save the solution and then start the application. Click the **Total Value** button (or press **Alt+t**). The total value of the games appears in a message box, as shown in Figure 12-48.

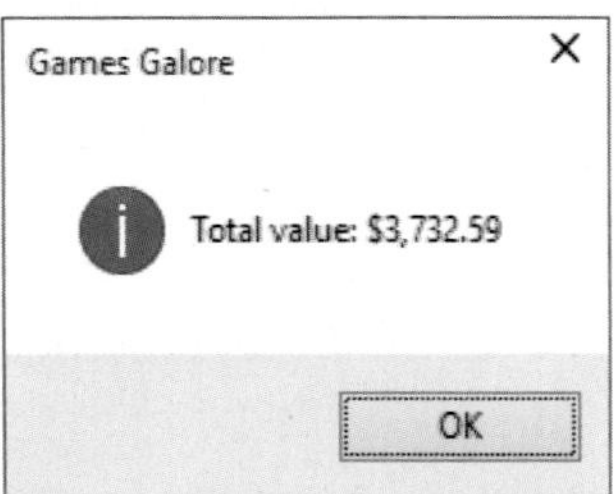

Figure 12-48 Message box showing the total value of the games

3. Close the message box and then close the application. Close the Code Editor window and then close the solution. Figure 12-49 shows the code for the Games Galore application.

```
' Project name:         Games Project
' Project purpose:      Displays all records or only those
'                       for a specific platform. Also displays
'                       the total value of the games in the store.
' Created/revised by:   <your name> on <current date>

Option Explicit On
Option Strict On
Option Infer On ' using LINQ

Public Class MainForm
    Private Sub TblGamesBindingNavigatorSaveItem_Click(
    sender As Object, e As EventArgs
    ) Handles TblGamesBindingNavigatorSaveItem.Click
        Try
            Me.Validate()
            Me.TblGamesBindingSource.EndEdit()
            Me.TableAdapterManager.UpdateAll(Me.GamesDataSet)
            MessageBox.Show("Changes saved", "Games Galore",
                            MessageBoxButtons.OK,
                            MessageBoxIcon.Information)
        Catch ex As Exception
            MessageBox.Show(ex.Message, "Games Galore",
                            MessageBoxButtons.OK,
                            MessageBoxIcon.Information)
        End Try
    End Sub

    Private Sub MainForm_Load(sender As Object, e As EventArgs
    ) Handles MyBase.Load
        'TODO: This line of code loads data into the
        'GamesDataSet.tblGames' table. You can move,
        or remove it, as needed.
        Me.TblGamesTableAdapter.Fill(Me.GamesDataSet.tblGames)

    End Sub

```

Figure 12-49 Code for the Games Galore application *(continues)*

(continued)

```
    Private Sub goButton_Click(sender As Object, e As EventArgs
    ) Handles goButton.Click
        ' display records for a specific platform

        Dim records = From game In GamesDataSet.tblGames
                      Where game.Platform.ToUpper Like
                          platformTextBox.Text.ToUpper & "*"
                      Select game
        TblGamesBindingSource.DataSource = records.AsDataView
    End Sub

    Private Sub totalButton_Click(sender As Object, e As EventArgs
    ) Handles totalButton.Click
        ' display the total value of the games

        Dim total As Double =
            Aggregate game In GamesDataSet.tblGames
                Select game.Quantity * game.Price
                    Into Sum
        MessageBox.Show("Total value: " &
                        total.ToString("C2"),
                        "Games Galore",
                        MessageBoxButtons.OK,
                        MessageBoxIcon.Information)
    End Sub
End Class
```

Figure 12-49 Code for the Games Galore application

PROGRAMMING EXAMPLE

Cartwright Industries Application

The sales manager at Cartwright Industries records the item number, name, and price of the company's products in a database named Items. The Items database is stored in the Items.accdb file, which is contained in the VbReloaded2015\Chap12\Access Databases folder. The tblItems table in the database contains 10 records, each composed of three fields. The ItemNum and ItemName fields contain text, and the Price field contains numbers. Create an application that displays the records in a DataGridView control. The application should allow the user to select records whose ItemNum field matches the one or more characters entered by the user. Use the following names for the solution and project, respectively: Cartwright Solution and Cartwright Project. Save the application in the VbReloaded2015\Chap12 folder. Change the form file's name to Main Form.vb. See Figures 12-50 through 12-53.

ItemNum	ItemName	Price
ABX12	Chair	$45.00
CSR14	Desk	$175.00
JTR23	Table	$65.00
NRE09	End Table	$46.00
OOE68	Bookcase	$100.00
PPR00	Coffee Table	$190.00
PRT45	Lamp	$30.00
REZ04	Love Seat	$200.00
THR98	Side Chair	$133.00
WKP10	Sofa	$273.00

Figure 12-50 Contents of the tblItems table in the Items database

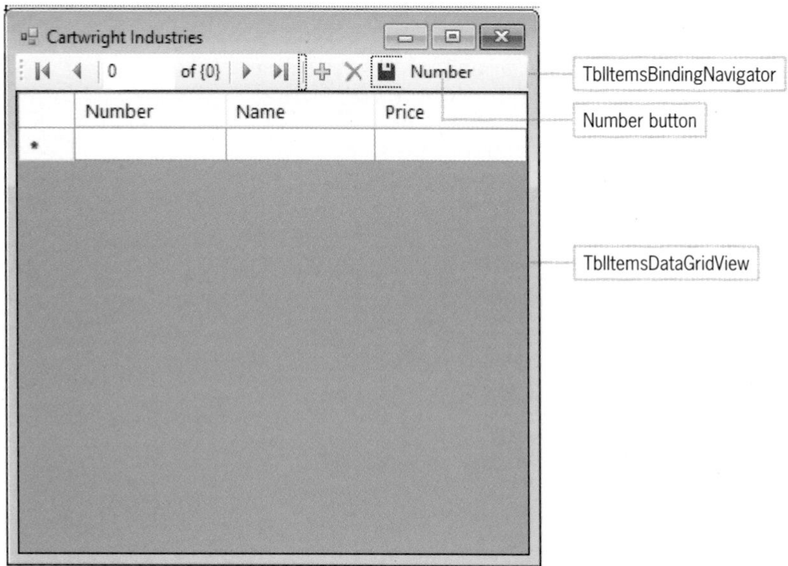

Figure 12-51 MainForm

Object	Property	Setting
MainForm	Font StartPosition Text	Segoe UI, 10pt CenterScreen Cartwright Industries
TblItemsDataGridView	AutoSizeColumnsMode	Fill
ItemNum column	HeaderText	Number
ItemName column	HeaderText	Name
Price column	DefaultCellStyle	Format: N2 Alignment: MiddleRight
Number button	Name DisplayStyle Text	numberButton Text Number

Figure 12-52 Objects, properties, and settings

PROGRAMMING EXAMPLE

```
' Project name:         Cartwright Project
' Project purpose:      Displays all records from a dataset
'                       or those matching an item number
' Created/revised by:   <your name> on <current date>

Option Explicit On
Option Strict On
Option Infer On

Public Class MainForm
    Private Sub TblItemsBindingNavigatorSaveItem_Click(
      sender As Object, e As EventArgs
      ) Handles TblItemsBindingNavigatorSaveItem.Click
        Try
            Me.Validate()
            Me.TblItemsBindingSource.EndEdit()
            Me.TableAdapterManager.UpdateAll(Me.ItemsDataSet)
            MessageBox.Show("Changes saved",
                            "Cartwright Industries",
                            MessageBoxButtons.OK,
                            MessageBoxIcon.Information)
        Catch ex As Exception
            MessageBox.Show(ex.Message,
                            "Cartwright Industries",
                            MessageBoxButtons.OK,
                            MessageBoxIcon.Information)
        End Try
    End Sub

    Private Sub MainForm_Load(sender As Object, e As EventArgs
    ) Handles MyBase.Load
        'TODO: This line of code loads data into the
        'ItemsDataSet.tblItems' table. You can move, or
        remove it, as needed.
        Me.TblItemsTableAdapter.Fill(Me.ItemsDataSet.tblItems)

    End Sub

    Private Sub numberButton_Click(sender As Object,
    e As EventArgs) Handles numberButton.Click
        ' displays records matching an item number

        Dim itemNum As String
        Const Prompt As String = "One or more characters " &
            "(leave empty to retrieve all records):"

        ' get item number
        itemNum = InputBox(Prompt, "Item Number")
        itemNum = itemNum.ToUpper.Trim
        ' select records matching item number
        Dim records = From item In ItemsDataSet.tblItems
            Where item.ItemNum.ToUpper Like itemNum & "*"
            Select item
        TblItemsBindingSource.DataSource = records.AsDataView
    End Sub
End Class
```

Figure 12-53 Code

Chapter Summary

- You can use Visual Basic to access the data stored in databases created by many different database management systems.
- Databases created by Microsoft Access are relational databases. A relational database can contain one or more tables. Each table consists of rows and columns, similar to a spreadsheet.
- Most tables contain a primary key that uniquely identifies each record.
- The data in a relational database can be displayed in any order, and you can control the amount of information you want to view.
- To access the data stored in a database, you first connect an application to the database. Doing this creates a dataset that contains objects, such as table objects and field objects.
- You can display the information contained in a dataset by binding one or more of the objects in the dataset to one or more controls in the application's interface.
- A TableAdapter object connects a database to a DataSet object.
- A BindingSource object connects a DataSet object to the bound controls on a form.
- The DataGridView control displays data in a row and column format, similar to a spreadsheet. The intersection of a column and a row is called a cell.
- In most applications, the statement to fill a dataset with data is entered in the form's Load event procedure.
- You can use the Try...Catch statement to handle any exceptions that occur while an application is running. A description of the exception is stored in the Message property of the Catch block's `ex` parameter.
- A database file's Copy to Output Directory property determines when and if the file is copied from the project folder to the project folder's bin\Debug folder each time the application is started.
- The BindingSource object uses an invisible record pointer to keep track of the current record in the dataset. The location of the record pointer is stored in the object's Position property.
- You can use the BindingSource object's Move methods to move the record pointer in a dataset.
- You can access the value stored in a field object in a dataset.
- You can use LINQ to select and arrange the records in a dataset. LINQ also provides the Average, Sum, Count, Min, and Max aggregate operators.
- You can include additional items, such as text boxes and drop-down buttons, on a BindingNavigator control. You can also delete items from the control.

Key Terms

Aggregate operator—an operator that returns a single value from a group of values; LINQ provides the Average, Count, Max, Min, and Sum aggregate operators

AutoSizeColumnsMode property—determines the way the column widths are sized in a DataGridView control

Binding—the process of connecting an object in a dataset to a control on a form

BindingNavigator control—can be used to move the record pointer from one record to another in a dataset and also to add, delete, and save records

BindingSource object—connects a DataSet object to the bound controls on a form

Bound controls—the controls connected to an object in a dataset

Cell—the intersection of a row and a column in a DataGridView control

Child table—a table linked to a parent table

Computer database—an electronic file that contains an organized collection of related information

Copy to Output Directory property—a property of a database file; determines when and if the file is copied from the project folder to the project folder's bin\Debug folder each time the application connected to the database is started

DataGridView control—displays data in a row and column format, similar to a spreadsheet

Dataset—a copy of the data (database fields and records) that can be accessed by an application

DataSet object—stores the information you want to access from a database

Exception—an error that occurs while an application is running

Foreign key—the field used to link a child table to a parent table

Language Integrated Query—LINQ; the query language built into Visual Basic

LINQ—the acronym for Language Integrated Query

Move methods—methods of a BindingSource object; used to move the record pointer to the first, last, next, or previous record in a dataset

Order By clause—used in LINQ to arrange (sort) the records in a dataset

Parent table—a table linked to a child table

Position property—a property of a BindingSource object; stores the position of the record pointer

Primary key—the field that uniquely identifies each record in a table

Query—specifies the records to select in a dataset and the order in which to arrange the records

Relational database—a database that stores information in tables composed of columns (fields) and rows (records)

Table—a group of related records

TableAdapter object—connects a database to a DataSet object

TableAdapterManager object—handles saving data to multiple tables in a dataset

Try...Catch statement—used for exception handling in a procedure

Where clause—used in LINQ to limit the records you want to view in a dataset

Review Questions

Each Review Question is associated with one or more objectives listed at the beginning of the chapter.

1. The ____________ property stores an integer that represents the location of the record pointer in a dataset. (4, 7)
   a. BindingNavigator object's Position
   b. BindingSource object's Position
   c. BindingSource object's Location
   d. TableAdapter object's Location

2. If the record pointer is positioned on record number 5 in a dataset, which of the following will move the record pointer to record number 4? (4, 7)
   a. `TblBooksBindingSource.GoPrevious()`
   b. `TblBooksBindingSource.Move(4)`
   c. `TblBooksBindingSource.MovePrevious()`
   d. `TblBooksBindingSource.PositionPrevious()`

3. The ____________ object provides the connection between a DataSet object and a control on a form. (3, 4)
   a. Bound
   b. Binding
   c. BindingSource
   d. Connecting

4. The process of connecting a control to an object in a dataset is called ____________. (3)
   a. assigning
   b. binding
   c. joining
   d. none of the above

5. Which of the following will select only records whose LastName field begins with an uppercase letter A? (9)

   a.
   ```
   Dim records = From name In NamesDataSet.tblNames
        Where name.LastName Like "A*"
        Select name
   ```
   b.
   ```
   Dim records = From NamesDataSet.tblNames
        Select LastName Like "A*"
   ```
   c.
   ```
   Dim records = From tblNames
        Where tblName.LastName Like "A*"
        Select name
   ```
   d.
   ```
   Dim records = From name In NamesDataSet.tblNames
        Where tblName.LastName Like "A*"
        Select name
   ```

6. Which of the following calculates the sum of the values stored in a numeric field named JulySales? (11)

   a.
   ```
   Dim total As Double =
        From sales In SalesDataSet.tblSales
        Select sales.JulySales Into Sum
   ```

b.
```
Dim total As Double =
     Aggregate sales In SalesDataSet.tblSales
     Select sales.JulySales Into Sum
```

c.
```
Dim total As Double =
     From sales In SalesDataSet.tblSales
     Aggregate sales.JulySales Into Sum
```

d.
```
Dim total As Double =
     From sales In SalesDataSet.tblSales
     Sum sales.JulySales
```

7. The tblCities table contains a numeric field named Population. Which of the following statements selects all cities having a population that exceeds 15,000? (9)

a.
```
Dim records = From city In CitiesDataSet.tblCities
     Where Population > 15000
     Select city
```

b.
```
Dim records = From city In CitiesDataSet.tblCities
     Select city.Population > 15000
```

c.
```
Dim records = From city In CitiesDataSet.tblCities
     Where city.Population > 15000 Select city
```

d.
```
Dim records = Select city.Population > 15000
     From tblCities
```

8. Which clause is used in a LINQ statement to limit the records that will be selected? (9)

a. Limit
b. Order By
c. Select
d. Where

9. Which of the following determines the number of records in the tblBooks table? (11)

a.
```
Dim num As Integer =
     Aggregate book In BooksDataSet.tblBooks
     In Count
```

b.
```
Dim num As Integer =
     Aggregate book In BooksDataSet.tblBooks
     Into Count
```

c.
```
Dim num As Integer =
     Aggregate book In BooksDataSet.tblBooks
     Into Sum
```

d.
```
Dim num As Integer =
     Aggregate book From BooksDataSet.tblBooks
     Into Counter
```

10. An application's BindingSource, BindingNavigator, DataSet, and table objects are named TblCustsBindingSource, TblCustsBindingNavigator, CustomersDataSet, and tblCusts, respectively. Which of the following assigns the value stored in the first record's City field to the `cityName` variable? (8)
    a. `cityName = TblCustsBindingNavigator.tblCusts(0).City`
    b. `cityName = tblCusts(0).City`
    c. `cityName = TblCustsBindingSource.City(0)`
    d. `cityName = CustomersDataSet.tblCusts(0).City`

Each Exercise is associated with one or more objectives listed at the beginning of the chapter.

Exercises

Pencil and Paper

INTRODUCTORY

1. Write a statement that assigns the location of a dataset's record pointer to an Integer variable named `recNum`. The BindingSource object's name is TblCityBindingSource. (7)

INTRODUCTORY

2. Write a statement that moves the record pointer to the last record in the dataset. The BindingSource object's name is TblCityBindingSource. (7)

INTRODUCTORY

3. The tblBooks table contains five fields. The BookNum, Price, and QuantityInStock fields are numeric; the Title and Author fields contain text. The dataset's name is BooksDataSet. (9)
    a. Write a LINQ statement that arranges the records in ascending order by the Author field.
    b. Write a LINQ statement that selects records having a price of at least $12.75.
    c. Write a LINQ statement that selects records having more than 100 books in inventory.
    d. Write a LINQ statement that selects the books written by George Marten and arranges them in descending order by the book's price.

INTERMEDIATE

4. Using the information from Pencil and Paper Exercise 3, write a LINQ statement that selects books whose name begins with the letter T (in either uppercase or lowercase). Also write a LINQ statement that calculates the total number of books in the store's inventory. (9, 11)

Computer

MODIFY THIS

5. Open the Adalene Solution (Adalene Solution.sln) file contained in the VbReloaded2015\Chap12\Adalene Solution-Labels folder. Modify the nextButton_Click and previousButton_Click procedures to use the Position property rather than the MoveNext and MovePrevious methods. Save the solution and then start and test the application. Close the solution. (4, 7)

6. If necessary, complete the Trivia Game application from this chapter's Programming Tutorial 1, and then close the solution. Use Windows to make a copy of the Trivia Solution folder. Rename the folder Trivia Solution-ModifyThis. Open the solution file contained in the Trivia Solution-ModifyThis folder. Display the question number (from 1 through 9) along with the word "Question" in a label control in the interface. Add another button to the interface. The button should allow the user to start a new game. Allow the user to click the New Game button only after he or she has answered all nine questions. Save the solution and then start and test the application. Close the solution. (2–4, 7, 9)

MODIFY THIS

7. Open the Adalene Solution (Adalene Solution.sln) file contained in the VbReloaded2015\Chap12\Adalene Solution-ListBox folder. Unlock the controls and then delete the numberLabel control from the form. Also delete the Previous Record and Next Record buttons and their Click event procedures. Add a list box to the form. Set the list box's Name, DataSource, and DisplayMember properties to numberListBox, TblStoresBindingSource, and StoreNum, respectively. Lock the controls and then reset the tab order. Save the solution and then start and test the application. Close the solution. (4)

MODIFY THIS

8. Open the Adalene Solution (Adalene Solution.sln) file contained in the VbReloaded2015\Chap12\Adalene Solution-DropDownButton folder. (9–11)

MODIFY THIS

   a. Add a DropDownButton to the BindingNavigator control. Change the DropDownButton's Name, DisplayStyle, and Text properties to ownerDropDownButton, Text, and &Owner, respectively.

   b. Use the DropDownItems property to add two menu items to the DropDownButton's menu: Company-Owned and Franchisee. Be sure to change each menu item's name as well as its DisplayStyle and Text properties. The Company-Owned menu item should display (in a message box) the number of company-owned stores. The Franchisee menu item should display (in a message box) the number of franchisees. Code each menu item's Click event procedure. Save the solution and then start and test the application. Close the solution.

9. If necessary, complete the Games Galore application from this chapter's Programming Tutorial 2, and then close the solution. Use Windows to make a copy of the Games Solution folder. Rename the copy Games Solution-Rating. Open the solution file contained in the Games Solution-Rating folder. Add a DropDownButton to the TblGamesBindingNavigator. The DropDownButton should allow the user to display only the games for a specific rating: M, E10+, T, or E. The ratings are stored in the Rating field. (The M, E10+, T, and E stand for Mature, Everyone 10 and over, Teen, and Everyone, respectively.) Save the solution and then start and test the application. Close the solution. (9–11)

MODIFY THIS

10. If necessary, complete the Games Galore application from this chapter's Programming Tutorial 2, and then close the solution. Use Windows to make a copy of the Games Solution folder. Rename the copy Games Solution-NewUsed. Open the solution file contained in the Games Solution-NewUsed folder. Add a DropDownButton to the TblGamesBindingNavigator. The DropDownButton should allow the user to display either new games or used games. The game's status (new or used) is stored in its NewUsed field. Save the solution and then start and test the application. Close the solution. (9–11)

MODIFY THIS

MODIFY THIS

11. If necessary, complete the Games Galore application from this chapter's Programming Tutorial 2, and then close the solution. Use Windows to make a copy of the Games Solution folder. Rename the copy Games Solution-TotalGames. Open the solution file contained in the Games Solution-TotalGames folder. Add a button to the TblGamesBindingNavigator. The button should display three values in a message box: the number of new games available for sale, the number of used games available for sale, and the total number of games available for sale. The quantity of each game is stored in its Quantity field. Save the solution and then start and test the application. Close the solution. (9–11)

INTRODUCTORY

12. Diamond Spa records the ID, name, and price of each of its services in a database named Services. The Services database, which is stored in the VbReloaded2015\Chap12\Access Databases\Services.accdb file, contains a table named tblServices. Open the Diamond Solution (Diamond Solution.sln) file contained in the VbReloaded2015\Chap12\Diamond Solution-DataGridView folder. Connect the application to the Services database. Change the database file's Copy to Output Directory property to Copy if newer. Bind the table to a DataGridView control, and then make the necessary modifications to the control. Enter the Try...Catch statement in the Save Data button's Click event procedure; include appropriate messages. Save the solution and then start and test the application. Close the solution. (2–6)

INTRODUCTORY

13. Diamond Spa records the ID, name, and price of each of its services in a database named Services. The Services database, which is stored in the VbReloaded2015\Chap12\Access Databases\Services.accdb file, contains a table named tblServices. Open the Diamond Solution (Diamond Solution.sln) file contained in the VbReloaded2015\Chap12\Diamond Solution-Labels folder. Connect the application to the Services database. Bind the appropriate objects to the existing label controls. Code the nextButton_Click and previousButton_Click procedures. Save the solution and then start and test the application. Close the solution. (2–4, 7)

INTRODUCTORY

14. Open the MusicBox Solution (MusicBox Solution.sln) file contained in the VbReloaded2015\Chap12\MusicBox Solution-DataGridView folder. Connect the application to the MusicBox database. The database, which is stored in the VbReloaded2015\Chap12\Access Databases\MusicBox.accdb file, contains a table named tblBox. Change the database file's Copy to Output Directory property to Copy if newer. Bind the table to a DataGridView control, and then make the necessary modifications to the control. Enter the Try...Catch statement in the Save Data button's Click event procedure; include appropriate messages. Save the solution and then start and test the application. Close the solution. (2–6)

INTRODUCTORY

15. Open the MusicBox Solution (MusicBox Solution.sln) file contained in the VbReloaded2015\Chap12\MusicBox Solution-Labels folder. Connect the application to the MusicBox database. The database, which is stored in the VbReloaded2015\Chap12\Access Databases\MusicBox.accdb file, contains a table named tblBox. Bind the appropriate objects to the existing label controls. Code the nextButton_Click and previousButton_Click procedures. Save the solution and then start and test the application. Close the solution. (2–4, 7)

INTRODUCTORY

16. Open the Magazine Solution (Magazine Solution.sln) file contained in the VbReloaded2015\Chap12\Magazine Solution-Introductory folder. The application is connected to the Magazines database, which is stored in the Magazines.accdb file. The database contains a table named tblMagazine. The table's Cost field is numeric;

its Code and MagName fields contain text. Start the application to view the records contained in the dataset, and then stop the application. Open the Code Editor window. The codeButton_Click procedure should display the record whose Code field exactly matches the user's entry. The nameButton_Click procedure should display the records whose MagName field begins with the one or more characters entered by the user. The allButton_Click procedure should display all of the records. Code the procedures and then test the application appropriately. (9)

17. Open the Magazine Solution (Magazine Solution.sln) file contained in the VbReloaded2015\Chap12\Magazine Solution-Intermediate folder. The application is connected to the Magazines database, which is stored in the Magazines.accdb file. The database contains a table named tblMagazine. The table's Cost field is numeric; its Code and MagName fields contain text. Start the application to view the records contained in the dataset, and then stop the application. Open the Code Editor window. Code the allButton_Click procedure so that it displays all of the records. Code the costButton_Click procedure so that it displays records having a cost equal to or greater than the amount entered by the user. Code the avgButton_Click procedure so that it displays (in a message box) the average cost of a magazine. Save the solution and then start and test the application. Close the solution. (9, 11) INTERMEDIATE

18. Open the MusicBox Solution (MusicBox Solution.sln) file contained in the VbReloaded2015\Chap12\MusicBox Solution-LINQ folder. The application is connected to the MusicBox database, which is stored in the MusicBox.accdb file. The tblBox table in the database contains four text fields. Start the application to view the records contained in the dataset, and then stop the application. Open the Code Editor window. Code the allButton_Click procedure so that it displays all of the records. Code the shapeButton_Click procedure so that it displays the records for music boxes having the shape selected by the user. Code the sourceButton_Click procedure so that it displays the records for music boxes either received as gifts or purchased by the user. Code the countButton_Click procedure to display the number of music boxes in the dataset. Save the solution and then start and test the application. Close the solution. (9, 11) INTERMEDIATE

19. In this exercise, you use a Microsoft Access database named Trips. The database, which is stored in the VbReloaded2015\Chap12\Access Databases folder, keeps track of a person's business and pleasure trips. The database contains one table named tblTrips. Each record has the following four text fields: TripDate, Origin, Destination, and BusinessPleasure. The user should be able to display the number of trips from a specific origin to a specific destination, such as from Chicago to Atlanta. He or she should also be able to display the total number of business trips and the total number of pleasure trips. (7, 9) INTERMEDIATE

    a. Create a Windows Forms application. Use the following names for the solution and project, respectively: Trips Solution and Trips Project. Save the application in the VbReloaded2015\Chap12 folder. Change the form file's name to Main Form.vb.

    b. Connect the application to the Trips database and then drag the tblTrips object to the form. Make the appropriate modifications to the DataGridView control. The user should not be able to add, edit, delete, or save records.

c. Open the Code Editor window and code the application. (Hint: You can use a logical operator in the Where clause.) Use the application to answer the following questions:

How many trips were made from Chicago to Nashville?
How many trips were made from Atlanta to Los Angeles?
How many business trips were taken?
How many pleasure trips were taken?

d. Close the solution.

SWAT THE BUGS

20. Open the Debug Solution (Debug Solution.sln) file contained in the VbReloaded2015\Chap12\Debug Solution folder. The application is connected to the Friends database stored in the Friends.accdb file. The database contains one table named tblFriends. The table contains nine records. Open the Code Editor window and review the existing code. Correct the code to remove the jagged line that appears below one of the lines of code. Save the solution and then start and test the application. Click the Fill button and then click the Next and Previous buttons. Notice that the application is not working correctly. Correct the application's code. When the application is working correctly, close the solution. (7)

Case Projects

Modified Trivia Game

If necessary, complete the Trivia Game application from this chapter's Programming Tutorial 1, and then close the solution. Use Windows to make a copy of the Trivia Solution folder. Rename the folder Trivia Solution-Case Project. Open the Trivia Solution (Trivia Solution.sln) file contained in the Trivia Solution-Case Project folder. Modify the application to allow the user to answer the questions in any order and also to change his or her answers. (You can modify the interface to include additional buttons.) The modified application should display the number of incorrect answers only when the user requests that information. Make the appropriate modifications to the code. Save the solution and then start and test the application. Close the solution. (2–4, 7, 8)

College Courses

In this Case Project, you use a Microsoft Access database named Courses. The database is stored in the VbReloaded2015\Chap12\Access Databases\Courses.accdb file. The database contains one table named tblCourses. Each record has the following four fields: ID, Title, CreditHours, and Grade. The CreditHours field is numeric; the other fields contain text. Create an application that allows the user to display the records for a specific grade (A, B, C, D, or F). The user should also be able to display all of the records. Display the records in a DataGridView control. The application should not allow the user to add, edit, delete, or save records. Include a Calculate GPA button on the BindingNavigator control. The button's Click event procedure should display the student's GPA. An A grade is worth 4 points, a B is worth 3 points, and so on. Use the following names for the solution and project, respectively: College Courses Solution and College Courses Project. Save the application in the VbReloaded2015\Chap12 folder. Change the form file's name to Main Form.vb. (2–11)

Political Awareness Organization

During July and August of each year, the Political Awareness Organization (PAO) sends a questionnaire to the voters in its district. The questionnaire asks the voter for his or her political party (Democratic, Republican, or Independent) and age. From the returned questionnaires, the organization's secretary tabulates the number of Democrats, Republicans, and Independents in the district. The secretary wants an application that she can use to save each respondent's information (political party and age) in a database named PAO. The PAO database is stored in the VbReloaded2015\Chap12\Access Databases\PAO.accdb file. The database contains one table named tblQuestionnaire. Each record has a text field named Party and two numeric fields named Id and Age. The application should also allow the secretary to edit and delete records as well as to calculate and display the number of voters in each political party. Use a DataGridView control in the interface. Use the following names for the solution and project, respectively: PAO Solution and PAO Project. Save the application in the VbReloaded2015\Chap12 folder. Change the form file's name to Main Form.vb. (2–6, 9, 11)

The Fiction Bookstore

Jerry Schmidt, the manager of the Fiction Bookstore, uses a Microsoft Access database named Books to keep track of the books in his store. The database is stored in the VbReloaded2015\Chap12\Access Databases\Books.accdb file. The database has one table named tblBooks. The table has five fields. The BookNumber, Price, and QuantityInStock fields are numeric. The Title and Author fields contain text. Mr. Schmidt wants an application that he can use to enter an author's name (or part of a name) and then display only the titles of books written by the author. Display the information in a DataGridView control; however, don't allow the user to add, delete, edit, or save records. In this application, you need to allow the user to specify the records he or she wants to select while the application is running. Add a text box and a button to the BindingNavigator control. Mr. Schmidt will use the text box to specify the records he wants to select. He will use the button to tell the computer to display the selected records. Mr. Schmidt also wants to display the total value of the books in his store. Use the following names for the solution and project, respectively: Fiction Bookstore Solution and Fiction Bookstore Project. Save the application in the VbReloaded2015\Chap12 folder. Change the form file's name to Main Form.vb. (2–6, 9–11)

Counting Calories

In this Case Project, you use a Microsoft Access database named Calories. The database is stored in the VbReloaded2015\Chap12\Access Databases\Calories.accdb file. The database contains one table named tblCalories. Each record has the following six fields: Day, Breakfast, Lunch, Dinner, Dessert, and Snack. The Day field contains text; the other fields are numeric. Create an application that allows the user to display the total number of calories consumed in the entire dataset. The user should also be able to add, delete, and edit records, as well as to display the total calories consumed for a specific meal, such as the total calories consumed for breakfasts, lunches, dinners, desserts, or snacks. In addition, the user should be able to display the total calories consumed on a specific day, the number of days in which more than 1,200 calories were consumed, and the average number of calories consumed per day. Use the following names for the solution and project, respectively: Calorie Counter Solution and Calorie Counter Project. Save the application in the VbReloaded2015\Chap12 folder. Change the form file's name to Main Form.vb. Use the application to answer the questions listed below. (2–6, 9, 11)

How many calories were consumed in the entire dataset?
How many calories were consumed for desserts?
How many calories were consumed on 12/21/2017?
On how many days were more than 1,200 calories consumed?
What is the average number of calories consumed per day?

CHAPTER 13

Creating Simple Web Applications

After studying Chapter 13, you should be able to:

1. Define basic Web terminology
2. Create a Web Site application
3. Add Web pages to an application
4. Customize a Web page
5. Code a control on a Web page
6. Start a Web application
7. Close and open a Web application
8. Use hyperlink and image controls (Programming Tutorial 1)
9. Add a table to a Web page (Programming Tutorial 2)
10. Use label, text box, button, and validator controls (Programming Tutorial 2)

Web Site Applications

The Internet is the world's largest computer network, connecting millions of computers located all around the world. One of the most popular features of the Internet is the World Wide Web, often referred to simply as the Web. The Web consists of documents called **Web pages** that are stored on Web servers. A **Web server** is a computer that contains special software that "serves up" Web pages in response to requests from client computers. A **client computer** is a computer that requests information from a Web server. The information is requested and subsequently viewed through the use of a program called a Web browser or, more simply, a **browser**. Currently, the most popular browsers are Google Chrome, Mozilla Firefox, and Microsoft Internet Explorer.

Many Web pages are static. A **static Web page** is a document whose purpose is merely to display information to the viewer. Static Web pages are not interactive. The only interaction that can occur between static Web pages and the viewer is through links that allow the viewer to "jump" from one Web page to another.

Figures 13-1 and 13-2 show examples of static Web pages created for The Fishbowl Emporium. The Web page in Figure 13-1 shows the store's name, address, and telephone number. The page also provides a link to the Web page shown in Figure 13-2. That page shows the store's business hours and provides a link for returning to the first Web page. You will create both Web pages in Programming Tutorial 1.

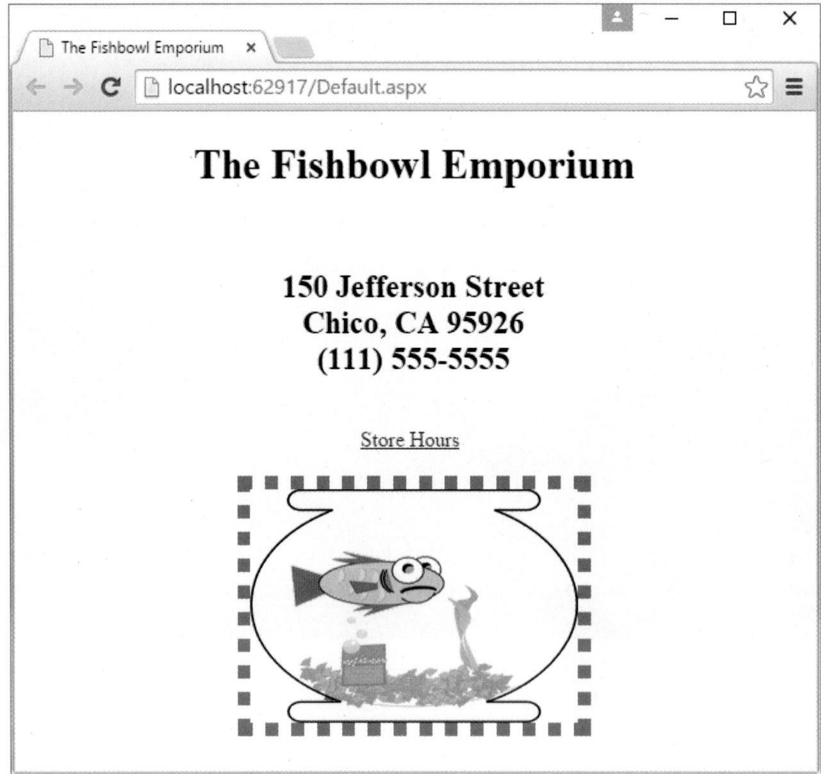

Figure 13-1 Example of a static Web page displayed using Google Chrome

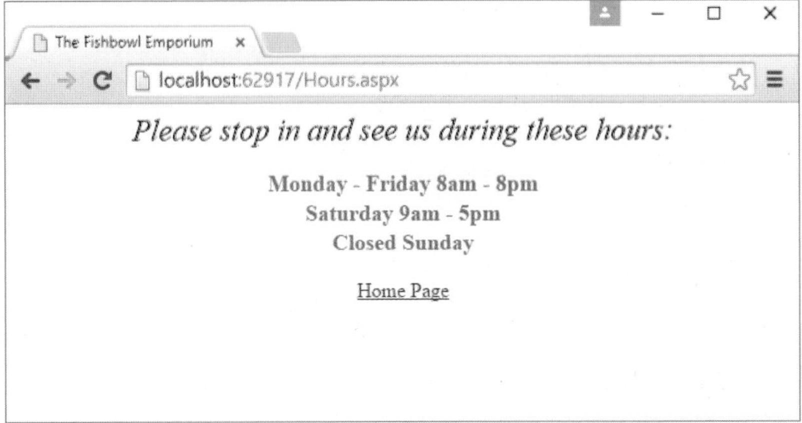

Figure 13-2 Another example of a static Web page displayed using Google Chrome

Although static Web pages provide a means for a store to list its location and hours, a company wanting to do business on the Web must be able to do more than just list information: It must be able to interact with customers through its Web site. The Web site should allow customers to submit inquiries, select items for purchase, and submit payment information. It should also allow the company to track customer inquiries and process customer orders. Tasks such as these can be accomplished using dynamic Web pages.

Unlike a static Web page, a **dynamic Web page** is interactive in that it can accept information from the user and also retrieve information for the user. Examples of dynamic Web pages include forms for purchasing merchandise online and for submitting online résumés. Figure 13-3 shows an example of a dynamic Web page that calculates the number of gallons of water a rectangular aquarium holds. To use the Web page, you enter the length, width, and height of the aquarium and then click the Submit button. The button's Click event procedure displays the corresponding number of gallons on the Web page. You will create the Aquarium Calculator Web page in Programming Tutorial 2.

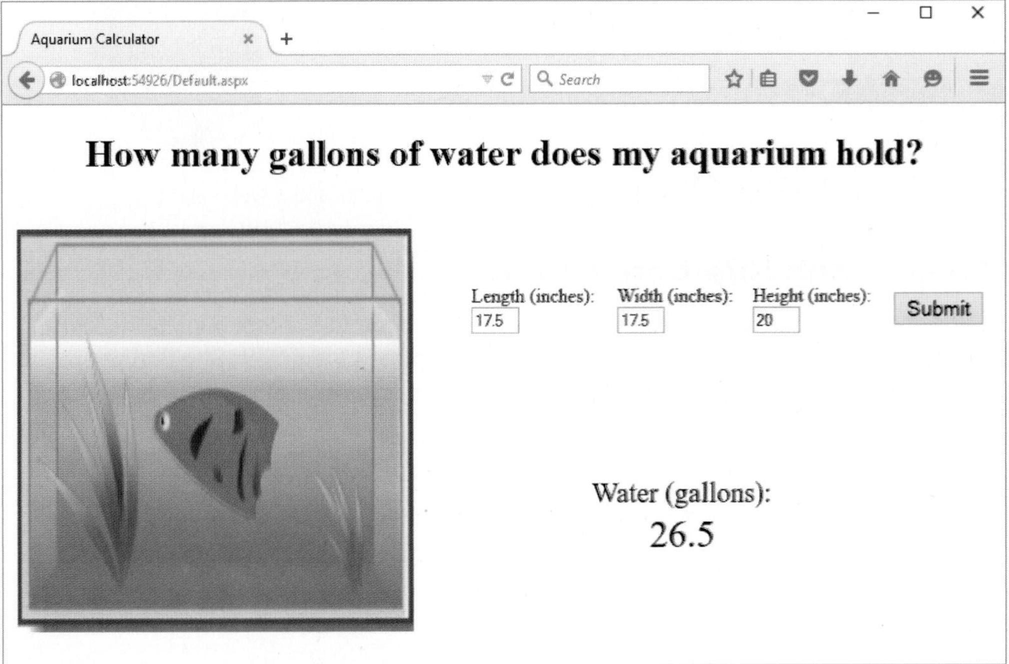

Figure 13-3 Example of a dynamic Web page displayed using Mozilla Firefox

The Web applications created in this chapter use a technology called ASP.NET 5. **ASP** stands for "active server page" and refers to the type of Web page created by the ASP technology. All ASP pages contain HTML (Hypertext Markup Language) tags that tell the client's browser how to render the page on the computer screen. For example, the instruction <h1>Hello</h1> uses the opening <h1> tag and its closing </h1> tag to display the word "Hello" as a heading on the Web page. Many ASP pages also contain ASP tags that specify the controls to include on the Web page. In addition to the HTML and ASP tags, dynamic ASP pages contain code that tells the objects on the Web page how to respond to the user's actions. In this chapter, you will write the appropriate code using the Visual Basic programming language.

When a client computer's browser sends a request for an ASP page, the Web server locates the page and then sends the appropriate HTML instructions to the client. The client's browser uses the instructions to render the Web page on the computer screen. If the Web page is a dynamic one, like the Aquarium Calculator page shown in Figure 13-3, the user can interact with the page by entering data. In most cases, the user then clicks a button on the Web page to submit the page and data to the server for processing. Using Web terminology, the information is "posted back" to the server for processing; this event is referred to as a **postback**.

When the server receives the information from the client computer, it executes the Visual Basic code associated with the Web page. It then sends back the appropriate HTML, which now includes the result of processing the code and data, to the client for rendering in the browser window. Notice that the Web page's HTML is interpreted and executed by the client computer, whereas the program code is executed by the Web server. Figure 13-4 illustrates the relationship between the client computer and the Web server.

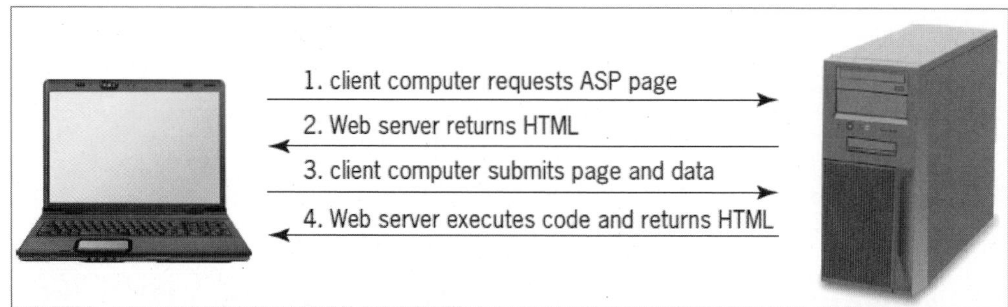
1. client computer requests ASP page
2. Web server returns HTML
3. client computer submits page and data
4. Web server executes code and returns HTML

Figure 13-4 Illustration of the relationship between a client computer and a Web server

Creating a Web Site Application

Figure 13-5 lists the steps for creating an empty Web Site application using Visual Studio Community 2015. It also includes an example of a completed New Web Site dialog box. (Your dialog box may look slightly different if you are using a different edition of Visual Studio.)

HOW TO Create an Empty Web Site Application

1. Start Visual Studio Community 2015.
2. Click File on the menu bar, and then click New Web Site to open the New Web Site dialog box. If necessary, click Visual Basic in the Installed Templates list. Click ASP.NET Empty Web Site in the middle column of the dialog box.
3. If necessary, change the entry in the Web location box to File System. The File System selection allows you to store your Web application in any folder on either your computer or a network drive.
4. In the box that appears next to the Web location box, enter the location where you want the Web application saved. (See figure below.)
5. Click the OK button to close the New Web Site dialog box.

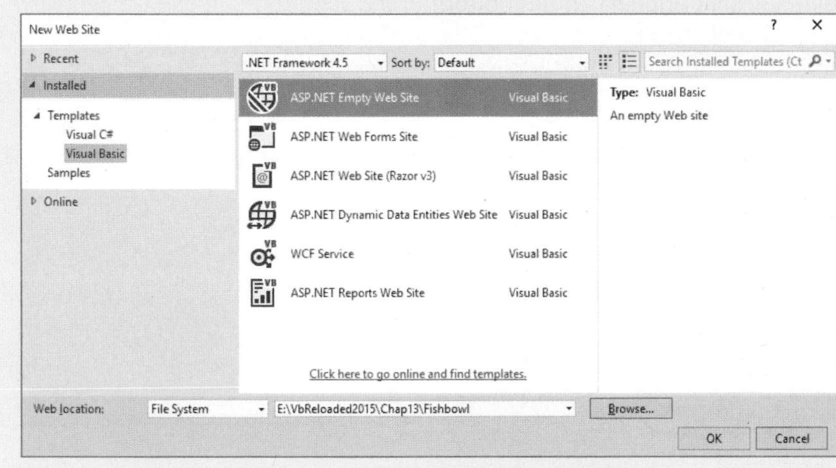

Figure 13-5 How to create an empty Web Site application

Adding a Web Page to an Application

After creating an empty Web application, you need to add a Web page to it. The first Web page added to an application is usually named Default.aspx. The .aspx file contains the instructions for rendering the visual elements on the Web page. Figure 13-6 lists the steps for adding a new Web page to an application. It also shows an example of a completed Add New Item dialog box as well as the Default.aspx Web page in Design view. (Your dialog box and screen may look slightly different if you are using a different edition of Visual Studio.)

HOW TO Add a New Web Page to an Application

1. If necessary, open the Web application. Click Website on the menu bar, and then click Add New Item to open the Add New Item dialog box. (If Website does not appear on the menu bar, click the Web application's name in the Solution Explorer window.)
2. If necessary, click Visual Basic in the Installed list. Click Web Form in the middle column of the dialog box. Verify that the Place code in separate file check box is selected, and that the Select master page check box is not selected. (See first figure below.)
3. If necessary, change the name in the Name box.
4. Click the Add button to display the Web page in the Document window. If necessary, click the Design tab that appears at the bottom of the IDE. You can use Design view to add text and controls to the Web page. (See second figure below.)
5. If you need to display the Formatting toolbar, click View on the menu bar, point to Toolbars, and then click Formatting.

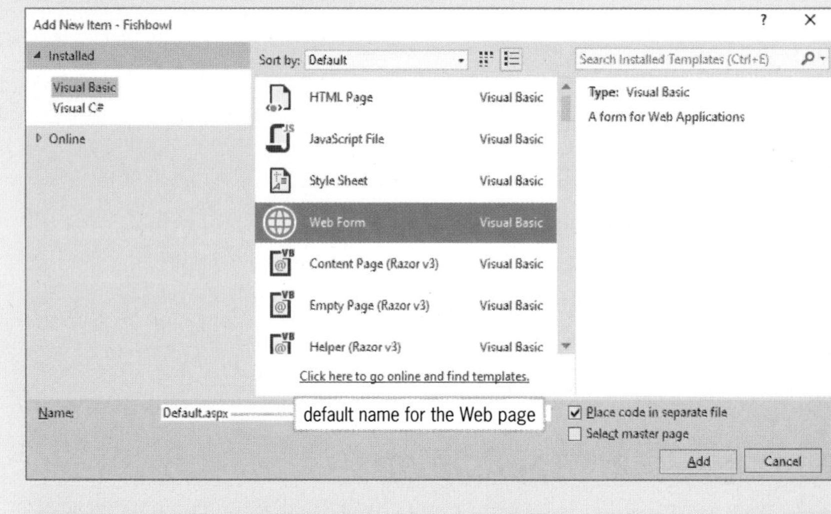

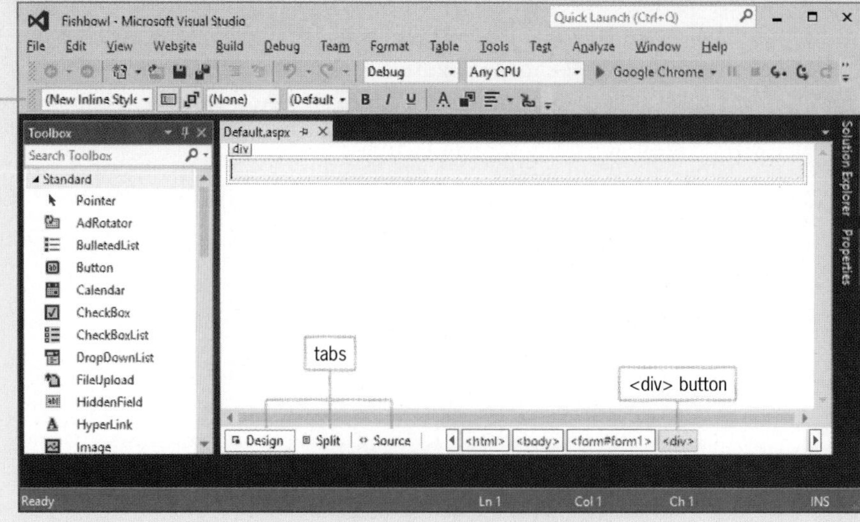

Figure 13-6 How to add a new Web page to an application

Figure 13-7 lists the steps for adding an existing Web page to an application.

HOW TO Add an Existing Web Page to an Application

1. If necessary, open the Web application. Click Website on the menu bar, and then click Add Existing Item to open the Add Existing Item dialog box. (If Website does not appear on the menu bar, click the Web application's name in the Solution Explorer window.)
2. Locate and then click the name of the file that contains the Web page. The filename will end with .aspx.
3. Click the Add button to display the Web page in the Document window. If necessary, click the Design tab that appears at the bottom of the IDE.

Figure 13-7 How to add an existing Web page to an application

Customizing a Web Page

Figure 13-8 shows different ways of customizing a Web page. As the figure indicates, you can add a title, controls, and text to a Web page. You can also format the **static text**, which is text that the user is not allowed to edit, and controls.

HOW TO Customize a Web Page

To add a title, which will appear on the page's tab in the browser window:
Click DOCUMENT in the Properties window's Object box, click Title in the Properties list, type the title, and then press Enter.

To add a control:
Use the tools provided in the Toolbox window. Like Windows controls, Web controls have properties that are listed in the Properties window. However, unlike Windows controls, Web controls have an ID property rather than a Name property.

To add static text, which is text the user cannot edit:
Either type the text directly on the Web page, or drag a label control from the toolbox to the Web page and then set the control's Text property.

To format the static text or controls:
Use either the Format menu or the Formatting toolbar (shown here). You can display the Formatting toolbar by clicking View on the menu bar, pointing to Toolbars, and then clicking Formatting.

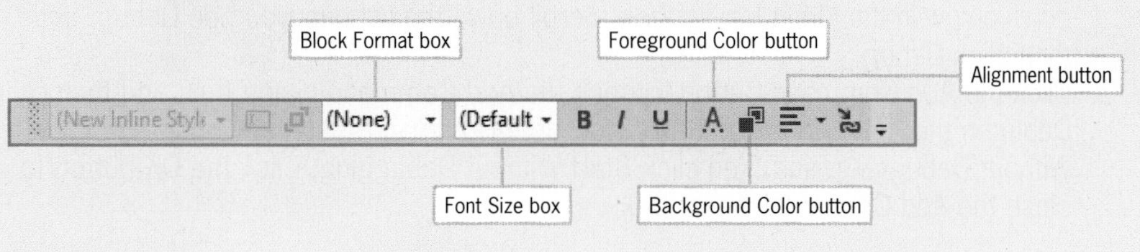

Figure 13-8 How to customize a Web page

Coding the Controls on a Web Page

Like the controls on a Windows form, the controls on a Web page can be coded to perform tasks when a specific event occurs. The submitButton_Click procedure shown in Figure 13-9, for example, will display the message "The Submit button was clicked." in the messageLabel when the user clicks the Submit button on the Web page. You enter the code in the Code Editor window. The code is saved in a file whose filename extension is .aspx.vb. The .aspx.vb extension indicates that the file contains the Visual Basic code for a Web page. The .aspx.vb file is commonly referred to as the code-behind file because it contains the code "behind" the Web page.

```
Protected Sub submitButton_Click(sender As Object, e As EventArgs
                                 ) Handles submitButton.Click
    messageLabel.Text = "The Submit button was clicked."
End Sub
```

Figure 13-9 Code entered in the submitButton_Click procedure

Starting a Web Application

Figure 13-10 shows the steps for starting a Web application. Notice that you can use either the Ctrl+F5 shortcut keys or the Start Without Debugging option on the Debug menu. However, if you want to use the menu option, you might need to add it to the menu because it is not automatically included on the menu. You can add the option to the menu by performing the steps listed in Figure 13-11.

HOW TO Start a Web Application

1. Use the browser box on the Standard toolbar to select the appropriate browser.
2. Either press Ctrl+F5 or click the Start Without Debugging option on the Debug menu. (If necessary, use the steps listed in Figure 13-11 to add the option to the menu.)

Figure 13-10 How to start a Web application

HOW TO Add the Start Without Debugging Option to the Debug Menu

1. Click Tools on the menu bar, and then click Customize to open the Customize dialog box.
2. Click the Commands tab. The Menu bar radio button should be selected. Click the down arrow in the Menu bar list box. Scroll down the list until you see Debug, and then click Debug.
3. Click the Add Command button to open the Add Command dialog box, and then click Debug in the Categories list. Scroll down the Commands list until you see Start Without Debugging, and then click Start Without Debugging. Click the OK button to close the Add Command dialog box.

Figure 13-11 How to add the Start Without Debugging option to the Debug menu *(continues)*

(continued)

4. Click the Move Down button until the Start Without Debugging option appears below the Start / Continue option.
5. Click the Close button to close the Customize dialog box.

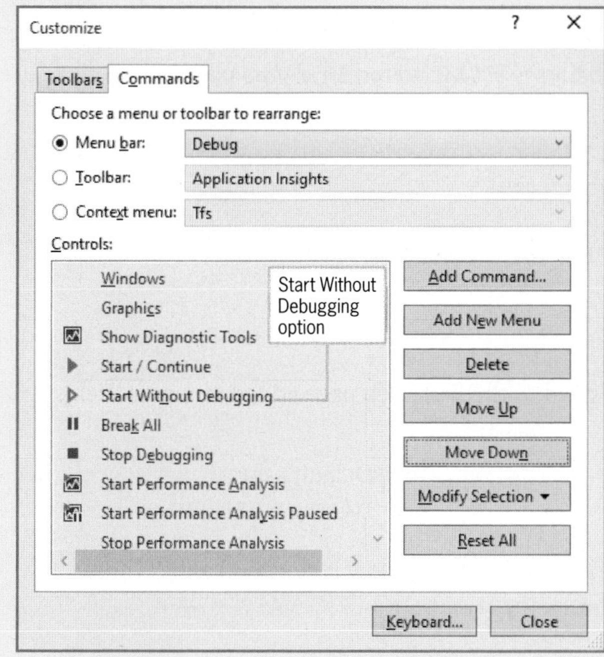

Figure 13-11 How to add the Start Without Debugging option to the Debug menu

Closing and Opening an Existing Web Application

You can use the File menu to close and also open an existing Web application. Figure 13-12 lists the steps for performing both tasks.

HOW TO Close and Open an Existing Web Application

<u>To close an existing Web application:</u>
Click File on the menu bar, and then click Close Solution.

<u>To open an existing Web application:</u>
1. Click File on the menu bar, and then click Open Web Site to open the Open Web Site dialog box. If necessary, click the File System button.
2. Click the name of the Web site, and then click the Open button.
3. If necessary, right-click the Web page's name in the Solution Explorer window and then click View Designer.

Figure 13-12 How to close and open an existing Web application

The answers to Mini-Quiz questions are located in Appendix A. Each question is associated with one or more objectives listed at the beginning of the chapter.

Mini-Quiz 13-1

1. A computer that requests an ASP page from a Web server is called a ____________ computer. (1)
   a. browser
   b. client
   c. requesting
   d. none of the above
2. A ____________ is a program that uses HTML to render a Web page on the computer screen. (1)
   a. browser
   b. client
   c. server
   d. none of the above
3. A Web page's HTML instructions are processed by the ____________. (1)
   a. client computer
   b. Web server
4. What name is automatically assigned to the first Web page added to a new Web site project? (3)
   a. Form1.aspx
   b. Default.vb
   c. Default.aspx
   d. WebForm1.vb
5. The code entered in a Web page's Code Editor window is stored in a file whose filename extension is ____________. (5)
   a. asp
   b. aspx
   c. aspx.vb
   d. vb.aspx

You have completed the concepts section of Chapter 13. The Programming Tutorial section is next.

PROGRAMMING TUTORIAL 1

Creating the Fishbowl Emporium Web Site Application

In this tutorial, you will create a Web Site application for The Fishbowl Emporium. The application contains the two Web pages shown earlier in Figures 13-1 and 13-2 in the chapter. The Web pages contain static text, an image control, and two hyperlink controls.

To create the Web Site application:

1. Start Visual Studio 2015. Open the Solution Explorer and Properties windows, and auto-hide the Toolbox window.
2. Click **File** on the menu bar and then click **New Web Site** to open the New Web Site dialog box. If necessary, click **Visual Basic** in the Installed Templates list. Click **ASP.NET Empty Web Site** in the middle column of the dialog box.
3. If necessary, change the entry in the Web location box to **File System**. The File System selection allows you to store your Web application in any folder on either your computer or a network drive.

4. In this step, you will be instructed to store the Web application in the VbReloaded2015\Chap13 folder on the E drive. However, you should use the letter for the drive where your data is stored, which might not be the E drive. In the box that appears next to the Web location box, replace the existing text with **E:\VbReloaded2015\Chap13\Fishbowl**. See Figure 13-13.

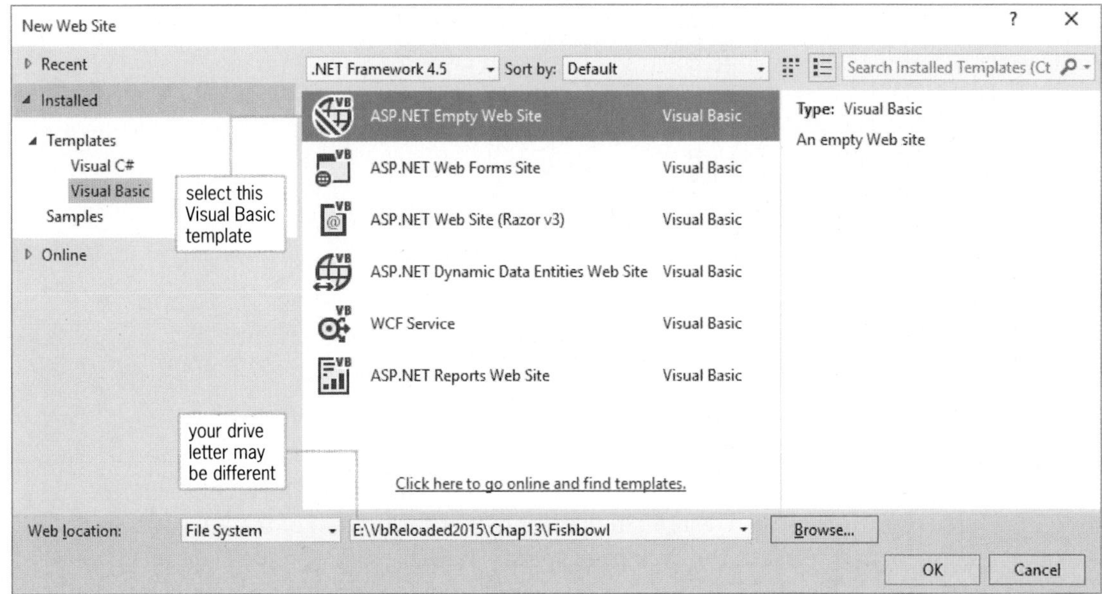

Figure 13-13 New Web Site dialog box

5. Click the **OK** button to close the dialog box. The computer creates an empty Web application named Fishbowl.

Adding a Web Page to the Project

After creating an empty Web application, you need to add a Web page to it.

To add a Web page to the application:

1. Click **Website** on the menu bar, and then click **Add New Item** to open the Add New Item dialog box. (If Website does not appear on the menu bar, click the Web application's name—in this case, Fishbowl—in the Solution Explorer window.)
2. If necessary, click **Visual Basic** in the Installed list. Click **Web Form** in the middle column of the dialog box. Verify that the Place code in separate file check box is selected and that the Select master page check box is not selected. As indicated in Figure 13-14, the Web page will be named Default.aspx.

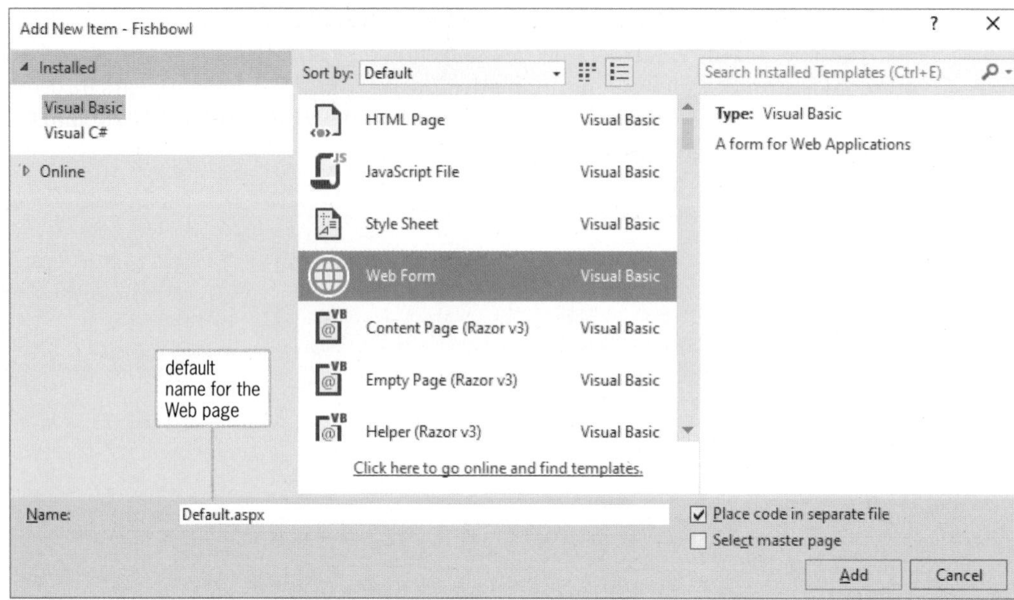

Figure 13-14 Add New Item dialog box

3. Click the **Add** button to display the Default.aspx page in the Document window. If necessary, click the **Design** tab that appears at the bottom of the IDE. When the Design tab is selected, the Web page appears in Design view in the Document window, as shown in Figure 13-15. You can use Design view to add text and controls to the Web page. If the div tag does not appear in the Document window, click the **<div>** button at the bottom of the IDE. If the Formatting toolbar does not appear on your screen, click **View** on the menu bar, point to **Toolbars**, and then click **Formatting**.

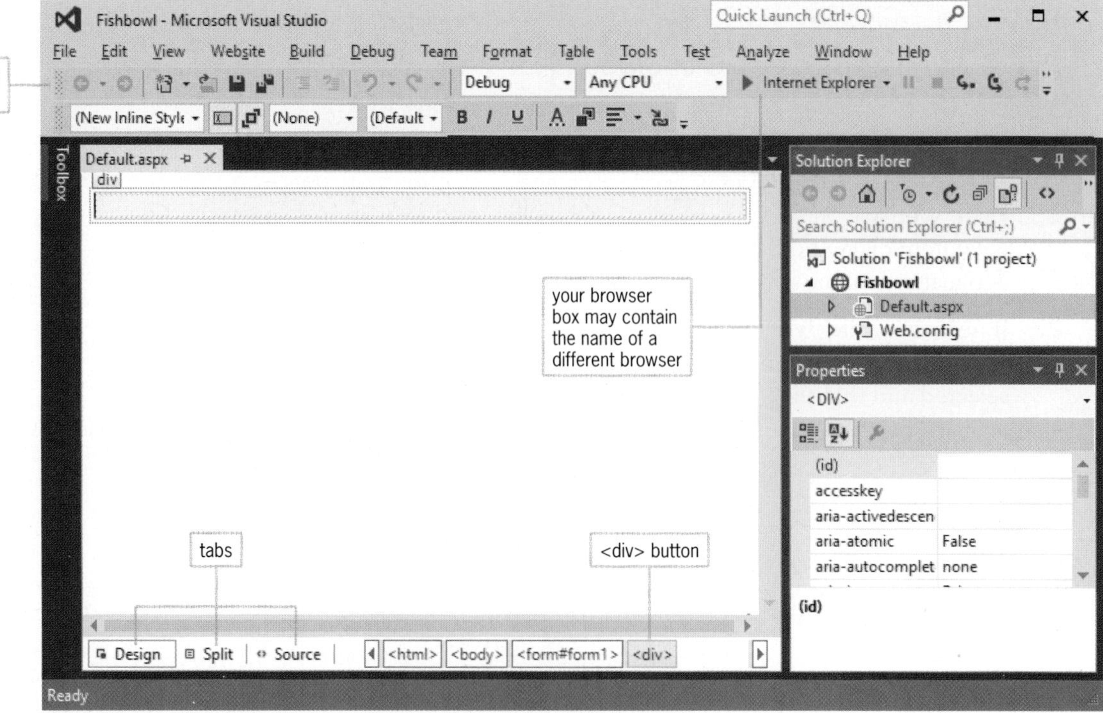

Figure 13-15 Default.aspx Web page shown in Design view

PROGRAMMING TUTORIAL 1

4. Click the **Source** tab to display the Web page in Source view. This view shows the HTML and ASP tags that tell a browser how to render the Web page. The tags are automatically generated as you are creating the Web page in Design view. Currently, the Web page contains only HTML tags.
5. Click the **Split** tab to split the Document window into two parts. The upper half displays the Web page in Source view, and the lower half displays it in Design view.
6. Click the **Design** tab to return to Design view, and then auto-hide the Solution Explorer window.

Adding a Title to the Web Page

In the following set of steps, you will change the Web page's Title property to The Fishbowl Emporium. When a Web page is displayed in a browser, the value stored in its Title property appears on the page's tab in the browser window.

To change the Title property:

1. Click the **down arrow** button in the Properties window's Object box, and then click **DOCUMENT** in the list. (If DOCUMENT does not appear in the Object box, click the Design tab.) The DOCUMENT object represents the Web page.
2. If necessary, click the **Alphabetical** button in the Properties window to display the properties in alphabetical order. Click **Title** in the Properties list. Type **The Fishbowl Emporium** in the Settings box, and then press **Enter**.
3. Auto-hide the Properties window. Save the application by clicking either the **Save All** button on the Standard toolbar or the **Save All** option on the File menu.

Customizing a Web Page

In the following set of steps, you will add static text to the Web page and then use the Formatting toolbar to format the text. Recall that static text is text that the user is not allowed to edit.

To add static text to the Web page:

1. If necessary, click **inside the rectangle** that appears below the div tag at the top of the Document window. The div tag defines a division in a Web page. (If the div tag does not appear in the Document window, click the <div> button at the bottom of the IDE.)
2. Enter the following four lines of text. Press **Enter** twice after typing the last line.

   The Fishbowl Emporium
   150 Jefferson Street
   Chico, CA 95926
   (111) 555-5555
3. Select (highlight) the first line of text on the Web page. Click the **down arrow** in the Block Format box on the Formatting toolbar. See Figure 13-16.

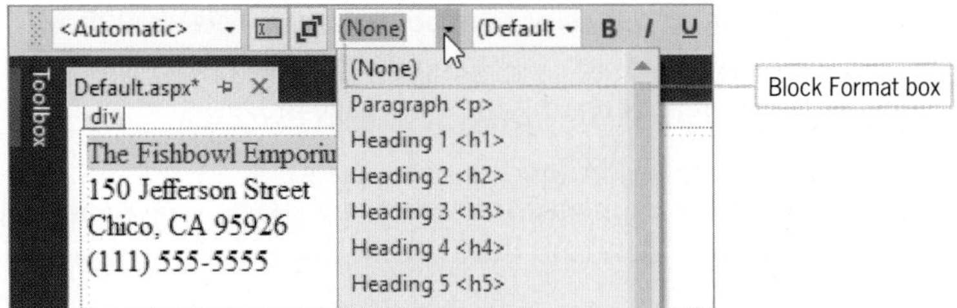

Figure 13-16 Result of clicking the arrow in the Block Format box

4. Click **Heading 1 <h1>**.
5. Select the address and phone number text on the Web page. Click the **down arrow** in the Block Format box and then click **Heading 2 <h2>**.
6. Next, you will use the Formatting toolbar's Alignment button to center the static text. Select all of the static text on the Web page, and then click the **down arrow** on the Alignment button. See Figure 13-17.

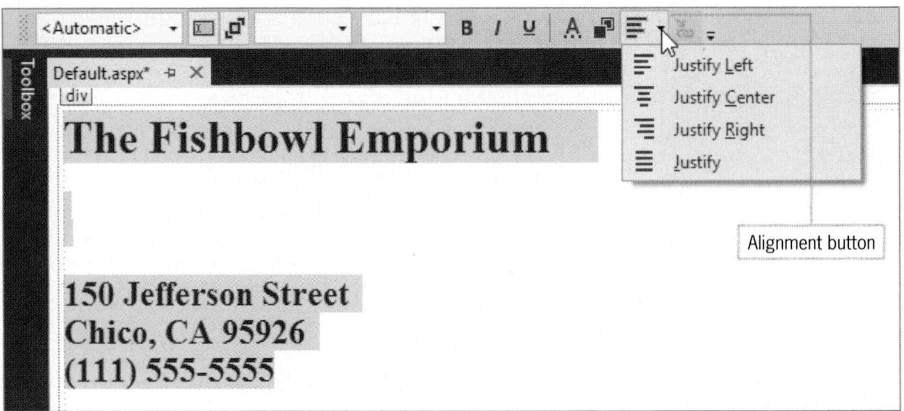

Figure 13-17 Result of clicking the arrow on the Alignment button

7. Click **Justify Center**. The selected text appears centered horizontally on the Web page. Click **anywhere below the phone number** to deselect the text, and then save the application.

Adding Another Web Page to the Application

In the next set of steps, you will add a second Web page to the application. The Web page will display the store's hours of operation.

To add another Web page to the application:

1. Click **Website** on the menu bar, and then click **Add New Item**. (If Website does not appear on the menu bar, click Fishbowl in the Solution Explorer window.)
2. If necessary, click **Visual Basic** in the Installed list. Click **Web Form** in the middle column of the dialog box. Change the filename in the Name box to **Hours** and then click the **Add** button. The computer appends the .aspx extension to the filename and then displays the Hours.aspx Web page in the Document window.

3. Temporarily display the Solution Explorer window. Notice that the window now contains the Hours.aspx filename.
4. Click the **Hours.aspx** tab, and then temporarily display the Properties window. Click the **down arrow** button in the Properties window's Object box, and then click **DOCUMENT** in the list. Change the Web page's Title property to **The Fishbowl Emporium**.
5. Click the **Hours.aspx** tab. The blinking insertion point should be inside the rectangle that appears below the div tab. (If the div tag does not appear in the Document window, click the <div> button at the bottom of the IDE.) Type **Please stop in and see us during these hours:** and then press **Enter** twice.
6. Enter the following three lines of text. Press **Enter** twice after typing the last line.

   Monday – Friday 8am – 8pm
   Saturday 9am – 5pm
   Closed Sunday
7. Select the first line of text on the Web page. Click the **down arrow** in the Font Size box on the Formatting toolbar, and then click **x-large (24pt)**. Also click the ***I*** (Italic) button on the toolbar.
8. Select the three lines of text that contain the store hours. Click the **down arrow** in the Font Size box and then click **large (18pt)**. Also click the **B** (Bold) button.
9. Next, you will change the color of the selected text. Click the **Foreground Color** button on the Formatting toolbar to open the More Colors dialog box. Click **any red hexagon** and then click the **OK** button.
10. Select all of the static text on the Web page. Click the **down arrow** on the Alignment button, and then click **Justify Center**.
11. Click the **second blank line** below the store hours to deselect the text, and then save the application.

Adding a Hyperlink Control to a Web Page

In the next set of steps, you will add a hyperlink control to both Web pages. Each **hyperlink control** will allow the user to "jump" from one page to another. The hyperlink control on the Default.aspx page will display the Hours.aspx page. The hyperlink control on the Hours.aspx page will return the user to the Default.aspx page.

To add a hyperlink control to both Web pages:

1. First, you will add a hyperlink control to the Hours.aspx page. Permanently display the Toolbox window. Expand the **Standard** node (if necessary) and then click the **Hyperlink** tool. Drag your mouse pointer to the location shown in Figure 13-18, and then release the mouse button.

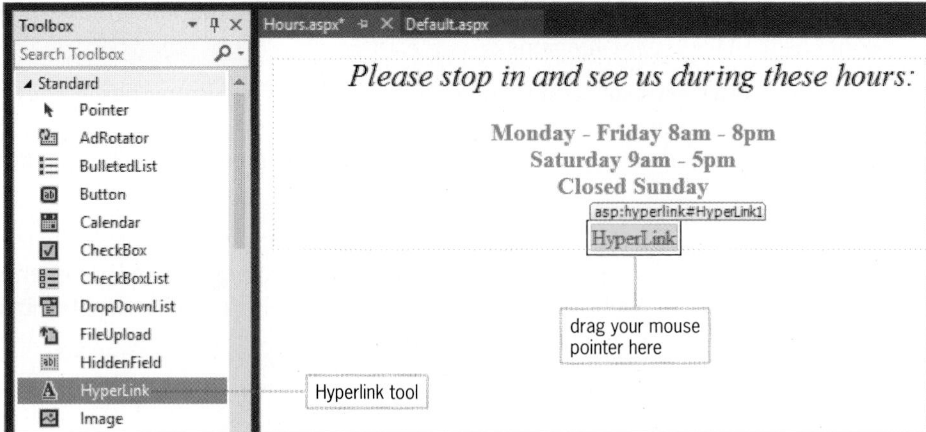

Figure 13-18 Hyperlink control added to the Hours.aspx page

2. Temporarily display the Properties window. Change the control's Text property to **Home Page**. Click **NavigateUrl** in the Properties list, and then click the **...** (ellipsis) button to open the Select URL dialog box. Click **Default.aspx** in the Contents of folder list. See Figure 13-19.

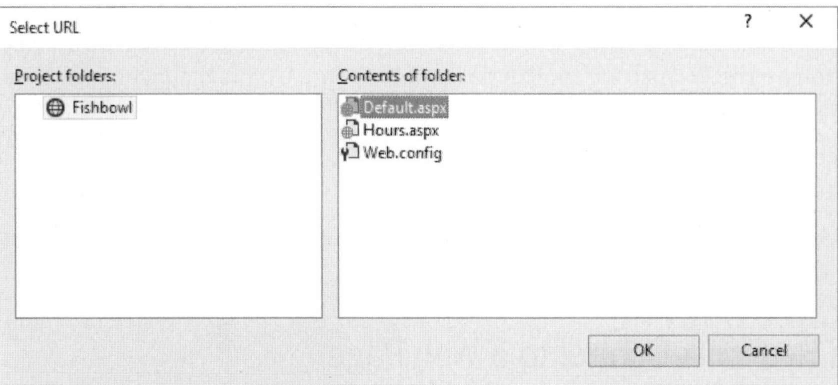

Figure 13-19 Select URL dialog box

3. Click the **OK** button to close the dialog box, and then click the **Hours.aspx** tab.
4. Next, you will add a hyperlink control to the Default.aspx page. Click the **Default.aspx** tab. Click the **Hyperlink** tool. Drag your mouse pointer to the location shown in Figure 13-20, and then release the mouse pointer.

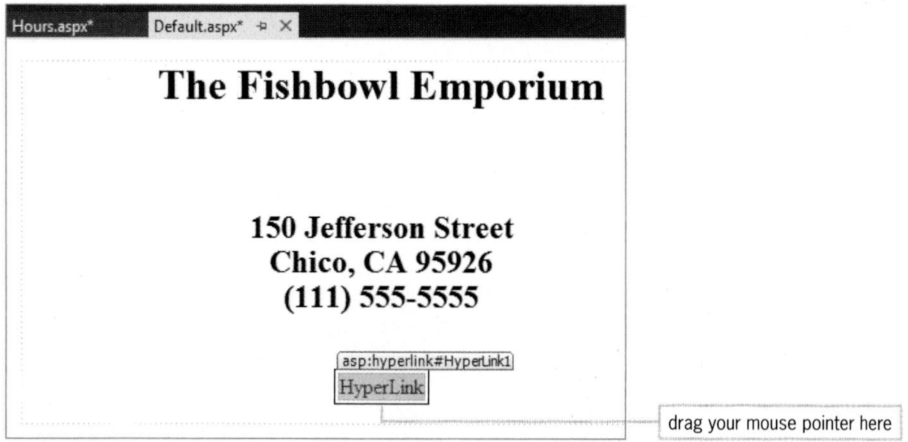

Figure 13-20 Hyperlink control added to the Default.aspx page

5. Temporarily display the Properties window. Change the control's Text property to **Store Hours** and then change its NavigateUrl property to **Hours.aspx**. Click the **OK** button to close the Select URL dialog box.
6. Click the **Default.aspx** tab, and then save the application.

Starting the Web Application

As mentioned earlier, you can start a Web application either by pressing Ctrl+F5 or by clicking the Start Without Debugging option on the Debug menu. If you prefer to use the menu option rather than the shortcut keys, you may need to add the option to your Debug menu. You can add the option by following the next set of steps. However, if you prefer to use the Ctrl+F5 shortcut keys, you can skip the following set of steps.

To add the Start Without Debugging option to the Debug menu:

1. First, you will determine whether your Debug menu already contains the Start Without Debugging option. Click **Debug** on the menu bar. If the menu contains the Start Without Debugging option, close the menu by clicking **Debug** again, and then skip the remaining steps in this set of steps.
2. If the Debug menu does *not* contain the Start Without Debugging option, close the menu by clicking **Debug** again. Click **Tools** on the menu bar, and then click **Customize** to open the Customize dialog box.
3. Click the **Commands** tab. The Menu bar radio button should be selected. Click the **down arrow** in the Menu bar list box. Scroll down the list until you see Debug, and then click **Debug**.
4. Click the **Add Command** button to open the Add Command dialog box, and then click **Debug** in the Categories list. Scroll down the Commands list until you see Start Without Debugging, and then click **Start Without Debugging**. Click the **OK** button to close the Add Command dialog box.
5. Click the **Move Down** button until the Start Without Debugging option appears below the Start / Continue option. See Figure 13-21.

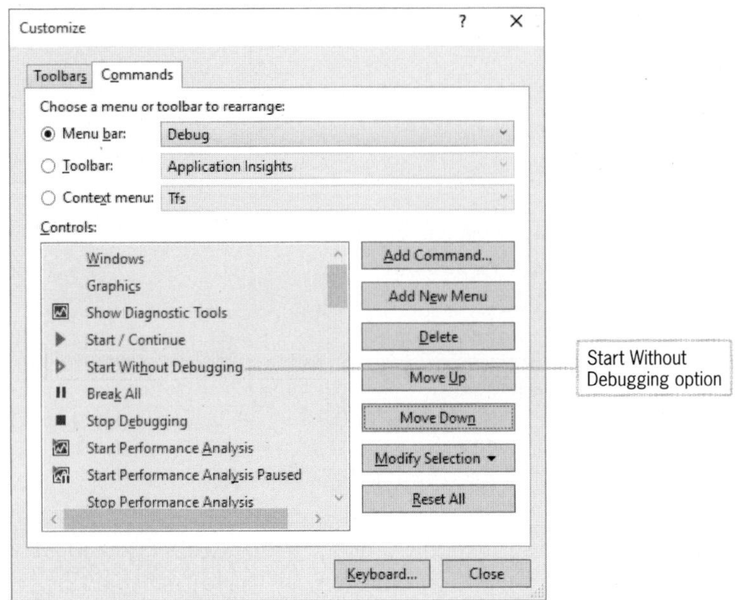

Figure 13-21 Customize dialog box

6. Click the **Close** button to close the Customize dialog box.

When you start a Web application, the computer creates a temporary Web server (on your local machine) that allows you to view your Web page in a browser. Keep in mind, however, that your Web page will need to be placed on an actual Web server for others to view it.

To start the Web application:

1. Use the browser box (shown earlier in Figure 13-10) to select the browser you want to use.
2. Either press **Ctrl+F5** or click the **Start Without Debugging** option on the Debug menu. Your browser requests the Default.aspx page from the local Web server. The server locates the page and then sends the appropriate HTML instructions to your selected browser for rendering on the screen. The value in the page's Title property appears on the page's tab in the browser window. See Figure 13-22.

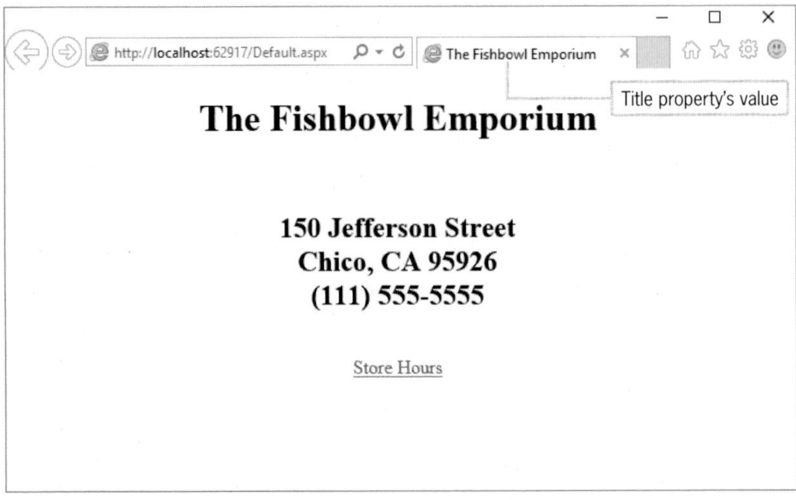

Figure 13-22 Default.aspx page displayed using Internet Explorer

3. Click the **Store Hours** hyperlink to display the Hours.aspx page. See Figure 13-23.

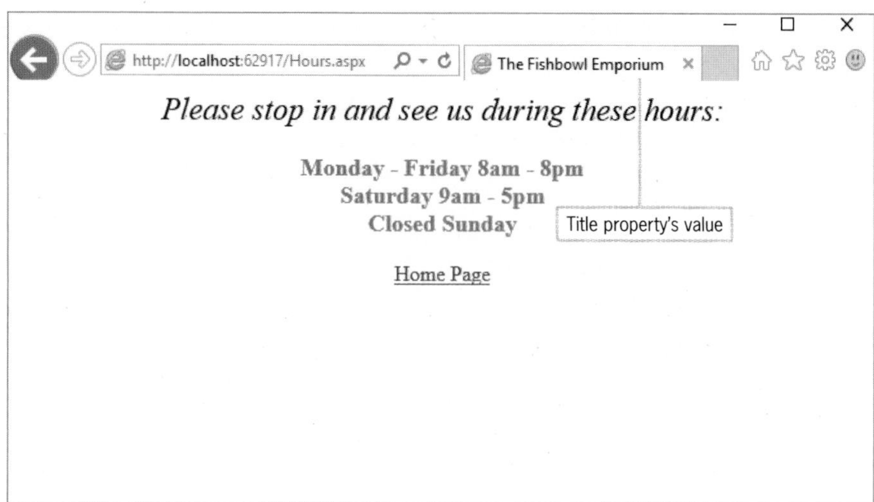

Figure 13-23 Hours.aspx Web page displayed using Internet Explorer

4. Click the **Home Page** hyperlink to display the Default.aspx page, and then close the browser window by clicking the **Close** button on its title bar.

Adding an Image Control to a Web Page

In the next set of steps, you will add an image control to the Default.aspx page. The control will display the image stored in the VbReloaded2015\Chap13\FishInBowl.png file.

To add an image control to the Web page:

1. First, you need to add the FishInBowl.png file to the application. Click **Website** on the menu bar, and then click **Add Existing Item**. Open the VbReloaded2015\Chap13 folder. Click the **down arrow** in the box that controls the file types, and then click **All Files (*.*)** in the list. Click **FishInBowl.png** in the list of filenames, and then click the **Add** button.
2. Click the **blank line** below the Store Hours hyperlink control. (If necessary, insert a blank line below the control.) Press **Enter** to insert another blank line. Click the **Image** tool in the toolbox. Drag your mouse pointer to the location shown in Figure 13-24, and then release the mouse button.

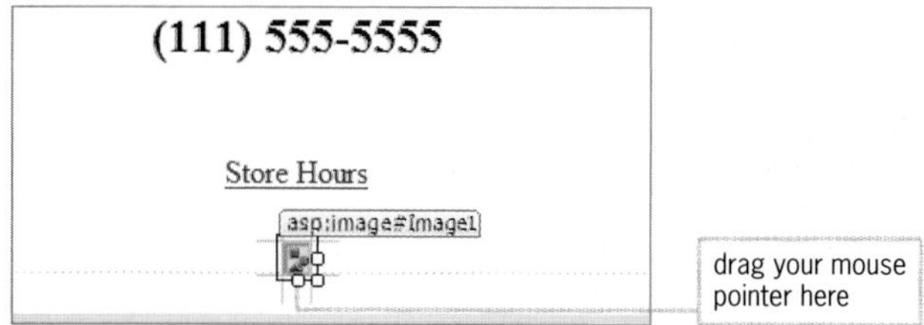

Figure 13-24 Image control added to the Default.aspx page

3. Temporarily display the Properties window. If necessary, click **ImageUrl** in the Properties list. Click the property's **...** (ellipsis) button to open the Select Image dialog box. Click **FishInBowl.png** in the Contents of folder section, and then click the **OK** button.

4. Place your mouse pointer on the lower-right corner of the image control, and then drag the control to make it smaller. See Figure 13-25. (The width and height measurements of the image in the figure are approximately 255px and 175px, respectively.)

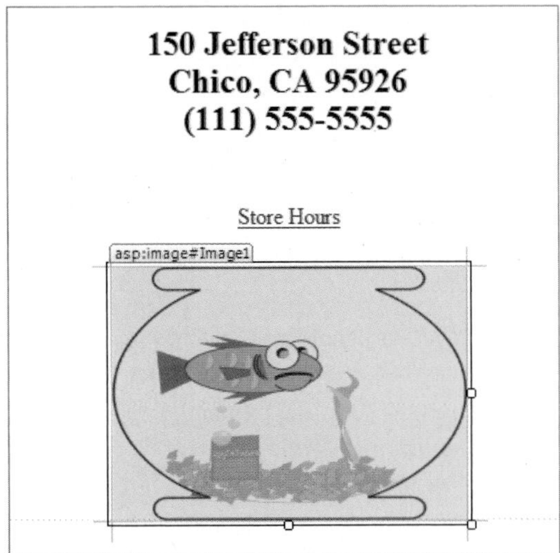

Figure 13-25 Resized image control

5. Next, you will put a border around the image control and also change the border's width to 10 pixels. Change the image control's BorderStyle property to **Dotted**, and then change its BorderWidth property to **10**. Press **Enter** after typing the number 10.

6. Now, you will change the color of the image's border to green. Click **BorderColor** in the Properties list and then click the **...** (ellipsis) button. When the More Colors dialog box opens, click **any green hexagon**. Click the **OK** button to close the dialog box, and then click the **Default.aspx** tab.

7. Auto-hide the toolbox. Save and then start the project. See Figure 13-26.

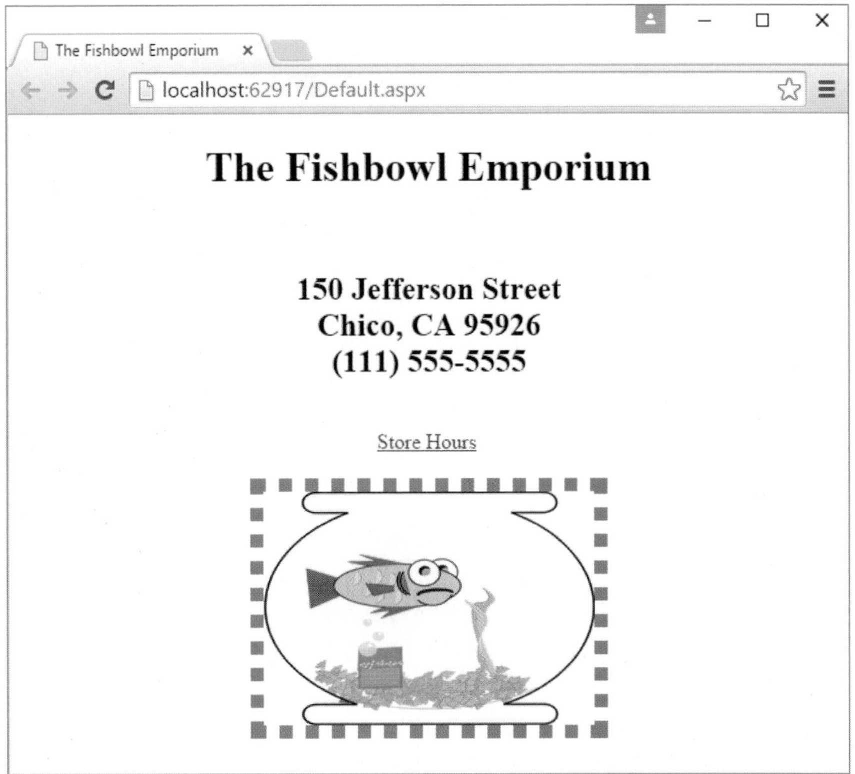

Figure 13-26 Default.aspx page displayed using Google Chrome

8. Verify that the browser window is not maximized. Place your mouse pointer on the window's right border, and then drag the border to the left to make the window narrower. Notice that the text and image remain centered in the visible portion of the window. Now, drag the right border to the right to make the window wider. Here, again, the text and image remain centered in the visible portion of the window.
9. Close the browser window.

Closing and Opening an Existing Web Application

You can use the File menu to close and also to open an existing Web application.

To close and then open the Web application:

1. Click **File** on the menu bar, and then click **Close Solution** to close the application.
2. Next, you will open the application. Click **File** on the menu bar, and then click **Open Web Site** to open the Open Web Site dialog box. If necessary, click the **File System** button. Locate the VbReloaded2015\Chap13\Fishbowl folder. Click the **folder** and then click the **Open** button.
3. Temporarily display the Solution Explorer window to verify that the application is open. If the Default.aspx page is not open in the Document window, right-click **Default.aspx** in the Solution Explorer window and then click **View Designer**.

Repositioning a Control on a Web Page

At times, you may want to reposition a control on a Web page. In this section, you will move the image and hyperlink controls to different locations on the Default.aspx page. First, however, you will create a copy of the Fishbowl Emporium application.

To create a copy of the Fishbowl Emporium application:

1. Close the Fishbowl Emporium application. If you are prompted to save the .sln file, click the **No** button.
2. Use Windows to make a copy of the VbReloaded2015\Chap13\Fishbowl folder. Rename the folder **Modified Fishbowl**.

Now, you will open the application contained in the Modified Fishbowl folder and then move the two controls to different locations on the Default.aspx Web page.

To open the application and then move the controls:

1. Open the Modified Fishbowl Web site. Right-click **Default.aspx** in the Solution Explorer window and then click **View Designer**.
2. First, you will move the image control from the bottom of the page to the top of the page. If necessary, position the insertion point **immediately before the letter T** in the store's name. Press **Enter** to insert a blank line above the name.
3. Click the **image control** on the Web page. Drag the image control to the blank line immediately above the store's name, and then release the mouse button.
4. Next, you will move the hyperlink control to the empty area below the store's name. Click the **hyperlink control**. Drag the control to the empty area below the store's name, and then release the mouse button.
5. Click **File** on the menu bar, and then click **Save Default.aspx**.
6. Start the application. See Figure 13-27.

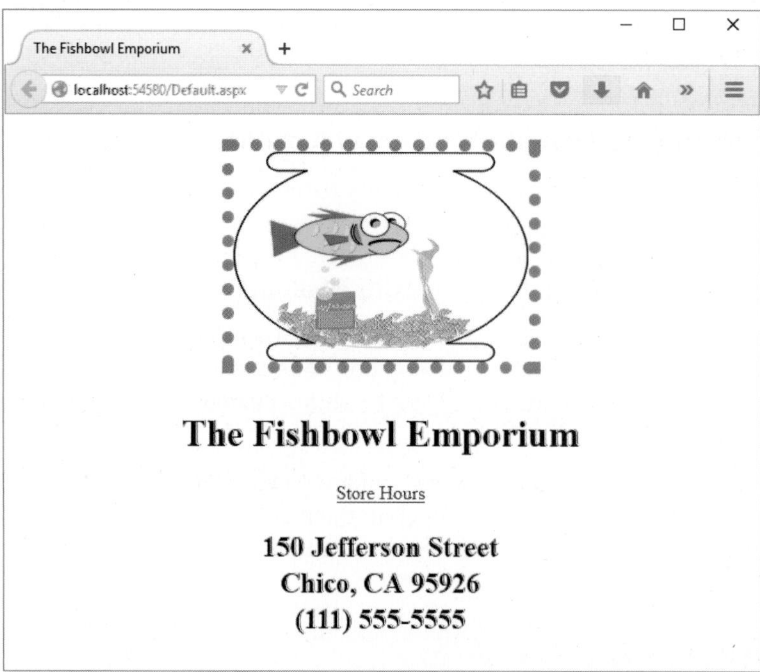

Figure 13-27 Modified Default.aspx page displayed using Mozilla Firefox

7. Close the browser window. Click **File** on the menu bar, and then click **Close Solution**. If you are prompted to save the .sln file, click the **No** button.

PROGRAMMING TUTORIAL 2

Creating the Aquarium Calculator Web Site Application

In this tutorial, you will create a Web Site application that displays the number of gallons of water a rectangular aquarium holds. The application contains the dynamic Web page shown earlier in Figure 13-3. The Web page contains static text, a table, and the following controls: an image, three text boxes, a label, and a button.

To create the application and then add a Web page and an image file to it:

1. Start Visual Studio 2015. Open the Solution Explorer, Properties, and Toolbox windows.
2. Use the New Web Site option on the File menu to create an empty Web Site application named Aquarium. Save the application in the VbReloaded2015\Chap13 folder. If you need help, refer to the How To box shown earlier in Figure 13-5.
3. Use the Add New Item option on the Website menu to add a Web page named Default.aspx to the application. If you need help, refer to the How To box shown earlier in Figure 13-6.
4. Click **Website** on the menu bar, and then click **Add Existing Item**. Open the VbReloaded2015\Chap13 folder. Click the **down arrow** in the box that controls the file types, and then click **All Files (*.*)** in the list. Click **Aquarium.png** in the list of filenames, and then click the **Add** button.

In the next set of steps, you will customize the Web page by adding static text and controls to it.

To customize the Web page:

1. If necessary, click **DOCUMENT** in the Properties window's Object box. Change the DOCUMENT object's Title property to **Aquarium Calculator**.
2. If necessary, click the **Design** tab to view the page in Design view. (If the div tag does not appear in the Document window, click the <div> button at the bottom of the IDE.)
3. If necessary, click **inside the rectangle** that appears below the div tag at the top of the Document window. Type **How many gallons of water does my aquarium hold?** and then press **Enter**.
4. Select (highlight) the static text, and then use the Block Format box to format the text to **Heading 1 <h1>**. Now, use the Alignment button to **center** the static text.
5. Click **anywhere below the static text** to deselect the text.
6. Position the blinking insertion point as shown in Figure 13-28.

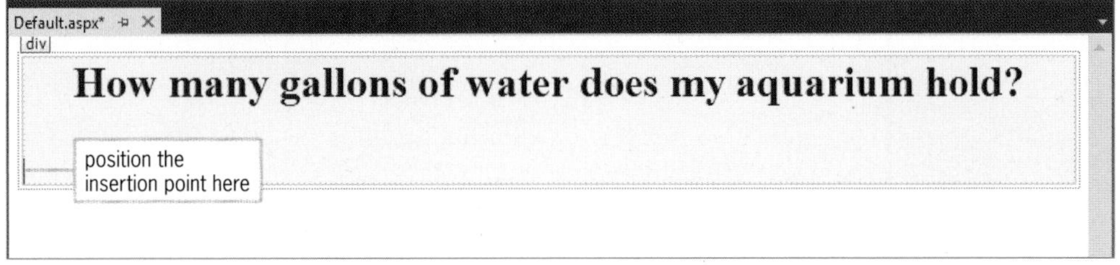

Figure 13-28 Default.aspx page

PROGRAMMING TUTORIAL 2

7. Click **Table** on the menu bar, and then click **Insert Table** to open the Insert Table dialog box. In the Size section of the dialog box, change the number of columns to **5**. In the Layout section, click the **In pixels** radio button, and then change the width to **850**. See Figure 13-29.

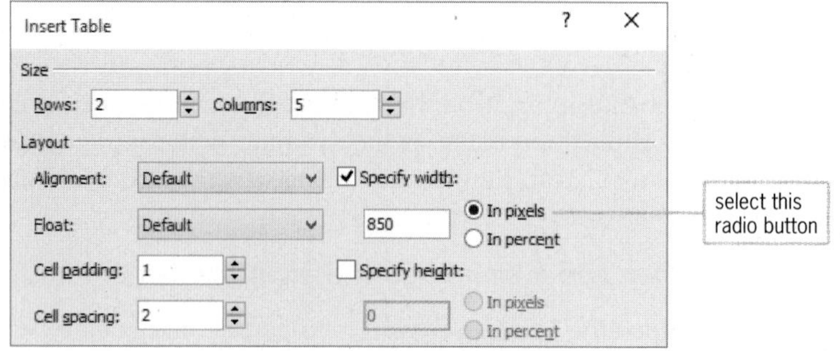

Figure 13-29 Insert Table dialog box

8. Click the **OK** button to close the dialog box. Select the two cells contained in the first column of the table. See Figure 13-30.

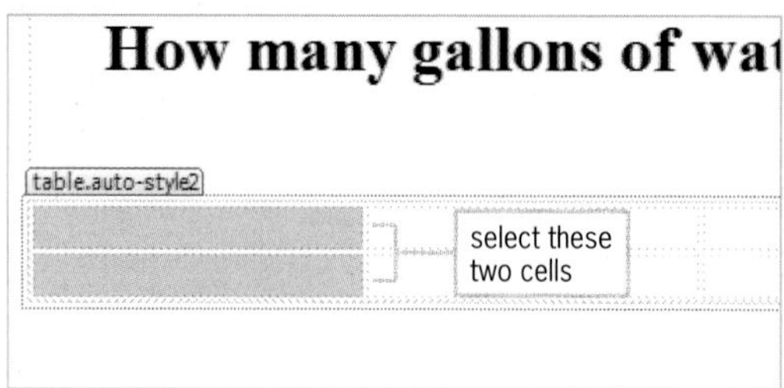

Figure 13-30 Two cells selected in the first column of the table

9. Click **Table** on the menu bar, point to **Modify**, and then click **Merge Cells**. The first column of the table now contains one large cell.
10. Drag an image control from the Standard section of the toolbox into the first column of the table, and then set its ImageUrl property to **Aquarium.png**. Also set its Height and Width properties to **335px** and **340px**, respectively.
11. Position the insertion point in the top cell in the second column, as shown in Figure 13-31.

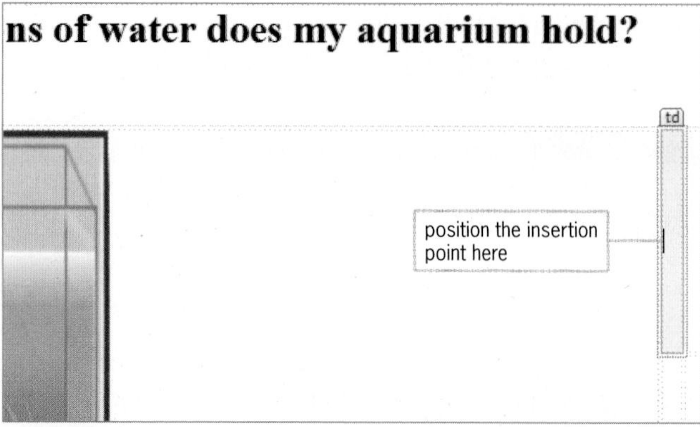

Figure 13-31 Insertion point positioned in the top cell in the second column

PROGRAMMING TUTORIAL 2

12. Type **Length (inches):** and press **Enter**. Click **TextBox** in the toolbox. Drag a text box control to the top cell in the second column, positioning it immediately below the Length (inches): text. Set the text box's Width property to **35px**. Unlike Windows controls, Web controls have an ID property rather than a Name property. Set the text box's ID property (which appears at the top of the Properties window) to **lengthTextBox**.
13. Position the insertion point in the top cell in the third column. Type **Width (inches):** and press **Enter**. Drag a text box control immediately below the Width (inches): text, and then set its ID and Width properties to **widthTextBox** and **35px**, respectively.
14. Position the insertion point in the top cell in the fourth column. Type **Height (inches):** and press **Enter**. Drag a text box control immediately below the Height (inches): text, and then set its ID and Width properties to **heightTextBox** and **35px**, respectively.
15. Next, you will add a Button control to the table. Position the insertion point in the top cell in the fifth (last) column. Click **Button** in the toolbox, and then drag your mouse pointer into the cell. Release the mouse button. Set the button's ID and Text properties to **submitButton** and **Submit**, respectively. Expand the **Font** node in the Properties window, click the **Size** arrow, and then click **Large**.
16. Select the bottom cells in the second through fourth columns. See Figure 13-32.

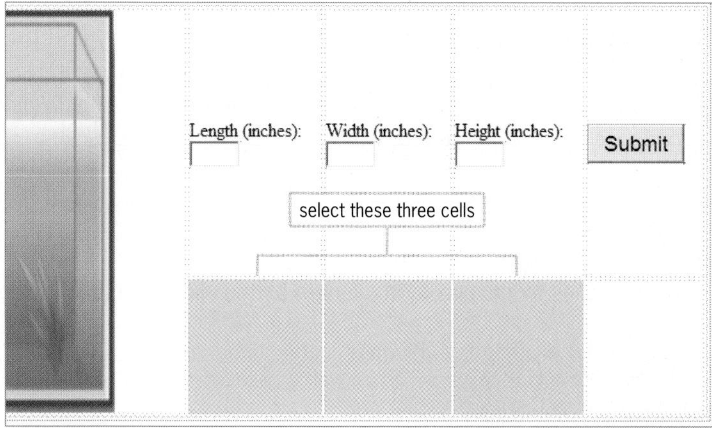

Figure 13-32 Three cells selected in the table

17. Click **Table** on the menu bar, point to **Modify**, and then click **Merge Cells**. The three selected cells become one large cell. Click the **large cell**, type **Water (gallons):**, and then press **Enter**.
18. Select the **Water (gallons):** text. Use the Font Size box on the Formatting toolbar to change the text's size to **x-large (24 pt)**. Then use the Alignment button on the Formatting toolbar to **center** the text.
19. Click **Label** in the toolbox. Drag a label control immediately below the Water (gallons): text. Set the control's ID, Font/Size, Height, and Width properties to **gallonsLabel**, **XX-Large**, **35px**, and **105px**, respectively.
20. Remove the contents of the label's Text property. When you clear the Text property, the control's ID appears in brackets. Click the Web page to deselect the label control.
21. Auto-hide the Toolbox, Solution Explorer, and Properties windows. Click **File** on the menu bar, and then click **Save Default.aspx**. The completed interface is shown in Figure 13-33.

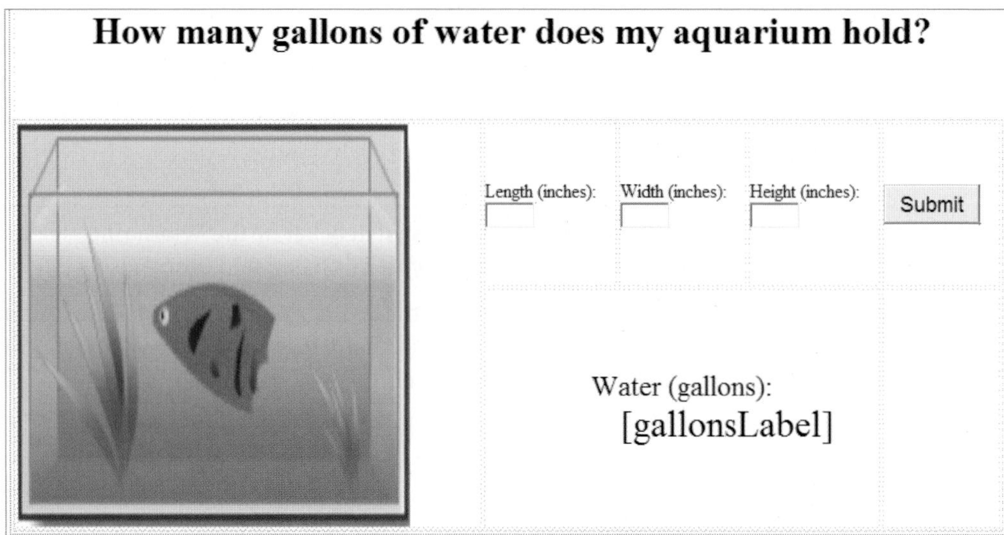

Figure 13-33 Completed interface

Coding the Submit Button's Click Event Procedure

When the user clicks a button on a Web page, a postback occurs automatically and the button's Click event procedure is sent to the server for processing. In the next set of steps, you will code the submitButton_Click procedure to calculate and display the number of gallons of water. Figure 13-34 shows the procedure's pseudocode and variables.

<u>submitButton Click event procedure</u>
1. store user input (length, width, and height) in variables
2. calculate the volume in cubic inches by multiplying the length by the width and then multiplying the result by the height
3. calculate the number of gallons by dividing the volume in cubic inches by 231 (There are 231 cubic inches in a gallon.)
4. display the number of gallons in gallonsLabel

Variable names	Stores
`length`	the aquarium's length in inches
`width`	the aquarium's width in inches
`height`	the aquarium's height in inches
`volume`	the volume in cubic inches
`gallons`	the number of gallons of water

Figure 13-34 Pseudocode and variables for the submitButton_Click procedure

To code and then test the submitButton_Click procedure:

1. Right-click the **Web page**, and then click **View Code** to open the Code Editor window. As the window's tab indicates, the code entered in this window will be saved in the Default.aspx.vb file. Recall that a Web page's .aspx.vb file is referred to as the code-behind file because it contains code that supports the Web page. Temporarily display the Solution Explorer window. If necessary, expand the **Default.aspx** node. See Figure 13-35.

PROGRAMMING TUTORIAL 2

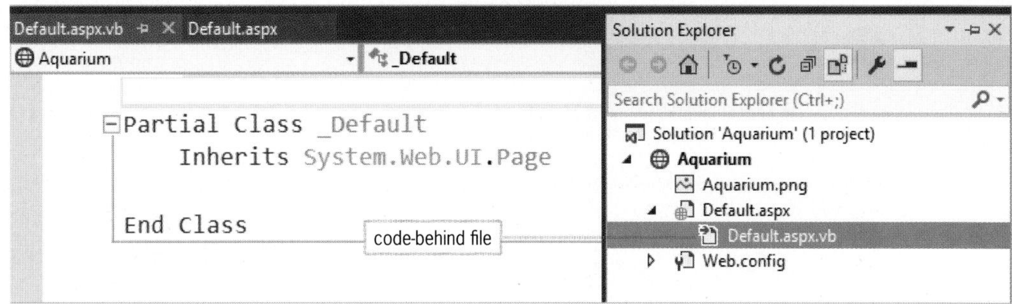

Figure 13-35 Code Editor and Solution Explorer windows

2. Click the **first blank line** in the Code Editor window. Enter the following comments, replacing <your name> and <current date> with your name and the current date, respectively. Press **Enter** twice after typing the last comment.

   ' Name: Aquarium
   ' Purpose: Display number of gallons
   ' Created/revised by: <your name> on <current date>

3. Enter the following Option statements:

   Option Explicit On
   Option Strict On
   Option Infer Off

4. Open the code template for the submitButton_Click procedure. Type the following comment and then press **Enter** twice:

   ' displays number of gallons

5. Enter the Dim statements to declare the five Double variables listed earlier in Figure 13-34. Press **Enter** twice after typing the last Dim statement.
6. The first step in the procedure's pseudocode is to store the input items in variables. Enter the appropriate TryParse methods. Press **Enter** twice after typing the last TryParse method.
7. The second step in the pseudocode calculates the volume of the aquarium in cubic inches. Enter the appropriate assignment statement.
8. The third step in the pseudocode calculates the number of gallons of water in the aquarium. Enter the appropriate assignment statement.
9. The last step in the pseudocode displays the number of gallons of water. Enter the appropriate assignment statement. Display the number of gallons with one decimal place.
10. Save the application.
11. Use the browser box (shown earlier in Figure 13-10) to select the browser you want to use, and then start the application. Your browser requests the Default.aspx page from the local Web server. The server locates the page and then sends the appropriate HTML instructions to your selected browser for rendering on the screen.
12. Type **30**, **20**, and **15.5** in the Length, Width, and Height boxes, respectively. Click the **Submit** button, which submits your entry to the server along with a request for additional services. At this point, a postback has occurred. The server processes the code contained in the submitButton_Click procedure and then sends the appropriate HTML to the browser for rendering on the screen. As Figure 13-36 indicates, the aquarium holds 40.3 gallons of water.

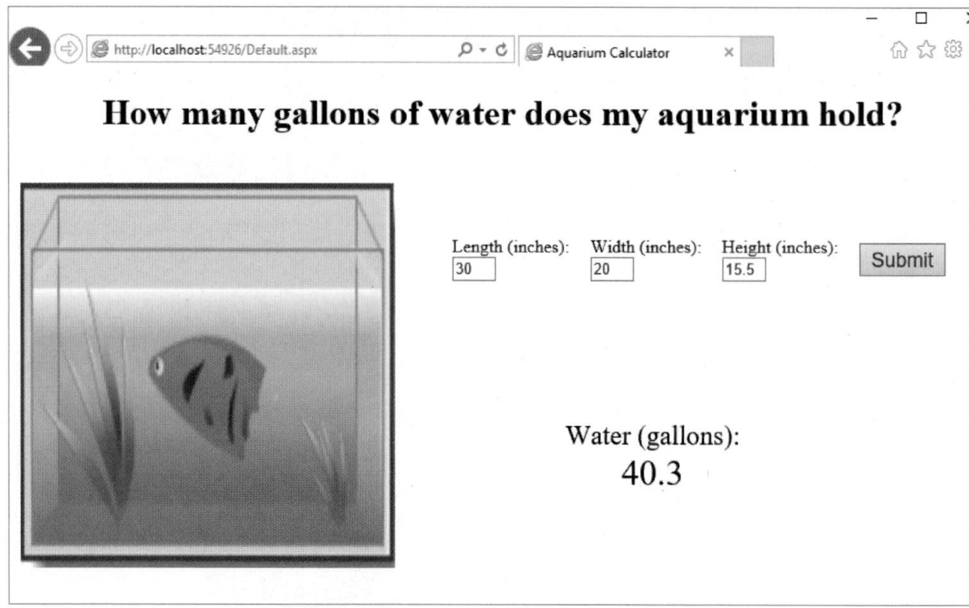

Figure 13-36 Default.aspx page displayed using Internet Explorer

13. Close the browser window and then close the Code Editor window.

Validating User Input

The Validation section of the toolbox provides several **validator tools** for validating user input. The name, purpose, and important properties of each validator tool are listed in Figure 13-37. In the Aquarium application, you will use RequiredFieldValidator controls to verify that the user entered the three input items.

HOW TO Use the Validator Tools

Name	Purpose	Properties
CompareValidator	compare an entry with a constant value or the property stored in a control	ControlToCompare ControlToValidate ErrorMessage Operator Type ValueToCompare
CustomValidator	verify that an entry passes the specified validation logic	ClientValidationFunction ControlToValidate ErrorMessage
RangeValidator	verify that an entry is within the specified minimum and maximum values	ControlToValidate ErrorMessage MaximumValue MinimumValue Type

Figure 13-37 How to use the validator tools *(continues)*

PROGRAMMING TUTORIAL 2

(continued)

RegularExpressionValidator	verify that an entry matches a specific pattern	ControlToValidate ErrorMessage ValidationExpression
RequiredFieldValidator	verify that a control contains data	ControlToValidate ErrorMessage
ValidationSummary	display all of the validation error messages in a single location on a Web page	DisplayMode HeaderText

Figure 13-37 How to use the validator tools

To verify that the user entered the three input values:

1. Click **to the immediate right of the lengthTextBox**, and then press **Enter**.
2. Permanently display the Toolbox window. If necessary, expand the Validation section. Click the **RequiredFieldValidator** tool and then drag the mouse pointer to the Web page, positioning it immediately below the lengthTextBox. Release the mouse button. The RequiredFieldValidator1 control appears on the Web page.
3. Temporarily display the Properties window. Set the RequiredFieldValidator1 control's ControlToValidate and ErrorMessage properties to **lengthTextBox** and **Required**, respectively. Click **ForeColor** in the Properties window, click the **...** (ellipsis) button, click a **red hexagon**, and then click the **OK** button to close the More Colors dialog box.
4. Click **to the immediate right of the widthTextBox**, and then press **Enter**. Drag a required field validator control below the widthTextBox. Set the RequiredFieldValidator2 control's ControlToValidate and ErrorMessage properties to **widthTextBox** and **Required**, respectively. Also set its ForeColor property using the same red hexagon used in Step 3. Click the **OK** button to close the More Colors dialog box.
5. Click **to the immediate right of the heightTextBox**, and then press **Enter**. Drag a required field validator control below the heightTextBox. Set the RequiredFieldValidator3 control's ControlToValidate and ErrorMessage properties to **heightTextBox** and **Required**, respectively. Also set its ForeColor property using the same red hexagon used in Step 3. Click the **OK** button to close the More Colors dialog box.
6. Click the **Default.aspx** tab, and then auto-hide the Toolbox window. Click **File** on the menu bar and then click **Save Default.aspx**.
7. Start the application by pressing **Ctrl+F5**. If the error message shown in Figure 13-38 appears, close the browser window; otherwise, skip to Step 10.

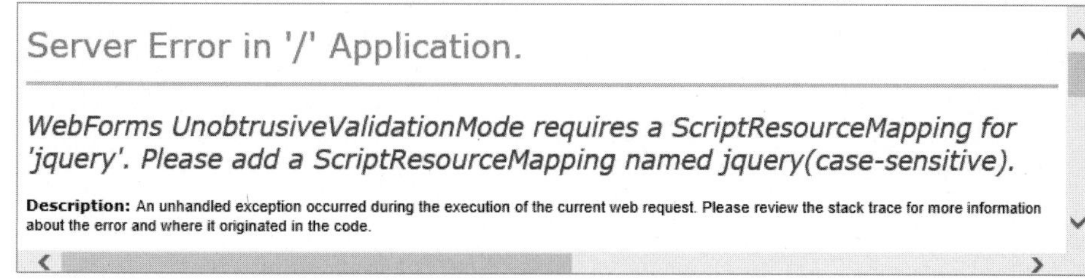

Figure 13-38 Error message that might appear

8. If you received the error message shown in Figure 13-38, right-click **Web.config** in the Solution Explorer window, and then click **Open**. Now use one of the two solutions shown in Figure 13-39.

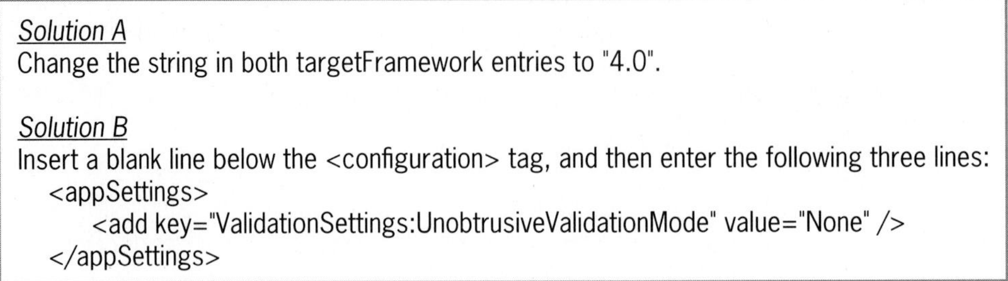

Solution A
Change the string in both targetFramework entries to "4.0".

Solution B
Insert a blank line below the <configuration> tag, and then enter the following three lines:

```
<appSettings>
    <add key="ValidationSettings:UnobtrusiveValidationMode" value="None" />
</appSettings>
```

Figure 13-39 Solutions to the error message shown in Figure 13-38

9. Click **File** on the menu bar, and then click **Save Web.config**. Close the Web.config window, and then press **Ctrl+F5**.

10. Click the **Submit** button without entering any values. Each RequiredFieldValidator control displays the "Required" message, as shown in Figure 13-40. (The Web page in the figure is displayed using Internet Explorer.)

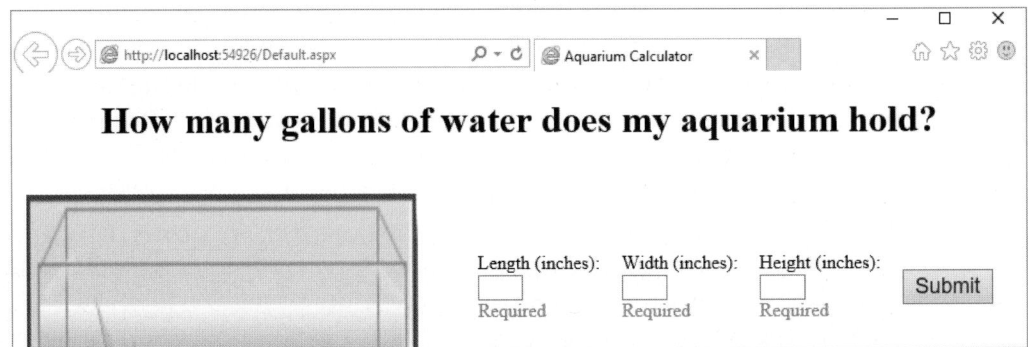

Figure 13-40 Result of clicking the Submit button when the text boxes are empty

11. Type **16** in the Length box, and then press **Tab** to move the insertion point into the Width box. Notice that the "Required" message below the Length box disappears.

12. Type **8** and **10** in the Width and Height boxes, respectively. Click the **Submit** button. The Web page indicates that the aquarium holds 5.5 gallons of water.

13. Close the browser window, and then close the application. If you are asked whether you want to save the .sln file, click the **No** button. Figure 13-41 shows the application's code.

```
' Name:               Aquarium
' Purpose:            Display number of gallons
' Created/revised by: <your name> on <current date>

Option Explicit On
Option Strict On
Option Infer Off

```

Figure 13-41 Code for the Aquarium Calculator application *(continues)*

(continued)

```
Partial Class _Default
    Inherits System.Web.UI.Page

    Private Sub submitButton_Click(sender As Object, e As EventArgs
    ) Handles submitButton.Click
        ' displays number of gallons

        Dim length As Double
        Dim width As Double
        Dim height As Double
        Dim volume As Double
        Dim gallons As Double

        Double.TryParse(lengthTextBox.Text, length)
        Double.TryParse(widthTextBox.Text, width)
        Double.TryParse(heightTextBox.Text, height)

        volume = length * width * height
        gallons = volume / 231
        gallonsLabel.Text = gallons.ToString("N1")

    End Sub
End Class
```

Figure 13-41 Code for the Aquarium Calculator application

PROGRAMMING EXAMPLE

Multiplication Calculator Web Site Application

Create an empty Web Site application named Multiplication. Save the application in the VbReloaded2015\Chap13 folder. Add a new Web page named Default.aspx to the application. Change the DOCUMENT object's Title property to Multiplication Calculator. Create the Web page shown in Figure 13-42. The calculator image is stored in the VbReloaded2015\Chap13\Calculator.png file. The Calculate button should display the product of the two numbers entered by the user. The application's code is shown in Figure 13-43.

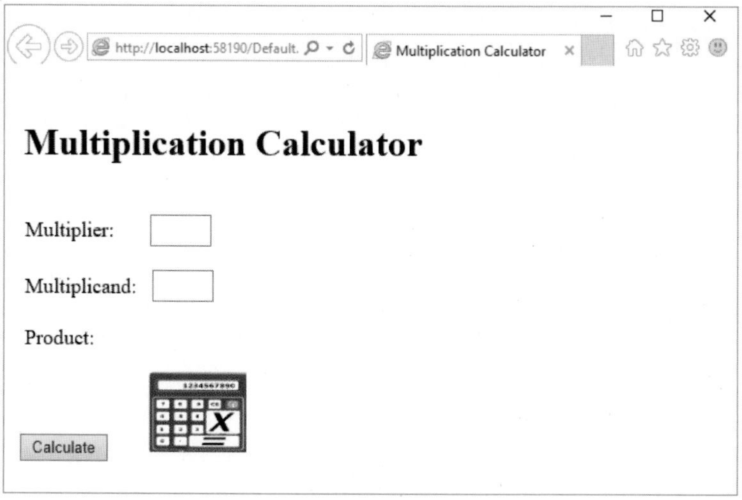

http://localhost:58190/Default.
Multiplication Calculator

Multiplication Calculator

Multiplier:

Multiplicand:

Product:

Calculate

Figure 13-42 Default.aspx Web page

```
' Name:                  Multiplication
' Purpose:               Display the product of two numbers
' Created/revised by:    <your name> on <current date>

Option Explicit On
Option Strict On
Option Infer Off

Partial Class _Default
   Inherits System.Web.UI.Page

   Protected Sub calcButton_Click(sender As Object, e As EventArgs) Handles calcButton.Click
       ' calculates the product of two numbers

       Dim multiplier As Double
       Dim multiplicand As Double
       Dim product As Double

       Double.TryParse(multiplierTextBox.Text, multiplier)
       Double.TryParse(multiplicandTextBox.Text, multiplicand)

       product = multiplier * multiplicand
       productLabel.Text = product.ToString("N2")
   End Sub
End Class
```

Figure 13-43 Code

Chapter Summary

- A client computer uses a browser to request a Web page from a Web server. It also uses the browser to view the Web page.
- Web pages can be either static or dynamic (interactive).
- HTML tags tell the browser how to render a Web page on the computer screen. ASP tags specify the controls to include on a Web page.
- Dynamic Web pages contain code that is processed by the Web server.
- You can add static text and controls to a Web page. Like Windows controls, Web controls have properties, and they can be coded to perform tasks when an action (such as clicking) occurs. However, unlike Windows controls, Web controls have an ID property rather than a Name property. You use the ID property to refer to the control in code.
- The .aspx file contains the instructions for rendering the visual elements on the Web page. The .aspx.vb file contains the Web page's code and is referred to as the code-behind file.
- You use the Hyperlink tool in the toolbox to add a hyperlink control to a Web page. You then set the control's Text and NavigateUrl properties.
- You use the Image tool to add an image control to a Web page. You then set the control's ImageUrl property.

Key Terms

ASP—the acronym for "active server pages"

Browser—a program that allows a client computer to request and view Web pages

Client computer—a computer that requests information from a Web server

Dynamic Web page—an interactive document that can accept information from the user and also retrieve information for the user

Hyperlink control—allows the user to "jump" from one Web page to another

Postback—occurs when the information on a dynamic Web page is sent (posted) back to a server for processing

Static text—text that the user is not allowed to edit

Static Web page—a noninteractive document whose purpose is merely to display information to the viewer

Validator tools—used to validate user input

Web pages—the documents stored on Web servers

Web server—a computer that contains special software that "serves up" Web pages in response to requests from client computers

Review Questions

Each Review Question is associated with one or more objectives listed at the beginning of the chapter.

1. An online form used to purchase a product is an example of a ____________ Web page. (1)
   a. dynamic
   b. static
2. ASP stands for ____________. (1)
   a. always special page
   b. active special page
   c. active server page
   d. active server product
3. Which of the following filenames indicates that the file contains the Visual Basic code associated with a Web page? (2, 3, 5)
   a. Default.aspx.vb
   b. Default.aspx
   c. Default.vb
   d. Default.vb.aspx
4. In code, you refer to a control on a Web page using the control's ____________ property. (5)
   a. Caption
   b. ID
   c. Name
   d. Text
5. The HTML instructions in a Web page are processed by the ____________. (1)
   a. client computer
   b. Web server
6. The Visual Basic code in a Web page is processed by the ____________. (1)
   a. client computer
   b. Web server

7. You can use a ____________ control to verify that a control on a Web page contains data. (10)
   a. RequiredFieldValidator
   b. RequiredField
   c. RequiredValidator
   d. RequiredData
8. You can use a ____________ control to verify that an entry on a Web page is within minimum and maximum values. (10)
   a. MinMaxValidation
   b. MaxMinValidation
   c. EntryValidator
   d. RangeValidator
9. The text that appears on a Web page's tab in the browser window is determined by the DOCUMENT object's ____________ property. (4)
   a. Name
   b. Title
   c. TabName
   d. WindowTitle
10. A ____________ is a program that uses HTML to render a Web page on the computer screen. (1)
   a. browser
   b. client
   c. server
   d. none of the above

Exercises

Pencil and Paper

INTRODUCTORY
1. Explain the difference between a static Web page and a dynamic Web page. (1)

INTRODUCTORY
2. Explain the relationship between a client computer and a Web server. (1)

Computer

MODIFY THIS
3. If necessary, complete the Multiplication Calculator application from this chapter's Programming Example, and then close the application. (2–8, 10)
   a. Use Windows to make a copy of the Multiplication folder. Rename the folder Modified Multiplication.
   b. Open the Modified Multiplication Web site. Right-click Default.aspx in the Solution Explorer window, and then click View Designer.
   c. Add two RequiredFieldValidator controls to the Web page. Associate the controls with the two text boxes. The controls should display the message "Required entry" (without the quotes) when their respective text box is empty.
   d. Save the application, and then start and test it. Close the browser window and then close the application.

4. Create an empty Web Site application named Caroline. Save the application in the VbReloaded2015\Chap13 folder. Add a new Web page named Default.aspx to the application. Change the DOCUMENT object's Title property to Caroline's Pet Shoppe. Create a Web page similar to the one shown in Figure 13-44. The static text should be centered, horizontally, on the page. Save and then start the application. Close the browser window and then close the application. (2–4, 6, 7)

INTRODUCTORY

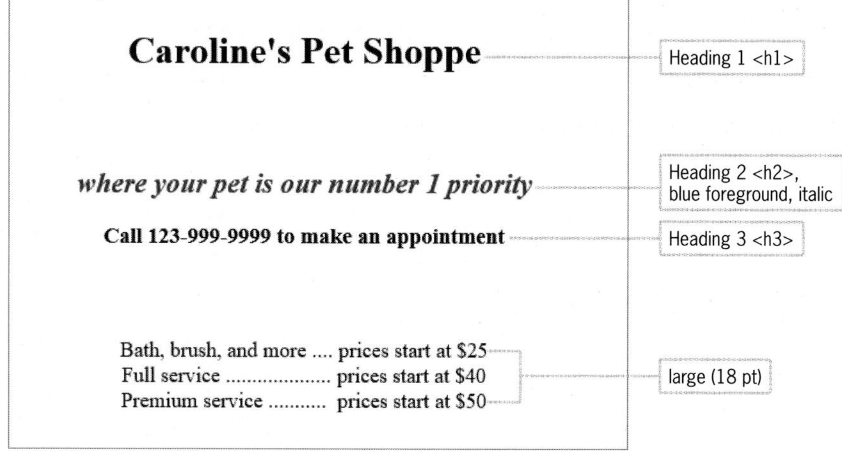

Figure 13-44 Default.aspx page for Exercise 4

5. Create an empty Web site project named Carnival. Save the application in the VbReloaded2015\Chap13 folder. Add a new Web page named Default.aspx to the application. Change the DOCUMENT object's Title property to Brookfield. Create a Web page similar to the one shown in Figure 13-45. The image on the Web page is stored in the VbReloaded2015\Chap13\Carnival.png file. (Hint: To position the image as shown in the figure, click the image, click Format on the menu bar, click Position, and then click the Left button in the Wrapping style section of the Position dialog box.) Save and then start the application. Close the browser window and then close the application. (2–4, 6–8)

INTRODUCTORY

Brookfield Carnival

Come join us on July 4th for our annual carnival. Buy a $10 ticket and get unlimited rides and a chance to win a grand prize of $500. There will be games and great food. At 9pm, the fireworks show will begin. Don't miss it!

Sam Jenkins
Brookfield City Manager

Figure 13-45 Default.aspx page for Exercise 5

INTERMEDIATE

6. Create an empty Web Site application named Tips. Save the application in the VbReloaded2015\Chap13 folder. Add a new Web page named Default.aspx to the application. Change the DOCUMENT object's Title property to Tip Calculator. Use Figure 13-46 as a guide when designing the Web page. In the Code Editor window, enter comments to document the application's name and purpose as well as your name and the current date. Also enter the appropriate Option statements. Code the Calculate Tip button's Click event procedure. Display the tips with a dollar sign and two decimal places. Save the application, and then start and test it. Close the browser window. Close the Code Editor window and then close the application. (2–7, 9, 10)

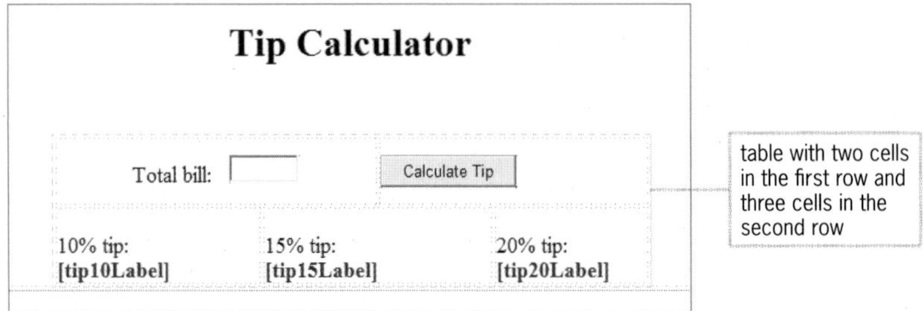

Figure 13-46 Web page for Exercise 6

INTERMEDIATE

7. Create an empty Web Site application named Measurement. Save the application in the VbReloaded2015\Chap13 folder. Add a new Web page named Default.aspx to the application. Change the DOCUMENT object's Title property to "Inches to Centimeters" (without the quotes). The Web page should provide a text box for the user to enter the number of inches. When the user clicks a button on the Web page, the button's Click event procedure should display the number of inches converted to centimeters. Save and then start and test the application. Close the browser window. Close the Code Editor window and then close the application. (2–7, 9, 10)

INTERMEDIATE

8. Create an empty Web Site application named Hearthstone. Save the application in the VbReloaded2015\Chap13 folder. Add two new Web pages named Default.aspx and Message.aspx to the application. Change each DOCUMENT object's Title property to Hearthstone Heating and Cooling. Create Web pages similar to the ones shown in Figures 13-47 and 13-48. The image on the Default.aspx page is stored in the VbReloaded2015\Chap13\Thermostat.png file. (Hint: To position the image as shown in the figure, click the image, click Format on the menu bar, click Position, and then click the Left button in the Wrapping style section of the Position dialog box.) The static text and hyperlink control on the Default.aspx page should be centered, horizontally, on the page. Save and then start the application. Close the browser window and then close the application. (2–4, 6–8, 10)

Figure 13-47 Default.aspx Web page for Exercise 8

We can handle all of your heating and cooling needs. We have been in business for 25 years and are fully licensed and insured. Call us now for a free estimate. For your peace of mind, we offer 24-hour emergency service.

Karen and Jake Jones

Previous Page

Figure 13-48 Message.aspx Web page for Exercise 8

Case Projects

Spa Monique

Create an empty Web Site application named Spa. Save the application in the VbReloaded2015\Chap13 folder. Add a new Web page named Default.aspx to the application. Change the DOCUMENT object's Title property to Spa Monique. Create a Web page similar to the one shown in Figure 13-49. The Spa Monique image is contained in the VbReloaded2015\Chap13\Spa.png file. Save and then start and test the application. Close the browser window and then close the application. (2–4, 6–8)

Spa Monique at Glen Springs

Take time for a relaxing and healing experience. You deserve it!

Massages

Swedish .... 50 minutes $100

Stress reliever .... 30 minutes $50

Herbal .... 50 minutes $115

Stone .... 40 minutes $90

Mom-to-be .... 50 minutes $100

Figure 13-49 Default.aspx page for Spa Monique

The Corner Market

Create an empty Web Site application named Market. Save the application in the VbReloaded2015\Chap13 folder. Add three new Web pages named Default.aspx, Apples.aspx, and Oranges.aspx to the application. Change each DOCUMENT object's Title property to Corner Market. Create Web pages similar to the ones shown in Figures 13-50 through 13-52. The images are stored in the Apple.png and Orange.png files contained in the VbReloaded2015\Chap13 folder. Save and then start and test the application. Close the browser window and then close the application. (2–8)

The Corner Market

75 Roberts Road
Hendersonville, TN 37075

We sell the freshest apples and oranges in the state. Want to see which varieties we have in stock today? Click the Apples or Oranges link below.

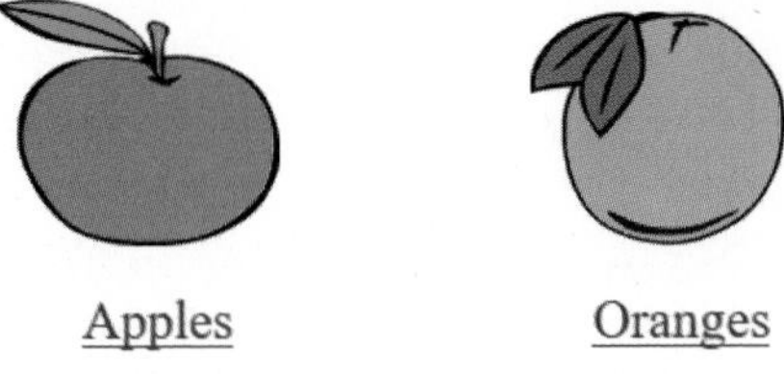

Apples Oranges

Figure 13-50 Default.aspx page for The Corner Market

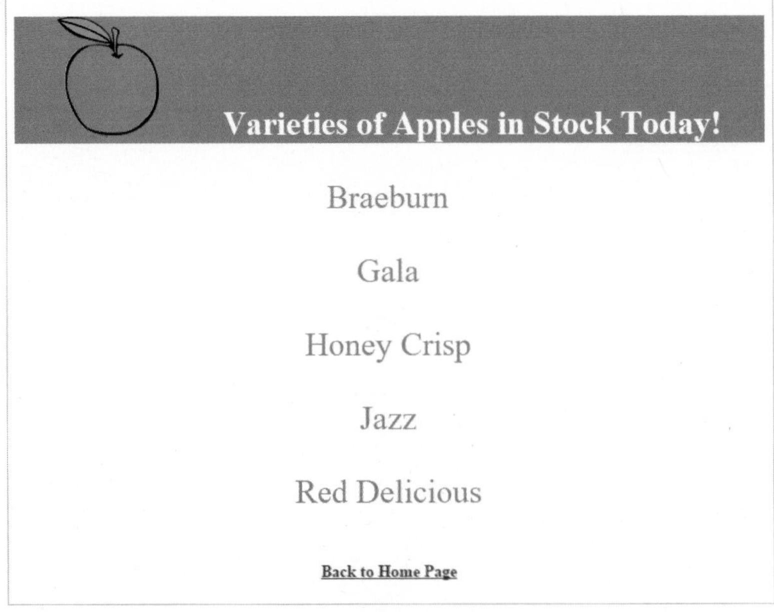

Figure 13-51 Apples.aspx page for The Corner Market

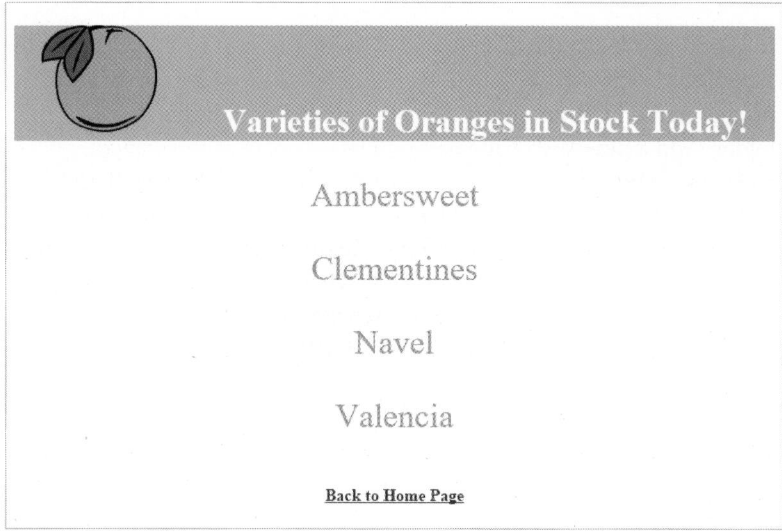

Figure 13-52 Oranges.aspx page for The Corner Market

Circle Area Calculator

Create an empty Web Site application named Circle. Save the application in the VbReloaded2015\Chap13 folder. Add a new Web page named Default.aspx to the application. Change the DOCUMENT object's Title property to Circle Area. Create a Web page similar to the one shown in Figure 13-53. The circle image is contained in the VbReloaded2015\Chap13\Circle.png file. Open the Code Editor window. Use comments to document the application's name and purpose as well as your name and the current date. Enter the Option statements. Code the Calculate Area button's Click event procedure. Use 3.14 as the value for Pi. Display the area with one decimal place. Save and then start and test the application. Close the browser window and then close the application. (2–10)

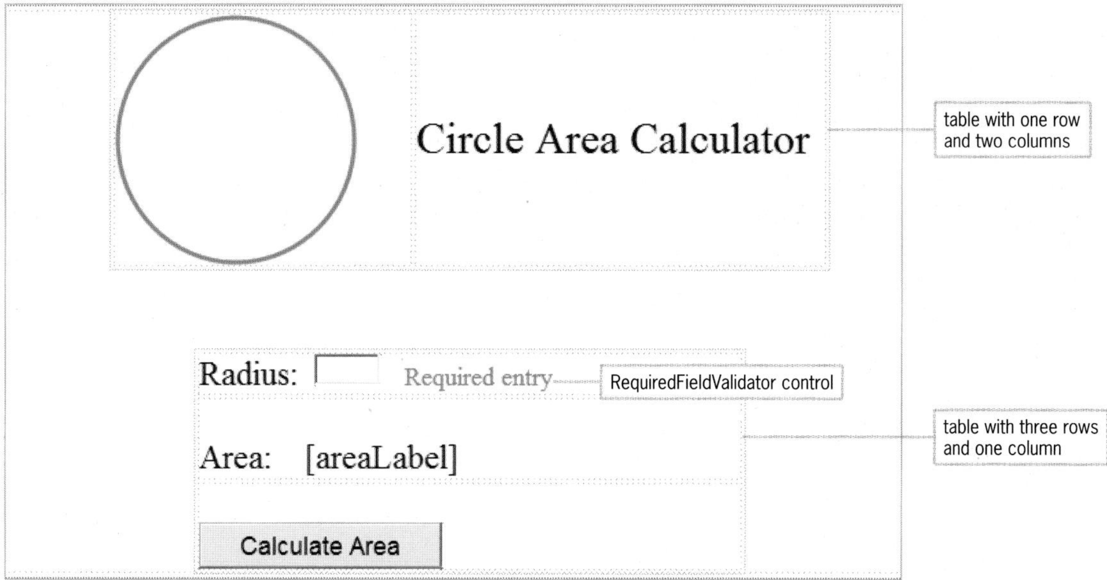

Figure 13-53 Default.aspx page for the Circle Area Calculator application

Cheap Loans

Create an empty Web site project named Cheap Loans. Save the application in the VbReloaded2015\Chap13 folder. Add a new Web page named Default.aspx to the project. Change the DOCUMENT object's Title property to Cheap Loans. Create a Web page that provides text boxes for the user to enter the amount of a loan, the annual interest rate, and the term of the loan (in years). Associate each text box with its own RequiredFieldValidator control. When the user clicks a button on the Web page, the button's Click event procedure should display the monthly payment. Code the procedure. Save and then start and test the project. Close the browser window and then close the application. (2–7, 9, 10)

Meyer's Purple Bakery

Create an empty Web Site application named Bakery. Save the application in the VbReloaded2015\Chap13 folder. Add a new Web page named Default.aspx to the application. Change the DOCUMENT object's Title property to Meyer's. The application should allow the user to enter two items: the number of doughnuts ordered and the number of muffins ordered. The application should display the total number of items ordered and the total sales amount, including a 5% sales tax. A doughnut costs $0.50; a muffin costs $0.75. Create an appropriate Web page, and then code the application. Save and then start and test the application. Close the browser window and then close the application. (2–10)

CHAPTER 14

Creating Classes and Objects

After studying Chapter 14, you should be able to:

1. Explain the terminology used in object-oriented programming
2. Create a class
3. Instantiate and utilize an object
4. Add Property procedures to a class
5. Include data validation in a class
6. Create default and parameterized constructors
7. Include methods other than constructors in a class
8. Include a ReadOnly property in a class
9. Create an auto-implemented property
10. Overload a method in a class

Object-Oriented Programming Terminology

As you learned in Chapter 1, Visual Basic 2015 is an **object-oriented programming language**, which is a language that allows the programmer to use objects to accomplish a program's goal. Recall that an **object** is anything that can be seen, touched, or used. In other words, an object is nearly any *thing*. The objects used in an object-oriented program can take on many different forms. The text boxes, list boxes, and buttons included in most Windows applications are objects, and so are the application's named constants and variables. An object can also represent something found in real life, such as a wristwatch or a car.

Every object in an object-oriented program is created from a **class**, which is a pattern that the computer uses to create the object. The class contains the instructions that tell the computer how the object should look and behave. Using object-oriented programming (**OOP**) terminology, objects are **instantiated** (created) from a class, and each object is referred to as an **instance** of the class. A button control, for example, is an instance of the Button class. The button is instantiated when you drag the Button tool from the toolbox to the form. A String variable, on the other hand, is an instance of the String class and is instantiated the first time you refer to the variable in code. Keep in mind that the class itself is not an object. Only an instance of a class is an object.

Every object has **attributes**, which are the characteristics that describe the object. Attributes are also called properties. Included in the attributes of buttons and text boxes are the Name and Text properties. List boxes have a Name property as well as a Sorted property.

In addition to attributes, every object also has behaviors. An object's **behaviors** include methods and events. **Methods** are the operations (actions) that the object is capable of performing. For example, a button can use its Focus method to send the focus to itself. Similarly, a String variable can use its ToUpper method to temporarily convert its contents to uppercase. **Events**, on the other hand, are the actions to which an object can respond. A button's Click event, for instance, allows the button to respond to a mouse click.

A class contains—or, in OOP terms, it **encapsulates**—all of the attributes and behaviors of the object it instantiates. The term *encapsulate* means to enclose in a capsule. In the context of OOP, the "capsule" is a class.

Creating a Class

In previous chapters, you instantiated objects using classes that are built into Visual Basic, such as the TextBox and Label classes. You used the instantiated objects in a variety of ways in many different applications. In some applications, you used a text box to enter a name; in other applications, you used it to enter a sales tax rate. Similarly, you used label controls to identify text boxes and also to display the result of calculations. The ability to use an object for more than one purpose saves programming time and money—an advantage that contributes to the popularity of object-oriented programming.

You can also define your own classes in Visual Basic and then create instances (objects) from those classes. You define a class using the **Class statement**, which you enter in a class file. Figure 14-1 shows the statement's syntax and lists the steps for adding a class file to an open project. The figure also includes an example of the Class statement entered in a class file. The three Option statements included in the figure have the same meaning in a class file as they have in a form file. Although it is not a requirement, the convention is to use Pascal case for the class name. The names of Visual Basic classes (for example, Integer and TextBox) also follow this naming convention.

The creation of a good class, which is one whose objects can be used in a variety of ways by many different applications, requires a lot of planning.

HOW TO Define a Class

Syntax
Public Class *className*
    attributes section
    behaviors section
End Class

Adding a class file to an open project
1. Click Project on the menu bar, and then click Add Class. The Add New Item dialog box opens with Class selected in the middle column of the dialog box.
2. Type the name of the class (using Pascal case) followed by a period and the letters vb in the Name box, and then click the Add button.

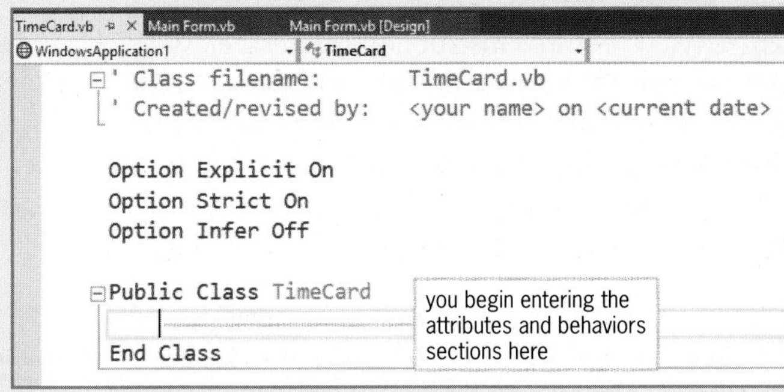

Figure 14-1 How to define a class

Within the Class statement, you define the attributes and behaviors of the objects the class will create. In most cases, the attributes are represented by Private variables and Public properties. The behaviors are represented by methods, which are usually Sub or Function procedures. (You can also include Event procedures in a Class statement. However, that topic is beyond the scope of this book.)

After you define a class, you can use either of the syntax versions in Figure 14-2 to instantiate one or more objects. In both versions, *variableName* is the name of a variable that will represent the object. The difference between the versions relates to when the object is actually created. The computer creates the object only when it processes the statement containing the `New` keyword, which you will learn about later in this chapter. Also included in Figure 14-2 is an example of using each version of the syntax.

HOW TO Instantiate an Object from a Class

Syntax—Version 1
{**Dim** | **Private**} *variableName* **As** *className*
variableName = **New** *className*

Syntax—Version 2
{**Dim** | **Private**} *variableName* **As New** *className*

Figure 14-2 How to instantiate an object from a class *(continues)*

(continued)

Example 1 (using Syntax version 1)
```
Private hoursInfo As TimeCard
hoursInfo = New TimeCard
```
The Private instruction creates a TimeCard variable named `hoursInfo`. The assignment statement instantiates a TimeCard object and assigns it to the `hoursInfo` variable.

Example 2 (using Syntax version 2)
```
Dim hoursInfo As New TimeCard
```
The Dim instruction creates a TimeCard variable named `hoursInfo`. The statement also instantiates a TimeCard object, which it assigns to the `hoursInfo` variable.

Figure 14-2 How to instantiate an object from a class

In Example 1, the `Private hoursInfo As TimeCard` instruction creates a class-level variable that can represent a TimeCard object; however, it does not create the object. The object isn't created until the computer processes the `hoursInfo = New TimeCard` statement, which uses the TimeCard class to instantiate a TimeCard object. The statement assigns the object to the `hoursInfo` variable. In Example 2, the `Dim hoursInfo As New TimeCard` instruction creates a procedure-level variable named `hoursInfo`. It also instantiates a TimeCard object and assigns it to the variable.

The answers to Mini-Quiz questions are located in Appendix A. Each question is associated with one or more objectives listed at the beginning of the chapter.

Mini-Quiz 14-1

1. A class is considered an object. (1)
   a. True
   b. False
2. You enter the Class statement in a class file whose filename extension is ____________. (2)
   a. .cla
   b. .cls
   c. .vb
   d. none of the above
3. Which of the following instantiates an Animal object and assigns it to the dog variable? (3)
   a. `Dim dog As Animal`
   b. `Dim dog As New Animal`
   c. `Dim dog As Animal`
      `dog = New Animal`
   d. both b and c

In the remainder of this chapter, you will view examples of class definitions and also examples of code in which objects are instantiated and used. The first example is a class that contains attributes only, with each attribute represented by a Public variable.

Example 1—A Class That Contains Public Variables Only

In its simplest form, the Class statement can be used in place of the Structure statement, which you learned about in Chapter 11. Like the Structure statement, the Class statement groups related items into one unit. However, the unit is called a class rather than a structure.

Figure 14-3 shows how you could code the Painters Paradise application from Chapter 11 using a class rather than a structure. As you may remember, the application displays the company's gross profit. Figure 14-3 also includes a sample run of the application.

If you want to experiment with the Painters Paradise application, open the solution contained in the Try It 1! folder.

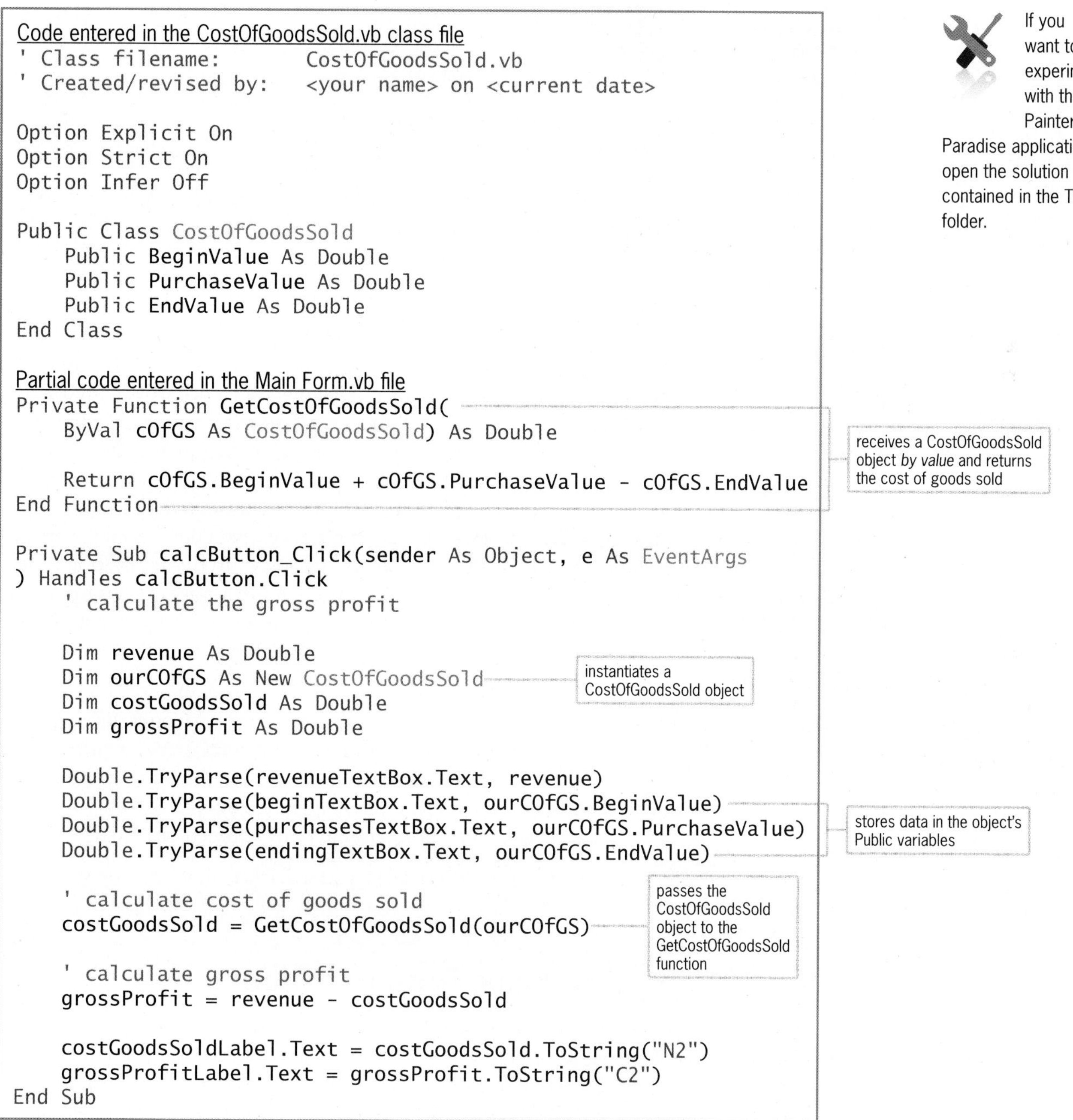

Code entered in the CostOfGoodsSold.vb class file

```
' Class filename:        CostOfGoodsSold.vb
' Created/revised by:    <your name> on <current date>

Option Explicit On
Option Strict On
Option Infer Off

Public Class CostOfGoodsSold
    Public BeginValue As Double
    Public PurchaseValue As Double
    Public EndValue As Double
End Class
```

Partial code entered in the Main Form.vb file

```
Private Function GetCostOfGoodsSold(
    ByVal cOfGS As CostOfGoodsSold) As Double

    Return cOfGS.BeginValue + cOfGS.PurchaseValue - cOfGS.EndValue
End Function

Private Sub calcButton_Click(sender As Object, e As EventArgs
) Handles calcButton.Click
    ' calculate the gross profit

    Dim revenue As Double
    Dim ourCOfGS As New CostOfGoodsSold
    Dim costGoodsSold As Double
    Dim grossProfit As Double

    Double.TryParse(revenueTextBox.Text, revenue)
    Double.TryParse(beginTextBox.Text, ourCOfGS.BeginValue)
    Double.TryParse(purchasesTextBox.Text, ourCOfGS.PurchaseValue)
    Double.TryParse(endingTextBox.Text, ourCOfGS.EndValue)

    ' calculate cost of goods sold
    costGoodsSold = GetCostOfGoodsSold(ourCOfGS)

    ' calculate gross profit
    grossProfit = revenue - costGoodsSold

    costGoodsSoldLabel.Text = costGoodsSold.ToString("N2")
    grossProfitLabel.Text = grossProfit.ToString("C2")
End Sub
```

receives a CostOfGoodsSold object *by value* and returns the cost of goods sold
instantiates a CostOfGoodsSold object
stores data in the object's Public variables
passes the CostOfGoodsSold object to the GetCostOfGoodsSold function

Figure 14-3 Painters Paradise application using a class *(continues)*

(continued)

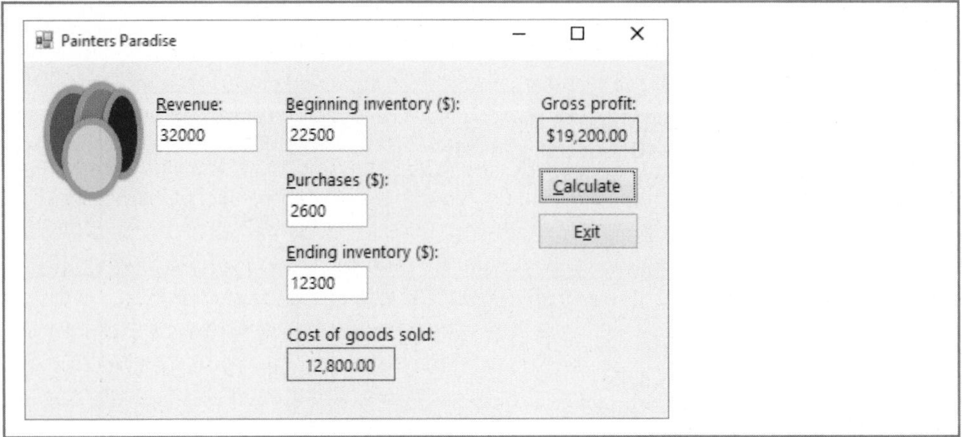

Figure 14-3 Painters Paradise application using a class

Comparing the original code from Figure 11-6 with the code shown in Figure 14-3, you will notice that the Structure statement has been replaced with the Class statement. Unlike the Structure statement, which is entered in the MainForm's Declarations section, the Class statement is entered in a class file named CostOfGoodsSold.vb. The Class statement defines the three attributes of a CostOfGoodsSold object; each attribute is represented by a Public variable. A class's Public variables can be accessed by any application that contains an instance of the class. Using OOP terminology, the Public variables are "exposed" to the application. The convention is to use Pascal case for the names of the Public variables in a class. This is because the Public variables represent properties that will be seen by anyone using an object instantiated from the class. The properties of Visual Basic objects, such as the Text and StartPosition properties, also follow this naming convention.

When comparing both versions of the code, you will also notice that the `Dim ourCOfGS As CostOfGoodsSold` statement in Figure 11-6 is replaced with the `Dim ourCOfGS As New CostOfGoodsSold` statement in Figure 14-3. (Notice the `New` keyword in the latter statement.) The Dim statement in Figure 11-6 declares a structure variable named `ourCOfGS`, whereas the Dim statement in Figure 14-3 instantiates a CostOfGoodsSold object named `ourCOfGS`.

Before viewing the second example of classes and objects, you will learn about Private variables, Public properties, and methods.

Private Variables and Public Property Procedures

Although you can define a class that contains only attributes represented by Public variables—like the CostOfGoodsSold class shown in Figure 14-3—that is rarely done. The disadvantage of using Public variables in a class is that a class cannot control the values assigned to its Public variables. As a result, the class cannot validate the values to ensure they are appropriate for the variables.

Rather than declaring a class's variables using the `Public` keyword, most programmers declare them using the `Private` keyword. When naming the Private variables, many programmers use the underscore as the first character in the name and then camel case for the remainder of the name, like this: `_side`, `_bonus`, and `_annualSales`.

Unlike a class's Public variables, its Private variables are not visible to applications that contain an instance of the class. Using OOP terminology, the Private variables are "hidden" from the application. Because of this, the names of the Private variables will not appear in the IntelliSense list as you are coding the application, nor will they be recognized within the application's code. A class's Private variables can be used only by instructions within the class itself.

For an application to assign data to or retrieve data from a Private variable in a class, it must use a Public property. In other words, an application cannot directly refer to a Private variable in a class. Rather, it must refer to the variable indirectly, through the use of a Public property.

You create a Public property using a **Property procedure**, whose syntax is shown in Figure 14-4. A Public Property procedure creates a property that is visible to any application that contains an instance of the class. In most cases, a Property procedure header begins with the keywords `Public Property`. However, as the syntax indicates, the header can also include one of the following keywords: `ReadOnly` or `WriteOnly`. The **ReadOnly keyword** indicates that the property's value can be retrieved (read) by an application, but the application cannot set (write to) the property. The property would get its value from the class itself rather than from the application. The **WriteOnly keyword** indicates that an application can set the property's value, but it cannot retrieve the value. In this case, the value would be set by the application for use within the class.

As Figure 14-4 shows, the name of the property follows the `Property` keyword in the header. You should use nouns and adjectives to name a property and enter the name using Pascal case, as in Side, Bonus, and AnnualSales. Following the property name is an optional *parameterList* enclosed in parentheses, the keyword `As`, and the property's *dataType*. The dataType must match the data type of the Private variable associated with the Property procedure.

HOW TO Create a Property Procedure

<u>Syntax</u>

Public [**ReadOnly** | **WriteOnly**] **Property** *propertyName*[**(***parameterList***)**] **As** *dataType*
  Get
    [*instructions*]
    Return *privateVariable*
  End Get
  Set(value As *dataType***)**
    [*instructions*]
    privateVariable = {**value** | *defaultValue*}
  End Set
End Property

<u>Example 1—an application can both retrieve and set the Side property's value</u>

```
Private _side As Integer

Public Property Side As Integer
    Get
        Return _side
    End Get
    Set(value As Integer)
        If value > 0 Then
            _side = value
        Else
            _side = 0
        End If
    End Set
End Property
```

Figure 14-4 How to create a Property procedure *(continues)*

(continued)

Example 2—an application can retrieve, but not set, the Bonus property's value
```
Private _bonus As Double

Public ReadOnly Property Bonus As Double
    Get
        Return _bonus
    End Get
End Property
```

Example 3—an application can set, but not retrieve, the AnnualSales property's value
```
Private _annualSales As Decimal

Public WriteOnly Property AnnualSales As Decimal
    Set(value As Decimal)
        _annualSales = value
    End Set
End Property
```

Figure 14-4 How to create a Property procedure

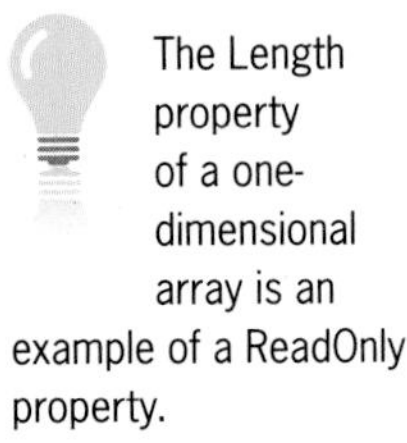

The Length property of a one-dimensional array is an example of a ReadOnly property.

Between a Property procedure's header and footer, you include a Get block of code, a Set block of code, or both Get and Set blocks of code. The appropriate block or blocks of code to include depends on the keywords contained in the procedure header. If the header contains the `ReadOnly` keyword, you include only a Get block of code in the Property procedure. The code contained in the **Get block** allows an application to retrieve the contents of the Private variable associated with the property. In the Property procedure shown in Example 2 in Figure 14-4, the `ReadOnly` keyword indicates that an application can retrieve the contents of the Bonus property, but it cannot set the property's value. The value can be set only by a procedure within the class.

If the header contains the `WriteOnly` keyword, on the other hand, you include only a Set block of code in the procedure. The code in the **Set block** allows an application to assign a value to the Private variable associated with the property. In the Property procedure shown in Example 3 in Figure 14-4, the `WriteOnly` keyword indicates that an application can assign a value to the AnnualSales property, but it cannot retrieve the property's contents. Only a procedure within the class can retrieve the value.

If the Property procedure header does not contain the `ReadOnly` or `WriteOnly` keywords, you include both a Get block of code and a Set block of code in the procedure, as shown in Example 1 in Figure 14-4. In this case, an application can both retrieve and set the Side property's value.

The Get block in a Property procedure contains the **Get statement**, which begins with the Get clause and ends with the End Get clause. Most times, you will enter only the `Return` *privateVariable* instruction within the Get statement. The instruction returns the contents of the Private variable associated with the property. In Example 1 in Figure 14-4, the `Return _side` statement returns the contents of the `_side` variable, which is the Private variable associated with the Side property. Similarly, the `Return _bonus` statement in Example 2 returns the contents of the `_bonus` variable, which is the Private variable associated with the Bonus property. Example 3 does not contain a Get statement because the AnnualSales property is designated as a WriteOnly property.

The Set block contains the **Set statement**, which begins with the Set clause and ends with the End Set clause. The Set clause's `value` parameter temporarily stores the value that is passed to the property by the application. The `value` parameter's *dataType* must match the data type of the Private variable associated with the Property procedure. You can enter one or more instructions between the Set and End Set clauses. One of the instructions should assign the contents of the `value` parameter to the Private variable associated with the property. In Example 3 in Figure 14-4, the `_annualSales = value` statement assigns the contents of the property's `value` parameter to the Private `_annualSales` variable.

In the Set statement, you often will include instructions to validate the value received from the application before assigning it to the Private variable. The Set statement in Example 1 in Figure 14-4 includes a selection structure that determines whether the side measurement received from the application is greater than 0. If it is, the `_side = value` instruction assigns the integer stored in the `value` parameter to the Private `_side` variable. Otherwise, the `_side = 0` instruction assigns a default value (in this case, 0) to the variable. The Property procedure in Example 2 does not contain a Set statement because the Bonus property is designated as a ReadOnly property.

Constructors

Most classes contain at least one constructor. A **constructor** is a class method, always named New, whose sole purpose is to initialize the class's Private variables. Constructors never return a value, so they are always Sub procedures rather than Function procedures. The syntax for creating a constructor is shown in Figure 14-5. Notice that a constructor's *parameterList* is optional. A constructor that has no parameters, like the constructor in Example 1, is called the **default constructor**. A class can have only one default constructor. A constructor that contains one or more parameters, like the constructor in Example 2, is called a **parameterized constructor**. A class can have as many parameterized constructors as needed. However, the parameterList in each parameterized constructor must be unique within the class. The method name (in this case, New) combined with its optional parameterList is called the method's **signature**.

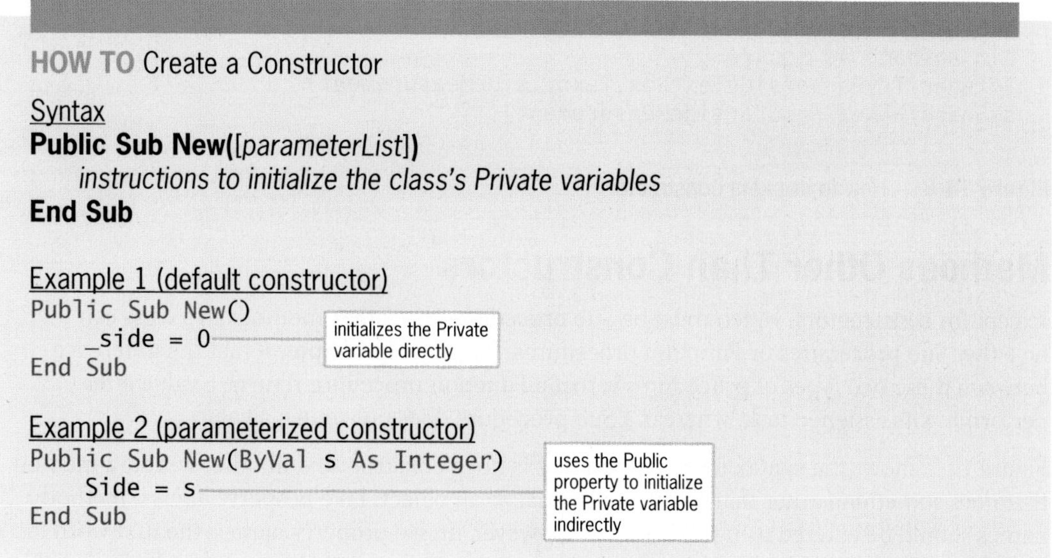

HOW TO Create a Constructor
Syntax
Public Sub New([parameterList])
instructions to initialize the class's Private variables
End Sub
Example 1 (default constructor)
Public Sub New()
_side = 0
End Sub
initializes the Private variable directly
Example 2 (parameterized constructor)
Public Sub New(ByVal s As Integer)
Side = s
End Sub
uses the Public property to initialize the Private variable indirectly

Figure 14-5 How to create a constructor

A default constructor is allowed to initialize the class's Private variables directly, as indicated in Example 1 in Figure 14-5. Parameterized constructors, on the other hand, should use the class's Public properties to access the Private variables indirectly. This is because the values passed to a parameterized constructor come from the application rather than from the class itself. Using a Public property to access a Private variable ensures that the Property procedure's Set block, which may contain validation code, is processed. The parameterized constructor shown in Example 2 in Figure 14-5, for instance, uses the class's Public property to initialize its Private variable, thereby invoking the property's validation code (shown earlier in Figure 14-4).

When an object is instantiated, the computer uses one of the class's constructors to initialize the class's Private variables. If a class contains more than one constructor, the computer determines the appropriate constructor by matching the number, data type, and position of the arguments in the statement that instantiates the object with the number, data type, and position of the parameters listed in each constructor's parameterList. The code in Examples 1 and 2 in Figure 14-6 will invoke the default constructor because the statements containing the `New` keyword do not have any arguments. The code in Examples 3 and 4 will invoke the parameterized constructor because the statements containing the `New` keyword have one argument whose data type is Integer. (Recall that the statement containing the `New` keyword instantiates the object.)

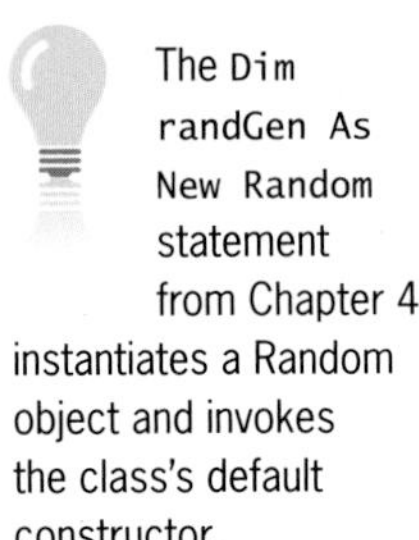

The `Dim randGen As New Random` statement from Chapter 4 instantiates a Random object and invokes the class's default constructor.

HOW TO Invoke a Constructor

Example 1—invokes the default constructor
```
Dim sqShape As New Square
```

Example 2—invokes the default constructor
```
Dim sqShape As Square
sqShape = New Square
```

Example 3—invokes the parameterized constructor
```
Dim sqShape As New Square(15)
```

Example 4—invokes the parameterized constructor
```
Dim sqShape As Square
Integer.TryParse(sideTextBox.Text, sideMeasurement)
sqShape = New Square(sideMeasurement)
```

Figure 14-6 How to invoke a constructor

Methods Other Than Constructors

Except for constructors, which must be Sub procedures, the other methods in a class can be either Sub procedures or Function procedures. Recall from Chapter 8 that the difference between these two types of procedures is that a Function procedure returns a value after performing its assigned task, whereas a Sub procedure does not return a value.

Figure 14-7 shows the syntax for a method that is not a constructor—in other words, a method that does something other than create and initialize an object. Like property names, method names should be entered using Pascal case. However, unlike property names, the first word in a method name should be a verb, and any subsequent words should be nouns and adjectives.

(Visual Basic's SelectAll and TryParse methods follow this naming convention.) Figure 14-7 also includes two examples of a method that allows a Square object to calculate its area. Notice that you can write the method as either a Function procedure or a Sub procedure.

HOW TO Create a Method That Is Not a Constructor

Syntax
Public {**Sub** | **Function**} *methodName*(**[***parameterList***]**) **[As** *dataType***]**
instructions
End {**Sub** | **Function**}

Example 1—Function procedure
```
Public Function GetArea() As Integer
    Return _side * _side
End Function
```

Example 2—Sub procedure
```
Public Sub GetArea(ByRef sqArea As Integer)
    sqArea = _side * _side
End Sub
```

Figure 14-7 How to create a method that is not a constructor

Example 2—A Class That Contains Private Variables, Public Properties, and Methods

Figure 14-8 shows the definition of the Rectangle class, which the Carpets Galore application uses to instantiate a Rectangle object that represents a floor in a room. The figure also shows the application's calcButton_Click procedure, which displays the floor's area (in square yards) and the cost of carpeting the floor. The figure also includes a sample run of the application.

Class statement entered in the Rectangle.vb class file
```
' Class filename:        Rectangle.vb
' Created/revised by:    <your name> on <current date>

Option Explicit On
Option Strict On
Option Infer Off

Public Class Rectangle
    Private _length As Double
    Private _width As Double

    Public Property Length As Double
        Get
            Return _length
        End Get
```

Figure 14-8 Carpets Galore application *(continues)*

If you want to experiment with the Carpets Galore application, open the solution contained in the Try It 2! folder.

(continued)

```
        Set(value As Double)
            If value > 0 Then
                _length = value
            Else
                _length = 0
            End If
        End Set
    End Property

    Public Property Width As Double
        Get
            Return _width
        End Get
        Set(value As Double)
            If value > 0 Then
                _width = value
            Else
                _width = 0
            End If
        End Set
    End Property

    Public Sub New()
        _length = 0
        _width = 0
    End Sub

    Public Sub New(ByVal len As Double, ByVal wid As Double)
        Length = len
        Width = wid
    End Sub

    Public Function GetArea() As Double
        Return _length * _width
    End Function
End Class
```

calcButton_Click procedure entered in the MainForm.vb file

```
Private Sub calcButton_Click(sender As Object, e As EventArgs
) Handles calcButton.Click
    ' displays square yards and cost of carpet

    ' instantiate a Rectangle object
    Dim floor As New Rectangle

    ' declare variables
    Dim priceSqYd As Double
    Dim sqYards As Double
    Dim cost As Double

    ' assign values
    Double.TryParse(lengthListBox.SelectedItem.ToString, floor.Length)
    Double.TryParse(widthListBox.SelectedItem.ToString, floor.Width)
    Double.TryParse(priceListBox.SelectedItem.ToString, priceSqYd)
```

uses the default constructor to instantiate a Rectangle object

uses the object's Public properties to assign values to its Private variables

Figure 14-8 Carpets Galore application *(continues)*

(continued)

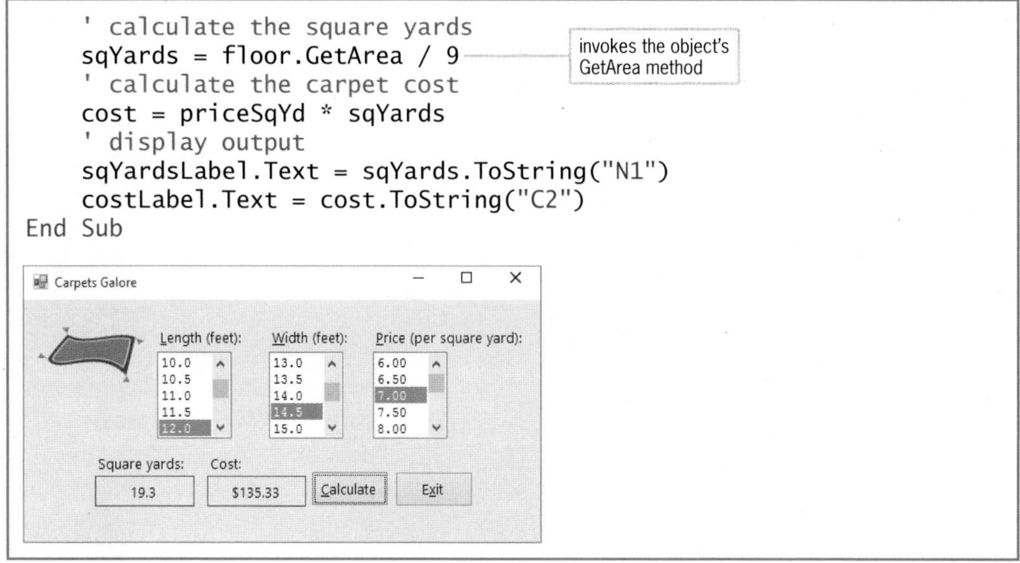

```
    ' calculate the square yards
    sqYards = floor.GetArea / 9
    ' calculate the carpet cost
    cost = priceSqYd * sqYards
    ' display output
    sqYardsLabel.Text = sqYards.ToString("N1")
    costLabel.Text = cost.ToString("C2")
End Sub
```


Figure 14-8 Carpets Galore application

The `Dim floor As New Rectangle` instruction in the calcButton_Click procedure instantiates a Rectangle object, using the class's default constructor to initialize the object's Private variables to the number 0. The first two TryParse methods in the procedure use the object's Public properties to assign values to its Private variables. The procedure then uses the object's GetArea method to calculate and return the area of the floor (in square feet).

Figure 14-9 shows how you could code the calcButton_Click procedure using the parameterized constructor rather than the default constructor used in Figure 14-8. The modifications made to the code are shaded in the figure.

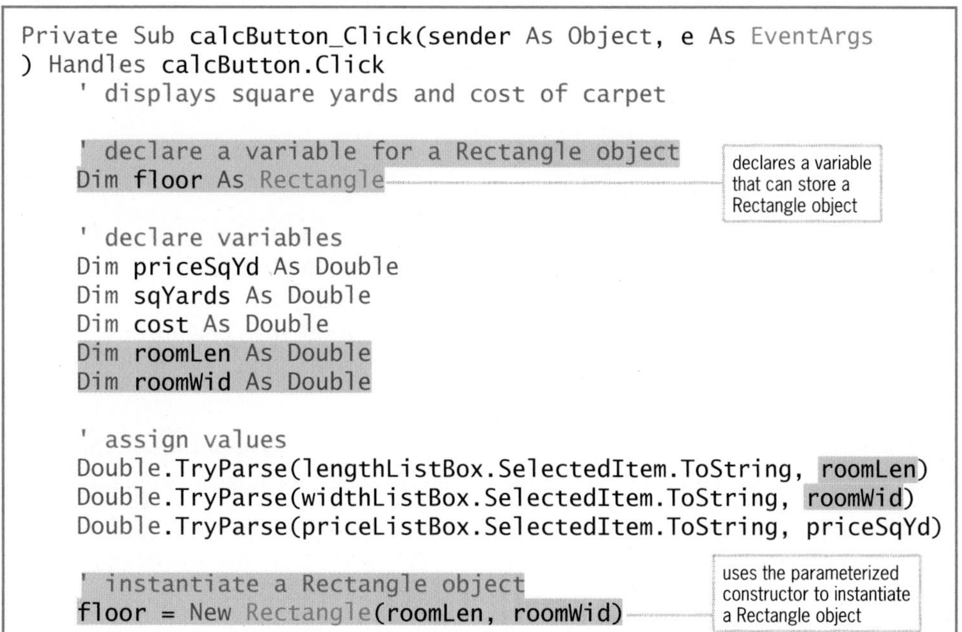

```
Private Sub calcButton_Click(sender As Object, e As EventArgs
) Handles calcButton.Click
    ' displays square yards and cost of carpet

    ' declare a variable for a Rectangle object
    Dim floor As Rectangle

    ' declare variables
    Dim priceSqYd As Double
    Dim sqYards As Double
    Dim cost As Double
    Dim roomLen As Double
    Dim roomWid As Double

    ' assign values
    Double.TryParse(lengthListBox.SelectedItem.ToString, roomLen)
    Double.TryParse(widthListBox.SelectedItem.ToString, roomWid)
    Double.TryParse(priceListBox.SelectedItem.ToString, priceSqYd)

    ' instantiate a Rectangle object
    floor = New Rectangle(roomLen, roomWid)
```


Figure 14-9 calcButton_Click procedure using the parameterized constructor *(continues)*

If you want to experiment with this version of the Carpets Galore application, open the solution contained in the Try It 3! folder.

(continued)

```
    ' calculate the square yards
    sqYards = floor.GetArea / 9
    ' calculate the carpet cost
    cost = priceSqYd * sqYards
    ' display output
    sqYardsLabel.Text = sqYards.ToString("N1")
    costLabel.Text = cost.ToString("C2")
End Sub
```

Figure 14-9 calcButton_Click procedure using the parameterized constructor

In this version of the procedure, the `Dim floor As Rectangle` instruction creates a variable that can store a Rectangle object, but it does not create the object. The object is created when the computer processes the `floor = New Rectangle(roomLen, roomWid)` instruction, which passes its two Double arguments (*by value*) to the parameterized constructor (shown earlier in Figure 14-8). The parameterized constructor stores the values it receives in its `len` and `wid` parameters. The assignment statements in the constructor then assign the parameter values to the Rectangle object's Public Length and Width properties.

When you assign a value to a property, the computer passes the value to the property's Set statement, where it is stored in the Set statement's `value` parameter. In this case, the selection structure in the Length property's Set statement (shown earlier in Figure 14-8) compares the value stored in the `value` parameter with the number 0. If the value is greater than 0, the selection structure's True path assigns the value to the Private `_length` variable; otherwise, its False path assigns the number 0 to the variable. The selection structure in the Width property's Set statement works the same way, except it assigns the appropriate number to the Private `_width` variable.

Notice that a parameterized constructor uses the class's Public properties to access the Private variables indirectly. This is because the values passed to a parameterized constructor come from the application rather than from the class itself. As mentioned earlier, values that originate outside of the class should always be assigned to the Private variables indirectly through the Public properties. Doing this ensures that the Property procedure's Set block, which typically contains validation code, is processed.

Example 3—Reusing a Class

In Example 2, you used the Rectangle class to instantiate an object that represented the floor in a room. In this example, you will use the Rectangle class to instantiate an object that represents a square pizza. A square is simply a rectangle that has four equal sides. As mentioned earlier, the ability to use an object—in this case, a Rectangle object—for more than one purpose saves programming time and money, which contributes to the popularity of object-oriented programming.

Figure 14-10 shows the calcButton_Click procedure in the Pete's Pizzeria application. The procedure uses the Rectangle class from Figure 14-8. The figure also includes a sample run of the application.

If you want to experiment with the Pete's Pizzeria application, open the solution contained in the Try It 4! folder.

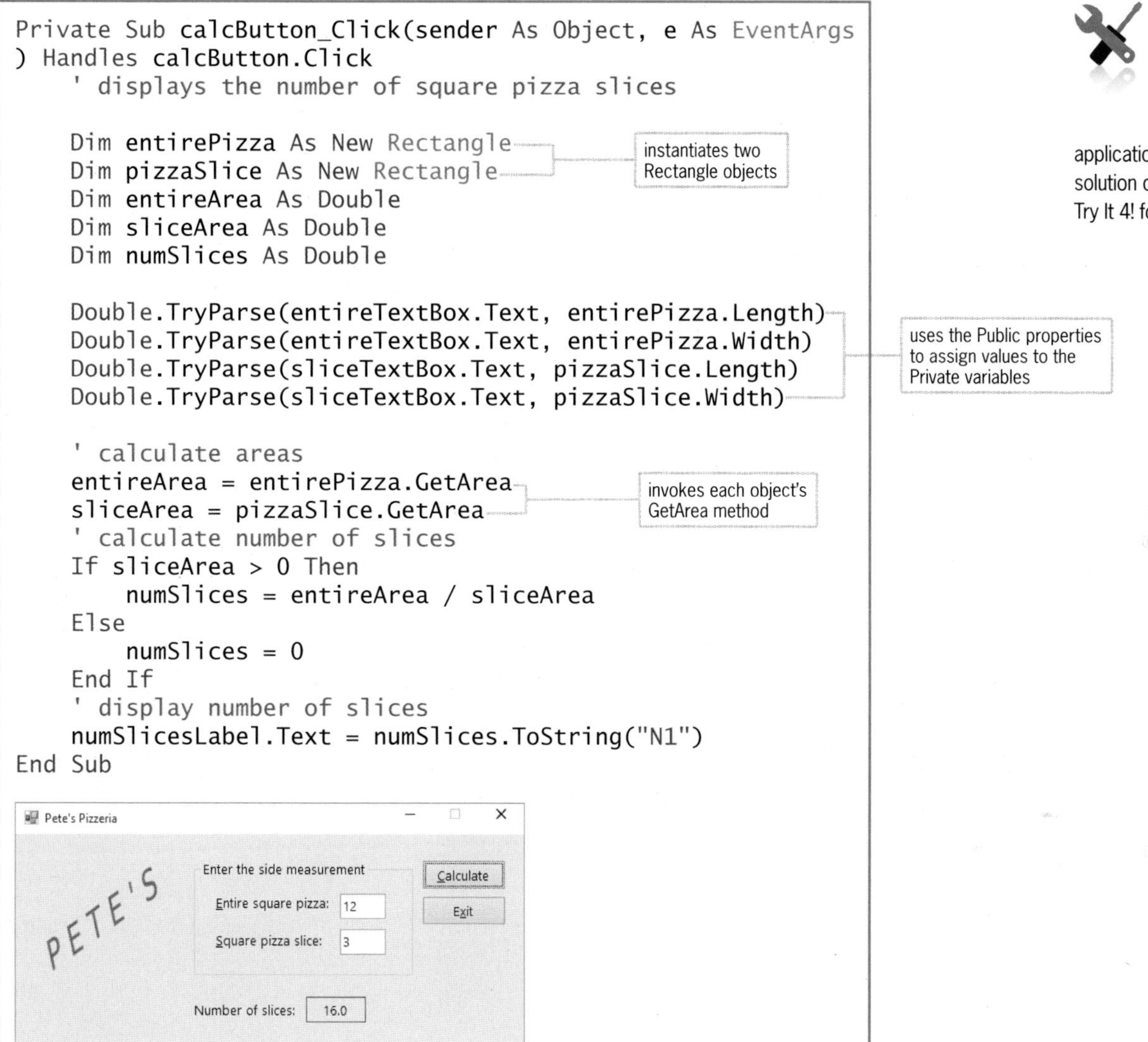
```
Private Sub calcButton_Click(sender As Object, e As EventArgs
) Handles calcButton.Click
    ' displays the number of square pizza slices

    Dim entirePizza As New Rectangle
    Dim pizzaSlice As New Rectangle
    Dim entireArea As Double
    Dim sliceArea As Double
    Dim numSlices As Double

    Double.TryParse(entireTextBox.Text, entirePizza.Length)
    Double.TryParse(entireTextBox.Text, entirePizza.Width)
    Double.TryParse(sliceTextBox.Text, pizzaSlice.Length)
    Double.TryParse(sliceTextBox.Text, pizzaSlice.Width)

    ' calculate areas
    entireArea = entirePizza.GetArea
    sliceArea = pizzaSlice.GetArea
    ' calculate number of slices
    If sliceArea > 0 Then
        numSlices = entireArea / sliceArea
    Else
        numSlices = 0
    End If
    ' display number of slices
    numSlicesLabel.Text = numSlices.ToString("N1")
End Sub
```


Figure 14-10 Pete's Pizzeria application

Example 4—A Class That Contains a ReadOnly Property

As you learned earlier, the `ReadOnly` keyword in a Property procedure's header indicates that the property's value can only be retrieved (read) by an application; the application cannot set (write to) the property. A ReadOnly property gets its value from the class itself rather than from the application. The CourseGrade class shown in Figure 14-11 contains a ReadOnly property named Grade. The property gets its value from the class's DetermineGrade method. The figure also shows the displayButton_Click procedure in the Grade Calculator application. The procedure instantiates a CourseGrade object and then uses the object's DetermineGrade method to determine the student's grade. The procedure displays the grade in the gradeLabel, as shown in the sample run included in the figure.

Class statement entered in the CourseGrade.vb class file

```
' Class filename:       CourseGrade.vb
' Created/revised by:   <your name> on <current date>

Option Explicit On
Option Strict On
Option Infer Off

Public Class CourseGrade
    Private _score1 As Integer
    Private _score2 As Integer
    Private _grade As String

    Public Property Score1 As Integer
        Get
            Return _score1
        End Get
        Set(value As Integer)
            _score1 = value
        End Set
    End Property

    Public Property Score2 As Integer
        Get
            Return _score2
        End Get
        Set(value As Integer)
            _score2 = value
        End Set
    End Property

    Public ReadOnly Property Grade As String
        Get
            Return _grade
        End Get
    End Property

    Public Sub New()
        _score1 = 0
        _score2 = 0
        _grade = String.Empty
    End Sub

    Public Sub DetermineGrade()
        Select Case _score1 + _score2
            Case Is >= 180
                _grade = "A"
            Case Is >= 160
                _grade = "B"
            Case Is >= 140
                _grade = "C"
            Case Is >= 120
                _grade = "D"
            Case Else
                _grade = "F"
```

ReadOnly property

Figure 14-11 Grade Calculator application *(continues)*

(continued)

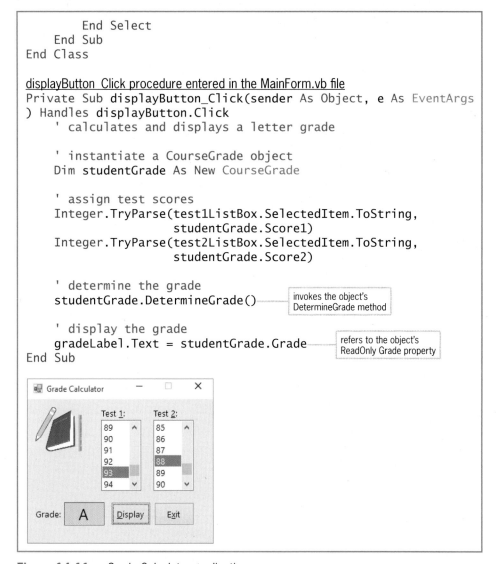

```
        End Select
    End Sub
End Class
```

displayButton_Click procedure entered in the MainForm.vb file

```
Private Sub displayButton_Click(sender As Object, e As EventArgs
) Handles displayButton.Click
    ' calculates and displays a letter grade

    ' instantiate a CourseGrade object
    Dim studentGrade As New CourseGrade

    ' assign test scores
    Integer.TryParse(test1ListBox.SelectedItem.ToString,
                     studentGrade.Score1)
    Integer.TryParse(test2ListBox.SelectedItem.ToString,
                     studentGrade.Score2)

    ' determine the grade
    studentGrade.DetermineGrade()

    ' display the grade
    gradeLabel.Text = studentGrade.Grade
End Sub
```

invokes the object's DetermineGrade method

refers to the object's ReadOnly Grade property

Grade Calculator

Test 1: 89 90 91 92 93 94

Test 2: 85 86 87 88 89 90

Grade: A

Display Exit

Figure 14-11 Grade Calculator application

Example 5—A Class That Contains Auto-Implemented Properties

The **auto-implemented properties** feature in Visual Basic enables you to specify the property of a class in one line of code, as shown in Figure 14-12. When you enter the line of code in the Code Editor window, Visual Basic automatically creates a hidden Private variable that it associates with the property. It also automatically creates hidden Get and Set blocks. The Private variable's name will be the same as the property's name, but it will be preceded by an underscore. For example, if you create an auto-implemented property named City, Visual Basic will create a hidden Private variable named `_City`. Although the auto-implemented properties feature provides a shorter syntax for you to use when creating a class, keep in mind that you will need to use the standard syntax if you want to add validation code to the Set block, or if you want the property to be either ReadOnly or WriteOnly.

HOW TO Create an Auto-Implemented Property

Syntax
Public Property *propertyName* **As** *dataType*

Example 1
`Public Property City As String`
creates a Public property named City, a hidden Private variable named `_City`, and hidden Get and Set blocks

Example 2
`Public Property Sales As Double`
creates a Public property named Sales, a hidden Private variable named `_Sales`, and hidden Get and Set blocks

Figure 14-12 How to create an auto-implemented property

Figure 14-13 shows how you could use the auto-implemented properties feature in the CourseGrade class from the previous section. The code pertaining to the two auto-implemented properties (Score1 and Score2) is shaded in the figure. You cannot use the auto-implemented properties feature for the class's Grade property because that property is ReadOnly. (You will create this class in Programming Tutorial 1.)

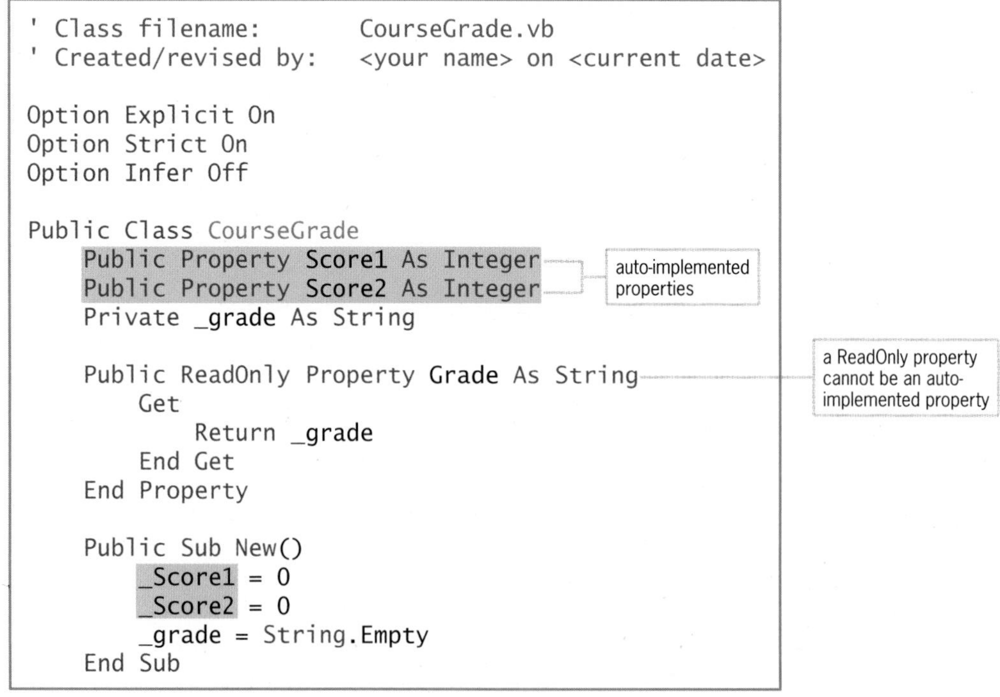

```
' Class filename:        CourseGrade.vb
' Created/revised by:    <your name> on <current date>

Option Explicit On
Option Strict On
Option Infer Off

Public Class CourseGrade
    Public Property Score1 As Integer
    Public Property Score2 As Integer
    Private _grade As String

    Public ReadOnly Property Grade As String
        Get
            Return _grade
        End Get
    End Property

    Public Sub New()
        _Score1 = 0
        _Score2 = 0
        _grade = String.Empty
    End Sub
```

auto-implemented properties
a ReadOnly property cannot be an auto-implemented property

Figure 14-13 CourseGrade class using auto-implemented properties *(continues)*

(continued)

```
    Public Sub DetermineGrade()
        Select Case _Score1 + _Score2
            Case Is >= 180
                _grade = "A"
            Case Is >= 160
                _grade = "B"
            Case Is >= 140
                _grade = "C"
            Case Is >= 120
                _grade = "D"
            Case Else
                _grade = "F"
        End Select
    End Sub
End Class
```

Figure 14-13 CourseGrade class using auto-implemented properties

Example 6—A Class That Contains Overloaded Methods

In this example, you will use a class named Employee to instantiate an object. Employee objects have the attributes and behaviors listed in Figure 14-14.

Attributes of an Employee object
employee number
employee name

Behaviors of an Employee object
1. An employee object can initialize its attributes using values provided by the class.
2. An employee object can initialize its attributes using values provided by the application in which it is instantiated.
3. An employee object can calculate and return the gross pay for salaried employees, who are paid twice per month. The gross pay is calculated by dividing the salaried employee's annual salary by 24.
4. An employee object can calculate and return the gross pay for hourly employees, who are paid weekly. The gross pay is calculated by multiplying the number of hours the employee worked during the week by his or her pay rate.

Figure 14-14 Attributes and behaviors of an Employee object

Figure 14-15 shows the Employee class defined in the Employee.vb file. The class contains two auto-implemented properties and four methods. The two New methods are the class's default and parameterized constructors. The default constructor initializes the class's Private variables directly, while the parameterized constructor uses the class's Public properties to initialize the Private variables indirectly. As you learned earlier, using a Public property in this manner ensures that the computer processes any validation code associated with the property. Even though the EmpNumber and EmpName properties in Figure 14-15 do not have any validation code, you should use the properties in the parameterized constructor in case validation code is added to the class in the future.

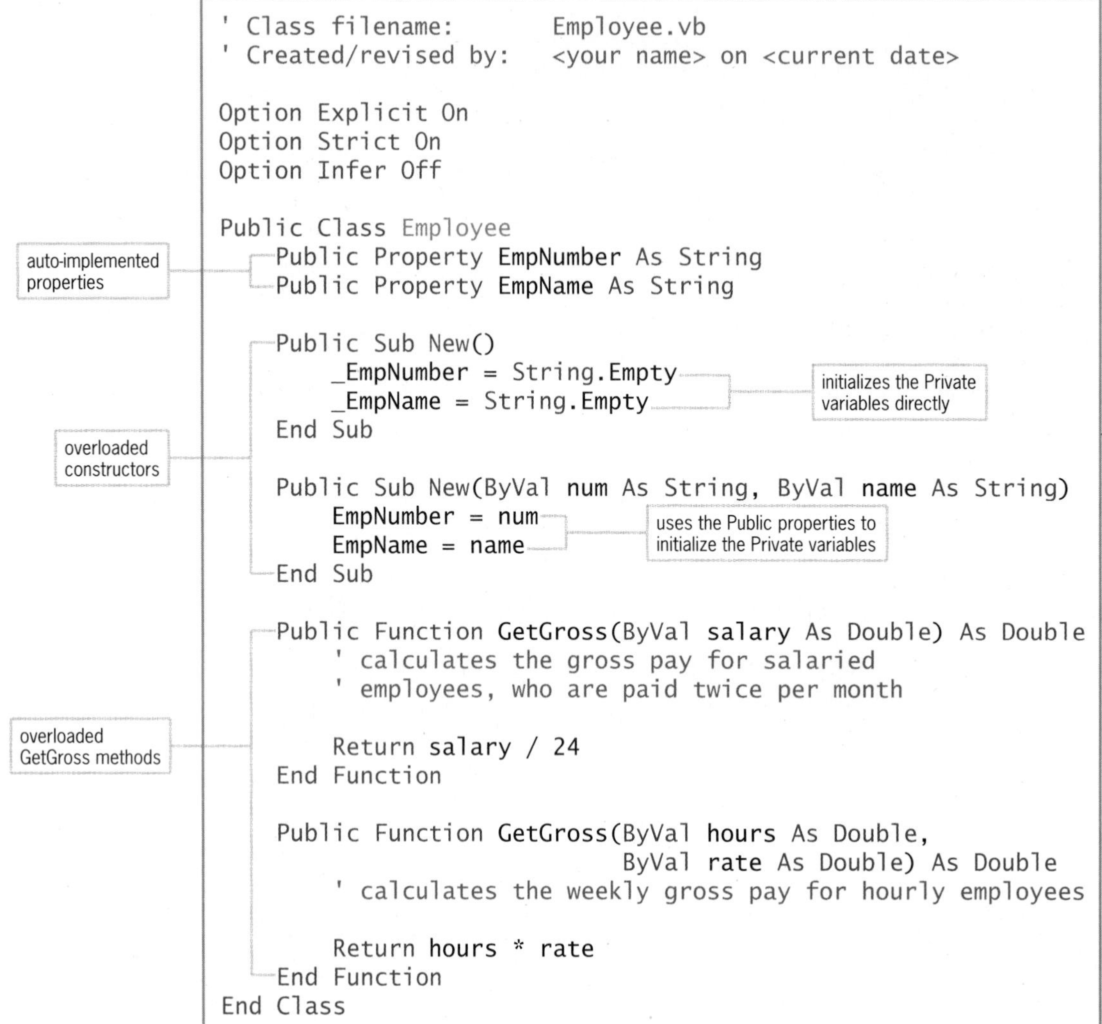

```
' Class filename:       Employee.vb
' Created/revised by:   <your name> on <current date>

Option Explicit On
Option Strict On
Option Infer Off

Public Class Employee
    Public Property EmpNumber As String
    Public Property EmpName As String

    Public Sub New()
        _EmpNumber = String.Empty
        _EmpName = String.Empty
    End Sub

    Public Sub New(ByVal num As String, ByVal name As String)
        EmpNumber = num
        EmpName = name
    End Sub

    Public Function GetGross(ByVal salary As Double) As Double
        ' calculates the gross pay for salaried
        ' employees, who are paid twice per month

        Return salary / 24
    End Function

    Public Function GetGross(ByVal hours As Double,
                             ByVal rate As Double) As Double
        ' calculates the weekly gross pay for hourly employees

        Return hours * rate
    End Function
End Class
```

auto-implemented properties
initializes the Private variables directly
overloaded constructors
uses the Public properties to initialize the Private variables
overloaded GetGross methods

Figure 14-15 Employee class definition

When two or more methods have the same name but different parameters, the methods are referred to as **overloaded methods**. The two constructors in Figure 14-15 are considered overloaded methods because each is named New and each has a different parameterList. You can overload any of the methods contained in a class, not just constructors. The two GetGross methods in the figure are also overloaded methods because they have the same name but a different parameterList.

In previous chapters, you used several of the overloaded methods built into Visual Basic, such as the ToString, TryParse, Convert.ToDecimal, and MessageBox.Show methods. When you enter an overloaded method in the Code Editor window, the Code Editor's IntelliSense feature displays a box that allows you to view a method's signatures, one signature at a time. Recall that a method's signature includes its name and optional parameterList. The list box shown in Figure 14-16 displays the first of the MessageBox.Show method's 21 signatures. You use the up and down arrows in the box to display the other signatures. If a class you create contains overloaded methods, the signatures of those methods will also be displayed in the IntelliSense box.

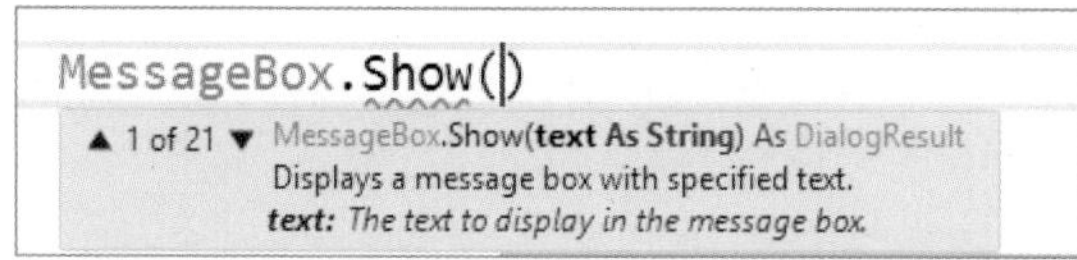

Figure 14-16 First of the MessageBox.Show method's 21 signatures

Overloading is useful when two or more methods require different parameters to perform essentially the same task. Both overloaded constructors in the Employee class, for example, initialize the class's Private variables. However, the default constructor does not need to be passed any information to perform the task, while the parameterized constructor requires two items of information (the employee number and name). Similarly, both GetGross methods in the Employee class calculate and return a gross pay amount. However, the first GetGross method performs its task for salaried employees and requires an application to pass it one item of information: the employee's annual salary. The second GetGross method performs its task for hourly employees and requires two items of information: the number of hours the employee worked and his or her rate of pay. Rather than using two overloaded GetGross methods, you could have used two methods having different names, such as GetSalariedGross and GetHourlyGross. The advantage of overloading the GetGross method is that you need to remember the name of only one method.

The Employee class is used in the Woods Manufacturing application, which displays the gross pay for salaried and hourly employees. Salaried employees are paid twice per month. Therefore, each salaried employee's gross pay is calculated by dividing his or her annual salary by 24. Hourly employees are paid weekly. The gross pay for an hourly employee is calculated by multiplying the number of hours the employee worked during the week by his or her hourly pay rate. The application also displays a report showing each employee's number, name, and gross pay. Figure 14-17 shows the application's calcButton_Click procedure and includes two sample runs of the application.

If you want to experiment with the Woods Manufacturing application, open the solution contained in the Try It 5! folder.

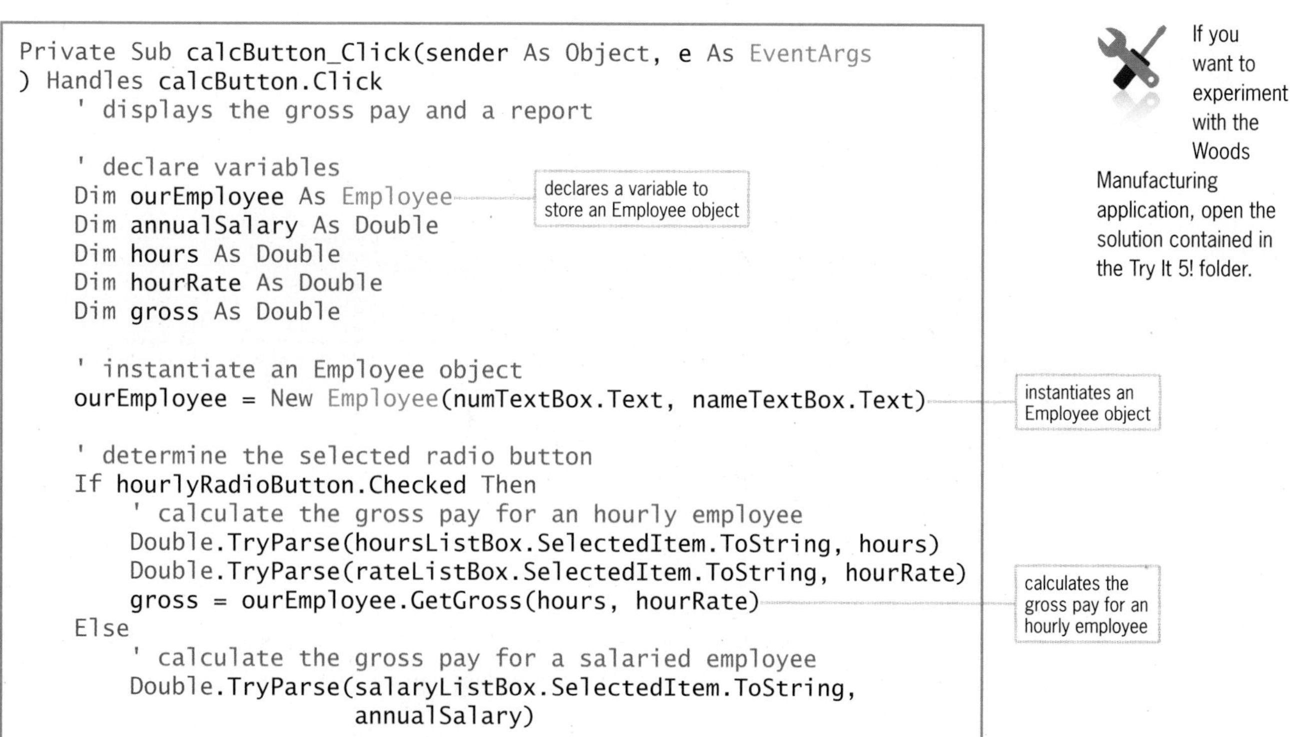

```
Private Sub calcButton_Click(sender As Object, e As EventArgs
) Handles calcButton.Click
    ' displays the gross pay and a report

    ' declare variables
    Dim ourEmployee As Employee
    Dim annualSalary As Double
    Dim hours As Double
    Dim hourRate As Double
    Dim gross As Double

    ' instantiate an Employee object
    ourEmployee = New Employee(numTextBox.Text, nameTextBox.Text)

    ' determine the selected radio button
    If hourlyRadioButton.Checked Then
        ' calculate the gross pay for an hourly employee
        Double.TryParse(hoursListBox.SelectedItem.ToString, hours)
        Double.TryParse(rateListBox.SelectedItem.ToString, hourRate)
        gross = ourEmployee.GetGross(hours, hourRate)
    Else
        ' calculate the gross pay for a salaried employee
        Double.TryParse(salaryListBox.SelectedItem.ToString,
                        annualSalary)
```


Figure 14-17 calcButton_Click procedure and two sample runs *(continues)*

(continued)

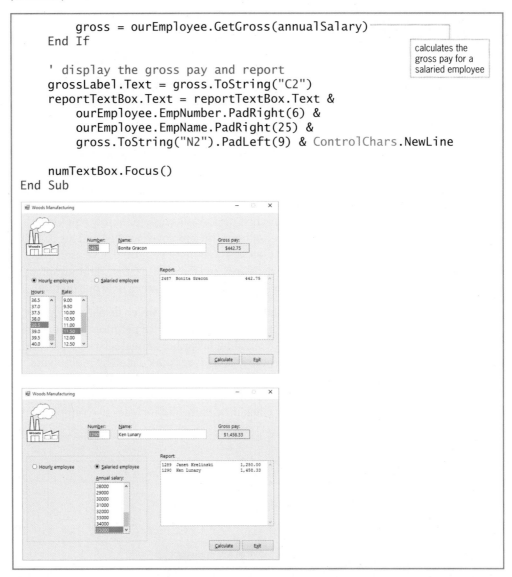

```
        gross = ourEmployee.GetGross(annualSalary)
    End If

    ' display the gross pay and report
    grossLabel.Text = gross.ToString("C2")
    reportTextBox.Text = reportTextBox.Text &
        ourEmployee.EmpNumber.PadRight(6) &
        ourEmployee.EmpName.PadRight(25) &
        gross.ToString("N2").PadLeft(9) & ControlChars.NewLine

    numTextBox.Focus()
End Sub
```

calculates the gross pay for a salaried employee

Figure 14-17 calcButton_Click procedure and two sample runs

The answers to Mini-Quiz questions are located in Appendix A. Each question is associated with one or more objectives listed at the beginning of the chapter.

Mini-Quiz 14-2

1. Some constructors return a value. (6)

   a. True b. False

2. A Private variable in a class can be accessed directly by a Public method in the same class. (6, 7)

   a. True b. False

3. The name of the default constructor for a class named Animal is ____________. (6)

   a. Animal
   b. AnimalConstructor
   c. Constructor
   d. none of the above

4. The validation code is entered in the ____________ block in a Property procedure. (5)

   a. Assign
   b. Get
   c. Set
   d. Validate

You have completed the concepts section of Chapter 14. The Programming Tutorial section is next.

PROGRAMMING TUTORIAL 1

Coding the Grade Calculator Application

In this tutorial, you will create an application that displays a student's grade. The grade is based on two tests whose scores can be from 0 through 100. The grading scale is shown in Figure 14-18 along with the application's TOE chart and MainForm. The MainForm contains four labels, two list boxes, a picture box, and two buttons.

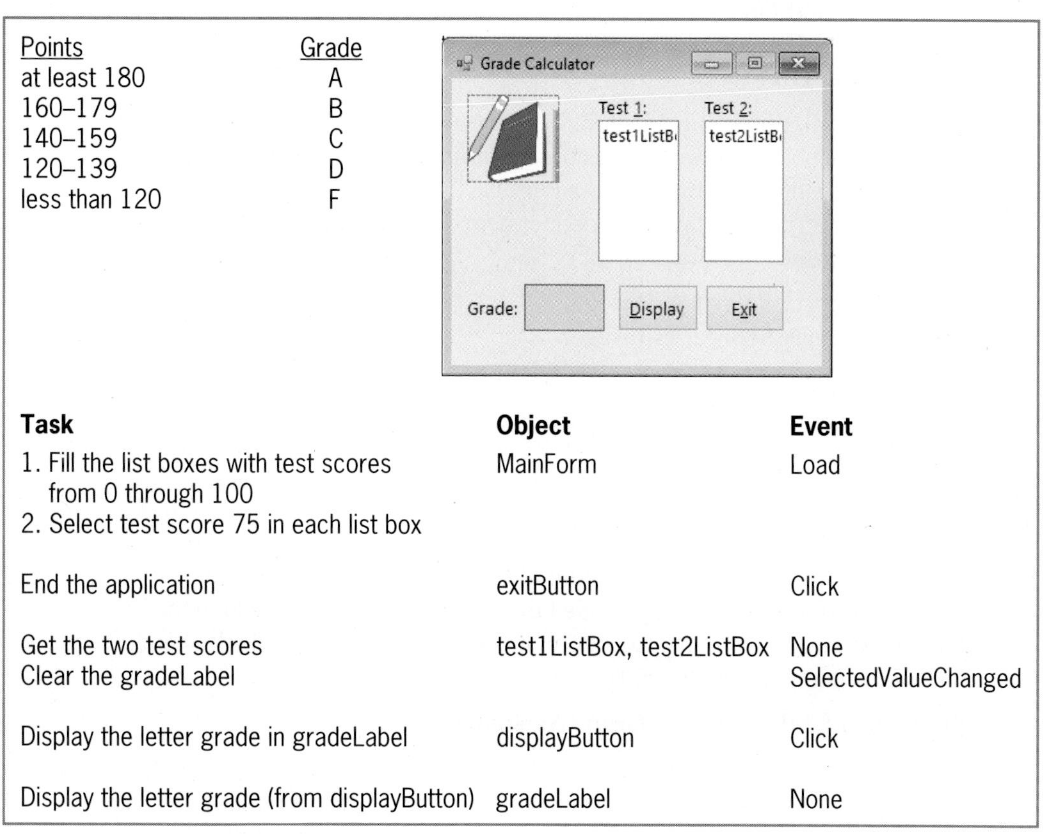

Points	Grade
at least 180	A
160–179	B
140–159	C
120–139	D
less than 120	F

Task	Object	Event
1. Fill the list boxes with test scores from 0 through 100 2. Select test score 75 in each list box	MainForm	Load
End the application	exitButton	Click
Get the two test scores Clear the gradeLabel	test1ListBox, test2ListBox	None SelectedValueChanged
Display the letter grade in gradeLabel	displayButton	Click
Display the letter grade (from displayButton)	gradeLabel	None

Figure 14-18 Grading scale, TOE chart, and MainForm for the Grade Calculator application

Creating the CourseGrade Class

First, you will open the Grade Calculator application and then create the CourseGrade class shown earlier in Figure 14-13. The CourseGrade class contains three attributes: two test scores and a letter grade. It also contains a default constructor that initializes the test scores to 0 and initializes the letter grade to the empty string. In addition, it contains the DetermineGrade method, which determines the appropriate letter grade based on the sum of both test scores.

To open the application and create the CourseGrade class:

1. Start Visual Studio. Open the **Grade Solution** (**Grade Solution.sln**) file contained in the VbReloaded2015\Chap14\Grade Solution folder. If necessary, open the designer window.
2. Click **Project** on the menu bar and then click **Add Class**. The Add New Item dialog box opens with Class selected in the middle column. Change the entry in the Name box to **CourseGrade.vb** and then click the **Add** button.
3. Press **Enter** to insert a blank line above the Public Class clause. Beginning in the blank line, enter the following two comments, replacing <your name> and <current date> with your name and the current date, respectively. Press **Enter** twice after typing the second comment.

   ```
   ' Class filename:      CourseGrade.vb
   ' Created/revised by:  <your name> on <current date>
   ```

4. Enter the following Option statements:

   ```
   Option Explicit On
   Option Strict On
   Option Infer Off
   ```

5. Click the **blank line** below the Public Class clause. The application that uses a CourseGrade object will be responsible for verifying that the two test scores are within the required range of 0 through 100. Because the class will not need to validate its two test score attributes, you can define them using the auto-implemented properties feature. Enter the following lines of code:

   ```
   Public Property Score1 As Integer
   Public Property Score2 As Integer
   ```

6. The third attribute is the letter grade, which will be determined by the class itself. The user should not be allowed to change the letter grade after it has been determined, so you will need to define the attribute using a Private variable and a Public ReadOnly property. Type the following line of code, and then press **Enter** twice:

   ```
   Private _grade As String
   ```

7. Enter the following Property procedure header and Get clause. When you press Enter after typing the Get clause, the Code Editor will automatically include the End Get and End Property clauses in the procedure. It will not enter the Set block of code because the header contains the `ReadOnly` keyword.

   ```
   Public ReadOnly Property Grade As String
   Get
   ```

8. As you learned in the chapter, the Get statement typically contains an instruction that returns the contents of the property's Private variable. Type the following statement, but don't press Enter:

   ```
   Return _grade
   ```

9. Next, you will enter the default constructor in the class. The default constructor will initialize the Private variables when a CourseGrade object is instantiated. Insert **two blank lines** above the End Class clause. Beginning in the blank line immediately above the clause, enter the following default constructor:

```
Public Sub New()
    _Score1 = 0
    _Score2 = 0
    _grade = String.Empty
End Sub
```

10. Finally, you will enter the DetermineGrade method, which will assign the appropriate grade to the Private `_grade` variable. The method will be a Sub procedure because it will not need to return a value to the application that invokes it. Insert **two blank lines** above the End Class clause, and then enter the following procedure header in the blank line immediately above the clause:

```
Public Sub DetermineGrade()
```

11. Now, enter the following Select Case statement:

```
Select Case _Score1 + _Score2
   Case Is >= 180
      _grade = "A"
   Case Is >= 160
      _grade = "B"
   Case Is >= 140
      _grade = "C"
   Case Is >= 120
      _grade = "D"
   Case Else
      _grade = "F"
End Select
```

12. Save the solution, and then close the CourseGrade.vb window.

Coding the displayButton's Click Event Procedure

According to the application's TOE chart (shown earlier in Figure 14-18), the following procedures need to be coded: the MainForm's Load event procedure, the Click event procedures for the two buttons, and the SelectedValueChanged procedure for the two list boxes. All but the displayButton_Click procedure have already been coded for you.

To code and then test the displayButton_Click procedure:

1. Open the MainForm's Code Editor window. In the comments that appear in the General Declarations section, replace <your name> and <current date> with your name and the current date, respectively.
2. Locate the displayButton_Click procedure, and then click the **blank line** below the `' instantiate a CourseGrade object` comment. Enter the following Dim statement:

```
Dim studentGrade As New CourseGrade
```

3. The procedure will use the object's Public properties to assign the test scores, which are selected in the list boxes, to the object's Private variables. Click the **blank line** below the `' assign test scores` comment, and then enter the following assignment statements:

```
Integer.TryParse(test1ListBox.SelectedItem.ToString,
                 studentGrade.Score1)
Integer.TryParse(test2ListBox.SelectedItem.ToString,
                 studentGrade.Score2)
```

PROGRAMMING TUTORIAL 1

4. Next, the procedure will use the object's DetermineGrade method to determine the appropriate grade. Click the **blank line** below the `' determine the grade` comment, and then enter the following statement:

   studentGrade.DetermineGrade()

5. Finally, the procedure will use the object's ReadOnly Grade property to display the grade stored in the Private `_grade` variable. Click the **blank line** below the `' display the grade` comment. Type the following code (including the second period), but don't press Enter.

   gradeLabel.Text = studentGrade.

6. Click **Grade** in the IntelliSense list. See Figure 14-19. The message that appears next to the IntelliSense list indicates that the Grade property is ReadOnly.

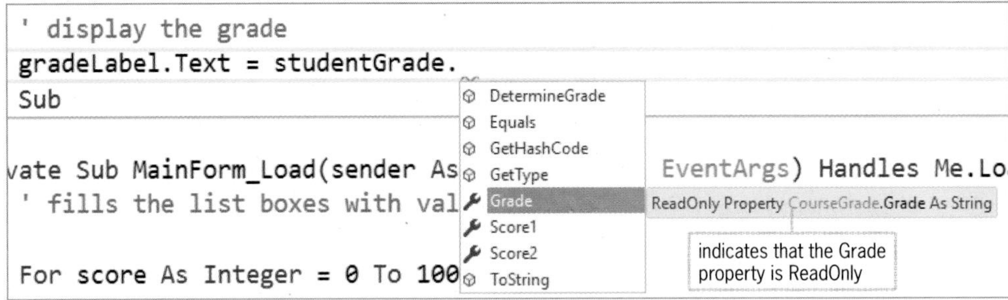

Figure 14-19 ReadOnly property message

7. Press **Tab** to include the Grade property in the assignment statement.

8. Save the solution and then start the application. Click **93** in the Test 1 box and then click **88** in the Test 2 box. Click the **Display** button. The letter A appears in the Grade box. See Figure 14-20.

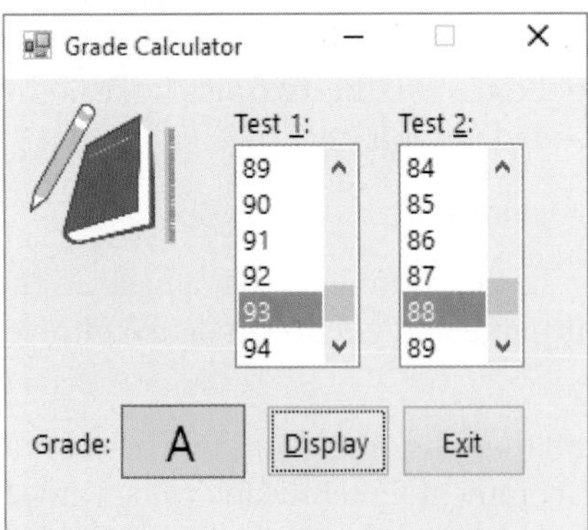

Figure 14-20 Grade shown in the interface

9. On your own, test the application using different test scores. When you are finished, click the **Exit** button. Close the Code Editor window and then close the solution. Figure 14-21 shows the code entered in the CourseGrade.vb and MainForm.vb files.

Class statement entered in the CourseGrade.vb class file

```
' Class filename:         CourseGrade.vb
' Created/revised by:     <your name> on <current date>

Option Explicit On
Option Strict On
Option Infer Off

Public Class CourseGrade
    Public Property Score1 As Integer
    Public Property Score2 As Integer
    Private _grade As String

    Public ReadOnly Property Grade As String
        Get
            Return _grade
        End Get
    End Property

    Public Sub New()
        _Score1 = 0
        _Score2 = 0
        _grade = String.Empty
    End Sub

    Public Sub DetermineGrade()
        Select Case _Score1 + _Score2
            Case Is >= 180
                _grade = "A"
            Case Is >= 160
                _grade = "B"
            Case Is >= 140
                _grade = "C"
            Case Is >= 120
                _grade = "D"
            Case Else
                _grade = "F"
        End Select
    End Sub
End Class
```

Code entered in the MainForm.vb file

```
' Project name:           Grade Project
' Project purpose:        Displays a grade based on two test scores
' Created/revised by:     <your name> on <current date>

Option Explicit On
Option Strict On
Option Infer On

Public Class MainForm
    Private Sub displayButton_Click(sender As Object, e As EventArgs) Handles displayButton.Click
        ' calculates and displays a letter grade

```

Figure 14-21 Code for the Grade Calculator application *(continues)*

(continued)

```
        ' instantiate a CourseGrade object
        Dim studentGrade As New CourseGrade

        ' assign test scores
        Integer.TryParse(test1ListBox.SelectedItem.ToString,
                         studentGrade.Score1)
        Integer.TryParse(test2ListBox.SelectedItem.ToString,
                         studentGrade.Score2)

        ' determine the grade
        studentGrade.DetermineGrade()

        ' display the grade
        gradeLabel.Text = studentGrade.Grade
    End Sub

    Private Sub MainForm_Load(sender As Object, e As EventArgs
    ) Handles Me.Load
        ' fills the list boxes with values

        For score As Integer = 0 To 100
            test1ListBox.Items.Add(score.ToString)
            test2ListBox.Items.Add(score.ToString)
        Next score

        test1ListBox.SelectedItem = "75"
        test2ListBox.SelectedItem = "75"
    End Sub

    Private Sub exitButton_Click(sender As Object, e As EventArgs
    ) Handles exitButton.Click
        Me.Close()
    End Sub

    Private Sub ClearLabel(sender As Object, e As EventArgs
    ) Handles test1ListBox.SelectedValueChanged,
    test2ListBox.SelectedValueChanged
        gradeLabel.Text = String.Empty
    End Sub
End Class
```

Figure 14-21 Code for the Grade Calculator application

PROGRAMMING TUTORIAL 2

Modifying the Lucky Number Game Application

In this tutorial, you will modify the Lucky Number Game application from Chapter 6's Programming Tutorial 1. The modified application will use a class named PairOfDice.

To open the application and create the PairOfDice class:

1. Start Visual Studio. Open the **Lucky Solution** (**Lucky Solution.sln**) file contained in the VbReloaded2015\Chap14\Lucky Solution folder. If necessary, open the designer window.

2. Use the Project menu to add a new Class to the project. Name the class file **PairOfDice.vb**.
3. Insert a **blank line** above the Public Class clause. Enter the following comments, replacing <your name> and <current date> with your name and the current date, respectively. Press **Enter** twice after typing the second comment.

   ' Class filename: PairOfDice.vb
   ' Created/revised by: <your name> on <current date>
4. Now, enter the appropriate Option statements.
5. The PairOfDice class should contain two Private Integer variables named `_die1` and `_die2`. Click the **blank line** below the Public Class clause and then enter the appropriate statements. Press **Enter** twice after typing the last statement.
6. Enter Public Property procedures for the two Private variables. The properties should be ReadOnly. Name the properties Die1 and Die2.
7. Enter the default constructor, which should initialize the Private variables to 0.
8. Enter a Public method named RollDice. The method should be a Sub procedure that generates two random integers from 1 through 6. The random integers should be assigned to the class's Private variables.
9. Save the solution, and then close the PairOfDice.vb window.

Now, you will modify the code contained in the rollButton_Click procedure.

To modify the rollButton_Click procedure:

1. Open the MainForm's Code Editor window. In the comments that appear in the General Declarations section, replace <your name> and <current date> with your name and the current date, respectively.
2. Locate the rollButton_Click procedure. Replace the `Dim random1 As Integer` and `Dim random2 As Integer` statements with a Dim statement that declares a PairOfDice variable named `dice`. The Dim statement should also instantiate a PairOfDice object.
3. Replace the two statements that assign values to the `random1` and `random2` variables with a statement that invokes the PairOfDice object's RollDice procedure.
4. Replace `random1` in the first Select Case clause with the PairOfDice object's Die1 property.
5. Replace `random2` in the second Select Case clause with the PairOfDice object's Die2 property.
6. Replace `random1` and `random2` in the first If clause with the appropriate properties.
7. Save the solution and then start the application. Click the **Roll 'Em** button. See Figure 14-22. Because random numbers determine the images assigned to the two picture boxes, your application might display different images than those shown in the figure. Also, if the sum of the dots on both of your dice equals 7, your Points box will contain the number 12 rather than the number 9.

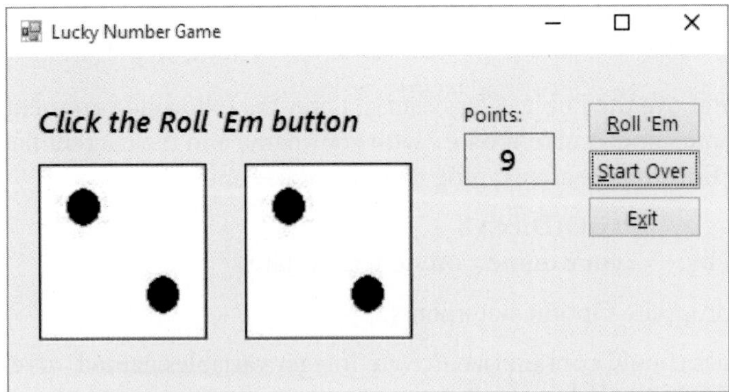

Figure 14-22 Sample run of the Lucky Number Game application

8. Click the **Exit** button. Close the Code Editor window and then close the solution. Figure 14-23 shows the code entered in the PairOfDice.vb file. It also shows the modified rollButton_Click procedure. The changes made to the original procedure are shaded in the figure.

Class statement entered in the PairOfDice.vb class file

```
' Class filename:        PairOfDice.vb
' Created/revised by:    <your name> on <current date>

Option Explicit On
Option Strict On
Option Infer Off

Public Class PairOfDice
    Private _die1 As Integer
    Private _die2 As Integer

    Public ReadOnly Property Die1 As Integer
        Get
            Return _die1
        End Get
    End Property

    Public ReadOnly Property Die2 As Integer
        Get
            Return _die2
        End Get
    End Property

    Public Sub New()
        _die1 = 0
        _die2 = 0
    End Sub

    Public Sub RollDice()
        Dim randGen As New Random
        _die1 = randGen.Next(1, 7)
        _die2 = randGen.Next(1, 7)
    End Sub
End Class
```

Figure 14-23 PairOfDice class and rollButton_Click procedure *(continues)*

(continued)

rollButton Click event procedure entered in the MainForm.vb file

```
Private Sub rollButton_Click(sender As Object, e As EventArgs) Handles rollButton.Click
    ' simulates the Lucky Number Game

    Dim randGen As New Random
    Dim dice As New PairOfDice

    ' remove images
    firstDiePictureBox.Image = Nothing
    secondDiePictureBox.Image = Nothing

    ' disable Roll 'Em button
    rollButton.Enabled = False

    ' refresh form and then delay execution
    Me.Refresh()
    System.Threading.Thread.Sleep(1000)

    ' generate two random integers from 1 through 6
    dice.RollDice()

    ' display appropriate image in firstDiePictureBox
    Select Case dice.Die1
        Case 1
            firstDiePictureBox.Image = dot1PictureBox.Image
        Case 2
            firstDiePictureBox.Image = dot2PictureBox.Image
        Case 3
            firstDiePictureBox.Image = dot3PictureBox.Image
        Case 4
            firstDiePictureBox.Image = dot4PictureBox.Image
        Case 5
            firstDiePictureBox.Image = dot5PictureBox.Image
        Case Else
            firstDiePictureBox.Image = dot6PictureBox.Image
    End Select

    ' display appropriate image in secondDiePictureBox
    Select Case dice.Die2
        Case 1
            secondDiePictureBox.Image = dot1PictureBox.Image
        Case 2
            secondDiePictureBox.Image = dot2PictureBox.Image
        Case 3
            secondDiePictureBox.Image = dot3PictureBox.Image
        Case 4
            secondDiePictureBox.Image = dot4PictureBox.Image
        Case 5
            secondDiePictureBox.Image = dot5PictureBox.Image
        Case Else
            secondDiePictureBox.Image = dot6PictureBox.Image
    End Select

```

Figure 14-23 PairOfDice class and rollButton_Click procedure *(continues)*

(continued)

```
    ' check sum of random numbers
    If dice.Die1 + dice.Die2 = 7 Then
        Dim count As Integer = 1
        Do While count <= 10
            numberLabel.Visible = Not numberLabel.Visible
            Me.Refresh()
            System.Threading.Thread.Sleep(200)
            count += 1
        Loop
        points += 2
    Else
        points -= 1
        If points = 0 Then
        MessageBox.Show("Sorry, you lost all of your points! " &
                "Click the Start Over button to try again.",
                "Lucky Number Game", MessageBoxButtons.OK,
                MessageBoxIcon.Information)
        End If
    End If
    ' display points
    pointsLabel.Text = points.ToString
    ' enable Roll 'Em button
    rollButton.Enabled = True

    End Sub
```

Figure 14-23 PairOfDice class and rollButton_Click procedure

PROGRAMMING EXAMPLE

Kessler Landscaping Application

Create an application that estimates the cost of laying sod. Use the following names for the solution and project, respectively: Kessler Solution and Kessler Project. Save the application in the VbReloaded2015\Chap14 folder. Change the form file's name to Main Form.vb. Add a new class file named Rectangle.vb to the project. See Figures 14-24 through 14-29.

Task	Object	Event
1. Calculate the area of the rectangle 2. Calculate the total price 3. Display the total price in the totalLabel	calcButton	Click
End the application	exitButton	Click
Display the total price (from calcButton)	totalLabel	None
Get the length in feet	lengthTextBox	None
Get the width in feet	widthTextBox	None
Get the price of the sod per square yard	priceTextBox	None

Figure 14-24 TOE chart *(continues)*

(continued)

Clear the contents of the totalLabel	lengthTextBox, widthTextBox, priceTextBox	TextChanged
Select the existing text		Enter

Figure 14-24 TOE chart

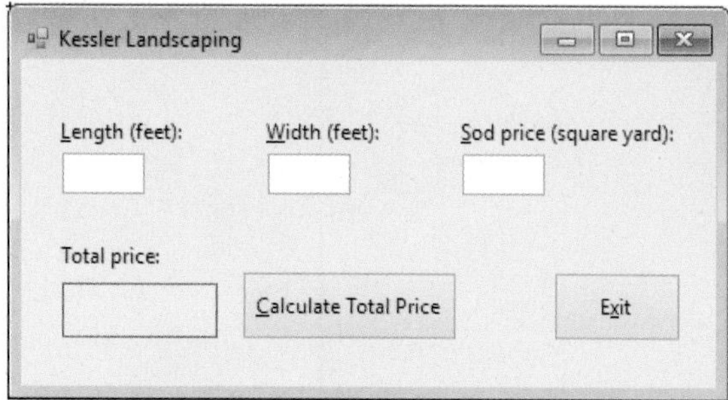

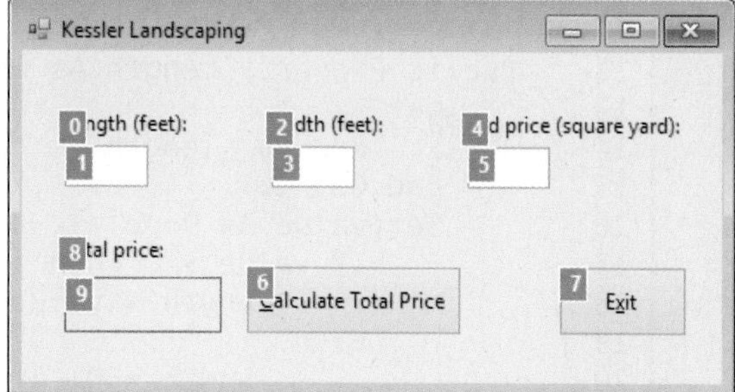

Figure 14-25 MainForm and tab order

Object	**Property**	**Setting**
MainForm	Font StartPosition Text	Segoe UI, 10pt CenterScreen Kessler Landscaping
totalLabel	AutoSize BorderStyle TextAlign	False FixedSingle MiddleCenter

Figure 14-26 Objects, properties, and settings

<u>exitButton Click event procedure</u>
close the application

<u>calcButton Click event procedure</u>
1. instantiate a Rectangle object
2. store the length and width entries in the Rectangle object's Public properties
3. store the sod price in a variable
4. use the Rectangle object's GetArea method to calculate the rectangle's area in square feet
5. calculate the rectangle's area in square yards
6. calculate the total price of the sod
7. display the total price of the sod in the totalLabel

<u>lengthTextBox, widthTextBox, and priceTextBox TextChanged event procedures</u>
clear the contents of the totalLabel

<u>lengthTextBox, widthTextBox, and priceTextBox Enter event procedures</u>
select the text box's existing text

Figure 14-27 Pseudocode

```
' Class filename:       Rectangle.vb
' Created/revised by:   <your name> on <current date>

Option Explicit On
Option Strict On
Option Infer Off

Public Class Rectangle
   Private _length As Double
   Private _width As Double

   Public Property Length As Double
       Get
           Return _length
       End Get
       Set(value As Double)
           If value > 0 Then
               _length = value
           Else
               _length = 0
           End If
       End Set
   End Property

   Public Property Width As Double
       Get
           Return _width
       End Get
       Set(value As Double)
           If value > 0 Then
               _width = value
           Else
               _width = 0
           End If
       End Set
   End Property

   Public Sub New()
       _length = 0
       _width = 0
   End Sub

   Public Sub New(len As Double, wid As Double)
       Length = len
       Width = wid
   End Sub

   Public Function GetArea() As Double
       Return _length * _width
   End Function
End Class
```

Figure 14-28 Code for the Rectangle.vb file

```
' Project name:          Kessler Project
' Project purpose:       Displays the cost of laying sod
' Created/revised by:    <your name> on <current date>

Option Explicit On
Option Strict On
Option Infer Off

Public Class MainForm
   Private Sub SelectText(sender As Object, e As System.EventArgs
   ) Handles lengthTextBox.Enter, widthTextBox.Enter,
   priceTextBox.Enter
       Dim thisTextBox As TextBox
       thisTextBox = TryCast(sender, TextBox)
       thisTextBox.SelectAll()
   End Sub

   Private Sub ClearLabel(sender As Object, e As System.EventArgs
   ) Handles lengthTextBox.TextChanged, widthTextBox.TextChanged,
   priceTextBox.TextChanged
       totalLabel.Text = String.Empty
   End Sub

   Private Sub exitButton_Click(sender As Object, e As System.EventArgs
   ) Handles exitButton.Click
       Me.Close()
   End Sub

   Private Sub calcButton_Click(sender As Object, e As System.EventArgs
   ) Handles calcButton.Click
       ' calculates the cost of laying sod

       Dim lawn As New Rectangle
       Dim sodPrice As Double
       Dim area As Double
       Dim totalPrice As Double

       Double.TryParse(lengthTextBox.Text, lawn.Length)
       Double.TryParse(widthTextBox.Text, lawn.Width)
       Double.TryParse(priceTextBox.Text, sodPrice)

       ' calculate the area (in square yards)
       area = lawn.GetArea / 9

       ' calculate and display the total price
       totalPrice = area * sodPrice
       totalLabel.Text = totalPrice.ToString("C2")
   End Sub
End Class
```

Figure 14-29 Code for the MainForm.vb file

Chapter Summary

- The objects used in an object-oriented program are instantiated (created) from classes.
- A class encapsulates (contains) the attributes that describe the object it creates. The class also contains the behaviors that allow the object to perform tasks and respond to actions.
- You use the Class statement to define a class. Class names are entered using Pascal case. You enter a class definition in a class file, which you can add to the current project using the Project menu.
- The `Option Explicit On`, `Option Strict On`, and `Option Infer Off` statements have the same meaning in a class file as they do in a form file.
- The names of the user-defined Private variables in a class usually begin with the underscore character. Subsequent characters in the name are entered using camel case. The names of the Private variables created by auto-implemented properties also begin with the underscore. However, the underscore is followed by the name of the Public property defined by the user.
- When an object is instantiated in an application, the Public members of the class are exposed to the application. The Private members, on the other hand, are hidden from the application.
- An application must use a Public property to either assign data to or retrieve data from a Private variable in a class. You create a Public property using a Public Property procedure. The names of the properties in a class should be entered using Pascal case and consist of nouns and adjectives.
- In a Property procedure header, the `ReadOnly` keyword indicates that the property's value can be retrieved (read) by an application, but it cannot be set by the application. The `WriteOnly` keyword, on the other hand, indicates that the property's value can be set by the application, but it cannot be retrieved by the application.
- The Get block in a Property procedure allows an application to access the contents of the Private variable associated with the property. The Set block, on the other hand, allows an application to assign a value to the Private variable. The Set block can contain validation code.
- A class can have one or more constructors. All constructors are Sub procedures that are named New. Each constructor must have a different parameterList (if any).
- A constructor that has no parameters is the default constructor. A class can contain only one default constructor. Constructors that contain parameters are called parameterized constructors.
- The computer processes the constructor whose parameters match (in number, data type, and position) the arguments contained in the statement that instantiates the object.
- The names of the methods in a class should be entered using Pascal case. You should use a verb for the first word in the name, and nouns and adjectives for any subsequent words in the name.
- Values that originate outside of a class should always be assigned to the class's Private variables indirectly, through the Public properties.
- When you create an auto-implemented property, Visual Basic automatically creates the property's Private variable and its (hidden) Get and Set blocks of code. An auto-implemented property cannot contain validation code. It also cannot be ReadOnly or WriteOnly.
- You can overload the methods in a class.

Key Terms

Attributes—the characteristics that describe an object

Auto-implemented properties—the feature that enables you to specify the property of a class in one line of code

Behaviors—an object's methods and events

Class—a pattern that the computer follows when instantiating (creating) an object

Class statement—the statement used to define a class in Visual Basic

Constructor—a method whose instructions are automatically processed each time the class instantiates an object; initializes the class's variables; always a Sub procedure named New

Default constructor—a constructor that has no parameters; a class can have only one default constructor

Encapsulates—an OOP term that means "contains"

Events—the actions to which an object can respond

Get block—the section of a Property procedure that contains the Get statement

Get statement—appears in a Get block in a Property procedure; contains the code that allows an application to retrieve the contents of the Private variable associated with the property

Instance—an object created from a class

Instantiated—the process of creating an object from a class

Methods—the actions that an object is capable of performing

Object—anything that can be seen, touched, or used; an instance of a class

Object-oriented programming language—a programming language that allows the use of objects to accomplish a program's goal

OOP—the acronym for object-oriented programming

Overloaded methods—two or more class methods that have the same name but different parameterLists

Parameterized constructor—a constructor that contains parameters

Property procedure—used to create a Public property that an application can use to indirectly access a Private variable in a class

ReadOnly keyword—used when defining a Property procedure; indicates that the property's value can only be retrieved (read) by an application

Set block—the section of a Property procedure that contains the Set statement

Set statement—appears in a Set block in a Property procedure; contains the code that allows an application to indirectly assign a value to the Private variable associated with the property; may also contain validation code

Signature—a method's name combined with its optional parameterList

WriteOnly keyword—used when defining a Property procedure; indicates that an application can only set the property's value

Each Review Question is associated with one or more objectives listed at the beginning of the chapter.

Review Questions

1. Two or more methods that have the same name but different parameterLists are referred to as ____________ methods. (1, 7, 10)

   a. loaded
   b. overloaded
   c. parallel
   d. signature

2. The Product class contains a Private variable named `_price`. The variable is associated with the Public Price property. An application instantiates a Product object and assigns it to a variable named `item`. Which of the following can be used by the application to assign the number 45 to the `_price` variable? (3, 4)

   a. `_price = 45`
   b. `Price = 45`
   c. `_price.item = 45`
   d. `item.Price = 45`

3. The Product class in Review Question 2 also contains a Public method named GetNewPrice. The method is a Function procedure. Which of the following can be used by the application to invoke the GetNewPrice method? (3, 7)

   a. `newPrice = Call GetNewPrice()`
   b. `newPrice = Price.GetNewPrice`
   c. `newPrice = item.GetNewPrice`
   d. `newPrice = item.GetNewPrice(_price)`

4. An application can access the Private variables in a class ____________. (2–4)

   a. directly
   b. using properties created by Public Property procedures
   c. through Private procedures contained in the class
   d. none of the above

5. To expose a variable or method contained in a class, you declare the variable or method using the keyword ____________. (1, 2)

   a. `Exposed`
   b. `Private`
   c. `Public`
   d. `Viewable`

6. The method name combined with the method's optional parameterList is called the method's ____________. (1, 6, 7)

   a. autograph
   b. inscription
   c. signature
   d. statement

7. A constructor is ____________. (6)

   a. a Function procedure
   b. a Property procedure
   c. a Sub procedure
   d. either a Function procedure or a Sub procedure

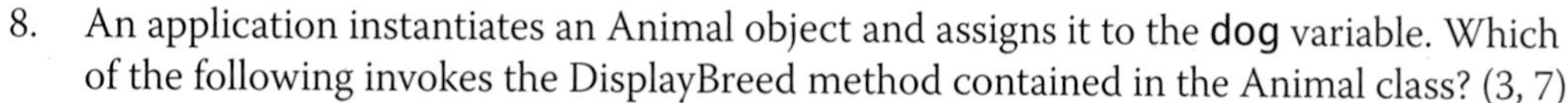

8. An application instantiates an Animal object and assigns it to the `dog` variable. Which of the following invokes the DisplayBreed method contained in the Animal class? (3, 7)
   a. `Animal.DisplayBreed()`
   b. `DisplayBreed.Animal()`
   c. `DisplayBreed.Dog`
   d. `dog.DisplayBreed`
9. An application instantiates a MyDate object and assigns it to the `payDate` variable. The MyDate class contains a Public Month property that is associated with a Private String variable named `_month`. Which of the following can be used by the application to assign the number 12 to the Month property? (3, 4)
   a. `payDate.Month = "12"`
   b. `payDate.Month._month = "12"`
   c. `payDate._month = "12"`
   d. `MyDate.Month = "12"`
10. The Return statement is entered in the ____________ block in a Property procedure. (4)
    a. Get
    b. Set
11. A class contains a Private variable named `_capital`. The variable is associated with the Public Capital property. Which of the following is the best way for a parameterized constructor to assign the value stored in its `capName` parameter to the variable? (2, 6)
    a. `_capital = capName`
    b. `Capital = capName`
    c. `_capital.Capital = capName`
    d. none of the above
12. A class can contain only one constructor. (2, 6)
    a. True
    b. False
13. The Purchase class contains a ReadOnly property named Tax. The property is associated with the Private `_tax` variable. A button's Click event procedure instantiates a Purchase object and assigns it to the `currentSale` variable. Which of the following is valid in the Click event procedure? (4, 8)
    a. `taxLabel.Text = currentSale.Tax.ToString("C2")`
    b. `currentSale.Tax = sales * .1`
    c. `currentSale.Tax = 50`
    d. all of the above
14. A class contains an auto-implemented property named Title. Which of the following is the correct way for the default constructor to assign the string "Unknown" to the variable associated with the property? (2, 9)
    a. `_Title = "Unknown"`
    b. `_Title.Title = "Unknown"`
    c. `Title._Title = "Unknown"`
    d. none of the above

15. A ReadOnly property can be an auto-implemented property. (2, 8, 9)
    a. True
    b. False

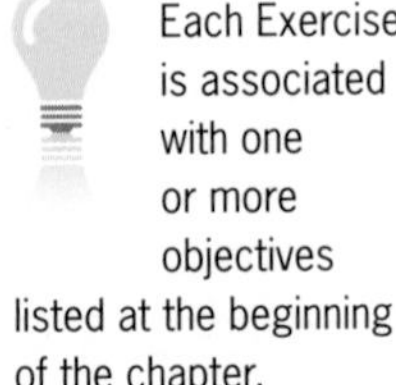
Each Exercise is associated with one or more objectives listed at the beginning of the chapter.

Exercises

Pencil and Paper

INTRODUCTORY

1. If a class contains more than one constructor, how does the computer determine the appropriate one to use when an object is instantiated? (3, 6)

INTRODUCTORY

2. What are overloaded methods and why are they used? (10)

INTRODUCTORY

3. Write a Class statement that defines a class named Book. The class contains three Public variables named `Title`, `Author`, and `Price`. The `Title` and `Author` variables have the String data type. The `Price` variable has the Decimal data type. Then use the syntax shown in Version 1 in Figure 14-2 to declare a variable that can store a Book object; name the variable `fiction`. Also write a statement that instantiates a Book object and assigns it to the `fiction` variable. (2, 3)

INTRODUCTORY

4. Rewrite the Class statement from Pencil and Paper Exercise 3 so that it uses Private variables rather than Public variables. Be sure to include the Property procedures and default constructor. Then, rewrite the Class statement using auto-implemented properties. (2, 4, 6, 9)

INTRODUCTORY

5. Write a Class statement that defines a class named SongInfo. The class contains three Private String variables named `_songName`, `_artist`, and `_songlength`. Name the corresponding properties SongName, Artist, and SongLength. Be sure to include the default constructor. Then, use the syntax shown in Version 2 in Figure 14-2 to create a Song object, assigning it to a variable named `hipHop`. (2–4, 6)

INTRODUCTORY

6. The Car class definition is shown in Figure 14-30. Write a Dim statement that uses the default constructor to instantiate a Car object in an application. The Dim statement should assign the object to a variable named `nissan`. Next, write assignment statements that the application can use to assign the string "370Z" and the number 30614.75 to the Model and Price properties, respectively. Finally, write an assignment statement that the application can use to invoke the GetNewPrice function. Assign the function's return value to a variable named `newPrice`. (3)

```
Public Class Car
    Private _model As String
    Private _price As Double

    Public Property Model As String
        Get
            Return _model
        End Get
        Set(value As String)
            _model = value
        End Set
    End Property
```

Figure 14-30 Car class definition *(continues)*

(continued)

```
    Public Property Price As Double
        Get
            Return _price
        End Get
        Set(value As Double)
            _price = value
        End Set
    End Property

    Public Sub New()
        _model = String.Empty
        _price = 0
    End Sub

    Public Sub New(ByVal type As String, ByVal cost As Double)
        Model = type
        Price = cost
    End Sub

    Public Function GetNewPrice() As Double
        Return _price * 1.15
    End Function
End Class
```

Figure 14-30 Car class definition

7. Using the Car class from Figure 14-30, write a Dim statement that uses the parameterized constructor to instantiate a Car object. Pass the string "Fusion" and the number 22560.99 to the parameterized constructor. The Dim statement should assign the object to a variable named `rentalCar`. (3) INTRODUCTORY

8. An application contains the statement `Dim myCar As Car`. Using the Car class from Figure 14-30, write an assignment statement that instantiates a Car object and initializes it using the `modelType` and `modelPrice` variables. The statement should assign the object to the `myCar` variable. (3) INTRODUCTORY

9. Write the Property procedure for a ReadOnly property named `Sales`, which is associated with the `_sales` variable. The property's data type is Decimal. (4, 8) INTERMEDIATE

10. Write the code for an auto-implemented property named Commission. The property's data type is Double. (9) INTERMEDIATE

11. Write the class definition for a class named Worker. The class should include Private variables and Property procedures for a Worker object's name and salary. The salary may contain a decimal place. The class should also contain two constructors: the default constructor and a parameterized constructor. (2, 6) INTERMEDIATE

12. Rewrite the code from Paper and Pencil Exercise 11 using auto-implemented properties. (9) INTERMEDIATE

13. Add a method named GetNewSalary to the Worker class from Pencil and Paper Exercise 12. The method should calculate a Worker object's new salary, which is based on a raise percentage provided by the application using the object. Before calculating the new salary, the method should verify that the raise percentage is greater than or equal to 0. If the raise percentage is less than 0, the method should assign 0 as the new salary. (5, 7) INTERMEDIATE

Computer

MODIFY THIS

14. Open the Painters Solution (Painters Solution.sln) file contained in the VbReloaded2015\Chap14\Painters Solution folder. Modify the CostOfGoodsSold class so that it uses Public auto-implemented properties rather than Public variables. Include a default constructor in the class. Save the solution and then start and test the application. Close the solution. (6, 9)

MODIFY THIS

15. Open the Pizzeria Solution (Pizzeria Solution.sln) file contained in the VbReloaded2015\Chap14\Pizzeria Solution. Modify the calcButton_Click procedure to use the Rectangle class's parameterized constructor. Save the solution and then start and test the application. Close the solution. (3)

INTRODUCTORY

16. Open the Square Solution (Square Solution.sln) file contained in the VbReloaded2015\Chap14\Square Solution folder. Add a new class file named Square.vb to the project. The Square class should have one attribute: a side measurement. The side measurement may contain a decimal place and should always be greater than or equal to 0. The class should also have three behaviors: a default constructor, a function that calculates and returns the square's area, and a function that calculates and returns the square's perimeter. Code the Square class. Then, open the form's Code Editor window and complete the calcButton_Click procedure. Display the calculated results with two decimal places. Save the solution and then start and test the application. (2–7)

INTRODUCTORY

17. Open the Sweets Solution (Sweets Solution.sln) file contained in the VbReloaded2015\Chap14\Sweets Solution folder. Add a new class file named Salesperson.vb to the project. The Salesperson class should have two attributes: a salesperson's ID and a sales amount. The ID and sales amount should have the String and Decimal data types, respectively. The class should also have a default constructor. Code the Salesperson class. Then, open the form's Code Editor window and complete the saveButton_Click procedure. The procedure should save the ID and sales amount in a sequential access file. Save the solution and then start and test the application. Be sure to verify that the sales.txt file contains the IDs and sales amounts that you entered. Close the solution. (2–6)

INTRODUCTORY

18. Open the Salary Solution (Salary Solution.sln) file contained in the VbReloaded2015\Chap14\Salary Solution folder. Open the Worker.vb class file and then enter the class definition from Pencil and Paper Exercises 12 and 13. Save the solution and then close the Worker.vb window. Open the MainForm's Code Editor window. Use the comments to enter the missing instructions. Save the solution and then start the application. Test the application by entering your name, a current salary amount of 54000, and a raise percentage of 10 (for 10%). The new salary should be $59,400.00. Close the solution. (2–7)

INTERMEDIATE

19. Open the Circle Area Solution (Circle Area Solution.sln) file contained in the VbReloaded2015\Chap14\Circle Area Solution folder. Add a new class file named Circle.vb to the project. The Circle class should contain one attribute: the circle's radius. It should also contain a default constructor, a parameterized constructor, and a method that calculates and returns the circle's area. Use the following formula to calculate the area: 3.141592 * $radius^2$. Code the Circle class. Save the solution and then close the Circle.vb window. Next, open the form's Code Editor window. The calcButton_Click procedure should display the circle's area, using the radius entered by the user. Display the area with two decimal places. Code the procedure. Save the solution and then start and test the application. Close the solution. (2–7)

20. In this exercise, you will create an application that can be used to calculate the cost of installing a fence around a rectangular area. (2–7)

INTERMEDIATE

a. Create a Windows Forms application. Use the following names for the solution and project, respectively: Fence Solution and Fence Project. Save the application in the VbReloaded2015\Chap14 folder. Change the form file's name to Main Form.vb.

b. Use Windows to copy the Rectangle.vb file from the VbReloaded2015\Chap14 folder to the Fence Solution\Fence Project folder. Use the Project menu to add the Rectangle.vb class file to the project. Add a method named GetPerimeter to the Rectangle class. The method should calculate and return the perimeter of a rectangle. To calculate the perimeter, the method will need to add together the length and width measurements and then multiply the sum by 2.

c. Create the interface shown in Figure 14-31. The image for the picture box is stored in the VbReloaded2015\Chap14\Fence.png file.

d. Code the application, which should calculate and display the cost of installing the fence.

e. Save the solution and then start the application. Test the application using 120 feet as the length, 75 feet as the width, and 10 as the cost per linear foot of fencing. The installation cost should be $3,900.00. Close the solution.

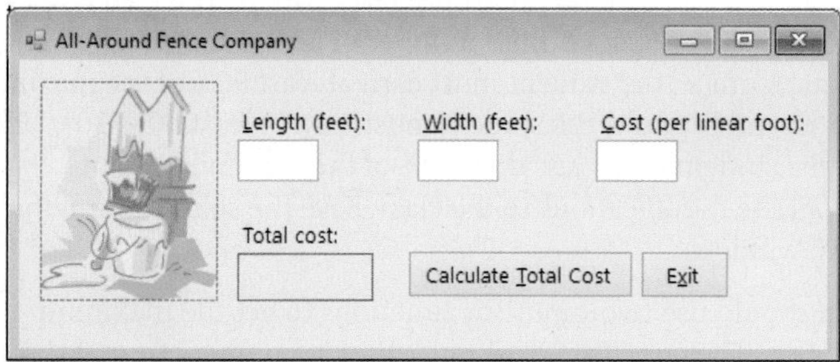

Figure 14-31 Interface for Exercise 20

21. In this exercise, you will define a Triangle class. You will also create an application that allows the user to display either a Triangle object's area or its perimeter. The formula for calculating the area of a triangle is 1/2 * *base* * *height*. The formula for calculating the perimeter of a triangle is $a + b + c$, where a, b, and c are the lengths of the sides. (2–7)

INTERMEDIATE

a. Create a Windows Forms application. Use the following names for the solution and project, respectively: Triangle Solution and Triangle Project. Save the application in the VbReloaded2015\Chap14 folder. Change the form file's name to Main Form.vb.

b. Create the interface shown in Figure 14-32. The image for the picture box is stored in the VbReloaded2015\Chap14\Triangle.png file.

c. Add a new class to the project. Name the class file Triangle.vb. The Triangle class should verify that the dimensions are greater than 0 before assigning the values to the Private variables. Include a default constructor in the class. The class should also include a method to calculate the area of a triangle, and a method to calculate the perimeter of a triangle. Save the solution and then close the Triangle.vb window.

d. Open the MainForm's Code Editor window. Use the InputBox function to get the appropriate data from the user. Save the solution and then start and test the application. Close the solution.

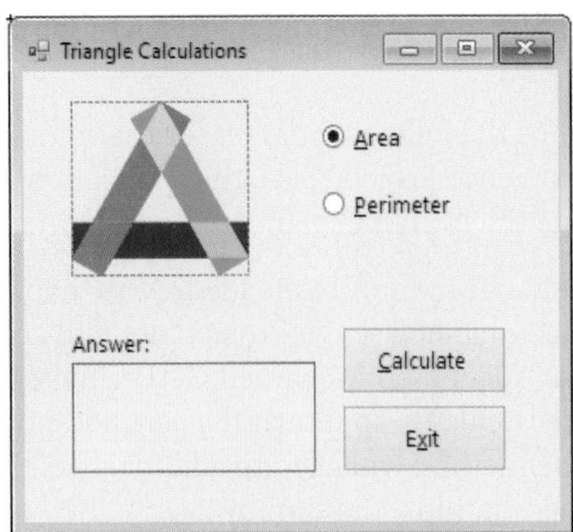

Figure 14-32 Interface for Exercise 21

ADVANCED

22. If necessary, complete the Grade Calculator application from this chapter's Programming Tutorial 1, and then close the solution. Use Windows to make a copy of the Grade Solution folder. Rename the folder Grade Solution-Advanced. Open the solution file contained in the Grade Solution-Advanced folder. (2–7)

    a. Open the CourseGrade.vb file. Currently, the maximum number of points that can be earned on both tests is 200 (100 points per test). Modify the DetermineGrade method so that it accepts the maximum number of points that can be earned on both tests. For an A grade, the student must earn at least 90% of the maximum points. For a B, C, and D grade, the student must earn at least 80%, 70%, and 60%, respectively. If the student earns less than 60% of the maximum points, the grade is F. Make the appropriate modifications to the class. Save the solution, and then close the CourseGrade.vb window.

    b. The application should use two InputBox functions to get the maximum number of points for each test. The test1ListBox should display numbers from 0 through the maximum number of points associated with the first test. The test2ListBox should display numbers from 0 through the maximum number of points associated with the second test.

    c. Open the MainForm's Code Editor window. Make the necessary modifications to the code. Save the solution and then start and test the application. Close the solution.

SWAT THE BUGS

23. Open the Debug Solution (Debug Solution.sln) file contained in the VbReloaded2015\Chap14\Debug Solution folder. Open the form's Code Editor window and the class's Code Editor window. Correct the calcButton_Click procedure to remove the squiggles (jagged lines). Save the solution and then start and test the application. Notice that the application is not working correctly. Locate and correct the errors in the code. When the application is working correctly, close the solution. (2–7)

Case Projects

Glasgow Health Club

Each member of Glasgow Health Club must pay monthly dues that consist of a basic fee and one or more optional charges. The basic monthly fee for a single membership is $50; for a family membership, it is $90. If the member has a single membership, the additional monthly charges are $30 for tennis, $25 for golf, and $20 for racquetball. If the member has a family membership, the additional monthly charges are $50 for tennis, $35 for golf, and $30 for racquetball. The application should display the member's basic fee, additional charges, and monthly dues. Use the following names for the solution and project, respectively: Glasgow Solution and Glasgow Project. Save the application in the VbReloaded2015\Chap14 folder. Change the form file's name to Main Form.vb. You can either create your own interface or create the one shown in Figure 14-33. Be sure to use a class in the application. (2–7)

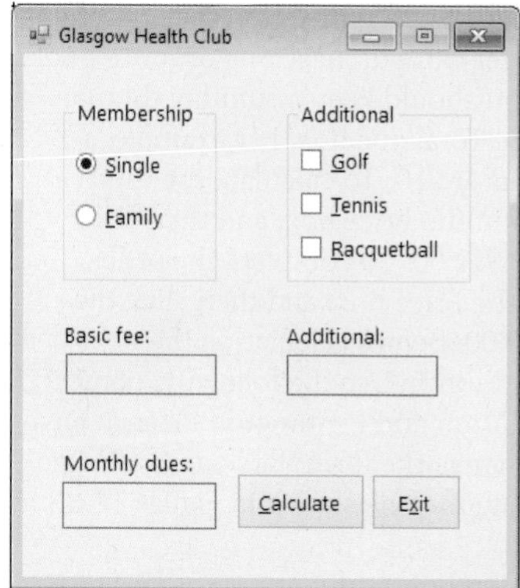

Figure 14-33 Sample interface for the Glasgow Health Club application

Serenity Photos

The manager of the Accounts Payable department at Serenity Photos wants an application that keeps track of the checks written by her department. More specifically, she wants to record (in a sequential access file) the check number, date, payee, and amount of each check. Use the following names for the solution and project, respectively: Serenity Solution and Serenity Project. Save the application in the VbReloaded2015\Chap14 folder. Change the form file's name to Main Form.vb. You can either create your own interface or create the one shown in Figure 14-34. The image is stored in the VbReloaded2015\Chap14\Flower.png file. Be sure to use a class in the application. (2–7)

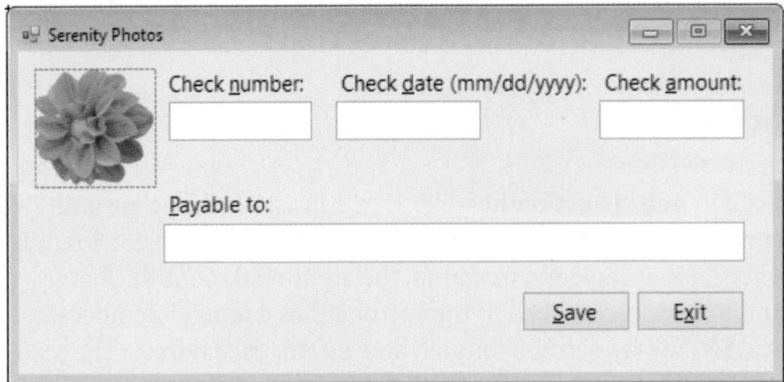

Figure 14-34 Sample interface for the Serenity Photos application

Pennington Book Store

Shelly Jones, the manager of the Pennington Book Store, wants an application that calculates and displays the total amount a customer owes. A customer can purchase one or more books at either the same price or different prices. The application should keep a running total of the amount the customer owes and display the total in the Total due box. For example, a customer might purchase two books at $6 and three books at $10. To calculate the total due, Shelly will need to enter 2 in the Quantity box and 6 in the Price box, and then click the Add to Sale button. The Total due box should display $12.00. To complete the order, Shelly will need to enter 3 in the Quantity box and 10 in the Price box, and then click the Add to Sale button. The Total due box should display $42.00. Before calculating the next customer's order, Shelly will need to click the New Order button. Use the following names for the solution and project, respectively: Pennington Solution and Pennington Project. Save the application in the VbReloaded2015\Chap14 folder. Change the form file's name to Main Form.vb. You can either create your own interface or create the one shown in Figure 14-35. Be sure to use a class in the application. (2–7)

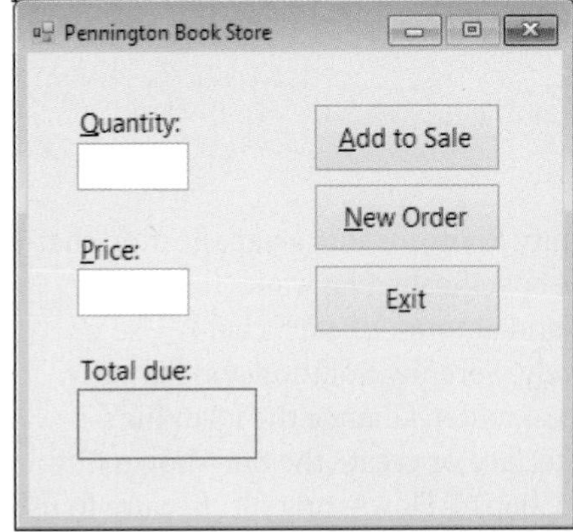

Figure 14-35 Sample interface for the Pennington Bookstore application

Playground

Create an application that displays the area of a triangular playground in square feet. It should also display the cost of covering the playground with artificial grass. Use the following names for the solution and project, respectively: Playground Solution and Playground Project. Save the application in the VbReloaded2015\Chap14 folder. Create a suitable interface. Provide list boxes for the user to enter the playground's base and height dimensions in yards. Both list boxes should display numbers from 20 to 50 in increments of 0.5. Also, provide a list box for entering the price per square foot of artificial grass. This list box should display numbers from 1 to 6 in increments of 0.5. Create a class named Triangle. The class should verify that the base and height dimensions are greater than 0 before assigning the values to the Private variables. (Although the dimensions come from list boxes in this application, the class might subsequently be used in an application whose dimensions come from text boxes.) The class should include a default constructor, a parameterized constructor, and a method to calculate the area of a triangle. (2–7)

Bingo Game

Create an application that simulates the game of Bingo. Use the following names for the solution and project, respectively: Bingo Solution and Bingo Project. Save the application in the VbReloaded2015\Chap14 folder. You can either create your own interface or create the one shown in Figure 14-36. Be sure to use a class in the application. (2–7)

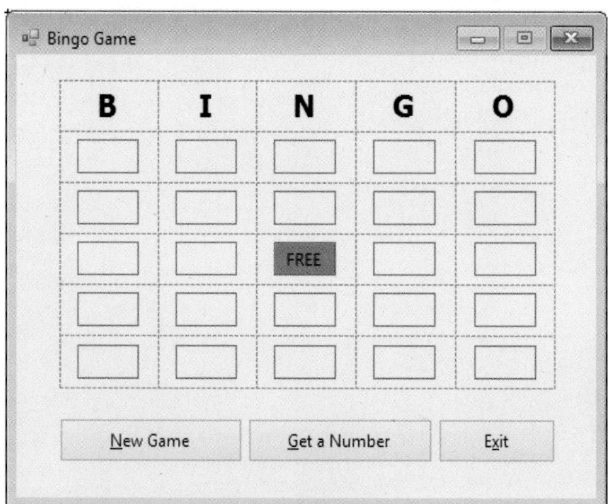

Figure 14-36 Sample interface for the Bingo Game application

Parking Lot

Create an application that displays the total cost of paving the parking lot shown in Figure 14-37. Use the following names for the solution and project, respectively: Parking Solution and Parking Project. Save the application in the VbReloaded2015\Chap14 folder. Create a suitable interface. Code the application by using a class to instantiate a parking lot object. (2–7)

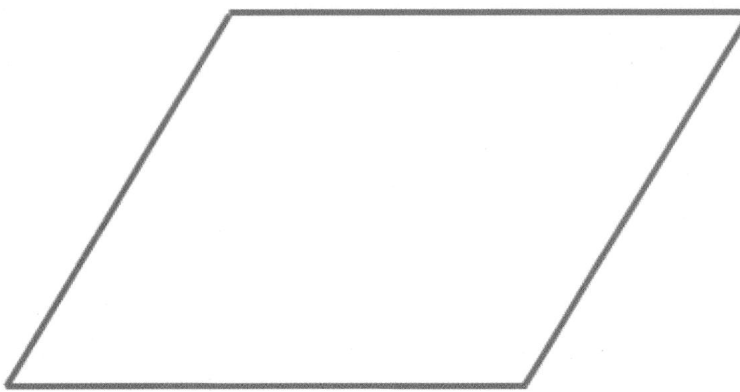

Figure 14-37 Parking lot for the Parking Lot application

APPENDIX A

Answers to Mini-Quizzes

Chapter 1

Mini-Quiz 1-1

1. d. all of the above
2. You auto-hide a window by clicking the Auto Hide (vertical pushpin) button on the window's title bar.
3. You temporarily display an auto-hidden window by clicking the window's tab.
4. To reset the windows in the IDE, click Window on the menu bar, click Reset Window Layout, and then click the Yes button.
5. c. Text
6. a. StartPosition

Mini-Quiz 1-2

1. To delete a control from a form, select the control in the designer window and then press the Delete key.
2. c. label
3. d. all of the above
4. b. Image
5. You should select the Label4 control first.
6. c. TextAlign

Mini-Quiz 1-3

1. b. Close Solution
2. c. startup
3. b. `Me.Close()`
4. c. `cityLabel.Text = "Nashville"`
5. c. debugging

Chapter 2

Mini-Quiz 2-1

1. d. tasks
2. b. False
3. c. text box

Mini-Quiz 2-2

1. a. book title capitalization
2. d. all of the above
3. c. sentence capitalization

Mini-Quiz 2-3

1. a. 0
2. c. 3
3. c. Alt+t
4. b. False

Mini-Quiz 2-4

1. d. all of the above
2. b. `PrintForm1.Print()`
3. c. .wav

Chapter 3

Mini-Quiz 3-1

1. a. only one item
2. c. `sales_2018`
3. `Dim payRate As Double`
4. `Dim counter As Integer = 1`

Mini-Quiz 3-2

1. b. `state = "TN"`
2. c. `age = 21`
3. b. `Integer.TryParse(inStock, quantity)`
4. a. `price = Convert.ToDecimal(75.63)`

Mini-Quiz 3-3

1. c. 16
2. b. 32
3. a. `counter += 1`

Mini-Quiz 3-4

1. d. procedure
2. b. Class-level
3. c. `Static score As Integer`
4. a. `Private Const Job As String = "Coach"`

Mini-Quiz 3-5

1. a. `Option Explicit On`
2. c. `Double.TryParse(salesTextBox.Text, sales)`
3. The computer will promote the contents of the `commRate` variable to Double and then multiply the result by the contents of the `sales` variable. Finally, it will assign the product to the `commission` variable.

Mini-Quiz 3-6

1. c. process
2. d. both a and b
3. a. `clearButton.Focus()`
4. b. `bonusLabel.Text = bonus.ToString("C2")`

Chapter 4

Mini-Quiz 4-1

1. b. False
2. c. both its True and False paths
3. b. False
4. a. diamond

Mini-Quiz 4-2

1. d. only the False path in the If...Then...Else statement
2. a. `If sales >= 450.67 Then`
3. a. `"Do they live in " & state & "?"`
4. b. `item.ToLower`
5. a. Checked

Mini-Quiz 4-3

1. a. True
2. False
3. False
4. b. `Dim randGen As New Random`

Chapter 5

Mini-Quiz 5-1

1. a. membership status, day of the week
2. if the golfer is a club member
   display $5
   else
   if the day is Monday through Thursday
   display $15
   else
   display $25
   end if
   end if

```
if the golfer is a club member
    display $5
else
    if the day is Monday through Thursday
          display $15
    else
          display $25
    end if
end if
```

3\.

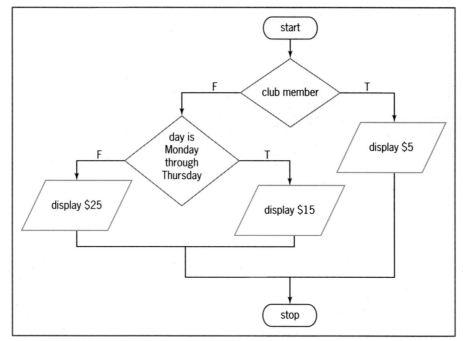

start
club member
F
T
display $5
day is Monday through Thursday
F
T
display $25
display $15
stop

4\.

```
If memberCheckBox.Checked Then
   feeLabel.Text = "$5"
Else
   If dayNum >= 1 AndAlso dayNum < 5 Then
         feeLabel.Text = "$15"
   Else
         feeLabel.Text = "$25"
   End If
End If
```

(Note: You can also use `If memberCheckBox.Checked = True Then`.)

Mini-Quiz 5-2

1. b. `Case "1", "2", "3", "4"`
2. a. `Case 10, 11, 12, 13, 14, 15`
3. a. True

Mini-Quiz 5-3

1. d. `ControlChars.Back`
2. a. Checked
3. c. `DialogResult.Abort`
4. b. `e.Handled = True`

Chapter 6

Mini-Quiz 6-1

1. b. pretest
2. b. loop exit
3. a. looping

Mini-Quiz 6-2

1. d. all of the above
2. `sum += score` (or `sum = sum + score`)
3. `numValues += 5` (or `numValues = numValues + 5`)
4. `numItems -= 1` (or `numItems += -1` or `numItems = numItems - 1` or `numItems = numItems + -1`)

Mini-Quiz 6-3

1. a. Multiline
2. b. within
3. d. `zip = InputBox("ZIP code:", "ZIP")`

Mini-Quiz 6-4

1. a. Add
2. b. Items
3. c. SelectedIndex
4. c. `System.Threading.Thread.Sleep(2000)`

Chapter 7

Mini-Quiz 7-1

1. d. all of the above
2. c. 13
3.
```
For num As Integer = 6 To 1 Step -1
    numListBox.Items.Add(num.ToString)
Next num
```

Mini-Quiz 7-2

1. c. either a pretest loop or a posttest loop
2. a. nested, outer
3. b. outer, nested

Mini-Quiz 7-3

1. c. `-Financial.Pmt(.04 / 12, 24, 5000)`
2. `cityTextBox.SelectAll()`
3. d. all of the above

Mini-Quiz 7-4

1. a. Add
2. b. False
3. c. `stateComboBox.Items.Count`
4. `ImageList1.Images.Item(1)`

Chapter 8

Mini-Quiz 8-1

1. a. True
2. b. `Private Sub DisplayMessage()`
3. d. `DisplayMessage()`

Mini-Quiz 8-2

1. b. `Private Sub Display(ByVal x As String, ByVal y As String)`
2. a. `Private Sub Calc(ByVal x As Integer, ByRef y As Double)`
3. b. `Calc(sales, bonus)`

Mini-Quiz 8-3

1. d. `Handles nameTextBox.TextChanged, salesTextBox.TextChanged`
2. a. `Private Function Calc() As Decimal`
3. c. one value only
4. b. `currentLabel = TryCast(sender, Label)`
5. a. `Math.Round(number, 3)`

Chapter 9

Mini-Quiz 9-1

1. a. `Dim letters(3) As String`
2. d. both a and b
3. a. `cities(4) = "Scottsburg"`

Mini-Quiz 9-2

1. b.
```
For Each scoreElement As Integer In scores
    total += scoreElement
Next scoreElement
```

2.
```
For subscript As Integer = 0 To 4
     total += scores(subscript)
Next subscript
```
(Note: You can also use either `scores.Length - 1` or `scores.GetUpperBound(0)` in place of the 4 in the For clause.)

3.
```
Dim subscript As Integer
Do While subscript <= 4
     total += scores(subscript)
     subscript += 1
Loop
```
(Note: You can also use either `scores.Length - 1` or `scores.GetUpperBound(0)` in place of the 4 in the For clause. Or, you can use `< 5`, `< scores.Length`, or `< scores.GetUpperBound + 1` in place of the `<= 4` in the For clause.)

4. `Array.Sort(scores)`

Mini-Quiz 9-3

1. d. all of the above
2. b. `testAnswers(2, 0) = True`
3. b. `highCol = population.GetUpperBound(1)`

Chapter 10

Mini-Quiz 10-1

1. a. `numChars = stateTextBox.Text.Length`
2. d. all of the above
3. b. `state = state.Insert(0, "North ")`

Mini-Quiz 10-2

1. d. False
2. b. 10
3. d. `footType = restaurant.Substring(9, 6)`
4. d. all of the above

Mini-Quiz 10-3

1. b. `modelNum Like "##[A-Z]##[A-Z]"`
2. a. `salesTextBox.Text Like "*,*"`
3. c. `rateTextBox.Text Like "*%"`

Chapter 11

Mini-Quiz 11-1

1. a. Declarations section
2. b. `address.city = "Miami"`
3. d. `inventory(4).quantity = 100`

Mini-Quiz 11-2

1. d. both a and b
2. b. `outFile.WriteLine(cityTextBox.Text)`
3. `outFile.Close()`

Mini-Quiz 11-3

1. c. OpenText
2. b. `msg = inFile.ReadLine`
3. `inFile.Close()`
4. the character

Mini-Quiz 11-4

1. c. `address = city & Strings.Space(10) & state`
2. a. `e.Cancel = True`
3. b. `customer = inFile.ReadLine.Split("$"c)`

Chapter 12

Mini-Quiz 12-1

1. a. database
2. b. relational
3. d. all of the above

Mini-Quiz 12-2

1. d. TableAdapter
2. d. `Me.TblFriendsTableAdapter.Fill(Me.FriendsDataSet.tblNames)`
3. c. `ex.Message`
4. d. all of the above

Mini-Quiz 12-3

1. c.
```
Dim records =
        From store In StoresDataSet.tblStores
        Where store.City.ToUpper Like "L*"
        Select store
```
2. a.
```
Dim total As Integer =
        Aggregate city In CitiesDataSet.tblCities
            Select city.population Into Sum
```
3. b. Order By

Chapter 13

Mini-Quiz 13-1

1. b. client
2. a. browser
3. a. client computer
4. c. Default.aspx
5. c. aspx.vb

Chapter 14

Mini-Quiz 14-1

1. b. False
2. c. .vb
3. d. both b and c

Mini-Quiz 14-2

1. b. False
2. a. True
3. d. none of the above
4. c. Set

APPENDIX B

How To Boxes

How to	Chapter	Figure
Access an item in a list box	6	6-23
Access characters in a string	10	10-6
Access the value stored in a field	12	12-23
Add a control to a form	1	1-14
Add a new Web page to an application	13	13-6
Add an existing Web page to an application	13	13-7
Add images to an image list control's Images collection	7	7-22
Add the Start Without Debugging option to the Debug menu	13	13-11
Align columns of information	11	11-22
Align the characters in a string	10	10-4
Assign a value to an existing variable	3	3-5
Assign a value to an object's property during run time	1	1-29
Assign the contents of a LINQ variable to a BindingSource object	12	12-25
Assign the result of an arithmetic expression to a variable	3	3-12
Associate a procedure with different objects and events	8	8-11
Bind an object in a dataset	12	12-7
Change the executable file's name in the Project Designer window	1	1-27
Check the denominator in an expression	4	4-8
Clear (remove) the items from a list box	6	6-21
Clear the Text property of a control	3	3-37
Close a solution	1	1-32
Close an input sequential access file	11	11-18
Close an output sequential access file	11	11-12
Close and open an existing Web Site application	13	13-12
Compare strings that contain digits and special characters	4	4-15
Concatenate strings	4	4-13
Configure Visual Studio Community 2015	1	1-2
Connect an application to an Access database	12	12-4
Create a constructor	14	14-5
Create a Function procedure	8	8-13
Create a method that is not a constructor	14	14-7

(continues)

(continued)

How to	Chapter	Figure
Create a Property procedure	14	14-4
Create a StreamReader object	11	11-14
Create a StreamWriter object	11	11-10
Create a Visual Basic 2015 Windows Forms application	1	1-5
Create an auto-implemented property	14	14-12
Create an empty Web Site application	13	13-5
Create and call an independent Sub procedure	8	8-2
Customize a BindingNavigator control	12	12-26
Customize a Web page	13	13-8
Declare a named constant	3	3-21
Declare a one-dimensional array	9	9-2
Declare a StreamReader variable	11	11-13
Declare a StreamWriter variable	11	11-9
Declare a structure variable	11	11-2
Declare a two-dimensional array	9	9-15
Declare a variable	3	3-4
Define a class	14	14-1
Define a structure	11	11-1
Determine the highest subscript in a one-dimensional array	9	9-6
Determine the highest subscripts in a two-dimensional array	9	9-17
Determine the number of characters in a string	10	10-1
Determine the number of elements in an array	9	9-5
Determine the number of items in a list box	6	6-24
Determine the order in which operators are evaluated	4	4-25
Determine whether a file exists	11	11-15
End a running application	1	1-28
Evaluate expressions containing a logical operator	4	4-22
Evaluate expressions containing arithmetic and comparison operators	4	4-7
Evaluate expressions containing operators with the same precedence	3	3-11
Format a number using the ToString method	3	3-34
Generate random integers	4	4-26
Insert characters in a string	10	10-3
Instantiate an object from a class	14	14-2
Invoke a constructor	14	14-6
Invoke a function	8	8-14
Make a control blink	6	6-40
Manage the windows in the IDE	1	1-8
Manipulate the controls on a form	1	1-15
Name a variable	3	3-2
Open an existing solution	1	1-33
Open the Code Editor window	1	1-18
Plan an application	2	2-1
Play an audio file	2	2-16
Preview the contents of a dataset	12	12-6
Print the code and interface during design time	1	1-31

(continues)

(continued)

How to	Chapter	Figure
Read data from a sequential access file	11	11-16
Read records from a sequential access file	11	11-24
Refer to a member variable in an array element	11	11-8
Refer to an image in the Images collection	7	7-23
Remove an item from a list box or combo box	11	11-21
Remove characters from a string	10	10-2
Save a solution	1	1-22
Search a string	10	10-5
Select the default list box item	6	6-26
Send the focus to a control	3	3-38
Set the TabIndex property using the Tab Order option	2	2-11
Specify a range of values in a Case clause	5	5-10
Specify the startup form	1	1-23
Start a Web application	13	13-10
Start an application	1	1-25
Start Visual Studio Community 2015	1	1-1
Store data in a one-dimensional array	9	9-4
Store data in a two-dimensional array	9	9-16
Swap the contents of two variables	4	4-11
Traverse a one-dimensional array	9	9-7
Traverse a two-dimensional array	9	9-18
Update counters and accumulators	6	6-10
Use a member variable	11	11-4
Use comparison operators in a condition	4	4-6
Use LINQ to select and arrange records in a dataset	12	12-24
Use logical operators in a condition	4	4-21
Use pattern matching to compare strings	10	10-7
Use the arithmetic assignment operators	3	3-13
Use the Array.Sort and Array.Reverse methods	9	9-13
Use the basic syntax of the TryParse method	3	3-6
Use the BindingSource object's Move methods	12	12-21
Use the BindingSource object's Position property	12	12-20
Use the Convert class methods	3	3-8
Use the Copy to Output Directory property	12	12-17
Use the Do...Loop statement	6	6-5
Use the Financial.FV method	7	7-32
Use the Financial.Pmt method	7	7-11
Use the For Each...Next statement	9	9-8
Use the For...Next statement	7	7-2
Use the Format menu to align/size/center controls	1	1-17
Use the FormClosing event procedure	11	11-19
Use the If...Then...Else statement	4	4-5
Use the InputBox function	6	6-12
Use the integer division and Mod operators	3	3-10
Use the Items collection's Add method	6	6-17

(continues)

(continued)

How to	Chapter	Figure
Use the KeyPress event to control the characters accepted by a text box	5	5-17
Use the LINQ aggregate operators	12	12-28
Use the Math.Round function	8	8-19
Use the MessageBox.Show method	5	5-13
Use the MessageBox.Show method's return value	5	5-15
Use the Peek method	11	11-17
Use the Refresh and Sleep methods	6	6-31
Use the Select Case statement	5	5-9
Use the SelectAll method	7	7-13
Use the SelectedItem and SelectedIndex properties	6	6-25
Use the ToUpper and ToLower methods	4	4-14
Use the Try...Catch statement	12	12-16
Use the TryCast operator	8	8-18
Use the type conversion rules with Option Strict On	3	3-22
Use the validator tools	13	13-37
Write data to a sequential access file	11	11-11
Write records to a sequential access file	11	11-23

APPENDIX C

Most Commonly Used Properties of Objects

Windows Form

AcceptButton	specify a default button that will be selected when the user presses the Enter key
CancelButton	specify a cancel button that will be selected when the user presses the Esc key
ControlBox	indicate whether the form contains the Control box, as well as the Minimize, Maximize, and Close buttons
Font	specify the font to use for text
FormBorderStyle	specify the appearance and behavior of the form's border
MaximizeBox	specify the state of the Maximize button
MinimizeBox	specify the state of the Minimize button
Name	give the form a meaningful name
Size	specify the form's size
StartPosition	indicate the starting position of the form
Text	specify the text that appears in the form's title bar

Button

Enabled	indicate whether the button can respond to the user's actions
Font	specify the font to use for text
Image	specify the image to display on the button's face
ImageAlign	indicate the alignment of the image on the button's face
Name	give the button a meaningful name
TabIndex	indicate the position of the button in the Tab order
Text	specify the text that appears on the button

CheckBox

Checked	indicate whether the check box is selected or unselected
Font	specify the font to use for text
Name	give the check box a meaningful name
TabIndex	indicate the position of the check box in the Tab order
Text	specify the text that appears inside the check box

ComboBox

DropDownStyle	indicate the style of the combo box
Font	specify the font to use for text
Name	give the combo box a meaningful name
SelectedIndex	get or set the index of the selected item
SelectedItem	get or set the value of the selected item
Sorted	specify whether the items in the list portion are sorted
TabIndex	indicate the position of the combo box in the Tab order
Text	get or set the value that appears in the text portion

DataGridView

AutoSizeColumnsMode	control the way the column widths are sized
DataSource	indicate the source of the data to display in the control
Dock	define which borders of the control are bound to its container
Name	give the data grid view control a meaningful name

GroupBox

Name	give the group box a meaningful name
Padding	specify the internal space between the edges of the group box and the edges of the controls contained within the group box
Text	specify the text that appears in the upper-left corner of the group box

Hyperlink (Web)

NavigateUrl	specify the page to display
Text	specify the hyperlink's text

Image (Web)

ImageUrl	specify the image to display

ImageList

ColorDepth	specify the number of bits per pixel allocated for the image color
Images	indicate the collection of images to store in the control
ImageSize	indicate the dimensions for the images
TransparentColor	specify the color to treat as transparent when an image is rendered

Label

AutoSize	enable/disable automatic sizing
BorderStyle	specify the appearance of the label's border
Font	specify the font to use for text
Name	give the label a meaningful name
TabIndex	specify the position of the label in the Tab order
Text	specify the text that appears inside the label
TextAlign	specify the position of the text inside the label

ListBox

Font	specify the font to use for text
Name	give the list box a meaningful name
SelectedIndex	get or set the index of the selected item
SelectedItem	get or set the value of the selected item

SelectionMode	indicate whether the user can select zero choices, one choice, or more than one choice
Sorted	specify whether the items in the list are sorted

Panel

BorderStyle	specify the appearance of the panel's border
Font	specify the font to use for the text and controls inside the panel

PictureBox

Image	specify the image to display
Name	give the picture box a meaningful name
SizeMode	specify how the image should be displayed
Visible	hide/display the picture box

RadioButton

Checked	indicate whether the radio button is selected or unselected
Font	specify the font to use for text
Name	give the radio button a meaningful name
Text	specify the text that appears inside the radio button

TableLayoutPanel

Name	give the table layout panel a meaningful name
CellBorderStyle	specify whether the table cells have a visible border
ColumnCount	indicate the number of columns in the table
Columns	specify the style of each column in the table
Padding	specify the internal space between the edges of the table layout panel and the edges of the controls contained within the table layout panel
RowCount	indicate the number of rows in the table
Rows	specify the style of each row in the table

TextBox

BackColor	indicate the background color of the text box
CharacterCasing	specify whether the text should remain as is or be converted to either uppercase or lowercase
Font	specify the font to use for text
ForeColor	indicate the color of the text inside the text box
Name	give the text box a meaningful name
MaxLength	specify the maximum number of characters the text box will accept
Multiline	control whether the text can span more than one line
PasswordChar	specify the character to display when entering a password
ReadOnly	specify whether the text can be edited
ScrollBars	indicate whether scroll bars appear on a text box (used with a multiline text box)
TabIndex	specify the position of the text box in the Tab order
TabStop	indicate whether the user can use the Tab key to give focus to the text box
Text	get or set the text that appears inside the text box

Timer

Name	give the timer a meaningful name
Enabled	stop/start the timer
Interval	indicate the number of milliseconds between each Tick event

APPENDIX D

Visual Basic Conversion Functions

This appendix lists the Visual Basic conversion functions. As mentioned in Chapter 3, you can use the conversion functions (rather than the Convert methods) to convert an expression from one data type to another.

Syntax	Return data type	Range for expression
CBool(*expression*)	Boolean	Any valid String or numeric expression
CByte(*expression*)	Byte	0 through 255 (unsigned)
CChar(*expression*)	Char	Any valid String expression; value can be 0 through 65535 (unsigned); only the first character is converted
CDate(*expression*)	Date	Any valid representation of a date and time
CDbl(*expression*)	Double	−1.79769313486231570E+308 through −4.94065645841246544E-324 for negative values; 4.94065645841246544E-324 through 1.79769313486231570E+308 for positive values
CDec(*expression*)	Decimal	+/−79,228,162,514,264,337,593,543,950,335 for zero-scaled numbers (that is, numbers with no decimal places); for numbers with 28 decimal places, the range is +/−7.9228162514264337593543950335; the smallest possible nonzero number is 0.0000000000000000000000000001 (+/−1E-28)
CInt(*expression*)	Integer	−2,147,483,648 through 2,147,483,647; fractional parts are rounded
CLng(*expression*)	Long	−9,223,372,036,854,775,808 through 9,223,372,036,854,775,807; fractional parts are rounded
CObj(*expression*)	Object	Any valid expression
CSByte(*expression*)	SByte (signed Byte)	−128 through 127; fractional parts are rounded
CShort(*expression*)	Short	−32,768 through 32,767; fractional parts are rounded
CSng(*expression*)	Single	−3.402823E+38 through −1.401298E-45 for negative values; 1.401298E-45 through 3.402823E+38 for positive values
CStr(*expression*)	String	Depends on the expression
CUInt(*expression*)	UInt	0 through 4,294,967,295 (unsigned)
CULng(*expression*)	ULng	0 through 18,446,744,073,709,551,615 (unsigned)
CUShort(*expression*)	UShort	0 through 65,535 (unsigned)

APPENDIX E

Finding and Fixing Program Errors

After studying Appendix E, you should be able to:

1. Locate syntax errors using the Error List window
2. Locate a logic error by stepping through the code
3. Locate logic errors using breakpoints
4. Fix syntax and logic errors
5. Identify a run time error

Finding and Fixing Syntax Errors

As you learned in Chapter 1, a syntax error occurs when you break one of a programming language's rules. Most syntax errors are a result of typing errors that occur when entering instructions, such as typing `Intger` instead of `Integer`. The Code Editor detects syntax errors as you enter the instructions. However, if you are not paying close attention to your computer screen, you may not notice the errors. In the next set of steps, you will observe what happens when you start an application that contains a syntax error.

To start debugging the Total Sales Calculator application:

1. Start Visual Studio 2015. Open the **Total Sales Solution** (**Total Sales Solution.sln**) file contained in the VbReloaded2015\AppE\Total Sales Solution folder. The application calculates and displays the total of the sales amounts entered by the user. See Figure E-1.

Figure E-1 Total Sales Calculator application

2. Open the Code Editor window. Replace <your name> and <current date> in the comments with your name and the current date, respectively. Figure E-2 shows the code entered in the calcButton_Click procedure. The red jagged lines, called squiggles, alert you that three lines of code contain a syntax error. The green squiggle warns you of a potential problem in your code.

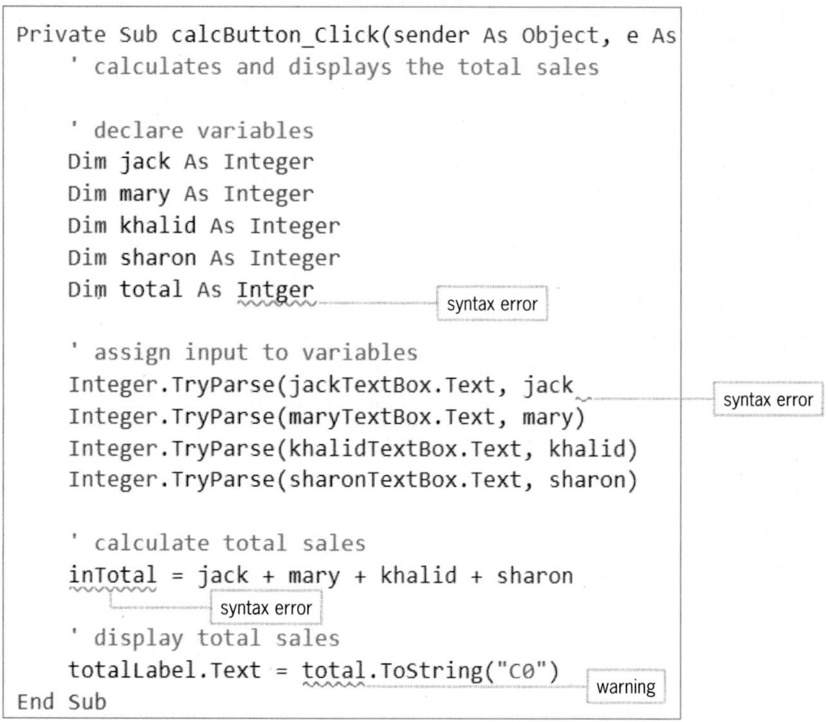

Private Sub calcButton_Click(sender As Object, e As
' calculates and displays the total sales
' declare variables
Dim jack As Integer
Dim mary As Integer
Dim khalid As Integer
Dim sharon As Integer
Dim total As Intger
syntax error
' assign input to variables
Integer.TryParse(jackTextBox.Text, jack
syntax error
Integer.TryParse(maryTextBox.Text, mary)
Integer.TryParse(khalidTextBox.Text, khalid)
Integer.TryParse(sharonTextBox.Text, sharon)
' calculate total sales
inTotal = jack + mary + khalid + sharon
syntax error
' display total sales
totalLabel.Text = total.ToString("C0")
warning
End Sub

Figure E-2 calcButton_Click procedure in the Total Sales Calculator application

3. Press **F5** to start the application. If the dialog box shown in Figure E-3 appears, click the **No** button.

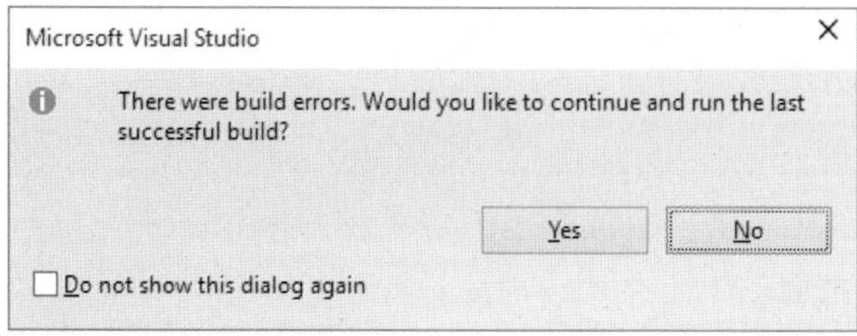

There were build errors. Would you like to continue and run the last successful build?

Do not show this dialog again

Figure E-3 Dialog box

4. The Error List window opens at the bottom of the IDE. If necessary, use the window's Auto Hide button to permanently display the window. See Figure E-4. The Error List window indicates that the code contains three errors and one warning, and it provides both a description and the location of each in the code. When debugging your code, always correct the syntax errors first because doing so will often remove the warning.

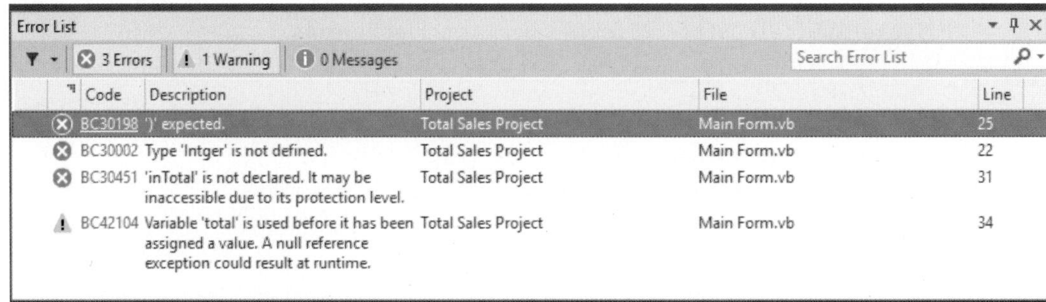

Figure E-4 Error List window

Note: You can change the size of the Error List window by positioning your mouse pointer on the window's top border until the mouse pointer becomes a vertical line with an arrow at the top and bottom. Then press and hold down the left mouse button while you drag the border either up or down.

5. Double-click the **description of the error associated with Line 22** in the Error List window. A LightBulb indicator appears in the margin. Hover your mouse pointer over the light bulb until a list arrow appears, and then click the **list arrow**. A list of suggestions for fixing the error appears. See Figure E-5.

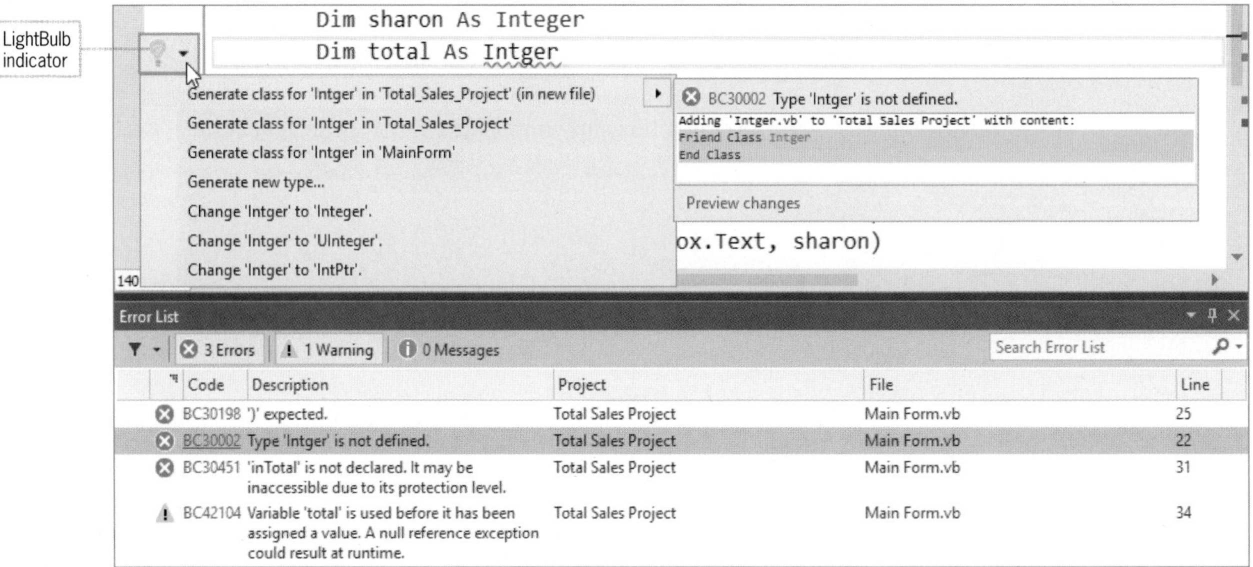

Figure E-5 Result of clicking the LightBulb indicator's list arrow

6. The first error is simply a typing error; the programmer meant to type Integer. You can either type the missing letter e yourself or click the appropriate suggestion in the list. Click **Change 'Intger' to 'Integer'.** in the list. The Code Editor makes the change in the Dim statement and also removes the error, as well as the warning, from the Error List window.

7. The Error List window now indicates that there is a missing parenthesis in the statement on Line 25. Double-click the **first error's description** in the Error List window. The Code Editor places the insertion point at the end of the first TryParse method. Hover your mouse pointer over the red squiggle. See Figure E-6.

```
' assign input to variables
Integer.TryParse(jackTextBox.Text, jack
Integer.TryParse(maryTextBox.Text, mary)   (local variable) jack As Integer
Integer.TryParse(khalidTextBox.Text, kha
Integer.TryParse(sharonTextBox.Text, sha   ')' expected.   error
```

Figure E-6 Result of double-clicking the error description for Line 25

8. Type). The Code Editor removes the error from the Error List window.
9. The description of the remaining error indicates that the Code Editor does not recognize the name `inTotal`. Double-click the **error's description**, hover your mouse pointer over the light bulb, and then click the **list arrow**. This error is another typing error; the variable's name is `total`, not `inTotal`. Click **Change 'inTotal' to 'total'.** in the list. The Code Editor removes the error from the Error List window.
10. Close the Error List window. Save the solution and then start the application. Test the application using **125600** as Jack's sales, **98700** as Mary's sales, **165000** as Khalid's sales, and **250400** as Sharon's sales. Click the **Calculate** button. The total sales are $639,700.
11. Click the **Exit** button. Close the Code Editor window and then close the solution.

Finding and Fixing Logic Errors

Unlike syntax errors, logic errors are much more difficult to find because they do not trigger an error message from the Code Editor. A logic error can occur for a variety of reasons, such as forgetting to enter an instruction or entering the instructions in the wrong order. Some logic errors occur as a result of calculation statements that are correct syntactically but incorrect mathematically. For example, consider the statement `sum = num1 * num2`, which is supposed to calculate the sum of two numbers. The statement's syntax is correct, but it is incorrect mathematically because it uses the multiplication operator rather than the addition operator. In the next two sections, you will debug two applications that contain logic errors.

To debug the Discount Calculator application:

1. Open the **Discount Solution** (**Discount Solution.sln**) file contained in the VbReloaded2015\AppE\Discount Solution folder. See Figure E-7. The application calculates and displays three discount amounts, which are based on the price entered by the user.

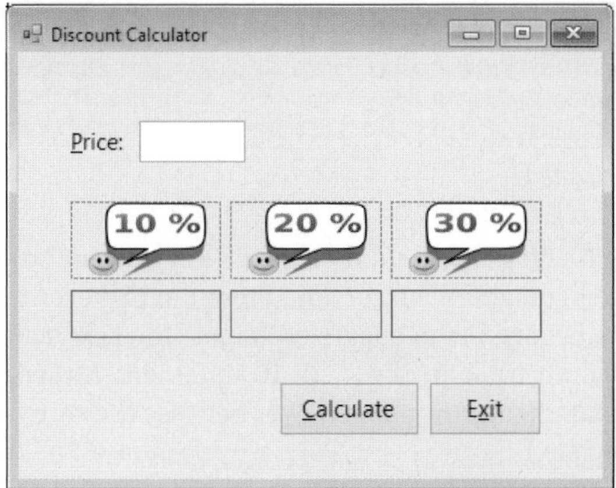

Figure E-7 Discount Calculator application

2. Open the Code Editor window. Figure E-8 shows the calcButton_Click procedure.

```
Private Sub calcButton_Click(sender As Object, e As
    ' calculates and displays a 10%, 20%, and
    ' 30% discount on an item's price

    ' declare variables
    Dim price As Decimal
    Dim discount10 As Decimal
    Dim discount20 As Decimal
    Dim discount30 As Decimal

    ' calculate discounts
    discount10 = price * 0.1D
    discount20 = price * 0.2D
    discount30 = price * 0.3D

    ' display discounts
    disc10Label.Text = discount10.ToString("N2")
    disc20Label.Text = discount20.ToString("N2")
    disc30Label.Text = discount30.ToString("N2")
End Sub
```

Figure E-8 calcButton_Click procedure in the Discount Calculator application

3. Start the application. Type **100** in the Price box and then click the **Calculate** button. The interface shows that each discount is 0.00, which is incorrect. Click the **Exit** button.

4. You will use the Debug menu to run the Visual Basic debugger, which is a tool that helps you locate the logic errors in your code. Click **Debug** on the menu bar. The menu's Step Into option will start your application and allow you to step through your code. It does this by executing the code one statement at a time, pausing immediately before each statement is executed. Click **Step Into**. Type **100** in the Price box and then click the **Calculate** button. The debugger highlights the first instruction to be executed, which is the calcButton_Click procedure header. In addition, an arrow points to the instruction, as shown in Figure E-9, and the code's execution is paused.

```
Private Sub calcButton_Click(sender As Object, e
    ' calculates and displays a 10%, 20%, and
    ' 30% discount on an item's price
```

Figure E-9 Procedure header highlighted

5. You can use either the Debug menu's Step Into option or the F8 key on your keyboard to tell the computer to execute the highlighted instruction. Press the **F8** key. After the computer processes the procedure header, the debugger highlights the next statement to be processed, which is the `discount10 = price * 0.1D` statement. It then pauses execution of the code. (The Dim statements are skipped over because they are not considered executable by the debugger.)

6. While the execution of a procedure's code is paused, you can view the contents of controls and variables that appear in the highlighted statement and also in the statements above it in the procedure. Before you view the contents of a control or variable, however, you should consider the value you expect to find. Before the highlighted statement is processed, the `discount10` variable should contain its initial value, 0. (Recall that the Dim statement initializes numeric variables to 0.) Place your mouse pointer on `discount10` in the highlighted statement. The variable's name and current value appear in a small box, as shown in Figure E-10. At this point, the `discount10` variable's value is correct.

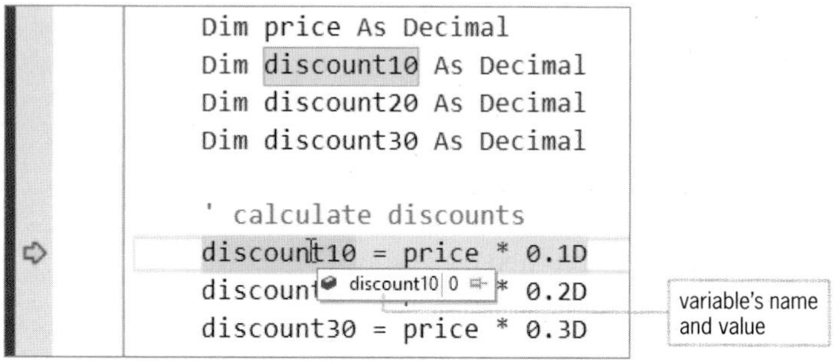

```
Dim price As Decimal
Dim discount10 As Decimal
Dim discount20 As Decimal
Dim discount30 As Decimal

' calculate discounts
discount10 = price * 0.1D
discoun[discount10 0] * 0.2D
discount30 = price * 0.3D
```

variable's name and value

Figure E-10 Value stored in the variable before the highlighted statement is executed

7. Now consider the value you expect to find in the `price` variable. Before the highlighted statement is processed, the variable should contain the number 100, which is the value you entered in the Price box. Place your mouse pointer on `price` in the highlighted statement. The variable contains 0, which is its initial value. The value is incorrect because no statement above the highlighted statement assigns the Price box's value to the `price` variable. In other words, a statement is missing from the procedure.

8. Click **Debug** on the menu bar and then click **Stop Debugging** to stop the debugger. Click the **blank line** below the last Dim statement and then press **Enter** to insert another blank line. Enter the following comment and TryParse method:

   'assign price to a variable
   Decimal.TryParse(priceTextBox.Text, price)

9. Save the solution. Click **Debug** on the menu bar and then click **Step Into**. Type **100** in the Price box and then click the **Calculate** button. Press **F8** to process the procedure header. The debugger highlights the first TryParse method and then pauses execution of the code.

10. Before the TryParse method is processed, the priceTextBox's Text property should contain 100, which is the value you entered in the Price box. Place your mouse pointer on `priceTextBox.Text` in the TryParse method. The box shows that the Text property contains the expected value. The 100 is enclosed in quotation marks because it is considered a string.

11. The `price` variable should contain its initial value, 0. Place your mouse pointer on `price` in the TryParse method. The box shows that the variable contains the expected value.

12. Press **F8** to process the TryParse method. The debugger highlights the `discount10 = price * 0.1D` statement before pausing execution of the code. Place your mouse pointer on `price` in the TryParse method, as shown in Figure E-11. Notice that after the method is processed by the computer, the `price` variable contains the number 100, which is correct.

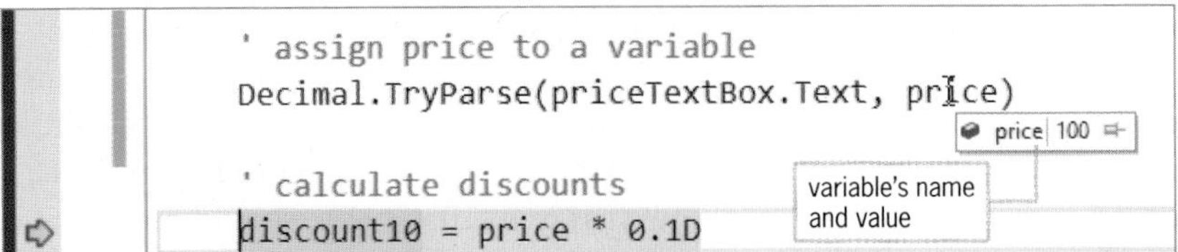

Figure E-11 Value stored in the variable after the TryParse method is executed

13. Before the highlighted statement is processed, the `discount10` variable should contain its initial value, and the `price` variable should contain the value assigned to it by the TryParse method. Place your mouse pointer on `discount10` in the highlighted statement. The box shows that the variable contains 0, which is correct. Place your mouse pointer on `price` in the highlighted statement. The box shows that the variable contains 100, which also is correct.

14. After the highlighted statement is processed, the `price` variable should still contain 100. However, the `discount10` variable should contain 10, which is 10% of 100. Press **F8** to execute the highlighted statement, and then place your mouse pointer on `discount10` in the statement. The box shows that the variable contains 10.0, which is correct. On your own, verify that the `price` variable in the statement contains the appropriate value (100).

15. To continue program execution without the debugger, click **Debug** on the menu bar and then click **Continue**. This time, the correct discount amounts appear in the interface. See Figure E-12.

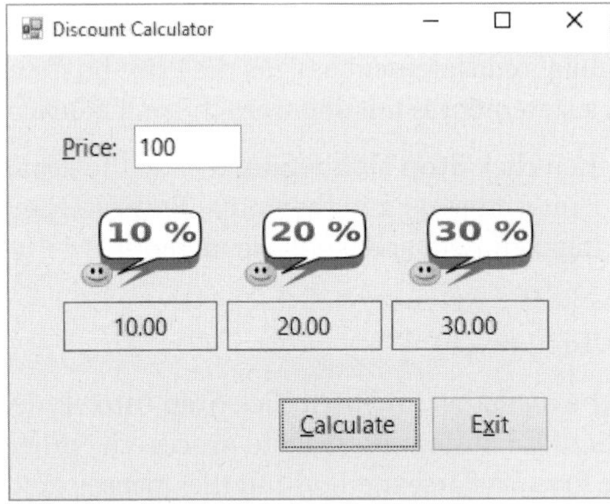

Figure E-12 Sample run of the Discount Calculator application

16. Click the **Exit** button. Close the Code Editor window and then close the solution.

Setting Breakpoints

Stepping through code one line at a time is not the only way to search for logic errors. You can also use a breakpoint to pause execution at a specific line in the code. You will learn how to set a breakpoint in the next set of steps.

To begin debugging the Hours Worked application:

1. Open the **Hours Worked Solution** (**Hours Worked Solution.sln**) file contained in the VbReloaded2015\AppE\Hours Worked Solution folder. See Figure E-13. The application calculates and displays the total number of hours worked in four weeks.

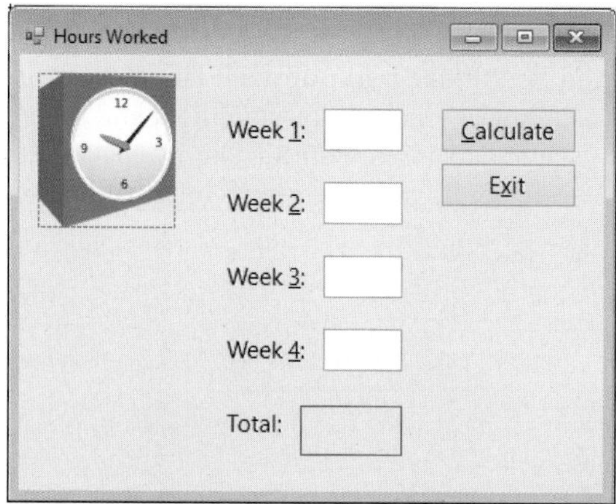

Figure E-13 Hours Worked application

2. Open the Code Editor window. Figure E-14 shows the calcButton_Click procedure.

```
Private Sub calcButton_Click(sender As Object, e A
    ' calculates and displays the total number
    ' of hours worked during 4 weeks

    ' declare variables
    Dim week1 As Double
    Dim week2 As Double
    Dim week3 As Double
    Dim week4 As Double
    Dim total As Double

    ' assign input to variables
    Double.TryParse(week1TextBox.Text, week1)
    Double.TryParse(week2TextBox.Text, week2)
    Double.TryParse(week3TextBox.Text, week2)
    Double.TryParse(week4TextBox.Text, week4)

    ' calculate total hours worked
    total = week1 + week2 + week3 + week4

    ' display total hours worked
    totalLabel.Text = total.ToString("N1")
End Sub
```

Figure E-14 calcButton_Click procedure in the Hours Worked application

3. Start the application. Type **10.5**, **25**, **33**, and **40** in the Week 1, Week 2, Week 3, and Week 4 boxes, respectively, and then click the **Calculate** button. The interface shows that the total number of hours is 83.5, which is incorrect; it should be 108.5. Click the **Exit** button.

The statement that calculates the total number of hours worked is not giving the correct result. Rather than having the computer pause before processing each line of code in the procedure, you will have it pause only before processing the calculation statement. You do this by setting a breakpoint on the statement.

To finish debugging the application:

1. Right-click the **calculation statement**, point to **Breakpoint**, and then click **Insert Breakpoint**. (You can also set a breakpoint by clicking the statement and then using the Toggle Breakpoint option on the Debug menu, or you can simply click in the gray margin next to the statement.) The debugger highlights the statement and places a circle next to it, as shown in Figure E-15.

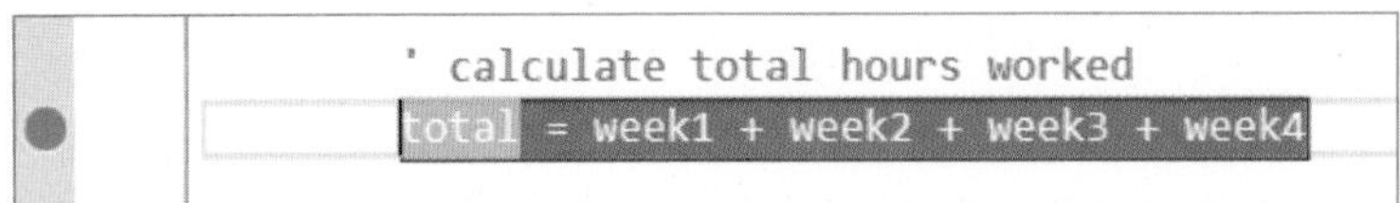

Figure E-15 Breakpoint set in the procedure

2. Start the application. Type **10.5**, **25**, **33**, and **40** in the Week 1, Week 2, Week 3, and Week 4 boxes, respectively, and then click the **Calculate** button. The computer begins processing the code contained in the calcButton_Click procedure. It stops processing when it reaches the breakpoint statement, which it highlights. The highlighting indicates that the statement is the next one to be processed. Notice that a yellow arrow now appears in the red dot next to the breakpoint. See Figure E-16.

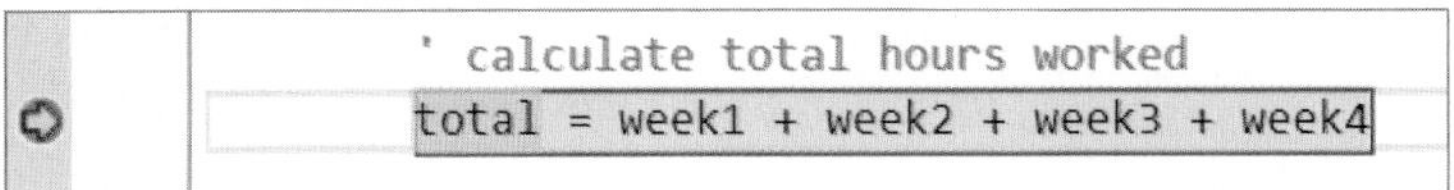

Figure E-16 Result of the computer reaching the breakpoint

3. Before viewing the values contained in each variable in the highlighted statement, consider the values you expect to find. Before the calculation statement is processed, the `total` variable should contain its initial value (0). Place your mouse pointer on `total` in the highlighted statement. The box shows that the variable's value is 0, which is correct. (You can verify the variable's initial value by placing your mouse pointer on `total` in its declaration statement.)
4. The other four variables should contain the numbers 10.5, 25, 33, and 40, which are the values you entered in the text boxes. On your own, view the values contained in the `week1`, `week2`, `week3`, and `week4` variables. Notice that two of the variables (`week1` and `week4`) contain the correct values (10.5 and 40). The `week2` variable, however, contains 33 rather than 25, and the `week3` variable contains its initial value (0) rather than the number 33.
5. Two of the TryParse methods are responsible for assigning the text box values to the `week2` and `week3` variables. Looking closely at the four TryParse methods in the procedure, you will notice that the third one is incorrect. After converting the contents of the week3TextBox to a number, the method should assign the number to the `week3` variable rather than to the `week2` variable. Click **Debug** on the menu bar, and then click **Stop Debugging**.
6. Change `week2` in the third TryParse method to **week3**.
7. Click the **breakpoint circle** to remove the breakpoint.

8. Save the solution and then start the application. Type **10.5**, **25**, **33**, and **40** in the Week 1, Week 2, Week 3, and Week 4 boxes, respectively, and then click the **Calculate** button. The interface shows that the total number of hours is 108.5, which is correct. See Figure E-17.

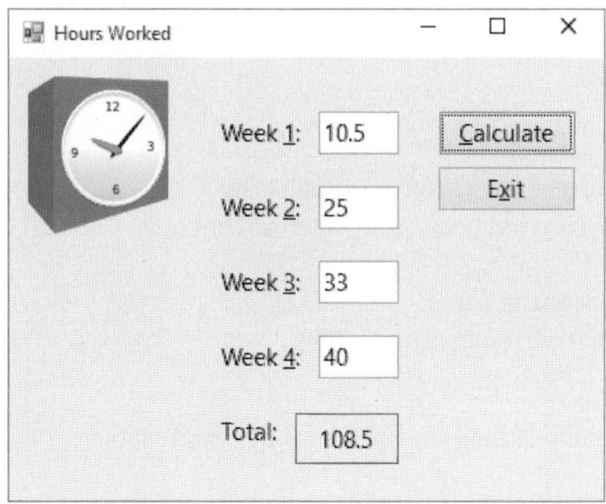

Figure E-17 Sample run of the Hours Worked application

9. On your own, test the application using other values for the hours worked in each week. When you are finished testing, click the **Exit** button. Close the Code Editor window and then close the solution.

Run Time Errors

In addition to syntax and logic errors, programs may also have run time errors. A run time error is an error that occurs while an application is running. As you will observe in the following set of steps, an expression that attempts to divide a value by the number 0 will result in a run time error if the expression's numerator and/or denominator has the Decimal data type.

To use the Quotient Calculator application to observe a run time error:

1. Open the **Quotient Solution** (**Quotient Solution.sln**) file contained in the VbReloaded2015\AppE\Quotient Solution folder. See Figure E-18. The interface provides two text boxes for the user to enter two numbers. The Calculate button's Click event procedure divides the number in the numeratorTextBox by the number in the denominatorTextBox and then displays the result, called the quotient, in the quotientLabel.

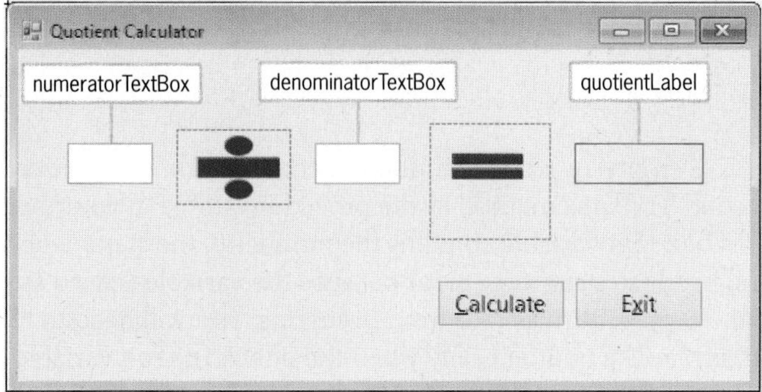

Figure E-18 Quotient Calculator application

2. Open the Code Editor window. Figure E-19 shows the calcButton_Click procedure.

```
Private Sub calcButton_Click(sender As Object, e As EventAr
    ' display the result of dividing two numbers

    Dim numerator As Decimal
    Dim denominator As Decimal
    Dim quotient As Decimal

    Decimal.TryParse(numeratorTextBox.Text, numerator)
    Decimal.TryParse(denominatorTextBox.Text, denominator)

    quotient = numerator / denominator
    quotientLabel.Text = quotient.ToString("N2")
End Sub
```

Figure E-19 calcButton_Click procedure in the Quotient Calculator application

3. Start the application. Type **100** and **5** in the numeratorTextBox and denominatorTextBox, respectively, and then click the **Calculate** button. The interface shows that the quotient is 20.00, which is correct.

4. Delete the **5** from the denominatorTextBox and then click the **Calculate** button. A run time error occurs. The Error Correction window indicates that the highlighted statement, which also has an arrow pointing to it, is attempting to divide by 0. The troubleshooting tips section of the window advises you to "Make sure the value of the denominator is not zero before performing a division operation." See Figure E-20.

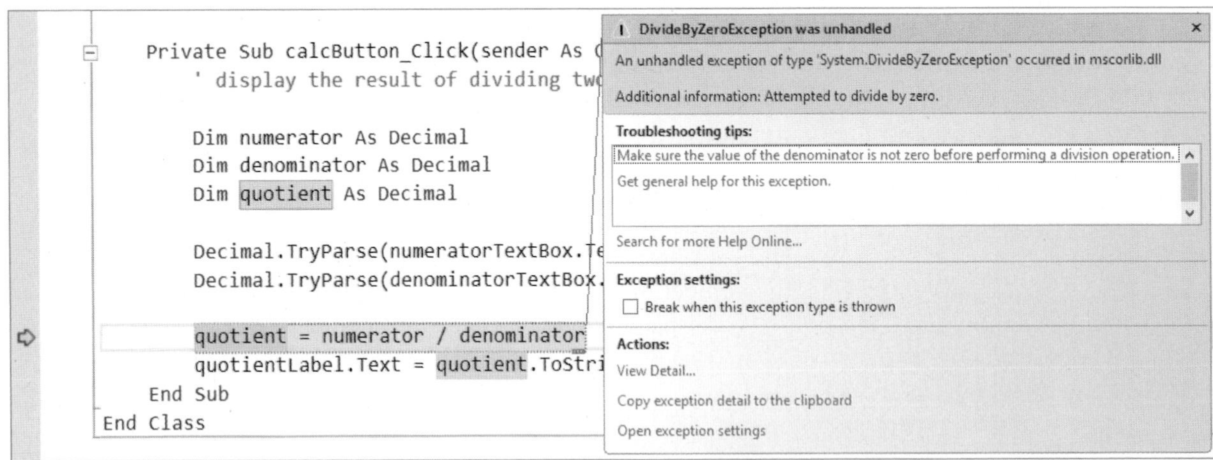

Figure E-20 Run time error caused by attempting to divide by 0

When the denominatorTextBox is empty, or when it contains a character that cannot be converted to a number, the second TryParse method in the procedure stores the number 0 in the `denominator` variable. When that variable contains the number 0, the statement that calculates the quotient will produce a run time error because the variable is used as the denominator in the calculation. To prevent this error from occurring, you will need to tell the computer to calculate and display the quotient only when the `denominator` variable does not contain the number 0; otherwise, it should display the "N/A" message. You do this using a selection structure, which is covered in Chapter 4 in this book.

To add a selection structure to the calcButton_Click procedure:

1. Click **Debug** on the menu bar and then click **Stop Debugging**.
2. Enter the selection structure shown in Figure E-21. Be sure to move the statements that calculate and display the quotient into the selection structure's true path, as shown.

```
Private Sub calcButton_Click(sender As Object, e As EventAr
    ' display the result of dividing two numbers

    Dim numerator As Decimal
    Dim denominator As Decimal
    Dim quotient As Decimal

    Decimal.TryParse(numeratorTextBox.Text, numerator)
    Decimal.TryParse(denominatorTextBox.Text, denominator)

    If denominator <> 0 Then
        quotient = numerator / denominator
        quotientLabel.Text = quotient.ToString("N2")
    Else
        quotientLabel.Text = "N/A"
    End If
End Sub
```

enter this selection structure

Figure E-21 Selection structure entered in the procedure

3. Start the application. Type **100** and **5** in the numeratorTextBox and denominatorTextBox, respectively, and then click the **Calculate** button. The interface shows that the quotient is 20.00, which is correct.
4. Now, delete the **5** from the denominatorTextBox and then click the **Calculate** button. Instead of a run time error, N/A appears in the interface. See Figure E-22.

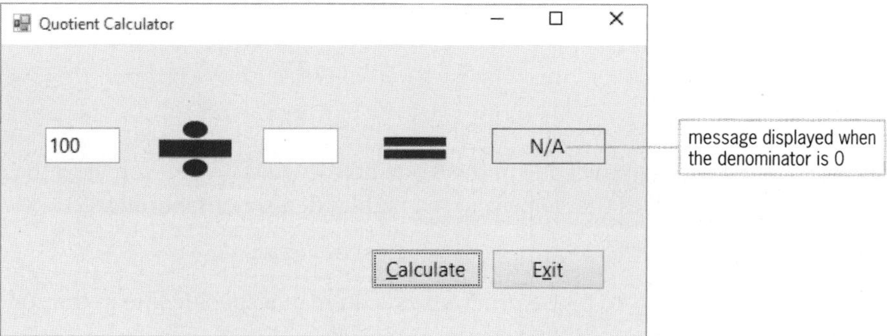

Figure E-22 Result of including the selection structure in the calcButton_Click procedure

5. Click the **Exit** button. Close the Code Editor window and then close the solution.

Summary

- To find the syntax errors in a program, look for squiggles (jagged lines) in the Code Editor window. Or, start the application and then look in the Error List window.
- To find the logic errors in a program, either step through the code in the Code Editor window or set a breakpoint.
- You can step through your code using either the Step Into option on the Debug menu or the F8 key on your keyboard.
- To set a breakpoint, right-click the line of code on which you want to set the breakpoint. Point to Breakpoint and then click Insert Breakpoint. You can also click the line of code and then use the Toggle Breakpoint option on the Debug menu. In addition, you can click in the gray margin next to the line of code.
- To remove a breakpoint, right-click the line of code containing the breakpoint, point to Breakpoint, and then click Delete Breakpoint. You can also simply click the breakpoint circle in the margin.
- You can use a selection structure to determine whether a variable contains the number 0.

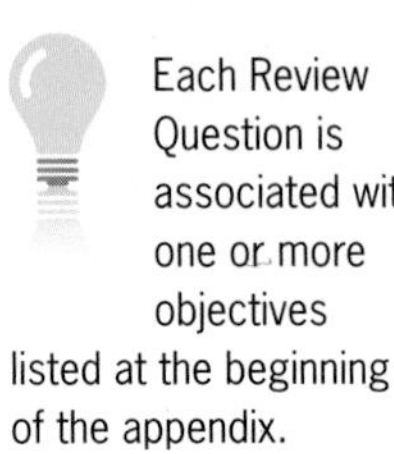

Each Review Question is associated with one or more objectives listed at the beginning of the appendix.

Review Questions

1. While stepping through code, the debugger highlights the statement that ______________. (2)
   a. was just executed
   b. will be executed next
   c. contains the error
   d. none of the above
2. Logic errors are listed in the Error List window. (1, 2)
   a. True
   b. False
3. Which key is used to step through code? (2)
   a. F5
   b. F6
   c. F7
   d. F8
4. While stepping through the code in the Code Editor window, you can view the contents of controls and variables that appear in the highlighted statement only. (2)
   a. True
   b. False
5. You use ______________ to pause program execution at a specific line in the code. (3)
   a. a breakpoint
   b. the Error List window
   c. the Step Into option on the Debug menu
   d. the Stop Debugging option on the Debug menu
6. The statement `Constant Rate As Double` is an example of a ______________. (1)
   a. correct statement
   b. logic error
   c. syntax error
   d. run time error

7. When entered in a procedure, which of the following statements will result in a syntax error? (1)
   a. `Me.Clse()`
   b. `Integer.TryPars(hoursTextBox.Text, hours)`
   c. `Dim taxRate as Decimel`
   d. all of the above

Exercises

1. Open the Commission Calculator Solution (Commission Calculator Solution.sln) file contained in the VbReloaded2015\AppE\Commission Calculator Solution folder. Use what you learned in the appendix to debug the application. (1–5) INTRODUCTORY
2. Open the New Pay Solution (New Pay Solution.sln) file contained in the VbReloaded2015\AppE\New Pay Solution folder. Use what you learned in the appendix to debug the application. (1–5) INTRODUCTORY
3. Open the Hawkins Solution (Hawkins Solution.sln) file contained in the VbReloaded2015\AppE\Hawkins Solution folder. Use what you learned in the appendix to debug the application. (1–5) INTRODUCTORY
4. Open the Allenton Solution (Allenton Solution.sln) file contained in the VbReloaded2015\AppE\Allenton Solution folder. Use what you learned in the appendix to debug the application. (1–5) INTRODUCTORY
5. Open the Martins Solution (Martins Solution.sln) file contained in the VbReloaded2015\AppE\Martins Solution folder. Use what you learned in the appendix to debug the application. (1–5) INTERMEDIATE
6. Open the Average Score Solution (Average Score Solution.sln) file contained in the VbReloaded2015\AppE\Average Score Solution folder. Use what you learned in the appendix to debug the application. (1–5) INTERMEDIATE
7. Open the Beachwood Solution (Beachwood Solution.sln) file contained in the VbReloaded2015\AppA\Beachwood Solution folder. Use what you learned in the appendix to debug the application. (1–5) ADVANCED
8. Open the Framington Solution (Framington Solution.sln) file contained in the VbReloaded2015\AppA\Framington Solution folder. Use what you learned in the appendix to debug the application. (1–5) ADVANCED

Index

Note: Page numbers in **boldface** indicate definitions of key terms.

Q

R

S